Questions of Gender

PERSPECTIVES AND PARADOXES

Dina L. Anselmi
Trinity College

Anne L. Law
Rider University

Boston   Burr Ridge, IL   Dubuque, IA   Madison, WI   New York   San Francisco
St. Louis   Bangkok   Bogotá   Caracas   Lisbon   London   Madrid   Mexico City
Milan   New Delhi   Seoul   Singapore   Sydney   Taipei   Toronto

McGraw-Hill

A Division of The McGraw·Hill Companies

QUESTIONS OF GENDER: PERSPECTIVES AND PARADOXES

Copyright © 1998 by The McGraw-Hill Companies, Inc. All rights reserved. Printed in the United States of America. Except as permitted under the United States Copyright Act of 1976, no part of this publication may be reproduced or distributed in any form or by any means, or stored in a data base or retrieval system, without the prior written permission of the publisher.

 This book is printed on recycled, acid-free paper containing 10% postconsumer waste.

1 2 3 4 5 6 7 8 9 0 QPF/QPF 9 0 9 8 7

ISBN 0–07–006017–7

Editorial director: *Jane E. Vaicunas*
Sponsoring editor: *Beth Kaufman*
Marketing manager: *James Rozsa*
Project manager: *Cathy Ford Smith*
Production supervisor: *Sandra Hahn*
Cover designer: *Laurie Jean Entringer*
Cover illustration: © *Jose Ortega/SIS*
Compositor: *Shepherd, Inc.*
Typeface: *Times New Roman*
Printer: *Quebecor Printing/Fairfield*

Credits begin on page 784 and are considered part of the copyright page.

Library of Congress Cataloging-in-Publication Data:

Anselmi, Dina.
    Questions of gender : perspectives and paradoxes / Dina Anselmi,
Anne L. Law.—1st ed.
        p.   cm.
    Includes index.
    ISBN 0-07-006017-7
    1. Sex.   2. Sex role.   3. Gender identity.   I. Law, Anne L.
II. Title.
BF692.2.A584   1998
155.3—dc21   97-31723
                                                    CIP

www.mhhe.com

*To the joys of friendship
and collaboration*

CONTENTS

CHAPTER THREE

Biology and Gender
111

CHAPTER FOUR

Gender and Culture
155

CHAPTER FIVE

Gender Roles and Stereotypes
195

CHAPTER SIX

Gender Identity Development
247

CHAPTER SEVEN

Gender and Sexuality
307

CHAPTER EIGHT

Gendered Behavior in a Social Context
357

CHAPTER NINE

Gender, Cognition, and Education
419

CHAPTER TEN

The Paradox of Relationships
483

CHAPTER ELEVEN

Gender and Reconceptualizing the Family
533

CHAPTER TWELVE

Social Institutions and Gender
593

CHAPTER THIRTEEN

Gender and Health
665

CHAPTER FOURTEEN

Gender, Mental Health, and Psychopathology
727

PREFACE

Welcome to *Questions of Gender: Perspectives and Paradoxes,* a project we began nearly two years ago with the goal of creating an alternative teaching and research tool for one of our favorite courses. As we are writing this preface, we are reminded of the pervasiveness of gender in our lives and the society in which we live. Although we sometimes think that after two years of intense focus on gender we have developed a special X-ray vision for gender implications, see if you do not recognize the importance of sex and gender in some of these events:

- There has been continuous debate over the integration of the last two all-male military schools, the Citadel and the Virginia Military Institute. During the winter of 1997, the Citadel lost two of its first four female cadets with charges of harassment. VMI has spent the last year preparing for its first gender-integrated class and women are included in the class of 2001.
- In the spring of 1997, major newspapers and magazines devoted considerable coverage to new research on hermaphrodism, conditions of ambiguous genitalia, as questions of sex and gender perplexed our culture. Late at night we can watch the RuPaul talk show, where the 6-foot, cross-dressing male model interviews celebrities and other guests.
- The summer of 1997 marked the twenty-fifth anniversary of Title IX, federal legislation banning discrimination based on sex in schools. While politicians proclaim Title IX a success, an evaluation of funding, especially in athletics, suggests that women still lag far behind in dollars spent on scholarships, programs and facilities.
- Gender inequity notwithstanding, the WNBA (Women's National Basketball Association)

playing its first season appears on its way to success, complete with male cheerleaders.

At a more informal level, we witness gender interactions at every turn. Both men and women follow certain rules—men are assertive, women defer, men take risks, women are careful, men open doors, women go in first, and so on. Of course, thankfully, not everyone follows these sorts of rules all the time, however, we do depend on men and women to behave predictably. Our observations of gender capture even the earliest moments of life, when newborns are capped in either pink or blue and parents make plans for little league or dance lessons. We could go on, but you probably get the point— gender is inescapable and endlessly fascinating. From development to social behavior, stereotype to culture, relationships to sexuality, biology to health, social institutions to psychopathology—various disciplines offers considerable insight into the dynamics of gender. This book is primarily about understanding gender using the focus of psychology, since we are both psychologists. We have added other academic perspectives, especially those from biology, anthropology, and sociology, because we believe that the perspectives offered by these disciplines broaden and deepen the psychological understanding of gender. Ultimately, questions of gender can only be understood from the interwoven contexts of many disciplinary threads.

WHY THIS BOOK?

In order to help you use this book most effectively we would like to introduce ourselves and our book. Whether you are a student, instructor, or interested layperson, we hope you will take the time to read our introductory remarks. The purpose of this book is to introduce you to contemporary scholarship on gender, and to help you develop a critical attitude toward understanding questions of gender. We have based this book on a model we use in teaching: having a set of core readings linked by lecture and discussion. We believe it is critical for students to learn how to read research and theory in the words of the scholars who provide the information that supports our understanding of gender. To turn this belief into a book, we have written introductory essays that provide an overview of the critical issues that we believe define the topics in each chapter. We have used a conversational style, similarly to how we would introduce some of these issues in teaching. We have added features such as questions and summaries as guides for discussion or for readers to use to self-check their comprehension. We have imagined this project as a dialogue, so while we cannot really engage in a conversation with each of you, we hope you will treat this book with some give and take— ask questions, agree and disagree, be surprised at what you learn, be skeptical, try to remember the central points, and most of all, do not treat anything as the final word.

We have tried to write our introductory essays with one voice. Although we hope we succeeded, we want you to know that we did not always agree on every reading or on every issue related to gender as we initially outlined the book. But through lengthy conversation, and, mostly gentle argument, we came to consensus about issues and ideas. This book is about thinking about gender, it is not about having the final say on an extremely complex individual, interpersonal, social, and cultural phenomena. As we have told the many people who have asked our opinion on a variety of gender related questions since we began writing this book, "if we really knew all the answers we'd be on Oprah." So while we do believe strongly in the point of view we will offer you, it is just that, a point of view, a way of thinking about complex questions, a guide so that you can become a critical thinker about gender in your life and in the world around you.

THE APPROACH OF THIS BOOK

We have carefully chosen several original articles for each chapter using some specific criteria for selection. First, most of the articles in this book have been published within the last five years—this is the newest scholarship on gender. The articles that are a bit older, generally, are classic treatments of an issue or have not been surpassed by something more recent. We searched very hard for articles that would represent a diverse point of view, although in many areas we were limited by the few choices available. Here is an interesting example of our dilemma. Chapter Five is about gender role stereotypes and we really wanted an article that would compare gender, race, and ethnic stereotypes: What are they? How are they different and how are they the same? You can imagine the interesting questions that might be asked by this comparison, except we never found such an article. After reviewing hundreds of choices for this volume, we learned that sometimes the most interesting questions have not yet been asked, much less answered. Of course, we had other criteria for selections to consider for inclusion in the final volume. We wanted good readable choices on the critical issues in gender studies. We wanted to represent the experiences of both men and women, and at the same time, recognize that discrimination has unfairly affected women. This issue is compounded by the fact that Men's Studies is a relatively new academic endeavor, while Women's Studies and feminist psychology are well established. We hope that we have done justice to the many important issues of gender, and most importantly, have shown you that understanding gender is for, and about, everyone.

We are both committed teachers of a variety of psychology courses. In addition to Psychology of Gender, we teach a range of courses in human development and special topics in research methods, culture, and gender issues. Inevitably our choice of readings for this book, and ways of presenting the critical issues, are influenced by our overall perspective on psychology. We are committed to furthering a point of view that recognizes the complex interaction among biological, social, cultural and individual factors. We have tried to represent all of these influences and to suggest ways to think about their interaction throughout the book. We strongly believe that psychology has failed to give full consideration to the range of human experience, and has often neglected or misrepresented the lives and experiences of different racial and ethnic groups, economically disadvantaged individuals, and women. While a recognition of this neglect has begun to influence the direction of psychology in this decade, our knowledge base has not caught up; we are, therefore, left with critical questions about the diversity of human experiences unanswered. As much as possible we have tried to at least raise these questions to make you aware of them and to provide some tentative answers when possible. We value the empirical evidence provided by psychological research, and we rely heavily on conclusions supported by evidence in our analysis of issues in this book. We, however, also take a critical stand on empirical methods, which, while central in psychological research, are often flawed. We also recognize and have tried to represent, several newer and often controversial approaches to the study of gender. Our most important goal is to share with you our enthusiasm for the ways psychology can offer answers to the questions of gender.

NOTE TO STUDENTS

We expect that you are probably an experienced reader of college textbooks. You have probably developed some reading habits that aid you in your education, and we suspect that you may have also developed some habits that do not always take full advantage of what a book has to offer. We believe that our book is somewhat unique among the books you might have used and we want to familiarize you with it before you begin reading. This book includes articles by well-known scholars in psychology and gender studies and original essays we have written to introduce each chapter. We suggest that you plan to read our essay first and then review the essay again after reading the articles. One goal of each essay is to introduce you to the critical issues of the area; the essay can also serve to help you review and reinforce your understanding of each article. We have included some features to direct your reading and to make it easier to re-read. Each chapter begins with a list of questions, which identify the issues to be covered in the chapter and which you should be able to answer after reading the entire chapter. Each section ends with a checkpoint, which is a summary point or two from the preceding section. Use the checkpoints to confirm that you recognize and understand these as brief summaries of arguments made by the previous article(s). Following the checkpoints are one or two thought questions to prepare you for reading the subsequent article(s). We encourage you to develop the habit of actively reviewing and evaluating what you have learned from your reading.

Most importantly, we hope that you will come to see the relationship between the issues raised in this book and your own experience. We introduce you to many of the nuances of how psychologists approach the issue of defining and understanding gender. These issues involve semantics, research methodology, recognizing the interaction among biological, social, cognitive, and institutional forces in our lives, and the political meaning of scientific explanations. It will be a challenge to understand the necessity of grappling with these complex issues in order to understand how important gender is to such everyday experiences as children's social interactions, aggression, emotions, education, family relationships, employment, or health care. When you finish reading this book, we believe you will never accept the simplistic view of men and women that portrays them as living on different planets or speaking different languages. Gender is a central element in many of our experiences in the world, but it is not a war between the sexes.

NOTE TO INSTRUCTORS

The book is structured around fourteen topics that build from the nuts and bolts of research methods and biology to the pervasive phenomena of culture, stereotypes and development, and concludes with a variety of topics where gender is a central issue including cognition and education, relationships and family, social institutions, health, and psychopathology. Each chapter begins with an essay written to introduce readers to the critical issues we believe define the chapter topics. These essays provide additional background that will facilitate the reading of the articles and should help in understanding the connections among the articles in the chapter. While the individual articles usually address a specific topic or question, our essays are broader in their coverage of each chapter's issues.

We believe it would be best to treat each chapter as a package—the introductory essay provides the big picture, each article addresses a central element of the topic, and the questions and summaries integrate these elements. It is also important to consider the interrelationships among the chapters, referencing other places in the book where there are related points. While we have divided the issues in a reasonable, and we hope, logical fashion, we recognize that the issues are related to each other in complex ways. Since we have provided comprehensive coverage of gender from a psychological point of view, many instructors will not have enough time in their course to cover all of these topics. You may choose to use only the chapters that best suit your course or you may select only some articles in a particular chapter for your students to read. Our essays can be read without the articles or as an introduction to the chapter topic.

An important feature of this book package that we are especially pleased with is the Instructor's Manual and Test Bank, authored by Elizabeth Paul. From our first conversations with her, it was clear that Beth has a vision of pedagogy that is creative, well grounded in psychology, and sensitive to the diverse needs of instructors. The Instructor's Manual includes summary points from each article and ideas for lecture/discussion topics (keyed to appropriate pages in the textbook, small group discussion topics, ideas for short and long projects, starters for journal entries or in-class free-write exercises, and a variety of exam questions. There are two features that are innovative and can significantly enhance your teaching of this course. First, for each chapter, Beth has identified a number of internet links related to the chapter. This is a terrific resource for broadening students' exposure to related topics and information—there are discussion groups, web pages, reference sources, and literary and first person accounts related to the topics of each chapter. Second, Beth has identified an empirical article for many of the chapters that can be examined for its use of sex and gender in its methodology. The article is summarized in the Instructor's Manual and a number of critical questions are provided which can be used to direct students in evaluating the article and its methods. Altogether, the resources in this Instructor's Manual provide thousands of ideas for teaching a course on gender; we urge you to review it carefully.

ACKNOWLEDGEMENTS

There are many people to whom we owe many thanks for their contributions to making this project a reality. Throughout the process we have had helpful reviews from the following colleagues:

Bonka Beneva
University of Pittsburgh

Patricia Donat
Mississippi University for Women

Susan Dutch
Westfield State University

Irene Frieze
University of Pittsburgh

Jack Meacham
State University of New York at Buffalo

Catherine Murray
St. Joseph's University

Elizabeth Paul
The College of New Jersey

Cheryl Rickabaugh
University of Redlands

Their insights and recommendations provided much food for thought and many of their good ideas are incorporated into this final version. In particular, Cheryl Rickabaugh, after serving as a reviewer for our complete set of articles, volunteered to review a draft of Chapter One and yet another revision of the set of articles. Her comments were most welcome and helped us evaluate our ideas as they developed. Finally, Elizabeth Paul did an extraordinary job as a reviewer and we are delighted that she agreed to write the Instructor's Manual to accompany this book. As you may have noted from our comments above we believe that this Instructor's Manual is a superb complement to our pedagogical vision for this book. We are fortunate to have an Instructor's Manual which both accurately represents our vision and strengthens the opportunity instructors have to fully address the complexities of these issues. Of course, we claim sole responsibility for all errors and examples of bad judgment.

Many students and colleagues made contributions both large and small to our work. We were especially fortunate to have several students who provided assistance: At Trinity College, we thank Joan Kreie for her efforts tracking down references, Arayna Albert who conducted many literature searches and read many articles, and Robyn Schiffman who read and commented on every article in our first table of contents. Robyn's knowledge of gender issues, comments on specific articles, as well as her enthusiasm for the merits of the project was very helpful as we revised our selection of articles. Kim Tarallo pitched in at the end of this project in a big way, helping to proofread each chapter with care and a wickedly fun sense of humor. At Rider University, we thank Shirrel McDowell and Beth Kuna who spent considerable time in the library constructing literature searches and finding articles, and who read many articles and provided us with written feedback. Brian Hall read and commented on many articles, provided good ideas for organization and helped shape our perception of our audience. In the fall of 1996, Anne's Psychology of Gender class used an early version of our set of readings and periodically wrote reviews of articles. These commentaries were instrumental in helping us make decisions about eliminating

pieces, and helped shape our essays as we worked to make each article accessible to students. We have also had the support of colleagues who read and offered comments on various parts of the text. Maurice Wade and Jerry Watts, in particular, read and provided feedback on many of the thorny concepts in Chapter One. We take full responsibility for not always heeding their insightful advice. Dan Lloyd offered many creative ideas for examples in our essays. We are grateful to several colleagues in other disciplines who helped us track down references, especially Johnny Williams who came through with help in a pinch.

We were introduced to McGraw-Hill, separately, Dina by Janie Pittendreigh and Anne by Debby Seme. These introductions led us to a terrific experience with a wonderful staff. Thanks Janie and Debby for your confidence and advice, we are very pleased with the outcome. Most especially, our editor Beth Kaufman had been a constant source of enthusiasm, creativity, and support. She believed in our ideas about teaching and gender and has patiently shepherded us through a complex project from start to finish. We could not be more fortunate. Jane Vaicunas, Editorial Director, was kind enough to meet with us and provide us with a plethora of ideas not only for this book but for future projects. We were very lucky to have a Permissions Editor, Maria Leon Maimone, who expertly tracked down every permission and kept track of hundreds of details, there is no doubt if we had to do her job this book would not be published until well after the new millenium. Cathy Smith, Project Manager, patiently explained and re-explained every detail of the production process. Thank you, Cathy, we may finally understand how you make a book—which page is *verso* again? In the last few weeks of writing, Adrienne D'Ambrosio, Editorial Coordinator was especially helpful coordinating ideas for the cover design. The design by Laurie Entringer is outstanding and we are delighted by it. Karen Dorman who provided the copyediting did a superb job of interpreting and simplifying our prose. If our essays seem slightly less than pedantic and academic, it is due in large measure to Karen's efforts. Thank you to the many other staff members at McGraw-Hill who have contributed to the development and production of this book, we are very appreciative.

As with all projects we encountered many practical problems especially during the Spring of 1997 while Dina was teaching in Italy. Providing a supportive environment and facilitating her work were Livio Pistelli and Francesco Ciccarelli. Dawn Zorgdrager provided much assistance in all of our long-distance collaboration. At Trinity, John Langeland and Benjamin Todd shared our urgency when attached files arrived as gibberish, and we wanted to read them immediately; to each of you we offer "molte grazie."

One of the most gratifying aspects of this project has been the level of interest people have expressed in our work. If, before we began, we were uncertain of how very interesting gender is, we now know that everyone is interested in gender. When we began brainstorming for a new title (our original clever version was Psychology and Gender, very catchy) we were inundated with ideas, a few that we did not choose are: He/she: What Will it Be, Genderology, and Genderizing. We loved some of the choices, and most especially the level of interest they expressed. Unfortunately, we have not written the book where men and women are different species or versions of aliens, and so, friends, we never will make it to Oprah. Thanks, however, for the considerable support and enthusiasm we received in many conversations with friends and acquaintances.

We especially thank Angelyn Arden, Kate Wilson, David Breault, Diane Zannoni, John Suler and Wendy Heath for their intellectual guidance, emotional support and timely humor, particularly when deadlines seemed impossible to keep. A special note of gratitiude goes to Jerry Watts, not only for his unfailing and forceful encouragement of this project but for his dogged insistence on the importance of being public intellectuals.

We owe our greatest debt to our families who have been a constant source of support and help.

Anne's parents, Bernard and Gertrude Oden, have repeatedly stepped in to make sure that their grandchildren were well taken care of—they have car pooled, prepared meals, babysat, and throughout the time we have worked they have been excited about our progress and a bit worried about missed deadlines. Dina's parents, Edward and Edna Anselmi, were not only supportive of the project, but were quite understanding about missed visits during the long summer months that it took to finish. Other family members were equally generous by always inquiring about the project without asking the perennial question of when we would be finished. Karen McCaffrey, Rachel McCaffrey, Ken and Cynthia Anselmi, and Heather and Ken Law deserve a special note of thanks because, in some moment of filial weakness, they all promised to read the book rather than just let it collect dust on a shelf.

Elizabeth and Katherine Law have been a constant reality check on how well we really understand gender and development. They are always willing to share their views on gender (summarized as "yes," boys and girls probably are from different planets), and more importantly, they have willingly shared their home and mother, and proudly told everyone that Mom and Aunt Dina are writing a book. Finally, Gene Law has been our staunchest supporter and greatest friend. He has encouraged, prodded, and kept us focused on our goal and never faltered in his belief that this was a worthwhile endeavor. He has solved more problems than we could name and gone to unimagined lengths to make our work easier. Thank you Gene—you have helped both of us understand that gender equality is an obtainable goal.

Dina L. Anselmi
dina.anselmi@trincoll.edu
Anne L. Law
PsychMom2@aol.com

CHAPTER ONE

Defining Sex and Gender

QUESTIONS TO THINK ABOUT

- **What is gender?**
- **What is the relationship between sex and gender?**
- **Why is there confusion about the use of the terms** *sex* **and** *gender*?
- **Are male and female mutually exclusive alternatives of a category "sex"?**
- **How have scientists studied the biology of race and sex?**
- **Are race and sex biological categories?**
- **What are "social categories"?**
- **Are race and sex social categories?**
- **What is the relationship between race and gender?**
- **How do essentialist and social constructionist views of the origins of gender differ?**
- **What are the political meanings of sex and gender?**

QUESTIONS OF DEFINITION

One of the first challenges of your reading will be to understand what is meant by **gender.** Certainly you have some ideas about what gender is—femininity or masculinity? maleness or femaleness? We often begin our understanding of gender rooted in the dichotomy of sex—male and female. In most Western cultures, sex operates as a category with two mutually exclusive alternatives. Gender is most certainly related to sex and is often treated as though it derives naturally from being either male or female. We begin by challenging this categorical notion of sex and gender and by looking carefully at how psychologists use the terms *sex* and *gender*.

The categories of sex and gender influence our everyday interactions (e.g., men open doors for women) as well as our larger social organization (e.g., women care for children more frequently than do men), but these categories also structure how psychologists have treated sex and gender. An examination of the history of research on sex and gender clearly shows that researchers frequently differ about the meaning of sex and gender (for the history of the biology of sex, see Ruth Hubbard's article in this chapter). The consequence of such disagreements is that researchers often approach their research from very different vantage points in terms of the nature of the phenomena to be studied, how to study the phenomena, and how to explain the findings. Questions about methodology are the major focus of chapter 2, but we mention the problem here because it is important to realize that the meaning of terms used may reflect the **epistemology**—or system of beliefs and values—that a researcher holds. For example, a researcher who defines sex as two distinct biological categories will be more likely to assume that any differences found between men and women reflect underlying biological differences, whereas a researcher who defines sex as a social category is more likely to assume that any differences found between men and women relate to how we create social perceptions and social arrangements. The first three readings introduce you to the prevailing epistemologies used to understand questions of sex and gender.

Research and Epistemological Beliefs

Although all researchers function with either an implicit or explicit epistemology, researchers often do not articulate their epistemological perspective. Only recently, as the traditional scientific enterprise has been challenged from a variety of perspectives, has the issue of a researcher's belief system come to the forefront. In particular, feminist scholars have been willing to publicly examine and debate the various assumptions that influence their research agenda. In a similar vein, researchers for years either did not bother to make clear what they meant when they used the terms *sex* and *gender,* or they assumed that we all understood what was meant by such terms (Unger, 1979). Recently there has been an increasing recognition of the necessity to clarify meaning.

The discussion of the meaning of sex and gender begins with the acknowledgment that *sex and gender are not synonymous terms,* but confusion remains about the precise meaning of the two terms. In the simplest version, the term **sex** is associated with characteristics of an individual that are rooted in biology, i.e., chromosomes and genes that allow for differences in physical appearance and, therefore, for the two categories of male and female. In contrast, **gender** refers to how social and cultural factors shape our reality and our sense of identity. In this view, gender is a **social category** of shared meanings about characteristics of maleness and femaleness and the behaviors, attitudes, and feelings associated with those characteristics. How we view ourselves and how others treat us will often be directly influenced by what position in the social category of gender we reside. For example,

in traditional heterosexual dating relationships, there are roles assigned to males and females. Typically men initiate the date, make the plans, and pay for both his and her expenses. Women respond to male initiatives. Of course, not everyone follows these social roles. When these roles are violated, however, people are often acutely aware that their behavior or the behavior of others is in violation of a social expectation. Clearly these social roles have no biological mandate—we are not hardwired to either pay or not pay for a movie or dinner, to respond "yes" or "no" to an invitation to a party, or to open doors or smile at bad jokes.

Does the distinction between sex and gender help us sort out how to use the terms *sex* and *gender,* and does it avoid the distortions in meaning that often crop up in common usage when the term *gender* is used as a more "politically correct" version of the term *sex*? This substitution of *gender* for *sex* can be particularly misleading. For example, a workshop leader refers to "the gender of all the participants as female," or a survey asks respondents to record their "gender." In both cases, the intention is to describe the sex of the person or people—according to the conventional biological distinction. Confounding sex and gender implies that the two are interchangeable.

The first article in this chapter, *Just What are Sex and Gender, Anyway?* by Douglas Gentile, makes clear that tremendous confusion still exists in both everyday usage and in the research literature about the meaning of the terms *sex* and *gender*. In this article, Gentile discusses the different ways that the terms *sex* and *gender* have been used by researchers and the confusions that have resulted from such usage. To clarify the semantic ambiguities he identifies, Gentile proposes the use of five terms: **sex, biologically sex-linked, gender-linked traits, sex-and-gender-linked traits,** and **sex-correlated traits.** The essential distinction that underlies all these terms for Gentile is between sex as a biological entity and gender as a sociocultural entity. Furthermore, Gentile proposes terminology that isolates causality as either biological, sociocultural, or indeterminate. Gentile believes that if researchers would identify whether they are examining phenomena that are caused either by biological or sociocultural factors, and then use *sex* to refer to biologically-based phenomena and *gender* to refer to sociocultural-based phenomena, the confusion among terms would be eliminated. He calls on researchers to use terminology in such a way as to make explicit their view of causality.

In their responses to Gentile's article, Rhoda Unger and Mary Crawford *(Sex and Gender—The Troubled Relationship Between Terms and Concepts)* and Kay Deaux *(Sorry, Wrong Number—A Reply to Gentile's Call)* respond to the claim that more precise language would eliminate the confusion over sex and gender and would clarify assumptions of causality. They contend that the issues at stake in this discussion are not merely of a semantic nature but relate to the different epistemological and conceptual frameworks that researchers have. Several related reasons explain why the use of a standard vocabulary will not readily alleviate the existing confusion. First, the confusion in meaning between the terms *sex* and *gender* often results from implicit assumptions about causality held not just by the researcher but by the *reader* of that research. Furthermore, the requirement that biological attributes be linked with sex and sociocultural attributes with gender may lead readers to assume that the causes of sex differences are solely biological and the causes of gender differences are cultural. Even more problematic is the naive view that sex differences cause gender differences. There is serious disagreement about the nature of the relationship between sex and gender. The use of the terms *biologically sex-linked* and *gender-linked,* as proposed by Gentile, will not clarify researchers' presuppositions about *how* sex and gender are related. A second related issue is that this simple and somewhat compelling focus on terminology obscures the difficult task facing researchers in explaining the complexity of the relationship between biological and sociocultural influences. Like most researchers today, we believe that both sex and gender emerge from a complex interaction of biological and sociocultural factors that cannot be divided up in terms of a specific contribution from nature and nurture. The challenge facing

researchers is to provide a detailed account of this interaction. This challenge will not be resolved by a researcher's choice of terminology.

A third issue is that gender exists at many different levels of analysis. In part, the level of analysis chosen by researchers reflects the discipline from which they work. Psychologists are interested in explanations that focus on processes within the individual or that focus on interactions between individuals (intrapsychic or interpersonal explanations). Other disciplines, such as sociology, anthropology, or political science, focus on institutional, social, or cultural explanations. Clearly all types of explanations aid our understanding of gender, and we use the research from these other disciplines in this book, although our emphasis is on *psychological* explanations. One very influential perspective that illustrates a different level of analysis is offered by West and Zimmerman (1987). They contend that gender is not primarily related to individuals but is created out of institutional allocation of resources and the social status and identities that particular social arrangements demand. According to their view, we do not "have a gender," rather, we are always engaged in the act of gender, namely, "doing gender," because gender arrangements pervade our social interactions and cultural arrangements. Their work shows how the level of analysis that researchers use significantly influences their conceptualization of gender, which in turn influences the kinds of questions researchers will ask.

Finally, the standardization of terminology that Gentile proposes will not ameliorate the usage dilemma because underlying the terminology (*sex* vs. *gender*) may be unstated beliefs about the causes of sex and gender. Therefore, the meaning of each term could shift in accord with who was using the term.

SEX AND GENDER: DICHOTOMY OR CONTINUUM?

Much of the research in psychology uses sex as a means of dividing the population into two groups or categories, which is defined as treating **sex as a**

subject variable. This approach is used in almost all the sex differences research. There are, however, some serous limitations to the use of sex as a subject variable. One concern about the comparison of males and females is that a finding of a sex difference is often accompanied by an assumption that sex differences arise from biological factors. Also, the practice of dividing research subjects by sex treats the resulting groups of males and females as though they are *categorically* different—meaning that there would be no overlap in the characteristics of people labeled female versus male and that the behavior of males and females could be easily distinguished based solely on membership of one of the sex categories. You should recognize that these are false assumptions. Of course there are similarities between males and females, and of course we cannot accurately predict someone's behavior simply by knowing their sex.

Challenging Categories

Western culture typically classifies humans as either male or female based on reproductive capacity, but this dichotomy does not capture the experiences of individuals in all cultures nor does it apply to all members of the animal kingdom (Unger and Crawford, 1996). One example that illustrates the variability in the relationship between sex and behavior are people called berdache, who are members of several northwestern American Indian societies. According to Williams (1986), the berdache are individuals who, although biologically male, embrace certain "female" customs and behaviors, often engage in sexual relations with other men, and are accorded special status within their society. Williams discusses other variations on the sex/gender continuum, such as amazon women, also North American Indians, who were women, but who dressed as men, married women, and could achieve social status as hunters. Important distinctions for both berdache and amazons are that sexuality is not a defining characteristic related to gender and that both berdache and amazons might, over the course of a lifetime, have sexual relationships with both men and women. According to Williams, American Indians considered sexuality a private matter, and sexual identity, unlike gender identity, was of little importance. This variability demonstrates that we should not assume a universal relationship between sex and gender.

The berdache and amazons represent variations in the relationship between sex and gender; however, anatomically they are males and females, respectively. There are people whose anatomy varies from the categories of male and female. The article by Anne Fausto-Sterling, *The Five Sexes: Why Male and Female Are Not Enough,* presents several cases of individuals who can be classified as **intersexed** because they possess varying amounts of male and female biological characteristics. They can be grouped into three categories: **true hermaphrodites** are individuals who have the reproductive organs of both males and females (one ovary and one testis), **male pseudohermaphrodites** are individuals who have testes and some female genital characteristics but no ovaries, and **female pseudohermaphrodites** are individuals who have ovaries and some male genital characteristics but no testes. There are, as you might expect, wide variations in the exact biological makeup of individuals in each category, and even more significantly, we have very little empirical evidence about their lives and experiences. Fausto-Sterling asserts that the variations of intersexuality provide evidence that sex is not a dichotomous variable but rather is better conceived of as a continuum.

Why does the inclination to categorize people persist so strongly? Certainly intersexuality is not a new phenomenon, and individuals have lived their lives as intersexed people. The reason, according to Fausto-Sterling, is that Western culture has such a strong ideological stake in the categorical distinction between male and female that any deviations that occur are immediately treated medically so that the individual conforms as much as possible to one of the sex categories. In actuality, writes Fausto-Sterling, before the evolution of medical technology, individuals born intersexed seemed to have identities that successfully incorporated their anatomical variations. The cases described by Fausto-Sterling suggest that these individuals were not particularly unhappy or distressed about their sexuality or gender identity.

Currently, the use of chromosomal tests virtually guarantees that physicians will assign an infant to one of the sex categories if that infant's appearance is ambiguous. In order to "create" an identity that is consistent with the infant's assigned sex, the child may undergo surgery and hormonal therapies so that anatomy and sex identity are as closely matched to one of the two sex categories as possible. Thus, a child born today is unlikely to live with an ambiguous sex identity because of ambiguous genitals or reproductive capacity. The examples presented by Fausto-Sterling illustrate the complexity involved in understanding the relationship between chromosomes, reproductive capacity, genital appearance, and identity as either male or female.[1] It is important to understand the role that culture plays in influencing expectations, and Western cultures convey a powerful expectation that genital appearance will conform to one of two sex identities. A further expectation is that sex identity will determine a person's sexual orientation and preferred gender role. Thus sex, gender, and sexuality are closely *prescribed* in our society.

There are individuals whose identities do not closely match cultural conventions with regard to gender. For example, **transsexual,** or **transgendered,** individuals have a sex identity that is different from their biological sex (e.g., men who believe they are, or should be, women). Another manifestation of the variations in the relationship between sex and gender is the phenomena of "gender blending" described by Devor (1989). The gender blenders interviewed by Devor are women who are commonly mistaken for men. Most of these women have been routinely mistaken for men (or boys) since childhood, and each has a distinctly masculine appearance and manner. These women all have a female gender identity (meaning that they all "know" themselves to be women, and none, at the time of Devor's research, desired to change that), although they vary in their sexual orientation; some are exclusively heterosexual, some are lesbian, and others have changed from heterosexual or bisexual to lesbian. For these women, the relationship between appearance and sexuality illustrates some of the fluid nature of gender and sexuality. One woman describes her conflict between her masculine appearance and her sexual attraction to men. At one point in her life, she thought about undergoing a sex change operation but also realized that she would then become a gay man. For her, sexual attraction transcended her appearance as well as how other people perceived her. Other women underwent shifts in their sexual partners, from heterosexual to lesbian. For these women, the relationship between their appearance and their sexual experiences shifted their perceptions of their sexual orientation.

These gender blenders vary, also, in their reactions to being perceived as a man. For some women, being identified as a man is liberating—they feel freed from the constraints of the feminine gender role, and they enjoy the power and privilege of being male. For other women, the reasons for the mistaken identity seem mysterious or elusive—they are unsure why people mistake them for men, and they see the solution to be a slavish adherence to exaggerated femininity. They feel that social acceptance for women is dependent on an ultrafeminine appearance. Rejecting this, they are resigned to being mistaken for men but do not see it as an advantage.

The interplay between self-perception and the perception of others is constantly at the forefront in the lives of these women. But what about those of us who will never experience these sorts of confusions; is our experience shaped by how we see ourselves and how others see us? We believe the gender blenders highlight many of the ways we all experience gender. Women and men are treated differently and this treatment is both pervasive and subtle. We may not even be aware of it, unless, like gender blenders, we experience both sides.

We can look to science and scientific analysis as both a cause and consequence of treating sex as a dichotomy. In her article *Race and Sex as Biological Categories,* Ruth Hubbard documents the efforts of scientists to uncover the biological basis of race and sex. In both cases, scientists have gone to extraordinary lengths to "create" differences where none can be detected. So nineteenth- and twentieth-century biologists sought to find distinctions between blacks and whites, males and females, in ways that would conform to prevailing social and cultural standards. Creating a hierarchy of intelligence, psychologists in the 1920s argued that blacks and ethnic minority immigrants were inherently inferior to whites while ignoring vast differences in literacy, economic opportunities, and education (Gould, 1981). According to Hubbard, there is no biological basis for the categorization of race—because of extensive interbreeding, human populations are genetically similar as a species, with about 90 percent of genetic variation shared by all national, racial, or ethnic groups. The simple fact is that biology does not provide us with a means to distinguish African Americans from Caucasian Americans. If race is not a distinct biological entity, then what is it? Race, like gender, is a social category. Individual identity is marked by physical characteristics, e.g., skin tone, hair texture, facial features for race; presence or absence of breasts, hair length and style, height, breadth of shoulders, posture for gender. We are perceived by others to belong to one of the social categories of race and sex, and assumptions about us and treatment based on social stereotypes about race and gender follow from this categorization.

With regard to gender, Hubbard argues that biological arguments about sex often resort to descriptions of reproductive function that are laden with cultural meaning but little biological reality. Hormones are described as male (androgens, meaning "generator of male") and female (estrogens, meaning "gadfly") when in fact both males and females secrete all hormones and in relatively similar proportions. Race and sex represent social categories that are laden with historical and cultural meaning and are related to positions of privilege and power in our society. The scientific analysis of race and sex is not likely to succeed without accounting for differences among people based on economic opportunity, cultural context, and the social meaning attributed to race and sex.

DEFINING WHO WE ARE: INTERSECTIONS OF RACE, CLASS, ETHNICITY, AND GENDER

The first readings in this chapter help you understand the complexities involved in defining sex and gender. Gender is only a part of our identity; we are also known by and know ourselves by other social categories, such as race, social class, ethnic group, religion, or age. We need to recognize that these aspects of identity are related to gender. In the last reading (*Toward a New Vision: Race, Class, and Gender as Categories of Analysis and Connection*), Patricia Hill Collins offers an examination of how race, class, and gender intersect and interact. Our culture makes distinctions among people based on such characteristics as race, social class, ethnic group, and age. To understand the impact of gender on identity, we must also understand it with regard to other dimensions that are significant in the formation of individual identity as well as highly salient in influencing what expectations others have of us and how we will be treated. Collins provides insight into how to think about the relationship among the various dimensions that make up individual identity. Most importantly, identity cannot be divided neatly into category membership (e.g., black vs. white, Latino vs. Anglo, male vs. female) because each person is a unique blending of features. Thus, the social perception of individuals as representative of membership in a category misrepresents the complex and unique features of identity. Collins argues that we should not reduce individual identity to any particular social category.

Collins treats these aspects of identity as interlocking facets of social oppression. In her analysis of oppression, she argues that the categorizing of individuals—black versus white, male versus female, poor versus rich—promotes false dichotomies that reduce complex identities to superficial characteristics. Many times, one characteristic may be made visible at the same time that other equally significant characteristics may be made invisible, such as when behavior is analyzed according to sex while ignoring race and social class. Collins proposes that we pay careful attention to the intersections of race, class, and gender, aiming at understanding the ways in which these dimensions interact with each other and with systems of power and privilege.

Social Categories and Power

Collins argues that identity and experiences are shaped by the relationship of the individual's identity to power and privilege in society. For individuals, their awareness of different aspects of identity may reflect their experiences with systems of power and oppression. An African American man who has been repeatedly stopped by the police for questioning may be very conscious of his identity with regard to both race and sex. He may be very much aware that the police find him especially suspicious because he is both black and male. Neither African American women nor white men or women are likely to share that experience, although each will interpret and understand his experience from their unique vantage point. This example illustrates the inextricable links between race and gender in terms of how they are experienced by the individual and how they are perceived by others. Power is an important dimension of human interaction and a feature of gender relationships. In subsequent chapters, we discuss power in analyzing stereotypes, interpersonal relationships, and social institutions. Power is also an important part in the interrelationship of race, class, and gender. People's experiences with power vary in relationship to the complexities of their identity.

One manifestation of power is seen in the way that some social categories are considered normative in society. The language by which we refer to the relationship of one social group to another shows this power—for example, *majority versus minority, dominant culture, mainstream society* all reflect the idea of one "standard" culture against which all others will be judged. In her analysis of "white privilege and male privilege," McIntosh (1988) argues that there are unacknowledged privileges associated with being white and/or male in our society. She offers numerous examples of her experiences with the privileges of being white, such as being free to move into any neighborhood without the fear of resentment by neighbors, being in the majority in most public settings, never

being treated as representative of her race, or readily finding greeting cards that portray people that look like her. These examples show the pervasive and subtle forms of privilege that define race and gender identity. In a similar vein, the recent furor over admission of women to The Citadel and the Virginia Military Institute exemplifies the powers of male privilege. After bitter legal battles and facing the loss of the substantial federal money that supported their institutions, both have agreed to admit women. Immediately each institution issued statements that "nothing would change" and that women would have to conform to the male standards—all hair would be cut above the ears, everyone would have to meet the existing physical fitness requirements, only a few accommodations for privacy, such as doors and window shades, would be made. We were struck that there was no question that the existing norms would remain the same. Why is *normal* assumed to be the male standard? No attempt would be made to redefine the institution norms now that women would be admitted: Why not, for example, require all cadets to wear skirts, institute new courses in cooperative learning, or set physical fitness standards to require endurance or pain tolerance?

Often, these power dynamics are not governed by conscious attempts of people or groups of people to defend their privileges; rather, members of privileged classes exist with relative ease and comfort in our society because their identity is considered normative. This analysis is helpful because considerations of power and privilege are often misunderstood to imply that "all men" or "all whites" exert power over women or blacks. Not only is this assumption not true, but individuals of these privileged groups—male and white—may themselves be subject to social class, religious, or ethnic discrimination or may be victimized by homophobia.[2] Pleck (1981) argues that among men, compulsive heterosexuality creates power distinctions such that gay men are discriminated against and are often denied access to typical masculine privilege. The relationship between heterosexuality and male power is so strong that when men avoid competition or share their power, they may be assumed to be gay. Power hierarchies, therefore, exist among men as well as between men and women.

According to Frankenburg, "whiteness" in our society operates as an "unmarked" category (Frankenburg, 1993). Frankenburg describes middle-class, white feminists who, when asked to describe the uniqueness of their cultural heritage, were at a loss, sometimes resorting to sarcasm or humor by answering "Wonder Bread" or "Heinz 57." For these women, their cultural heritage so represented the cultural mainstream that they were unaware of it and could not comfortably name it. Frankenburg argues that the relative power of their position (vis-à-vis race and social class) allows for the privilege of asserting their nonawareness of their "category membership." With regard to gender, maleness has often been accorded the privilege of being an unmarked category.

In psychology, much of the development of theory and research excluded women (Bohan, 1993). In this way, white male behavior has been held to be the standard against which others might be judged. The consequence of this standard is that the search for differences is shaped by a narrow perspective on what would be considered normative. Using white, male behavior as the norm, that which is feminine or represents other racial or ethnic perspectives is considered different or deviant or deficient. When social categories are defined as normative, such as *white* and *male* are, they often are treated as prescriptive—the way people are "supposed" to be. The reality of people's life experience rarely conforms to these social prescriptions. Attending to the intersections and interactions among sex, gender, class, ethnicity, and race may make it possible to develop a more complex and nuanced portrait of the influence of social categories on behavior and experience.

THE ROOTS OF DIFFERENCE: ESSENTIALISM VERSUS SOCIAL CONSTRUCTION

An examination of the social categories of gender inevitably leads to questions of difference—Are women and men different from each other? In what ways and how significant are these differences? Psychologists have studied sex differences between men and women in many areas—emotions, social behavior, aggression, cognitive ability, personality. The debate over the existence and magnitude of differences is vigorous, as is the question of whether to study sex differences at all. Both these issues are examined in detail in chapter 2. Two contrasting perspectives can be used to understand the study of differences. One contrasting perspective is the differences between **essentialism** and **social constructionism.** The second is the contrast between **maximalists** and **minimalists.** We use these contrasting perspectives in many places later in the book, and you will want to understand their definitions and be alert for examples of each as you read the articles in this book.

The contrast between essentialism and social constructionism refers to the underlying meaning of observed sex differences. One belief is that observations of behavioral differences must reveal essential sex differences. This position is known as essentialism. Essentialism portrays gender as resident within the individual and inextricably linked to that individual's sex. Essentialist theories about sex differences portray those differences as qualities of individuals that exist in all situations and generally are separable from the social and cultural context of life. Most psychologists, but not all, who represent the essentialist perspective assume that differences between females and males are biological in origin, and they study the neurological, hormonal, or evolutionary bases of sex differences. In addition to biological evidence, essentialists use cross-cultural similarities as evidence to support the argument for universal sex differences. From the essentialist point of view, cross-cultural similarities may be used to support the notion that there are *essential* qualities associated with sex. The important distinction of this point of view is that gender is seen as a characteristic of individuals, most likely caused by underlying biological factors that distinguish women from men. (See Bohan, 1993, for a more detailed analysis of essentialism.)

Social constructionism represents another perspective on the meaning of sex and gender differences. Rather than search for universal sex differences, social constructionists argue that gender is a product of social or cultural transactions or arrangements. According to the social constructionist perspective, gender differences emerge out of social arrangements that shape the experiences of people, sometimes in relationship with one's sex. The study of sex differences from the social constructionist perspective would examine the *conditions* under which a difference is more or less likely to occur, would examine the *beliefs* of individuals with regard to sex role stereotypes, or would consider cross-cultural *variation* as evidence that gender is socially constructed.

An initial understanding of the contrast between essentialism and social constructionism might inappropriately compare it to the classic nature/nurture dichotomy in which essentialism would be compared to nature and social constructionism would be compared to nurture. The nature/nurture debate, however, revolves around the *causes* of gender—biological or social—whereas the dichotomy between essentialism and social constructionism is about the *location* of gender—within the individual (essentialism) or within social arrangements (social constructionism). The processes referred to as nurture (socialization, parental treatment, enculturation) may contribute to the social construction of gender, but they, by themselves, are not responsible for gendered behavior. Let's consider an example that illustrates some of the important differences between essentialism and social constructionism.

A behavioral observation that both essentialists and social constructionists might make is that women are often more involved in taking care of children than are men. The two psychologists would offer very different explanations for this observation, and herein lies the basic difference between these two perspectives. The essentialist would cite the biological differences between men and women as accounting for this difference in behavior. Women give birth and nurse babies, men do not. She might posit the existence of a maternal instinct and thereby claim that the behavior of women is rooted in their biological nature. The social con-

structionist would cite various social institutions, cultural traditions, social constraints, or opportunities to account for this difference in behavior. She might note the various ways in which women are rewarded for taking care of children, or stigmatized for not doing so, as among the many social forces that originate and sustain this behavioral difference. Traditional social arrangements are such that women are more likely to care for infants than are men—but nothing in the nature of either men or women dictates this social arrangement. According to the social constructionist view, social changes such as increased economic opportunities for women might lead to an increase in men taking primary responsibility for child care. Nothing in the biological nature of men prevents them from being caretakers, and nothing in the biological nature of women compels them to be caretakers.

The second contrast that we use to understand the study of sex differences is the difference between maximalists and minimalists. This dichotomy refers to the *emphasis* placed on the meaning of differences. Gender maximalists claim to observe large differences between the behavior of men and women and often believe that these differences are deeply rooted. These psychologists are likely to believe that differences are highly resistant to efforts to change them. Gender minimalists claim that differences between women and other women, and between men and other men, are larger than the observed differences between women and men. They deny that the gender "divide" has either the depth or the breath that gender maximalists describe. This distinction is not the same as the distinction between essentialism and social constructionism. Some essentialists and some social constructionists may regard the gender divide as very wide and very deep despite their differences about the origins of the divide. Similarly, some essentialists and some social constructionists may agree that the gender divide is not very wide or very deep while disagreeing about the causes for the narrow and shallow divide that they both acknowledge. Each of these distinctions, essentialism versus social constructionism and gender maximalism versus gender minimalism, are important to keep in mind while reading the articles in this book. How psychologists approach the study of gender can be significantly influenced by their (often unstated and implicit) assumptions concerning these distinctions.

SOCIAL CHANGE AND POLITICAL AGENDAS

The readings in this chapter are all consistent on one point—gender can mean many different things. By close examination we can become aware of the presuppositions that underlie differing meanings of gender. All the perspectives introduced in these readings have political and social meanings. The belief that sex and gender are ordered so that sex determines gender implies that social change in gender relationships may be either impossible, undesirable, or unnatural. On the other hand, the belief that gender is socially constructed from social and cultural prescriptions suggests that changes in the relationship between gender and behavior may be possible or even inevitable, arising from changing historical, social, cultural, or economic conditions.

Understanding the political implications of different theoretical positions is important because gender relationships are not equal. Many characteristics attributed to men, such as intelligence, bravery, persuasiveness, strength, power, and so on, are highly prized, and men are often valued because of their presumed masculinity. (Of course, the discovery that a particular man does not always possess such characteristics may have negative consequences for him because it undermines his presumed masculinity.) On the other hand, characteristics often deemed feminine—dependence, empathy, compromise, sensitivity, emotionality—in some circumstances are not highly valued. Women may suffer as a result of their association with femininity. Women and men are judged on the degree to which they conform to traditional gender roles. We should also note that people have differing experiences with what are presumed to be social prescriptions about gender roles. Historically, African American women would be unlikely to become dependent or emotionally frail—these qualities are inconsistent with the social and economic constraints on their lives. Thus, qualities of femininity, by which women are judged, are not of equal value or equally accessible under all circumstances. In a similar vein, as you will read in chapter 4, Lazur and Majors (1995) argue that men of color develop versions of masculinity that are consistent with their particular cultural perspective, although they are challenged to conform to the larger social norms of male dominance, economic success, and power. One example these authors offer is that of Native American men, who strive for economic autonomy and success under political conditions that have systematically denied them access to paths for economic progress. Native American men may struggle with their tribal identity, which stresses interdependence and community, and the larger American cultural ideal, which stresses independence and autonomy.

In general, however, men have a position of advantage in this society, whereas women are subject to disadvantages because of their sex. When sexism exerts itself in a pervasive way, it becomes a form of social oppression. The fact that women did not achieve the right to vote until 1920 represents not only sexism but social oppression. A more contemporary observation, that most women who are murdered are killed by their husbands or partners, is another example of oppression. Women's relative lack of political power and social value can be linked to this social pattern.

Sexism arises out of social organizations that favor men and masculinity over women and femininity. Although most of us can identify obvious sexism— for example, women are forbidden from working in a particular factory because the work is deemed too strenuous—we are often in disagreement over subtler forms of discrimination. Is it discriminatory to reduce a woman's job responsibilities when she returns to work following the birth of a child? Is it discriminatory to pay the highly successful coach of a college football team more than the equally successful coach of a softball team? The analyses presented in this chapter suggest that sexism can only be understood fully by taking into account the complex nature of identity—both from the point of view of the individual's experience and from the social perspective that categorizes and objectifies individuals. **Feminism** is one attempt to redress sexism and provide alternative explanations for gendered phenomena. Feminism is not for women only. Many new scholars work in an area known as Men's Studies, and many of them consider themselves feminist (Kimmel and Messner, 1995). One perspective of this new scholarship on men uses a social constructionist framework to discover the impact of socially prescribed gender roles on the experiences of men.

Social oppression is complex and related to multiple facets of individual experience, most especially social class, race, ethnicity, and sexual orientation. As Patricia Hill Collins points out, it is important to consider sexism, racism, classism, ethnocentrism, or heterosexism from the point of view of the individual's experience. This perspective can be invaluable in helping us understand how various facets of identity are experienced. Throughout this book, we urge caution in generalizing about gender without taking into account differences and similarities among people. Unfortunately researchers have not always been so careful about incorporating diversity into their analyses, and therefore our knowledge of how gender interacts with other features of identity is limited (Landrine, 1995). Feminist psychologists have identified many biases in theory and research and provide alternative explanations for gendered phenomena. Feminist psychology has also responded positively to the charge that psychology has been centered on the experiences of largely white, middle-class women, and newer analyses of gender pay attention to social, racial, ethnic, and sexual diversity (Landrine, 1995). New ways of thinking about the intersection of identity may also facilitate social change. Collins advocates building coalitions across the boundaries of identity that allow people to examine the common elements of their experience. A feminist perspective on gender is helpful in this regard because it encourages us to assess the effects of sexism on individual experience and social organization.

THE PERSPECTIVE OF THIS BOOK

Before you begin your journey through the study of gender, you should know a bit about our point of view. We are both developmental psychologists and that perspective has deeply influenced how we look at gender. In chapter 6 *(Gender Identity Development)* you learn about gender from this perspective and in other places through the book when we examine how adults change over time. We are also feminists, which means that we recognize the existence of biases in the way women have been treated, both in psychology and the world at large. As feminist psychologists, we hope to link new ways of understanding the influences of gender with new models for relationships among people, especially as they impact the treatment of women. This does not mean that we will dictate to you what social changes we advocate, nor does it mean that we are not interested in social change that will improve social conditions for men. Rather, we will present to you areas in which change may be beneficial, and we hope you will begin to develop your own ideas about social change. We believe that you will come to see that social change will inevitably influence the experiences of women and men and that social change is not a win-lose proposition that pits men against women.

This chapter introduces you to the complexities of defining the terms *sex* and *gender*. We want to clarify our usage of these terms. We use *sex* when referring to research in which people have been divided into the categories of male and female. We also use *sex* when the intended distinction is between individuals who differ in anatomy. We use *gender* when talking about sociocultural stereotypes or prescriptions related to sex. We look upon those characteristics that can be thought of as masculine and feminine as representative of gender. For example, when describing the process whereby children come to identify themselves categorically as male or female and adopt socially proscribed behaviors in accord with that knowledge, we use the term *gender identity*. A person can "do gender" by responding in a gendered way in a particular circumstance.

Gendered behavior may reflect a person's socialization (e.g., when young boys play competitive games, and as adult men, treat interpersonal interactions as a win-lose game) or it may be elicited by circumstances (e.g., the death of a loved one elicits tears of grief). Our usage of the terms *sex* and *gender* follows the tradition of Deaux and Unger and Crawford. You should be aware that not all the authors whose work we have selected for this book follow the same guidelines for usage, and you will want to be alert to nuances of differences and underlying meaning in the terms.

We have emphasized to you that it is important to understand the theoretical perspective of a researcher, that is, his/her epistemological position. Consequently, here are our own thoughts about the essentialist versus social constructionist distinction. Many aspects of social constructionism appeal to us. We are certainly persuaded that there is no *essential* relationship between sex and gendered behavior, and the social constructionist perspective offers a way to contextualize gendered behavior and experiences that reflects the position that gender does not reside within the individual. However, there are weaknesses of the social constructionist point of view that we believe are noteworthy. In its strictest form, social constructionism holds life experience to be continually constructed and reconstructed by the individual, and therefore, empirically derived generalizations would not be a valid source of understanding. Social constructionism also calls into question the notion of a stable individual identity—identity is continually constructed through social transactions. Two of the most central elements of psychology—the value of generalizing from carefully conducted empirical research and the notion of the individual—are challenged by social constructionism (Unger, 1995). Although we detail for you in chapter 2 the difficulties of conducting empirical research on sex and gender, we do believe in its potential value to contribute useful information to the study of gender. Like Unger, we would like to see an increase in research on gender that is mindful of the diversity of people's experience and identity. With regard to the issue of a "stable identity," as developmental psychologists, we accept the notion that individuals change; however, the social constructionist perspective implies that each individual's history and circumstances are always unique, and therefore it is impossible to find elements of comparison across people or groups. While we are enthusiastic about efforts to distinguish the uniqueness of individual identity, we believe, like Patricia Hill Collins, that it is important to build coalitions across groups by finding common elements in their experiences. We would hope that, carefully utilized, some of the tools of traditional psychological research would advance this effort. Thus we are scientists who are interested in observations, questionnaires, and experiments and in the traditional statistical analysis of the results of such research. In chapter 2, you learn more about traditional empirical research—its weakness and potential value. We are also enthusiastic about the addition of feminist methods to psychology and value the contributions added by qualitative and phenomenological approaches as well as ethnomethodology. With regard to the role of biology in understanding sex and gender, we believe it is naive to assume that biology plays no role in our understanding of gender. We are not essentialists, however, and believe that many biological phenomena interact with gender in complex and nontransparent ways. We believe that researchers should seek to understand the nature of this interaction and not assume that any discussion of biological factors inevitably leads to biological determinism.

Throughout the book, we have tried to represent diverse points of view; however, in some cases points that may be controversial are not necessarily articulated concisely and clearly in an article we might have included for reading. We alert you to areas of conflict or disagreement among scholars, and you may want to read further about issues raised in our selections. Most of all, we hope that this collection of readings introduces you to some unexplored areas of psychology, encourages you to think critically about research in psychology, and helps you understand yourself and others as gendered people in a gendered society.

NOTES

1. We use the term **sex identity** to refer to a person's labeling of themselves as either male or female.
2. In this context, **homophobia** refers to the fear among men of being thought by others to be gay or of association with gay men. **Heterosexism** refers to the presumption that all people are, or should be, heterosexual. Both of these are manifestations of power and represent different aspects of discrimination based on sexual orientation. Some critics object to the use of the term *homophobia* because of the implications that homosexuality is something to be feared (Herek, 1995).

REFERENCES

Bohan, J. (1993). Regarding gender: Essentialism, constructionism, and feminist psychology. *Psychology of Women Quarterly, 17,* 5–21.

Devor, H. (1989). *Gender blending: Confronting the limits of duality.* Indianapolis, IN: Indiana University Press.

Frankenburg, R. (1993). *White women, race matters: The social construction of whiteness.* Minneapolis: University of Minnesota Press.

Gould, S. J. (1981). *The mismeasure of man.* New York: Norton.

Herek, G. M. (1995). Psychological heterosexism in the United States. In A. R. D'Augelli & C. J. Patterson (Eds.), *Lesbian, gay, and bisexual identities over the lifespan: Psychological perspectives.* Washington, DC: American Psychological Association.

Kimmel, M. S., & Messner, M. A. (1995). *Men's lives.* (3rd ed.). Boston: Allyn and Bacon.

Landrine, H. (Ed.). (1995). *Bringing cultural diversity to feminist psychology.* Washington, DC: American Psychological Association.

Lazur, R. F., & Majors, R. (1995). Men of color: Ethnocultural variations of male gender role strain. In R. F. Levant & S. Pollack (Eds.), *A new psychology of men* (pp. 337–358). New York: Basic Books.

McIntosh, P. (1988). *White privilege and male privilege: A personal account of coming to see correspondences through work in Women's Studies* (Working Papers). Wellesley, MA: Wellesley College Center for Research on Women.

Pleck, J. (1981). *The myth of masculinity.* Cambridge, MA: MIT Press.

Unger, R. K. (1979). Toward a redefinition of sex and gender. *American Psychologist, 34,* 1085–1094.

Unger, R. (1995). Conclusion: Cultural diversity and the future of feminist psychology. In H. Landrine (Ed.), *Bringing cultural diversity to feminist psychology: Theory, research and practice* (pp. 413–432). Washington, DC: American Psychological Association.

Unger, R., & Crawford, M. (1996). *Women and gender: A feminist psychology.* (2nd ed.). New York: McGraw-Hill.

West, C., & Zimmerman, D. H. (1987). Doing gender. *Gender & Society, 1,* 125–151.

Williams, W. L. (1986). *The spirit and the flesh: Sexual diversity in American Indian culture.* Boston: Beacon Press.

Just What Are Sex and Gender, Anyway?
A Call for a New Terminological Standard

DOUGLAS A. GENTILE

Abstract—*The terms sex and gender have come to be used as synonyms in the social sciences literature. However, nothing has been gained by the use of the term gender except confusion. This article identifies five meanings for which social scientists often use the terms sex or gender and proposes a distinct term for each of those five meanings. The terms proposed are (1) sex: to refer to the biological function; (2) biologically sex-linked: to refer to traits or conditions that are causally biologically related to being male or female; (3) gender-linked: to refer to traits or conditions that are causally linked with maleness or femaleness but are culturally based as opposed to biologically based; (4) sex- and gender-linked: to refer to traits or conditions that are causally related to both a biological component and a cultural component; and (5) sex-correlated: to refer to traits or conditions that are related to being male or female without asserting a causal relation to either biology or culture (because we do not wish to make such an assertion or cannot do so confidently). It is hoped that adopting a terminological standard will reduce the confusion resulting from nonspecific language use.*

As I read the literature, I find that when an author uses either the term *sex* or the term *gender,* I am usually at a loss for its intended meaning. We in the behavioral sciences use the terms sex and gender in at least five distinct ways. It is unfortunate that it is rarely clear which meaning of the term is intended. The purpose of the present article is twofold. First, I wish to draw attention to the lack of terminological

Address correspondence to Douglas A. Gentile, Institute of Child Development, 51 East River Rd., Minneapolis, MN 55455; e-mail: gentile@turtle.psych.umn.edu.

clarity as it currently exists and the difficulties presented by this lack of clarity. Second, I wish to propose a standard vocabulary for each of the meanings to help solve the problem.

Sex, as the word is commonly used in the journals, can mean one of at least five things:

1. Sexual intercourse and related behavior.
2. Traits or conditions that are causally biologically linked with the condition of being male or female and are often carried genetically on sex chromosomes.
3. Traits or conditions that are causally linked with maleness or femaleness but are culturally based rather than biologically based.
4. Traits or conditions that are causally linked with both a biological component and a cultural component.
5. Traits or conditions that are linked with being male or being female but for which no claim is made for a causal relation with either culture or biology (because the author does not wish to make such an assertion or because no causal relation is known).

The term gender is used increasingly to mean each of the latter four meanings above. Thus, the terms are becoming synonymous and losing what unique meaning they originally had (described below). This lack of technical specificity causes confusion, for both authors and readers. For example, if an author is investigating "the relationship between sex and mathematics performance," it is unclear whether the investigation concerns sociocultural issues (such as differential treatment of boys and girls in school), biological issues (such as the heritability of mathematical aptitude), or other issues (such as whether self-reports of the frequency of sex are related to math performance).

This confusion can be remedied in one of two ways. Either authors can explain the theoretical beliefs underlying their use of the words sex and gender in everything they write, or they can adopt a common vocabulary which will make clear what the authors mean.

The former suggestion has the merit of increasing clarity, but it also increases the wordiness of publications and still leaves each author with his or her own definitions of sex and gender. Thus, I favor the latter suggestion. I propose that we adopt a vocabulary standard such that when a researcher speaks of a "gender difference," we all understand automatically what the researcher's theoretical position is. There is nothing radical in this suggestion. Professionals in all fields define their vocabularies so that they can speak to other professionals and understand each other. I devote the remainder of this article to exploring the histories of the words sex and gender (and their derivatives) and then suggesting a distinct technical term for each of the five distinct meanings.

The word sex in English can be traced back to at least 1312 meaning "either of the two divisions of organic beings distinguished as male and female respectively; the males or the females (of a species, etc., esp. of the human race) viewed collectively" (*Oxford English Dictionary, OED,* 1989, Vol. XV, p. 107). This meaning has had the longest history in English. Furthermore, this meaning has had the richest history. The first, second, and third definitions of sex in the *OED* (1989) all have to do with the quality of being biologically male or female. Some examples follow:

> 1382 Wyclif *Gen.* vi. 19 Of alle thingis hauynge sole of ony flehs, two thow shalt brynge into the ark, that maal sex and femaal lyuen with thee. [Rough translation: Of all things having soul or flesh, two thou shalt bring into the ark, the male sex and the female.] (Vol. XV, p. 107)
>
> 1865 Dickens *Mut. Fr.* II. i, It was a school for both sexes. (Vol. XV, p. 107)

The third definition, part b, is sexual intercourse.

The fifth definition concerns the many combination words, a few of which are germane here: sex difference, sex stereotype, sex typed, sex role. Thus, the word sex has long been used referring to the maleness or femaleness of human beings.[1]

Gender, in contrast, has only recently come to be used in this manner. The first definition of gender is "kind, sort, class; also, genus as opposed to species" (*OED,* 1989, Vol. VI, p. 427). The second definition refers to gender as a technical linguistic term: "each of the three (or in some languages two) grammatical 'kinds', corresponding more or less to the distinctions of sex (and absence of sex) in the objects denoted . . . discriminated according to the nature of the modification they require . . ." (*OED,* 1989, Vol. VI, p. 427). These uses of gender also trace their history back to the 14th century.

Only within the past 30 years has gender started to become a synonym for sex. "In mod[ern] (esp. feminist) use, [the term gender is] a euphemism for the sex of a human being, often intended to emphasize the social and cultural, as opposed to the biological, distinctions between the sexes" (*OED,* 1989, Vol. VI, p. 428). Examples follow:

> 1963 A. Comfort *Sex in Society* ii. 42 The gender role learned by the age of two years is for most individuals almost irreversible, even if it runs counter to the physical sex of the subject. (Vol. VI, p. 428)
>
> 1972 A. Oakley *Sex, Gender & Society* viii. 189 Sex differences may be 'natural', but gender differences have their source in culture. (Vol. VI, p. 428)

Many professionals seem to have embraced this distinction between sex and gender. Grossly speaking, sex refers to biology and gender refers to environment. This distinction is reasonable. Unfortunately, this distinction was also breaking down as gender entered the vernacular.

Gender has come to be used as a euphemistic synonym for all the meanings of sex except sexual intercourse. As I assess the situation, this usage has come about out of some sense that the word gender is somehow more polite (or more politically correct) than the word sex. Thus, on questionnaires, I frequently see respondents asked to indicate their gender, that is, whether they are biologically male or female. This sloppy usage has become quite prevalent. University presidents have begun using the term this way: "equal rights and protections . . . regardless of race, religion, color, gender, national origin, disability, age, veteran status or sexual orientation" (Hasselmo, 1990, p. 7). Geraldine Ferraro referred to herself as "the first of her gender" to achieve nomination to the vice presidency (cited in Safire, 1984). I personally find this usage of the term to be the most damaging. No distinction between the two words is being made. In these examples, the word gender is used to refer to biological sex—whether people are male or female. I fail to see any reason to change the meaning of a word because it is more "polite." However, personal distaste aside, this usage only further obfuscates the meanings of both sex and gender. In these cases, we do not gain anything through the use of the term gender as opposed to sex. There is no new nuance of meaning nor any recently emerged phenomenon that the word gender now denotes. Under this usage, neither term has any unique meaning. Given that there are at least five distinct meanings of these terms among which we wish to distinguish, we should have five terms that have distinct meanings.

I have argued that the behavioral and social sciences need a new vocabulary standard so that we can better understand one another. I now attempt to propose and justify such a standard.

The first definition of sex I distinguished was the biological function, sexual intercourse and related behavior. I do not know what term other than "sex" could be used for this.

The second definition I distinguished was that of traits biologically linked with being male or female. Examples of such traits are hemophilia and color blindness. For this definition, I propose the term "biologically sex-linked" traits. I admit that this phrase is somewhat cumbersome, but it is unambiguous.

In defense of this term, I note first that the *OED* (1989) defines the term sex-linked primarily as "being or determined by a gene that is carried on a sex chromosome" (Vol. XV, p. 112). Examples of this usage date back to at least 1905.

The major distinction I propose to make between sex and gender is one of biology versus culture. Thus, a person's sex is a matter of biological fact. A person's gender is a matter of cultural relativity. "Biological sex" is therefore redundant to me. However, it appears to be useful to use the modifier biological in order to make the distinction perfectly explicit.

The third definition I distinguished was that of traits that are linked with being male or female and that have a cultural or societal basis. For example, American men are supposed to be more aggressive than American women, and women are supposed to be more nurturing than men. For this definition, I propose the term "gender-linked" traits.

In defense of this term, as stated earlier, the *OED* does define gender as a modern euphemism emphasizing the social and cultural distinctions between males and females. Furthermore, this usage of gender is already common among many social scientists.[2]

The fourth definition I distinguished was that of traits that are linked with being male or female and that have both a biological and a societal basis. An example might be that women are typically the primary caregivers for children. For this definition, I propose the term "sex- and gender-linked" traits.

This proposed term is my least favorite, but it has the advantage of being logically consistent with the previous terms. Furthermore, it is explicit that the trait in question is theoretically expected to have both biological and cultural bases.

The fifth definition I distinguished was that of traits correlationally linked with being male or female, but having an unknown basis (or perhaps a basis one is not interested in asserting). An example might be any serendipitously found "sex difference" for which one does not want to claim a theoretical position on biology versus culture. For this definition, I propose the term "sex-correlated" trait.

In defense of this term, I assert that often this is all we know in the behavioral and social sciences. We usually find some difference between the males and females, but do not have enough evidence to "prove" that this difference is due to genes or the environment. When this is the case, all we know is that the difference found is correlated with the biological sex of the subjects.

However, it should be mentioned that researchers often have a theoretical reason for believing that a difference found is biologically based or culturally based. In these cases, the researcher is encouraged to use the terms biologically sex-linked or gender-linked, as described above. In general, the distinction I am proposing is that sex- or gender-*linked* implies a causal relation, whereas sex-*correlated* does not.

To summarize, social scientists study and write about sex, biologically sex-linked traits or differences, gender-linked traits or differences, sex- and gender-linked traits or differences, and sex-correlated traits or differences. Unfortunately, however, the vocabulary used by authors has not been standardized. This state of affairs has caused problems of not being able to understand easily whether an author is making a theoretical distinction about the cause of the partic-

ular sex-correlated difference found. A vocabulary standard has been proposed. At its core is the distinction between the terms sex and gender. Sex is taken as a biological property (e.g., maleness/femaleness). Gender is taken as a cultural-societal property (e.g., masculinity/femininity). It would be beneficial to the science to adopt the proposed terms or any other set of distinct terms and use them consistently.

I have discussed the terminology in relation to traits or differences. However, the proposed terms can easily be modified when writing about other sex-correlated behaviors, attitudes, roles, and norms. I hope that the proposed vocabulary distinctions will be helpful to authors, readers, and the social sciences.

Acknowledgments—I would like to thank J. Ronald Gentile, Anne Pick, and Willard Hartup for their helpful comments on earlier drafts. The writing of this article was supported by a Graduate School Fellowship from the University of Minnesota.

NOTES

1. The definitions I have not provided are not particularly relevant to the discussion here. However, they all are related to issues of division or biology (e.g., definition 4: "used, by confusion, in senses of *sect*"; *OED,* 1989, Vol. XV, p. 108).

2. I am, however, tempted to propose facetiously the term "group sex" to refer to socially produced gender roles. Knowing that this would only engender further confusions, I have resisted the inclination.

REFERENCES

Hasselmo, N. (1990, December 3). The U community is not living up to its ideals. *The Minnesota Daily,* p. 7.

Oxford English Dictionary (2nd ed.). (1989). Oxford: Clarendon Press.

Safire, W. (1984, August 5). Goodbye sex, hello gender. *The New York Times,* section 6, p. 8.

Commentary: Sex and Gender—
The Troubled Relationship Between Terms and Concepts

RHODA K. UNGER AND MARY CRAWFORD

Gentile (this issue) indicates that there is great confusion among social scientists about the appropriate use of the terms sex and gender and calls for a new terminological standard. Researchers who have been conducting studies in this area for many years can easily document examples of such confusion. For example, one of the leading journals concerned with the psychology of women and gender is called *Sex Roles*. And, occasionally, one can find a study in which rats are described as having a "gender," although it is hard to imagine that they have pink or blue bows on their tails as they run the maze (Unger & Crawford, 1992).

We do not believe, however, that simply tightening up our linguistic labels will reduce the confusion in this area. In this commentary, we review briefly the history of efforts to change terminology. The consequences of these efforts suggest that the problems are conceptual rather than terminological (Unger, 1983). Therefore, the issues must be addressed in terms of differing epistemologies involving sex-related causality that coexist within the field.

DEFINITIONS OF SEX AND GENDER: A BRIEF REVIEW

Gender was originally used as a term in linguistics to describe the formal rules that follow from masculine or feminine designation. In the mid-1970s, however, feminist scholars began to use the term to refer to the social organization of the relationship between the

sexes. They did so to insist upon the fundamental social quality of distinctions based on sex and to denote a rejection of the biological determinism implicit in the use of such terms as sex or sexual difference (Unger, 1979).

The connection to grammar is both explicit and full of unexamined epistemological possibilities (Scott, 1986). One of these unexamined possibilities is the fact that in many Indo-European languages, there is a third category—unsexed, or neuter. And there is some evidence to suggest that the existence of a third linguistic category can influence the way people think about sexual identity (Gailey, 1987; Herdt & Davidson, 1988).

In grammar, moreover, gender is understood as a way of classifying phenomena—a socially agreed upon system of distinctions rather than an objective description of inherent traits. However, masculine or feminine qualities may be assigned even to inanimate objects on the basis of their designated sex (Tobach, 1971). Similarly, societies prescribe particular characteristics for males and females on the basis of assigned sex (Vaughter, 1976; Weisstein, 1968). Thus, gender must be examined as a cultural as well as a linguistic phenomenon.

When cultural and biological distinctions are confused, researchers have tended to search for universal and essential biological differences between females and males (Russett, 1989; Shields, 1975; Unger, 1979). Therefore, the term gender has become popular with those individuals who wish to force a critical reexamination of the premises and standards of existing scholarly work (Crawford & Marecek, 1989; Hare-Mustin & Marecek, 1990; Unger, 1992). They see this term as a vehicle by which disciplinary paradigms can be fundamentally transformed.

Address correspondence to Rhoda K. Unger, Department of Psychology, Montclair State College, Upper Montclair, NJ 07043.

FEMINIST REEVALUATIONS OF THE SEX-GENDER DISTINCTION

Gender Is More Than Just Sex

The use of the term gender is complicated by the fact that it can be used at several different levels of analysis. Thus, gender-related processes have been shown to influence behavior, thoughts, and feelings within the person as well as interactions among individuals (Deaux & Major, 1987). In addition, gender helps to determine the structure of social institutions (Unger & Crawford, 1992). Confusions among these levels may obscure analyses of the origins of sex-related differences and the processes that maintain them.

Feminist psychologists were, for example, interested in the concept of androgyny because it allowed them to view the healthy individual as someone who possessed traits considered stereotypically appropriate for both sexes (Bem, 1974). But androgyny can be limiting if one does not consider the social context in which gender-related behaviors are played out (Lott, 1981). Traditional masculine traits such as instrumentality are highly valued in our society. They are rewarded in women as well as men. Thus, instrumental traits appear to contribute to self-esteem more than affective qualities do (Whitley, 1983). This finding might lead one to conclude that androgyny is good for women but not for men. But it is sex-asymmetrical social transactions that account for this difference rather than the traits themselves. With this kind of analysis, there is no need to reify traditional male-female dichotomies.

Other feminist researchers have also explored the situational nature of sex-gender differences (Deaux, 1984; Eagly, 1987). While their findings are much too extensive to recount in a brief article, it is important to note that sex-related differences are more likely to emerge under public scrutiny than in private, that they are more likely to be found as a function of roles than as a function of sexual categories, and that they are often a product of social expectations and the self-fulfilling prophecy (cf. O'Leary, Unger, & Wallston, 1985).

Psychologists have been most interested in aspects of gender that operate at the intrapsychic level. Other social scientists have been more interested in gender at the structural level. Gender and social roles are often confused because roles are sex segregated. Gender as a social distinction also influences access to power and resources (Sherif, 1982). Such confounds have led to an overemphasis on internal sources of variability. Thus, the biological and personological sources of sex-related differences are stressed and cultural factors may be ignored.

The Nature-Nurture Controversy

Although the distinction between sex and gender has proved to be conceptually provocative, it has not resolved most of the epistemological issues in the field. Unfortunately, the distinction (as well as the more elaborated categories proposed by Gentile) continues to reify a dichotomy between nature and nurture. With the possible exception of very specific reproductive behaviors, however, it is not possible to determine how much of a particular trait or behavior is influenced by biological versus social factors (Money, 1987). Complex interactions are the rule, not the exception.

Distinctions between sex and gender also assume that whereas gender is problematic, sex-related effects are consistent and stable. There is considerable evidence, however, that sex is neither simply dichotomous nor necessarily internally consistent in most species (Unger, in press). Physicians concerned with the medical management of sexual anomalies in young infants appear to recognize that they may construct a child's sex while, at the same time, they attempt to convey information about essential sex to concerned parents (Kessler, 1990).

Studies of sexually dysphoric individuals (also known as transsexuals) also suggest that sex as well as gender may be socially constructed. Surgical treatment of transsexuals confirms traditional social constructions of maleness and femaleness (Eichler, 1980; Raymond, 1979). It opts for massive, permanent changes in the body rather than acceptance of the idea that roles and bodies may be independent. It ignores the possibility that the connection between biology and behavior is imposed by the cultural standards for each sex.

TOWARD AN EXPLICIT DISCUSSION OF CAUSALITY

The problem of distinctions between sex and gender is due to unresolved conflicts within psychology about the causality of various sex-linked phenomena rather than to the terms used. As noted earlier, feminist scholars tend to use the term gender because they prefer to emphasize social and cultural explanations for most differences between females and males. They also recognize that "biological" does not mean immutable and that biology-behavior interactions work in both directions.

Some other researchers in the area have come to use the term gender apparently because they believe that the term sex has become somehow politically incorrect. Still others appear to use the two terms interchangeably, as synonyms. What vocabulary people use seems to be driven by their assumptions about causality. It is possible, therefore, to find instances of the same trait or behavior described in different terms by different groups of investigators.

Attempts to clarify terminology in this area have not met much success. The addition of new terms to the mix will probably not prove to be any more effective until issues of causality are made more explicit. Since, however, all of us would agree that most human behaviors include both biological and sociocultural components, a conservative recommendation is that psychologists continue to modify terminology. We recommend that they use language that indicates relatedness and avoid terms such as sex difference or sexually dimorphic. These practices will enable us all to get on with the task of analyzing the multidimensional causes of all human variability.

REFERENCES

Bem, S. L. (1974). The measurement of psychological androgyny. *Journal of Consulting and Clinical Psychology, 42,* 155–162.

Crawford, M., & Marecek, J. (1989). Psychology reconstructs the female. *Psychology of Women Quarterly, 13,* 147–166.

Deaux, K. (1984). From individual differences to social categories: Analysis of a decade's research on gender. *American Psychologist, 39,* 105–116.

Deaux, K., & Major, B. (1987). Putting gender into context: An interactive model of gender-related behavior. *Psychological Review, 94,* 369–389.

Eagly, A. H. (1987). *Sex differences in social behavior: A social-role interpretation.* Hillsdale, NJ: Erlbaum.

Eichler, M. (1980). *The double standard: A feminist critique of feminist social science.* New York: St. Martin's Press.

Gailey, C. W. (1987). Evolutionary perspectives on gender hierarchy. In B. B. Hess & M. M. Ferree (Eds.). *Analyzing gender: A handbook of social science research* (pp. 32–67). Newbury Park, CA: Sage.

Hare-Mustin, R. T., & Marecek, J. (Eds.). (1990). *Making a difference: Psychology and the construction of gender.* New Haven, CT: Yale University Press.

Herdt, G. H., & Davidson, J. (1988). The Sambra "Turnim-man": Sociocultural and clinical aspects of gender formation in male pseudohermaphrodites with 5 alpha-reductase deficiency in Papua New Guinea. *Archives of Sexual Behavior, 17,* 33–56.

Kessler, S. J. (1990). The medical construction of gender: Case management of intersexed infants. *Signs, 16,* 3–26.

Lott, B. (1981). A feminist critique of androgyny: Toward the elimination of gender attributions for learned behavior. In C. Mayo & N. M. Henley (Eds.). *Gender and nonverbal behavior* (pp. 171–180). New York: Springer-Verlag.

Money, J. (1987). Propaedeutics of diecious G-I/R: Theoretical foundations for understanding dimorphic gender-identity/role. In J. M. Reinisch, L. A. Rosenblum, & S. S. Sanders (Eds.), *Masculinity/femininity: Basic perspectives* (pp. 13–28). New York: Oxford University Press.

O'Leary, V. E., Unger, R. K., & Wallston, B. S. (Eds.). (1985). *Women, gender, and social psychology.* Hillsdale, NJ: Erlbaum.

Raymond, J. (1979). *The transsexual empire: The making of the she-male.* Boston: Beacon Press.

Russett, D. N. (1989). *Sexual science.* Cambridge, MA: Harvard University Press.

Scott, J. W. (1986). Gender: A useful category of historical analysis. *American Historical Review, 91,* 1053–1075.

Sherif, C. W. (1982). Needed concepts in the study of gender identity. *Psychology of Women Quarterly, 6,* 375–398.

Shields, S. A. (1975). Functionalism, Darwinism, and the psychology of women: A study in social myth. *American Psychologist, 30,* 739–754.

Tobach, E. (1971). Some evolutionary aspects of human gender. *American Journal of Orthopsychiatry, 41,* 710–715.

Unger, R. K. (1979). Toward a redefinition of sex and gender. *American Psychologist, 34,* 1085–1094.

Unger, R. K. (1983). Through the looking glass: No Wonderland yet! (The reciprocal relationship between methodology and models of reality). *Psychology of Women Quarterly, 8,* 9–32.

Unger, R. K. (1992). Will the real sex difference please stand up? *Feminism & Psychology, 2,* 231–238.

Unger, R. K. (in press). Alternative conceptions of sex (and sex differences). In M. Haug, R. Whalen, C. Aron, & K. L. Olsen (Eds.), *The development of sex differences and similarities in behavior.* Dordrecht, The Netherlands: Kluwer Academic.

Unger, R. K., & Crawford, M. (1992). *Women and gender: A feminist psychology.* Philadelphia: Temple University Press.

Vaughter, R. M. (1976). Review essay: Psychology. *Signs, 2,* 120–146.

Weisstein, N. (1968). *Kinder, Kirche, Kuche as scientific law: Psychology constructs the female.* Boston: New England Free Press.

Whitley, B. E., Jr. (1983). Sex role orientation and self-esteem: A critical meta-analytic review. *Journal of Personality and Social Psychology, 44,* 765–785.

QUESTIONS OF DEFINITION

Commentary: Sorry, Wrong Number— A Reply to Gentile's Call

KAY DEAUX

Gentile (this issue) calls for a new terminological standard for the use of the terms sex and gender, suggesting that current usage is inconsistent, confusing, and scientifically uninformative. Although his reference list, consisting of one college newspaper, *The New York Times,* and the *Oxford English Dictionary,* provides no hint, many social scientists have debated how these terms should best be used (e.g., Deaux, 1985; Gould, 1980; Sherif, 1982; Unger, 1979).

My own preference, first stated in 1985, is to use sex when one is referring to any study or finding in which people are selected on the basis of the demographic categories of male and female. Thus, if one compares women with men, girls with boys, or male with female rats, one is making a sex comparison.[1] However, I advocate the use of gender when one is making judgments or inferences about the nature of femaleness and maleness, of masculinity and femininity. Thus, I argue for terms such as gender identity, gender stereotypes, and gender roles. Unger (1979) made a similar distinction in discussing differences between sex as a subject variable and as a stimulus variable. As she noted, "Gender may be used for those traits for which sex acts as a stimulus variable, independently of whether those traits have their origin with the subject or not" (1979, p. 1086).

Neither of these analyses presupposes the origins of any observed similarities or differences. For many people, however, the sex-versus-gender debate does connote causal assumptions. Thus, some would restrict the term sex to those behaviors that are biologically determined, and gender to those that are societally influenced.[2] This desire to identify causal factors also motivates Gentile to offer his resolution. Whatever appeal such a state of certainty may have, it is fundamentally unattainable.

Address correspondence to Kay Deaux, Graduate School and University Center, City University of New York, 33 West 42nd St., New York, NY 10036–8099.

Gentile's proposed solution substitutes five distinct but somewhat cumbersome terms for the currently popular two. He uses the first of his terms, "sex," to refer to biological functions. (Although Gentile is at a loss to find any other term for this domain, I suggest that "sexual behavior" is both explicit and widely understood.) Gentile's remaining four terms are intended to denote the causal basis of an observed difference between women and men. Thus, he offers the terms "biologically sex-linked" and "gender-linked" when the cause is known to be exclusively biological or sociocultural, respectively; "sex- and gender-linked" when both causes are known to contribute to the observed difference; and "sex-correlated" when the origin of an observed difference is unknown.

The critical question, of course, is how does one know? Science is a dynamic process, and the certainty of yesterday can easily be replaced by ambiguity today, or vice versa. In Gentile's scheme, such shifts in understanding would require changes in terminology. Thus, the biologically sex-linked behavior of one decade could be the gender-linked behavior of another, and the sex- and gender-linked behavior of yet another period. Or consider the case in which a difference thought to be biologically determined is modified by training (e.g., Conner, Schackman, & Serbin, 1978). Should such a pattern be called a biologically linked difference before training and a gender-linked similarity after training?

Gentile argues that when a researcher describes findings in areas related to sex and gender, the reader should always "understand automatically what the researcher's theoretical position is." I strongly disagree. For terminology to depend on theoretical stance when demographic categories are at issue only exacerbates confusion and proliferates terms. Why should the term sex be tied to a specific theoretical position any more than age, or sexual orientation, or linguistic grouping? Further, the belief that these terms can be linked to a specific set of circumstances belies the social construction processes that shape these categories.

I believe there is some value in using a term such as sex-correlated or sex-related (as distinct from sex-linked, which as Gentile shows is defined by the *Oxford English Dictionary* in terms of chromosomes). As an alternative to the term sex differences, the use of the term sex-related, as well as such conceptually similar terms as age-related, should signal the reader that sex is being used as a marker rather than a causal statement. Scientific caution would thus prevail over deterministic theories. The field of sex and gender has had more than its share of simplistic and wrongheaded assumptions over the past 100 years (e.g., Shields, 1975, 1982). Arguing for specific terminology on an assumption of scientific certainty risks adding to the record of misguided pronouncements.

NOTES

1. This distinction ignores, but does not preclude the existence of, individuals whose sex categorization is more ambiguous.
2. A similar debate is possible with regard to the use of race versus ethnicity. Again, these terms have often been used interchangeably although there is some tendency to use race when biological factors are implicated, and ethnicity when socialization is the dominant explanation (P.T. Reid, personal communication, September 23, 1992).

REFERENCES

Conner, J. M., Schackman, M., & Serbin, L. A. (1978). Sex-related differences in response to practice on a visual-spatial test and generalization to a related test. *Child Development, 49,* 24–29.

Deaux, K. (1985). Sex and gender. *Annual Review of Psychology, 36,* 49–81.

Gould, M. (1980). The new sociology. *Signs, 5,* 459–467.

Sherif, C. W. (1982). Needed concepts in the study of gender identity. *Psychology of Women Quarterly, 6,* 375–398.

Shields, S. A. (1975). Functionalism, Darwinism, and the psychology of women: A study in social myth. *American Psychologist, 30,* 739–754.

Shields, S. A. (1982). The variability hypothesis: The history of a biological model of sex differences in intelligence. *Signs, 7,* 769–797.

Unger, R. K. (1979). Toward a redefinition of sex and gender. *American Psychologist, 34,* 1085–1094.

CHECKPOINTS

1. Gentile argues that psychologists need to clarify their use of the terms *sex* and *gender*. He proposes five new terms that would identify researchers' beliefs about the causes of sex and gender—biological or social.

2. Unger and Crawford, in their response to Gentile, assert that the use of terminology is not standard because scholars differ in their views of the causes of sex and gender.

3. Deaux argues that science is dynamic and questions the assumption that scientists would know beforehand whether they were discussing biological or social causes of sex or gender.

To prepare for reading the next section, think about these questions: Is everyone either male or female?

1. What is the relationship between one's identity as male or female and one's identity as masculine or feminine?

2. Is race a biological category—such that people can be unequivocally sorted by their racial identity?

3. Why do scientists study race and sex differences?

4. Is science biased?

The Five Sexes:
Why Male and Female Are Not Enough

ANNE FAUSTO-STERLING

In 1843 Levi Suydam, a twenty-three-year-old resident of Salisbury, Connecticut, asked the town board of selectmen to validate his right to vote as a Whig in a hotly contested local election. The request raised a flurry of objections from the opposition party, for reasons that must be rare in the annals of American democracy: it was said that Suydam was more female than male and thus (some eighty years before suffrage was extended to women) could not be allowed to cast a ballot. To settle the dispute a physician, one William James Barry, was brought in to examine Suydam. And, presumably upon encountering a phallus, the good doctor declared the prospective voter male. With Suydam safely in their column the Whigs won the election by a majority of one.

Barry's diagnosis, however, turned out to be somewhat premature. Within a few days he discovered that, phallus notwithstanding, Suydam menstruated regularly and had a vaginal opening. Both his/her physique and his/her mental predispositions were more complex than was first suspected. S/he had narrow shoulders and broad hips and felt occasional sexual yearnings for women. Suydam's "feminine propensities, such as a fondness for gay colors, for pieces of calico, comparing and placing them together, and an aversion for bodily labor, and an inability to perform the same, were remarked by many," Barry later wrote. It is not clear whether Suydam lost or retained the vote, or whether the election results were reversed.

Western culture is deeply committed to the idea that there are only two sexes. Even language refuses

This article is reprinted by permission of THE SCIENCES and is from the March/April 1993 issue. Individual subscriptions are $21 per year in the U.S. Write to: The Sciences, 2 East 63rd Street, New York, NY 10021.

other possibilities; thus to write about Levi Suydam I have had to invent conventions—*s/he* and *his/her*—to denote someone who is clearly neither male nor female or who is perhaps both sexes at once. Legally, too, every adult is either man or woman, and the difference, of course, is not trivial. For Suydam it meant the franchise; today it means being available for, or exempt from, draft registration, as well as being subject, in various ways, to a number of laws governing marriage, the family and human intimacy. In many parts of the United States, for instance, two people legally registered as men cannot have sexual relations without violating anti-sodomy statutes.

But if the state and the legal system have an interest in maintaining a two-party sexual system, they are in defiance of nature. For biologically speaking, there are many gradations running from female to male; and depending on how one calls the shots, one can argue that along that spectrum lie at least five sexes—and perhaps even more.

For some time medical investigators have recognized the concept of the intersexual body. But the standard medical literature uses the term *intersex* as a catch-all for three major subgroups with some mixture of male and female characteristics: the so-called true hermaphrodites, whom I call herms, who possess one testis and one ovary (the sperm- and egg-producing vessels, or gonads); the male pseudohermaphrodites (the "merms"), who have testes and some aspects of the female genitalia but no ovaries; and the female pseudohermaphrodites (the "ferms"), who have ovaries and some aspects of the male genitalia but lack testes. Each of those categories is in itself complex; the percentage of male and female characteristics, for instance, can vary enormously among members of the same subgroup. Moreover, the inner lives of the people in each subgroup—their special needs and their problems, attractions and repulsions—have gone unexplored by science. But on the basis of what is known about them I suggest that the three intersexes, herm, merm and ferm, deserve to be considered additional sexes each in its own right. Indeed, I would argue further that sex is a vast, infinitely malleable continuum that defies the constraints of even five categories.

Not surprisingly, it is extremely difficult to estimate the frequency of intersexuality, much less the frequency of each of the three additional sexes: it is not the sort of information one volunteers on a job application. The psychologist John Money of Johns Hopkins University, a specialist in the study of congenital sexual-organ defects, suggests intersexuals may constitute as many as 4 percent of births. As I point out to my students at Brown University, in a student body of about 6,000 that fraction, if correct, implies there may be as many as 240 intersexuals on campus—surely enough to form a minority caucus of some kind.

In reality though, few such students would make it as far as Brown in sexually diverse form. Recent advances in physiology and surgical technology now enable physicians to catch most intersexuals at the moment of birth. Almost at once such infants are entered into a program of hormonal and surgical management so that they can slip quietly into society as "normal" heterosexual males or females. I emphasize that the motive is in no way conspiratorial. The aims of the policy are genuinely humanitarian, reflecting the wish that people be able to "fit in" both physically and psychologically. In the medical community, however, the assumptions behind that wish—that there be only two sexes, that heterosexuality alone is normal, that there is one true model of psychological health—have gone virtually unexamined.

The word *hermaphrodite* comes from the Greek names Hermes, variously known as the messenger of the gods, the patron of music, the controller of dreams or the protector of livestock, and Aphrodite, the goddess of sexual love and beauty. According to Greek mythology, those two gods parented Hermaphroditus, who at age fifteen became half male and half female when his body fused with the body of a

nymph he fell in love with. In some true hermaphrodites the testis and the ovary grow separately but bilaterally; in others they grow together within the same organ, forming an ovo-testis. Not infrequently, at least one of the gonads functions quite well, producing either sperm cells or eggs, as well as functional levels of the sex hormones—androgens or estrogens. Although in theory it might be possible for a true hermaphrodite to become both father and mother to a child, in practice the appropriate ducts and tubes are not configured so that egg and sperm can meet.

In contrast with the true hermaphrodites, the pseudohermaphrodites possess two gonads of the same kind along with the usual male (XY) or female (XX) chromosomal makeup. But their external genitalia and secondary sex characteristics do not match their chromosomes. Thus merms have testes and XY chromosomes, yet they also have a vagina and a clitoris, and at puberty they often develop breasts. They do not menstruate, however. Ferms have ovaries, two X chromosomes and sometimes a uterus, but they also have at least partly masculine external genitalia. Without medical intervention they can develop beards, deep voices and adult-size penises. . . .

Intersexuality itself is old news. Hermaphrodites, for instance, are often featured in stories about human origins. Early biblical scholars believed Adam began life as a hermaphrodite and later divided into two people—a male and a female—after falling from grace. According to Plato there once were three sexes—male, female and hermaphrodite—the third sex was lost with time.

Both the Talmud and the Tosefta, the Jewish books of law, list extensive regulations for people of mixed sex. The Tosefta expressly forbids hermaphrodites to inherit their fathers' estates (like daughters), to seclude themselves with women (like sons) or to shave (like men). When hermaphrodites menstruate they must be isolated from men (like women); they are disqualified from serving as witnesses or as priests (like women), but the laws of pederasty apply to them.

In Europe a pattern emerged by the end of the Middle Ages that, in a sense, has lasted to the present day: hermaphrodites were compelled to choose an established gender role and stick with it. The penalty for transgression was often death. Thus in the 1600s a Scottish hermaphrodite living as a woman was buried alive after impregnating his/her master's daughter.

For questions of inheritance, legitimacy, paternity, success to title and eligibility for certain professions to be determined, modern Anglo-Saxon legal systems require that newborns be registered as either male or female. In the U.S. today sex determination is governed by state laws. Illinois permits adults to change the sex recorded on their birth certificates should a physician attest to having performed the appropriate surgery. The New York Academy of Medicine, on the other hand, has taken an opposite view. In spite of surgical alterations of the external genitalia, the academy argued in 1966, the chromosomal sex remains the same. By that measure, a person's wish to conceal his or her original sex cannot outweigh the public interest in protection against fraud.

During this century the medical community has completed what the legal world began—the complete erasure of any form of embodied sex that does not conform to a male-female, heterosexual pattern. Ironically, a more sophisticated knowledge of the complexity of sexual systems has led to the repression of such intricacy.

In 1937 the urologist Hugh H. Young of Johns Hopkins University published a volume titled *Genital Abnormalities, Hermaphroditism and Related Adrenal Diseases.* The book is remarkable for its erudition, scientific insight and open-mindedness. In it Young drew together a wealth of carefully documented case histories to demonstrate and study the medical treatment of such "accidents of birth." Young did not pass judgment on the people he studied, nor did he attempt to coerce into treatment those intersexuals who rejected that option. And he showed unusual even-handedness in referring to those people who had had sexual experiences as both men and women as "practicing hermaphrodites."

One of Young's more interesting cases was a hermaphrodite named Emma who had grown up as a female. Emma had both a penis-size clitoris and a vagina, which made it possible for him/her to have "normal" heterosexual sex with both men and women. As a teenager Emma had had sex with a number of girls to whom s/he was deeply attracted; but at the age of nineteen s/he had married a man. Unfortunately, he had given Emma little sexual pleasure (although *he* had had no complaints), and so throughout that marriage and subsequent ones Emma had kept girlfriends on the side. With some frequency s/he had pleasurable sex with them. Young describes his subject as appearing "to be quite content and even happy." In conversation Emma occasionally told him of his/her wish to be a man, a circumstance Young said would be relatively easy to bring about. But Emma's reply strikes a heroic blow for self-interest:

> Would you have to remove that vagina? I don't know about that because that's my meal ticket. If you did that, I would have to quit my husband and go to work, so I think I'll keep it and stay as I am. My husband supports me well, and even though I don't have any sexual pleasure with him, I do have lots with my girlfriends.

Yet even as Young was illuminating intersexuality with the light of scientific reason, he was beginning its suppression. For his book is also an extended treatise on the most modern surgical and hormonal methods of changing intersexuals into either males or females. Young may have differed from his successors in being less judgmental and controlling of the patients and their families, but he nonetheless supplied the foundation on which current intervention practices were built.

By 1969, when the English physicians Christopher J. Dewhurst and Ronald R. Gordon wrote *The Intersexual Disorders,* medical and surgical approaches to intersexuality had neared a state of rigid uniformity. It is hardly surprising that such a hardening of opinion took place in the era of the feminine mystique—of the post–Second World War flight to the suburbs and the strict division of family roles according to sex. That the medical consensus was not quite universal (or perhaps that it seemed poised to break apart again) can be gleaned from the near-hysterical tone of Dewhurst and Gordon's book, which contrasts markedly with the calm reason of Young's founding work. Consider their opening description of an intersexual newborn:

One can only attempt to imagine the anguish of the parents. That a newborn should have a deformity . . . [affecting] so fundamental an issue as the very sex of the child . . . is a tragic event which immediately conjures up visions of a hopeless psychological misfit doomed to live always as a sexual freak in loneliness and frustration.

Dewhurst and Gordon warned that such a miserable fate would, indeed, be a baby's lot should the case be improperly managed; "but fortunately," they wrote, "with correct management the outlook is infinitely better than the poor parents—emotionally stunned by the event—or indeed anyone without special knowledge could ever imagine."

Scientific dogma has held fast to the assumption that without medical care hermaphrodites are doomed to a life of misery. Yet there are few empirical studies to back up that assumption, and some of the same research gathered to build a case for medical treatment contradicts it. Francies Benton, another of Young's practicing hermaphrodites, "had not worried over his condition, did not wish to be changed, and was enjoying life." The same could be said of Emma, the opportunistic hausfrau. Even Dewhurst and Gordon, adamant about the psychological importance of treating intersexuals at the infant stage, acknowledged great success in "changing the sex" of older patients. They reported on twenty cases of children reclassified into a different sex after the supposedly critical age of eighteen months. They asserted that all the reclassifications were "successful," and they wondered then whether reregistration could be "recommended more readily than [had] been suggested so far."

The treatment of intersexuality in this century provides a clear example of what the French historian Michel Foucault has called biopower. The knowledge developed in biochemistry, embryology, endocrinology, psychology and surgery has enabled physicians to control the very sex of the human body. The multiple contradictions in that kind of power call for some scrutiny. On the one hand, the medical "management" of intersexuality certainly developed as part of an attempt to free people from perceived psychological pain (though whether the pain was the patient's, the parents' or the physician's is unclear). And if one accepts the assumption that in a sex-divided culture people can realize their greatest potential for happiness and productivity only if they are sure they belong to one of only two acknowledged sexes, modern medicine has been extremely successful.

On the other hand, the same medical accomplishments can be read not as progress but as a mode of discipline. Hermaphrodites have unruly bodies. They do not fall naturally into a binary classification; only a surgical shoehorn can put them there. But why should we care if a "woman," defined as one who has breasts, a vagina, a uterus and ovaries and who menstruates, also has a clitoris large enough to penetrate the vagina of another woman? Why should we care if there are people whose biological equipment enables them to have sex "naturally" with both men and women? The answers seem to lie in a cultural need to maintain clear distinctions between the sexes. Society mandates the control of intersexual bodies because they blur and bridge the great divide. Inasmuch as hermaphrodites literally embody both sexes, they challenge traditional beliefs about sexual difference: they possess the irritating ability to live sometimes as one sex and sometimes the other, and they raise the specter of homosexuality.

But what if things were altogether different? Imagine a world in which the same knowledge that has enabled medicine to intervene in the management of intersexual patients has been placed at the service of multiple sexualities. Imagine that the sexes have multiplied beyond currently imaginable limits. It would have to be a world of shared powers. Patient and physician, parent and child, male and female, heterosexual and homosexual—all those oppositions and others would have to be dissolved as sources of division. A new ethic of medical treatment would arise, one that would permit ambiguity in a culture that had overcome sexual division. The central mission of medical treatment would be to preserve life. Thus hermaphrodites would be concerned primarily not about whether they can conform to society but about whether they might develop potentially life-threatening conditions—hernias, gonadal tumors, salt imbalance caused by adrenal malfunction—that sometimes accompany hermaphroditic development. In my ideal world medical intervention for intersexuals would take place only rarely before the age of reason; subsequent treatment would be a cooperative venture between physician, patient and other advisers trained in issues of gender multiplicity.

I do not pretend that the transition to my utopia would be smooth. Sex, even the supposedly "normal," heterosexual kind, continues to cause untold anxieties in Western society. And certainly a culture that has yet to come to grips—religiously and, in some states, legally—with the ancient and relatively uncomplicated reality of homosexual love will not readily embrace intersexuality. No doubt the most troublesome arena by far would be the rearing of children. Parents, at least since the Victorian era, have fretted, sometimes to the point of outright denial, over the fact that their children are sexual beings.

All that and more amply explains why intersexual children are generally squeezed into one of the two prevailing sexual categories. But what would be the psychological consequences of taking the alternative road—raising children as unabashed intersexuals? On the surface that tack seems fraught with peril. What, for example, would happen to the intersexual child amid the unrelenting cruelty of the school yard? When the time came to shower in gym class, what horrors and humiliations would await the intersexual as his/her anatomy was displayed in all its nontradi-

tional glory? In whose gym class would s/he register to begin with? What bathroom would s/he use? And how on earth would Mom and Dad help shepherd him/her through the mine field of puberty?

In the past thirty years those questions have been ignored, as the scientific community has, with remarkable unanimity, avoided contemplating the alternative route of unimpeded intersexuality. But modern investigators tend to overlook a substantial body of case histories, most of them compiled between 1930 and 1960, before surgical intervention became rampant. Almost without exception, those reports describe children who grew up knowing they were intersexual (though they did not advertise it) and adjusted to their unusual status. Some of the studies are richly detailed—described at the level of gym-class showering (which most intersexuals avoided without incident); in any event, there is not a psychotic or a suicide in the lot.

Still, the nuances of socialization among intersexuals cry out for more sophisticated analysis. Clearly, before my vision of sexual multiplicity can be realized, the first openly intersexual children and their parents will have to be brave pioneers who will bear the brunt of society's growing pains. But in the long view—though it could take generations to achieve—the prize might be a society in which sexuality is something to be celebrated for its subtleties and not something to be feared or ridiculed.

Race and Sex as Biological Categories

RUTH HUBBARD

The laws made of skin and hair fill the statute books in Pretoria. . . . Skin and hair. It has mattered more than anything else in the world.

—*Nadine Gordimer,* A Sport of Nature

Scientists, whose business it is to investigate things that matter in the world, have put a good deal of effort into examining the biological basis of differences not only in skin and hair but also in other characteristics that are assigned cultural and political significance. And they have sometimes made it appear as though the differences in power, encoded in the statute books (and not only those in Pretoria), were no more than the natural outcomes of biological differences. This became critically important in the eighteenth century, when support for the aims of the revolutions fought for liberty, equality, fraternity and for the Rights of Man needed to be reconciled with the obvious inequalities between nations, the "races," and the sexes.

As late as the sixteenth century some authors described the peoples of Africa as superior in wit and intelligence to the inhabitants of northern climes, arguing that the hot, dry climate "enlivened their temperament,"[1] and two centuries later Rousseau still rhapsodized about the Noble Savage. Yet beginning in the fifteenth century Africans became human chattel, hunted and sold as part of the resources Europeans extracted from that "dark and primitive" continent. The industrialization of Europe and North America depended on the exploitation of the native populations of the Americas and Africa, and so it became imperative to draw distinctions between that small number of men who were created equal and everyone else. By the nineteenth century the Noble Savage was a lying, thieving Indian, and Africans and their enslaved descendants were ugly, slow, stupid, and in every way inferior to Caucasians. Distinctions also needed to be drawn between women and men, since, irrespective of class and race, women were not included among "all men" who had been created equal.

Although there are many similarities in the ways biologists have rationalized the inequalities between the races and sexes (and continue to do so to this day), this discussion will be clearer if we look at the arguments separately.

THE RACES OF MAN

Allan Chase[2] dates scientific racism from the publication of Malthus's *Essay on Population* in 1798 and argues that it focused on class distinctions among Caucasians rather than on distinctions between Caucasians and the peoples of Africa, America, and Asia. On the other hand, Stephen Jay Gould[3] points to Linnaeus (1758) for the first scientific ranking of races. Linnaeus arranged the races into different subspecies and claimed that Africans, whom he called *Homo sapiens afer,* are "ruled by caprice," whereas Europeans *(Homo sapiens europaeus)* are "ruled by customs." He also wrote that African men are indolent and that African women are shameless and lactate profusely.

Both dates occur more than two centuries after the beginning of the European slave trade, which became an important part of the economies of Europe and the Americas. But they are contemporary with the intellectual and civic ferment that led to the American and French revolutions (1776 and 1789, respectively) and to the revolution that overthrew slavocracy in Haiti (1791). As Walter Rodney has pointed out,[4] it is wrong to think "that Europeans enslaved Africans for racist reasons." They did so for economic reasons, since without a supply of free African labor they would not have been able "to open up the New World and to use it as a constant generator of wealth. . . . Then, having become utterly dependent on African labour, Europeans at home and abroad found it necessary to rationalize that exploitation in racist terms."

Nineteenth-century physicians and biologists helped with that effort by constructing criteria, such as skull volume and brain size, by which they tried to prove scientifically that Africans are inferior to Caucasians. Gould's *Mismeasure of Man* describes some of the measurements and documents their often patently racist intent. Gould also illustrates the apparent naïveté with which, for example, the famous French scientist Paul Broca discarded criteria (such as the ratio of lengths of the long bones in the lower and upper arm, because it is greater in apes than humans) when he could not make them rank white men at the top. And he shows how Broca and the U.S. craniometer Samuel George Morton fudged and fiddled with their data in order to make the rankings come out as these men knew they must: white men on top, next Native American men, then African-American men. Women were problematic: though clearly white women ranked below white men, were they to be above or below men of the other races? A colleague of Broca's wrote in 1881, "Men of the black races have a brain scarcely heavier than that of white women."[5]

In 1854 an American physician, Dr. Cartwright, wrote in an article entitled "Diseases and Peculiarities of the Negro" that a defect in the "atmospherization of the blood conjoined with a deficiency of cerebral matter in the cranium . . . led to that debasement of mind which has rendered the people of Africa unable to take care of themselves."[6] And racialist biologisms did not end with slavery. Jim Crow theorizing and practices survived until past the passage of the Civil Rights Act of 1957. Writing during World War II, Gunnar Myrdal marveled that the American Red Cross "refused to accept Negro blood donors. After protests it now accepts Negro blood but segregates it to be used exclusively for Negro soldiers. This is true at a time when the United States is at war, and the Red Cross has a semi-official status."[7] The American Red Cross continued to separate the blood of whites and African Americans until December 1950, when the binary classification into "Negro" and "white" was deleted from the donor forms. As Howard Zinn remarks, "It was, ironically, a black physician named Charles Drew who developed the blood bank system."[8]

What can we in the 1990s say about the biology of race differences? Looking at all the evidence, there are none.[9] Demographers, politicians, and social scientists may continue to use "race" to sort people, but, as a biological concept, it has no meaning. The fact is that, genetically, human beings *(Homo sapiens)* are a relatively homogeneous species. If Caucasians were to disappear overnight, the genetic composition of the species would hardly change. About 75 percent of known genes are the same in all humans. The remaining 25 percent exist in more than one form, but all these forms occur in all groups, only sometimes in different proportions.[10] Another way to say it is that, because of the extent of interbreeding that has happened among human populations over time, our genetic diversity is pretty evenly distributed over the entire species. The occasional, relatively recent mutation may still be somewhat localized within a geographic area, but about 90 percent of the variations known to occur among humans as a whole occur also among the individuals of any one national or racial group.[11]

Another important point is that, for any scientific measurement of race difference, we first have to construct what we mean by race. Does the least trace of African origins make someone black, or does the least trace of Caucasian origins make someone white? The U.S. census for 1870 contained a third category, "Mulatto," for "all persons having any perceptible trace of African blood" and warned that "important scientific results depend on the correct determination of this class."[12] The U.S. census for 1890 collected information separately for "quadroons and octoroons"—that is, people who have one grandparent or one great-grandparent who is African, respectively, "while in 1930, any mixture of white and some other race was to be reported according to the race of the parent who was not white." Finally, in 1970 the Statistical Policy Division of the Office of Management and Budget warned that racial "classifications should not be interpreted as being scientific or anthropological in nature."[13] We need only look at the morass of legalisms in apartheid South Africa to abandon any notion that there are clear racial differences.

Yet we read such statistics as that "black men under age 45 are ten times more likely to die from the effects of high blood pressure than white men," that "black women suffer twice as many heart attacks as white women," and that "a variety of common cancers are more frequent among blacks . . . than whites."[14] At the same time some scientists and the media keep stressing the genetic origin of these diseases. So, must we not believe once again that there are inherent, biological differences between blacks and whites, as groups?

A closer look again leads us to answer no. What is misleading is that U.S. health statistics are usually presented in terms of the quasibiological triad of age, race, and sex, without providing data about employment, income, housing, and the other prerequisites for healthful living. Even though there are genetic components to skin color, as there are to eye or hair color, there is no biological reason to assume that any one of these is more closely related to health status than any other. Skin color ("race") is no more likely to be related biologically to the tendency to develop high blood pressure than is eye color.

On the other hand, the median income of African Americans since 1940 has been less than two-thirds that of whites. Disproportionate numbers of African Americans live in more polluted and rundown neighborhoods, work in more polluted and stressful workplaces, and have fewer escape routes out of these living and work situations than whites have. Therefore, it is not surprising to find large discrepancies in health outcomes between these groups.

Mary Bassett and Nancy Krieger, looking at mortality risks from breast cancer, have found that the black-white differential of 1.35 drops to 1.10 when they look at African-American and white women of comparable social class, as measured by a range of social indicators.[15] And within each "racial" group

social class is correlated with mortality risk. Thus, although it is true that African-American women, as a group, are at greater risk of dying from breast cancer than white women are, women of comparable class standing face a similar risk within these groups as well as between them. In other words, because of racial oppression, being black is a predictor of increased health risk, but so is being poor, no matter what one's skin color may be.

SEX DIFFERENCE

That having been said, what about sex? Here, too, it can be argued that, since in our society any muting of differences between women and men is intolerable, this insistence may exaggerate biological differences and, therefore, enhance our impressions of them.[16] (Note the use of the phrase "the opposite sex" instead of "the other sex.") In fact, women and men exhibit enormous overlaps in body shape and form, strength, and most other parameters. The diversity within the two groups is often as large as the differences between them. Yet biological differences exist as regards women's and men's procreative capacities. Our society may exaggerate and overemphasize them, but the fact is that people who procreate need to be of two kinds. Therefore, the question I want to look at is to what extent ideological commitments to the differences our society ascribes to women and men in the social and political spheres influence the ways biologists describe the differences that are involved in procreation.

To do this it is useful to start with a quick look at Darwin's theory of sexual selection, which embedded Victorian preconceptions about the differences between women and men in modern biology. Sex is important to Darwin's theory of evolution by natural selection because the direction evolution takes is assumed to depend crucially on who mates with whom. This is why Darwin needed to invent the concept of sexual selection—the ways sex partners choose each other. Given the time in which he was writing, it is not surprising that he came up with the Victorian paradigm of the active, passionate, sexually undiscriminating male who competes with every other male in his pursuit of every available female, while females, though passive, coy, and sexually unenthusiastic, are choosy and go for "the winner." Darwin theorized that this makes for greater competition among males than females, and, since competition is what drives evolution by natural selection, males are in the vanguard of evolution. Females get pulled along by mating with the most successful males. The essentials of this interpretation have been incorporated into modern sociobiology.[17] Only in the last few years feminist sociobiologists, such as Sarah Blaffer Hrdy, have revised this canon and pointed out that females also can be active, sexually aggressive, and competitive and that males can nurture and be passive. Among animals as well as among people females do not just stand by and wait for the most successful males to come along.[18]

I have criticized the Darwinian paradigm of looking at sex differences elsewhere.[19] The point I want to stress here is that, until quite recently, the active male–passive female dyad has been part of biological dogma and is the metaphor that informs standard descriptions of procreative biology at every level.

For example, the differentiation of the sex organs during embryonic development is said to proceed as follows: the embryo starts out sexually bipotential and ambiguous, but early during embryonic development in future males something happens under the influence of the Y chromosome which makes part of the undifferentiated, primitive gonads turn into fetal testes. These then begin to secrete fetal androgens (called male hormones), which are instrumental in masculinizing one set of embryonic ducts so that they develop into the sperm ducts and external male genitalia (the scrotal sac and penis), whereas another set of ducts atrophies. The story goes on to say that, if at this critical point no Y chromosome is present, then *nothing happens.* In that case somewhat later, and without special hormonal input, another part of the undifferentiated fetal gonad differentiates into ovaries, and, since these do *not* secrete androgens, the other set of fetal ducts differentiates into the fallopian tubes, uterus, vagina, and the external female genitalia (the labia and clitoris).

Notice that in this description male differentiation is active and triggered by the Y chromosome and by so-called male hormones; female differentiation happens because these triggering mechanisms are absent.[20] Of course, this cannot be true. All differentiation is active and requires multiple inputs and decision points. Furthermore, the so-called sex hormones are interconvertible, and both males and females secrete all of them and, for considerable parts of our lives, in not very different proportions. Diana Long Hall has described the history of the discovery of these hormones and the ways gender ideology was incorporated into designating them "male" and "female."[21] Anne Fausto-Sterling has noted that the Greek names that scientists gave them are also ideology laden. The "male" hormone is called androgen, the "generator of males," but there is no gynogen, or generator of females. Instead, the "female" analogue of androgen is called estrogen, from *oestrus,* which means "frenzy" or "gadfly."[22]

The standard description of fertilization again follows the traditional script.[23] Ejaculation launches sperm on its dauntless voyage up the female reproductive tract. In contrast, eggs are "released," or "shed," from the ovary to sit patiently in the fallopian tubes until a sperm "penetrates" and "activates" them. Given that fertilization is an active process in which two cells join together and their nuclei fuse, why is it that we say that a sperm *fertilizes* the egg, whereas eggs are fertilized? In 1948 Ruth Herschberger caricatured this scenario in her delightful book *Adam's Rib,*[24] but that did not change the standard biological descriptions.

Of course, both sessile eggs and sprightly sperm are fabrications. Eggs, sperm, and the entire female reproductive tract must participate if fertilization is to take place, and infertility can result from the malfunctioning of any one of them. Also, a good deal goes on in eggs both before and after fertilization. It is interesting that modern biologists have been so focused on the role of the sperm and on chromosomes and genes that they have paid much more attention to the fact that, during fertilization, eggs and sperm contribute the same number of chromosomes than to the important part the egg's cytoplasm plays in the differentiation and development of the early embryo. The egg contributes much more than its nuclear chromosomes; it contributes all its cell contents—the cytoplasm, with its complement of cytoplasmic DNA and its subcellular structure and metabolic apparatus.

Finally, let us turn to the surely objective realm of DNA molecules. Here we find an article, published in December 1987 in the professional journal *Cell* and immediately publicized in the weekly scientific magazine *Science* and in the daily press, entitled "The Sex-Determining Region of the Human Y Chromosome Encodes a Finger Protein."[25] The authors claimed, and the magazines and newspapers promptly reported, that sex is determined by a single gene, located on the Y chromosome. The X chromosome, the authors wrote, has a similar gene, but it has nothing to do with sex differentiation. Reading the article more closely, we see that the authors identified a region of the Y chromosome which seemed to be correlated with the differentiation of testes. When this region was missing no testes developed; when it was present they did. By this argument the presence or absence of testes determines sex: people who have testes are male; people who don't are female.

More recently, in December 1989, two other groups of scientists claimed that the region on the Y chromosome which the previous group had identified as "determining sex" does not "determine" either maleness or sex because males can develop testes in its absence,[26] but that has simply refocused the search for *the sex* gene elsewhere on the Y chromosome. None of these authors points out that being female implies more than not having testes and that the differentiation of sex organs, whether female or male, requires processes of differentiation in which many genes as well as other metabolites must be involved.

CONCLUSIONS

I have selected these examples to illustrate the ways in which our particular cultural preoccupations with race and sex penetrate the biological sciences. But I do not want this analysis to suggest that it is useless to attempt to describe nature or, indeed, society in scientific ways. In fact, throughout this article I have drawn on scientific work to argue against scientific claims that exhibit racial or gender bias. Science remains one of the better ways we have of trying to understand what goes on in the world. But when we use it to investigate subjects such as race and sex, which are suffused with cultural meanings and embedded in power relationships, we need to be wary of scientific descriptions and interpretations that sustain or enhance the prevailing political realities.

To look critically at these kinds of data and interpretations, we need to bear in mind that in any society that is stratified by gender or race the fact that we are born with "female" or "male" genitals and "black" or "white" skin means that we will live different lives. Yet our biology and how we live are dialectically related and interpenetrate each other. The differences in our genital anatomy or in the color of our skin affect the ways we live, and our ways of life affect our biology.

For these reasons the scientific methodology of research into sex or race differences is intrinsically flawed. Scientists cannot vary genital anatomy or skin color and hold the environment constant, nor can they switch the cultural conditions that differentiate the environments of African Americans and whites or of women and men. Therefore, scientists cannot sort the effects of biology from societal influences. Scientists can catalog similarities and differences between women and men and between African Americans and whites, but they cannot establish their causes.[27]

One last point: I have looked at race and sex as separate categories, but we must not forget that they have also been combined to generate the cultural images of the eroticized, exotic African, male and female, and of the debased, sexualized African American, the black rapist, pimp, and whore. Social scientists and philosophers have only begun to explore the significance and ramifications of this melding of racism and sexism.[28] Scientists, and indeed all of us, need to become aware of the multiple meanings of these images and metaphors and to grasp the extent to which they penetrate our consciousness, collectively and as individuals, if we are to free the ways we think about race, sex, and gender from the subtle as well as the more blatant stereotypes that permeate our culture.

NOTES

1. Londa Schiebinger, *The Mind Has No Sex? Women and the Origins of Modern Science* (Cambridge: Harvard University Press, 1989), 165.

2. Allan Chase, *The Legacy of Malthus: The Social Costs of the New Scientific Racism* (New York: Alfred Knopf, 1977).

3. Stephen Jay Gould, *The Mismeasure of Man* (New York: W.W. Norton, 1981), 35.

4. Walter Rodney, *How Europe Underdeveloped Africa* (Dar-es-Salaam: Tanzania Publishing House, 1972), 99–100.

5. Gould, *Mismeasure of Man,* 103.

6. Cited in Dorothy Burnham, "Black Women as Producers and Reproducers for Profit," in *Woman's Nature: Rationalizations of Inequality,* ed. Marian Lowe and Ruth Hubbard (New York: Pergamon Press, 1983), 35.

7. Gunnar Myrdal, *An American Dilemma: The Negro Problem and Modern Democracy* (New York: Harper and Brothers, 1944), 1367.

8. Howard Zinn, *A People's History of the United States* (New York: Harper and Row, 1980), 406.

9. Leo Kuper, ed., *Race, Science and Society* (Paris: UNESCO Press, 1975).

10. R. C. Lewontin, Steven Rose, and Leon J. Kamin, *Not in Our Genes: Biology, Ideology, and Human Nature* (New York: Pantheon, 1984), esp. 119–29.

11. Richard Lewontin, *Human Diversity* (New York: Scientific American Books, 1982).

12. Janet L. Norwood and Deborah P. Klein, "Developing Statistics to Meet Society's Needs," *Monthly Labor Review* (October 1989).

13. Norwood and Klein, "Developing Statistics."

14. Nancy Krieger and Mary Bassett, "The Health of Black Folk: Disease, Class, and Ideology in Science," *Monthy Review* 38, no. 3 (July-August 1986): 74.

15. Mary T. Bassett and Nancy Krieger, "Social Class and Black-White Differences in Breast Cancer Survival," *American Journal of Public Health* 76, no. 12 (1986): 1400–1403.

16. Suzanne J. Kessler and Wendy McKenna, *Gender: An Ethnomethodological Approach* (Chicago: University of Chicago Press, 1978).

17. Edward O. Wilson, *Sociobiology: The Modern Synthesis* (Cambridge: Harvard University Press, 1975).

18. Sarah Blaffer Hrdy, "Empathy, Polyandry, and the Myth of the Coy Female," in *Feminist Approaches to Science,* ed. Ruth Bleier (New York: Pergamon Press, 1986).

19. Ruth Hubbard, *The Politics of Women's Biology* (New Brunswick, N.J.: Rutgers University Press, 1990), 87–118.

20. Anne Fausto-Sterling, *Myths of Gender: Biological Theories about Women and Men* (New York: Basic Books, 1985).

21. Diana Long Hall, "Biology, Sex Hormones, and Sexism in the 1920s," in *Women and Philosophy: Toward a Theory of Liberation,* ed. Carol C. Gould and Marx W. Wartofsky (New York: G. P. Putnam's Sons, 1976), 81–96.

22. Anne Fausto-Sterling, "Society Writes Biology / Biology Constructs Gender," *Daedalus* 116 (1987): 61–76.

23. Emily Martin, "The Egg and the Sperm," *Signs* 16 (1991): 485–501.

24. Ruth Herschberger, *Adam's Rib* (New York: Harper and Row, 1948).

25. David C. Page et al., "The Sex-Determining Region of the Human Y Chromosome Encodes a Finger Protein," *Cell* 51 (24 December 1987): 1091–1104.

26. M. S. Palmer et al., "Genetic Evidence that ZFY Is Not the Testis-Determining Factor." *Nature* 342, nos. 21–28 (December 1989): 937–39; Peter Koopman et al., "Zfy Gene Expression Patterns Are Not Compatible with a Primary Role in Mouse Sex Determination," *Nature* 342, nos. 21–28 (December 1989): 940–42.

27. Hubbard, *Politics of Women's Biology,* 128–29, 136–40.

28. Angela Y. Davis, *Women, Race, and Class* (New York: Random House, 1981); Henry Louis Gates, Jr., ed., *Race, Writing, and Difference* (Chicago: University of Chicago Press, 1986); Sander Gilman, *Difference and Pathology: Stereotypes of Sexuality, Race, and Madness* (Ithaca: Cornell University Press, 1985); Donna Haraway, *Primate Visions: Gender, Race, and Nature in the World of Modern Science* (New York: Routledge, 1989); Nancy Stepan, "Race and Gender: The Role of Analogy in Science," *Isis* 77: 261–77.

CHECKPOINTS

1. The examples of intersexuality described by Fausto-Sterling suggest that sex is not categorical, but that there are many gradations of biological maleness and femaleness.

2. Fausto-Sterling suggests that Western cultures are based on a clear distinction between male and female.

3. Hubbard provides evidence that science has not been objective in defining race and sex as biological entities.

4. Social inequalities between races and sexes have been supported by biased scientific evidence.

5. The scientific analysis of gender cannot be separated from the political, social, and cultural meanings of masculinity and femininity.

To prepare for reading the next section, think about these questions:

1. Are people either privileged or disadvantaged by their identities as male/female, white/black, wealthy/poor?

2. What is the relationship between race, gender, ethnicity, and social class as facets of identity?

3. Do race, sex, ethnicity, and social class create barriers between people?

INTERSECTIONS OF GENDER, RACES, AND CLASS

Toward a New Vision: Race, Class, and Gender as Categories of Analysis and Connection
PATRICIA HILL COLLINS

The true focus of revolutionary change is never merely the oppressive situations which we seek to escape, but that piece of the oppressor which is planted deep within each of us.

—*Audre Lorde,* Sister Outsider, *123*

Audre Lorde's statement raises a troublesome issue for scholars and activists working for social change. While many of us have little difficulty assessing our own victimization within some major system of oppression, whether it be by race, social class, religion, sexual orientation, ethnicity, age or gender, we typically fail to see how our thoughts and actions uphold someone else's subordination. Thus, white feminists routinely point with confidence to their oppression as women but resist seeing how much their white skin privileges them. African-Americans who possess eloquent analyses of racism often persist in viewing poor White women as symbols of white power. The radical left fares little better. "If only people of color and women could see their true class interests," they argue, "class solidarity would eliminate racism and sexism." In essence, each group identifies the type of oppression with which it feels most comfortable as being fundamental and classifies all other types as being of lesser importance.

Oppression is full of such contradictions. Errors in political judgment that we make concerning how we teach our courses, what we tell our children, and which organizations are worthy of our time, talents and financial support flow smoothly from errors in theoretical analysis about the nature of oppression and activism. Once we realize that there are few pure victims or oppressors, and that each one of us derives varying amounts of penalty and privilege from the multiple systems of oppression that frame our lives, then we will be in a position to see the need for new ways of thought and action.

To get at that "piece of the oppressor which is planted deep within each of us," we need at least two things. First, we need new visions of what oppression is, new categories of analysis that are inclusive of race, class, and gender as distinctive yet interlocking structures of oppression. Adhering to a stance of comparing and ranking oppressions—the proverbial, "I'm more oppressed than you"—locks us all into a dangerous dance of competing for attention, resources, and theoretical supremacy. Instead, I suggest that we examine our different experiences within the more fundamental relationship of damnation and subordination. To focus on the particular arrangements that race or class or gender take in our time and place without seeing these structures as sometimes parallel and sometimes interlocking dimensions of the more fundamental relationship of domination and subordination may temporarily ease our consciences. But while such thinking may lead to short term social reforms, it is simply inadequate for the task of bringing about long term social transformation.

While race, class and gender as categories of analysis are essential in helping us understand the structural bases of domination and subordination, new ways of thinking that are not accompanied by new ways of acting offer incomplete prospects for change. To get at that "piece of the oppressor which is planted deep within each of us," we also need to change our daily behavior. Currently, we are all enmeshed in a complex web of problematic relationships that grant our mirror images full human subjec-

tivity while stereotyping and objectifying those most different than ourselves. We often assume that the people we work with, teach, send our children to school with, and sit next to . . . will act and feel in prescribed ways because they belong to given race, social class or gender categories. These judgments by category must be replaced with fully human relationships that transcend the legitimate differences created by race, class and gender as categories of analysis. We require new categories of connection, new visions of what our relationships with one another can be. . . .

[This discussion] addresses this need for new patterns of thought and action. I focus on two basic questions. First, how can we reconceptualize race, class and gender as categories of analysis? Second, how can we transcend the barriers created by our experiences with race, class and gender oppression in order to build the types of coalitions essential for social exchange? To address these questions I contend that we must acquire both new theories of how race, class and gender have shaped the experiences not just of women of color, but of all groups. Moreover, we must see the connections between these categories of analysis and the personal issues in our everyday lives, particularly our scholarship, our teaching and our relationships with our colleagues and students. As Audre Lorde points out, change starts with self, and relationships that we have with those around us must always be the primary site for social change.

HOW CAN WE RECONCEPTUALIZE RACE, CLASS AND GENDER AS CATEGORIES OF *ANALYSIS?*

To me, we must shift our discourse away from additive analyses of oppression (Spelman, 1982; Collins, 1989). Such approaches are typically based on two key premises. First, they depend on either/or, dichotomous thinking. Persons, things and ideas are conceptualized in terms of their opposites. For example, Black/White, man/woman, thought/feeling, and fact/opinion are defined in oppositional terms. Thought and feeling are not seen as two different and interconnected ways of approaching truth that can coexist in scholarship and teaching. Instead, feeling is defined as antithetical to reason, as its opposite. In spite of the fact that we all have "both/and" identities, (I am both a college professor and a mother—I don't stop being a mother when I drop my child off at school, or forget everything I learned while scrubbing the toilet), we persist in trying to classify each other in either/or categories. I live each day as an African-American woman—a race/gender specific experience. And I am not alone. Everyone has a race/gender/class specific identity. Either/or, dichotomous thinking is especially troublesome when applied to theories of oppression because every individual must be classified as being either oppressed or not oppressed. The both/and position of simultaneously being oppressed and oppressor becomes conceptually impossible.

A second premise of additive analyses of oppression is that these dichotomous differences must be ranked. One side of the dichotomy is typically labeled dominant and the other subordinate. Thus, Whites rule Blacks, men are deemed superior to women, and reason is seen as being preferable to emotion. Applying this premise to discussions of oppression leads to the assumption that oppression can be quantified, and that some groups are oppressed more than others. I am frequently asked, "Which has been most oppressive to you, your status as a Black person or your status as a woman?" What I am really being asked to do is divide myself into little boxes and rank my various statuses. If I experience oppression as a both/and phenomenon, why should I analyze it any differently?

Additive analyses of oppression rest squarely on the twin pillars of either/or thinking and the necessity to quantify and rank all relationships in order to know where one stands. Such approaches typically see African-American women as being more oppressed than everyone else because the majority of Black women experience the negative effects of race, class and gender oppression simultaneously. In essence, if you add together separate oppressions, you are left with a grand oppression greater than the sum of its parts.

I am not denying that specific groups experience oppression more harshly than others—lynching is certainly objectively worse than being held up as a sex object. But we must be careful not to confuse this issue of the saliency of one type of oppression in people's lives with a theoretical stance positing the interlocking nature of oppression. Race, class and gender may all structure a situation but may not be equally visible and/or important in people's self-definitions. In certain contexts, such as the antebellum American South and contemporary South America, racial oppression is more visibly salient, while in other contexts, such as Haiti, El Salvador and Nicaragua, social class oppression may be more apparent. For middle class White women, gender may assume experiential primacy unavailable to poor Hispanic women struggling with the ongoing issues of low paid jobs and the frustrations of the welfare bureaucracy. This recognition that one category may have salience over another for a given time and place does not minimize the theoretical importance of assuming that race, class and gender as categories of analysis structure all relationships.

In order to move toward new visions of what oppression is, I think that we need to ask new questions. How are relationships of domination and subordination structured and maintained in the American political economy? How do race, class and gender function as parallel and interlocking systems that shape this basic relationship of domination and subordination? Questions such as these promise to move us away from futile theoretical struggles concerned with ranking oppressions and towards analyses that assume race, class and gender are all present in any given setting, even if one appears more visible and salient than the others. Our task becomes redefined as one of reconceptualizing oppression by uncovering the connections among race, class and gender as categories of analysis.

I. Institutional Dimension of Oppression

Sandra Harding's contention that gender oppression is structured along three main dimensions—the institutional, the symbolic, and the individual—offers a useful model for a more comprehensive analysis encompassing race, class and gender oppression (Harding, 1986). Systemic relationships of domination and subordination structured through social institutions such as schools, businesses, hospitals, the work place, and government agencies represent the institutional dimension of oppression. Racism, sexism and elitism all have concrete institutional locations. Even though the workings of the institutional dimension of oppression are often obscured with ideologies claiming equality of opportunity, in actuality, race, class and gender place Asian-American women, Native American men, White men, African-American women, and other groups in distinct institutional niches with varying degrees of penalty and privilege.

Even though I realize that many . . . would not share this assumption, let us assume that the institutions of American society discriminate, whether by design or by accident. While many of us are familiar with how race, gender and class operate separately to structure inequality, I want to focus on how these three systems interlock in structuring the institutional dimension of oppression. To get at the interlocking nature of race, class and gender, I want you to think about the antebellum plantation as a guiding metaphor for a variety of American social institutions. Even though slavery is typically analyzed as a racist institution, and occasionally as a class institution, I suggest that slavery was a race, class, gender specific institution. Removing any one piece from our analysis diminishes our understanding of the true nature of relations of domination and subordination under slavery.

Slavery was a profoundly patriarchal institution. It rested on the dual tenets of White male authority and White male property, a joining of the political and the economic within the institution of the family. Heterosexism was assumed and all Whites were expected to marry. Control over affluent White women's sexuality remained key to slavery's survival because property was to be passed on to the legitimate heirs of the slave owner. Ensuring affluent White women's virginity and chastity was deeply intertwined with maintenance of property relations.

Under slavery, we see varying levels of institutional protection given to affluent White women, working class and poor White women, and enslaved African women. Poor White women enjoyed few of the protections held out to their upper class sisters. Moreover, the devalued status of Black women was key in keeping all White women in their assigned places. Controlling Black women's fertility was also key to the continuation of slavery, for children born to slave mothers themselves were slaves.

African-American women shared the devalued status of chattel with their husbands, fathers and sons. Racism stripped Blacks as a group of legal rights, education, and control over their own persons. African-Americans could be whipped, branded, sold, or killed, not because they were poor, or because they were women, but because they were Black. Racism ensured that Blacks would continue to serve Whites and suffer economic exploitation at the hands of all Whites.

So we have a very interesting chain of command on the plantation—the affluent White master as the reigning patriarch, his White wife helpmate to serve him, help him manage his property and bring up his heirs, his faithful servants whose production and reproduction were tied to the requirements of the capitalist political economy, and largely propertyless, working class White men and women watching from afar. In essence, the foundations for the contemporary roles of elite White women, poor Black women, working class White men, and a series of other groups can be seen in stark relief in this fundamental American social institution. While Blacks experienced the most harsh treatment under slavery, and thus made slavery clearly visible as a racist institution, race, class and gender interlocked in structuring slavery's systemic organization of domination and subordination.

Even today, the plantation remains a compelling metaphor for institutional oppression. Certainly the actual conditions of oppression are not as severe now as they were then. To argue, as some do, that things have not changed all that much denigrates the achievements of those who struggled for social change before us. But the basic relationships among Black men, Black women, elite White women, elite White men, working class White men and working class White women as groups remain essentially intact.

A brief analysis of key American social institutions most controlled by elite White men should convince us of the interlocking nature of race, class and gender in structuring the institutional dimension of oppression. For example, if you are from an American college or university, is your campus a modern plantation? Who controls your university's political economy? Are elite White men overrepresented among the upper administrators and trustees controlling your university's finances and policies? Are elite White men being joined by growing numbers of elite White women helpmates? What kinds of people are in your classrooms grooming the next generation who will occupy these and other decision-making positions? Who are the support staff that produce the mass mailings, order the supplies, fix the leaky pipes? Do African-Americans, Hispanics or other people of color form the majority of the invisible workers who feed you, wash your dishes, and clean up your offices and libraries after everyone else has gone home?

If your college is anything like mine, you know the answers to these questions. You may be affiliated with an institution that has Hispanic women as vice-presidents for finance, or substantial numbers of Black men among the faculty. If so, you are fortunate. Much more typical are colleges where a modified version of the plantation as a metaphor for the institutional dimension of oppression survives.

2. The Symbolic Dimension of Oppression

Widespread, societally-sanctioned ideologies used to justify relations of domination and subordination comprise the symbolic dimension of oppression. Central to this process is the use of stereotypical or controlling images of diverse race, class and gender groups. In order to assess the power of this dimension of oppression, I want you to make a list, either on paper or in your head, of "masculine" and "feminine" characteristics. If your list is anything like that compiled by most people, it reflects some variation of the following:

Masculine	Feminine
aggressive	passive
leader	follower
rational	emotional
strong	weak
intellectual	physical

Not only does this list reflect either/or dichotomous thinking and the need to rank both sides of the dichotomy, but ask yourself exactly which men and women you had in mind when compiling these characteristics. This list applies almost exclusively to middle class White men and women. The allegedly "masculine" qualities that you probably listed are only acceptable when exhibited by elite White men, or when used by Black and Hispanic men against each other or against women of color. Aggressive Black and Hispanic men are seen as dangerous, not powerful, and are often penalized when they exhibit any of the allegedly "masculine" characteristics. Working class and poor White men fare slightly better and are also denied the allegedly "masculine" symbols of leadership, intellectual competence, and human rationality. Women of color and working class and poor White women are also not represented on this list, for they have never had the luxury of being "ladies." What appear to be universal categories representing all men and women instead are unmasked as being applicable to only a small group.

It is important to see how the symbolic images applied to different race, class and gender groups interact in maintaining systems of domination and subordination. If I were to ask you to repeat the same assignment, only this time, by making separate lists for Black men, Black women, Hispanic women and Hispanic men, I suspect that your gender symbolism would be quite different. In comparing all of the lists, you might begin to see the interdependence of symbols applied to all groups. For example, the elevated images of White womanhood need devalued images of Black womanhood in order to maintain credibility.

While the above exercise reveals the interlocking nature of race, class and gender in structuring the symbolic dimension of oppression, part of its importance lies in demonstrating how race, class and gender pervade a wide range of what appears to be universal language. Attending to diversity in our scholarship, in our teaching, and in our daily lives provides a new angle of vision on interpretations of reality thought to be natural, normal and "true." Moreover, viewing images of masculinity and femininity as universal gender symbolism, rather than as symbolic images that are race, class and gender specific, renders the experiences of people of color and of non-privileged White women and men invisible. One way to dehumanize an individual or a group is to deny the reality of their experiences. So when we refuse to deal with race or class because they do not appear to be directly relevant to gender, we are actually becoming part of some one else's problem.

Assuming that everyone is affected differently by the same interlocking set of symbolic images allows us to move forward toward new analyses. Women of color and White women have different relationships to White male authority and this difference explains the distinct gender symbolism applied to both groups. Black women encounter controlling images such as the mammy, the matriarch, the mule and the whore, that encourage others to reject us as fully human people. Ironically, the negative nature of these images simultaneously encourages us to reject them. In contrast, White women are offered seductive images, those that promise to reward them for supporting the status quo. And yet seductive images can be equally controlling. Consider, for example, the views of Nancy White, a 73-year-old Black woman, concerning images of rejection and seduction:

> My mother used to say that the black woman is the white man's mule and the white woman is his dog. Now, she said that to say this: we do the heavy work and get beat whether we do it well or not. But the white woman is closer to the master and he pats them on the head and lets them sleep in the house, but he ain't gon' treat neither one like he was dealing with a person. (Gwaltney, 1980, p. 148)

Both sets of images stimulate particular political stances. By broadening the analysis beyond the confines of race, we can see the varying levels of rejection and seduction available to each of us due to our race, class and gender identity. Each of us lives with an allotted portion of institutional privilege and penalty, and with varying levels of rejection and seduction inherent in the symbolic images applied to us. This is the context in which we make our choices. Taken together, the institutional and symbolic dimensions of oppression create a structural backdrop against which all of us live our lives.

3. The Individual Dimension of Oppression

Whether we benefit or not, we all live within institutions that reproduce race, class and gender oppression. Even if we never have any contact with members of other race, class and gender groups, we all encounter images of these groups and are exposed to the symbolic meanings attached to those images. On this dimension of oppression, our individual biographies vary tremendously. As a result of our institutional and symbolic statuses, all of our choices become political acts.

Each of us must come to terms with the multiple ways in which race, class and gender as categories of analysis frame our individual biographies. I have lived my entire life as an African-American woman from a working class family and this basic fact has had a profound impact on my personal biography. Imagine how different your life might be if you had been born Black, or White, or poor, or of a different race/class/gender group than the one with which you are most familiar. The institutional treatment you would have received and the symbolic meanings attached to your very existence might differ dramatically from what you now consider to be natural, normal and part of everyday life. You might be the same, but your personal biography might have been quite different.

I believe that each of us carries around the cumulative effect of our lives within multiple structures of oppression. If you want to see how much you have been affected by this whole thing, I ask you one simple question—who are your close friends? Who are the people with whom you can share your hopes, dreams, vulnerabilities, fears and victories? Do they look like you? If they are all the same, circumstance may be the cause. For the first seven years of my life I saw only low income Black people. My friends from those years reflected the composition of my community. But now that I am an adult, can the defense of circumstance explain the patterns of people that I trust as my friends and colleagues? When given other alternatives, if my friends and colleagues reflect the homogeneity of one race, class and gender group, then these categories of analysis have indeed become barriers to connection.

I am not suggesting that people are doomed to follow the paths laid out for them by race, class and gender as categories of analysis. While these three structures certainly frame my opportunity structure, I as an individual always have the choice of accepting things as they are, or trying to change them. As Nikki Giovanni points out, "we've got to live in the real world. If we don't like the world we're living in, change it. And if we can't change it, we change ourselves. We can do something" (Tate 1983, p. 68). While a piece of the oppressor may be planted deep within each of us, we each have the choice of accepting that piece or challenging it as part of the "true focus of revolutionary change."

HOW CAN WE TRANSCEND THE BARRIERS CREATED BY OUR EXPERIENCES WITH RACE, CLASS AND GENDER OPPRESSION IN ORDER TO BUILD THE TYPES OF COALITIONS ESSENTIAL FOR SOCIAL CHANGE?

Reconceptualizing oppression and seeing the barriers created by race, class and gender as interlocking categories of analysis is a vital first step. But we must transcend these barriers by moving toward race, class and gender as categories of connection, by building relationships and coalitions that will bring about social change. What are some of the issues involved in doing this?

I. Differences in Power and Privilege

First, we must recognize that our differing experiences with oppression create problems in the relationships among us. Each of us lives within a system that vests us with varying levels of power and privilege. These differences in power, whether structured along axes of race, class, gender, age or sexual orientation, frame our relationships. African-American writer June Jordan describes her discomfort on a Caribbean vacation with Olive, the Black woman who cleaned her room:

> . . . even though both "Olive" and "I" live inside a conflict neither one of us created, and even though both of us therefore hurt inside that conflict, I may be one of the monsters she needs to eliminate from her universe and, in a sense, she may be one of the monsters in mine (1985, p. 47).

Differences in power constrain our ability to connect with one another even when we think we are engaged in dialogue across differences. Let me give you an example. One year, the students in my course "Sociology of the Black Community" got into a heated discussion about the reasons for the upsurge of racial incidents on college campuses. Black students complained vehemently about the apathy and resistance they felt most White students expressed about examining their own racism. Mark, a White male student, found their comments particularly unsettling. After claiming that all the Black people he had ever known had expressed no such beliefs to him, he questioned how representative the viewpoints of his fellow students actually were. When pushed further, Mark revealed that he had participated in conversations over the years with the Black domestic worker employed by his family. Since she had never expressed such strong feelings about White racism, Mark was genuinely shocked by class discussions. Ask yourselves whether that domestic worker was in a position to speak freely. Would it have been wise for her to do so in a situation where the power between the two parties was so unequal?

In extreme cases, members of privileged groups can erase the very presence of the less privileged.

When I first moved to Cincinnati, my family and I went on a picnic at a local park. Picnicking next to us was a family of White Appalachians. When I went to push my daughter on the swings, several of the children came over. They had missing, yellowed and broken teeth, they wore old clothing and their poverty was evident. I was shocked. Growing up in a large eastern city, I had never seen such awful poverty among Whites. The segregated neighborhoods in which I grew up made White poverty all but invisible. More importantly, the privileges attached to my newly acquired social class position allowed me to ignore and minimize the poverty among Whites that I did encounter. My reactions to those children made me realize how confining phrases such as "well, at least they're not Black," had become for me. In learning to grant human subjectivity to the Black victims of poverty, I had simultaneously learned to demand White victims of poverty. By applying categories of race to the objective conditions confronting me, I was quantifying and ranking oppressions and missing the very real suffering which, in fact, is the real issue.

One common pattern of relationships across differences in power is one that I label "voyeurism." From the perspective of the privileged, the lives of people of color, of the poor, and of women are interesting for their entertainment value. The privileged become voyeurs, passive onlookers who do not relate to the less powerful, but who are interested in seeing how the "different" live. Over the years, I have heard numerous African-American students complain about professors who never call on them except when a so-called Black issue is being discussed. The students' interest in discussing race or qualifications for doing so appear unimportant to the professor's efforts to use Black students' experiences as stories to make the material come alive for the White student audience. Asking Black students to perform on cue and provide a Black experience for their White classmates can be seen as voyeurism at its worst.

Members of subordinate groups do not willingly participate in such exchanges but often do so because members of dominant groups control the institutional and symbolic apparatuses of oppression. Racial/ethnic groups, women, and the poor have never had the luxury of being voyeurs of the lives of the privileged. Our ability to survive in hostile settings has hinged on our ability to learn intricate details about the behavior and world view of the powerful and adjust our behavior accordingly. I need only point to the difference in perception of those men and women in abusive relationships. Where men can view their girlfriends and wives as sex objects, helpmates and a collection of stereotyped categories of voyeurism—women must be attuned to every nuance of their partners' behavior. Are women "naturally" better in relating to people with more power than themselves, or have circumstances mandated that men and women develop different skills? . . .

Coming from a tradition where most relationships across difference are squarely rooted in relations of domination and subordination, we have much less experience relating to people as different but equal. The classroom is potentially one powerful and safe space where dialogues among individuals of unequal power relationships can occur. The relationship between Mark, the student in my class, and the domestic worker is typical of a whole series of relationships that people have when they relate across differences in power and privilege. The relationship among Mark and his classmates represents the power of the classroom to minimize those differences so that people of different levels of power can use race, class and gender as categories of analysis in order to generate meaningful dialogues. In this case, the classroom equalized racial difference so that Black students who normally felt silenced spoke out. White students like Mark, generally unaware of how they had been privileged by their whiteness, lost that privilege in the classroom and thus became open to genuine dialogue. . . .

2. Coalitions Around Common Causes

A second issue in building relationships and coalitions essential for social change concerns knowing the real reasons for coalition. Just what brings people together? One powerful catalyst fostering group solidarity is the presence of a common enemy. African-American, Hispanic, Asian-American, and women's studies all share the common intellectual heritage of challenging what passes for certified knowledge in the academy. But politically expedient relationships and coalitions like these are fragile because, as June Jordan points out:

> It occurs to me that much organizational grief could be avoided if people understood that partnership in misery does not necessarily provide for partnership for change: When we get the monsters off our backs all of us may want to run in very different directions (1985, p. 47).

Sharing a common cause assists individuals and groups in maintaining relationships that transcend their differences. Building effective coalitions involves struggling to hear one another and developing empathy for each other's points of view. The coalitions that I have been involved in that lasted and that worked have been those where commitment to a specific issue mandated collaboration as the best strategy for addressing the issue at hand.

Several years ago, masters degree in hand, I chose to teach in an inner city, parochial school in danger of closing. The money was awful, the conditions were poor, but the need was great. In my job, I had to work with a range of individuals who, on the surface, had very little in common. We had White nuns, Black middle class graduate students, Blacks from the "community," some of whom had been incarcerated and/or were affiliated with a range of federal anti-poverty programs. Parents formed another part of this community, Harvard faculty another, and a few well-meaning White liberals from Colorado were sprinkled in for good measure.

As you might imagine, tension was high. Initially, our differences seemed insurmountable. But as time passed, we found a common bond that we each brought to the school. In spite of profound differences in our personal biographies, differences that in other settings would have hampered our ability to relate to one another, we found that we were all deeply committed to the education of Black children. By learning to value each other's commitment and by recognizing that we each had different skills that were essential to actualizing that commitment, we built an effective coalition around a common cause. Our school was successful, and the children we taught benefitted from the diversity we offered them.

. . . None of us alone has a comprehensive vision of how race, class and gender operate as categories of analysis or how they might be used as categories of connection. Our personal biographies offer us partial views. Few of us can manage to study race, class and gender simultaneously. Instead, we each know more about some dimensions of this larger story and less about others. . . . Just as the members of the school had special skills to offer to the task of building the school, we have areas of specialization and expertise, whether scholarly, theoretical, pedagogical or within areas of race, class or gender. We do not all have to do the same thing in the same way. Instead, we must support each other's efforts, realizing that they are all part of the larger enterprise of bringing about social change.

3. Building Empathy

A third issue involved in building the types of relationships and coalitions essential for social change concerns the issue of individual accountability. Race, class and gender oppression form the structural backdrop against which we frame our relationship—these are the forces that encourage us to substitute voyeurism . . . for fully human relationships. But while we may not have created this situation, we are each responsible for making individual, personal choices concerning which elements of race, class and gender oppression we will accept and which we will work to change.

One essential component of this accountability involves developing empathy for the experiences of individuals and groups different than ourselves. Empathy begins with taking an interest in the facts of other people's lives, both as individuals and as groups. If you care about me, you should want to know not only the details of my personal biography but a sense of how race, class and gender as categories of analysis created the institutional and symbolic backdrop for my personal biography. How can you hope to assess my character without knowing the details of the circumstances I face?

Moreover, by taking a theoretical stance that we have all been affected by race, class and gender as categories of analysis that have structured our treatment, we open up possibilities for using those same constructs as categories of connection in building empathy. For example, I have a good White woman friend with whom I share common interests and beliefs. But we know that our racial differences have provided us with different experiences. So we talk about them. We do not assume that because I am Black, race has only affected me and not her on that because I am a Black woman, race neutralizes the effect of gender in my life while accenting it in hers. We take those same categories of analysis that have created cleavages in our lives, in this case, categories of race and gender, and use them as categories of connection in building empathy for each other's experiences.

Finding common causes and building empathy is difficult, no matter which side of privilege we inhabit. Building empathy from the dominant side of privilege is difficult, simply because individuals from privileged backgrounds are not encouraged to do so. For example, in order for those of you who are White to develop empathy for the experiences of people of color, you must grapple with how your white skin has privileged you. This is difficult to do, because it not only entails the intellectual process of seeing how whiteness is elevated in institutions and symbols, but it also involves the often painful process of seeing how your whiteness has shaped your personal biography. Intellectual stances against the institutional and symbolic dimensions of racism are generally easier to maintain than sustained self-reflection about how racism has shaped all of our individual biographies. Were and are your fathers, uncles, and grandfathers really more capable than mine, or can their accomplishments be explained in part by the racism members of my family experienced? Did your mothers stand silently by and watch all this happen? More importantly, how have they passed on the benefits of their whiteness to you?

These are difficult questions, and I have tremendous respect for my colleagues and students who are trying to answer them. Since there is no compelling reason to examine the source and meaning of one's own privilege, I know that those who do so have freely chosen this stance. They are making conscious efforts to root out the piece of the oppressor planted within them. To me, they are entitled to the support of people of color in their efforts. Men who declare themselves feminists, members of the middle class who ally themselves with anti-poverty struggles, heterosexuals who support gays and lesbians, are all trying to grow, and their efforts place them far ahead of the majority who never think of engaging in such important struggles.

Building empathy from the subordinate side of privilege is also difficult, but for different reasons. Members of subordinate groups are understandably reluctant to abandon a basic mistrust of members of powerful groups because this basic mistrust has traditionally been central to their survival. As a Black woman, it would be foolish for me to assume that White women, or Black men, or White men or any other group with a history of exploiting African-American women have my best interests at heart. These groups enjoy varying amounts of privilege over me and therefore I must carefully watch them and be prepared for a relation of domination and subordination.

Like the privileged, members of subordinate groups must also work toward replacing judgments by category with new ways of thinking and acting. Refusing to do so stifles prospects for effective coalition and social change. Let me use another example from my own experiences. When I was an undergraduate, I had little time or patience for the theorizing of the privileged. My initial years at a private, elite institution were difficult, not because the coursework was challenging (it was, but that wasn't what distracted me) or because I had to work while my classmates lived on family allowances (I was used to work). The adjustment was difficult because I was surrounded by so many people who took their privilege for granted. Most of them felt entitled to their wealth. That astounded me.

I remember one incident of watching a White woman down the hall in my dormitory try to pick out which sweater to wear. The sweaters were piled up on her bed in all the colors of the rainbow, sweater after sweater. She asked my advice in a way that let me know that choosing a sweater was one of the most important decisions she had to make on a daily basis. Standing knee-deep in her sweaters, I realized how different our lives were. She did not have to worry about maintaining a solid academic average so that she could receive financial aid. Because she was in the majority, she was not treated as a representative of her race. She did not have to consider how her classroom comments or basic existence on campus contributed to the treatment her group would receive. Her allowance protected her from having to work, so she was free to spend her time studying, partying, or in her case, worrying about which sweater to wear. The degree of inequality in our lives and her unquestioned sense of entitlement concerning that inequality offended me. For a while, I categorized all affluent White women as being superficial, arrogant, overly concerned with material possessions, and part of my problem. But had I continued to classify people in this way, I would have missed out on making some very good friends whose discomfort with their inherited or acquired social class privileges pushed them to examine their position.

Since I opened with the words of Audre Lorde, it seems appropriate to close with another of her ideas. . . .

> Each of us is called upon to take a stand. So in these days ahead, as we examine ourselves and each other, our works, our fears, our differences, our sisterhood and survivals, I urge you to tackle what is most difficult for us all, self-scrutiny of our complacencies, the idea that since each of us believes she is on the side of right, she need not examine her position (1985).

I urge you to examine your position.

REFERENCES

Butler, Johnnella. 1989. "Difficult Dialogues." *The Women's Review of Books 6,* no. 5.

Collins, Patricia Hill. 1989. "The Social Construction of Black Feminist Thought." *Signs.* Summer 1989.

Gwaltney, John Langston. 1980. *Drylongso: A Self-Portrait of Black America.* New York: Vintage.

Harding, Sandra. 1986. *The Science Question in Feminism.* Ithaca, New York: Cornell University Press.

Jordan, June. 1985. *On Call: Political Essays.* Boston: South End Press.

Lorde, Audre. 1984. *Sister Outsider.* Trumansberg, New York: The Crossing Press.

———. 1985. "Sisterhood and Survival." Keynote address, conference on the Black Woman Writer and the Diaspora, Michigan State University.

Spelman, Elizabeth. 1982. "Theories of Race and Gender: The Erasure of Black Women." *Quest 5:* 32–36.

Tate, Claudia, ed. 1983. *Black Women Writers at Work.* New York: Continuum.

CHECKPOINTS

1. Collins urges readers to think about race, class, gender, and ethnicity as interlocking facets of identity.

2. Recognizing the interrelatedness of race, class, and gender creates opportunities for social change by creating new categories of connection.

3. Everyone lives in a complex system of power and privilege connected to their racial, ethnic, social class, and gender identity.

Defining Sex and Gender

QUESTIONS FOR REFLECTION

1. Should we adopt new terminology for the existing terms *sex* and *gender*?
2. How can we replace the understanding of sex and race as biological categories with a view of sex and race that takes into account the socially constructed meaning of these concepts?
3. Is it possible to study gender without taking a position on the political, social, and cultural meanings of masculine and feminine?

CHAPTER APPLICATIONS

1. List all the ways your personal identity is both privileged and oppressed. What connections can you see between yourself and others who are different from you in terms of sex, race, or social class?
2. You are the new parent of a child who is born intersexed. You do not have access to medical or surgical intervention to bring the child's appearance into conformity to one of the sex categories. How will you raise this child? What special issues of gender identity and sexual orientation will you have to address? Fausto-Sterling implies that the intersexed individuals she describes led fulfilled and happy lives—do you believe that? Why?

CHAPTER TWO
Studying Gender

QUESTIONS TO THINK ABOUT

- **How do psychologists study sex and gender differences?**
- **How do feminists critique research on sex and gender?**
- **What are the goals of feminist Men's Studies?**
- **Can you study sex/gender without studying race, ethnicity, or social class?**
- **What is the social construction of knowledge?**
- **How do feminist methodologies provide a research alternative?**
- **How can methods of science be sensitive to diversity?**
- **Why and how do psychologists study sex differences?**
- **What are the problems with the study of sex differences?**

HOW WE STUDY GENDER

Suppose you wanted to know what types of information people reveal about themselves in personal ads. You might be interested in descriptions of age, appearance, race, religion, occupation, income, hobbies, and other personal details. You may also wonder what kinds of descriptions people respond to in personal ads. You might be curious about whether there are sex differences in these areas and if so, what explanations might account for any differences. How would you go about answering these questions? You might begin by developing a hypothesis and then figuring out a way to test that hypothesis.[1] For example, you might speculate that men are more likely to respond to ads that reveal positive physical characteristics whereas women are more likely to respond to ads that reveal positive personal attributes. Or you might believe that men tend to reveal less about themselves in ads than do women. To test

any one of these hypotheses, you might examine ads placed by men and women in several sources to see if any of these differences emerged. As another strategy, you could interview men and women and ask them to explain the types of information that they would use to describe themselves in personal ads. Or you could ask different individuals to explain what importance they attach to personal ads and how they interpret the information in such ads.

Which one of these approaches is the best? As we discussed in chapter 1, how we study gender in large part depends on our epistemological perspective. What counts as knowledge and how we go about discovering that knowledge are significant points of contention in the contemporary psychological study of gender as well as in other areas of psychology.

In psychology, the laboratory experiment has been the gold standard for scientific knowledge. If a researcher wanted to conduct research on the effects of noise on conversation among men and women, he/she could create two conditions in the laboratory (noisy vs. quiet) and then measure the amount of conversation (number of words spoken during a fixed period of time). In an experiment, the researcher controls the variable that is presumed to cause an effect. This variable is known as an independent variable, and in this experiment, "noise versus quiet" is the independent variable. The behavior that results from the manipulation of the independent variable is known as the dependent variable, and in this experiment, the dependent variable would be the amount of conversation.

Variations of this method would include experimentation in settings outside the laboratory (creating noisy vs. quiet classrooms and measuring the amount of conversation between students), questionnaires and surveys (asking people to rate the noise in various settings and to estimate the amount of conversation in those settings), and observational research in laboratory or field settings (counting the number of people talking at baseball games vs. symphony concerts). All these methods allow for the quantification of both the causal variables (noise) and the dependent variables (conversation). Each type of method results in a different quantified version of the same variable. Researchers, however, are not in agreement over how to quantify all aspects of human behavior, and this example illustrates that, depending on your research question, it is possible to quantify the same variable in many different ways.

Is quantification the only reliable way to gather information, as traditional approaches to science contend, or does a quantitative focus distort or ignore critical information, including the voices of research participants? In order for such voices to be heard, some researchers have suggested the necessity of using *qualitative* methods for a fully adequate understanding of any question. Qualitative methods do not reduce behavior and situations to discrete variables that can be measured. Rather, qualitative methods try to provide detailed description and may allow a researcher to analyze very complex issues or problems. Unstructured interviews or case studies are qualitative methods. For example, a researcher who

wanted to understand the transition to parenthood for women and men might conduct detailed interviews of expectant parents. The researcher might also ask his/her participants to keep a diary during the period before and after an infant's birth. Both these approaches involve the use of relatively few participants and the collection of information that might be *subjective* and not easily summarized or reduced to numbers. The advantage of such methods is that they place the "voice" of the participants in the foreground, preserving the language, understanding, experiences, or relationships of the participants as the primary source of information.

Qualitative methods do not substitute for quantitative methods, and they do not answer the same types of questions. Quantitative methods are best used for answering cause and effect questions, whereas qualitative methods are best used for an understanding of context, for the elaboration of individual experiences, or for addressing issues or questions in which experimentation (or other quantifiable methods) would be ethically questionable (Rabinowitz & Sechzer, 1993).

Serious debate is also taking place about the content of questions that researchers ask. Are all questions of equal legitimacy? How a question is posed may influence the methods used as well as the type of answer obtained. This point is clearly illustrated in our earlier example of the study of personal ads. We might ask if men and women use different adjectives to describe themselves. This would be a question about sex differences. A different type of question is: do people who provide descriptions of their appearance also request information about personal appearance from those responding to their ad? Notice that this question does not specify an answer in terms of sex differences. Sex and gender differences may emerge but they are not assumed to exist by the study's hypothesis. One contentious debate concerns the question of whether we should study sex differences. Surprisingly, some psychologists have proposed that we should abandon the study of sex differences. Several readings in this chapter introduce you to the varying points of view on the study of sex differences.

TRADITIONAL METHODS OF SCIENCE

As Stephanie Riger points out in the first article in this chapter (*Epistemological Debates, Feminist Voices: Science, Social Values, and the Study of Women*), the methods that define modern science have been around for at least four centuries and have marked a significant break with the philosophical and moral traditions of medieval times. Before the advent of the scientific approach, the final arbiter of truth was either the church or the reigning political authority.[2] The modern scientific enterprise is based on the independence of science from political or moral influence. Science operates from several premises that define its *subject* matter, its *procedures*, its *measurement*, and its *generalizability* to other settings or subjects. Most of the premises of modern science that support research in the social and behavioral sciences can be linked to the logical positivist movement (McGrath, Kelly, & Rhodes, 1993).

The application of the scientific method to philosophical questions about human beings was a significant factor in the emergence of psychology as an academic discipline. Allegiance to the methods of science allowed the newly emerging discipline to achieve the status accorded to other disciplines in the natural sciences. As a result of this historical legacy, psychologists have considerable loyalty to the traditions of science.

One major assumption is the belief in science as an objective endeavor, which suggests that we can distinguish between the object of study and the person carrying out the study. The process of discovery exists apart from the researcher. The methods of science are thought to allow the researcher to transcend his/her particular point of view and achieve an objective, unbiased standpoint. This view connects to the idea that science is value free and that knowledge and truth are uncovered without regard to any political, social, and cultural values. Science is therefore a value-free activity that scientists engage in without consequence to the applied or political ramifications of their work. Knowledge of the world is gained through objective, quantitative measurements like those found in laboratory experiments, allowing for replication, a hallmark of the experimental method. The results of research are thought to be universally generalizable. For example, principles of learning discovered in the animal laboratory have been generalized to human behavior, and findings from male subjects have been generalized to females.

CRITICISMS OF THE SCIENTIFIC METHOD

To reiterate, there are four critical assumptions of the scientific method: (a) science is an objective enterprise; (b) science is value neutral; (c) science is empirical, distinguished in psychology by experimentation or other quantifiable approaches; (d) research results are universally applicable.

As you might expect, scholars have critically analyzed each of the underlying assumptions of the traditional scientific method. In particular, feminist scholars have articulated thorough criticisms of scientific empiricism (Unger, 1983). Feminists have not been the only group to criticize the scientific method; however, feminist criticism has revolutionized the study of gender.[3] In addition, feminist critiques of science have been successful in articulating alternative models of generating knowledge—what have become known as **feminist methods.** This success may be attributed, in part, to the commitment of feminists to the successful analysis of social issues that impact women and the development of solutions to circumstances of gender inequity (McGrath, Kelly, & Rhodes, 1993).

Some of the earliest criticisms of scientific psychology were addressed at the exclusion of women from the methods and practice of psychology (Weisstein, 1968; Shields, 1975). Two significant issues are raised by these criticisms. One issue is the almost exclusive use of male participants in research. The belief that research subjects were generic humans permeated much of twentieth-century psychology and served as the rationale for excluding women as participants. The second issue is the *androcentric* bias believed to be inherent in a science dominated by men. The exclusion of women from the academic ranks has been documented by historians of psychology and supports the view that much of the development of the discipline was left to privileged, well-educated, white male academic psychologists. Topics of research, choice of methods, definitions of variables, interpretations of data, and development of theory all occurred in this androcentric context.

Psychology is unique among social sciences in its reliance on laboratory experiments as its preferred method. In the laboratory setting, behavior is divorced from its natural ongoing social context in order to isolate the behaviors of interest from contextual influences (often known as extraneous variables). In many experiments, the research participants have little interaction with the researcher and rarely see or interact with other participants. Participants' behavior is often highly constrained by the design of the experiment. The researcher typically has no interest in the participants' personal history, interpretation of the experimental setting, beliefs about the research question, range of social behaviors, or interpretation of the behavior of others.[4] The feminist critique of this limited view of human behavior argues that context is a key element to developing a full understanding of behavior. Feminist psychologists take the view that men and women have not always experienced social, political, and historical events in the same ways, and therefore it is essential to understand the relationship between context and behavior. The feminist critique would argue for the necessity of accounting for context, although feminists are not always in agreement about what methods will achieve this goal.

Another criticism of traditional methods in psychology has been the treatment of sex as a subject variable, or independent variable. This issue was discussed in chapter 1, especially by Unger and Crawford, as one reason why conceptual confusion continues to exist in the use of the terms *sex* and *gender*. In experimental research, the researcher establishes the independent variables of the experiment, traditionally by manipulation. As we defined for you earlier, the independent variables are those variables being examined for their effects on the dependent variables (the variables measured as outcomes). Some variables that

are presumed to cause an effect cannot be truly manipulated; for example, age, race, or social class may all exert an independent influence on an outcome of interest, but researchers cannot randomly assign participants to conditions of age, race, or social class. The same is true of sex. Researchers who study such variables typically divide their subject population into what are considered appropriate categories, such as, young versus old, black versus white, poor versus wealthy, or male versus female. Notice that in each case, the researcher is responsible for determining membership in each category. Some categorization may be made empirically. Researchers can collect information on chronological age and then limit their participants based on membership in the desired age range. For example, young subjects could be defined as those between the ages of 18 and 22 and old subjects as those between the ages of 70 and 75. In order to assign subjects to categories of social class, researchers could collect information on income, wealth, or education.[5] Although these variables cannot be manipulated, and therefore causation cannot be readily determined, researchers can be more precise about how they assign participants to categories. As we discussed in chapter 1, both race and sex are typically treated as dichotomous categories, but in reality the distinctions between categories are blurred. Subjects are assigned to one of the two categories of sex based on the researcher's determination of the subject's membership in one of the categories—male or female. As was seen in chapter 1, not everyone can be unequivocally categorized as either male or female. Although this situation may only apply to a small number of people, another issue raised by the use of sex as a subject variable has very broad implications. The use of subject variables is part of the search for cause-and-effect relationships—the independent variable(s) are hypothesized to cause the dependent variable(s). The inclusion of sex as an independent variable is, therefore, an assertion that sex is causally related to whatever outcome is being studied. As Unger and Crawford (1996) point out, a sex difference is a description, not an explanation. However, following the logic of scientific methods, the finding of a sex difference requires a cause-and-effect explanation. Feminist psychologists have repeatedly challenged this model of the inclusion of sex in research.

Another challenge to the assumptions of the scientific method is the belief that science is value free. Feminist critiques of science recognize that science is a human activity and, as such, is inevitably influenced by human social interactions, beliefs, and interpretations. In particular, feminist criticisms emphasize that psychology, as a discipline, has developed in a privileged, male-dominated, largely North American, twentieth-century context. One of the most deeply embedded assumptions of psychological research is the positioning of the white male as the normative standard against which others are judged. Tavris (1992), in her account of the history and meaning of sex differences research, presents many examples of how the language of scientific explanations portray women as different, deficient, or deviant. In an example from research on hemispheric lateralization of the brain, female brains were described as "less specialized." Tavris comments that the researchers could have chosen to describe the findings alternatively— as male brains being "less integrated." Notice that the chosen description not only poses the female outcome in comparison with the male standard, but also implies a female deficiency. Neither of these descriptions with their corresponding interpretations are appropriate. Critics argue that we need to be alert for underlying political or social implications masked by the guise of scientific objectivity. Scientific terminology is not value free because science is a product of its social/cultural context, not removed from it.

Feminist criticisms of the scientific method have had an impact on the growing study of masculinity. The problem of generalizing research findings from male subjects to females raises the broader question of the representativeness of many research samples. The general population of males is diverse, and researchers are increasingly aware that white, male, college-age populations do not match this larger, more diverse reality. In the second article in this chapter (*Theorizing Masculinities in Contemporary Social Science*), Scott Coltrane discusses the relation-

ship between feminist criticisms of science and the development of theories of masculinity. In agreement with feminist criticism, Coltrane urges psychologists to examine *masculinity* using a social constructionist framework. Coltrane argues that feminist criticisms of science can enlighten the study of men and masculinity by helping uncover the ways in which gender structures the experiences of men. For Coltrane, the social goal of feminism, that is, to reduce social inequalities based on gender, should be shared by scholars interested in masculinity.

THE NEED FOR ADDITIONAL VOICES

The development of a feminist perspective on masculinity is only part of a larger dialogue calling for increased recognition of diversity among individuals. In their analysis of research on the psychology of women, Reid and Kelly (1994) argue that feminist psychologists have promoted a fiction of the homogeneity of women, often excluding or marginalizing women of color or poor women. These authors identify two failures embedded in the increased attention to women's issues in psychology. The first failure is the nearly exclusive focus on white, largely college-age women. The second failure is seen when researchers include participants varying in race, culture, or social class, and the resulting research marginalizes or pathologizes the participants. This point is illustrated by the inclusion of women of color most often in research on teen pregnancy, low self-esteem, victimization, poverty, or single-parenthood.

In an analysis of the integration of cultural diversity into feminist psychology, Landrine (1995) suggests that psychological theory has been dominated by a mechanistic model of human behavior that reduces complex, multilayered relationships among the many facets of culture, identity, and behavior to simplistic, context-free behavioral differences. This model is best exemplified by the proliferation of differences research (e.g., sex differences, race differences, ethnic differences), which are largely atheoretical and superficial. Landrine advocates a contextualized model of behavior in which behavior and its context are treated as a single unit and the meaning of behavior can only be discerned by an analysis of its sociocultural context. This issue is further emphasized in chapter 4 as we examine how culture and gender are related.

Landrine (1995) offers an example of a contextualized analysis of gender and ethnic differences in adolescent smoking. Data indicate that ethnic minority boys and girls begin smoking later and in smaller numbers than do European Americans, with the highest rate of smoking and the fastest increase of smoking within the population of European American girls.[6] Focusing on the meaning of smoking within a sociocultural context reveals that the European American girls who smoked also showed an increased interest in weight control and were more likely to engage in perpetual dieting and other means of weight control. This focus was not found among nonsmoking European American girls and boys and ethnic minority boys and girls (smokers or nonsmokers). Only among European American girls who smoked was smoking defined as a means of weight control. Thus, the cultural meaning of this behavior varies, and attempts to understand smoking must be contextually sensitive.

Efforts to increase diversity in research by including varied research participants will not succeed if the resulting research does not attend to the meaning of race, culture, and class in the experiences of these participants. As Patricia Hill Collins explained in the article you read for chapter 1, a complete analysis of gender depends on understanding the interlocking relationships among many aspects of identity.

THE FEMINIST PERSPECTIVE ON SCIENCE

The first article in this chapter, by Riger (1992), analyzes feminist challenges to the scientific methodology as practiced in psychology. She is particularly concerned with the interaction between recommendations for methodological change and feminist values. She describes three alternative feminist challenges to traditional empiricism. According to Riger, the meaning of feminism is not universal, and therefore we should not expect consensus to emerge from feminist criticisms. It is important to note that although feminist scholars have had a central role in the development of each of the approaches described by Riger, these approaches are not exclusively feminist.

Feminist Empiricism

Many feminist psychologists are loyal to the traditions of empirical science while acknowledging how bias can influence the process. The adherence to the methods of scientists while adopting a critical feminist perspective is known as **feminist empiricism** (Harding, 1986). Working within the empirical framework, feminist empiricists try to reshape and reformulate scientific practices. The biases of sexism have been identified at all stages of the research process: formulating a hypothesis, choosing and defining variables, choosing participants and researchers, implementing research procedures, interpreting data, and communicating research findings (McHugh, Koeske, & Frieze, 1986). The feminist empiricist position recognizes the importance of the inclusion of diversity among both scientists and research participants. Diverse points of view can be useful for generating alternative research hypotheses and creating new audiences for the products of an improved, *nonsexist* science.

Two related strategies best represent the feminist empiricist tradition. The first strategy is a series of recommendations designed to help researchers identify and correct gender bias in the research process. Several extensive guides for reducing sexist bias in research have been published (Caplan & Caplan, 1994; Denmark, Russo, Frieze, & Sechzer, 1988; McHugh, Koeske, & Frieze, 1986). Among other recommendations, researchers are cautioned to consider that the sex of the researcher may influence the outcome of the research—people respond differently to men versus women.

The second strategy is the development of statistical methods to evaluate the magnitude of sex differences estimated across several research studies. This procedure is known as meta-analysis. Feminist empiricists believe that this method is an important tool because of the high credibility accorded to statistical evidence by scientific psychologists (Hyde, 1994a). Hyde argues that meta-analysis can serve feminist goals by challenging long-held stereotypes about sex differences with quantitative evidence for the actual size (or in many cases lack of size) of sex differences.

Feminist empiricists do not reject the premise of traditional science but rather seek to reform its practices from within the system. In a critique of feminist empiricism, Harding (1991) contends that science is not an objective enterprise. All scientists operate from a framework of experience in which history and culture shapes their work and cannot be divorced from this work. Adding more women and minorities, or changing research practices so that they are nonsexist, although laudable goals, will not change the power relationship that exists between the researcher and the researcher participants. In the traditional research scenario, the underlying assumption is that only the researcher holds an understanding of the research endeavor, and research subjects provide data for the researcher to analyze and interpret.

Feminist Standpoint Theory

A second position, described as **feminist standpoint theory,** challenges the belief in scientific objectivity (Harding, 1986). Its goal is to move away from the distinction between researcher and subject by placing the subject, in this case women, at the center of study. This theory contends that those who have historically been in a less powerful position have a unique perspective to provide to science. The feminist standpoint perspective places women's experiences at the center of study and does not reformulate them in accord with researchers' preconceptions and beliefs. Working from this premise, researchers attempt to base their analyses on their interactions with research participants and to not define a priori their categories of analysis. Successful research depends on a collaborative relationship between researcher and participant and relies on qualitative analyses that give voice to the ways in which women define their own experience. Experiences of oppression, which have characterized many groups including women, have the potential to reveal important aspects of knowledge that might otherwise remain invisible to a researcher operating from a position of power and privilege.

Feminist standpoint methodologies do not simply substitute the feminist perspective for the traditional masculine one that has dominated science. Rather, multiple feminist standpoints each represent varying positions of powerlessness. Clearly one challenge for feminist standpoint theory is to represent these varying positions while not minimizing differences among women nor reducing the analysis to the subjective experiences of one or a few individuals.

An interesting example of gender research using a standpoint methodology is a study of poor, elderly, Black, and White women living in rural Maryland (Andersen, 1997). In her research, Andersen shows both a concern for the power dynamics in the relationship between researcher and subject and a concern for the perspective of her participants. Andersen was interested in the ways in which these women have experienced race relations in their small community through their lifetimes. She wanted to successfully cross age, race, and education boundaries that might separate her from the participants and to develop a firsthand account of their experiences and perceptions. She engaged the women in many hours of informal conversation, in their homes and in a local senior citizens center, and through this process gained their cooperation and interest in the project. Although initially skeptical, the participants came to trust Andersen, and she valued that trust, became a volunteer aide in the senior center, and shared her life story with her participants. As an example of standpoint theory research, Andersen's research illustrates a project in which the researcher is *not* the expert, does *not* determine the direction of the research, and does *not* assume a guise of objectivity. In describing this method, Andersen says: "feminist and qualitative research shows that emotion, the engagement of self, and the relationship between the knower and the known all guide research, just as they guide social action" (p. 76).

Postmodernism and Science

As described by Riger, **postmodernism** is an emerging alternative to rational, empirical analysis. A fundamental assumption of postmodernism is that science "creates" reality through the imposition of a preconceived view of reality. According to the postmodern perspective, science is perceived as the ultimate truth, and its vision often dominates society, especially women and minorities. Postmodernists are more concerned with analyzing power relationships than with uncovering empirical truths, which they claim do not exist. Postmodernism is closely allied with social constructionism, sharing the view that gender is multiply constructed.

From the perspective of postmodernism, many methods might be appropriate. Traditional methods might be useful for illustrating a particular version of reality but would not be used as evidence to reify that view of reality. Postmodernists might also advocate methods not traditionally used in social science, such as text analysis, as a means to understand the multiple and shifting meanings of experience.

In a postmodern analysis of gender, Gergen (1997) uses autobiographical narratives to explore the lives of men and women. Gergen believes that gendered life stories are acquired and projected onto the story of one's life when retold. Put more directly, the experience of being male or female shapes one's understanding of, and subjective experience of, one's life, and this experience in turn is visible in one's narration of one's life. Gergen searches autobiographical narratives for illustrations of "manstories" and "womanstories." As an example of a manstory, Gergen uses the theme of heroism in the narrative of Lee Iacocca, who explains that his upwardly mobile career at Ford Motor Corporation occurred at the same time that his wife was dying from complications associated with diabetes. In a similar vein, physicist Richard Feynman describes re-

turning after the death of his young wife during World War II, to continue his work on the Manhattan Project. Gergen's heroic theme is a pattern of facing crises, following an individual quest, and achieving success. As a postmodernist, Gergen recognizes the subjectivity in both her analysis and the subjects of her analysis. Although she articulates the basis for her understanding, Gergen sees her view as an illustration. She urges others to provide their interpretations, both competing and complementary.

The success of a postmodern analysis is not judged according to the criteria used to judge an empirical analysis. Theory and research can be judged by moral criteria or by the pragmatic utility of the research in achieving a desired outcome (Gergen, 1985; Unger, 1983). Because feminism is a social and political philosophy that advocates challenges to prevailing power dynamics, research that allows progress toward these goals would be valued. From a postmodern perspective, it is not meaningful to pose questions about sex differences because the categories of male and female are based on a preconceived dualism, the analysis of which serves to reproduce these categories. The study of gender as sex differences also obscures important differences in power among women and among men (Fine & Gordon, 1989).

The postmodern alternative does not reject empiricism; rather, it rejects the notion that empiricism offers a more accurate view of reality. Concepts deeply valued by empirical scientists, such as objectivity, reliability, validity, and generalizability, are challenged because they are assumed to be mechanisms that serve to reinforce the position that science offers the best lens for viewing reality. Adopting a postmodern perspective on gender forces us to reevaluate preexisting categories and forms of knowledge and to seek alternative knowledge that is situated in ongoing, dynamic power relationships.

Postmodernism has been criticized especially by those researchers who find its focus and methods unhelpful for providing causal explanations (Unger, 1988). Another problem that has been associated with postmoderism is that, in its emphasis on the subjective importance of individual experiences and in its denial of individual agency, it can undermine attempts to promote gender equality.

ALTERNATIVE METHODS—IS THERE ONE FEMINIST METHOD?

Feminists' criticisms of the scientific method in psychology have existed for nearly thirty years and have led to a variety of suggestions for changes to traditional psychology. These responses have ranged from making changes in journal editorial policies that require nonsexist language in scientific writing and developing guidelines for nonsexist research (McHugh, Koeske, & Frieze, 1986) to advocating the abandonment of experimental methods in favor of more qualitative and contextualized research methods (Gergen, 1988). Some research methods have become closely associated with feminist criticism. In particular, methods that focus on description or are qualitative are sometimes thought of as feminist methods.

Peplau and Conrad (1989) consider Riger's question of whether certain methods should be known as feminist. These authors conclude that it is risky for feminist psychologists to endorse some methods and reject others. If the core of feminism is advocacy for social equality, then evaluation of methods should be made on the merits of a nonsexist approach to research. They argue that research is feminist because of the issues under consideration—exploring questions that are important to women and including aspects of experience and a range of people not typically addressed by psychological research. According to these authors, any method can be used to forward feminist values, while methods sometimes identified as feminist, such as nonexperimental methods, might undermine the goals of gender equity. Certainly a sexist interpretation could be offered of the results of an interview, or a female researcher could replicate the traditional power dynamics in a research setting.

The analysis by Coltrane in this chapter is in agreement with the conclusion of Peplau and Conrad that methods should not be labeled as *feminist*.

Coltrane further argues that feminist critics should not label traditional methods in psychology as *masculinist*. This labeling establishes false dichotomies such as experimental versus nonexperimental, quantitative versus qualitative, empirical versus nonempirical, deductive versus inductive, and masculine versus feminine reminiscent of the essentialist dichotomy between male and female that we described for you in chapter 1. According to Coltrane, the benefit of a feminist analysis of masculinity is not the addition of new methodologies, but rather a focus on the relationship between men and masculinity.

Coltrane contrasts the essentialist view of masculinity with a social constructionist view of masculinity. He argues that the adoption of a social constructionist framework to understand masculinity aligns men's studies scholars with feminist scholars. Both are focused on understanding how gender organizes the experiences of men and women. Both recognize the power typically accorded to men in Western cultures, and both advocate the reduction of the importance of gender and power conferred by gender. Using the position of standpoint theory, Coltrane argues that men should be involved in research on women's issues, and women should be involved in research on men's issues. Of course, by engaging in such research, men must be careful not to reproduce an androcentric approach to research questions or findings. As an example, Coltrane suggests that men's standpoint is essential in fully understanding how and why men exclude women from many situations. The unique vantage point men and women bring to their research would enrich the study of gender as well as specific men's and women's issues. Coltrane would agree that men can be and often are feminists, whereas methods are not gendered.

SHOULD PSYCHOLOGISTS STUDY SEX DIFFERENCES?

If psychologists have ignored the importance of gender in both the development of the discipline and its resulting portrayal of human behavior, they have not neglected the study of sex differences. According to Sherif (1987), research on sex differences was part of the earliest empirical psychology and had continued through the twentieth century despite frequent criticism. The issue of sex differences goes beyond how similar or different males and females are, it extends to the social and political meaning of difference. The second half of this chapter is devoted to a critical analysis of the study of sex differences.

We have selected four articles for you to read from a special issue of a journal called *Feminism and Psychology*. Several prominent psychologists were asked to respond to the question "Should Psychologists Study Sex Differences?"[7] The responses are: Janet Hyde, *Yes, With Some Guidelines;* Alice Eagly, *On Comparing Women and Men;* Diane Halpern, *Stereotypes, Science, Censorship, and the Study of Sex Differences;* and Rachel Hare-Mustin and Jeanne Marecek, *Asking the Right Questions: Feminist Psychology and Sex Differences*. The three "yes" answers and one "no" answer represent a broad range of positions on both methodology and epistemology. We now introduce you to some of the themes that emerge in these articles. As you read the articles, keep in mind how each author explores the themes of methods and epistemology.

The explosion of research on sex differences, coupled with ongoing concern about the meaning of such differences, makes it especially hard to interpret research on sex differences. Two broad questions need to be addressed. The first question is: Are there sex differences that would help us understand the nature and meaning of gender? The second question is: What kind of question is a "sex difference" question? This latter question is derived from our concern with epistemology—what kinds of knowledge are generated from questions about sex differences? To add to the complexity, questions about the size and significance of sex differences are related both to the methodological and epistemological positions described early in this essay.

Researchers in the study of sex differences have often taken a minimalist or a maximalist position.

You will recall from chapter 1 that these terms refer to an epistemological position on the general meaning and magnitude of sex differences. Some answers to the question about whether to study sex differences focus on the usefulness of research findings that either contrast differences between males and females (maximizer position) or show similarities between males and females (minimizer position). The position taken by many feminist psychologists on the minimalist/maximalist continuum is related to their perception of the political or social significance of sex differences research. Feminist psychologists are well aware that research on sex differences is among the most heavily cited in the popular literature. Newspapers and newsmagazines are replete with articles providing evidence that demonstrates sex differences (Tavris, 1992). Concerns that have been raised about this popularization of sex differences are that women are often portrayed negatively and that the complexity of the relationship between sex and gender is not adequately explained in most popular accounts. Short reports of complex research are unlikely to explore the many caveats and cautions that a researcher would present and are also unlikely to contextualize the findings so that readers might know when and how the findings are relevant.

Questions about sex differences are also related to one's understanding of the relationship between sex and gender. According to the *essentialist* view, observations of sex differences can be explained by factors intrinsic to each sex. Gender is assumed to be a quality of people that can be observed or measured by studying male-female differences. From the *social constructionist* point of view, gender is a process that emerges from particular kinds of social arrangements and circumstances. Observations of sex differences, in and of themselves, do not reveal gender-related behaviors. Furthermore, an emphasis on sex differences without attention to social and cultural context may tend to misleadingly imply that gender is a product of sex differences.

Researchers also do not agree on the presumed relationship between biology and gender. Awareness that biological explanations for sex differences are common and concern that evidence that shows a sex difference will be treated as evidence for biologically based gender differences has led some researchers to urge caution in continuing to explore sex differences (Hyde, 1994b).

A final issue has to do with the relationship between power and gender. One argument against sex differences research is that continued emphasis on sex differences serves to divert attention away from a critical analysis of gender and power. Without an analysis of how race, ethnicity, sexual orientation, and social class are related to gender and systems of power, psychology reproduces power asymmetries rather than challenges existing systems of power (Fine & Gordon, 1989). Consistent with this focus on power and gender is the position of Coltrane, who argues that to understand gender oppression, researchers must examine masculinity and its relationship with race, class, and sexual orientation. With regard to power and masculinity, Coltrane argues that men experience the contradictory feelings of personal powerlessness and the power accorded their maleness by society. To understand this contradictory experience, he advocates the examination of masculinity from varied points of view of men's lived experience. From a critical feminist standpoint position, research on sex differences will not uncover this complex relationship between gender and power.

The issues addressed by the four responses to the question of studying sex differences focus on the practical considerations of how to improve empirical research, on the political and social meaning of sex differences, and on the varied meanings of sex differences questions. In a compelling analysis of the sex similarities versus sex differences debate within psychology, Kimball (1995) argues that both traditions should continue, with feminist psychologists adopting a double vision. She advocates a plurality of methods and active resistance to premature foreclosure on either position. Recognizing the social and political consequences of both emphasizing and minimizing sex differences, Kimball suggests

that better understanding will emerge from continued work from both perspectives. Thus, support can be advocated for any of the four arguments answering the question: should psychologists continue to do research on sex differences?

EVALUATING THE EVIDENCE

The debates over how to formulate questions about gender and what methods to use in studying gender are intense. We have introduced you to the range of answers to these questions and to the variety of methodologies that have developed as responses to criticisms of the scientific method. As you read the articles in this chapter, refer to the contrasting positions we introduced in chapter 1: social constructionism versus essentialism and minimalism versus maximalism. Try to identify the position of each author on each of these dimensions. This scrutiny will alert you to the epistemological position of each author, that is, their position on knowledge. What *kind* of knowledge are they searching for?

Another critical question that this chapter addresses is: should psychologists study sex differences? After reading the opinions of each author, you may find that you are confused. How could there be so many answers to one question? To develop your own perspective on the issue of studying sex differences, ask yourself the following: What kinds of questions about sex differences does each author address? What methods would these questions rely on? What is the relationship between the researcher and the research participants? What are the political or social implications of the question being posed or the type of answer being offered? These readings will help you become more sensitive to the relationships among question, method, and interpretation. Keep all these relationships in mind as you read each succeeding article in this book. Rather than tell you what methods psychologists should use, we want you to develop an attitude toward research on gender that is both open-minded and discerning.

NOTES

1. A hypothesis is a prediction of the outcome of a scientific study made by researchers before they begin their research. At the conclusion of the study, researchers compare the actual outcome of the research to the hypothesis and draw conclusions.

2. Probably the best known example of this control was the imprisonment of Galileo for his advocacy of the theory of Copernicus that the sun is the center of the solar system.

3. For an intriguing analysis of the relationship between feminist and other radical criticisms of science, we refer you to Fee (1986).

4. In 1985, 78 percent of published research in major social psychological journals was conducted in a laboratory, and 83 percent of research participants in these studies were white undergraduate students (Fine & Gordon, 1989).

5. In practice, considerable variation exists in how social class is defined, and the use of social class as an independent variable is not without controversy.

6. Note: In the use of terms for racial and ethnic variations, we rely on the language used by the author to whose work we are referring. In her article, Landrine uses *European American* and *ethnic minority*.

7. Altogether, five answers were offered to this question, accompanied by an introductory essay. Because of space limitations, we have chosen four answers; however, you may want to read the entire issue to get the full flavor of the discussion (*Feminism and Psychology,* vol. 4, 1994). We have chosen three articles that answer "yes" and one that answers "no," but this does not reflect our position on the relative merits of each position. The "yes" answers to the question each offer slightly different methodological solutions to sex bias, while the "no" answer seemed to us to succinctly address that point of view.

REFERENCES

Andersen, M. (1997). Studying across difference: Race, class, and gender in qualitative research. In M. Baca Zinn, P. Hondagneu-Sotelo, & M. A. Messner (Eds.), *Through the prism of difference: Readings on sex and gender.* Boston: Allyn and Bacon.

Caplan, P. J., & Caplan, J. B. (1994). *Thinking critically about research on sex and gender.* New York: HarperCollins.

Denmark, F. L., Russo, N. F., Frieze, I. H., & Sechzer, J. A. (1988). Guidelines for avoiding sexism in psychological research: A report of the APA ad hoc committee on nonsexist research. *American Psychologist, 43,* 582–585.

Fee, E. (1986). Critiques of modern science: The relationship of feminism to other radical epistemologies. In R. Bleier (Ed.), *Feminist approaches to science* (pp. 42–56.) New York: Pergamon.

Fine, M., & Gordon, S. M. (1989). Feminist transformations of/despite psychology. In M. Crawford & M. Gentry (Eds.), *Gender and thought* (pp. 146–174). New York: Springer-Verlag.

Gergen, K. (1985). The social constructionist movement in modern psychology. *American Psychologist, 40,* 266–275.

Gergen, K. J. (1988). Feminist critique of science and the challenge of social epistemology. In M. M. Gergen (Ed.), *Feminist thought and the structure of knowledge* (pp. 27–48). New York: New York University Press.

Gergen, M. (1997). Life stories: Pieces of a dream. In M. Gergen & S. Davis (Eds.), *Toward a new psychology of gender: A reader.* London: Routledge.

Harding, S. (1986). *The science question in feminism.* Ithaca, NY: Cornell University Press.

Harding, S. (1991). *Whose science? Whose knowledge? Thinking from women's lives.* Ithaca, NY: Cornell University Press.

Hyde, J. S. (1994a). Can meta-analysis make feminist transformations in psychology? *Psychology of Women Quarterly, 18,* 451–462.

Hyde, J. S. (1994b). I. Should psychologists study gender differences? Yes, with some guidelines. *Feminism & Psychology, 4,* 507–512.

Kimball, M. M. (1995). *Feminist visions of gender similarities and differences.* New York: Harrington Park Press.

Landrine, H. (Ed.). (1995). *Bringing cultural diversity to feminist psychology.* Washington, DC: American Psychological Association.

McGrath, J. E., Kelly, J. R., & Rhodes, J. E. (1993). A feminist perspective on research methodology: Some meta-theoretical issues, contrasts, and choices. In S. Oskamp & M. Constanzo (Eds.), *Gender issues in contemporary society* (pp. 19–37). Newbury Park, CA: Sage Publications.

McHugh, M. C., Koeske, R. D., & Frieze, I. N. (1986). Issues in conducting nonsexist psychological research: A guide for researchers. *American Psychologist, 41,* 879–890.

Peplau, L. A., & Conrad, E. (1989). Beyond nonsexist research. *Psychology of Women Quarterly, 13,* 379–400.

Rabinowitz, V. C., & Sechzer, J. A. (1993). Feminist perspectives on research methods. In F. L. Denmark & M. A. Paludi (Eds.), *Psychology of women: A handbook of issues and theories.* Westport, CT: Greenwood Press.

Reid, P. T., & Kelly, E. (1994). Research on women of color: From ignorance to awareness. *Psychology of Women Quarterly, 18,* 477–486.

Riger, S. (1992). Epistemological debates, feminist voices: Science, social values, and the study of women. *American Psychologist, 47,* 730–738.

Sherif, C. W. (1987). Bias in psychology. In S. Harding (Ed.), *Feminism & methodology.* Bloomington: Indiana University Press.

Shields, S. A. (1975). Functionalism, Darwinism, and the psychology of women: A study in social myth. *American Psychologist, 30*, 739–754.

Tavris, C. (1992). *Mismeasure of women.* New York: Simon & Schuster.

Unger, R. (1983). Through the looking glass: No Wonderland yet! (The reciprocal relationship between methodology and models of reality). *Psychology of Women Quarterly, 8*, 9–32.

Unger, R. (1988). Psychological, feminist, and personal epistemology. In M. M. Gergen (Ed.), *Feminist thought and the structure of knowledge* (pp. 124–141). New York: New York University Press.

Unger, R., & Crawford, M. (1996). *Women and gender: A feminist psychology* (2nd ed.). New York: McGraw-Hill.

Weisstein, N. (1968). *Kinder, Kirche, Kuche as scientific law: Psychology constructs the female.* Boston: New England Free Press.

ON READING AND UNDERSTANDING RESEARCH ON SEX DIFFERENCES

As this chapter has made clear, understanding and interpreting research findings can be controversial. Through the readings in this book, you will encounter many reports of research used as evidence for various points about gender. Some of the research you will read uses descriptive methods such as ethnographic observations or interviews, some uses feminist empirical methods, while some uses traditional empirical methods. To aid you in interpreting the empirical results you will encounter, we have prepared some general guidelines to keep in mind when you encounter research reporting statistical sex differences. These guidelines have been drawn from the analyses of Halpern (1992, 1995), Kimball (1995), and McHugh, Koeske, and Frieze (1986).

Reports of sex differences rely almost exclusively on statistical tests that compare the average (known statistically as the **mean**) performance of females to males. A statistically significant sex difference shows us that, within the confines of the research being considered, the average score of the male and female groups were reliably different. The average performance of each group does not tell you what the range of scores within each group was (the within group range), nor does it tell you the degree to which the two groups overlap. When the two groups overlap considerably, most of the scores for both men and women will fall within the same range. Let us look at a practical example of a sex difference and some common, false reasoning about sex differences. Some research indicates that women outperform men on specific tests of verbal fluency; how-

ever, the difference is small. This means that the range of scores of the two populations overlap substantially. It is not unusual to encounter someone who argues, based on these findings, that men are not as verbal as women or that because a particular person is a male, we should expect lower verbal skills. Although there is a statistically significant difference between the average performance of the female and male groups, it is not accurate to conclude that *as a group* men and women are different, nor is it possible to predict someone's performance by knowing their sex.

In interpreting a statistically significant difference between males and females, you might want to know the answers to the following questions:

1. What is the range of scores within the female and male populations?

2. What are the shapes of the distribution of scores for each group? That is, are the scores evenly spread out across the range, or are they narrowly distributed around the mean?

3. How many participants were included in the research?

4. What does the magnitude of the difference mean in practical terms?

5. What populations of individuals were studied?

6. Did the researchers study any other factors such as race, ethnicity, sexual orientation, or age? Do these factors influence the observed sex difference?

7. Are all alternative explanations evaluated, or does the researcher rely on an essentialist view of sex differences?

ON READING AND UNDERSTANDING META-ANALYSIS

In this chapter's discussion of feminist empiricist methods, we introduce the use of a particular statistical technique called meta-analysis. In this book, you will encounter several reports of research summaries using meta-analysis, and you will need to know how to interpret these results. Meta-analysis makes it possible to estimate the magnitude of a sex difference from a collection of research studies on the same topic. To conduct a meta-analysis, a researcher collects and analyzes all the studies done on a particular question, such as aggression, verbal ability, or empathy. The procedure takes into account the number of subjects in each study, the average score of the male and female groups, and the variability within each group. The result is a statistic known as d, which can be averaged across all the studies to produce an overall estimate known as an "effect size." This effect size allows one to judge the magnitude of a sex difference across all the known studies on a particular topic. Of particular importance for you, as you read this book, are some guidelines for judging the magnitude of the d statistic.

There are no definite rules for interpreting the d statistic; however, there are some rules of thumb that most researchers use in judging the magnitude of a sex difference. When you read research that reports the d statistic, keep in mind that the average of d is 0, a value of about .20 is considered a small sex difference, .50 is considered moderate, and .80 is considered large (Hyde, 1996). You should keep in mind that meta-analysis does not take into account any criticisms of the individual pieces of research, and the result of the meta-analysis will only be useful to the extent that each individual study has been carefully conducted.

These guidelines are only a beginning to understanding and critically evaluating research findings. Any piece of research is subject to criticism, just as any piece of research might fill in a missing piece of the gender puzzle. Whether these readings, and the research therein, successfully address the issues raised in this book depends, in part, on your ability to discern the adequacy of the findings. We encourage you to keep these guidelines in mind and refer back to them as you read the various studies reported in this book.

REFERENCES

Halpern, D. F. (1992). *Sex differences in cognitive abilities* (2nd ed.). Hillsdale, NJ: Erlbaum.

Halpern, D. (1995). Cognitive sex differences: Why diversity is a critical research issue. In H. Landrine (Ed.), *Bringing cultural diversity to feminist psychology* (pp. 77–92). Washington, DC: American Psychological Association.

Hyde, J. (1996). Where are the gender differences? Where are the gender similarities? In D. M. Buss & N. M. Malamuth (Eds.), *Sex, power, conflict: Evolutionary and feminist perspectives* (pp. 107–118). New York: Oxford University Press.

Kimball, M. M. (1995). *Feminist visions of gender similarities and differences.* New York: Harrington Park Press.

McHugh, M. C., Koeske, R. D., & Frieze, I. N. (1986). Issues in conducting nonsexist psychological research: A guide for researchers. *American Psychologist, 41,* 879–890.

Epistemological Debates, Feminist Voices: Science, Social Values, and the Study of Women

STEPHANIE RIGER

Feminist criticisms of the neglect, distortion, and exclusion of women in psychological research reflect three epistemological positions: feminist empiricism, feminist standpoint epistemologies, and postmodern feminism. On the basis of these criticisms, some argue that there is a need for a uniquely feminist method. This article critically examines these claims and calls for a new vision of the psychological study of women that construes gender as a product of social interaction and links women's agency with the shaping power of the sociocultural, historical, and political context.

Modern scientific methods, invented in the 16th century, were not only a stunning technical innovation, but a moral and political one as well, replacing the sacred authority of the Church with science as the ultimate arbiter of truth (Grant, 1987). Unlike medieval inquiry, modern science conceives itself as a search for knowledge free of moral, political, and social values. The application of scientific methods to the study of human behavior distinguished American psychology from philosophy and enabled it to pursue the respect accorded the natural sciences (Sherif, 1979).

The use of "scientific methods" to study human beings rested on three assumptions:

(1) Since the methodological procedures of natural science are used as a model, human values enter into the study of social phenomena and conduct only as objects; (2) the goal of social scientific investigation is to construct laws or lawlike generalizations like those of physics; (3) social science has a technical character, providing knowledge which is solely instrumental. (Sewart, 1979, p. 311)

Critics recently have challenged each of these assumptions. Some charge that social science reflects not only the values of individual scientists but also those of the political and cultural milieux in which science is done, and that there are no theory-neutral "facts" (e.g., Cook, 1985; Prilleltensky, 1989; Rabinow & Sullivan, 1979; Sampson, 1985; Shields, 1975). Others claim that there are no universal, ahistorical laws of human behavior, but only descriptions of how people act in certain places at certain times in history (e.g., K. J. Gergen, 1973; Manicas & Secord, 1983; Sampson, 1978). Still others contend that knowledge is not neutral; rather, it serves an ideological purpose, justifying power (e.g., Foucault, 1980, 1981). According to this view, versions of reality not only reflect but also legitimate particular forms of social organization and power asymmetries. The belief that knowledge is merely technical, having no ideological function, is refuted by the ways in which science has played handmaiden to social values, providing an aura of scientific authority

Michael S. Pallack served as action editor for this article.

The use of first names herein is intended to highlight the contributions of women to psychology. I am grateful to Dan A. Lewis for comments and discussion on numerous iterations of this article; to Marilyn Yalom, Karen Offen, and other members of the Affiliated and Visiting Scholars Seminar of the Institute for Research on Women and Gender of Stanford University; to Sandra Bartky, Cynthia Fuchs Epstein, Christopher Keys, Jane Mansbridge, and Shula Reinharz for helpful comments; and to Rondi Cartmill for outstanding research assistance. An extended version of this article will appear in *Psychology of Women: Biological, Psychological and Social Perspectives* (Riger, in preparation).

Correspondence concerning this article should be addressed to Stephanie Riger, Women's Studies Program (M/C 360), University of Illinois at Chicago, Box 4348, Chicago, IL 60680.

to prejudicial beliefs about social groups and giving credibility to certain social policies (Degler, 1991; Shields, 1975; Wittig, 1985).

Within the context of these general criticisms, feminists have argued in particular that social science neglects and distorts the study of women in a systematic bias in favor of men. Some contend that the very processes of positivist science are inherently masculine, reflected even in the sexual metaphors used by the founders of modern science (Keller, 1985; Merchant, 1980). To Francis Bacon, for example, nature was female, and the goal of science was to "bind her to your service and make her your slave" (quoted in Keller, 1985, p. 36). As Sandra Harding (1986) summarized.

> Mind vs. nature and the body, reason vs. emotion and social commitment, subject vs. object and objectivity vs. subjectivity, the abstract and general vs. the concrete and particular—in each case we are told that the former must dominate the latter lest human life be overwhelmed by irrational and alien forces, forces symbolized in science as the feminine. (p. 125)

Critics see the insistence of modern science on control and distance of the knower from the known as a reflection of the desire for domination characteristic of a culture that subordinates women's interests to those of men (Hubbard, 1988; Reinharz, 1985). Some go so far as to claim that because traditional scientific methods inevitably distort women's experience, a new method based on feminist principles is needed (M. M. Gergen, 1988). Others disagree, claiming that the problem in science is not objectivity itself, but rather lack of objectivity that enables male bias to contaminate the scientific process (Epstein, 1988). The first part of this article summarizes feminist charges against standard versions of science; the second part explores three possibilities for a distinctly "feminist" response to those charges: *feminist empiricism, feminist standpoint epistemologies,* and *feminist postmodernism.* (By feminist, I refer to a system of values that challenges male dominance and advocates social, political, and economic equity of women and men in society.)

BIAS WITHIN PSYCHOLOGY IN THE STUDY OF WOMEN

Since Naomi Weisstein denounced much of psychology as the "fantasy life of the male psychologist" in 1971, numerous critics have identified the ways that gender bias permeates social science (summarized in Epstein, 1988, pp. 17–45; Frieze, Parsons, Johnson, Ruble, & Zellman, 1978, pp. 11–27; Hyde, 1991, pp. 7–15; Lips, 1988, pp. 64–75; Millman & Kanter, 1975; Wilkinson, 1986). For many years, subjects of relevance to women, such as rape or housework, have been considered either taboo topics or too trivial to study, marginal to more central and prestigious issues, such as leadership, achievement, and power (Epstein, 1988; McHugh, Koeske, & Frieze, 1986; Farberow, 1963; Smith, 1987). Women's invisibility as subjects of research extends to their role as researchers as well, with relatively few women in positions of power or prestige in science (Rix, 1990). Even today, women make up only 25% of the faculty in psychology departments and only 15% of editors of psychological journals (Walker, 1991). When women are studied, their actions often are interpreted as deficient compared with those of men. Even theories reflect a male standard (Gilligan, 1982). The classic example dates back to Freud's (1925/1961) formulation in 1925 of the theory of penis envy.

Over the last two decades, critics have compiled a long and continually growing list of threats to the validity of research on women and sex differences (see Jacklin, 1981). For example, a great many studies have included only male samples. Sometimes women are included only as the stimulus, not the subject of study—they are seen but not heard—but conclusions are generalized to everyone (Meyer, 1988). Sex-of-experimenter effects contaminate virtually every area of research (Lips, 1988), and field studies yield different findings than laboratory research on the same phenomenon (Unger, 1981). Multiple meanings of the term *sex* confound biological sex differences with factors that vary by sex (i.e., sex-*related* differences) and are more appropriately labeled *gender* (McHugh et al., 1986; Unger 1979). Sex is treated as an independent variable in studies of gender difference, even though people cannot be randomly assigned to the "male" or "female" group (Unger, 1979). The emphasis on a "difference" model obscures gender similarities (Unger, 1979); this emphasis is built into the methods of science because experiments are formally designed to reject the null hypothesis that there is no difference between the experimental group and the control group. When a difference is found, it is usually small, but the small size is often overshadowed by the fact that a difference exists at all (Epstein, 1988). A focus on between-gender differences and a lack of attention to within-gender differences reflects a presupposition of gender polarity that frames this research (Fine & Gordon, 1989).

Findings of the magnitude of sex differences have diminished over time, perhaps because of an increasing willingness to publish results when such differences are not significant (Hyde, 1990), or perhaps because of a reduction in operative sex role stereotypes. For example, findings of differences in cognitive abilities appear to have declined precipitously over the past two decades (Feingold, 1988), and researchers have found greater influenceability among women in studies published prior to 1970 than in those published later (Eagley, 1978). Carol Jacklin (1981) pointed out that the more carefully a study is carried out, the less likely it is that gender differences will be found: "With fewer variables confounded with sex, sex will account for smaller percentages of variance. Thus, paradoxically, the better the sex-related research, the less useful sex is as an explanatory variable" (p. 271). The decline in findings of difference suggest either that increasing care in designing studies has eliminated differences that were artifacts of bias, or that historical factors, rather than ahistorical, universal laws, shape behavior, whether of subjects or experimenters. In fact, so many studies find no sex differences that this research might more appropriately be called the study of sex similarities (Connell, 1987).

Psychological research on women often contains another source of bias, the lack of attention to social context. The purpose of the laboratory experiment is to isolate the behavior under study from supposedly extraneous contaminants so that it is affected only by the experimental conditions. The experimental paradigm assumes that subjects leave their social status, history, beliefs, and values behind as they enter the laboratory, or that random assignment vitiates the effects of these factors. The result is to abstract people's action from social roles or institutions (Fine & Gordon, 1989; Parlee, 1979; Sherif, 1979). Instead of being contaminants, however, these factors may be critical determinants of behavior. By stripping behavior of its social context, psychologists rule out the study of sociocultural and historical factors, and implicitly attribute causes to factors inside the person. Moreover, an absence of consideration of the social context of people's actions is not limited to laboratory research (Fine, 1984). In an ironic reversal of the feminist dictum of the 1960s, when social context is ignored, the political is misinterpreted as personal (Kitzinger, 1987).

Ignoring social context may produce a reliance on presumed biological causes when other explanations of sex differences are not obvious, even when the biological mechanisms that might be involved are not apparent (Lips, 1988). Social explanations become residual, although sociocultural determinants may be just as robust and important as biological causes, if not more so (Connell, 1987). Although biological differences between the sexes are obviously important, it is critical to distinguish between biological difference and the social meaning attached to that difference (Rossi, 1979).

Alice Eagley (1987) raised a different objection to experimentation. She disagreed that the psychological experiment is context-stripped, and contended instead that it constitutes a particular context. An experiment typically consists of a brief encounter among strangers in an unfamiliar setting, often under the eye of a psychologist. The question is whether this limited situation is a valid one from which to make generalizations about behavior. To Eagley, the problem is that social roles (such as mother, doctor, or corporation president) lose their salience in this setting, bringing to the foreground gender-related expectations about behavior.

Cynthia Fuchs Epstein (1988) stated that "Much of the bias in social science reporting of gender issues comes from scientists' inability to capture the social context or their tendency to regard it as unnecessary to their inquiry—in a sense, their disdain for it" (p. 44). In psychology, this disdain has at least two sources (Kahn & Yoder, 1989; Prilleltensky, 1989). First, psychology focuses on the person as he or she exists at the moment. Such a focus leads the researcher away from the person's history or social circumstances. Second, the cultural context in which psychology is practiced (at least in the United States) is dominated by an individualistic philosophy (Kitzinger, 1987; Sampson, 1985). The prevailing beliefs assume that outcomes are due to choices made by free and self-determining individuals; the implication is that people get what they deserve (Kahn & Yoder, 1989). Not only assumptions of individualism, but also those of male dominance are often so taken for granted that we are not aware of them. Recognition that supposedly scientific assertions are permeated with ideological beliefs produces, in Shulamit Reinharz's (1985) words, a condition of "feminist distrust." Perhaps one of the most difficult challenges facing social scientists is to disengage themselves sufficiently from commonly shared beliefs so that those beliefs do not predetermine research findings (McHugh et al., 1986).

FEMINIST RESPONSES TO THE CRITICISMS OF SCIENCE

Challenges to the neutrality of science have long been a concern to those who study women, and have prompted three different reactions among feminists (Harding, 1986). Some remain loyal to scientific traditions, attempting to rise above the cultural embeddedness of these traditions by adhering more closely to the norms of science (e.g., Epstein, 1988; McHugh et al., 1986). Others seek to redress the male-centered bias in science by giving voice to women's experience and by viewing society from women's perspective (e.g., Belenky, Clinchy, Goldberger, & Tarule, 1986; Gilligan, 1982; Smith, 1987). Still others abandon traditional scientific methods entirely (e.g., Hare-Mustin, 1991). Philosopher of science Sandra Harding (1986) labeled these three approaches, respectively, feminist empiricism, feminist standpoint science, and postmodernism (see also Morgan's, 1983, distinction among positivist, phenomenological, and critical/praxis-oriented research paradigms). Next, I examine the manifestations of these three positions in the study of the psychology of women.

Feminist Empiricism

The psychologists who identified the problem of experimenter effects did not reject experimentation. Instead, they recommended strategies to minimize the impact of the experimenter (Rosenthal, 1966). Likewise, feminist empiricists advocate closer adherence to the tenets of science as the solution to the problem of bias. From this perspective, bias is considered error in a basically sound system, an outbreak of irrationality in a rational process. Scrupulous attention to scientific methods will eliminate error, or at least minimize its impact on research findings (Harding, 1986). Once neutrality is restored, scientific methods, grounded in rationality, will give access to the truth.

Maureen McHugh et al. (1986) presented a set of guidelines for eliminating bias. In addition to obvious corrections of the problems described earlier, other steps can be taken to ensure that the impact of the researcher's values is minimized, such as specifying the circumstances in which gender differences are found (because contexts tend to be deemed more appropriate for one sex than the other) and assessing experimental tasks for their sex neutrality (because many tasks are perceived to be sex linked; Deaux, 1984). The sex composition of the group of participants in research also may affect behavior because individuals act differently in the presence of females or males (Maccoby, 1990). Finally, attention ought to be paid to findings of sex similarities as well as sex differences, and the magnitude of such differences reported.

These suggestions are intended to produce gender-fair research using traditional scientific methods. The assumption is that a truly neutral science will produce unbiased knowledge, which in turn will serve as a basis for a more just social policy (Morawski, 1990). Yet the continuing identification of numerous instances of androcentric bias in research has lead some to conclude that value-free research is impossible, even if it is done by those of good faith (Hare-Mustin & Maracek, 1990). Technical safeguards cannot completely rule out the influence of values; scientific rigor in testing hypotheses cannot eliminate bias in theories or in the selection of problems for inquiry (Harding, 1986, 1991). Hence critics assert that traditional methods do not reveal reality, but rather act as constraints that limit our understanding of women's experiences.

Feminist Standpoint Epistemologies

Feminist empiricism argues that the characteristics of the knower are irrelevant to the discovery process if the norms of science are followed. In contrast, feminist standpoint epistemologies claim that we should center our science on women because "what we know and how we know depend on who we are, that is, on the knower's historical locus and his or her position in the social hierarchy" (Maracek, 1989, p. 372). There are several justifications for this viewpoint (see Harding, 1986). First, some argue that women's cognitive processes and modes of research are different than men's. It has been suggested that a supposedly feminine communal style of research that emphasizes cooperation of the researcher and subjects, an appreciation of natural contexts, and the use of qualitative data contrasts with a supposedly masculine agentic orientation that places primacy on distance of the researcher from the subjects, manipulation of subjects and the environment, and the use of quantitative data (Carlson, 1972; cf. Peplau & Conrad, 1989). Evelyn Fox Keller (1985) attempted to provide grounds for this position in a psychoanalytic view of child development. She argued that the male child's need to differentiate himself from his mother leads him to equate autonomy with distance from others (see also Chodorow, 1978). The process of developing a masculine sense of self thus establishes in the male a style of thinking that both reflects and produces the emphasis in science on distance, power, and control. Keller identifies an alternative model of science based not on controlling but rather on "conversing" with nature.

Keller's (1985) argument that science need not be based on domination is salutary, but her explanation is problematic. She presumes, first, that male and female infants have quite different experiences and, second, that those early experiences shape the activities of adult scientists, but she does not substantiate these claims. The supposedly masculine emphasis on separation and autonomy may be a manifestation of Western mainstream culture rather than a universal distinction between women and men. Black men and women who returned from northern U.S. cities to live in the rural South manifest a relational as opposed to autonomous self-image (Stack, 1986), and both Eastern and African world views see individuals as interdependent and connected, in contrast to the Western emphasis on a bounded and independent self (Markus & Oyserman, 1989). Identifying a masculine cognitive style as the grounds for scientific methods seems to doom most women and perhaps non-White men to outsider status. Furthermore, an emphasis on cognitive style ignores the role played by social structure, economics, and politics in determining topics and methods of study (Harding, 1986). Experimental methods in psychology characterized by control and objectivity are accorded prestige partly because they emulate the highly valued physical sciences (Sherif, 1979). Within social science, the prestige of a study mirrors the prestige of its topic (Epstein, 1988). Sociocultural factors such as these seem more likely as determinants of the shape of science than individual psychology.

A more plausible basis for a feminist standpoint epistemology is the argument that women's life experiences are not fully captured in existing conceptual schemes. Research often equates *male* with the general, typical case, and considers *female* to be the particular—a subgroup demarcated by biology (Acker, 1978). Yet analytical categories appropriate for men may not fit women's experience. Dorothy Smith (1987) argued that women are alienated from their own experience by having to frame that experience in terms of men's conceptual schemes; in Smith's terms they have a "bifurcated consciousness"—daily life grounded in female experience but only male conceptual categories with which to interpret that experience.

Starting our inquiries from a subordinate group's experience will uncover the limits of the dominant group's conceptual schemes where they do not fully fit the subordinates (see also Miller, 1986). Accordingly, a science based on women's traditional place in society not only would generate categories appropriate to women, but also would be a means of discovering the underlying organization of society as a whole (see also Code, 1981).

In contrast to traditional social science in which the researcher is the expert on assessing reality, an interpretive-phenomenological approach permits women to give their own conception of their experiences. Participants, not researchers, are considered the experts at making sense of their world (Cherryholmes, 1988). The shift in authority is striking. Yet phenomenological approaches are limited in at least two ways. First, they require that the subjects studied be verbal and reflective (Reinharz, 1992); second, they run the risk of psychological reductionism (attributing causation simply to internal, psychological factors: Morawski, 1988).

Carol Gilligan's (1982) theory of women's moral development is the most influential psychological study in this tradition. Her work asserting that women stress caring in the face of moral dilemmas in contrast to men's emphasis on justice has been criticized because other researchers have found no sex differences in moral reasoning using standardized scales (e.g., Greeno & Maccoby, 1986; Mednick, 1989). Gilligan (1986) retorted that women's responses on those scales are not relevant to her purposes:

> The fact that educated women are capable of high levels of justice reasoning has no bearing on the question of whether they would spontaneously choose to frame moral problems in this way. My interest in the way people *define* moral problems is reflected in my research methods, which have centered on first-person accounts of moral conflict. (p. 328)

Although standardized scales might tell us what women have in common with men, they will not reveal the way women would define their own experiences if given the opportunity to do so. The absence (and impossibility) of a comparison group of men in Gilligan's definitive study of 29 women considering abortions raises questions about whether moral orientations are sex linked, however (Crawford, 1989; Epstein, 1988, pp. 81–83).

The feminist standpoint epistemologies aim not simply to substitute "woman centered" for "man centered" gender loyalties, but rather to provide a basis for a more accurate understanding of the entire world. Howard Becker (1967) claimed that

> In any system of ranked groups, participants take it as given that members of the highest group have the right to define the way things really are. . . . Credibility and the right to be heard are differentially distributed through the ranks of the system. (p. 241)

Feminist standpoint epistemologies argue that traditional methods of science give credibility only to the dominant group's views. Listening to subordinates reveals the multifocal nature of reality (Riger, 1990). The term *subjugated knowledges* describes the perspectives of those sufficiently low on the hierarchy that their interpretations do not reflect the predominant modes of thought (Foucault, 1980, p. 81). Giving voice to women's perspective means identifying the ways in which women create meaning and experience life from their particular position in the social hierarchy.

Moreover, women (and minorities) sometimes have a better vantage point to view society than do majorities because minority status can render people socially invisible, thus permitting them access to the majority group that is not reciprocated (Merton, 1972). Accordingly, incorporating subordinates' experience will not only "add" women and minorities to existing understandings, it will add a more thorough understanding of the dominant group as well. For example, Bell Hooks (1984) described African Americans living in her small Kentucky hometown as having a double vision. They looked from the outside in at the more affluent White community across the railroad tracks, but their perspective shifted to inside out when they crossed those tracks to work for White employers. Movement across the tracks was regulated, however: Whites did not cross over to the

Black community, and laws ensured that Blacks returned to it.

The arguments for feminist standpoint epistemologies have stimulated rich and valuable portrayals of women's experience. Yet there are problems with a feminist standpoint as the basis for science. First, assuming a commonality to all women's experience glosses over differences among women of various racial and ethnic groups and social classes (Spelman, 1988). The life experience of a woman wealthy enough to hire childcare and household help may have more in common with her spouse than with a poor woman trying to raise her children on a welfare budget. Standpoint epistemology can recognize multiple subjugated groups demarcated by gender, race, social class, sexual orientation, and so on. Yet carried to an extreme, this position seems to dissolve science into autobiography. A critical challenge for feminist standpoint epistemology is to identify the commonalities of subjugated experience among different groups of women without losing sight of their diversity. Moreover, those who are subjugated may still adhere to a dominant group's ideology.

Furthermore, we each have multiple status identities (Merton, 1972). The poet Audre Lorde (1984) described herself as "a forty-nine-year-old Black lesbian feminist socialist mother of two, including one boy, and a member of an interracial couple" (p. 114). Each of these identities becomes salient in a different situation; at times, they conflict within the same situation. The hyphenated identities that we all experience in different ways—Black feminist, lesbian mother, Asian American, and so on—call into question the unity of the category of woman, making it difficult to generalize about "women's experience" (Harding, 1987).

Nonetheless, feminist standpoint epistemologies do not claim that social status alone allows the viewer clarity. Reasonable judgments about whether views are empirically supported are still possible. Rather than proclaiming the one true story about the world, feminist standpoint epistemologies seek partial and less distorted views. These partial views, or situated knowledges, can be far less limited than the dominant view (Haraway, 1988).

Feminist Postmodernism

A number of perspectives, including Marxism, psychoanalysis, and postmodernism, share a challenge to the primacy of reason and the autonomy of the individual. Here I focus on postmodernism and, in particular, poststructuralism, because of its influence on an emerging stream of feminist psychology (e.g., Hare-Mustin & Maracek, 1990; Wilkinson, 1986). A traditional social scientist entering the terrain of poststructuralism at times feels a bit like Alice falling into a Wonderland of bewildering language and customs that look superficially like her own yet are not. Things that seem familiar and stable—the meaning of words, for example—become problematic. What once were nouns (e.g., privilege, valor, foreground) now are verbs. Even the landscape looks different, as words themselves are chopped up with parentheses and hyphens to make visible their multiple meanings. What is most unsettling, perhaps, is the fundamental poststructuralist assertion that science does not mirror reality, but rather creates it (i.e., making science a process of invention rather than discovery; Howard, 1991). Many scientists would agree that an unmediated perception of reality is impossible to obtain, and that research findings represent (rather than mirror) reality. However, they would maintain that some representations are better than others. The traditional scientific criteria of validity, generalizability, and so forth determine how close research findings come to actual truth. In contrast, poststructuralists reject traditional notions of truth and reality, and claim instead that power enables some to define what is or is not considered knowledge. Expressing our understanding of experience must be done through language, but language is not a neutral reflection of that experience because our linguistic categories are not neutral:

> If statements and not things are true or false, then truth is necessarily linguistic: if truth is linguistic, then it is relative to language use (words, concepts, statements, discourses) at a given time and place; therefore, ideology, interests, and power arrangements at a given time and place are implicated in the production of what counts as "true." (Cherryholmes, 1988, p. 439)

Or, as Humpty Dumpty said to Alice in *Through the Looking Glass:*

> "When I use a word," Humpty Dumpty said, in a rather scornful tone, "it means just what I choose it to mean—neither more or less."
> "The question is," said Alice, "whether you can make words mean so many different things."
> "The question is," said Humpty Dumpty, "which is to be master—that's all." (Carroll, 1872/1923, p. 246)

The central question in poststructuralism is not how well our theories fit the facts, or how well the facts produced by research fit what is real. Rather, the question is which values and social institutions are favored by each of multiple versions of reality (i.e., discourses). Of critical concern is whose interests are served by competing ways of giving meaning to the world (Weedon, 1987). Feminists of a postmodern bent claim that positivism's neutral and disinterested stance masks what is actually the male conception of reality; this conception reflects and maintains male power interests (Gavey, 1989). As legal scholar Catherine MacKinnon (1987) put it, "Objectivity— the nonsituated, universal standpoint, whether claimed or aspired to—is a denial of the existence of potency of sex inequality that tacitly participates in constructing reality from the dominant point of view" (p. 136). In MacKinnon's view, rather than being neutral, "the law sees and treats women the way men see and treat women" (p. 140). The same criticism can be made about traditional social science in its exclusion, distortion, and neglect of women.

The social constructionist stance, as poststructuralism is known within psychology (K. J. Gergen, 1985), offers a particular challenge to the psychology of women. In contrast to feminist empiricism, the central question no longer asks whether sex or gender differences exist. Knowing the truth about difference is impossible (Hare-Mustin & Maracek, 1990). Varying criteria of differentness can produce divergent findings, for example, when conclusions based on averages contradict those based on the amount of overlap of scores of men and women (Luria, 1986). When an assumed difference is not scientifically supported,

the argument simply shifts to another variable (Unger, 1979), and similar findings can be interpreted in opposing ways. Given the impossibility of settling these questions, poststructuralism shifts the emphasis to the question of difference itself (Scott, 1988):

> What do we make of gender differences? What do they mean? Why are there so many? Why are there so few? Perhaps we should be asking: What is the point of differences? What lies beyond difference? Difference aside, what else is gender? The overarching question is choice of question. (Hare-Mustin & Maracek, 1990, pp. 1–2)

One goal of a feminist constructionist science is "disrupting and displacing dominant (oppressive) knowledges" in part by articulating the values supported by alternate conceptions of reality (Gavey, 1989, p. 462). An analysis of contrasting perspectives on sex differences demonstrates the relationship among values, assumptive frameworks, and social consequences. According to Rachel Hare-Mustin and Jeanne Maracek (1988), the received views of men and women tend either to exaggerate or to minimize the differences between them. On the one hand, the tendency to emphasize differences fosters an appreciation of supposedly feminine qualities, but it simultaneously justifies unequal treatment of women and ignores variability within each sex group. The consequence of emphasizing difference, then, is to support the status quo. On the other hand, the tendency to minimize differences justifies women's access to educational and job opportunities, but it simultaneously overlooks the fact that equal treatment is not always equitable, because of differences in men's and women's position in a social hierarchy. Gender-neutral grievance procedures in organizations, for example, do not apply equally to men and women if men are consistently in positions of greater power (Riger, 1991).

Researchers have widely different interpretations of the implications of poststructural critiques for social science methods. Some use empirical techniques for poststructuralist ends. Social constructionists see traditional research methods as a means of providing "objectifications" or illustrations, similar to vivid photographs, that are useful in making an argument persuasive rather than in validating truth claims (K. J. Gergen, 1985). Traditional methods can also help identify varying versions of reality. For example, Celia Kitzinger (1986, 1987) used Q-sort methodology to distinguish five separate accounts of lesbians' beliefs about the origin of their sexual orientation. Techniques of attitude measurement can also be used to assess the extent to which people share certain versions of reality. Rhoda Unger and her colleagues used surveys to assess belief in an objectivist or subjectivist epistemology, finding that adherence to a particular perspective varied with social status (Unger, Draper, & Pendergrass, 1986).

Others propose that we treat both psychological theories and people's actions and beliefs as texts (i.e., discursive productions located in a specific historical and cultural context and shaped by power), rather than as accounts, distorted or otherwise, of experience (Cherryholmes, 1988; Gavey, 1989). Methods developed in other disciplines, particularly literary criticism, can be used to analyze these texts. For example, through careful reading of an interview transcript with an eye to discerning "discursive patterns of meaning, contradictions, and inconsistencies," Nicola Gavey (p. 467) identified cultural themes of "permissive sexuality" and "male sexual needs" in statements by a woman about her experiences of heterosexual coercion (see also Hare-Mustin, 1991; Walkerdine, 1986). A particular technique of discourse analysis, deconstruction, can be used to expose ideological assumptions in written or spoken language, as Joanne Martin (1990) did to identify forces that suppress women's achievement within organizations. Deconstruction highlights the revealing quality not just of what is said, but rather of what is left out, contradictory, or inconsistent in the text. Deconstruction offers a provocative technique for analyzing hidden assumptions. Yet it is a potentially endless process, capable of an infinite regress, inasmuch as any deconstruction can itself be deconstructed (Martin, 1990).

The absence of any criteria for evaluation means that the success of accounts of social construction "depend primarily on the analyst's capacity to invite,

compel, stimulate, or delight the audience, and not on criteria of veracity" (K. J. Gergen, 1985, p. 272). This raises the possibility that what Grant (1987) said in another context could apply here: "Such theories risk devolving into authoritarian non-theories more akin to religions" (p. 113). The relativism of poststructuralism can be countered, however, by the identification of moral criteria for evaluation (K. J. Gergen, 1985; Unger, 1983). Theory and research can be assessed in terms of their pragmatic utility in achieving certain social and political goals, rather than the allegedly neutral rules of science (Gavey, 1989). However, because feminists disagree about whether celebrating women's difference or emphasizing the similarity of the sexes is most likely to change women's basic condition of subordination (Snitow, 1990), agreement about criteria for evaluation seems unlikely.

What poses perhaps the greatest dilemma for feminists is the view of the subject advocated by poststructuralist theory. Poststructuralists consider the attribution of agency and intentionality to the subject to be part of a deluded liberal humanism, complicit with the status quo. The multiple discourses of selfhood, intentionality, and so forth that are present in our culture compete for dominance; those that prevail constitute individual subjectivity. Social cognition on the part of the individual is channeled into certain ways of thinking that dominate society (although resistance is possible). Those discourses antedate our consciousness and give meaning to our experience, which otherwise has no essential meaning (Weedon, 1987). In contrast, feminist standpoint epistemologies consider individuals to be the active construers of their reality, albeit within a particular social and historical context; women's subjectivity is considered an important source of information about their experience. Poststructuralism's rejection of intentionality on the part of the individual seems to deny the validity of women's voices, just at a time when women are beginning to be heard (see also Hartsock, 1987).

Poststructuralism offers a provocative critique of social science and makes us critically aware of the relationship of knowledge and power. Yet the focus on "problematizing the text" of our disciplines, although admirably self-reflexive, can lead to an inward emphasis that neglects the study of women in society. In a parallel manner, poststructuralism's emphasis on language as determining consciousness can lead to the disregard of other determinants, such as women's position in a social hierarchy (Segal, 1986). Furthermore, Rhoda Unger (1988) identified a dilemma for social scientists who reject traditional empirical methods:

> The attempt to infer cause-and-effect relationships about human behavior using the tools of empiricism is one of the few unique contributions that psychology as a discipline can offer to the rest of scholarship. If such tools may not be used by feminist psychologists there is little likelihood that their insights will be taken seriously by the rest of the discipline. (p. 137)

Feminist foremothers in psychology, such as Helen Thompson (Woolley) and her colleagues, at the turn of this century, used traditional scientific methods to contest social myths about women (Reinharz, 1992; Rosenberg, 1982); they may still serve that purpose today. Poststructuralists would likely retort that the fact that Thompson's insights have had to be repeatedly rediscovered (or, rather, reinvented) demonstrates that power, not truth, determines which version of reality will prevail.

IS THERE A FEMINIST METHOD?

On the basis of multiple critiques of the social sciences, some propose an alternative research method based on feminist values. The lack of consensus on what values are feminist makes this a daunting project, yet many would agree on the need for more interactive, contextualized methods in the service of emancipatory goals (cf. Peplau & Conrad, 1989). A feminist method should produce a study not just *of* women, but also *for* women, helping to change the world as well as to describe it (Acker, Barry, & Esseveld, 1983; Wittig, 1985). Mary Gergen (1988) advocated the following as central tenets of a feminist method (see also Wilkinson, 1986):

1. recognizing the interdependence of experimenter and subject;
2. avoiding the decontextualizing of the subject or experimenter from their social and historical surroundings;
3. recognizing and revealing the nature of one's values within the research context;
4. accepting that facts do not exist independently of their producers' linguistic codes;
5. demystifying the role of the scientists and establishing an egalitarian relationship between science makers and science consumers. (p. 47)

Joan Acker et al. (1983) attempted to implement some of these principles in a study of women who had primarily been wives and mothers and were starting to enter the labor market. Interviews became dialogues, a mutual attempt to clarify and expand understandings. Often friendships developed between researchers and the women in the study. Acker and her colleagues discovered that these methods are not without problems, however. The researcher's need to collect information can (perhaps inadvertently) lead to the manipulation of friendship in the service of the research. Methods that create trust between researchers and participants entail the risk of exploitation, betrayal, and abandonment by the researcher (Stacey, 1988). Acker's study took place over a number of years, and participant's interpretations of their lives were constantly changing in hindsight, raising problems of validity in the research. The desire to give participants an opportunity to comment on researchers' interpretations of the interviews became a source of tension when disagreements arose. The solùtion to these dilemmas reached by Acker and her colleagues—to report the women's lives in their own words as much as possible—was not satisfactory to the women in the study who wanted more analysis of their experience. Finally, it was difficult to determine if this research experience had an emancipatory effect on participants. Intending to create social change is no assurance of actually doing so.

The conflict between the researcher's perspective and that of the participants in this study raises a critical issue for those who reject positivism's belief in the scientist as expert. Because a feminist method (at least according to the principles listed) assumes that there is no neutral observer, whose interpretations should prevail when those of the researcher and the people under study conflict? Feminism places primacy on acknowledging and validating female experience (Wilkinson, 1986), yet postmodern perspectives challenge the authority of the individual (Gavey, 1989; Weedon, 1987). Consider, for example, Margaret Andersen's (1981) study of 20 corporate wives. She disbelieved their claims of contentment and attributed their lack of feminism to *false consciousness,* a Marxist term meaning that these women identified with (male) ruling class interests against their own (female) class interests. The women wrote a rebuttal rejecting Andersen's interpretation. In response, Andersen revised her position to accept the women's statements of satisfaction with their lives. Instead of treating them as deluded or insincere, she looked for sources of their contentment in their position in the social hierarchy. Lather (1986, 1988) recommended this kind of dialogic process to avoid imposing on research participants interpretations that disempower them (see also Kidder, 1982). Without it, we grant privilege to the authority of the researcher, even if on postmodern rather than positivist grounds.

CONCLUSION

Although the strategies intended as a feminist method overcome some of the objections to traditional social science, they raise as many problems as they solve (see Reinharz, 1992). No method or epistemology seems devoid of limitations or perfectly true to feminist values, which are themselves contested (e.g., Jagger & Struhl, 1978). Feminism is most useful as a set of questions that challenge the prevailing asymmetries of power and androcentric assumptions in science and society, rather than as a basis for a unique method (Reinharz, 1992). Feminism thus identifies "patterns and interrelationships and causes and effects and implications of questions that nonfeminists have not seen and still do not see" (Lorber, 1988, p. 8).

The psychological study of women emerged from the field of individual differences. Dominated by the question of sex differences, this tradition assumes that an inner core of traits or abilities distinguishes women from men (Buss, 1976). Such a conceptualization no longer seems useful. Few gender differences in personality or abilities have been reliably demonstrated (Feingold, 1988; Hyde, 1990), and factors other than individual dispositions influence our behavior (Maccoby, 1990). A more appropriate strategy for the study of women would consider the ways in which gender is created and maintained through interpersonal processes (Deaux & Major, 1987).

From this perspective, gender does not reside within the person. Instead, it is constituted by the myriad ways in which we "do" rather than "have" gender; that is, we validate our membership in a particular gender category through interactional processes (West & Zimmerman, 1987). Gender is something we enact, not an inner core or constellation of traits that we express; it is a pattern of social organization that structures the relations, especially the power relations, between women and men (Connell, 1985, 1987; Crawford & Maracek, 1989): "In doing gender, men are also doing dominance and women are doing deference" (West & Zimmerman, 1987, p. 146). Transsexuals know well that merely altering one's sex organs does not change one's gender. Membership in the category of "male" or "female" must be affirmed continuously through social behavior (see, e.g., Morris, 1974).

Each of the epistemological positions described can contribute to this perspective, despite their contradictions. An interactional conceptualization of gender recognizes that the behavior and thoughts of men and women are channeled into certain sociocultural forms, as poststructuralism claims. As Peter Manicas and Paul Secord (1983) stated:

> Social structures (e.g., language) are reproduced and transformed by action, but they preexist for individuals. They enable persons to become persons and to act (meaningfully and intentionally), yet at the same time, they are "coercive," limiting the ways we can act. (p. 408)

The dominant ideology of a society is manifested in and reproduced by the social relations of its members (Unger, 1989). Unlike poststructuralism, however, an interactional view of gender also acknowledges individual agency in the production and transformation of social forms. Such a perspective would regard the person as an initiator of action and construer of meaning within a context composed not only of varying modes of interpreting the world but also of structural constraints and opportunities (see, e.g., Buss, 1978; Riegel, 1979; Sampson, 1978; Unger, 1983), as standpoint epistemologies claim.

Diverse methods, evaluated by reasonable criteria, are needed to capture the rich array of personal and structural factors that shape women and girls, and in turn are shaped by them. What is critical is that we are aware of the epistemological commitments—and value assumptions—we make when we adopt a particular research strategy (Unger, 1983). Moreover, rather than abandoning objectivity, systematic exami-

nation of assumptions and values in the social order that shape scientific practices can strengthen objectivity (Harding, 1991).

Epistemological debates in recent years have shattered the traditional picture of science as neutral, disinterested, and value free and have replaced it with a view of knowledge as socially constructed. Feminists' contributions to this debate highlight not only the androcentric nature of social science, but also its collusion in the perpetuation of male dominance in society. To assume that the multiple voices of women are not shaped by domination is to ignore social context and legitimate the status quo. On the other hand, to assume that women have no voice other than an echo of prevailing discourses is to deny them agency and, simultaneously, to repudiate the possibility of social change. The challenge to psychology is to link a vision of women's agency with an understanding of the shaping power of social context.

REFERENCES

Acker, J. (1978). Issues in the sociological study of women's work. In A. Stromberg & S. Harkness (Eds.), *Women working* (pp. 134–161). Palo Alto, CA: Mayfield.

Acker, J., Barry, K., & Esseveld, J. (1983). Objectivity and truth: Problems in doing feminist research. *Women's Studies International Forum, 6,* 423–435.

Andersen, M. (1981). Corporate wives: Longing for liberation or satisfied with the status quo? *Urban Life, 10,* 311–327.

Becker, H. S. (1967). Whose side are we on? *Social Problems, 14,* 239–247.

Belenky, M. F., Clinchy, B. M., Goldberger, N. R., & Tarule, J. M. (1986). *Women's ways of knowing: The development of self, voice, and mind.* New York: Basic Books.

Buss, A. R. (1976). Galton and sex differences: An historical note. *Journal of the History of the Behavioral Sciences, 12,* 283–285.

Buss, A. R. (1978). The structure of psychological revolutions. *Journal of the History of the Behavioral Sciences, 14,* 57–64.

Carlson, R. (1972). Understanding women: Implications for personality theory and research. *Journal of Social Issues, 28,* 17–32.

Carroll, L. (1923). *Alice's adventures in Wonderland; and Through the looking glass.* Philadelphia: Winston. (Original work published 1872).

Cherryholmes, C. H. (1988). Construct validity and the discourses of research. *American Journal of Education, 96,* 421–457.

Chodorow, N. (1978). *The reproduction of mothering.* Berkeley: University of California Press.

Code, L. B. (1981). Is the sex of the knower epistemologically significant? *Metaphilosophy, 12,* 267–276.

Connell, R. W. (1985). Theorizing gender. *Sociology, 19,* 260–272.

Connell, R. W. (1987). *Gender and power: Society, the person and sexual politics.* Stanford, CA: Stanford University Press.

Cook, T. D. (1985). Postpositivist critical multiplism. In L. Shotland & M. M. Mark (Eds.), *Social science and social policy* (pp. 21–62). Beverly Hills, CA. Sage.

Crawford, M. (1989). Agreeing to differ: Feminist epistemologies and women's ways of knowing. In M. Crawford & M. Gentry (Eds.), *Gender and thought: Psychological perspectives* (pp. 128–145). New York: Springer-Verlag.

Crawford, M., & Maracek, J. (1989). Psychology reconstructs the female, 1968–1988. *Psychology of Women Quarterly, 13,* 147–165.

Deaux, K. (1984). From individual differences to social categories. *American Psychologist, 39,* 105–116.

Deaux, K., & Major, B. (1987). Putting gender into context: An interactive model of gender-related behavior. *Psychological Review, 94,* 369–389.

Degler, C. (1991). *In search of human nature.* New York: Oxford University Press.

Eagley, A. H. (1978). Sex differences in influenceability. *Psychological Bulletin, 1978, 85,* 86–116.

Eagley, A. H. (1987). *Sex differences in social behavior: A social-role interpretation.* Hillsdale, NJ: Erlbaum.

Epstein, C. F. (1988). *Deceptive distinctions: Sex, gender and the social order.* New Haven, CT: Yale University Press.

Farberow, N. L. (1963). *Taboo topics.* New York: Atherton Press.

Feingold, A. (1988). Cognitive gender differences are disappearing. *American Psychologist, 43,* 95–103.

Fine, M. (1984). Coping with rape: Critical perspectives on consciousness. *Imagination, Cognition, and Personality: The Scientific Study of Consciousness, 3,* 249–67.

Fine, M., & Gordon, S. M. (1989). Feminist transformations of/despite psychology. In M. Crawford & M. Gentry (Eds.), *Gender and thought: Psychological perspectives* (pp. 146–174). New York: Springer-Verlag.

Foucault, M. (1980). *Power/knowledge: Selected interviews and other writings, 1972–1977* (C. Gordon, Ed. and Trans.). New York: Pantheon Books.

Foucault, M. (1981). *The history of sexuality: Vol. 1. An introduction.* Harmondsworth, England: Viking.

Freud, S. (1961). Some psychical consequences of the anatomical distinctions between the sexes. In J. Strachey (Ed. and Trans.), *The complete psychological works of Sigmund Freud* (Vol. 19, pp. 248–258). London: Hogarth Press. (Original work published 1925).

Frieze, I. H., Parsons, J. E., Johnson, P. B., Ruble, D. N., & Zellman, G. L. (1978). *Women and sex roles: A social psychological perspective.* New York: Norton.

Gavey, N. (1989). Feminist poststructuralism and discourse analysis: Contributions to a feminist psychology. *Psychology of Women Quarterly, 13,* 459–476.

Gergen, K. J. (1973). Social psychology as history. *Journal of Personality and Social Psychology, 26,* 309–320.

Gergen, K. J. (1985). The social constructionist movement in modern psychology. *American Psychologist, 40,* 255–265.

Gergen, M. M. (1988). Building a feminist methodology. *Contemporary Social Psychology, 13,* 47–53.

Gilligan, C. (1982). *In a different voice.* Cambridge, MA: Harvard University Press.

Gilligan, C. (1986). Reply by Carol Gilligan. *Signs: Journal of Women in Culture and Society, 11,* 324–333.

Grant, J. (1987). I feel therefore I am: A critique of female experience as the basis for a feminist epistemology. In M. J. Falco (Ed.), *Feminism and epistemology: Approaches to research in women and politics* (pp. 99–114). Binghampton, NY: Haworth Press.

Greeno, C. G., & Maccoby, E. E. (1986). How different is the "different voice"? *Signs: Journal of Women in Culture and Society, 11,* 310–316.

Haraway, D. (1988). Situated knowledges: *The science question in feminism* and the privilege of partial perspective. *Feminist Studies, 14,* 575–599.

Harding, S. (1986). *The science question in feminism.* Ithaca, N.Y.: Cornell University Press.

Harding, S. (1987). Introduction: Is there a feminist method? In S. Harding (Ed.), *Feminism and methodology: Social science issues* (pp. 1–14), Bloomington: Indiana University Press.

Harding, S. (1991). *Whose science? Whose knowledge?* Ithaca, NY: Cornell University Press.

Hare-Mustin, R. T. (1991). Sex, lies, and headaches: The problem is power. In T. J. Goodrich (Ed.), *Women and power: Perspectives for therapy.* New York: Norton.

Hare-Mustin, R. T., & Maracek, J. (1988). The meaning of difference: Gender theory, postmodernism, and psychology. *American Psychologist, 43,* 355–464.

Hare-Mustin, R. T., & Maracek, J. (1990). *Making a difference: Psychology and the construction of gender.* New Haven, CT: Yale University Press.

Hartsock, N. (1987). Epistemology and politics: Minority vs. majority theories. *Cultural Critique, 7,* 187–206.

Hooks, B. (1984). *Feminist theory: From margin to center.* Boston: South End Press.

Howard, G. S. (1991). Culture tales: Narrative approach to thinking, cross-cultural psychology, and psychotherapy. *American Psychologist, 46,* 187–197.

Hyde, J. (1990). Meta-analysis and the psychology of gender differences. *Signs: Journal of Women in Culture and Society, 16,* 55–73.

Hyde, J. (1991). *Half the human experience: The psychology of women* (4th ed.). Lexington, MA: Heath.

Hubbard, R. (1988). Some thoughts about the masculinity of the natural sciences. In M. M. Gergen, *Feminist thought and the structure of knowledge* (pp. 1–15). New York: New York University Press.

Jacklin, C. N. (1981). Methodological issues in the study of sex-related differences. *Developmental Review, I,* 266–273.

Jaggar, A., & Struhl, P. R. (1978). *Feminist frameworks: Alternative theoretical accounts of the relations between women and men.* New York: McGraw-Hill.

Kahn, A. S., & Yoder, J. D. (1989). The psychology of women and conservatism: Rediscovering social change, *Psychology of Women Quarterly, 13,* 417–432.

Keller, E. F. (1985). *Reflections on gender and science.* New Haven, CT: Yale University Press.

Kidder, L. (1982). Face validity from multiple perspectives. In D. Brinberg & L. Kidder (Eds.), *Forms of validity in research* (pp. 41–58). San Francisco: Jossey-Bass.

Kitzinger, C. (1986). Introducing and developing Q as a feminist methodology: A study of accounts of lesbianism. In S. Wilkinson (Ed.), *Feminist social psychology: Developing theory and practice* (pp. 151–172). Milton Keynes, England: Open University Press.

Kitzinger, C. (1987). *The social construction of lesbianism.* London: Sage.

Lather, P. (1986). Research as praxis. *Harvard Educational Review, 56,* 257–277.

Lather, P. (1988). Feminist perspectives on empowering research methodologies. *Women's Studies International Forum, 11,* 569–581.

Lips, H. (1988). *Sex and gender: An introduction.* Mountain View, CA: Mayfield.

Lorber, J. (1988). From the editor. *Gender & Society, 1,* 5–8.

Lorde, A. (1984). *Sister outsider: Essays and speeches.* New York: Crossing.

Luria, Z. (1986). A methodological critique. *Signs: Journal of Women in Culture and Society, 11,* 316–320.

Maccoby, E. E. (1990). Gender and relationships: A developmental account. *American Psychologist, 43,* 513–520.

MacKinnon, C. A. (1987). Feminism, Marxism, method and the state: Toward feminist jurisprudence. In S. Harding (Ed.), *Feminism and methodology: Social science issues* (pp. 135–156). Bloomington: Indiana University Press.

Manicas, P. T., & Secord, P. F. (1983). Implications for psychology of the new philosophy of science. *American Psychologist, 38,* 399–413.

Maracek, J. (1989). Introduction: Theory and method in feminist psychology [Special issue]. *Psychology of Women Quarterly, 13,* 367–377.

Markus, H., & Oyserman, D. (1989). Gender and thought: The role of the self-concept. In M. Crawford & M. Gentry (Eds.), *Gender and thought: Psychological perspectives* (pp. 100–127). New York: Springer-Verlag.

Martin, J. (1990). Deconstructing organizational taboos: The suppression of gender conflict in organizations. *Organizational Science, 5,* 339–359.

McHugh, M., Koeske, R., & Frieze, I. (1986). Issues to consider in conducting nonsexist psychological research: A guide for researchers. *American Psychologist, 41,* 879–890.

Mednick, M. T. (1989). On the politics of psychological constructs: Stop the bandwagon, I want to get off. *American Psychologist, 44,* 1118–1123.

Merchant, C. (1980). *The death of nature: Women, ecology, and the scientific revolution.* New York: Harper & Row.

Merton, R. (1972). Insiders and outsiders: A chapter in the sociology of knowledge. *American Journal of Sociology, 78,* 9–47.

Meyer, J. (1988). Feminist thought and social psychology. In M. Gergen (Ed.), *Feminist thought and the structure of knowledge* (pp. 105–123). New York: New York University Press.

Miller, J. B. (1986). *Toward a new psychology of women* (2nd ed.). Boston: Beacon.

Millman, M., & Kanter, R. (Eds.). (1975). *Another voice: Feminist perspectives on social life and social sciences.* Garden City, NY: Anchor Books.

Morawski, J. G. (1988). Impasse in feminist thought? In M. M. Gergen (Ed.), *Feminist thought and the structure of knowledge* (pp. 182–194). New York: New York University Press.

Morawski, J. G. (1990). Toward the unimagined: Feminism and epistemology in psychology. In R. L. Hare-Mustin & J. Maracek, *Making a difference: Psychology and the construction of gender* (pp. 150–183). New Haven, CT: Yale University Press.

Morgan, G. (Ed.). (1983). Toward a more reflective social science. In G. Morgan (Ed.), *Beyond method: Strategies for social research* (pp. 368–376). Beverly Hills, CA: Sage.

Morris, J. (1974). *Conundrum.* New York: Harcourt, Brace, Jovanovich.

Parlee, M. (1979). Psychology and women. *Signs: Journal of Women in Culture and Society, 5,* 121–133.

Peplau, L. A. & Conrad, E. (1989). Feminist methods in psychology. *Psychology of Women Quarterly, 13,* 379–400.

Prilleltensky, I. (1989). Psychology and the status quo. *American Psychologist, 44,* 795–802.

Rabinow, P., & Sullivan, W. M. (1979). The interpretive turn: Emergence of an approach. In P. Rabinow & W. M. Sullivan (Eds.), *Interpretive social science: A reader* (pp. 1–21). Berkeley: University of California Press.

Reinharz, S. (1985). Feminist distrust: Problems of context and context in sociological work. In D. N. Berg & K. K. Smith (Eds.), *The self in social inquiry: Researching methods* (pp. 153–172). Beverly Hills, CA: Sage.

Reinharz, S. (1992). *Feminist methods in social research.* New York: Oxford University Press.

Reigel, K. F. (1979). *Foundations of dialectical psychology.* San Diego, CA: Academic Press.

Riger, S. (1990). Ways of knowing and organizational approaches to community research. In P. Tolan, C. Keys, F. Chertok, & L. Jason (Eds.), *Researching community psychology* (pp. 42–50). Washington, DC: American Psychological Association.

Riger, S. (1991). Gender dilemmas in sexual harassment policies and procedures. *American Psychologist, 46,* 497–505.

Riger, S. (in preparation). *Psychology of women: Biological, psychological and social perspectives.* New York: Oxford University Press.

Rix, S. E. (Ed.). (1990). *The American woman, 1990–1991.* New York: Norton.

Rosenberg, R. (1982). *Beyond separate spheres.* New Haven, CT: Yale University Press.

Rosenthal, R. (1966). *Experimenter effects in behavioral research.* New York: Appleton-Century-Crofts.

Rossi, A. (1979). Reply by Alice Rossi. *Signs: Journal of Women in Culture and Society, 4,* 712–717.

Sampson, E. E. (1978). Scientific paradigms and social values: Wanted—A scientific revolution. *Journal of Personality and Social Psychology, 36,* 1332–1343.

Sampson, E. E. (1985). The decentralization of identity: Toward a revised concept of personal and social order. *American Psychologist, 40,* 1203–1211.

Scott, J. W. (1988). Deconstructing equality-versus-difference: Or, the uses of poststructuralist theory for feminism. *Feminist Studies, 14,* 33–50.

Segal, L. (1986). *Is the future female? Troubled thoughts on contemporary feminism.* London: Virago.

Sewart, J. J. (1979). Critical theory and the critique of conservative method. In S. G. McNall (Ed.), *Theoretical perspectives in sociology* (pp. 310–322). New York: St. Martin's Press.

Sherif, C. W. (1979). Bias in psychology. In J. A. Sherman & E. T. Beck (Eds.), *A prism of sex: Essays in the sociology of knowledge* (pp. 93–133). Madison: University of Wisconsin Press.

Shields, S. (1975). Functionalism, Darwinism, and the psychology of women: A study in social myth. *American Psychologist, 30,* 739–754.

Smith, D. (1987). *The everyday world as problematic.* Boston: Northeastern University Press.

Snitow, A. (1990). A gender diary. In M. Hirsch & E. F. Keller (Eds.), *Conflicts in feminism* (pp. 9–43). New York: Routledge.

Spelman, E. V. (1988). *Inessential woman: Problems of exclusion in feminist thought.* Boston: Beacon Press.

Stacey, J. (1988). Can there be a feminist ethnography? *Women's Studies International Forum, 11,* 21–27.

Stack, C. (1986). The culture of gender: Women and men of color. *Signs: Journal of Women in Culture and Society, 11,* 321–324.

Unger, R. K. (1979). Toward a redefinition of sex and gender. *American Psychologist, 34,* 1085–1094.

Unger, R. K. (1981). Sex as a social reality: Field and laboratory research. *Psychology of Women Quarterly, 5,* 645–653.

Unger, R. K. (1983). Through the looking glass: No wonderland yet! (The reciprocal relationship between methodology and models of reality). *Psychology of Women Quarterly, 8,* 9–32.

Unger, R. K. (1988). Psychological, feminist, and personal epistemology: Transcending contradiction. In M. M. Gergen (Ed.), *Feminist thought and the structure of knowledge* (pp. 124–141). New York: New York University Press.

Unger, R. K. (1989). Sex, gender, and epistemology. In M. Crawford & M. Gentry (Eds.), *Gender and thought: Psychological perspectives* (pp. 17–35). New York: Springer-Verlag.

Unger, R. K., Draper, R. D., & Pendergrass, M. L. (1986). Personal epistemology and personal experience. *Journal of Social Issues, 42,* 67–79.

Walker, L. (1991). The feminization of psychology. *Psychology of Women Newsletter of Division 35, 18,* 1, 4.

Walkerdine, V. (1986). Post-structuralist theory and everyday social practices: The family and the school. In S. Wilkinson (Ed.), *Feminist social psychology: Developing theory and practice* (pp. 57–76). Milton Keynes, England: Open University Press.

Weedon, C. (1987). *Feminist practice and poststructuralist theory.* New York: Basil Blackwell.

Weisstein, N. (1971). *Psychology constructs the female: Or, the fantasy life of the male psychologist.* Boston: New England Free Press.

West, C., & Zimmerman, D. H. (1987). Doing gender. *Gender & Society, I,* 125–151.

Wilkinson, S. (1986). Sighting possibilities: Diversity and commonality in feminist research. In S. Wilkinson (Ed.), *Feminist social psychology: Developing theory and practice* (pp. 7–24). Milton Keynes, England: Open University Press.

Wittig, M. A. (1985). Metatheoretical dilemmas in the psychology of gender. *American Psychologist, 40,* 800–811.

CHECKPOINTS

1. According to Riger, numerous gender biases in psychological research compromise our understanding of sex and gender. Feminist critiques of science emerge from attempts to address gender biases.

2. There is no single feminist alternative to science; rather, there are three prevailing feminist views of science: feminist empiricism, feminist standpoint theory, and feminist postmodernism.

To prepare for reading the next section, think about these questions:

1. Are there other biases in psychological science other than those described by Riger?

2. Can you imagine a feminist Men's Studies? How would it be defined?

Theorizing Masculinities in Contemporary Social Science

SCOTT COLTRANE

Life is not determined by consciousness, but consciousness by life . . . circumstances make men just as much as men make circumstances.

—*Karl Marx, 1846/1978a*

Not, then, men and their moments. Rather moments and their men.

—*Erving Goffman, 1967*

Living a century apart and working at different levels of analysis, Karl Marx and Erving Goffman made unique contributions to the understanding of social life. Although their works are rarely mentioned together, these passages resonate with each other and raise two issues that deserve the attention of scholars who study gender. The first is that both men used what is now called "sexist" language. Both subsumed all of humanity under the term *men,* effectively minimizing the experiences of women and ignoring the importance of gender in men's lives. One might excuse their linguistic transgressions because they were following social customs, but one ought not lose sight of the fact that gender, though considered elsewhere in their writings, was of secondary importance to them. In that sense, these two theorists teach by negative example and remind scholars that they are breaking new ground by explicitly focusing on gender when studying men.

On the second issue, the models of society presented by Marx and Goffman highlight the importance of social structure at the macro- and microlevels. Social structure is the patterned repetition of the same types of events happening over and over again, involving many different people spread out across many different locations (Collins, 1988).

Marx's and Goffman's ideas about social structure have fallen out of fashion in the recent postmodern turn toward discourse analysis and historical particularity, but their insights into the dialectical nature of social processes and their emphasis on systemic patterns of social relations have much to offer contemporary gender scholars. The macrohistorical view from Marx reminds one that individual choice is constrained by material circumstances, especially the unequal distribution of wealth and access to the means of production. The microinteractionist view from Goffman is a reminder that routine social experiences shape consciousness and define individual identities. Both theorists conceived of complex reciprocal relationships between structure and agency, but both ultimately gave priority to patterned systems of social relations. For Marx, "men" made history, but not under conditions of their own choosing. Rather, historically variable social and economic conditions shaped peoples' consciousness and constrained their actions according to identifiable patterns (Marx, 1851/1978b). For Goffman, men and women actively engaged in impression management, but they were held hostage to routine ritual observances and the collaborative production of selves (Goffman, 1967).

Few would argue that Marx privileged social structure over individual choice, but Goffman, too, gave precedence to the structure of situations. He conceived of "moments" as historically situated events that followed a loosely patterned sequence, carried normative prescriptions, and, most important, created an emergent sense of self. More than most social scientists of his day, Goffman acknowledged the importance of individual initiative in shaping society, but his fundamental assumption was that moments created "men" rather than the reverse. Although he did not attempt an explicit study of masculinity, Goffman began to write about gender before he died in 1982, and his analytical scheme, coupled with some of Marx's insights, provides the foundations for a promising microstructural approach to the study of gender (Goffman, 1977, 1979). In this chapter, I emphasize the continuing heuristic value of the concept of social structure and suggest that a microstructural approach to the study of masculinities can help guide one through some difficult epistemological and political dilemmas.

Marx and Goffman were criticized for departing from the accepted research protocols of their times, but they both advocated empirical research that seems rather scientific and conventional by today's standards. In contrast, many recent critical scholars advocate abandoning conventional sociological approaches to the study of gender on the grounds that these methods tend to favor a masculinist individualism, mask diversity, and perpetuate inequality. Conventional social science has favored the interests of dominant men and slighted the influence of gender, but the call for its abandonment carries some dangers of its own. A more reformist strategy would acknowledge the sexism of past research, but continue to use a range of objectivist and subjectivist methods to document patterned regularity in systems of inequality. Underlying this position is the belief that the critical insights of Goffman and Marx can be coupled with conventional social science methods to further the understanding of men and masculinities. Toward that end, I describe some of the epistemological issues raised by recent gender scholarship and suggest how a microstructural analysis of masculinities might be both politically and intellectually satisfying. Rather than focusing on one specific issue in detail, this chapter surveys potential and actual problems in the field and closes with a few suggestions for ways to incorporate men's standpoints into gender studies.

PAST RESEARCH ON MEN AND MASCULINITY

Research on men is as old as scholarship itself, but a focus on masculinity, or men as explicitly gendered individuals, is relatively recent (Morgan, 1981). As the women's movement was gaining momentum in the 1970s, men began writing about how boys were socialized to be tough and competitive and how men had trouble expressing their emotions (Goldberg, 1976; Nichols, 1975). Often confessional, therapeutic, and ignorant of the power dimension of gender relations, this style of research on men continued through the 1980s and into the 1990s. Some writers focused on their personal experiences caring for a child (Clary, 1982), or on middle-aged men's longing for their fathers (Osherson, 1986), and many emphasized how men suffered from confining masculine stereotypes and were misunderstood by women (Farrell, 1986). These popular books helped men develop their sensitivities, but paid little attention to those who suffered at the hands of dominant men's privileged position. Recent best-selling authors in this tradition include Robert Bly (1990) who blends mythical storytelling with pop psychology in a celebration of tribal male bonding. Books like this posit timeless natural differences between men and women, and although these authors often portray themselves as part of a progressive men's movement, their writing often resembles the antiwoman rhetoric of reactionary men's rights activists (Coltrane & Hickman, 1992).

In response to, and in support of, the women's movement, a different group of men scholars and activists adopted an explicitly feminist perspective in their early explorations of masculinity. The defining feature of this approach to men's studies was its attention to men's power over women (Pleck, 1977/1981; Sattel, 1976). During the 1980s, critical studies of men became more sophisticated and scholars developed concepts such as "hegemonic masculinity" to highlight the multidimensional and socially constructed aspects of male dominance (Connell, 1987). Recent scholarship on men uses insights from feminist theories, highlights diversity in masculinities, includes a focus on gay men, and promotes an understanding of what Kaufman (1993) calls "men's contradictory experiences of power" (Brod, 1987; Hearn & Morgan, 1990; Kaufman, 1987; Kimmel & Messner, 1989). Many current scholars use postmodern critiques of value-free social science, apply critical Marxist and feminist standpoint epistemologies, and attempt to move beyond older structuralist theoretical frameworks (Jackson, 1990; Messner, 1990; Seidler, 1989).

At the risk of oversimplification, there are thus two conflicting styles of men writing about masculinity: One celebrates male bonding and tells men they are OK, and the other focuses on issues of power using academic feminist interpretive frameworks. The former approach sells many books and receives much media attention. The latter approach, of which this volume is an example, focuses on the contradictory meanings and experiences of manhood and aligns itself with the women's movement. Of concern in this chapter, however, is the observation that neither approach makes extensive use of conventional social science methods to bolster its arguments.

For most profeminist academics, the choice to forsake positivist social science is intentional, for the traditions that spawned it are held accountable for a ubiquitous style of masculinity that is detached, unemotional, authoritarian, and prone to violence and destruction (Easlea, 1981). Nevertheless, critiques of "masculinist" social science leave unanswered some difficult questions about how to study men. For example, how does one determine what are masculinist research methods, and on what basis should they be rejected? Similarly, what counts as "feminist" research, and how is this determined? If men want to study masculinity using feminist insights, can they avoid reproducing patriarchal consciousness simply by adopting a style of discourse common among women's studies scholars? These questions plague contemporary male scholars researching men, even if the reasons for and the implications of their methodological choices remain unarticulated. For those who celebrate masculinity and tend to avoid issues of power and dominance, these epistemological questions are typically of little concern. But for profeminist men studying masculinities, these questions remain critical.

GOALS OF FEMINIST MEN'S STUDIES

Criticism of male scholars who focus on "men's studies" or call their work "feminist" has come from different quarters. In the tradition of patriarchal dominance, some colleagues (mostly men) find gender studies superfluous and suggest that conventional academic subjects are more worthy of scholarly attention. Feminist colleagues also question men's intentions when they focus on gender, and some worry about the potential patriarchal usurpation of women's studies' initiatives (Canaan & Griffin, 1990; Jardine & Smith, 1987; Reinharz, 1992). Given a discouraging and sometimes hostile academic environment, why, then, would men want to study masculinity from a feminist perspective? The short answer is that gender is too important to ignore and that feminist theories explain more about gender than other theories.

Although there are many different reasons for studying gender and a variety of theoretical and methodological approaches to its study, one key feminist assumption has inspired much research. In a very general sense, gender carries undue importance in the social world, and its salience tends to reinforce men's power over women. Most feminists agree that gender is socially constructed and that its form and relative importance are subject to change. Many, like Judith Lorber, the founding editor of *Gender & Society,* promote the idea that women and men ought to be socially interchangeable: "The long-term goal of feminism must be no less than the eradication of gender as an organizing principle of postindustrial society" (Lorber, 1986, p. 568). Paradoxically, one of the ways to work toward this long-term political goal of reducing the importance of gender is for scholars to call attention to it. Many feminists thus focus on gender as an analytical category in the study of women's lives, but do so, ultimately, to reduce its importance in everyday life.

For men to concur that gender should be unimportant in everyday life, however, opens them to criticism because men have often blithely assumed that gender could be ignored, or at least argued that competence, rather than mere biology, provided them with special privileges. Historically, men's experiences have been universalized, allowing them to overlook discrimination against women and legitimate male dominance (Kimmel, 1990). Many profeminist men avoid this regressive potential by highlighting gender and paying attention to men's overt and subtle exercise of power. By placing gender at the center of their analyses, they attempt to overcome past tendencies to view men as generically human. By linking the ways that men create and sustain gendered selves with the ways that gender influences power relations and perpetuates inequality, feminist men's studies support and compliment the critical perspectives of women's studies.

Because gender is one of the most important organizing principles of societies throughout the world, and because male scholars have too often ignored its influence on men, an explicit focus on masculinities is clearly warranted. Nonetheless, highlighting gender in the study of men carries some risks of its own. Sometimes academic claims about the importance of gender are addressed by adding "sex" to a long list of competing independent variables. When this is coupled with the pressure to publish statistically significant differences (rather than similarities), one ends up with widely reported sex differences that are relatively meaningless. Other researchers use clinical reports, interpretive methods, and ethnographic techniques to contrast the lives and perceptions of men with those of women. The findings of difference that emerge from these studies tend to legitimate taken-for-granted assumptions about dissimilarity and reinforce the importance of gender in everyday life. Thus, the use of gender as an analytic category can work against the political goal of reducing its salience. I am not suggesting that one ignore gender because of this risk. Gender carries so much weight in most social and institutional settings that it needs to be studied explicitly, even at the risk of overemphasizing its importance. Nevertheless, it is useful to consider the political implications of adopting research methods or embracing theories that stress gender differences.

ESSENTIALIST CLAIMS ABUT GENDER

Despite research and theories to the contrary, most people continue to conceive of gender differences as innately given, reflecting some underlying essential dichotomy between men and women. Early feminist scholarship, whether it focused on women or men, assumed that biological sex differences could not account for the social meaning of gender or the relative distribution of power and prestige between and among men and women. In the 1980s, academic discourse frequently moved "beyond" debunking the false unity of sex and gender, as if popular essentialist notions had already been transformed. It might seem "old" to continue to argue against the innateness of masculinity or femininity, but the distinction between sex (biological) and gender (social) deserves frequent repetition. The assumption of natural and God-given differences between men and women is so firmly embedded in habits of thought and social institutions that to focus on difference instead of similarity carries political risks.

The tendency to essentialize gender differences is not limited to the political or religious right, or even to men. Some contemporary women writers celebrate gender differences that are characterized as fundamental and timeless. For example, some French feminists (Irigaray, 1981), cultural and eco-feminists (Griffin, 1978), neoconservative feminists (Elshtain, 1981), and biosocial feminists (Rossi, 1985) conflate sex and gender by positing universal sex differences based on females' reproductive functions and putative closeness to nature (Stacey, 1983). A similar essentialist argument about men can be found in Robert Bly's *Iron John.* Bly worries that modern men have lost touch with their "Zeus energy" and recommends all-male retreats and rituals to restore the natural order (Bly, 1990). The form of community that Bly conjures up with visions of Zeus energy, however, has misogynist overtones. Women in ancient Greece, for all its democratic ideals, were relegated to the home and prohibited from participating fully in public life. This points to one of the central flaws in mythopoetic and other essentialist approaches to gender: They reduce historically and culturally specific myths and practices to universal psychological or biological truths, thereby ignoring the social structural conditions that produced them. One should question the assumption that reinstituting ancient male initiation rites will heal modern men and rescue a declining culture. In fact, reenacting ancient chest-pounding rituals on a grand scale would probably increase gender antagonism rather than pro-moting some idyllic balance between fierce men and yielding women. Accepting the notion of a natural masculine fierceness and an inborn "need" for mascu-line validation reaffirms gender difference and carries the very real danger of perpetuating violence against women and other men.

Robert Bly's account is only one among many that invoke images of fundamental, timeless, and natural gender differences stemming from biological sex. Many of these accounts rely on biblical passages or call up primordial images of tribal societies to verify their version of natural gender differences. Authorita-tive males and nurturing females from ancient times come to stand for some underlying masculinity or femininity that supposedly resides deep within hu-mans. Unfortunately, this imagery resonates so closely with Western culture's gender ideology that most people accept the tribal portrayals as evidence for the inevitability of patriarchal power and feminine frailty. This is a fundamentally false assumption based on an inaccurate reading of human history and a profound misuse of biological and anthropological evidence. For instance, feminist anthropologists, biol-ogists, and historians of science have demonstrated how an oversimplified "Man-the-Hunter" interpreta-tion of human evolution based on sociobiology (Tiger, 1969; Wilson, 1975) ignores important evi-dence in its quest to rationalize women's domesticity (Bleier, 1984; Haraway, 1978).

USING COMPARATIVE RESEARCH TO REFUTE ESSENTIALIST CLAIMS

To evaluate essentialist claims about masculinity or male dominance, it is helpful to rely on the concept of social structure and attend to cross-cultural varia-tion in the organization and expression of gender. Early versions of comparative research on women sought to locate the "origins" of gender inequality by looking at so-called primitive peoples (Engels, 1891/1978). Like natural law theorists before them, these scholars were prone to fabricate a past in order to justify their vision of the future. Later researchers

attempting to understand the position of women in nonindustrial societies have generally concluded that male dominance was widespread, but that women's subordination is not a unitary phenomenon that ap-pears the same at all times and in all places. Rather, the status of women appears to be multidimensional and subject to change due to a variety of factors (e.g., Blumberg, 1984; Chafetz, 1984; Leacock, 1981; Ort-ner & Whitehead, 1981; Sanday, 1981). Although comparative cross-cultural studies of gender are fraught with epistemological difficulties, they are one of the few reliable and convincing ways to refute popular essentialist theories of gender.

There are two basic ways to evaluate theories using comparative cross-cultural research: extensive and intensive approaches (Ragin, 1987). Extensive approaches tend to compare whole cultures, societies, or nations; typically include a large number of cases; reduce social phenomena to variables; seek patterns of association via statistical analyses; and are good for testing universals (as well as generating some false universals of their own). The emphasis in exten-sive comparative research is usually to identify cross-cultural similarities between different instances of general outcomes and to isolate structural correlates of social phenomena. Though not necessarily re-quired, extensive comparative research also tends to use quantitative data and statistical analysis. Much extensive comparative research is nomothetic, seek-ing causal explanations for why observed phenomena occur. For some, the goal is to test competing theo-ries and determine "laws" of social organization. Others have less grandiose goals and use extensive comparative research more inductively. In these cases, researchers are attempting to isolate which so-cial features might be idiosyncratic; which structures, ideologies, or associations might be historically or culturally specific; and which might be considered common features of the general social phenomenon under study.

Intensive comparative studies, in contrast, con-tain just a few cases and tend to be idiographic, re-lying on thick description of historically specific oc-currences. This small-scale case study approach seeks to interpret specific instances of some phenomenon and is an excellent means of identifying cross-cultural difference (though it is prone to over-generalizing from atypical cases). Intensive comparative studies are attuned to historically situated phenomena and because they are more detailed than extensive comparisons, they pay more attention to the specific contexts of social practices. In the late 1980s and early 1990s historians, anthropologists, and increasing numbers of sociologists (including most feminists) tended to favor the intensive approach to comparative studies (cf. Kohn, 1989). Intensive and extensive comparative approaches can coexist, and the distinction between them is sometimes blurred, as when intensive researchers refer to similar "types" of cases (Kandiyoti, 1991) or when extensive researchers use detailed illustrative examples (Coltrane, 1992).

There is no "right way" to do cross-cultural or comparative research, and both of the approaches outlined help to explicate social structures. Intensive studies are in some ways more fundamental, because secondary analysis of the extensive sort depends on initial detailed ethnographies or historical case studies. Intensive comparative studies are especially useful for showing how some individuals or groups depart from a falsely universalizing conception of gender, but they are open to the claim that the few cases selected are atypical. Extensive comparisons can isolate cross-cultural variation among many different societies and can link that variation with specific sets of social structural conditions. The heuristic value and political import of such linkages should not be underestimated. When one documents cross-cultural and historical variation in gender relations and can isolate the conditions under which various divisions of labor and distributions of wealth and prestige occur, one is better able to understand how gender systems operate and how gender shapes peoples' everyday lives. Perhaps even more important, with large-scale comparisons and causal explanations, one can argue convincingly that gender is socially constructed and be in a better position to transform gender relations to make them more equal. My own research provides an example.

FATHER-CHILD RELATIONSHIPS AND WOMEN'S STATUS

In two extensive comparative studies of nonindustrial societies, I isolated some of the conditions under which men tend to dominate women. Coded data on about a hundred societies were used in each study, including cultures from all major geographic regions of the world and representing societies ranging from small-scale hunter-gatherers to populous feudal agrarian states. One study looked at men's ritualized displays of manliness—boastful demonstrations of strength, aggressiveness, and sexual potency of the type idealized by Robert Bly (Coltrane, 1992). This study also looked at the conditions associated with other micropolitical aspects of gender relations, such as women deferring to men by bowing, giving up their seats, or following men's orders; husbands dominating their wives; and belief systems considering women to be inferior to men. Several explanations positing various causes for these behaviors were tested, and strong support was found for two types of theories: materialist and psychodynamic. Significantly fewer displays of manliness, less wifely deference, less husband dominance, and less ideological female inferiority were evident in societies where men participated in child rearing and women controlled property. The associations with men's dominance were statistically significant even when controlling for a host of other potentially causal social, economic, and environmental factors.

The other extensive comparative study attempted to isolate the impact of men's participation in child care on women's public status. The extent to which women participated in public decision making and whether they could hold leadership roles was evaluated with respect to a variety of potential causal factors (Coltrane, 1988). Father-child relationships were measured with reference to the frequency of father-child proximity, the amount of routine child care performed by men, and the likelihood of men expressing emotional warmth or support toward children. As in the other study, the association between close father-child relationships and women's public status was statistically robust, even when controlling for other factors. The results are consistent with Nancy Chodorow's (1978) theory that exclusive child rearing by mothers produces young men with psychological needs to differentiate from women and denigrate the feminine in themselves. Other interesting findings from this study concerned the importance of focusing on fraternal interest groups in analyzing women's access to public power and, following Sanday (1981), an association between men's child care and gender-balanced origin symbolism. Societies with distant fathers told myths about distant, sky-dwelling, all-powerful male gods like Zeus, whereas societies with nurturing fathers tended to tell stories about both male and female gods.

Extensive cross-cultural studies like these counter the essentialist claims of writers like Robert Bly. Although one cannot say much about specific causal paths from this sort of correlational analyses (much less "prove" causality or locate origins), one can at least rule out some improbable explanations and focus attention on theories that seem most plausible. These studies suggest that regardless of the ultimate reasons for fathers being involved with their children, when they are, it has important consequences for a social psychology of gender equality. In societies where men develop and maintain close relationships with young children, hypermasculine displays, competitive posturing, and all-male enclaves are rare. These societies allow both women and men to hold office and participate in public decisions, rarely require women to publicly pay homage to men, and tend to conceive of men and women as inherently equal.

Systematically comparing social structural patterns across diverse settings or historical periods allows one to consider the implications of a cultural emphasis on gender difference. By defining themselves as essentially different from women, men in some societies have excluded women from positions of power and dominated them in more intimate relationships. Belief in essential gender difference helps men maintain microstructures of inequality. Seen from this perspective, mythopoetic calls for reinstituting ancient male initiation rites carry regressive, not progressive, potential. The practices that accompany all-male initiation rites and everyday affirmations of masculine strength and fortitude typically work to the disadvantage of women and nondominant men. Although ritual gender segregation and celebration of difference may not theoretically or inherently imply male domination, in practice this is what tends to occur. Cross-cultural analysis suggests that the key to minimal gender dominance and deference is ongoing gender cooperation in child rearing and property control, not carving out separate domains for men and women.

CAN "MASCULINIST" METHODS SERVE FEMINIST GOALS?

The conventional sociological practices used in the previously mentioned studies, including comparing disparate societies, using large data sets, reducing social phenomena to numbers, and performing statistical tests, are sometimes criticized as "masculinist" or "colonialist." I am not alone in using such mainstream research methods to argue against sexist notions (Chafetz, 1984;; Jayaratne, 1983; Sanday, 1981), but many researchers studying gender prefer qualitative, theoretical, oppositional, and standpoint methodologies (Reinharz, 1992). For instance, Dorothy Smith (1992) states that "when we employ standard sociological methods of work, we inadvertently realign the issues that concern us with those of the relations of ruling" (p. 96). At issue is whether one ought to use data that were collected without attention to limiting ethnocentric and androcentric biases; whether one can compare societies that are so different from one another; whether the use of variables and statistical associations can reveal anything of value; whether such methods manufacture false universals and promote evolutionary theorizing; whether such methods objectify, exploit, and alienate their "subjects"; and whether findings from such studies necessarily serve the dominant interests of men and colonial powers. These are not new concerns to anthropologists—who generally accept them—and they are concerns familiar to most feminist sociologists, though many conventional social scientists would reject these criticisms as too political or subjective.

For those who agree that past cross-cultural scholarship, and social science in general, has neglected women and perpetuated white Western men's understandings of the world, these criticisms are indeed quite serious. They have motivated numerous studies that place women's experiences in the foreground and provide richly detailed descriptions of the ways that women have exercised authority, struggled against patriarchy, and been active agents of change. These complex, multidimensional descriptive studies are theoretically rich and illuminating in their own right, but one ought to be able to generalize from them as well. In addition to conducting feminist ethnographies, case histories, and experiential studies, one can pursue an integrative and systematic understanding of social life that comes from explicitly comparative research designs with an emphasis on social structure. Feminist anthropologists, sociologists, and historians have illustrated that the meaning of womanhood or manhood is historically and culturally unique. This does not mean that one should forsake attempts to compare across these unique viewpoints to formulate synthetic theories in an effort to understand the consistent and pervasive features of gender.

An emphasis on social structure is both illuminating and politically expedient. Such an approach does not require the claim that abstracted comparative knowledge is value free or inherently more objective than more interpretive or idiographic ways of knowing. Extensive comparative studies and other conventional social science techniques such as experiments and mathematical modeling allow one to generalize to larger populations, seek causal explanations, and formulate general principles of social organization. New studies using these techniques could be used against women and oppressed peoples, but this tendency is not inherent to the method. The danger stems, instead, from political causes, from the self-interested standpoints of those in power who use conventional methods to invoke pseudo-objectivity and ignore issues of inequality and domination. This political threat is perhaps the most compelling reason

that gender scholars should not abandon conventional methodologies to those who would maintain the status quo. Even if it should not be so, results of quantitative studies carry more weight in policy arenas than isolated personal accounts or even the best in-depth qualitative studies. Another compelling reason to use conventional social science methods to study gender is that when the right questions are asked, the knowledge generated helps to identify those issues and projects with the greatest potential for realizing social change.

SCIENTISM AND POSTMODERNISM

Scientism is the prejudice that science objectively deals only with observable facts and that any investigation that does not employ natural science-like methods is "merely" subjective and therefore not explanatory (Lloyd, 1989). In the post-Kuhnian academy, one might hope that scientism would be dead, but it is still the dominant paradigm in many social science disciplines (Kuhn, 1970). In the interests of brevity, I will not restate why scientism, in its various forms, is intellectually false and politically dangerous. Instead, I turn to one of its main challengers, postmodernism.

Unifying a disparate number of feminist and nonfeminist scholars under the label "postmodernism" is itself misleading, but I do so to question some emergent idealist and particularist tendencies in gender studies. Postmodern approaches are enlightening because they attempt to deconstruct false dualisms of mind/body, culture/nature, man/woman, modern/primitive, reason/emotion, subject/object, and so forth. Images of "fractured," "decentered," and "reflexive" selves that appear in postmodernist writing help to critically evaluate overly simple concepts and categories. In its more extreme forms, however, postmodernism's focus is solely on language and its role in the perception of reality. Discourse and cognition are important, but there is much more than this to social life. If one focuses too much on language as constructing reality, solutions to injustice tend to be clever word games, and the concrete bases of social inequality are slighted. Describing the social world as floating fields of symbols, manipulated by reflexive agents probably captures a phenomenological "reality," but one needs to ground such analyses in patterns of material conditions (Coltrane & Hickman, 1992). By relying too heavily on deconstructionism, one too easily overlooks persistence and oppression in favor of historical, symbolic, and subjective particularity.

The postmodern tendency to ignore social structure undermines sociological attempts to understand gender inequality. It is now increasingly common to reject a sociology that seeks systematic regularities and patterns of causality. For example, most feminist researchers caricature role theory or set up structural-functionalism or structural-Marxism as rhetorical "straw persons." Although many feminist sociologists retain a revised concept of social structure, other gender scholars show disdain for even middle-level theoretical abstraction as they attempt to honor diversity and give voice to silenced women. My fear is that the heuristic value of social structure could be lost by failing to generalize across situations, even if those situations include diverse peoples living unique lives.

The postmodern emphasis on particularity and language also discourages one from seeking causal explanations. Without some concept of social causality, one can only describe a multitude of unique experiences and talk endlessly about talk. Kuhn and his successors were right in pointing out that science has no special claim to truth, but one still needs to look for causal patterns in the social world and ask why things happen as they do. Theories need to remain causal, even if most of the research methods cannot adequately prove causality (Lieberson, 1985). Perhaps one should reject both scientism and postmodernism while simultaneously relying on their contradictory root assumptions. In researching masculinities, one might look for both regularized similarity and particularistic difference. By using multiple methods and relying on diverse ways of knowing, one might move closer to some tentative conclusions about which theoretical explanations for gender inequality are most plausible.

Rejecting conventional social science methods and liberal philosophic traditions is provocative, but it carries some internal contradictions. Descartes, Bacon, Hobbes, Rousseau, and the others were "sexist" and "elitist," and their ideas are suspect because of it. Nevertheless, Western liberalism can be seen as providing the impetus for the civil rights movement as well as the women's movement. Similarly, science has emancipatory as well as destructive potential (Jansen, 1990; Olson, 1990). New false dichotomies are created by branding specific research techniques (i.e., quantitative sociology) as inherently "male" or "masculinist" (O'Brien, 1989; Seidler, 1989). Critiques of masculinist science as stemming from Western men's proclivity to objectify and dominate others (Easlea, 1981) provide insights into relationships between knowledge and power, but attributing some essential gendered nature to these specific research practices is misleading.

If one takes seriously recent calls to situate and historicize the sociological analyses of gender, then one should avoid the false dichotomy between "male" and "female" research. *Quantitative/empirical/ deductive/explanatory* research such as mathematical data analysis, random sample surveys, extensive cross-cultural comparisons, and experiments are not necessarily masculine. *Qualitative/intuitive/ inductive/exploratory* research such as ethnography, interviewing, participant observation, oral histories, and intensive case studies are not necessarily feminine. Even if there are proportionately more men doing the former and proportionately more women doing the latter, one should remember that the association with gender is historically specific and socially constructed. For example, in the early part of the century, quantitative social science methods were first advocated by women, and for a time they were considered "feminine" (Deegan, 1988). It was only later that surveys and mathematical modeling became associated with men and masculinity.

Research findings are also employed for political purposes. Study methods that produce easily understood conclusions about the causes and consequences of gender inequality become increasingly important as fundamentalist and backlash movements call for reinstating patriarchal privileges. Pseudoscientific studies carry especially high credibility with policy makers. To abandon conventional social science to those who would support existing patterns of gender stratification would be a grave political mistake. Similarly, to ignore the knowledge created by systematic empirical inquiry because others have made a fetish of science would be a profound intellectual error. How, then, might one retain some aspects of conventional social science in studying masculinities, while at the same time integrating recent feminist insights?

STANDPOINT THEORIES AND MEN'S STUDIES

From what standpoint should men (or women) study masculinity? Women studying gender can begin from a feminist standpoint, from the "actualities of women's lives," the "concrete, relational, subjugated activities" of women (Smith, 1987). Feminist standpoint theorists argue that this perspective affords them a more encompassing and empowering grasp of social life than conventional social science that represents the views of dominant men (Harding, 1986; Hartsock, 1983; Smith, 1992). Standpoint theories favor process over static categorizing and treat the personal as both political and theoretically enlightening. What can standpoint theories tell about how to study men and masculinities?

The most basic insight from standpoint theories is that everyday life—the concrete activities people do—structure perception, attitudes, and ways of knowing. Where one stands shapes what one can see and how one can understand it. One way to use standpoint theories is to focus on how activities conventionally performed by women (e.g., child care) might structure the consciousness and behavior of mothers and fathers in similar fashion (Coltrane, 1989; Risman, 1987) or how couple dynamics might respond to similar power inequities regardless of gender or sexual preference (Blumstein & Schwartz, 1983). This type of analysis, by focusing on how gender and its related standpoints are socially constructed under specific microstructural conditions, can tell much

about the creation and maintenance of gender difference and gender inequality.

If one focuses on the lived reality of most men's lives, however, one also runs the risk of reproducing patriarchal consciousness. Focusing on men's standpoints will typically produce a picture of men's felt powerlessness. One must be careful to acknowledge that these same men exercise considerable power in their lives, particularly over women, but also over other men. This contradictory coexistence of felt powerlessness and actual (if latent) power is quite common for men. For instance, family violence researchers are finding that men's subjective sense of lost or slipping control is often a precursor to wife beating. The "partial and perverse perspective" (Harding, 1986) that has come from men studying men in the past may be recreated by contemporary scholars if they adopt an uncritical stance that treats men as victims. In contrast, Messner (1990) identifies an emergent genre in the sociology of sports that integrates the personal experience of male victimization with the promise of masculine privilege. He notes that concrete examination of men's lives can reveal the social mechanisms through which men's power over women is constructed but also recognizes the political tension around emphasizing too much the costs, rather than the benefits, of masculinity. The "tricky balancing act" (Messner, 1990, p. 145) of profeminist men's studies is open to attack because men scholars share institutional power and privilege and because any emphasis on the victimization of men can be seen as detracting from the business of exposing women's oppression (Harding, 1986; Jardine & Smith, 1987). Messner advocates an inclusive profeminist approach that integrates analyses of masculinity with class, race, and sexual inequalities and, above all, highlights gender oppression. This follows Connell's (1987) call for a focus on history, process, and struggle surrounding hegemonic and subordinated masculinities.

In order to illuminate how gendered interaction and power are socially structured, I suggest that researchers attempt to integrate men's standpoints into gender studies in at least three ways: (a) by focusing on men's emotions, (b) by studying men in groups, and (c) by placing men's experiences in a structural context. First, one needs to get men talking about their emotional lives in some detail, even if, or perhaps especially because, they may lack a vocabulary for doing so. Researchers cannot afford to accept men's superficial characterizations of their internal states and need to push them for self-reflection. Many men are motivated by fears and insecurities that conventional sociological research strategies do not easily capture. For example, a man who runs court-referral groups for abusing men told me how he uses a "freeze-frame" technique to get men to talk about, and thus become aware of, their emotions. He stops the men while they are presenting accounts of battering instances and repeatedly demands that they tell him details about what they are feeling at certain key moments. The emotion he hears most, particularly the one men report having just before they hit women, is fear (see also Lisak, 1991). Researchers need to be able to specify the types of insecurities (and senses of self-importance) men report in various circumstances and begin to document their behavioral counterparts. By looking at how men experience, organize, and talk about their emotions, one might begin to build bridges between interactionist, psychodynamic, and power-based theories of gender.

I am not suggesting a simplistic acceptance of emotional or autobiographical material as epistemologically privileged discourse. Much writing in men's studies is autobiographical or confessional, but rarely gets past the insight that men are taught to be competitive and have trouble expressing their emotions. One should guard against the tendency in some scholarly writing to accept one's felt emotions or bodily sensations as somehow superior or more authentic than other ways of knowing, because emotions and bodily experiences are also socially constructed, often in the service of power and domination. I think researchers should focus on men's emotionality, not because it is epistemologically privileged, but because it may be an illuminating fault line for men between what is and what should be (Smith, 1987).

A second way to take men's unique standpoints into account is to focus on how men create difference, exclude women, and use privileged informa-

tion. Feminist scholars have countered androcentric scholarship by bringing the women back in, focusing on their experiences and giving voice to their silenced concerns. One reason to focus on men's standpoints is to find out how and why they exclude women. Men are in a unique position to do research on groups of men and to identify processes through which men create rituals, reaffirm symbolic difference, establish internal hierarchy, and exclude, belittle, dominate, and stigmatize women and nonconforming men. Locker rooms, playing fields, board rooms, shop floors, the military, and fraternal organizations of all types provide access to the relations of ruling (Goode, 1982; Smith, 1992). Investigating men's standpoints allows the examination of privileged sources of information that, although incomplete and falsely universalizing, can contribute to the understanding of the exercise of men's power.

Men should not be the only ones to study masculinity, because women's standpoints are also necessary for a full understanding of gender relations. Thus, my third focus concerns the relational context of gender and brings me back to the need to highlight power and identify structural patterns. Individual actors and their experiences are obviously important, but researchers also need a focus on patterns of relationships between men and women, among men, and among women. One fruitful way to validate both difference and similarity and highlight both agency and structure is to identify the conditions under which gender becomes salient in everyday life. What types of settings and interactions are likely to call for participants to use gender in understanding or expressing their thoughts, feelings, and actions? Who brings up gender in social interaction and when is it subtly inferred? One should attempt to determine when gender is invoked as a prerogative-maintaining move by men, when and how gender is used by men in group settings, and what relationship the use of gender has to felt insecurity.

If one can identify the typical purposes and costs of men's and women's use of gender as an interactional resource, one will better understand how it facilitates or inhibits social interaction and at whose expense those interactions occur. One might also focus on internal conversations about gendered feelings or behaviors. This relatively "micro" approach follows Goffman (1977) and West and Zimmerman (1987) by conceptualizing gender as an actively constructed accomplishment of ongoing interaction, but it also suggests a focus on contextual, structural, and psychodynamic correlates of such activities. Such an approach might render the "doing" of gender amenable to conventional sociological research practices because one could focus on identifying the common features of situations that called for gender to become salient. Researchers need to document and categorize the microstructures (Risman & Schwartz, 1989) under which men and women use gender in particular ways. Systematic studies are also needed of "gender strategies" (Hochschild, 1989) to assess the extent to which they are uniquely crafted and to identify broad patterns of regularity in their form and use across historical, cultural, geographic, economic, and institutional context. By using comparative sociological methods, focusing on the concept of social structure, and paying attention to gender as an interactional resource, one can better understand how gender is actively constructed by social actors. Documenting how power and material conditions are associated with women's and men's standpoints can counter essentialist claims, contribute to public debates about gender, and ultimately transform society. By not forsaking traditional social science practices, perhaps scholars can literally, not just figuratively, deconstruct gender inequality.

REFERENCES

Bleier, R. (1984). *Science and gender*. New York: Pergamon.

Blumberg, R. L. (1984). A general theory of gender stratification. In R. Collins (Ed.), *Sociological theory* (pp. 23–101). San Francisco: Jossey-Bass.

Blumstein, P., & Schwartz, P. (1983). *American couples*. New York: William Morrow.

Bly, R. (1990). *Iron John: A book about men*. Reading, MA: Addison-Wesley.

Brod, H. (Ed.). (1987). *The making of masculinities*. Boston: Unwin Hyman.

Canaan, J., & Griffin, C. (1990). The new men's studies. In J. Hearn & D. Morgan (Eds.), *Men, masculinities and social theory* (pp. 206–214). London: Unwin Hyman.

Chafetz, J. S. (1984). *Sex and advantage*. Totowa, NJ: Rowman & Allanheld.

Chodorow, N. (1978). *The reproduction of mothering*. Berkeley: University of California Press.

Clary, M. (1982). *Daddy's home*. New York: Seaview.

Collins, R. (1988). The micro contribution to macro sociology. *Sociological Theory, 6*, 242–253.

Coltrane, S. (1988). Father-child relationships and the status of women. *American Journal of Sociology, 93*, 1060–1095.

Coltrane, S. (1989). Household labor and the routine production of gender. *Social Problems, 36*, 473–490.

Coltrane, S. (1992). The micropolitics of gender in nonindustrial societies. *Gender & Society, 6*, 86–107.

Coltrane, S., & Hickman, N. (1992). The rhetoric of rights and needs. *Social Problems, 39*, 401–421.

Connell, R. W. (1987). *Gender and power*. Cambridge: Polity.

Deegan, M. J. (1988). *Jane Addams and the men of the Chicago school, 1892–1918*. New Brunswick, NJ: Transaction Books.

Easlea, B. (1981). *Science and sexual oppression*. London: Weidenfeld & Nicolson.

Elshtain, J. B. (1981). *Public man, private woman*. Princeton, NJ: Princeton University Press.

Engels, F. (1978). The origin of the family, private property and the state. In R. Tucker (Ed.), *The Marx-Engels reader* (pp. 734–759). New York: Monthly Review Press. (Original work published 1891)

Farrell, W. (1986). *Why men are the way they are*. New York: McGraw-Hill.

Goffman, E. (1967). *Interaction ritual*. New York: Anchor.

Goffman, E. (1977). The arrangement between the sexes. *Theory and Society, 4*, 301–331.

Goffman, E. (1979). *Gender advertisements*. New York: Harper & Row.

Goldberg, H. (1976). *The hazards of being male*. Ithaca, NY: Cornell University Press.

Goode, W. J. (1982). Why men resist. In B. Thorne & M. Yalom (Eds.), *Rethinking the family* (pp. 131–150). New York: Longman.

Griffin, S. (1978). *Woman and nature*. New York: Harper Colophon.

Haraway, D. (1978). Animal sociology and a natural economy of the body politic. *Signs, 4*, 21–60.

Harding, S. (1986). *The science question in feminism*. Ithaca, NY: Cornell University Press.

Hartsock, N. (1983). The feminist standpoint. In S. Harding & M. Hintikka (Eds.), *Discovering reality* (pp. 283–310). Boston: Reidel.

Hearn, J., & Morgan, D. (Eds.). (1990). *Men, masculinities and social theory*. London: Unwin Hyman.

Hochschild, A. (1989). *The second shift*. Berkeley: University of California Press.

Irigaray, L. (1981). And the one doesn't stir without the other. *Signs, 7,* 56–79.

Jackson, D. (1990). *Unmasking masculinity*. London: Unwin Hyman.

Jansen, S. C. (1990). Is science a man? *Theory and Society, 19,* 235–246.

Jardine, A., & Smith, P. (1987). *Men in feminism*. New York: Metheun.

Jayaratne, T. E. (1983). The value of quantitative methodology for feminist research. In G. Bowles & R. D. Klein (Eds.), *Theories of women's studies* (pp. 140–161). London: Routledge & Kegan Paul.

Kandiyoti, D. (1991). Bargaining with patriarchy. *Gender & Society, 2,* 274–290.

Kaufman, M. (Ed.). (1987). *Beyond patriarchy*. Toronto: Oxford University Press.

Kaufman, M. (1993). *Cracking the armour: Power, pain, and the lives of men*. Toronto: Penguin/Viking.

Kimmel, M. (1990). After fifteen years. In J. Hearn & D. Morgan (Eds.), *Men, masculinities and social theory* (pp. 93–109). London: Unwin Hyman.

Kimmel, M., & Messner, M. (Eds.). (1989). *Men's lives*. New York: Macmillan.

Kohn, M. (Ed.). (1989). *Cross-national research in sociology*. Newbury Park, CA: Sage.

Kuhn, T. (1970). *The structure of scientific revolutions*. Chicago: University of Chicago Press.

Leacock, E. (1981). *Myths of male dominance*. New York: Monthly Review Press.

Lieberson, S. (1985). *Making it count*. Berkeley: University of California Press.

Lisak, D. (1991). Sexual aggression, masculinity, and fathers. *Signs, 16,* 238–262.

Lloyd, C. (1989). Realism, structurism, and history. *Theory and Society, 18,* 451–494.

Lorber, J. (1986). Dismantling Noah's ark. *Sex Roles, 14,* 567–580.

Marx, K. (1978a). The German ideology. In R. Tucker (Ed.), *The Marx-Engels reader* (pp. 146–200). New York: Monthly Review Press. (Original work published 1846)

Marx, K. (1978b). The eighteenth brumaire of Louis Bonaparte. In R. Tucker (Ed.), *The Marx-Engels reader* (pp. 594–617). New York: Monthly Review Press. (Original work published 1851)

Messner, M. (1990). Men studying masculinity. *Sociology of Sport Journal, 7,* 136–153.

Morgan, D. (1981). Men, masculinity and the process of sociological enquiry. In H. Roberts, *Doing feminist research* (pp. 83–113). London: Routledge & Kegan Paul.

Nichols, J. (1975). *Men's liberation*. New York: Penguin.

O'Brien, M. (Ed.). (1989). *Reproducing the world: Essays in feminist theory*. Boulder, CO: Westview.

Olson, R. (1990). Historical reflections on feminist critiques of science. *History of Science, 28,* 125–147.

Ortner, S., & Whitehead, H. (1981). *Sexual meanings*. Cambridge, UK: Cambridge University Press.

Osherson, S. (1986). *Finding our fathers*. New York: Free Press.

Pleck, J. (1981). Men's power with women, other men, and society. In R. A. Lewis (Ed.), *Men in difficult times* (pp. 234–244). Englewood Cliffs, NJ: Prentice Hall. (Original work published 1977)

Ragin, C. (1987). *The comparative method*. Berkeley: University of California Press.

Reinharz, S. (1992). *Feminist methods in social research*. New York: Oxford University Press.

Risman, B. J. (1987). Intimate relationships from a microstructural perspective. *Gender & Society, 1,* 6–32.

Risman, B., & Schwartz, P. (Eds.). (1989). *Gender in intimate relationships*. Belmont, CA: Wadsworth.

Rossi, A. (Ed.). (1985). *Gender and the lifecourse*. New York: Aldine.

Sanday, P. R. (1981). *Female power and male dominance*. Cambridge, UK: Cambridge University Press.

Sattel, J. (1976). Men, inexpressiveness, and power. *Social Problems, 23,* 469–477.

Seidler, V. (1989). *Rediscovering masculinity*. London: Routledge.

Smith, D. E. (1987). *The everyday world as problematic*. Boston: Northeastern University Press.

Smith, D. E. (1992). Sociology from women's experience. *Sociological Theory, 10,* 88–98.

Stacey, J. (1983). The new conservative feminism. *Feminist Studies, 9,* 559–583.

Tiger, L. (1969). *Men in groups*. New York: Vintage.

West, C., & Zimmerman, D. H. (1987). Doing gender. *Gender & Society, 1,* 125–151.

Wilson, E. O. (1975). *Sociobiology*. Cambridge, MA: Belknap.

CHECKPOINTS

1. Coltrane argues that feminist critiques of science can serve the study of men and masculinity.
2. Coltrane uses a social constructionist framework to study men and masculinity, and he argues that masculinity is related to systems of social power.

To prepare for reading the next section, think about these questions:
1. Are sex differences central to the understanding of gender?
2. Could psychologists eliminate the study of sex differences?

SHOULD PSYCHOLOGISTS STUDY SEX DIFFERENCES?

Should Psychologists Study Gender Differences? Yes, With Some Guidelines

JANET SHIBLEY HYDE

In 1887 Romanes argued that women were less intelligent than men and that this was a result of women's brains being smaller than men's. One hundred years later, in 1987, Kimura argued that there are gender differences[1] in the brain and that these brain factors create gender differences in abilities (see also Kimura, 1992). Psychologists and other scientists have a history of studying gender differences and attributing them to biological causes. In this article I contend that, like it or not, psychologists will continue to study gender differences and the media will continue to publicize the findings; the best course of action, then, is to institute guidelines so that the study of gender differences will be carried out in a manner

that meets the highest standards of science and at the same time is not detrimental to women (for other discussions of this issue, see Baumeister, 1988; Rothblum, 1988).

THE NEVER-ENDING SEARCH FOR GENDER DIFFERENCES

The media and the lay public alike are greatly intrigued with gender differences. For example, within the last five years, *Time* (20 January 1992), *Newsweek* (28 May 1990), and *US News and World Report* (8 August 1988) have all carried cover stories on the question of psychological gender differences.

As noted at the beginning of this article, psychologists have studied gender differences from the very beginning of psychology in the late 1800s (Shields, 1975). Research and theorizing on gender differences, some of it by feminists and some by others, continued throughout the first six decades of the 20th century, including Helen Thompson Woolley's excellent early

Janet Shibley HYDE is Professor of Psychology and Women's Studies at the University of Wisconsin-Madison. She is the author of the undergraduate textbook *Half the Human Experience: The Psychology of Women* (4th ed., Lexington, MA: D.C. Heath, 1991), and has been working on meta-analyses of psychological gender differences. Her ADDRESS is: Department of Psychology, 1202 W. Johnson Street, University of Wisconsin, Madison, WI 53706, USA.

feminist review of the literature (1910), the famous psychologist Lewis Terman's study *Sex and Personality* (1936) and Eleanor Maccoby's edited volume of theory and empirical research (1966).

Beginning around 1970, stimulated in part by the feminist movement's emphasis on gender, there was a virtual explosion of theory and research on gender differences. This research has been reviewed in volumes such as those by Maccoby and Jacklin (1974), Hyde and Linn (1986), Halpern (1992), Eagly (1987a) and Hall (1984).

In short, the study of gender differences in psychology has been nothing but a growth industry. It shows no sign of declining. It's here to stay. The question then becomes one of how can we regulate this somewhat unruly growth industry so that it (1) becomes better science and (2) is used on behalf of women rather than against women.

PROBLEMS WITH EXISTING RESEARCH ON GENDER DIFFERENCES

A number of pernicious problems in the study of gender differences must be addressed if this research literature is to meet the twin goals of becoming better science and becoming beneficial to women.

The first problem is *publication bias,* a general bias in psychology toward publishing significant findings and not publishing null findings. This bias applies to the study of gender differences. It implies that there is a bias toward publishing findings of significant gender differences. A study finding nonsignificant gender differences may not be published. If the study is on another topic and the researchers conduct a routine test for gender differences, they are likely to report the finding if the difference is significant and make no mention of it if it is non-significant. The result of this bias is a general impression that there is a multitude of psychological gender differences and few gender similarities, because the latter tend not to be reported.

The second problem, related to the first, is the proliferation of *unreplicated findings of gender differences.* As a result of the tendency to report significant findings of gender differences, and the fascination of

psychologists and the media with differences, a single report of a finding of a gender difference may receive widespread media coverage. Ten independent investigators may try to replicate the finding and all fail, i.e., all obtain a non-significant gender difference. These studies may not find their way into print or, if they do, they will attract no media attention. As a result, the original study reporting the difference stands as authoritative, with no recognition of the contradictory evidence.

The third problem is *failure to report effect sizes, so that tiny gender differences are given more attention than they merit.* An example comes from the extensive research on gender differences in mathematics performance. This gender difference has, for decades, been thought to be reliable and important— and, by implication, large. Yet meta-analysis shows the magnitude of the difference to be at most 0.15 standard deviation (Hyde et al., 1990). Had researchers all along reported the effect size d (Hyde et al., 1990) for their gender differences, we might have known long ago that the difference was small.

The fourth problem is that *findings of gender differences are often interpreted as indicating female deficits.* For example, there is a fairly consistent gender difference in self-confidence; on tasks such as estimating how many points they think they earned on an exam before the actual grades are known, females estimate fewer points, on the average, than males do (Hyde, 1991; Lenney, 1977). This finding has often been interpreted as indicating that females lack self-confidence—that is, that they have a deficit. An alternative interpretation might be that males are unrealistically over-confident. In fact, when estimated scores are compared with actual scores, it turns out that males overestimate their performance about as much as females underestimate theirs, although some studies find girls' estimates to be accurate and boys' to be inflated (Berg and Hyde, 1976; Crandall, 1969; Hyde, 1991). Therefore, there is little basis for saying that females have a deficit in self-confidence.

A fifth problem is that *findings of gender differences, when not reported and applied carefully, may be used in a manner that is harmful to females.* As an example, in a 1980 *Science* article, Benbow and Stanley made much of a very lopsided gender ratio (far more males than females) in their sample of highly mathematically precocious seventh graders. The media picked up this report and it appeared in national and international newspapers. Jacobs and Eccles (1985) were in the midst of a longitudinal study in which they had just asked parents for their estimates of their child's mathematical ability. They re-interviewed the parents following the publicity over the Benbow and Stanley report. They found that the media coverage had adversely affected the mothers of daughters. Mothers who had heard the media coverage had significantly lower estimates of their daughters' abilities than mothers who had not heard the media coverage. And, the mothers exposed to the media coverage, gave estimates that were lower than they had been before the media coverage. Mothers' confidence in their daughters' abilities, of course, is very important to girls' developing confidence in their own mathematical ability. In essence, then, the reporting of the Benbow and Stanley results, partly because of a lack of appropriate scientific caveats by the researchers, created outcomes that could be demonstrated to be harmful to females.

Finally, a sixth problem is that *gender differences are often interpreted as being due to biological factors in the absence of appropriate biological data.* An example is the Benbow and Stanley (1980) study reporting far more males than females among the mathematically gifted. Benbow and Stanley speculated that the difference was due to biological factors, when they actually had collected no biological measures.

GUIDELINES FOR NON-SEXIST RESEARCH ON GENDER DIFFERENCES

In order to address the problems previously listed, I propose the following guidelines for non-sexist research on gender differences (for related guidelines, see Denmark et al., 1988; McHugh et al., 1986):

1. Researchers should routinely conduct the appropriate significance tests for gender differences on all major measures in their study (Eagly, 1987b). Furthermore, researchers should take responsibility for reporting and publishing findings of non-significant gender differences, so they are reported on an equal basis with findings of significant gender differences.

2. Journal editors should take care to publish findings of non-significant gender differences, provided the study meets appropriate scientific standards.

3. Researchers should be required to report an effect size (such as *d:* cf. Hyde et al., 1990) for all findings of gender differences, whether significant or not, so that the reader is informed of the magnitude of the difference.

4. Researchers should be alert to the manner in which they interpret findings of gender differences. Interpretations implying a female deficit should always be questioned to see whether there is an equally tenable interpretation that does not imply a female deficit.

5. Biological explanations for gender differences should be made with great caution. Biological explanations should not be invoked when no biological measures were collected.

6. Researchers should apply appropriate scientific standards of conduct in ensuring that their data are appropriately interpreted so that the risk of the data being used inappropriately, in a manner detrimental to women, is minimized as much as possible.

CONCLUSION

I contend that psychologists will surely continue to do research on gender differences, the media will continue to publicize and glamorize the findings and the lay public will continue to be fascinated and influenced by these reports. It would be unwise in the extreme for feminist psychologists to abandon this area, thereby losing their power to influence it. It is of utmost importance to institute guidelines for non-sexist gender differences research. The six guidelines listed here should be very useful in remedying current problems in gender differences research.

NOTE

1. It seems safe to say that there is controversy and no consensus among feminist psychologists about the best system of nomenclature in using the terms 'sex' and 'gender'. One fairly common system is to use 'sex differences' to refer to innate or biologically produced differences between females and males (e.g., there are sex differences in the genitals) and to use 'gender differences' to refer to male–female differences that result from learning and the social roles of females and males (e.g., Unger, 1979). The problem with this terminology is that in many cases we do not know whether a particular male–female difference is biologically caused or culturally caused, and we should hold out the possibility of biology-environment interactions, with both contributing. In the latter case, the terminology becomes impossible.

I have adopted an alternative terminology that has worked well in my writing and conceptualizing. I use 'sex' to refer to sexual behaviors and anatomy, and 'gender' to the state of being male or female (e.g., Hyde, 1979). One advantage of this terminology is that it overcomes the ambiguous use of the term 'sex' in English, since it sometimes refers to sexuality and sometimes to maleness and femaleness. For example, does the book *Sex and Temperament in Three Primitive Societies* address the question of whether sexual expression influences one's temperament or does it address the question of gender roles and temperament? I therefore use 'gender differences' consistently to refer to male–female differences, leaving aside the issue of whether the differences are biologically or environmentally caused, or both, since we typically do not know the answer to this question.

REFERENCES

Baumeister, R. F. (1988). 'Should We Stop Studying Sex Differences Altogether?', *American Psychologist* 43: 1092–5.

Benbow, C. P., and Stanley, J. C. (1980). 'Sex Differences in Mathematical Ability: Fact or Artifact?', *Science* 210: 1262–4.

Berg, P., and Hyde, J. S. (1976). 'Gender and Race Differences in Causal Attributions'. Paper presented at the September meeting of the American Psychological Association, Washington, DC.

Crandall, V. C. (1969). 'Sex Differences in Expectancy of Intellectual and Academic Reinforcement', in C. P. Smith (ed.) *Achievement-Related Motives in Children.* New York: Russell Sage Foundation.

Denmark, F., Russo, N. F., Frieze, I. H., and Sechzer, J. A. (1988). 'Guidelines for Avoiding Sexism in Psychological Research', *American Psychologist* 43: 582–5.

Eagly, A. H. (1987a). *Sex Differences in Social Behavior: A Social-Role Interpretation.* Hillsdale; NJ: Erlbaum.

Eagly, A. H. (1987b). 'Reporting Sex Differences', *American Psychologist* 42: 756–7.

Hall, J. A. (1984). *Nonverbal Sex Differences.* Baltimore: Johns Hopkins University Press.

Halpern, D. G. (1992). *Sex Differences in Cognitive Abilities,* 2nd ed. Hillsdale, NJ: Erlbaum.

Hyde, J. S. (1979). *Understanding Human Sexuality.* New York: McGraw-Hill.

Hyde, J. S. (1991). *Half the Human Experience: The Psychology of Women,* 4th ed. Lexington, MA: D.C. Heath.

Hyde, J. S., Fennema, E., and Lamon, S. J. (1990). 'Gender Differences in Mathematics Performance: A Meta-Analysis,' *Psychological Bulletin* 107: 139–55.

Hyde, J. S., and Linn, M. C., eds. (1986). *The Psychology of Gender: Advances Through Meta-Analysis.* Baltimore: Johns Hopkins University Press.

Jacobs, J., and Eccles, J. S. (1985). 'Science and the Media: Benbow and Stanley Revisited', *Educational Researcher* 14: 20–5.

Kimura, D. (1987). 'Are Men's and Women's Brains Really Different?', *Canadian Journal of Psychology* 37: 19–35.

Kimura, D. (1992). 'Sex Differences in the Brain', *Scientific American* 267(3): 118–25.

Lenney, E. (1977). 'Women's Self-Confidence in Achievement Settings', *Psychological Bulletin* 84: 1–13.

Maccoby, E. E., ed. (1966). *The Development of Sex Differences.* Stanford, CA: Stanford University Press.

Maccoby, E. E., and Jacklin, C. N. (1974). *The Psychology of Sex Differences.* Stanford, CA: Stanford University Press.

McHugh, M. C., Koeske, R. D., and Frieze, I. H. (1986). 'Issues to Consider in Conducting Nonsexist Psychological Research: A Guide for Researchers', *American Psychologist* 41: 879–90.

Romanes, G. J. (1887). 'Mental Differences Between Men and Women', *Nineteenth Century* 21(123): 654–72.

Rothblum, E. D. (1988). 'More on Reporting Sex Differences,' *American Psychologist* 43: 1095.

Shields, S. A. (1975). 'Functionalism, Darwinism, and the Psychology of Women: A Study in Social Myth', *American Psychologist* 30: 739–54.

Terman, L. M. (1936). *Sex and Personality.* New York: McGraw-Hill.

Unger, R. (1979). ''Toward a Redefinition of Sex and Gender', *American Psychologist* 34: 1085–94.

Woolley, H. T. (1910). 'A Review of the Recent Literature on the Psychology of Sex', *Psychological Bulletin* 7:335–42.

On Comparing Women and Men

ALICE H. EAGLY

The practice of comparing the sexes in scientific data has been hotly debated by feminists in recent years. The controversy stems, at least in part, from the failure of the findings of empirical research to tell the story that we hoped that they would. When some of us started studying gender in the late 1960s and early 1970s from a feminist perspective that reflected our commitment to furthering equality between the sexes, we anticipated that research would serve the aims of our social movement. Implicit or explicit in the majority of this work was the expectation that feminists' comparisons of women and men would help to raise women's status by dispelling people's stereotypes about women. Much of our gender research reflected two missions: revealing people's damaging stereotypes and attitudes concerning women (e.g., Broverman et al., 1972); and displaying the absence of stereotypic sex differences in behavior, traits and abilities (e.g., Maccoby and Jacklin, 1974). We hoped to explain women's disadvantaged social position through people's negative stereotypes and attitudes. Our research on sex differences would shatter these stereotypes and change people's attitudes by proving that women and men are essentially equivalent. However admirable our goals, scientific research has presented us with a considerably more challenging set of findings.

Before describing some of the complexities of contemporary research findings, a note on terminology is appropriate. Consistent with ordinary usage in

Alice H. EAGLY is a Professor of Psychology at Purdue University. Her interests include syntheses of research comparing women and men as well as studies of attitudes and stereotypes about the sexes. ADDRESS: 1364 Psychological Sciences Building, Department of Psychological Sciences, Purdue University, West Lafayette, IN 47907-1364, USA. E-mail address is EAGLY@BRAZIL.PSYCH.PURDUE.EDU.

scientific psychology, the term 'sex difference' refers in this article to any observed difference between females and males, without any implications for the causes of the difference (see Eagly, 1987b). Others prefer the more complex terms 'sex-correlated' or 'sex-related' for this purpose (e.g., Deaux, 1993; Gentile, 1993). Whether or not the 'correlated' or 're-lated' feature is added to the term 'sex,' using 'sex' to mark group membership is consistent with typical dictionary definitions of the term as referring to the division of beings into male and female categories. Moreover, treating sex as a marker variable explicitly departs from the artificial 'nature versus nurture' dichotomy furthered by psychologists who attach the term 'sex' to biology and the term 'gender' to culture (e.g., Unger, 1979). Surely an observed difference should not be labeled a 'sex' or 'gender' difference, depending on whether psychologists wish to think about it as biologically caused or culturally induced. The causation of differences between women and men cannot usefully be addressed merely by labeling observed differences by terms intended to connote particular causal factors. Instead, theoretically understanding of the causes of differences and similarities is an end point of effective scientific research.

THE STATE OF THE EVIDENCE

Caught up in the passions of our feminist social movement in the 1960s and 1970s, many of us had a simple vision of what empirical research on sex differences would yield. Not anticipating how thoroughly our findings would require us to expand and refine this vision, we created a formidable body of scientific knowledge by comparing women and men on a wide range of measures in many different types of research. As the amount of research grew, integrating it to answer questions about similarities and differences became increasingly difficult as long as authors applied informal, narrative methods to the task of overviewing the field. Beginning in the late 1970s, a methodological revolution occurred in the integration of research findings as psychologists turned to the quantitative techniques known as meta-analysis (see Hyde, 1990).

These more sophisticated and reliable methods of aggregating findings describe differences and similarities on a continuum and thus avoid the artificial dichotomization of research findings as demonstrating either sameness or difference. In order to address the global question of the extent to which the behavior of men and women differs in a domain (e.g., aggression), the meta-analyst thus averages the effect sizes from the individual studies and then interprets their central tendency. This central tendency is located somewhere along a continuum that runs from no difference to large differences and thus does not provide a simple 'yes' or 'no' answer to the question of whether, in general, men differ from women.

Even more important than this escape from a simplistic debate about 'sameness versus difference' is the ability of quantitative syntheses to describe sex differences in each domain by a set of effect sizes, each representing a particular study. The set of effect sizes is ordinarily much more important and informative than their central tendency because the effect sizes vary in magnitude (and often in direction as well). This observed variability in the effect sizes is an invitation to theory-building because the principal job of the meta-analyst is to explain *why* these effect sizes differ—that is, why the magnitude of the sex difference varies across the studies (see Eagly and Wood, 1991).

Contrary to our expectations that quantitative syntheses would challenge stereotypes, the majority of them have conformed in a general way to people's ideas about the sexes (Eagly, 1987b, 1993; Eagly and Wood, 1991). Relevant to the accuracy of gender stereotypes are meta-analyses in which student judges estimated the extent to which men and women would or would not differ in each of the studies that had provided a comparison of men's and women's behavior in a particular domain. The correlations between these estimates, which represented students' gender stereotypes, and the actual behavioral sex differences in the studies, assessed by their effect sizes, were positive and significant (e.g., Eagly and Crowley, 1986: Table 5; Eagly and Karau, 1991: Table 6; Eagly and Steffen, 1986: Table 5). In addition, compelling evidence of the general accuracy of people's gender stereotypes was provided by Swim's (1994) demonstration that subjects' perceptions of differences between the sexes predicted with considerable success the aggregated sex differences that had been obtained in prior quantitative syntheses of research (e.g., in cognitive abilities, non-verbal behaviors, social behaviors such as aggression and helping). Moreover, Swim's respondents tended either to be accurate about the magnitude of sex differences or to underestimate them. There was no tendency for subjects to overestimate the magnitude of differences between female and male behavior. Although the issue of stereotype accuracy invites further analysis (see Judd and Park, 1993), this evidence suggests that lay people, once maligned in much feminist writing as misguided holders of gender stereotypes, may be fairly sophisticated observers of female and male behavior.

It is not surprising that many feminist psychologists have been less than enthusiastic about this new wave of research on sex differences. Feminists had already enjoyed considerable success in shaping a consensus about the triviality of sex differences and the inaccuracy of gender stereotypes, a consensus tailored to serve feminist political goals. Attesting to feminist achievements, these views have become 'politically correct' in many circles and strongly influence most textbook presentations, despite a counter-theme in feminist writing emphasizing women's distinctive communal characteristics (e.g., Gilligan, 1982).

When contending with the onslaught of meta-analyzed empirical findings, many feminists have been extremely reluctant to accept the subtlety of conceptualizing differences and similarities along a continuum. The holding action of many feminist psychologists has been to argue for the very small size of virtually *all* sex differences as well as for their inconsistency across studies (e.g., Archer, 1987; Deaux, 1984; Lott, 1991). Feminists have also pointed out the multiple ways that science is socially constructed (e.g., Hare-Mustin and Marecek, 1988, 1990; see also this issue, pp. 531–7).

Advocates of the small-size position often used percent variance accounted for by sex as an index of effect magnitude and then argued that this number was typically small. However, in the very same year that Deaux (1984) suggested that 5 percent of the variance is an 'upper boundary' for the magnitude of sex differences. Hall (1984) reviewed numerous research literatures on non-verbal behavior and found that many such behaviors had average effect sizes that exceeded this boundary, some by substantial amounts (see Hall, 1984: Table 11.1). Other feminist psychologists exhorted scientists to accompany any reports of sex comparisons with the percent-variance 'tag' attached to them (McHugh et al., 1986). In the face of methodological writing explaining why the percent-variance metric is easily misinterpreted and why differences that appear small by this metric can have considerable practical importance (e.g., Abelson, 1985; Prentice and Miller, 1992; Rosenthal and Rubin, 1979), the consensus about small size should have been eroded. Also devastating to the small-size verdict are the comparisons that can now be made between meta-analyzed sex comparisons and meta-analyzed findings associated with hypotheses unrelated to gender (see Eagly, 1987b). These comparisons suggest that the magnitudes of sex-difference findings are, on the whole, typical of findings produced in psychological research by manipulating variables experimentally or classifying people by other personal characteristics (e.g., personality attributes). In fact, relative to most other findings in psychology, sex-difference findings in some domains are large (see Ashmore, 1990: Table 19.1; Helpern, 1992: 86–7).

The inconsistencies in the magnitude of sex-difference findings (and sometimes in their direction) are their most challenging feature. This feature was obscured by the traditional practice of comparing findings across studies merely by their statistical significance. Inconsistencies suggested by differing significance levels are illusory to the extent that they reflect differences in studies' statistical power (e.g., in sample size). Comparisons of effect sizes are considerably more informative because effect sizes are independent of studies' sample sizes.

Most of the inconsistencies in effect sizes revealed by quantitative syntheses are explicable in terms of methodological dissimilarities between studies (e.g., differences in measuring instruments or in the social settings or role relationships examined). Between-studies inconsistencies such as these demonstrate the contextual quality of findings—that is, their tendency to differ in magnitude (and sometimes in direction) depending on the particular context in which a behavior is elicited. Quantitative reviewers test hypotheses about the contextual quality of sex-difference findings by calculating statistical models that use studies' contextual features to predict effect sizes. For example, Eagly and Crowley's (1986) synthesis of helping behavior studies examined, among other features, the presence versus absence of an audience of people who could observe research participants' helpful behavior.

It is quite startling to find that psychologists critical of work on sex differences still claim that context is neglected in this work. Perhaps these critics have not actually studied contemporary syntheses of sex-difference findings or have been prevented from understanding these syntheses by technical barriers (e.g., specialized meta-analytic statistics). Claims that context is ignored are inaccurate and may reflect a stereotype based on these critics' reading of pre-1980s research. It is important not only to understand the strong emphasis on context in much contemporary research on sex differences, but also to appreciate that context-dependence is not unique to sex-difference findings. Rather, it is another typical feature of the findings of psychological research. As Rosnow and Rosenthal (1989: pp. 1280) wrote: 'there is growing awareness in psychology that just about everything under the sun is context dependent in one way or another.' The context-dependence of our empirical findings should encourage us to offer contextually-qualified generalizations about gender, but it should not prevent us from drawing conclusions from our research.

A social constructionist position has frequently been contrasted with a logical positivist position ascribed by some feminists to those researchers who study sex differences empirically (e.g., Mednick, 1991; Hare-Mustin and Marecek, this issue, pp. 531–7). The feminist message that science is biased appears to be directed to psychologists who are thought to believe that science is objective (see Crawford and Marecek, 1989). However, it would be startling to find a modern social scientist who would fail to agree that science is socially constructed or who would maintain that science is objective or value-free. There are virtually no empirical researchers adopting a feminist perspective who would neglect to scrutinize research for masculinist methodological and theoretical biases. Although it is appropriate to sow uneasiness about science through emphasizing its social construction, science remains a rule-bound set of social activities that provides a powerful tool for examining relations between variables and for testing theories about these relations. Science is ultimately strengthened and improved by feminist psychologists' many analyses of the failures of science to live up to its rules (e.g., Sherif, 1979; Shields, 1975).

Given the rediscovery of the once-banished sex differences, comparing the sexes is newly regarded by some feminists as a possibly dangerous and potentially subversive activity that feminists should avoid. Mednick's (1991) summary of her survey of a selected sample of feminist psychologists suggests that these negative views about research comparing women and men are quite widespread. Given that comparisons of the sexes do not shatter stereotypes in the simple fashion we had hoped, the faint of heart among feminists seem ready to abandon such comparisons. Considerably more palatable to many feminist psychologists is the targeting of our empirical research to study people's ideas about gender—in effect, an emphasis on only the 'damaging stereotype' aspect of our original dual-purpose research agenda.

A RECOMMENDATION FOR ACTION

How should we proceed as feminist scientists? We should not discourage sex-difference research by calling for its censorship and close regulation, as some have done (e.g., Baumeister, 1988; McHugh et al., 1986). Such a closed-minded approach would only undercut the feminist agenda in the long run. Feminist psychologists ought, instead, to consider whether the advantages of fostering comparisons of the sexes outweigh the risks. More radically, we might encourage *all* scientists to share openly their comparisons of male and female research participants. As I have suggested earlier (Eagly, 1987a), comparisons of the sexes might become a routine part of scientific reports, until such time that these reports are merely redundant with established knowledge and therefore no longer of interest. This recommendation does not imply an emphasis on these comparisons in research reports—only that investigators make them accessible for archival purposes.

There are numerous political and scientific arguments in favor of full and open reporting of comparisons between women and men (see Eagly, 1987a, 1990). Fundamentally important is the point that more data would produce a richer and more differentiated picture of gendered behavior and, in particular, would reveal its contextual patterning. This patterning lends itself to understanding the ways in which behavior is constrained by its social context and, in particular, by men's more dominant social position (e.g., Eagly and Crowley, 1986; Eagly and Johnson, 1990; Eagly and Karau, 1991; Eagly and Steffen, 1986; Wood and Rhodes, 1992). Reports of sex comparisons provide a magnificent lens for revealing gender to the extent that many such comparisons are accessible from a wide variety of studies that have established differing social settings and used different methods. Such data sets are a rich lode for theory building (Eagly and Wood, 1991) and belie the criticism that 'using sex as a subject variable is essentially atheoretical' (Archer, 1987: pp. 89). Indeed, it is quite puzzling to find that critics of sex-difference research believe that such work is atheoretical. On the contrary, the flowering of theories to explain sex differences and similarities is the most exciting feature of research in the area, especially during the last five or so years.

Although some critics acknowledge the theory-driven quality of contemporary research, they sometimes offer a different and equally puzzling claim—namely, that theories produced to explain sex differences and similarities presume that the causes of differences are inherent in the individual or that they arise from biology or early socialization (e.g., Kahn and Yoder, 1989). On the contrary, feminist social scientists, especially social psychologists, routinely offer theories that stress the shaping of behavior by people's expectations, which are in turn shaped by the roles that women and men play in society and by the social hierarchies within which gender is enacted (e.g., Deaux and Major, 1987; Eagly, 1987b; Ridgeway, 1992). Such theories mesh well with the feminist political commitment to change in social arrangements.

Finally, feminist social scientists should consider the consequences of abandoning research comparing the sexes. Would any other scientists continue this work? Most assuredly the answer to this question is affirmative. Particularly important are the efforts of biologically-oriented scientists, whose interest in sex differences is even more intense than that of social scientists in the modern period (e.g., Haug et al., 1993; Hoyenga and Hoyenga, 1993; Kimura, 1992). Although feminism has a voice among biologists and biopsychologists (e.g., Gowaty, 1992; Lancaster, 1991), most biological theories foster interpretations of sex differences as relatively ingrained. For example, sociobiologists and evolutionary psychologists view behavioral sex differences as arising primarily from the differing roles of women and men in reproduction (see Buss, 1989; Buss and Schmitt, 1993; Daly and Wilson, 1983; Kenrick, 1994). Such theories tend to have more troubling implications for feminist political goals.

The most important outcome of sex-difference research is not the placement of sex comparisons along a continuum of magnitude, but the interpretation that scientists give to differences and similarities. To the extent that scientists' interpretations become accepted by the public, they will affect everyday behavior as well as public policy. Feminist theoretical positions would only be weakened by constraints on the reporting of comparisons between the sexes, because it is the rich diversity of findings that allows compelling arguments to be made for these theories. Our comparisons of women and men have turned out somewhat differently than we had anticipated, but we can meet this challenge by providing effective theories of female and male behavior. These theories must withstand rigorous scientific scrutiny.

Feminists be bold! Let us be active, smart scientists who welcome new research findings and who enter the theoretical fray as powerful contenders.

Acknowledgments—Thanks are extended to Carolyn Jagacinski and Janice Kelly for comments on a draft of this article.

REFERENCES

Abelson, R. P. (1985). 'A Variance Explanation Paradox: When a Little is a Lot', *Psychological Bulletin* 97:128–32.

Archer, J. (1987). Beyond Sex Differences: Comments on Borrill and Reid,' *Bulletin of the British Psychological Society* 40: 88–90.

Ashmore, R. D. (1990). 'Sex, Gender, and the Individual', in L. A. Pervin (ed.) *Handbook of Personality: Theory and Research,* pp. 486–526. New York: Guilford Press.

Baumeister, R. F. (1988). 'Should We Stop Studying Sex Differences Altogether?', *American Psychologist* 42: 1092–5.

Broverman, I. K., Vogel, S. R., Broverman, D. M., Clarkson, F. E., and Rosenkrantz, P. S. (1972). 'Sex-role Stereotypes: A Current Appraisal,' *Journal of Social Issues* 28(2): 59–78.

Buss, D. M. (1989). 'Sex Differences in Human Mate Preferences: Evolutionary Hypotheses Tested in 37 Cultures', *Behavioral and Brain Sciences* 12: 1–49.

Buss, D. M., and Schmitt, D. P. (1993). 'Sexual Strategies Theory: An Evolutionary Perspective on Human Mating', *Psychological Review* 100: 204–32.

Crawford, M., and Marecek, J. (1989). 'Psychology Reconstructs the Female, 1968–1988', *Psychology of Women Quarterly* 13: 147–65.

Daly, M., and Wilson, M. (1983). *Sex, Evolution and Behavior,* 2nd ed. Boston: Willard Grant Press.

Deaux, K. (1984). 'From Individual Differences to Social Categories: Analysis of a Decade's Research on Gender', *American Psychologist* 39: 105–16.

Deaux, K. (1993). 'Commentary: Sorry, Wrong Number—a Reply to Gentile's Call', *Psychological Science* 4: 125–6.

Deaux, K., and Major, B. (1987). 'Putting Gender into Context: An Interactive Model of Gender-related Behavior', *Psychological Review* 94: 369–89.

Eagly, A. H. (1987a). 'Reporting Sex Differences', *American Psychologist* 42: 756–7.

Eagly, A. H. (1987b). *Sex Differences in Social Behavior: A Social-role Interpretation.* Hillsdale, NJ: Erlbaum.

Eagly, A. H. (1990). 'On the Advantages of Reporting Sex Comparisons', *American Psychologist* 45: 560–2.

Eagly, A. H. (1993). 'Sex Differences in Human Social Behavior: Meta-analytic Studies of Social Psychological Research', in M. Haug, R. Whalen, C. Aron and K. Olsen (eds.). *The Development of Sex Differences and Similarities in Behaviour,* pp. 421–36. London: Kluwer Academic.

Eagly, A. H., and Crowley, M. (1986). 'Gender and Helping Behavior: A Meta-analytic Review of the Social-psychological Literature', *Psychological Bulletin* 100: 283–308.

Eagly, A. H., and Johnson, B. T. (1990). 'Gender and Leadership Style: A Meta-analysis', *Psychological Bulletin* 108: 233–56.

Eagly, A. H., and Karau, S. (1991). 'Gender and the Emergence of Leaders: A Meta-analysis', *Journal of Personality and Social Psychology* 60: 685–710.

Eagly, A. H., and Steffen, V. J. (1986). 'Gender and Aggressive Behavior: A Meta-analytic Review of the Social-psychological Literature', *Psychological Bulletin* 100: 309–30.

Eagly, A.H., and Wood, W. (1991). 'Explaining Sex Differences in Social Behavior: A Meta-analytic Perspective', *Personality and Social Psychology Bulletin* 17: 306–15.

Gentile, D. A. (1993). 'Just What Are Sex and Gender, Anyway? A Call for a New Terminological Standard', *Psychological Science* 4(2): 120–4.

Gilligan, C. l(1982). *In a Different Voice: Psychological Theory and Women's Development.* Cambridge, MA: Harvard University Press.

Gowaty, P. A. (1992). 'Evolutionary Biology and Feminism', *Human Nature* 3: 217–49.

Hall, J. A. (1984). *Nonverbal Sex Differences: Communication Accuracy and Expressive Style.* Baltimore, MD: Johns Hopkins University Press.

Halpern, D. F. (1992). *Sex Differences in Cognitive Abilities,* 2nd ed. Hillsdale, NJ: Erlbaum.

Hare-Mustin, R. T., and Marecek, J. (1988). 'The Meaning of Difference: Gender Theory, Postmodernism, and Psychology', *American Psychologist* 43: 455–64.

Hare-Mustin, R. T., and Marecek, J., eds. (1990). *Making a Difference: Psychology and the Construction of Gender.* New Haven: Yale University Press.

Haug, M., Whalen, R., Aron, C., and Olsen, K., eds. (1993). *The Development of Sex Differences and Similarities in Behaviour.* London: Kluwer Academic.

Hoyenga, K. B., and Hoyenga, K. T. (1993). *Gender-Related Differences: Origins and Outcomes.* Boston: Allyn and Bacon.

Hyde, J. (1990). 'Meta-analysis and the Psychology of Gender Differences', *Signs: Journal of Women in Culture and Society* 16: 55–73.

Judd, C. M., and Park, B. (1993). 'Definition and Assessment of Accuracy in Social Stereotypes', *Psychological Bulletin* 100: 109–28.

Kahn, A. S., and Yoder, J. D. (1989). 'The Psychology of Women and Conservatism: Rediscovering Social Change', *Psychology of Women Quarterly* 13: 417–32.

Kenrick, D. T. (1994). 'Evolutionary Social Psychology: From Sexual Selection to Social Cognition', in M. P. Zanna (ed.). *Advances in Experimental Social Psychology,* Vol. 26, pp. 75–121. San Diego, CA: Academic Press.

Kimura, D. (1992). 'Sex Differences in the Brain', *Scientific American* 267(3): 118–25.

Lancaster, J. B. (1991). 'A Feminist and Evolutionary Biologist Looks at Women', *Yearbook of Physical Anthropology* 34: 1–11.

Lott, B. (1991). 'Social Psychology: Humanist Roots and Feminist Future', *Psychology of Women Quarterly* 15: 505–19.

Maccoby, E. E., and Jacklin, C. N. (1974). *The Psychology of Sex Differences.* Stanford, CA: Stanford University Press.

McHugh, M. D., Koeske, R. D., and Frieze, I. H. (1986). 'Issues to Consider in Conducting Non-sexist Psychological Research: A Guide for Researchers', *American Psychologist* 41: 879–90.

Mednick, M. T. (1991). 'Currents and Futures in American Feminist Psychology: State of the Art Revisited', *Psychology of Women Quarterly* 15: 611–21.

Prentice, D. A., and Miller, D. T. (1992). 'When Small Effects are Impressive', *Psychological Bulletin* 112: 160–4.

Ridgeway, C. L., ed. (1992). *Gender, Interaction, and Inequality.* New York: Springer-Verlag.

Rosenthal, R., and Rubin, D. (1979). 'A Note on Percent Variance Explained as a Measure of the Importance of Effects', *Journal of Applied Social Psychology* 9: 395–6.

Rosnow, R. L., and Rosenthal, R. (1989). 'Statistical Procedures and the Justification of Knowledge in Psychological Science', *American Psychologist* 44: 1276–84.

Sherif, C. W. (1979). 'Bias in Psychology', in J. A. Sherman and E. T. Beck (eds.). *The Prism of Sex: Essays in the Sociology of Knowledge,* pp. 93–133. Madison, WI: University of Wisconsin Press.

Shields, S. A. (1975). 'Functionalism, Darwinism, and the Psychology of Women: A Study in Social Muth', *American Psychologist* 30: 739–54.

Swim, J. K. (1994). 'Perceived Versus Meta-analytic Effect Sizes: An Assessment of the Accuracy of Gender Stereotypes', *Journal of Personality and Social Psychology* 66: 21–36.

Unger, R. K. (1979). 'Toward a Redefinition of Sex and Gender', *American Psychologist* 34: 1085–94.

Wood, W., and Rhodes, N. (1992). 'Sex Differences in Interaction in Task Groups', in C. L. Ridgeway (ed.). *Gender, Interaction, and Inequality,* 97–121. New York: Springer-Verlag.

Stereotypes, Science, Censorship, and the Study of Sex Differences

DIANE F. HALPERN

Research on sex differences is front-page news, often in the prestigious 'above the fold' section that is visible when the paper is folded. This is where the general public learns about studies like the one that found few females among mathematically-gifted youth (Benbow, 1988) and the one that found that women's fine motor and cognitive performance vary over the menstrual cycle (Hampson and Kimura, 1988). The bold headlines that proclaim these differences are based on the belief that news of sex differences, like sex itself, sells. The news media treat complex issues—like whether, when and how much females and males differ—simplistically, with a heavy emphasis on controversies (they're more interesting than agreements) and colorful quotes that are typically unrelated to their merit. The reports of these studies often bear little resemblance to the actual findings of the research because the usual rules of scientific evidence and reasoning don't apply in the media world, where deadlines and interest value reign supreme and rebuttal is frequently absent. Should reputable psychologists be contributing to the media circus that molds public opinion with sound bites and simplistic analyses of complex problems? Yes, we not only should, but we must.

Diane F. HALPERN is a cognitive psychologist who has written extensively on individual differences in cognition and ways of using the principles of cognitive psychology to improve our ability to think critically. Her books include *Sex Differences in Cognitive Abilities* (2nd ed); *Thought and Knowledge: An Introduction to Critical Thinking* (2nd ed); *Changing College Classrooms: New Teaching and Learning Strategies for an Increasingly Complex World and Enhancing Thinking Skills in the Sciences and Mathematics*. She can be contacted at the Department of Psychology, California State University, 5500 University Parkway, San Bernardino, CA 92407–2397, USA.

STEREOTYPES AND SCIENCE

Critics of sex-differences research argue that such research legitimizes negative stereotypes of women by creating an emphasis on the way the sexes differ while slighting the multitude of similarities. These critics often propose that psychologists should study only similarities because similarities are more important than differences. But, when we examine this argument closely, we find that it contains several unstated assumptions that don't hold up under scrutiny and tell more about negative stereotypes about women than the research that it criticizes. Stereotypes about any group (e.g., women, Latinos, men in college fraternities, New Yorkers) are not created as a result of systematic studies of group similarities and differences. Stereotypes about women and men existed long before psychologists applied their research skills to understanding the unique and shared aspects of group membership. Empirical research doesn't create stereotyping, as its critics imply; the systematic study of sex differences using scientific rules of evidence is the only way to dispel stereotypes and to understand legitimate differences.

The argument against research on the many questions of sex differences ignores the fact that we cannot study similarities without also studying differences. If we had not studied the way the sexes respond in different situations, we would not know, for example, that situational variables are more important in determining how a person will respond in most situations than individual variables like sex (Eagly, 1987). The insistence that we study only similarities creates a false dichotomy because research on similarities is not separable from the study of differences.

THE 'WOMEN HAVE LESS' FALLACY

Another unstated assumption often implied by those opposed to the study of sex differences is that, if the truth were known, the results would reveal female deficiencies. This sort of unstated assumption can often be found in arguments against the biological bases of female and male differences. In my recent book on this subject (Halpern, 1992), I called this belief 'the women have less fallacy.' Many researchers have found that there are sex differences that are unrelated to reproduction that have large and practically-significant effects, and some of these differences cannot be completely explained without recognizing the biological differences between females and males. There are numerous examples of carefully controlled research where the data clearly show the effect of biological variables on non-reproductive differences between females and males. Although the literature on such differences is too large and too technical in nature to summarize here, I will briefly list some of these studies. I will limit my examples to those that pertain to cognitive abilities because this is the area that I know best, but there are numerous other areas where large sex differences are found that have, at least in part, a biological component (e.g. the overwhelming majority of acts of violence are committed by males; the ratio of males to females diagnosed with Attention Deficit Disorder is 10:1; and eating disorders are much more likely in females than males [American Psychiatric Association, 1987]). Because of space limitations, my summary is very brief and interested readers will need to consult the original studies and literature reviews for a more complete understanding.

Several researchers have found that certain cognitive abilities vary in a cyclical fashion over the menstrual cycle. For example, in a series of carefully controlled studies of normal women (using women without cyclical variations in 'sex hormones' as controls), Hampson and Kimura (Hampson, 1990a, 1990b; Hampson and Kimura, 1988) found that performance on visual-spatial tasks declined during the period in the monthly cycle when quantities of estrogen and progesterone are low, and verbal fluency and manual dexterity tasks improved during the portion of the monthly cycle when quantities of estrogen and progesterone are high. Many other studies have shown that perception also varies as a function of monthly changes in female hormones (e.g. Goolkasian, 1980). Although the magnitude of these differences is small, the systematic covariation with the ebb and flow of monthly hormones cannot be explained without acknowledging that these hormones can affect cognition.

Numerous studies involving individuals with hormone abnormalities also show the involvement of biological variables on cognition. Males with androgen deficiencies at puberty show severe deficits in spatial abilities with normal functioning on other cognitive tasks (Hier and Crowley, 1982). Similarly, females with Turner's syndrome, an abnormality in which they have very low levels of 'sex hormones,' have severe deficits in visual-spatial abilities with normal abilities on verbal tasks (e.g. Hines, 1982). Females who have been exposed to high levels of androgens during pre-natal development show increased aggression and activity, preference for 'boy-typical' toys and high levels of spatial ability (Berenbaum and Hines, 1992; Newcombe et al., 1983; Reinisch, 1981).

There is also clear evidence that there are some differences in the brain structures of normal females and males and that these differences are evident *in-utero* (e.g. de Lacoste-Utamsing and Holloway, 1982; Kimura, 1987). Of course, the fact that there are brain differences doesn't imply that these differences *cause* sex-related differences in cognition, but there is a large body of other sorts of data that support this contention. For example, cognitive abilities vary as both a function of one's sex and one's preferred hand. Handedness (extent to which an individual is right- or left-handed) is a rough indicator of brain organization, and there are sex differences in handedness (see, for example, Casey and Brabeck, 1989; Coren and Halpern, 1991; Halpern and Coren, 1993). Careful manipulations of pre-natal and post-natal hormones with non-human mammals clearly show that these hormones affect a wide range of non-reproductive behaviors (e.g. Denenberg et al., 1988). Ancillary evidence that supports this viewpoint was recently presented by Masters and Sanders (1993), who found that the extremely large effect size for some spatial tasks (close to one standard deviation between female and male means) has remained stable over the past 17 years, despite substantial changes in the number of women in higher education and changes in sex roles. The ability to produce fluent speech is much more likely to be a problem for males than females. There are three to four times more male stutterers than female stutterers (Skinner and Shelton, 1985). Males are also 10 times more likely to be severely dyslexic than are females (Sutaria, 1985). Finally, there have been numerous replicated studies that show that sexual orientation also covaries with specific cognitive abilities in predictable ways (e.g. Gladue et al., 1990; Sanders and Ross-Fields, 1986).

Although there is a huge body of evidence showing that sex-related differences do exist, there is nothing in these studies to suggest that either females or males have the overall advantage. Differences are not deficiencies, and there is no logical reason for labeling those characteristics that are associated with being female, as 'less' valuable than those that are associated with being male. For example, girls are, on the average, more cooperative (less aggressive) than boys and score much higher, on the average, on tests of manual dexterity and the production of fluid speech (Hines, 1990). Thus, from an abilities perspective, we might expect that a majority of surgeons, mechanics and politicians would be female. That they are not is unrelated to their abilities and must have its origin in social variables. Boys, on the average, excel at other tasks such as the mental manipulation of shapes (see Halpern, 1992, for a review of these studies). If society labels those traits that are associated with being female as negative and those associated with being male as positive, then the problem lies in societal values, not in the fact that females and males differ or in the fact that researchers found these differences. We need to separate differences from the evaluation of the way in which people differ. This is an important message because we live in a diverse world where sex is only one way in which people differ. It makes no more sense to argue over which sex has the better intellectual skills than to argue over which sex has the better genitals or which race has the best skin color or shape of their eyes. Sex differences research is not a zero sum game with a winner and a loser. We can learn to appreciate differences and to value the uniqueness of individuals without denying the fact that males and females differ in many ways including some aspects of both nature, nurture and their interaction.

KNOWLEDGE IS POWER

It is a fact that males score an average of 47 to 50 points higher than females on the mathematics portion of the Scholastic Aptitude Test (SAT-M), a difference that has remained constant for the last 25 years. If any part of this huge difference is due to sex-related differences in abilities, it is extremely small because the sex differences on other tests of mathematics ability are much smaller. Thus, sex differences research is critical in understanding and improving female performance on the SAT-M. The SAT-M is an important test because it is used in making decisions about college admissions in thousands of colleges in North America. We can and should argue about the reasons for, and consequences of, this huge difference, but this is an argument that we could not have if psychologists had never studied sex differences on the SAT-M. We could not address, or redress, the fact that this test results in lower scores for girls if the studies that show this difference had not been conducted. The only alternative to the knowledge that studies of sex differences provide is ignorance, and ignorance will not advance females or any other group.

A PSYCHOLOGY OF WOMEN

Like many of my feminist colleagues, I have taught a course entitled 'Psychology of Women' for many years. If we were to abandon the study of sex differences, then we would lose the theoretical underpinnings of courses like this one and all of the other women's studies courses. When we talk about the psychology of women, or their history, or literature, or women's 'place' in other academic disciplines, we are always putting women in some context and making comparisons with men, just as studies of minority groups make implicit and explicit comparisons with other ethnic groups. The notion of sex differences is at the heart of these courses because if there were not differences then there would be no need for a psychology of women. The alternative to the study of differences is to conclude that there is nothing distinct about women's psychology. The alternative is a return to the normative use of males for studies designed to explore human nature, an alternative that few feminists would advocate. This would be a giant step backward to a not-too-distant past where males were used as subjects in almost all areas of research including psychological and medical research. For example, it was only a little over 15 years ago when all of the studies on aging conducted by federally-funded United States agencies used only male subjects despite the fact that a majority of the elderly is female. The exclusive use of male subjects was based on the tacit assumptions that sex differences should not be studied and males would yield data that would be applicable to all people. Of course, statistics about any group cannot be applied to individuals, especially when there is a great deal of variability in the data. We can only make group-level statements about 'on the average' differences, and it is important that this fact be clearly communicated whenever sex differences are discussed.

PSYCHOBIOSOCIAL MODELS

Despite the fact that I believe that we must encourage the study of sex differences, I also understand the concerns of those who hold opposing opinions. We must all remember that research takes place in a social context and every aspect of our work, ranging from the types of research questions that we consider important, to the way we interpret data, is influenced by this context. Turn-of-the-century scientists found 'evidence' for the intellectual inferiority of women and it was 'well established' that intellectual tasks would drain the blood needed for menstruation which

would somehow be harmful to women's health: sexist conclusions that were acceptable because of the social context in which they were presented (reported in Shields, 1980).

A feminist perspective on sex differences research is crucial for proposing new models and research paradigms for the study of women's psychology. Such models and paradigms recognize the reciprocal and interactive effects of psychology, sociology and biological factors—a model in which the influence of environmental factors on biology, and the way biological variables influence environmental factors, work jointly with a host of other variables to create sex-related differences and similarities. The answer to the questions about sex differences can never be 'either-or'; we must seek answers that allow for multiple determinants. There is ample evidence that biological and environmental variables exert mutual effects—the types of activities in which we engage alter brain structures and brain structures, in turn, are likely to influence those activities in which we choose to engage (e.g. Diamond, 1988; Greenough et al., 1987).

TOWARD A NEW MODEL OF FEMINISM

Like many of my colleagues, I shudder every time I hear a female college student proclaim that she is not a feminist. After many lengthy discussions and informal 'focus groups,' I have concluded that so many young women eschew feminism because they believe that much of it is rigid and conformist. To some extent, I have also seen this drift toward a single admissible point of view. For example, there are many colleagues who refuse to consider the possibility that some women might lie about rape, incest or abuse. The importance of the issue of violence against women cannot be overemphasized, and it is feminists who must ensure counseling, medical care, legal assistance, education and shelter for the many victims whose only crime is being female. But this does not mean that no woman ever lies about violence. Similarly, feminists must ensure that cultural and other environmental factors are considered in our understanding of the ways in which females and males are similar and different. We must also fight vigorously against the misuse and biased interpretation of data. But this does not mean that we must reject the substantial body of evidence that says that biological variables are also involved in some of the differences. In other words, we must move toward a more tolerant and more inclusive feminism. We cannot pretend that data supporting biological factors do not exist. We also cannot ignore the overwhelming body of evidence showing that, while some sex differences are non-existent or very small, there are also some extremely large and meaningful differences.

The new feminism I am calling for will welcome debate and will encourage a careful and open-minded analysis of all the evidence that pertains to important issues. This would be a healthy change, signalling that feminism is strong enough to allow dissent and that 'truth' is not predetermined before the data are collected. Otherwise, we run the danger of becoming as myopic and dogmatic as those who believe that all sex differences are due to biological factors.

I hope that at least half of those future scientists who will propose and test these new models will be females who are proud to call themselves feminists, and I hope that they will understand that the misuse of research in the past is not a reason for censoring the science of the future. Censorship, even self-censorship, is the wrong response to past abuses. If we do not conduct research on sex differences, then we are left with stereotypes and the status quo.

REFERENCES

American Psychiatric Association (1987). *Diagnostic and Statistical Manual of Mental Disorders,* 3rd rev. ed. Washington, DC: American Psychiatric Association.

Benbow, C. P. (1988). 'Sex Differences in Mathematical Reasoning Ability in Intellectually Talented Preadolescents: Their Nature, Effects, and Possible Causes', *Behavioral and Brain Sciences* 11: 169–232.

Berenbaum, S. A., and Hines, M. (1992). 'Early Androgens are Related to Childhood Sex-typed Toy Preferences', *Psychological Science* 3: 203–6.

Casey, M. B., and Brabeck, M. M. (1989). 'Exception to a Male Advantage on a Spatial Task: Family Handedness and College Major as Factors Identifying Women who Excel', *Neuropsychologia* 27: 689–96.

Coren, S., and Halpern, D. F. (1991). 'Left-handedness: A Marker for Decreased Survival Fitness', *Psychological Bulletin* 109: 90–106.

de Lacoste-Utamsing, M. C., and Holloway, R. L. (1982). 'Sexual Dimorphism in the Human Corpus Callosum', *Science* 216: 1431–2.

Denenberg, V. H., Berrebi, A. S., and Fitch, R. H. (1988). 'A Factor Analysis of the Rat's Corpus Callosum', *Brain Research* 497: 271–9.

Diamond, M. C. (1988). *Enriching Heredity: The Impact of the Environment on the Anatomy of the Brain.* New York: Free Press.

Eagly, A. H. (1987). *Sex Differences in Social Behavior: A Social-role Interpretation.* Hillsdale, NJ: Erlbaum.

Gladue, B. A., Beatty, W. W., Larson, J., and Staton, R. D. (1990). 'Sexual Orientation and Spatial Ability in Men and Women', *Psychobiology* 18: 101–8.

Goolkasian, P. (1980). 'Cyclic Changes in Pain Perception: An ROC Analysis', *Perception and Psychophysics* 27: 499–504.

Greenough, W. T., Black, J. E., and Wallace, C. S. (1987). 'Experience and Brain Development', *Child Development* 58: 539–59.

Halpern, D. F. (1992). *Sex Differences in Cognitive Abilities,* 2nd ed. Hillsdale, NJ: Erlbaum.

Halpern, D. F., and Coren, S. (1993). 'Left-handedness and Life Span: A Reply to Harris', *Psychological Bulletin* 114: 235–41.

Hampson, E. (1990a). 'Estrogen-related Variations in Human Spatial and Articulatory-motor Skills', *Psychoneuroendocrinology* 15: 97–111.

Hampson, E. (1990b). 'Variations in Sex-related Cognitive Abilities Across the Menstrual Cycle', *Brain and Cognition* 14: 26–43.

Hampson, E., and Kimura, D. (1988). 'Reciprocal Effects of Hormonal Fluctuations on Human Motor and Perceptual-Spatial Skills', *Behavioral Neuroscience* 102: 456–95.

Hier, D. B., and Crowley, W. F., Jr. (1982). 'Spatial Ability in Androgen-deficient Men', *The New England Journal of Medicine* 306: 1202–5.

Hines, M. (1982). 'Prenatal Gonadal Hormones and Sex Differences in Human Behavior', *Psychological Bulletin* 92: 56–80.

Hines, M. (1990). 'Gonadal Hormones and Human Cognitive Development', in J. Balthazart (ed.). *Hormones, Brain and Behavior in Vertebrates, Vol. 1, Sexual Differentiation, Neuroanatomical Aspects, Neurotransmitters and Neuropeptides,* pp. 51–63. Basel: Karger.

Kimura, D. (1987). 'Are Men's and Women's Brains Really Different?', *Canadian Psychology* 28: 133–47.

Masters, M. S., and Sanders, B. (1993). 'Is the Gender Difference in Mental Rotation Disappearing?', *Behavior Genetics* 23: 337–41.

Newcombe, N., Bandura, M., and Taylor, D. G. (1983). 'Sex Differences in Spatial Ability and Spatial Activities', *Sex Roles* 9: 377–86.

Reinisch, J. (1981). 'Prenatal Exposure to Synthetic Progestins Increases Potential for Aggression in Humans', *Science* 211: 1171–3.

Sanders, G., and Ross-Field, L. (1986). 'Sexual Orientation and Visual–Spatial Ability', *Brain and Cognition* 5: 280–90.

Shields, S. A. (1980). 'Nineteenth-century Evolutionary Theory and Male Scientific Bias', In G. W. Barlow and J. Silverberg (eds.). *Sociobiology: Beyond Nature/Nurture,* pp. 489–502. Boulder, CO: Westview Press.

Skinner, P. H., and Shelton, R. L. (1985). *Speech, Language, and Hearing: Normal Processes and Disorders,* 2nd ed. New York: Wiley.

Sutaria, S. D. (1985). *Specific Learning Disabilities: Nature and Needs.* Springfield, IL: Charles C. Thomas.

SHOULD PSYCHOLOGISTS STUDY SEX DIFFERENCES?

Asking the Right Questions: Feminist Psychology and Sex Differences

RACHEL T. HARE-MUSTIN AND JEANNE MARECEK

In asking how basic gender differences are, we are also asking how basic we want them to be (Di Stefano, 1990: 66).

If they get you to ask the wrong questions, they don't need to worry about your answers (Anonymous).

Should psychologists study sex differences? Our answer, simply put, is no. Our 'no' is a situated refusal, reflecting our time and place. The question of sex differences has been important in the past, but we believe that feminist psychology should now put it aside.

The issue of sex differences has been fraught with mystification and conflict since psychology's earliest

days. Historically, the search for sex differences was closely aligned with the quest by male theorists to understand 'woman's nature.' Then, as now, men served as the unmarked reference group, and male behavior was the norm or standard of comparison. The implicit question was whether women are the same as, different from, or even as good as men. As early as 1910, Helen Thompson Woolley concluded her review of the 'motley mass' of sex difference research in psychology with the declaration that 'martyred' logic, 'flagrant personal bias' and 'even sentimental rot and drivel' run riot throughout the literature (1910: pp. 340). Today, nearly 85 years later, questions about sex differences are far from settled. Moreover, accusations of bias are now issued by feminists and antifeminists alike.

Rachel T. Hare-Mustin is a feminist theorist and clinical psychologist in private practice at 139 Rose Lane, Haverford, PA 19041 USA.

Jeanne Marecek is Professor of Psychology and Women's Studies at Swarthmore College, 500 College Avenue, Swarthmore, PA 19081 USA.

Like any human endeavor, the discipline of psychology is situated within the matrix of culture and society. This matrix lends urgency to particular issues, authorizes the scientific scrutiny of certain questions and selects certain answers for professional and popular dissemination. Thus, whatever the intentions of individual researchers, research cannot be neutral, value-free or apolitical. Since Woolley's time, assertions about sex difference have been used to argue women's inferiority, to limit their spheres of action, and to restrict their autonomy and freedom of movement. To rebut such claims, some feminists have argued that women's differences from men are insignificant or even non-existent. But asserting that women are no different from men does not serve feminist interests in every case. Paradoxically, assertions of no difference can sometimes deny women equitable treatment. Consider, for example, equal or sex-blind treatment of the work force. Such treatment fails to recognize that women, but not men, can become pregnant and that, in most cases, it is women who bear the major responsibility for infant care. When such differences are disregarded, equal treatment is not equitable.

Some feminists have asserted women's difference from, and superiority over, men in the domains of caregiving, morality and emotional connection. Yet even these assertions of superiority can readily be appropriated by traditionalists to urge a return to conventional roles and to discourage women's striving for agency, autonomy and social power (Hare-Mustin and Marecek, 1990). What we conclude is that assertions about male-female differences and similarities do not have a single, fixed meaning; instead, they serve as raw material for constructing a variety of contested interpretations, cultural meanings and political agendas.

DIFFERENCE RESEARCH AND ESSENTIALISM

The complex relationship between feminism, antifeminism, difference and sameness prompts us to step back and examine the assumptions underlying difference research. Difference research presupposes an essentialist model of gender. As Bohan (1993: pp. 7) says, essentialism locates gender within the person and portrays it 'in terms of fundamental attributes that are conceived as internal, persistent, and generally separate from ongoing experience . . .' Consider the following statements: 'Females are more likely to experience math anxiety'; 'Women excel in helpfulness in long-term situations'; 'girls are more fearful, timid, and anxious than boys'.[1] Such statements (and difference research more generally) construe gender in terms of stable, inner qualities and thus reaffirm an essentialist model. One reading of the ambiguous phrase 'the psychology of women' is 'women's psychology.' This reading, an essentialist one, suggests that women (a unitary group) have a shared psychology (an array of inner qualities, traits and capacities, either innate or learned) that presumably produces behavior. The widespread use of terms like 'psychology of women' and 'women's psychology' reflects the extent to which essentialist thought pervades the whole discipline of psychology, including feminist psychology.[2]

Sex difference research assumes that there is such a thing as Woman, and further that 'Womanness' can be defined in terms of inherent qualities (e.g. cognitive skills, emotions, 'ways of knowing' or gendered 'voice'). It highlights the ways in which women differ from men and overlooks the differences among women. Moreover, when gender is construed in terms of the abstracted qualities of individuals, the circumstances and experiences of varying groups of women become irrelevant and can be set aside. In this way, feminist psychologists have too often mistaken the experiences of white middle-class women as the experiences of all women. As Elizabeth Spelman notes, 'the claim of commonality can be very arrogant indeed' (1988: pp. 139).

The difference paradigm, with its reliance on essentialized qualities, disregards the complexity and dynamism of gendered behavior, which is situated within the ebb and flow of ongoing social relations. It 'collapses a "play of differences that is always on the move" [in Edward Snow's compelling phrase] into static and exaggerated dualisms' (Thorne, 1993: pp. 91). Social constructionism focuses directly on the 'play of differences' in an effort to produce a more adequate account of gender. Among the questions that frame constructionist inquiry are: How is gender produced and sustained by human agents in interaction with one another? How do the organizational features and symbolic aspects of social situations bear upon and get worked out through gender relationships? Through what institutional structures, social practices, cultural representations, linguistic codes and patterns of social interchange is gender accomplished as a social fact (Butler, 1990; West and Zimmerman, 1987)? Such concerns underlie our opening quotation: 'In asking how basic gender differences are, we are also asking how basic we want them to be' (Di Stefano, 1990: pp. 66). Further questions are: how is gender made to seem natural, and how are the practices that produce gender rendered invisible, leaving us with the conviction that we have freely chosen who we are, and that our choices are deeply expressive of an inner self?

DIFFERENCE RESEARCH AND FEMINISM

The practical and political implications of sex difference research are also of concern. Some feminist psychologists conduct sex difference research with the aim of combating invidious gender stereotypes (see, for example, Halpern, this issue pp. 523–30), a goal we share. But sex difference research has other pragmatic and political consequences that we find problematic. First, the question of sex differences is a 'received' question and, by accepting this question, feminist psychologists divert their energy and attention from issues of their own choosing. Second, participating in the debate about women's nature prolongs that protracted debate still further. Furthermore, research on sex differences—like research on age or race differences—is merely descriptive; it does not illuminate the processes involved in the psychological phenomena under scrutiny. In addition, although sex difference research yields results that are only descriptive, such results are often granted prescriptive force. By claiming to know what men and women are, sex difference researchers seem to proclaim what they ought to be. Must a woman be empathic in order to be a woman?

Feminist psychologists are being challenged to attend to the experiences of women who have been disregarded (Landrine et al., 1992; Reid, 1993). In our view, this requires that feminist psychology relinquish the 'difference' paradigm, along with its essentialism and categoricalism. Race, ethnicity, class and sexual orientation cannot be studied by dividing women into categories and searching for the essential attributes that distinguish the normative member of each category (e.g. 'the' working-class woman, 'the' Latina). Such research programs can only produce another 'motley mass' of assertions about difference, with problems similar to those noted by Woolley 85 years ago. That is, these assertions are likely to be laced with 'bias' and 'martyred' logic, this time about Other women, as in the following: 'Lesbians had significantly higher self-esteem than college women'; 'Black women reported a lower level of functioning than Black men. White women, and White men.' We join with Aida Hurtado (1989) in calling for feminist psychologists to move beyond this categoricalism. In its stead, we urge the study of ongoing relations of privilege, power, subordination and rebellion among individuals provisionally demarcated by their gender, class membership, race/ethnicity and sexual orientation.

Another concern about difference research is the model of change it implies. Often, the conclusions drawn from difference research suggest that women's place in the social hierarchy, and their misfortunes, result from their 'psychology.' For example, if women are held to be less assertive than men, then this gender-linked deficiency could be used to explain women's lack of corporate advancement, thus diverting attention from institutional sexism. The feminist dictum 'the personal is political' is subverted by rendering gender once again merely personal. Too often difference research implies a feminist praxis that leaves the context unexamined, and instead centers on personal transformation, e.g. therapy, education and self-help (cf. Kitzinger and Perkins, 1993). Such modes of personal transformation are usually available only to the well-off, and thus do little to promote social justice.

THE SOCIAL CONSTRUCTION OF PSYCHOLOGICAL KNOWLEDGE

Sex difference researchers have typically taken the categories of psychological knowledge to be self-evident and unproblematic. Thus, a researcher might study male-female differences in aggression, independence, orgasmic frequency, persuasibility or verbal ability without questioning the meanings of the categories themselves. Moreover, sex difference research (whether it takes place in the laboratory or elsewhere) assumes that constructs such as aggression and independence are bounded and stable, and refer to real psychological phenomena.

Social constructionists are skeptical of the categories of knowledge, viewing them as accounts of experience shaped in accordance with cultural dictates. As Sampson (1993) points out, the definitions and categories that go unexamined, and that are accepted as natural, are typically those held by dominant groups. When psychological categories have been scrutinized through a feminist lens, many have been shown to reflect male-centered views of human experience, to privilege ways of being and behaving that are associated with men or to valorize aspects of women's behavior that benefit men (Hare-Mustin, 1994). Leonore Tiefer (in press), for instance, has identified the male-centered model of sexuality underlying the official diagnostic categories of sexual dysfunction. Others have argued that conventional definitions of independence and autonomy conceal the extent to which men depend on women for material and emotional sustenance, as well as the extent to which women cannot rely on men in return (Hare-Mustin and Marecek, 1986; Lerner, 1983). Others have interrogated such constructs as assertiveness, field dependence, aggression and humor (Crawford and Gressley, 1991; Frodi et al., 1977; Gervasio and Crawford, 1989; Haaken, 1988). In sum, for a feminist social constructionist, the psychological literature on male-female differences is not a record of cumulative knowledge about the 'truth' of what men and women are 'really' like. Rather, it is a repository of accounts of gender organized within particular assumptive frameworks and reflecting various interests.

CONCLUSION

Feminist theorists, in concert with other social theorists, have mounted challenges to many of the modernist assumptions of psychology, including its essentialism, its individualism and its faith in positivism (Marecek, in press). We cannot imagine ways to reform sex difference research that meet such challenges. For us, the sex difference question has become the proverbial 'wrong question.'

NOTES

1. These are quotations from current 'psychology of women' textbooks. We omit citations because it is not our intent to criticize individual scholars.
2. 'Psychology of women' is the customary title of courses offered in hundreds of US colleges and universities. It is also the designation of a Division (Section) of the American Psychological Association (as well as its journal and newsletter), and of a parallel group within the British Psychological Society. Such a designation may have been selected in order to gain acceptance within an established discipline (cf. Burns and Wilkinson, 1989). Nonetheless, the designation supports the idea of essential differences.

REFERENCES

Bohan, Janis S. (1993). 'Regarding Gender: Essentialism, Constructionism, and Feminist Psychology', *Psychology of Women Quarterly* 17: 5–21.

Burns, Jan, and Wilkinson, Sue. (1989). 'What's in a Name?', *British Psychological Society Psychology of Women Section Newsletter* 5: 35–8.

Butler, Judith P. (1990). *Gender Trouble*. New York: Routledge.

Crawford, Mary and Gressley, Diane. (1991). 'Creativity, Caring and Context: Women's and Men's Accounts of Humor Preferences and Practices', *Psychology of Women Quarterly* 15: 201–31.

Di Stefano, Christine. (1990). 'Dilemmas of Difference; Feminism, Modernity, and Postmodernism', in Linda J. Nicholson (ed.). *Feminism/Postmodernism,* pp. 63–82. New York: Routledge.

Frodi, Ann, Macaulay, Jacqueline, and Thome, Pauline R. (1977). 'Are Women Always Less Aggressive than Men? A Review of the Experimental Literature', *Psychological Bulletin* 84: 634–60.

Gervasio, Amy H., and Crawford, Mary. (1989). 'The Social Evaluation of Assertion: A Critique and Speech Act Reformulation', *Psychology of Women Quarterly* 13: 1–25.

Haaken, Janice. (1988). 'Field Dependence Research: A Historical Analysis of a Psychological Construct', *Signs* 13: 311–30.

Hare-Mustin, Rachel T. (1994). 'Discourses in the Mirrored Room: A Postmodern Analysis of Therapy', *Family Process* 33: 19–35.

Hare-Mustin, Rachel T., and Marecek, Jeanne. (1986). 'Autonomy and Gender: Some Questions for Therapists', *Psychotherapy* 23: 205–12.

Hare-Mustin, Rachel T., and Marecek, Jeanne. (1990). *Making a Difference: Psychology and the Construction of Gender.* New Haven, CT: Yale University Press.

Hurtado, Aida. (1989). 'Relating to Privilege: Seduction and Rejection in the Subordination of White Women and Women of Color', *Signs* 14: 833–55.

Kitzinger, Celia, and Perkins, Rachel. (1993). *Changing Our Minds: Lesbian Feminism and Psychology.* New York: New York University Press and London: Onlywomen Press.

Landrine, Hope, Klonoff, Elizabeth A., and Brown-Collins, Alice. (1992). 'Cultural Diversity and Methodology in Feminist Psychology', *Psychology of Women Quarterly* 16: 145–63.

Lerner, Harriet Goldhor. (1983). 'Female Dependency in Context', *American Journal of Orthopsychiatry* 53: 697–705.

Marecek, Jeanne (in press). 'Psychology and Feminism: Can This Relationship Be Saved?', in Domna Stanton and Abigail J. Stewart (eds.). *Feminisms in the Academy: Rethinking the Disciplines.* Ann Arbor, MI: University of Michigan Press.

Reid, Pamela Trotman. (1993). 'Poor Women in Psychological Research: Shut Up and Shut Out', *Psychology of Women Quarterly* 17: 133–50.

Sampson, Edward E. (1993). *Celebrating the Other: A Dialogic Account of Human Nature.* Boulder, CO: Westview Press.

Spelman, Elizabeth V. (1988). *Inessential Woman.* Boston: Beacon Press.

Thorne, Barrie. (1993). *Gender Play: Girls and Boys in School.* New Brunswick, NJ: Rutgers University Press.

Tiefer, Leonore (in press). *Sex Is Not a Natural Act, and Other Essays.* Boulder, CO: Westview Press.

West, Candace and Zimmerman, Don H. (1987). 'Doing Gender', *Gender and Society* I: 125–51.

Woolley, Helen Thompson. (1910). 'A Review of Recent Literature on the Psychology of Sex', *Psychological Bulletin* 7: 335–42.

CHECKPOINT

1. A broad range of issues is raised in the answer to the question "Should psychologists study of sex differences," including concern about the use of biological explanations, understanding how sex difference findings would impact social change, advocating new methodologies, and concern about censorship of unpopular findings.

Studying Gender

QUESTIONS FOR REFLECTION

1. What criticisms could you offer to the various feminist alternatives to the traditional scientific method?
2. In what ways is the question of "sex differences" the same as, or different from, the question of "gender differences"?

CHAPTER APPLICATIONS

1. Find any empirical study of sex or gender differences in a psychology journal, analyze the methods, and then redesign them using one of the feminist approaches described in these readings.
2. Explain to your mother or father why questions of sex and gender differences are so difficult to ask and answer.

CHAPTER THREE
Biology and Gender

QUESTIONS TO THINK ABOUT

- **What is the relationship between biology and sex?**
- **What are biological sex differences?**
- **What is the relationship between prenatal hormones, morphology, anatomy, reproductive function, and gender?**
- **What is biological determinism?**
- **How does evolutionary psychology explain sex and gender differences?**
- **How can we describe the relationship between biology and social/cultural factors in understanding sex and gender?**
- **In what ways are biological theories also political arguments?**
- **How do essentialism and social constructionism view biology and gender?**

THE RELATIONSHIP BETWEEN BIOLOGY AND GENDER

A central issue in defining sex and gender is identifying the role of biology. For some researchers, biology provides the key in distinguishing between sex and gender (recall the definitions offered by Gentile in chapter 1). For other researchers, biological variation is a critical factor in understanding why sex is not a dichotomous category (recall the examples of hermaphrodism offered by Fausto-Sterling in chapter 1). In examining the methodology of studying sex and gender presented to you in chapter 2, you discovered that researchers' choice of method may depend in large part on their preexisting beliefs about the relationship between sex and gender. A researcher who believes that sex and gender are roughly synonymous might conclude that sex differences, rooted in the biological distinctions between male and female, account for gender differences. We might refer to work of this sort as reflecting an *implicit* biological view of sex and gender.[1] On the other hand, a researcher whose primary concern is in understanding how the social context influences the behavior of men and women may not believe that the biology of sex provides any useful data for the question of interest. Working from this point of view, this researcher may not even acknowledge the presence of biological influences. Both these perspectives shortchange the complex relationship between biology and gender. This chapter shows you many theories of biological influences on gender and alternative ways to conceptualize the relationship between biology and gender. It is not sufficient to naively assume that biology causes behavior, just as it is not appropriate to assume that in the study of social context we can ignore biology.

One question that complicates an understanding of biology and gender is the distinction between sex and gender. Chapter 1 presented some alternative views on the definitions of sex and gender. The position advocated by Gentile is that the terms *sex differences* and *biologically sex-linked* be used for phenomena in which the biological connection to behavior is established. However, as critics point out, in many cases of sex differences, researchers do not know the precise biological causes, if any even exist. Furthermore, the assumption that biological causes and environmental causes are entirely separable ignores the more likely possibility—an interaction between biological and environmental causes. This introduction describes several kinds of biological theories as well as different ways that biology can interact with social/cultural factors. You will come to appreciate that simple assumptions about biology and gender are not sufficient to provide any satisfactory explanation of how gender develops or is maintained.

Different Biological Mechanisms

To begin studying biological explanations for gender, we need to identify the exact biological mechanisms that are under study. Biological explanations encompass a wide range of structures, mechanisms, or processes. They can operate alone or in conjunction with other factors, but the key point to recognize is that in describing biological mechanisms, we are often looking at different levels of analysis. Fundamental to any biological explanation of gender is the chromosomal distinction between XX (female) and XY (male) individuals. Under conditions of normal fetal development, individuals who are XX and XY will develop the reproductive systems, patterns of hormone production, and external genitalia that are characteristic of females and males, respectively. Explanations that rely on mechanisms related to these structures or processes are **genetic explanations,** whose foundation is the reliance on differences linked to the chromosomal distinction between males and females. For example, explanations that would examine factors tied to the Y chromosome fall under the rubric of genetic theories. A further

analysis of genetic explanations describes the many layers of complexity necessary to understand the mechanisms that derive from genetics, ranging from an articulation of the complex chemical coding of DNA to specifying a sequence of events related to this code and to understanding the observable consequences of these events. You need to be aware, and it will be the mantra of this chapter, that this entire genetic sequence occurs in the context of a dynamic environment. According to Fausto-Sterling (1992), "genes alone do not determine human behavior. They work in the presence and under the influence of a set of environments" (p. 71). Theories that explain gender or sex differences by examining hormones, brain mechanisms, lateralization, or structure are all rooted in a *genetic* perspective on difference.

Another type of biological explanation used to explain sex and gender differences is based on **evolutionary theory.**[2] Applying Darwin's principles of natural selection, changes in morphology (body structures) are attributed to the relative adaptiveness of certain characteristics that favor the survival of organisms within the context of particular environments. To explain human sex differences, evolutionary psychologists have drawn on a less well-known principle proposed by Darwin—**sexual selection.** The principle of sexual selection proposes that characteristics that favor reproductive advantage will flourish. Reproductive advantage refers to strategies that increase the likelihood of successful reproduction. According to this chapter's article by David Buss, *Psychological Sex Differences: Origins Through Sexual Selection* (1995), many sex differences can be explained by differences in reproduction strategy related to different adaptive problems faced by men versus women. In human reproduction, the roles of males and females are different, and therefore different strategies for achieving success in reproduction have evolved. Evolutionary psychologists rely on evidence from anthropology, paleontology, and cross-cultural and cross-species comparisons to support the view that differences in behavior patterns between women and men are rooted in evolution.

We have identified two major variations of biological theory—genetic explanations that examine chromosomal, hormonal, or neurological mechanisms and evolutionary theory that postulates how sex differences have evolved to suit the particular reproductive roles of males and females. Our distinction among biological theories is partly a heuristic one, to allow you to clearly see the proposed biological mechanisms that might be used to explain gender. In reality, biological theories draw on these mechanisms in complex, interrelated ways. For example, Kimura (1992) relates sex differences in the brain to evolutionary theory, whereas evolutionary psychology can provide explanations of genetic-related sex differences (Hoyenga & Hoyenga, 1993). We would add that most cases are largely hypothesized relationships between evolution and neural organization. Critical analyses of all biological theories, even those that propose complex interactions among biological factors, have urged attention to context and environment, with the particular environmental features varying in accord with the theoretical propositions under consideration. In this chapter, you will read evidence for a variety of biological mechanisms that are related to a wide range of sex and gender differences; this evidence varies in its complexity.

If it seems to you that we have raised more questions than we have answered, you are correct. The issues of definition, and of how questions are asked, are central in understanding gender. Additional questions are raised when we consider the many different forms that biological explanations can take. These questions are not easy to answer; they have no clearly agreed upon answers. Our goal is for you to understand what questions to ask and what types of answers address these questions. The way that biological explanations have been used to understand sex and gender is one of the most controversial issues in the study of gender (Fausto-Sterling, 1992). Understanding how a particular research finding follows from the way a researcher poses a question is as important as learning all the research findings. The articles in this chapter provide a range of perspectives on the relationship between biology and gender. The question underlying all of the issues in this area is, what is the contribution of nature *and* nurture? We turn first to the different ways that we can describe the relationship between nature and nurture.

WHAT IS THE RELATIONSHIP BETWEEN BIOLOGY AND ENVIRONMENT?

The classic debate of nature and nurture revolves around explanations of the contributions of biology and environment to behavior. In the simplest view of nature and nurture, biology causes sex and gender differences. This relationship should be familiar to everyone because it is the basis for many of our commonsense assumptions about gender. Whenever we attribute a woman's emotional reactions to "the time of the month" or a man's angry outburst to a "testosterone rush," we are making an argument that biology causes some behavior. Both are examples of behaviors that are assumed to distinguish men and women at some basic biological level.

Another view of biology and environment is that biology and environment each make separate contributions to gender. Some aspects of gender are rooted in biology, whereas others are the result of environment. This model relates to Gentile's suggestion (see chapter 1) that researchers use the terms *biologically sex-linked* for phenomena explained by biology and *gender-linked* for phenomena explained by social factors. This view sees biology and environment as either/or alternatives. Examining differences *between* men and women on a given trait and attributing these differences to XX and XY genetic differences while allowing that environmental variation would explain variations in the same trait *within* the XX and XY subgroups represents a view of nature and nurture as separable influences. Unlike the first model, in which biology is used to explain some behaviors and environment is used to explain other behaviors, this view of nature and nurture is aimed at the same behavior. We offer the following example to illustrate this type of reasoning. It is essential that you are aware of conflicting evidence for this example, so we are *not* suggesting that the conclusions as described are valid. As an explanation for human aggression, a researcher might want to account for sex differences between men and women as well as for individual differences within each group. To account for the observation that men on average are more aggressive than women, biological evidence related to differential levels of hormones might be evaluated; whereas to explain why some men are less aggressive and some women are more aggressive than average, evidence from differential socialization practices might be given.

A third view of nature and nurture suggests that they interact with one another such that both exert an influence on gender as well as on each other. In one type of interaction model, biological influences might be conceptualized as setting limits on behavior or channeling behavior into a range of behavioral expressions, whereas the environment is thought to facilitate or inhibit the biological mechanisms. An example of this type of interaction between nature and nurture would be the relationship between biological processes and environment in menstruation. The onset and duration of menstruation involves brain functions (e.g., the hypothalamus), hormones (e.g., pituitary gland), and reproductive organs (e.g., ovaries and uterus). These processes, however, are influenced by the environment. Poor nutrition or malnutrition are both associated with irregularities of the menstrual cycle or the cessation of menstruation. This environmental influence does not have a uniform influence on all women. One important aspect of an interaction is that both nature and nurture are simultaneously involved in the behavior of interest.

A more dynamic model of interaction argues that the influences of nature and nurture change over time and place (Sternberg, 1993).[3] According to this model, nature and nurture are both fully involved in gender-related behaviors, attitudes, and feelings, which may change over time and across cultures. We see this dynamic influence in a further analysis of menstruation. Among women in the United States, there has been a downward trend in the age of menarche,[4] largely attributed to improvements in nutrition. Also, the age of menarche varies cross-culturally. An additional variation in the timing of menstruation occurs among women who live together. A growing body of research demonstrates that some women living together, as in a college dormitory, will over time begin to menstruate together,

with this synchrony more likely among women who are sensitive to others' emotions. This type of synchrony is less likely to occur among women who work together but live and sleep with men (Hoyenga & Hoyenga, 1993). Thus, we see historical, interpersonal, and cultural influences on the nature/nurture interaction with regard to menstruation. Not only do we have biological and environmental influences interacting with each other, as in the first example, but by considering the influences of historical time, setting, or geographic location, we can see that the interaction between biology and environment itself is subject to change. In her article, *The Political Nature of Human Nature,* Ruth Hubbard describes this change as dialectical, which means that the changes in the nature/nurture relationship may also bring about changes in the nature and nurture phenomena themselves.

Biological Determinism

The various perspectives on the nature/nurture relationship that we have described with regard to gender are related to researchers' perspectives on **determinism.** Theories that emphasize biology as playing an essential role in gender-related behaviors can be characterized as biological determinist theories. This perspective on the role of biology assumes that biological evidence alone is sufficient to explain whatever behavior is of interest. Some biological evidence, and many popularized accounts of sex differences, are presented as biological deterministic accounts of differences. As an example of the popular use of biological evidence, ABC television broadcast a show titled "Boys and Girls Are Different: Men, Women, and the Sex Difference" in 1995. The central argument of the show was that despite parents' efforts to treat children equally, powerful sex differences in behavior emerge in childhood. The show concluded that biology must be more important than childrearing in the development of sex differences. We could offer many criticisms of this show and of these sorts of naive arguments. You should be wary of simplistic biological explanations, especially those that a priori give biology precedence over other factors. As you encounter accounts of the biological evidence with regard to gender, keep in mind that various relationships between biology and environment can be proposed and that researchers can vary in the degree to which they interpret their evidence in a deterministic fashion. We encourage you to evaluate every explanation with careful consideration of all factors that might be significant in forming a full explanation of gender.

GENETIC THEORIES: CHROMOSOMAL, HORMONAL, OR BRAIN DIFFERENCES (OR SIMILARITIES)?

In the first reading in this chapter, *Where It All Begins: The Biological Bases of Gender*, Holly Devor examines the role of biology in the development of gender. In her account of the biological events that are related to gender, Devor attempts to accomplish two goals. Her first goal is to provide a description of the role of chromosomes and hormones on gender throughout the life span. Her second goal is to evaluate the presumed relationship between biology and gender by examining the cases of individuals with chromosomal or hormonal abnormalities. In reading this selection, you should attend to the alternative interpretations that can be made from the same data; these interpretations show how important it is to examine various hypotheses about the relationship between biology and gender.

Devor cautions the reader to consider two issues that are reminiscent of the issues raised in chapter 2. First, many researchers have a preexisting belief that people can be divided unequivocally into groups of males and females, which leads to the research practice of using sex as a subject variable. The consequence of this practice is that researchers find sex differences because their study is designed in such a way that a sex difference finding is the only conclusion possible. The second problem relates to the practice of generalizing from animal research to human behavior. This practice often results in unquestioned analogies being drawn between the behaviors of rodents or primates and humans, which masks the complex social and cultural organizations that characterize each group.

What Are Sex Hormones?

For obvious reasons, researchers have looked at sex hormones for evidence of biological differences between men and women and at the related consequences of these differences on behavior. It is commonly believed that male and female hormones influence prenatal and adolescent development and are related to reproduction. What are these hormones, and are they really "male" and "female" sex hormones? The sex hormones are estrogens, androgens, and progestins. Beginning prenatally, these hormones are produced by the gonads and the adrenal glands (Hoyenga & Hoyenga, 1993).[5] Males and females produce all three of these hormones, although the relative amounts of each vary, with males producing more androgens and females producing more estrogens and progestins. Significantly, the range of hormones for any individual varies developmentally across the life span and cyclically during the day and throughout the year (Bleier, 1984; Fausto-Sterling, 1992). The production of these hormones is controlled by the hypothalamus via chemical messages that influence the pituitary. Researchers have focused on the levels of hormones present in males versus females and on the activity of the hypothalamus as a likely source of sex differences. For example, sex hormones affect neurological development, both pre- and postnatally, and therefore, researchers have theorized a relationship between the hormonal environment, brain development, and sex differences. However, as Bleier points out, it is difficult to isolate specific hormonal effects because of the presence of all three hormones in both men and women. Each of the sex hormones has several different metabolized forms, each of which might be linked to different physiological effects; therefore, isolating behavioral consequences that might result from hormonal causes can be very difficult if not impossible.

Numerous studies have demonstrated that hormones play a significant role in the differentiation of males and females prenatally (Hoyenga & Hoyenga, 1993). The hormonal environment of the fetus varies depending on the XY or XX chromosomal combination, and hormones are being produced by both the fetus and its mother.[6] Through a complex process of inhibition and facilitation, estrogens in XX fetuses and androgens in XY fetuses are related to the development of external genitalia. According to the evidence that Devor summarizes, changes in hormone secretion occur over the life span. During the prenatal period and for a few months after birth, and again during puberty, there are substantial sex differences in hormone production. In childhood, both boys and girls develop under the influence of similar and relatively low levels of these hormones. Hormone production in adults is somewhat different for males and females and varies in cyclic patterns.

Chromosomes, Hormones, and Gender

Hormones, as influenced by one's chromosomal sex, are related to some circumscribed aspects of sex differentiation, the development of secondary sex characteristics at puberty, and reproductive capacity. These aspects are all examples of behaviors or functions that some researchers characterize as sex-related. But how are chromosomes and hormones related to gender (which, you will remember, we have defined as sociocultural stereotypes), socially prescribed roles (often related to one's sex), and the development of an identity as either male or female and related preferences for activities deemed masculine or feminine? Are biological factors related in any systematic way to these socially and culturally defined characteristics?

Devor examines several kinds of evidence to answer this question. She considers the role of chromosomes in human development of gender identity; she reviews animal research on hormones, in which experimental manipulation of the hormonal environment is possible; she considers case studies of individuals who have been exposed prenatally to prescription hormones taken by their mothers; and she evaluates evidence on the relationship between brain development and hormones. Central to her analyses is the consideration of individuals whose development does *not* follow the typical pattern in which chromosomal sex, genital appearance and reproductive capacity, sex as perceived by others, and sex and gender identity of the individual are all consistent.[7] By evaluating variations from the typical pattern of development, we are able to critically evaluate the causal links in a biological explanation of gender.

In one example of biological variation, Devor describes individuals whose biological development is not determined by an XX or XY chromosomal complement. There are several patterns of chromosomal abnormality that Devor describes: Turner's Syndrome (XO), women who develop a typical female identity; Androgen Insensitivity Syndrome (XY), genetic males whose bodies do not respond to androgen, develop female genitalia, and are often strongly feminine in both appearance and identity; and Klinefelter's Syndrome (XXY), male-appearing infants whose development is somewhat feminized at puberty but whose identity is masculine. Devor's conclusion is that gender identity, both as perceived by others and internalized by the individual, is not directly related to chromosomal status. In fact, one's *appearance* as male or female seems to play a significant role in gender identity. For Devor, the evidence seems to point to a dynamic interaction between biological factors and environmental factors, with the environment exerting considerable influence both on the production of hormones and in establishing boundaries for gender identity.

EVOLUTIONARY PSYCHOLOGY: ARE HUMAN SEX DIFFERENCES ROOTED IN OUR EVOLUTIONARY PAST?

The theoretical mechanism that links biology and gender is somewhat more straightforward from the evolutionary perspective. Rather than examine mechanisms at the cellular or biochemical level, evolutionary psychologists study behavior to explain human sex differences. In his article in this chapter, David Buss summarizes the position of evolutionary psychology and the evidence that supports this view. According to evolutionary psychologists, human sex differences reflect the different evolutionary pressures facing males and females in the quest for successful reproduction. Women and men show different reproduction strategies, based on different adaptive problems faced by men and women. As an example, men face the problem of paternity uncertainty because in evolutionary history males were not able to determine whether or not offspring were their children. As a response to this uncertainty, according to evolutionary theory, certain sex differences evolved. Men are more sexually jealous than women in order to preserve their exclusive relationship with a given woman (Kendrick & Trost, 1993). An example of an adaptive problem faced by women is the need to identify a mate who is willing to invest time and resources to support her through a pregnancy and lactation.[8] According to Buss, this example explains why women place a greater value on men who have financial resources and the ability to provide protection than do men. Rossi (1994) argues that the emphasis on physical attractiveness for women, women's preferences for taller men, and the greater likelihood that men will initiate a sexual encounter all evolved as sex differences in reproductive strategies.

Evolutionary theory has been used to explain an enormous array of human behavior, from attraction to infants (Rossi, 1994) to the reported sex difference in spatial rotation (Buss, 1995). As Buss's article illustrates, evolutionary psychologists organize many findings of sex differences to support the hypotheses of their theory. Hyde (1996) argues that these researchers may fail to account for alternative interpretations of these same data. For example, evolutionary psychologists argue that men and women hold different attitudes toward casual sexual activity because of the relative differences in their roles in reproduction. Hyde, however, suggests that the **social cost** of casual sex is also very different for men and women. In observations of contemporary behavior, it becomes impossible to separate factors such as social cost and evolutionary cost. Evolutionary psychologists rely on an array of evidence from cross-cultural comparisons to cross-species comparisons. The logic for using such evidence is that the finding of either cross-cultural or cross-species similarities would provide evidence for an evolutionary solution to a common

problem. This assumption, fundamental to evolutionary theory, has been challenged by several researchers. A critical point to understand is that the same behavior may not result from a common cause (Bleier, 1984), and therefore, the observation of a cross-cultural similarity is no guarantee that these seemingly similar behaviors are a result of a common evolutionary heritage. In their evaluations of cross-species comparisons, many biologists and psychologists point out that primates show wide variety in their mating and parental behaviors (Hrdy, 1994; Silverstein, 1996; Smuts & Gubernick, 1992). According to Silverstein, a feminist interpretation of the variety of behaviors shown by both primates and humans would argue for an interactionist view rather than a strict evolutionary account. Related to this point, says Silverstein, is evolutionary psychology's emphasis on sex differences, which obscures the overlap and similarities between males and females. Critics of evolutionary theory are also concerned about the definitions of culture used by evolutionary psychologists (Derry, 1996). As you will see in chapter 4, adequate definitions of culture are as complex as adequate definitions of biology, and therefore the use of culture as a unitary variable is a questionable practice.

Explanations of gender-related phenomena using evolutionary psychology have proliferated. In support of evolutionary explanations, Jacklin and Reynolds (1993) address the concern, often leveled at evolutionary explanations, that such explanations are used as a defense of the status quo, which may perpetuate gender stereotypes and sexism. These authors argue that biological explanations themselves do not control social change or limit movements for social equality. The finding of a sex difference, rooted in biology, does not imply that a particular difference justifies discrimination or that social conditions could not lead to behavioral change. In fact, environmental theories, with no regard for evolution or other biological factors, provide no greater insight into the mechanisms that lead to change in behavior than do evolutionary theories. Kendrick and Trost (1993) argue that cultures have evolved in conjunction with humans, are not infinitely different, and themselves cannot be understood without reference to human genetics and evolution. Evolution should be expected to exert pressures on culture, while culture may act against biological predispositions.

CONDITIONS FOR AN ADEQUATE BIOLOGICAL THEORY

Clearly the relationship between biology and gender is an intricate one, requiring explanations that account for the complex interactions among genes, hormones, neural mechanisms, human evolution, *and* social interaction, culture, and individual development. Although it is unlikely that any single theory or even broad theoretical perspective can do all of this, we can establish some criteria by which we judge the adequacy of biological explanations.

The article by biologist Ruth Hubbard in this chapter introduces you to the relationship between political ideology and biological theories. Hubbard shows how deeply embedded scientific arguments are in social/political contexts. Understanding biological arguments requires that we acknowledge the multiple and shifting meanings of concepts and terms. As you read Hubbard's article, look for the examples she presents of ambiguity in meaning and the way social or political meaning is transferred to a biological construct. One example is using the concept of energy expenditure to explain the level of investment men versus women have in their biological offspring. According to evolutionary psychology, men invest relatively little energy (e.g., sperm production, sexual intercourse) in the creation of offspring, whereas women expend enormous energy (e.g., ovulation, sexual intercourse, pregnancy, lactation). Hubbard critiques the meaning of energy expenditure, suggesting that we know relatively little about the effort required by males and females in these biological processes yet we assume that fertility, pregnancy, and lactation has tremendous *physiological* cost to women and that this cost would, therefore, provide a stronger biological motive for women's attention to their offspring. Hubbard's article illustrates the underlying political significance of many biological concepts.

One argument central to Hubbard's analysis is that the distinctions we make among levels of analysis, such as the interaction among genes, hormones, neural mechanisms, and social interaction, are artificial distinctions among categories created by scientists and do not necessarily reflect the reality of biological phenomena. The processes that constitute different levels of analysis occur simultaneously and constitute one reality. At a political level, these arbitrary divisions are strengthened by distinctions made among scientists. Biologists, biochemists, psychobiologists, cognitive psychologists, social psychologists, and cultural anthropologists have all weighed in on the nature/nurture debate while often representing only one particular view of reality. We would further argue that biological arguments are not the only explanations that may contain political meanings. Certainly interpersonal, social, and cultural explanations must be examined for the intended and unintended ways in which they use terms and constructs laden with multiple meanings. Critics of biological theories recommend a careful examination of the deeply held belief that the biological sciences are objective and of the guise of scientific methods and terminology that often masks the social and political meaning that those methods contain. From a theoretical standpoint, social constructionism must also be examined carefully for social and political meanings.

We have taken a critical stance on how some biological evidence is presented. We do believe that it is imperative to continue to understand and evaluate the biological evidence, and no theory of gender will be complete without incorporating biological factors. We are often exposed to simplistic biological arguments that either assume that biological evidence eliminates the need to continue to search for social or cultural evidence or that presumes that biological evidence somehow provides a more adequate or superior explanation of behavior. Both Devor and Hubbard argue for accounts of biological evidence that are integrated with relevant cultural and psychological evidence. Furthermore, we claim in this essay that the appropriate model for understanding behavior recognizes the mutual effect of biological and environmental factors on each other and of their dynamic, ongoing interaction with social/historical context. This type of model yields a complex portrait of gender; one that is likely to demonstrate both sex differences and similarities, and one that may change or shift over time and place. The remaining chapters in this book elaborate on the many social, interpersonal, and cultural elements that help construct gender. You should prepare to read about the many aspects of the social/cultural construction of gender, mindful that they interact with biological factors in complex and multifaceted ways.

NOTES

1. *Implicit* because the researcher is not positing a specific biological mechanism (an explicit biological theory); rather, the researcher is simply assuming that biology must account for sex differences.
2. Evolutionary psychology is a variant of the broader theory known as sociobiology.
3. We refer to this as a **dynamic** model of the nature/nurture interaction; however, it may also be referred to as a **reciprocal** model, and in her article reprinted in this chapter, Hubbard uses the terms *dialectical* and *transformationism*. We believe all these models share enough similarities to be considered variations of the same reasoning, with the terms *dynamic* or *reciprocal* being our preferred usage.
4. Menarche is the onset of menstruation.
5. Gonads are sex glands, which are undifferentiated during the first few weeks after conception but which in XY fetuses will typically develop into male testes and in XX fetuses will develop into ovaries.
6. It is possible that chromosomal abnormalities or variations in the prenatal hormonal environment (or both in combination) could lead to variations from the typical pattern of development, and in rare cases, this does happen.
7. For example, typically, individuals who are XX will develop female genitalia, be perceived by others to be female, will become fertile adult women, will identify themselves as women, and to varying degrees will adopt some of the culturally determined behaviors identified as feminine. In this sequence of events, the greatest variability is found in the adoption of gender-related behaviors by the individual.
8. Be aware that the motives of males and females are not considered conscious nor intentional. In the case of the female's preference for men who will invest resources, evolutionary psychology assumes that pregnant and lactating women, in early history, would have been vulnerable and required protection.

REFERENCES

Bleier, R. (1984). *Science and gender*. New York: Pergamon Press.

Buss, D. M. (1995). Psychological sex differences: Origins through sexual selection. *American Psychologist, 50,* 164–68.

Devor, H. (1989). *Gender blending: Confronting the limits of duality*. Indianapolis: Indiana University Press.

Derry, P. S. (1996). Buss and sexual selection: The issue of culture. *American Psychologist, 51,* 159–160.

Fausto-Sterling, A. (1992). *Myths of gender: Biological theories about women and men* (2nd ed.). New York: Basic Books.

Hoyenga, K. B., & Hoyenga, K. T. (1993). *Gender related differences: Origins and outcomes*. Boston: Allyn & Bacon.

Hrdy, S. B. (1994). What do women want? In T. A. Bass (Ed.), *Reinventing the future: Conversations with the world's leading scientists* (pp. 7–25). Reading, MA: Addison-Wesley.

Hubbard, R. (1990). The political nature of "human nature." In D. L. Rhode (Ed.), *Theoretical perspectives on sexual difference* (pp. 63–73). New Haven, CT: Yale University Press.

Hyde, J. (1996). Where are the gender differences? Where are the gender similarities? In D. M. Buss & N. M. Malamuth (Eds.), *Sex, power, conflict: Evolutionary and feminist perspectives* (pp. 107–118). New York: Oxford University Press.

Jacklin, C. N., & Reynolds, C. (1993). Gender and childhood socialization. In A. E. Beall & R. J. Sternberg (Eds.), *The psychology of gender* (pp. 197–214). New York: Guilford Press.

Kendrick, D. T., & Trost, M. R. (1993). The evolutionary perspective. In A. E. Beall & R. J. Sternberg (Eds.), *The psychology of gender* (pp. 148–172). New York: Guilford Press.

Kimura, D. (1992, September). Sex differences in the brain. *Scientific American*, pp. 119–125.

Rossi, A. S. (Ed.). (1994). *Sexuality across the life course*. Chicago: University of Chicago Press.

Silverstein, L. B. (1996). Evolutionary psychology and the search for sex differences. *American Psychologist, 51,* 160–161.

Smuts, B., & Gubernick, D. J. (1992). Male-infant relationships in nonhuman primates: Paternal investment or mating effort. In B. S. Hewlett (Ed.), *Father-child relations: Cultural and biosocial contexts* (pp. 1–30). New York: Aldine de Gruyter.

Sternberg, R. J. (1993). What is the relation of gender to biology and environment? An evolutionary model of how what you answer depends on just what you ask. In A. E. Beall & R. J. Sternberg (Eds.), *The psychology of gender* (pp. 1–8). New York: Guilford Press.

Where It All Begins
The Biological Bases of Gender

HOLLY DEVOR

BIOLOGICAL QUESTIONS

Whenever people stop to think about what makes men men, women women, and some people neither, their thoughts inevitably lead to questions of genetics, hormones, and our inheritance from lower animals. Few people today would maintain that we are entirely the product of either a set of biological instructions, or of our socialization. Still, arguments rage about just how much of human behavior is controlled by genetic coding and hormonal functioning, or to what degree social factors influence the daily actions, thoughts, and desires of women and men, girls and boys. Scientific investigations of the interactions between genetics, anatomy, and physiology, on the one hand, and the social-psychological influences of gender attribution, gender identity, and gender role, on the other, help to clarify the relationship between biological sex and social gender. But no matter how detailed an investigation science has thus far made, it is still not possible to draw a clear dividing line even between male and female. The biological sciences, at best, provide only strong suggestions about why human females and males act the way they do. Human sex differences can only be described in terms of averages, tendencies, and percentages rather than clear-cut absolutes. As a result, there remains a tension between the desire for clear sex/gender distinctions in everyday life and the evidence being uncovered by the biological sciences.

In an effort to begin to understand our biological heritage, it is instructive to first look at what science has been able to determine concerning the development of human beings from conception to maturity. By examining the information available on this subject, it is possible to come to some understanding of the degree of human malleability from the time of conception and on through the maturation process. Some information presented here is fairly well accepted and documented by extensive research; some is controversial.

When reviewing reports of this research, it is important to keep in mind that researchers unintentionally carry the biases of their everyday attitudes into their work. Even the most scrupulous research is unable to entirely avoid this pitfall, because all humans, by virtue of being social entities, hold certain "incorrigible beliefs" which they carry with them, unchallengeable, throughout all of their actions.[1] These incorrigible beliefs remain invisible to the research and so fall outside of the strict discipline of the scientific method.

Incorrigible beliefs show up in research about both human and animal behavior in various ways. A common example is the assumption underlying almost all work on sex and gender that all subjects must be either male or female. This shows up in the routine practice of dividing subjects into these two groups before studying them. The very act of dividing a group of subjects in this fashion prejudices the results of any further investigation, because researchers who make this their first criterion are implicitly stating that they have already determined that there are certain sex-typed differences and that they are recognizable to them without the aid of empiricism. If one is seeking to determine the differences between the sexes, then this method does not allow for proper controls and a double blind situation.

There is also a great deal of interpretation in sex/gender research which is presented as impartial observation. Aggressive behavior, for example, is one topic which has received a great deal of attention. In the everyday world we have a commonsense understanding of what aggressive behavior is and a dictionary for further clarification. But in scientific research, terms are usually given very specific technical meanings for the purposes of exactness and repeatability. In behavioral research, it is common to see the term *aggression* used as a synonym for *fighting*. More specifically, aggression in the research reports generally means male-to-male fighting, usually for a position in a dominance hierarchy. Other forms of fighting are just as often not recognized as aggressive behavior. What this means in practice is that subjects are first divided into male groups and female groups and then fighting behavior is noted; male/male dominance fighting is noted as aggressive behavior while female/male fighting is noted as sexual in nature and female/female fighting may or may not be noted at all, or may be classified as related to the care of young, or as play, or as another nonaggressive type of behavior.[2] In ways such as these, research too often becomes self-fulfilling prophecy in support of, and based on, invisible incorrigible beliefs.

In most of the literature on the subject of gender, it is possible to find information based on actual human evidence, but it is also common to find conclusions concerning human development that are based almost entirely on evidence from animal studies. When reviewing this body of research, one must always question the applicability of animal studies to human situations. There is a great deal of research profitably undertaken on animals which could not morally or ethically be considered using human subjects. The conclusions of this kind of work are generalized to humans on the basis that we are simply highly developed animals; our instincts and biological mechanisms are assumed to be very closely related to those of our less developed cousins. No doubt there is a great deal of truth to this claim although, in this case, cautionary concerns seem compelling: it has been repeatedly and clearly demonstrated that social conditioning and human will can overshadow biological tendencies relating to sex and gender.[3] While animal studies may be, in some instances, quite firm in their findings, the transferability of animal results to

human situations is, at best, highly tentative. Nonetheless, research conducted on rats and monkeys is routinely used as the basis for hypotheses attempting to explain human behavior ranging from makeup to the missionary position. It is not at all uncommon to see an analogy made between rat mounting behavior or lordosis* and human "tomboyism" and homosexuality.[4]

The fact that a body of research has faults and problems within it or that it has occasionally been used in spurious ways does not invalidate it. No research is without its flaws, nor is any evidence totally beyond question. There will always be unanswered questions and alternative interpretations of data. An overview of the present state of knowledge concerning the interplay of biological sex and social gender is necessary for an understanding of the process of the creation of gender.

THE USUAL ROUTE

The process of creating human life begins when a sperm cell joins an egg cell. Under normal circumstances, when a sperm cell and an egg cell meet there are two possibilities: if both carry X chromosomes, the resulting baby will be born bearing ovaries, uterus, and vulva; if the egg cell carries an X chromosome and the sperm cell carries a Y chromosome, the resulting baby will be born equipped with penis and testes. During the development of the fetus from two cells to human baby, hormones (produced by the fetus itself, produced by its mother, or introduced into the fetal environment from external sources) influence the developing structures of parts of the brain, central nervous system, and reproductive organs.** These structures develop along different lines

---

*The pattern of behavior of the female rat in sexual encounter with the male rat.
**Sex hormones are grouped into three general categories: estrogens, progestins, and androgens. Females secrete all three types, although they secrete more estrogen and progestins than androgens. Males also secrete all three kinds of sex hormones, although they secrete more androgens than progestins or estrogens.

according to whether the fetus has XX or XY chromosomes, and as a result of the fetal hormonal environment. Many researchers maintain that once these sex differences are established in the fetus, they are irreversible. They propose that these physical differences cause male and female humans to have different sensitivities and propensities throughout life, somewhat analogous to instincts in the lower animals. Their position is that patterns established before birth account for later differences found at puberty and throughout maturity. Others believe the human animal to be far more plastic.

All human embryos start out with the potential to develop either female or male internal reproductive organs, external genitals, and behavior patterns. By the third to fourth month of fetal life fetuses start to differentiate in either the female or male direction. Fetuses with two X chromosomes normally develop into female babies whether or not functioning fetal ovaries are present, because the fetal hormonal environment provided by the mother alone is sufficient to produce a female baby in the absence of contravening masculinizing influences. The presence of a Y chromosome is normally sufficient to turn development away from the female path, to create a male baby. Shortly after an XY fetus develops properly functioning testes, they begin to secrete testosterone and a chemical called Mullerian Inhibiting Substance (MIS). If the body of the fetus responds to testosterone in a normal male fashion, the testosterone prompts the fetal external reproductive organs to grow into penis and scrotum, and MIS causes rudimentary female structures to wither.

In the first few months after birth, both male and female infants experience production spurts of some hormones. In particular they both generate higher quantities of two pituitary hormones (LH and FSH)* which in turn stimulate the secretion of the major sex hormones. Males also produce almost as much testosterone in their first few postnatal months as some men do as adults. Beyond these first few months, both fe-

male and male children grow up under the influence of roughly the same consistently low levels of all sex hormones.[5] As there is very little sex hormone production in either males or females past the first few months of life, it must be concluded that childhood gender development is the result of the effects of largely prenatal hormonal influences, overlaid with many years of postnatal socialization experiences.

At puberty, the bodies of young men and women again begin to produce significant quantities of sex hormones. Males begin to produce vastly greater amounts of testosterone than they had produced during childhood. At puberty, female androgen production also rises, but only slightly. Male testosterone levels jump by roughly ten to thirty times their childhood levels, whereas female levels only increase by, at most, a factor of two.[6] In both sexes, increased androgen production leads to an increased sex drive, a deepening of the voice, and an increase in body hair. The large amounts secreted by young males also account for the maturation of their genitals and the development of masculine bony structures and musculature.

Estrogen production also increases at puberty in both males and females. Male estrogen secretions increase to, at most, twice their childhood levels, whereas female estrogen secretions begin to follow a cyclical pattern whose peaks are approximately ten times childhood levels. Any effects which the slight increase in estrogen production in males might have at this time are entirely drowned in the sea of testosterone being produced by pubescent boys' bodies, while estrogens produced by young women's ovaries have marked effects on their physical appearances. Estrogens are responsible for the growth of hips and breasts and a general increase in subcutaneous body fat. The combined effects of hormone production stimulation from the hypothalamus-pituitary system and ovarian estrogens and progestins prompt the changes which turn young girls into women capable of conceiving and bearing children.

During puberty, as children physically mature into young women and men, the changes that their bodies undergo are accompanied by changes in their social relations. Their physical changes act as catalysts for

*LH and FSH stimulate ovulation in females. In males, LH stimulates secretion of testosterones and FSH stimulates the production of sperm.

emotional upheavals and as signals to those around them that they must no longer be treated as children. Under normal circumstances, puberty is a time of marked growth and change precipitated largely by hormonal changes but enhanced and given meaning by corresponding alterations in social roles, experiences, and expectations.

Sex hormone levels in adults normally differ in that females produce estrogens and progestins in a cyclical menstrual cycle, which allows them to conceive and bear children, while males produce these hormones in smaller and more consistent quantities. Males and females both produce testosterone at vastly different, but relatively steady, levels. But even those hormone secretions usually thought of as being tonic, or acyclical, actually do regularly vary through daily cycles in both women and men.[7]

In addition, sex hormone secretion levels can affect, and be affected by, people's emotional experiences in their environments. Elevations of progestins and estrogens associated with the menstrual cycle, pregnancy, and childbirth have been linked to mood changes, while elevated androgen levels have been tied to increases in the sex drive, aggression, and dominance in both men and women. Although it is commonly believed that the actions of sex hormones on the bodies of men and women cause the emotional changes that have been correlated with changing hormone levels, this has yet to be proven; and in certain circumstances, discussed later in this chapter, the evidence is strongly in the favor of the reverse causation.

Old age brings with it changes in sex hormone secretion patterns. Females undergo menopause, during which the ovaries gradually decrease in size and ability to produce ova and hormones. These changes are accompanied by a cessation of menstrual cycles and a loss of fertility. As female production of estrogens and progestins decreases, the effects of adrenal androgens become stronger. The combined effects of these two processes can often be seen in physical changes which accompany menopause, such as loss of fullness in the breasts and increased facial hair. Males also undergo a menopausal-like climacteric in which they too experience a decrease in the productive activity of the gonads. In a similar fashion as ex-

perienced by females, the effects of male estrogens and progestins become stronger as androgen levels drop. These changes in hormone levels result in such physical changes as a gradual loss of potency and muscle tone, and increases in subcutaneous body fat. These physical changes in men and women as they age are also accompanied by changes in social statuses, roles, and expectations.

Thus it would seem that, throughout the life cycle, physical structure and function, behavior, and emotional state are affected to varying degrees by the actions of sex hormones on the body. In the prenatal period, sex chromosomes give direction to the cells of the fetal tissue, telling them what structures to form. The secretions of those structures and the fetal hormonal environment play a major role in determining whether a normal male or female child develops. In the years between birth and puberty, the production of sex hormones, and therefore their effects, are slight and roughly equivalent in both males and females. During that stage, most gender development takes place under the influence of factors other than sex hormones.

At puberty, the effects of sex hormones are dramatically dimorphic. They account for the transformation of children into adult women and men. The physical transformations which take place at this stage of development are accompanied by very strong social changes. It is therefore difficult to say with certainty exactly how much of the emotional and behavioral changes of adolescence are the result of biological changes and what part are the results of intense social pressures felt by that age group.

Adulthood brings with it a relative hormonal consistency. Females settle into monthly cycles, usually punctuated by childbirth and its associated hormonal changes. Both males and females also undergo individual daily hormonal rhythms. During this stage of life, emotional states and behavioral activities vary with hormonal vacillations. In some cases, hormonal changes are probably instigated by human perceptions of their experiences in the world; in some cases the reverse is no doubt true.

Old age brings with it a final adjustment in hormonal patterns. As men and women move into seniority, their hormonal levels shift so that the relationship between the dominant and less influential sex hormones becomes more equal. In men, androgen levels decrease and the effects of estrogens normally become more pronounced, while in women the effects of estrogens and progestins are diminished and those of androgens are advanced. As in other life transitions, old age carries with it new and different social demands and expectations. Here too it seems clear that while physical changes affect behavior and emotion, so too do social changes.

Normal human development thus can be seen as a number of steps beginning at conception and proceeding through to old age and death. Sex chromosomes set a developmental process in motion which is then carried through its various stages under the encouragement of the differing amounts of the sex hormones produced by the bodies of boys and girls, men and women, at each of those stages. Throughout the life cycle, hormonal messages are accompanied by social and environmental experiences. The messages of those social experiences work with, or against, the developmental programs set out by chromosomes and hormones to create the totality of a human life experience.

EXCEPTIONS TO THE RULES

Not all people follow the usual route. The study of persons whose development is in some way abnormal can uncover information concerning some of the questions which remain unclear in the study of normal developmental processes. By examining the exceptions to the rules, it sometimes becomes possible to better understand causes and effects in more usual cases.

When discussing human development it is important to bear in mind the distinction between sex and gender. Sex is usually decided by scientists on the basis of chromosomal sex. XX individuals are classified as female, XY individuals as male. In cases where this test of sex is not conclusive, a variety of methods are employed to enable a person to be classified as either male or female. In general the presence

of at least one Y chromosome is sufficient to merit a male classification.

Gender is usually divided into the two categories of men (boys) and women (girls). Gender is recognized on the basis of social behavior and commonly believed to be congruent with sex. The actual characteristics used to define gender are infinitely variable over time and place. Those characteristics which might be defined as feminine in one location or time period are not the same ones as may be defined as such in another. Gender functions as the intra- and interpersonal understanding of what it means to be a female or a male. In most chromosomally normal people, gender identity and sex match. Gender role is not always in complete alignment, but usually gender role, gender identity, and sex all more or less agree.

In individuals with chromosomal or hormonal abnormalities, this easy constellation can fall apart. It is tempting to look at the normal course of human development and assume that because things usually unfold in a particular order, they do so because they must. Many people simplistically draw the conclusion that because most people with XX chromosomes become mothers, there must be something in their XX chromosomes driving them to do so; or that because there is a strong correlation between testosterone and aggression, testosterone causes aggression. Although there can be no argument that these correlations are indeed strong, the evidence of research into chromosomal and hormonal abnormalities, brain development and functioning, and gender dysphorias shows that the question of causation is far from resolved.

CHROMOSOMES AND GENDER

While under normal circumstances, humans have either XX or XY sex chromosomes, a look at the cases of people who do not fit this pattern shows that, although chromosomes appear to be causative of a wide variety of sex and gender characteristics, neither sex nor gender follow slavishly from chromosomal instructions.

When a fetus develops with only one sex chromosome present in all or most of its cells, it has a condition known as Turner's Syndrome. This configuration is referred to as $_{45}$XO, or simply as XO. All Turner's Syndrome individuals are born with a female body type and are often thought to be unremarkable females at birth, but they lack normal female internal sexual organs. What can usually be found upon internal examination is a streaklike mass of tissue, which has never developed into gonads, and an underdeveloped uterus. As a result, Turner's Syndrome females develop fetally only under the influence of maternal hormones and do not grow up under the influence of any gonadal hormones of their own.

At puberty, Turner's Syndrome females find themselves shorter than most other girls and lacking in pubertal development. This syndrome, which is usually discovered at this point if it has not already been identified, is treated by the administration of estrogens. This may result in the onset of menses if the reproductive organs are sufficiently developed, and will promote the development of breasts, body hair, and the distribution of subcutaneous fat usually associated with female puberty.[8] The administration of estrogens at puberty enables XO females to live feminine lives from birth through adulthood. They develop feminine identities and gender roles, and in some cases XO females have even been described as hyperfeminine.[9] They differentiate a clearly feminine gender identity in spite of the fact that they have only one sex chromosome rather than the normal two.

There is no analogous situation where a fetus develops only a Y chromosome. The YO condition will not sustain life. There is, however, a condition in which an XY individual is unable to use androgens and thus, although producing normally sufficient quantities of androgens, does not develop under their influence. This condition is known as Androgen Insensitivity Syndrome (AIS), or Testicular Feminization. In such cases, an XY baby is born with normal-looking female external genitalia, male internal reproductive organs, and a short vagina that does not lead to a cervix or uterus. Testes may be present inside the abdomen or may be palpable within the labia. Such children appear as normal female infants at birth. Parents and medical personnel see only a female baby, and children born this way are raised as such. They grow up as apparently normal females whose condition usually only becomes recognizable at puberty.

Even their puberty is in most respects normal for a female; they develop breasts and hips and a normal female distribution of body fat. The difference is that they have no menses, as there is no uterus, and body hair is slight to nonexistent. The hormonal source of this feminine puberty in XY individuals is the small amount of estrogen secreted by the testes and adrenal glands.[10] The testes do secrete testosterone in quantities normal for a male, but the bodies of AIS individuals are unable to use it and thus are not affected by it.[11]

These chromosomally male individuals grow up with gender identities similar to the XO females in that they show themselves to be good examples of traditional femininity. Money and Ehrhardt reported on a study they conducted of ten such XY girls. They compared them with fifteen Turner's Syndrome females and with a control group of normal XX females. They compared them on the basis of identity as a tomboy, expressed satisfaction with the female role, athletic interests and skills, preference for male or female playmates, clothing preferences, and attitudes toward the maternal role. The results of their comparisons showed that both the XO and AIS XY children were as feminine as, or more feminine than, the control group in all respects.[12]

In both Turner's Syndrome and the Androgen Insensitivity Syndrome, children are unquestioningly identified by medical personnel as female at birth and reared in accordance with that assignment. In Turner's Syndrome there is only one sex chromosome, and there are no endogenous gonadal hormones to reinforce femininity, either from their prenatal effects or throughout childhood. In the Androgen Insensitivity Syndrome, a child is also assigned to the female sex at birth and reared as such. During childhood and throughout life, an AIS female has XY chromosomes, testes, and testosterone, to no apparent effect on the social or psychological functioning of an individual living wholly as a female. In both of these cases, the major restriction that their condition puts on their ability to live fully feminine lives is their infertility, a problem they share with many "normal" women.

Thus, femaleness is not determined in these cases by chromosomes (or gonadal hormones) but rather by the social implications of a judgment, made at birth, on the basis of genital appearances.

These examples demonstrate that there need not be a direct link between chromosomal status and gender identity or gender role. These syndromes illustrate that it is not necessary to be an XX individual to be socially acceptable as a female, and that having XY chromosomes does not always make a person into a man. Humans may develop apparently normal female bodies in the presence of the typically male chromosomal arrangement or with a shortage of sex chromosomes. Gender identity in these cases follows from the sex assigned to a newborn baby on the basis of appearance of its genitals at the time of its birth.

Other chromosomal abnormalities include individuals with more than two sex chromosomes or with different patterns of sex chromosomes in different cells of the body.* In Klinefelter's Syndrome an individual has two or more X chromosomes combined with a single Y chromosome. Such individuals are born with normal looking male genitals. On that basis they are assigned to the male sex at birth and raised as boys. At puberty, they fail to fully develop normal male characteristics: the testes often shrink in size and breasts develop, body hair is usually light, and the voice deepens. These boys are often fertile and capable of normal male sexual activity despite their small testes and characteristically female breasts. Individuals with more than two sex chromosomes, in any combination, show increasing degrees of mental retardation with increasing number of chromosomes.[13]

The XXY chromosomes of persons with Klinefelter's Syndrome might conceivably make them females with one Y chromosome or males with an extra X chromosome. As was the case with Turner's Syndrome XO individuals and androgen insensitive XY people, the sex and gender identities of these people follow from their sex assignment at birth and from their rearing. When they reach puberty and experience difficulties, they experience them as adolescent boys, not as boys who are suddenly turning into girls.

Individuals found to have one X chromosome and more than one Y chromosome are born with the appearance of a normal male. As they mature they tend to grow to be unusually tall (generally well over six feet) but are otherwise physically normal.[14] As with other chromosomal abnormalities, the tendency to mental retardation increases with the number of sex chromosomes present. Their extra Y chromosome(s) do not make them into "super-males" in any sense of the word.[15]

Persons whose sex chromosomes show variety throughout the body are known as mosaics. These individuals exhibit many characteristics similar to those outlined in descriptions of other sex chromosome syndromes. Just as their sex chromosomes are a mixture, so too are their symptoms,[16] but their sex identities, gender identities, and behavior follow their sex assignment at birth and the rearing that comes with it, regardless of often apparently contradictory chromosomal complements.

Persons with chromosomal abnormalities have been estimated to account for three out of every 1,000 births. They are twice as common as Down's Syndrome individuals but generally move in society as unremarkable females and males.[17] From the fact of the unremarkableness of their fit with the gender requirements of society it must be concluded that "although the sex chromosome complement provides the initial stimulus for normal male or normal female sexual development, an abnormal sex chromosome complement seldom influences sexual development in such a way that the individual's social sex is in doubt."[18] Sex chromosomes may or may not lead to a particular body type, hormonal set, or behavior pattern. Chromosomes exert an influence on sex but they do not prove to be the single determining factor governing future developmental patterns and gender behavior.

HORMONES AND GENDER

Sex hormones play a major role in the development of physical and behavioral patterns. Experiments using animal subjects have manipulated hormonal levels in

---

*In normal individuals sex chromosomes are present in all cells of the body and they are the same in all cells.

fetuses and adults in an attempt to isolate the effects of individual hormones at specific periods of maturation. In particular, a great deal of work has focused on the effects of excessive doses of androgens on fetuses and older animals. To a lesser degree, attention has been turned to the effects of estrogens and progestins on both XX and XY fetuses and adult humans.

When examining the literature on the effects of hormones, it is important to keep in mind certain cautions. Although experiments are conducted using known quantities of drugs, it is not fully understood how they are used by the body. Chemical pathways in the body often convert one sex hormone to another before the hormone is actually used by the body. As well, all of the sex hormones are quite similar in chemical structure and can cause similar effects. The situation is further complicated by the fact that the action of sex hormones in combination can either be inhibitory or enhancing.[19] So although an experiment may be a controlled one, the results may not directly reflect the action of the hormone which has been manipulated, but rather the action of some hormone further along in a chain of reactions.

Part of the complexity of the question lies in the fact that androgens may be converted by the brains of primates into estrogens.[20] As a result, at this point in our knowledge of sex hormones we cannot say with certainty whether it is estrogens or androgens which are functionally operative in the brain. It is also believed that sensitivity to estrogen, at least in lower animals, is related to both the amounts of estrogen already retained by the body and to the amounts of progestins and androgens circulating in the organism.[21] We cannot therefore reliably determine the effects of hormones by means of simple quantitative measurement of circulating hormones without having available more detailed information concerning hormonal balance, sensitivity, and hormonal history.

The situation is still further complicated by the fact that sex hormones circulate in the body in two main states, bound or unbound. When a sex hormone is in its bound state, it is circulating in the blood stream attached to another chemical substance. A sex hormone must be in its free, or unbound state, in order for the body to be able to process it at a recep-

tor site. Receptor sites can most easily be pictured as keyholes. A sex hormone in a bound state will not fit the keyhole and therefore cannot unlock the series of responses of an organ. Unbound hormones will release a chemical response when they bind to a receptor site, which in turn will set off other reactions which may eventually result in physical changes or behavioral responses. Males and females have different concentrations of receptor sites in various parts of their bodies which may result in dimorphic sensitivities to stimuli.

Often quoted statistics comparing hormones and hormone levels in males and females can, as a result, be misleading. John Money, a prominent, prolific, and highly respected authority on sex differences, whose work stands among the major references in the field, explains the differences in hormonal levels between female and male humans by quoting figures which "do not discriminate between bound and free circulating blood levels of the hormone but," he adds, "they do indicate the relativity of the amount secreted."[22] So although we know that women have on the average between 6 percent and 20 percent of the circulating androgens that men do, or that men have the same progesterone levels as premenstrual women and approximately 30 percent of the estrogen level of postmenstrual women, we do not yet know exactly what impact these hormones have on the development, maintenance, or sensitivity of human receptor sites.[23]

Animal studies expose important questions for research into human conditions. Animal sex-typed behavior studied in hormone research is usually divided along the lines of mounting behavior and presenting behavior. Masculinity is defined in terms of mounts and femininity is defined in terms of sexual presentations. Other behaviors which are less clearly related to actual sexuality are also divided along sex lines: activity levels, exploratory behavior, and fighting, to name a few. Human behavior patterns commonly used in hormone studies as indicators of biologically based femininity include: interest in weddings and marriage, preference for marriage over career, interest in infants and children, and an enjoyment of childhood play with dolls.[24] Evidence of biologically based masculinity is defined in terms of childhood enjoyment of toys and games requiring high levels of activity, in self-assurance, and in holding career aspirations as more important than parenting.[25] Clearly the criteria used for investigations involving humans are even more highly socially determined than those used for animals.

Many studies have been done of animals whose fetal development has been surgically manipulated. Gonads have been removed from both male and female animals, pregnant mothers have been injected with androgens or estrogens, or submitted to situations of high physical stress. It has been well established that when XX fetuses in lower animals are exposed to unusually high doses of androgens (most often testosterone), they develop into hermaphrodites who have male genitals and female internal reproductive organs. Female monkeys exposed to androgens in utero become "predisposed to the acquisition and expression of patterns of behavior that are normally characteristic of the genetic male."[26]

While not questioning the validity of these findings, it is important to recognize that monkeys are social creatures with personalities and rules governing group behavior. While admittedly their behavior is governed more by biological imperatives than is that of humans, it is still correct to say that much of their behavior is socially learned. Harry Harlow, an authority on the behavior patterns of the rhesus monkey, reports that though the rhesus monkey appears to be born with a repertoire of mating gestures available to it, it must have "good emotional bonds with its mother and peers" or else it will not "learn from them how to use these inborn gestures appropriately."[27] Thus, although research results linking prenatal androgens to masculinized female monkeys may be reliable, the interpretation of those results may overemphasize biological factors. Monkey mothers have been observed to carefully inspect the genitals of their newborn infants, presumably to determine the infants' sex.[28] Androgens may well cause masculinized external reproductive organs, but the social response of adults to those genitals may play the major role in the determination of gendered behavior pattern formation even among monkeys.

The results gained from the study of animals are usually used as a jumping off point for studies of humans. Of course, it is not possible to administer androgens to pregnant women for experimental purposes. Instead scientists study incidents in nature which they believe to most closely resemble situations that they would like to experimentally induce.

Two groups of XX individuals have been studied to this end. One group are XX individuals whose mothers took the anti-miscarriage drug diethylstilbestrol (DES) while they were in utero, and who were born with some degree of masculinization of the genitals. Some were born with what was considered at birth to be an enlarged clitoris and were assigned as females at birth, some were born with what was considered to be an undersized penis and were assigned as males at birth, and some were born with what were considered to be normal male genitals and were thus unquestioningly assigned as males at birth.[29]

In the years between 1945 and 1971 a large number of fetuses were exposed to this drug, which is often considered an androgenizing agent despite the fact that it is a progestin.[30] Progestins do move through a stage of being androgens but are used by the body in their final state as estrogens.[31] The cells of the body, including brain cells, convert both androgens and progestins into estrogens, which may be the final and useful form of all sex hormones.[32] The inclusion of DES studies with androgenizing syndromes perhaps seems more understandable in light of the fact that androgens are masculinizing hormones, and in a small number of cases, XX babies born to mothers treated with DES were born with some degree of virilization of the genitals.[33] It is important to note, however, that these children represent only a minute percentage out of the estimated 980,000 to 4.5 million children exposed to this drug in the U.S. alone.[34]

The gender identity and gender role of DES exposed and masculinized chromosomal females has been the subject of much study in an attempt to determine if their behavior was masculinized along with their genitals. There are a number of problems with this course of research: (1) As has been pointed out, DES is *not* an androgen.[35] (2) Conclusions drawn from studies regarding the effects of DES on the fetus are representative of only a tiny fraction of the individuals actually affected by this drug. If the effects in question were resultant from this drug, why have so few come to the attention of the medical establishment? (3) In all of the cases under study there was at least partial masculinization of the genitals. It is therefore impossible to say with certainty whether any masculine behavior was resultant from chemical effects on the central nervous system and other physical mechanisms or from a masculine gender identity based on the physical evidence of male-looking genitals.

Excessive prenatal exposure to progestins does not always masculinize the external sexual organs of an XX fetus. Reinisch and Karow studied girls who were exposed to excessive progestins prenatally but were not physically virilized. They compared these girls to a group of girls known to have been prenatally exposed to excess estrogens. The progestin group was found to be more independent, more self-assured, more self-sufficient, more individualistic, and more sensitive, as well as being more inner directed in their thoughts and having a tendency to feel their way through things rather than think in a dry, objective, and cognitive way.[36] The description that Reinisch and Karow gave of girls fetally exposed to high doses of progestins is one which could easily be interpreted as the personality type of a masculinized girl, yet progestins are not normally considered to be "masculine" hormones. The action of DES and other progestins are lumped together with those of androgens because of the incorrigible beliefs of researchers that some of the behavior they observe is "men's" behavior despite the fact that it is common among women and appears to be caused by what is usually referred to as a type of pregnancy hormone. This suggests that although hormones may affect behavior, the interpretation of those behavioral effects can be skewed by social definitions and constructs.

A second human group studied in an attempt to shed light on the action of hormones on humans, is XX individuals with Congenital Adrenal Hyperplasia (CAH), also called the Adrenogenital Syndrome (AGS). In this syndrome the adrenal glands of the fetus, and later the child and adult, do not function properly. The adrenal cortex fails to make cortisol in

sufficient amounts. This signals the pituitary to secrete adrenocorticotrophic hormone (ACTH) in larger amounts. ACTH causes the adrenals to increase in size and the enlarged adrenals secrete more of all of their hormones including adrenal androgens.

In this syndrome the fetus becomes partially masculinized, and if uncorrected, the child and adult will continue to live under the influence of excessive amounts of adrenal androgens. This syndrome does offer a good facsimile to the studies conducted on lower animals, but the correspondence is not perfect. In the animal experiments the androgen used is some form of testosterone; in the human "experiments" the androgen is adrenal in origin.

AGS XX individuals, when born with normal-looking male genitals, live their lives with a male gender identity and behave in accordance with the masculine gender role despite their XX chromosomes and normal estrogen secretions. AGS XX individuals born with subsized genitals of a male appearance who are assigned at birth as males also live their lives with a male gender identity and behave in accordance with the masculine gender role. They may have anxieties about their abilities to perform sexually, but they show no doubts concerning their actual status as males and no lack of interest in the masculine role, again demonstrating that sex assignment at birth, and rearing, are more important in producing gender than are chromosomes.

AGS XX individuals assigned at birth as females require extensive surgery at several stages in their lives and are sustained throughout life on cortisol hormone therapy.[37] It is impossible to accurately assess the effect of this process on a girl's self-image. It is also as yet unknown what effect a lifetime of cortisol treatment might have on physiology or personality. Thus, in the study of AGS females it is difficult to separate the precise effects of adrenal androgens from other results of their abnormal hormonal condition.

Ehrhardt and Baker, and Money and Ehrhardt studied groups of AGS girls and concluded that they were more often long-term "tomboys" than the females in their control groups. The parameters that they used as positive indicators of tomboyism were: rough-and-tumble play or intense energy expenditure;

preference for stereotypical boys' toys and male play-mates; lack of interest in clothing and adornment; lack of interest in infants, motherhood, and marriage; and an interest in career for later life.[38] But these researchers used the label "tomboy" to support a finding of increased masculinity in girls exposed to either progestins or androgens in utero, while at the same time noting that the behavior pattern that they identified as tomboyism is in no way abnormal for the female gender role.[39]

Childhood tomboyism is so much a part of the normal female gender role pattern that it is present to a comparable degree in many females with no history of prenatal or postnatal hormonal abnormalities. In one sample of heterosexual women, 50 percent reported that they had been tomboys in their youth, while 75 percent of the lesbians studied reported childhood tomboyism. Another study similarly found 75 percent of the lesbian respondents reporting childhood tomboyism.[40] When these figures are compared with those reported by Ehrhardt and Baker in their major study of AGS girls, the implications of the phenomenon of tomboyism among AGS girls are weak. Ehrhardt and Baker reported that 59 percent of the girls that they studied were persistent tomboys.[41] This figure represents only a slightly higher rate than has been found among heterosexual females, and a considerably lower rate than has been found among lesbians. Yet these and similar results are used to support a hypothesis that both the Adrenogenital Syndrome and prenatal progestin exposure result in masculinization of the behavior of females. A more logical conclusion would take into account the fact that tomboyism is a normal feature of the feminine gender role.[42] More rationally, the female gender role could be redefined to include what are common and unremarkable facts of childhood: self-centeredness and the desire of children to play active and physical games. Thus, rather than masculinizing girl children, the effects of progestins and the AGS Syndrome might be interpreted as supporting behaviors inherent within the normal female range.

"Normal femininity," of the psychological-test variety, may actually be a rare commodity. In one study of college aged females, only 15 percent of the heterosexual sample tested as feminine on a widely accepted sex role inventory. The remaining 85 percent of heterosexual females scored as either masculine or as some combination of masculine and feminine. In the same study, only 7 percent of the lesbians scored as feminine, while the other 93 percent were rated as exhibiting some gender role which was not predominantly feminine.[43] A similar study found a less dramatic distribution among both heterosexual women and lesbian women. In a total heterosexual sample of 790 women, 41 percent were rated as feminine while 59 percent were rated as not predominantly feminine. In a smaller lesbian sample, 14 percent were found to score in the feminine range, while more than 85 percent of the lesbian sample scored as not feminine.[44] Thus it can be seen that few females of any hormonal history are particularly feminine by these standards, and the claim of hormonally induced masculinity is not well supported.

The question of the influence of prenatal hormones on human behavior is obscured by social definitions of masculinity and femininity. There are many characteristics which both males and females share, yet they are often designated by researchers as appropriate, or even natural, for only one sex and not the other. When a behavior pattern is exhibited by members of the sex deemed inappropriate to that behavior, researchers set off in search of a biological basis for that "abnormal" behavior. But prenatal influences on postnatal behavior are very difficult to isolate among the totality of human experience. Social definition of infants starts from the moment they are identified as members of one sex and not the other. Even in the absence of a designation of sex, most adults will presume one sex or the other and proceed to interact with an infant according to their own understanding of sex and gender.[45] The effects of this social response to assigned sex are so strong that hermaphrodites whose physical bodies are similarly equipped, but who have been assigned to different sexes, have gender identities which follow their assigned sex, and gender roles which follow their gender identities. Although two hermaphrodites, in such cases, may have genitals, gonads, and hormones of the same type, they will grow up to be accepted and function in society as the different sexes they were assigned to at birth.[46] Thus it can be seen that although prenatal hormones have some influence on gender behavior patterns, the ability of researchers to isolate those influences is confused by the ambiguity of the social definitions and the meanings of gender roles. Clearly, research into the effects of excessive exposure to prenatal progestins and androgens is infused with incorrigible gender stereotypes which color what questions are asked and how results are interpreted.

Hormone levels in adult animals and humans have also been linked to behavior patterns and sensitivities. It has long been known that hormone levels in humans and other primates are responsive to events perceived by individuals in their environment. The "fight or flight" response of the adrenals is learned by every schoolchild. But the relationship between the sex hormones and environmental events is less clear. One area of investigation has centered on sex differences in hormonal responses to stress. This work has shown that in both humans and monkeys, males respond to stress both differently from females and to a greater degree than females. Contrary to popular misconceptions, male androgen levels are more excitable in stressful situations than are female hormone levels.[47]

Rose et al. studied the behavior and androgen levels of rhesus monkeys in changing dominance situations. They found that testosterone levels of male monkeys respond markedly to environmental variables. Testosterone levels in their experimental groups were highest when male monkeys were in situations where they were able to be most dominant. In the experiment, the testosterone levels of a group of male animals became elevated when they were exposed to sexually receptive females who granted them sexual access, thus allowing them to reach the top of the dominance hierarchy in that situation. When the same males were exposed to a new group of males where they were not able to establish dominance and were in fact physically overpowered, their testosterone levels fell below the baseline or pre-test level. The hormonal effects of defeat and failure were reversed entirely when the same group of males was returned to the presence of the receptive females.[48]

Similar results have been noted in observations of female monkeys and human males and females. Primate female testosterone levels rise with an elevation of their dominance rank. Human male testosterone levels have been found to rise in response to situations perceived by subjects as demonstrating their personal achievement.[49] Similarly, human females who view themselves as self-directed, action-oriented, resourceful people have also been found to have higher testosterone levels than more conventional and less self-confident women.[50]

In related work, both emotional stress and surgical stress have been shown to depress testosterone levels in humans.[51] Emotional stress in the form of depression, though, has a different effect on human males than it does on females. Depressed females decrease their secretion of adrenal androgens, while male estrogen secretion is increased by depression. This would seem to imply that when a human is in a situation which is experienced as one of high dominance or achievement, androgen levels respond by rising, and that when a human is in a situation which is perceived as one of low dominance or failure, the endocrine system responds to this external stimulus by lowering the secretion rate of androgens and raising the secretion rate of estrogens.[52]

It would not seem unreasonable then to hypothesize that situations that either encourage or allow a perception of dominance or achievement in humans actually promote the secretion of androgens. Although the link between androgens and aggressive dominance-seeking behavior has not been unequivocally established, there is a great deal of research devoted to clarifying this issue, most of which points toward a positive connection.[53]

HORMONES AND THE BRAIN

The hormones circulating through the bodies of normal male and female fetuses are also thought, by many researchers, to have a strong influence on the development of the central nervous system. In particular a great deal of attention has centered on the hypothalamus of the brain. The hypothalamus is the control center for the endocrine system in general and the sex hormones in particular. Much of hypothalamic research has been done with a variety of animals, but examinations of human subjects have also been made within the bounds of ethical constraints.[54]

The hypothalamus is a very small body consisting of a number of nuclei. It is located in the brain stem directly above the pituitary gland and between the two branches of the optic nerve. Some endocrinologists see its functioning as so intricately tied with that of the pituitary gland that the two are studied as a unit, but this is not the majority approach. The hypothalamus is normally different in males and females. It is generally believed that differences in the structures of the hypothalami of males and females are the result of fetal hormonal baths during gestation and account for the later cyclical release of sex hormones in adult females and the acyclical, or tonic, release of sex hormones in males.

The hypothalamus acts as a regulator of hormone levels through feedback mechanisms. The hypothalamus stimulates or inhibits the secretion of endocrine hormones by other organs on the basis of a constant monitoring of the levels of various substances which circulate in the blood and pass through hypothalamic centers. Human secondary sex characteristics and reproductive behaviors are regulated by the action and sensitivity of the hypothalamus. Many argue that the "maleness" or "femaleness" of the hypothalamus and the hormonal systems it controls are permanently set by well-timed hormonal baths during fetal life.

It has been shown that in lower animals the hypothalamus is capable of learning responses to repeated environmental stimuli,[55] resulting in measurable physical changes in the structure of the hypothalamus. Such changes in the hypothalamus can then result in different response patterns than those initially fostered in the fetal environment. Panksepp speculated that these changes can be subtle enough that they occur before actual behavioral changes are perceptible to investigators. He suggested that behavioral changes are affected through a cycle of sensory input, hypothalamic response, hormonal response

and/or motor response, and back to hypothalamic response. Panksepp argued that "the presence of cells in the hypothalamus which rapidly learn environmental contingencies suggests that the hypothalamus may extract the value of environmental events and analyze reward contingencies so that rudimentary motor output can be changed to increase the recurrence of rewards."[56]

Siegel and Edinger proposed that the hypothalamus serves a gatekeeping function between sensory inputs which have elicited behavioral responses in the past and neural messages which prompt motor centers to respond in a similar fashion again. Siegel and Edinger suggested that sex hormones sensitize the hypothalamus to such input: "The scheme presented here suggests that [sex] hormones act to increase or decrease hypothalamic excitability levels and thereby alter the bias exerted on the cortical mechanisms from which the motor patterns associated with aggressive behavior are elaborated."[57] The pattern suggested by this research is that the learning of certain behaviors is strongly mediated by the hypothalamus and that the hypothalamus itself is both mediated by, and the mediator of, the flow of sex hormones.

Gupta et al. pointed out that the sensitivity of the hypothalamic-pituitary system decreases with age.[58] But evidence presented by Arnold and Breedlove strongly suggests that the actions of sex hormones on the adult brain can still cause both permanent morphological changes to the brain and long-term reversible behavioral changes. Sex hormone effects on the brain can include alterations in the size, form, and speed of neuron growth and changes in sex hormone secretion and usage. Arnold and Breedlove further suggested that there may be critical periods, past the neonatal stages, during which the organism is most receptive to these effects.[59] Thus the evidence suggests that environmental factors can affect sensitivity and response patterns of the hormonal system and that these changes in hormonal functioning can have far-reaching effects throughout the lifetime of an organism.

It would seem then that the differing structures of the hypothalami of male and female animals, resultant from fetal endocrine baths, may be either a starting point for sex-related behaviors or a step on a twisting path. The research presented here suggests that although the intrauterine hormonal environment may predispose the endocrine-hypothalamic system to certain sensitivities, those sensitivity levels and the behaviors that they direct are subject to environmental influences throughout life. Both behavior patterns *and* their neuroendocrine correlates may be significantly shaped by the experiences of an animal in its environment both before and after birth.

This evidence suggests a pattern. Fetal hormonal secretions and environments establish a first level of hypothalamic sensitivity to environmental and hormonal stimuli, partially on the basis of genetic programming. External environmental factors then begin their direct influences at birth, and are most potent closest to the time of birth.[60] They act to reinforce or block hypothalamic activity patterns, receptor site sensitivities, and hormonal secretion patterns. Changing environmental demands may increase or obstruct secretions of hormones. The resulting changes in circulating hormones may then increase or inhibit receptor site sensitivity. Receptor site sensitivities may in turn increase or diminish hypothalamic sensitivity to environmental stimuli.[61] Thus, over time, lesser or greater environmental demands may produce lesser, equal, or greater behavioral results depending on the direction of the effects at each stage of the process.[62]

Thus it may be concluded that human experiences, and the meanings given to those experiences, play a role in the development of hormonal production and sensitivity patterns. It seems possible that forms of human social organization not only can constrain the social experiences of individuals in their worlds, but may even shape some part of our abilities to physically perceive and respond to the people and events of our world. In the final analysis, it may well turn out that much as our social selves are limited by our flesh and blood, so too are our corporal selves molded by our social experiences and the meanings that we attach to them. Chronic defeat and failure, or success and dominance, may leave far more than psychic marks—our bodies may

themselves be shaped by the roles that we play every day of our lives.

TRANSSEXUALISM

Transsexuals offer an interesting window on gender because they constitute a striking example of discordance between sex and gender. It is not uncommon, among the general public, to find examples of individuals who do not conform well with their socially expected gender role, but in physiologically normal females and males (other than transsexuals), sex and gender identity match: females are either girls or women, and males are either boys or men. Normally, people unquestioningly accept that they are, and should be, the sex assigned to them at birth. In the case of transsexuals this is not so. Transsexuals believe that they are persons of one gender mistakenly born into the body of the wrong sex, e.g., real men in female bodies by mistake.[63]

Transsexuals are not transvestites. For transvestites, sex and gender identity match; nonetheless, transvestites periodically dress and behave according to another gender role, i.e., males who think of themselves as men but who, for brief periods of time, dress and act like women. Transsexuals differ from transvestites in that gender identity and gender role conform to one another but are discordant with sex, e.g., female-to-male transsexuals identify and act as men but were born to the female sex. Transsexuals dress and act as they do because that is the appropriate role for persons of their gender identity; transvestites dress and act as they do to assume another role. Transsexuals are persons whose morphological sex and chromosomal sex are in agreement but whose gender identity and social gender differ from their sex. As such, they present a formidable challenge to the assumption that sex-based biological factors determine gender. Transsexual people appear to be biologically normal members of their birth sex, yet in all social respects they belong to the opposite gender and take whatever steps they can to alter their sexual status to conform to their gender.

In retrospective, reports of their childhoods given by transsexuals and their family members, transsexuals are reported to have exhibited gender characteristics discordant with their assigned sex from very early childhood. Their accounts report that they expressed desires to change sex from as young as three years of age. As children they persist strongly in the belief that they can change sex and exhibit a marked preference for a gender role discordant with their assigned sex as well as an aversion to the gender role considered appropriate to their assigned sex. Around the time of puberty they usually develop sexual and romantic interests in persons who are of the same sex as themselves but of a different gender. If they do engage in sex, they see themselves as entirely heterosexual and attempt to choose partners who also see themselves as engaging in heterosexual activities. Generally they have a great dislike for their own genitals and any of their own physical characteristics which remind them of their birth sex. Transsexuals avoid reminders of their sex status and attempt to override sex status with gender status. Eventually, many transsexuals present themselves to doctors with the request that their bodies be made to conform to their gender.[64]

By definition, a transsexual is a person whose physical sex is unambiguous, and whose gender identity is unambiguous, but whose sex and gender do not concur. The existence of such people challenges the belief that gender is necessarily linked to chromosomes or anatomical features, and that males are masculine and females are feminine.[65] Scientists have turned to investigations of the hormonal status of transsexuals in an attempt to locate a biological source of their abnormality.

These studies have taken two approaches. The more common approach is to simply assay the hormonal levels of transsexuals. Testosterone levels are usually investigated in search of depressed testosterone levels in male-to-female transsexuals and elevated testosterone levels in female-to-male transsexuals.[66] The major authors on the subject of transsexualism report that hormonal assays have found normal levels of all sex hormones in both male-to-female and female-to-male transsexuals,[67]

although there have been isolated reports of elevated testosterone levels in transsexuals, which have not been widely replicated.[68] These results strongly suggest that if there is a hormonal reason for this condition, it is not so simply or direct a cause as mismatched testosterone levels.

An alternate, and less common, approach is to investigate the ways that transsexuals process the hormones in their bodies.[69] Seyler et al. took this second approach and studied hormone processing in female-to-male transsexuals. They found that female-to-male transsexuals responded differently to experimentally administered progestins than did either average females or average males. Heterosexual women responded to ingested DES with increased blood concentrations of both luteinizing hormone (LH) and follicle stimulating hormone (FSH). Heterosexual men responded with decreased blood concentrations of both of these hormones. The female-to-male transsexuals in this study exhibited a response which was intermediate in both pattern and intensity between the average male and female responses.[70]

Midgeon et al. found similar results in their study of male-to-female transsexuals. In that study, male-to-female transsexuals, average males, and average females were administered estrogens and their responses monitored. Estrogen normally acts as an anti-testosterone agent in the sense that it increases the binding of testosterone to other molecules, thus rendering it unusable at receptor sites. Estrogen administered to either males or females will, under normal conditions, lower the blood concentration of free testosterone and increase the concentration of bound testosterone in the blood. Male-to-female transsexuals were found to react dramatically to the administered estrogens. Their blood levels of unbound testosterone were found to decrease to the point that their concentrations were even lower than those of the normal females studied.[71]

These studies indicate that transsexuals process the hormones in their bodies in an abnormal way. Seyler et al. suggested two possible explanations for the results of their investigation: first, "that the changes observed in estrogen responses are acquired due either to psychological or other disturbance. Psychological state is known to influence gonadotropic function;"[72] and second, "that the anomalous pituitary sensitization responses of transsexual women suggest that there may have been an abnormality in hormonal milieu during fetal life."[73] Other studies have demonstrated the ability of hypothalami to learn responses to external stimuli. The pituitary is controlled by the hypothalamus and the functioning of the entire endocrine system is controlled by the hypothalamic-pituitary system. These facts, combined with the widely accepted understanding that hormonal cycling in the female can be disrupted by psychological factors, strongly suggest the first hypothesis. If the second explanation offered by Seyler et al. were to be valid it would be logical to expect to find an increased incidence of transsexualism among females known to have been masculinized in utero. All studies of AGS and DES girls have found that gender identity follows sex of assignment. There have been no reports of increased incidence of transsexualism among these populations.[74] Thus, these studies add weight to the contention that human gender role behavior and environmental experience may have some causative influence on hormonal production and response mechanisms.

A model which might be used to explain the transsexual phenomenon, and possibly the gender phenomena of the everyday world, would have to account for the interactions of physiology and environment. It has been shown that among humans,[75] and perhaps among animals as well,[76] social interaction begins to shape personality from the moment of birth. Neonates enter this world with the heritage of their chromosomal influences and prenatal hormonal environment. At birth they are assigned to a sex; in every way this assignment colors the events of the remainder of their lives.

External environmental experiences set into motion a momentum which may be in continuation of prenatal influences, or in contradiction to them. In either case, social factors may be capable of overriding most, if not all, prenatal influences.[77] Social influences may actually reset the direction which future development of a hormonal system will take. They may act to suppress or enhance biological predispositions. If social forces continue to exert pressure over long periods of time, a chronic situation can develop which may crystallize into relatively stable physical configurations that reflect the direction of social pressures. In this way, hormonal abnormalities might be seen to be the result of chronic social abnormalities.

In the same way, one might interpret the gross hormonal differences between socially normal men and women as being a result, rather than a cause, of the chronic social pressures which males and females undergo in the process of becoming socially normal men and women. Thus the interaction between the hormonal systems and the environment can be seen to function as a feedback loop. If the loop is a positive one, the hormonal system and the environment reinforce one another and thus enhance the predispositions suggested by the prenatal experience. If it is a negative feedback loop, the effects of environmental experience may be capable of overriding prenatal influences to such an extent that the original impetus may become overshadowed by the demands of social environment.

The ongoing requirements of everyday social interaction may be powerful enough, in their long-term effects, to be of greater importance than hormones in shaping the behavioral sex differences found among humans. The constant feedback and reinforcement of behavior might have some determining effect on the hormonal levels in humans. The net result could well be that not only are human minds capable of learning behavioral patterns but so too are human brains and the endocrine systems which they control. Thus, although the endocrine glands and their secretions may have a controlling influence on gendered human behavior patterns, they are in a dynamic relationship with the experience of the social organism through the mediation of the brain. Not only is the human mind in dynamic interaction with its environment, constantly learning and changing, so too is the human body changing, learning, and growing through its experience within its environment.

NOTES

1. Incorrigible beliefs are those concepts which people believe so strongly that nothing can cause them to question their veracity. At one time the idea that the world was flat was such a belief. H. Mehan and H. Wood, *The Reality of Ethnomethodology* (New York: John Wiley and Sons, 1975), p. 9.

2. R. Bleier, "Social and Political Bias in Science: An Examination of Animal Studies and Their Generalizations to Human Behavior and Evolution," in *Genes and Gender II: Pitfalls in Research on Sex and Gender,* ed. R. Hubbard and M. Lowe (New York: Gordian Press, 1979), pp. 49–69.

3. A. A. Ehrhardt, "Maternalism in Fetal Hormonal and Related Syndromes," in *Contemporary Sexual Behavior: Critical Issues of the 1970's,* ed. J. Zubin and J. Money (Baltimore: Johns Hopkins University Press, 1973), p. 113; A. Lev-Ran, "Gender Role Differentiation in Hermaphrodites," *Archives of Sexual Behavior* 3 (1974), pp. 391–424, esp. p. 391; R. J. Stoller, *Sex and Gender: On the Development of Masculinity and Femininity* (New York: Science House, 1968), p. 83.

4. Gunter Dorner, "Sexual Differentiation of the Brain," *Vitamins and Hormones* 38 (1980), pp. 325–81, esp. pp. 360–69.

5. Charles H. Doering, "The Endocrine System," in *Constancy and Change in Human Development,* ed. O. G. Brim Jr. and J. Kagan (Cambridge, Mass.: Harvard University Press, 1980) pp. 229–71, esp. p. 251.

6. Ibid., p. 251.

7. Ibid., p. 238.

8. C. J. Dewhurst and R. R. Gordon, *The Intersexual Disorders* (London: Bailliere, Tindall and Cassell, 1969), pp. 111–13.

9. J. Money and A. A. Ehrhardt, *Man and Woman, Boy and Girl: The Differentiation and Dimorphism of Gender Identity from Conception to Maturity* (Baltimore: Johns Hopkins University Press, 1972), pp. 105–108.

10. Ibid., p. 109.

11. Dewhurst and Gordon, pp. 58–60.

12. Money and Ehrhardt, pp. 105–14.

13. When females are born with more than two X chromosomes they likewise share a tendency toward low IQ with increasing numbers of chromosomes, but show no other physical or behavioral abnormalities. Dewhurst and Gordon, pp. 114–16.

14. Dewhurst and Gordon estimate that as many as half of all males having more than one Y chromosome are over six feet tall. See Dewhurst and Gordon, p. 116.

15. W. M. C. Brown, P. A. Jacobs, and W. H. Price, "Sex Chromosome Aneuploidy and Criminal Behavior," in *Genetic and Environmental Influences on Behavior,* ed. J. M. Thoday and A. S. Parkes (New York: Plenum Press, 1968), pp. 180–93, esp. p. 185.

16. Mosaic chromosome arrangements can be any combination of XX, XY, XO, XXY, XYY etc.; mosaic combinations are notated as XX/XY, XO/XY, XX/XXY, XY/XYY etc. Mosaics are often hermaphrodites whose physical characteristics are a mixture of normal female and male characteristics. See Dewhurst and Gordon, pp. 116–20.

17. Suzanne Kessler and Wendy McKenna, *Gender: An Ethnomethodological Approach* (New York: John Wiley and Sons, 1978), p. 78 note.

18. Dewhurst and Gordon, p. 12.

19. Androgens and estrogens are thought to inhibit the action of one another while estrogens and progestins can enhance each other's actions. These effects act in relation to relative quantities of the hormones involved and there may be minimum quantity thresholds that must be surpassed for the effects to occur. See R. D. Lisk and L. A. Rueter, "Hypothalamic and Sexual Behavior: Progesterone Modulation of Estrogen Sensitivity," in *Current Studies in Hypothalamic Function: Metabolism and Behavior,* vol. 2, ed. W. L. Veale and K. Lederers (New York: Karger, 1978), pp. 183–94, esp. pp. 190–91; A. C. Petersen, "Hormones and Cognitive Functioning," in *Sex Related Differences in Cognitive Functioning: Developmental Issues,* ed. M. A. Wittig and A. C. Petersen (New York: Academic Press, 1979), pp. 189–214, esp. pp. 191–92.

20. J. A. Rosko, "Fetal Hormones and Development of the Central Nervous System in Primates," in *Regulatory Mechanisms Affecting Gonadal Hormone Action,* ed. J. A. Thomas and R. L. Singhal (Baltimore: University Park Press, 1977), pp. 138–68, esp. p. 162; M. J. Baum et al., "Hormonal Basis of Proceptivity and Receptivity in Female Primates," *Archives of Sexual Behavior* 6 (1977), pp. 173–92, esp. p. 184.

21. Lisk and Rueter, pp. 190–91; Petersen, p. 192.

22. John Money, *Love and Love Sickness: The Science of Sex, Gender Difference and Pair Bonding* (Baltimore: Johns Hopkins University Press, 1980), p. 138.

23. Ibid., p. 137.

24. A. A. Ehrhardt and S. W. Baker, "Fetal Androgens, Human Central Nervous System Differentiation and Behavior Sex Differences," in *Sex Differences in Behavior,* ed. R. Friedman et al. (New York: John Wiley and Sons, 1974), pp. 33–52, esp. p. 42.

25. Money and Ehrhardt, p. 10.

26. J. M. Reinisch, "Fetal Hormones, the Brain, and Human Sex Differences: A Heuristic, Integrative Review of the Recent Literature," *Archives of Sexual Behavior* 3 (1974), pp. 51–90, esp. p. 67.

27. Interview with Harry Harlow in A. Keller, *Sexuality and Homosexuality: A New View* (New York: W. Norton, 1971), p. 401.

28. Money, *Love and Love Sickness,* p. 25.

29. DES babies assigned as males require little or no corrective surgery. DES babies assigned as females usually require surgery to decrease the size of their clitoris and possibly to correct abnormalities of the labia. The assignment of such ba-

bies to the male or the female sex is largely based on the size of the clitoris; if it is large enough, in the opinion of doctors, to be serviceable as a penis, the infant is assigned as male. If not, the child is assigned as female.

30. Money and Ehrhardt actually refer to the progestin DES as androgenizing XX fetuses. See Money and Ehrhardt, pp. 49, 95; Ehrhardt and Baker, p. 35.

31. Money and Ehrhardt, p. 290.

32. R. Bleier, "Bias in Biological and Human Sciences: Some Comments" *Signs* 4 (1978), pp. 159–62; Bleier, "Social and Political Bias," pp. 52–53; Rosko, p. 162.

33. Male DES babies also suffer abnormalities of the urinogenital tract, most commonly undescended testes and infertility. See K. Nuefeld, "DES Exposure: What You Should Know," *HERizons* (March, 1983), pp. 20–23.

34. J. M. Reinisch and W. G. Karow, "Prenatal Exposure to Synthetic Progestins and Estrogens: Effects on Human Development," *Archives of Sexual Behavior* 6 (1977), pp. 257–88, esp. p. 262.

35. Money and Ehrhardt consider DES girls in their discussion of androgenized females. See Money and Ehrhardt, pp. 98 ff.

36. Reinisch and Karow, pp. 257–88.

37. AGS individuals assigned as males require hormone therapy as well. If untreated they will experience premature puberty. Some also elect for minor cosmetic surgery to implant artificial testes in the empty scrotum.

38. Ehrhardt and Baker, pp. 40–44; Money and Ehrhardt, pp. 98–103.

39. Ehrhardt and Baker, p. 44.

40. V. R. Brooks, *Minority Stress in Lesbian Women* (Toronto: Lexington Books, 1981), pp. 27–28.

41. Ehrhardt and Baker, p. 43.

42. As a normal feature it seems a misnomer to refer to this cluster of behaviors as "tomboyism" a word which originally meant "a rude, boisterous or forward boy." See B. Fried, "Boys Will Be Boys: The Language of Sex and Gender," in *Women Look at Biology Looking at Women: A Collection of Feminist Critiques,* ed. R. Hubbard, M. S. Henifin, and B. Fried (Cambridge, Mass.: Schenkman, 1979), pp. 37–59, esp. p. 37.

43. A. Heilbrun and N. Thompson, "Sex-Role Identity and Male and Female Homosexuality," *Sex Roles* 3 (1977), pp. 65–79, esp. p. 71.

44. S. Oldham, D. Farnill, and I. Ball, "Sex-Role Identity of Female Homosexuals," *Journal of Homosexuality* 8 (1982), pp. 41–46.

45. C. Seavey, P. Katz, and S. R. Zalk, "Baby X: The Effects of Gender Labels on Adult Responses to Infants," *Sex Roles* 2 (1975), pp. 103–109.

46. Money and Ehrhardt, p. 9; Money and Ehrhardt report the interesting case of the entirely normal identical twin baby boy whose penis was irretrievably damaged in a circumcision accident. The parents and doctors of the boy decided to reassign him as a a girl. Corrective surgery and a name change were undertaken and the baby subsequently grew up to be acceptably female as a young child but experienced gender role difficulties as an adolescent. The girl's twin brother showed no signs of femininity, thus allowing for a control of sorts. See Money and Ehrhardt pp. 118–23; Milton Diamond, "Sexual Identity, Monozygotic Twins Reared in Discordant Sex Roles and a BBC Follow-up," *Archives of Sexual Behavior* 11 (1982), pp. 181–86.

47. C. N. Jacklin, "Epilogue," in *Sex Related Differences in Cognitive Functioning: Developmental Issues,* ed. M. A. Wittig and A. C. Petersen (New York: Academic Press, 1979), pp. 357–71, esp. p. 364.

48. R. Rose, T. Gordon, and I. Bernstein, "Plasma Testosterone Levels in the Male Rhesus: Influences of Sexual and Social Stimuli," *Science* (November 10, 1972), pp. 643–45.

49. Allen Mazur and Theodore A. Lamb, "Testosterone, Status, and Mood in Human Males," *Hormones and Behavior* 14 (1980), pp. 236–46; Arthur Kling, "Testosterone and Aggressive Behavior in Man and Nonhuman Primates," in *Hormonal Correlates of Behavior Volume I: A Lifespan View,* ed. Basil E. Eleftheriou and Richard L. Sprott (New York: Plenum Press, 1975), pp. 305–23; J. Raymond, *The Transsexual Empire: The Making of the She-Male* (Boston: Beacon Press, 1979), p. 57.

50. D. H. Baucom, P. K. Besch, S. Callahan, "Relation between Testosterone Concentration, Sex Role Identity, and Personality among Females," *Journal of Personality and Social Psychology* 48 (1985), pp. 1218–26.

51. H. F. L. Meyer-Bahlburg, "Aggression, Androgens, and the XYY Syndrome," in *Sex Differences in Behavior,* ed. R. Friedman et al. (New York: John Wiley and Sons, 1974), pp. 433–53, esp. p. 444.

52. Petersen comments that in humans the link between stress and hormones "is a contingent correlation dependent upon the presence of a stimulating or provocative situation." See Petersen, p. 200; Doering et al. found that there was "a significant correlation between . . . average levels of self-perceived depression and the average concentration of plasma testosterone" in men. Human males may respond to depression as if provoked to action or as if defeated. These, and many other possible responses to depression might evoke different hormonal reactions. See C. H. Doering et al., "Plasma Testosterone Levels and Psychologic Measures in Men over a Two Month Period," in *Sex Differences in Behavior,* ed. R. Friedman et al. (New York: John Wiley and Sons, 1974), pp. 413–33, esp. p. 430.

53. Kenneth E. Moyer, "Sex Differences in Aggression," in *Sex Differences in Behavior,* ed. R. Friedman et al. (New York: John Wiley and Sons, 1974), pp. 335–72, esp. p. 345.

54. K. Sano et al., "Results of Stimulation and Destruction of the Posterior Hypothalamus in Man," *Journal of Neurosurgery* 33 (1970), pp. 689–707; G. Schmidt and E. Schorsch, "Psychosurgery of Sexually Deviant Patients: Review and Analysis of New Empirical Findings," *Archives of Sexual Behavior* 10 (1981), pp. 301–23.

55. J. Panksepp, "Hypothalamic Integration of Behavior: Rewards, Punishments, and Related Psychological Processes," in *Behavioral Studies of the Hypothalamus,* ed. P. Morgane and J. Panksepp (New York: Marcel Dekker, 1981), pp. 289–431.

56. Panksepp, p. 304.

57. A. Siegel and H. Edinger, "Neural Control of Aggression and Rage Behavior," in *Behavioral Studies of the Hypothalamus,* ed. P. Morgane and J. Panksepp (New York: Marcel Dekker, 1981), pp. 230–40, esp. p. 230.

58. D. Gupta et al., "Hypothalamic-Pituitary-Testicular Feedback Mechanism during Mammalian Sexual Maturation," in *Hypothalamic Hormones: Structure, Synthesis and Biological Activity,* ed. D. Gupta and W. Voelter (Weinheim, Germany: Verlag Chemie, 1975), pp. 179–206, esp. p. 179.

59. Arthur P. Arnold and Marc Breedlove, "Organizational and Activational Effects of Sex Steroids on Brain and Behavior: A Reanalysis," *Hormones and Behavior* 19 (1985), pp. 469–98.

60. Gupta et al., p. 179.

61. Research done by J. M. Reinisch, R. Gandelman, and F. S. Spiegel indicated that there are differences in perceptual abilities between men and women and that these differences are linked to hormonal status. They cite examples in the perception of odors and sounds. They speculate that "at the most basic level it is possible that environmental stimuli have different 'meanings' for males and females. Thus, it may be that males and females are essentially quite different creatures whose perceptions of the world differ markedly, even when confronted with similar physical environments." See "Prenatal Influences in Cognitive Abilities: Data from Experimental Animals and Human Genetic and Endocrine Syndromes," in *Sex Related Differences in Cognitive Functioning: Developmental Issues,* ed. M. A. Wittig and A. C. Petersen (New York: Academic Press, 1979), pp. 215–39, esp. p. 234.

62. The shifting of dominance status during the aging process might be a partial explanation for the decrease in androgen secretion by both men and women as they age, the decrease in estrogen secretion in aging women, and the increase in estrogen secretion in elderly men. As women grow older in our society they do not move up the dominance hierarchy so far as to reach a position of dominance, but maturity often brings with it some feeling of control over one's life. Elderly men often retain much of the status of their youth but understand themselves to be losing status to younger men.

63. Transsexuals assigned at birth to the male sex will be referred to as male-to-female transsexuals. Transsexuals assigned at birth as females will be referred to as female-to-male transsexuals. These designations will be maintained regardless of their hormonal or surgical status.

64. R. Green, *Sexual Identity Conflict in Children and Adults* (New York: Basic Books, 1974), pp. 82–116; Stoller, *Sex and Gender,* pp. 89–92.

65. As the definition of transsexual excludes the question of chromosomal abnormalities, hermaphrodites and other persons of ambiguous chromosomal status are defined out of the transsexual group. See L. M. Lothstein, *Female to Male Transsexualism: Historical, Clinical and Theoretical Issues* (Boston: Routledge and Kegan Paul, 1983), p. 62.

66. G. Fulmer, "Testosterone Levels in Female to Male Transsexualism," Letter to the Editor, *Archives of Sexual Behavior* 2 (1973), pp. 399–400; Green, p. 38; J. Jones and J. Saminy, "Plasma Testosterone Levels in Female Transsexualism," *Archives of Sexual Behavior* 2 (1973), pp. 251–56; C. J. Midgeon, M. A. Rivarola, and M. G. Forest, "Studies of Androgens in Male Transsexual Subjects: Effects of Estrogen Therapy," in *Transsexualism and Sex Reassignment,* ed. R. Green and J. Money (Baltimore: Johns Hopkins University Press, 1969), pp. 203–11; I. Sipova and L. Starka, "Plasma Testosterone Values in Transsexual Women," *Archives of Sexual Behavior* 6 (1977), pp. 477–81.

67. Green, p. 38; D. Hunt, J. Carr, and J. Hampson, "Cognitive Correlates of Biological Sex and Gender Identity in Transsexualism," *Archives of Sexual Behavior* 10 (1981), pp. 65–77; Jones and Saminy, p. 255; Midgeon et al., p. 209; Money and Ehrhardt, p. 231; Stoller, *Sex and Gender,* p. 66.

68. Fulmer, p. 399; Sipova and Starka, p. 477.

69. Green, p. 38; Midgeon et al., p. 203–11; L. E. Seyler et al., "Abnormal Gonadotropin Secretory Responses to LRH in Transsexual Women after Diethylstilbestrol Priming," *Journal of Clinical Endocrinology and Metabolism* 47 (1978), pp. 176–83.

70. Seyler et al., pp. 176–83.

71. Midgeon et al., pp. 203–11.

72. Seyler et al., p. 181.

73. Ibid., p. 181.

74. J. Money, "Sex Reassignment as Related to Hermaphroditism and Transsexualism," in *Transsexualism and Sex Reassignment,* ed. R. Green and J. Money (Baltimore: Johns Hopkins University Press, 1969), pp. 91–113, esp. p. 102.

75. Seavey, Katz, and Zalk; J. D. Lichtenberg, *Psychoanalysis and Infant Research* (Hillside, New Jersey: The Analytic Press, 1983), pp. 3–27; Gupta et al., p. 179; N. Ross, "On the Significance of Infant Sexuality," in *On Sexuality: Psychoanalytic Observations,* ed. T. B. Karasu and C. W. Socarides (New York: International University Press, 1979), pp. 47–60, esp. pp. 48–49.

76. Keller, p. 401.

77. Money and Ehrhardt, pp. 4, 16, 18.

CHECKPOINTS

1. Devor's article describes how biological and environmental factors operate in concert through chromosomes and hormones to affect gender.
2. Devor considers variations in the development of sex and gender to be informative in constructing a thorough biological theory of gender.
3. Devor cautions readers to be aware of underlying assumptions that researchers bring to their study.

To prepare for reading the next section, think about these questions:

1. What role might evolution play in explaining sex and gender differences?
2. What factors would an adequate biological theory of gender have to account for?

EVOLUTIONARY PSYCHOLOGY—EXPLANATION FOR HUMAN SEX DIFFERENCES

Psychological Sex Differences Origins Through Sexual Selection

DAVID M. BUSS
University of Michigan

Men and women clearly differ in some psychological domains. A. H. Eagly (1995) shows that these differences are not artifactual or unstable. Ideally, the next scientific step is to develop a cogent explanatory framework for understanding why the sexes differ in some psychological domains and not in others and for generating accurate predictions about sex differences as yet undiscovered. This article offers a brief outline of an explanatory framework for psychological sex differences—one that is anchored in the new theoretical paradigm of evolutionary psychology. Men and women differ, in this view, in domains in which they have faced different adaptive problems over human evolutionary history. In all other domains, the sexes are predicted to be psychologically similar. Evolutionary psychology jettisons the false dichotomy between biology and environment and provides a powerful metatheory of why sex differences exist, where they exist, and in what contexts they are expressed (D. M. Buss, 1995).

Evolutionary psychology predicts that males and females will be the same or similar in all those domains in which the sexes have faced the same or similar adaptive problems. Both sexes have sweat glands because both sexes have faced the adaptive problem of thermal regulation. Both sexes have similar (although not identical) taste preferences for fat, sugar, salt, and particular amino acids because both sexes have faced similar (although not identical) food consumption problems. Both sexes grow callouses when they experience repeated rubbing on their skin because both

Correspondence concerning this article should be addressed to David M. Buss, Department of Psychology, University of Michigan, Ann Arbor, MI 48109–1109.

sexes have faced the adaptive problem of physical damage from environmental friction.

In other domains, men and women have faced substantially different adaptive problems throughout human evolutionary history. In the physical realm, for example, women have faced the problem of childbirth; men have not. Women, therefore, have evolved particular adaptations that are absent in men, such as a cervix that dilates to 10 centimeters just prior to giving birth, mechanisms for producing labor contractions, and the release of oxytocin in the blood stream during childbirth.

Men and women have also faced different information-processing problems in some adaptive domains. Because fertilization occurs internally within the woman, for example, men have faced the adaptive problem of uncertainty of paternity in putative offspring. Men who failed to solve this problem risked investing resources in children who were not their own. All people descend from a long line of ancestral men whose adaptations (i.e., psychological mechanisms) led them to behave in ways that increased their likelihood of paternity and decreased the odds of investing in children who were putatively theirs but whose genetic fathers were other men. This does not imply, of course, that men were or are consciously aware of the adaptive problem of compromised paternity.

Women faced the problem of securing a reliable or replenishable supply of resources to carry them through pregnancy and lactation, especially when food resources were scarce (e.g., during droughts or harsh winters). All people are descendants of a long and unbroken line of women who successfully solved this adaptive challenge—for example, by preferring mates who showed the ability to accrue resources and the willingness to provide them for particular women (Buss, 1994). Those women who failed to solve this problem failed to survive, imperiled the survival chances of their children, and hence failed to continue their lineage.

Evolutionary psychologists predict that the sexes will differ in precisely those domains in which women and men have faced different sorts of adaptive problems (Buss, 1994). To an evolutionary psychologist, the likelihood that the sexes are psychologically identical in domains in which they have recurrently confronted different adaptive problems over the long expanse of human evolutionary history is essentially zero (Symons, 1992). The key question, therefore, is not whether men and women differ psychologically. Rather, the key questions about sex differences, from an evolutionary psychological perspective, are (a) In what domains have women and men faced different adaptive problems? (b) What are the sex-differentiated psychological mechanisms of women and men that have evolved in response to these sex-differentiated adaptive problems? (c) Which social, cultural, and contextual inputs moderate the magnitude of expressed sex differences?

SEXUAL SELECTION DEFINES THE PRIMARY DOMAINS IN WHICH THE SEXES HAVE FACED DIFFERENT ADAPTIVE CHALLENGES

Although many who are not biologists equate evolution with natural selection or survival selection, Darwin (1871) sculpted what he believed to be a second theory of evolution—the theory of sexual selection. Sexual selection is the causal process of the evolution of characteristics on the basis of reproductive advantage, as opposed to survival advantage. Sexual selection occurs in two forms. First, members of one sex can successfully outcompete members of their own sex in a process of intrasexual competition. Whatever characteristics lead to success in these same-sex competitions—be they greater size, strength, cunning, or social skills—can evolve or increase in frequency by virtue of the reproductive advantage accrued by the winners through increased access to more numerous or more desirable mates.

Second, members of one sex can evolve preferences for desirable qualities in potential mates through the process of intersexual selection. If members of one sex exhibit some consensus about which qualities are desirable in the other sex, then members of the other sex who possess the desirable qualities will gain a preferential mating advantage. Hence, the desirable qualities—be they morphological features such as antlers or plumage or psychological features such as a lower threshold for risk taking to acquire resources—can evolve by virtue of the reproductive advantage attained by those who are preferentially chosen for possessing the desirable qualities. Among humans, both causal processes—preferential mate choice and same-sex competition for access to mates—are prevalent among both sexes, and probably have been throughout human evolutionary history (Buss, 1994).

HYPOTHESES ABOUT PSYCHOLOGICAL SEX DIFFERENCES FOLLOW FROM SEXUAL ASYMMETRIES IN MATE SELECTION AND INTRASEXUAL COMPETITION

Although a detailed analysis of psychological sex differences is well beyond the scope of this article (see Buss, 1994), a few of the most obvious differences in adaptive problems include the following.

Paternity Uncertainty Because fertilization occurs internally within women, men are always less than 100% certain (again, no conscious awareness implied) that their putative children are genetically their own. Some cultures have phrases to describe this, such as "Mama's baby, papa's maybe." Women are always 100% certain that the children they bear are their own.

Identifying Reproductively Valuable Women Because women's ovulation is concealed and there is no evidence that men can detect when women ovulate, ancestral men had the difficult adaptive challenge of identifying which women were more fertile. Although ancestral women would also have faced the problem of identifying fertile men, the problem is considerably less severe (a) because most men remain fertile throughout their life span, whereas fertility is steeply age graded among women and (b) because women invest more heavily in offspring, making them the more "valuable" sex, competed for more intensely by men seeking sexual access. Thus, there is rarely a shortage of men willing to contribute the sperm necessary for fertilization, whereas from a man's perspective, there is a pervasive shortage of fertile women.

Gaining Sexual Access to Women Because of the large asymmetry between men and women in their minimum obligatory parental investment—nine months gestation for women versus an act of sex for men—the direct reproductive benefits of gaining sexual access to a variety of mates would have been much higher for men than for women throughout human evolutionary history (Symons, 1979; Trivers, 1972). Therefore, in social contexts in which some short-term mating or polygynous mating were possible, men who succeeded in gaining sexual access to a variety of women, other things being equal, would have experienced greater reproductive success than men who failed to gain such access (see also Greiling, 1993, for adaptive benefits to women of short-term mating).

Identifying Men Who Are Able to Invest Because of the tremendous burdens of a nine-month pregnancy and subsequent lactation, women who selected men who were able to invest resources in them and their offspring would have been at a tremendous advantage in survival and reproductive currencies compared with women who were indifferent to the investment capabilities of the man with whom they chose to mate.

Identifying Men Who Are Willing to Invest Having resources is not enough. Copulating with a man who had resources but who displayed a hasty postcopulatory departure would have been detrimental to the woman, particularly if she became pregnant and faced raising a child without the aid and protection of an investing father. A man with excellent resource-accruing capacities might channel resources to another woman or pursue short-term sexual opportunities with a variety of women. A woman who had the ability to detect a man's willingness to invest in her and her children would have an adaptive advantage compared with women who were oblivious to a man's willingness or unwillingness to invest.

These are just a few of the adaptive problems that women and men have confronted differently or to differing degrees. Other examples of sex-linked adaptive problems include those of coalitional warfare, coalitional defense, hunting, gathering, combating sex-linked forms of reputational damage, embodying sex-linked prestige criteria, and attracting mates by fulfilling the differing desires of the other sex— domains that all have consequences for mating but are sufficiently wide-ranging to span a great deal of social psychology (Buss, 1994). It is in these domains that evolutionary psychologists anticipate the most pronounced sex differences—differences in solutions to sex-linked adaptive problems in the form of evolved psychological mechanisms.

PSYCHOLOGICAL SEX DIFFERENCES ARE WELL DOCUMENTED EMPIRICALLY IN THE DOMAINS PREDICTED BY THEORIES ANCHORED IN SEXUAL SELECTION

When Maccoby and Jacklin (1974) published their classic book on the psychology of sex differences, knowledge was spotty and methods for summarizing the literature were largely subjective and interpretive (Eagly, this issue). Since that time, there has been a veritable explosion of empirical findings, along with quantitative meta-analytic procedures for evaluating them (e.g., Eagly, 1995; Feingold, 1990; Hall, 1978; Hyde, in press; Oliver & Hyde, 1993; Rosenthal, 1991). Although new domains of sex differences continue to surface, such as the recently documented female advantage in spatial location memory (Silverman & Eals, 1992), the outlines of where researchers find large, medium, small, and no sex differences are starting to emerge more clearly.

A few selected findings illustrate the heuristic power of evolutionary psychology. Cohen (1977) used the widely adopted d statistic as the index of magnitude of effect to propose a rule of thumb for evaluating effect sizes: 0.20 = "small," 0.50 = "medium," and 0.80 = "large." As Hyde (in press) has pointed out in a chapter titled "Where Are the Gender Differences? Where Are the Gender Similarities?,"

sex differences in the intellectual and cognitive ability domains tend to be small. Women's verbal skills tend to be slightly higher than men's ($d = -0.11$). Sex differences in math also tend to be small ($d = 0.15$). Most tests of general cognitive ability, in short, reveal small sex differences.

The primary exception to the general trend of small sex differences in the cognitive abilities domain occurs with spatial rotation. This ability is essential for successful hunting, in which the trajectory and velocity of a spear must anticipate correctly the trajectory of an animal as each moves with different speeds through space and time. For spatial rotation ability, $d = 0.73$. Other sorts of skills involved in hunting also show large magnitudes of sex differences, such as throwing velocity ($d = 2.18$), throwing distance ($d = 1.98$), and throwing accuracy ($d = 0.96$; Ashmore, 1990). Skilled hunters, as good providers, are known to be sexually attractive to women in current and traditional tribal societies (Hill & Hurtado, 1989; Symons, 1979).

Large sex differences appear reliably for precisely the aspects of sexuality and mating predicted by evolutionary theories of sexual strategies (Buss & Schmitt, 1993). Oliver and Hyde (1993), for example, documented a large sex difference in attitudes toward casual sex ($d = 0.81$). Similar sex differences have been found with other measures of men's desire for casual sex partners, a psychological solution to the problem of seeking sexual access to a variety of partners (Buss & Schmitt, 1993; Symons, 1979). For example, men state that they would ideally like to have more than 18 sex partners in their lifetimes, whereas women state that they would desire only 4 or 5 ($d = 0.87$; Buss & Schmitt, 1993). In another study that has been replicated twice, 75% of the men but 0% of the women approached by an attractive stranger of the opposite sex consented to a request for sex (Clark & Hatfield, 1989).

Women tend to be more exacting than men, as predicted, in their standards for a short-term mate ($d = 0.79$). Women tend to place greater value on good financial prospects in a mate—a finding confirmed in a study of 10,047 individuals residing in 37 cultures located on six continents and five islands from around the world (Buss, 1989a). More so than men, women especially disdain qualities in a potential mate that signal inability to accrue resources, such as lack of ambition ($d = 1.38$) and lack of education ($d = 1.06$). Women desire physical protection abilities more than men, both in short-term mating ($d = 0.94$) and in long-term mating ($d = 0.66$).

Men and women also differ in the weighting given to cues that trigger sexual jealousy. Buss, Larsen, Westen, and Semmelroth (1992) presented men and women with the following dilemma: "What would upset or distress you more: (a) imagining your partner forming a deep emotional attachment to someone else or (b) imagining your partner enjoying passionate sexual intercourse with that other person" (p. 252). Men expressed greater distress about sexual than emotional infidelity, whereas women showed the opposite pattern. The difference between the sexes in which scenario was more distressing was 43% ($d = 0.98$). These sex differences have been replicated by different investigators (Wiederman & Allgeier, 1993) with physiological recording devices (Buss et al., 1992) and have been replicated in other cultures (Buunk, Angleitner, Oubaid, & Buss, 1994).

These sex differences are precisely those predicted by evolutionary psychological theories based on sexual selection. They represent only a sampling from a larger body of supporting evidence. The sexes also differ substantially in a wide variety of other ways that are predicted by sexual selection theory, such as in thresholds for physical risk taking (Wilson & Daly, 1985), in frequency of perpetrating homicides (Daly & Wilson, 1988), in thresholds for inferring sexual intent in others (Abby, 1982), in perceptions of the magnitude of upset people experience as the victims of sexual aggression (Buss, 1989b), and in the frequency of committing violent crimes of all sorts (Daly & Wilson, 1988). As noted by Donald Brown (1991), "it will be irresponsible to continue shunting these [findings] aside, fraud to deny that they exist" (p. 156). Evolutionary psychology sheds light on why these differences exist.

CONCLUSIONS

Strong sex differences occur reliably in domains closely linked with sex and mating, precisely as predicted by psychological theories based on sexual selection (Buss, 1994). Within these domains, the psychological sex differences are patterned in a manner that maps precisely onto the adaptive problems men and women have faced over human evolutionary history. Indeed, in most cases, the evolutionary hypotheses about sex differences were generated a decade or more before the empirical tests of them were conducted and the sex differences discovered. These models thus have heuristic and predictive power.

The evolutionary psychology perspective also offers several insights into the broader discourse on sex differences. First, neither women nor men can be considered "superior" or "inferior" to the other, any more than a bird's wings can be considered superior or inferior to a fish's fins or a kangaroo's legs. Each sex possesses mechanisms designed to deal with its own adaptive challenges—some similar and some different—and so notions of superiority or inferiority are logically incoherent from the vantage point of evolutionary psychology. The metatheory of evolutionary psychology is descriptive, not prescriptive—it carries no values in its teeth.

Second, contrary to common misconceptions about evolutionary psychology, finding that sex differences originated through a causal process of sexual selection does not imply that the differences are unchangeable or intractable. On the contrary, understanding their origins provides a powerful heuristic to the contexts in which the sex differences are most likely to be manifested (e.g., in the context of mate competition) and hence provides a guide to effective loci for intervention if change is judged to be desirable.

Third, although some worry that inquiries into the existence and evolutionary origins of sex differences will lead to justification for the status quo, it is hard to believe that attempts to change the status quo can be very effective if they are undertaken in ignorance of sex differences that actually exist. Knowledge is power, and attempts to intervene in the absence of knowledge may resemble a surgeon operating blindfolded—there may be more bloodshed than healing (Tooby & Cosmides, 1992).

The perspective of evolutionary psychology jettisons the outmoded dualistic thinking inherent in much current discourse by getting rid of the false dichotomy between biological and social. It offers a truly interactionist position that specifies the particular features of social context that are especially critical for processing by our evolved psychological mechanisms. No other theory of sex differences has been capable of predicting and explaining the large number of precise, detailed, patterned sex differences discovered by research guided by evolutionary psychology (e.g., Bailey, Gaulin, Agyei, & Gladue,

1994; Buss & Schmitt, 1993; Daly & Wilson, 1988; Ellis & Symons, 1990; Gangestad & Simpson, 1990; Greer & Buss, 1994; Kenrick & Keefe, 1992; Symons, 1979). Evolutionary psychology possesses the heuristic power to guide investigators to the particular domains in which the most pronounced sex differences, as well as similarities, will be found. People grappling with the existence and implications of psychological sex differences cannot afford to ignore their most likely evolutionary origins through sexual selection.

I thank Jill Becker, Kent Berridge, Bram Buunk, Sarah Moldenhauer, Richard Nisbett, Lance Sandelands, and Don Symons for helpful suggestions on earlier versions of this article.

REFERENCES

Abby, A. (1982). Sex differences in attributions for friendly behavior. Do males misperceive females' friendliness? *Journal of Personality and Social Psychology, 32,* 830–838.

Ashmore, R. D. (1990). Sex, gender, and the individual. In L. A. Pervin (Ed.), *Handbook of personality: Theory and research* (pp. 486–526). New York: Guilford Press.

Bailey, J. M., Gaulin, S., Agyei, Y., & Gladue, B. A. (1994). Effects of gender and sexual orientation on evolutionarily relevant aspects of human mating psychology. *Journal of Personality and Social Psychology, 66,* 1074–1080.

Brown, D. (1991). *Human universals.* Philadelphia: Temple University Press.

Buss, D. M. (1989a). Sex differences in human mate preferences: Evolutionary hypotheses tested in 37 cultures. *Behavioral and Brain Sciences, 12,* 1–49.

Buss, D. M. (1989b). Conflict between the sexes: Strategic interference and the evocation of anger and upset. *Journal of Personality and Social Psychology, 56,* 735–747.

Buss, D. M. (1994). *The evolution of desire: Strategies of human mating.* New York: Basic Books.

Buss, D. M. (1995). Evolutionary Psychology: A new paradigm for psychological science. *Psychological Inquiry, 6,* 1–30.

Buss, D. M., Larsen, R., Westen, D., & Semmelroth, J. (1992). Sex differences in jealousy: Evolution, physiology, and psychology. *Psychological Science, 3,* 251–255.

Buss, D. M., & Schmitt, D. P. (1993). Sexual strategies theory: An evolutionary perspective on human mating. *Psychological Review: 100,* 204–232.

Buunk, B., Angleitner, A., Oubaid, V., & Buss, D. M. (1994). *Sexual and cultural differences in jealousy: Tests from the Netherlands, Germany, and the United States.* Manuscript submitted for publication.

Clark, R. D., and Hatfield, E. (1989). Gender differences in receptivity to sexual offers. *Journal of Psychology and Human Sexuality, 2,* 39–55.

Cohen, J. (1977). Statistical power analysis for the behavioral sciences. San Diego, CA: Academic Press.

Daly, M., & Wilson, M. (1988). *Homicide.* New York: Aldine de Gruyter.

Darwin, C. (1871). *The descent of man and selection in relation to sex.* London: Murray.

Eagly, A. H. (1995). The science and politics of comparing women and men. *American Psychologist, 50,* 145–158.

Ellis, B. J., & Symons, D. (1990). Sex differences in sexual fantasy: An evolutionary psychological approach. *Journal of Sex Research, 27,* 527–556.

Feingold, A. (1990). Gender differences in effects of physical attractiveness on romantic attraction: A comparison across five research paradigms. *Journal of Personality and Social Psychology, 59,* 981–993.

Gangestad, S. W., & Simpson, J. A. (1990). Toward an evolutionary history of female sociosexual variation. *Journal of Personality, 58,* 69–96.

Greer, A., & Buss, D. M. (1994). Tactics for promoting sexual encounters. *Journal of Sex Research, 5,* 185–201.

Greiling, H. (1993, June). *Women's short-term sexual strategies.* Paper presented at the Conference on Evolution and the Social Sciences. London School of Economics, London, England.

Hall, J. A. (1978). Gender effects in decoding nonverbal cues. *Psychological Bulletin, 85,* 845–852.

Hill, K., & Hurtado, M. (1989). Hunter-gatherers of the new world. *American Scientist, 77,* 437–443.

Hyde, J. S. (in press). Where are the gender differences? Where are the gender similarities? In D. M. Buss & N. Malamuth (Eds.), *Sex, power, conflict: Feminist and evolutionary perspectives.* New York: Oxford University Press.

Kenrick, D. T., & Keefe, R. C. (1992). Age preferences in mates reflect sex differences in reproductive strategies. *Behavioral and Brain Sciences, 15,* 75–133.

Maccoby, E. E., & Jacklin, C. N. (1974). *The psychology of sex differences.* Stanford, CA: Stanford University Press.

Oliver, M. B., & Hyde, J. S. (1993). Gender differences in sexuality: A meta-analysis. *Psychological Bulletin, 114,* 29–51.

Rosenthal, R. (1991). *Meta-analytic procedures for social research* (rev. ed.). Newbury Park, CA: Sage.

Silverman, I., & Eals, M. (1992). Sex differences in spatial abilities: Evolutionary theory and data. In J. Barkow, L. Cosmides, & J. Tooby (Eds.), *The adapted mind: Evolutionary psychology and the generation of culture* (pp. 539–549). New York: Oxford University Press.

Symons, D. (1979). *The evolution of human sexuality.* New York: Oxford University Press.

Symons, D. (1992). On the use and misuse of Darwinism in the study of human behavior. In J. Barkow, L. Cosmides, & J. Tooby (Eds.), *The adapted mind: Evolutionary psychology and the generation of culture* (pp. 137–159). New York: Oxford University Press.

Tooby, J., & Cosmides, L. (1992). Psychological foundations of culture. In J. Barkow, L. Cosmides, & J. Tooby (Eds.), *The adapted mind: Evolutionary psychology and the generation of culture* (pp. 119–136). New York: Oxford University Press.

Trivers, R. (1972). Parental investment and sexual selection. In B. Campbell (Eds.), *Sexual selection and the descent of man* (pp. 136–179). New York: Aldine de Gruyter.

Wiederman, M. W., & Allgeier, E. R. (1993). Gender differences in sexual jealousy: Adaptationist or social learning explanation? *Ethology and Sociobiology, 14,* 115–140.

Wilson, M., & Daly, M. (1985). Competitiveness, risk taking, and violence: The young male syndrome. *Ethology and Sociobiology, 6,* 59–73.

CHECKPOINTS

1. Men and women experienced different challenges in adaptation to the environment, and sex differences evolved to meet those differing challenges.

2. According to Buss, the primary evidence in support of an evolutionary explanation of psychological sex differences comes from cross-cultural and cross-species comparisons.

To prepare for reading the next section, think about these questions:

1. After reading the first two articles, what concerns do you have about biological theories?

2. How might biological theories be influenced by history and culture?

The Political Nature of "Human Nature"

RUTH HUBBARD

Biologists, social scientists, and philosophers have speculated about human nature. Is there such a thing, and if so, how does one describe it? Fortunately I do not need to review the history of such speculations, since Alison Jaggar has provided a lucid discussion of the main issues and has located the debates in their historical and political contexts.[1] What I can do is evaluate the biological suppositions that underlie the concept of a human nature.

The ambiguity of the term *biology* is at the heart of questions about what scientists do when they try to examine nature. We use the word to denote what scientists tell us about the nature of organisms and also the living experience. When I speak of "my biology," I am usually referring to how I experience my biological functions, not to what scientists tell me about them. I can also use the word as the name of the scientific discipline, as in "I am studying biology." These multiple meanings for *biology* reflect confusions and ambiguities about the connections between scientific descriptions and the phenomena in the real world that scientists try to describe. It is important that we be aware of this ambiguity when we think about "human nature." Are we describing the natures of real people—you and me—or an abstraction or reification that biologists construct? "Human nature" does not describe people It is a normative concept that incarnates historically based beliefs about what human beings are and how they should behave.

Biologists' claims about human nature are embedded in the ways they learn about and describe living organisms. Most biologists, like other scientists, accept the notion that nature can best be described in terms of different levels of organization. These levels extend from ultimate particles, through atoms and molecules, to cells, tissues, and organs, to organisms considered individually, and then to groups of organisms—societies. Biology nowadays is concerned with the range of levels from atoms and molecules through organisms, and also with groups of organisms and their relations with each other over time (evolution) and space (animal behavior and ecology). Some biologists learn about organisms by taking them apart; others observe whole organisms in the laboratory or the field. Yet these levels are not credited with equal authority. Most biologists (as well as chemists and physicists) believe that the "lower" atomic and molecular levels are more basic and have intrinsically greater explanatory potential. Thus we find scientists and science writers describing genes (which are molecules) as keys to "the secret of life" or as "blueprints" of the organism. Numerous biologists believe that we would understand a great deal more about ourselves and other animals if we knew the composition and sequence of all the genes on our chromosomes. This belief in the superior explanatory content of "lower" levels is usually referred to as *reductionism,* and at this time reductionism is the dominant mode of thinking among biologists.

Reductionists assert that the study of organs, tissues, and molecules can yield important information about how organisms, and hence societies, operate. For example, they attribute the existence of crime to the "criminal personality," and criminals are said to behave as they do because they have diseased brains, too much or too little of certain hormones or other critical substances, or defective genes. Reductionism is a hierarchical theory that proceeds from the bottom up.

The converse is sometimes called *holism.* It can be based on a similar analysis that accepts hierarchies of levels, but it assigns superior authority to the "higher" levels, the organism as a whole or the organism in its surroundings. It is a less popular system of explanation among scientists, but one that carries considerable weight among practitioners of "alternative" methods of healing such as acupuncture and massage, and among feminists and environmentalists. They see reductionist ways of conceptualizing nature as a threat to people and our environment because these focus on specific areas of interest as though they could be isolated from their context.

Biodeterminism is a form of reductionism that explains individual behavior and characteristics of societies in terms of biological functions. Feminists know it best in the form of Freud's notorious statement, "Biology is destiny." During the nineteenth and twentieth centuries, biologists have produced numerous biodeterminist explanations for the obvious differences in women's and men's access to social, economic, and political power. Among them are Darwin's descriptions of the greater "vigour" and more highly developed weapons of males, acquired over eons of evolution through competition among males for access to females. At the same time, Darwin claimed, females sharpened their skills at discerning the most fit among their suitors and acquired coyness and the other wiles needed to captivate the best males. Biodeterminism has also prompted comparisons between the sizes of men's and women's brains and between brains of men of different races—which scientists used to "prove" the superiority of Caucasian men over men of other races and over all women.

A good deal of present-day research into presumed causes of social and behavior differences between women and men relies upon reductionist explanations. These draw on hypothesized differences in hormone levels of female and male fetuses or on hypothetical genes for spatial skills, mathematical ability, and competitiveness and aggression in men and for domesticity and nurturance in women. The most pervasive and comprehensive of contemporary biodeterminist theories is sociobiology, which has as its project "the systematic study of the *biological basis* of all social behavior" (my italics).[2] Sociobiologists claim that the fundamental elements of human nature can be identified in traits that characterize all people (and selected animals as well) irrespective of their cultural or historical differences. Once these supposedly universal traits have been identified, for example, male aggression and female nurturance, sociobiologists argue that their universality is evidence that they are adaptive. The term *adaptive* in this context means that individuals who exhibit these traits leave more descendants than do other individuals and that they pass the traits on to their descendants. In this way the genes for more adaptive traits come to outnumber the genes for less adaptive ones until the more adaptive traits become universal.

Sociobiologists argue that animals, including humans, do things that help spread their genes about. Behaviors that let them do that most effectively become universal traits. Among males, these are behaviors that lead them to inseminate as many females as possible, hence male promiscuity; for females they are behaviors that optimize the ability to spot and attach themselves to genetically well endowed males and to take good care of the few precious offspring they can produce in their lifetime, hence female fidelity and nurturance.

This basic difference between male and female reproductive strategies is said to arise from the fact that males can produce large numbers of small sperm, whereas females can produce fewer but larger eggs.[3] From this seemingly trivial asymmetry, sociobiologists draw two conclusions that they assume are crucial for the evolution of important differences between females and males: (1) females are the scarce resource (few eggs) and (2) females invest more energy in each egg than males do in each sperm.

But there is no reason to believe that females expend more energy (whatever that means) in the biological components of reproduction than males do. Among mammals, females indeed produce fewer eggs than males do sperm, and females gestate the embryos, but it is not obvious how to translate these facts into energy expenditures. Is it reasonable to count only the energy males require to produce the few sperm that actually end up fertilizing eggs, or should one not count the total energy they expend in producing and ejaculating semen (that is, sperm plus spermatic fluid) throughout their lives (however one would do that)? What is more, a woman's eggs are laid down ("produced") while she is still in her mother's womb. So should they be credited to her mother's energy expenditures or to her own (however one might calculate them)?

There are other puzzles. Sociobiologists describe the growth of a fetus as an investment of energy on the part of the pregnant woman. But the metabolism of a mammalian embryo is part of a pregnant woman's metabolic functions. As she eats, breathes, and metabolizes, some of the food she takes in is used to build the embryo. Why does that represent an investment of *her* energies? I can see that an embryo that grows inside an undernourished woman may be a drain on her because it uses her body for its growth. But healthy, well nourished women have been known to live normal active lives, create art, compete in Olympic events, and feel "energized" rather than drained by their pregnancies.

In the nineteenth century, physicians argued that girls would not be able to grow up to bear children if they diverted the energy required by their developing reproductive organs to their brains by going to school and becoming educated, like boys.[4] And they spoke of menstruation and pregnancy requiring energy as part of the self-serving ideology by which they portrayed all female reproductive functions as diseases that required medical (hence, of course, male) supervision. Sociobiological arguments that posit differences in the energy women and men invest in procreation to explain why men take less responsibility for the care of their children than women do may ring with scientific plausibility. But there is no way even to specify the variables, much less to do the necessary calculations to turn such hand-waving into scientific statements.

Sociobiologist Richard Dawkins takes sociobiological reductionism to its extreme by asserting that organisms are merely the gene's way of making more genes. He claims that everything organisms do is done out of self-interest, since organisms are only living manifestations of "selfish genes" engaged in the process of replicating themselves.[5] One of the obvious problems with this kind of formulation is that genes do not replicate *themselves*. Nor do eggs or sperm. Even many organisms do not reproduce themselves—at least not organisms that procreate sexually, like humans and most other animals discussed

by sociobiologists. Sexual procreation involves a coming together of individuals with different genetic makeups, who produce individuals who are genetically different from their parents and from each other. This has made it difficult for biologists to know how to analyze the ways in which even simple Mendelian traits that involve differences in only one gene become established in a population, not to speak of the ill-defined behaviors that sociobiologists label selfishness, aggression, or nurturance.

Sociobiology can be criticized on many levels. Even within the reductionist, biodeterminist paradigm, human sociobiology allows far too much leeway for identifying and naming traits that are observed in different cultures and under different historical circumstances as the same and hence "universal," especially when these "same" traits are generalized to animals as well. In such an exercise, everything—from sharp business practices and warfare to toddlers and young animals roughhousing to interactions scientists have observed among animals in the field, in zoos, or in crowded laboratory cages—becomes "aggression." The term *rape*, which refers ordinarily to the violent, sexualized assertion of power men impose on unconsenting women and occasionally on other men, has been used by sociobiologists as though it denoted nothing more sinisters than males' efforts to spread their genes around. Hence sociobiologists have described what they choose to call rape among birds, fishes, insects, and even plants.[6] Contexts and cultural meanings are erased, and all that is left is reified traits, which are universalized when the same name is given to a multiplicity of behaviors. In this way sociobiological reductionism leads to absurd extremes of lumping diverse behaviors together and naming them to suit the scientist's purpose.

Obviously similarities exist between the ways animals and people behave. But the variety of animal behaviors on which to draw for models of human behavior is so great that one can prove any human behavior is "natural" if the criterion is merely that one can point to an animal that behaves that way. This brings me to a crucial problem with efforts to construct lines of evolutionary descent for behaviors among animals, as well as between animals and people. In attempting to establish continuities between different species that may be of historical—evolutionary—significance, biologists have learned to distinguish between two types of similarities: analogies and homologies. Analogies are similarities in appearance or function that have diverse biological origins. Examples are the wings of birds, bats, and insects, and the eyes of frogs, lobsters, and octopuses. Homologous structures may look less similar, but they exhibit important similarities of structure and function that point to a common ancestry. An example is the scales of reptiles and the feathers of birds. To establish lines of historical continuity, analogies are irrelevant. One must look for homologies, which usually requires culling the fossil record.

Behavior leaves no fossils. There are only observations of how contemporary animals (including people) act and interpretations of what their actions signify. This offers too much leeway for postulating connections and imagining possible lines of descent for similar behaviors in particular groups of people and kinds of animals. If we want to use biological observations to try to trace and describe our natural history (which is what sociobiologists want to do), we have to follow more rigorous rules. Resemblances in the ways different animals and people act should not alone lead us to conclude that a behavior has evolutionary significance and is genetically determined.

INTERACTIVE, DIALECTICAL, AND COMPLEMENTARY MODELS OF NATURE

To get away from reductionism *and* holism and from futile arguments about whether nature or nurture is more significant in shaping behavior, a number of scientists have stressed that both genetics and environment are important, and that their effects cannot be separated. The simplest model suggests that the effects are additive. On the basis of that kind of model Arthur Jensen and Richard Herrnstein have argued that 80 percent of intelligence is inherited, 20 percent due to environment.

Other scientists have pointed out that this interpretation is too simplistic and that nature and nurture interact in ways that cannot be numerically quantified because they are not additive but simultaneous, and always act together. For example, Lewontin has argued that we can assess the separate contributions of genetic and environmental factors that act jointly only under strictly controlled conditions that permit the experimenter to change just one variable at a time.[7] On the basis of such experiments one can construct graphs called norms of reaction that describe how specific changes in each variable affect the phenomenon under observation (such as the growth of a plant in various types of soil and under various conditions of moisture, temperature, and cultivation). But these graphs do not permit one to predict the reactions of different varieties of the same organism under the same experimental conditions, or the reactions of a single variety under conditions that one has not yet measured. Such experiments illustrate the complexity of the situation but do not yield information about the real world, in which changes do not occur one variable at a time or in controlled or controllable ways.

More recently, Lewontin, Rose, and Kamin, as well as Birke, have argued that this kind of interactive model, though less limited than simple additive ones, is still too static.[8] Lewontin, Rose, and Kamin propose a dialectical model that acknowledges levels of organization, such as the ones I have enumerated. They argue that no one level is more fundamental than any other. None "causes" or "determines" another, but all are related dialectically, mutually drawing upon and modifying the changes that may be produced at any particular level. Properties observed at a particular level cannot be inferred form properties at other levels because the levels are related dialetically. For example, one cannot predict the physic and chemistry of water from the properties of hydrogen and oxygen atoms. Nor can one predict the structures and functions of proteins from the properties of the amino acids of which they are composed, and even less from the properties of the atoms that make up the amino acids. This is not because we do not know enough about atoms or amino acids, but because new properties emerge when atoms or amino acids come together in different combinations. These properties must be discovered empirically. The same goes for the relationships between organisms and their genes or between societies and the individuals who live in them.

I like to call the dialectical model *transformationism,* an awkward term, but one that tries to signify that biological and environmental factors can utterly change an organism so that it responds differently to other concurrent or subsequent, biological or environmental changes than it might have done. At the same time, the organism transforms its environment, which includes other organisms.

We can visualize this kind of interaction or transformation by thinking about the interplay between biological and cultural factors that affects the ways boys and girls grow up in our society. If a society puts half its children into short skirts and warns them not to move in ways that reveal their panties, while putting the other half into jeans and overalls and encouraging them to climb trees, play ball, and participate in other vigorous outdoor games; if later, during adolescence, the children who have been wearing trousers are urged to "eat like growing boys," while the children in skirts are warned to watch their weight and not get fat; if the half in jeans runs around in sneakers or boots, while the half in skirts totters about on spike heels, then these two groups of people will be biologically as well as socially different. Their muscles will be different, as will their reflexes, posture, arms, legs and feet, hand-eye coordination, and so on. Similarly, people who spend eight hours a day in an office working at a typewriter or a visual display terminal will be biologically different from those who work on construction jobs. There is no way to sort the biological and social components that produce these differences. We cannot sort nature from nurture when we confront group differences in societies in which people from different races, classes, and sexes do not have equal access to resources and power, and therefore live in different environments. Sex-typed generalizations, such as that men are heavier, taller, or stronger than women, obscure the diversity among women and among men and the extensive overlaps between them for all traits except those directly involved with procreation. Most

women and men fall within the same range of heights, weights, and strengths, three variables that depend a great deal on how we have grown up and live. We all know that first-generation Americans, on average, are taller than their immigrant parents and that men who do physical labor, on average, are stronger than male college professors. But we forget to look for the obvious reasons for differences when confronted with assertions like "Men are stronger than women." We should be asking: "Which men?" and "What do they do?" There may be biologically based average differences between women and men, but these are interwoven with a host of social differences from which we cannot disentangle them.

Recently some of us have begun to use yet another model to look at the different levels of organization, a model that draws on Niels Bohr's principle of complementarity. Bohr proposed complementarity as a way to think about the fact that light and other electromagnetic radiation can be described equally well as bursts of particles (quanta) or as waves spreading out from a point source. Classical physicists argued over which they really are: Bohr and other quantum theorists asserted that they are both. By complementarity Bohr meant that they are both at all times, not sometimes one, sometimes the other. Which description is appropriate depends on the instruments an observer uses to examine the radiation. When observed with a phototube or a photoelectric cell, light looks like a random succession of packets of energy; with a diffraction grating or a prism, it looks like waves.

Complementarity provides a fruitful model to integrate the different levels of organization and describe living organisms. The phenomena we observe at the subatomic, atomic, molecular, cellular, organismic, and societal levels are all taking place simultaneously and constitute a single reality. The distinctions between them are not part of nature. It is an outcome of Western cultural history and of the history of professionalization that we have developed separate academic specialties that describe these levels as though they were different phenomena. The only reason we think in terms of such levels is that we have developed specialties that draw distinctions between them. But physicists do not have access to more fundamental truths than molecular biologists have, and molecular biologists do not provide more basic descriptions than do the biologists who study cells or organisms. Biologists do not probe deeper realities than anthropologists or historians, only different ones. The fact that academic professionals value the explanatory power of these disciplines differently tells us something about the history and sociology of professionalization and about the alliances different disciplines have been able to forget with economic and political power, not about nature.

HUMAN NATURE

It is questionable whether the concept of human nature means anything. People's "nature" can be described only by looking at the things we do. To try to abstract or reify a human essence from the ways in which different groups of people have grappled with issues of survival in the range of geographical, ecological, and demographic settings that our species has populated is a dubious enterprise, because what one labels as "natural" depends on one's experience and viewpoint. People with different backgrounds are not likely to agree. Margaret Mead pointed out years ago that in societies with different, even opposite, sexual divisions of labor, people tend to believe that what women and men do follows from inherent differences in our natures.[9]

Sociobiologists presume that certain traits are inherent in our biological nature. Primary among them is selfishness, since it supposedly gets us to perpetuate our genes. A variant on selfishness is altruism of the kind that benefits the altruist (something like, "I'll scratch your back if you'll scratch my children's"). Then there are territoriality and a tendency toward establishing dominance hierarchies, which entered descriptions of animal behavior around the beginning of World War I, when a so-called pecking order was described among barnyard chickens,[10] a not very "natural" population. There are also the sex-differentiated characteristics of male aggressiveness and competitiveness and female coyness and nurturance, which

supposedly follow from the asymmetry in our reproductive interests that I questioned earlier. Wilson includes in "human nature" various behaviors that make sexual relationships between women and men emotionally satisfying, such as fondling and kissing, religious and spiritual aspirations that generate the need to believe in something beyond oneself, and the incest taboo.[11] He acknowledges cultural influences but insists that biology contributes a "stubborn kernel" that "cannot be forced without cost."[12] Because sociobiologists posit that "kernel" of biological traits, honed over eons of evolutionary history, their human nature theories tend to be conservative and portray competitive, hierarchical, capitalist societies in which men dominate women and a small, privileged group of men dominates everyone else as the natural outcome of inborn biological propensities.[13] But competition and dominance hierarchies do not characterize all human societies,[14] and there is no reason to believe that our biology determines the ways we construct them.

Stimulated in part by insights gained in the women's liberation movement, a number of sociobiologists have recently published accounts that round out the traditional descriptions of female animals as reproducers.[15] They present females as active participants in the social life of the group, as aggressive, competitive, involved in dominance hierarchies of their own, and as initiators of sexual contact and promiscuous. It seems that the sexual revolution has overtaken the dominant, competitive male and the coy, submissive female.

In his chapter in this collection, Carl Degler points out that sociobiologists as individuals have a range of political views and commitments. This is true, but the sociobiological definition of human nature lends itself to conservative politics. It is not inconsistent for a sociobiologist to assert that Marxism is "based on an inaccurate description of human nature,"[16] or that women's liberation is doomed because "human societies have evolved toward sexual domination as though sliding down a ratchet,"[17] and that "even with identical education and equal access to all professions, men are likely to play a disproportionate role in political life, business, and science."[18]

Biology imposes limits on what people can do, but when we feel the need we usually try to overcome them—at times all too recklessly. Bareskinned, we live in the arctic; wingless we fly; we live under water without benefit of gills. In view of the ingenuity with which we have overcome our limitations, it might seem odd that scientists call on sometimes quite subtle hypothetical differences between women and men to explain gender inequalities and that research into sex differences arouses so much scientific and public interest. We must recognize that differences among people are of interest only if they are correlated with differences in power. Little, if any, research is done on biological or psychosocial correlates of differences in height, although folk wisdom suggests there may be some. But when it comes to dark-skinned and light-skinned people or women and men, every possibility of difference is explored—and always some scientists predict that it will be hard to overcome.

Yet people have undergone substantial physical as well as psychological changes during times of major political and economic transformation. For example, as a result of rationing and the social policies the British government enacted during World War II, a generation of children grew up in Britain that was healthier and looked significantly different from any that had gone before. People who participate in major political or personal changes that drastically alter the ways they live often experience simultaneous changes in the ways their bodies function—changes in their ability to work and concentrate, in sleep and eating patterns, muscle mass, shape and strength, body weight, skin color and texture, and many others. It is not that changes in our way of life *cause* our biology to change. All the changes are interconnected: *we* change. Women who have participated in the women's liberation movement are well aware of such changes—changes in our bodies as well as in our lives.

Another example: We tend to think of menstruation as purely biological, yet menstrual patterns and experiences are profoundly affected by the ways women live, and the menstrual and reproductive patterns of women whose ways of life differ can be very different. Research conducted with female college athletes has demonstrated menstrual changes induced by exercise and diet.[19] !Kung women who forage for food in the Kalahari desert in southern Africa have entirely different menstrual and reproductive histories from the ones we are accustomed to think of as normal or natural. These women walk a great deal as part of their foraging and eat food that, although nutritionally adequate, supplies very different proportions and kinds of carbohydrates, fats and proteins than do our Western diets. Also, they nurse their babies for longer times and much more frequently than we do.[20] As a result, the !Kung establish patterns of ovulation and menstruation that produce only four or five pregnancies and very few menstruations in a lifetime.[21] It seems quite possible that the regular monthly cycle that some Western ideologies have put at the core of female personality is an accompaniment of ways of life that have developed in the last few thousand years. During this time increasing numbers of people have ceased to live as nomadic foragers and have begun to cultivate land, form settlements, and build the kinds of cultural and political structures that have yielded historical records.[22] But even now, women (and no doubt men) in different parts of the world live diverse biological, as well as social and economic, lives. As I have tried to say, these aspects of our lives cannot be separated.

Biological differences between the sexes prevent us from achieving gender equality only in procreation, narrowly defined. To date, only men can produce sperm and only women can produce eggs and gestate. Women *and* men can now feed infants reasonably healthful imitations of mother's milk, at least in affluent societies. People's capacities to work at socially useful tasks and to nurture children and form nonexploitative and mutually satisfying relationships are not limited by biology, but by discriminatory economic and social practices.

I want to thank Robin M. Gillespie for critical comments and discussion.

NOTES

1. Alison Jaggar, *Feminist Politics and Human Nature* (Totowa, N.J.: Rowman and Allanheld, 1983).
2. Edward O. Wilson, *Sociobiology: The New Synthesis* (Cambridge: Harvard University Press, 1975), 4.
3. George C. Williams, *Sex and Evolution* (Princeton: Princeton University Press, 1975).
4. Edward H. Clarke, *Sex in Education* (Boston: James R. Osgood, 1874).
5. Richard Dawkins, *The Selfish Gene* (Oxford: Oxford University Press, 1976).
6. David Barash, *The Whispering Within* (New York: Harper & Row, 1979).
7. R. C. Lewontin, "The Analysis of Variance and the Analysis of Causes," *American Journal of Human Genetics* 26 (1974): 400–11.
8. R. C. Lewontin, Steven Rose, and Leon J. Kamin, *Not in Our Genes* (New York: Pantheon, 1984); Lynda Birke, *Women, Feminism and Biology* (New York: Methuen, 1986).
9. Margaret Mead, *Male and Female* (New York: Dell, 1949).
10. Donna Haraway, "Signs of Dominance," *Studies in History of Biology* 6 (1983): 129–219.
11. Edward O. Wilson, *On Human Nature* (Cambridge: Harvard University Press, 1978).
12. Wilson, *On Human Nature,* 147.
13. Idem, *Sociobiology,* chap. 27; "Human Decency Is Animal," *New York Times Magazine* (October 12, 1975).
14. Eleanor Burke Leacock, *Myths of Male Dominance* (New York: Monthly Review Press, 1981).
15. Samuel K. Wasser, ed., *Social Behavior of Female Vertebrates* (New York: Academic, 1983); Sarah Blaffer Hrdy, "Empathy, Polyandry, and the Myth of the Coy Female," in Ruth Bleier, ed., *Feminist Approaches to Science* (New York: Pergamon, 1986), 119–46.
16. Wilson, *On Human Nature,* 190.
17. Ibid., 134.
18. Wilson, "Human Decency Is Animal."
19. Rose Frisch et al., "Delayed Menarche and Amenorrhea of College Athletes in Relation to Age of Onset of Training," *Journal of the American Medical Association* 246 (1981): 1559–63.
20. Melvin Konner and Carol Worthman, "Nursing Frequency, Gonadal Function, and Birth Spacing among !Kung Hunter-Gatherers," *Science* 207 (1980): 788–90.
21. Nancy Howell, *Demography of the Dobe !Kung* (New York: Academic, 1979).
22. Barbara B. Harrell, "Lactation and Menstruation in Cultural Perspective," *American Anthropologist* 83 (1982): 796–823.

CHECKPOINTS

1. Biological explanations are not devoid of political implications.
2. Dialectical models best explain the relationship between biology and gender.
3. According to Hubbard, sociobiological explanations are weakened by lack of clarity of concepts, politically laden terminology, and inadequate evidence.

Biology and Gender

QUESTIONS FOR REFLECTION

1. Prior to reading this chapter, what role did you think chromosomes and hormones played in sex and gender differences? Has your view changed?
2. What would be the best evidence in favor of an evolutionary explanation for sex and gender differences? What is the strongest criticism of evolutionary explanations?

CHAPTER APPLICATIONS

1. Find one newspaper or magazine account of sex and gender differences. How does the article treat the relationship between nature and nurture? What model of the relationship does the author use?

CHAPTER FOUR

Gender and Culture

QUESTIONS TO THINK ABOUT

1. **What is culture?**
2. **What is the relationship among sex, gender, and culture?**
3. **Why is gender considered a "cultural construction"?**
4. **Are there universal characteristics of gender roles?**
5. **What are the differences among patriarchal, matriarchal, and egalitarian societies?**
6. **How do researchers' belief systems influence their interpretation of their observations?**
7. **How are access to production and reproduction related to gender?**
8. **How do race and ethnicity relate to gender roles in the United States?**
9. **What are some cultural constructions of masculinity?**
10. **How might masculinity create psychological distress for men in the United States?**

THE INFLUENCE OF CULTURE ON GENDER

The readings in chapter 3 address the search for the relationship between gender and biology. Culture is often viewed as the alternative to a biological explanation. We have argued earlier that biological factors interact with culture in complex ways that lead to the different gender arrangements that we observe throughout the world. Culture, however, has proved to be an elusive and knotty concept to define. Culture has often been defined as race, nationality, ethnicity, or even religion. These everyday notions of culture illustrate both the complexity and ambiguity in how we use the term *culture*. Is culture who we are, where we are from, or what we believe? Or is it some complex mix of these?

The Meaning of Culture in Research on Gender

Many researchers, especially those interested in cross cultural issues, will refer to *cross-national* comparisons of behavior, attitudes, values, or beliefs. Cross-cultural comparisons such as these treat culture as an independent variable.[1] Examining culture in this way assumes some similarity among members of a particular cultural, ethnic, or racial group. The assumption that cultures are homogeneous may not be valid; this use of culture as a unitary variable ignores the complex nature of culture (Betancourt & Lopez, 1993; Matsumoto, 1996). Differences across cultures might arise because of differences in geography, natural resources, patterns of migration, history, religion, political systems, or many other factors that distinguish one location from another.

Cross-national comparisons of behavior or beliefs should be accompanied by an analysis of the factors within a culture that might explain the findings, but this analysis is seldom included. Identifying the elements of culture that might account for differences among people may be even more complex in studies of culture within the United States. Our multicultural society is not distinguished by differences that serve to separate one nation from another; rather, the differences within the United States, largely due to the complex history of colonialism, slavery, immigration, and migration, have led to variations in cultural identity.[2] Differences in national origin, history, religious practices, or other factors are sometimes related to cultural subgroups in the United States. For example, Americans of Irish ancestry might be distinguished from Americans of Japanese ancestry in terms of religion, shared history, and certain features of social and family orientation. We need to be careful, however, not to assume that all people of the same ancestry will share the same sense of identity and beliefs. It is not easy, nor straightforward, to identify who will belong to various cultural subgroups in the United States, because part of subcultural identity results from self-identity, such that many members of American society have a complex and varied multiracial or multiethnic heritage and therefore, by tradition or choice, may identify more or less with particular elements of their heritage. Not surprisingly, this identification further complicates the study of culture. Psychological anthropologists such as LeVine (1984) argue that the analysis of culture must attend to the many layers of meaning of culture and that observers should not be deceived by surface disparities or similarities.

Defining Culture

The concept of culture goes beyond representations of race, nationality, or ethnicity to include psychological and symbolic meanings. Culture involves a system of shared meanings and ideas. It includes both public aspects, such as customs, institutions, and language, and private aspects, such as

feelings and thoughts (LeVine, 1984). Not all dimensions of a culture are obvious even to the members of that culture. Rather, some elements of a culture exist at such a deep level that they often remain hidden or invisible to its members. LeVine contends that surface differences among people within a culture often obscure consensus at deeper levels of ideas, beliefs, or perceptions.

One metaphor that is used to describe the invisibility of culture, especially to its members, is that of a cultural lens. Culture shapes our perceptions and provides us with a shared lens to view reality (Veroff & Goldberger, 1995). Through the acquisition of culture, we learn, albeit implicitly, what our culture defines as important, and we become what Bem (1993) calls a cultural native. According to Bem, the transmission of cultural imperatives about gender is a nonconscious process whereby children come naturally to incorporate into their worldview their particular culture's gender organization—the behaviors, attitudes, and characteristics attributed to males and females as well as the nature and types of relationships between males and females. The invisibility of culture to its participants helps explain why certain cultural arrangements such as gender classifications are so hard to recognize and may appear to be essential characteristics of individuals and their social arrangements, rather than constructions emerging from culture.

One goal of this chapter is to lead you to carefully consider the meaning of culture. We have included readings that offer cross-national comparisons as well as cultural variations within the United States. To understand the relationship between culture and gender, you should look at how culture and gender are related by examining the mechanisms by which culture might influence gender. In many Islamic countries, for example, women wear veils, either by choice or by law. Although this attire may have its origins in Islamic teaching, it is also deeply embedded in these societies and influences family and social interactions. Often only husbands are permitted to see a woman unveiled; strangers and acquaintances rarely see the faces of women. The veil is one example of how, in many Middle Eastern countries, men and women live largely separate lives (Ward, 1996). In this example, sex strongly differentiates the experiences of men and women, which are then related to systems of power and privilege within the society. In her analysis of Islamic customs, Ward cautions observers not to use Western standards of social organization to judge the practice of the veil; she provides evidence that the segregation of women and men empowers women within a highly gendered social organization.

GENDER AS A CULTURAL CONSTRUCTION

Many contemporary views of gender and culture portray gender as a cultural construction. Individual cultures provide people with a body of knowledge that serves to explain the world, structure social interactions, and establish beliefs and attitudes. Thus knowledge, beliefs, attitudes, and behaviors related to gender vary according to cultural tradition and worldview. In Western cultures, gender traditionally has been divided into two categories, male and female, based on an individual's sex. However, societies in Asia, the South Pacific, and among North American Indians recognize other gender constructions. In chapter 1, we described the berdache of the North American Indians. Another example is found among the Hua people in Papua New Guinea, who see masculine people as high status but physically powerless and weak. Masculinity is lost by men as they age and gained by women through childbearing. A woman who has born at least three children may participate in the discussions and rituals of men, and as she ages she gains authority; however, she must adhere carefully to dietary restrictions because of the physical vulnerability attributed to masculinity. Thus while Huas' relationship with masculinity is partially determined by sex, it is dramatically influenced by age and life events (Renzetti & Curran, 1995). Considerable cross-cultural similarity as well as variability can be found in the meaning ascribed to gender. The readings for this chapter consider the search for cross-cultural universals as well as observations of cultural differences.

THE SEARCH FOR UNIVERSALS

The task of searching for similarities across cultures is intriguing and would seem to provide an answer to questions about the essential nature of females and males. Do men and women act in similar ways in different societies? Are men always (or usually) more aggressive than women? Are women always (or usually) caretakers of children? Are men dominant while women are subservient? As you have already learned in chapter 3, the evolutionary psychology approach would lead to affirmative responses to these questions premised on evolutionary differences in mating strategies. Can evidence from cross-cultural studies shed some light on these questions? One research area that has uncovered considerable similarities has examined cross-cultural agreement in stereotypes of men and women. As part of their research, Williams and Best (1990)[3] asked participants in 25 countries to indicate to what degree each of 300 adjectives applied to either men, women, or both equally. There was strong agreement on 49 stereotypes that were largely attributed to men (e.g., active, adventurous, aggressive autocratic, robust, strong, independent), while there was high agreement on 25 items attributed largely to women (e.g., affectionate, dreamy, emotional, sensitive, sentimental, submissive, superstitious, weak). Although this research reveals considerable cross-cultural similarity in individual's stereotypes of men and women, it does not address the actual relationship of these perceptions to behavior because it examined stereotyped beliefs, not actual behavior. An additional factor to consider is the perceived value of each trait within different countries. Williams and Best's research revealed considerable variability in the favorability of male and female stereotypes. In Australia, Brazil, and Italy, stereotypes of males were seen as unfavorable while in Japan, Nigeria, and South Africa, stereotypes of men were favorable. These findings emphasize the importance of considering the *level of analysis*. One level of analysis is the comparison across cultures, in which we see similarity in the attribution of stereotypes to men and women. At another level of analysis—the favorability of gender stereotypes within each culture—we see differences across cultures.

THE MEANING OF CROSS-CULTURAL SIMILARITIES

The observance of similarities across cultures might seem to provide evidence for a biological foundation for gender and for the sociobiologists' view that gender differences are rooted in evolution. This view is not the conclusion that Best and Williams (1993) suggest. They emphasize the interactive nature of biology and culture and consider how several features of culture might be related to their results. One part of their research examined children's knowledge of sex-role stereotypes and degree of belief in these stereotypes. Variations in parental and cultural socialization practices were related to variations in children's behavior and sex-role attitudes. For example, in Muslim countries, in which there is substantial segregation by sex, children learn sex stereotypes at an earlier age. Williams and Best also observed that the presence of a conservative religious ideology in a country predicted stronger adherence to stereotypes and earlier learning of stereotypes by children. In contrast, the sex-role ideology of children ages 5 to 8 tended to be less conservative and stereotyped in countries that were more technologically developed and more urbanized. Best and Williams suggest that their results show *both* strong cross-cultural similarity, which could be used as evidence for a biological basis for gender roles, and variations within and between cultures, which could be used to argue for the cultural influence on gender roles. Thus, culture and biology act and interact differently in different cultural settings.

In the first article in this chapter, *The Longest War: Gender and Culture,* Carole Wade and Carol Tavris discuss the search for essential differences between men and women. These authors caution readers that researchers have often used their own cultural lenses when viewing behavior in different

societies. In addition to the examples provided by Wade and Tavris, an analysis of hunter-gatherer societies shows the ways in which the cultural lens of researchers has influenced their findings. These traditional societies have been offered as evidence for the evolution of modern culture in which there is strong division of labor by sex and in which male activities are more highly valued. According to this analysis, male dominance is rooted in a division of labor in which men were responsible for hunting. This theory posits that women were dependent upon men for survival, and therefore, loyalty to men, prestige accorded to male activities, and male dominance have an evolutionary history that is carried forward into contemporary societies. This analysis has been so widely accepted that it has been used to explain such disparate phenomena as the lack of interest in parenting by males, male aggression, and female interest in homemaking and child care. In a reanalysis of these foraging societies, Gailey (1987) points out that the assumption that hunting was more important to survival than was the foraging and gathering of foodstuffs represents an androcentric twentieth-century bias. Researchers ignored the skills necessary to successfully forage and have underestimated the degree to which survival was dependent on reliable food gathering (as opposed to occasional big kills during hunting). Researchers also minimized the involvement of women and children in hunting by interpreting early tools such as knives and scrapers as having been developed for use in hunting when considerable evidence suggests that these tools may have been used equally in the preparation of plant-based foods. Gailey draws the following conclusion: "To make the male activity the driving force of human evolution interprets the paleontological data with tunnel vision and simply ignores the role of both gathering and hunting in known foraging societies" (p. 41). As we have emphasized, it is important to know the point of view that a researcher brings to the task of collecting, analyzing, and interpreting information in order to understand what that researcher's findings mean and what alternative hypotheses are possible.

ELEMENTS OF CULTURE THAT INFLUENCE GENDER ROLES

Researchers examining cross-cultural patterns of behavior and attitudes agree that a division of labor by sex is nearly universal and that the pattern of dividing work according to sex underlies the forms of gender hierarchy that pervade many societies (Bem, 1993; Burn, 1996; Gailey, 1987; Renzetti & Curran, 1995). However, no universal agreement exists on the *specific* labor of women and men. According to Renzetti and Curran, there are few tasks from which men or women are excluded, although those tasks that are mostly male dominant include hunting large sea animals, metalworking, and lumbering while those tasks that are predominantly female include cooking, laundering, and preparing vegetables. Many tasks, cross-culturally, are shared relatively equally, including generating fire, basket weaving, preparing animal skins, gathering small animals, planting, and harvesting.

According to Wade and Tavris in the article you will read, cross-cultural similarity does not necessarily mean that a behavior or belief is universal. The best example of this approach is the widespread belief that men are universally more aggressive than women. This chapter's second article by Maria Lepowsky, *Women, Men, and Aggression in an Egalitarian Society,* describes in detail a society with very little aggression and no sex differences in aggression. Her research provides a strong challenge to the view that males are universally more aggressive than females and to the underlying assumption that aggression is an essential characteristic rooted in biological differences between males and females.

It is important to recognize that similarities across cultures might arise for different reasons. Wade and Tavris argue that special features of each culture might explain particular behaviors or attitudes related to gender. Political systems, economic systems, weather, geography, and environmental pressures to produce children or control reproduction might provide explanations for gender roles and beliefs. In particular, Wade and Tavris claim that the access men and women have to the means of production of goods and services will strongly influence gender or-

ganization within a culture. Conditions of extreme segregation in work and limited access to natural resources seem to heighten competition between men and women and strengthen sex role distinctions. One example provided by Wade and Tavris is the highland people of New Guinea who live under harsh conditions and show extreme sex segregation. On the other hand, a different tribe in New Guinea with a great deal of uncultivated land and with convenient access to natural resources shows a pattern of gender organization in which antagonism between men and women is relatively low.

THE CONSTRUCTION OF GENDER AND SPECIFIC FEATURES OF CULTURE

One way to examine the relationship between specific features of a culture and how gender is represented within that culture is to conduct detailed observations of one particular society. This approach, known as ethnography, is the mainstay of anthropological research. Maria Lepowsky's article is an example of ethnographic research; she spent many months, across several years, on Vanatinai, a small island off the coast of New Guinea, observing and documenting the interpersonal, social, economic, and political organization of men and women (see Lepowsky, 1993).

Social Organization and Gender

Gender relationships on Vanatinai are **egalitarian,** meaning that both women and men have equal access to means of production and have equal opportunities for prestigious social roles and that all children are socialized toward highly valued traits such as assertiveness and autonomy. Although the division of labor shows a marked degree of overlap, some tasks are not always equally shared, so that Vanatinai is not a perfectly egalitarian society. There are few known completely egalitarian societies in the world.

The most prevalent form of social organization is patriarchy, in which males control the distribution of resources and dominate the social hierarchy and in which inheritance is often traced through the male line. Relatively few societies are matriarchies, in which women control the majority of the resources and hold most of the power. However, about one third of human societies are matrilineal, which describes a kinship system in which inheritance is traced though the maternal line. Often, matrilineal societies highlight female kinship relationships and may involve mother-centered or female-centered households, although the occurrence of matriarchal power structures is *not* associated with matrilineal inheritance (Ward, 1996). Thus, the relationship between sex and the organization of power within a society can be diverse, although patriarchy predominates worldwide.

Whereas labels such as patriarchy, matriarchy, or egalitarian describe the access to power and prestige of men and women, a closer examination of social organization reveals little universality accorded the roles of men and women. Not only does the specific labor of men and women vary, but the value accorded to those behaviors varies. The same or similar behaviors, observed cross-culturally, may actually represent differences across cultures. Renzetti and Curran (1995) describe a variety of ways that hunter-gatherer societies are organized. One type, exemplified by Eskimo people, divides labor strictly by sex—men hunt and women process food. Hunting is associated with power and prestige largely because it provides the dietary staples of meat and fish, and a basis for trade with non-Eskimos. The work of women is indispensable in this process because they provide needed clothing and tools for hunting, and the roles of men and women are complementary, not interchangeable. The social organization would be described as patriarchal. The !Kung of the Kalahari desert also have a strict division of labor for hunting—men and boys hunt large animals, while women and children gather the foodstuffs, that provide 70 to 80 percent of the society's nutrition. Women are particularly valued for their ability to discriminate among the many plants and vegetables and for the valuable information about the habits of animals that they provide to hunters. Unlike Eskimos, however, the division of labor by sex is not rigid, and men are likely to share chores with women, especially child

care. Therefore, while in one society, hunting is a central component of a rigid, patriarchal gender hierarchy, in another, hunting is a male-dominated activity in a nonauthoritarian, nonpatriarchal social structure.

Maria Lepowsky describes the management of aggression within the Vanatinai. This is a particularly intriguing issue because of the prevailing stereotypes about aggression and the rarity of egalitarian cultures. Certainly you are aware that aggression is viewed as a male-dominated activity—this view is a widely shared stereotype. In the Williams and Best (1990) survey respondents in 24 of 25 countries associated aggression with males. We will return to stereotypes about male aggression in chapter 5, *Gender Roles and Stereotypes,* and to the reality of male aggression in the United States in chapter 12, *Social Institutions.* This chapter looks at the relationship between social organization, gender, and aggression.

Lepowsky, in many months of observation among the Vanatinai, observed only five instances of physical aggression. She attributes the lack of violence to the convergence of a number of factors, including the use of sorcery and witchcraft to manage conflict and the access to power and prestige available to both men and women. As you read the article, keep track of the aspects of Vanatinai culture that contribute to its egalitarian character as well as those features that represent a gender hierarchy. You should be alert to the temptation to view these as exotic people. Rather, use this example as an illustration of a social organization very different from your own. By contrasting this society with technological cultures such as the United States, we can see the complexity and contradictory nature of gender roles worldwide. After reading Lepowsky's article, you may see more features that contribute to gender hierarchies in your own culture.

THE RELATIONSHIP AMONG CULTURE, ETHNICITY, AND GENDER

Unlike Vanatinai, the United States is a society within which many different racial, ethnic, and religious traditions coexist. Such heterogeneity makes it difficult to speak of one uniform culture. There are, however, some dominant elements of our society to which all members are exposed and that shape the experiences of individuals. One example is the patriarchal nature of American society, in which men have greater access to power, privilege, and opportunity. Thus, the male role accords men more power and socializes men toward the attainment of power. Other hierarchies—for example, race, social class, and ethnicity—also structure access to power and privilege. Not all men have equal access to systems of power and privilege. As we pointed out in chapter 1, men of color and gay men often are subjected to subtle and overt forms of harassment and discrimination.

The third article in this chapter, *Men of Color: Ethnocultural Variations of Male Gender Role Strain* by Richard Lazur and Richard Majors, examines male gender role socialization and its consequences for men from four cultures of color in the United States: African American, Latino, American Indian, and Asian American.[4] We have chosen this article in order to highlight the diversity of culture in the United States and its effect on the lives of different groups of men. The article introduces another element of the relationship between culture and gender. Whereas the first two articles describe how features of culture connect to the social organization of gender and related patterns of behavior, this article discusses the psychological consequences of the conflict between the dominant culture's construction of masculinity and the sense of identity shaped by being a member of a specific ethnic or racial community.

THE MEANING OF MASCULINITY

What is masculinity? What are the goals of socializing boys into men? Brannon (1976) has identified four themes of traditional masculinity in the United States: (a) antifemininity—avoiding that which is feminine, including the expression of emotion, sexual feelings for men, and vulnerability; (b) status and achievement—striving for success in sports and work and earning the respect of others through achievement; (c) inexpressiveness and indepen-

dence—maintaining self-composure, solving problems, and dislike of weakness; (d) adventurousness and aggressiveness—risk taking and violence. This definition of masculinity has provided the foundation for considerable research on masculinity and its consequences. For example, both lack of emotional expressiveness and limited self-disclosure have been linked to masculinity (Kilmartin, 1994).

Men in the United States are raised to be unemotional and oriented toward success and achievement. A popular bumper sticker that reads "He who dies with the most toys wins" (often fastened to the back of a red Jeep Cherokee) is probably not written using the generic masculine but really applies only to men. Masculine, successful men are strongly admired by others. The traditional man is a breadwinner who adheres to his masculinity through financial provisions for his family. According to Kilmartin, substantial contributions to society in science and engineering related to improvements in our overall quality of life.

One important challenge that has been raised to this definition of masculinity and the analysis of its consequences is that this definition assumes a white, middle-class, middle-age, heterosexual male. If men of color, of varying ages, from different social classes, or who are gay or bisexual depart from this prescription of masculinity, they may be labeled as different or deviant. Researchers now recognize that masculinity is not monolithic, uniform, nor static. Kimmel and Messner (1995) describe how masculinities can be thought of as a matrix of possibilities organized by race, ethnicity, social class, age, and sexual orientation.

The Consequences of Masculinity

Recent research on masculinity has focused on several negative consequences of masculinity. Pleck (1976) has developed a theory of masculine gender role strain that proposes that socialization pressures encourage boys encourage and men to live up to a standard of masculinity. The efforts of men to achieve masculinity can have three negative consequences: (a) low self-esteem or other negative psychic consequences when one's perceived success at masculinity is not matched by the cultural standard, (b) successful fulfillment of the male gender role through traumatic socialization, which has lifelong consequences, (c) successful fulfillment of the male gender role with negative consequences because the desired qualities have negative properties, for example, little contact with children (Pleck, Sonnenstein, & Ku, 1993). Pleck further proposes that the degree to which a man endorses traditional masculine ideology will impact the emotional consequences of his achievement of masculinity.

The article by Lazur and Majors considers the implications of gender role strain for four groups of men of color. Using ethnographic research in each community, the authors describe the standards of masculinity that each group prescribes for men and compares that to the dominant culture's prescriptions of masculinity. This article shows that one difficulty in demonstrating how these differing views of masculinity impact men is understanding the competing aspiration to achieve what may be contradictory versions of masculinity. This article illustrates the complexity of accounting for diversity in cultural identity while focusing on gender as the object of analysis.

CULTURE AND GENDER

The articles in this chapter make clear the innumerable ways that culture shapes and molds our social and psychological reality. Culture, in interaction with biological factors, provides us with a powerful gender lens that brings into distinctive focus our experiences, feelings, and thoughts. Our notions of ourselves as gendered beings emerges out of our cultural experiences. By understanding the powerful hold that culture has on each one of us, we can begin to uncover the ways in which we are engaged in "doing gender" (West & Zimmerman, 1987). We urge you to search for the many layers of culture that surround us all in order to fully appreciate the ways it shapes us as individuals as well as how it shapes our institutions and social organization. We are not suggesting that we believe that culture is the most important influence on gender. Nor is culture, rather than biology, easier to mold and change. As we argued in chapter 3, it is important to recognize the dynamic and reciprocal relationship between biological and cultural factors in describing and understanding gender. As you move on to the remaining chapters in this book, you should actively seek explanations that emphasize these sorts of complex interactions.

NOTES

1. This treatment is similar to how researchers treat sex as a subject variable. This was discussed in chapter 2, and the criticisms that we offered there also apply to cross-cultural comparisons, which treat nations or countries as unitary entities.
2. You should be aware that the United States is not the only multicultural nation; other examples would include, to varying degrees, Australia, Canada, South Africa, and Brazil.
3. The results summarized here are only a small portion of a complex cross-national comparison of sex-role stereotypes, sex-role ideologies, and sex-role socialization conducted by Williams and Best (1990).
4. The choice of labels for ethnic and racial groups has become a difficult and sensitive issue. When discussing a specific article, either reprinted here or used for background, we will use the terminology used by those authors.

REFERENCES

Bem, S. L. (1993). *The lenses of gender: Transforming the debate on sexual inequality.* New Haven: Yale University Press.

Best, D., & Williams, J. E. (1993). A cross-cultural viewpoint. In A. E. Beall & R. J. Sternberg (Eds.), *The psychology of gender.* New York: Guilford Press.

Betancourt, H., & Lopez, S. W. (1993). The study of culture, ethnicity, and race in American psychology. *American Psychologist, 48,* 629–637.

Brannon, R. (1976). The male sex role: Our culture's blueprint of manhood, and what it's done for us lately. In D. David & R. Brannon (Eds.), *The forty-nine percent majority.* Reading, MA: Addison-Wesley.

Burn, S. M. (1996). *The social psychology of gender.* New York: McGraw-Hill.

Gailey, C. W. (1987). Evolutionary perspectives on gender hierarchy. In B. B. Hess & M. M. Ferree (Eds.), *Analyzing gender: A handbook of social science research.* Newbury Park, CA: Sage.

Kilmartin, C. T. (1994). *The masculine self.* New York: Macmillan.

Kimmel, M. S., & Messner, M. A. (1995). Introduction. In M. S. Kimmel & M. A. Messner (Eds.), *Men's lives* (3rd ed.). Boston: Allyn & Bacon.

Lazur, R. F., & Majors, R. (1995). Men of color: Ethnocultural variations of male gender role strain. In R. F. Levant & S. Pollack (Eds.), *A new psychology of men.* New York: Basic Books.

Lepowsky, M. (1993). *Fruit of the motherland: Gender in an egalitarian society.* New York: Columbia University Press.

Lepowsky, M. (1994). Women, men, and aggression in an egalitarian society. *Sex Roles, 30,* 199–211.

LeVine, R. (1988). Human parental care: Universal goals, cultural strategies, individual behaviors. In R. A. LeVine, P. M. Miller, & M. M. West (Eds.), *Parental behavior in diverse societies* (pp. 3–13). San Francisco: Jossey-Bass.

Matsumoto, D. (1996). *Culture and psychology.* Pacific Grove, CA: Brooks/Cole.

Pleck, J. H. (1976). The male sex role: Definitions, problems, and sources of change. *Journal of Social Issues, 32,* 155–164.

Pleck, J. H., Sonenstein, F. L., & Ku, L. C. (1993). Masculinity ideology and its correlates. In S. Oskamp & M. Costanzo (Eds.), *Gender issues in contemporary society* (pp. 85–113). Newbury Park, CA: Sage Publications.

Renzetti, C. M., & Curran, D. J. (1995). *Women, men, and society* (3rd ed.). Boston: Allyn & Bacon.

Veroff, J. B., & Goldberger, N. R. (1995). What's in a name: The case for 'intercultural' psychology. In N. R. Goldberger & J. B. Veroff (Eds.), *Culture and Psychology* (pp. 3–21). New York: New York University Press.

Wade, C., & Tavris, C. (1994). The longest war: Gender and culture. In W. Lonner & R. Malpass (Eds.), *Psychology and culture.* Needham Heights, MA: Allyn & Bacon.

Ward, M. C. (1996). *A world full of women.* Boston, MA: Allyn & Bacon.

West, C., & Zimmerman, D. H. (1987). Doing gender. *Gender & Society, 1,* 125–151.

Williams, J., & Best, D. (1990). *Measuring sex stereotypes: A multination study.* Beverly Hills, CA: Sage.

The Longest War: Gender and Culture

CAROLE WADE AND CAROL TAVRIS

A young boy notices, at an early age, that he seems different from other boys. He prefers playing with girls. He is attracted to the work adult women do, such as cooking and sewing. He often dreams at night of being a girl, and he even likes to put on the clothes of girls. As the boy enters adolescence, people begin to whisper that he's "different," that he seems feminine in his movements, posture, and language. One day the boy can hide his secret feelings no longer, and reveals them to his parents.

The question: How do they respond?
The answer: It depends on their culture.

In twentieth-century North America and Europe, most parents would react with tears, anger, or guilt ("Where did we go wrong?"). After the initial shock, they might haul their son off to a psychiatrist, who would diagnose him as having a "gender identity disorder" and begin intensive treatment. In contrast, if

Carole Wade earned her Ph.D. in cognitive psychology at Stanford University; taught at the University of New Mexico, where she initiated a course on gender; was professor of psychology at San Diego Mesa College; and currently teaches at College of Marin in California. She is co-author, with Carol Tavris, of *The Longest War: Sex Differences in Perspective* and of *Psychology,* the first textbook to emphasize critical thinking and to mainstream research on culture and gender into the introductory course. Wade is also co-author, with Sarah Cirese, of *Human Sexuality.*

Carol Tavris earned her Ph.D. in Social Psychology at the University of Michigan, where she first became interested in cross-cultural psychology and gender studies. She has taught at the New School and UCLA and is widely known as a writer and lecturer on many social issues. In addition to her books with Carole Wade, she is author of *The Mismeasure of Woman* and *Anger: The Misunderstood Emotion.*

their daughter wanted to be "more like a man," the parents' response would probably be far milder. They might view a girl's desire to play hockey or become a construction worker as a bit unusual, but they probably wouldn't think she had a mental disorder.

These reactions are not universal. Until the late 1800s, in a number of Plains Indians and western Indian tribes, parents and other elders reacted with sympathy and understanding when a young person wanted to live the life of the other sex. The young man or woman was often given an honored status as a shaman, a person with the power to cure illness and act as an intermediary between the natural and spiritual worlds. A boy was permitted to dress as and perform the duties of a woman, and a girl might become a warrior. In some Native American cultures, the young man would be allowed to marry another man, the young woman to marry another woman.

In the Sambian society of Papua New Guinea, parents would react still differently. In Sambia, reports anthropologist Gilbert Herdt (1984), all adolescent boys are *required* to engage in oral sex with older men as part of their initiation into manhood. Sambians believe that a boy cannot mature physically or emotionally unless he ingests another man's semen over a period of several years. However, Sambian parents would react with shock and disbelief if a son said he wanted to live as a woman. Every man and woman in Sambian society marries someone of the other sex and performs the work assigned to his or her own sex; no exceptions.

What these diverse reactions tell us is that although anatomical *sex* is universal and unchangeable (unless extraordinary surgical procedures are used), *gender,* which encompasses all the duties, rights, and behaviors a culture considers appropriate for males and females, is a social invention. It is gender, not anatomical sex, that gives us a sense of personal identity as male or female. Cultures have different notions about what gender roles should entail, how flexible these roles ought to be, and how much leeway males and females have to cross the gender divide.

Perhaps, however, there is something essential about the sexes, something lying *beneath* the veneer of culture, immutable and eternal. That assumption is certainly widespread, and it has guided the research of social scientists as well as the beliefs of laypersons. Let us examine this assumption more closely. Are there some aspects of masculinity and femininity that occur at all times and in all places? If certain characteristics are common, why is that so? What determines how men and women should act toward each other, what their rights and obligations should be, and what it means, in psychological terms, to be female or male?

SEARCHING FOR THE ESSENTIAL MAN AND WOMAN

By comparing and contrasting different cultures around the world, social scientists have tried to identify those aspects of gender that are universally male or female. Their efforts may sound pretty straightforward. However, because researchers, like everyone else, are influenced by their own deeply felt perceptions and convictions about gender, the topic has been one of the most complex to study cross-culturally.

For many years American and European researchers looked for and found evidence that primate males (human and ape) were "by nature" competitive, dominant, and promiscuous, whereas primate females were "by nature" cooperative, submissive, and monogamous (Tavris, 1992). Because of their own preconceptions about male and female roles, based on their own cultural experiences, these observers often overlooked the evidence that contradicted their assumptions, even when the evidence was in front of their noses.

For example, many years ago the famous anthropologist Bronislaw Malinowski wrote a book on the Trobriand Islanders, in which he concluded that males controlled the economic and political life of the community. (Another of his biases is glaringly apparent in the title he gave his book: *The Sexual Life of Savages*.) But when Annette Weiner went to live among the Trobrianders many years later, she learned, by talking to the women, what Malinowski had not: that there was an important economic underground controlled by the labor and exchanges of women.

Similarly, in 1951, another famous anthropologist, E. E. Evans-Pritchard, reported that among the Nuer, a tribe living in the Sudan, husbands, had unchallenged authority over their wives. Yet he himself described incidents in Nuer family life that contradicted his conclusion:

> [Should a Nuer wife] in a quarrel with her husband disfigure him—knock a tooth out, for example—her father must pay him compensation. I have myself on two occasions seen a father pay a heifer to his son-in-law to atone for insults hurled at the husband's head by his wife when irritated by accusations of adultery.

We don't approve of domestic violence, nor do we think the wife's actions cancel out men's political power over women in Nuer culture. However, as anthropologist Micaela di Leonardo observes, a husband's authority in the home is not absolute if his wife can insult him and knock his teeth out, and all he can do is demand that his father-in-law fork over a cow!

Many early researchers not only assumed that male dominance and aggression were universally the province of men; they also assumed that female nurturance was universally the province of women. Because of this assumption, Western researchers often overlooked the nurturing activities of men, or even *defined* nurturance in a way that excluded the altruistic, caring actions of men. When anthropologist David Gilmore (1991) examined how cultures around the world define manhood, he expected to find masculinity equated with selfishness and hardness. Instead he found that it often entails selfless generosity and sacrifice. "Women nurture others directly," notes Gilmore. "They do this with their bodies, with their milk and their love. This is very sacrificial and generous. But surprisingly, 'real' men nurture, too, although they would perhaps not be pleased to hear it put this way." Men nurture their families and society, he observes, by "bringing home food for both child and mother . . . and by dying if necessary in faraway places to provide a safe haven for their people" (pp. 229–230).

Our own cultural stereotypes, then, affect what we see in other cultures and how we interpret what we see. Still, a few common themes—not universal, mind you, but common—do emerge from the cross-cultural study of gender. Generally speaking, men have had, and continue to have, more status and more power than women, especially in public affairs. Generally speaking, men have fought the wars and brought home the meat. If a society's economy includes hunting large game, traveling a long way from home, or making weapons, men typically handle these activities. Women have had the primary responsibility for cooking, cleaning, and taking care of small children.

Corresponding with this division of jobs, in many cultures around the world people regard masculinity as something that boys must achieve through strenuous effort. Males must pass physical tests, must endure pain, must confront danger, and must separate psychologically and even physically from their mothers and the world of women. Sometimes they have to prove their self-reliance and courage in bloodcurdling initiation rites. Femininity, in contrast, tends to be associated with responsibility, obedience, and childcare, and it is seen as something that develops naturally, without any special intervention from others.

THE INVENTION OF GENDER

From these commonalities, some theorists have concluded that certain fundamental aspects of gender must be built into our genes. Biological factors—the fact that women are (so far) the only sex that gets pregnant and that men, on the average, have greater upper body strength—undoubtedly play some role in the sexual division of labor in many societies. But biology takes us only so far, because, when we remove our own cultural blinders and look at the full cross-cultural picture, the range of variation among men and women, in what they do and in how they regard one another, is simply astonishing.

For instance, in some places women are and have been completely under the rule of men, an experience reflected in the haunting words of the Chinese poet Fu Hsuan: "How sad it is to be a woman! Nothing on earth is held so cheap." Women in Saudi Arabia today are not allowed to drive a car; many girls in India submit to arranged marriages as early as age nine; girls and women in the Sudan and other parts of Africa are subjected to infibulation (the practice of cutting off the clitoris and much of the labia, and stitching together the vaginal opening), allegedly to assure their virginity at marriage. Yet elsewhere women have achieved considerable power, influence, and sexual independence. Among the Iroquois, some of the older wives played an important role in village politics. Although they could not become members of the Council of Elders, the ruling body, they had a major say in its decisions. In this century, women have been heads of State in England, Israel, India, Sri Lanka, Iceland, and elsewhere.

Thus it is an oversimplification to say that men are the dominant sex, women the subordinate one. The status of women has been assessed by measures of economic security, educational opportunities, access to birth control and medical care, degree of self-determination, participation in public and political life, power to make decisions in the family, and physical safety. According to these indexes, the status of women worldwide is highest in Scandinavian countries and lowest in Bangladesh, with tremendous variation in between.

Similarly, cultures vary in many other aspects of male-female relations:

- The *content* of what is considered "men's work" and "women's work" differs from culture to culture. In some cultures, men weave and women do not; in others, it's the opposite. In many cultures women do the shopping and marketing, but in others marketing is men's work.

- In many cultures, women are considered the "emotional" sex and are permitted to express their emotions more freely than men. But in cultures throughout the Middle East and South America, men are permitted (and expected) to be as emotionally expressive as women, or even more so, whereas many Asian cultures expect *both* sexes to control their emotions. Moreover, the rules about which sex gets to display which emotion are quite variable. In one major international study, Israeli and Italian men were more likely than women to control feelings of sadness, but British, Spanish, Swiss, and German men were *less* likely than women to inhibit this emotion.

- Cultures differ in the degree of daily contact that is permitted between the sexes. In many farm communities and in most modern occupations in North America and Europe, men and women work together in close proximity. At the other end of the continuum, some Middle Eastern societies have a tradition of *purdah,* the veiling of women and the seclusion of wives from all male eyes except those of their relatives.

- In some cultures, as in Iran or the Sudan, women are expected to suppress all sexual feeling (and certainly behavior) until marriage, and premarital or extramarital sex is cause for the woman's ostracism from the community or even death. In others, such as Polynesia, women are expected to have sex before marriage. In still others, such as the Toda of India, women were allowed to have extramarital affairs (as long as they told their husbands and didn't sneak around).

Perhaps no society challenges our usual assumptions about the universal nature of psychological maleness and femaleness as profoundly as Tahiti. For over two centuries, Western visitors to Tahiti have marveled at the lack of sexual differentiation among its peaceful inhabitants. Early European sailors who arrived on the island reported that Tahitian women were free to do just about everything the men did. Women could be chiefs, they could take part in all sports, including wrestling, and they enjoyed casual sex with many different partners.

In the 1960s, anthropologist Robert Levy lived among the Tahitians and confirmed that they didn't share Westerners' ideas about gender. Men in Tahiti were no more aggressive than women, nor were women gentler or more maternal than men. Men felt no obligation to appear "manly" or defend "male honor," and women felt no pressure to be demure and "womanly." The Tahitians seemed to lack what psychologist Sandra Bem has called a "gender schema," a network of assumptions about the personalities and moral qualities of the two sexes. To Tahitians, Levy found, gender was just no big deal. Even the Tahitian language ignores gender: Pronouns are not different for males and females, and most traditional Tahitian names are used for both sexes.

The existence of cultures such as Tahiti, together with the wide variations in gender roles that exist around the world, suggest that the qualities that cultures link with masculinity and femininity are not innately male or female. Instead. they are, in the language of social science, *socially constructed.* As David Gilmore puts it, "gender ideologies are social facts, collective representations that pressure people into acting in certain ways."

WHERE DO THE RULES OF GENDER COME FROM?

When most people read about the customs of other cultures, they are inclined to say, "Oh, boy, I like the sexual attitudes of the Gorks but I hate the nasty habits of the Dorks." The point to keep in mind is that a culture's practices cannot easily be exported elsewhere, like cheese, or surgically removed, like a tumor. *A culture's attitudes and practices regarding gender are deeply embedded in its history, environment economy, and survival needs.*

To understand how a society invents its notions of gender, we need to understand its political system, and its economy, and how that economy is affected by geography, natural resources, and even the weather. We need to know who controls and distributes the resources, and how safe a society is from interlopers. We need to know the kind of work that people do, and how they structure that work. And we need to know whether there is environmental pressure on a group to produce more children, or to have fewer of them. In short, we need to know about *production* and *reproduction.*

For example, David Gilmore found that rigid concepts of manhood tend to exist wherever there is a great deal of competition for resources—which is to say, in most places. For the human species, life has usually been harsh. Consider a tribe trying to survive in the wilds of a South American forest; or in the dry and unforgiving landscape of the desert; or in an icy Arctic terrain that imposes limits on the number of people who can survive by fishing. When conditions like these exist, men are the sex that is taught to hunt for large game, compete with each other for work, and fight off enemies. (As we've noted, this division of labor may originally have occurred because of men's relatively greater upper-body muscular strength and the fact that they do not become pregnant or nurse children.) Men will be socialized to resist the impulse to avoid confrontation and retreat from danger. They will be "toughened up" and pushed to take risks, even with their lives.

How do you get men to do all this? To persuade men to wage war and risk death, argues anthropologist Marvin Harris (1974), societies have to give them something—and the something is prestige, power, and women. That in turn means you have to raise obedient women; if the King is going to offer his daughter in marriage to the bravest warrior, she has to go when given. In contrast, David Gilmore finds, in cultures such as Tahiti, where resources are abundant and there are no serious hazards or enemies to worry about, men don't feel they have to prove themselves or set themselves apart from women.

The economic realities of life also affect how men and women regard each other. Ernestine Friedl has described the remarkable differences between two tribes in New Guinea. One tribe, living in the highlands, believes that intercourse weakens men, that women are dangerous and unclean, and that menstrual blood can do all sorts of terrifying things. Sex is considered powerful and mysterious; if it is performed in a garden, the act will blight the crops. Antagonism between the sexes runs high; men often delay marriage and many remain single. Not far away, another tribe has an opposite view of women and sex. People in this tribe think sexual intercourse is fun and that it revitalizes men. Sex, they say, *should* take place in gardens, as it will foster the growth of plants. Men and women do not live in segregated quarters, as they do in the highlands, and they get along pretty well.

One possible explanation for these differences is that the highland people have been settled a long time and have little new land or resources. If the population increased, food would become scarce. Sexual antagonism and a fear of sexual intercourse help keep the birth rate low. The sexy tribe, however, lives in uncultivated areas and needs more members to work the land and help defend the group. Encouraging positive attitudes toward sex and early marriage is one way to increase the birth rate.

Cross-cultural studies find that when the sexes are mutually dependent and work cooperatively, as in husband-wife teams, sexual antagonism is much lower than when work is organized along sex-segregated lines. Among the Machiguenga Indians of Peru, where the sexes cooperate in growing vegetables, fishing, and recreation, husbands and wives feel more solidarity with each other than with their same-sex friends. Among the Mundurucu, however, women and men work in same-sex groups, and friendships rarely cross sexual lines; women therefore feel a sense of solidarity, with other women, men with men.

In our own culture, changing conditions have profoundly influenced our ideas about gender as well as our family relationships. According to Francesca Cancian (1987), before the nineteenth century, the typical household was a cooperative rural community in which both spouses shared responsibility for the material and emotional well-being of the family. Men didn't "go to work"; work was right there, and so was the family. Women raised both chickens and children. This is not to say that the two sexes had equal rights in the public domain, but in psychological terms they were not seen as opposites.

But with the onset of the industrial revolution, shops and factories began to replace farming, and many men began to work apart from their families. This major economic change, argues Cancian, created a rift between "women's sphere," at home, and "men's sphere," at work. The masculine ideal adjusted to fit the new economic realities, which now required male competitiveness and the suppression of any signs of emotional "weakness." The feminine ideal became its opposite: Women were now seen as being "naturally" nurturant, emotional, and fragile.

WHAT'S AHEAD?

In the twentieth century, two profound changes in production and reproduction are occurring that have never before happened in human history. Most jobs in industrial nations, including military jobs, now involve service skills and brainwork rather than physical strength. Reproduction, too, has been revolutionized; although women in many countries still lack access to safe and affordable contraceptives, it is now possible for women to limit reliably the number of children they will have and to plan when to have them. The "separate spheres" doctrine spawned by the industrial revolution is breaking down in this post-industrial age, which requires the labor of both sexes.

As these changes unfold, ideas about the "natural" qualities of men and women are also being transformed. It is no longer news that a woman can run a country, be a Supreme Court justice or a miner, or walk in space. It is no longer news that many men,

whose own fathers would no more have diapered a baby than jumped into a vat of boiling oil, now want to be involved fathers.

What a cross-cultural, historical perspective teaches us, then, is that gender arrangements, and the qualities associated with being male and female, are not arbitrary. Our ideas about gender are affected by the practical conditions of our lives. These conditions are far more influential than our hormones in determining whether men are expected to be fierce or gentle, and whether women are expected to be financially helpless or Wall Street whizzes.

The cross-cultural perspective reminds us too that no matter how entrenched our own notions of masculinity and femininity are, they can be expected to change—as the kind of work we do changes, as technology changes, and as our customs change. Yet many intriguing questions remain. Do men and women need to feel that they are psychologically different from one another in some way? Will masculinity always rest on male achievements and actions, and femininity on merely being female? Since most of us cannot move to Tahiti, but must live in a world in which wars and violence persist, is it wise or necessary to make sure that at least one sex—or only one sex—is willing to do the dangerous work?

Marvin Harris has argued that male supremacy was "just a phase in the evolution of culture," a phase that depended on the ancient division of labor that put men in charge of war and women in charge of babies. Harris predicts that by the 21st century, male supremacy will fade and gender equality will become, for the first time in history, a real possibility.

Is he right? How will gender be constructed by our own culture in the next century? What do you think?

REFERENCES

Cancian, Francesca (1987). *Love in America: Gender and self-development.* Cambridge, England: Cambridge University Press.

Gilmore, David (1991). *Manhood in the making.* New Haven, CT: Yale University Press.

Harris, Marvin (1974). *Cows, pigs, wars, and witches: The riddles of culture.* New York: Random House.

Herdt, Gilbert H. (1984). *Ritualized homosexuality in Melanesia.* Berkeley: University of California Press.

Kimmel. Michael S. (1987). *Changing men: New directions in research on men and masculinity.* Beverly Hills, CA: Sage.

Tavris, Carol (1992). *The mismeasure of woman.* New York: Simon & Schuster.

CHECKPOINTS

1. Wade and Tavris argue that gender is constructed by culture and related to specific features of cultures.
2. Researchers have interpreted their observations of different cultures in terms of their cultural prescriptions about gender.
3. Two features that are related to the status of women in a society are access to means of production and control over reproduction.

To prepare for reading the next section, think about these questions:

1. What would an egalitarian society be like?
2. On what basis would you compare a remote, isolated, horticultural society to the mobile, technological society of the United States?

THE INFLUENCE OF CULTURE ON BEHAVIOR—THE CASE OF AGGRESSION

Women, Men, and Aggression in an Egalitarian Society[1]

MARIA LEPOWSKY[2]
University of Wisconsin, Madison

Vanatinai, a small island society off New Guinea, is egalitarian, with no indigenous formal systems of rank or authority. Assertiveness and autonomy are highly valued as personal qualities and equivalent for males and females. Overt aggression is condemned and violence is rare. Women were the aggressors in four out of five incidents over ten years. Sexual jealousy was the dominant motif in all five cases. This article considers, in historical contexts, indigenous concepts of the gendered person and their relations to anger, violence, and the supernatural aggression of sorcery and witchcraft. The Vanatinai case is evidence that the rarity of intragroup violence, especially of attacks by men on women, is a characteristic of egalitarian societies.

Vanatinai is a small and remote island in the South Pacific, where women still wear coconut leaf skirts, and where men and women alike sail outrigger ca-noes to distant islands, seeking the shell-disc necklaces and axe blades of polished greenstone exchanged in feasts honoring the dead. Part of the independent nation of Papua New Guinea, the island, which lies about 200 miles southeast of the New Guinea mainland, is also a striking contrast to Western societies because of the absence of any indigenous ideologies of male superiority or of any formal authority of men over women.

Except through colonial legal systems and, since 1975, national law, sporadically enforced by outsiders such as government officers, nobody on Vanatinai has a recognized right to tell another adult what to do. Both girls and boys are socialized to be confident and assertive. Unmarried young people have equal rights to control their own sexual behavior. Women choose their own marriage partners and can divorce at will. Women and men have equivalent control of their own persons. Women are central to the island's matrilineal kinship system and are considered to be the "owners of the gardens," controlling the distribution of most staple foods. As adults, both sexes can, if they want to, accumulate ceremonial valuables from exchange partners and then host lavish feasts. By giving away enormous quantities of food and valuables they earn the gender-blind title of *gia,* literally, "giver," or big woman/big man. The same personal qualities of strength, wisdom, and generosity are admired in both women and men.

Ideologies of power are inherently gendered because those who exercise power, or who are supposed to, are gendered beings. In all societies, most of the sacred and religious powers that justify or potentiate the powers of humans have a gender valence as well. In a culture with prevailing ideologies of gender equality, no indigenous system of formal authority, and a high value on assertiveness and personal autonomy for both sexes, do concepts of female and male personal power differ? What happens when these strong-willed, autonomous people have conflicts?

I focus here on gendered constructions of the person and personal power as revealed by physical aggression and by the supernatural attacks of sorcery and witchcraft. The example of Vanatinai in the late twentieth century generally supports the position that overt anger—and the physical aggression with which it is often associated—are less prevalent in egalitarian societies (see Burbank, this issue; Myers, 1988). But I further argue that we must place our cultural examples in historical contexts.

In the case of Vanatinai, we need to examine the implications for gender ideologies and roles related to aggression of the British and Australian colonial suppression of indigenous warfare. Even though the position of the island on the distant periphery of two colonial empires and a nation-state have resulted in relatively little surveillance of and interference with island affairs, the imposition of colonial and national legal codes have made indigenous warfare and intra-hamlet violence criminal behavior. One consequence has been an efflorescence of supernatural aggression through sorcery and witchcraft (Lepowsky, 1993).

Overt physical aggression by either men or women is extremely rare on Vanatinai. Since 1943, in

a population of about 2000, there has been one murder by a Vanatinai person: in the 1950s a man hit his wife in a jealous rage and killed her, then tried to weight her body in the lagoon. Also in the 1950s an Australian trader went berserk and killed two island men with a shotgun. Both killers were reported to Australian colonial authorities, charged with murder, and sentenced to prison. I have never observed or heard about two men engaged in a physical fight. Nor have I heard of or seen two children, of either sex, in a physical fight. These are significant negative instances, compared to any representative eighteen months of residence in a North American or European community, that suggest the distinct absence of any "culture of violence" on Vanatinai. A tolerance for overt interpersonal violence seems to correlate cross-culturally with a widespread prevalence of violence against women (Levinson, 1989, 40–45, 84; Mitchell, 1992, 90; Tracy and Crawford, 1992, 30).

On Vanatinai physical abuse of a woman by any man, including her husband, is very unusual, and it is abhorred. Levinson (1989, 84), based on a cross-cultural study of ninety small-scale and peasant societies, concludes that "gender-based economic inequality," along with a general propensity toward "violent conflict resolution," are the key contextual factors in societal patterns of widespread violence against wives. The rarity or absence of violence against women has in itself been suggested as a significant index cross-culturally of high female autonomy or the absence of a male supremacist complex (Schlegel, 1972; Divale and Harris, 1976; Sanday, 1981; cf. Lepowsky, 1990a).

In more than a decade since my first field research, I have only heard about five acts of violence. While others may well have occurred, it seems to be highly unusual behavior. Of these five incidents, four of the aggressors were women, two attacking other women and two their husbands. The fifth was a man who hit his wife. In four of the cases, the aggressors felt the strong social disapproval of neighbors and the shame of their own kinspeople, and they feared retaliation through supernatural attack by the victim's kin. I explain the reasons for the one exception below. The government Officer-in-Charge, in each case a man from another part of Papua New Guinea residing at the government station twenty miles away, never heard about any of these acts of violence, all of them crimes under the legal code inherited from Australian colonial administration at independence.

The motif of sexual jealousy runs through all of these incidents. This is congruent with the finding in Victoria Burbank's (1987) cross-cultural study of female aggression that female "rivals in sex and marriage are the most common victims" (cf. Kerns, 1992, 128) and that husbands are the most common male targets of female attacks. Male sexual jealousy, and male accusations of female adultery or sexual infractions, are among the most common precursors of acts of violence against women in all human societies (Daly and Wilson, 1988, 200; Levinson, 1989, 34, 84; Brown, 1992, 3–4, 8; Campbell, 1992, 235, 245).

The first violent incident I heard about on Vanatinai occurred after I had lived on the island for some months. A woman I knew, in her early twenties — call her Urupo (all names in this article have been changed)—had been having an adulterous intrigue. Women, and men, often use their friends as third parties to arrange rendezvous, and I had heard Urupo discussing details with a mutual woman friend, who was reluctant to get involved because she liked Urupo's husband. I had also seen Urupo meet another lover a month earlier one night when we were at a feast in another hamlet and all sleeping in the same house. One morning, her husband came into the house where I lived with a local family with his wrist broken and an ugly, infected burn on his chest. The night before, Urupo had flown into a jealous rage, accusing her husband of meeting a lover, which he repeatedly denied. Finally she seized a burning brand from the fire, struck him hard on the wrist, and then lunged forward and burned him.

The neighbors were appalled, and her kinfolk were ashamed. Public opinion held that the husband was innocent and that Urupo, in fact, was the adulterer, who suspected him of her own wrongdoing, an indigenous model of projection. Her kin and friends were also afraid, not of physical retaliation but of the supernatural retaliation of his mother's witchcraft on the violent and adulterous wife, whom the mother had never liked. The couple divorced the following year.

Unmarried people are expected to have many lovers, but married people have exclusive sexual rights over one another. Many marriages, especially those of people in their twenties, break up because one or the other spouse cannot make this transition and continues to seduce others or respond to their invitations. Both women and men make sexual propositions.

Success in love is believed due to the practice of love magic, by either sex, that makes a person dazzlingly attractive and renders others negenege, or dizzy with desire, and helpless to defend themselves against the will of the seducer. Human powers in all types of magic, sorcery, and witchcraft flow primarily from a person's secret knowledge of how to gain the assistance of male and female ancestor spirits or place spirits (see Lepowsky, 1993).

The principle of seduction also operates in the magic of ceremonial exchange. Vanatinai and neighboring islands are part of a regional, interisland system of ritual exchange linking people speaking a dozen different languages. They travel by sailing canoe in quest of ceremonial valuables such as shell-disc necklaces and greenstone axe blades as well as pigs, baskets of yams, clay pots, and other household goods. This exchange network was made famous in anthropology by the pioneering work of Bronislaw Malinowski (1922) in 1915–1918 in the Trobriand Islands, 300 miles northwest of Vanatinai, where it is known as kula. On Vanatinai, exchange visitors, male and female, beautify themselves and use magic, based on the power of ancestor and other spirits, to render the host and exchange partner of either sex negenge and eager to part with a prized valuable, metaphorically the genitals of a seduced lover. Vanatinai magic, then, which also underlies success in gardening, healing, and all other important endeavors, often operates on the principle of aggressive intrusion into the person and subversion of the will of another. I will come back to this point.

A second incident, again of a woman striking her husband, is the exception I mentioned to the pattern of shame and disgust with violent behavior felt by kinspeople and neighbors. In this case, a middle-aged man, well known throughout the region for his success in ceremonial exchange, announced to his wife of twenty years that he planned to take a second wife, a slightly younger widow with whom he had been having an affair. Polygyny is permissible on Vanatinai, but it is rare, and the man must have his wife's consent to take a co-wife. As in this instance, the permission is not always forthcoming. Furious, the wife hit her husband once with her hand, without injuring him, and told him that he was welcome to take another wife, but that if he did, she was leaving him. The man never did take a second wife, and in fact he ended his affair. This story was told to me by a witness, a young kinswoman of the wife, who recounted it in tones of admiration (with a tinge of amusement) for a woman who asserted herself. If the wife had actually injured her husband, I think her kinspeople would have been ashamed of her behavior, even though they believed she acted with provocation.

Neither of the Vanatinai cases of violence against a husband occurred in the context of a "mutually violent relationship or in self-defense" as postulated by Campbell (1992, 230–32) and Levinson (1989) based upon comparisons of human societies cross-culturally. Violence against husbands may well be related to, or triggered by, wife abuse where there is a well-developed "culture of violence" and where spouse abuse is more common and more tolerated, but it was not in these two rare incidents, both triggered by female sexual jealousy, on Vanatinai.

In two other incidents of violence, which I recount below, a woman attacked "the other woman" with whom her husband or lover was having an affair. In the last incident, a man accused his wife of adultery and then punched her once in the jaw, loosening her teeth. Again, as in the first case of the violent wife, public opinion held that the violent spouse, the husband, was the adulterous one and the victim was innocent. (I myself saw the husband slip away into the darkness with a young widow during the midnight dancing at a feast a few months earlier).

The man was publicly shamed by his kin later, and many of his neighbors avoided him long afterward, a person revealed as volatile and dangerous. The woman left her husband for a while, taking her young children, but then the couple reconciled. They remained married for several more years with no further episodes of violence but finally divorced. Neither has remarried.

My view of Vanatinai is located at a particular historical moment, in the late twentieth century. A hundred years ago there was a gold rush on the island and, as a result, in 1888, the new colony of British New Guinea was annexed. (It became the Australian Territory of Papua in 1906.) In the usual imperial irony, the British immediately began asserting their exclusive right to aggressive behavior (using naval cannons and the occasional hanging), and they believed that warfare among islanders was suppressed by 1888. In fact, raids continued until as late as 1942, after the Battle of the Coral Sea, fought in the seas and skies of the archipelago between the Japanese and the Americans and Australians (Lepowsky 1989, 1990b, 1993).

Nevertheless, the former male role of *asiara,* or champion warrior, was by mid-century an avenue to prestige and influence for younger men—one that excluded all women as well as male elders—that belonged to a legendary past. Interpretations of the past made by people in the present emphasize not the attacks of the *asiara* of old against others but their heroic defense of kinfolk and neighbors against attacks by men of other districts and other islands.

Men and women tell you today, "Before we killed with spears. Now we kill with sorcery." What is now prevalent on Vanatinai is supernatural violence. Vanatinai is known for hundreds of miles as the home of powerful sorcerers. Almost every death, serious illness, or injury is said to be due to sorcery or, more rarely, witchcraft. These are two separate magical traditions. Sorcerers, called *ribiroi,* or poisoner, after one of their killing techniques, are mostly male. Female *ribiroi* wear the customary male dress of a decorated palm leaf drawn between the legs and secured with a cord around the hips. Sorcery is a conscious and malevolent practice of destruction that usually involves the firing of magical projectiles" into a victim's body or the manipulation of personal leavings (but not physical poisoning, these days). It is based on the power of ancestor spirits and place spirits, petitioned through secret magical spells learned in a long apprenticeship.

Most witches are female. Chronic or wasting illnesses are generally attributed to witchcraft. Witches leave their bodies behind, seemingly sleeping or dozing, while their spirits fly to distant hamlets and islands, sometimes visible at sea trying to capsize a sailing canoe or on land perching on the roof of a victim's house. They often attack a person's entrails, leaving him or her to die slowly. A witch will either eat her victim or bring the body to other witches at a supernatural cannibal feast, the way humans bring pigs, and the others will owe her a debt of human flesh, mirroring the normal rules of exchange. Witches also attack their own children and matrilineal kin, a terrifying supernatural subversion of the nurturing roles of mother and matrilineal kinswoman. People say that your kinfolk own you and can either nurture or kill you. Witchcraft is generally inherited from mother to daughter. But witches also act consciously, learning their trade from others, male and female, stealing a victim's image in a stream or mirror, or seeking revenge in anger (for more on sorcery and witchcraft see Lepowsky, 1990c, 1993).

Women accused, markedly less often than men, of destructive magic after deaths or misfortunes befall the community, are usually called witches, not sorcerers. On one peaceful afternoon I saw a two year old boy, the son of a friend, stumbling after the bigger children in the hamlet plaza. By midnight he was dead. We found out shortly afterward when we woke, frightened and groggy, to the eerie cries of ritual wailing piercing the silence of a moonless night. We dressed hastily and ran up the hill, following the sound, to the house where the little boy lay dead surrounded by his distraught relatives.

That evening, we learned, the child had developed a high fever and gone into convulsions, dying hours later from what sounded to me like cerebral malaria. The shock of this sudden death demanded explanation, and my neighbors almost immediately began to piece the story together. Iviowa, his young mother, was separated from her husband. Just a few days earlier she had marched grimly into another hamlet

about a mile away and publicly confronted a young divorcée who lived there. Flying into a rage, Iviowa accused the other woman of having sex with her husband and trying to steal him away from her. Then Iviowa began hitting the young woman on the face and body until she was pulled off by the woman's mother. News of this ugly incident had traveled quickly to all the nearby hamlets and had horrified and disturbed everyone. Iviowa's kinfolk had been deeply ashamed. Now it was clear to all that her little boy had been killed as a result, probably through witchcraft. The most likely killer was not the other woman but the woman's mother, well known for her knowledge of custom and ritual, although never previously accused of, or thought to know, witchcraft by her neighbors.

The child was buried the next day. I heard Iviowa's father say to her, in a low and passionate voice, "You see, I warned you to curb your temper. Now you see what you have caused." Iviowa, in a trance of grief, seemed not to hear. A few minutes later she had to be physically prevented by her brother and other kinsmen from throwing herself into the little boy's grave.

Iviowa and her husband have reconciled and separated several times since then. When I last saw her a few years ago, she had a small daughter, but she and her husband were living apart.

This tragic story was read by my neighbors as a parable about the dangers of aggression. It did not matter that Iviowa's husband was probably sleeping with the pretty divorcée. Iviowa should not have assaulted or even confronted her. It was a selfish act because it exposed her little boy to a retaliatory supernatural attack. This is the kind of reason why both men and women with young children do not usually become highly visible in ceremonial exchange at that life stage. They would inevitably excite the envy and rage of a rival and expose not only themselves but their children to sorcery or witchcraft.

What Iviowa should have done, I was told, was acquire some especially potent love magic to defeat her rival and lure her husband's mind until his thoughts were occupied only with her. Magic, then, even when it is beneficial to you, is often a supernatural form of aggression that subverts the autonomy and will of others.

The last case of physical aggression I know of involved a fifty year old woman, Bwaragha, who was widely regarded as one of the most powerful people in the district. She was the most knowledgeable person in her lineage, performing the public, ritual prayers to ancestor spirits at communal yam plantings. This is the analogue to the well-known ethnographic example of the Trobriand Island yam garden magician, with the significant difference that Trobriand garden magicians are exclusively male (Malinowski, 1935).

Bwaragha also knew sorcery and witchcraft. She flouted the basic rule of Vanatinai custom by living openly with a man who, by my reckoning, was her matrilineal second cousin but by local perception was her own uncle. A few years later, this man began an affair with a widow in her forties (he confided in a relative, who told me). Those of us who knew about it, who also included people in the widow's hamlet, some miles away, kept quiet, either from general discretion or out of fear of Bwaragha's rage.

But one day she walked down out of the mountains and through the coastal swamp to the widow's house and found her sitting outside on the ground with her neighbors. Those who were there say Bwaragha violently attacked her. The most shocking thing she did was to deliberately mutilate the younger woman by ripping away the lobe of her ear. People's ears are pierced in infancy, and it is a mark of attractiveness in both men and women to wear a row of small round tortoise-shell earrings. By middle age there is a large hole in the ear and the lobe droops with the weight of the earrings. This looks especially beautiful, according to custom, and this is what Bwaragha tore.

Bwaragha's act of rage was that of a person confident she could withstand the retaliatory sorcery and witchcraft sure to follow her violent attack. Even her close kin were horrified and, of course, deeply ashamed. But she was used to ignoring the censure of others, for she lived in what they all saw as an incestuous union. Her man stopped seeing the widow and continued to live with Bwaragha for the rest of her life.

When I would ask why most sorcerers were men, or why women should not hunt with spears, people would explain, "Because women are the ones who give life and men the ones who take it." This is a common, though far from universal, theme in human philosophies of gender (cf. Rosaldo and Atkinson, 1975). But one of the most significant contradictions in Vanatinai gender ideologies is between this often-stated ideal of woman as life-giver and the belief that women kill through witchcraft and, more rarely and in male dress, as sorcerers.

Vanatinai images of females, particularly of mothers, can be multivalent and contradictory. The witch subverts two closely related and cherished images: those of the nurturing and life-giving mother and of the sheltering and protecting matrilineage. A witch kills and eats her victims, who are prototypically her own children or people of her own matrilineage. In this she is committing the ultimate anti-social act, making her children into food and devouring them instead of giving them food and caring for them (cf. Munn, 1986).

In Vanatinai custom witchcraft comes from somewhere else, the islands that stretch immediately to the northwest. It is the women of other places, people say, who are more likely to attack their own kinfolk. But this belief coexists with the attribution of witchcraft powers to many Vanatinai women, both prominent and weak, elders and unmarried young. Paradoxically, this power, like the power of male sorcery, simultaneously inspires fear and protects its suspected possessor, and her or his associates, from the physical and supernatural violence of others.

Both sorcery and witchcraft are projections of the person, the ultimate aggressive violations of the autonomy of others. The witch leaves the boundaries of her body behind and flies over great distances to attack, invading her victim's body and eating the entrails. The sorcerer hides his body with invisibility magic, or uses powerful spells to assume the shape of a snake. He knows special traveling magic to transport himself almost instantly from his home, or a secret spot in the forest, to the other side of the island. Sorcerers fire projectiles into the bodies of their victims, or invade them with poison. Both sorcerers and witches kill for the selfish and perverse pleasure of feeling their own power.

Theirs is the ultimate personal autonomy played out in the imposition of one individual will upon another. Nancy Munn (1986, 233) writes of Gawa Island, some 200 miles to the north, that "Gawans experience the individualistic egalitarianism of their society, as domination, in the shape of the witch." On Vanatinai as well, a strong cultural emphasis on personal autonomy and the strength of individual will, in a society with no indigenous formal authority, appears as the coercion of the individual sorcerer or witch. Thus, even though islanders frequently say that women are the givers of life and men the givers of death, both male and female, father and mother are simultaneously symbols of nurture and destruction.

The identification of woman as life-giver is further at odds with women's hunting of small animals such as marsupials and monitor lizards—the only restriction on female hunting is that they may not hunt with spears. Women also participated, in earlier generations, in war magic, the field of battle, and decisions to make war, as well as to make peace or give compensation. This is epitomized in the ultimate female signal to start, or stop; a battle: a woman untying and throwing her outer skirt on the ground between male antagonists. In an archetypal image of woman as peace-maker, which does fit nicely into the theme of woman as life-giver, if a son or brother persisted in throwing his spear, my friends said, and metaphorically pierced her skirt, it would be as if he were committing incest. He would be too ashamed and would have to contain his anger. But the same dramatic female sign of the skirt flung on the ground is also a signal for attack.

A man in his role as father is a life-giving and nurturing figure on Vanatinai. His cumulative acts of love and generosity to his children, who belong to a different matrilineage, are ritually compensated for after his death when his children give shell-disc necklaces and greenstone axe blades to the father's matrilineal heirs. Nevertheless, in island gender ideologies, men are, and were, closely associated with death and violence, through warfare, hunting, and sorcery, epitomized by the exclusively male symbols of the forcefully thrown spear of the warrior and hunter and the magical projectile of the sorcerer that penetrates his victim's body.

Before the coming of Europeans, physical aggression, through intergroup violence, was much more prevalent, although violence against women, people tell me, has always been rare, and heavily sanctioned. In fact, the last interhamlet violence on southwestern Vanatinai took place early in this century after a man struck his wife on the head and severely injured her, causing bleeding from her nose, mouth, and ears. Her kinsmen, in revenge, killed not only the husband but all of his nearby relatives, except for one small boy, his nephew, and one woman. The little boy was later tricked into eating a mouthful of his own mother's brother, whose body had been cooked by the victors for a ritual cannibal feast. The wife's kin offered compensation (three shell-disc necklaces, thirty greenstone axe blades, and ten poles of processed sago starch) to members of the husband's clan who lived in other settlements to ward off retaliation. But their compensation payment was rejected, and the attackers and all of their kinspeople living with them were slaughtered in a surprise attack, except for two women who managed to escape. None of this bloodshed appears in the sparse colonial records of the time, when the island was only visited by colonial officers two or three times each decade. This cautionary tale of the danger of open aggression, and the cycle of violence it may initiate, which involves the grandparents of people in middle age today, also shows the error of making unqualified statements about the lack of violence on Vanatinai, or anywhere else, without specifying historical periods and political contexts.

Strathern (1988) emphasizes the value of close attention to indigenous constructions of male and female sociality for making sense of local gender relations. The image of the warrior used to be the most dramatically and exclusively male on Vanatinai. Nowadays, apart from the public one of the nurturing and loving father, it is that of the sorcerer, alone in the forest gathering herbs and leaves for his secret spells, walking, cloaked by invisibility magic, his breath scented with ginger, to the shore on moonless nights to drink saltwater, hoarding betel nut skins left on the ground by a careless victim, and firing fishbones or shell discs into a rival's body. People often say their own kinsmen use magical knowledge as counter-sorcery, through traditional healing or as protection from the attacks of others, just as the warriors of earlier generations are remembered today as heroic defenders rather than aggressors. But Vanatinai people live in constant dread of sorcery, as English gold miner David White wrote in 1893, and the sorcerer is the essence of socially unmediated masculinity, a taker of life (see Lepowsky 1993 for a more detailed discussion of Vanatinai gender symbolism).

In Vanatinai constructions of the gendered person, males and females experience equally strong emotions of envy, jealousy, frustrated desire, and rage. There is no perception that a man's feelings of anger are any stronger than a woman's. But both men and women, unlike small children, should learn to control not the internal experience of anger but its public expression in angry words or violent behavior (cf. Briggs, 1970). The very word for anger, *gaizi,* also means war.

Even angry words are dangerous, for they signal the desire to commit violence through supernatural attack. They will trigger the anger of their hearer, who is likely to seek revenge or compensation for his or her rage or humiliation through sorcery or witchcraft. The option of supernatural violence, available to both men and women on Vanatinai, is a way of sublimating public anger and avoiding open interpersonal violence.[3]

A distinctive characteristic of Vanatinai understandings of the person is the notion that it is impossible to know what another is thinking. It is therefore impossible to explain overt behavior by reference to someone else's private thoughts. Both men and women are assumed to experience strong emotions of anger and desire, but this is their business, "something of theirs," as people say. And both sexes act on these emotions at times through covert use of love or exchange magic that subverts the will of another or through acts of sorcery and witchcraft. This channeling of anger and frustration into supernatural acts of aggression, and the strong fear of supernatural attacks by others, are Vanatinai people's explanations for why there is so little physical aggression on the island.

In spite of the historical particulars of the Vanatinai case, and its distinctively Melanesian cultural flavor, the example of Vanatinai offers evidence that the rarity of intragroup violence, especially of attacks by men on women, is a characteristic of egalitarian societies.

NOTES

1. An earlier version of this paper was read at the Session on Female Aggression at the American Anthropological Association Annual Meeting, Chicago, in November 1991. I would like to thank session participants, Douglas Fry, Victoria Burbank, Robert Lepowsky, Florence Lepowsky, and the anonymous reviewers for *Sex Roles* for their helpful comments at various points. The fieldwork in Papua New Guinea on which this paper is based was carried out over a total of eighteen months in 1977–1979, 1981, and 1987. 1 gratefully acknowledge the financial support of the National Science Foundation, Chancellor's Patent Fund and Department of Anthropology of the University of California, Berkeley, the Papua New Guinea Institute of Applied Social and Economic Research, the National Institute of Child Health and Human Development of the National Institutes of Health, the Wenner-Gren Foundation, and the Graduate School of the University of Wisconsin, Madison.

2. To whom correspondence should be addressed at Department of Anthropology, University of Wisconsin, Madison, 1180 Observatory Drive, Madison, WI 53706.

3. The incidence of violence against women is also reported as low in four other small-scale societies where the possibility of supernatural attack is a culturally validated option for both sexes: the Garifuna of Belize (Kerns, 1992, 127, 131, 133), the islanders of Mayotte, in the Western Indian Ocean (Lambek, 1992, 159–60), the islanders of Ujelang, in Micronesia (Carucci, 1992, 113, 119–20), and the Wape of New Guinea (Mitchell, 1992, 92–93).

REFERENCES

Briggs, J. (1970). *Never in anger: Portrait of an Eskimo family.* Cambridge, MA: Harvard University Press.

Brown, J. (1992). Introduction: Definitions, assumptions, themes, and issues. In D. Counts, J. Brown, & J. Campbell (Eds.), *Sanctions and sanctuary: Cultural perspectives on the beating of wives.* Boulder, CO: Westview Press.

Burbank, V. (1987). Female aggression in cross-cultural perspective. *Behavior Science Research 21,* 70–100.

Burbank, V. (1994). Cross-Cultural Perspectives on Aggression in Women and Girls: An Introduction. *Sex Roles, 30,* 169–176.

Campbell, J. (1992). Wife-battering: Cultural contexts versus Western social science. In D. Counts, J. Brown, & J. Campbell (Eds.), *Sanctions and sanctuary: Cultural perspectives on the beating of wives.* Boulder, CO: Westview Press.

Carucci, L. (1992). Nudging her harshly and killing him softly: Displays of disenfranchisement on Ujelang atoll. In D. Counts, J. Brown, & J. Campbell (Eds.), *Sanctions and sanctuary: Cultural perspectives on the beating of wives.* Boulder, CO. Westview Press.

Daly, M., & Wilson. M. (1988). *Homicide.* New York: Aldine de Gruyter.

Divale, W., & Harris, M. (1976). Population, warfare, and the male supremacist complex. *American Anthropologist, 78,* 521–538.

Kerns, V. (1992). Preventing violence against women: A Central American case. In D. Counts, J. Brown, & J. Campbell (Eds.), *Sanctions and sanctuary: Cultural perspectives of the beating of wives.* Boulder, CO: Westview Press.

Lambek, M. (1992). Like tooth biting tongue: The proscription and practice of spouse abuse in Mayotte. In D. Counts, J. Brown, & J. Campbell (Ed.), *Sanctions and sanctuary: Cultural perspectives on the beating of wives.* Boulder, CO: Westview Press.

Lepowsky, M. (1989). Soldiers and spirits: The impact of World War II on a Coral Sea island. In G. White & L. Lindstrom (Eds.), *The Pacific theater: Island representations of World War II.* Pacific Monograph Series Volume 8. Honolulu University of Hawaii Press.

Lepowsky, M. (1990a). Gender in an egalitarian society: Lessons from a Coral Sea island. In P. Sanday & R. Goodenough (Eds.), *Beyond the second sex: New directions in the anthropology of gender.* Philadelphia: University of Pennsylvania Press.

Lepowsky, M. (1990b). Big men, big women, and cultural autonomy. *Ethnology, 29,* 35–50.

Lepowsky, M. (1990c). Sorcery and penicillin: treating illness on a Papua New Guinea island. *Social Science and Medicine, 30,* 1049–1063.

Lepowsky, M. (1993). *Fruit of the motherland: Gender in an egalitarian society.* New York: Columbia University Press.

Levinson, D. (1989). *Family violence in cross-cultural perspective.* Newbury Park, CA: Sage Publications.

Malinowski, B. (1922). *Argonauts of the Western Pacific.* New York: E. P. Dutton.

Malinowski, B. (1935).*Coral gardens and their magic* (Two volumes). New York: American Book Company.

Mitchell, W. (1992). Why Wape men don't beat their wives: Constraints toward domestic tranquility in a New Guinea society. In D. Counts, J. Brown, & J. Campbell (Eds.), *Sanctions and sanctuary: Cultural perspectives on the beating of wives.* Boulder, CO: Westview Press.

Munn, N. (1986). *The fame of Gawa: A symbolic study of value transformation in a Massim {Papua New Guinea) society.* Cambridge: Cambridge University Press.

Myers, F. (1988). The logic and meaning of anger among Pintupi Aborigines. *Man, 23,* 589–610.

Rosaldo, M., & Atkinson, J. (1975). Man the hunter and woman: Metaphors for the sexes in Ilongot magical spells. In R. Willis (Ed.), *The interpretation of symbolism.* New York: John Wiley.

Sanday, P. (1981). *Female power and male dominance: On the origins of sexual inequality.* Cambridge: Cambridge University Press.

Schlegel, A. (1972). *Male dominance and female autonomy: Domestic authority in matrilineal societies.* New Haven, CT: HRAF Press.

Strathern, M. (1988). *The gender of the gift: Problems with women and problems with society in Melanesia.* Berkeley: University of California Press.

Tracy, K., & Crawford, C. (1992). Wife abuse: Does it have an evolutionary origin? In D. Counts, J. Brown, & J. Campbell (Eds.), *Sanctions and sanctuary: Cultural perspectives on the beating of wives.* Boulder, CO: Westview Press.

White, D. (1893). Descriptive account by David L. White, Esquire, of the customs, etc. of the natives of Sudest Island. *British New Guinea Annual Reports,* Appendix U. 73–76.

CHECKPOINTS

1. Men and women on Vanatinai are socialized to be independent and confident. Both are thought to experience anger, jealousy, and sexual desire and to channel these strong emotions appropriately.

2. Magic, sorcery, and witchcraft are used to control aggressive impulses and sexual jealousy. Very few incidents of physical aggression occur among the Vanatinai people.

To prepare for reading the next section, think about these questions:

1. What is masculinity in the United States?

2. Does identity as a man of color in the United States, alter a man's perception of masculinity?

3. How could masculinity cause psychological pain?

CULTURE AND VARIATIONS IN GENDER ROLES

Men of Color: Ethnocultural Variations of Male Gender Role Strain

RICHARD F. LAZUR AND RICHARD MAJORS

INTRODUCTION

Male gender roles vary from race to race and from culture to culture (Kimmel & Messner, 1992). They vary as a man develops, matures, and acquires his place in the world. Yet despite this social constructionist understanding, men of color have often been overlooked in the study of male gender roles and their effects upon the quality of life. This chapter examines how men of four cultures of color in the United States—African-American, Latino, American-Indian,[1] and Asian-American—express gender role strain. From the social constructionist perspective, it addresses how these men remain true to their cultural values while adapting to the demands of the dominant society.

Constrained by economic roadblocks and societal discrimination, men of color are frequently considered foreigners by the dominant culture. Often limited by educational opportunities, they are subtly but effectively kept in a subservient status. To be a man of color means confrontation between ethnic identity and demands from the popular culture. Power, success, and even providing for his family are defined within the context of the dominant racial and cultural belief systems. Reconciling cultural and male identities with economic and social obstacles is critical for men of color.

Among ethnic groups, certain attitudes and behaviors are valued and expected among the members. To belong, an individual adopts these perspectives and behaviors. While individual men integrate the male gender role in their own unique ways, the culture of the ethnic group offers survival techniques to guard against inferior status and feelings of oppression. African-American males have adopted distinctive actions and attitudes known as "cool pose" (Majors, 1983, 1986, 1988, 1990, 1991, 1994; Majors &

Mancini Billson, 1992). Emphasizing honor, virility, and physical strength, the Latino male adheres to a code of machismo (Ruiz, 1981; Stevens, 1973; Valdés, Barón, & Ponce, 1987). The American-Indian male struggles to maintain contact with a way of life and the traditions of elders while faced with economic castration and political trauma (Braveheart-Jordan, 1993; Schacht, 1993; Schroeder, 1991). Asian-American men resolve their uncertainty privately, in order to save face, and surrender personal autonomy to family obligations and needs (Huang & Ying, 1989, Sue & Sue, 1993). While individual differences and wide variations exist within social classes, these characteristics reflect male gender role strain and socialization across these four cultures of color in the United States.

In his seminal work, *The Myth of Masculinity* (1981), Pleck examined traditionally held beliefs about male gender roles and offers an alternative paradigm from which to view them. From a social constructionist perspective, Pleck suggested that gender roles are operationally defined by widely shared beliefs about what these roles should be. Both men and women maintain notions of what the expected behaviors are for their own and the opposite sex. However, work and family demands make it difficult, if not impossible, to strictly adhere to these prescriptive behaviors. Gender roles are contradictory and inconsistent. Pleck observed that violations frequently occur, and that when they do, they incur social condemnation. This consequence causes people to overconform. He also noted that certain prescribed characteristics, like male aggression and emotional inhibition, are dysfunctional and provoke negative psychological consequences.

Being a man reflects an individual psychology that has integrated attitudes and behaviors from a lifetime of interaction with the world. If a man's personal world encompasses a dominant culture different from his own, he must acknowledge the similarities and differences between his own culture and the dominant one and come to terms with a suitable personal fit (Atkinson, Morton, & Sue, 1993). In such a way, a man of color comes to experience his own unique male gender role.

THE ROLE OF CULTURE

Men are not born, growing from infants through boyhood to manhood, to follow a predetermined biological imperative, encoded in their physical organization. To be a man is to participate in social life as a man, as a gendered being. . . . Our sex may be male, but our identity as men is developed through a complex process of interaction with the culture in which we both learn the gender scripts appropriate to our culture and attempt to modify those scripts to make them more palatable. (Kimmel & Messner, 1992, pp. 8, 9)

The social constructionist view asserts that "the meaning of masculinity varies from culture to culture" (Kimmel & Messner, 1992, p. 9) and, within a given culture, is modified over time. Men of the same age but different cultures, and ethnicity experience their masculinity differently. As a man matures, his concept of masculinity is modified and redefined according to his life experiences and his interchanges with the environment. The male gender role varies according to location, time, and popular beliefs.

Family, friends, and societal expectations play an integral role in the development of gender roles. Cultural norms affect how the individual male comes to know his role in society. He learns the expectations and adopts and modifies them to his unique person. He carries them out in his everyday behaviors. He interacts with those around him. Through this interaction with his environment, a man projects an image of self to the world, which responds to that image and offers feedback. The environment lets him know whether his behaviors are acceptable or not. Lazur (1983, 1992) calls this interaction a "conversation." It involves a give-and-take between the individual and the world. Each person projects a particular self-image through self-presentation (Goffman, 1959). These presentations are influenced by societal norms that govern what is acceptable and what is not (Goffman, 1955). The norms become incorporated into the individual and dictate behaviors, thus influencing one's culture.

It is the norms of the culture that define gender roles. *"Sex role norms* are widely shared prescriptive beliefs about what the sexes ideally *should be"* (Pleck, 1981, p. 11). Each culture has its own set of beliefs. While similarities may exist, "ethnic groups within races differ in cultural content. . . . People of the same racial origin and of the same ethnic groups differ in their cultural matrices. All browns, or blacks, or whites, or yellows, or reds, are not alike in the culture in which they live and have their being" (Moore. 1974, p. 41).

Through interaction with the culture, a man masters the male gender role. The conversation he engages in with the culture helps him to define his unique fit between personal needs and societal expectations. In the process of the conversation, he comes to know what it means to be a man within his cultural context. It is this mercurial variation for the individual that powers gender role strain. Work and family demands require responses from the individual man on their own merits, not only because of gender role expectations. Life experiences, level of maturity, and comfort with self also influence how the individual adheres to gender role expectations. Although a member of the culture, each man expresses his own unique masculinity. In his conversation with the world, he assesses gender role expectations, compares them with his needs, and responds in a way that balances both his needs and societal prescriptions. His response, in turn, is evaluated by the social environment as to how it meets that environment's needs. Feedback is offered in terms of either acceptance or disapproval.

Through his conversation with the culture, a man operationalizes gender role norms. He sees their inconsistencies and conflicting demands. At times, a response is required that opposes his natural inclination. This is especially true in work or family settings where the prescribed behaviors are dysfunctional. Not wishing to perpetuate the dysfunction, he violates the gender role. He does so at the risk of provoking social condemnation and/or negative psychological consequences. He engages in conversation with the world and offers alternative behaviors that can either be integrated into the social norms or put him at risk of being perceived as nonconforming and suffering the social consequences. It is through this process that a man defines his meaning-making system. He interconnects with the culture but defines his own individual male gender role.

For a man of color, defining his own gender role involves integration of the dominant society's restrictions. Measuring himself against the standard that dictates the male gender role for the dominant culture yet denies equal access to the opportunities that sustain that standard evokes in the man of color frustrations, unexpressed emotions, and a drive for survival. Whether African-American, Latino, American-Indian, or Asian-American, he feels oppressed and at a disadvantage because his skin color, physical characteristics, and family heritage are not of the dominant culture. Despite federal legislation and politically correct lip service from those around him, he is understood from his meaning-making system only insofar as it reflects the norms of the dominant culture. If he displays attitudes or conduct discordant with the dominant culture—even though they may be vital to his family's culture—he is proscribed. That is, if he acts according to *his* culture, those in the dominant culture view him as "different," bar his access to resources, and may even engage in acts of violence against him. If he acts according to the prescriptions of the dominant culture, he ascribes to a system that, in effect, negates him, and he is considered by his own people to have "sold out ." Whatever his choice, a man of color is constantly faced with the challenge of dealing with the consequences of how he acts. This pressure creates in him additional stress and conflict in fulfilling the male gender role.

Notwithstanding this treacherous reality of life in the United States, a man of color has to find a way to not only survive but to flourish. He has to identify and acknowledge the similarities and differences between his own and the dominant culture. He has to take into account the obstacles that interfere with his acceptance. The conflict and stress arise from the task of finding the suitable personal fit: deciding how he is going to integrate, if at all, his two different cultures. He must identify for himself and those around him what is important to him as a male, and he must express it in his everyday actions. He must develop his own meaning-making system with regard to the male gender role.

THE AFRICAN-AMERICAN MALE

Generations of discrimination, oppression, and racism have left their mark on African-American men. With the highest rates of mortality, substance abuse, unemployment, and imprisonment among all groups, they have been labeled an "endangered species" (Gibbs, 1984, 1989). One belief of the male gender role identity paradigm is that "Black males are particularly vulnerable to gender role identity problems" (Pleck, 1981, p. 25). Believed to have been emasculated by slavery, to be an irresponsible breadwinner and parent, and relegated to menial jobs, the African-American male is perceived as having to prove his manhood. Building his hypothesis on this belief, Moynihan (1965) attributed the social problems found in African-American families to the absence of men and the dependence on women as heads of household, ignoring political and economic realities. By focusing on gender roles, Moynihan sidestepped the societal issues of racism, oppression, and injustice.

However, those realities exist. It was not apathy or gender role confusion that caused African-American men to fail to provide for their families; they failed because financially they could not do so (Frazier, 1939). Economically and politically impotent, African-American males lack adequate access to the educational, commercial, and social resources historically mastered by European-American men. Yet despite these obstacles, African-American men continue to define the male gender role for themselves in the terms of the dominant culture. This inability to acquire what is valued and possessed by the other culture results in feelings of frustration, alienation, bitterness, and rage. No longer willing to accept what is doled out, African-American men attempt to achieve the goals of the male gender role by defending against exploitation and expressing their distrust toward the dominant society.

By adopting "a ritualized form of masculinity that entails behaviors, scripts, physical posturing, impression management, and carefully crafted performances that deliver a single, critical message: pride, strength, and control" (Majors & Mancini Billson,

1992, p. 4), the African-American male embraces a coping strategy of cool pose (Majors, 1983, 1986, 1988, 1990, 1991, 1994; Majors & Mancini Billson, 1992). He proclaims to the world that he is an African-American male.

The goals of cool pose are social competence, protection, and conveying a sense of pride. Creating, acting, and redefining himself through handshakes, walking, eye work, body stance, and facial expressions, the African-American male proclaims to the world that he is proud, in control, powerful, and strong. It is his way of countering stress and adapting to environmental circumstances. Cool pose also expresses bitterness, anger, and distrust toward the dominant culture and preserves an African-American man's sense of dignity, pride, and respect.

Kochman (1981) observed a difference between the styles of the dominant and African-American cultures. European-American behavior is low-stimulus, impersonal, nonchallenging, and dispassionate, while the African-American mode is high-stimulus, emotional, rhythmic, animated, and assertive. "While blacks are more interested in expressing than controlling their impulses, whites value self-restraint, understatement, and diffusion of intense situations" (Majors & Mancini Billson, 1992, p. 53). This difference in styles creates judgments, anxieties, and misgivings between the races, especially in urban areas at night. The resultant disquietude perpetuates a cycle of power/control. While cool pose signifies distrust of the dominant culture, it also engenders pride, self-respect, and social competence. It encapsulates masculinity for some African-American males but is not the sole means of expressing the male gender role.

The African-American male's attempt to maintain his identity comes at a cost. By protecting himself against the dominant society, his behaviors often interfere with authentic heterosexual relationships. Cool pose behaviors impede his attempts to develop an open, expressive emotional relationship with a woman. While some African-American women may find his display of power and virility exciting, it can hinder emotional intimacy. Not able to turn the cool pose behaviors off and on at will, the African-American male has difficulty disclosing himself or expressing feelings in a meaningful way to those with whom he wishes to be close. He proves himself at the cost of intimacy.

Another cost is mistreatment of self and other African-Americans. Not able to express his feelings, fears, or worries, yet constantly under pressure to prove his manhood, his emotions burst forth in expressions of assault, accident, or homicide or are buried in alcoholism or substance abuse. "For many Black men, heavy drinking is the norm and is perceived as an attribute of manhood and camaraderie" (Parham & McDavis, 1987, p 25). Longtime racism, discrimination, and oppression have resulted in homicide, drug abuse, suicide, and accidents being the leading causes of death among African-American men. Alcoholism, diabetes, hypertension, neglect of other treatable diseases, and inadequate health care (Gibbs, 1984, 1989; Parham & McDavis, 1987) have shortened the African-American male's average life span. Pent-up frustrations and unexpressed emotions have the potential to explode against others, especially other African-Americans. Parham and McDavis (1987) observed that the majority of perpetrators of crimes against African-American males are also African-American. If cool pose behavior guards against oppression and second-class treatment from European-American males, it takes its toll on African-Americans.

The toll is most evident on African-American adolescent males. Adopting cool pose tenets, the African-American adolescent male distances himself from uncool activities like achieving success in school. In the midst of developing an identity yet full of self-doubt, confused about how to express himself, and confronted by the contrast between self and the dominant culture, the adolescent male often seeks identity refuge in a gang. Promoting a masculine culture, the gang embraces initiation rites, displays of strength and daring, camaraderie, and even fashion.

> The gang can become a family that offers belonging, pride, respect, and empowerment that may be absent in the home or denied by society. . . . African-American gang members have their own rules and culture. They are consumed with sym-

bols that identify and promote a masculine cultural display: distinctive handshakes, hairstyles, stance, walks, battle scars, turf wars, hand signals, language, and nicknames. (Majors & Mancini Billson, 1992, pp. 50, 51)

The costs are often immense. Gang warfare, crime, possession and use of weapons, substance abuse, dropping out of school, and risk-taking behaviors are destructive and endanger the next generation of African-Americans, both male and female. Continuing to overcome centuries of oppression, African-American adolescent males fight to find a way to leave their mark on the world, often at the price of their lives.

The African-American man redefines and operationalizes his male gender role in the struggle to better his life and the lives of those he loves. He attempts to gain status and economic parity. He wards off the power differential with the dominant culture by adopting a certain physical style of interacting with the world. He proclaims his competence, projects his pride, and protects himself. It is one of the few ways he can assert his manhood in the dominant culture.

THE LATINO MALE

Lending the English language a word to describe the essence of virility, *machismo* involves "physical strength, sexual attractiveness, virtue, and potency" (Ruiz, 1981, p. 191). With this clear definition of what it means to be masculine, men of various Hispanic countries attempt to integrate the cultural demands of their heritage into the male gender role. Mexican-Americans, Puerto Ricans, Cubans, and the men of South American nations all have masculine identifications and behaviors prescribed by their societies.[2]

When the term is applied by non-Latinos, however, "'macho' often is defined in terms of physical aggression, sexual promiscuity, dominance of women, and excessive use of alcohol" (Ruiz, 1981, p. 192).

What has happened over the years is that English has usurped the word and reworked the definition, turning it into the functional equivalent of male chauvinism. The sociological and psychological impact of this has been to stereotype unfairly Hispanic men as being exaggeratedly masculine in their behavior. While there is no doubt that chauvinism and sexism occur among Hispanic men, we doubt that they exist to a greater degree than in other groups. (Valdés, Barón, & Ponce, 1987, p. 210)

Latinos are the fastest-growing group in the United States, owing in part to immigration and high fertility rates (Gibbs, 1989). In addition to their cultural diversity, they exhibit

variation in racial characteristics. Hispanics represent a mixture of several racial groupings. Some families trace their bloodlines directly back to Spain and consequently retain Caucasian features. Other families share multiple bloodlines comprising [the] Native-American, African, and Caucasian races. (Valdés, Barón, & Ponce, 1987, p. 209)

Naturally then, Latino men express male gender roles in various ways. Shifts occur across generations as Puerto Rican families acculturate (Inclan & Herron, 1989). Moving from an agrarian to an industrial economy changes the Puerto Rican family: Where once children would have stayed within the family, they now live in a culture that encourages individual autonomy. This change creates stress and conflict within the family. "The first generation tends to uphold its culture of origin and values in the new host culture" (Inclan & Herron, 1989, p. 256), while second and third generations have a foot in both the culture of origin and the new environment.

Prior to the development of capitalism, the home was the center and focus of all human activity—work, recreation, family life, etc., and all members of the family—men women, children—participated alike. Capitalism brought with it a split . . . [and] wage-labor . . . now began to be performed at the work center and was primarily the responsibility of men. . . . Characteristics such as unemotionality, toughness, and performance-

minded[ness] became institutionalized and reinforced as male characteristics while the realm of the emotional, personal life was valued in women. (Inclan, 1983, p. 6)

While traditionally Latino males were expected to be strong and forceful, to withhold affectionate emotions, and to be the provider and protector of the family (Ramirez, 1989), male dominance among Mexican-Americans is part of

the status structure within which their interactions occur. This emphasis is crucial because it alerts us to the importance of structural variables in understanding sex stratification. Furthermore, it casts doubt on interpretations which treat culture (the systems of shared beliefs and orientations unique to a group) as the cause of male dominance. If male dominance is universal, then it cannot be reduced to the culture of a particular category of people. (Baca Zinn, 1982, p. 30)

Although machismo influences the patriarchal structure, gender roles may still vary, as Ramirez and Arce (1981) observed. They espoused traditional values, but when observed during real life, Mexican-American men tend to share the day-to-day decision-making with women, and there is greater equality and opportunity for women in this culture than its traditional values would lead one to expect. True, some families remain patriarchal with domineering husbands, while others are matriarchally dominated with docile males (Falicov, 1982), but there appears to be movement toward an egalitarian system.

Confronted with the male gender role demands of the dominant culture yet denied economic and political access to its resources, Latino men have undergone increasing stress. Alcohol has been viewed as providing relief from the sense of powerlessness, inferiority, and subordination. "Hispanic men have markedly higher rates of alcoholism, arrest for drunken behavior, deaths due to cirrhosis of the liver, and deaths due to alcohol-related traffic accidents than do non-Latino American males" (Panitz, McConchie, Sauber, & Fonseca, 1983, p. 31). The high incidence of poverty, cultural pride in the manufacture of alcohol in the homeland, absence of religious structures, responsibility for extended family members, and the machismo ethos are cited as major influences.

In an attempt to lease out the significance of machismo, Neff, Prihoda, and Hoppe (1991) found that while Mexican-American and African-American males are more likely to be highly macho, Mexican-Americans are more likely to be heavy drinkers (5–6 drinks at a sitting) than either European-American or African-American males. For these groups, high machismo was generally associated with a low probability of heavy drinking. The authors cite a model of powerlessness wherein the individual compensates for what he does not yet have. "Machismo is no more strongly related to alcohol use among Mexican-Americans than among Anglos or blacks" (Neff, Prihoda, & Hoppe, 1991, p. 461).

The study also found that high macho males are more likely to have low self-esteem than are low macho males. Neff et al. argue that, "although 'machismo,' per se, is typically not discussed as a core element of Anglo culture, machismo effects are significant in all Anglo subgroups" (p. 461).

Using dominoes as a metaphor of how Puerto Rican males interact, Inclan (1983, 1991) has observed a cultural shift with the advent of industrialization as means to economic development. With the change in the social structure, dominoes came to represent a way for men to connect outside the worksite and to express a full spectrum of "interpersonal possibilities—from aggresivity [*sic*] and competition to support and collaboration—all framed in the 'pretend' language of playing a game" (1983, p. 7). At times serving as respite from conflict at home, dominoes represent loyalty and partnership among Puerto Rican men. During play, a "no talking" rule exists. "It's a structure where communication and affect can be exchanged in safe and metaphorical ways. It is one of a variety of responses that a people has developed to deal with male-male relationships in their special set of historical circumstances" (1983, p. 14).

Within the various cultures of the Latino community, the male gender role also varies according to the nationality, ethnic identity, acculturation into the dominant culture, responsibilities to the extended family, poverty, and machismo of the individual man. The progressive aspects of machismo can be celebrated. However, as Pleck (1981) noted, violation of gender roles lead to social condemnation and negative psychological consequences. Baca Zinn (1982) observed: "Perhaps manhood takes on greater importance for those who do not have access to socially valued roles. Being male is one sure way to acquire status when other roles are systematically denied by the workings of society" (p. 39).

The Latino man draws upon his culture of machismo to define his male gender role in the face of the demands of the dominant culture. Confronted with economic and social obstacles that impede his access to power and success, he attempts to reconcile the differences and integrate the standards of his own culture with those of the dominant one. However, he pays the price in stress, which takes its toll not only on him but on those he loves and on the community in which he lives.

THE AMERICAN-INDIAN MALE

An ethnic group indigenous to the North American continent and the only one legally defined by Congress (Trimble & Fleming 1989), "American-Indians" are a highly heterogeneous people "comprised of approximately 530 distinct tribes of which 478 are recognized by the U.S. government" (Sue & Sue, 1990, p. 176). Even though differences in family structure, language, and customs exist between tribes, an individual with 25% Indian blood is considered American-Indian (Trimble, 1988; Sue & Sue, 1990).[3] Culture plays an important role in the definition of gender roles for the American-Indian, but little has been written about those roles and how the changes within the culture affect American-Indian men. Once the providers of food and game for the community, American-Indian males have been run over by the dominant culture (Braveheart-Jordan, 1993; Schroeder, 1991), leading to the unavailability of male role models and the conflict of living in a dominant culture that is frequently incompatible with the core identity.

Cooperative by nature, the American-Indian tribe plays an important role in individual identity. Seeing themselves individually as extensions of the tribe, "this identity provides them with a sense of belonging and security, with which they form an interdependent system" (Sue & Sue, 1990, p. 177). Everyone is essential to the tribe's functioning (Schacht, 1993). Individual behaviors are judged according to how they benefit the tribe. If others benefit from the behavior, then it is good. In Eskimo villages above the Arctic Circle, whale hunters are revered for bringing food to the entire community.

Establishing a sense of affinity, the tribe encourages interdependence. Grandparents, aunts, uncles, and cousins play instrumental roles in teaching the child how to function. Skills are taught and customs passed through the generations by oral tradition. Maternal uncles are frequently responsible for instructing boys in the skills, traditions, and cultural values necessary for survival and spiritual harmony. The life force of nature is honored and esteemed within others and within the self. The duality of forces, the masculine and feminine, which beget energy and channel life, is venerated. Even in hunting, the animal's life is honored for the good it offers to others.

However, as government regulations have restricted the use of land, American-Indians have been confined and the traditions of the past changed. The traditional male roles of hunter, warrior, teacher, and leader have been nullified. The dominant culture holds power, prestige, and influence, which it exerts in ways that are antithetical to American-Indian tradition. "As members of a conquered nation, they have replaced ancient behaviors in service of survival, often at the cost of health" (Schroeder, 1991).

Examining the cumulative trauma for multiple generations when a way of life that had existed for thousands of years was wiped out in a single generation, Perez (1993) attributes current problems of American-Indian life to the stress incurred by dependence on a dominant foreign force. Heart disease, accidents, cancer, chronic liver disease and cirrhosis, and suicide are the leading causes of death among American-Indian males (U.S. Department of Health and Human Services, 1992). One-third of American-

Indian males in the state of New Mexico die before reaching age 35 (DeBruyn, 1993). The rate of suicide among Alaska Native American males is 10 times the national average. Within a 16-month period, one village of 550 people experienced "eight suicides [one of whom was female], dozens of attempts, two murders, and four drownings" (Weaver, 1988 p. A2). Alcohol, the destruction of the subsistence lifestyle, poor educational opportunities, and few jobs have made an impact. American-Indian males have lost the core activities that were integral to their identity.

A Tsimshian Indian, Doug Modig, declared, "Our culture has been destroyed" (Weaver, 1988, p. A3). Another, Thelkla Hootch, said, "The men are not what they were. Men had dog teams, they'd go out in the morning. Everybody helped each other. My grandfather would go hunt ducks and seals. They don't do that anymore. They're on welfare, food stamps. . . . It's not like it used to be" (Weaver, 1988, p. A3). The effects of the dominant culture have been profound.

Rectifying the distortions of history—distortions often internalized by American-Indians themselves—DeBruyn (1993) clarifies the role of the Lakota warrior. Warriors were the protectors willing to bravely sacrifice themselves to defend their people. War was the last resort, not a thing of glory, as depicted by European-American culture. Schacht (1993) suggests that when the American-Indian male was unable to fill the protector role, he lost an important identity. Losing relatives and friends to the invasion by the dominant culture was extremely painful. Unable to do his job of protecting the community led to self-hatred and a learned helplessness in the realization that there was no escape from the pain.

Unable to counteract the intrusions of the dominant culture, American Indian males have found that their attempts to integrate into it have been equally destructive. "Frequent relocation, substandard living conditions, and chronic unemployment in both urban and reservation areas have taken their toll on Indian people" (La Fromboise & Graff Low, 1989, p. 116). Denied access to the resources necessary for a subsistence lifestyle and to educational and economic opportunities, the American-Indian male is often compelled to work in the city, leaving behind his culture and ancient ways of life. Faced with racism, stereotypic images (Trimble, 1988), and the great number of people in a city, many feel overwhelmed and unable to cope. Despite these hardships, the economic future appears to be better for American-Indians in urban areas, and the majority of American-Indians live outside of trust lands, villages, pueblos, and reservations (La Fromboise & Graff Low, 1989).

However, in leaving, they become unavailable for tribal ceremonies. Traditional practice holds that everyone is essential to the tribe's function. If they leave, they will not be present during crucial times in ceremonial events. The community feels abandoned, creating a conflict that makes it difficult to function (Schacht, 1993) and presents a difficult choice: loyalty to the tribe, or economic survival.

Drawing a parallel to domestic violence in a family, Schroeder (1991) likens the dominant culture to the powerful father who beats a boy's mother, the American-Indian culture. Witnessing this abuse and uncertain about their cultural identity, American-Indian males lack adequate male gender role models. Wanting to protect his mother but fearing retaliation, the boy regards the father with disgust and hatred; however, as a male, he looks to the father as his primary source of socialization as a man. Wanting to connect with his mother but also believing that she should be able to protect him, the boy feels contempt for her. "As a culture, as Native-American males have witnessed this desecration of the traditional values, they have very much wanted to defend that, yet have been unable, to with the understandable results of powerlessness, hopelessness, and depression—self-defeating behaviors that would happen in an individual transferred to a cultural level" (Schroeder, 1991).

The effects have been profound. Calling it the "great invisible wound of this country," Schacht (1993) acknowledges the American-Indians' cumulative unresolved grief, which has been ignored by society. "It's never talked about. Nobody is even standing over the graves saying, 'This is a terrible tragedy and something ought to be done about it.'" A way of life, a culture, was destroyed. Children were shipped to boarding schools, provider and protector roles were stripped from the men, and language and customs were extinguished. Adrift, individuals were caught between two worlds. Pent-up feelings could not be expressed. The American-Indians suffer unresolved cultural grief and anger as a people.

A case can be made for calling what is happening to the American-Indians genocide. DeBruyn (1993) applies to the history of American-Indians the definition spelled out by the United Nations 1948 General Assembly's Convention on Genocide.

> Genocide means any of the following acts committed with intent to destroy in whole or in part a national, ethnical, racial, or religious group and includes five types of criminal actions:
> - killing members of the group,
> - causing serious bodily or mental harm to members of the group,
> - deliberately inflicting on the group conditions of life calculated to bring about its physical destruction in whole or in part,
> - imposing measures intended to prevent births within the group, and
> - forcibly transferring children of the group to another group.

These acts have been committed against American-Indians. The effects have been felt by generations of American-Indians seeking their identity as a people. For healing to occur, the anger, grief, and other unexpressed emotions need to be acknowledged and proclaimed.

Drawing upon the grief work done with survivors of the Holocaust, Braveheart-Jordan (1993) proposes that the American-Indian male confront the past, learn the history of his people, and acknowledge his anger and other feelings as he begins the grief process. She and her colleagues lead workshops in which men come to understand and internalize the concept of the "survivor syndrome." Collective responses reduce the sense of isolation and victim-blaming, normalize the experience, and put the blame where it belongs. By sharing a cathartic group experience with other members of the tribal community, survivors are able to share their feelings and mobilize and channel them in individual constructive actions. In such a way, community/cultural values are restored.

Perhaps as American-Indian men grieve the losses of their culture, they will draw upon the amazing strength and resources of previous generations. Then they will be able to use that strength to define the male gender role in such a way as to continue to contribute to the welfare of their people. In so doing, they will reclaim their place in American life.

THE ASIAN-AMERICAN MALE

Observing that members of the dominant culture are unable to distinguish among Asian subgroups and treat all Asian-Americans the same, with no regard for individual and ethnic differences, Chan (1992) distinguishes "thirty separate and distinct ethnic groups, each with their own values, customs, languages, behavior and tradition" (p. 8). Though they all have cultural roots in Confucian and Buddhist traditions, Chinese, Korean, Japanese, and Taiwanese customs differ from each other and from Cambodian, Laotian, and Vietnamese customs. Degree of acculturation also leads to differences: The obligations of a fourth-generation Chinese-American differ from those of an immigrant. To address all Asian-American male gender roles the same would be simplistic; however, little research has been published on any Asian-American male's experience of gender roles. Consequently, this section attempts to integrate the information—much of it found in counseling literature—that is available.

Although customs and religions vary, Sue and Sue (1993) found several similarities between the various Asian-American cultures. Parents instill a sense of obligation to family that is maintained throughout life. Family needs supersede personal autonomy. Even if married, sons maintain a strong allegiance to parents. Emotions are restrained, especially in public. Authority is rooted in a patriarchal system; males are highly valued. "The father's behavior in relationship to other family members is generally dignified, authoritative, remote, and aloof" (Sue and Sue, 1993, p. 200).

Influenced by the teachings of Confucius, Chinese home life is governed by a strict sense of order, with prescribed roles. In return for ensuring the family's economic well-being and social status, the father has unchallenged authority and the loyalty and respect of all family members. Emotional well-being is the responsibility of the mother. Firstborn sons are "the most valued child, [and] received preferential treatment as well as more familial responsibilities. . . . [They are] expected to provide emotional support to the mother, assume responsibility for the educational and character development of younger siblings, and bring honor and financial support to the family" (Huang & Ying, 1989, pp. 36, 42). These expectations place extreme pressure on firstborn Asian-American males (Hirasma, 1980; Lee, 1982).

A hierarchical family structure characterized by male authority, restrictive emotional displays, and family obligation is also evident in Japanese-American families (Nagata, 1989). For instance:

> It was not uncommon for third generation (Sansei) children to have acquired only the most basic and straightforward facts about their elders' internment experience [during World War II]. . . . They gained little understanding of the personal and group impact of being abruptly removed from homes and incarcerated in desolate locales . . . or of the extent of racial hatred and wartime hysteria that prevailed. (Nakanishi, 1988, p. 167)

The effects upon Japanese-American families, especially males, of such stoicism has been profound (Sue & Sue, 1990).

Both Chinese- and Japanese-Americans tend to be well educated and to exceed the national median income and have low rates of delinquency, divorce, and psychiatric contact (Sue & Sue, 1990). While they reflect an image of success, closer analysis indicates that poverty is equally prevalent among these groups, more than one wage earner often contributes to the family income, and wages are often not commensurate with education and training. Because disgrace and shame are often associated with public acknowledgment of problems, they are more often resolved within the context of the family rather than through outside resources.

Based on Confucian traditions but influenced by Roman Catholic missionaries, Vietnamese culture values the family as the basic social unit. Extended family interdependence is important. Roles and responsibilities within the family hierarchy are clearly delineated. Elders are respected, and children are seen as the future. "Both children and adults feel a sense of inferiority if children do not achieve goals set by the family" (Huang, 1989, p. 295).

Less socially prescribed, Cambodian culture is influenced by Buddhist teachings. In this patriarchal society, the extended family is acknowledged but the family structure is formed by the couple. Buddhist tradition upholds respect for life in all its forms, the presence of suffering, and the importance of honesty and gentleness. This morality, codified by Cambodian civil law, counterbalances the father's sovereignty as head of the family. Even though he is highly regarded, the husband shares authority with his wife (Huang, 1989).

Noting the plight of Cambodian, Laotian, and Vietnamese immigrants following the Vietnam War, Huang (1989) determined that although loss and culture shock are integral components of the refugee experience, children rate their fathers "as slightly more willing to 'Americanize'" (Huang, 1989, p. 290) than mothers, who are the least happy family members. Physical and sexual assault by sea pirates had a profound impact upon the children, and "adolescent males [were] overwhelmed by fear, shame, rage" (Huang, 1989, p. 292). Many teenage boys, "detached from the native culture and unable to secure a niche in American society, [would] group together [into a gang] for reasons of identity, protection, and economics" (Huang, 1989, p. 292).

Whether he is recently emigrated or several generations acculturated makes a difference in the Asian-American man's attitude and response to the male gender role. It is the balance between the family and the dominant culture that influences how individual Asian-American males prescribe the role for themselves. As Chan (1992) differentiates:

The distinction between the public and private self is really the very important concept in Asian cultures. The public self is that which conforms to gendered and familial role expectations. The public self behaves in a manner which follows social norms, which seeks to avoid actions which would bring shame upon one's family and one's community. . . . The private self is never seen by anyone other than one's most intimate relationships. (Chan, 1992, p. 9)

Integrating the public and private selves, an Asian-American man's attitude and response to the male gender role differs depending on the amount of time he has spent in this culture. Family values and loyalties, religious philosophy, and economic pursuits are integral parts of male gender role strain. The individual man attempts to make sense of his gender role for himself within the context of his culture and the demands of the world at large.

DISCUSSION

Men of color must overcome societal prejudices, economic obstacles, educational constraints, and, at times, acts of violence to assert their place in the dominant culture. Motivated by the same goals that impel men of the dominant culture, men of color forge the male gender role by balancing personal needs with cultural demands and the expectations of the world at large. However, to date that effort has been ignored by the men's studies literature.

As Kimmel and Messner (1992) have articulated, male gender roles vary from culture to culture and are modified over time within a culture. Even more evident, within a culture, there are variations as well as individual differences. Gender roles are operationally defined by widely shared beliefs (Pleck, 1981). These widely shared beliefs are part of the cultural attitudes. As such, they are important ingredients in the individual man's definition of his gender role.

Through an interaction with the environment, a man comes to know what others expect of him. Family, peers, and societal demands prescribe attitudes and behaviors that comprise his gender role. There is a give-and-take, a conversation, in which the individual projects his particular self-image into the environment. The congruence of this image with societal expectations regulates the environment's response to him. If he is congruent, the feedback is positive and he is accepted. While some differences are tolerated, if he is widely divergent from societal expectations of the male gender role, he is more likely to be ostracized.

This is what constitutes gender role strain. Widely shared beliefs create a norm against which the man and the environment are likely to compare and contrast his attitudes and behaviors. In addition to these norms, stereotypic perceptions of the way each gender acts operationally define gender roles. However, life-cycle inconsistencies, historical changes, and other contradiction make it difficult if not impossible to conform to gender roles (Pleck, 1981). Violations occur. The degree of the violation dictates environmental sanctions. While some behaviors can be tolerated by the environment, if they are too divergent, negative consequences are imposed. If a man fails to live up to critical aspects of the male gender role, or is imagined to have so failed; the environment dictates that he compensate. Often he does so by over-conforming (Pleck, 1981).

Through his conversation with the environment, a man evaluates the expectations, compares them with his own needs, determines the risks of noncompliance, and acts accordingly, attempting to balance gender role prescriptions with his own needs. A conversation between the individual and the environment (including cultural attitudes and expectations) assists the man in defining how he wants to live the male gender role possibilities. While men have been criticized for adhering to rigid gender role definitions, it is the rigidity of the expectations and restrictions placed on women that has brought attention to how men fulfill gender roles. Many qualities of male gender roles are highly adaptive for society; however, the constrictions needlessly block the fulfillment of human potential.

As men in the dominant culture examine the usefulness of these constrictions, it is assumed that men of color should do the same. Applying the same paradigm, no matter how useful to one culture, to different cultures is to implicitly deny the importance of the differences and the value of alternative ways of viewing the same kind of life event. Different cultures have different expectations. Not to honor these differences is tantamount to oppression.

For a man of color, a paradigm for understanding gender roles must emerge from his culture and be relevant to it. More research, along with increased dialogue between the culture and dominant expectations, are needed. Without both these contributions to understanding, the differences will be exaggerated and misunderstanding will predominate.

Racism in its various forms needs to be confronted in his essay "why [sic] is this men's movement so white?" Gordon (1993) raises the issue of European-Americans' fear of African-American men. "But with your fear around confronting male power, I also feel you are afraid of me. *Are you afraid of me?* Are you afraid of who and what I represent? Are you afraid of my blackness?" (p. 15). "For black Americans, racism has been a fact of life for over three centuries (Jones, 1988, p. 126). Suggesting that racism needs to be addressed on both the individual and institutional levels, Jones asserts that "the dual power to define difference as deficient and to reinforce conformity to prevailing standards is the essential character of cultural racism" (p. 131). He adds, "Two basic beliefs are necessary to convert the problem of racism to our collective advantage: there is strength in diversity and . . . we are no stronger as a nation than the weakest among us" (p. 133).

For men of color to confront the male gender role, European-American men must also be aware of how facets of their role in the dominant culture suppress and restrain men who are not part of the dominant culture. For too long the dominant culture has preserved economic, educational, and societal obstacles that have restricted and effectively maintained men of color in a subservient position. Just as European-American males are becoming increasingly aware of the repression of women, so too is it necessary to examine the power differential and their resulting economic supremacy over other males.

The end result is going to be disruptive. Whenever there is a shift in power, those who perceive they are losing it become entrenched and seek to restabilize the equilibrium in their favor. While the dominant culture may give lip service to parity, little has been done to accept, much less integrate, cultures of color in the power structure of the United States.

To do so would create conflict and pain. It would mean changing how things are done and examining traditional and current models, finding the similarities and differences with those of other cultures. In effect, it would mean that the European-American male would have to do what a man of color has always had to do: examine himself to determine how he fits in, if at all.

Economic factors will have to be examined. Traditionally valued as the breadwinner, men have long felt that making money is an essential component of the traditional male gender role. However, men of color have long been discriminated against in this arena. Denied access to the economic opportunities of the dominant culture, men of color have had to work harder, longer, and against greater odds to accomplish less than their European-American counterparts. And when men of color do succeed, the perception that their color gave them an unfair advantage diminishes their sense of accomplishment and self-worth.

By the year 2000, two-thirds of the American workforce will be people of color and women (Johnston, 1987). The effects on business will be profound. European-American men will be faced with one of the most demanding challenges to their identity: The source of power and control will be threatened by the very people needed to sustain it!

While elaboration of these issues is outside the purview of this chapter, the issues themselves need to be raised. In addressing the context, perhaps some understanding of the impact of male gender role strain on men of color can be attained. However, more research needs to be done.

Data needs to be collected on the expression of male gender roles across cultures in the United States. While African-American, Latino, American-Indian, and Asian-American are four common cultures of color in the United States, they certainly are not the only ones. In reviewing the literature for this chapter, the authors were unable to find information on several cultures, and what was available was limited. Many cultural attributes are generalizations, and each culture is characterized by wide variation within social class and among individual males in their understanding of the male gender role. More participants representing these cultures would add a dialogue of exploration and discovery to the men's studies literature.

Paradigms of other worldviews need to be integrated into the definition of male gender roles; what works in one culture may not apply in another. Other perspectives need to be offered. Changes in definitions as individual men mature and redefine their male gender roles also needs to be respected. Longevity studies within a culture need to be done. Most important, men of the dominant culture need to listen to their brothers of color and learn from their experiences. Regardless of culture, a man participates in an interactive process of defining and redefining his awareness, behaviors, and beliefs about his male gender role. There is much work left to be done. This is just a beginning.

NOTES

1. While many readers may prefer the term "Native American," the authors wish to honor the tradition of the "American-Indian," a term that has returned to popular usage.
2. While more than 20 nationalities can be categorized as Latino, only those in a majority in the United States—Mexican-Americans, Puerto Ricans, and Cubans—will be considered here. Stevens (1973) observed a difference between those cultures affected by "outside" conquering cultures and those where indigenous autonomy prevails. Machismo prevails in the former, whereas the latter honor the matrilineal family structure.
3. The authors recognize the uniqueness of the individual American-Indian cultures. Unfortunately, space does not allow for a more detailed description of the individual peoples; only salient shared characteristics are considered here. Clearly, more work in this area needs to be done.

REFERENCES

Atkinson, D. R., Morton, G., & Sue, D. W. (1993). *Counseling American minorities: A cross-cultural perspective* (4th ed.). Dubuque, IA: William C. Brown.

Baca Zinn, M. (1982). Chicano men and masculinity. *Journal of Ethnic Studies, 10*(2), 29–44.

Braveheart-Jordan, M. (1993, August). Healing historical trauma in Native-American men. In J. Perez (Chair), *Impact of historical trauma on Native-American men.* Symposium presented at the annual meeting of the American Psychological Association, Toronto.

Chan, C. (1992). What's love got to do with it? Sexual/gender identities. *American Psychological Association Division 44 Newsletter, 8*(3), 8–11, 18.

DeBruyn, L. (1993, August). Historical factors impacting the mental health of Native-American men. In J. Perez (Chair), *Impact of historical trauma on Native-American men.* Symposium presented at the annual meeting of the American Psychological Association, Toronto (cassette recording no. 93-083).

Falicov, C. J. (1982). Mexican families. In M. McGoldrick, J. K. Pearce, & J. Giordano (Eds.), *Ethnicity and family therapy* (pp. 164–186). New York: Guilford Press.

Frazier, E. (1939). *The Negro family in the United States.* Chicago: University of Chicago Press.

Gibbs, J. T. (1984). Black adolescents and youth: An endangered species. *American Journal of Orthopsychiatry, 54,* 6–21.

Gibbs, J. T. (Ed.). (1989). *Children of color: Psychological interventions with minority youth.* San Francisco: Jossey-Bass.

Goffman, E. (1955). On face—work. *Psychiatry, 18,* 213–231.

Goffman, E. (1959). *The presentation of self in everyday life.* New York: Doubleday/Anchor.

Gordon, M. D. (1993, Summer/Fall). why [*sic*] is this men's movement so white? *Changing Men, 26,* 15–17.

Hirasma, T. (1980). Minority group children and behavior disorders: The case of Asian-American children. *Behavior Disorders, 5*(3), 186–196.

Huang, L. N. (1989). Southeast Asian refugee children and adolescents. In J. T. Gibbs (Ed.), *Children of color: Psychological interventions with minority youth* (pp. 278–321). San Francisco: Jossey-Bass.

Huang, L. N., & Ying, Y. W. (1989). Chinese-American children and adolescents. In J. T. Gibbs (Ed.), *Children of color: Psychological interventions with minority youth* (pp. 30–66). San Francisco: Jossey-Bass.

Inclan, J. E. (1983, February). *Interpersonal relations among Puerto Rican men; or, why so much dominoes?* Paper presented at the meeting of the Association of Anthropological Study of Play, Baton Rouge, LA.

Inclan, J. E. (1991, March). *Playing dominoes: Relationships among Latino men.* Paper presented at the midwinter meeting of the American Psychological Association, divisions of psychotherapy, independent practice, and family psychology, San Antonio, TX.

Inclan, J. E., & Herron, D. G. (1989). Puerto Rican adolescents. In J. T. Gibbs (Ed.), *Children of color: Psychological interventions with minority youth* (pp. 251–277). San Francisco: Jossey-Bass.

Johnston. W. B. (1987). *Workforce 2000: Work and workers for the 21st century.* Indianapolis: Hudson Institute.

Jones, J. M. (1988). Racism in black and white: A bicultural model of reaction and evolution. In P. A. Katz & D. A.Taylor (Eds.), *Eliminating racism: Profiles in controversy* (pp. 117–135). New York: Plenum.

Kimmel, M., & Messner, M. (1992). *Men's lives* (2nd ed.). New York: Macmillan.

Kochman, T. (1981). *Black and white styles in conflict.* Chicago: University of Chicago Press.

LaFramboise, T. D., & Graff Low, K. (1989). American-Indian children and adolescents. In J. T. Gibbs (Ed.), *Children of color: Psychological interventions with minority youth* (pp. 114–147). San Francisco: Jossey-Bass.

Lazur, R. F. (1983). *What it means to be a man: A phenomenological study of masculinity.* Unpublished doctoral dissertation, Massachusetts School of Professional Psychology, Newton.

Lazur, R. F. (1992, August). Warrior child: Narcissistic injuries of the male sex role. In M. R. Wong (Chair), *Snips and snails and puppy dog tails: Men and shame.* Symposium presented at the centennial meeting of the American Psychological Association, Washington, DC.

Lee, L. (1982). Social systems approach to assessment and treatment for Chinese-American families. In M. McGoldrick, J. K. Pearce, & J. Giordano (Eds.), *Ethnicity and family therapy* (pp. 164–186). New York: Guilford Press.

Majors, R. (1983). *Cool pose: A new hypothesis in understanding antisocial behavior in lower socioeconomic status males.* Unpublished manuscript, University of Illinois, Urbana.

Majors, R. (1986). Cool pose: The proud signature of black survival. *Changing Men: Issues in Gender, Sex, and Politics, 17,* 5–6.

Majors, R. (1988). Cool pose: A new approach toward systemic understanding and studying of black male behavior. *Dissertation Abstracts International, 49–01, 259B.*

Majors, R. (1990). Cool pose: Black masculinity and sport. In M. Messner & D. Sabo (Eds.), *Sport, men, and the gender role: Critical feminist perspectives* (pp. 109–114). Champaign, IL: Human Kinetics.

Majors, R. (1991). Nonverbal behavior and communications styles among African Americans. In R. Jones (Ed.), *Black psychology* (3rd ed.) (pp. 269–294). Berkeley, CA: Cobb & Henry.

Majors, R. (1994). *The American black male: His present status and future.* Chicago: Nelson & Hall.

Majors, R., & Mancini Billson, J. (1992). *Cool pose: The dilemmas of black manhood in America.* New York: Lexington Books.

Moore, B. M. (1974). Cultural differences and counseling perspectives. *Texas Personnel and Guidance Association Journal, 3,* 39–44.

Moynihan, D. (1965). *The Negro family: The case for national action.* Washington, DC: U.S. Government Printing Office.

Nagata, D. K. (1989). Japanese American children and adolescents. In J. T. Gibbs (Ed.), *Children of color: Psychological interventions with minority youth* (pp. 67–113). San Francisco: Jossey-Bass.

Nakanishi, D. T. (1988). Convergence in race relations research: Japanese-Americans and the resurrection of the internment. In P. A. Katz & D. A. Taylor (Eds.), *Eliminating racism: Profiles in controversy* (pp. 159–180). New York: Plenum.

Neff, J. A., Prihoda, T. S., & Hoppe, S. K. (1991). "Machismo," self-esteem, education and high maximum drinking among Anglo, black, and Mexican-American male drinkers. *Journal of Social Studies, 52*(5), 458–463.

Panitz, D. R., McConchie, R. D., Sauber, S. R., & Fonseca, J. A. (1983). The role of machismo and the Hispanic family in the etiology and treatment of alcoholism in Hispanic American males. *American Journal of Family Therapy, 11*(1), 31–44.

Parham, T. A., & McDavis, R. J. (1987). Black men, an endangered species: Who's really pulling the trigger? *Journal of Counseling and Development, 66,* 24–27.

Perez, J. (Chair). (1993, August). *Impact of historical trauma on Native American men.* Symposium presented at the annual meeting of the American Psychological Association, Toronto.

Pleck, J. (1981). *The myth of masculinity.* Cambridge, MA: MIT Press.

Ramirez, O. (1989). Mexican-American children and adolescents. In J. T. Gibbs (Ed.), *Children of color: Psychological interventions with minority youth* (pp. 224–250). San Francisco: Jossey-Bass.

Ramirez, O., & Arce, C. H. (1981). The contemporary Chicano family: An empirically based review. In A. Barón, Jr. (Ed.), *Explorations in Chicano psychology* (pp. 3–35). New York: Praeger.

Ruiz, R. A. (1981). Cultural and historical perspective in counseling Hispanics. In D.W. Sue (Ed.), *Counseling the culturally different: Theory and practice* (pp. 186–215). New York: Wiley.

Schacht, A. (1993, August). Psycholgocial and behavioral consequences of historical trauma in Native-American men. In J. Perez (Chair), *Impact of historical trauma on Native-American men.* Symposium presented at the annual meeting of the American Psychological Association, Toronto.

Schroeder, J. (1991, August). Gone are the buffalo: Gender role stress in Native American men. In R. F. Lazur (Chair), *Buffalo, dominoes, and machismo: Exploring racial and cultural male sex roles.* Symposium presented at the annual meeting of the American Psychological Association, San Francisco.

Stevens, E. (1973). Machismo and marianismo. *Society, 10,* 57–63.

Sue, D., & Sue, D. W. (1993). Ethnic identity: Cultural factors in the psychological development of Asians in America. In D.W. Atkinson, G. Morten, & D.W. Sue (Eds.), *Counseling American minorities: A cross-cultural perspective* (4th ed.). Dubuque, IA: William C. Brown.

Sue, D. W. & Sue, D. (1990). Counseling the culturally different: Theory and practice (2nd ed.). New York: Wiley.

Trimble, J. E. (1988). Stereotypic images, American Indians, and prejudice. In P. A. Katz & D. A. Taylor (Eds.), *Eliminating racism: Profiles in controversy* (pp. 181–202). New York: Plenum.

Trimble, J. E. & Fleming, C. M. (1989). Providing counseling services for Native-American Indians: Client, counselor, and community characteristics. In P. B. Pedersen, J.G. Draguns, W. J. Lonner, & J. E. Trimble (Eds.), *Counseling across cultures* (3rd ed.) (pp. 177–204). Honolulu: University of Hawaii Press.

Valdés. L. F. Barón, A. Jr., & Ponce, F. Q. (1987). Counseling Hispanic men. In M. Scher, M. Stevens, G. Good, & G. A. Eichenfield (Eds.), *Handbook of counseling and psychotherapy with men* (pp. 203–217). Newbury Park, CA: Sage.

U.S. Department of Health and Human Services (1992). *Health United States 1991* (DHHS Publication No. PHS 92-1232). Washington, DC: U.S. Government Printing Office.

Weaver, H. (1988, January 10). A people in peril: A generation of despair. *Anchorage Daily News,* pp. A2, 3.

CHECKPOINTS

1. Men of color are frequently blocked in their attempts to achieve a masculine identity according to the dominant's cultures standards for masculinity.

2. Constructions of masculinity vary in accord with a man's ethnic or racial identity; some of these features of masculinity may conflict with the dominant culture's version of masculinity.

3. Psychologists need to examine the ethnocentrism and racism in their theories of masculinity and in their understanding of the consequences of the male gender role.

Gender and Culture

QUESTIONS FOR REFLECTION

1   How can cross-cultural examples of gender constructions help us understand gender in our multicultural, technological, mobile, Western culture?
2. What are some cultural prescriptions for femininity and what do you think are the consequences of the feminine gender role for women in the United States? How might these gender role prescriptions vary with ethnic and racial identity?

CHAPTER APPLICATIONS

1. Tavris and Wade argue that historical changes in the division of labor are related to changes in gender roles. What changes might you predict for the future of gender roles? How could evidence from cross-cultural examples be used to promote increased equality in gender roles?
2. If you had the opportunity to observe gender roles in an isolated and little-known society, what features of behavior and culture would you observe?

CHAPTER FIVE

Gender Roles and Stereotypes

QUESTIONS TO THINK ABOUT

- **What are gender roles?**
- **What are stereotypes?**
- **How are gender roles and stereotypes related to masculinity?**
- **Define "kernel of truth."**
- **What is the relationship between gender stereotypes and race and ethnic stereotypes?**
- **What is the relationship between gender stereotypes and heterosexism?**
- **Does gender stereotyping lead to sex discrimination?**
- **What is social role theory?**

GENDER ROLES—PRESCRIPTIONS FOR IDENTITY?

From your reading in the last chapter you are certainly aware of the pervasive nature of gender roles in our everyday experience. The articles you read highlighted the search for universal aspects of behavior as well as observations of differences across cultures. In this chapter, we discuss the concepts of gender roles from the vantage point of social psychology, whose primary research focus is in studying the relationship among social arrangements, interpersonal interactions, and behavior. In accord with the social psychological literature, we define **gender roles** as socially and culturally defined prescriptions and beliefs about the behavior and emotions of men and women. Gender roles influence both our perceptions of others as well as our behavior and feelings, just as stereotypes do. We define **stereotypes** as overgeneralized beliefs about people based on their membership in one

of many social categories. Gender roles are closely related to stereotypes, and one goal of this chapter is to elaborate on the relationship between these concepts. Gender roles and stereotypes cannot always be clearly distinguished from one another. Some theories suggest that cultural gender roles lead to stereotyping, whereas other theories suggest that stereotypes form the basis of gender roles. We do not believe it is possible to conclude that gender roles cause stereotyping or vice versa. This dilemma is like the proverbial chicken and egg question.[1] Clearly, however, gender roles and stereotypes exert a mutual influence on each other, and it is not possible to understand one without recognizing the influence of the other.

Differing Views of Gender Roles

The contrast between essentialism and social constructionism can be useful in understanding different views of gender roles. Early research on gender roles considered masculinity and femininity to be personality characteristics. It was thought that masculinity and femininity were characteristics that described aspects of individuals' personality, with men exhibiting masculinity and women exhibiting femininity, both in varying degrees. It was further assumed that these characteristics represented the healthy, normal organization of one's personality. Men who were not high in masculinity or showed characteristics of femininity were viewed as abnormal, as were women who were not feminine or who showed characteristics of masculinity. Masculinity and femininity, and the elements that contributed to each, were viewed as oppositional traits (Ashmore, 1990). You may recognize this attitude as an essentialist position, which parallels the essentialist view of the relationship between sex and gender.

Ashmore (1990) recounts the history of the study of masculinity/femininity as a personality variable and shows that this research moved through several permutations. From the 1930s until the 1970s, the view of masculinity and femininity as opposite traits prevailed. As criticism of this view grew, two alternative perspectives emerged—the androgyny model proposed by Bem (1974) and the gender identity model of Spence (Spence & Helmreich, 1978). These two perspectives shared the following criticisms of the trait approach: (a) Rather than viewing masculinity and femininity as opposite ends of a continuum, these perspectives viewed masculinity and femininity as separate and independent characteristics; (b) they challenged the assumption that good psychological health is related to sex-typing; (c) they defined masculinity and femininity in terms of cultural norms about gender roles rather than attempting to identify consistent sex differences in behavior. All these challenges emphasized the role of cultural values and norms in defining gender roles.

The most significant event in the evolution of the study of gender roles, during this period, was the development of the concept of androgyny. Androgyny was proposed by Bem (1974) as an alternative to the belief that individuals can be characterized as either masculine or feminine. Recognizing that individuals

might endorse both masculine and feminine characteristics, Bem proposed **androgyny**—having both masculine and feminine characteristics—as a way of addressing the problems associated with the trait approach. In its early uses, androgyny was treated as a third kind of gender role, and used in this way, androgyny would still be characterized as an essentialist view of gender roles. Both Bem and Spence worked toward refining the techniques for measuring gender roles through the development of self-evaluation scales. Spence, too, incorporated the notion of androgyny in her view of gender roles, and her subsequent work has been directed toward understanding the multiple meanings of gender identity and to developing measurement tools for assessing the dimensions of gender roles (Ashmore, 1990). For Bem, the scale items were related to cultural ideals about masculinity and femininity, while for Spence, scale items were judged to be gender role stereotypes.[2] The measurement of masculinity, femininity, and androgyny and the relationship of one's gender role to many other aspects of behavior provided much of the research on gender roles through the 1980s. Morawski (1987), in an influential critique of the entire androgyny enterprise, argued that the measurement of gender roles perpetuates the assumption that gender roles are an unchanging aspect of personality. Similarly, Ashmore contends that the gender-role-as-personality view oversimplifies the multiple and shifting meanings of gender and fails to connect gender roles as a characteristic of the individual to actual behavior.

Although the introduction of the construct of androgyny significantly altered the research landscape on gender roles, its use as a theoretical model has declined. More importantly, there has been a shift away from viewing gender roles through an essentialist lens to a more social constructionist perspective. Kay Deaux, *Psychology Constructions of Masculinity and Femininity,* argues that an adequate account of masculinity/femininity first must clearly explain the relationship between the elements that make up masculinity/femininity and actual behavior, and second must allow for the fact that situations exert substantial influence in an individual's display of gendered behaviors. In a more radical critique, Morawski (1987) suggests that psychologists need to abandon their search for the categories of masculinity, femininity, and androgyny and focus instead on the social institutions and interpersonal interactions that construct gender. The social constructionist framework for understanding gender roles, which recognizes the relationship among social structures, and the positions of women and men in social organizations and in systems of power, has led to new lines of research on gender roles (see Gergen & Davis, 1997).

Gender Roles and Identity

Although the social constructionist criticism eschews the view that gender roles are a stable, unidimensional, essential element of personality, many theorists continue to believe that gender roles play a role in an individual's construction of identity. According to Ashmore (1990), the challenge in developing an understanding of individual gender identity is to provide an account of the relationship between an individual's experiences and gender role identity that incorporates the influence of gendered contexts and the variability of individual behavior. For Ashmore, **gender identity**[3] is one component of a multiplicity model of gender role identity that includes the social construction of gender, the biological elements of sex and gender, beliefs about men and women, and attitudes toward men and women. Thus gender roles, internalized as an aspect of identity, are subject to these multiple influences and would not be a stable, unchanging element of identity. Gender roles are perhaps best represented by an ongoing reciprocal relationship between the individual's beliefs and values with regard to gender, the immediate social context, and the larger cultural construction of gender. Nonetheless, gender roles, as they are internalized by the individual and acted on by others, have a subjective stability in people's experiences. We emphasize, in future chapters, the process by which children construct a stable sense of gender identity (chapter 6) and the emotional value of gender identity in sexuality and interpersonal relationships (chapters 7, 10, and 11).

One Consequence of Gender Roles—The Case of Masculinity

In chapter 4, you read about the potential negative consequences of the male gender role for men of color in the United States. We described the development of the theory of male gender role strain, which argues that Western views of masculinity encourage men to deny their emotions and to be oriented toward public success. The article in this chapter by David Gilmore, *Manhood*, presents his anthropological observations of how masculinity expresses itself in different cultures. In many societies, boys can only achieve manhood through painful rituals or public challenges. Gilmore was struck by the variety of such rituals and the many settings in which they occur. Although there are no such dramatic rituals in the United States, there are intriguing parallels in the public performances or displays during athletics that characterize the behavior of young men. Gilmore questions the function of such hard-won masculinity. His conclusion, that the public displays of manhood he describes represent a kind of nurturing that parallels the private nurturing most associated with the feminine gender role, is both intriguing and, for many, controversial. Embedded in this idea is perhaps the broader notion that those characteristics that are often posited as opposites (e.g., aggressive vs. passive, independent vs. nurturing, emotional vs. detached) may represent different responses to similar human needs.

WHAT ARE STEREOTYPES?

We are all familiar with stereotypes of race, ethnicity, age, nationality, social class, sexual orientation, region of the country, religion, and of course, gender. Stereotypes hold an odd position in our thinking. We readily acknowledge their existence, many of us denounce their usage, we are urged to treat everyone as an individual, and yet we cannot escape the presence of stereotypes or their influence on us. Stereotypes surround us in many ways: advertising, television, movies, music, literature. Consider your beliefs about attractiveness, body image, romance, work, child rearing, aging—and ask yourself where these beliefs come from. Do they come from your experience with real, unique, individual people? Or are your beliefs based on the cultural images that bombard us daily? Stereotypes abound in children's books, where women are mommies, children live at home with two parents, and people are white and where boys are active, have adventures, and solve problems while girls are passive, dependent, and fearful. From the time we are born—and dressed in either blue or pink—and throughout our lives, we live in a world that constantly defines and reinforces particular ways that men and women should behave, act, and think. Is it little wonder that our thinking about sex and gender is structured around such generalizations?

Research on Stereotypes

Social psychologists have a long history of research on stereotypes and several theoretical approaches have emerged (Ashmore & Del Boca, 1986). One point of view used to examine stereotypes is a sociocultural perspective, which emphasizes the development of a shared belief system held by a cultural group. As we have seen in chapter 4, gender roles are developed in a cultural context, and gender stereotypes may have different meanings across cultures. A second perspective emphasizes motivational factors and the relationship between stereotypes and prejudice. From this point of view, researchers have been interested in the relationship between gender stereotypes, the evaluation of men and women, and sex or gender discrimination. A third perspective incorporates cognitive factors into sociocultural theory so that stereotyping is seen as a basic aspect of information processing, adding the recognition that the content and meaning of gender stereotypes may vary according to social and cultural context (Deaux & Kite, 1994).

The contemporary incorporation of cognitive theory into social psychology views stereotypes as a kind of mental concept known as a *fuzzy set* (Deaux & Kite, 1994). Concepts are a form of mental organization in which different examples of objects,

things, people, animals, and so on are organized by their similar properties; for example, robin, blue jay, and hummingbird are exemplars of the concept of bird. Cognitive theories have proposed several different types of mental concepts such as prototype, category, or schema, all of which describe different ways that information can be organized and accessed mentally. There is evidence to suggest that gender is not a mental category in which masculine and feminine are mutually exclusive and opposite, despite our everyday use of the term *opposite sex*. Because we recognize that the borders between the attributes that define masculinity and femininity sometimes overlap and that it is impossible to determine every attribute associated with each concept, these sorts of categories are described as fuzzy (Maccoby, 1987).

It appears that people view the characteristics associated with masculinity and femininity as more or less likely to be associated with men versus women. Attributes such as competitive, independent, unemotional, and objective are viewed as highly likely to be associated with men, while attributes such as emotional, talkative, gentle, and sensitive are viewed as highly likely to be associated with women (Basow, 1992). Research on gender stereotypes has revealed that people also recognize that attributes such as competitive, independent, or unemotional, are not exclusively male, just as emotional, gentle, and sensitive are not exclusively female attributes. We may expect that a person who is competitive or unemotional will be a male, but we know that will not always be the case. Gender stereotypes do not describe categories of people, male or female, but instead function as *probabilities*. People use these probabilities to estimate the likelihood that men or women will act in particular ways or possess particular characteristics.

The Content of Gender Stereotypes

Deaux's article in this chapter reviews the research on gender stereotypes and concludes that stereotypes are composed of the following four components: *traits* (e.g., independent, emotional), *role behaviors* (e.g., financial provider, cares for children), *physical characteristics* (e.g., muscular, graceful) and *occupations* (e.g., engineer, elementary school teacher). Each component contains characteristics more likely to be associated with men and characteristics more likely to be associated with women. Research on how people use stereotypes shows that information about someone on one component influences assumptions about other components. For example, a woman described as a source of emotional support who takes care of children and manages a household (*role behaviors*) is more likely to be judged as emotional and gentle (*traits*) and as an elementary school teacher (*occupation*) than she is to be judged as unemotional, aggressive, or a banker. When making judgments about others, research participants rely more on information about role behavior and physical appearance than they do on information about biological sex. However, when information about role behavior violates stereotypes for a person's sex (e.g., a male who cooks and decorates the house), then that person is more likely to be judged as homosexual than would a person described in gender-stereotypic ways (Deaux & Kite, 1994).

Research also shows that there are sex differences in the application and use of stereotypes. Judgments of men tend to be harsher, with the expectation of rigid adherence to the masculine gender role (Hudak, 1993; Williams & Best, 1990). Both women and men use more stereotyped terms to describe men. Men, however, tend to apply stereotypes to both men and women more stringently than do women. Men seem to be more judgmental of violations of stereotypes, whereas there is some evidence that women do not view nontraditional men negatively (Deaux & Kite, 1994; Williams & Best, 1990).

Gender Stereotypes and Racial/Ethnic Identity

Most research on stereotypes is based on the results of research participants who are asked to judge the characteristics or behaviors of *hypothetical* men or women. What exactly do you suppose are the other characteristics of these hypothetical people? Given that most research participants are college students who are predominantly young, white, and middle class, it is a safe assumption that the basis for their judgments would be individuals like themselves. How do these stereotypes apply to diverse racial and ethnic groups? Do the characteristics associated with masculine and feminine stereotypes apply to those people who are not like the homogenized, hypothetical person? Are gender roles based on stereotypes different for people whose identity does not match this mythical norm?

The answer, not surprisingly, is complex. Our predominantly white society does hold certain stereotypes of women and men of color. In an analysis of racial and ethnic stereotypes, Davenport and Yurich (1991) examined the stereotypes associated with two groups in the United States: African Americans and Mexican Americans. These authors observed that the gender stereotypes describing each of these groups are not the same as the gender stereotypes of European Americans. Mexican American men often are portrayed as domineering and oppressive, while Mexican American women are portrayed as self-sacrificial and passive. Accompanying these stereotypic views of Mexican Americans are rapidly changing gender roles within the community. These changes in gender roles are partially related to the level of exposure to European American culture. These findings suggest that it is important to consider stereotypes and actual behavior simultaneously.

Stereotypes of African Americans are rooted in the historical experiences of slavery and postslavery economic discrimination. African American women are stereotyped as domineering while African American men are viewed as irresponsible. The reality, according to Staples (1982), is that African Americans do define gender roles somewhat differently than the white norm. African American women endorse "being a good provider" as an important quality for being a good mother, and both men and women share somewhat more egalitarian attitudes toward women and men.

Research by Landrine, Klonoff, and Brown-Collins (1992) illustrates the complexity of the relationship between ethnic identity and gender stereotypes. They asked a sample of women to rate gender stereotypic self-descriptive phrases.[4] The participants were white, black, Asian, and Latina. The researchers were also interested in the meaning attributed to each characteristic by the women, so following the rating, participants were given a choice of several possible definitions and asked to circle the one that best matched the attribute. In the first analysis, which looked at differences in self-rating for the different attributes, no differences among the four groups of women were found.

The analysis of the meaning attributed to the traits did show differences in two intriguing ways. First, there were differences across ethnic groups in the meaning attributed to some of the traits. For example, Latina and Asian American women were more likely to define *assertive* as "say what's on my mind," white women were more likely to define it as "standing up for myself," and black women were more likely to choose "standing up for myself" or "aggressive." The second difference was that the rating on a given trait depended on the definition given to that trait. For example, white women who defined *sensitive* as "doing what others want" rated themselves as less sensitive than white women who chose "care about others" or "understand other's point of view." These data illustrate a powerful point about the complexity of stereotypes—similarities across ethnic groups or for men and women may not indicate agreement on the meaning of the stereotype in question. It is, therefore, critical to understand that the same behavior or trait may not necessarily represent a universally agreed upon meaning (Landrine, Klonoff, & Brown-Collins, 1992).

The third article in this chapter, *Overcoming Stereotypes of Mothers in the African American Context* by Elizabeth Sparks, considers the personal implications of stereotypes for African American women. Sparks highlights some of the historical differences between the experiences of African American women and white women, especially in connection with slavery and the postslavery treatment of African American women. One important issue for Sparks, in her work as a clinical psychologist, is the *internalization* of stereotypes. The internalization of stereotypes describes a process whereby people incorporate into their identity stereotyped images or characteristics. For Sparks, many of the images of

African American women regarding motherhood, sexuality, and employment have either been highly negative (e.g., promiscuous, indifferent to her children, unwilling to work) or have imposed unrealistic standards, such as a superwoman who is ultracompetent in work, motherhood, and community service. Whereas the negative stereotypes are hurtful, socially oppressive, and represent the prejudices of the dominant society, the more positive stereotype originates from efforts within the African American community to counter these negative images. The consequences of this more positive stereotype are still harmful. In particular, Sparks is concerned with the negative self-image, depression, and low self-esteem that may result when African American women judge themselves against this internalized standard.

There are some interesting comparisons between Sparks's analysis and the analysis of the male gender role presented in the article by Gilmore. While they describe very different cultural constructions of masculinity and femininity, both authors address the social and individual consequences of gender roles. For Gilmore, broad cultural pressures define manhood in particular ways that distinguish it from things that are feminine. For Sparks, stereotypes emerge from the justification of patterns of social oppression against African American women. Both analyses agree that cultural gender roles or cultural stereotypes can perpetuate oppression—especially when they function as prescriptions for one's gender identity.

Gender Stereotypes and Sexual Orientation

Stereotypes about homosexuality are a special case of the interaction between gender stereotypes and stereotypes about sexuality. Among the general population, perhaps the most penetrating stereotype of homosexuals is the view that gay men are feminine and lesbians are masculine. This stereotype gained scientific validity as psychologists sought to verify it through the measurement of gay men's femininity, using scales of masculinity/femininity (Lewin, 1984). According to Lewin, research on this (called the inversion theory) was a dismal failure, finding no relationship between gay men and femininity, yet the stereotype persisted. This stereotype is so pervasive that men and women whose behavior or appearance is not stereotypically masculine or feminine are likely to be assumed to be homosexual (Herek, 1995). The stereotypes about homosexuality operate in two powerful ways—one when inappropriate assumptions about one's gender role are made based on knowledge of sexual orientation, and the other when judgments are made about sexual orientation based on the violation of gender role prescriptions.

Heterosexism is defined as beliefs, attitudes, or values that discriminate or stigmatize any nonheterosexual behavior or identity. Herek (1995) describes the heterosexist bias in Western societies and its relationship to stereotyping along two salient dimensions. Cultural heterosexism is a belief system whereby social institutions, customs, and practices are based on a heterosexual norm, excluding all other possibilities, and individual heterosexism is a belief system held by individuals that repudiates or denigrates homosexuals. Heterosexist beliefs are highly resistant to change and are perpetuated by the unwillingness of many heterosexuals to associate with homosexuals. The strong biases against gay men, exhibited by many heterosexual men, are perpetuated by elements of the masculine gender role.[5] The prescription to avoid that which is feminine coupled with the stereotype of gay men as feminine is related to a pervasive intolerance of homosexuality by many heterosexual men.

There are many negative consequences of heterosexism for nonheterosexuals. Faced with discrimination and prejudice, many gay people have hidden their identities. Furthermore, the overt prejudice, which has been linked to violence against gay men and lesbians, has made the risks of an open identity even greater. According to Herek (1995), one survey reported that the average length of time between the private acknowledgment of one's gay identity and coming out to family was 4.6 years, and between 23 and 40 percent of another group surveyed had never told any member of their family. This discrepancy between public and private identity can force individuals to live with a level of painful dis-

honesty about their identity—perhaps participating in heterosexist conversations, laughing at jokes, or hiding many aspects of one's private life. This result is in sharp contrast to some of the other consequences of gender stereotypes that we have discussed. Although sexism may exert negative influences on women, it does not deny their identity as women. And although the interaction of sexism and racism may converge into narrower gender role prescriptions for African American women, these phenomena do not deny one's identity as an African American and a woman. It would be completely counterproductive to rank discrimination, but it is worthwhile to acknowledge the differences among forms of discrimination.

Are Stereotypes True? The Kernel of Truth Hypothesis

Clearly there are some circumstances in which stereotypes are gross distortions with little relationship to reality. The stereotypes of sexuality present in pornography fit that description (Cowan & Campbell, 1994) as do the distorted views of masculinity and femininity present in heterosexism. Other stereotypes may derive from generalizations that do, in some way, represent reality. Deaux and Kite (1994) argue that some objective sex differences in behavior or preferred activities correspond to stereotypes. Men, for example, are more likely to play competitive sports (although this sex difference has changed considerably in the last twenty years). Women are more likely to have experience caring for children, and many occupations are highly sex segregated—construction, engineering, nursing, clerical work. To the extent that stereotypes do represent a hypothetical average or typical example, there is a certain kind of truth to the stereotype. In her article in this chapter, Deaux refers to this approach as the "kernel of truth" of some stereotypes. Many stereotypes do not pass this kernel of truth test. Generalizations about personal qualities, beliefs, or emotions do not seem well supported by evidence.

The most troubling aspect of the reality of stereotypes is that they may be used to judge individuals or as prescriptions of "what should be." There may be a kernel of truth to the view that women are more likely to be teachers, secretaries, or nurses. The judgment, however, that a woman who repairs computers or builds furniture is therefore "not feminine" is unwarranted, just as the judgment that a man who is a teacher, secretary, or nurse is "effeminate" is also misplaced. There is wide variation among both men and women in preferred activities, skills, and interests.

THE CONSEQUENCES OF STEREOTYPES— DISCRIMINATION

To the extent that stereotypes misrepresent groups or impose prescriptions on individuals, discrimination may occur. Gender discrimination occurs when people are treated unfairly because of expectations based on gender. Expectations and beliefs about gender have had an impact on employment opportunities for women. Discrimination in hiring has been, to some extent, addressed by affirmative action (see the article by Eberhardt and Fiske in chapter 12); however, there are still disparities in promotions, or in women breaking into the upper echelon, a phenomenon known as the *glass ceiling* (Stroh, Brett, & Reilly, 1992). You may wonder how men have fared in traditionally female occupations. Some research suggests that men have a very high success rate in nontraditional occupations, a phenomenon recently named the *glass escalator* (Williams, 1992).

The article in this chapter by Fiske and Stevens, *What's So Special About Sex: Gender Stereotyping and Discrimination*, examines the relationship between gender stereotypes and discrimination against women in employment. The authors describe two different kinds of discrimination. The first is a case of the sexual harassment of a woman employed as a welder in a shipyard; the second case concerns a woman manager in an accounting firm who was denied partnership. The sexual harassment in the first case can be linked to the presence of only a few women in an environment that was described as "men only." The woman in the second case was described by her male evaluators as "not feminine

enough." The behaviors in these two incidents are radically different. In the first case, subjecting a female employee to repeated exposure to explicit sexual material and harassing comments, and in the second case, denying a promotion because of the female's lack of adherence to feminine stereotypes.

Fiske and Stevens analyze the contribution of gender stereotypes to these incidents. They identify five ways in which gender stereotypes are unique and provide a basis for establishing that gender discrimination is different from other forms of discrimination such as age, race, or ethnic discrimination. According to Fiske and Stevens, gender stereotypes share the following unique characteristics: (a) gender stereotypes are highly prescriptive, (b) differences in social status between men and women are linked to differences in access to power, (c) men and women live highly gender-integrated lives, (d) interpersonal interactions between men and women occur in a biological and sexual context, and (e) the expression of sexism has undergone rapid historical change. In reading their article, you should be alert for definitions and examples of these characteristics of gender stereotypes. Although Fiske and Stevens identify the unique elements of gender stereotypes that contribute to gender discrimination, you do not want to be misled into believing that gender stereotypes and gender discrimination are somehow qualitatively worse in their impact on individuals or society than other types of discrimination.

The unique characteristics of gender stereotypes help us understand some of the complex interactions among gender, race, ethnicity, and sexual orientation in gender stereotypes and gender roles that were revealed in the research by Landrine and in the analysis by Herek that we described earlier. Gender stereotypes do share some characteristics with stereotypes of race, ethnicity, and sexual orientation despite the emphasis by Fiske and Stevens on the distinctive features of gender stereotypes. All these stereotypes are characterized by power differences in the social roles of people—men versus women, White versus African American, European American versus ethnic minority, gay versus straight, and so on.[6] Often accompanying these power differences are economic disparities—these social groups do not have equal access to economic resources. Finally, gender, race, ethnic, and sexual orientation stereotypes are steeped in historical, cultural, and social conditions that support the perpetuation of these stereotypes. Gender stereotypes can be distinguished from the other stereotypes in two profound ways. First, men and women share complex intimate relationships with one another—in families, in the workplace, in education, and perhaps in intimate sexual relationships—and therefore gender roles and stereotypes are a constant backdrop to human interactions. Second, according to Fiske and Stevens, unlike race and ethnic stereotypes, which are purely social in nature, gender role stereotypes may be explained in part by the evolution of sex differences. Although a comparison of different social stereotypes may provide a useful heuristic by which we can examine different facets of social identity (e.g., race, gender, ethnicity, sexual orientation), the insistence on rigid distinctions among stereotypes may serve to further essentialist views of identity. The reality of stereotypes is that they will interact with each other and with social settings in complex ways.

STEREOTYPES AND GENDER ROLES—AGENIC AND COMMUNAL QUALITIES

One of the most influential models of the relationship between gender stereotypes and gender roles is the social role theory developed by Eagly (1987). According to Eagly, gender roles result from the sexual division of labor, from sex-typed behaviors and skills related to the division of labor, and from behavioral and role expectations based on social stereotypes. The characteristics contained in gender stereotypes can be summarized as two dimensions: communal and agenic. The communal role includes the following elements: caring, nurturant, affectionate, interpersonally sensitive, concerned with the welfare of others, and emotionally expressive. This role is more likely to be associated with women. The agenic role would be described as assertive, controlling, forceful, independent, leading, ambitious, and dominant. This role is more

likely to be associated with men. Just as stereotypes do not neatly divide men and women into separate categories, gender roles likewise represent overlapping groups containing considerable individual variation both in behavioral preferences and in gender role identity. Eagly's theory attempts to account for some of the confusion in our understanding of gender roles and stereotypes. Stereotypes represent overgeneralizations about people, and gender roles are prescriptions that are tied to cultural images and views of men and women. Under what conditions do people endorse stereotypes, and under what conditions do people conform to gender role prescriptions? Recognizing that stereotypes and gender roles do not apply in all circumstances, Eagly's theory attempts to isolate some of the most salient characteristics of stereotypes and gender roles and to specify when and how both are actually used.

Citing evidence that men and women show considerable behavioral conformity to gender stereotypes, Eagly (1987) argues that gender stereotypes form the basis for gender roles. Gender roles become norms for the behavior of men and women and are treated as prescriptive. People are judged on the degree to which they conform to prescribed gender roles, and individuals internalize gender roles as a significant element of their identity. Certainly there are individual differences in the degree to which a person acts in accord with social gender roles as well as differences in circumstances that are likely to elicit specific stereotyped behaviors. Gender role norms are likely to exert a strong influence on behavior when there is wide agreement on the particular stereotype (e.g., men are leaders) and when there is a strong cultural expectation of gender role behavior (e.g., women are the providers of child care).

As we learned in chapter 4, the sexual division of labor is central to understanding the cultural construction of gender. Eagly emphasizes the traditional division of labor as the basis for gender stereotypes and gender roles. The core attributes of the communal social role are thought to derive from the domestic activities (e.g., homemaking and child care), performed predominantly by women. The core attributes of the agenic role emerge from activities in the public sphere (e.g., decision making, earning money), predominantly the world of work—and men. Wait a minute, you might say. Don't these represent stereotypes, not reality? In reality, aren't men and women both involved in the public and private realms? What about the dramatic increase of women in the workforce? These are all good questions that can be accounted for by Eagly's model. The strength of Eagly's argument is in her analysis of how power and responsibility are distributed to men and women in public versus domestic settings and how individual identity is constructed around these social roles.

In general, in the United States, the domestic role carries little status, prestige, and power. There is little motivation for men to share household responsibilities, and there is substantial evidence that among heterosexual married couples, women perform far more domestic work than do men, regardless of the women's employment status (see the article by Kurdek in chapter 11). Women have increased their participation in the workforce dramatically in the last twenty years. However, they have made few inroads into positions of power and influence and tend to be segregated in female-dominated positions such as teacher, nurse, clerical worker, and so on (U.S. Department of Labor, 1994). Although women are employed in greater numbers, they seldom occupy positions in which the development of characteristics related to the agenic role is likely.[7] According to Eagly, men continue to have greater status and decision-making power; furthermore, status, influence over others, and power are predictive of being perceived as agenic by others.

GENDER ROLES AND GENDER STEREOTYPES

As you can see, the concepts of gender roles and gender stereotypes do overlap, and the relationship between them is complex. The readings for this chapter introduce you to specific examples of the differing ways gender roles and stereotypes can be related. The position that gender roles are internalized as aspects of identity is represented by Gilmore's discussion of the universal aspects of manhood. The view that stereotypes may lead to the construction of a particular gender role is represented by Sparks, who writes about the negative consequences of stereotypes for African American women. Fiske and Stevens articulate the relationship between gender stereotypes and sex discrimination. Some common elements of these differing presentations include the notion that gender roles and stereotypes are composed of a culturally based belief system about gender, that we should not assume that behavior is clearly related to gender roles or stereotypes, and that gender roles and stereotypes have both systemic and individual negative consequences.

Deaux, in her review of the research on gender roles and gender stereotypes, provides you with three cautions that are important to remember as you think about the articles in this chapter: One should not oversimplify the complexity of gender roles and stereotypes; one should not assume that gender identity will be a unidimensional construct when the evidence is that it is multifaceted; and one should not assume stability of either gender roles or behavior because variability is the norm. We suggest an additional caution: Be aware that the concepts that we readily use in our everyday lives—stereotypes and gender roles—have shifting and multiple meanings.

NOTES

1. Part of the distinction between gender roles and stereotypes may also derive from semantics and tradition—psychologists interested in personality and culture as well as those interested in developmental issues have tended to use the term *gender roles,* whereas social psychologists use the term *stereotypes.*

2. The items on Bem's scale (Bem Sex-Role Inventory) were identified as characteristics desirable by either men, women, or both, and on Spence's scale (Personal Attributes Questionnaire), items were judged to be more typical of one sex than of the other.

3. In this chapter, we are referring to gender identity as it is used by social psychologists to describe the relationship between the individual and social arrangements. In the next chapter, we describe the development of gender identity using the perspective of developmental psychology.

4. I make decisions easily; I am sensitive to the needs of others; I am feminine; I am assertive; I am independent; I have leadership ability; I am passive.

5. Heterosexual men exhibit much higher levels of prejudice against homosexuals than do heterosexual women (Herek, 1995).

6. Remember that we are not asserting that all members of one group experience greater power than all members of the other group, but that power as distributed within our society reflects these broad differences.

7. Of course, some women have had access to positions of power and influence and may demonstrate agency as a result of their experiences. One analysis of the Fiske and Stevens example of Price Waterhouse versus Hopkins is that Hopkins's demonstration of agenic qualities violated social role expectations.

REFERENCES

Ashmore, R. D. (1990). Sex, gender, and the individual. In L. A. Pervin (Ed.), *Handbook of personality theory and research*. New York: Guilford Press.

Ashmore, R. D., & Del Boca, F. K. (Eds.). (1986). *The social psychology of female-male relations: A critical analysis of central concepts*. Orlando, FL: Academic Press.

Basow, S. A. (1992). *Gender stereotypes and roles* (3rd ed.). Pacific Grove, CA: Brooks/Cole.

Bem, S. L. (1974). The measurement of psychological androgyny. *Journal of Personality and Social Psychology, 42*, 155–162.

Cowan, G., & Campbell, R. R. (1994). Racism and sexism in interracial pornography. *Psychology of Women Quarterly, 18*, 323–338.

Davenport, D. S., & Yurich, J. M. (1991). Multicultural gender issues. *Journal of Counseling and Development, 70*, 64–71.

Deaux, K. (1987). Psychological constructions of masculinity and femininity. In J. Reinisch, L. Rosenblum, & S. Sanders (Eds.), *Masculinity/femininity: Basic perspectives* (pp. 289–303). New York: Oxford University Press.

Deaux, K., & Kite, M. (1994). Gender stereotypes. In F. Denmark & M. Paludi (Eds.), *Psychology of women: A handbook of issues and theories* (pp. 107–139). Westport, CT: Westview Press.

Eagly, A. H. (1987). *Sex differences in social behavior: A social role interpretation*. Hillsdale, NJ: Erlbaum.

Fiske, S. T., & Stevens, L. E. (1993). What's so special about sex? Gender stereotyping and discrimination. In S. Oskamp & M. Costanzo (Eds.), *Gender issues in contemporary society* (pp. 173–196). Beverly Hills, CA: Sage.

Gergen, M. M., & Davis, S. N. (Eds.). (1997). *Toward a new psychology of gender: A reader*. New York: Routledge.

Gilmore, D. D. (1990, June). Manhood. *Natural History*, pp. 6–10.

Herek, G. M. (1995). Psychological heterosexism in the United States. In A. R. D'Augelli & C. J. Patterson (Eds.), *Lesbian, gay, and bisexual identities over the lifespan: Psychological perspectives*. Washington, DC: American Psychological Association.

Hudak, M. A. (1993). Gender schema theory revisited: Men's stereotypes of American women. *Sex Roles, 28*, 279–293.

Landrine, H., Klonoff, E. A., & Brown-Collins, A. (1992). Cultural diversity and methodology in feminist methodology. *Psychology of Women Quarterly, 18*, 145–163.

Lewin, M. (1984). "Rather worse than folly?" Psychology measures femininity and masculinity. In M. Lewin (Ed.), *In the shadow of the past: Psychology portrays the sexes* (pp. 155–178). New York: Columbia University Press.

Maccoby, E. E. (1987). The varied meanings of "masculine" and "feminine". In J. M. Reinisch, L. A. Rosenblum, & S. A. Sanders (Eds.), *Masculinity/femininity: Basic perspectives*. New York: Oxford University Press.

Morawski, J. (1987). The troubled quest for masculinity, femininity, and androgyny. *Review of Personality and Social Psychology, 7*, 44–69.

Sparks, E. E. (1996). Overcoming stereotypes of mothers in the African American context. In K. F. Wyche & F. J. Crosby (Eds.), *Women's ethnicities: Journeys through psychology*. Boulder, CO: Westview Press.

Spence, J. T., & Helmreich, R. L. (1978). *Masculinity and femininity: Their psychological dimensions, correlates, and antecedents*. Austin: University of Texas Press.

Staples, R. (1982). *Black masculinity: The black male's role in American society*. San Francisco: The Black Scholar Press.

Stroh, L. K., Brett, J. M., & Reilly, A. (1992). All the right stuff: A comparison of female and male managers' career progression. *Journal of Applied Psychology, 77*, 251–260.

U.S. Department of Labor. (1994). *1993 Handbook on women workers: Trends and issues*. Washington, DC: U.S. Government Printing Office.

Williams, C. L. (1992). The glass escalator: Hidden advantages for men in the "female" professions. *Social Problems, 39*, 253–267.

Williams, J., & Best, D. (1990). *Measuring sex stereotypes: A multination study*. Beverly Hills, CA: Sage.

Psychological Constructions of Masculinity and Femininity

KAY DEAUX

The terms *masculinity* and *femininity* are rich in meaning and widespread in use, applied to a diversity of phenomena by both laypersons and scientists. In her recent appraisal of femininity, for example, Susan Brownmiller (1984) pointed to body, hair, clothes, voice, skin, movement, emotion, and ambition as equally important aspects of the concept. I suspect that a similar analysis of masculinity could yield an equally lengthy list.

Given the umbrella-like quality of both of these terms, it is perhaps inevitable that scientific discussions have displayed both confusion and misunderstanding. Different disciplines use different evidential bases, but across the disciplines the terms *masculinity* and *femininity* find continued use. I will not attempt to survey this broad conceptual range; instead, I will restrict my analysis to those uses of the term that are most distinctly psychological—or, perhaps even more narrowly, social psychological.

The terms *masculinity* and *femininity* have been used by investigators in personality and social psychology in at least three areas: (1) stereotypic views of males and females; (2) studies of sex differences and similarities in cognitive abilities, personality traits, and social behaviors; and (3) gender identity and self-reported masculinity and femininity. These three areas are equally important to an understanding of what is meant by masculinity and femininity, and research in each of the areas has been relatively vigorous, particularly in the past 10–15 years. I would like to outline some of the assumptions that underlie each of these approaches, noting representative research and raising some of the questions that each area implies.

PERCEPTIONS OF MALES AND FEMALES

A stereotype is, to use the definition offered by Ashmore and Del Boca (1979), "a structured set of beliefs about the personal attributes of a group of people" (p. 222). Originally imbued with both motivational processes and negative connotations, the concept of stereotype has recently been reinterpreted in terms more consistent with the newer work in social cognition. In adopting this theoretical framework, psychologists consider the stereotype in neutral terms, viewing it as simply one type of categorization that shares many features with other cognitive categories.

Stereotypes about women and men represent one particular set of beliefs, wherein males and females are the identifiable groups in question. Gender stereotypes have traditionally been defined in terms of the presence or absence of specific personality traits. Most commonly, a distinction has been made between expressive traits, viewed as more characteristic of women, and instrumental traits, seen as more characteristic of men (e.g., Broverman, Vogel, Broverman, Clarkson, & Rosenkrantz, 1972; Spence, Heimreich, & Stapp, 1974). Thus, women are typically viewed as being warm, gentle, and aware of the feelings of others, while men are described by traits such as independent, dominant, and assertive.

More recently, a number of investigators have begun to recognize that the content of gender stereotypes is not limited to trait adjectives (e.g., Ashmore & Del Boca, 1979; Ashmore, Del Boca, & Wohlers, 1986; Deaux & Lewis, 1983, 1984). Ashmore and Del Boca have suggested three classes of gender-related attributes: defining characteristics (consisting primarily of biological features), identifying characteristics (such as stature, clothing, and other externally visible signs), and ascribed characteristics (exemplified by trait adjectives).

In recent research on gender stereotypes, Laurie Lewis and I have identified four separate components that are reliably used by observers to distinguish males from females (Deaux & Lewis, 1983). These four components are traits, role behaviors, physical characteristics, and occupations. Within each of these component domains is one set of features seen as more characteristic of men than of women and another set seen as more characteristic of women than of men. For example, men are viewed as more likely than women to be strong, to be the financial provider in a household, to be an engineer, and to be competitive. In turn, women are rated more apt to have a soft voice, to take care of children, to be a secretary, and to be able to devote themselves to others. Although the probability attached to a particular characteristic is significantly different for men and women, the features are not viewed in dichotomous terms. The obtained probability of a male being independent, for example, is .77, while the comparable rating for a woman is .58. The pattern for other characteristics is similar, with differences ranging from 15 to 30 points on a 100-point probability scale. Thus, we should most appropriately consider gender stereotypes in terms of relative instead of absolute differences—or as fuzzy sets, in the terminology of cognitive psychologists.

Further complexity is added to the picture when we find that these components are not perfectly correlated with one another. These various components appear to function somewhat independent of one another, at least in the abstract. At the same time, learning that a person possesses a high degree of one component does lead to some convergence in other judgments, particularly when the information is counter to expectations for a particular individual (Deaux & Lewis, 1984). Thus a man who is described as being warm and emotional is also judged to be more likely to have feminine physical characteristics and to engage in more traditionally female role behaviors. Further, such seemingly simple coun-

terstereotypic trait information can also lead to a marked increase in the assessed probability that the man is homosexual.

The Deaux and Lewis research also points to the importance of physical characteristics in the construction of gender stereotypes. Although these obvious indicators have been slighted in most of the earlier research on stereotypy, their influence can not be ignored. Indeed, cues as to physical appearance have been found to carry the greatest weight in subsequent gender-related judgments, influencing inferences of traits, role behaviors, and occupational position (Deaux & Lewis, 1984). Thus, the male who is slight of build or whose voice is relatively soft may be particularly vulnerable to judgments of femininity and of homosexuality. The ready availability of information about physical characteristics thus serves as a point of initial inference—a point beyond which the casual observer may not pass. In other words, the stereotypic inference process may begin as soon as the visual information is available, and observers may not wait to find out whether their inferences are actually based in fact.

To the best of our knowledge, all societies have a set of beliefs (or schema) about gender. Comparison of gender stereotypes within the United States to stereotypic concepts held in other parts of the world reveals both similarities and differences. In perhaps the most extensive recent investigation, one involving data collections in 30 different nations, Williams and Best (1982) find "pancultural generality" in many aspects of gender stereotypes. Specifically, they report that men are typically viewed as stronger, more active, and higher in achievement, autonomy, and aggression. Women are seen as weaker, less active, and more concerned with affiliation, nurturance, and deference. Both patterns are obviously consistent with the instrumental-expressive distinction found in previous single-nation studies. This same pattern can be detected in Block's (1973) cross-cultural studies, wherein specific traits may differ across countries but the underlying instrumental and expressive dimensions remain constant. Other variations across country as a function of religious affiliation have been noted by Williams and Best (1982); in Catholic countries, for example, women are viewed more positively than they are in Protestant countries. Dwyer (1978) notes variations in Morocco based on age and social interaction, with a heavy element of sexuality contained in the female stereotype. Strathern (1976), basing her observations primarily on New Guinea cultures, notes apparent contradictions in some elements of gender stereotypes (for example, she points to views of women as both hard-headed and soft-brained). She also finds evidence for a multiple-component view of stereotypes, as do Deaux and Lewis (1983, 1984), with components often implicating one another.

Thus, the evidence suggests that male and female, or masculinity and femininity, are not simple unidimensional concepts. Instead, they are loosely constructed categories that contain, with varying degrees of probability, a variety of characteristics and associations. From the cognitive perspective, we could view these attributes as varying in their degree of prototypicality to the central concepts—concepts that are, at best, fuzzy sets instead of clearly delineated categories.

At the same time that the concepts of masculinity and femininity, considered separately, show evidence of multidimensionality, the two concepts themselves are typically viewed as opposite ends of a single dimension. Thus, a common perception exists that what is masculine is not feminine, and vice versa, a finding that has been demonstrated in a number of investigations (Deaux & Lewis, 1984; Foushee, Helmreich, & Spence, 1979; Major, Carnevale, & Deaux, 1981). The commonly used term *the opposite sex* captures this mode of thought, positing opposition to explain differences. Such a dialectic assumption is evident not only in lay conceptions, but also in the postulates of scientific investigators.

To summarize our knowledge of gender stereotypes, we can safely say that all known societies have constructed a set of beliefs that differentiate males and females along some dimensions. Most often, the general concepts of masculinity and femininity are viewed in terms of opposition, with the presence of one set of characteristics implying the absence of the other. In addition is a set of elements central to the gender stereotypes held in most cultures. One can speculate that certain defining or identifying characteristics of males and females support these distinctions; for example, the typically greater strength and stature of the male and the female's stronger link to childbearing may provide the seeds from which attributes such as instrumentality and nurturance develop. Considerable diversity, however, is in other ascribed attributes that are associated with masculinity and femininity. These attributes are formed in the context of the existent social system, and undoubtedly reflect both cause and consequence of the distribution of women and men into specific social roles (cf. Eagly, 1983; Eagly & Steffen, 1984). Such variations suggest caution in assuming a simple or universal gender stereotype; conceptions of male and female are elaborated in different ways depending on the cultural context in which they emerge.

SEX DIFFERENCES AND SIMILARITIES

Research on sex differences and similarities can be examined to determine whether perceived stereotypes are reflected in reality—that is, do gender stereotypes possess a kernel (or a larger portion) of truth? One possible hypothesis is that gender stereotypes develop as widely used cognitive categories because they accurately mirror the reality of male and female behavior. Such a hypothesis would be supported by evidence of reliable sex differences in specifically designated behaviors and would be strengthened by evidence of universality of beliefs. Alternatively, one might hypothesize that differences in the behavior of women and men are far less evident than the stereotypes would suggest. Cognitive processes such as biased scanning and preferential recall of category-consistent information might then be invoked to explain the persistence of gender stereotypes when they are not totally justified by experience. This perspective would be more compatible with evidence of variation in stereotypes across culture and changes in stereotypes across time. Suggestive of this approach is the statement of Strathern (1976): "Myths about masculinity and femininity (gender constructs) endure and change, as language endures and changes, because of their usefulness as symbols in the society at large" (p. 68).

The answers to these questions are less easily obtained than one might suppose. Leaving aside for the moment the relative contributions of biological and experiential determinants, one still finds a great deal of uncertainty as to what sex differences are reliable and stable. The uncertainty does not result from any lack of effort. Since before the turn of the century, investigators have explored various behavioral areas for evidence of sex differences, arriving at different conclusions throughout. Summaries of such findings have often been challenged, for both methodological and political reasons.

The most recent attempt to provide a broad-scale assessment of possible sex differences in behavior is that of Maccoby and Jacklin (1974). Their ambitious review of the literature pointed to only four areas in which reliable sex differences could be established— verbal, mathematical, and spatial abilities, and aggressive behavior. In many other areas, they stated that they had simply no evidence for sex differences in behavior, including sociability, suggestibility, self-esteem, and achievement. In still other areas, Maccoby and Jacklin concluded that the questions are still open, with insufficient data or ambiguous findings precluding conclusions in either direction. These unsettled areas included competitiveness, dominance, compliance, and nurturance (all areas that are closely tied to pervasive gender stereotypes).

Research in the past decade has probed these issues further, supporting some of Maccoby and Jacklin's conclusions and questioning others (see Block, 1976, for a general critique of the Maccoby and Jacklin analysis). Typically, investigators have focused on a narrower set of behaviors and applied meta-analytic procedures to determine the existence and extent of differences. Eagly, for example, has found evidence of sex differences in social influence and in prosocial behavior (Eagly & Carli, 1981; Eagly & Crowley, 1985). Hyde (1982) reports reliable sex differences in aggression. Yet these and other differences have also been found to be small, generally accounting for less than 5% of the variance. Within-sex variation is substantially greater than between-sex variance in these analyses. Furthermore, most of the behavioral differences are strongly affected by situational factors, cautioning against any sweeping statements about invariant sex differences.

These patterns of small but significant differences recommend caution but not dismissal. In constrained situations—what one might call the maximal performance setting of the psychological laboratory—sex differences appear to be rather limited. On many of the measures that psychologists have devised, males and females are capable of comparable performance. Furthermore, experimental studies indicate that most, if not all, of the behavioral differences observed in the laboratory are highly susceptible to variations in the situation and in experience. Thus, immutability can not be assumed.

One exception to this pattern of small sex differences in laboratory investigations concerns the case of self-report. Self-assessed tendencies by males and females often show stronger sex differences than do actual performance measures. Such a pattern has been reported both for analyses of aggression (Frodi, Macaulay, & Thome, 1977) and for empathy (Eisenberg & Lennon, 1983). These differences are difficult to interpret. On the one hand, sex differences of this type may reflect the operation of demand characteristics, with both males and females reflecting an awareness of prevailing gender stereotypes instead of accurately assessing their own behavior. Alternatively, one could hypothesize that in self-report, people are summarizing a broader range of experience than that tapped by the psychologist's repertoire of tasks— experience that may evidence differences in choices, if not in capability.

From a somewhat different perspective, Carol Gilligan (1982) has postulated fundamental sex differences on the basis of self-reported reactions to moral dilemmas. Men and women, Gilligan asserts, speak in "different voices"—men concerned with separation and women with attachment. These different voices have implications for developmental sequences, perceptions of self and other, language, thought, and moral choices. Although Gilligan acknowledges the existence of some overlap, her basic message speaks to the differences between the sexes. Her thesis thus affirms that there is a "masculine" and a "feminine" mode, quite different from each other, with implications for a wide range of human behavior. Researchers may question Gilligan's conclusions, and in particular the evidence on which her contentions are based (see Benton et al., 1983). Nonetheless, her thesis is important if for no other reason than it moves beyond the piecemeal investigations so characteristic of sex-difference research.

The constrained environment of the laboratory, although important in assessing differences between women and men on specific tasks, cannot remain the sole arbitrator of questions regarding sex differences. Observations in less constrained contexts provide more grist for the mill of sex differences. A simple glance at the social world shows considerable variation in the behavior of women and men. Occupational distributions, child-care practices, and other realms of social life suggest distinctly different male and female patterns (see Eagly, 1983; Eagly & Steffen, 1984). These situations, not the experimental laboratory, form the experiential base for the development of gender belief systems; here the evidence of behavioral differences is far more pervasive.

Thus, in assessing sex differences, a distinction must be made between what men and women *can* do, when put to the test by psychological investigators, and what they *do* do in situations that provide greater choice among options. The two settings pose different questions, and researchers may arrive at different answers. Concepts of masculinity and femininity must take both types of evidence into account—inherent capabilities and behavioral choices—but the distinction between the two needs to be acknowledged in any conceptualization.

QUESTIONS OF GENDER IDENTITY

Acknowledging the element of choice in the conceptualization of masculinity and femininity relates to the issue of self-definition by women and men. Questions of gender identity have been approached from two slightly different perspectives: developmentalists have focused on the initial acquisition of a sense of one's maleness or femaleness (e.g., Stoller, 1968; Money & Ehrhardt, 1972), while social and personality psychologists have emphasized the concomitants of the adult's self-defined masculinity and femininity. Within the tradition of developmental psychology, three major models have been postulated over the years: the psychoanalytic model, the social-learning model, and the cognitive-developmental model. Each model posits that the child acquires a relatively stable sense of gender identity at a fairly early age, but the models differ in the hypothesized processes leading to this acquisition.

For the psychoanalytic theorist, masculinity and femininity are the inevitable outcomes of biological givens. Events occurring during the well-known Oedipal period determine sex role identity, an identity that is believed to remain stable throughout life. Subsequent theorists in the psychoanalytic tradition, such as Karen Horney and Erik Erikson, suggested modifications of the original Freudian position, but they maintained adherence to the biological determinants and the stability of gender identity.

Social-learning theorists point to the environment instead of to biological factors as determinants of gender identity, but they are similar in their acceptance of a stable gender identity formed relatively early in life. The child's identification with the same-sex parent is the principal mechanism by which gender identity is established, and both direct reinforcement and observational learning are invoked to explain acquisition of gender-appropriate behaviors.

Cognitive-development theory, as proposed by Lawrence Kohlberg, is similar to psychoanalytic theory in its postulation of a universal and invariant sequence. Also similar is its assumption that a stable gender identity is formed by the time a child is 5 or 6 years of age. This theory differs, however, in its suggestion that the child first categorizes himself or herself as a boy or girl, and then structures experience to be consistent with this categorization. Thus, identification with same-sex parents is a consequence, not a cause, of gender identity.

Each of these models, described only briefly here, postulates fundamentally different patterns of male and female behavior, reflecting differences in masculine and feminine identity. Specific examples of gender-related behaviors are provided by each theory. In general, however, sufficient attention has not been paid to delineating the precise set of behaviors that should be considered ramifications of gender identity. Although one may be tempted to conclude, in ad hoc fashion, that any and all observed sex differences in behavior are reflections of basic differences in self-conceived masculinity and femininity, such an easy conclusion runs a heavy risk of circularity. As Spence (1985) has recently suggested, the influence of gender identity in guiding the acquisition of gender congruent behaviors may diminish with time, becoming less influential to the adult than it is to the developing child.

Such a position does not necessarily imply that a basic sense of gender identity is weakened. It does suggest that the link between gender identity and any specific behavior may be tenuous. Thus, the distinction must be maintained (or perhaps initially recognized) between the global concept of gender identity and the specific referents that are invoked. Individuals may, as Spence (1985) suggests, create their own calculus for assessing maleness or femaleness, "using those gender-appropriate behaviors and characteristics they happen to possess to confirm their gender identity and attempting to dismiss other aspects of their make-up as unimportant" (p. 84).

Similar problems in distinguishing between a global construct and specific attitudinal and behavioral referents can be detected in the measurement of self-described masculinity and femininity by investigators in the personality and psychometric traditions. Over the past 50 years, several instruments have been developed to assess these constructs. Implicit in most has been the assumption that masculinity and femininity are bipolar concepts that can be represented on a single dimension (Constantinople, 1973). Further inherent in many of the measures is the belief that masculinity is what males do and femininity is what females do. Thus, to cite one of my favorite examples, a preference for a shower to a bath is scored for indicating masculinity, while the reverse preference indicates femininity. Because males and females typically endorsed these two alternatives with different frequencies, the item became, by definition, a valid indicator of masculinity and femininity. (The cultural limitations of this definition should be obvious.)

Recent work in this area has abandoned the notion of a single construct. In its place are two orthogonal scales that are proposed to measure masculinity and femininity separately, thus allowing people to vary from high to low on one or both of the scales. The most prominent examples of this approach, among several that have surfaced, are the BSRI developed by Sandra Bem (1974) and the PAQ introduced by Spence, Helmreich, and Stapp (1974). For both scales, males have been found to score significantly higher than females on the masculinity dimension, and females to score higher than males on the femininity dimension. The differences are relatively small in absolute terms, however, and the overlap is considerable. Thus, substantial numbers of both males and females score high on both "masculinity" and "femininity," suggesting for some investigators (e.g., Bem, 1974) the utility of postulating an androgynous personality type that combines both attributes.

Note that the specific terms *masculinity* and *femininity* were included as items in the original version of the BSRI. As Pedhazur and Tetenbaum (1979) noted in their critique of the scale, self-ratings for these two items are typically far more polarized than are ratings by women and men on any of the other items. Further, as Bem acknowledges, these two items "are actually the worst two items on the scale" (1979, p. 1050). They do not correlate with other items presumed to measure concepts of masculinity and femininity, but are more directly linked to simple sex distinctions. Thus, males almost always report that they are highly masculine, and females almost always report that they are highly feminine, independent of their self-reported possession of other traits on the scale. This apparent discrepancy is less interesting as a methodological problem, which has been discussed at length in the literature, than as a conceptual issue relevant to the basic definitions of masculinity and femininity. What does it mean to consider oneself masculine or feminine, contingent on being a male or a female? If this self-designation bears little relationship to behavioral referents or to other hypothesized correlates of masculinity and femininity, exactly what can we conclude? In her penetrating critique of the masculinity-femininity construct, Constantinople observed, "We are dealing with an abstract concept that seems to summarize some dimension of reality important for many people, but we are hard pressed as scientists to come up with any clear definition of the concept or indeed any unexceptionable criteria for its measurement" (1973, p. 390).

The extensive debates as to precisely what is being assessed by the masculinity and femininity scales of the PAQ and BSRI reflect this uncertainty. Bem, as the title of her instrument implies, has conceptualized these dimensions as relevant to a broad range of sex-related role behaviors, including, in her more recent work, gender-belief systems and cognitive schemata for processing gender-related information (Bem, 1981). Spence and Helmreich, in contrast, have advocated a closer link between the traits being measured by the scale and their behavioral consequences. Hence, they are prone to speak of clusters of instrumental and expressive traits, eschewing more extended links to other gender-linked behaviors and attitudes. Evidence for strong relationships among various gender-related behaviors has not thus far been provided (Spence & Helmreich, 1980). Further, we have some evidence that simple biological sex is more predictive of choices of sex-linked tasks than are dimensions of masculinity and femininity (Helmreich, Spence, & Holahan, 1979).

As discussed earlier with respect to the development of gender identity, we should distinguish between the global concepts of masculinity and femininity and more specific referents that may or may not be associated with the self-defined masculine and feminine person (see Spence, 1985). Knowing that a person describes herself as feminine may offer little predictability for any specific gender-related behavior.

MASCULINITY AND FEMININITY: DICTUM OR DIVERSION?

Masculinity and femininity are indeed fuzzy sets, not only for the lay observer attempting to form meaningful categories, but also for the scientific investigator. The prototypical concepts of masculinity and femininity are comprised of a variety of associated characteristics, related to their prototypes with varying degrees of probability. Lulled into security by terms that everyone seemingly understands, we have tended to ignore the many signs of confusion and lack of clarity inherent in these concepts. Each of the three areas that I have reviewed points to problems in conceptualization. Two problems stand out most clearly: the assumption of unidimensionality and the absence of behavioral referents.

Psychologists in the past assumed that masculinity and femininity were opposite ends of a single dimension, an assumption that is still evident in lay conceptions. In recent years, the two concepts have been separated in experimental investigations, and empirical evidence supports the hypothesized orthogonality between the two dimensions. Although one loaf has become two, however, we have seen insufficient consideration of the homogeneity of each of these loaves. Both are most often assumed to be unidimensional concepts, incorporating a variety of gender-related traits and behaviors. Available evidence does not support this assumption. Recent studies of gender stereotypes demonstrate that a number of separate and identifiable components are only moderately correlated with one another. Assessment of the attitudes, self-descriptions, and behaviors of males and females shows these gender-related characteristics to be only weakly related. Cross-cultural work shows diverging patterns of gender stereotypes and considerable variation in the division of labor between males and females (e.g., Murdock, 1965). Taken together, these lines of evidence pose a strong indictment of the unidimensional assumptions that underpin much of the psychological research.

A second major weakness of most research on masculinity and femininity is the tendency to point to ephemeral concepts in the absence of clearly defined behavioral referents. In post hoc fashion, one can point to many behaviors as indicants of masculinity and femininity. Yet few attempts have been made to chart systematically the occurrence of these behaviors and to determine the relationships among them. Trait psychologists have often been criticized for their proclivity to lump diverse behaviors together without first assessing their co-occurrence, a habit nearly as evident today as in the often-maligned Freudian era. Behavioral ecologists may have much to offer in their display of caution when assuming interrelationships among behavior patterns (e.g., Daly & Wilson, 1983).

Also missing from most of the research dealing with masculinity and femininity is an appreciation of the fluidity of these concepts and the behaviors they presumably describe—a fluidity that is evident in animal behavior as well as human. Considerable variation across situations is exhibited in many behaviors—most certainly in that vast range of behaviors that are caught up in the masculinity-femininity net. Futhermore, an element of choice is in many aspects of an individual's gender display that defies assumptions of constancy and inevitability. Let me speak in just a bit of detail about these more social-psycological considerations.

Biological distinctions undoubtedly exist between male and female, many of which are addressed in this volume. Apart from the less visible differences that may be detected in neurological and hormonal analysis, we see more apparent signs of sex differences. Two features that may be most critical are the typically greater size and strength of the male, and the female's greater involvement in childbearing. Yet these basic differences can-not realistically account for the great diversity of traits and behaviors associated with masculinity and femininity, much less for the considerable overlap in virtually all behaviors associated with the concepts.

Many investigators have pointed to the range that masculinity and femininity may cover. Birdwhistell (1970), for example, in discussing nonverbal displays of masculinity and femininity, argues that although certain physical distinctions are common to males and females, the nonverbal displays are learned and do differ across cultures: "Let me stress again that these positions, movements and expressions are culturally coded—that what is viewed as masculine in one culture may be regarded as feminine in another" (Birdwhistell, 1970, p. 44). Goffman (1979), analyzing gender depictions in the medium of advertising within U.S. culture, makes an even stronger statement about the role of individual choice: "What the human nature of males and females really consists of, then, is the capacity to learn to provide and to read depictions of masculinity and femininity and a willingness to adhere to a schedule for presenting these pictures. . . . One might just as well say there is no gender identity. There is only a schedule for the portrayal of gender" (p. 8).

At a more micro level, we have growing evidence from social psychological experiments that people consciously choose to portray different aspects of themselves depending on situational influences. To cite just a few examples, potential reinforcement can affect the degree to which achievement behavior is enacted (Jellison, Jackson-White, Bruder, & Martyna, 1975), aggression is displayed (Bandura, Ross, & Ross, 1961) and makeup and feminine clothes are worn (von Baeyer, Sherk & Zanna, 1981). Thus, masculinity and femininity can be consciously selected, displayed in some situations and absent in others. These findings do not deny that the concepts of masculinity and femininity are in some sense understood and acted on by the individual. Yet at the same time, they caution against the more prevalent assumption that the concepts are static and uninfluenced by the environmental circumstances.

To summarize the arguments presented here, I contend that traditional conceptions of masculinity and femininity have oversimplified that which is not simple, have unidimensionalized that which is multidimensional, and have conveyed a sense of stability and permanence to that which is inherently flexible. Perhaps the concepts of masculinity and femininity can be maintained in our repertoire. Yet if they are to remain, important distinctions need to be made between the theoretical concepts of masculinity and femininity and specific gender-related behaviors and attitudes. We need to specify the exact features that the concepts are believed to incorporate, we need to pay much more attention to situations and environments that encourage or discourage gender displays, and we need to give more thought to the functions that such behaviors may serve. Analyses of possible differences between males and females have not been well served by the easy invocation of the concepts of masculinity and femininity, and recognition that these terms are not explanations but simply labels is a necessary step for further understanding.

Acknowledgments—This chapter was prepared while the author was a Fellow at the Center for Advanced Study in the Behavioral Sciences, supported in part by the John D. and Catherine T. MacArthur Foundation. A grant to the author from the National Science Foundation (BNS-8217313) is also gratefully acknowledged. Thanks are extended to Janet T. Spence for her helpful comments on an earlier version of this manuscript.

REFERENCES

Ashmore, R. D., and Del Boca, F. K. (1979). Sex stereotypes and implicit personality theory: Toward a cognitive-social psychological conceptualization. *Sex Roles, 5,* 219–248.

Ashmore, R. D., Del Boca, F. K., & Wohlers, A. J. (1986). Gender stereotypes. In R. D. Ashmore & F. K. Del Boca (Eds.), *The social psychology of female-male relations: A critical analysis of central concepts.* New York: Academic Press.

Bandura, A., Ross, D., & Ross, S. (1961). Transmission of aggression through imitation of aggressive models. *Journal of Abnormal and Social Psychology, 63,* 575–582.

Bem, S. L. (1974). The measurement of psychological androgyny. *Journal of Consulting and Clinical Psychology, 42,* 155–162.

Bem, S. L. (1979). Theory and measurement of androgyny: A reply to the Pedhazur-Tetenbaum and Locksley-Colten critiques. *Journal of Personality and Social Psychology, 37,* 1047–1054.

Bem, S. L. (1981). Gender schema theory: A cognitive account of sex typing. *Psychological Review, 88,* 354–364.

Benton, C. J., Hernandez, A. C. R., Schmidt, A., Schmitz, M. D., Stone, A. J., & Weiner, B. (1983). Is hostility linked with affiliation among males and with achievement among females? A critique of Pollak and Gilligan. *Journal of Personality and Social Psychology, 45,* 1167–1171.

Birdwhistell, R. L. (1970). *Kinesics and context: Essays on body motion communication.* Philadelphia: University of Pennsylvania Press.

Block, J. H. (1973). Conceptions of sex roles: Some cross-cultural and longitudinal perspectives. *American Psychologist, 28,* 512–526.

Block, J. H. (1976). Issues, problems, and pitfalls in assessing sex differences: A critical review of "The Psychology of Sex Differences." *Merrill Palmer Quarterly, 22,* 283–308.

Broverman, I. K., Vogel, S. R., Broverman, D. M., Clarkson, F. E., & Rosenkrantz, P. S. (1972). Sex-role stereotypes: A current appraisal. *Journal of Social Issues, 28*(2), 59–78.

Brownmiller, S. (1984). *Femininity.* New York: Linden Press/Simon & Schuster.

Constantinople, A. (1973). Masculinity-femininity: An exception to a famous dictum? *Psychological Bulletin, 80,* 389–407.

Daly, M., & Wilson, M. (1983). *Sex, evolution, and behavior* (2nd ed.). Boston: Willard Grant Press.

Deaux, K., & Lewis, L. L. (1983). Assessment of gender stereotypes: Methodology and components. *Psychological Documents, 13,* 25.

Deaux, K., & Lewis, L. L. (1984). The structure of gender stereotypes: Interrelationships among components and gender label. *Journal of Personality and Social Psychology, 46,* 991–1004.

Dwyer, D. H. (1978). *Images and self-images: Male and female in Morocco.* New York: Columbia University Press.

Eagly, A. H. (1983). Gender and social influence: A social psychological analysis. *American Psychologist, 38,* 971–981.

Eagly, A. H., & Carli, L. L. (1981). Sex of researchers and sex-typed communications as determinants of sex differences in influenceability: A meta-analysis of social influence studies. *Psychological Bulletin, 90,* 1–20.

Eagly, A. H., & Crowley, M. (in press). Gender and helping behavior: A meta-analytic review of the social psychological literature. *Psychological Bulletin.*

Eagly, A. H., & Steffen, V. (1984). Gender stereotypes stem from the distribution of women and men into social roles. *Journal of Personality and Social Psychology, 46,* 735–754.

Eisenberg, N., & Lennon, R. (1983). Sex differences in empathy and related capacities. *Psychological Bulletin, 94,* 100–131.

Foushee, H. C., Heimreich, R. L., & Spence, J. T. (1979). Implicit theories of masculinity and femininity: Dualistic or bipolar? *Psychology of Women Quarterly, 3,* 259–269.

Frodi, A., Macaulay, J., & Thome, P. R. (1977). Are women always less aggressive than men? A review of the experimental literature. *Psychological Bulletin, 84,* 634–660.

Gilligan, C. (1982). *In a different voice: Psychological theory and women's development.* Cambridge: Harvard University Press.

Goffman, E. (1979). *Gender advertisements.* New York: Harper & Row.

Helmreich, R. L., Spence, J. T., & Holahan, C. K. (1979). Psychological androgyny and sex-role flexibility: A test of two hypotheses. *Journal of Personality and Social Psychology, 37,* 1631–1644.

Hyde, J. S. (1984). How large are gender differences in aggression? A developmental meta-analysis. *Developmental Psychology, 20,* 722–736.

Jellison, J. M., Jackson-White, R., Bruder, R. A., & Martyna, W. (1975). Achievement behavior: A situational interpretation. *Sex Roles, 1,* 369–384.

Maccoby, E. E., & Jacklin, C. N. (1974). *The psychology of sex differences.* Stanford: Stanford University Press.

Major, B., Carnevale, P. J. D., & Deaux, K. (1981). A different perspective on androgyny: Evaluations of masculine and feminine personality characteristics. *Journal of Personality and Social Psychology, 41,* 988–1001.

Money, J., & Ehrhardt, A. A. (1972). *Man & woman, boy & girl.* Baltimore: Johns Hopkins University Press.

Murdock, G. P. (1965). *Culture and society.* Pittsburgh: University of Pittsburgh Press.

Pedhazur, E. J., & Tetenbaum, T. J. (1979). Bem Sex Role Inventory: A theoretical and methodological critique. *Journal of Personality and Social Psychology, 37,* 996–1016.

Spence, J. T. (1985). Gender identity and its implications for concepts of masculinity and femininity. *Nebraska symposium on motivation, 32,* 59–95. Lincoln: University of Nebraska Press.

Spence, J. T., & Helmreich, R. L. (1980). Masculine instrumentality and feminine expressiveness: Their relationship with sex role attitudes and behaviors. *Psychology of Women Quarterly, 5,* 147–163.

Spence, J. T., Helmreich, R., & Stapp, J. (1974). The personal attributes questionnaire: A measure of sex-role stereotypes and masculinity-femininity. *JSAS Catalog of Selected Documents in Psychology, 4,* 43. (MS No. 617).

Stoller, R. (1968). *Sex and gender: On the development of masculinity and femininity.* New York: Science House.

Strathern, M. (1976). An anthropological perspective. In B. Lloyd & J. Archer (Eds.), *Exploring sex differences* (pp. 49–70). New York: Academic Press.

von Baeyer, C. L., Sherk, D. L., & Zanna, M. P. (1981). Impression management in the job interview: When the female applicant meets the male (chauvinist) interviewer. *Personality and Social Psychology Bulletin, 7,* 45–51.

Williams, J. E., & Best, D. L. (1982). *Measuring sex stereotypes. A thirty-nation study.* Beverly Hills: Sage Publications.

CHECKPOINTS

1. Deaux provides an overview of the various meanings of masculinity and femininity and criticizes a unidimensional and simplistic view of these constructs.

2. According to Deaux, the four components of gender stereotype are traits, role behaviors, physical characteristics, and occupations. Each component contains characteristics more or less likely to be associated with men versus women.

To prepare for reading the next section, think about these questions:

1. How do the stereotypes of masculinity and femininity vary?

2. Why would stereotypes vary cross-culturally or with race and ethnicity?

Manhood:
Why Is Being a "Real Man" So Often a Prize to Be Won?

DAVID D. GILMORE

*Masculinity is not something given to you,
something you're born with, but something
you gain. . . . And you gain it by winning
small battles with honor.*

*—Normam Mailer, "Cannibals
and Christians"*

We Westerners have always been concerned with manhood as a matter of personal identity or reputation, but this concern is not confined to the West. On Truk Island, a little atoll in the South Pacific, for example, men are also obsessed with being masculine. Echoing Lady Macbeth, a common challenge there is: "Are you a man? Come, I will take your life now." In East Africa, young boys from cattle-herding tribes, including the Masai, Rendille, Jie, and Samburu, are taken away from their mothers and subjected to painful circumcision rites by which they become men. If the Samburu boy cries out while his flesh is being cut, if he so much as blinks an eye, he is shamed for life as unworthy of manhood. The Amhara, an Ethiopian tribe, have a passionate belief in masculinity called *wand-nat.* To show their *wand-nat,* Amhara youths are forced to engage in bloody whipping contests known as *buhe.* Far away, in the high mountains of Melanesia, young boys undergo similar trials before being admitted into the select club of manhood. They are torn from their mothers and forced to undergo a series of brutal rituals. These include whipping, bloodletting, and beating, all of which the boys must endure stoically. The Tewa people of New Mexico also believe that boys must be

"made" into men. Tewa boys are taken away from their homes, purified by ritual means, and then whipped mercilessly by the kachina spirits (their fathers in disguise). Each boy is lashed on the back with a crude yucca whip that draws blood and leaves permanent scars. "You are made a man," the elders tell them afterward.

Why must manhood be vindicated in so many cultures through tests and challenges? And how widespread are such rites of masculinity? My own interest in this subject arose through experiences in the field—in my case, a rural *pueblo* (town or village) in Andalusia, a region of southern Spain. There I noticed a heavy emphasis on being manly, or *macho* as Andalusians say, using the Spanish word for "male" (a word that, significantly, has worked its way into many languages as *machismo*). Hardly a day passed by when this subject went unmentioned. I found that it was hard to measure up in this regard. Indeed, it became a minor personal crisis when some male friends requested my company—rather insistently—on a nocturnal visit to a whorehouse so that I could prove that I was a "man."

Trained to see each culture as unique, cultural anthropologists emphasize human differences, but sometimes common themes draw them ineluctably to the contemplation of human similarities. As I pondered my friends' invitation, I experienced a curious sense of familiarity. I sensed affinity not only with the cultures described above but also with my own. I had grown up absorbing the manly fiction of Ernest Hemingway, Jack London, Norman

---

David D. Gilmore is a professor of anthropology at the State University of New York at Stony Brook.

Mailer, Tom McGuane, and James Dickey. Like many of my friends I, too, had gone to Pamplona to run with the bulls in imitation of Jake Barnes in *The Sun Also Rises,* a typical, if ersatz, rite of passage for college-age Americans. Later, when I returned home, I found the topic of manliness cropping up in discussions with colleagues. Almost every society, I found, has some specific notion about "true" manhood.

Sometimes, as in Andalusia, virility or potency is paramount; elsewhere, as among the Trukese and Amhara, physical toughness is more important. Sometimes economic "go-getting," athletic ability, or heavy drinking is the measure of a man. The ingredients vary, but in all these places a man has to pass some sort of test, measure up, accomplish something. Why is manhood a test in so many cultures? My quests for answers started in Spain.

There was a young man in the *pueblo* named Lorenzo. He was a perennial student and bachelor. A gentle character of outstanding native intelligence, Lorenzo was the only person from the *pueblo* ever to have gone to graduate school to pursue a doctorate, in this case in literature. But he was unable for various reasons ever to complete his dissertation, so he remained in a kind of occupational limbo, indecisive and feckless. Because of his erudition, Lorenzo was generally acknowledged as a sort of locally grown genius. Many people had high hopes for him. But the more traditionally minded were not among his admirers. In the very important matter of gender appropriateness, Lorenzo was eccentric, even deviant. "A grave case," as one man put it.

First, there were his living arrangements. Oddly, Lorenzo stayed indoors with his widowed mother, studying, reading books, rarely leaving his scholar's cloister. He had no discernible job. He lived off his uncomplaining old mother, hardworking but poor. Withdrawn and secretive, Lorenzo made no visible efforts to change this state of affairs; nor did he often, as men are supposed to do, enter the masculine world of the bars to drink or engage in the usual convivial banter. Rarely did he enter into the aggressive card games or the drunken bluster that men in his *pueblo* enjoy and expect.

Perhaps most bizarre, Lorenzo avoided women. He was actually intensely shy with girls. This is a very unusual dereliction indeed, one that is always greeted with real dismay by both men and women in Spain. Sexual shyness is more than a casual flaw; it is a serious, even tragic inadequacy. The entire village bemoans shyness as a personal calamity and collective disgrace. People said that Lorenzo was "afraid" of girls, afraid to try his luck. They believe that a real man must break down the wall of female resistance that separates the sexes. Otherwise there will be no children—God's gift to family, community, and nation. Being a sensitive soul, Lorenzo keenly felt the pressure to go out and run after women. He knew he was supposed to target a likely wife, get a paying job, and start a family. A cultural rebel by default, he felt himself to be a man of modern, "European" sensibilities, and he resisted.

One evening, after we had spent a pleasant hour talking about Cervantes, Lorenzo looked up at me with his great, melancholy eyes and confessed his cultural transgressions. He began by confiding his anxieties about the aggressive courting that is a man's presumed function. "I know you have to throw yourself violently at women," he said glumly, "but I prefer not to." Taking up a book, he shook his head with a shrug, awaiting a comforting word. It was obvious he was pathologically afraid of rejection.

Because he was a decent and honest man, Lorenzo had a small circle of friends in the town, all educated people, and he was the subject of much concern among them. They feared he would never marry, bachelorhood being accounted the most lamentable fate outside of blatant homosexuality. With the best intentions in mind, these people often asked me if I did not think it was sad that Lorenzo was so withdrawn and what should be done about him? Finally, one perceptive friend, discussing Lorenzo's case at length as we often did, summed up the problem in an unforgettable phrase. He noted his friend's debilitating unhappiness and social estrangement, and he told me in all seriousness that Lorenzo's problem was his failure "to be a man." When I asked him what he meant, he explained that in pursuing arcane knowledge, Lorenzo had "forgotten" how to be a man.

Shaking his head sadly, he uttered a lapidary diagnosis: *como hombre, no sirve* (literally, as a man he just doesn't "serve," or work).

Spoken by a concerned friend in a tone of commiseration rather than reproach, the phrase *no sirve* has much meaning. Loosely translated, it means that as a man Lorenzo fails muster in some practical way, the Spanish verb *servir* meaning getting things done, "working" in the sense of proficiency: serviceability. This emphasis on serviceability, on efficiency and competence, provides a common thread in manly imagery and a clue to its deeper meanings. How does Lorenzo fail the test of manhood?

I had the good fortune, also, to encounter the model man. The opposite of Lorenzo was Juan, known to everyone by his nickname, Robustiano, "the robust one." He was tall and energetic, a worker who toiled hard in the fields from dawn till dusk, "sacrificed," as they say, to support his huge family. He was a fearless labor organizer, too, and during the dark days of the Franco dictatorship he had kept the faith alive among the town's workers and peasants by openly defying the police. He went to jail often and suffered many beatings, but even the tough Civil Guards could not break his spirit. They said that he resembled a mule in stubbornness, but that he had more *cojones* (balls) than a mountain of ministers—a begrudging way of complimenting a political opponent. *Muy hombre,* they admitted as they beat him, "a lot of man." In addition, Robustiano had fathered many children, with five sons among his brood. Only in his forties, Robustiano was a kind of culture hero.

These negative and positive examples sum up the qualities of manliness in Andalusia. A real man is one who provides for his family, protects dependents, and produces babies. He is not a bully, never a wife beater. On the contrary, he is a supporting prop of his community; above all, he is competent, a doer. He is willing to absorb punishment in pursuit of approved civic goals. He is fearless. On a more abstract level, one might summarize by saying he reproduces and augments the highest values of his culture by force of will. He creates something from nothing. In this way, he serves. Lorenzo's main failure, by contrast, is his fickle recessiveness, his timidity.

How can we conceptualize this composite image of manhood in Spain? It seems a threefold threshold: "man the protector" is also "man the provider" and, of course, "man the impregnator." This trinity of competencies is a recurrent image of communal hope. The emphasis on productivity and on omnicompetence is a common denominator that unites men and women in the re-creation of core values. It is this deeper function of creating and buttressing, not the specifics of form, that opens the door to cross-cultural comparison. Let us take a few brief examples from other cultures, far from Spain.

Among the aboriginal Mehinaku, a Stone Age tribe of farmers and fishermen living in the Amazon Basin in Brazil, there are "real men" and there are effeminate "trash yard men." A real man is one who displays efficiency in all walks of life. He gets up early to go on long, arduous fishing expeditions over dangerous terrain, ignoring hostile tribes that wait in ambush. When he returns, sometimes days later, he marches ostentatiously to the middle of the village where he throws down his catch for everyone to share. He is a fierce competitor in games and sports, especially wrestling—a favorite tribal pastime. He fathers many children, has many lovers, and satisfies his wife sexually. An incompetent man, one who is stingy, weak, or impotent, is scorned as effeminate.

Among the nonviolent Bushmen of the Kalahari Desert in southwest Africa, boys are not granted their manhood until they stalk and kill a large antelope single-handedly. In this way they show that they are capable of providing meat for the entire band. Among the Sambia people of highland New Guinea, a boy cannot be a man until he has learned to disdain the sight of his own blood—basic training for the warrior's life that awaits him and upon which the security of the tribe depends. To be really a man, the Sambia tribesman must also father at least two children. Among the Masai of Kenya, a boy is not a man until he has stood up to a charging lion, established an independent household, and fathered more than one child. Among the Mende of West Africa, a boy is only a man when he shows he can survive unaided in the bush. In all these cases, the tests and accomplishments involved are those that will prepare boys and youths specifically for the skills needed in adult life to support, protect, and expand the living community. And it is only when these skills are mastered and displayed communally, in public, that manhood is conferred consensually upon the youth.

But still, we ask: why the stress and drama of manhood? Why is all this indoctrination needed, why the trials and tribulations? Why must males be literally pushed into such displays of performance? Here, as in most cases of human behavior where strong emotions are involved, we need a little guidance from psychological theory, and here, too, is where there is agreement with what feminists have said about the plasticity of gender roles. The key, I think, lies in the inherent weaknesses of human nature, in the inborn tendency of all human beings, male and female, to run from danger, to retreat from challenges, to return to the safety of the hearth and home. In psychoanalytic thinking, this tendency, exemplified perhaps by Lorenzo, is called psychic regression. It is defined as the tidal pull back toward the world of childhood, the pull back to the mother, the wish to return to the blissful, traumaless idyll of infancy.

Seen from this psychological perspective, we can interpret manhood as a moral instigation for performance—the moral force that culture erects against the eternal child in men, that makes retreat impossible by creating a cultural sanction literally worse than death: the theft of one's sexual identity.

Interestingly, manhood is not just a call to aggression. The brutal *machismo* of violent men is not real manhood in these cultures, but a meretricious counterfeit—the sign of weakness. A curious commonality is that true manhood is a call to nurturing. "Real" men are those who give more than they take, who, like "the robust one," serve others by being brave and protective. This "manly" nurturing is different from the female. It is less direct, more obscure; the "other" involved may be society in general rather than specific persons. Yet real men do nurture. They do this by shedding their blood, their sweat, their semen; by bringing home food, producing children, or dying if necessary in far away places to provide security for their families. But this masculine nurturing is paradoxical. To be supportive, a man must first be tough in order to ward off enemies; to be generous, he must first be selfish in order to amass goods; to be tender, he must be aggressive enough to court, seduce, "win" a wife.

Finally, with all this said, why should the challenges (and rewards) of these manhood codes be confined to males? We have seen that true manhood often means serving society: accepting challenges, taking risks, being expendable in the service of society. Why aren't women allowed to be real men too? Why can't women also earn the glory of a risk successfully taken? But here we have to stop, for this is a question for the philosopher, not the cultural anthropologist.

Overcoming Stereotypes of Mothers in the African American Context

ELIZABETH E. SPARKS

I am an African American, middle-aged professional woman who has spent the past twenty years thinking about and discussing with others what it means to be an African American woman in this society. Because of the clients with whom I have interacted over the years, I have been particularly interested in what it means to be an African American mother in contemporary America. My viewpoint has undergone changes during this time, and the perspective expressed in this chapter is the culmination of my personal experiences as an African American daughter (who is not a mother), experiences that I have shared with female kin and friends (most of whom are mothers), and from my work as a psychotherapist with African American mothers. We have all struggled to understand what it means to be a woman and mother, both within our own cultural context and as we are perceived by the White-majority culture. Our experiences of motherhood range from feeling strong and empowered because of who we are to feeling overwhelmed, burdened, and unfulfilled.

In this chapter I explore some of the stereotypes of African American women that have been promulgated by the White establishment and which have been internalized by at least some of my clients. In the first part of the chapter, I look at the historical roots of these images of motherhood and outline current stereotypical conceptualizations of African American women. I next present a set of case examples. In them, we see women who are struggling with difficult situations in their lives and whose recovery has been hindered by the internalization of these stereotypical images. In the third section, I discuss the personal journey required to free myself from these controlling images and my work in helping clients overcome the negative impact of this internal-

ization process. Finally, I argue for a new definition of African American motherhood and for rekindling the sense of collectivism that has been so highly valued within the African American community throughout its history.

STEREOTYPES

African Roots and Transformations During Slavery

The analysis of motherhood that is presented in this chapter incorporates the broader perspective of African American womanhood because of the intricate connection that exists between these two identities for African American women. In traditional African society, reproduction and mothering formed a valued and integral aspect of women's identity (Mbiti, 1969). The tradition involved not only nurturing one's biological offspring but also caring for other, often nonrelated children (Oppong, 1973). Child rearing was thought to be a shared responsibility of the community, and there was a common African practice of fostering children as a means of minimizing what was viewed as a dysfunctional emphasis on individualism within a communal setting (James, 1993; Sudarkasa, 1993). Although enslaved West Africans were unable to replicate traditional family and communal patterns and values in America, some traditions, including the emphasis on the interconnectedness and interdependence between families, appear to have been adapted as a means of coping with slavery's highly destructive system of exploitation and oppression (Gutman, 1976).

African American slave women played an integral role in the maintenance and survival of the family.

However, the control of motherhood (reproduction) and mothering (caretaking) was ultimately held by the White slave master. African American female slaves were generally not seen as women at all, but as beasts whose reproductive capacities (as well as their physical labor) were used to produce commodities for someone else's benefit (Fox-Genovese, 1988; Greene, 1994). In some instances, women were able to establish solid relationships with male partners and to provide caretaking for their children. Slave narratives provide stories of women who stole food and clothing from their White masters in order to supplement the meager provisions allocated for their children and stories of women who made valiant attempts to keep their children with them (Shaw, 1994). However, there was a darker side to this struggle between African American slave women and their White masters for the control of motherhood, which sometimes resulted in drastic measures being used by the slave women to influence the fate of their offspring. Documents written by slave owners during this era indicate that there were high rates of infant mortality, including deaths by natural causes and those that were the result of infanticide (Shaw, 1994). Some documents also indicate the use of self-induced abortions as a means of controlling reproduction.

Despite the attempts made by women to provide consistent caretaking for their children, slave owners' disregard for the sanctity and unity of the family often led to instability (James, 1993; Greene, 1994). It was against the law for African American slaves to marry; however, documents in counties throughout the South indicate that many couples who had been informally married and living together during slavery had their marriages legalized and registered after emancipation (Billingsley, 1992). Both official documents and slave narratives suggest that slaves created patterns of family life that were functionally integrative and that did more than prevent the destruction of personality. Family life also created the conditions out of which came African American pride, identity, culture, and community (Billingsley, 1992).

The conditions of slavery made it necessary for mothers and fathers to be psychologically prepared, and their children socialized, for possible separation.

This led to a conceptualization of "mother" that was collective. The term "mother" was used to refer to birthmothers and any other adult slave woman who provided basic caretaking for the child. Thus, the African tradition of fostering was adapted to meet the needs of the enslaved community in America, and the practice of "othermothering" played a critical role in child rearing (James, 1993). This tradition of women-centered units being primarily responsible for the nurturing and rearing of children has continued in the African American community since the times of slavery. It reflects both a continuation of West African culture values and functional adaptations to race and gender oppression faced by African Americans in this society (Tanner, 1974; Stack, 1974; Sudarkasa, 1981).

What is most important about these years in slavery, and the period of time immediately following emancipation, is the way in which African Americans developed their own socially constructed definition of family. This definition included those adults (whether birth parents, relatives, or fictive kin) who accepted responsibility for the nurturance and socialization of children and who shared strong feelings of loyalty and trust. The work of contemporary scholars such as Carol Stack (1974) and Joyce Aschenbrenner (1975) show that these patterns of cooperation have been a very important factor in the survival of African American families in cities as well as in rural areas throughout America. During slavery, othermothers cared for children orphaned by sale or death of their parents and children conceived through rape whose mothers were unable to bond with them. In more contemporary times, othermothers support children born into extreme poverty or to alcoholic or drug-addicted mothers, children of young mothers, as well as children who for other reasons cannot remain with their birthmothers (Young, 1970; Dougherty, 1978).

Although there is little discussion in the literature about the quality of the relationships between birthmothers and othermothers, the interactions are described as cooperative and seem to reflect the importance of women working together collectively to raise children successfully under oppressive conditions

(Collins, 1990). Cross-residential or transresidential cooperation among African Americans was, and continues to be, an important factor in rearing children, providing financial support in times of need, caring for aged family members, and providing shelter for various kinfolk who need it from time to time. Thus, many contemporary mothers rely on women-centered communities as their basis for support in caring for their children (Sudarkasa, 1993).

Stereotypical Images from Slavery to the Civil Rights Era

In addition to supporting each other and caring for their partners and children under severe conditions of racism, sexism, and oppression, African American women have also had to struggle to counteract negative stereotypes promulgated by the White-majority culture since the time of slavery (hooks, 1981; Greene, 1994). A stereotype is defined as a belief about a group of people that gives insufficient attention to individual differences among members of that group (Brislin, 1993). In situations where these stereotypes are negative, pervasive, and have existed for many generations, they become part of the culture into which children are socialized and reflect prejudicial feelings about this group. Throughout the history of this country, the White-majority culture has created negative stereotypes about African American women as mothers, and these stereotypes have been used to legitimize their oppression (Collins, 1990).

In her sociopolitical analysis of race, class, and gender bias in America and its impact on African American women, Patricia Hill Collins identifies stereotypes that seem to have penetrated the consciousness of African American women today. Collins's thesis represents a bringing together of sociological research, ideas of Black feminist theorists, her own experiences as an African American woman, and experiences of other women she has encountered in many different arenas. She examines the complexity of ideas that exist in both scholarly and everyday life and formulates a perspective that helps us understand the experiences of African American women as they attempt to find an authentic "voice" in the current social, political, and economic climate (Collins, 1990). In identifying these stereotypical images, Collins utilizes observations taken from African American literature, historical documents, the media, and research. She highlights the controlling nature of these stereotypical images and describes how each has contributed to the oppression and subjugation of African American women. Two of these images, "Mammy" and "Jezebel," were developed during slavery. Three others evolved later.

The stereotypical Mammy was portrayed as the faithful, obedient domestic servant who loved, nurtured, and cared for White children without any thought or attention to her own needs or to those of her family (Collins, 1990). This image not only characterized African American women as having exceptional nurturing and caretaking skills, but it also promoted the belief that she preferred to care for White children, even if this meant neglecting her own. Thus, the Mammy image was one that provided support for White superiority while it characterized African American women as both understanding and accepting of their subordinate place in society. The Mammy image buttressed the ideology of the cult of true womanhood, in which sexuality and fertility are severed. "Good" White mothers were expected to deny their female sexuality and to devote their attention to the moral development of their offspring. In contrast, Mammy was an asexual, surrogate African American mother who handled the more basic child care needs for White children (Collins, 1990). This image was used to justify the economic exploitation of African American women both as slaves and later as domestic workers (Gilkes, 1994).

In the Jezebel stereotype, African American women were portrayed as being sexually aggressive and responsible for their own sexual victimization. This image was created by Whites as a way of justifying the widespread sexual assaults on African American women by White males that occurred during slavery (Davis, 1991; hooks, 1981; White, 1985). By their acceptance of the Jezebel stereotype, the White establishment was able to rationalize using African American women as "breeders" for the financial gain of slaveholders. This stereotype has continued to be applied to African American women even in more modern times, as evidenced by the fact that White males who were accused of raping African American women received no legal sanctions in courts in many southern states from the time of emancipation through more than two-thirds of the twentieth century (White, 1985). In a similar way, the Jezebel stereotype was reflected in the treatment received by African American domestic workers in White homes during the early 1900s. According to narratives from women who were domestics during that time period, African American women often risked sexual harassment and victimization by White male employers. As one woman remarked in 1912: "I believe that nearly all White men take, and expect to take, undue liberties with their colored female servants—not only the fathers, but in many cases the sons also. Those servants who rebel against such familiarity must either leave or expect a mightily hard time, if they stay" (quoted in Mann, 1990, p. 148).

Although the Jezebel stereotype is not directly focused on mothers, as is the Mammy stereotype, it has affected the perception of African American mothers within the larger White-majority culture because of the complex, often contradictory, connection between sexuality and motherhood that exists in this society. Although children are conceived through sexual activity, the prevailing notion of motherhood is of one that is relatively asexual, with "good mothers" expected to have rigid control over their sexuality. As a result, women are often seen as being either a "Madonna," who is devoted, asexual mother figure, or as a "Whore," whose maternal feelings and instincts are thought to be minimal at best. The Jezebel stereotypical image portrays African American women as having excessive sexual appetites; therefore, it follows that these women could not possibly be good mothers because of their preoccupation with sexuality. During slavery, this stereotype contributed to the rationalizations used by the White establishment to legitimize separating slave children from their mothers, as these women were believed to have little, if any, commitment to mothering the children who resulted from their sexual activity. Although the Jezebel stereotype may have freed African American women from the rigid, puritanical attitudes toward sexuality that af-

fected the lives of most White women of that day, it ultimately made them vulnerable to sexual assault and held them responsible for their own sexual victimization and for the removal of their children.

The third stereotypical image, the "Matriarch," was constructed by the White establishment during the 1960s. She is an African American woman who has failed to fulfill her traditional "womanly" role by working outside the home and who is so negative and critical toward her male partner (or spouse) that he is unwilling to live with her (Collins, 1990). This stereotype presents African American women as bad mothers, since, according to this stereotype, their work outside of the home forces them to neglect their children, and their critical, negative interaction with the children's father causes him to abandon the family. Although the Matriarch image does present African American women as strong and powerful maternal figures, in opposition to the then prevailing cultural image of White women as being weak, passive, and submissive, it is nonetheless used as a means of controlling African American women.

The Matriarch stereotype allows the White establishment to blame African American women for the success or failure of their children and for the economic circumstances of African American families (Collins, 1990; Greene, 1994). White scholars, journalists, and policymakers have claimed that the African American family structure is the main cause of the high rates of crime, unemployment, school dropouts, teenage pregnancies, drug abuse, and disaffection among young people in the inner cities (Moynihan, 1967). This perspective, although challenged by many researchers of color (e.g., Billingsley, 1968; Hill, 1972; McAdoo, 1981), is an extremely difficult myth to overcome because many in this country, including some African Americans, believe the stereotype and accept it as truth (Sudarkasa, 1988).

Current Stereotypical Images

The fourth image is that of the "Welfare Mother," which labels the fertility of women who are not White and middle class as unnecessary and even dangerous to the values of this country (Collins, 1990). Unlike the Matriarch, who was seen as too aggressive, the Welfare Mother is not aggressive enough. She is seen as too lazy to work and as having repetitive pregnancies in order to collect more money from the state. She is portrayed as a mother who does not appropriately socialize her children to accept the societal values and normative behaviors surrounding the work ethic, thereby causing her family to remain in poverty. The Jezebel image can be seen underneath the Welfare Mother stereotype, since the latter is also seen as being sexually promiscuous and having little emotional connection to her offspring, who result from her heightened sexual activity. As with the other stereotypical images of African American women, the Welfare Mother image allows the White-majority culture to blame the victims for their own oppression and victimization and shifts the focus away from the institutional and structural factors that perpetuate poverty.

The final stereotypical image is that of the "Superwoman." Unlike the earlier stereotypes, which were constructed by the White establishment to justify its exploitative behavior toward African American women, the Superwoman image has been perpetuated by the African American community and is embraced by many as being an "idealized" image of motherhood. The Superwoman image requires that African American women sacrifice their own needs for those of their children and families, while being committed to maintaining the economic viability of their families by working and contributing to the advancement of the African American community as a whole through their participation in service work. Michele Wallace (1991) describes the Superwoman as follows:

[She is a woman] of inordinate strength, with an ability for tolerating an unusual amount of misery and heavy, distasteful work. This woman does not have the same fears, weaknesses, and insecurities as other women, but believes herself to be and is, in fact, stronger emotionally than most men. Less of a woman in that she is less "feminine" and helpless, she is really more of a woman in that she is the embodiment of Mother Earth, the quintessential mother with infinite sexual, life-giving, and nurturing reserves. In other words, she is a Superwoman. (p. 107)

The Superwoman image is deceptive because it builds on the efforts that African American women have made through the years to oppose negative stereotypes prevalent in the White-majority culture, particularly the Matriarch and Welfare Mother images. Because it appears to be positive and to represent the strengths of African American motherhood, it is one that many African American women have internalized (Boyd-Franklin, 1991; Greene, 1994). In the 1980s the Superwoman image was expanded to include another criterion—she must also be a highly educated, professional woman. This newer image has been labeled the "Super/Essence woman," after the popular magazine geared toward professional African American women (Edwards, 1992). The Super/Essence woman is expected to be a supportive, and at times submissive, partner to her spouse, a devoted mother who is actively involved in her children's lives, while also being aggressive, competent, and career-focused in her professional life. She must be able to create and maintain a viable marriage, while also being prepared to care for herself and her children alone if necessary.

This stereotype has a strong influence on mothering and on the mother-daughter relationship for African American women. Mothers strive to equip their daughters with the skills necessary to meet these expectations, making every effort to ensure that their daughters have the stability and emotional strength to overcome whatever obstacles are in their way (Collins, 1990).

With the Super/Essence woman image held up as an ideal, life for African American women can become a gauntlet race. Some succeed, but there are many casualties. The "wounded" are those women who make up the 42.8 percent (1988 figures) of Black female heads of households who live at or below the poverty level (Mullings, 1994). They are the mothers of the 70.1 percent of Black children who are living in families with incomes less than twice the poverty level (Edelman, 1985). These women head families that constitute what has been called the "underclass," which refers to those individuals who live in persistent poverty and who have "dropped out" of the struggle to attain economic stability and security. Many of these women living in poverty are young. Statistics indicate that the African American female head of household has become younger over the past forty years, which compounds the difficulties that these women and their children face. In 1980, figures indicated that 1 in 8 female-headed African American families were headed by women under twenty-five years of age (Smith, 1988). Among this number, three-fourths of these young women have never been married. They tend to be women from low-income families whose incomes are depressed even further as they form their own families out of wedlock (Smith, 1988). Clearly, teen mothers are quite disadvantaged in their capacity to attain the Super/Essence woman ideal. For those who have internalized the image, the result can be depression and guilt.

THE INTERNALIZATION OF STEREOTYPES

Case Examples

Claudine. Claudine is a 35-year-old African American woman who is the single parent for her two boys, ages 8 and 6. She was married to, and lived with, the boys' father for seven years, during which time he was physically and emotionally abusive to her. When Claudine left her husband, she had a high school education but no specific job-related skills. She applied for and received Aid to Families with Dependent Children (AFDC) and began living in an inner-city apartment near her mother and sisters. Once her children were in school all day, Claudine requested job training through the Welfare Department. She hoped to be able to find a job that would provide her with a livable income so that she would no longer need AFDC. Claudine was referred to a program that trained women to work as instrument technicians, preparing surgical kits for hospitals. She faithfully attended the training, and at graduation she received an award for being the most consistent and conscientious trainee in the program.

For six months after completing the training, Claudine applied for jobs in local hospitals. Although she received a few interviews, she was not hired. From time to time, Claudine found temporary work (usually during the Christmas season) in a local department store. However, she could never seriously consider taking a full-time position and terminating her AFDC benefits because the minimum-wage salary that she could earn would not be sufficient to compensate for the benefits she would lose. In addition to the stipend, Claudine's AFDC benefits included subsidized housing, Medicaid coverage for herself and the children, and food stamps.

Claudine is in therapy because one of her sons developed severe behavior problems following the parental separation. She actively participates in his treatment and in supportive sessions for herself. In her individual sessions, Claudine expresses frustration with her life. She very much wants to establish a "better life" for her children, and she blames herself for not being able to figure out a way to work and take care of her family. Although she does not want to return to her abusive husband, she sometimes wonders whether she caused him to be abusive, often blaming herself for some "defect" that made her a "failure" as a wife and mother.

Claudine's life situation reflects at least two of the prevailing stereotypes of African American women—that of the Matriarch and that of the Welfare Mother. She is a single head of household and feels personally responsible for the plight of her family and for the failure of her marriage. In many ways, Claudine has internalized these stereotypical images, which contributes to her feelings of worthlessness, guilt, and depression.

Annette. Annette is a 22-year-old African American young woman who has been in treatment since she was 14 years old. She was raised by her mother in a single-parent household and has a history of physical and sexual abuse. At age 15, Annette ran away from her mother and went to live with a family friend (she was Annette's fictive aunt). While in her aunt's home, she was raped, which resulted in her being placed in a Department of Social Services (DSS) foster home. Annette became pregnant during her senior year in high school and decided to keep her child. This disrupted her foster placement, and after the baby's birth, she (and her child) went to live with a biological aunt. Annette, with the help of an adult female cousin, was able to adequately parent the child for the first two years. She completed high school and was admitted to a small two-year college in the area. Annette's situation is complicated by the regulations of the social services system, which made her ineligible for AFDC benefits because she was still considered a foster child under the jurisdiction of DSS. The financial support Annette received from DSS was not sufficient to care for herself and her child, and the agency refused to provide support for the child since she was technically not in foster care. Although Annette's therapist attempted to advocate, she was unsuccessful. Eventually, Annette no longer had the financial resources or the emotional energy to continue both attending college and adequately parenting her child. After a great deal of deliberation, Annette released custody of the child to her cousin. She is currently attempting to complete her college education and is employed as a temporary worker.

In Annette's case, we see internalization of the Super/Essence woman image by a young, single mother who has had a problematic life history. Her decision to attend college was based on a firm belief that as an African American woman, she was expected to educate herself so that she could obtain a professional-level job in order to adequately care for herself and her child. Annette's early history and life experiences undoubtedly complicate her situation; however, she has continued to feel totally responsible for her plight. Annette faced tremendous stress, both emotionally and physically, when she tried to parent her daughter and attend college at the same time, but she frequently comments that other African American women have been able to do these things successfully. She blames herself (and feels that others also blame her) for this perceived failure. Annette gives little credence to the financial hardships she faced being unemployed and receiving a small stipend from the DSS and to the contradictions in the social services system that contributed to the problems she faced. The internalization of the Super/Essence woman stereotype is certainly not the only factor responsible for Annette's distress; however, it has contributed to her self-perception and expectations in a way that is detrimental.

Darlene. Darlene is a 35-year-old African American mother of four children. The children have two different fathers, and she has little consistent contact with either man. Darlene lost custody of her children two years prior to her entering treatment because of her chronic alcoholism and neglect. The children are placed with Darlene's mother, who altered her retirement plans in order to care for them. Darlene's relationship with her mother is strained, although they try to cooperate in the caretaking of the children. Darlene hopes to have her children returned to her care and custody some day, but she has been unable to consistently follow through with treatment for her alcoholism. She seems to have also internalized the Matriarch and Super/Essence woman images and blames herself for her situation. She suffers from depression, low self-esteem, and a sense of failure about her inability to appropriately take care of her children. Darlene believes that she has had every opportunity to "make it" in life and feels that she is solely responsible for her failure to be a strong, resilient woman who could overcome all of the obstacles inherent in the society in order to adequately care for herself and her children.

PROBLEMS WITH THE IMAGE

The Super/Essence woman stereotype, like the other negative stereotypes of African American women, attributes total responsibility for the status of one's life situation to the individual, while ignoring the prevailing sociopolitical conditions that have a negative impact on women's lives. In a society where almost 30 percent of all African American families live under oppressive conditions that threaten their survival, such as pervasive poverty, joblessness, drugs, and violence, the Super/Essence woman image can be used by the White establishment to once again blame African American women for their own (and their family's) plight. Those African American women who have been able to embody the Super/Essence woman image have been written about in many different sources, and their self-sacrifice, struggle, and commitment to family and to the broader community should not be discredited (Gilkes, 1994; Collins, 1990; Greene, 1990). However, maintaining this strength in the face of oppression and poverty is quite costly, and many African American mothers have not been able to successfully overcome these barriers (Collins, 1990).

The often difficult nature of motherhood within the African American cultural context explains the range that is found in women's reactions to motherhood and the ambivalence that many feel about mothering (Collins, 1990). In a unique way, some contemporary African American mothers are like the voices heard in slave narratives and the slave mothers portrayed in Toni Morrison's book *Beloved,* whose losses are so deep and pervasive that they are driven to desperate acts. African American women living in poverty are often overwhelmed by the task of caring for children, and they may experience motherhood as a challenge that they have no hope of winning. Some women may simply give up and let go of the attempt to nurture and provide for their children. They are the victims of the structural conditions of racism and discrimination that limit their access to adequate resources to care for themselves and their children and victims of the depression and hopelessness experienced as a result of their internalization of the stereotypes. African American women like the ones described in the above case examples represent those who have been unable to reach the stereotypical, idealized image of the Super/Essence woman. Even within the African American cultural context, their voices have seldom been recorded or heard (Weems, 1993).

The silence that has surrounded these African American mothers who are "not so sturdy bridges" for their children is a reaction within this community against the negative stereotypes that are prevalent in the White-majority culture. Some, however, have begun to speak out about this issue and to call for a deeper understanding of the complex experience of African American motherhood (Bell-Scott, Guy-Sheftall, Jones-Royster, Sims-Wood, DeCosta-Willis, and Fultz, 1991; Wade-Gayles, 1984; Weems, 1993). They suggest that it is critical that we not romanticize the struggles of African American mothers by failing to acknowledge and understand fully the psychological and physical costs to their survival (Greene,

1990). The mothers in the case examples would be considered failures in their attempts to achieve the Super/Essence woman ideal, and their internalization of the stereotype has contributed to their feelings of depression, guilt, and self-blame. In the treatment process, it is essential to find a way to counter-act these stereotypes, while helping the women construct a more comprehensive understanding of the experience of African American motherhood in order to facilitate positive growth and empowerment.

COUNTERACTING STEREOTYPICAL IMAGES

In clinical work with clients like Claudine, Annette, and Darlene, I try to find a way to effectively counter-act their internalization of stereotypical images. Most often this is done by providing information about the controlling nature of these stereotypes and explanations of how they have been used to blame African American women for their condition in life and for the plight of their families and the community. I have done most of my clinical work with low-income African American women who are struggling with economic and personal hardships and who are parenting alone. Therefore, I also inform them of the systemic and institutional forces that contribute to their continuing poverty and limited access to resources.

To be able to work with African American women in this way, I first had to struggle to counteract my own internalization of the Super/Essence woman stereotype. I was socialized to believe that this was an ideal image for an African American woman, and I began my professional career thinking that I would "have it all" by the time I was 35 years old—a husband, beautiful children, and a successful, exciting career. I knew that women sometimes were not able to achieve all of these things, but I felt that I had been taught how to effectively handle the stress involved and therefore would be one of the "successful" ones. I quickly learned that this was an almost impossible task. The amount of time involved in establishing and maintaining a successful professional career interfered with developing relationships, and I could never figure out when I would have the time to absent myself from work long enough to have a child. Gradually, I began to realize that all women (including African American women) must make choices about their lives and that often something had to be put "on hold." As I came to terms with this insight, I also realized that African American women (including myself) have been attempting to reach a mythical image, one that is not possible to achieve in reality. I began to understand that the sociopolitical forces that keep many of my African American clients in poverty also drive me to work extra hard to develop a professional career. I realize that I have purchased my professional success at a high price.

After gaining this personal perspective on the stereotypical nature of the Super/Essence woman image, I was ready to utilize my experiences to help clients better understand their lives. I decided to use the psychotherapeutic relationship to help strengthen their "psychological armor." This term describes the behavioral and cognitive skills used by African Americans and other persons of color to decrease their psychological vulnerability in encounters where there is a potential for racism (Faulkner, 1983; Greene, 1993). African American mothers socialize their daughters in such a way that they can make psychological sense out of the racist and sexist messages that they receive on a routine basis in this society, thereby creating a psychological barrier that protects one's self-esteem and identity.

Many of my clients have grown up in dysfunctional families where they have been deprived of an effective racial socialization process. Since they have not received the type of training that would prepare them to confront institutional barriers and negative stereotypes in an adaptive manner, my clients are especially vulnerable to the effects of racism. I see my job as helping them overcome the inadequate training they received, while strengthening their adaptive strategies for coping with racism.

Within the context of the therapeutic relationship, I engage with the client in a form of racial socialization. The therapy sessions are an opportunity for us to discuss appropriate responses to situations reflecting institutional racism that occur within a woman's life and to develop strategies for self-advocacy. The racial socialization process also involves my understanding of, and empathy for, the experiences of racism and sexism that occur in my clients' lives, and I provide emotional support for the feelings of anger and impotence that result from their attempts to overcome these barriers.

To see psychotherapy as the building of this psychological armor represents a culture-specific approach to treatment. In the more traditional models of psychodynamic psychotherapy, an individual's difficulties in functioning are thought to be the result of intrapsychic conflicts and anxiety that is not effectively being controlled because the client has poor coping skills or is using inappropriate defenses. Effective psychotherapy with African American clients requires that the therapist identify *both* the internal and external sources of stress and not just assume that the problem has an internal locus of etiology. The internal sources of stress are treated in much the same way as they would be in nonminority clients. There is a recognition, however, that the external sources of stress can exacerbate any internal conflicts that may be present. In working with African American mothers, the therapist must find a way to challenge the internalization of stereotypical images that can contribute to the client's feelings of frustration, anger, and helplessness. The therapeutic focus can then move beyond self-blame and feelings of helplessness toward helping the client envision ways to effectively maneuver around these barriers. In addition to psychological armoring, another adaptive strategy that is often observed in African Americans is "cultural paranoia" (Grier and Cobbs, 1968). Therapists working with African American clients need to understand that these behaviors, and the complex attitudes that accompany them, are necessary for survival in this society and should not conclude that their presence in the clinical picture is evidence of psychopathology.

THE NEED FOR A NEW DEFINITION OF MOTHERHOOD

In many instances, the clinical interventions that I provide for my African American female clients are helpful in facilitating their ability to understand the internalization of negative stereotypes and the mythical nature of the Super/Essence woman image. More than this is needed, however, to overcome the impact that these controlling images have on the psychological well-being of African American women. The Super/Essence woman stereotype must be challenged as an idealized image of African American motherhood. It does not acknowledge the negative impact that racism and discrimination have on the lives of African Americans or how these factors can inhibit a woman's ability to effectively care for her children. What is called for is a redefinition of motherhood: one that not only takes into account the strengths and resilience of African American women but also incorporates the sociopolitical and economic issues that act as barriers to success.

Prior to the civil rights movement of the 1960s there was an understanding in the African American community that poverty was directly attributable to the racist, discriminatory practices of the larger society. The changes in discriminatory laws and social policies that resulted from this movement have been accompanied by the attribution of complete personal responsibility for one's success or failure in life. Some segments of the African American community, along with the White-majority culture, seem to believe that equal opportunity exists for all, and they cite intraindividual deficits as the only causal factor involved when someone is chronically unemployed and living in pervasive poverty. This attribution of individual responsibility for success and failure in life underlies the Super/Essence woman stereotype.

The belief in intraindividual causality is only one thesis that has been proposed to explain chronic poverty. A related theory, the cultural-deficiency model, assumes that the African American culture holds a value system that is characterized by low aspirations and accepts female-headed families as normative (Corcoran, Duncan, Gurin, and Gurin, 1985). It attributes poverty to the disintegration of the traditional male-dominated family structure, embracing the notion that welfare creates disincentives to work and incentives to have children out of wedlock (Moynihan, 1967). From this perspective, the African American culture is seen as maladaptive and creating

thought processes within individuals that cause the continuation of poverty in the Black community (Zinn, 1990). This cultural-deficiency model is reflected in the stereotypes of the Matriarch and the Welfare Mother.

The structural model challenges this perspective and provides an alternative explanation for the existence of chronic poverty. It focuses on the socioeconomic conditions and institutional forces that work to keep ethnic-minority groups in poverty (Zinn, 1990; Wilson, 1987). Within this model, attention is drawn away from psychological and cultural issues and is focused on the social structures that allocate economic and social rewards (Zinn, 1990). The structural model explains such conditions as the prevalence of female-headed households in the African American community as being the result of poverty, not the cause of it. Researchers cite such statistics as the decline in the male-female ratio that occurs by ages 25 to 44 and attribute causality to early mortality (1 in 10 African American males dies before age 20), high levels of incarceration (1 in 4 African American males are either in prison or on parole), and the number of African Americans who marry outside of their ethnic group (Jenkins, 1994). They also suggest that the chronic joblessness experienced by many African American men contributes to the problem of female-headed families, since men who are unable to obtain consistent employment are unlikely to marry their partners (Wilson, 1987).

Utilizing this model, we can now begin to see how an African American woman's difficulties in caring for herself and her children are not solely the result of intrapersonal deficits but have roots in the socioeconomic conditions that limit access to employment, the amount of income she can earn even if employed, and the likelihood that she will be able to establish and maintain a viable marital partnership with an African American male. With clients who are low-income mothers living on welfare, I often discuss the structural model and use examples from their own lives to illustrate the fact that the conditions under which many African American women (and men) live are extremely vulnerable to economic change. The client is then able to understand that as an

African American mother living in poverty, she is being hampered in her efforts to rise out of this condition even when she follows all of the "rules" of the society. When she is able to work, she is the lowest paid among all employed individuals. If she is unable to find a job, which will most likely be the case if she resides in the inner city, the welfare benefits she receives will keep her at or below poverty level. And even if she longs for the traditionally female role of homemaker and nurturer of children, she is unlikely to have a male partner who is in a position to adequately provide for the family and with whom she can share the challenge of survival.

As a clinician, I am particularly concerned with African American women's internalization of the stereotypical images described above, since this can have a powerful negative effect on their psychological well-being (Greene, 1994; Jenkins, 1993). When women have internalized the Super/Essence woman stereotype, they often feel that they have somehow failed to attend appropriately to all of their burdens or to solve all of their family members' problems. These clients rarely wonder whether their responsibilities are too extensive or if their expectations of themselves are unrealistic. They express the fear that coming to therapy means that they are "weak" or "couldn't take it" and believe that it is "indulgent" to spend time talking about their own personal concerns (Childs, 1990; Jenkins, 1994; Greene, 1992). These women not only blame themselves for their inability to function, but they may also harbor attitudes and beliefs that interfere with their ability to seek and sustain important support and validation from other women (Greene, 1994). The conditions that exist today in the African American community highlight the need to return to women-centered communi-ties that care for children—in much the same way that they were needed during slavery. Yet, the Super/Essence woman image hinders the development of this sense of community.

The current idealized image of African American motherhood (the Super/Essence woman), buttressed by the negative stereotypes of poor African American mothers in the White-majority culture (the Matriarch and Welfare Mother), creates a dilemma for most women and makes it difficult for many to succeed.

Both low-income and professional women must struggle to deal with the controlling nature of each of these stereotypes, and their internalization contributes to feelings of guilt and shame, which complicate the treatment process. Further, the attribution of total individual responsibility for success or failure that underlies each of the stereotypes makes it difficult for African American women to join together across social class lines to form a collective sisterhood. Challenging the existing Super/Essence woman image and creating a new definition of African American motherhood should help to counteract the internalization of these stereotypes and to enhance cooperation and collective support for mothering. Although this new definition acknowledges the negative effects of institutional racism and other sociopolitical factors on the lives of African Americans, I am not suggesting that there should be no attribution of personal responsibility, since there is always a component of individual agency under even the most oppressive conditions. However, there is an interaction between these systemic forces and individual skills that must be taken into account if we are to truly understand the complexities of African American motherhood.

With the new definition that I am suggesting, it should be possible for African American mothers to overcome the arbitrary class divisions that have kept them apart and women would realize that we are all adversely affected by the sociopolitical and institutional conditions in society. This perspective should also help reduce the tendency to blame one segment of the community for its own victimization, thereby contributing to a more cooperative social climate. Communities of women (as birthmothers, othermothers, and community othermothers) could provide support and caring for each other while working together to nurture African American children in this hostile environment. This definition challenges us to remember, and to put into practice once again, the patterns of collectivism, mutual support, and interdependency that have been highly valued in the African American community throughout its history. These values helped African American families survive the most brutal years of our history in America. They can also effectively lead us through this modern-day maze of social ills.

REFERENCES

Aschenbrenner, J. (1975). *Black families in Chicago.* Prospect Heights, IL: Waveland Press.

Bell-Scott, P., Guy-Sheftall, B., Jones-Royster, J., Sims-Wood, J., DeCosta-Willis, M., and Fultz, L. P. (Eds.). (1991). *Double stitch.* New York, NY: HarperCollins.

Billingsley, A. (1968). *Black families in White America.* Englewood Cliffs, NJ: Prentice-Hall.

Billingsley, A. (1992). *Climbing Jacob's ladder.* New York, NY: Simon and Schuster.

Boyd-Franklin, N. (1991). Recurrent themes in the treatment of African American women in group therapy. *Women and Therapy, 11*(2), 25–40.

Brislin, R. (1993). *Understanding culture's influence on behavior.* New York, NY: Harcourt Brace Jovanovich.

Childs, E. K. (1990). Therapy, feminist ethic, and the community of color with particular emphasis on the treatment of Black women. In H. Lerman and N. Porter (Eds.), *Feminist Ethics in Psychotherapy* (pp. 195–203). New York, NY: Springer.

Collins, P. H. (1990). *Black feminist thought.* Boston, MA: Unwin Hyman.

Corcoran, M., Duncan, G. J., Gurin, G., and Gurin, P. (1985). Myth and reality: The causes and persistence of poverty. *Journal of Policy Analysis and Management, 4*(4), 516–536.

Davis, A. (1981). *Women, race and class.* New York, NY: Vintage.

Dougherty, M. C. (1978). *Becoming a woman in rural Black culture.* New York, NY: Holt, Rinehart and Winston.

Edelman, M. W. (1985). The sea is so wide and my boat is so small: Problems facing Black children today. In H. McAdoo and J. McAdoo (Eds.), *Black children: Social, educational and parental environments.* Newbury Park, CA: Sage.

Edwards, A. (1992). *Children of the dream: The psychology of Black success.* New York, NY: Doubleday.

Faulkner, J. (1983). Women in interracial relationships. *Women and Therapy 2,* 193–203.

Fox-Genovese, E. (1988). *Within the plantation household: Black and White women of the old south.* Chapel Hill, NC: University of North Carolina Press.

Gilkes, C. T. (1994). "If it wasn't for the women . . .": African American women, community work, and social change. In M. B. Zinn and B. Thorton Dill (Eds.), *Women of color in U.S. society.* Philadelphia, PA: Temple University Press.

Greene, B. (1990). What has gone before: The legacy of racism and sexism in the lives of Black mothers and daughters. *Women and Therapy, 9*(1–3), 207–230.

Greene, B. (1992). Black feminist psychotherapy. In E. Wright (Ed.), *Feminism and psychoanalysis.* Oxford, England: Blackwell.

Greene, B. (1993). Psychotherapy with African American women: Integrating feminist and psychodynamic models. *Journal of Training and Practice in Professional Psychology, 7*(1), 49–66.

Greene, B. (1994). Diversity and difference: The issue of race in feminist therapy. In M. Mirkin (Ed.), *Women in context: Toward a feminist reconstruction of psychotherapy.* New York, NY: Guilford.

Grier, W. H., and Cobbs, P. (1968). *Black rage.* New York, NY: Basic Books.

Gutman, H. G. (1976). *The Black family in slavery and freedom: 1750–1925.* New York, NY: Vintage Books.

Hill, R. B. (1972). *The strengths of Black families.* New York, NY: Emerson Hall.

hooks, b. (1981). *Black women and feminism.* Boston, MA: South End Press.

James, S. M. (1993). Mothering: A possible black feminist link to social transformation? In S. M. James and A.P.A. Busia (Eds.), *Theorizing Black feminisms: The visionary pragmatism of Black women* (pp. 44–54). New York, NY: Routledge.

Jenkins, L. (1994). African-American identity and its social context. In E. P. Salett and D. R. Koslow (Eds.), *Race, ethnicity and self: Identity in multicultural perspective* (pp. 63–88). Washington, DC: National Multicultural Institute.

Jenkins, Y. (1993). African American women: Ethnocultural variables and dissonant expectations. In J. L. Chin. V. De La Cancela, and Y. Jenkins (Eds.), *Diversity in psychotherapy: The politics of race, ethnicity and gender* (pp. 117–136). Westport, CT: Praeger.

Mann, S. A. (1990). Slavery, sharecropping, and sexual inequality. In M. R. Malson, E. Mudimbe-Boyi, J. F. O'Barr, and M. Wyer (Eds.), *Black women in America* (pp. 133–157). Chicago, IL: University of Chicago Press.

Mbiti, J. (1969). *African religions and philosophies.* New York, NY: Anchor.

McAdoo, H. P. (1981). *Black Families.* Beverly Hills, CA: Sage.

Moynihan, D. P. (1967). The Negro family: The case for national action. In L. Rainwater and W. L. Yancy (Eds.), *The Moynihan report and the politics of controversy* (pp. 39–132). Cambridge, MA: MIT Press.

Mullings, L. (1994). Images, ideology, and women of color. In M. B. Zinn and B. T. Dill (Eds.), *Women of color in U.S. society.* Philadelphia, PA: Temple University Press.

Oppong, C. (1973). *Growing up in Dagbon.* Tema, Ghana: Ghana Publishing Corporation.

Shaw, S. (1994). Mothering under slavery in the antebellum south. In E. N. Glenn, Chang, G., and Forcey, L. R. (Eds.), *Mothering: Ideology, experience and agency* (pp. 237–258). New York, NY: Routledge.

Smith, J. P. (1988). Poverty and the family. In G. Sandefur and M. Tienda (Eds.), *Divided opportunities: Minorities, poverty and social policy* (pp. 141–172). New York, NY: Plenum.

Stack, C. B. (1974). *All our kin: Strategies for survival in a Black community.* New York, NY: Harper and Row.

Sudarkasa, N. (1981). Interpreting the African heritage in Afro-American family organization. In H. P. McAdoo (Ed.), *Black families* (pp. 37–53). Beverly Hills, CA: Sage.

Sudarkasa, N. (1988). Interpreting the African heritage in Afro-American family organization. In H. P. McAdoo (Ed.), *Black families* (2d ed., pp. 27–43). Newbury Park, CA: Sage.

Sudarkasa, N. (1993). Female-headed African American households: Some neglected dimensions. In H. P. McAdoo (Ed.), *Family ethnicity: Strength in diversity* (pp. 81–89). Newbury Park, CA: Sage.

Tanner, N. (1974). Matrifocality in Indonesia and Africa and among Black Americans. In M. Z. Rosaldo and L. Lamphere (Eds.), *Women, culture, and society* (pp. 129–156). Stanford, CA: Stanford University Press.

Wade-Gayles, G. (1984, Fall). The truth of our mother's lives: Mother-daughter relationships in Black women's fiction. *Sage: A Scholarly Journal on Black Women, 1,* 8.

Wallace, M. (1991). *Black macho and the myth of the superwoman.* New York, NY: Verso Press.

Weems, R. J. (1993). *I asked for intimacy: Stories of blessings, betrayals, and birthings.* San Diego, CA: Lura Media.

White, D. G. (1985). *Ar'n't I a woman? Female slaves in the plantation south.* New York, NY: W. W. Norton.

Wilson, J. (1987). *The truly disadvantaged: The inner city, the underclass and public policy.* Chicago, IL: University of Chicago Press.

Young, V. H. (1970). Family and childhood in a southern Negro community. *American Psychologist, 72,* 269–288.

Zinn, M. B. (1990). Family, race, and poverty in the eighties. In M. R. Malson, E. Mudimbe-Boyi, J. F. O'Barr, and M. Wyer (Eds.), *Black women in America.* Chicago, IL: University of Chicago Press.

CHECKPOINTS

1. Gilmore provides cross-cultural examples of the meaning of masculinity.

2. Sparks describes the negative implications of cultural images of African American women on their internalized identity and self-esteem.

To prepare for reading the next section, think about this question:

1. How might gender stereotypes lead to discrimination?

THE CONSEQUENCES OF GENDER ROLES AND STEREOTYPES

What's So Special About Sex?[1]
Gender Stereotyping and Discrimination

SUSAN T. FISKE AND LAURA E. STEVENS

The Expert Witness: There are general stereotypes of what people particularly expect men to be like and typically expect women to be like. People typically expect women to be strong on the social dimensions. Women are generally expected to be more tender and understanding and concerned about other people, and soft.

The Court: You say that of people who have dealt with women expect that? People who have dealt with women in the business context expect that, or are you talking about people out on the farm?

—Price Waterhouse v. Hopkins, *1989, p. 543*

People all have their own opinions about gender stereotypes. Consequently, a social psychologist explaining the well-established research literature may find herself in the awkward position of disputing or at least elaborating the audience's commonsense judgments. Although common sense is the natural foil for all of social psychology given its domain (Kelley, 1992), it is particularly a problem in the field of gender stereotypes and discrimination, because of the special status of gender. This chapter addresses what makes sex special, that is, what makes gender-based responses more vulnerable to commonsense psychologizing than other types of category-based responses, stemming, for example, from race, age, or disability.

We will argue that gender is special (and especially awkward to evaluate in commonsense terms) because of (a) the heavily prescriptive aspects of gender stereotypes, (b) the inherent power asymmetries implied by gender differences in social status and average physical size, (c) the intimate communal relationships between members of the two groups, (d) the sexual and biological context of interpersonal interactions, and (e) the rapid historical change in the expression of sexism. As an illustration of these points let's begin with two case studies, drawn from the first author's experience as an expert witness. These cases depict superficially different but fundamentally similar cases of gender stereotyping and discrimination.

TALES OF TWO WOMEN

Lois Robinson worked as a welder in a certain Jacksonville, Florida, shipyard. Jacksonville Shipyards, Inc. (JSI) repairs U.S. Navy and commercial ships in dry dock in what is tough, sometimes dangerous work. The enterprise includes a wide variety of skilled craftworkers: welders, shipfitters, carpenters, electricians, machinists, boilermakers, sheetmetal workers, and more. The atmosphere is heavily identified with the Navy; many of the management had Navy careers before moving to the private sector. Women are less than 5% of the JSI work force, and less than half of 1% of the skilled craftworkers. What

Authors' Note: Portions of this chapter were presented at the meetings of the American Psychological Society (June 1991), the American Psychological Association (August 1992), and at Tulane University (October 1992).

this means from a practical point of view is that there are typically no or few women on any given shift, a minimum of none if business is slow, and a maximum of 8 to 10 out of 150 workers on a busy shift. Most often, there are 1 or 2 women out of 50 to 100 workers on shift, so a woman is likely to be the only woman in the crowd getting on the shipyard buses or at the time clock.

The JSI shipyard has been described as a boy's club, a man's world, and someone even painted "Men Only" on one of the work trailers. (When someone else complained, the sign was painted over, but in a cursory way.) It is perhaps best summarized as an atmosphere with a lot of joking and messing around. For example, one worker put a flashlight in his pants to show how well-endowed horses are; another carved the handle of a tool to resemble a penis, waving it in the faces of the women. There is open hostility to women on the part of a few men: "there's nothing worse than having to work around women; women are only fit company for something that howls." More often, there is simply a great deal of off-color joking (including one often-repeated joke about death by rape). Obscenity and profanity are routine.

Prominent in the visual environment (according to depositions, "every craft, every shop") are many calendars showing women in various states of undress and sexually explicit poses. Comparable magazines are widely shared, and pinups are torn out and posted spontaneously. Decorating various public walls are graffiti, both words and cartoons, with explicit sexual content depicting women. Note that there are of course no pictures, graffiti, or magazines depicting naked men. Note also that the workers are not allowed to bring other magazines on the job, and they are not allowed to post other material that is not work-related.

The few women workers are typically called by demeaning or sexually explicit names (honey, dear, baby, sugar, mamma, pussy, cunt, etc.). They are constantly teased, touched, humiliated, sexually evaluated, and propositioned; the incidents occur "every day all day" involving "all crafts," according to depositions.

Lois Robinson complained about the magazines and calendars, but she was brushed off, all the way up to the highest levels. A manager even pointed out that he had his own pinups. She eventually brought a lawsuit alleging sex discrimination due to sexual harassment in a hostile work environment; she won her case at the trial court level. An appeal by JSI is pending.

Let's move to the boardrooms of a Big Eight accounting firm, Price Waterhouse (PW), where one of the top managers brought in millions of dollars in accounts, worked more billable hours than anyone in that cohort, was well-liked by clients, and was described as aggressive, hard-driving, ambitious. But this exemplary manager was denied partnership because she was not feminine enough. Ann Hopkins was not accepted for partner because of "interpersonal skills problems" that would be corrected, a supporter informed her, by walking, talking, and dressing more femininely.

Although the setting was not exactly Jacksonville Shipyards, Inc., it encouraged stereotyping of women in several ways. First, Hopkins was in a firm that had about 1% female partners (7 of 662), and she was the only woman out of 88 people proposed for partner that year. The few women managers certainly stood out as women. Second, being a manager in a Big Eight firm is a stereotypically masculine job, calling for tough, aggressive behavior; consequently people think there is a lack of fit between being a woman and being a manager (Heilman, 1983). Third, gender stereotypes are more free to operate on ambiguous criteria, such as judgments of interpersonal skills, than they are on unambiguous counting criteria, such as number of billable hours. PW failed to guard against bias in these subjective judgments by even so minimal an effort as having a written policy against gender-based discrimination. And there were considerable differences of opinion about how to interpret Hopkins's hard-driving managerial behavior. Fourth, the partnership evaluations were based on ambiguous and scant information in many cases; hearsay and casual opinions were given substantial weight. Finally, the firm had no explicit policy against gender discrimination, although it did prohibit discrimination on the basis of age or health in partnership decisions (American Psychological Association [APA], 1989, details these points.)

Ann Hopkins also filed a lawsuit alleging sex discrimination, which she won, even though PW appealed it all the way to the Supreme Court.

WHAT'S SO SPECIAL ABOUT GENDER IN THESE CASES?

Could such cases have been brought by a plaintiff who was not a woman (for example, by a man or by a person of color)? The answer is "probably not," and explaining it provides some insight into what is so special about gender. After playing out several alternative scenarios, later sections of the chapter will elaborate the conceptual analysis and provide relevant references. For the moment, simply consider the overall argument.

Imagine the alternative scenario that the Robinson case had been brought by a man of color, alleging racial harassment in a hostile work environment. Legal issues aside, the character of the harassment would have been rather different in several ways, each of which we will spend the rest of the chapter elaborating.

1. The harassment would not have such a prescriptive element. "Be more sexually available," said to a woman, is a more plausible message than "be more musical" or "be more hip," said to an African American.

2. It would not have the same type of power dynamics. Although in both the actual and the hypothetical instance, the target would be vastly outnumbered and perhaps feel physically threatened on that account, there are two important differences: the individual male, white or black, is on average evenly matched on physical power. And the social power is at least theoretically equivalent; an apologist might dismiss sexual harassment as harmless by saying "boys will be boys," but it would be less normative to defend racial hostility by saying "white guys will be white guys." (This is not to say that racial harassment is not often dismissed or minimized as harmless using other stratagems.)

3. Another difference is that the sexual harassers have knowledge and expectations based on their wives, girlfriends, mothers, and daughters, whereas racial harassers are less likely to have intimates or relatives who are members of the targeted group.

4. Yet another major difference lies in the (overt at least) goal of sexual harassment, which supposedly is sexual favors. (Hostility is another possible agenda, shared with other types of harassment.) The double message of sexual harassment is clear: "I am sexually interested in you but I am ignoring your refusal."

5. Finally, the norms against expressing sexism are not the same as the norms against expressing racism.The presence of pictures and messages demeaning to women is far more common than comparable materials demeaning to other groups. People are more defensive about appearing racist than sexist (people react more strongly to being called a racist than a sexist), giving rise to all kinds of subtleties in the expression of racism that do not operate identically in sexism, as we will elaborate later. Thus a charge of racial harassment in the Robinson case probably would have looked quite different in several respects.[2]

Consider the Robinson case again, now from the perspective of a man alleging sexual harassment by women (leaving aside the possibility of sexual harassment by other men). Everything here hinges on power differences, both physical and social. There are three main reasons female sexual harassment is not likely to be as threatening: (a) The average physical size difference favors men. (b) The nature of male and female genital physiology makes it far more plausible for men to genitally rape an unwilling woman than for women to genitally rape an unwilling man. (c) Men have more power in society generally, so they have a broader background of power, against which any particular interaction is set. In short, although a man or a person of color could clearly be harassed on the basis of sexual or racial categories, the nature of the harassment would differ dramatically from sexual harassment because of fundamental features of gender stereotyping. These differences form the themes of our discussion in this chapter.

The dramatically different case of Ann Hopkins also highlights what is so special about gender, but in a superficially quite different setting. Consider the Hopkins case if it were brought by a man of color, praised for his competence but faulted for his interpersonal skills problems. To be comparable, the situation would have to entail a job requiring behavior considered antithetical to the stereotypic expectations (e.g., international sophistication for a stereotypic African American or social improvisation for a stereotypic Japanese American). At the same time, strong social prescriptions would require that the person not display such career-enhancing behavior, at the risk of making the decision makers personally uncomfortable. The tension between job requirements and stereotypic prescriptions would result in the career-oriented target being blamed for interpersonal difficulties. The main issue here is that the prescriptive aspect of racial stereotypes is less salient than that for gender stereotypes, so the racial version of *Hopkins* is less plausible. We will elaborate in a later section.

Finally, consider the Hopkins case from the perspective of a man alleging sex discrimination on the basis of stereotyping of his interpersonal skills. Suppose that he behaved in a "feminine" manner that was suited to his job but not suited to the tastes of his employers. Certainly, the prescriptions are strong against men behaving in stereotypically feminine ways. It is possible to imagine a male nurse, for example, faulted for being a mother hen. But the difference is that most stereotypically feminine behavior is not adaptive in most task settings; it is simply not competent behavior to be stereotypically feminine: emotional, passive, vulnerable, and dependent. Hence the configuration of female gender stereotypic behavior is not valued in the workplace, so few employees aspire to it. Essentially, this brings up the power dimension in yet another form; that is, the workplace values "masculine" traits but suppresses them in women.

The Robinson and Hopkins cases and their hypothetical alternative scenarios illustrate some central features of gender stereotyping that set it apart from other kinds of stereotyping. The next sections address each feature in turn.

GENDER STEREOTYPES ARE HEAVILY PRESCRIPTIVE

A stereotype has both a descriptive component and a prescriptive component. The descriptive component is composed of the attributes that constitute what people believe the typical group member to be like. For instance, the descriptive component of the female stereotype includes the following attributes: emotional, weak, dependent, passive, uncompetitive, and unconfident (Fiske, Bersoff, Borgida, Deaux, & Heilman, 1991). The prescriptive component of a stereotype is composed of the behaviors deemed suitable for the target group. In other words, prescriptions indicate how a member of the target group "should" behave. For example, the female stereotype includes the following prescriptions: A woman should have good interpersonal skills, she should be passive and docile, and she should cooperate with others.

Although all stereotypes include both descriptive aspects and prescriptive aspects, gender stereotypes are more prescriptive than other stereotypes. The many prescriptions characteristic of gender stereotypes are due in part to the amount of exposure people have to members of both gender categories. While observing and interacting with others, people develop a multitude of complex ideas about how members of each gender category actually do behave and how they would ideally behave. People are then able to incorporate these actual and ideal behaviors and formulate prescriptions or "shoulds" for each gender. These "shoulds" define behavior that is appropriate for members of each gender category (e.g., Terborg, 1977).

On the other hand, many people do not have much experience with the behavior of people in other categories. For example, many European-American people have not observed or interacted with African Americans often enough to have significant knowledge of their behavior. Thus it would be difficult for

these people to develop shoulds. However, they could still subscribe to the general descriptive aspect of the African-American stereotype: Blacks are athletic, talkative, religious, and musical (Dovidio & Gaertner, 1986; Stephan & Rosenfield, 1982). The descriptive aspect of a stereotype is more cognitive and could be easily learned from other people (think of all the people who endorse stereotypic descriptions about a category of people with whom they have never interacted). We would argue, however, that the prescriptive aspect of a stereotype is centrally based on experience with the target group.

Not only do people have more experience with gender categories than other categories, people also learn gender categories earlier than other categories. Though children only 24 months old have shown gender stereotyping of objects (Thompson, 1975), simple racial classification of black and white dolls does not emerge until around the age of 5 (Williams & Morland, 1976). In terms of gender stereotypes, by the time children are in preschool and kindergarten they ascribe gender stereotypic labels to toys, activities, and occupations without making many "errors." However, children do not seem to acquire knowledge of gender stereotypic descriptive traits until they are around 8 years old. Thus children apparently acquire knowledge of gender roles (i.e., stereotypic prescriptions) before they acquire knowledge of gender attributes (i.e., stereotypic descriptions) (Ruble & Ruble, 1982). Because the prescriptions people develop as a child are held for such a long time, it is likely that they are very strong.

The strength and complexity of the prescriptive aspects of gender stereotypes contribute to their saliency. Overall, gender is a more salient category than other categories. For instance, Fiske, Haslam, and Fiske (1991) found that people are more likely to confuse individuals of the same gender than individuals of the same age, race, role, or name. In addition, Stangor, Lynch, Duan, and Glass (1992) found people were more likely to categorize people according to their sex than their race. Because gender is such a salient category and the many prescriptive aspects are very strong, it follows that the prescriptive aspects of gender stereotypes will be more salient than the weaker prescriptive aspects of less salient categories. Therefore, people should be more likely to notice when a woman breaks with a stereotypic prescription than when, for example, a person fails to "act his or her age," thereby breaking with a stereotypic prescription.

Well-developed gender stereotypic prescriptions or shoulds limit both men's and women's behavior and, when the prescriptions are broken, it is particularly salient to observers. In addition, any behavior that violates gender prescriptions is generally negatively evaluated by others (Nieva & Gutek, 1980). This poses an especially difficult situation for working women. People will notice when working women do not meet the prescriptive demands of the female stereotype. Yet, as noted, these prescriptions are not usually adaptive for women in work settings (Bardwick & Donovan, 1971; Heilman, 1983). For example, if a female lawyer could not make up her mind, tended to behave in a passive and uncompetitive manner with her peers, and had publicly emotional reactions to both professional and personal experiences, she probably would not advance her career. Women are thus in a double bind. Do they behave in a way that will meet the sex stereotypic prescriptive demands to be feminine? Or, do they act competently and aggressively in order to fill job-specific demands? If they work to fill the job-specific demands, they run the risk of being evaluated negatively for displaying behavior antithetical to the stereotypic expectation for women. On the other hand, if they fill the gender-prescriptive demands, they run the risk of being viewed as incapable of having a successful career. Interestingly, both of these scenarios could result in sexual discrimination. In one case, discrimination would result from not behaving like a woman should and, in the other case, from behaving too much like a woman.

In sum, the prescriptive aspects of stereotypes are more central to gender stereotypes than they are to other stereotypes for a number of different reasons. First, people have more experience with members of each gender category than with members of other categories. This experience allows people to develop many complex prescriptions for gender. Second, people begin learning gender prescriptions at a very young age. These prescriptions are strong because they have been with people for so long. Finally, gender prescriptions are more salient than the prescriptions for other social categories. Unfortunately, the centrality and strength of gender prescriptions places working women in a sensitive situation that easily results in sexual discrimination.

GENDER STEREOTYPES ARE BASED ON DRAMATIC POWER DIFFERENCES

The illustrative hypothetical scenarios presented earlier in the chapter suggested the culturally unusual notion of a man bringing a sexual harassment suit, or a man wanting to behave in a feminine fashion to keep a job, but being prevented from doing so by female colleagues. Power is a core issue defining the implausibility of both hypotheticals. If we define *power* as the asymmetrical control over another person's outcomes (Dépret & Fiske, in press), then because men control a disproportionate share of outcomes valued in society (or at least in the workplace), men have power. It is common wisdom that this is so (e.g., Rohrbaugh, 1979), supported by sample statistics, such as the fact that women comprise a mere 3% of the top executive positions, with no increase over the last decade, and earning 72 cents for every dollar earned by men, with wage gaps even in female-dominated professions (Saltzman, 1991).

Sociologists have recognized these phenomena and their impact on gender differences, described in status theories such as expectation states theory (Berger, Conner, & Fisek, 1974; Berger, Fisek, Norman, & Zelditch, 1977). The basic premise is that expected performance (i.e., perceived competence) ranks people in interactions such that some people's contributions are expected to be more valuable than others. Those higher ranked people (e.g., men, European Americans) are then given more opportunities to contribute, receive deference, and so on (for a recent review and analysis, see Ridgeway & Diekema, 1992). Although this theory is designed to explain gender differences in communication styles, both verbal (Aries, 1987; Smith-Lovin & Robinson, 1992; Wood & Rhodes, 1992) and nonverbal (Ellyson, Dovidio, & Brown, 1992; Hall, 1987; Hall & Veccia, 1992), it also may be expanded to help us understand gender stereotyping.

The higher status of men in general leads to expectations that they will be more competent in general than women. But more specifically, the power and status differences can account for the differential valuing of male stereotypic traits (the competency cluster) and devaluing of female stereotypic traits (the social-emotional cluster), at least in task settings. In fact, the power itself may enable those people in power to define which traits are valuable. Because men have more status and power, their stereotypic traits are viewed as more deserving of respect. Which came first is unclear, but at least some of the variance is due to the power → respect sequence. This is not to say that people do not feel fond of others who display the social-emotional cluster stereotypic of women (Eagly & Mladinic, 1989). They often do, but this fondness may be accompanied by contempt (Kirchler, 1992). Fiske and Ruscher (in press) have argued that people seem to view women simultaneously as likable but also as unworthy of much respect (also see Freeman, 1971). Respect, which translates into rewards in the public marketplace, is differentially awarded to male stereotypic traits precisely because of their association with the group having more power and prestige.

The power and prestige asymmetry can also explain the prescription that women, the stereotypically less competent group, should limit themselves to their stereotypic (less valued) domains of expertise. And, clearly, it explains why men traditionally would not aspire to "feminine" traits, the devalued alternative. Indeed, as more women move into a given field, the status of the field may decline (Touhey, 1974).

In contrast to the status-and-power-differences argument, there is the role theory explanation of gender differences. Eagly (1987) argues that women take on the communal characteristics needed for

their traditional roles at home, and men conversely take on the agentic characteristics needed for their traditional roles in the work world. In effect, people are what they do and what other people expect them to be. Both individual and social experience contribute to gender differences. In this analysis, gender roles cause gender differences in behavior, and stereotypes reflect this process. However, this analysis does not account for the devaluing of women more generally in marketplace terms. Role theory does focus squarely on face-to-face interactions as people enact their traditional or nontraditional roles, and the more sociological status theory explanations are incorporating this level of analysis as well (Ridgeway & Diekema, 1992). Power dynamics in specific organizational settings are also important determinants of the extent of stereotyping. So, for example, solo status in an organization encourages stereotyping of individuals from the rare group (B. Mullen, personal communication, May 1992). This is consistent with a power-based explanation, whereby the outnumbered group has less power, and so it is not able to control as many resources. The lack of rewards available from the smaller group in turn decreases the motivation of the larger group to go beyond their initial stereotypes, and it also limits the power of the outnumbered group to alter those stereotypes. The larger, more powerful group in effect defines the norms (Kanter, 1977). Maccoby (1990) suggests that this may cause the disadvantaged group, that is, little girls, to withdraw and create their own subculture.

A final source of power differences results from relative physical size of men and women on average. For example, Dutton (1988) uses this as one among several explanations for the greater seriousness of wife assault than husband assault. This argument of course extends to other types of violence against women by men. It is important to note the physical size issue's contribution to male-female power asymmetries.

Power differences between men and women, then, are based on relative status, expected competence, common roles, relative numbers in the workplace, and average physical size.

GENDER STEREOTYPES DERIVE COMPLEXITY FROM CLOSE CONTACTS

Another characteristic of gender stereotypes that separates them from other category-based responses is their complexity. This complexity is derived from the numerous communal relationships between men and women. People have relationships with members of the "opposite" sex every day. Even if people do not have friends or co-workers of the other sex, members of their family are of the other sex. Women have fathers, boyfriends, husbands, and sons; men have mothers, girlfriends, wives, and daughters. Members of no other "minority group" have such routinely close relationships outside their group (Hacker, 1951). The mix of intimacy and discrimination can create profound ambivalence.

Furthermore, people generally have a great deal of time and effort invested in these personal relationships. In fact, some people may consider the behavior of their close friends, family members, and intimates to be the prototypical behavior for other members of the same gender category. They therefore derive expectations for members of the other sex from their personal experiences with these people. Some support for this lies in the fact that men in more egalitarian relationships have less traditional stereotypes of women than men in more traditional relationships (Peplau & Campbell, 1989). Even though these egalitarian partners may have chosen one another because they were each somewhat egalitarian, once in the relationship the expectations of the partners, in particular the male partners, also may have changed to become even more egalitarian.

This variety of close contact with family members, intimates, and friends of the other sex not only affects people's expectations for members of the other sex. It also increases the complexity of gender stereotypes by promoting the use of subtypes. *Subtypes* are "subcategories develop[ed] in response to isolated cases that disconfirm [a stereotype]" (Fiske & Taylor, 1991). For example, a man may have a female cousin who is a very aggressive and competent brain surgeon. She does not fit his female stereotype in many ways. Therefore, he may develop a subtype: female

doctors. In essence, he has "fenced off" (Allport, 1954) this family member who disconfirms his more global stereotype of women. In fact, this subtype gives him more information regarding his cousin's dispositions than would the other, broader category (Stangor et al., 1992).

The process of subtyping women is not a recent phenomenon. Women have been subtyped throughout history. Subtypes of women have ranged from love goddesses (e.g., the chivalric notion of the woman on the pedestal) to wholesome mother figures (e.g., the Christian ideal of Mother Mary) to inferior and evil creatures (e.g., the Chinese conception of the feminine nature, the Yin, which is evil and dark) (Rohrbaugh, 1979; Ruble & Ruble, 1982). In the 1970s, research began to address directly these more specific gender subtypes. For instance, Clifton, McGrath, and Wick (1976) discussed two different female stereotypes: "housewife" and "bunny." More recently, Deaux and her colleagues (Deaux, Kite, & Lewis, 1985; Deaux & Lewis, 1984) have also noted specific types of women, many based on job categories.

On the surface, subtyping may appear to be a good process, one that reduces stereotyping. After all, by subtyping, people are recognizing that not all people in a category are the same. For example, there are female doctors, female bunnies, and female leaders. Each of these subtypes has unique characteristics that separate it from the others and, to some degree, from the overall female stereotype. As promising as this line of thinking appears to be, however, it has not proven to be beneficial.

Subtyping or "fencing off" actually allows people to keep their overall stereotype intact (Hewstone, Hopkins, & Routh, 1992; Hewstone, Johnston, & Aird, 1992; Johnston & Hewstone, 1992). By separating people who disconfirm a stereotype into a subtype, people brand these disconfirmatory cases as atypical. If these disconfirmatory case are considered atypical, they will not affect the overall stereotype because the overall stereotype describes people who are *typical* members of the category.

Interestingly, even the subtypes people form to account for women who disconfirm the stereotype still incorporate gender. Women are not simply doctors or professors. They are *female* doctors or *female* professors. These category labels imply that there is something about being female that is relevant to role performance. One rarely says "male doctor" or "male professor." Moreover, one would think that gender would not be a part of the label of a category developed to classify women who disconfirm the gender stereotype.

So, what would be the best way to disconfirm and, subsequently, to change a stereotype that has a propensity for subtyping? Rothbart and John (1985) argue that disconfirming behaviors will only alter stereotypes if they are associated with people who are otherwise typical group members. In this way the overall category is activated and it is more difficult to subtype. The female fighter pilot who also has a husband, two children, and a big kitchen probably does more to counteract stereotypes than the unmarried female fighter pilot who hates to cook. Change of stereotypes is also promoted if the disconfirming behavior displayed by otherwise typical group members occurs repeatedly in many different settings. This reduces the chance that the disconfirming behavior will be attributed to environmental conditions. Women who are fighter pilots, rock climbers, and construction workers have undermined the old stereotype that women cannot do tough, demanding work. More recently, Hewstone and his colleagues have found support for the idea that dispersed inconsistent information promotes more stereotype change than does concentrated inconsistent information (Hewstone et al., 1992; Johnston & Hewstone, 1992).

One would think, with all the experiences shared between members of the two genders, that gender stereotypes would have changed. In particular, in recent years many American women have entered the work force and disconfirmed a number of stereotypic beliefs about women. Yet the basic, core contents of the female stereotype have not changed to any great degree over centuries (for a recent reference, see Eagly & Mladinic, 1989; for a review, see Ruble & Ruble, 1982). Perhaps men who subscribe to the traditional female stereotype think they are "experts" on women's behavior because they have had firsthand experience and they "know" how women should and do act. In other words, these men may have their own prescriptions and descriptions for women's behavior that they think must be appropriate and accurate because they have had many experiences that confirm their ideas. This poses two problems for stereotype change. First, the "experts" may simply refuse to accept that their stereotypes are inaccurate. Second, the group that believes it is an expert on the other group may have a sense of superior status and many studies on intergroup contact have indicated that stereotypes are not likely to change unless the two groups experience contact with one another under conditions of equal status (Stephan & Brigham, 1985).

Finally, the expectations sexual harassers have for people of the opposite sex, which are based on their friends, family members, and intimates, are complex and hard to change. Even sexual harassers who treat their female intimates respectfully are aware of both the more positive aspects of the female stereotype, which may lead to respect, and the more traditional aspects of the stereotype, which may promote harassing behavior in the workplace. Thus, because they have extremely complex and subtyped stereotypes of women, it may be even more difficult to change the stereotypes of "respectful" harassers than those of "consistent" harassers who have less complex and subtyped stereotypes.

On the other hand, racial harassers are less likely to have intimates who are members of the targeted group. Therefore, racial harassers' stereotypes should be less defined and less complex. Thus it may even be simpler to change racial harassers' stereotypes because they do not have a large number of subtypes that would need to be incorporated into the global stereotype. Of course, the problem of promoting equal status between the two groups would still exist.

In sum, gender stereotypes seem more complex than other stereotypes. The two genders share many experiences with one another. These experiences allow people to develop complex expectations for members of the other gender. In addition, this interaction promotes the use of subtypes. Unfortunately, stereotype change for gender stereotypes seems more difficult than for other categories because people have many subtypes for gender categories that would need to be integrated for change to occur.

GENDER STEREOTYPES DERIVE UNIVERSALITY FROM BIOLOGY

Men and women are biologically fated to intertwined lives. Nevertheless, that very same biology suggests that men and women may want different things from each other, and this is likely to affect their mutual perceptions. The potential impact of sexual biology tells us mostly about the evolution of our ancestors rather than about the social developments since that time or to come in the future. Social change is also part of the evolution of the species. Nevertheless, some evolutionary biological background sheds light on the near universality—but not inevitability—of certain cultural forms, including gender stereotypes.

From this standpoint, men and women regard each other primarily as potential mates, and sex differences in mate preferences suggest some important mismatched goals and stereotypes. Starting from the biological premise that females have more physical investment in each individual child than males do, females should value males who show signs of ability and willingness to invest in joint offspring (Buss, 1988, 1989). This suggests that women will look for men with financial resources. On the other hand, males can maximize their reproductive capability by finding fertile and nurturing females, and this suggests to sociobiologically oriented psychologists that men should value women who appear young and healthy. Other evolutionary sex differences can be similarly analyzed, but the basic contrast lies in women looking for mates showing evidence of resource acquisition and men looking for mates showing evidence of reproductive capacity (Buss, 1988; for a similar analysis, see Kenrick, 1989). Some of these preferences have been confirmed in samples from 37 different cultures (Buss, 1989).

Whatever the merits of the evolutionary argument, it certainly fits with the division of male and female prescriptive stereotypes into competency cluster for men (indicating the means to resource acquisition) and an attractiveness-nurturance cluster for women (signs of reproductive capacity). If the men in the Jacksonville Shipyard had only appreciated aspects of the women workers other than their reproductive readiness, and if the men at Price Waterhouse had only appreciated other aspects of Ann Hopkins than her apparent lack of nurturance, both environments would have been much more civilized. The women were foolish enough to believe that work was what mattered in the workplace; fortunately, the courts agreed with them, despite human evolutionary proclivities.

GENDER STEREOTYPES ARE HISTORICALLY SITUATED

Reviewing two decades of research on gender stereotypes (an enterprise not intended here, but see Deaux, 1985; Ruble & Ruble, 1982), one would see a sea-change in the message of the literature then and now. Either our research subjects or our psychological colleagues or both are changing their minds about the content and scope of gender stereotypes. The historical context has shifted from men and women being perceived as opposite sexes to men and women being perceived as overlapping on multiple dimensions and gender stereotypes being fleshed out in multiple subtypes. Whether we or our subjects are becoming more sophisticated almost does not matter, for some change is accomplished. (Perhaps our biology is not so fixed after all?)

One index of the change is the citation frequency of the classic article by Broverman, Vogel, Broverman, Clarkson, and Rosenkrantz (1972) documenting the content of gender stereotypes. From a steady buildup from 1972 to 1980, with a peak of nearly 80 citations in 1980, the citations dropped to less than half that in 1990 (according to citations listed in the *Social Science Citation Index*). Any article has a similar citation profile, assuming it is cited at all, but this article, as one of the catalysts of the research literature, is intrinsically diagnostic. Although there have been no replications of Broverman et al. (1972), there is evidence that people still endorse these gender stereotypes (e.g., Martin, 1987).

Another gender stereotype classic, the Goldberg (1968) study, illustrates the change in the overall message over time. Although the 1968 study seemed to demonstrate that the same work product was evaluated more favorably when attributed to a man than to a woman, the message has become more complex over time (Swim, Borgida, Maruyama, & Myers, 1989). The effect size was larger in studies published during 1968–1973, but not huge even then. Essentially the current message is that stereotyping is a function of many moderator variables, most of which have not been examined in enough detail to conduct a meta-analysis on the moderators. Swim et al. suggested several plausible moderators: particular subtypes activated, perceived diagnosticity of information, interaction between stereotype and information, goals or motives of the subject, and task demands.

When one collapses over various moderators, of course, one is averaging over (a) control conditions designed to show the baseline discriminatory effect (i.e., women are evaluated less favorably than comparable men) and (b) experimental conditions designed to eliminate the effect (i.e., the effect goes away if people are motivated to be more careful). It is not surprising then that an overall meta-analysis of the main effect concluded that the effect is small (Fiske, Bersoff, Borgida, Deaux, & Heilman, 1991). The interactions between the basic effect and the proposed moderator variables are being ignored.

One might examine the small main effects for gender and conclude that gender stereotyping has nearly vanished. Some textbook writers indeed are beginning to conclude that gender stereotyping is less of a problem than it used to be. Compare one of the best-selling social psychology texts in 1981: "As we have seen throughout this discussion, sexual stereotypes, and the discriminatory behaviors that accompany them, certainly persist at the present time" (Baron & Byrne, 1981, p. 182); and a decade later: "Together, all these findings point to substantial shifts toward a reduced incidence of sex discrimination in the world of work" (Baron & Byrne, 1991, p. 219). There is clearly some room for optimism at present; however, the experimental research is not an indicator of incidence per se, not being a representative sample survey, but rather having been designed

to study moderators and mediators of effects. In other words, current experiments show that stereotyping is a complex process but say little about how frequently it occurs.

An illustration of the role of subtypes in stereotyping serves to indicate the complexity of modern sexism. Ann Hopkins was a victim of gender stereotypes, but certainly not the stereotype that she was passive, incompetent, and emotional. Quite the contrary. And a recent meta-analysis bears (Eagly, Makhijani, & Klonsky, 1992) out the conclusions of the American Psychological Association's amicus brief (APA, 1989) and the Supreme Court:

> Women in leadership positions were devalued relative to their male counterparts when leadership was carried out in stereotypically masculine styles, particularly when this style was autocratic or directive. In addition, the devaluation of women was greater when leaders occupied male-dominated roles and when the evaluators were men. (Eagly, Makhijani, & Klonsky, 1992, p. 3)

In short, one would not expect a main effect such that all women are universally devalued; rather, certain women are devalued when gender-based subtypes interact with the features of a particular work environment.

Elsewhere, Fiske (1989) has argued that these people, who do not match widespread descriptive stereotypes, are faulted on subjective grounds because they make us uncomfortable by violating our notions of how such people should behave. This gives rise to the perception that one is dealing with a "difficult" person, someone who simply does not fit in. The point is that such people are stereotyped and the blame for their problems is laid at the door of their own personal attributes. Hopkins was certainly seen as a difficult person, and Lois Robinson also was faulted for not going along with the locker-room atmosphere. Both were perceived as difficult people.

Besides the increasing complexity of subtypes, gender stereotyping has the potential for another major historical shift. Such a shift has already occurred in the literature on racism, along with changing historical norms. Whereas early research indicated overt, old-fashioned racism (claiming blacks are inferior to whites), more recent efforts have tackled modern racism in several forms (See Pettigrew, 1985, for a review). For example, Sears and his colleagues (Sears, Hensler, & Speer, 1979) argued that people do not want to feel racist, so instead they attack issues symbolic of the out-group; thus, opposing all policies related to busing, affirmative action, welfare, and the like, would indicate symbolic racism. Similarly, Gaertner and Dovidio (1986) described aversive racism: the person's racism is aversive to his or her self-image, so the person behaves in a nondiscriminatory, even reverse discriminatory way, except when the behavior is covert or when there is an acceptable alternative explanation (an excuse) for the discriminatory behavior that would make it appear nonracist. Also, Katz and his colleagues (Katz, Wackenhut, & Hass, 1986) discussed at length the ambivalence and response amplification that may result when people hold simultaneously sympathetic and rejecting attitudes toward an out-group. All of these dynamics seem to us to be plausible accounts of what is beginning to happen with sexism as well; it has not vanished, just become less acceptable in many circles, so it has gone underground. Researchers need to pursue this parallel between modern racism and modern sexism.

Research topics go through a predictable development, and gender stereotyping research is no exception: from the heady days of first discoveries (the more counterintuitive or provocative, the better), to the replications and extensions, to the inevitable dissent, to the moderator variable stage. Gender stereotyping research has clearly arrived at the moderator variable stage. From there, research can fizzle if people decide "there is no there there" (too many contradictions, too many qualifications, too complicated,

too limited to one paradigm; whatever the complaint, the result is the same). Alternatively, research at this stage can spin off new theoretical approaches that synthesize previous work. Given the importance and interest value of gender as an enduring feature of the human landscape, we expect that the future will bring synthesis rather than fizzle.

SUMMARY

This chapter has argued that gender-based responses differ from other types of category-based responses in a variety of ways. First, gender stereotypes are heavily prescriptive. People acquire gender categories in the family, before they acquire other categories, and they therefore have more time to develop and motivation to invest in gender prescriptions. Second, gender stereotypes are based on dramatic power differences. Men are not only physically larger than women, but they also control a disproportionate share of the outcomes valued in society. Third, close contact between the two genders increases the complexity of gender stereotypes, and thus gender stereotypes may be characterized by more subtypes than other stereotypes. Fourth, gender stereotypes possess sexual and biological facets that other stereotypes do not have. And, finally, gender stereotypes change as a function of cultural change and scientific advance.

Every one of these distinctive characteristics of gender stereotypes has significant effects on interactions between people. As illustrated in the text of this chapter, they each affected the stereotyping of and discrimination against both Lois Robinson and Ann Hopkins. In addition, these characteristics influence the literature on gender. And, perhaps most importantly, they affect our everyday interactions with our friends, co-workers, relatives, and intimates.

NOTES

1. Technically, this part of the title should read "What's So Special About Gender?" However, we opted for the more eye-catching "What's So Special About Sex?"

2. We are merely trying to illustrate how sexism is different from racism. We are not saying that sexism is more important or more serious.

REFERENCES

Allport, G. W. (1954). *The nature of prejudice.* Reading, MA: Addison-Wesley.

American Psychological Association Brief for Amicus Curiae in Support of Respondent, *Price Waterhouse v. Hopkins,* 109 S. Ct. 1775 (1989).

Aries, E. (1987). Gender and communication. In P. Shaver & C. Hendrick (Eds.), *Review of personality and social psychology: Sex and gender* (Vol. 7, pp. 149–176). Newbury Park, CA: Sage.

Bardwick, J. M., & Donovan, E. (1971). Ambivalence: The socialization of women. In V. Gornick & B. K. Moran (Eds.), *Woman in sexist society* (pp. 147–159). New York: Basic Books. (Reprinted from J. M. Bardwick (Ed.), *Readings on the psychology of women* (pp. 52–58), Harper & Row, 1972).

Baron, R. A., & Byrne, D. (1981). *Social psychology: Understanding human interaction* (3rd ed.). Boston: Allyn & Bacon.

Baron, R. A., & Byrne, D. (1991). *Social psychology: Understanding human interaction* (6th ed.). Boston: Allyn & Bacon.

Berger, J., Conner, T. L., & Fisek, M. H. (1974). *Expectation states theory: A theoretical research program.* Cambridge, MA: Winthrop.

Berger, J., Fisek, M. H., Norman, R. Z., & Zelditch, M., Jr. (1977). *Status characteristics and social interaction.* New York: Elsevier.

Broverman, I. K., Vogel, S. R., Broverman, D. M., Clarkson, F. E., & Rosenkrantz, P. S. (1972). Sex-role stereotypes: A current appraisal. *Journal of Social Issues, 28*(2), 59–78.

Buss, D. M. (1988). Love acts: The evolutionary biology of love. In R. J. Sternberg & M. L. Barnes (Eds.), *The psychology of love* (pp. 100–118). New Haven, CT: Yale University Press.

Buss, D. M. (1989). Sex differences in human mate preferences: Evolutionary hypotheses tested in 37 cultures. *Behavioral and Brain Sciences, 12,* 1–49.

Clifton, A. K., McGrath, D., & Wick, B. (1976). Stereotypes of woman: A single category? *Sex Roles, 2,* 135–148.

Deaux, K. (1985). Sex and gender. *Annual Review of Psychology, 36,* 49–81.

Deaux, K., Kite, M. E., & Lewis, L. L. (1985). Clustering and gender schemata: An uncertain link. *Personality and Social Psychology Bulletin, 11,* 387–397.

Deaux, K., & Lewis, L. L. (1984). Structure of gender stereotypes: Interrelationships among components and gender label. *Journal of Personality and Social Psychology, 46,* 991–1004.

Dépret, E. F., & Fiske, S. T. (in press). Social cognition and power: Some cognitive consequences of social structure as a source of control deprivation. In G. Weary, F. Gleicher, & K. Marsh (Eds.), *Control motivation and social cognition.* New York: Springer.

Dovidio, J. F., & Gaertner, S. L. (1986). Prejudice, discrimination, and racism: Historical trends and contemporary approaches. In J. F. Dovidio & S. L. Gaertner (Eds.), *Prejudice, discrimination, and racism* (pp. 1–34). New York: Academic Press.

Dutton, D. G. (1988). Research advances in the study of wife assault etiology and prevention. *Law and Mental Health,* 161–219.

Eagly, A. H. (1987). *Sex differences in social behavior: A social-role interpretation.* Hillsdale, NJ: Lawrence Erlbaum.

Eagly, A. H., Makhijani, M. G., & Klonsky, B. G. (1992). Gender and the evaluation of leaders: A meta-analysis. *Psychological Bulletin, 111,* 3–22.

Eagly, A. H., & Mladinic, A. (1989). Gender stereotypes and attitudes toward women and men. *Personality and Social Psychology Bulletin, 15,* 534–558.

Ellyson, S. L., Dovidio, J. F., & Brown, C. E. (1992). The look of power: Gender differences and similarities in visual dominance behavior. In C. L. Ridgeway (Ed.), *Gender, interaction and inequality* (pp. 50–80). New York: Springer.

Fiske, A. P., Haslam, N., & Fiske, S. T. (1991). Confusing one person with another: What errors reveal about the elementary forms of social relations. *Journal of Personality and Social Psychology, 60,* 656–674.

Fiske, S. T. (1989, August). *Interdependence and stereotyping: From the laboratory to the Supreme Court (and back).* Invited address given at the 97th Annual Convention of the American Psychological Association, New Orleans.

Fiske, S. T., Bersoff, D. N., Borgida, E., Deaux, K., & Heilman, M. E. (1991). Social science research on trial: Use of sex stereotyping research in *Price Waterhouse v. Hopkins. American Psychologist, 46,* 1049–1060.

Fiske, S. T., & Ruscher, J. B. (in press). Negative interdependence and prejudice: Whence the affect? In D. M. Mackie & D. L. Hamilton (Eds.), *Affect, cognition, and stereotyping: Interactive processes in group perception.* New York: Academic Press.

Fiske, S. T., & Taylor, S. E. (1991). *Social cognition* (2nd ed.). New York: McGraw-Hill.

Freeman, J. (1971). Social construction of the second sex. In M. H. Garskof (Ed.), *Roles women play: Readings toward women's liberation* (pp. 123–141). Belmont, CA: Wadsworth.

Gaertner, S. L., & Dovidio, J. F. (1986). The aversive form of racism. In J. F. Dovidio & S. L. Gaertner (Eds.), *Prejudice, discrimination, and racism* (pp. 61–89). New York: Academic Press.

Goldberg, P. (1968). Are women prejudiced against women? *Transaction, 5,* 28–30.

Hacker, H. M. (1951). Women as a minority group. *Social Forces, 30,* 60–69.

Hall, J. A. (1987). On explaining gender differences: The case of nonverbal communication. In P. Shaver & C. Hendrick (Eds.),

Review of personality and social psychology: Sex and gender (Vol. 7, pp. 177–200). Newbury Park, CA: Sage.

Hall, J. A., & Veccia, E. M. (1992). Touch asymmetry between the sexes. In C. L. Ridgeway (Ed.), *Gender, interaction, and inequality* (pp. 81–96). New York: Springer.

Heilman, M. E. (1983). Sex bias in work settings: The lack of fit model. *Research in Organizational Behavior, 5,* 269–298.

Hewstone, M., Hopkins, N., & Routh, D. A. (1992). Cognitive models of stereotype change: Generalization and subtyping in young people's views of the police. *European Journal of Social Psychology, 22,* 219–224.

Hewstone, M., Johnston, L., & Aird, P. (1992). Cognitive models of stereotype change: Perceptions of homogeneous and heterogeneous groups. *European Journal of Social Psychology, 22,* 235–250.

Johnston, L., & Hewstone, M. (1992). Cognitive models of stereotype change: Subtyping and the perceived typicality of disconfirming group members. *Journal of Experimental Social Psychology 28,* 260–386.

Kanter, R. M. (1977). *Men and women of the corporation.* New York: Basic Books.

Katz, I., Wackenhut, J., & Hass, R. G. (1986). Racial ambivalence, value duality, and behavior. In J. F. Dovidio & S. L. Gaertner (Eds.), *Prejudice, discrimination, and racism* (pp. 35–59). New York: Academic Press.

Kelley, H. H. (1992). Common-sense psychology and scientific psychology. *Annual Review of Psychology, 43,* 1–23.

Kenrick, D. T. (1989). A biosocial perspective on mates and traits: Reuniting personality and social psychology. In D. M. Buss & N. Cantor (Eds.), *Personality psychology: Recent trends and emerging directions* (pp. 308–319). New York: Springer.

Kirchler, E. (1992). Adorable woman, expert man: Changing gender images of women and men in management. *European Journal of Social Psychology, 22,* 363–373.

Maccoby, E. E. (1990). Gender and relationships. *American Psychologist, 45,* 513–520.

Martin, C. L. (1987). A ratio measure of sex stereotyping. *Journal of Personality and Social Psychology, 52,* 489–499.

Nieva, V. F., & Gutek, B. A. (1980). Sex effects on evaluation. *Academy of Management Review, 5,* 267–276.

Peplau, L. A., & Campbell, S. M. (1989). The balance of power in dating and marriage. In J. Freeman (Ed.), *Women: A feminist perspective* (pp. 121–137). Mountain View, CA: Mayfield.

Pettigrew, T. F. (1985). New black-white patterns: How best to conceptualize them? *Annual Review of Sociology, 11,* 329–346.

Price Waterhouse v. Hopkins, 109 S. Ct. 1775 (1989).

Ridgeway, C. L., & Diekema, D. (1992). Are gender differences status differences? In C. L. Ridgeway (Ed.), *Gender, interaction, and inequality* (pp. 157–180). New York: Springer.

Rohrbaugh, J. B. (1979). *Women: Psychology's puzzle.* New York: Basic Books.

Rothbart, M., & John, O. P. (1985). Social categorization and behavioral episodes: A cognitive analysis of the effects of intergroup contact. *Journal of Social Issues, 41*(3), 81–104.

Ruble, D. N., & Ruble, T. L. (1982). Sex stereotypes. In A. G. Miller (Ed.), *In the eye of the beholder: Contemporary issues in stereotyping* (pp. 188–252). New York: Praeger.

Saltzman, A. (1991, June 17). Trouble at the top. *U.S. News and World Report,* pp. 40–48.

Sears, D. O., Hensler, C. P., & Speer, L. K. (1979). Whites' opposition to busing: Self-interest or symbolic politics? *American Political Science Review, 73,* 369–384.

Smith-Lovin, L., & Robinson, D. T. (1992). Gender and conversational dynamics. In C. L. Ridgeway (Ed.), *Gender, interaction, and inequality* (pp. 122–156). New York: Springer.

Stangor, C., Lynch, L., Dunn, C., & Glass, B. (1992). Categorization of individuals on the basis of multiple social features. *Journal of Personality and Social Psychology, 62,* 207–218.

Stephan, W. G., & Brigham, J. C. (1985). Intergroup contact: Introduction. *Journal of Social Issues, 41*(3), 1–8.

Stephan, W. G., & Rosenfield, D. (1982). Racial and ethnic stereotypes. In A. G. Miller (Ed.), *In the eye of the beholder: Contemporary issues in stereotyping* (pp. 92–136). New York: Praeger.

Swim, J., Borgida, E., Maruyama, G., & Myers, D. G. (1989). Joan McKay versus John McKay: Do gender stereotypes bias evaluations? *Psychological Bulletin, 105,* 409–429.

Terborg, J. R. (1977). Women in management: A research review. *Journal of Applied Psychology, 62,* 647–664.

Thompson, S. K. (1975). Gender labels and early sex role development. *Child Development, 46,* 339–347.

Touhey, J. C. (1974). Effects of additional women professionals on ratings of occupational prestige and desirability. *Journal of Personality and Social Psychology, 29,* 86–89.

Williams, J. E., & Morland, K. J. (1976). *Race, color and the young child.* Chapel Hill: University of North Carolina Press.

Wood, W., & Rhodes, N. (1992). Sex differences in interaction style in task groups. In C. L. Ridgeway (Ed.), *Gender, interaction, and inequality* (pp. 97–121). New York: Springer.

CHECKPOINT

1. Fiske and Stevens describe five characteristics that make gender stereotypes unique and that contribute to the perpetuation of stereotypes about women that lead to sex discrimination.

Gender Roles and Stereotypes

QUESTIONS FOR REFLECTION

1. How have gender, race, ethnic, and sexual orientation stereotypes changed over the last thirty years?
2. In your opinion, and based on your reading, what factors are central in changing gender stereotypes?
3. How are the communal and agenic roles expressed in cultural variations of masculinity and femininity?

CHAPTER APPLICATIONS

1. Write a list of stereotypes of men and women. Watch a television show and keep track of the frequencies of conformity to and violations of these gender stereotypes. Keep track of the race, ethnicity, and sexual orientation of the characters. Do these factors make a difference in gender stereotyping?
2. Fiske and Stevens describe how gender stereotypes lead to gender discrimination in the case of Ann Hopkins at Price Waterhouse and to sexual harassment in the case of Lois Robinson at the Jacksonville shipyards. How might these events have differed if Ann Hopkins were an African American woman and Lois Robinson a gay man? How could you defend these claims of discrimination based on stereotypes?

CHAPTER SIX

Gender Identity Development

QUESTIONS TO THINK ABOUT

- How do different theories describe the development of gender identity?
- Describe gender schema theory.
- What is the significance of sex segregation?
- What biological factors might be related to sex segregation?
- What is the relationship between gender and development?
- What are the important socialization and cognitive factors for gender identity development?
- How is development during adolescence both continuous and discontinuous with childhood?
- Do gender roles change across the lifespan?

THE SIGNIFICANCE OF GENDER

In 1990 I (A. L.) was pregnant for the second time. At one point prior to the baby's birth, a colleague of my husband's commented to him, "Well, you have a daughter, so you must *really* want a son this time." "No," he answered, "Now that I have a daughter, I *really* want another daughter." Our then-two-year-old daughter told everyone that she really wanted a baby sister (whom she would name Rainbow Sky), and I kept quiet (privately preferring another daughter).[1] Are we in the minority? Absolutely yes. The vast majority of American men, when asked whether they have a preference concerning the sex of their first child, state a preference for a son. A smaller percentage of women, but still a majority, also state a preference for a son (Williamson, 1976). This preference for sons can be so strong in some societies, notably India and China, that it leads to in-

fanticide of infant girls or selective abortions of female fetuses (Hrdy, 1988).

What might be the basis for such a strong preference? Certainly the reasons vary across cultures. In the United States, the answer may be related to one's perception of the role of the child and parent. For several years, both of us have asked students in various courses to conduct a small survey. The students asked male and female adults their preference for a first- and second-born child and the reason for their choice. Even with different samples (e.g., college students, married adults with and without children), the responses showed a consistent, strong preference for sons, especially for the firstborn child. Most interesting were the reasons given for this preference. Semester after semester, the project yielded the same patterns. Men preferred sons largely for the following reasons: "to carry on the family name," "to play sports with," "so I'll know what to do with him," "because girls are too fragile," or "I wouldn't know what to do with a daughter." Women preferred sons for the following reasons: "because my husband would probably prefer a son," "so if I had a daughter, she would have a big brother," and "because boys have it better." Notice that these answers depend on the sex of the adult and the role attributed to either sons or daughters. For prospective fathers, the role of a future son is tied to being a name carrier or a playmate. He expects the son to become like him, to share his interests, and to carry on the family traditions, especially the family name.[2] These prospective fathers seem to believe that as men, they have more to offer to a son. For prospective mothers, one important goal seems to be to fulfill the expectations of the baby's father. Mothers seem aware of the role of a son in the cultural community—either to be a "big brother" or because boys, in general, are more favored. Clearly these kinds of responses derive from the stereotypes and gender roles that we examined in chapter 5. How soon does stereotyping begin to influence a developing child? Based on our own informal study and on other research findings, the answer suggests that stereotyping occurs well before birth—perhaps long before conception!

QUESTIONS ABOUT DEVELOPMENT AND GENDER

When do children become aware of the importance of gender? What do children learn about gender? When and how do children come to see themselves as boys and girls? When do children develop preferences for certain activities, toys, and playmates that are preferred by others of their sex? If cultural stereotypes and parental expectations are in place before birth, how and when does a child come to share these cultural views and practices about gender?

Developmental psychologists have studied these questions about gender and development. In this chapter, we examine the role of gender in shaping children's experiences as they develop; we also look at how development shapes what children know about gender and how children come to incorporate gender into their identity. We further consider how gender identity interacts with development during adolescence and adulthood. Our perspective is that gender and development influence each other over the course of an individual's life such that we can only understand one by knowing the other. The question then becomes, how do gender and development interact? By studying how children change with age and by studying how children come to understand and use their knowledge of gender, we can begin to see the interaction between gender and development. The behaviors that reflect gender, a child's knowledge of gender, and the emotional significance of gender all appear different at various points in the developmental progression.

Many, although not all, children will develop preferences for playmates of the same sex and activities that are sex-typed. If you have had the opportunity to observe children of about age 4 or 5, you might have noticed these preferences. In a preschool classroom, many boys prefer to build with blocks while girls may play in a kitchen corner. Outside, boys and girls might separate themselves into segregated groups, sometimes playing games involving boys chasing girls (Thorne, 1990). One component of gender identity development is the process by which children acquire behaviors related to their sex. This process of mapping particular behaviors and attitudes onto children based on their biological sex is referred to as the acquisition of *gender roles*. As you saw in chapter 4, most cultures provide different social roles for boys and girls. Part of growing up involves acquiring the behaviors that are related to these culturally defined gender roles. Although not all children adopt all features of the prescribed gender role, there are differences in behaviors prescribed for the social roles of boys and girls. When and why do children come to prefer some activities, playmates, behaviors, hobbies, or styles of social interaction over others, and how much variation is there in these preferences? We will refer to these behaviors as the *social/behavioral* component of gender identity. All sorts of behaviors are related to the socialization of gender identity, such as classroom behavior, displays of emotion, parent-child interactions, or preferences for activities.

Another dimension of gender identity is the child's knowledge about gender, or the *cognitive* component of gender identity. Some children begin as young as age 2 to use the label "girl" or "boy" to describe themselves and others. What meaning is attached to this label for young children? As cognitive development progresses, the meaning and significance of the concept of gender begins to change. How does a child's understanding of gender change with development? We will see that contemporary theories of cognitive development can be used to understand a child's comprehension of gender.

A third component of gender identity is the *affective* component, which refers to what children feel about their identity as either male or female. Not only do children often prefer toys and playmates related to their gender, they often become deeply attached to the part of themselves they know as "girl" or "boy." Typically, both boys and girls prefer to be who they are with regard to their gender identity.[3] Often in middle childhood we see this affective component reflected in children's debates over who are better—boys or girls, with each group arguing for its own unique advantages. As children reach adolescence, the emotional significance of gender identity may intensify as physical changes intersect with cultural prescriptions to create pressures to adopt gender appropriate adult role behaviors (Huston & Alvarez, 1990).

Obviously, the development of gender identity must involve all three components—*social/behavioral, cognitive,* and *affective.* Children learn to think and act in ways that reflect their gender, and they develop strong feelings about themselves as gendered people. We now turn to the question of how psychologists have studied questions of gender and development and to the different theories that have been proposed to account for how children come to understand a gender identity.

THEORIES OF GENDER AND DEVELOPMENT

Three of the most influential perspectives in psychology have been used to explain gender identity development: psychoanalytic theory, social learning theory, and cognitive developmental theory. Each of these theories offers a different perspective on gender identity, and each has received varying levels of research support from psychological research. Each article in this chapter provides some information on one or more of these theories. Following is a brief introduction to these three theoretical perspectives so when you read the articles, you will better understand the points each author makes about these positions.

The Psychoanalytic Perspective on Gender Identity

Psychoanalytic theory, as proposed by Freud, positions the child's development of gender identity in the context of his/her relationship with the parent of the same sex. Gender identity is part of Freud's larger theory of psychosexual development, which begins during infancy and accounts for an individual's personality development. In Freud's view, both male and female children have their primary identification with their mother. For a male child, gender identity occurs through the resolution of the Oedipal Complex. This resolution occurs when the male child, realizing the father's superiority and fearing castration, internalizes the gender identity as well as the moral values of the father. Freud developed his views of gender identity around the relationship between boys and fathers, proposing that boys develop into men via their internalization of the masculinity and morality of their fathers. In comparison, girls are viewed as deficient because the motivation for their identification (penis envy) is less powerful than boys' motivation (castration anxiety) and involves less psychic energy to resolve, and the object of their identification remains with the mother, who is inherently less powerful than the father.[4] Freud's view of gender identity has been criticized since its initial formulation, most especially for its negative view of girls and women (Fast, 1993).[5] Psychoanalytic theories do not generalize well across cultures; they are based on the assumption that all children are raised in a two-parent nuclear family; and they assume that heterosexuality is normative (Reid, Haritos, Kelly, & Holland, 1995).

Despite the many criticisms of psychoanalytic theories, they call attention to three aspects of development that are essential to our understanding of gender identity. The first is the affective component of identity, including how we feel about who we are as men and women as well as how children come to attach an emotional significance to themselves as boys or girls. The second is the internalization of identity. In the Freudian view, the internalized self is developed through unconscious, conflicting motives. Whether unconscious or not, one's sense of oneself as a gendered person is partially internalized. The third focus of psychoanalytic theory highlights the relationship between identity and sexuality. It is important to recognize the complex relationship between gender identity, sexuality, and sexual orientation. In chapter 7, we review the development of both sexuality and sexual orientation, focusing on the importance of gender in understanding sexuality.

Social Learning Theory and Gender Role Development

Social learning theory examines the role of reinforcement and observational learning in the child's acquisition of sex-typed behaviors. Two primary mechanisms are used by social learning theory. The first mechanism is the presence or absence of rewards for gender-appropriate behavior and punishment for gender-inappropriate behavior. The second mechanism is the imitation, or modeling, of behavior demonstrated by same-sex models. Social learning theory is most associated with the social/behavioral component of gender identity. According to social learning theory, several factors should influence variations in children's acquisition of gender-related behaviors: the availability of same sex role models, the child's perception of the similarity between him/herself and the role model, and the child's perception of the likely consequences of his/her behavior. The parent of the same sex emerges as a likely

candidate for an appropriate model, and so researchers have examined the degree to which children attend to and imitate the behavior of parents of the same sex. Unfortunately, what seems to be an intuitively obvious and interesting mechanism by which children come to adopt gender-role behavior is not supported by research evidence. Children do not preferentially imitate their same-sex parent (Huston, 1983).

The other important mechanism proposed by the social learning perspective has received some empirical support. The role of differential reinforcement may play a part in children's adoption of gender role behavior. In many areas, parents do not treat sons and daughters differently; however, evidence shows that parents do encourage gender-typed activities (Jacklin & Reynolds, 1993). Social learning theory may help explain very early gender differences in behavior because parents perceive and treat children differently from birth based on the child's sex.

In their observations of their world, children are exposed to *gendered role models,* meaning that adults frequently engage in gender segregated behaviors. A child may observe his/her mother in the kitchen and father cutting the lawn, may see women as elementary school teachers and men as school principals, and may see male physicians and female nurses. According to social learning theory, the significance of such observations is that children may come to believe that because they are of a certain sex, they are similar to the person(s) they observe simply because of the person's sex. This perceived similarity may increase the likelihood that children will imitate the behavior of the person observed. This mechanism of social learning may be quite powerful because children are constant witnesses to the gendered divisions in our society, for example, what kinds of work men and women do, what kinds of characteristics men and women portray, what kinds of interests and activities men and women enjoy.

As a scientific theory, social learning offers many advantages over psychoanalytic theory. Testable predictions based on clearly specified relationships between a child's experience and potential outcomes have led to a large body of research from this perspective. In the second article in this chapter, *Psychosocial and Cognitive Determinants of Early Gender-Role Development*, Beverly Fagot reviews much of this research and summarizes what is known about early social influences on gender role. Although these social learning mechanisms are important, they are not sufficient to explain the complexities of gender identity development.

There are two fundamental weaknesses of social learning theory that limit its ability to explain all gender role development. First, we know that there is considerable variation in the degree to which individual boys and girls conform to gender role stereotypes. Within each sex, children vary substantially in their behavior, and across situations and circumstances, children vary in the degree to which they respond to gender role models. Variations in a child's adoption of gender role behaviors are not related to characteristics of the child's same-sex parent, as social learning theory would predict (Beal, 1994). Highly sex-typed children do not necessarily have highly sex-typed parents. The second criticism of social learning theory is that it does not account for the influences of development[6] in that it portrays the child as a passive and unvarying recipient of social influences. Considerable evidence shows that children are active participants in the socialization process and that they perceive and comprehend their experiences differently as they develop cognitively. Most current versions of social learning, recognizing the greater complexity of the learning task facing children, have incorporated cognitive mechanisms into their theories as a way of explaining how children come to imitate certain behaviors and not others. For example, Perry and Bussey (1979) suggest that children do not simply imitate their same-sex parent, but rather, they learn the appropriate behaviors of males and females by watching what behaviors, and how frequently these behaviors, are performed by males and females. In this view of social learning theory, what is imitated is a much more abstract version of male or female, making it necessary to delineate the cognitive processes that underlie learning.

Despite these criticisms, social learning theory represents a powerful framework from which to examine the adoption of gender role behaviors. Whereas psychoanalytic theory focuses our attention on the affective component of gender identity, social learning theory focuses attention on the social/behavioral component of gender identity. For both perspectives, identification with adults of the same sex (presumably parents) is an important component of gender identity development, although the mechanisms by which identification occurs are dramatically different for each perspective.

Cognitive Developmental Explanations of Gender Roles

The third approach to understanding gender role development is the cognitive developmental approach, in which the child's cognitive processing of gender takes center stage. This framework addresses the weakness of social learning theory by accounting for individual differences in gender role behavior and by accounting for developmental changes that might be related to gender role identity (Golombok & Fivush, 1994). Cognitive developmental theory predicts that a child's adoption of gender role behavior will be related to his/her understanding of gender as a social category. The cognitive developmental theory of gender was first articulated by Kohlberg (1966), who argued that children's understanding of gender can be described by three stages of cognitive change. At about age 2, children begin to use labels that indicate *gender identity;* they begin using gender labels to describe themselves and others. They base their categorizations on superficial characteristics, such as hair and clothing, and their use of labels is subject to errors. At about age 3, children move into a stage of *gender stability,* in which they realize that gender does not change over time. However, their reasoning is still subject to particular errors, because they believe that appearance and activities determine gender. By about age 5, most children have acquired *gender constancy,* recognizing that gender is permanent and determined by genitals and not clothing, hair style, or activity. Several aspects of Kohlberg's theory have been supported, including the idea that children develop a concept of gender identity before they understand the concept of constancy (Stangor & Ruble, 1987). It is clear that gender labeling is an important part of young children's understanding of gender. There is, however, controversy about the timing of the acquisition of gender-related knowledge, which seems to occur earlier than Kohlberg's theory would predict (Maccoby & Jacklin, 1987). Another criticism of Kohlberg's theory is that children appear to exhibit significant knowledge of gender-related behaviors well before they have acquired gender permanence. Therefore, gender constancy does not appear to be necessary for children's understanding of certain gender stereotypes.

Gender Schema Theory

A variation of cognitive developmental theory is gender schema theory. One version of gender schema theory is articulated by Sandra Bem in the first article in this chapter, *Gender Schema Theory and Its Implications for Child Development: Raising Gender-Aschematic Children in a Gender-Schematic Society.*[7] Bem's analysis of the specific elements of cognitive change that describe the development of gender identity are different from those proposed by Kohlberg, and in her article, Bem provides a critique of both the social learning and cognitive developmental perspectives. Bem's account recognizes the importance of social and cultural factors, although both theories are distinctly cognitive in their emphasis on the child's comprehension of the elements that contribute to sex and gender identity.

Central to the cognitive developmental perspective is the child's knowledge of gender. According to Bem, gender becomes a catalyst for children's cognitive organization of their experiences. The structure that develops is called a *schema,* a network of mental associations that functions to sort and simplify the vast amount of information about gender that is available to the child. Children come to categorize activities, objects, experiences, even themselves and others in terms of gender, and all such information becomes part of their gender schema. Because our culture provides overwhelming information not only about sex differences but also about all the associa-

tive characteristics of masculinity and femininity, children readily learn which attributes are related to their sex and, therefore, to themselves. This awareness is a critical point for Bem because it explains how "the two sexes become, in their own eyes, not only different in degrees, but different in kind" (Bem, 1985, p. 188). Because gender schema theory is concerned with the process of learning rather than the specific content of one's schemes, the composition of our gender schemas is linked directly to our cultural prescriptions of masculinity and femininity. In effect, our cultural stereotypes become the cognitive categories of reality, of how we view ourselves and others—our gender identity comes from gender stereotypes. This point parallels the relationship between gender roles and stereotypes articulated by Eagly (1987) in her social role theory (see chapter 5). Gender identity from the developmental perspective and gender roles and stereotypes from the social psychological perspective all influence how we come to act in gendered ways. Does this mean that all individuals are equally engendered? From your own experience, your answer to that question would probably be no. Bem would agree that there are significant differences between individuals. If you remember back to chapter 5, Bem's proposal for the measurement of psychological androgyny was made in response to the observation that men and women might be both masculine and feminine in varying degrees (Bem, 1974). What is of importance for understanding development is that children can acquire gender schemas that vary in degree from schematic to aschematic. Individuals who are schematic have well-developed gender schemas that they use to interpret information about gender. These individuals are highly gender typed. Aschematic individuals tend to have less well-developed schemas for gender and use other types of schemas when they process information about gender. In her article, Bem provides evidence for how schematic and aschematic individuals categorize information differently. Understanding those studies help clarify that although we all use gender schemas because we live in a highly gendered society, some individuals' gender schemas will be more stereotyped than others. Additionally, Fagot's article reviews the evidence for the acquisition of gender schemas and gender role behaviors in early development. Understanding the complexity of early experience with regard to gender-related development sheds some light on how individual differences in gender schemas and adherence to cultural stereotypes can develop.

Gender schema theory is highly regarded as a theory to explain how children come to see themselves as male or female and to adopt masculine or feminine gender roles. It places suitable emphasis on how children contribute to their own gender identity development in concert with the forces of socialization. Thus, gender schema theory provides a useful framework from which to understand how individual and environmental factors interact to determine gender identity, gender-typed behaviors, and gender roles. Reid, Haritos, Kelly, & Holland (1995) suggest that gender schema theory is particularly valuable for understanding racial and ethnic variations in gender roles. According to their argument, children's gender schemas reflect cultural norms, often as presented by family and other close representatives of the culture. To the extent that cultural beliefs about gender do not reflect the dominant culture, children would develop schemas that better represent their culture's portrayal of gender. One example you have read about are the culturally specific versions of masculinity described by Lazur and Majors in chapter 4. A developmental analysis would suggest that these versions of masculinity represent alternative gender schemas. Reid et al. suggest that African American families are less traditionally gender stereotyped and that women in particular are more independent and self-confident than is prescribed by the dominant gender role. Although there is no research directly examining African American children's knowledge of gender roles as related to family variations in the expression of gender roles, we can use some indirect evidence to infer potential differences in gender schemas between African American and white adolescent girls. African American girls are less likely to define femininity around body image and thinness, show less decline in self-esteem at adolescence, and are less likely to connect self-esteem and attractiveness (Powell & Kahn, 1995; Tashakkori, 1993). Gender schema theory could be a particularly valuable tool for examining racial and ethnic variations in gendered thinking, because it proposes a common mechanism by which children acquire and organize knowledge about gender while also allowing for variations in experiences, values, and behaviors in different communities.

One shortcoming of gender schema theory is that researchers have not always been able to find a clear link between the cognitive aspects of gender and specific gender-related behaviors (Bussey & Bandura, 1992). Furthermore, although gender schema theory is useful as a broad framework, its ability to explain the salience of different socializing factors in the development of gender identity has not yet materialized. For instance, we still know very little about what types of parenting attitudes, characteristics, and behaviors might lead to more or less gender schematic or aschematic thinking. A related problem is that gender schema theory mostly focuses on individual variables that lead to gendered thinking rather than on structural variables such as occupational segregation.

Elaborations of Gender Schema Theory

In the most recent version of her viewpoint, Bem (1993) elaborates on the relationship between the individual's cognitions (gender schemas) and the cultural construction of gender. Bem addresses the concern by focusing on three cultural forces (cultural lenses) that shape and maintain our notions of gender: biological essentialism, androcentrism (patriarchy), and gender polarization (maximization of gender differences). We have discussed these forces in previous chapters. The critical point for Bem is that each of these forces has permeated our culture so pervasively that we often are not aware of its effects. In chapter 4, we described the process of becoming a cultural native whereby children learn their culture's often unspoken worldview. Because gender is one basic categorical division in our culture, children become "gendered natives" as they are enculturated into our particular culture's androcentric and gender-polarized beliefs. Enculturation of the androcentric lens is particularly insidious because it implicates the individual in a social structure that privileges masculinity and devalues femininity.

In recent years, several researchers have revised their approach to gender schema theory to respond to new directions in research. Fagot's article in this chapter outlines some of the changes she sees as important in responding to weaknesses in the theory. One revision represented by the work of Martin (1993) proposes that gender schemas are more likely to be loosely organized cognitive components rather than hierarchically organized structures of information about maleness and femaleness. Because gender information comes from a variety of sources in many different forms, cognitive schemas operate as connections that integrate diverse gender stereotypic information in a less restricted manner. According to Fagot, one example of how gender schemas might operate as loose connections is when children maintain occupational stereotypes despite their own experiences with mothers or fathers who contradict such stereotypes. Studying young children's knowledge of gender scripts is another approach to gaining convergent information about children's knowledge of gender stereotypes. Extensive research shows that young children represent information in a generalized form called a script. One important finding that has emerged from this research is that children have better organized knowledge of the scripts for their own sex than for the other sex and that this knowledge difference is greater for boys than for girls (Levy & Fivush, 1993).

THE ROLE OF GENDER SEGREGATION

As the research presented by Fagot clearly shows, children's gender identity is well established by early childhood, entailing both knowledge of one's own sex and the commitment to and interest in same-sex behaviors, activities, and playmates. In the last article in this chapter, titled *Gender and Relationships: A Developmental Account*, Eleanor Maccoby describes in detail one phenomenon that has been studied ex-

tensively—preference for playmates of the same sex. Gender segregation appears to begin around age 3 and persists throughout childhood and adolescence. What factors account for this type of gender-segregated play? Interestingly, it is not involvement in sex-typed activities that explains this systematic preference. Nor is this preference based on adult organization of children's activities, because gender segregation represents the spontaneous interactions of even very young children. Maccoby suggests at least two major reasons why gender segregation occurs. First, the rough physical nature and competitive focus of boys' play does not appeal to girls. Second, it is difficult to influence boys, and therefore girls find it unpleasant to play with partners who are unresponsive to their attempts to influence behaviors or activities. What are the consequences of gender-segregated play? Simply stated, boys and girls develop different styles of interaction and interpersonal skills, which appear to be suited to same-sex partners rather than cross-sexed partners. Although spontaneous gender segregation continues into adolescence and even adulthood, males and females in our culture do spend considerable time with members of the opposite sex, as couples, as members of families, as coworkers. The ability to interact and communicate with one another is vital. Girls in their groups tend to emphasize cooperation, sensitivity to others, the fostering of interpersonal closeness. Boys in their groups tend to emphasize dominance, competition, the fostering of individual assertion. Both styles can lead to successful outcomes, although the style associated with girls may lead more easily to learning how to blend individual with group needs (Leaper, 1994). Maccoby (1994) contends, however, that males in same-sex groups also learn how to subordinate individual needs to groups needs, just in different ways. In addition, male same-sex groups can serve the important function of channeling male aggressiveness and assertiveness. We might also ask ourselves how boys and girls (and subsequently, men and women) view the interactional style of the other. Is greater status given to one style or the other? Given the highly gendered world we live in, Maccoby's analysis raises intriguing questions about how we successfully manage interactions with members of the same and opposite sex across a variety of situations (e.g., domestic, occupational, public).

Do Biological Factors Explain Gender Segregation?

According to Maccoby, gender segregation serves to explain a wide variety of gendered phenomena across the life span. In the article in this chapter, Maccoby discusses the role of gender segregation in the following areas: the social interaction styles of boys and girls and men and women; the classroom organization of boys and girls; activities and games preferred by boys and girls; gender segregation in leisure activities during adolescence and adulthood; mixed versus same-sex problem-solving behaviors; and interaction style in romantic relationships and parenting. Given the hypothetical centrality of gender segregation to such a wide array of behaviors, we would certainly want to know what factors govern the emergence and maintenance of same-sex peer groups. One possibility for understanding the pervasiveness of gender segregation is sex differences in the threshold for physiological arousal of emotions and the subsequent regulation of physiological arousal (Fabes, 1994). Fabes presents a complex model of how differences in arousal are not pervasive sex differences but emerge under particular circumstances. He describes one experiment, which showed no sex differences in arousal for preschool children during a nonstimulating activity (watching a relaxing film), whereas sex differences in arousal did occur when children were shown a film depicting a child being injured and then teased about the injury by other children. While watching this film, boys showed both greater emotional reactivity and slower return to baseline, as measured by skin conductance. Using this experiment and other evidence, Fabes concludes that boys and girls respond to different emotionally arousing contexts, and that boys and girls respond differently to each other's emotion states. For example, boys prefer rough-and-tumble play, which both girls and adults may have difficulty distinguishing from aggression. Girls

are more physiologically responsive to sympathy-inducing situations and use less evocative social responses, such as reciprocity and collaboration, in their peer interactions. Maccoby (1994) agrees that Fabes presents a thought-provoking explanation for gender segregation, although she points out some limitations in the existing data. In particular, she is concerned with how emotionally evocative situations are defined and how physiological arousal is measured.

Fabes's theory is a rare example of an effort to integrate biological with cognitive and social mechanisms in theories of gender role development. In her review of social and cognitive factors, Fagot notes that biological factors are not yet well understood with regard to gender role identity. In chapter 7, however, you read about interactive theories that are used to explain the development of sexual identity and sexual orientation.

GENDER ROLE DEVELOPMENT IN ADOLESCENCE

We have presented you with various accounts of how gender identity might be established, all of which suggest that children's gender identity is well established during childhood. By late childhood, children have both the knowledge of their own gender identity and highly developed preferences for same-sex activities and playmates. We have emphasized that both biological and socialization factors contribute to children's gender identity. Those reciprocal forces are also at work during adolescence, which marks an important transition period in the development of gender roles. Gender identity development in adolescence shows both continuity with the processes begun in childhood and some points of dramatic departure. The many forces that support gender roles, including parents, peers, school, and television, provide consistent socializing messages into adolescence. Given the changes that accompany adolescence (Beal, 1994). especially the dramatic biological and physical changes of puberty, there are also important ways in which gender roles during adolescence become further differentiated (Huston & Alvarez, 1990). We have already discussed some of the consequences of gender-segregated groupings for the development of different interactional styles for boys and girls. In her article, Maccoby speculates on the effects of these styles for adolescent and adult interactions. You want to consider Maccoby's analysis carefully, especially as it relates to some of the different experiences that confront adolescents.

Socialization of Adolescent Boys and Girls

There is no question that adolescents face different issues and challenges than do younger children, but those challenges are not equally shared between boys and girls. Are the new demands of adolescent gender roles more difficult for either boys or girls? Depending on which aspect of gender role acquisition you study, the answer is often girls but sometimes boys. Based on the findings of numerous research studies, it would appear that the socialization forces operating for adolescent girls convey the cultural message that males are considered the more valuable and competent sex (Huston & Alvarez, 1990). Whatever gender role flexibility girls possessed during childhood begins to decrease as they enter early adolescence.[8] The message sent to girls through parents, peer groups, schools, and the media, even more dramatically than in childhood, is that physical attractiveness is a highly valued characteristic that can make the difference between social acceptance and rejection (Adler, Kless, & Adler, 1992). It is not surprising that increased interest in physical appearance might be linked to many of the problems that adolescent girls experience, including loss of self-confidence, negative body image, and, in some cases, eating disorders. Brown and Gilligan (1992) interviewed preteen and teenage girls at both private and public schools and contend that these girls undergo a radical shift in self-perception during the adolescent years. Girls who were previously willing to express their ideas and feelings now become "silenced" as they see the costs, especially

for maintaining relationships, of speaking their minds and of not adopting feminine conventions. Brown and Gilligan label this silencing a loss of voice. Although it is unclear whether the type of silencing described by Brown and Gilligan characterizes the experiences of most adolescent girls, substantial evidence suggests that this time period serves to intensify gender differentiation (Hill & Lynch, 1983).

Sexuality and Gender Roles During Adolescence

Adolescence brings both a greater awareness of and an increased interest in sexuality. This interest, although related to changes at puberty, must be understood in the larger context of social and cultural factors. We know that significant gender segregation, most especially in friendship groups, continues to mark the adolescent years, but we also know that adolescents begin to develop an awareness of themselves as sexual beings as well as an interest in dating. For many parents, issues around dating and sexuality are the thorniest problems of adolescence. Parents are confronted with the delicate issue of how to encourage autonomy and independence while still maintaining control over adolescent behaviors. Cultural attitudes toward sexuality are clearly reflected in how information about sex is conveyed to adolescents. Even with the many changes brought by the sexual revolution, accountability for sexual behaviors is not the same for males and females. A double standard still exists for females in that they are judged more harshly for engaging in sexual behaviors than are males. In addition, many sex education programs focus on the mechanics of sex or contraceptive use and ignore any discussion of sexual feelings, especially for females. In an ethnographic analysis of teenage girls in public high school, Fine (1988) found that one of the most common themes of school-based health clinics is that of seeing women as victims of male sexual needs. According to Fine, missing from these programs was any recognition that girls may feel sexual desire, may want to discuss the meanings of such desire, and understand the consequences that could follow from acting on such desire. Fine argues that, because many of the girls she interviewed who got pregnant held traditional views of female roles and behaved passively in class, denying one's sexual feelings can have serious negative consequences. To understand how girls do, in fact, experience sexual desire, Tolman (1994) interviewed teenage girls and found that they expressed deep conflict between feelings of sexual desire and the negative ways in which such desire may be viewed by others. Our culture has not yet fully sanctioned the idea that girls and women have sexual desires and that sexual pleasure is as much a female experience as it is a male experience.

Physical attractiveness is also an important dimension in the development of adolescent boys. Teenage boys are most certainly concerned about their appearance, as can be attested to by any mother or father watching a son getting dressed for a date; the number of glances in the mirror tells a great deal about adolescent boys' interests. A disproportionate weight, however, is placed on the role of physical appearance in the feminine gender role, seen clearly in the number of fashion magazines devoted to girls' appearance. Boys are reinforced to engage in other pursuits, especially athletics and academics, activities that confer high status in our culture and are correlated with success. Many researchers, especially those working from the perspective of men's studies, suggest that although the traditional male gender role accords men and boys greater access to power and higher status, these gains are not made without significant psychological costs. In chapter 4, we delineated some of the characteristics associated with masculinity and introduced you to the gender role strain paradigm as articulated by Pleck (1976). Chapter 4's article by Lazur and Majors explained the effects of gender role strain for men of color. How does gender role strain affect adolescent boys? Pleck, Sonnenstein, and Ku (1993) found that problem behaviors of adolescent males (e.g., drug and alcohol use, being questioned by police) were significantly correlated with their support of traditional masculinity ideology (e.g.,

"I don't think a husband should have to do housework"). The Pleck et al. research shows that how adolescent males define themselves in terms of traditional masculinity is implicated in whether they engage in delinquent behaviors.

Concepts of masculinity assert themselves in other ways for adolescents. Sports are one rite of passage for many teenagers to prove their masculinity. For American society, sports represent a prime place for the public display of masculinity that Gilmore observed in different cultural settings (see Gilmore reading in chapter 5). If we conceptualize sports as a social institution, we can appreciate that it holds enormous power in socializing young boys and teenagers into the norms of masculinity. According to Sabo (1995), by playing sports, boys learn that it is acceptable to win at any cost, that aggression is a legitimate way to accomplish their goals, and that their emotions and sensitivity to others' needs must be suppressed in order to tolerate pain. These characteristics of traditional masculine ideology have led men to enormous success in our culture. But what is the cost to boys and men who fail at public displays of masculinity? Gilmore, in the reading in chapter 5, describes Lorenzo's failure to live up to the Andalusian concept of manhood because he did not demonstrate the ability to serve and to give something to the community. Although Lorenzo was treated only as a minor outcast in his society, Levant (1995) has described the psychological consequences of "failing" at masculinity in our culture as ranging from stress to sexual excesses, drug abuse, and violence, especially against women. The acquisition and maintenance of traditional male ideology is not without its developmental implications.

Sexuality and Sexual Orientation During Adolescence

Most of the literature on the emergence of sexuality in the teenage years has either focused on a population of heterosexual youths or has ignored the question of sexual orientation, assuming that all children and adolescents are heterosexual (Savin-Williams,

1995). How are gender roles expressed in adolescents who identify themselves as either gay, lesbian, or bisexual? In chapter 7 we discuss in detail questions of sexual orientation, including the complexities involved in understanding sexual orientation; here, we briefly consider what researchers know about sexual orientation and dating patterns. Adolescents who identify themselves as gay, lesbian, or bisexual face additional challenges from heterosexual youths in trying to forge a gender identity. In recognizing and identifying themselves, often with little or no adult support, these adolescents are accepting a sexual and gender identity that is perceived negatively by many in the dominant culture (Herdt, 1989). This acknowledgment makes peer interactions, and especially dating, somewhat difficult. Many gay and lesbian youth engage in heterosexual dating and sexual activity as they are exploring their sexual identity. Especially during adolescence, it may be hard for same-sex partners to find one another; moreover, if dating does occur, it is not likely to be perceived in a positive light by parents and peers (Savin-Williams, 1995). Despite these obstacles, many gay and lesbian youth are involved in romantic relationships. Research by Savin-Williams shows that a majority of lesbian women (80 percent) and gay men (67 percent) had romantic relationships in high school or college, with lesbian and bisexual women having had more relationships than gay men.

ADULTHOOD AND GENDER ROLES

In adulthood, many developmental milestones interact with an individual's gender identity and socially prescribed gender roles. The remaining chapters of this book describe in detail how issues such as sexuality, relationships, family and work, and health and mental illness can be understood from the perspective of adult gender identity and gender roles. Eagly's (1987) social role theory presented in chapter 5 is one explanation of how men and women come to act in ways consistent with cultural pre-

scriptions. Are we to assume, then, that gender roles acquired during childhood and adolescence remain constant throughout adulthood? Researchers have tried to answer just that question, but there does not seem to be one clear answer. Belsky (1992) argues that there is research to suggest that midlife contains a greater convergence of gender roles, with men endorsing more nurturant traits and women more assertive and independent traits. Some of this evidence is based on the cross-cultural analysis of Gutmann (1987), who postulated that traditional gender roles reflect a parental imperative and that as parenting responsibilities decrease, both men and women become freed from the rigid constraints of gender roles. This perspective has been criticized for failing to consider the way in which significant cultural changes in gender role expectations might account for any measurable gender differences (Costa & McCrae, 1980). For example, as more women combine paid work with parenthood and as men become more actively involved in parenting, gender roles based on a traditional division of labor may begin to lessen. This adjustment may lead to greater flexibility in gender roles for both men and women across the life span.

BECOMING GENDER ASCHEMATIC

Although life experiences may lead to changes in gender roles, the question remains, what would lead to changes in cognitive structures about gender? According to Bem (1983), the place to begin is during the time that gender schemas are developed. In her article in this chapter, Bem introduces her ideas about raising gender-aschematic children. She argues that parents need to intentionally alter the child-rearing environment in order to change the content of children's schemas. She believes that children need to learn about the biological elements of sex differences, such as differences in genitalia and reproduction, but not learn to associate a multitude of social stereotypes with biological sex. Bem further suggests that parents provide alternative schemas, such as an individual differences schema, whereby children learn to attribute the causes of people's behavior not to sex but to individual personality differences. For example, when encountering a boy in preschool who behaves aggressively, many parents might unwittingly reinforce gender stereotypes by suggesting to their child that "boys are like that" or "boys like to fight." Instead, parents should offer an individual differences attribution: "He is having trouble making friends" or "he needs to control his anger." Notice that both types of explanations help a child label and understand the other child's behavior, but one attribution roots the behavior in sex differences and the other looks elsewhere for the cause of the child's aggressiveness. As with any alteration to a prevailing social ideology, raising gender-aschematic children must be based on the parents' political commitment to reducing sex-typed thinking on the part of their child. For Bem, this alteration is the one solution to the powerful gender typing that occurs as children develop gender schemas. As you read Bem's description of raising gender-aschematic children, think about whether you believe, like Bem, that traditional gender schemas are harmful and serve to reproduce negative stereotypes about men and women. Then think about whether you agree with Bem's analysis of how to change gender schemas.[9]

THE SIGNIFICANCE OF DEVELOPMENT

During early development, children come to know themselves as gendered people, and they come to know a great deal about how their society organizes information about males and females. Behavior, thoughts, and emotions all come to take on particular meanings as children develop a gender identity. The evidence is strong that children are active participants in the construction of their own identity, as they seek appropriate information and experiences to reinforce their developing sense of self. They pay more attention to the behaviors and characteristics that they believe match their gender, and they generally prefer the company of children of their own sex. In this sense, gender identity, as Fagot claims in her article, is overdetermined. So many forces are working in concert that the process of gender development is probably not dependent on any single one. In adolescence, gender takes on new meanings as the child's established sense of identity interacts with the onset of puberty and the many social and biological meanings of sexual maturity. The context of adolescence is critical as youth are exposed to powerful messages from parents, peers, and the media about what is expected of boys versus girls. During adulthood and with aging, gender roles are often expressed through the many prescribed differences for men and women. Significant events through the life span, such as education, career development, romance, marriage, parenthood, retirement, and widowhood, interact with gender roles.

The perspective of developmental psychology suggests that age and maturity are accompanied by cognitive and behavioral changes. To use this perspective to understand gender, we need to understand the nature of these changes with regard to gender, and the readings in this chapter review our current knowledge of these issues. Beyond a description and analysis of development and gender, we want you to be aware of the deep significance of gender for individual identity. Gender identity has an emotional significance for people, which is expressed faithfully in our interactions with others, our understanding of our own behavior, our choices and opportunities throughout life, and the meaning given to our intimate relationships. In the remaining chapters of this book, you will read more specifically about how gender interacts with our experiences in the family, in school, in social institutions, and with mental and physical health. As you read about these issues, keep in mind the perspective of this chapter and how development can interact with social, cognitive, and biological factors to produce both continuity and discontinuity in our gender identities.

NOTES

1. End of the story: Daughter no. 2 arrived safely, was welcomed warmly, and was not named Rainbow Sky.
2. Even among women who have different last names from their husband, most often the children, especially a male child, takes the father's last name.
3. A notable exception are transgendered individuals, who either believe they belong to the other sex or wish they were the other sex.
4. Freud's view of early development and a child's identification with the parent of the same sex is very complex. A more elaborate description of Freud's theory of gender identity as well as contemporary revisions and criticisms can be found in any of the following: Beal, 1994; Fast, 1993; Golombok & Fivush, 1994; Unger & Crawford, 1996.
5. Following Freud, many variations of psychoanalytic theory have been articulated, including the feminist psychoanalytic theory of Nancy Chodorow (1978). This theory has been highly influential for many feminist's accounts of personality development.
6. For developmental psychologists, it is important to account for changes that accompany age and for factors that relate to increasing maturity. With age and with increasing cognitive, physical, and social maturity, children's physical competence increases, they understand their experiences in new ways, and their social interactions become more sophisticated.
7. Other theorists have proposed their own version of gender schema theory, most notably Martin and Halverson (1981).
8. Girls can engage in tomboy-type activities, such as playing boys' sports or dressing in boys' clothing, with fewer negative sanctions than can boys who engage in stereotypically girl activities, such as playing with dolls. Boys who engage in such behaviors are often called *sissies,* a term that continues to have highly negative connotations despite changing gender norms. In fact, evidence shows that many girls exhibit tomboy interests and that tomboyishness is associated with positive characteristics such as leadership (Hemmer & Kleiber, 1981). Young girls, therefore, are at greater liberty to exhibit both masculine and feminine characteristics.
9. Bem (1993), in her more recent writings, has suggested that beyond changes in children's gender schemas, we need to address the cultural lenses, such as patriarchy, that maintain the strong gender distinctions in our culture.

REFERENCES

Adler, P. A., Kless, S. J., & Adler, P. (1992). Socialization to gender roles: Popularity among elementary school boys and girls. *Sociology of Education, 65,* 169–187.

Beal, C. R. (1994). *Boys and girls: The development of gender roles.* New York: McGraw-Hill.

Belsky, J. (1992). The research findings on gender issues in aging men and women. In B. R. Wainrib (Ed.), *Gender issues across the lifespan* (pp. 163–172). New York: Springer.

Bem, S. L. (1974). The measurement of psychological androgyny. *Journal of Personality and Social Psychology, 42,* 155–162.

Bem, S. L. (1983). Gender schema theory and its implications for child development: Raising gender-aschematic children in a gender-schematic society. *Signs, 8,* 598–616.

Bem, S. L. (1985). Androgyny and gender schema theory: A conceptual and empirical integration. In T. Sonderegger (Ed.), *Nebraska Symposium on Motivation, 1984: Psychology and gender* (pp. 179–226). Lincoln: University of Nebraska Press.

Bem, S. L. (1993). *The lenses of gender: Transforming the debate on sexual inequality.* New Haven: Yale University Press.

Brown, L. M., & Gilligan, C. (1992). *Meeting at the crossroads.* New York: Ballantine Books.

Bussey, K., & Bandura, A. (1992). Self-regulatory mechanisms governing gender development. *Child Development, 63,* 1236–1250.

Chodorow, N. (1978). *The reproduction of mothering.* Berkeley: University of California Press.

Costa, P. T., & McCrae, R. R. (1980). Still stable after all these years: Personality as a key to some issues in adulthood and old age. In P. B. Baltes & O. G. Brim (Eds.), *Lifespan development and behavior* (Vol. 3, pp. 65–102). New York: Academic Press.

Eagly, A. H. (1987). *Sex differences in social behavior: A social role interpretation.* Hillsdale, NJ: Erlbaum.

Fabes, R. A. (1994). Physiological, emotional, and behavioral correlates of gender segregation. In C. Leaper (Ed.), *Childhood gender segregation: Causes and consequences* (pp. 19–34). San Francisco, CA: Jossey-Bass.

Fagot, B. I. (1995). Psychosocial and cognitive determinants of early gender-role development. In R. C. Rosen (Ed.), *Annual review of sex research* (Vol. 6). Mason City, IA: Society for the Scientific Study of Sexuality.

Fast, I. (1993). Aspects of early gender development: A psychodynamic perspective. In A. E. Beall & R. J. Sternberg (Eds.), *The psychology of gender* (pp. 173–196). New York: Guilford.

Fine, M. (1988). Sexuality, schooling, and adolescent females: The missing discourse of desire. *Harvard Educational Review, 58,* 29–53.

Golombok, S., & Fivush, R. (1994). *Gender development.* Cambridge, England: Cambridge University Press.

Guttman, D. (1987). *Reclaimed powers: Towards a new psychology of later life.* New York: Basic Books.

Hemmer, J. D., & Kleiber, D. A. (1981). Tomboys and sissies: Androgynous children? *Sex Roles, 7,* 1205–1217.

Herdt, G. (1989). Introduction: Gay and lesbian youth, emergent identities, and cultural scenes at home and abroad. In G. Herdt (Ed.), *Gay and lesbian youth* (pp. 1–42). New York: Harrington Park Press.

Hill, J. P., & Lynch, M. E. (1983). The intensification of gender related role expectations during early adolescence. In J. Brooks-Gunn & A. C. Peterson (Eds.), *Girls at puberty: Biological, psychological, and social perspectives* (pp. 201–228). New York: Plenum.

Hrdy, S. B. (1988, April) Daughters or sons. *Natural History* pp. 64–82.

Huston, A. C., & Alvarez, M. M. (1990). The socialization context of gender role development in early adolescence. In R. Montemayer, G. R. Adams, & R. P. Gullotta (Eds.), *From childhood to adolescence: A transitional period?* (Vol. 2, pp. 156–179). Newbury Park, CA: Sage.

Jacklin, C. N., & Reynolds, C. (1993). Gender and childhood socialization. In A. E. Beall & R. J. Sternberg (Eds.), *The psychology of gender* (pp. 197–214). New York: Guilford Press.

Kohlberg, L. (1966). A cognitive-developmental analysis of children's sex role concepts and attitudes. In E. E. Maccoby (Ed.), *The development of sex differences* (pp. 82–173). Stanford, CA: Stanford University Press.

Leaper, C. (1994). Exploring the consequences of gender segregation on social relationships. In C. Leaper (Ed.), *Childhood gender segregation: Causes and consequences* (pp. 67–86). San Francisco, CA: Jossey-Bass.

Levant, R. F. (1995). *Masculinity reconstructed: Changing the rules of manhood—at work, in relationships, and in the family life.* New York: Dutton.

Levy, G. D., & Fivush, R. (1993). Scripts and gender: A new approach for examining gender-role development. *Developmental Review, 13,* 126–146.

Maccoby, E. (1990). Gender and relationships: A developmental account. *American Psychologist, 45,* 513–520.

Maccoby, E. (1994). Commentary: Gender segregation in childhood. In C. Leaper (Ed.), *Childhood gender segregation: Causes and consequences* (pp. 87–98). San Francisco, CA: Jossey-Bass.

Maccoby, E., & Jacklin, C. N. (1987). Gender segregation in childhood. In E. H. Reese (Ed.), *Advances in child development and behavior* (Vol. 20, pp. 239–287). New York: Academic Press.

Martin, C. L. (1993). New directions for investigating children's gender knowledge. *Developmental Review, 13,* 184–204.

Martin, C. L., & Halverson, C. F. (1981). A schematic processing model of sex typing and stereotyping in children. *Child Development, 52,* 1119–1134.

Perry, D. G., & Bussey, K. (1979). The social learning theory of sex differences: Imitation is alive and well. *Journal of Personality and Social Psychology, 37,* 1699–1712.

Pleck, J. H. (1976). The male sex role: Definitions, problems, and sources of change. *Journal of Social Issues, 32,* 155–164.

Pleck, J. H., Sonnenstein, F. L., & Ku, L. C. (1993). Masculinity ideology and its correlates. In S. Oskamp & M. Costanzo (Eds.), *Gender issues in contemporary society* (pp. 85–113). Newbury Park, CA: Sage.

Powell, A. D., & Kahn, A. S. (1995). Racial differences in women's desire to be thin. *Journal of Eating Disorders, 17,* 191–195.

Reid, P. T., Haritos, C., Kelly, E., & Holland, N. E. (1995). Socialization of girls: Issues of ethnicity in gender development. In H. Landrine (Ed.), *Bringing cultural diversity to feminist psychology: Theory, research, and practice* (pp. 93–112). Washington, DC: American Psychological Association.

Sabo, D. (1995). Pigskin, patriarchy and pain. In M. S. Kimmel & M. A. Messner (Eds.), *Men's lives* (3rd ed., pp. 99–101). Boston: Allyn & Bacon.

Savin-Williams, R. C. (1995). Lesbian, gay male, and bisexual adolescents. In A. R. D'Augelli & C. J. Patterson (Eds.), *Lesbian, gay, and bisexual identities over the lifespan: Psychological perspectives* (pp. 165–189). Washington, DC: American Psychological Association.

Stangor, C., & Ruble, D. N. (1987). Development of gender role knowledge and gender constancy. In L. S. Liben & M. L. Signorella (Eds.), *Children's gender schemata* (Winter Vol., pp. 5–22). San Francisco, CA: Jossey-Bass.

Tashakkori, A. (1993). Gender, ethnicity, and the structure of self-esteem: An attitude theory approach. *Journal of Social Psychology, 133,* 479–488.

Thorne, B. (1990). Children and gender: Constructions of difference. *Theoretical perspectives on sexual difference* (pp. 100–113). New Haven, CT: Yale University Press.

Tolman, D. (1994). Doing desire: Adolescent girls' struggles for/with sexuality. *Gender and Society, 8,* 324–342.

Unger, R., & Crawford, M. (1996). *Women and gender: A feminist psychology* (2nd ed.). New York: McGraw-Hill.

Williamson, N. E. (1976). *Sons or daughters.* Beverly Hills, CA: Sage.

Gender Schema Theory and Its Implications for Child Development: Raising Gender-aschematic Children in a Gender-schematic Society

SANDRA LIPSITZ BEM

As every parent, teacher, and developmental psychologist knows, male and female children become "masculine" and "feminine," respectively, at a very early age. By the time they are four or five, for example, girls and boys have typically come to prefer activities defined by the culture as appropriate for their sex and also to prefer same-sex peers. The acquisition of sex-appropriate preferences, skills, personality attributes, behaviors, and self-concepts is typically referred to within psychology as the process of sex typing.

The universality and importance of this process is reflected in the prominence it has received in psychological theories of development, which seek to elucidate how the developing child comes to match the template defined as sex appropriate by his or her culture. Three theories of sex typing have been especially influential: psychoanalytic theory, social learning theory, and cognitive-developmental theory. More recently, a fourth theory of sex typing has been introduced into the psychological literature—gender schema theory.

This article is designed to introduce gender schema theory to feminist scholars outside the discipline of psychology. In order to provide a background for the conceptual issues that have given rise to gender schema theory, I will begin with a discussion of the three theories of sex typing that have been dominant within psychology to date.

Psychoanalytic Theory

The first psychologist to ask how male and female are transmuted into masculine and feminine was Freud. Accordingly, in the past virtually every major source book in developmental psychology began its discussion of sex typing with a review of psychoanalytic theory.[1]

Psychoanalytic theory emphasizes the child's identification with the same-sex parent as the primary mechanism whereby children become sex typed, an identification that results from the child's discovery of genital sex differences, from the penis envy and castration anxiety that this discovery produces in females and males, respectively, and from the successful resolution of the Oedipus conflict.[2] Although a number of feminist scholars have found it fruitful in recent years to work within a psychoanalytic framework,[3] the theory's "anatomy is destiny" view has been associated historically with quite conservative conclusions regarding the inevitability of sex typing.

Of the three dominant theories of sex typing, psychoanalytic theory is almost certainly the best known outside the discipline of psychology, although it is no longer especially popular among research psychologists. In part, this is because the theory is difficult to test empirically. An even more important reason, however, is that the empirical evidence simply does not justify emphasizing either the child's discovery of genital sex differences in particular[4] or the child's identification with his or her same-sex parent[5] as a crucial determinant of sex typing.

Social Learning Theory

In contrast to psychoanalytic theory, social learning theory emphasizes the rewards and punishments that children receive for sex-appropriate and sex-inappropriate behaviors, as well as the vicarious learning that observation and modeling can provide.[6] Social learning theory thus locates the source of sex typing in the sex-differentiated practices of the socializing community.

Perhaps the major virtue of social learning theory for psychologists is that it applies to the development of psychological femaleness and maleness the very same general principles of learning that are already known to account for the development of a multitude of other behaviors. Thus, as far as the formal theory is concerned, gender does not demand special consideration; that is, no special psychological mechanisms or processes must be postulated in order to explain how children become sex typed beyond those already used to explain how children learn other socialized behaviors.

Interestingly, the theory's generality also constitutes the basis of its appeal to feminist psychologists in particular. If there is nothing special about gender, then the phenomenon of sex typing itself is neither inevitable nor unmodifiable. Children become sex typed because sex happens to be the basis of differential socialization in their culture. In principle, however, any category could be made the basis for differential socialization.

Although social learning theory can account for the young child's acquiring a number of particular behaviors that are stereotyped by the culture as sex appropriate, it treats the child as the relatively passive recipient of environmental forces rather than as an active agent striving to organize and thereby to comprehend the social world. This view of the passive child is inconsistent with the common observation that children themselves frequently construct and enforce their own version of society's gender rules. It is also inconsistent with the fact that the flexibility with which children interpret society's gender rules varies predictably with age. In one study, for example, 73 percent of the four-year-olds and 80 percent of the nine-year-olds believed—quite flexibly—that there should be no sexual restrictions on one's choice of occupation. Between those ages, however, children held more rigid opinions, with the middle children being the least flexible of all. Thus, only 33 percent of the five-year-olds, 10 percent of the six-year-olds, 11 percent of the seven-year-olds, and 44 percent of

the eight-year-olds believed there should be no sexual restrictions on one's choice of occupation.[7]

This particular developmental pattern is not unique to the child's interpretation of gender rules. Even in a domain as far removed from gender as syntax, children first learn certain correct grammatical forms through reinforcement and modeling. As they get a bit older, however, they begin to construct their own grammatical rules on the basis of what they hear spoken around them, and they are able only later still to allow for exceptions to those rules. Thus, only the youngest and the oldest children say "ran"; children in between say "runned."[8] What all of this implies, of course, is that the child is passive in neither domain. Rather, she or he is actively constructing rules to organize—and thereby to comprehend—the vast array of information in his or her world.

COGNITIVE-DEVELOPMENTAL THEORY

Unlike social learning theory, cognitive-developmental theory focuses almost exclusively on the child as the primary agent of his or her own sex-role socialization, a focus reflecting the theory's basic assumption that sex typing follows naturally and inevitably from universal principles of cognitive development. As children work actively to comprehend their social world, they inevitably "label themselves—call it alpha—and determine that there are alphas and betas in the environment. Given the cognitive-motivational properties of the self, . . . the child moves toward other alphas and away from betas. That is, it is the child who realizes what gender he or she is, and in what behaviors he or she should engage."[9] In essence, then, cognitive-developmental theory postulates that, because of the child's need for cognitive consistency, self-categorization as female or male motivates her or him to value that which is seen as similar to the self in terms of gender. This gender-based value system, in turn, motivates the child to engage in gender-congruent activities to strive for gender-congruent attributes, and to prefer gender-congruent peers. "Basic self-categorizations determine basic valuings. Once the boy has stably identified himself as male, he then values positively those objects and acts consistent with his gender identity."[10]

The cognitive-developmental account of sex typing has been so influential since its introduction into the literature in 1966 that many psychologists now seem to accept almost as a given that the young child will spontaneously develop both a gender-based self-concept and a gender-based value system even in the absence of external pressure to behave in a sex-stereotyped manner. Despite its popularity, however, the theory fails to explicate why sex will have primacy over other potential categories of the self such as race, religion, or even eye color. Interestingly, the formal theory itself does not dictate that any particular category should have such primacy. Moreover, most cognitive-developmental theorists do not explicitly ponder the "why sex" question nor do they even raise the possibility that other categories could fit the general theory just as well. To the extent that cognitive-developmental psychologists address this question at all, they seem to emphasize the perceptual salience to the child of the observable differences between the sexes, particularly biologically produced differences such as size and strength.[11]

The implicit assumption here that sex differences are naturally and inevitably more perceptually salient to children than other differences may not have cross-cultural validity. Although it may be true that our culture does not construct any distinctions between people that we perceive to be as compelling as sex, other cultures do construct such distinctions, for example, distinctions between those who are high caste and those who are low caste, between those who are inhabited by spirits and those who are not, between those who are divine and those who are mortal, between those who are wet and those who are dry, or between those who are open and those who are closed.[12] Given such cross-cultural diversity, it is ironic that a theory emphasizing the child's active striving to comprehend the social world should not be more open to the possibility that a distinction other than sex might be more perceptually salient in another cultural context. What appears to have happened is that the universality and inevitability that the theory claims for the child's cognitive processes have been implicitly and gratuitously transferred to one of the many substantive domains upon which those processes operate: the domain of gender.

This is not to say, of course, that cognitive-developmental theory is necessarily wrong in its implicit assumption that all children have a built-in readiness to organize their perceptions of the social world on the basis of sex. Perhaps evolution has given sex a biologically based priority over many other categories. The important point, however, is that the question of whether and why sex has cognitive primacy is not included within the bounds of cognitive-developmental theory. To understand why children become *sex* typed rather than, say, race or caste typed, we still need a theory that explicitly addresses the question of how and why children come to utilize sex in particular as a cognitive organizing principle.

GENDER SCHEMA THEORY

Gender schema theory[13] contains features of both the cognitive-developmental and the social learning accounts of sex typing. In particular, gender schema theory proposes that sex typing derives in large measure from gender-schematic processing, from a generalized readiness on the part of the child to encode and to organize information—including information about the self—according to the culture's definitions of maleness and femaleness. Like cognitive-developmental theory, then, gender schema theory proposes that sex typing is mediated by the child's own cognitive processing. However, gender schema theory further proposes that gender-schematic processing is itself derived from the sex-differentiated practices of the social community. Thus, like social learning theory, gender schema theory assumes that sex typing is a learned phenomenon and, hence, that it is neither inevitable nor unmodifiable. In this discussion, I shall first consider in some detail what gender-schematic processing is and how it mediates sex typing; I shall then explore the conditions that produce gender-schematic processing, thereby providing an explicit account of why sex comes to have cognitive primacy over other social categories.

Gender-schematic Processing

Gender schema theory begins with the observation that the developing child invariably learns his or her society's cultural definitions of femaleness and maleness. In most societies, these definitions comprise a diverse and sprawling network of sex-linked associations encompassing not only those features directly related to female and male persons—such as anatomy, reproductive function, division of labor, and personality attributes—but also features more remotely or metaphorically related to sex, such as the angularity or roundedness of an abstract shape and the periodicity of the moon. Indeed, no other dichotomy in human experience appears to have as many entities linked to it as does the distinction between female and male.

But there is more. Gender schema theory proposes that, in addition to learning such content-specific information about gender, the child also learns to invoke this heterogeneous network of sex-related associations in order to evaluate and assimilate new information. The child, in short, learns to encode and to organize information in terms of an evolving gender schema.

A schema is a cognitive structure, a network of associations that organizes and guides an individual's perception. A schema functions as an anticipatory structure, a readiness to search for and to assimilate incoming information in schema-relevant terms. Schematic information processing is thus highly selective and enables the individual to impose structure and meaning onto a vast array of incoming stimuli. More specifically, schematic information processing entails a readiness to sort information into categories on the basis of some particular dimension, despite the existence of other dimensions that could serve equally well in this regard. Gender-schematic processing in particular thus involves spontaneously sorting attributes and behaviors into masculine and feminine categories or "equivalence classes," regardless of their differences on a variety of dimensions

unrelated to gender, for example, spontaneously placing items like "tender" and "nightengale" into a feminine category and items like "assertive" and "eagle" into a masculine category. Like schema theories generally,[14] gender schema theory thus construes perception as a constructive process in which the interaction between incoming information and an individual's preexisting schema determines what is perceived.

What gender schema theory proposes, then, is that the phenomenon of sex typing derives, in part, from gender-schematic processing, from an individual's generalized readiness to process information on the basis of the sex-linked associations that constitute the gender schema. Specifically, the theory proposes that sex typing results, in part, from the assimilation of the self-concept itself to the gender schema. As children learn the contents of their society's gender schema, they learn which attributes are to be linked with their own sex and, hence, with themselves. This does not simply entail learning the defined relationship between each sex and each dimension or attribute—that boys are to be strong and girls weak, for example—but involves the deeper lesson that the dimensions themselves are differentially applicable to the two sexes. Thus the strong-weak dimension itself is absent from the schema to be applied to girls just as the dimension of nurturance is implicitly omitted from the schema to be applied to boys. Adults in the child's world rarely notice or remark upon how strong a little girl is becoming or how nurturant a little boy is becoming, despite their readiness to note precisely these attributes in the "appropriate" sex. The child learns to apply this same schematic selectivity to the self, to choose from among the many possible dimensions of human personality only that subset defined as applicable to his or her own sex and thereby eligible for organizing the diverse contents of the self-concept. Thus do children's self-concepts become sex typed, and thus do the two sexes become, in their own eyes, not only different in degree, but different in kind.

Simultaneously, the child also learns to evaluate his or her adequacy as a person according to the gender schema, to match his or her preferences, attitudes, behaviors, and personal attributes against the prototypes stored within it. The gender schema becomes a prescriptive standard or guide,[15] and self-esteem becomes its hostage. Here, then, enters an internalized motivational factor that prompts an individual to regulate his or her behavior so that it conforms to cultural definitions of femaleness and maleness. Thus do cultural myths become self-fulfilling prophecies, and thus, according to gender schema theory, do we arrive at the phenomenon known as sex typing.

It is important to note that gender schema theory is a theory of process, not content. Because sex-typed individuals are seen as processing information and regulating their behavior according to whatever definitions of femininity and masculinity their culture happens to provide, the process of dividing the world into feminine and masculine categories—and not the contents of the categories—is central to the theory. Accordingly, sex-typed individuals are seen to differ from other individuals not primarily in the degree of femininity or masculinity they possess, but in the extent to which their self-concepts and behaviors are organized on the basis of gender rather than on the basis of some other dimension. Many non-sex-typed individuals may describe themselves as, say, nurturant or dominant without implicating the concepts of femininity or masculinity. When sex-typed individuals so describe themselves, however, it is precisely the gender connotations of the attributes or behaviors that are presumed to be salient for them.

Empirical Research on Gender-schematic Processing

Recent empirical research supports gender schema theory's basic contention that sex typing is derived from gender-schematic processing. In a variety of studies using different subject populations and different paradigms, female and male sex-typed individuals have been found to be significantly more likely than non-sex-typed individuals to process information—including information about the self—in terms of gender.[16]

One study, for example, used a memory task to determine whether gender connotations are, in fact, more "cognitively available" to sex-typed individuals than to non-sex-typed individuals, as gender schema theory claims.[17] The subjects in this study were forty-eight male and forty-eight female undergraduates who had described themselves as either sex typed or non-sex typed on the Bem Sex Role Inventory (BSRI).[18]

During the experimental session, subjects were presented with a randomly ordered sequence of sixty-one words that included proper names, animal names, verbs, and articles of clothing. Half of the proper names were female, half were male; one-third of the items within each of the other semantic categories had been consistently rated by undergraduate judges as feminine (e.g., butterfly, blushing, bikini), one-third as masculine (e.g., gorilla, hurling, trousers), and one-third as neutral (e.g., ant, stepping, sweater). The words were presented on slides at three-second intervals, and subjects were told that their recall would later be tested. Three seconds after the presentation of the last word, they were given a period of eight minutes to write down as many words as they could, in whatever order they happened to come to mind.

As expected, the results indicated that although sex-typed and non-sex-typed individuals recalled equal numbers of items overall, the order in which they recalled the items was different. Once having recalled a feminine item, sex-typed individuals were more likely than non-sex-typed individuals to recall another feminine item next rather than a masculine or a neutral item. The same was true for masculine items. In other words, the sequence of recall for sex-typed individuals revealed significantly more runs or clusters of feminine items and of masculine items than the sequence of recall for non-sex-typed individuals. Thinking of one feminine (or masculine) item could enhance the probability of thinking of another feminine (or masculine) item in this way only if the individual spontaneously encodes both items as feminine (or masculine), and the gender schema thereby links the two items in memory. These results thus confirm gender schema theory's claim that sex-typed individuals have a greater readiness than do non-sex-typed individuals to encode information in terms of the sex-linked associations that constitute the gender schema.

A second study tested the hypothesis that sex-typed individuals have a readiness to decide on the basis of gender which personal attributes are to be associated with their self-concepts and which are to be dissociated from their self-concepts.[19] The subjects in this second study were another set of forty-eight male and forty-eight female undergraduates who had also described themselves as sex typed or non-sex typed on the Bem Sex Role Inventory. During each of the individual experimental sessions, the sixty attributes from the BSRI were projected on a screen one at a time, and the subject was requested to push one of two buttons, "Me" or "Not Me," to indicate whether the attribute was or was not self-descriptive. Of interest in this study was the subject's response latency, that is, how long it took the subject to make a decision about each attribute.

Gender schema theory predicts and the results of this study confirm that sex-typed subjects are significantly faster than non-sex-typed subjects when endorsing sex-appropriate attributes and when rejecting sex-inappropriate attributes. These results suggest that when deciding whether a particular attribute is or is not self-descriptive, sex-typed individuals do not bother to go through a time-consuming process of recruiting behavioral evidence from memory and judging whether the evidence warrants an affirmative answer—which is presumably what non-sex-typed individuals do. Rather, sex-typed individuals "look up" the attribute in the gender schema. If the attribute is sex appropriate, they quickly say yes; if the attribute is sex inappropriate, they quickly say no. Occasionally, of course, even sex-typed individuals must admit to possessing an attribute that is sex inappropriate or to lacking an attribute that is sex appropriate. On these occasions, they are significantly slower than non-sex-typed individuals. This pattern of rapid delivery of gender-consistent self-descriptions and slow delivery of gender-inconsistent self-descriptions confirms gender schema theory's contention that sex-typed individuals spontaneously sort information into categories on the basis of gender, despite the existence of other dimensions that could serve equally well as a basis for categorization.

Antecedents of Gender-schematic Processing

But how and why do sex-typed individuals develop a readiness to organize information in general, and their self-concepts in particular, in terms of gender? Because gender-schematic processing is considered a special case of schematic processing, this specific question is superseded by the more general question of how and why individuals come to organize information in terms of any social category, that is, how and why a social category becomes transformed into a cognitive schema.

Gender schema theory proposes that the transformation of a given social category into the nucleus of a highly available cognitive schema depends on the nature of the social context within which the category is embedded, not on the intrinsic nature of the category itself. Given the proper social context, then, even a category like eye color could become a cognitive schema. More specifically, gender schema theory proposes that a category will become a schema if: (*a*) the social context makes it the nucleus of a large associative network, that is, if the ideology and/or the practices of the culture construct an association between that category and a wide range of other attributes, behaviors, concepts, and categories; and (*b*) the social context assigns the category broad functional significance, that is, if a broad array of social institutions, norms, and taboos distinguishes between persons, behaviors, and attributes on the basis of this category.

This latter condition is most critical, for gender schema theory presumes that the culture's insistence on the functional importance of the social category is what transforms a passive network of associations into an active and readily available schema for interpreting reality. We all learn many associative networks of concepts throughout life, many potential cognitive schemata, but the centrality or functional importance assigned by society to particular categories and distinctions animates their associated networks and gives these schemata priority and availability over others.

From the perspective of gender schema theory, then, gender has come to have cognitive primacy over many other social categories because the culture has made it so. Nearly all societies teach the developing child two crucial things about gender: first, as noted earlier, they teach the substantive network of sex-related associations that can come to serve as a cognitive schema; second, they teach that the dichotomy between male and female has intensive and extensive relevance to virtually every domain of human experience. The typical American child cannot help observing, for example, that what parents, teachers, and peers consider to be appropriate behavior varies as a function of sex; that toys, clothing, occupations, hobbies, the domestic division of labor—even pronouns—all vary as a function of sex.

Gender schema theory thus implies that children would be far less likely to become gender schematic and hence sex typed if the society were to limit the associative network linked to sex and to temper its insistence on the functional importance of the gender dichotomy. Ironically, even though our society has become sensitive to negative sex stereotypes and has begun to expunge them from the media and from children's literature, it remains blind to its gratuitous emphasis on the gender dichotomy itself. In elementary schools, for example, boys and girls line up separately or alternately; they learn songs in which the fingers are "ladies" and the thumbs are "men"; they see boy and girl paper-doll silhouettes alternately placed on the days of the month in order to learn about the calendar. Children, it will be noted, are not lined up separately or alternately as blacks and whites; fingers are not "whites" and thumbs "blacks"; black and white dolls do not alternately mark the days of the calendar. Our society seeks to deemphasize racial distinctions but continues to exaggerate sexual distinctions.

Because of the role that sex plays in reproduction, perhaps no society could ever be as indifferent to sex in its cultural arrangements as it could be to, say, eye color, thereby giving the gender schema a sociologically based priority over many other categories. For the same reason, it may even be, as noted earlier, that sex has evolved to be a basic category of perception for our species, thereby giving the gender schema a biologically based priority as well. Be that as it may,

however, gender schema theory claims that society's ubiquitous insistence on the functional importance of the gender dichotomy must necessarily render it even more cognitively available—and available in more remotely relevant contexts—than it would be otherwise.

It should be noted that gender schema theory's claims about the antecedents of gender-schematic processing have not yet been tested empirically. Hence it is not possible at this point to state whether individual differences in gender-schematic processing do, in fact, derive from differences in the emphasis placed on gender dichotomy in individuals' socialization histories, or to describe concretely the particular kinds of socialization histories that enhance or diminish gender-schematic processing. Nevertheless, I should like to set forth a number of plausible strategies that are consistent with gender schema theory for raising a gender-schematic child in the midst of a gender-schematic society.

This discussion will, by necessity, be highly speculative. Even so, it will serve to clarify gender schema theory's view of exactly how gender-schematic processing is learned and how something else might be learned in its place. As we shall see, many of the particular strategies recommended for raising gender-aschematic children are strategies that have already been adopted by feminist parents trying to create what is typically called a nonsexist or a gender-liberated form of child rearing. In these cases, what gender schema theory provides is a new theoretical framework for thinking about the psychological impact of various child-rearing practices. Sprinkled throughout the discussion will be examples taken from my own home. These are meant to be illustrations and not systematic evidence that such strategies actually decrease gender-schematic processing.

RAISING GENDER-ASCHEMATIC CHILDREN

Feminist parents who wish to raise gender-aschematic children in a gender-schematic world are like any parents who wish to inculcate their children with beliefs and values that deviate from those of the dominant culture. Their major option is to try to undermine the dominant ideology before it can undermine theirs. Feminist parents are thus in a difficult situation. They cannot simply ignore gender in their child rearing as they might prefer to do, because the society will then have free rein to teach their children the lessons about gender that it teaches all other children. Rather, they must manage somehow to inoculate their children against gender-schematic processing.

Two strategies are suggested here. First, parents can enable their children to learn about sex differences initially without their also learning the culture's sex-linked associative network by simultaneously retarding their children's knowledge of sex's cultural correlates and advancing their children's knowledge of sex's biological correlates. Second, parents can provide alternative or "subversive" schemata that their children can use to interpret the culture's sex-linked associative network when they do learn it. This step is essential if children are not simply to learn gender-schematic processing somewhat later than their counterparts from more traditional homes. Whether one is a child or an adult, such alternative schemata "build up one's resistance" to the lessons of the dominant culture and thereby enable one to remain gender-aschematic even while living in a gender-schematic society.

Teaching Children about Sex Differences

Cultural correlates of sex.—Children typically learn that gender is a sprawling associative network with ubiquitous functional importance through their observation of the many cultural correlates of sex existing in their society. Accordingly, the first step parents can take to retard the development of gender-schematic processing is to retard the child's knowledge of these cultural messages about gender. Less crudely put, parents can attempt to attenuate sex-linked correlations within the child's social environment, thereby altering the basic data upon which the child will construct his or her own concepts of maleness and femaleness.

In part, parents can do this by eliminating sex stereotyping from their own behavior and from the alternatives that they provide for their children, just as many feminist parents are already doing. Among other things, for example, they can take turns making dinner, bathing the children, and driving the car; they can ensure that all their children—regardless of sex—have both trucks and dolls, both pink and blue clothing, and both male and female playmates; and they can arrange for their children to see women and men in nontraditional occupations.

When children are quite young, parents can further inhibit cultural messages about gender by actually censoring books and television programs whose explicit or implicit message is that the sexes differ on nonbiological dimensions. At present, this tactic will eliminate many children's books and most television programming. Ironically, it will also temporarily eliminate a number of feminist books designed to overcome sex stereotypes; even a book which insists that it is wrong for William not to be allowed to have a doll by implication teaches a child who has not yet learned the associative network that boys and dolls do not normally go together.

To compensate for this censorship, parents will need to seek out—and to create—materials that do not teach sex stereotypes. With our own children, my husband and I got into the habit of doctoring books whenever possible so as to remove all sex-linked correlations. We did this, among other ways, by changing the sex of the main character; by drawing longer hair and the outline of breasts onto illustrations of previously male truck drivers, physicians, pilots, and the like; and by deleting or altering sections of the text that described females or males in a sex-stereotyped manner. When reading children's picture books aloud, we also chose pronouns that avoided the ubiquitous implication that all characters without dresses or pink bows must necessarily be male: "And what is this little piggy doing? Why, he or she seems to be building a bridge."

All of these practices are designed to permit very young children to dwell temporarily in a social environment where, if the parents are lucky, the cultural correlations with sex will be attenuated from, say, .96 to .43. According to gender schema theory, this attenuation should retard the formation of the sex-linked associative network that will itself form the basis of the gender schema. By themselves, however, these practices teach children only what sex is not. But children must also be taught what sex is.

Biological correlates of sex.—What remains when all of the cultural correlates of sex are attenuated or eliminated, of course, are two of the undisputed biological correlates of sex: anatomy and reproduction. Accordingly, parents can make these the definitional attributes of femaleness and maleness. By teaching their children that the genitalia constitute the definitive attributes of females and males, parents help them to apprehend the merely probabilistic nature of sex's cultural correlates and thereby restrict sex's associative sprawl. By teaching their children that whether one is female or male makes a difference only in the context of reproduction, parents limit sex's functional significance and thereby retard gender-schematic processing. Because children taught these lessons have been provided with an explicit and clear-cut rule about what sex is and when sex matters, they should be predisposed to construct their own concepts of femaleness and maleness based on biology, rather than on the cultural correlates to which they have been exposed. And to the extent that young children tend to interpret rules and categories rigidly rather than flexibly, this tendency will serve to enhance their belief that sex is to be narrowly defined in terms of anatomy and reproduction rather than to enhance a traditional belief that every arbitrary gender rule must be strictly obeyed and enforced. Thus there may be an irony, but there is no inconsistency, in the fact that an emphasis on the biological differences between the sexes should here be advocated as the basis for feminist child rearing.

The liberation that comes from having an unambiguous genital definition of sex and the imprisonment that comes from not having such a definition are nicely illustrated by the story of what happened to our son Jeremy, then age four, the day he decided to wear barrettes to nursery school. Several times that day, another little boy told Jeremy that he, Jeremy, must be a girl because "only girls wear barrettes." After trying to explain to this child that "wearing barrettes doesn't matter" and that "being a boy means having a penis and testicles," Jeremy finally pulled

down his pants as a way of making his point more convincingly. The other child was not impressed. He simply said, "Everybody has a penis; only girls wear barrettes."

In the American context, children do not typically learn to define sex in terms of anatomy and reproduction until quite late, and, as a result, they—like the child in the example above—mistakenly treat many of the cultural correlates of sex as definitional. This confusion is facilitated, of course, by the fact that the genitalia themselves are not usually visible and hence cannot be relied on as a way of identifying someone's sex.

Accordingly, when our children asked whether someone was male or female, we frequently denied certain knowledge of the person's sex, emphasizing that without being able to see whether there was a penis or a vagina under the person's clothes, we had no definitive information. Moreover, when our children themselves began to utilize nonbiological markers as a way of identifying sex, we gently teased them about that strategy to remind them that the genitalia—and only the genitalia—constitute the definition of sex: "What do you mean that you can tell Chris is a girl because Chris has long hair? Does Chris's hair have a vagina?"

We found Stephanie Waxman's picture book *What Is a Girl? What Is a Boy?* to be a superb teaching aid in this context.[20] Each page displays a vivid and attractive photograph of a boy or a girl engaged in some behavior stereotyped as more typical of or more appropriate for the other sex. The accompanying text says such things as, "Some people say a girl is someone with jewelry, but Barry is wearing a necklace and he's a boy." The book ends with nude photographs of both children and adults, and it explicitly defines sex in terms of anatomy.

These particular lessons about what sex is, what sex is not, and when sex matters are designed to make young children far more naive than their peers about the cultural aspects of gender and far more sophisticated than their peers about the biological aspects of sex. Eventually, of course, their naiveté will begin to fade, and they too will begin to learn the culture's sprawling network of sex-linked associations.

At that point, parents must take steps to prevent that associative network from itself becoming a cognitive schema.

Providing Alternative Schemata

Let us presume that the feminist parent has successfully produced a child who defines sex in terms of anatomy and reproduction. How is such a child to understand the many sex-linked correlations that will inevitably begin to intrude upon his or her awareness? What alternative schemata can substitute for the gender schema in helping the child to organize and to assimilate gender-related information?

Individual differences schema.—The first alternative schema is simply a child's version of the time-honored liberal truism used to counter stereotypic thinking in general, namely, that there is remarkable variability of individuals within groups as compared with the small mean differences between groups. To the child who says that girls do not like to play baseball, the feminist parent can thus point out that although it is true that some girls do not like to play baseball, it is also true that some girls do (e.g., your Aunt Beverly and Alissa who lives across the street) and that some boys do not (e.g., your dad and Alissa's brother Jimmy). It is, of course, useful for parents to supply themselves with a long list of counterexamples well in advance of such occasions.

This individual differences schema is designed to prevent children from interpreting individual differences as sex differences, from assimilating perceived differences among people to a gender schema. Simultaneously, it should also encourage children to treat as a given that the sexes are basically similar to one another and, hence, to view all glib assertions about sex differences as inherently suspect. And it is with this skepticism that feminist consciousness begins.

Cultural relativism schema.—As the child's knowledge and awareness grow, he or she will gradually begin to realize that his or her family's beliefs and attitudes about gender are at variance with those of the dominant culture. Accordingly, the child needs some rationale for not simply accepting the majority view as the more valid. One possible rationale is cultural relativism, the notion that "different people believe different things" and that the coexistence of even contradictory beliefs is the rule in society rather than the exception.

Children can (and should) be introduced to the schema of cultural relativism long before it is pertinent to the domain of gender. For example, our children needed the rationale that "different people believe different things" in order to understand why they, but not the children next door, had to wear seat belts; why our family, but not the family next door, was casual about nudity in the home. The general principle that contradictory beliefs frequently coexist seems now to have become a readily available schema for our children, a schema that permits them to accept with relative equanimity that they have different beliefs from many of their peers with respect to gender.

Finally, the cultural relativism schema can solve one of the primary dilemmas of the liberal feminist parent: how to give one's children access to the riches of classical literature—as well as to the lesser riches of the mass media—without abandoning them to the forces that promote gender-schematic processing. Happily, the censorship of sex-stereotyped materials that is necessary to retard the initial growth of the sex-linked associative network when children are young can end once children have learned the critical lesson that cultural messages reflect the beliefs and attitudes of the person or persons who created those messages.

Accordingly, before we read our daughter her first volume of fairy tales, we discussed with her the cultural beliefs and attitudes about men and women that the tales would reflect, and while reading the tales, we frequently made such comments as, "Isn't it interesting that the person who wrote this story seems to think that girls always need to be rescued?" If such discussions are not too heavy-handed, they can provide a background of understanding against which the child can thoroughly enjoy the stories themselves, while still learning to discount the sex stereotypes within them as irrelevant both to their own beliefs and to truth. The cultural relativism schema thus brings children an awareness that fairy tales are fairy tales in more than one sense.

Sexism schema.—Cultural relativism is fine in its place, but feminist parents will not and should not be satisfied to pretend that they think all ideas—particularly those about gender—are equally valid. At some point, they will feel compelled to declare that the view of women and men conveyed by fairy tales, by the mass media—and by the next-door neighbors—is not only different, but wrong. It is time to teach one's children about sexism.

Moreover, it is only by giving children a sexism schema, a coherent and organized understanding of the historical roots and the contemporaneous consequences of sex discrimination, that they will truly be able to comprehend why the sexes appear to be so different in our society: why, for example, there has never been a female president of the United States; why fathers do not stay home with their children; and why so many people believe these sex differences to be the natural consequence of biology. The child who has developed a readiness to encode and to organize information in terms of an evolving sexism schema is a child who is prepared to oppose actively the gender-related constraints that those with a gender schema will inevitably seek to impose.

The development of a sexism schema is nicely illustrated by our daughter Emily's response to Norma Klein's book *Girls Can Be Anything*.[21] One of the characters is Adam Sobel, who insists that "girls are always nurses and boys are always doctors" and that "girls can't be pilots, . . . they have to be stewardesses." After reading this book, our daughter, then age four, spontaneously began to label with contempt anyone who voiced stereotyped beliefs about gender an "Adam Sobel." Adam Sobel thus became for her the nucleus of an envolving sexism schema, a schema that enables her now to perceive—and also to become morally outraged by and to oppose—whatever sex discrimination she meets in daily life.

As feminist parents, we wish it could have been possible to raise our children with neither a gender schema nor a sexism schema. At this historical moment, however, that is not an option. Rather we must choose either to have our children become gender schematic and hence sex typed, or to have our children become sexism schematic and hence feminists. We have chosen the latter.

A COMMENT ON PSYCHOLOGICAL ANDROGYNY

The central figure in gender schema theory is the sex-typed individual, a shift in focus from my earlier work in which the non-sex-typed individual—the androgynous individual in particular—commanded center stage.[22] In the early 1970s, androgyny seemed to me and to many others a liberated and more humane alternative to the traditional, sex-biased standards of mental health. And it is true that this concept can be applied equally to both women and men, and that it encourages individuals to embrace both the feminine and the masculine within themselves. But advocating the concept of androgyny can also be seen as replacing a prescription to be masculine or feminine with the doubly incarcerating prescription to be masculine and feminine. The individual now has not one but two potential sources of inadequacy with which to contend. Even more important, however, the concept of androgyny is problematic from the perspective of gender schema theory because it is based on the presupposition that there is a feminine and a masculine within us all, that is, that "femininity" and "masculinity" have an independent and palpable reality and are not cognitive constructs derived from gender-schematic processing. Focusing on androgyny thus fails to prompt serious examination of the extent to which gender organizes both our perceptions and our social world.

In contrast, the concept of gender-schematic processing directs our attention to the promiscuous availability of the gender schema in contexts where other schemata ought to have priority. Thus, if gender schema theory has a political message, it is not that the individual should be androgynous. Rather, it is that the network of associations constituting the gender schema ought to become more limited in scope and that society ought to temper its insistence on the ubiquitous functional importance of the gender dichotomy. In short, human behaviors and personality attributes should no longer be linked with gender, and society should stop projecting gender into situations irrelevant to genitalia.

Department of Psychology
and the Women's Studies Program
Cornell University

NOTES

1. See, e.g., Paul H. Mussen, "Early Sex-Role Development," in *Handbook of Socialization Theory and Research,* ed. David A. Goslin (Chicago: Rand McNally & Co., 1969), pp. 703–31. For a more recent review that does not even mention psychoanalytic theory, see Aletha C. Huston, "Sex-Typing," to appear in *Carmichael's Manual of Child Psychology,* ed. Paul H. Mussen, 4th ed. (New York: John Wiley & Sons, in press).

2. Urie Bronfenbrenner, "Freudian Theories of Identification with Their Derivatives," *Child Development* 31, no. 1 (March 1960): 15–40; Sigmund Freud, "Some Psychological Consequences of the Anatomical Distinction between the Sexes (1925)," in *Collected Papers of Sigmund Freud,* ed. Ernest Jones, 5 vols. (New York: Basic Books, 1959), 5:186–97; Sigmund Freud, "The Passing of the Oedipus Complex (1924)," ibid., 2: 269–76.

3. E.g., Nancy Chodorow, *The Reproduction of Mothering: Psychoanalysis and the Sociology of Gender* (Berkeley: University of California Press, 1978); Gayle Rubin, "The Traffic in Women: Notes on the 'Political Economy' of Sex," in *Toward an Anthropology of Women,* ed. Rayna Reiter (New York: Monthly Review Press, 1975), pp. 157–210.

4. Lawrence Kohlberg, "A Cognitive-Developmental Analysis of Children's Sex-Role Concepts and Attitudes," in *The Development of Sex Differences,* ed. Eleanor E. Maccoby (Stanford, Calif.: Stanford University Press, 1966), pp. 82–173; Maureen J. McConaghy, "Gender Permanence and the Genital Basis of Gender: Stages in the Development of Constancy of Gender Identity," *Child Development* 50, no. 4 (December 1979): 1223–26.

5. Eleanor E. Maccoby and Carol N. Jacklin, *The Psychology of Sex Differences* (Stanford, Calif.: Stanford University Press, 1974).

6. Walter Mischel, "Sex-Typing and Socialization," in *Carmichael's Manual of Child Psychology,* ed. Paul H. Mussen, 2 vols. (New York: John Wiley & Sons, 1970), 2:3–72.

7. William Danion, *The Social World of the Child* (San Francisco: Jossey-Bass, 1977).

8. Courtney B. Cazden, "The Acquisition of Noun and Verb Inflections," *Child Development* 39, no. 2 (June 1968): 433–48; Herber H. Clark and Eve V. Clark, *Psychology and Language: An Introduction to Psycholinguistics* (New York: Harcourt Brace Jovanovich, 1977).

9. Michael Lewis and Jeanne Brooks-Gunn, *Social Cognition and the Acquisition of Self* (New York: Plenum Publishing Corp., 1979), p. 270.

10. Kohlberg, p. 89.

11. Kohlberg; Lewis and Brooks-Gunn; Dorothy Z. Ullian, "The Child's Construction of Gender: Anatomy as Destiny," in *Cognitive and Affective Growth: Developmental Interaction,* ed. Edna K. Shapiro and Evelyn Weber (Hillsdale, N.J.: Lawrence Erlbaum Associates, 1981), pp. 171–85.

12. For a discussion of the wet-dry distinction, see Anna S. Meigs, "Male Pregnancy and the Reduction of Sexual Opposition in a New Guinea Highlands Society," *Ethnology* 15, no. 4 (1976): 393–407; for a discussion of the open-closed distinction, see Sally Falk Moore, "The Secret of the Men: A Fiction of Chagga Initiation and Its Relation to the Logic of Chagga Symbolism," *Africa* 46, no. 4 (1976): 357–70.

13. Sandra L. Bem, "Gender Schema Theory: A Cognitive Account of Sex Typing," *Psychological Review* 88, no. 4 (July 1981): 354–64; and "Gender Schema Theory and Self-Schema Theory Compared: A Comment on Markus, Crane, Bernstein, and Siladi's 'Self-Schemas and Gender,'" *Journal of Personality and Social Psychology* 43, no. 6 (December 1982): 1192–94.

14. Ulric Neisser, *Cognition and Reality* (San Francisco: W. H. Freeman & Co., 1976); Shelley E. Taylor and Jennifer Crocker, "Schematic Bases of Social Information Processing," in *Social Cognition, the Ontario Symposium,* ed. E. Tory Higgins, C. Peter Herman, and Mark P. Zanna (Hillsdale, N.J.: Lawrence Erlbaum Associates, 1981), 1:89–135.

15. Jerome Kagan, "Acquisition and Significance of Sex Typing and Sex Role Identity," in *Review of Child Development Research,* ed. Martin L. Hoffman and Lois W. Hoffman (New York: Russell Sage Foundation, 1964), 1:137–67.

16. Susan M. Andersen and Sandra L. Bem, "Sex Typing and Androgyny in Dyadic Interaction: Individual Differences in Responsiveness to Physical Attractiveness," *Journal of Personality and Social Psychology* 41, no. 1 (July 1981): 74–86; Bem, "Gender Schema Theory"; Kay Deaux and Brenda Major, "Sex-related Patterns in the Unit of Perception," *Personality and Social Psychology Bulletin* 3, no. 2 (Spring 1977): 297–300; Brenda Girvin, "The Nature of Being Schematic: Sex-Role Self-Schemas and Differential Processing of Masculine and Feminine Information" (Ph.D. diss., Stanford University, 1978); Robert V. Kail and Laura E. Levine, "Encoding Processes and Sex-Role Preferences," *Journal of Experimental Child Psychology* 21, no. 2 (April 1976): 256–63; Lynn S. Liben and Margaret L. Signorella, "Gender-related Schemata and Constructive Memory in Children," *Child Development* 51, no. 1 (March 1980): 11–18; Richard Lippa, "Androgyny, Sex Typing, and the Perception of Masculinity-Femininity in Handwriting," *Journal of Research in Personality* 11, no. 1 (March 1977): 21–37; Hazel Markus et al., "Self-Schemas and Gender," *Journal of Personality and Social Psychology* 42, no. 1 (January 1982): 38–50; Shelley E. Taylor and Hsiao-Ti Falcone, "Cognitive Bases of Stereotyping: The Relationship between Categorization and Prejudice," *Personality and Social Psychology Bulletin* 8, no. 3 (September 1982): 426–32.

17. Bem, "Gender Schema Theory," pp. 356–58.

18. The Bem Sex Role Inventory, or BSRI, is an instrument that identifies sex-typed individuals on the basis of their self-concepts or self-ratings of their personal attributes. The BSRI

asks the respondent to indicate on a seven-point scale how well each of sixty attributes describes himself or herself. Although it is not apparent to the respondent, twenty of the attributes reflect the culture's definition of masculinity (e.g., assertive), and twenty reflect its definition of femininity (e.g., tender), with the remaining attributes serving as filler. Each respondent receives both a masculinity and a femininity score, and those who score above the median on the sex-congruent scale and below the median on the sex-incongruent scale are defined as sex typed. That is, men who score high in masculinity and low in femininity are defined as sex typed, as are women who score high in femininity and low in masculinity. The BSRI is described in detail in the following articles: Sandra L. Bem, "The Measurement of Psychological Androgyny," *Journal of Consulting and Clinical Psychology* 42, no. 2 (April 1974): 155–62; "On the Utility of Alternative Procedures for Assessing Psychological Androgyny," *Journal of Clinical and Consulting Psychology* 45, no. 2 (April 1977): 196–205; "The Theory and Measurement of Androgyny: A Reply to the Pedhazur-Tetenbaum and Locksley-Colten Critiques," *Journal of Personality and Social Psychology* 37, no. 6 (June 1979): 1047–54; and *A Manual for*

the Bem Sex Role Inventory (Palo Alto, Calif.: Consulting Psychologists Press, 1981).

19. Bem, "Gender Schema Theory," pp. 358–61.

20. Stephanie Waxman, *What Is a Girl? What Is a Boy?* (Culver City, Calif.: Peace Press, 1976).

21. Norma Klein, *Girls Can Be Anything* (New York: E. P. Dutton, 1973).

22. Sandra L. Bem, "Sex-Role Adaptability: One Consequence of Psychological Androgyny," *Journal of Personality and Social Psychology* 31, no. 4 (April 1975): 634–43; Sandra L. Bem, Wendy Martyna, and Carol Watson, "Sex-Typing and Androgyny: Further Explorations of the Expressive Domain," *Journal of Personality and Social Psychology* 34, no. 5 (November 1976): 1016–23; Sandra L. Bem, "Beyond Androgyny: Some Presumptuous Prescriptions for a Liberated Sexual Identity," in *The Future of Women: Issues in Psychology,* ed. Julia Sherman and Florence Denmark (New York: Psychological Dimensions, Inc., 1978), pp. 1–23; Sandra L. Bem and Ellen Lenney, "Sex-Typing and the Avoidance of Cross-Sex Behavior," *Journal of Personality and Social Psychology* 33, no. 1 (January 1976): 48–54.

CHECKPOINTS

1. Gender schemas organize and categorize information about gender and lead children to incorporate the stereotypes of males and females into their gender identity.

2. Bem believes that children's adoption of narrow gender identities can be reduced by encouraging children to organize their cognitions about sex and gender differently.

To prepare for reading the next section, think about these questions:

1. In what ways do parents, teachers, and peers influence gender identity?

2. What role does the child play in developing a gender identity?

Psychosocial and Cognitive Determinants of Early Gender-Role Development

BEVERLY I. FAGOT

The focus of this article is on the development of understanding about sex and gender from infants' earliest recognition of sex-related differences through the acquisition of gender knowledge and sex-typed behavior during early childhood. I will emphasize children's own construction of gender as they try to make sense of a sex-typed world, but children's part of the process cannot be understood without considering the socialization pressures and environmental influences to which they must respond. My underlying conviction that environmental influences are often more subtle and more powerful than has been asserted, and that the child's gender understanding is more complex and less concrete, has both shaped and been shaped by the work reported here. The environmental influences discussed in this paper are family, peers, and teacher/caregivers—the major influences in the life of the young child. Biological and hormonal variables will not be discussed, and readers who wish to explore this aspect of gender-role development can refer to the recent article by Hines and Collaer (1993), who reviewed research on endocrine systems and brain structure.

Gender is a category system made up of many interwoven levels. Physiology defines the most fundamental level, designating people as male or female on the basis of their observable sexual anatomy, but every known society surrounds the basic facts of sexual form and function with a system of social rules and customs concerning what males and females are supposed to be and do. As children master and internalize this system, they learn to discriminate and label themselves and others on the basis of sex, to recognize attributes, attitudes, and behaviors that are typical of or considered appropriate for each sex, and to learn how to do what is seen as appropriate and to

avoid what is not. What is more, the gender-category system is infused with affect to an extent few other knowledge bases can match, making it what is perhaps the most salient parameter of social categorization for the young child.

First, a word about *sex* and *gender*. These terms are neither completely interchangeable nor completely distinct. For the most part, sex will refer to the dichotomous classification of people as male or female, and *sex typing* and *sex roles* will refer to what is assigned to people on the basis of their sex. Gender will be used where the dimensions of masculinity and femininity come into play, as the location of attitudes and behaviors on these dimensions is not limited to the male-female dichotomy. The term *gender-role development* will be used to define the complex process by which children come to understand the societal ramifications of their sex.

There is probably no area in psychology in which so much has been written, with so little agreement, as the area of gender-role development. No single theory gives us a coherent account of the process of gender-role development. Mischel (1966) and other social learning theorists have emphasized the importance of environmental input in defining the differing worlds of boys and girls. Kohlberg (1966) and other cognitive-developmental theorists have pointed to regularities in children's understanding of gender. Freud and other psychodynamic theorists have alerted us to the importance of affect in the acquisition of gender knowledge. However, children's lives are not neatly divided into separate realms of experience. Children experience the contingencies of a sex-typed world, try to make sense of all they take in, care very much about their identity as a girl or boy, and strive to get it right.

The two major positions in the field have been social learning and cognitive development. There are many viewpoints within each broad area, and the two approaches have come closer together in the 1980s and 1990s, but research in psychology since 1960 has been shaped primarily by the two approaches. Social learning theorists have focused upon how the environment shapes boys' and girls' development. Children are wrapped from birth in sex-differentiated information. Researchers have confirmed that boys and girls receive different information from both home and school environments (Fagot, 1974; Rheingold & Cook, 1975; Serbin, O'Leary, Kent, & Tonick, 1973; Shakin, Shakin, & Sternglantz, 1985). Cognitive developmentalists, such as Kohlberg, have emphasized the regularities in the child's understanding of gender and developed a stage theory of gender-role development. Kohlberg (1966) emphasized the unfolding maturational process by which gender development takes place. He emphasized the sequence of identifying one's own sex (gender identity), of understanding that sex remained stable over time (gender stability), and of understanding that sex remained constant despite perceptual changes (gender constancy). Early work within the Kohlbergian framework was designed to test whether there was a consistent sequence to children's understanding, and, for the most part, it was confirmed that there was (Emmerich, Goldman, Kirsh, & Sharabany, 1977; Fagot, 1985a; Marcus & Overton, 1978). Social learning theory emphasizes the role of the environment, whereas cognitive development theory emphasizes the role of maturational changes. Both social learning and Kohlbergian theories portray the child as essentially passive in the development of gender role.

Beginning with Martin and Halverson's (1981) article, researchers started to show how children actively contribute to their own gender-role development. This view emphasized the normative nature of cognitive development, with gender presented as a special case. Martin and Halverson adopted the term *schema* to describe outcomes of the developmental process. A schema is an organized knowledge structure, and a gender schema is a knowledge structure organized around gender or sex. Researchers began to

study how children's understanding of gender influenced their memories and information processing, as well as their choice of toys and activities (Carter & Levy, 1988). As they try to understand all they see and hear, children begin to form categories that help organize the flood of information that inundates them. The distinction between female and male, feminine and masculine, provides a readily available organizing principle that is relevant to the child's own self. During the 1980s there were several attempts to bring together views from cognitive development and social learning theories as applied to children's gender-role development (Bem, 1981; Fagot, 1985b). Because children live in a sex-typed world, they develop gender schemas that guide the choice of "sex-appropriate" behaviors and the knowledge of the action patterns necessary for carrying them out. Gender-role adoption is expected to occur as the self-concept is assimilated to the gender schema and as children adopt standards of sex appropriateness in accordance with the information to which they are exposed. Schema formation undoubtedly depends upon the child's own mental effort and developmental status, but the information being processed must reflect the degree and importance of gender typing in the child's surroundings. Thus, schema theory offers a framework for describing and integrating the development of gender understanding with environmental information and values (Martin, 1991).

One of the first questions asked about a newborn child is its sex, and parents often show disappointment when the child is not the sex they preferred. Clearly, gender is laden with affect for parents. Researchers dealing with infants have witnessed the attempts of parents to visually label girl babies prior to the growth of hair—with ruffled pink overalls and bows pasted upon bald head—and have witnessed the distress and anger generated when the child's sex was wrongly identified. From infancy on, gender is a salient parameter of social categorization for the young child (Serbin & Sprafkin, 1986). Readers can almost feel the outrage of young children responding to Damon's (1977) questions concerning a boy who preferred girl's clothes and activities. Therefore, any study of gender-role development process needs to include measurement of the behavioral responses to gender-typed acts, the child's cognitive understanding, and the affect involved in the interaction. Until recently, affect has been the neglected parameter of gender studies, although there has been a good deal of discussion concerning differences in emotional socialization. Fortunately, there is a new emphasis on affect in the study of gender, which is bringing in more subjective emotional reactions and physiological measurement (Fabes, 1994).

THE ROLE OF THE ENVIRONMENT

From studies done in the home, daycare centers, and preschools by a number of researchers, as reviewed by Huston (1983), we are beginning to have a fairly clear picture of how the environment maintains gender roles. Parents react in gender-differentiated ways to children's behavior, in effect reinforcing gender stereotypes (Clarke-Stewart, 1978; Fagot, 1973b, 1974; Stoneman & Brody, 1981), and both teachers and peers react to children in ways that maintain gender-stereotyped behaviors (Carpenter & Huston, 1980; Etaugh, Collins, & Gerson, 1975; Fagot, 1973a; Fagot & Patterson, 1969; Serbin et al., 1973). There are numerous anecdotes in the developmental literature on the strength of societal stereotypes concerning gender. Any parent who has tried to raise a child to feel free to sample broad ranges of activities knows how strongly peer groups and the media work to maintain gender typing and how difficult attempts to work against stereotypes are. The question to be addressed in the next section is how the reactions of adults in the home and school relate to our stereotypical view of what boys and girls are like.

DIFFERENTIAL RESPONSES OF ADULTS IN THE ENVIRONMENT TO GENDER-TYPED BEHAVIORS

Mothers' and fathers' roles in the family. The traditional view of the family is one of the mother providing warmth and caregiving and the father providing discipline and support (Parsons & Bales, 1955).

These characterizations of family life do not appear to describe parenting today, and probably never did. Although mothers do spend more time with their children than fathers—and this is as true of mothers who work outside the home as of those who spend their days at home with the children (Pederson, 1980)—the roles of present day mothers and fathers appear to have evolved somewhat differently. Mothers do most of the routine caregiving, but the fathers' role is not that of the abstract disciplinarian; instead, the father appears to have taken over many of the qualities of playmate. Lamb (1977, 1981) found that, when fathers spent time with toddler-aged children, it was play time. Whenever the child needed some type of care, the child was returned to the mother.

Block (1976) suggested that fathers are more important to the gender-role development of children than mothers and that fathers interact with boys and girls in very different ways, whereas mothers will react in similar ways to boys and girls. She based this suggestion in part upon the *reciprocal role theory* of Johnson (1963, 1975), from which it is predicted that the father's behavior will promote typically gender-typed behavior in both boys and girls. Whereas both mothers and fathers are expected to encourage traditional gender typing, fathers will make greater distinctions between sons and daughters. Boys will be sought out by fathers and will be encouraged to take on an instrumental, independent style of behavior, whereas girls will be encouraged to seek help and to be more dependent. Though this viewpoint has received widespread acceptance in the psychological and lay literature, there is actually not a lot of support for this viewpoint. Much of our information concerning the role of fathers has come from mothers. What we know directly from fathers is biased toward well-educated fathers and concerns interactions in infancy and early childhood. There has been only modest support for a differential effect on later gender-role variables. Reviewing the research on mother-child and father-child relationships with children in middle childhood and early adolescence, Collins and Russell (1991) reported differences for both mothers and fathers in relationships with sons and daughters. However, what differences were found were more likely to be in respect to attitudes about the differences between boys and girls than in behavior toward boys and girls. There is still considerable controversy over the strength of parental differences in the socialization of the sexes. Maccoby and Jacklin (1974) concluded that parental differences, outside of socialization of specific behaviors with toys and domestic activities, were relatively minimal. Lytton and Romney (1991) examined studies of parent treatment of boys and girls and found that, out of the eight major socialization variables, the only consistent sex-differentiated parental reaction was in encouragement of sex-typed behaviors. The results of the Maccoby and Jacklin (1974) study as well as the Lytton and Romney (1991) meta-analysis should convince us that to look for sex-differentiated socialization in all parent reactions will not help us understand sex-role development or differences in boys and girls.

The Lytton and Romney (1991) analysis strongly suggests that age is a crucial variable (effect sizes were greater for younger children) and that the way we define and measure parent reactions and child behaviors will affect the outcome of our studies. Confirming the effect of age of child, Fagot and Hagan (1991) found that parents observed in the home showed considerable differences in response to 12- and 18-month-old boys and girls engaged in sex-typical activities, whereas there were few differences in parents' reactions to 5-year-old boys and girls. There is some indication that parents become more differentiated in their reactions to boys and girls at adolescence, and are more likely to react to sex-typed activities (Gjerde, 1986). At some points in the child's development the parents may be very concerned about conformity to cultural standards of sex-typing, but once such conformity is obtained, parents may well appear to be behaving more similarly than not to boys and girls.

In a summary article examining 39 published studies concerning differential socialization, Siegel (1987) concluded that some support exists for the uniqueness of the father's role; however, the effects were surprisingly small. Fathers were more likely to show gender-specific differences than mothers; however, the direction of the effects was contradictory among the studies, so it is difficult to interpret the findings. For example, with 1- and 2-year-old children, Weinraub and Frankel (1977) reported fathers talking more to sons, whereas Stoneman and Brody (1981) reported fathers talking more to daughters when mothers were present. What is suggested by these studies is that fathers may be more variable than mothers in responses to their children. Thus researchers may find that fathers differ in their responses to boys and girls, but, this may be a statistical artifact of greater variability rather than a finding based on a consistent paternal mode of responding. In work with somewhat older children, Russell and Russell (1988) reported that, when asked to explain their interactions with their child, fathers mostly used adult-centered explanations of their behavior, but mothers used child characteristics as an explanation more often than fathers. In a meta-analysis in which mother-child versus father-child dyads were examined, Collins and Russell (1991) reported that individual differences among parents outweighed the role differences between mothers and fathers.

Mothers and fathers in individual families vary in their childrearing styles, but as a group, mothers spend far more time with their children than do fathers, do most of the caregiving, and, if the family breaks up, are far more likely to rear children as single parents. Although there is some movement within the middle class for more involvement of the father in the family, even in families choosing an egalitarian type of childrearing in which both parents are employed outside the home, mothers continue to do most of the caregiving (Fagot & Leinbach, in press; Pederson, 1980). Patterson, Reid, and Dishion (1992) found that, in most studies, mother variables tend to be stronger predictors of child outcome than father variables even in two-parent families (i.e., the behavior of the mothers differentiated children but not the behavior of the fathers). Children in single-mother households, whether created by birth to a single mother or by divorce, tend to have more difficulties (Furstenberg, Brooks-Gunn, & Chase-Lonsdale, 1989; Hetherington & Clingempeel, 1992; Hetherington, Cox, & Cox, 1982), but in the studies of single-mother families, single-mother status has often been confounded with economic hardship and social stress, so it is difficult to know whether it is father absence or other variables that predict negative outcome. In a study that controlled for income level, Leve and Fagot (1995) found that single mothers and fathers had less traditional gender-role attitudes than mothers and fathers in two-parent families, but that children in single-parent families did not differ in gender-role preference or knowledge from children in two-parent families. Leve and Fagot also found that mothers and fathers reported more negative behavior from opposite-sex children than from same-sex children; boys in single-mother families and girls in single-father families may appear to have more problems because there is no balancing report from a same-sex parent. Interestingly enough, single parents report more positive behavior from their children than do parents in two-parent families, and they tend to use more problem-solving techniques with their children. In general, however, fathers with sons use fewer problem-solving techniques than fathers with daughters or mothers with either sex. Stevenson and Black (1988) conducted a meta-analysis on the sex-role development of children in a total of 67 studies comparing father-absent and father-present families. The effects were found primarily for boys and were not easy to interpret. Preschool boys from father-absent families were less sex-stereotyped in their choice of toys and activities; however, older boys from father-absent families were more sex-stereotyped, particularly in the area of aggression. Stevenson and Black found that effect size covaried with age of child, socioeconomic status of the family, reason for father absence, and race. The study is perhaps best summarized by the authors, who begin their discussion with the sentence "Overall, the differences between father absent and father present samples were not large" (p. 805). They also made the point that father-absent families are a very heterogeneous group, as many, if not most, of the children in the father-absent group had some access to their fathers and often spent a considerable amount of time with them.

The questions of socialization of sex differences and the differential roles of mothers and fathers are still open. In broad-scale meta-analyses of research, effect sizes appear relatively small (Lytton & Romney, 1991; Siegel, 1987; Stevenson & Black, 1988); however, meta-analysis makes clear that one must attend to age differences, setting differences, and measurement variables. In studies using natural settings, where the participants are not constrained by the experimenter, larger effect sizes have been found, as is also the case in studies with young children, and those rated of higher quality. In studies of more molar qualities of families (such as who attends teacher conferences, who takes the children if the family splits up, who leaves work to take the child to the doctor), it is clear that mothers are more involved in child care than fathers. However, explaining gender differences only as a function of parental socialization would be foolish. What parents do is provide information about the importance of gender, both in terms of their reactions to the child and in terms of family organization. As discussed later, that information, along with other sources of information, will help the child construct categories, labels, scripts, and theories about gender. It is important to remember that parents are not the only source of information for even very young children; the role of teachers and peers will be discussed in the next sections.

Adult reactions in daycare and school. Boys and girls receive somewhat different reactions to their behaviors in daycare and school situations from the time they are very young. To take one example, teachers of 12- to 16-month-old children responded to the sex of the child, giving more attention to boys engaged in assertive acts and to girls engaged in communication acts, even though there were no differences in the frequency with which boys and girls engaged in these acts (Fagot, Hagan, Leinbach, & Kronsberg, 1985). One year later, these same boys engaged in more aggression, and the girls engaged in more communication with teachers, even though teachers now responded to the children in terms of their actual behavior rather than the gender of the child. In the school and daycare environments, peers appear to take over the role of maintaining gender-role standards somewhere around 30 months of age. For boys in particular, attempting to engage in cross-sex activities brings a good deal of negative feedback from male peers (Fagot, 1977). Serbin, Tonick, and Sternglanz (1977) attempted to have teachers shape cooperative cross-sex play, which was successful as long as the teachers maintained a heavy reward schedule; however, once the program ended, cross-sex play dropped to preintervention levels. Fagot (1985b) showed that boys responded and changed their behavior when rewarded or punished by male peers but did not respond to girls or teachers, whereas girls responded to both other girls and teachers.

Serbin et al. (1973) reported that girls clustered around teachers, whereas boys played at the edges of the classrooms. As the teachers in the Serbin et al. study were female, Fagot (1981) examined both male and female teachers and found that girls clustered around both male and female teachers, whereas boys continued to play around the edges of classrooms even when male teachers were available. Fagot also compared inexperienced teachers and experienced teachers. Inexperienced teachers, both male and female, were more likely to join ongoing activities of children including the behavior of boys on the edges of the classroom, whereas experienced teachers, both male and female, concentrated their interactions around table play, book reading, and art activities. As suggested by Lee and Kedar-Voivodas (1977), experienced preschool teachers react more to children in the pupil role than they do to children playing in other types of activities. Pupil behaviors overlap more with feminine-preferred behaviors (e.g., many kinds of table games) than with male-preferred behaviors (e.g., large motor activities). Moreover, teachers fail to react to either boys or girls involved in traditional gender-typed behaviors (e.g., rough-and-tumble play or doll play, respectively).

Differences in boys' and girls' preference for high- or low-structured activities influence more than the child's gender-role development. Carpenter and Huston (1980) found that children of either sex who preferred high-structured activities were more compliant and used toys in less novel ways. In contrast, children who preferred less structure interacted more

with peers. Because more boys than girls took part in low-structured activities, boys were more likely to interact with other boys. Gender segregation may therefore be encouraged by these gender differences in activity preference. Carpenter (1983) suggested that long-term and continued participation in low- or high-structured activities teach different styles of interaction with the environment. High-structured activities contribute to the learning of rules and the accommodation of the child to the environment, whereas low-structured activities may force children to adapt in new ways to the environment. Block (1983) took this beyond preschool and suggested that, in general, girls are taught to accommodate to rules, whereas boys are forced to adapt to a lack of rules. Maccoby (1988) noted that girls prefer the protection from boys that teachers provide and that girls' flocking toward the teacher may be more an avoidance of boys than a preference for the teacher. It should be noted that children who prefer greater structure are learning the rules of schooling, and this preference for higher structure may be one reason that girls outperform boys in early school years. Smith and Connolly (1980) found that high structure inhibited both aggression and rough-and-tumble play, but it appeared that the children—boys in particular—were not learning self-control, for in unstructured situations the same children remained aggressive and boisterous.

Gender differences in preschool are then not confined just to play with different toys in gender-segregated groups. Girls spend a great deal more time with their teachers (Fagot & Patterson, 1969; Serbin et al., 1973), and consequently teachers interact more with girls. Girls also respond more to teachers' directions (Fagot, 1985b; Serbin, Connor, & Citron, 1981) and avail themselves more of teachers' consolations (Feldbaum, Christenson, & O'Neal, 1980). Teachers tend to react positively and to help children when they are engaged in art and school-typed behaviors (Fagot & Patterson, 1969; Lee & Kedar-Voivodas, 1977), so that children engaged in such activities get more teacher attention. During the 1960s and 1970s there was a discussion in the literature concerning the possible feminization of boys in schools because teachers interact more with children in behaviors that are preferred by girls (Sexton, 1968), but Brophy and Good (1974), in a review of teacher-child interaction, could find no indication that boys became more feminine with increased schooling. Today, reviewing much of the same literature, there has been a media debate concerning school's unfairness to girls (Sadker & Sadker, 1994). How can the same studies be used to support exactly opposite positions? In part, it is due to selective use of particular parts of studies. For instance, the often cited study of Serbin et al. (1973) has been used to support both sides (i.e., that boys are feminized by preschools, and that girls are treated unfairly by preschool teachers). The feminization supporters report the finding that girls receive more attention overall from teachers because girls spend more time with teachers and that boys receive more negatives due to more active misbehaviors. The unfairness-to-girls supporters pick up on the finding that when boys did interact with teachers, they received a higher proportion of attention, totally ignoring the fact that this attention was both positive and negative. What we can say from the literature is that boys and girls do have different experiences with their preschool teachers, which is dictated in part by differences in behaviors and interests of the children and in part because teachers see that a large portion of their role is to help children learn behaviors that are necessary for future school performance.

Peer reactions to sex-typed behaviors. By the time they are 3 years old, boys and girls around the world participate in different activities and show different behavioral styles (Whiting & Edwards, 1988); they play more with same-sex peers and avoid opposite-sex peers (Maccoby, 1988). Different cultures have very different ideas about the capabilities of the young child, and in many cultures, preschool-age children are not considered capable of learning through instruction (Whiting & Edwards, 1988). In such cultures, children are often taught their social roles through guided participation in ongoing family social groups (Rogoff, 1990) rather than being placed in formal school settings.

Goodall (1986) noted that young female chimpanzees are kept much closer to their mothers and are not allowed to join the free roaming playgroups of males. Female chimp friendships are more closely tied to family groups, and the females play in smaller groups than do the males. As documented by Whiting and Edwards (1988), there are cultures in which the family segregates young boys and girls from a very early age. However, in Western culture, there is actually little family pressure for gender segregation of young children, but in nursery schools, which often promote a lack of gender segregation, researchers have long noted that much of the children's play is in same-sex groups (Maccoby, 1988). Charlesworth and Hartup (1967) documented these differences in one of the first observational studies examining this phenomenon. Fagot and Patterson (1969) and Fagot (1977) showed that boys spent much more time playing in same-sex groups than did girls. Boys who attempted to play in groups of girls or in activities favored by girls received a good deal more peer criticism than boys who did not. In addition, such criticism continued even when the boys then attempted to play in male-typical activities. Fagot (1985b) showed that girls received more positive feedback when playing with other girls, but it was all right for girls to play in male activities. Boys, on the other hand, received positive feedback only when engaged with other boys and when engaged in male activities. Serbin et al. (1981) showed that it is very difficult to change the pattern of boys' play through teacher intervention but relatively easy to change girls' play. In a German sample, boys did not value female activities and disliked boys who did, whereas girls valued female activities but did not react negatively when other girls tried out male activities (Trautner, Helbing, & Sahm, 1985).

Gender segregation, which is the separation of boys and girls into single-sex groups, exists from early childhood and in fact continues throughout life. Maccoby and Jacklin (1987) suggested several possible reasons behind this separation, ranging from play style compatibility to behavioral incapability in terms of boys' preference for rougher play styles. Boys and girls do spend a good portion of their time in different activities. Maccoby (1994) reviewed some of the support mechanisms behind gender segregation. She concluded that gender segregation is most probably overdetermined, in that there may be physiological differences that result in behavioral incompatibility, there are certain play preferences, and there are probably cognitive processes that influence children's choices. Each of these variables has been found to be present in preschool children. Sex differences in toy and activity preference among preschool children have been documented in different cultures (O'Brien & Huston, 1985; Smith & Connolly, 1980; Trautner et al., 1985). Differences in behavioral styles and distancing from adult figures have been noted by observers in several different cultures and in nonhuman primates (Blurton-Jones, 1972; DiPietro, 1981). In particular, young males engage in more rough-and-tumble play, even though there are minimal sex differences in large motor activity.

Gender segregation and the resulting differences in activity choice have implications for cognitive skills. Block (1983) used Piaget's mechanism of adaptation to discuss the play of young children. Block suggested that boys engage in activities that require them to change their own structures. She suggested that boys' toys and boys' activities allow them to solve problems in new and creative ways. Girls, on the other hand, were more likely to engage in activities that imitated life roles and that did not require them to change but allowed them to rehearse cultural roles; therefore, girls might actually know more about the expectations of the culture. Block (1983) suggested that these differences in early play styles lead to differences in intellectual and emotional development. Block suggested that girls make use of existing cognitive and social structures that are modified by incremental steps. They are given toys that encourage learning social rules and imitation of behaviors, such as dolls, and imitation domestic toys, such as vacuum cleaners and stoves, and are encouraged by adults to keep in close contact. Boys, on the other hand, according to Block, are given toys that force them to develop their own schemas and to find out how the toys work, such as building toys, chemistry sets, and model plane sets. Boys are also encouraged to engage more in activities with peers and not with adults. Block hypothesized that, as a conse-

quence of these differences in play styles and differences in interactions with adults and peers, girls' development is more stable than boys' because girls can draw upon adults for help. Boys' development is less stable because they do not use adult help as effectively, but they are forced to restructure more often and to produce their own unique solutions. Leaper (1994) suggested that gender segregation contributes to the fostering of differential skills in both the cognitive and social domains, but also sounded a warning about assuming a simple dichotomy. Girls' groups may be more concerned with affiliation and cooperation, but they also are concerned with assertion and dominance although they may use different methods to maintain dominance. Leaper also pointed out that gender segregation is multiply determined and that it is not something imposed by parents and teachers, but that children themselves work hard to maintain the segregation. In the next section of this paper, I will explore the child's part in the development of gender roles.

THE CHILD'S CONTRIBUTION

Beginnings of the process. The differentiation process by which infants are exposed to gender information begins in the newborn period; differential treatment by gender starts as soon as the infant's sex is known. The newborn nursery provides color-coded blankets, identification bracelets, and diapers. Gifts to the child are carefully selected by gender, with girls receiving pastel outfits, sometimes beruffled, whereas boys are given tiny jeans and bold colors. Indeed, although parents seldom mention sex-appropriateness when asked about clothing choices for their infants, most infants are dressed in gender-typed clothing (Shakin et al., 1985). Several researchers have examined adult responses to babies in terms of gender stereotypes. The findings of these so-called Baby X studies are that, when adults do not have additional information about the infant, they fall back on gender stereotypes to describe physical attributes and personality traits (Condry & Condry, 1976). In the real world there is no lack of information with which to identify or discriminate the sexes, and adults use whatever information they have available. However, we do not know with any precision when infants come to recognize males and females as categorically distinct.

In order to demonstrate categorical recognition in infants, we must first show that they can make discriminations that differentiate the sexes. But discrimination alone is not enough. It is necessary to show that the discrimination is categorical; that is, that women in general evoke responses from the infants that are different from the responses evoked by men. One currently accepted criterion for demonstrating categorical perception involves habituating infants to discriminably different instances of one category, then testing for dishabituation with a new instance of the familiar category and an exemplar of the contrast category. Recovery of interest only in response to the contrast category indicates that infants have lost interest in the familiar category as a whole while retaining the potential for responding to the contrast category.

What kinds of differences between men and women might a young infant be able to detect? Vision and hearing have provided the primary means of access to infant knowledge, but although the senses of smell and touch are quite well developed at birth, we know of no attempts to investigate either smell or tactile sensitivity in connection with gender recognition. A discrimination task using men's and women's voices provides the earliest evidence in which categorical perception concerning the sexes has been demonstrated. Two-month-old infants habituated to syllables spoken by a series of talkers of one sex can detect a change to the same syllables spoken by members of the opposite sex (Jusczyk, Pisoni, & Mullinnex, 1992). By 7 months, infants can readily learn to respond differentially to male and female voices (Miller, Younger, & Morse, 1982). Miller (1983) further showed that, at 6 months, infants generalized habituation to the voices of either sex to novel members of the habituated gender category, indicating that they were truly responding to male and female voices categorically rather than simply discriminating any new voice. Miller also showed that by 7 months infants were sensitive to other differ-

ences between male and female voices in addition to differences in pitch. These differences remain to be identified but may include known differences in intonation patterns (Brend, 1971) and formant frequencies (Sachs, 1975).

Researchers of habituation and visual preference have shown that infants well under 1 year of age can discriminate individual male and female faces (Cornell, 1974; Fagan, 1976) and that the features that define faces as male or female contribute more to 5- and 6-month-old infants' ability to recognize whether a face is familiar than does the lack of feature similarity (Fagan & Singer, 1979). However, although the discrimination of individual male and female faces undoubtedly underlies recognition of them as members of separate categories, it does not demonstrate possession of the categories.

The possibility of early categorical responding to female faces has been indicated (Cohen & Strauss, 1979). At 7 months, infants who had been habituated to a series of female faces in various orientations generalized habituation to a familiar face in a new orientation and to an entirely new female face as well. Although this widely cited study has been credited by some authors with showing categorical perception of females and males (e.g., Gibson & Spelke, 1983), only female faces were used. These infants could have been habituated to faces in general rather than to female faces as a category. The possibility of categorical perception of female faces was not ruled out; had a male face been presented, it might well have been perceived as novel. The need to clarify this issue prompted a study to use faces of both sexes in a partial replication and extension of Cohen and Strauss's (1979) study.

Leinbach and Fagot (1993) used Cohen and Strauss's (1979) infant-controlled procedure to habituate infants at 5, 7, 9, and 12 months of age to a series of faces of one sex (familiar category), then tested them with a new face from the familiar category and, as a contrast category, a face of the opposite sex. At both 9 and 12 months, fixation times were greater for the contrast test than for the familiar test or the posthabituation mean. On the basis of the group data, we can say with certainty only that, by

9 months, infants demonstrated categorical perception of male and female faces. However, even at 5 and 7 months of age, some individual infants indicated clear recovery of interest when the face from the contrast category appeared. Consequently, adapting Reznick and Kagan's (1983) criterion for recovery of interest (dishabituation), Leinbach and Fagot (1993) credited infants with categorical perception of male and female faces if their fixation time to the contrast test exceeded their mean fixation times for the familiar test and the mean of their posthabituation test by 20% or more. This is a fairly strong criterion in that it attempts to avoid attributing dishabituation to infants whose contrast fixation time is within the range of fixation times shown after habituation. By this standard, 75% of the infants at 12 months, 50% at 9 months, 20% at 7 months, and 35% at 5 months indicated categorical perception of male and female faces.

Intons-Peterson (1988) found that hair length was a major cue for recognition of the sexes in children. Leinbach and Fagot (1993) used the habituation procedure described above to investigate the relative importance of hair and clothing cues in 12-month-old infants' categorical discrimination of male and female faces. The same stimulus materials were used as in the first study, with the following changes. One group of 20 infants saw the pictures with clothing altered so that men and women alike appeared to be wearing dark, turtle-necked shirts. A second group saw the same set of faces, but with the women's hair carefully trimmed so that men's and women's hair appeared approximately the same length. A third group saw the same faces, with clothing altered as for the first group and women's hair trimmed as for the second. The 12-month-old infants in the previous study, who saw the unaltered stimuli, served as a control group. All procedures and criteria for habituation and dishabituation remained as before. Sixty-five percent of the children seeing pictures with hair untrimmed met the criterion for dishabituation; this proportion is not significantly different from the 75% dishabituation rate in the control condition. When hair only was altered, 40% dishabituated, and when both hair and clothing were altered, 25% dishabitu-

ated; these proportions differed significantly from the control condition but not from each other. Results for the hair-altered groups suggest that some infants' "gender categories" could consist mainly of long- and short-haired people. This calls for caution in attributing categorical discrimination of gender in infants who may be responding to fairly superficial features rather than to conceptual categories. This is an issue that begs for further investigation. Another pressing issue involves the identification of cues infants use in discriminating males and females. In Fagan and Singer's (1979) study, infants between 5 and 6 months of age could apparently tell the difference between a bald-headed baby and a bald-headed man, and between an adult brother and sister, both with short hair, who resembled each other strongly. Just which aspects of facial structure infants are sensitive to remains to be seen. We believe that infants at the end of their first year have clearly begun the process of categorizing people according to gender, but the step from recognizing or perceiving the sexes categorically to conscious awareness of this distinction is a large one.

Single-modality studies of voice and face perception indicate early recognition of certain male and female attributes, but in the real world, faces, voices, and tactile cues are all of a piece. There is some evidence that infants respond cross-modally to voice and visual cues. Therefore, we would expect that infants would respond differentially to real men and women even more readily than to the disembodied stimuli used in empirical studies. Fagot and Leinbach (1994) did not find any relation between the gender-typed traditionality of the home environment and the child's habituation to faces, so that there is still much work to be done in understanding the beginnings of the gender process. We have evidence that infants are attending to gender cues, that they associate the relation among some environmental cues (i.e., hair length and gender), but prior to 12 months the process of gender categorization is mostly dependent upon the infant's processing capacities rather than socialization variables.

The next step: The importance of gender labels. Maccoby (1980) stated that the first step toward knowing what it means to be male or female consists of self-labeling, an ability unlikely to be secure before the age of two. Such a statement reflects the cognitive-developmental view that young children construct their knowledge of the world at the level their mental capabilities permit, an approach that assumes that acquisition of sex-typical behaviors and attitudes comes after the child's self-perceived identity as a boy or girl. However, in emphasizing attainment of successively higher levels of reasoning, cognitive-developmental theory appears to overestimate the degree of understanding children must possess before knowledge of sex typing can be shown and can begin to affect behavior. Tests of gender knowledge have been constructed to ensure that achievement of a particular level is not credited unless a correct judgment of a child's gender can be held fast in the face of perceptual transformation of the stimulus. Such stringent criteria tend to mask early knowledge and to leave children under 3 years old looking curiously incompetent with regard to gender. An example of such a test is the Slaby and Frey (1975) interview, in which children are asked a series of items starting with the question of whether they are a boy or girl. The children are asked the question three times with different wording, which confuses young children. Recent investigators indicate that children's knowledge of categories is greater than their typically poor performance on classification tasks would suggest, and that even young children use category labels to support inductive inferences about category members. In particular, children who are unable to classify objects on the basis of shared properties are often quite adept at inferring properties when presented with category labels (Gelman & Markman, 1986). Gelman, Collman, and Maccoby (1986) have extended this finding to early gender knowledge. They taught children that boys had "andro" in their blood whereas girls had "estro." Young children without gender constancy had no difficulty saying that a child labeled as a boy, even though the picture looked feminine, would have "andro" and not "estro" in his blood, but children had extreme difficulty with the same picture if they were simply told that a child had "andro" in its blood and asked to name the sex of the child. Gelman et al.

(1986) proposed that even very young children can recognize gender category labels as important pieces of information that permit inferences about enduring properties of the category members.

Even before other children can be categorized accurately, a child may be acquiring information about what boys and girls are supposed to look like or do. When gender labels can be used to designate self and others correctly, children should be able to use whatever gender knowledge they have to inform their own behavior and interpret that of others around them. Thus, we see labeling as a milestone on the road to gender understanding, a milestone that signals a change from perceptual discrimination and tacit knowledge to conscious awareness of the separate categories and the ability to use this information deliberately.

Ascertaining the onset of accurate labeling calls for a testing procedure that takes the toddler's limited verbal ability into account and is sensitive to the beginning of competence. Children just learning to talk seem to understand much more than they can say and must be given a simple task and nonverbal response mode if they are to demonstrate what they know.

Using a modified version of Thompson's (1975) gender labeling task, in which children were asked to point to paired pictures of men and women or boys and girls, Fagot (1985a) tested 64 children between 20 and 30 months of age. The children were also given the gender identity questions from the Slaby and Frey (1975) interview. The results identified three levels of gender knowledge. One group of children gave the correct gender label to 75% of the pictures on the gender labeling task and answered the Slaby and Frey (1975) gender identity questions correctly. The second group gave the correct gender labels but failed the gender identity questions. The third group neither gave correct gender labels nor answered the gender identity questions correctly. Fagot (1985a) then compared the groups with regard to adoption of sex-typed behaviors in playgroups. Children of both sexes in groups 1 and 2 spent an average of 80% of their time in same-sex groups, whereas children who did not have gender labels spent only 50% of their time in same-sex groups. There were no differences in the performance of children who knew only gender labels and those who knew gender labels and answered the gender identity questions correctly.

For other sex-typical behaviors, the relation to labeling was more complicated. For girls, the three groups did not differ in the amount of time spent with male-typical and female-typical toys. For boys, there was no significant difference in amount of time spent with male-typical toys, but boys who did not know gender labels spent more time with female-typical toys than boys who knew the labels. In particular, boys without knowledge of gender labels or gender identity played with dolls at rates about equal to girls' rates, but this behavior was almost nonexistent in boys who showed some knowledge of gender labels. Because the effects of age differences were not assessed, and because the criterion for passing the gender labeling task was not strong (75% of the items correct on a two-choice test), these results may be regarded as suggestive but not definitive.

The need for a better way to assess early gender knowledge led us to develop a gender labeling task for young children (Leinbach & Fagot, 1986). The task was designed to be simple to administer and psychometrically sound and, at the same time, easy and nonthreatening enough to reveal what knowledge of gender labels the child might have. It involved showing the child a series of pictures of the two sexes (head and shoulders only) and assessing the child's ability to choose the named member of each pair more consistently than chance responding would predict. Because pilot work indicated that many children can discriminate men and women before they can identify boys and girls, separate sets of adult and child stimulus pictures were prepared. To ensure that the children were able to follow instructions and to point to pictures (so that failure could be attributed to lack of gender knowledge rather than inability to perform the task), a pretest consisting of pictures of familiar objects and animals was also prepared.

There were no sex differences in performance on the gender tasks. Nearly all of the children had mastered the adult discrimination before they were able to discriminate boys and girls, a result which is consistent with the findings of Weinraub et al. (1984).

Fewer than 8% of the children younger than the group's median age of 26 months passed the child picture task, whereas 50% of those older than 26 months passed. For the adult test, 55% of the children younger and 97% of those older than 26 months passed. This difference in the age of mastery is not surprising considering the importance of parents to young children; these children could surely recognize their own parents, and label them as well (labels for adults are usually in use by 16 months of age). In addition, adults are undoubtedly more discriminable than children in that they show greater differences in facial features, clothing, and hairstyles.

The age ranges of the children succeeding at each test varied greatly. Some passed the child labeling test as early as 24 months, but failure occurred as late as 40 months. For the adult discrimination, success occurred as early as 19 months, and no child older than 27 months failed. The greater variability in the age at which the sex of children is discriminated may stem from the child's family experience. Although parents who are strongly sex typed, especially fathers, may foster earlier awareness of gender in their children, as Weinraub et al. (1984) have suggested, we need to know more about the correlates of gender label acquisition.

Although the development of gender labeling is an interesting issue in its own right, an even more important question concerns how the acquisition of gender labels is related to sex-typed behavior. Fagot, Leinbach, and Hagan (1986) investigated the relation between gender labeling and naturally occurring sex-typed behavior during the period in which labeling begins and behavioral sex differences appear in areas over which the child can exert some control. The gender labeling task (Leinbach & Fagot, 1986) was used to measure the child's understanding of labels for adults and children. Three categories of behavior (preference for same-sex rather than opposite-sex playmates, aggressive actions, and choice of sex-typed toys) were designated for naturalistic observation. These categories were chosen because they represented areas in which evidence for early sex typing had been found most consistently and because they involve purposeful behavior on the part of the child.

We hypothesized that the ability to label boys and girls correctly would be related to the adoption of sex-typed behaviors. Specifically, we predicted that boys and girls who used the labels accurately would exhibit greater same-sex peer preference and toy choice than those who did not. Because males at all ages exhibit more aggression than females (Maccoby & Jacklin, 1980; Zahn-Waxler, 1993; Zoccolillo, 1993), and as a society we expect this to be so, learning to conform to prevailing standards of behavior would move aggression scores for boys and girls in opposite directions. Thus, we expected rates of aggression for boys who used the labels accurately to remain stable or rise and rates for girls who used the labels accurately to decline.

We found again that children could make adult discriminations earlier than child discriminations, and again there was more variability in the age at which children passed the child task. The ability to label adults was not related to any measure of adoption of sex-typed behaviors. Two of the predictions concerning the relation between gender labeling of children and adoption of sex-typed behaviors were confirmed. Children who labeled the pictures of boys and girls correctly played significantly more with same-sex playmates than did children who failed to label correctly. In addition, girls who passed the labeling task behaved significantly less aggressively than girls who failed the task. However, although boys avoided female-typed toys and played with male-typed toys significantly longer than girls, sex-typed toy choice was not related to gender labeling. Thus, we failed to replicate Fagnot's (1985b) finding that labeling preceded preference for sex-typed toys and supported the findings of Weinraub et al. (1984) that self-reported preference for sex-typed toys preceded gender categorization and gender identity.

The data in the Fagot et al. (1986) study were cross-sectional, and some of the children who were tested may well have had gender labels for some time. Therefore, the exact nature of the relation between sex-typed behavior and gender labeling remains an open question. To untie contextual effects from gender labeling effects, a definitive study would need to examine children's contact with each other over time. To do this, Fagot (1990) used a longitudinal sample followed from age 18 months to 4 years. The findings of Fagot et al. (1986) were replicated, as was the expected change in same- and opposite-sex play, with boys dropping opposite-sex play almost completely after gender labels were learned, and both boys and girls increasing same-sex play. Again, gender segregation increased after the learning of labels, and aggression dropped for girls.

Fagot and Leinbach (1989) used the same longitudinal sample of children followed from 18 months to 4 years of age to examine the development of gender labeling and its relation to parenting behaviors and to children's adoption of sex-typed behaviors. Children who know correct child gender labels before 27 months of age (early labelers) had parents who gave more emotionally charged reactions (both positive and negative) to the children's sex-typed behaviors at 18 months. Fathers of early labelers had more traditional attitudes toward sex roles than fathers of late labelers. At 18 months, the children did not differ in their activities; by 27 months early labelers played more with sex-typed toys; the girls were less aggressive and communicated more with adults. At age 4, children who were early labelers knew more about gender categories, but they did not necessarily have stronger preferences for same-sex activities. Preference tests may be more sensitive than knowledge tests to socialization pressures of the moment, and less related to cognitive processing.

I interpret the results of this group of studies as indicating that early labeling is promoted by parental attention when the child is involved in sex-typed play and by greater parental endorsement of traditional sex typing, especially by fathers. This may sensitize the child to gender information and make gender a more salient aspect of everyday life. Early labelers may encounter more situations in which to practice sex-typed behaviors, suggesting a broader knowledge base from which to elaborate gender schemas. Thus, the early labeler has a longer period of time spent in a more sex-typed atmosphere in which to practice sex-typed behaviors and consolidate sex-typed knowledge and attitudes. As Staub (1979) noted with regard to prosocial behavior, direct participation—rehearsal of the behavior in question—may determine to a great extent whether delayed repetition and generalization of the behavior occurs. This, in turn, provides an important source of learning. Although it is true that the later labelers catch up, the enduring consequences and other correlates of early labeling should be investigated further, along with the cognitive processes underlying the progression from early discrimination of males and females to the advent of accurate labeling.

GENDER SCHEMA THEORY

Martin and Halverson (1981) and Bem (1981) proposed that specific cognitive processes would influence children's gender-related beliefs and behavior. These theorists assumed that children's developing cognitive abilities or knowledge structures would shape children's beliefs and behaviors. The research since 1981 has shown that children develop information about gender in a fashion consistent with their cognitive capacities; however, a consistent effect on behavior or even on beliefs has not been found. Martin (1993) proposed that gender information is not organized in the hierarchical fashion proposed by early schema proponents, but instead is organized into components. Information is organized into context domains, such as family-role behaviors and occupations, and the components are placed into two overriding groups, male and female. Because the information can come from different sources and at different times, the components are not necessarily highly related but instead are loosely held together by the overriding categories of male and female. Gender schemas then are not tightly organized hierarchies of information but are instead loosely organized components of information from many different sources. Children make inferences across components on the basis of the broad categories of male and female, and some of the memory failures and overgeneralizations we see are a consequence of using one component to infer another. For instance, we have many examples of children whose parent is in a job that contradicts sex stereotypes stating that only one sex can do the job, stating that only women can be nurses or only men can be carpenters, even though their own parent contradicts the stereotype. It is almost as if the power of the gender schema overrides what the child knows about his or her own individual world.

What might the earliest form of gender schema contain? Children's use of object and activity stereotypes is well documented (Kuhn, Nash, & Brucken, 1977; Martin & Little, 1990), but there is more to stereotyping than accumulating knowledge about who has or does what. Perhaps it is time to move beyond testing children on the conventional "dolls are for girls, trucks are for boys" stereotyping of earlier studies. Gender schemas must also include dimensions of meaning that underlie the concepts of masculinity and femininity. Leinbach, Fagot, and Hort (in press) found suggestions of such dimensions in preschoolers. Four-year-old children assigned bears, fire, and something rough to boys and men, and butterflies, hearts, and flowers to women and girls. We strongly doubt that such notions are taught directly. True, children may observe women, more often than men, with or wearing flowers, but do they see men in the company of bears or women with butterflies? It is at least plausible that these youngsters have begun to associate qualities such as strength or dangerousness with males, and gentler qualities with females, whether or not they can name the attributes involved. The recent surge of interest in metaphor as a cognitive process makes this suggestion somewhat less outlandish than it would have seemed a few years ago.

Johnson (1987) departed from traditional views of category and concept formation to assert that metaphorical projections based on our experience, particularly the constraints on experience imposed by the kind of body we live in, constitute a primary way of understanding the world. As Johnson (1987) put it, "Our reality is shaped by the patterns of our bodily movement, the contours of our spatial and temporal orientation, and the forms of our interaction with objects" (p. xix). If this notion is correct, then the "metaphorical" associations with gender Bem (1981) decries, such as the roundedness or angularity of an abstract shape, may have their roots in the infant's different sensory experience of men and women—their shape and texture, the sounds they make, their movement patterns, and so on.

Children do appear to make rather abstract assumptions on the basis of appearance. C. L. Martin (personal communication, October 19, 1990) described a study in which children were shown "creatures from outer space" with two different head shapes. Children assigned gender to these creatures on the basis of the different head shapes, seeming to believe that if things look different they must be different in other ways as well. Because sex is a well known, salient category for children, they then went on from their knowledge of gender to derive complex rules about these creatures. Martin suggested that it is almost as though children can formulate extremely abstract rules or theories from their body of information about gender, and she hypothesized that children learn to generalize from their metaphorical knowledge to more abstract planes.

THE WORKING OUT OF GENDER SCRIPTS

Children begin organizing their knowledge at a very young age by categorizing and labeling, but as children move beyond infancy, the way gender knowledge is organized becomes more complex. One interesting line of gender research concerns children's use of gender scripts. Within the general study of cognitive development, scripts have been posited as one way in which children facilitate many cognitive skills. A script is seen as a generalized or temporally ordered representation (Nelson, 1981). Children as young as 3 years possess generalized and well-organized knowledge about familiar events (Hudson & Nelson, 1983; Nelson & Gruendel, 1981). The paradigm has been to present children with scrambled events and ask them to order them in terms of time. It is clear that the child's cognitive capacities and social experiences both influence that child's abilities to perform these tasks. For instance, Fivush and Mandler (1985) used a familiar event, such as going to McDonald's, versus an unfamiliar event, such as going parachute jumping, to study the in-

creasing cognitive skills of children from 4 to 6. Younger children could sequence familiar events but had a much harder time with unfamiliar events, suggesting that the younger children needed familiar cues to help them perform such tasks. Boston and Levy (1991) examined 4- and 5-year-old children's ability to sequence scrambled masculine and feminine scripts. Older children were more competent at providing the correct sequence of events. Girls were equally accurate on feminine and masculine scripts, whereas boys were more accurate on masculine scripts. Even the youngest children showed some ability to correctly sequence the gender scripts. As predicted by the work of Nelson (1981), taxonomic knowledge, as represented by the Sex Role Knowledge score on the Sex Role Learning Inventory (Edelbrock & Sugawara, 1978), was not correlated with correct sequencing. The finding that girls appear to attend to the gender scripts for both their own and the other sex more equally than do boys was confirmed by Bauer (1992) with 24- to 26-month-old children. Both the Bauer, and Boston and Levy (1991) findings show an avoidance of feminine scripts by boys rather than just more knowledge of the male stereotype by boys. It is therefore difficult to untangle the cognitive understanding of the child from the motivation to perform. This study is consistent with the behavioral data reported by O'Brien and Huston (1985) that boys tend to avoid female play behavior at an earlier age than girls avoid male play behaviors. We know that boys are given more negative feedback when they perform opposite-sex play behaviors than girls (Fagot, 1977, 1989), so we have some suggestions that boys' greater adherence to male knowledge and stereotypes is at least in part motivational.

Individual differences in children's ability to sequence gender scripts correctly has not been studied in relation to social aspects of the child's environment. It would be interesting to know if children from more traditional homes are better at sequencing gender scripts or if perhaps such children would avoid other-sex scripts. However, we cannot assume that environmental differences would have such an impact, given the findings of Boston and Levy (1991) that gender knowledge was not related to scripts, which once again confirmed the findings of Sears, Rau, and Alpert (1965) and Hort, Leinbach, and Fagot (1991) that different measures of gender may not be related in an easy-to-understand, linear fashion.

SUMMARY

The study of gender development has come a long way since Mischel (1966) and Kohlberg (1966) presented supposedly opposing theories of gender-role development. Today, few researchers would say that gender should be studied as strictly a socialization or strictly a cognitive process. Instead, during the past 10 years, there have been many attempts to understand how the environment works upon the child in collaboration with the child's own construction of the environment. At this point, the psychological literature does not interface with the biological findings reported by Hines and Collaer (1993). However, as we are beginning to develop behavioral tests for intact brain functioning, it seems that the moment to bring together the biological underpinnings of cognitive

and affective processes that are related to gender differences may have come.

Why are young children so consistent in their gender role development? The answer of this article is that gender-role development is overdetermined. The environmental information received by the child is relatively consistent. We may argue over effect sizes for socialization differences, but we do not argue about the direction of the differences. In addition, the regularity of children's cognitive development leads them to use environmental information in very specific ways. Once the patterns of thinking and patterns of behavior are adopted, then the culture, particularly the peer group, maintains them. Children learn that it is perilous to try out behaviors of the other sex, although less so for girls than for boys. It is important though to understand that when we talk about sex differences we are discussing the content of gender schema and not differences in the process by which they come to put these schema together. Boys and girls may receive different messages from the environment, but the way they use their knowledge is a function of their underlying human abilities to process information.

REFERENCES

Bauer, P. A. (1992). Memory for gender consistent and inconsistent event sequences by 25-month-old children, *Child Development, 64,* 285–297.

Bem, S. L. (1981). Gender schema theory: A cognitive account of sex typing. *Psychological Review, 88,* 354–364.

Block, J. H. (1976). Issues, problems, and pitfalls in assessing sex differences: A critical review of "The psychology of sex differences." *Merrill-Palmer Quarterly, 22,* 283–308.

Block, J. H. (1983). Differential premises arising from conjectures. *Child Development, 54,* 1335–1354.

Blurton-Jones, N. G. (Ed.). (1972). *Ethological studies of child behavior.* London: Cambridge University Press.

Boston, M. B., & Levy, G. D. (1991). Changes and differences in preschoolers' understanding of gender scripts. *Cognitive Development, 6,* 417–432.

Brend, R. M. (1971). Male-female intonation patterns in American English. *Proceedings of the Seventh International Congress of Phonetic Sciences,* 866–869. The Hague: Mouton.

Brophy, J., & Good, T. L. (1974). *Teacher-student relationships: Causes and consequences.* New York: Holt, Rinehart and Winston.

Carpenter, C. J. (1983). Activity structure and play: Implications for socialization. In M. B. Liss (Ed.), *Social and cognitive skills: Sex roles and children's play* (pp. 117–145). New York: Academic Press.

Carpenter, C. J., & Huston, A. J. (1980). Activity structure and sex-typed behavior in preschool children. *Child Development, 51,* 862–872.

Carter, D. B., & Levy, G. D. (1988). Cognitive aspects of early sex-role development: The influence of gender schemas on preschoolers' memories and preferences for sex-typed toys and activities, *Child Development, 59,* 782–792.

Charlesworth, R., & Hartup, W. W. (1967). Positive social reinforcement in the nursery school peer group. *Child Development, 38,* 315–320.

Clarke-Stewart, F. A. (1978). And daddy makes three: The father's influence on mother and young child. *Child Development, 49,* 466–478.

Cohen, L. B., & Strauss, M. S. (1979). Concept acquisition in the human infant. *Child Development, 50,* 419–424.

Collins, W. A., & Russell, G. (1991). Mother-child and father-child relationships in middle childhood and adolescence. *Developmental Review, 11,* 99–136.

Condry, J., & Condry, S. (1976). Sex differences: A study of the eye of the beholder. *Child Development, 47,* 812–819.

Cornell, E. (1974). Infants' discriminations of photographs following redundant presentations. *Journal of Experimental Child Psychology, 18,* 98–106.

Damon, W. (1977). *The social world of the child.* San Francisco: Jossey-Bass.

DiPietro, J. (1981). Rough and tumble play: A function of gender. *Developmental Psychology, 17,* 50–58.

Edelbrock, C., & Sugawara, A. I. (1978). Acquisition of sex-typed preferences in preschool-aged children. *Developmental Psychology, 14,* 614–623.

Emmerich, W., Goldman, K., Kirsh, B., & Sharabany, R. (1977). Evidence for a transitional phase in the development of gender constancy. *Child Development, 48,* 930–936.

Etaugh, C., Collins, G., & Gerson, A. (1975). Reinforcement of sex-typed behaviors of two-year-old children in a nursery school setting. *Developmental Psychology, 11,* 255.

Fabes, R. A. (1994). Physiological, emotional, and behavioral correlates of gender segregation. In C. Leaper (Vol. Ed.), W. Damon (Series Ed.), *New directions for child development: The development of gender and relationships* (pp. 19–24). San Francisco: Jossey-Bass.

Fagan, J. F. (1976). Infants' recognition of invariant features of faces. *Child Development, 47,* 627–638.

Fagan, J. F., & Singer, L. T. (1979). The role of simple feature differences in infant recognition of faces. *Infant Behavior and Development, 2,* 39–46.

Fagot, B. I. (1973a). Influence of teacher behavior in the preschool. *Developmental Psychology, 9,* 198–206.

Fagot, B. I. (1973b). Sex-related stereotyping of toddlers' behaviors. *Developmental Psychology, 9,* 429.

Fagot, B. I. (1974). Sex differences in toddlers' behavior and parental reaction. *Developmental Psychology, 10,* 554–558.

Fagot, B. I. (1977). Consequences of moderate cross-gender behavior in preschool children. *Child Development, 48,* 902–907.

Fagot, B. I. (1981). Male and female teachers: Do they treat boys and girls differently? *Sex Roles, 7,* 263–271.

Fagot, B. I. (1985a). Changes in thinking about early sex role development. *Developmental Review, 5,* 83–98.

Fagot, B. I. (1985b). Beyond the reinforcement principle: Another step toward understanding sex role development. *Developmental Psychology, 21,* 1092–1104.

Fagot, B. I. (1989). Cross-gender behavior and its consequences for boys. *Italian Journal of Clinical and Cultural Psychology, 1,* 79–84.

Fagot, B. I. (1990). A longitudinal study of gender segregation: Infancy to preschool. In F. Strayer (Chair), *Determinants of gender differences in peer relations.* Symposium presented at the International Conference on Infant Studies, Montreal, Canada.

Fagot, B. I., & Hagan, R. (1991). Observations of parent reactions to sex-stereotyped behavior: Age and sex effects. *Child Development, 62,* 617–628.

Fagot, B. I., Hagan R., Leinbach, M. D., & Kronsberg, S. (1985). Differential reactions to assertive and communicative acts of toddler boys and girls. *Child Development, 56,* 1499–1505.

Fagot, B. I., & Leinbach, M. D. (1989). The young child's gender schema: Environmental input, internal organization. *Child Development, 60,* 663–672.

Fagot, B. I., & Leinbach, M. D. (1994). Gender-role development in young children. In M. Stevenson (Ed.), *Gender roles through the life span* (pp. 3–24). Muncie, IN: Ball State University Press.

Fagot, B. I., & Leinbach, M. D. (1995). Gender knowledge in egalitarian and traditional families, *Sex Roles, 32,* 513–526.

Fagot, B. I., Leinbach, M. D., & Hagan, R. (1986). Gender labeling and adoption of sex-typed behaviors. *Developmental Psychology, 22,* 440–443.

Fagot, B. I., & Patterson, G. R. (1969). An in vivo analysis of reinforcing contingencies for sex-role behaviors in the preschool child. *Developmental Psychology, 1,* 563–568.

Feldbaum, C. L., Christenson, T. E., & O'Neal, E. C. (1980). An observational study of the assimilation of the newcomer to the preschool. *Child Development, 51,* 497–507.

Fivush, R., & Mandler, J. M. (1985). Developmental changes in the understanding of temporal sequences. *Child Development, 56,* 1437–1446.

Furstenberg, F., Brooks-Gunn, J., & Chase-Lonsdale, L. (1989). Teenage pregnancy and childbearing. *American Psychologist, 44,* 313–320.

Gelman, S., Collman, P., & Maccoby, E. E. (1986). Inferring properties from categories versus inferring categories from properties: The case of gender. *Child Development, 57,* 396–404.

Gelman, S. A., & Markman, E. M. (1986). Categories and induction in young children. *Cognition, 23,* 183–209.

Gibson, E. J., & Spelke, E. S. (1983). The development of perception. In J. H. Flavell & E. M. Markman (Eds.), P. H. Mussen (Series Ed.), *Handbook of child psychology, Vol. 3. Cognitive development* (pp. 1–76). New York: Wiley.

Gjerde, P. F. (1986). The interpersonal structure of family interaction settings: Parent-adolescent relations in dyads and triads. *Developmental Psychology, 22,* 297–304.

Goodall, J. (1986). *The chimpanzees of Gombe: Patterns of behavior.* Cambridge, MA: Harvard University Press.

Hetherington, E. M., & Clingempeel, W. G. (1992). Coping with marital transitions: A family systems perspective. *Monographs of the Society for Research in Child Development, 57*(2–3, Serial No. 227).

Hetherington, E. M., Cox, M., & Cox, R. (1982). Effects of divorce on parents and children. In M. E. Lamb (Ed.),

Nontraditional families (pp. 233–288). Hillsdale, NJ: Lawrence Erlbaum.

Hines, M., & Collaer, M. L. (1993). Gonadal hormones and sexual differentiation of human behavior: Developments from research on endocrine systems and studies of brain structure. *Annual Review of Sex Research, 4,* 1–48.

Hort, B. E., Leinbach, M. D., & Fagot, B. I. (1991). Is there coherence among the components of gender acquisition? *Sex Roles, 24,* 195–207.

Hudson, J., & Nelson, K. (1983). Effects of script structure on children's story recall. *Developmental Psychology, 19,* 623–635.

Huston, A. C. (1983). Sex-typing. In P. H. Mussen (Series Ed.), E. M. Hetherington. (Vol. Ed.), *Handbook of child psychology: Vol. 4. Socialization, personality, and social development* (pp. 387–467). New York: Wiley.

Intons-Peterson, M. J. (1988). *Children's concepts of gender.* Norwood, NJ: Ablex.

Johnson, M. (1987). *The body in the mind.* Chicago: University of Chicago Press.

Johnson, M. M. (1963). Sex role learning in the nuclear family. *Child Development, 34,* 315–333.

Johnson, M. M. (1975). Fathers, mothers, and sex typing. *Sociological Inquiry, 45,* 15–26.

Jusczyk, P. W., Pisoni, D. B., & Mullinnex, J. (1992). Some consequences of stimulus variability on speech processing by 2-month-old infants. *Cognition, 43,* 253–291.

Kohlberg, L. (1966). A cognitive-developmental analysis of children's sex-role concepts and attitudes. In E. Maccoby (Ed.), *The development of sex differences* (pp. 82–173). Stanford, CA: Stanford University Press.

Kuhn, D., Nash, S. C., & Brucken, L. (1977). Sex role concepts of two- and three-year-olds. *Child Development, 49,* 445–451.

Lamb, M. E. (1977). Father-infant and mother-infant interaction in the first year of life. *Child Development, 48,* 167–181.

Lamb, M. E. (1981). The development of father-infant relationships. In M. E. Lamb (Ed.), *The role of the father in child development* (Rev. ed., pp. 459–488). New York: Wiley.

Leaper, C. (1994). Exploring the consequences of gender segregation on social relationships. In C. Leaper (Vol. Ed.), W. Damon (Series Ed.), *New directions for child development: The development of gender and relationships* (pp. 67–86). San Francisco: Jossey-Bass.

Lee, P. C., & Kedar-Voivodas, G. (1977). Sex role and pupil role in early childhood education. In L. Katz (Ed.), *Current topics in early childhood education. Vol. 1* (pp. 105–118). Norwood, NJ: Ablex.

Leinbach, M. D., & Fagot, B. I. (1986). Acquisition of gender labeling: A test for toddlers. *Sex Roles, 15,* 655–666.

Leinbach, M. D., & Fagot, B. I. (1993). Categorical habituation to male and female faces: Gender schematic processing in infancy. *Infant Behavior and Development, 16,* 317–332.

Leinbach, M. D., Fagot, B. I., & Hort, B. (in press). Bears are for boys: "Metaphorical" associations in the young child's gender schema. *Cognitive Development.*

Leve, L., & Fagot, B. I. (1995). *The role of parental marital status, parent gender, and child gender on sex-role traditionality and discipline practices.* Manuscript submitted for publication.

Lytton, H., & Romney, D. M. (1991). Parents' sex-related differential socialization of boys and girls: A meta-analysis. *Psychological Bulletin, 109,* 267–296.

Maccoby, E. E. (1980). *Social development: Psychological growth and the parent-child relationship.* New York: Harcourt Brace.

Maccoby, E. E. (1988). Gender as a social category. *Developmental Psychology, 24,* 755–765.

Maccoby, E. E. (1994). Commentary: Gender segregation in childhood. In C. Leaper (Vol. Ed.), W. Damon (Series Ed.), *New directions for child development: The development of gender and relationships* (pp. 87–98). San Francisco: Jossey-Bass.

Maccoby, E. E., & Jacklin, C. N. (1974). *The psychology of sex differences.* Stanford, CA: Stanford University Press.

Maccoby, E. E., & Jacklin, C. N. (1980). Sex differences in aggression: A rejoinder and reprise. *Child Development, 51,* 964–980.

Maccoby, E. E., & Jacklin, C. N. (1987). Gender segregation in childhood. In H. A. Reese (Ed.), *Advances in child behavior and development* (Vol. 20, pp. 239–287). San Diego: Academic Press.

Marcus, D., & Overton, W. F. (1978). The development of cognitive gender constancy and sex role preferences. *Child Development, 49,* 434–444.

Martin, C. A. (1991). The role of cognition in understanding gender effects. *Advances in Child Development and Behavior, 23,* 113–149.

Martin, C. A. (1993). New directions for investigating children's gender knowledge. *Developmental Review, 13,* 184–204.

Martin, C. A., & Halverson, C. F. (1981). A schematic processing model of sex typing and stereotyping in children. *Child Development, 52,* 1119–1134.

Martin, C. A., & Little, J. K. (1990). The relation of gender understanding on children's sex-typed preferences and gender stereotypes. *Child Development, 61,* 1427–1439.

Miller, C. L. (1983). Developmental changes in male/female voice classification by infants. *Infant Behavior and Development, 6,* 313–330.

Miller, C. L., Younger, B. A., & Morse, P. A. (1982). The categorization of male and female voices in infancy. *Infant Behavior and Development, 5,* 143–159.

Mischel, W. (1966). A social-learning view of sex differences in behavior. In E. E. Maccoby (Ed.), *The development of sex differences* (pp. 56–81). Stanford, CA: Stanford University Press.

Nelson, K. (1981). Social cognition in a script framework. In J. H. Flavell & L. Ross (Eds.). *Social cognitive development: Frontiers and possible selves* (pp. 97–118). New York: Cambridge university Press.

Nelson, K., & Gruendel, J. (1981). Generalized event representations: Basic building blocks of cognitive development. In M. E. Lamb & A. L. Brown (Eds.). *Advances in developmental psychology* (Vol. 1, pp. 131–158). Hillsdale, NJ: Lawrence Erlbaum.

O'Brien, M., & Huston, A. C. (1985). Development of sex-typed play behaviors in toddlers. *Developmental Psychology, 21,* 866–871.

Parsons, T., & Bales, R. (1955). *Family socialization and interactive process.* Glencoe, IL: Free Press.

Patterson, G. R., Reid, J. B., & Dishion, T. J. (1992). *Antisocial boys.* Eugene, OR: Castalia.

Pederson, F. A. (1980). *The father-infant relationship: Observational studies in the family setting.* New York: Praeger.

Reznick, J. S., & Kagan, J. (1983). Category detection in infancy. In L. P. Lipsett & C. K. Rovee-Collier (Eds.), *Advances in infancy research* (Vol. 2, pp. 79–111). Norwood, NJ: Ablex.

Rheingold, H. L., & Cook, K. V. (1975). The contents of boys' and girls' rooms as an index of parent behavior. *Child Development, 46,* 459–463.

Rogoff, B. (1990). *Apprenticeship in thinking: Cognitive development in social context.* New York: Oxford University Press.

Russell, A., & Russell, G. E. (1988). Mothers' and fathers' explanations of observed interactions with their children. *Journal of Applied Developmental Psychology, 9.* 421–440.

Sachs, J. (1975). Cues to the identification of sex. In B. Thorne & N. Henley (Eds.). *Language and sex: Difference and dominance* (pp. 152–171). Rowley, MA: Newbury House.

Sadker, M., & Sadker, D. (1994). *Failing at fairness: How America's schools cheat girls.* New York: Scribners.

Sears, R. R., Rau, L., & Alpert, R. (1965). *Identification and child rearing.* Stanford, CA: Stanford University Press.

Serbin, L. A., Connor, J. M., & Citron, C. C. (1981). Sex differentiated free play behavior: Effect of teacher modeling, location and gender. *Developmental Psychology, 17,* 640–646.

Serbin, L. A., O'Leary, K. D., Kent, R. N., & Tonick, I. J. (1973). A comparison of teacher response to preacademic and problem behavior of boys and girls. *Child Development, 44,* 796–804.

Serbin, L. A., & Sprafkin, C. (1986). The salience of gender and the process of sex-typing in three- to seven-year-old children. *Child Development, 57,* 1188–1199.

Serbin, L. A., Tonick, I. J., & Sternglanz, S. H. (1977). Shaping cooperative cross-sex play. *Child Development, 48,* 924–929.

Sexton, P. C. (1968). Schools and effeminacy. *School and Society, 96,* 273–274.

Shakin, M. Shakin, D., & Sternglanz, S. H. (1985). Infant clothing: Sex labeling for strangers. *Sex Roles, 12,* 955–963.

Siegel, M. (1987). Are sons and daughters treated more differently by fathers than by mothers? *Developmental Review, 7,* 183–209.

Slaby, R. G., & Frey, K. S. (1975). Development of gender constancy and selective attention to same-sex models. *Child Development, 46,* 849–856.

Smith, P. K., & Connolly, K. J. (1980). *The ecology of preschool behaviour.* Cambridge: Cambridge University Press.

Staub, E. (1979). *Positive social behavior and morality* (Vol. 2). New York: Academic Press.

Stevenson, M. R., & Black, K. N. (1988). Paternal absence and sex role development: A meta-analysis. *Child Development, 59,* 793–814.

Stoneman, Z., & Brody, G. H. (1981). Two's company, three makes a difference: An examination of mothers' and fathers' speech to their young children. *Child Development, 52,* 705–707.

Thompson, S. K. (1975). Gender labels and early sex role development. *Child Development, 46,* 339–347.

Trautner, H. M., Helbing, N., & Sahm, W. B. (1985). *Schlussbericht uber des VW-Projeckt 'Geschlechtstypisierung'.* Frankfurt: Munster.

Weinraub, M., Clements, L. P., Sockloff, A., Ethridge, T., Gracely, E., & Myers, B. (1984). The development of sex role stereotypes in the third year: Relationships to gender labeling, gender identity, sex typed toy preferences. *Child Development, 55,* 1493–1503.

Weinraub, M., & Frankel, J. (1977). Sex differences in parent-infant interaction during free play, departure, and separation. *Child Development, 48,* 1240–1249.

Whiting, B. B., & Edwards, C. P. (1988). *Children of different worlds: The formation of social behavior.* Cambridge: Harvard University Press.

Zahn-Waxler, C. (1993). Warriors and worriers: Gender and psychopathology. *Developmental Psychopathology, 5,* 79–90.

Zoccolillo, M. (1993). Gender and the development of conduct disorder. *Development and Psychopathology, 5,* 65–78.

CHECKPOINTS

1. Young children's gender role development is *overdetermined,* meaning that patterns of thinking, treatment by adults, and peer interactions all converge in gender role identity.

2. Recent evidence seems to suggest that knowledge about gender stereotypes and roles is not organized in a tight categorical fashion, thus allowing children to hold beliefs about gender that contradict their experience. This loose organization also explains why children so readily overgeneralize about sex and gender.

To prepare for reading the next section, think about these questions:

1. Do children, adolescents, and adults prefer same-sex versus opposite-sex companions?

2. What interactional skills would a child need to develop in order to be comfortable in same-sex versus opposite-sex groups?

GENDER SEGREGATION: CHILDHOOD, ADOLESCENCE, ADULTHOOD

Gender and Relationships
A Developmental Account

ELEANOR E. MACCOBY
Stanford University

Abstract—This article argues that behavioral differentiation of the sexes is minimal when children are observed or tested individually. Sex differences emerge primarily in social situations, and their nature varies with the gender composition of dyads and groups. Children find same-sex play partners more compatible, and they segregate themselves into same-sex groups, in which distinctive interaction styles emerge. These styles are described. As children move into adolescence, the patterns they developed in their childhood same-sex groups are carried over into cross-sex encounters in which girls' styles put them at a disadvantage. Patterns of mutual influence can become more symmetrical in intimate male-female dyads, but the distinctive styles of the two sexes can still be seen in such dyads and are subsequently manifested in the roles and relationships of parenthood. The implications of these continuities are considered.

Author's note. Correspondence concerning this article should be addressed to Eleanor E. Maccoby, Department of Psychology, Stanford University, Jordan Hall, Bldg. 420, Stanford, CA 94305-2130.

Historically, the way we psychologists think about the psychology of gender has grown out of our thinking about individual differences. We are accustomed to assessing a wide variety of attributes and skills and giving scores to individuals based on their standing relative to other individuals in a sample population. On most psychological attributes, we see wide variation among individuals, and a major focus of research has been the effort to identify correlates or sources of this variation. Commonly, what we have done is to classify individuals by some antecedent variable, such as age or some aspect of their environment, to determine how much of the variance among individuals in their performance on a given task can be accounted for by this so-called *antecedent* or *independent* variable. Despite the fact that hermaphrodites exist, almost every individual is either clearly male or clearly female. What could be more natural for psychologists than to ask how much variance among individuals is accounted for by this beautifully binary factor?

Fifteen years ago, Carol Jacklin and I put out a book summarizing the work on sex differences that had come out of the individual differences perspective (Maccoby & Jacklin, 1974). We felt at that time that the yield was thin. That is, there were very few attributes on which the average values for the two sexes differed consistently. Furthermore, even when consistent differences were found, the amount of variance accounted for by sex was small, relative to the amount of variation within each sex. Our conclusions fitted in quite well with the feminist zeitgeist of the times, when most feminists were taking a minimalist position, urging that the two sexes were basically alike and that any differences were either illusions in the eye of the beholder or reversible outcomes of social shaping. Our conclusions were challenged as having both overstated the case for sex differences (Tieger, 1980) and for having understated it (Block, 1976).

In the last 15 years, work on sex differences has become more methodologically sophisticated, with greater use of meta analyses to reveal not only the direction of sex differences but quantitative estimates of their magnitude. In my judgment, the conclusions are still quite similar to those Jacklin and I arrived at in 1974: There are still some replicable sex differences, of moderate magnitude, in performance on tests of mathematical and spatial abilities, although sex differences in verbal abilities have faded. Other aspects of intellectual performance continue to show gender equality. When it comes to attributes in the personality-social domain, results are particularly sparse and inconsistent. Studies continue to find that men are more often agents of aggression than are women (Eagly, 1987; Huston, 1985; Maccoby & Jacklin, 1980). Eagly (1983, 1987) reported

in addition that women are more easily influenced than men and that men are more altruistic in the sense that they are more likely to offer help to others. In general, however, personality traits measured as characteristics of individuals do not appear to differ systematically by sex (Huston, 1985). This no doubt reflects in part the fact that male and female persons really are much alike, and their lives are governed mainly by the attributes that all persons in a given culture have in common. Nevertheless, I believe that the null findings coming out of comparisons of male and female individuals on personality measures are partly illusory. That is, they are an artifact of our historical reliance on an individual differences perspective. Social behavior, as many have pointed out, is never a function of the individual alone. It is a function of the interaction between two or more persons. Individuals behave differently with different partners. There are certain important ways in which gender is implicated in social behavior—ways that may be obscured or missed altogether when behavior is summed across all categories of social partners.

An illustration is found in a study of social interaction between previously unacquainted pairs of young children (mean age, 33 months; Jacklin & Maccoby, 1978). In some pairs, the children had same-sex play partners; in others, the pair was made up of a boy and a girl. Observers recorded the social behavior of each child on a time-sampling basis. Each child received a score for total social behavior directed toward the partner. This score included both positive and negative behaviors (e.g., offering a toy and grabbing a toy; hugging and pushing; vocally greeting, inviting, protesting, or prohibiting). There was no overall sex difference in the amount of social behavior when this was evaluated without regard to sex of partner. But there was a powerful interaction between sex of the subject and that of the partner: Children of each sex had much higher levels of social behavior when playing with a same-sex partner than when playing with a child of the other sex. This result is consistent with the findings of Wasserman and Stern (1978) that when asked to approach another child, children as young as age three stopped farther away when the other child was of the opposite sex, indicating awareness of gender similarity or difference, and wariness toward the other sex.

The number of time intervals during which a child was simply standing passively watching the partner play with the toys was also scored. There was no overall sex difference in the frequency of this behavior, but the behavior of girls was greatly affected by the sex of the partner. With other girls, passive behavior seldom occurred; indeed, in girl-girl pairs it occurred less often than it did in boy-boy pairs. However when paired with boys, girls frequently stood on the sidelines and let the boys monopolize the toys. Clearly, the little girls in this study were not more passive than the little boys in any overall, trait-like sense. Passivity in these girls could be understood only in relation to the characteristics of their interactive partners. It was a characteristic of girls in cross-sex dyads. This conclusion may not seem especially novel because for many years we have known that social behavior is situationally specific. However, the point here is that interactive behavior is not just situationally specific, but that it depends on the gender category membership of the participants. We can account for a good deal more of the behavior if we know the gender mix of dyads, and this probably holds true for larger groups as well.

An implication of our results was that if children at this early age found same-sex play partners more compatible, they ought to prefer same-sex partners when they entered group settings that included children of both sexes. There were already many indications in the literature that children do have same-sex playmate preferences, but there clearly was a need for more systematic attention to the degree of sex segregation that prevails in naturally occurring children's groups at different ages. As part of a longitudinal study of children from birth to age six, Jacklin and I did time-sampled behavioral observation of approximately 100 children on their preschool playgrounds, and again two years later when the children were playing during school recess periods (Maccoby & Jacklin, 1987). Same-sex playmate preference was clearly apparent in preschool when the children were approximately 4½. At this age, the

children were spending nearly 3 times as much time with same-sex play partners as with children of the other sex. By age 6½, the preference had grown much stronger. At this time, the children were spending 11 times as much time with same-sex as with opposite-sex partners.

Elsewhere we have reviewed the literature on playmate choices (Maccoby, 1988; Maccoby & Jacklin, 1987), and here I will simply summarize what I believe the existing body of research shows:

1. Gender segregation is a widespread phenomenon. It is found in all the cultural settings in which children are in social groups large enough to permit choice.
2. The sex difference in the gender of preferred playmates is large in absolute magnitude, compared to sex differences found when children are observed or tested in nonsocial situations.
3. In a few instances, attempts have been made to break down children's preferences for interacting with other same-sex children. It has been found that the preferences are difficult to change.
4. Children choose same-sex playmates spontaneously in situations in which they are not under pressure from adults to do so. In modern co-educational schools, segregation is more marked in situations that have not been structured by adults than in those that have (e.g., Eisenhart & Holland, 1983). Segregation is situationally specific, and the two sexes can interact comfortably under certain conditions, for example, in an absorbing joint task, when structures and roles are set up by adults, or in nonpublic settings (Thorne, 1986).
5. Gender segregation is not closely linked to involvement in sex-typed activities. Preschool children spend a great deal of their time engaged in activities that are gender neutral, and segregation prevails in these activities as well as when they are playing with dolls or trucks.
6. Tendencies to prefer same-sex playmates can be seen among three-year-olds and at even earlier ages under some conditions. But the preferences

increase in strength between preschool and school and are maintained at a high level between the ages of 6 and at least age 11.

7. The research base is thin, but so far it appears that a child's tendency to prefer same-sex playmates has little to do with that child's standing on measures of individual differences. In particular, it appears to be unrelated to measures of masculinity or femininity and also to measures of gender schematicity (Powlishta, 1989).

Why do we see such pronounced attraction to same-sex peers and avoidance of other-sex peers in childhood? Elsewhere I have summarized evidence pointing to two factors that seem to be important in the preschool years (Maccoby, 1988). The first is the rough-and-tumble play style characteristic of boys and their orientation toward issues of competition and dominance. These aspects of male-male interaction appear to be somewhat aversive to most girls. At least, girls are made wary by male play styles. The second factor of importance is that girls find it difficult to influence boys. Some important work by Serbin and colleagues (Serbin, Sprafkin, Elman, & Doyle, 1984) indicates that between the ages of 3½ and 5½, children greatly increase the frequency of their attempts to influence their play partners. This indicates that children are learning to integrate their activities with those of others so as to be able to carry out coordinated activities. Serbin and colleagues found that the increase in influence attempts by girls was almost entirely an increase in making polite suggestions to others, whereas among boys the increase took the form of more use of direct demands. Furthermore, during this formative two-year period just before school entry, boys were becoming less and less responsive to polite suggestions, so that the style being progressively adopted by girls was progressively less effective with boys. Girls' influence style was effective with each other and was well adapted to interaction with teachers and other adults.

These asymmetries in influence patterns were presaged in our study with 33-month-old children: We found then that boys were unresponsive to the vocal prohibitions of female partners (in that they did not withdraw), although they would respond when a vocal prohibition was issued by a male partner. Girls were responsive to one another and to a male partner's prohibitions. Fagot (1985) also reported that boys are "reinforced" by the reactions of male peers—in the sense that they modify their behavior following a male peer's reaction—but that their behavior appears not to be affected by a female's response.

My hypothesis is that girls find it aversive to try to interact with someone who is unresponsive and that they begin to avoid such partners. Students of power and bargaining have long been aware of the importance of reciprocity in human relations. Pruitt (1976) said, "Influence and power are omnipresent in human affairs. Indeed, groups cannot possibly function unless their members can influence one another" (p. 343). From this standpoint, it becomes clear why boys and girls have difficulty forming groups that include children of both sexes.

Why do little boys not accept influence from little girls? Psychologists almost automatically look to the nuclear family for the origins of behavior patterns seen in young children. It is plausible that boys may have been more reinforced for power assertive behavior by their parents, and girls more for politeness, although the evidence for such differential socialization pressure has proved difficult to come by. However, it is less easy to imagine how or why parents should reinforce boys for being unresponsive to *girls*. Perhaps it is a matter of observational learning: Children may have observed that between their two parents, their fathers are more influential than their mothers. I am skeptical about such an explanation. In the first place, mothers exercise a good deal of managerial authority within the households in which children live, and it is common for fathers to defer to their judgment in matters concerning the children. Or, parents form a coalition, and in the eyes of the children they become a joint authority, so that it makes little difference to them whether it is a mother or a father who is wielding authority at any given time. Furthermore, the asymmetry in children's cross-sex influence with their peers appears to have its origins at quite an early age—earlier, I would suggest, that children have a very clear idea about the connection between their own sex and that of the same-sex parent. In other words, it seems quite unlikely that little boys ignore girls' influence attempts because little girls remind them of their mothers. I think we simply do not know why girls' influence styles are ineffective with boys, but the fact that they are has important implications for a variety of social behaviors, not just for segregation.

Here are some examples from recent studies. Powlishta (1987) observed preschool-aged boy-girl pairs competing for a scarce resource. The children were brought to a playroom in the nursery school and were given an opportunity to watch cartoons through a movie-viewer that could only be accessed by one child at a time. Powlishta found that when the two children were alone together in the playroom, the boys got more than their share of access to the movie-viewer. When there was an adult present, however, this was no longer the case. The adult's presence appeared to inhibit the boys' more power-assertive techniques and resulted in girls having at least equal access.

This study points to a reason why girls may not only avoid playing with boys but may also stay nearer to a teacher or other adult. Following up on this possibility, Greeno (1989) brought four-child groups of kindergarten and first-grade children into a large playroom equipped with attractive toys. Some of the quartets were all-boy groups, some all-girl groups, and some were made up of two boys and two girls. A female adult sat at one end of the room, and halfway through the play session, moved to a seat at the other end of the room. The question posed for this study was: Would girls move closer to the teacher when boys were present than when they were not? Would the sex composition of a play group make any difference to the locations taken up by the boys? The results were that in all-girl groups, girls actually took up locations *farther* from the adult than did boys in all-boy groups. When two boys were present, however, the two girls were significantly closer to the adult than were the boys, who tended to remain at intermediate distances. When the adult changed position halfway through the session, boys'

locations did not change, and this was true whether there were girls present or not. Girls in all-girl groups tended to move in the opposite direction when the adult moved, maintaining distance between themselves and the adult; when boys were present, however, the girls tended to move *with* the adult, staying relatively close. It is worth noting, incidentally, that in all the mixed-sex groups except one, segregation was extreme; both boys and girls behaved as though there was only one playmate available to them, rather than three.

There are some fairly far-reaching implications of this study. Previous observational studies in preschools had indicated that girls are often found in locations closer to the teacher than are boys. These studies have been done in mixed-sex nursery school groups. Girls' proximity seeking toward adults has often been interpreted as a reflection of some general affiliative trait in girls and perhaps as a reflection of some aspect of early socialization that has bound them more closely to caregivers. We see in the Greeno study that proximity seeking toward adults was *not* a general trait in girls. It was a function of the gender composition of the group of other children present as potential interaction partners. The behavior of girls implied that they found the presence of boys to be less aversive when an adult was nearby. It was as though they realized that the rough, power-assertive behavior of boys was likely to be moderated in the presence of adults, and indeed, there is evidence that they were right.

We have been exploring some aspects of girls' avoidance of interaction with boys. Less is known about why boys avoid interaction with girls, but the fact is that they do. In fact, their cross-sex avoidance appears to be even stronger. Thus, during middle childhood both boys and girls spend considerable portions of their social play time in groups of their own sex. This might not matter much for future relationships were it not for the fact that fairly distinctive styles of interaction develop in all-boy and all-girl groups. Thus, the segregated play groups constitute powerful socialization environments in which children acquire distinctive interaction skills that are adapted to same-sex partners. Sex-typed modes of interaction become consolidated, and I wish to argue that the distinctive patterns developed by the two sexes at this time have implications for the same-sex and cross-sex relationships that individuals form as they enter adolescence and adulthood.

It behooves us, then, to examine in somewhat more detail the nature of the interactive milieus that prevail in all-boy and all-girl groups. Elsewhere I have reviewed some of the findings of studies in which these two kinds of groups have been observed (Maccoby, 1988). Here I will briefly summarize what we know.

The two sexes engage in fairly different kinds of activities and games (Huston, 1985). Boys play in somewhat larger groups, on the average, and their play is rougher (Humphreys & Smith, 1987) and takes up more space. Boys more often play in the streets and other public places; girls more often congregate in private homes or yards. Girls tend to form close, intimate friendships with one or two other girls, and these friendships are marked by the sharing of confidences (Kraft & Vraa, 1975). Boys' friendships, on the other hand, are more oriented around mutual interests in activities (Erwin, 1985). The breakup of girls' friendships is usually attended by more intense emotional reactions than is the case for boys.

For our present purposes, the most interesting thing about all-boy and all-girl groups is the divergence in the interactive styles that develop in them. In male groups, there is more concern with issues of dominance. Several psycholinguists have recorded the verbal exchanges that occur in these groups, and Maltz and Borker (1983) summarized the findings of several studies as follows: Boys in their groups are more likely than girls in all-girl groups to interrupt one another; use commands, threats, or boasts of authority; refuse to comply with another child's demand; give information; heckle a speaker; tell jokes or suspenseful stories; top someone else's story; or call another child names. Girls in all-groups, on the other hand, are more likely than boys to express agreement with what another speaker has just said, pause to give another girl a chance to speak, or when starting a speaking turn, acknowledge a point previously made by another speaker. This account indicates that among boys, speech serves largely egoistic functions and is used to establish and protect an individual's turf. Among girls, conversation is a more socially binding process.

In the past five years, analysts of discourse have done additional work on the kinds of interactive processes that are seen among girls, as compared with those among boys. The summary offered by Maltz and Borker has been both supported and extended. Sachs (1987) reported that girls soften their directives to partners, apparently attempting to keep them involved in a process of planning a play sequence, while boys are more likely simply to tell their partners what to do. Leaper (1989) observed children aged five and seven and found that verbal exchanges among girls more often take the form of what he called "collaborative speech acts" that involve positive reciprocity, whereas among boys, speech acts are more controlling and include more negative reciprocity. Miller and colleagues (Miller, Danaher, & Forbes, 1986) found that there was more conflict in boys' groups, and given that conflict had occurred, girls were more likely to use "conflict mitigating strategies," whereas boys more often used threats and physical force. Sheldon (1989) reported that when girls talk, they seem to have a double agenda: to be "nice" and sustain social relationships, while at the same time working to achieve their own individual ends. For boys, the agenda is more often the single one of self-assertion. Sheldon (1989) has noted that in interactions among themselves, girls are *not* unassertive. Rather, girls do successfully pursue their own ends, but they do so while toning down coercion and dominance, trying to bring about agreement, and restoring or maintaining group functioning. It should be noted that boys' confrontational style does not necessarily impede effective group functioning, as evidenced by boys' ability to cooperate with teammates for sports. A second point is that although researchers' own gender has been found to influence to some degree the kinds of questions posed and the answers obtained, the summary provided here includes the work of both male and female researchers, and their findings are consistent with one another.

As children move into adolescence and adulthood, what happens to the interactive styles that they developed in their largely segregated childhood groups? A first point to note is that despite the powerful attraction to members of the opposite sex in adolescence, gender segregation by no means disappears. Young people continue to spend a good portion of their social time with same-sex partners. In adulthood, there is extensive gender segregation in workplaces (Reskin, 1984), and in some societies and some social-class or ethnic groups, leisure time also is largely spent with same-sex others even after marriage. The literature on the nature of the interactions that occur among same-sex partners in adolescence and adulthood is quite extensive and cannot be reviewed here. Suffice it to say in summary that there is now considerable evidence that the interactive patterns found in sex-homogeneous dyads or groups in adolescence and adulthood are very similar to those that prevailed in the gender-segregated groups of childhood (e.g., Aries, 1976; Carli, 1989; Cowan, Drinkard, & Mac-Gavin, 1984; Savin-Williams, 1979).

How can we summarize what it is that boys and girls, or men and women, are doing in their respective groups that distinguishes these groups from one another? There have been a number of efforts to find the major dimensions that best describe variations in interactive styles. Falbo and Peplau (1980) have factor analyzed a battery of measures and have identified two dimensions: one called direct versus indirect, the other unilateral versus bilateral. Hauser et al. (1987) have distinguished what they called *enabling* interactive styles from *constricting* or *restrictive* ones, and I believe this distinction fits the styles of the two sexes especially well. A restrictive style is one that tends to derail the interaction—to inhibit the partner or cause the partner to withdraw, thus shortening the interaction or bringing it to an end. Examples are threatening a partner, directly contradicting or interrupting, topping the partner's story, boasting, or engaging in other forms of self-display. Enabling or facilitative styles are those, such as acknowledging another's comment or expressing agreement, that support whatever the partner is doing and tend to keep the interaction going. I want to suggest that it is

because women and girls use more enabling styles that they are able to form more intimate and more integrated relationships. Also I think it likely that it is the male concern for turf and dominance—that is, with not showing weakness to other men and boys—that underlies their restrictive interaction style and their lack of self-disclosure.

Carli (1989) has recently found that in discussions between pairs of adults, individuals are more easily influenced by a partner if that partner has just expressed agreement with them. In this work, women were quite successful in influencing one another in same-sex dyads, whereas pairs of men were less so. The sex difference was fully accounted for by the fact that men's male partners did not express agreement as often. Eagly (1987) has summarized data from a large number of studies on women's and men's susceptibility to influence and has found women to be somewhat more susceptible. Carli's work suggests that this tendency may not be a general female personality trait of "suggestibility" but may reflect the fact that women more often interact with other women who tend to express reciprocal agreement. Carli's finding resonates with some work with young children interacting with their mothers. Mary Parpal and I (Parpal & Maccoby, 1985) found that children were more compliant to a mother's demands if the two had previously engaged in a game in which the child was allowed to give directions that the mother followed. In other words, maternal compliance set up a system of reciprocity in which the child also complied. I submit that the same principle applies in adult interactions and that among women, influence is achieved in part by being open to influence from the partner.

Boys and men, on the other hand, although less successful in influencing one another in dyads, develop group structures—well-defined roles in games, dominance hierarchies, and team spirit—that appear to enable them to function effectively in groups. One may suppose that the male directive interactive style is less likely to derail interaction if and when group structural forces are in place. In other words, men and boys may *need* group structure more than women and girls do. However, this hypothesis has yet to be tested in research. In any case, boys and men in their groups have more opportunity to learn how to function within hierarchical structures than do women and girls in theirs.

We have seen that throughout much of childhood and into adolescence and adulthood as well, people spend a good deal of their social time interacting with others of their own gender, and they continue to use distinctive interaction styles in these settings. What happens, then, when individuals from these two distinctive "cultures" attempt to interact with one another? People of both sexes are faced with a relatively unfamiliar situation to which they must adapt. Young women are less likely to receive the reciprocal agreement, opportunities to talk, and so on that they have learned to expect when interacting with female partners. Men have been accustomed to counterdominance and competitive reactions to their own power assertions, and they now find themselves with partners who agree with them and otherwise offer enabling responses. It seems evident that this new partnership should be easier to adapt to for men than for women. There is evidence that men fall in love faster and report feeling more in love than do women early in intimate relationships (Huston & Ashmore, 1986). Furthermore, the higher rates of depression in females have their onset in adolescence, when rates of cross-sex interaction rise (Nolen-Hoeksema, in press). Although these phenomena are no doubt multidetermined, the asymmetries in interaction styles may contribute to them.

To some degree, men appear to bring to bear much the same kind of techniques in mixed-sex groups that they are accustomed to using in same-sex groups. If the group is attempting some sort of joint problem solving or is carrying out a joint task, men do more initiating, directing, and interrupting than do women. Men's voices are louder and are more listened to than women's voices by both sexes (West & Zimmerman, 1985); men are more likely than women to lose interest in a taped message if it is spoken in a woman's rather than a man's voice (Robinson & MacArthur, 1982). Men are less influenced by the opinions of other group members than are women. Perhaps as a consequence of their greater assertiveness, men have more influence on the group process (Lockheed,

1985; Pugh & Wahrman, 1983), just as they did in childhood. Eagly and colleagues (Eagly, Wood, & Fishbaugh, 1981) have drawn our attention to an important point about cross-sex interaction in groups: The greater resistance of men to being influenced by other group members is found only when the men are under surveillance, that is, if others know whether they have yielded to their partners' influence attempts. I suggest that it is especially the monitoring by other *men* that inhibits men from entering into reciprocal influence with partners. When other men are present, men appear to feel that they must guard their dominance status and not comply too readily lest it be interpreted as weakness.

Women's behavior in mixed groups is more complex. There is some work indicating that they adapt by becoming more like men—that they raise their voices, interrupt, and otherwise become more assertive than they would be when interacting with women (Carli, 1989; Hall & Braunwalk, 1981). On the other hand, there is also evidence that they carry over some of their well-practiced female-style behaviors, sometimes in exaggerated form. Women may wait for a turn to speak that does not come, and thus they may end up talking less than they would in a women's group. They smile more than the men do, agree more often with what others have said, and give nonverbal signals of attentiveness to what others—perhaps especially the men—are saying (Duncan & Fiske, 1977). In some writings this female behavior has been referred to as "silent applause."

Eagly (1987) reported a meta-analysis of behavior of the two sexes in groups (mainly mixed-sex groups) that were performing joint tasks. She found a consistent tendency for men to engage in more task behavior—giving and receiving information, suggestions, and opinions (see also Aries, 1982)—whereas women are more likely to engage in socioemotional behaviors that support positive affective relations within the group. Which style contributes more to effective group process? It depends. Wood, Polek, and Aiken (1985) have compared the performance of all-female and all-male groups on different kinds of tasks, finding that groups of women have more success on tasks that require discussion and negotiation, whereas male groups do better on tasks where success depends on the volume of ideas being generated. Overall, it appears that *both* styles are productive, though in different ways.

There is evidence that women feel at a disadvantage in mixed-sex interaction. For example, Hogg and Turner (1987) set up a debate between two young men taking one position and two young women taking another. The outcomes in this situation were contrasted with a situation in which young men and women were debating against same-sex partners. After the cross-sex debate, the self-esteem of the young men rose, but that of the young women declined. Furthermore, the men liked their women opponents better after debating with them, whereas the women liked the men less. In other words, the encounter in most cases was a pleasurable experience for the men, but not for the women. Another example comes from the work of Davis (1978), who set up get-acquainted sessions between pairs of young men and women. He found that the men took control of the interaction, dictating the pace at which intimacy increased, whereas the women adapted themselves to the pace set by the men. The women reported later, however, that they had been uncomfortable about not being able to control the sequence of events, and they did not enjoy the encounter as much as the men did.

In adolescence and early adulthood, the powerful forces of sexual attraction come into play. When couples are beginning to fall in love, or even when they are merely entertaining the possibility of developing an intimate relationship, each is motivated to please the other, and each sends signals implying "Your wish is my command." There is evidence that whichever member of a couple is more attractive, or less in love, is at an advantage and is more able to influence the partner than vice versa (Peplau, 1979). The influence patterns based on the power of interpersonal attraction are not distinct in terms of gender; that is, it may be either the man or the woman in a courting relationship who has the influence advantage. When first meeting, or in the early stages of the acquaintance process, women still may feel at some disadvantage, as shown in the Davis study, but this situation need not last. Work done in the 1960s indicated that in many couples, as relationships become deeper and more enduring, any overall asymmetry in influence diminishes greatly (Heiss, 1962; Leik, 1963; Shaw & Sadler, 1965). Most couples develop a relationship that is based on communality rather than exchange bargaining. That is, they have many shared goals and work jointly to achieve them. They do not need to argue over turf because they have the same turf. In well-functioning married couples, both members of the pair strive to avoid conflict, and indeed there is evidence that the men on average are even more conflict-avoidant than the women (Gottman & Levenson, 1988; Kelley et al., 1978). Nevertheless, there are still carry-overs of the different interactive styles males and females have acquired at earlier points in the life cycle. Women seem to expend greater effort toward maintaining harmonious moods (Huston & Ashmore, 1986, p. 177). With intimate cross-sex partners, men use more direct styles of influence, and women use more indirect ones. Furthermore, women are more likely to withdraw (become silent, cold, and distant) and/or take unilateral action in order to get their way in a dispute (Falbo & Peplau, 1980), strategies that we suspect may reflect their greater difficulty in influencing a male partner through direct negotiation.

Space limitations do not allow considering in any depth the next set of important relationships that human beings form: that between parents and children. Let me simply say that I think there is evidence for the following: The interaction styles that women have developed in interaction with girls and other women serve them well when they become mothers. Especially when children are young, women enter into deeper levels of reciprocity with their children than do men (e.g., Gleason, 1987; Maccoby & Jacklin, 1983) and communicate with them better. On the other hand, especially after the first two years, children need firm direction as well as warmth and reciprocity, and fathers' styles may contribute especially well to this aspect of parenting. The relationship women develop with young children seems to depend very little on whether they are dealing with a son or a daughter; it builds on maternal response to the characteristics and needs of early childhood that are found in both boys and girls to similar degrees. Fathers, having a less intimate relationship with individual children, treat young boys and girls in a somewhat more gendered way (Siegal, 1987). As children approach middle childhood and interact with same-sex other children, they develop the interactive styles characteristic of their sex, and their parents more and more interact with them as they have always done with same-sex or opposite-sex others. That is, mothers and daughters develop greater intimacy and reciprocity; fathers and sons exhibit more friendly rivalry and joking, more joint interest in masculine activities, and more rough play. Nevertheless, there are many aspects of the relationships between parents and children that do not depend on the gender of either the parent or the child.

Obviously, as the scene unfolds across generations, it is very difficult to identify the point in the developmental cycle at which the interactional styles of the two sexes begin to diverge, and more important, to identify the forces that cause them to diverge. In my view, processes within the nuclear family have been given too much credit—or too much blame—for this aspect of sex-typing. I doubt that the development of distinctive interactive styles has much to do with the fact that children are parented primarily by women, as some have claimed (Chodorow, 1978; Gilligan, 1982), and it seems likely to me that children's "identification" with the same-sex parent is more a consequence than a cause of children's acquisition of sex-typed interaction styles. I would place most of the emphasis on the peer group as the setting in which children first discover the compatibility of same-sex others, in which boys first discover the requirements of maintaining one's status in the male hierarchy, and in which the gender of one's partners becomes supremely important. We do not have a clear answer to the ultimate question of why the segregated peer groups function as they do. We need now to think about how it can be answered. The answer is important if we are to adapt ourselves successfully to the rapid changes in the roles and relationships of the two sexes that are occurring in modern societies.

REFERENCES

Aries, E. (1976). Interaction patterns and themes of male, female, and mixed groups. *Small Group Behavior, 7,* 7–18.

Aries, E. J. (1982). Verbal and nonverbal behavior in single-sex and mixed-sex groups: Are traditional sex roles changing? *Psychological Reports, 51,* 127–134.

Block, J. H. (1976). Debatable conclusions about sex differences. *Contemporary Psychology, 21,* 517–522.

Carli, L. L. (1989). Gender differences in interaction style and influence. *Journal of Personality and Social Psychology, 56,* 565–576.

Chodorow, N. (1978). *The reproduction of mothering.* Berkeley, CA: University of California Press.

Cowan, C., Drinkard, J., & MacGavin, L. (1984). The effects of target, age and gender on use of power strategies. *Journal of Personality and Social Psychology, 47,* 1391–1398.

Davis, J. D. (1978). When boy meets girl: Sex roles and the negotiation of intimacy in an acquaintance exercise. *Journal of Personality and Social Psychology, 36,* 684–692.

Duncan, S., Jr., & Fiske, D. W. (1977). *Face-to-face interaction: Research, methods and theory.* Hillsdale, NJ: Erlbaum.

Eagly, A. H. (1983). Gender and social influence. *American Psychologist, 38,* 971–981.

Eagly, A. H. (1987). *Sex differences in social behavior: A social role interpretation.* Hillsdale, NJ: Erlbaum.

Eagly, A. H., Wood, W., & Fishbaugh, L. (1981). Sex differences in conformity: Surveillance by the group as a determinant of male nonconformity. *Journal of Personality and Social Psychology, 40,* 384–394.

Eisenhart, M. A., & Holland, D. C. (1983). Learning gender from peers: The role of peer group in the cultural transmission of gender. *Human Organization, 42,* 321–332.

Erwin, P. (1985). Similarity of attitudes and constructs in children's friendships. *Journal of Experimental Child Psychology, 40,* 470–485.

Fagot, B. I. (1985). Beyond the reinforcement principle: Another step toward understanding sex roles. *Developmental Psychology, 21,* 1097–1104.

Falbo, T., & Peplau, L. A. (1980). Power strategies in intimate relationships. *Journal of Personality and Social Psychology, 38,* 618–628.

Gilligan, C. (1982). *In a different voice: Psychological theory and women's development.* Cambridge, MA: Howard University Press.

Gleason, J. B. (1987). Sex differences in parent-child interaction. In S. U. Phillips, S. Steele, & C. Tanz (Eds.), *Language, gender and sex in comparative perspective* (pp. 189–199). Cambridge, England: Cambridge University Press.

Gottman, J. M., & Levenson, R. W. (1988). The social psychophysiology of marriage. In P. Roller & M. A. Fitzpatrick (Eds.), *Perspectives on marital interaction* (pp. 182–200). New York: Taylor & Francis.

Greeno, C. G. (1989). *Gender differences in children's proximity to adults.* Unpublished doctoral dissertation, Stanford University, Stanford, CA.

Hall, J. A., & Braunwalk, K. G. (1981). Gender cues in conversation. *Journal of Personality and Social Psychology, 40,* 99–110.

Hauser, S. T., Powers, S. I., Weiss-Perry, B., Follansbee, D. J., Rajapark, D., & Greene, W. M. (1987). *The constraining and enabling coding system manual.* Unpublished manuscript.

Heiss, J. S. (1962). Degree of intimacy and male-female interaction. *Sociometry, 25,* 197–208.

Hogg, M. A., & Turner, J. C. (1987). Intergroup behavior, self stereotyping and the salience of social categories. *British Journal of Social Psychology, 26,* 325–340.

Humphreys, A. P., & Smith, P. K. (1987). Rough and tumble friendship and dominance in school children: Evidence for continuity and change with age in middle childhood. *Child Development, 58,* 201–212.

Huston, A. C. (1985). The development of sex-typing: Themes from recent research. *Developmental Review, 5,* 1–17.

Huston, T. L., & Ashmore, R. D. (1986). Women and men in personal relationship. In R. D. Ashmore & R. K. Del Boca (Eds.), *The social psychology of female-male relations.* New York: Academic Press.

Jacklin, C. N., & Maccoby, E. E. (1978). Social behavior at 33 months in same-sex and mixed-sex dyads. *Child Development, 49,* 557–569.

Kelley, H. H., Cunningham, J. D., Grisham, J. A., Lefebvre, L. M., Sink, C. R., & Yablon, G. (1978). Sex differences in comments made during conflict in close relationships. *Sex Roles, 4,* 473–491.

Kraft, L. W., & Vraa, C. W. (1975). Sex composition of groups and pattern of self-disclosure by high school females. *Psychological Reports, 37,* 733–734.

Leaper, C. (1989). *The sequencing of power and involvement in boys' and girls' talk.* Unpublished manuscript (under review), University of California, Santa Cruz.

Leik, R. K. (1963). Instrumentality and emotionality in family interaction. *Sociometry, 26,* 131–145.

Lockheed, M. E. (1985). Sex and social influence: A meta-analysis guided by theory. In J. Berger & M. Zelditch (Eds.), *Status, attributions, and rewards* (pp. 406–429). San Francisco, CA: Jossey-Bass.

Maccoby, E. E. (1988). Gender as a social category. *Developmental Psychology, 26,* 755–765.

Maccoby, E. E., & Jacklin, C. N. (1974). *The psychology of sex differences.* Stanford, CA: Stanford University Press.

Maccoby, E. E., & Jacklin, C. N. (1980). Sex differences in aggression: A rejoinder and reprise. *Child Development, 51,* 964–980.

Maccoby, E. E., & Jacklin, C. N. (1983). The "person" characteristics of children and the family as environment. In D. Magnusson & V. L. Allen (Eds.), *Human development: An interactional perspective* (pp. 76–92). New York: Academic Press.

Maccoby, E. E., & Jacklin, C. N. (1987). Gender segregation in childhood. In H. W. Reese (Ed.), *Advances in child development and behavior* (Vol. 20, pp. 239–288). New York: Academic Press.

Maltz, D. N., & Borker, R. A. (1983). A cultural approach to male-female miscommunication. In John A. Gumperz (Ed.), *Language and social identity* (pp. 195–216). New York: Cambridge University Press.

Miller, P., Danaher, D., & Forbes, D. (1986). Sex-related strategies for coping with interpersonal conflict in children aged five and seven. *Developmental Psychology, 22,* 543–548.

Nolen-Hoeksema, S. (in press). *Sex differences in depression.* Stanford, CA: Stanford University Press.

Parpal, M., & Maccoby, E. E. (1985). Maternal responsiveness and subsequent child compliance. *Child Development, 56,* 1326–1334.

Peplau, A. (1979). Power in dating relationships. In J. Freeman (Ed.), *Women: A feminist perspective* (pp. 121–137). Palo Alto, CA: Mayfield.

Powlishta, K. K. (1987, April). *The social context of cross-sex interactions.* Paper presented at biennial meeting of the Society for Research in Child Development, Baltimore, MD.

Powlishta, K. K. (1989). *Salience of group membership: The case of gender.* Unpublished doctoral dissertation. Stanford University, Stanford, CA.

Pruitt, D. G. (1976). Power and bargaining. In B. Seidenberg & A. Snadowsky (Eds.), *Social psychology: An introduction* (pp. 343–375). New York: Free Press.

Pugh, M. D., & Wahrman, R. (1983). Neutralizing sexism in mixed-sex groups: Do women have to be better than men? *American Journal of Sociology, 88.* 746–761.

Reskin, B. F. (Ed.). (1984). *Sex segregation in the workplace: Trends, explanations and remedies.* Washington, DC: National Academy Press.

Robinson, J., & McArthur, L. Z. (1982). Impact of salient vocal qualities on causal attribution for a speaker's behavior. *Journal of Personality and Social Psychology, 43,* 236–247.

Sachs, J. (1987). Preschool boys' and girls' language use in pretend play. In S. U. Phillips, S. Steele, & C. Tanz (Eds.), *Language, gender and sex in comparative perspective* (pp. 178–188). Cambridge, England: Cambridge University Press.

Savin-Williams, R. C. (1979). Dominance hierarchies in groups of early adolescents. *Child Development, 50,* 923–935.

Serbin, L. A., Sprafkin, C., Elman, M., & Doyle, A. (1984). The early development of sex differentiated patterns of social influence. *Canadian Journal of Social Science, 14,* 350–363.

Shaw, M. E., & Sadler, O. W. (1965). Interaction patterns in heterosexual dyads varying in degree of intimacy. *Journal of Social Psychology, 66,* 345–351.

Sheldon, A. (1989, April). *Conflict talk: Sociolinguistic challenges to self-assertion and how young girls meet them.* Paper presented at the biennial meeting of the Society for Research in Child Development. Kansas City.

Siegal, M. (1987). Are sons and daughters treated more differently by fathers than mothers? *Developmental Review, 7,* 183–209.

Thorne, B. (1986). Girls and boys together, but mostly apart. In W. W. Hartup & L. Rubin (Eds.), *Relationships and development* (pp. 167–184). Hillsdale, NJ: Erlbaum.

Tieger, T. (1980). On the biological basis of sex differences in aggression. *Child Development, 51,* 943–963.

Wasserman, G. A., & Stern, D. N. (1978). An early manifestation of differential behavior toward children of the same and opposite sex. *Journal of Genetic Psychology, 133,* 129–137.

West, C., & Zimmerman, D. H. (1985). Gender, language and discourse. In T. A. van Dijk (Ed.), *Handbook of discourse analysis: Vol. 4, Discourse analysis in society* (pp. 103–124). London: Academic Press.

Wood, W., Polek, D., & Aiken, C. (1985). Sex differences in group task performance. *Journal of Personality and Social Psychology, 48,* 63–71.

CHECKPOINTS

1. Boys' strong preference for rough-and-tumble play and the inability of girls to influence the activities of boys account for self-selected sex segregation by children.

2. As a result of disproportionate time spent with same-sex peers in childhood, adolescents and adults show interactional styles that are often geared to members of the same sex and that are not always successful with members of the opposite sex.

Gender Identity Development

QUESTIONS FOR REFLECTION

1. How can parents and educators respond to self-selected sex segregation and promote the goal of gender equality?
2. How would social learning theory and gender schema theory explain the development of transsexual or transgendered identity?

CHAPTER APPLICATION

1. In a preschool, school playground, or local park, observe children in free play. Note the rates of same-sex and opposite-sex play. Keep track of the activities and types of interactions among the children. How do your observations compare with Maccoby's description? Did you observe both stereotyped and nonstereotyped play? If possible, interview a few of the children and ask them about their preferences for playmates. How do children describe and explain play group preferences?

CHAPTER SEVEN

Gender and Sexuality

QUESTIONS TO THINK ABOUT

• **Define sexuality, sexual identity, and sexual orientation.**
• **Distinguish between sexual orientation and sexual identity.**
• **How do biological theories explain sexuality and sexual orientation?**
• **How do social/cultural theories explain sexuality and sexual orientation?**
• **Describe how biological and social/cultural factors could interact to explain sexuality and sexual orientation.**
• **What are some political implications of different explanations for sexuality and sexual orientation?**
• **How is sexuality fluid?**
• **How do psychologists explain the development of sexuality?**
• **How do relationships provide a context for sexual experiences?**

GENDER, SEXUALITY, AND SEXUAL ORIENTATION

In chapter 2, we asked you to think about how a researcher might use personal ads to study the question of what types of information people are willing to reveal in personal ads. We would now like you to think about personal ads in a different way. Imagine you are reading the Sunday newspaper's personal ads. You find ads for women seeking men, men seeking women, women seeking women, and men seeking men. People placing these ads usually identify some characteristics they would like in a partner—appearance, hobbies, personal qualities, age, religion, and so on. What can you tell about someone from these ads? When someone places a personal ad, are they always seeking a

sexual relationship? Are the people who are seeking persons of the same sex always homosexual? Are the people who are seeking persons of the opposite sex always heterosexual? Do men and women look for different qualities in a partner? Are there differences between people interested in same-sex versus opposite-sex partners? Here are some samples with pertinent information deleted; see what you can infer:

1. Single, (?) psychologist, 36, witty, gentle, affectionate, emotional, passionate, analytical, caring, nice looking. Seeks similar single, (?) for long-term relationship.
2. Easygoing (?), 38, enjoys dining out, movies, quiet times at home. Seeking same for flea markets, get togethers, fun times.

3. Passionate (?), 39, great sense of humor, honest, sincere, loves cooking, movies, music, beach walks. Seeking (?) for friendship, enjoying life, more. The sky's the limit. Age open.

4. Professional, good looking (?), 33, introspective, witty, sensual, very attentive. Seeks open minded, 24–49 (?) for some tenderness, laughs, mutual support, and lifelong friendship.

5. Be on the lookout for this vegetarian, (?), 39. Considered adventurous, creative, huggable, and dangerously fun. Armed with a mischievous spirit. Reward for capture.

6. A life of laughter, honesty, respect, love, friendship, commitment, and various activities. Youthful, attractive, intelligent, professional, 47 (?), Seeks kind (?), 38+, for the same.

7. Sincere (?), 54, brown/green eyes, professional, caring, nonsmoker, nondrinker, enjoys travel, dinner out, jazz, classical music. Seeks (?) with similar qualities and interests.

8. (?), 36, attractive, professional, adventurous is seeking out attractive (?) 28–40 to share special times with me at my home.[1]

Perhaps your guesses were accurate, but with the identifying information removed, it is hard to tell who has written these ads. What can be learned from this exercise? One answer is that some of our assumptions about sexuality, personal preferences, and gender may be based more on stereotype than reality. Without the framework provided by the identity of the writer, we may find that it is difficult to categorize the writer as man or woman, gay or straight. As we have emphasized in earlier discussions, categories about sex (male vs. female) and gender (feminine vs. masculine) do not adequately describe reality. In the same way, categories of sexuality such as heterosexual, homosexual, bisexual may be inadequate to describe human sexual expression.

Gender and sexuality are intimately related. Sexuality is partially an expression of gender identity. According to Leonore Tiefer and Brunhild Kring in the first article in this chapter, *Gender and the Organization of Sexual Behavior*, gender provides the best predictor of sexual feelings and values. Sexuality is often learned through experiences that differentiate male and female gender identity. For example, one aspect of feminine identity places a high value on relationships; therefore, maintaining a relationship may become a motive for sexual activity. Sexuality may also be seen as an aspect of identity; sometimes individuals are known by their sexual identity. In the last twenty years, we have seen a cultural revolution in the public acknowledgment of gay, lesbian, and bisexual identities. Sometimes sex is embedded in the complexities of male-female relationships. Men and women live and work together under almost all circumstances, and these nonintimate relationships are sometimes tinged with sexual overtones. These overtones range from Freud's assertion that opposite-sex parent-child relationships contain a sexual element to recent charges that playground teasing among boys and girls is evidence of sexual harassment, or to flirtatious behavior by men or women in work settings.[2] Sexuality is essential for human reproduction, and procreative sex occurs in the context of relationships between men and women. Sexual expression is not limited to reproduction or to male-female, female-female, or male-male relationships. One important aspect of sexuality is physical arousal and orgasm; however, sexuality can occur without desire or pleasure. In sum, sexuality is related to gender identity, reproduction, intimate relationships, and physical pleasure. None of these aspects of sexuality mandates the form of sexual expression, and none explains the complexities of sexuality. Sexual behavior is both individually and culturally constructed. Particular life experiences of individuals as well as the more general attitudes, norms, and gender roles as defined by culture exert a joint influence on sexuality. The experience of sexual pleasure is both physiological and subjective. Although a variety of physiological mechanisms contribute to sexuality, one's interpretation of pleasure, desire, satisfaction, need, revulsion, distaste, disinterest, passion, obligation (and on and on) is powerfully subjective. Our portrayal of sexuality and gender emphasizes the flexible nature of sexual behaviors, a reciprocal relationship between biology and behavior, and the importance of cultural context.

There are very few *universal* elements of sexuality (Tiefer, 1995). This fact may seem surprising, because penile-vaginal intercourse would seem essential to human survival. Certainly, sex for procreation is universal across cultures, if not individuals. Beyond reproduction, however, there is enormous variety in the experiences and activities that people find erotic. According to Tiefer and Kring in this chapter, kissing is totally absent or considered disgusting in some societies, whereas in Western societies, it is a widespread and usually pleasurable sexual behavior. Cultures exert significant influence over sexual expression. The behaviors that people enjoy or object to; the conditions under which sexual expression is considered appropriate or inappropriate; the partners one has available; and the meaning of sexuality, whether for procreation, recreation, or obligation—all these aspects of sexuality vary across cultures. Furthermore, cultures assign different roles to men and women concerning sexuality.

In the preceding chapters, we have emphasized the importance of understanding the meanings that are given to particular terms. Gender, sex, sexuality, sexual identity, and sexual orientation are all different aspects of understanding sexuality and gender. You should be aware of different meanings that you may come across in discussions of these issues, especially in the popular press, and realize that there is not universal agreement on the definition of these terms. In this chapter, we define **sexuality** as behaviors and/or thoughts with erotic meaning. An essentialist perspective on sexuality views it as an entity, integral to one's identity; whereas in a social constructionist account, sexuality emerges from relationships that themselves exist in a cultural and historical context (Tiefer, 1995). **Sexual orientation** describes the pattern of one's sexual attraction and, in Western culture, is typically associated with the labels *heterosexual, homosexual,* and *bisexual.* **Sexual identity** refers to the self-ascribed label one adopts to describe one's sexuality. Sexual identity and sexual orientation are not always the same. For instance, some individuals who identify themselves as heterosexual may have had same-sex sexual experiences or may have erotic attractions to people of the same sex

(Bailey, 1995). Researchers who investigate sexuality may use definitions of sexuality, sexual orientation, and sexual identity that reflect either an essentialist or social constructionist view, and thus the nature of the research questions and the meaning attributed to the results may be influenced by their underlying ideology. The implications of different ideological perspectives are discussed later in this introduction.

While reading the articles in this chapter, you should remember that sexuality intersects both gender and sexual orientation and that sexuality, sexual orientation, and sexual identity may not always cohere according to the patterns with which you are most familiar. For example, we may expect females to identify themselves as women, to prefer sexual experiences with men, and to adopt a feminine gender role with regard to sexual behaviors, whereas in reality, there is significant variation among each of these factors, both within individuals and among groups of people. As you review various accounts of sexuality, be aware that some explanations are directed at understanding variations in sexual orientation and other explanations are aimed at understanding variations in sexual practices.

APPROACHES TO THE STUDY OF SEXUALITY

The Biological/Medical Approach to the Study of Sexuality

Significant research attention has been devoted to studying sexuality from a biological or medical perspective. Several different types of biological explanations have been offered for sexuality. Some biological/medical theories have examined different sorts of biological mechanisms for their role in sexual behavior or sexual orientation; other theories have taken a more clinical focus, examining sexual behavior from a medical point of view. Implicit in most of these approaches is an essentialist belief that sexuality constitutes some core component related to biology. As we describe these research approaches, we alert you to the kinds of biological mechanisms studied and whether this approach is aimed more at sexual behavior or sexual orientation or both.

The evolutionary approach considers mate selection and reproduction to be at the core of human sexuality, especially sex differences, which are theorized to have evolved as mechanisms that enhance the success of reproduction. Evolutionary researchers focus on sex differences in sexual patterns that include the number of sexual relationships men and women have over their lifetime. From the evolutionary perspective, the finding that men have more sexual partners than women is explained as motivated by the goal of achieving reproductive success. Because the purpose of sexuality is to ensure reproduction, sexual behaviors by women and men have evolved to ensure that offspring are conceived and survive, and any observed sex differences are interpreted as complementary solutions to the problem of successful reproduction (Rossi, 1994). Rossi evaluates the role of physical attractiveness in sexuality and concludes that physical appearance and adornment are key elements in sexual attraction between men and women. Her summary of these data supports the claim of evolutionary theorists that women prefer older, taller men while men prefer younger, smaller women who meet cultural standards for beauty (Buss, 1989; Rossi, 1994). One criticism of evolutionary theory that we made in chapter 3 is that it often does not specify how culture and evolution act together in the service of reproduction. Rossi suggests that one example of this interplay is in the emergence of the concept of recreational sex that occurred with the advent of reliable contraception. Cultural ideas about sexuality, therefore, evolved to respond to changes in the social control of reproduction.

Another biological approach has examined neuroanatomical, genetic, or hormonal influences on sexuality. One area in this approach that has piqued popular interest is the role of biological and genetic factors in determining sexual orientation. An example of research that reflects the search for underlying biological causes of sexual orientation is the work of LeVay (1991). LeVay's initial results were based on postmortem examinations of the anterior hypothalamus of a sample of gay and heterosexual men. Based on these comparisons, LeVay concluded that there is a significant size difference in this brain structure be-

tween the two groups. The published results of this research have generated much debate, and there are competing explanations for LeVay's finding. One explanation is that differences in brain structure may reflect a biological difference that causes (or is related to the causes of) sexual orientation. Another interpretation is that this difference is a result of the different life experiences of homosexual and heterosexual men. There is ample evidence that biological structures both cause behaviors and are altered by behavior, and LeVay's evidence does not distinguish between these two alternatives (Bailey, 1995).

In a different approach to the study of sexual orientation, Hamer, Hu, Magnuson, Hu, and Pattatucci (1993) have developed a research program that examines genetic models of the inheritance of male sexual orientation. In particular, they have proposed that male homosexuality is linked to the X chromosome, and using data from a study of families with two gay brothers, they are searching for DNA markers, which might support this hypothesis. One methodological problem with this research is the exclusion of heterosexual brothers of gay men. This exclusion makes it impossible to determine if the same genetic markers are present in both homosexual and heterosexual brothers, which would provide evidence for environmental influences on sexual orientation (Byne, 1994). Although the investigation of genetic factors is progressing at a rapid pace, many technical and methodological issues still need to be resolved before this research approach can be considered fully reliable (Bailey, 1995; Gladue, 1994).

The final biological/medical approach we discuss has been characterized as the medical study of sexuality and is best represented by the work of researchers such as Kinsey and his colleagues and Masters and Johnson. The focus of their research was on the sexual behavior of men and women, especially the orgasmic experience (Kinsey, Pomeroy, & Martin, 1948; Kinsey, Pomeroy, Martin, & Gebhard, 1953; Masters & Johnson, 1966, 1970). These researchers studied sexuality through clinical observations of couples during sexual intercourse. This approach emphasizes the "naturalness" of orgasm as a physiological reflex. These researchers and others representing the study of sexology focus on anatomy, often disregarding the cultural and interpersonal elements involved in sexual expression. In fact, they contend that sexuality can only be understood when the biases imposed by culture and socialization have been eliminated (Tavris, 1992).

Beginning with Kinsey and continued by Masters and Johnson, this medical approach has emphasized the equality of sexual potential of men and women, focusing on the pleasurable aspects of sexuality. This research culminated in the publication of Masters and Johnson's model of sexuality, the human sexual response cycle (1966), which describes four stages of sexual responsiveness that they claimed were universal. The model presents men and women as essentially equivalent in their sexual responsiveness, with the four stages representing an orderly progression of events during sexual intercourse, driven by deep-seated biological mechanisms. This model has been widely cited and used by therapists as a basis for helping individuals overcome various sexual dysfunctions. In her critique of the human sexual response cycle, Tiefer (1995) argues that Masters and Johnson only used research participants whose sexual behavior conformed to their model, that these participants consisted of upper middle class, heterosexual, orgasmic couples, and that the researchers also acted as sex therapists, instructing subjects in sexual performance and thereby altering their sexual behavior during the research. It now appears that the sexual response cycle, rather than being a discovery drawn from objective observations, was a theory for which observations were constructed to conform.

Although the biological models we have discussed are all distinctly different, they share a view of sexuality that is somewhat disconnected from human interactions, especially relationships. By treating sex as a biological event, these theories offer little or no understanding of the impact of social roles and culture on sexual behavior and meaning. By giving little consideration to the social and interpersonal elements of sexuality and by emphasizing a universalist theme, these models do not effectively account for the variability of human sexual behaviors and experiences. It is clear that there is variation of sexual behaviors across cultures, that sexuality varies with sexual orientation, and that gender roles influence the production and experience of sexuality.

Social/Contextual Models of Sexuality

Not surprisingly there are psychological theories of sexuality that emphasize social and cultural elements. These models can be distinguished from the biological models we have presented by the types of descriptions they offer to explain sexual orientation, sex differences in sexual behaviors, and cultural variations in the expression of sexuality.

For some psychologists, sexuality is no different from any complex behavior, and they would explain sexual phenomena in terms of current psychological models of human behavior. For instance, social learning theory, which you were introduced to in chapter 6, would predict sexual behavior based on the processes of imitation of same-sex behavior (Oliver & Hyde, 1993). According to this approach, children are differentially attracted to models of the same sex and are more likely to exhibit the behaviors and attitudes of those same-sex models. Critical to social learning theory are the opportunities one has to observe models of the same sex, and examples of behavior presented in television and movies provide especially salient sources of culturally determined patterns of sexual behavior. Oliver and Hyde claim that social learning theory can explain sex differences in attitudes toward casual sex, and sex differences in the frequency of sexual activity, based on cultural images in the media, which present examples of such sex differences and provide vicarious reinforcement for conforming to this pattern. Social learning theory, as a general mechanism to explain how people acquire patterns of behavior, is well supported, but it does have weaknesses that limit its utility for understanding sexuality. First, it does not provide a means to understand the role of biological mechanisms such as the effects of prenatal hormones. Second, it does not adequately explain the wide variation of sexual patterns and preferences *within* each sex—and how these are acquired and maintained in the face of limited opportunities to observe such variations.

Another view of how social and cultural factors influence sexual behavior argues that human cognitive processes organize patterns of behavior and attitudes into *social roles* and *scripts,* which reflect both social behaviors and thoughts about sexuality. According to social role theory (Eagly, 1987), which was introduced in chapter 5, sex differences in behavior can be explained by the general differences in the roles—and the characteristics associated with those roles—assigned to men and women in our culture. The communal role, typically associated with women, exhibits a concern for others, is emotionally expressive, and is interpersonally sensitive. The agenic role, typically associated with men, is independent, forceful, and dominant. In the context of sexual relationships, we see some patterns of sex differences that correspond to these differences in social roles. In a study that looked at sex differences in motives for sexual intercourse, women and men were asked the following question: "What would be your motives for having sexual intercourse?" Typical answers for women included: "My motives . . . would be all due to the love and commitment I feel for my partner" or "love, to feel loved, to express love to someone," while typical answers for men included "need it," "gratification," and "when I'm tired of masturbation" (Carroll, Volk, & Hyde, 1984). These responses appear to reflect differences tied to communal versus agenic qualities. Social role theory would predict that women would demonstrate a stronger orientation toward the relational aspects of sexuality and research by Kurdek (1994) supports this contention. In comparisons of gay, lesbian, and heterosexual couples, both lesbian and heterosexual women showed greater interest in the overall quality of their relationships than did men.

Scripts about sexuality are detailed information about the events surrounding sexual behavior, including culturally defined parameters that describe dating, romance, marriage. Scripts often contain information about the context within which particular behaviors are likely to occur as well as ways of interpreting the behavior of others. In research that examined male and female scripts for a first date, Rose and Frieze (1989) found many elements in common between the groups, such as planning what to wear, being nervous, getting to know the date, and trying to impress the date. There were some differences as well. Men were more likely to mention initiating the date, planning the date, checking money, and initiating physical contact; women were more likely to mention concern with appearance, introducing date to parents, and telling friends or family about date.

The elaboration of personal scripted knowledge about sexuality is complemented by cultural scripts about love and romance. Popular culture, by way of romance novels, soap operas, fairy tales, and television movies, portrays love and romance in highly formulaic ways that women are more likely to read or watch. Some of the formula elements in these romantic scripts include a dominant man and submissive woman, a woman rescued by a male hero, a woman giving up her identity for romance and marriage, and a woman engaged in sex only in the context of either a relationship or marriage. In their analysis of sexuality and intimate relationships (which is the last article in this chapter, *Intimate Relationships and the Creation of Sexuality*), Philip Blumstein and Pepper Schwartz argue that women, through these socializing experiences, develop a view of sexuality that links it to attachment, love, and romance. Erotic feelings, for women, often emerge out of relationships—just as the cultural script for sex and love would predict. According to Blumstein and Schwartz, the reverse is often true for men, who are first erotically attracted to someone and then intimate feelings and a desire for a relationship emerge from those erotic feelings. In their article, Blumstein and Schwartz describe some of the ways in which sexuality is linked to individual experience and culture, and they contrast the experiences of men and women in heterosexual, gay, lesbian, or bisexual relationships.

Cultures vary in the social organization of sex and sexuality, and this variation is reflected in different cultural scripts for sex, love, and romance. Research by Dion and Dion (1993), from an article that you will read in chapter 10, shows that college students of Asian background held different views of love than did students of European background.

In particular, the students of Asian heritage defined love around friendship and companionship and stressed the value of marriage as a means to sustain the interdependence of the extended family. Students of European heritage defined love in more erotic terms, stressing the benefit of marriage for individual satisfaction. Dion and Dion suggest that cultures define the meaning of intimate relationships and that differing views of intimate relationships contribute to culture-bound meanings for concepts such as romance, love, and sexuality. Jacobs and Cromwell (1992), in their cross-cultural review of variations in sex and gender, argue that cultures often construct views of sexuality that control or limit women's sexual expression. Legal and social sanctions against women engaging in premarital or extramarital sex continue to be present in many cultures.

The theories of social roles and social scripts encourage us to look closely at particular social prescriptions for sexual behavior. These theories would predict specific differences between men and women, such as attitudes toward casual sex, and specific similarities in social scripts for dating and romance. Sexual scripts can also help us understand how gender influences sexual attitudes and values irrespective of sexual orientation, as in women's greater interest in the relational elements of an intimate relationship. The successful application of social role and script theories to explain sexual phenomena will depend, in part, on the further elaboration of research that describes people's experience based on cultural background, race, and ethnicity.

Interactionist Models of Sexuality

Interactionist models of sexuality incorporate both biological and social/cultural factors. These models differ in the particular biological factors of interest and in their conceptualization of the social and cultural environment. The second article in this chapter, *Sexual Orientation and Development: An Interactive Approach* by Michael Kauth and Seth Kalichman, describes a variety of interactionist theories of sexuality as they pertain to sexual orientation.

One interactive theory that has been enormously influential is the model of sexual identity developed by Money (1987, 1988). During a very long research career, Money has studied many variations of human hermaphrodism, used animal models, and examined hormonal and genetic variations in human development in an attempt to explain human sexuality. Money's research addresses the development of both sexual orientation and sexual identity. His work is concerned with the development of preferences for sexual partners as well as with the development of one's sense of self-identity as male or female. Money argues that human sexuality is predisposed toward heterosexuality, influenced by prenatal hormones, and facilitated by experiences that reinforce heterosexuality. Therefore, sexual orientation, like handedness or native language, has a strong biological basis but its ultimate expression is shaped by an individual's experiences. Prenatal exposure in males to androgen should predispose them to be sexually attracted to females, and the absence of androgens in females should predispose them to be sexually attracted to men. An error in this process, so that a male fetus, for example, does not receive enough androgen, may lead to a predisposition to be sexually attracted to men. Events during pregnancy, such as high levels of maternal stress, may be part of what leads the prenatal system to err according to Money. In an interactive model, it is important to remember that predispositions do not lead to inevitable outcomes. Money claims that environmental factors such as adult perceptions of an infant's sex based largely on genitalia and childhood sexual play influence the final outcome of one's sexual orientation. There is significant controversy about the different factors proposed by Money to explain the development of sexual orientation. Kauth and Kalichman's article provides a detailed critique of Money's account of sexual orientation, showing how there is weak evidence for many of the specific factors in Money's account as well as how Money's theory reflects many ideological biases.

Money's model of sexual orientation is only one part of his larger theory of sexual identity. Although also controversial, this larger theory has several aspects worth noting. For Money, the development of sexual identity is strongly related to children's body morphology, or outward appearance as male or female. Money argues that this outward appearance influences how others treat children as either male or female. Among the important variables in Money's theory, the treatment one receives based on morphology is a powerful force in shaping individuals' sexual self-definition.[3]

An alternative, interactive model is favored by Kauth and Kalichman—the epigenetic-biosexual potentiality model. Their goal is to account for both biological influences and cultural variation with a model that is truly dynamic and reciprocal. Kauth and Kalichman claim that hormonal influences vary in timing, degree, and duration, and the effects may predict a much wider array of potential sexual outcomes than is typically recognized. Their analysis also incorporates cross-cultural observations of a variety of sexual behaviors and sexual orientations to explain how social and cultural factors shape sexual expression. They provide a comprehensive definition of sexuality that includes sexual fantasy, emotional attachment, sexual behavior, and viewing sexual orientation as a circular rather than a linear phenomenon. Each of these elements is subject to change over time, and therefore, according to Kauth and Kalichman, sexuality is fluid and potentially wide ranging for both men and women.

THE POLITICS OF RESEARCH ON SEXUALITY AND SEXUAL ORIENTATION

The study of sexuality and sexual orientation provides one of the best windows on the interplay between research and ideology. To understand this interplay, we return to the perspectives of essentialism and social constructionism as they relate to sexuality and sexual orientation. Perhaps the most contentious issue relates to the different explanations for sexual orientation, and in particular, how those explanations connect to the question of whether sexual orientation is fixed or is a choice. For individuals in our strongly heterosexist culture to identify themselves as other than heterosexual involves confronting the prevailing political, moral, and social climate regarding gender and sexuality.[4] This climate has undergone major changes in the last thirty years as discrimination based on sexual orientation has reached the public discourse through several high-profile examples such as the military "don't ask, don't tell policy," the Defense of Marriage Act, and spouse equivalent employee benefits. The gay rights movement of the 1970s and 1980s, as part of a larger effort to end discrimination based on sexual orientation, presented sexual orientation as an alternative lifestyle, advocating open acknowledgment of sexual orientation and a recognition of the gay community. This "alternative" to heterosexuality was discussed as a "sexual preference." The choice of language served as a rhetorical device to remove the stigma from prevailing assumptions that cast homosexual behavior as deviant or pathological. The grounds of the political debate were civil rights and the status of sexual identity. Although the gay rights movement's efforts to destigmatize nonheterosexuality has had a political impact, it has also become clear that the rhetoric of choice cast sexual orientation as a matter of individual preference, or voluntary choice, and not as an identity status. Ironically, this connotation does not necessarily serve the larger political goal of equality, because the conservative political interpretation is to argue that a behavior that is a choice is not deserving of civil rights. The language used to describe nonheterosexuality has begun to shift, and the most politically neutral term today for many activists is *sexual orientation*. The movement away from sexual preference, or choice, is related both to the political meanings of these terms and to the growing evidence that sexual orientation, for many individuals, emerges very early in life and is not perceived or experienced by them as a choice. Essentialist, biological arguments that root sexual orientation in neuroanatomy or genetics serve the political motives of equality and provide evidence for individuals' subjective experiences that sexual orientation is not a choice.

This, however, is not the entire story of sexual orientation and the political meanings of scientific explanations. During the 1980s and 1990s, new accounts of nonheterosexual identity emerged to challenge the essentialist view of sexual orientation. Feminist critics have countered that the development of lesbian identities can be described by several different trajectories, and there is no consistent agreement that women recollect their sexual orientation emerging very early in life (Levine & Evans, 1991). Based on Levine and Evans's review of the evidence, the development of lesbian identity is different from the development of gay male identity. There is greater variability in the age at which women become aware of their attraction to women, and in general, women act on their erotic attractions to women at a later age than men act on their attractions to men. Kitzinger and Wilkinson (1995) describe the experiences of a sample of 80 women who, during adulthood and after a substantial period of commitment to heterosexuality, transitioned to a lesbian identity. This evidence does not support the notion that sexual orientation is a fixed entity within people, and essentialist, biological models would have difficulty explaining such evidence. For some women, the adoption of a lesbian identity has a political meaning that serves as an ideological statement against sexism and repressive gender role norms for women (Heyl, 1996), and for some lesbians, the political agenda precedes sexual orientation. Here we see a different intersection between ideology and the nature of a scientific explanation. A social constructionist analysis is more compatible with the evidence that shows changes within an individual's sexual identity (e.g., from heterosexual to lesbian) as well as with evidence that shows different developmental pathways toward sexual orientation. The strong version of social constructionism would claim that any attempt to label identity as a fixed biological identity is flawed and that humans have no stable, fundamental sexuality (Kitzinger, 1995). Debates between social constructionism and essentialism have dominated much of the literature on sexual orientation for the last fifteen years (Kitzinger, 1995; Gross, 1996). These issues are embedded in the politics of gender, because the meaning of sexual orientation is contested not just as a theoretical question but in the ways it affects the lives of gay men, lesbians, and bisexuals.

As we have argued in previous chapters, political motives and ideological beliefs structure how questions will be asked and what sorts of answers will fit into a researcher's belief system. We have briefly chronicled some of the important issues in the debate over the question of the origins of sexual orientation and the implications of whether individuals can and do exercise control over their sexual orientation. Other aspects of sexuality can be viewed from the lenses of essentialism and social constructionism. For example, the perspective that a researcher adopts will lead to varying answers to questions about sexual experiences and whether women and men have similar sexual response systems (presumably biologically driven) or differing sexual response systems (presumably socially constructed via cultural scripts) and about the universality of sexuality versus the culturally and socially constructed meaning of sexuality. An understanding of these perspectives should help you decipher why certain questions and issues are addressed and others remain unanswered.

SEXUALITY IS FLUID

All the articles in this chapter present a view of sexuality that emphasizes flexibility and fluidity. Sexual behaviors, erotic attractions, emotional attachments all vary across cultures, across sexes, and within individuals. Despite its variability, we would argue that sexuality is not infinitely flexible. Biology, culture, and gender roles all interact to constrain the variety of expressions of sexuality. Cultural variations follow discernable patterns that reflect the specific gender arrangements of a particular culture. In our society, as the gender roles of men emphasize independence, autonomy, and power, the consequences for sexuality are that men will initiate sex and will be more experienced and more knowledgeable sexually in comparison with female partners. Because the gender roles of women focus on relationships, nurturance, and intimacy, the consequence for sexuality is that women will connect sexual behaviors to conditions of love and commitment in relationships. In other cultures, in which the roles of men and women are different, their respective prescriptions for sexuality are also different. For instance, Muslim concepts of female sexuality emphasize the dangerous nature of femininity and women are seen as sexual aggressors, so women's sexuality tends to be highly controlled (Mernissi, 1987). Besides culturally constructed gender roles, sexuality may also be influenced by cultural pressures regarding fertility. Brettell and Sargent (1997) suggest that when children are highly valued, cultures place constraints on sexuality outside of marriage, and barriers to procreation such as birth control or homosexuality may be seen as evil. In societies in which procreation is less important, sexuality has many more socially acceptable forms, and sexuality is seen as an expression of individual identity and not simply a vehicle for parenthood.

You have already seen that individuals' concepts of sexuality may vary across their life. Erotic attractions and the sexual behaviors that follow from such attractions do not always follow a linear path. Some gay men's and many lesbians' initial sexual experiences are in the context of heterosexual relationships. These experiences may well reflect cultural constraints, and as gay and lesbian identities become part of the mainstream, this type of fluidity may decrease. On the other hand, as cultural restrictions on sexuality are lessening, we are seeing a marked increase in individuals labeling themselves as bisexual, which is why we need to interpret fluidity in many contexts, including historical, cultural, and political. Furthermore, situating sexuality in the context of relationships is vital to understanding the fluid nature of sexuality, according to Blumstein and Schwartz. In their article in this chapter, they present an example of a man who had a happy, successful, monogamous marriage to a woman. After she died unexpectedly, this man became in touch with his homoerotic feelings and entered into a relationship with another man. The critical point here is that this man did not see any disjunction between these two relationships and felt that both represented an integral part of his sexuality.

THE EMERGENCE OF SEXUALITY

Tiefer's article in this chapter reviews events across the life span as they are related to the construction of gender and sexuality. The question of the emergence of sexuality, its timing and significance during development, have run deeply through psychology beginning with Freud's formulations of early childhood sexuality. Unlike Freud, who postulated sex to be a basic biological drive, Tiefer believes that adult sexuality is the result of an individual's construction of gender in conjunction with cultural values and practices of sexuality. In her article, Tiefer presents many illustrations of how gender and sexuality relate. Two key points will help you understand these illustrations. First, the socialization of girls and boys around sexuality and relationships is substantially different. The expectations, values, beliefs, and behaviors ascribed to each sex differ, which accounts for many of the difficulties in communication and in sexual relationships that occur in adulthood. The second issue is that gender identity is such a central feature of one's overall sense of self that it motivates sexual activity. Rather than portray sexual behavior as a result of drives, instincts, or urges, as it has often been cast, Tiefer believes that sexual behaviors serve to maintain and reinforce individuals' sense of themselves as gendered members of a society. Thus social and cultural scripts about sexuality may themselves become key elements in one's identity, and failure to live up to these prescriptions may have painful consequences for feelings of self-worth.

Tiefer presents these consequences in her discussion of individuals whose identity does not match conventional descriptions. She argues that all variations of gender dysphoria[5]—including transsexualism (a persistent cross-gender identity), transvestitism (cross-dressing), and fetishism (use of a ritualized object, often women's garments, for sexual arousal)—represent a disjunction between gender identity and sexual scripts. According to Tiefer, gender identity confusion leads to mixed consequences for sexuality; some individuals seek to create a body that matches their gender identity (sex-change surgery), whereas others develop a transgendered identity that may include cross-gendered behavior without surgical treatment. Although sexual experiences vary widely, there is a consistent tendency to construct a sexual identity that best matches the gender identity of the individual. To reiterate, Tiefer's argument is that gender identity powerfully shapes one's search for sexual experiences that, in one way or another, match one's gender identity.

SEXUALITY AND RELATIONSHIPS

In the final reading in this chapter, Blumstein and Schwartz discuss the context within which much sexuality occurs, intimate relationships. Their article reviews the experiences of gay, lesbian, and heterosexual couples concerning sexuality. They contrast an essentialist view of sexuality and sexual orientation with their own position that sexuality is socially constructed and given meaning by individuals in the context of intimate relationships. From this perspective, it is important to consider how gender roles define sexuality and how the social organization of everyday life structures opportunities for sexual expression. For Blumstein and Schwartz, sexuality is situationally constructed and subject to modification through one's lifetime. Their analysis is supported by many examples of how gender roles and opportunities interact to construct sexual experiences. The social organization of college and university life is one example. Powerful social expectations for male-female interactions accompany mixed-sex living arrangements and freedom from parental supervision. It is not surprising that sexual behaviors such as one-night stands occur or that students engage in unusual sleeping arrangements that would have different meanings at other times of life. According to Blumstein and Schwartz, marriage provides another set of constraints on the organization of sexuality. Expectations for monogamy and gender role prescriptions create sexual patterns in which men initiate sex, sexual frequency between the couple declines over time, and men are more likely to fantasize about sex outside the relationship. Blumstein and Schwartz further suggest that the prevailing cultural models of sexuality have been dominated by a masculine perspective that emphasizes the frequency of sex, the timing of sex, and sexual fantasy. Another perspective, more reflective of the feminine gender role, would urge attention to attraction, love, and attachment and would recognize the degree to which eroticization occurs as a consequence of love and attachment. Further attention to the dynamic elements of relationships should yield a deeper understanding of how sexuality emerges from social and interpersonal experiences.

THE CONTRADICTIONS OF SEXUALITY

The study of sexuality has to account for some puzzling contradictions. Rooted in the imperatives of human reproduction, sexual behavior worldwide shows surprising variability. Biological processes and experiences that may show similarity across the sexes may also be distinguished by the experiences and roles of male and female. For many individuals, identity of sex, gender, and sexual orientation are in agreement, but this harmony is not true for everyone. Finally, what seems to be a fixed characteristic of people—the preference for sexual partners—may shift and change with age, experience, and opportunity. The relationship among sex, gender, and sexuality is complex. As you read the articles in this chapter, keep in mind the importance of accounting for individual differences in sexuality among people, differences rooted in both biology and culture and often expressed in the context of intimate relationships. These readings should help answer many questions about sexuality and gender and prepare you for addressing the relationship between gender and interpersonal relationships, social behavior, family, and health—all to be addressed in upcoming chapters.

NOTES

1. The answers are: 1. man seeking woman; 2. man seeking man; 3. woman seeking woman; 4. man seeking woman; 5. woman seeking man; 6. woman seeking man; 7. man seeking man; 8. woman seeking woman.
2. By using these examples, we are not claiming that any of these relationships necessarily has a sexual component.
3. As you have read in chapter 1, pseudohermaphrodism is a variation in the normal pattern of development. According to Money, the ambiguity of morphological characteristics is what leads others to treat pseudohermaphrodite children in ways that may contribute to the development of an ambiguous sexual identity.
4. We intentionally use the term **nonheterosexual** here in order to resist labeling identity as gay, lesbian, or bisexual—for some people, and for some explanations of sexual orientation, these labels are apt. However, for others, these labels are rooted in the heterosexist bias of our cultural view of sexuality.
5. Gender dysphoria refers to the class of experiences in which gender identity, sexual identity, and sexual orientation are in some way inconsistent with typical cultural patterns.

REFERENCES

Bailey, J. M. (1995). Biological perspectives on sexual orientation. In A. R. D'Augelli & C. J. Patterson (Eds.), *Lesbian, gay, and bisexual identities over the lifespan: Psychological perspectives* (pp. 102–135). New York: Oxford University Press.

Blumstein, P., & Schwartz, P. (1989). Intimate relationships and the creation of sexuality. In B. J. Risman & P. Schwartz (Eds.), *Gender in intimate relationships: A microstructural approach* (pp. 120–129). Belmont, CA: Wadsworth.

Brettell, C. B., & Sargent, C. F. (1997). *Gender in cross-cultural perspective.* Upper Saddle River, NJ: Prentice Hall.

Buss, D. M. (1989). Sex differences in human mate preferences: Evolutionary hypotheses tested in 37 cultures. *Behavioral and Brain Sciences, 12,* 1–14.

Byne, W. (1994, May). The biological evidence challenged. *Scientific American,* pp. 50–55.

Carroll, J., Volk, K., & Hyde, J. S. (1984). Differences between males and females in motives for engaging in sexual intercourse. *Archives of Sexual Behavior, 14,* 131–139.

Dion, K., & Dion, K. L. (1993). Individualistic and collectivistic perspectives on gender and the cultural context of love and intimacy. *Journal of Social Issues, 49,* 53–69.

Eagly, A. H. (1987). *Sex differences in social behavior: A social role interpretation.* Hillsdale, NJ: Erlbaum.

Gladue, B. A. (1994). The biopsychology of sexual orientation. *Current directions in psychological science, 3,* 150–154.

Gross, L. (1996). Identity politics, coming out and coming together. In M. E. Roger (Ed.), *Multicultural experiences, multicultural theories* (pp. 248–260). New York: McGraw-Hill.

Hamer, D. H., Hu, S., Magnuson, V. L., Hu, N., & Pattatucci, A. M. L. (1993, July 16). A linkage between DNA markers on the X chromosome and male sexual orientation. *Science, 261,* 321–327.

Heyl, B. S. (1996). Homosexuality: A social phenomenon. In K. E. Rosenblum & T. C. Travis (Eds.), *The meaning of difference: American constructions of race, sex and gender, social class, and sexual orientation* (pp. 120–130). New York: McGraw-Hill.

Jacobs, S. E., & Cromwell, J. (1992). Visions and revisions of reality: Reflections on sex, sexuality, gender, and gender variance. *Journal of Homosexuality, 23,* 43–69.

Kauth, M. R., & Kalichman, S. C. (1995). Sexual orientation and development: An interactive approach. In L. Diamant & R. D. McAnulty (Eds.), *The psychology of sexual orientation, behavior, and identity* (pp. 81–103). Westport, CT: Greenwood Press.

Kinsey, A. C., Pomeroy, W. B., & Martin, C. E. (1948). *Sexual behavior in the human male.* Philadelphia: W. B. Saunders.

Kinsey, A. C., Pomeroy, W. B., Martin, C. E., & Gebhard, P. H. (1953). *Sexual behavior in the human female.* Philadelphia: W. B. Saunders.

Kitzinger, C. (1995). Social constructionism: Implications for lesbian and gay psychology. In A. R. D'Augelli & C. J. Patterson (Eds.), *Lesbian, gay, and bisexual identities over the lifespan: Psychological perspectives* (pp. 136–164). Washington, DC: American Psychological Association.

Kitzinger, C., & Wilkinson, S. (1995). Transitions from heterosexuality to lesbianism: The discursive production of lesbian identities. *Developmental Psychology, 31,* 95–104.

Kurdek, L. A. (1994). The nature and correlates of relationship quality in gay, lesbian, and heterosexual cohabiting couples: A test of the contextual, investment, and discrepancy models. In B. Greene & G. M. Herek (Eds.), *Lesbian and gay psychology: Theory, research, and clinical applications* (pp. 133–155). Thousand Oaks, CA: Sage.

LeVay, S. (1991). A difference in hypothalamic structure between heterosexual and homosexual men. *Science, 253,* 1034–1037.

Levine, H., & Evans, N. J. (1991). The development of gay, lesbian, and bisexual identities. In K. E. Rosenblum & T. C. Travis (Eds.), *The meaning of difference: American construction of race, sex and gender, social class, and sexual orientation* (pp. 130–136). New York: McGraw-Hill.

Masters, W. H., & Johnson, V. E. (1966). *Human sexual response.* Boston: Little, Brown.

Masters, W. H., & Johnson, V. E. (1970). *Human sexual inadequacy.* Boston: Little, Brown.

Mernissi, F. (1987). *Beyond the veil: Male-female dynamics in modern Muslim society*. Bloomington and Indianapolis: Indiana University Press.

Money, J. (1987). Sin, sickness, or status? Homosexual gender identity and psychoneuroendrocrinology. *American Psychologist, 42*, 384–399.

Money, J. (1988). *Gay, straight, and in-between: the sexology of erotic orientation*. New York: Oxford University Press.

Oliver, M. B., & Hyde, J. S. (1993). Gender differences in sexuality: A meta-analysis. *Psychological Bulletin, 114*, 29–51.

Rose, S., & Frieze, I. H. (1989). Young singles' scripts for a first date. *Gender & Society, 3*, 258–268.

Rossi, A. S. (Ed.). (1994). *Sexuality across the life course*. Chicago: University of Chicago Press.

Tavris, C. (1992). *Mismeasure of women*. New York: Simon & Schuster.

Tiefer, L. (1995). *Sex is not a natural act & other essays*. Boulder, CO: Westview Press.

Tiefer, L., & Kring, B. (1995). Gender and the organization of sexual behavior. *Clinical Sexuality, 18*, 25–37.

Gender and the Organization of Sexual Behavior

LEONORE TIEFER, PHD, AND BRUNHILD KRING, MD

SEX, GENDER, AND SEXUAL BEHAVIOR

Relationships among "sex," "gender," and "sexual behavior" are more complicated than one might expect because the terms are not clear, and because the ideas behind the terms are not really clear either. Terms that seem in ordinary usage to be simple become complicated when the physician or clinician examines real people's real lives. The wise clinician pays attention to the lives and does not have assumptions based on the terms.

Some authors make a clean nature/culture split in discussing the relationship between "sex" and "gender." For example, Levine[18] suggests that

. . . gender is the experience of oneself or another person as male or female, and masculine and feminine. It is different from 'sex,' which refers to the biological distinction between females and males. *Sex* refers to such bodily matters as vagina, penis, lactation, and ejaculation. *Gender* refers to the psychological experience of these anatomical and physiological distinctions (p. 26).

This makes it sound as if both sex and gender are dichotomous classifications, with sex being the objective aspect and gender the subjective aspect.

But, often, perhaps even usually, neither sex nor gender fit neatly into binary categories. Persons with genetic intersex conditions or pseudohermaphroditic hormonal conditions, for example, are obvious sexual anomalies, because they have inconsistencies among their chromosomal sex, fetal gonadal sex, fetal hormonal sex, and sex of internal and external genitalia, making simply binary classification impossible. Even for "ordinary" people, when biologic sex is assigned at birth by either the presence or absence of a penis, it is assumed without examination that all the other biologic and physiologic variables are perfectly consistent. Multiple physical indicators are collapsed into a simple binary classification, and it is assumed that a judgment made on the basis of brief inspection of the external genitalia reflects genes, hormones, and internal anatomy. In fact, given the multiple physiologic variables, it is likely that were everything to be measured carefully, there would be several sexual categories, not just two. A person is assigned one of the two sexes at birth because there are only two categories in our vocabulary—there is no room for degrees of mixture.

Likewise, "gender" has multiple dimensions and takes a wide range of forms in real life. People rarely fall 100% into the masculine or feminine camps, whether we are talking about "gender identity" or "gender role." The original definition of the former emphasized subjective identity, "the sameness, unity, and persistence of one's individuality as male, female or ambivalent (p. 4),"[21] with the inclusion of "ambivalent" foreshadowing some of the complexities we see in clinical work.

Our society teaches each child how to answer the common question, "Are you a little girl or boy?" by swiftly "correcting" any "mistakes" that are made; e.g., "No, Bobby, you can't be a little girl, you are a little boy." A child's subjective experience of gender identity, then, becomes based on internalizing an an-

From the Departments of Urology (LT) and Psychiatry (LT, BK), Albert Einstein College of Medicine; and the Departments of Urology (LT) and Psychiatry (LT, BK), Montefiore Medical Center, Bronx, New York.

Address reprint requests to: Leonore Tiefer, Ph.D., Department of Urology, Montefiore Medical Center, 111 East 210th Street, Bronx, NY 10467.

swer that is based on adult identification of the newborn's external genitalia. When an individual's feelings, talents, and interests are compatible with the "gender role" associated with the sex of assignment, there is no disruption to such identity. This is often not the case, however.

One definition of gender role stresses "the traits and behaviors stereotypically expected of males and females in a culture (p. 5)"[1] and, the authors add, "people vary in the extent to which they incorporate these expected roles into their own personalities (ibid.)." This added qualifier again directs our attention toward thinking of gender as a mosaic of possibilities rather than a simple dichotomy, and alerts us as clinicians to remember that when an individual does not "match" the social stereotypes for his or her gender *role,* there may be repercussions in terms of secure gender *identity.*

Thus, when we look at the relationship between gender and sexual behavior we must begin with a mind open to multiple arrangements and possibilities, not just a two-category system, "men" and "women," or "male" and "female." As will be discussed later in this article, the revolution in gender roles that has affected expectations in the worlds of work, politics, family, sports, religion, the arts, and so on, has begun to extend even to gender identity, creating "gender-blending," "gender-bending," or "transgenderist" as new categories. But we are getting ahead of our story. We still need to introduce "sexual behavior."

Sexual behavior is no easier to define in a simple fashion than are "sex" or "gender." We certainly want a definition wider than just "the sexual act" or coitus; i.e., heterosexual penis-vagina intercourse. Nor do we want to expand this just to include acts of "foreplay" (because such acts could be anything); e.g., caressing, kissing, oral-genital contact, anal stimulation, genital masturbation, breast stimulation, dancing, prolonged eye contact, pressing together the soles of the feet, or synchronized breathing. Such a list would be very arbitrary. In some cultures, for example, kissing is considered an important sexual behavior, whereas in others it is considered a disgusting exchange of germs.[29] We could define sexual behavior as any behavior that produced genital arousal and

orgasm, or maybe just even genital arousal, or was erotic or romantic, but there are certainly many instances in which people engage in acts they would call sexual that they are doing for money, or as a favor, and do not experience arousal, romance, or eroticism.

The plain fact is that there are no universal sexual behaviors besides just the procreative act because sexuality is a social and cultural construction. Research may distort the subjective reality of people's lives by only counting genital contacts. By excluding affectionate cuddling or nongenital body contact, such research definitions result, for example, in lesbian couples having far less frequent sexual activity than gay male couples or heterosexual couples.[2]

In fact, what constitutes the range of sexual behaviors in a particular culture or subculture may be as distinctive as what a culture considers as music or as food. And, as with eating or enjoying or performing music, motivations to behave sexually are very broad, including strong emotional feelings ("passion"), the wish for attachment, the urge to feel valued in one's masculinity or femininity, or even fear, hatred, or the wish for domination. We will define sexual behavior and experience, then, in a subjective way, as whatever an individual or culture defines as sexual behavior.[13] The contents of this category tend to vary over the life span of an individual as well as among cultures.

THE IMPORTANCE OF GENDER TO SEXUAL BEHAVIOR

Gender is so obviously, but often so invisibly, related to sexuality that we may actually take its importance for granted. It needs to be stated quite boldly, therefore, that you cannot overestimate the importance of gender with regard to sexuality. If you know nothing about a person except his or her gender, you can make better predictions about sexual feelings and values than if you know the person's religion, health status, or sexual orientation, to choose three factors that also significantly relate to sexuality. Comparative studies of gay, straight, and lesbian couples, for example, suggest more similarities than differences in the sexual values and preferences of same-gendered people regardless of their homosexual or heterosexual relationships.[2]

Gender identity and gender role acquire and retain this primal influence because people learn all their attitudes and values and have all their personal experiences in a "gendered world" of sexual expression; i.e., a world of sexual possibilities that is thoroughly and inextricably colored and imbued with gender. It is difficult for us to even imagine a sexual act or relationship in which a person would not be continually aware of gender, and cross-cultural studies suggest this interpenetration is not unique to our society. All societies, however, are not equally or identically engendered. Compared with less industrialized societies, for example, modern Western societies are less gendered in terms of occupational roles, child care, clothing style, and certain social and recreational activities. Yet, gender differentiation still can be found throughout the way we "dress, sit, walk, talk, work, and play (p. 17)"[16] and, as the examples below show, throughout the way we learn about, think about, and conduct ourselves sexually.

Since to completely document the relationship between gender and sexuality would take an encyclopedic effort, let us illustrate the connections, and how they develop over the life span, with a potpourri of examples (mostly North American). The clinically astute reader will notice in these examples the seeds of two very common psychological problems. First, the fact that girls and boys are reared with markedly different expectations and values about sexuality makes communication between the sexes difficult, and predicts that misunderstandings will be common. Second, because gender is so important psychologically, the motivation for sexual activity, as for many other daily and lifetime choices and activities, is often at least partly to affirm gender identity and role, rather than simply for pleasure or intimacy or tension release. Sexual activity may even become the single most important activity to affirm identity; i.e., "the mainstay of identity."[23] As a consequence, a person having problems with sexual experience or performance can feel devastated and highly threatened and may think, "I'm not a *real* man or woman."

Let us see now how gender and sexuality evolve together and become inextricably intertwined.

Life Span Examples

Infancy   Numerous studies using deceptive birth announcements have shown that adults' descriptions of newborns' behavior and adults' behavior toward newborns are based on assumptions about the babies' sex, rather than their actual sex or their objective behavior.[31] It seems that adults want to know what sex a baby is before they know how to interact.

Then, throughout the early months of life, the tactile and kinesthetic experiences of baby girls and boys differ, as from the earliest age little girls are more often caressed and patted whereas baby boys are more often tickled and rough-housed.[32] Presumably, at least some of the ways adults experience bodily pleasure, comfort, and intimacy can be related to early physical experiences such as these, and to a sense of "rightness" about ways of being touched and held, which becomes part of the body ego.

Early Childhood   American children grow up in a highly gendered world. Their toys, games, clothes, conduct, and personalities are expected to show predictably gendered differences, and rewards and punishments (or at least strong discouragements) are meted out accordingly. Especially relevant to later sexual experience is the emphasis placed on physical appearance and "prettiness" in the lives of little girls from their earliest years, setting up a preoccupation of looks and standards of beauty that creates a lifetime of sexual concern about desirability, deservingness, and competence.[4]

Girls are permitted more latitude in their choice of clothes, toys, and activities than boys, as "tomboys" in our culture are more acceptable than "sissy boys."[24] Consequently, boys show more stereotyped preferences than girls at every age, and go to great lengths to avoid "girl-stuff." The sense that men's gender role depends on knowing and performing the correct behaviors and avoiding at all cost being seen as girlish or womanish becomes one of the central elements of adult masculinity, with extensive ramifications for "appropriate" sexual behavior and enjoyment.[14]

One of the tasks of early childhood is to learn the names of parts of the body. Lerner[16] has discussed the long-term consequences of "parental mislabeling" of female genitals. That is, little girls are universally taught that they have a mysterious internal organ called a vagina, but not that they have a vulva, labia, or, especially, a clitoris. Boys, if they are told anything about girls, are also usually taught that girls' genitals consist of "a vagina." Lerner speculates that this omission occurs because parents fear that telling girls that sexual pleasure is the main purpose of a part of their body might encourage precocious sexualization or sexual misconduct. She provides numerous adult case examples of how shame, sexual inhibition, and the absence of a sense of sexual permission is related to this silencing. All of us who provide sex therapy services use anatomic models and drawings to educate female and male patients about the names of women's genital organs as part of our work to reverse the cognitive and emotional effects of this repression.

The extreme example of this silencing, of course, is the practice of traumatic genital mutilation still commonly forced on young girls in parts of Asia and Africa, and even practiced in the United States by some immigrants from these regions.[19] The purpose of the operation, in which at least the clitoris is excised, and sometimes large sections of the labia and vulva are removed and the remaining genital region sutured with only a pinhole opening, is to ensure women's sexual modesty and fidelity. This is an example of how sexual pleasure and capacity can be sacrificed completely to the social demands of gender role, a situation we may compare to some of the surgical choices made by individuals with gender identity conflicts discussed later in this article.

Later Childhood   Children's gendered fantasies about sexual life remarkably prefigure lifelong sexual values and feelings. One study showed that many stories spontaneously made up by children aged 5 to 10 years had sexual or romantic themes; however, only boys told sexually explicit stories, and girls far outnumbered boys in telling romantic stories.[28] This gender difference can be followed directly up through adolescent intercourse experiences in which most sexually experienced 15-year-old girls but few sexually experienced 15-year-old boys expect to marry their current sexual partners.[6] The same pattern is shown in gender differences in sexual versus romantic motives for extramarital sexual affairs.[2] This fundamental difference between men and women in the motives for and the meaning of sexual relations is one of the most stable and significant aspects of the gendered experience of sexuality we are describing in this article, and it probably is the biggest source of difficulties in understanding and communication between the sexes.

Adolescence   Beginning in childhood, girls are taught to feel sexually vulnerable and endangered. The message intensifies in adolescence, highlighted by differences in the sexual encouragement offered to adolescent girls and boys. A central theme of school-based sexuality education holds that men and teenage boys "naturally" have strong sexual needs and are aggressive in fulfilling them, and that girls and women are responsible for protecting themselves from victimization.[8] It is no surprise, then, that surveys show significant differences in every age and ethnic group between men and women concerning how safe they feel in the world; e.g., in laundromats, walking in their neighborhood at night, walking through parks, going alone to the movies.[11] Most girls and women worry frequently about rape, and beginning in early adolescence, they shape their dress, conduct, choice of escort, recreation, travel, and even marriage and vocational plans around issues of sexual safety. The reality of rape and sexual assault cannot be minimized in terms of its effects on women's sense of sexuality, with the latest national statistics suggesting that one fourth of all women have suffered either attempted or completed rape by the end of their teenage years.[15]

Gender roles become intensified around the time of puberty, with physical changes leading to changes in self-image and the expectations of others.[12] Norms of courtship and sexual initiative-taking, importance of attractiveness, and motives for sexual activity (e.g., peer acceptance, keeping a relationship) become based on gender-differentiated stereotypes, and fixed in sexual identity and values.[1]

Recent research suggests that the double standard is undergoing some modification, such that boys and girls report comparable experience with many sexual acts (age at first intercourse, frequency of sexual fantasies and masturbation, and so on), but do not report equal comfort with sexual expression, do not have the same motives for engaging in sexual activity, and do not make the same sexual interpretations of nonverbal aspects of a dating relationship.[5] Girls are more likely to report sadness, ambivalence, or dissatisfaction after their first intercourse experience than are boys.[6] Teenage boys gain more in social status by experiencing coitus and telling their friends about it than do girls. This peer affirmation for sexuality reinforces the boy for pursuing and initiating sexual activity as a mainstay of his gender identity whereas the girl is reinforced for attractiveness and desirability as central to her gender identity.

Early Adulthood   Sexual activity in adulthood is governed largely by culturally appropriate sexual scripts.[10] Like scripts for plays, although far less detailed, sexual scripts specify who does and says what, when, and why. There are scripts for first sexual encounters, for paid sexual encounters, and for sexual encounters with familiar partners. Sexual scripts specify appropriate erogenous zones, forms of arousal, ways to initiate intercourse or other genital activities, and ways to terminate them.

Gender roles are among the primary elements in sexual scripts, and by the time individuals reach adulthood they usually have internalized the norms of sexual conduct appropriate for their gender in various circumstances. Norms have become somewhat less gender-differentiated in recent decades, but research shows that being appropriate to one's gender role often takes precedence over the specifically sexual satisfactions of arousal and orgasm. Women who identify with a traditional gender role are reluctant to initiate sexual activities, are less ac-

tive during sexual activities (e.g., not choosing the top position during coitus or actively thrusting against their partner), and are less likely to report being focused on their own sexual sensations, yet such women report psychological satisfaction with their sexual activities.[25]

Sexual conquest is so central to the young man's peer-based gender role that marital sexual satisfaction may seem bland. The quantitative ("scorecard") aspects of sexual experience (how many? how long?) continue to dominate even when there is only one partner, and successful sexual experiences become defined by erection and ejaculation performance scores. Consequently, men with complaints of sexual dysfunction report devastating effects on their gender self-esteem. One patient with erection problems said, "I can't go into a bar anymore; I just don't feel like one of the guys." The ready adoption of invasive treatments such as penile prostheses and intracavernosal injections for erectile dysfunction can be attributed to this gender role devastation and the quest for erectile security to restore masculinity.[30] Imagine the irony of a situation in which invasive surgery is sought to correct a gender disturbance! It is similar to the situation ot transsexualism we discuss later.

Awareness and disclosure of feelings during sex remain elusive for many well-socialized men. Many men fail in their ability to fuse affection with sexual satisfaction (many never try) because of early gender training and internalized adolescent sexual norms that require that they be willing and able to perform sexually at all times and under all circumstances.[34] Performance anxiety and sexual dysfunction are common outcomes as men continue to tune out their emotions and act as if the penis were not attached to the heart. They have no way other than symptomatically to express feelings such as shyness, fear of women, or disinterest in sex.

A study of 100 well-educated, self-defined "happy" married couples revealed high frequencies (more than half the respondents) of sexual dysfunctions (arousal and orgasm problems) and sexual difficulties; e.g., partner chooses inconvenient time, inability to relax, too little foreplay.[9] Women had more of both types of complaints, but wives were far more aware of their husbands' complaints than their husbands were of their wives' complaints. Even in these happy couples, communication about sexual activities was greatly lacking.

Later Adulthood   As people age, they require gender role flexibility to adapt to the inevitable physical changes affecting sexual interest, arousal, and orgasm.[20] If sexual scripts are governed too rigidly by early gender role training, then the body's age-related changes may prohibit continued sexual activity. If youthful ideals of attractiveness or youthful standards of performance persist as central features of gender role, then individuals and couples will cease sexual activity rather than risk failure in their own eyes.

Gendered demographic realities of later life challenge sexuality as much as the physiologic changes. Women live longer than men, which means there are many more women than men in older age groups, and many widows, as wives tend to be younger than their husbands. Widowers tend to remarry, whereas widows, surviving their husbands by an average of 18 years, do not.[32] The earlier death of men means also that many wives spend asexual years caring for a declining husband. The sexual prospects of older women are limited by their own gender role training (older women are less likely to masturbate or switch to lesbian activities) and by that of younger men, an available age group that generally is not attracted to older women.

SEXUALITY AND INDIVIDUALS WITH ATYPICAL GENDER IDENTITIES

Because of our inescapable adherence to sexual scripts, we cannot have sexual feelings without simultaneously being aware of gender identity and role. Subtle conflicts about gender identity may give rise to sexual nervousness or more serious sexual anxieties or other problems. The expectations a person internalizes from the social norms must match his or her own wishes and needs in order for a person to feel comfortable during sexual activity. And a person's behavior must match the partner's expectations for both people to feel appropriate and comfortable. Partners may go along with the sexual styles of their lovers or spouses, but these styles may not arouse their own feelings of desire because they do not match a script for gender appropriateness. Because few couples ever openly discuss their sexual longings and reactions, such discrepancies may remain unacknowledged through decades of sexual activity.

In our society there is a spectrum of subjective gender nonconformity and overt experimentation with gender roles. The most relevant syndromes for the clinician are fetishism, transvestitism, gender dysphoria, transgenderism, and transsexualism. The common denominator for these overlapping forms of sexual expression is some degree of gender identity confusion and some urge to dress in the clothes socially appropriate to the other gender.

The use of a fetishistic object (e.g., women's lingerie) during sexual behavior can be seen as a way for a man to overcome and master episodes of childhood humiliation and anxiety that left him with an uncertain sense of his masculinity. Stoller[27] argues that sexual perversions are more common in men because many boys fail at the difficult task of separating from "peaceful symbiosis" with the mother and developing a masculine identity.

Transvestitism is related to fetishism in that a specific set of objects is necessary for sexual arousal. Most transvestites are men with male gender identity, male gender role, and heterosexual orientation who dress occasionally in women's clothes for purposes of sexual arousal, anxiety management, or self-soothing. A common cause for periodic cross-dressing derives from the use of women's garments to console the man against the dreaded loss of the mother; i.e., it assuages separation anxiety.[3]

Transvestites have an insecure sense of masculinity. Cross-dressing behavior constitutes an attempt at mastery as the man, in fantasy, transforms the experience of a childhood sexual trauma into an adult triumph.[26] To ward off threats to his masculinity and avoid anxiety in the interaction with women, the transvestite embodies the woman for the arousal of his masculine self. As Docter[7] explains

> Nothing more clearly provides a clue to the experience of the transvestite than does the mirror. The cross dresser never wants to perceive himself as his male self in the mirror; he wants to see images, stimuli, and many variations of his dream girl. The mirror offers him endless reflections of his ideal pin-up; the one "girl" who will never reject or disappoint; a predictable, reliable partner in the adventures of sex (p. 208).[7]

When male transvestites marry, their sexual scripts have to accommodate their sexual fantasy scenarios. Obviously, with all major roles already cast, their wives are relegated to the status of audience or extras.

One might imagine that variations such as the use of female garments could be integrated easily in the lovemaking repertoire of two consenting adults. Questionnaire studies with the wives of transvestites indicate, however, that the female partners have mixed reactions to their husbands' peculiar (or particular) sexual script requirements.[7] The majority of respondents disliked the cross-dressing behavior, despite acknowledging and appreciating the heightened sexual arousal it inspired. The greatest concern of the wives centered around keeping the cross-dressing secret from children and neighbors, and they resented risk-taking episodes of cross-dressing in public. Mental coping strategies included denial ("close your eyes and let him do it" p. 177),[7] avoidance of sexual intimacy, rationalization that this will contribute to personal growth, tolerance out of a maternal attitude, and suppression of honest feelings.

Transsexualism provides a striking example in which the unity of gender, gender identity, and gender role has fallen apart. Transsexuals have a profound and persistent cross-gender identification. The DSM-IV specifies that this syndrome is characterized by a repeatedly stated desire to be the opposite sex, insistence on cross-dressing, strong and persistent preferences for cross-sex roles in fantasy play, preference for games and playmates of the other gender, discomfort with one's assigned gender role, and rejection of one's genitals.

The disowning of one's male or female body and its secondary sexual characteristics goes so far that the affected individuals insist on surgically modifying their body (mastectomy, hysterectomy, penectomy, orchiectomy, vaginoplasty, phalloplasty) in order to tailor it to their own inner sense of masculinity or femininity.

What is the sexual life of such individuals? Gender dysphoria has profound but inconsistent effects on sexual behavior, sexual desire, sexual self-esteem, and erotic attachments. Some transsexuals are asexual, some bisexual, and some monosexual (with partners of one or the other sex). It is often hard to tell, however, what their spontaneous attitudes are because so many transsexuals shape their narrated histories to conform to what they think will gain approval for sex reassignment surgery. Attempts to conform to the "correct" presentation for a transsexual may be motivated not only by a calculating attitude, but also by a sometimes desperate attempt to escape generalized identity confusion. Patients with chaotic and painful histories may focus on gender reassignment as the solution for many kinds of internal confusion, and may be bitter and depressed postoperatively when feelings of confusion remain.

Because society insists that each of us be unambiguously one gender or the other, a person with vague or confused or "in-between" gender identity fits nowhere. The recent growth, however, of the "transgenderist" category of persons with significant cross-dressing history who seek hormonal but not surgical treatment may represent the realization of "mixed" gender identity.

SEXUALITY AND ATYPICAL GENDER IDENTITIES IN ANTHROPOLOGIC PERSPECTIVE

Alternative gender concepts in cultures different from ours (e.g., the berdache of Native American groups or the Hijras of India) shed further light on the complexities of gender and sexuality, and the options provided in different cultural settings.

Institutionalized religious sex reversal within Native American groups was reported by European explorers and early travelers in the Americas with both fascination and abhorrence. Bisexual shamans were called "berdaches" and were documented in every region in North America. Berdaches were men-women whose gender status was defined by the tasks they performed rather than by anatomic phenotype. Berdaches performed female food-gathering, cared for the sick, educated the young, buried the dead, and were sexual partners to warriors and married men. Native American groups may have regulated male-male sexual relationships with the institution of the berdache because, although sexual contact between two men was not prohibited, men were encouraged to have sex instead with a berdache.

Having only two gender categories based on anatomy, and prejudiced against sodomy, Spanish conquistadors and English and French settlers failed to understand the Native American third gender category, and made every effort to eradicate the berdache tradition.[33]

The Hijras of India represent yet another configuration of gender and sexuality.[22] In a ceremony of commitment to a religious life, biologic men are surgically emasculated. They live, dress, and act as women, and in their religious capacity they perform at birth celebrations and weddings. Their religious income, however, is inadequate, and economic hardship leads many of them into prostitution with male clients. Again, the opportunity to have sex with a Hijra may serve as a way to avoid homosexuality in the community.

SUMMARY

Gender socialization seems important in every culture although the precise nature of gender categories and the specifics of gender roles differ across societies. Gender socialization produces in most people a compulsion to behave according to appropriate rules and expectations, and a grave anxiety about not being considered by others, or by themselves, truly male or female. Sexual performance is tightly tied to appropriate gender role behavior, and the need to conform to conventional scripts probably inhibits most people from expressing individual desires and interests. The gratification obtained from gender affirmation, however, may compensate for any lost erotic or intimate rewards.

Our society is in the throes of major changes in gender roles, and many of the frequent public debates about sexual issues (e.g., impact of pornography, prevalence of sexual abuse and harassment, advisability of public sex education, propriety of homosexuals in the military) reflect insecurities about the effect of these new roles on sexual behavior. Present knowledge suggests that any change in gender roles is bound to have a major effect on sexual behavior, both within the life of an individual and within a society. Insecurities and adjustment difficulties are likely to remain normative, and to be part of the problems brought to every mental health clinician.

REFERENCES

1. Allgeier, E. R., McCormick, N. B. *Changing Boundaries: Gender Roles and Sexual Behavior.* Palo Alto, Mayfield Publishing, 1983.
2. Blumstein, P., Schwartz, P. *American Couples.* New York, Morrow, 1983.
3. Bradley, S. J. *Gender disorders in childhood: A formulation.* In Steiner, B. W. (ed). *Gender Dysphoria: Development, Research, Management.* New York, Plenum, 1985, pp. 175–188.
4. Chapkis, W. *Beauty Secrets.* Boston, South End Press, 1986.
5. Christopher, F. S., Roosa, M. W. Factors affecting sexual decisions in the premarital relationships of adolescents and young adults. *In* McKinney, K., Sprecher, S. (eds). *Sexuality in Close Relationships.* Hillsdale, NJ: Lawrence Erlbaum, 1991.
6. Coles, R., Stokes, G. *Sex and the American Teenager.* New York, Harper and Row, 1985.
7. Docter, R. F. *Transvestites and Transsexuals: Toward a Theory of Cross-Gender Behavior.* New York, Plenum, 1988.
8. Fine, M. Sexuality, schooling, and adolescent females: The missing discourse of desire. *Harvard Educational Review 58,* 29–53, 1988.
9. Frank, E., Anderson, C., Rubinstein, D. Frequency of sexual dysfunction in "normal" couples. *N Engl J Med 299,* 111–115, 1978.
10. Gagnon, J. H. Scripts and the coordination of sexual conduct. *Nebraska Symposium on Motivation,* 21: 27–60, 1973.

11. Gordon, M. T., Riger, S. *The Female Fear: The Social Cost of Rape.* Urbana, IL, University of Chicago Press, 1989.

12. Hill, J. P., Lynch, M. E. The intensification of gender-related role expectations during early adolescence. *In* Brooks-Gunn, J., Petersen, A. C. (eds). *Girls at Puberty.* New York, Plenum Press, 1983, p. 201.

13. Katchadourian, H. A. The terminology of sex and gender. In *Human Sexuality: A Comparative and Developmental Perspective.* Berkeley, University of California Press, 1979, pp. 8–34.

14. Kimmel, M. S. (ed). *Changing Men: New Directions in Research on Men and Masculinity.* Newbury Park, Sage, 1987.

15. Koss, M. P., Gidyez, C. A., Wisniewski, N. The scope of rape: Incidence and prevalence of sexual aggression and victimization in a national sample of higher education students. *J Consult Clin Psychol 55,* 162–170, 1987.

16. Lerner, H. G. *Women in Therapy.* Northvale, NJ, Jason Aronson, 1988.

17. Levine, S. *Sex Is Not Simple.* Columbus, OH, Psychology Publishing Company, 1988.

18. Levine, S. *Sexual Life: A Clinician's Guide.* New York, Plenum Press, 1992.

19. Lightfoot-Klein, H. *Prisoners of Ritual: An Odyssey into Female Genital Circumcision in Africa.* New York, Harrington Park Press, 1989.

20. Masters, W. H., Johnson, V. E. *Human Sexual Response.* Little, Brown, 1966.

21. Money, J., Ehrhardt, A. A. *Man and Woman, Boy and Girl.* Baltimore, Johns Hopkins University Press, 1972.

22. Nanda, S. *Neither Man Nor Woman: The Hijras of India.* Belmont, CA, Wadsworth, 1990.

23. Person, E. S. Sexuality as the mainstay of identity: Psychoanalytic perspectives. *Signs 5,* 605–630, 1980.

24. Plumb, P., Cowan, G. A developmental study of de-stereotyping and androgynous activity preferences of tomboys, nontomboys, and males. *Sex Roles 10,* 703–712, 1984.

25. Radlove, S. Sexual response and gender roles. *In* Allgeier, E. R., McCormick, N. B. (eds). *Changing Boundaries: Gender Roles and Sexual Behavior.* Palo Alto, CA, Mayfield Publishing, 1983, p. 87.

26. Stoller, R. *Perversion: The Erotic Form of Hatred.* New York, Pantheon, 1975.

27. Stoller, R. *Presentations of Gender.* New Haven, Yale University Press, 1985.

28. Sutton-Smith, B., Abrams, D. M. Psychosexual material in the stories told by children. *In* Gemme, R., Wheeler, C. C. (eds). Progress in Sexology. New York, Plenum Press, 1977.

29. Tiefer, L. The kiss. *Human Nature 1,* 28–37, 1994.

30. Tiefer, L. The medicalization of impotence: Normalizing phallocentrism. *Gender and Society 8,* 363–378, 1994.

31. Unger, R. K. *Female and Male: Psychological Perspectives.* New York, Harper and Row, 1979.

32. Unger, R., Crawford, M. *Women and Gender: A Feminist Psychology.* New York, McGraw-Hill, 1992.

33. Williams, W. L. *The Spirit and the Flesh.* Boston, Beacon Press, 1986.

34. Zilbergeld, B. *The New Male Sexuality.* New York, Bantam, 1992.

CHECKPOINTS

1. Gender is critically, but invisibly, related to sexuality. According to Tiefer and Kring, sexual behavior is largely an expression of a culture's prescriptions for men and women.

2. Examples of transgendered individuals show how difficult it is to construct a sexual identity when sex and gender identity are discordant.

To prepare for reading the next section, think about these questions:

1. What do you think is the relationship between sexuality and sexual orientation?

2. Do you believe sexual orientation is biologically determined or socially constructed?

Sexual Orientation and Development: An Interactive Approach

MICHAEL R. KAUTH AND SETH C. KALICHMAN

DEFINING SEXUAL ORIENTATION

It is difficult to imagine any other culture that has been as consumed by sexuality as modern Western society during the past century. Rather than a general interest in sexuality, the West has demonstrated an obsession with homosexuality and once-taboo practices such as masturbation and oral sex. Despite claims of scientific objectivism, most theories of sexual attraction are stereotypes about homosexual development cloaked in scientific jargon. Kuhn (1970) charged that scientific theories reflect the socially accepted assumptions of their day and therefore are bound by their sociological and historical context. When theoretic anomalies become numerous, a scientific revolution occurs. Current thought about sexual orientation is on the threshold of such a revolution as it struggles to incorporate data from DNA studies, family prevalence studies, and cross-cultural and transhistorical observations. This chapter shifts away from single-factor theories toward a more comprehensive interactive model of sexual orientation.

Many ancient writers mused on the nature of attraction to one gender or the other, or to both, without interference of social stigma or assignment of sexual identity (Boswell 1980, 1994). Although *sexual orientation* is a loaded Western concept, the term is still a useful one, if we avoid imposing Western thoughts and meanings associated with our language on non-Western, noncontemporary cultures.

By sexual orientation, we mean the cumulative experience and interaction of erotic fantasy, romantic-emotional feelings, and sexual behavior directed toward one or both genders. These three somewhat independent and parallel dimensions are traditionally conceived as being overlaid on a plane of sexual orientation (Bell & Weinberg 1978; Weinberg, Williams & Pryor 1994; cf. Kinsey et al., 1948, 1953) (figure 1). Opposite-sex attraction is located on one end and same-sex attraction on the other. This model suggests that sexual orientation is not static and may vary throughout the course of a lifetime. Dimensional concordance for one gender (monosexuality) refers to exclusive homosexuality or heterosexuality. Gender divergence or dimensional concordance for both genders refers to bisexuality. Celibate individuals may identify as falling somewhere on this plane based on their feelings, fantasies, or political views. The cultural milieu determines the meaning of any given set of sexual feelings, fantasies, and behaviors. People who have sexual feelings or engage in stigmatized behaviors may proclaim or be assigned a social identity (Ross 1987). In repressive cultures, public sexual behavior may be inconsistent with personal attraction or identity, and socially unacceptable feelings may be suppressed or unrecognized for years.

Figure I *Kinsey Scale of Sexual Orientation*

Traditional theories of sexual orientation have often assumed default development of heterosexuality and presented a "sickness model" of homosexuality. Most theories have proposed single or few etiological factors, either constitutional or imposed, implying that humans somehow develop outside the influence of their biologic or social context. In addition, a great deal of current thinking about human sexual orientation comes from observations of nonhuman animal sexual development. Nonhuman sexual behavior is treated as homologous to human sexual orientation, although development between the two markedly differs, and reflexive nonhuman animal sexual behavior has little to do with human cognitive-affective experience.

While nonhuman animal observations raise many interesting questions about human experience, they answer few. To understand human behavior, we must study humans—and not only those with atypical or aberrant developmental histories. We must focus on what goes "right" with sexuality across a variety of populations. Anthropologist Ruth Benedict (1938) argued that the "facts of nature" are not "natural" for humans, for culture serves as nature's mediator. By comparing cultural influences on sexual experience at different historical periods, we can begin to map out a range of human sexual expressions and identify culture-constant regularities. A useful theory of sexual orientation will merge findings from the laboratory and the field into a transhistorical and interactive model.

What are the range and forms of gender attraction and sexual behavior across culture and time? Briefly, whether sanctioned or stigmatized or ignored, same-sex sexual behavior and thus for many, bisexuality, is not uncommon to most human societies. Heterosexual and homosexual behavior may occur concurrently or sequentially. Aristocratic men in ancient Japan and classical Athens practiced concurrent bisexuality (Bullough 1976), maintaining parallel sexual relationships with men and women. In Athens, male citizens were expected to marry and produce children, and as long as these social obligations were fulfilled, there was no stigma associated with simultaneous sexual relationships with men. In fact, in the *Sympo-*

sium, Plato proclaimed that profound love and intellectual intimacy are possible only with other men. Although the ideal affectional relationship was an older, married male with a younger, single male (Dover 1978), in noted cases the *erastes* ("lover") and *eromenos* ("beloved") were close in age (Achilles and Patroklos), the beloved was older (as was Socrates to Alcibiades), or the relationship continued past puberty (again, Socrates and Alcibiades; Boswell 1980). Furthermore, despite the custom of bisexuality, some men maintained only monosexual relationships and experienced not a small degree of harassment for their actions. While a few men may have been limited in their pool of sexual partners, it is curious that in a society that encouraged sexual activity with both genders, a minority of people had partners of only one. For ancient Greek women, same-sex sexual behavior has been documented, although it is unclear whether relationships were age structured or concurrent for both genders. Although there are many dissimilarities between the two cultures, men and women today in the United States who identify as bisexual often practice concurrent bisexuality and may or may not be in a heterosexual marriage (Weinberg, Williams, & Pryor, 1994).

Sequential bisexuality refers to alternating sexual relationships with one gender, then the other, but not both at the same time. An example of this type of sexual expression is present-day Melanesian societies and related cultures in the Pacific (Herdt 1984). At about age 9, Melanesian boys leave their families and reside exclusively with men until marriage or approximately 19 years of age. During this time, they acquire their manhood and sexual potency by regularly fellating to orgasm older males who are themselves married. A similar male fertility ritual among Sambians of New Guinea may last from age 7 to 30 years of age (Herdt 1981). Upon marrying, Melanesian and Sambian men maintain almost exclusive heterosexual relationships, with the exception that married men provide semen to young males. Observations often depict ritualized sexual behavior in these cultures as erotic and imply that emotional attachments between male pairs sometimes develop (Herdt 1981, 1984). In both Melanesian and Sambian cultures, women are perceived as inherently fertile. Therefore no procedure is necessary to acquire it, which is not to say that same-sex sexual behavior does not occur for other reasons among women in these cultures.

Nondevelopmental examples of sequential bisexuality include modern bisexual men and women who do not have concurrent relationships (Weinberg, Williams & Pryor 1994) and sexual behavior among men (and less often women) in same-sex living conditions such as military institutions (Berrube 1990; Shilts 1993). Among military personnel, neither party may identify as gay, and later each may engage in exclusive heterosexual behavior, although some do not. While most same-sex sexual activity among single-gender populations is viewed as situational and about sexual release, this explanation avoids the question of why celibacy or masturbation is not an option and ignores evidence of affectional relationships, some of which continue outside the restrictive environment.

A third expression of sexual orientation is *monosexuality,* meaning sexual feelings and interest in one gender. Heterosexual or homosexual relationships may be concurrent or sequential. Ideal heterosexual relationships involve marriage (and only one sexual partner), although most do not. Homosexuality as an identity is unique to the past century (Halperin 1990). In 1869, the term *homosexual* was first used to refer to men who love men and who enjoy receptive anal intercourse (Bullough 1976). The word was later applied to women who love women, and, finally, the terms *gay men* and *lesbians* were employed to represent same-sex attraction, as well as a political identity. Most modern societies influenced by the West have citizens who identify as gay or lesbian, including the United States, Great Britain, Canada, Australia, Germany, Denmark, and Norway. The last two countries recognize same-sex marriage. While at any given time a significant proportion of gay men and lesbians are in relationships (McWhirter & Mattison 1984; Peplau & Amaro 1982), a few may have more than one partner, and many may have no partner at all.

Simply because one form of sexuality (e.g., heterosexuality) is upheld as the ideal does not indicate that the ideal is typical or preferable or that other forms of behavior are uncommon. Variety in sexual expression, development, and social norms is one of the most striking features across different cultures. Keep this variety in mind while examining the following single-factor theories of sexual orientation and later two interactive approaches.

OVERVIEW OF SINGLE-FACTOR THEORIES OF SEXUAL ORIENTATION

Biologic Models: Homosexuals Are Born

Most biologic models of sexual orientation are founded on dichotomous categories (Ross 1987): masculine-feminine, active-passive, normal-abnormal, and heterosexual-homosexual. Biologic theories also assume that hormonalization, development, and sexual desires and behavior express (heterosexual) gender roles. *Gender role* may be defined as the public expression of what society considers maleness, femaleness, or ambivalence (Money 1988, 1991). (Although Money allowed for ambivalent identity and androgyny, these characteristics are either ignored or considered "cross-gendered" in his text.) Biologic theory holds "normal" sexual development to be heterosexual. Androgens are thought to make "men," and the absence of androgen and/or presence of estrogen makes "women." Heterosexual gender role dictates that men act "masculine" and women act "feminine." Men are perceived as independent and active (the inserter) in the sexual role with women, while "women" are dependent and sexually passive (receptive) with men. All sexual dyads are conceived as expressions of heterosexual gender roles.

When the heterosexual gender role bias is applied to nonheterosexuals, it reads like this: Sexual attraction to men is what women do; therefore, men who like men are more like women ("feminine"). By contrast, attraction to women is what men do; therefore, women who like women are more like men ("masculine"). In a patriarchal society, men who are like women are less than "men," and women who are like men are a threat. This misogynist reasoning employs negative stereotypes about women to devalue gay men and lesbians. An interesting paradox within the heterosexual gender role bias is that gay men who perform in the active sexual role are viewed as more "masculine" and somehow less gay. Bisexuality is difficult, if not impossible, to explain with a gender-roled model.

Assuming for the moment that there are stark contrasts between (heterosexual) men and women, researchers reason that they may discover the source of these differences by examining sexual differentiation. Furthermore, if gay people are cross-gendered in sexual attraction, then gay men should have much in common with heterosexual women, and lesbians should be similar to heterosexual men. The following sections examine the degree to which data from hormonal, neuroanatomic, genetic, and twin-family studies confirm these presuppositions and support a biologic model of sexual orientation. (For a comprehensive review of biologic data, see . . . Byne & Parsons 1993.)

Hormonal Studies   Considerable research has produced evidence that sexually dimorphic reproductive behaviors are organized perinatally or prenatally by gonadal steroid hormones in laboratory animals. The premise behind hormonal studies is that human sexual orientation is determined by hormonalization and that all mammals develop similarly. Most hormonal studies focus on homosexual behavior in laboratory animals.

The prenatal hormonal hypothesis, based on studies with rats, purports that mammalian brain development is female and introduction of androgens by the male fetus differentiates the male brain. Unlike differentiation of external genitalia, loss of female characteristics and development of male characteristics in the brain is independent. In some species, testosterone has a direct effect on androgen receptors, while, among others, androgen must be converted to estrogen by aromatase enzymes in the brain. Presenting behavior, or lordosis, is displayed by female rats or by genetic males castrated perinatally and is dependent on gonadal hormones. Mounting and thrusting behavior is displayed by intact male rats or by genetic females exposed to androgens in early

development. Thus, the prenatal theory holds that male heterosexuality and female homosexuality are products of prenatal exposure to androgens, while male homosexuality and female heterosexuality result from insensitivity to or lack of androgens. One would then predict that most gay men would evidence syndromes of androgen insensitivity or deficiency and lesbians would show signs of prenatal androgen exposure. However, extensive literature reviews by Meyer-Bahlburg (1984) and Byne and Parsons (1993) found no evidence of significant gonadal or hormonal dysfunction in gay men or lesbians. Although Meyer-Bahlburg cited three studies suggesting gay men had lower levels of testosterone, twenty studies found no difference.

There also was no evidence that progesterone-related compounds used during pregnancy to prevent miscarriage—which may have a demasculinizing effect on the brain—influence sexual orientation (Gooren 1990; Meyer-Bahlburg 1984; Ehrhardt, Meyer-Bahlburg, Feldman & Ince 1984; Beral & Colwell 1981; Kester, Green, Finch & Williams, 1980; Hines 1982). Although one group of researchers (Ehrhardt et al. 1984) found an increase in bisexuality and homosexuality in women exposed to a potent progesterone, this finding is contrary to what is known about sexual differentiation of the brain, which is *not* mediated by estrogen. Another set of researchers (Dittmann, Kappes & Kappes 1992; Money, Schwartz & Lewis 1984) concluded that a genetic recessive condition in women, congenital virilizing adrenal hyperplasia (CVAH), which androgenizes development, increased the likelihood of homosexuality. However, the impact of having obviously masculinized genitals (an enlarged clitoris and shallow vagina) and knowledge about their condition were not assessed.

Support for prenatal hormonal theory has been sought in postnatal hormonal feedback mechanisms. In adult female rats, estrogen acts on the hypothalamus to exert positive and negative feedback on release of luteinizing hormone (LH) for regulation of ovulation. In normal adult male rats, estrogen has only a negative feedback on LH release, presumably because of early exposure to androgens. Therefore, the theory goes, if gay men were insufficiently andro-genized prenatally, they should show a stronger posi-tive feedback to estrogen than do heterosexual men. Although two groups of researchers reported that gay men do show a slight, positive feedback (Gladue, Green & Hellman 1984; Dorner, Rhode, Stall, Krell & Masius 1975), better-controlled studies demon-strated that the type of feedback response is deter-mined by the hormonal status of the individual at the time of estrogen challenge rather than by genetic sex or sexual orientation (Gooren 1986a, 1986b). Among matched groups of homosexual and heterosexual men, no differences were found to estrogen chal-lenge. Gooren suggested that previous supportive studies were influenced by differences in testicular function and that a true positive feedback response cannot be demonstrated in gonadally intact men (Gooren 1986b, 1990).

In sum, incomplete or disconfirming evidence has been found for a prenatal theory of human sexual ori-entation or, at least, homosexuality. There is no evi-dence that hormonalization and sexual development in rats is comparable to human development, and other data suggest that prenatal hormonalization dif-fers in its process and effects across species (Money 1988, 1991). Consistent with the heterosexual gender role bias, laboratory observers viewed lordotic male rats and mounting females as homosexual, but male rats who mounted males were labeled heterosexual.

Neuroanatomic Studies The idea behind neuro-anatomic studies is that prenatal hormonalization re-sults in sexually dimorphic brain structures or nuclei, which in turn affect sexual orientation and behavior. Recent attention has focused on a group of cells called the interstitial nuclei 2 through 4 of the ante-rior hypothalamus (INAH2, etc.). Two studies found differences in INAH3 (Allen, Hine, Shryne & Gorski 1989; LeVay 1991). Popular attention has been given to LeVay's study, which reported that INAH3 was smaller for gay men than for heterosexual men. LeVay speculated that INAH3 is comparable to the sexually dimorphic nucleus of the preoptic area (SDN-POA) in rats, which regulates sexual behavior and lordosis in male rats. In male rats, size of the

SDN-POA is related to frequency of mounting. LeVay suggested that INAH3 operates similarly in gay men. Aside from conceptual problems and lack of supportive evidence from prenatal hormonal the-ory, LeVay's hypothesis fails to account for gay men who do not engage in receptive anal intercourse, for bisexuals, or for lesbians. Methodological concerns also render his conclusions premature and question-able. Sexual histories of subjects were incomplete, several subjects died of AIDS, and the size of INAH3 may depend on adult levels of testosterone that de-crease during end-stage AIDS.

Other brain sites that have been purported to influ-ence sexual orientation are the suprachiasmatic nu-cleus in the hypothalamus, the anterior commissure, and the corpus callosum. To date there is no indica-tion how these structures influence sexual behavior. Anatomic correlates of sexual orientation do not in themselves denote a biologic origin. Experience is known to alter the physiology and structure of the brain in laboratory animals (Bhide & Bedi 1984; Turner & Greenough 1985; Kraemer, Ebert, Lake & McKinney 1984).

Twin and Family Studies Despite weak data from hormonal and neuroanatomic studies, twin and family studies have produced supportive evidence for a bio-logic basis of sexual orientation. In a series of studies, Bailey and Pillard reported a significant correlation for homosexuality among monozygotic (MZ) and dizygotic twins (DZ). Among fifty-six MZ male twin probands and fifty-four DZ male twin probands, 52 percent of MZ co-twins and 22 percent of DZ co-twins were concordant for homosexuality (Bailey & Pillard 1991). Concordance for nontwin biologic brothers and unrelated adoptive brothers was 9.2 per-cent and 11.0 percent, respectively. Among seventy-one MZ female twin probands and thirty-seven DZ female twin probands, forty-eight percent of MZ co-twins and 16 percent of DZ co-twins were concordant for homosexuality, and 14 percent of nontwin bio-logic sisters and 6 percent of adoptive sisters of les-bians were also gay or bisexual (Bailey, Pillard, Neale & Agyei 1993). Significantly more women than men identified as bisexual. Bailey and colleagues concluded that there is strong support for a genetic, although independent, etiology for sexual orientation among gay men and lesbians. Although there were a large number of discordant MZ twins in these studies despite shared genes and similar environments, the authors questioned whether we can ever assume an equal environment for MZ twins.

Other studies have found that families with a homosexual member are more likely to have other homosexual relatives. Pillard and Weinrich (1986) reported that gay men were four times more likely than heterosexual men to have gay brothers, and Hamer and colleagues (1993) observed that their sample of seventy-six gay men were three to seven times more likely to have gay brothers. Hamer and associates also found a higher prevalence of homosexuality among maternal uncles (7.3 percent) and sons of maternal aunts (7.7 percent) and concluded that some forms of male homosexuality may be inherited via the mother's X chromosome. No hypothesis was proffered concerning a genetic mechanism for female homosexuality.

Genetic Studies   Hamer and colleagues (1993) compared twenty-two DNA markers on the X chromosome of forty gay sibling pairs using a polymerase chain reaction procedure to replicate genes quickly. Five consecutive markers on the long arm of Xq28 evidenced a .82 correlation. No matches were found outside this area. The authors speculated that recombination of adjacent repeated sequences, or between active and inactive sequences on the X and Y chromosomes, could produce a high rate of DNA sequence variants and could generate a trait that may reduce reproduction. It is not clear what mechanisms these markers may activate to influence sexual orientation. Although seven (18 percent) sibling pairs were not similar for all five genetic markers, Hamer and colleagues suggested that this discrepancy may be due to genetic variability or nongenetic variation in sexual orientation. Additional research is necessary to identify common DNA sequences between gay men and heterosexual brothers and between lesbians and heterosexual sisters before stronger conclusions can be drawn.

Summary of Biologic Data

A heterosexual gender role bias and reliance on non-human laboratory data have resulted in biologic theorists' drawing many premature conclusions; however, supportive data from twin and family studies argue for a reconception of biology's role. It may be that genetic or hormonal events form a predisposition that requires environmental events to shape and develop fully.

Psychoanalytic Models: Homosexuals Are Fixated and Perverse

A chronology of the development of psychoanalytic and psychodynamic theories of homosexuality is well described. . . . Briefly, Sigmund Freud's (1905, 1920) concept of a bisexual constitution was rejected after his death, and homosexuality was pathologized. "Normal" sexual orientation was declared to be heterosexual (Bergler 1947), and revised theories hypothesized that fixation during the early stages of psychosexual development predisposed or directly resulted in adult homosexuality and psychopathology. From case studies, theorists concluded that gay men fail to separate from their mothers in early childhood, fail to individualize fully (Socarides 1968; Socarides & Volkan 1990), and grow up in dysfunctional families (Bieber et al. 1962; Rado 1940; Wiedeman 1974). Yet empirical support for the notion that gay men or lesbians come from dysfunctional families or experience more psychopathology as adults is lacking. Hooker (1956) demonstrated that psychological functioning of well-adjusted homosexual men was indistinguishable from heterosexuals as assessed by the Rorschach. Consistent with this finding, Isay (1989) also reported that psychopathology was not prevalent among a sample of highly functional gay men.

Proponents of psychoanalytic theories of sexual orientation have offered circular stories, anecdotal evidence from case histories, or data from poorly controlled studies to support their (a priori) claims. No intrapsychic etiology of sexual orientation has been demonstrated. Unfortunately, homosexuality as a pathology has only recently been removed from the standards of psychiatric diagnosis and remains a part of psychoanalytic conceptual models, as well as biomedical models (Willerman & Cohen, 1990).

Learning/Conditioning Models: Homosexuals Are Made

A history of learning theories of sexual orientation is presented. . . . [R]adical behaviorists have claimed that accidental stimulation of infant genitals by the same-sex caregiver, punishment following genital stimulation by the opposite-sex parent, negative messages about heterosexual relations, attention from a same-sex person, lack of an opposite-sex partner when aroused, and poor heterosocial skills may promote adult homosexuality (Barlow & Agras 1973; Green 1985, 1987; Greenspoon & Lamal 1987). However, self-reported histories of gay men, lesbians, and heterosexuals have not shown these experiences to be predictive of later sexual orientation (Bell, Weinberg & Hammersmith 1981), and we know of no data that find that gay men and lesbians lack sufficient social skills for intimacy.

While acknowledging that they have not identified the relevant variables that contribute to and maintain homosexuality (Greenspoon & Lamal 1987), many behavioral clinicians in the 1960s and early 1970s proclaimed that gay men could be "cured" through reorientation or aversion therapies (Barlow & Agras 1973; Feldman & MacCulloch 1971; Marks & Gelder 1967). Despite claims of "success" (cf. Feldman & MacCulloch 1971; Masters & Johnson 1979), conversion therapies have demonstrated that heterosexual arousal does not make a "heterosexual," that many people are capable of bisexual responses, and that behavioral or physiological changes but not necessarily changes in erotic thoughts or desires that constitute sexual orientation may occur for highly motivated individuals and are not generally maintained outside the laboratory (Haldeman 1991).

Learning theorists evoke popular stereotypes when alluding to an older homosexual seducer, the lonely and desperate prehomosexual, the fragility of heterosexuality against which we must defend, and the highly reinforcing nature of same-sex sex (cf. Feldman & MacCulloch 1971; Greenspoon & Lamal 1987). Behaviorists sound curiously like psychoanalytic theorists when discussing the homosexual's fear and avoidance of heterosexual sex (cf. Bieber et al., 1962). However, several studies have reported that many gay men and lesbians have a great deal of heterosexual experience (Kinsey et al. 1948, 1953; Bell & Weinberg 1978), and bisexuals continue to do so (Weinberg, Williams & Pryor 1994).

The most obvious and damaging criticism of learning theorists with regard to sexual orientation is their lack of discussion about how society shapes sexuality. Westerners such as Americans grow up in an antihomosexual society and in families that do not encourage but rather explicitly and implicitly punish homosexual tendencies. Advertising, music, television, movies, and organized social functions remind us constantly that heterosexual behavior is rewarded, despite moral prohibitions against adolescent or premarital sexuality. At best, a few social messages about homosexuality may be ambiguous, although promotion of heterosexuality is loud, clear, and consistent. Within such a society, it seems unlikely that there should be more than occasional same-sex sexual behavior, and people who prefer such activities should be quite rare. Prevalence of gay men, lesbians, and bisexuals in Western societies suggests that same-sex sexual behavior is not uncommon. Furthermore, given the benefits of heterosexual behavior in the West, it is difficult to imagine why reorientation therapies have been so unsuccessful, if only conditioning principles were operative in the development of sexual orientation.

INTERACTIVE THEORIES OF SEXUAL ORIENTATION AND DEVELOPMENT

An interactive theory of sexual orientation must be able to account for all forms of gender attraction, explain cross-cultural variations in sexual behavior, and distinguish between development of an identity (heterosexual, bisexual, or gay) and sexual behavior (Ross 1987). An interactive theory also must be able to show how biologic mechanisms and environment influence each other to produce the spectrum of human sexual behavior. Bound less by hormone levels or cycles or seasons, people are aroused by a variety of sexual and nonsexual stimuli in the environment or through their imagination. Once aroused, unlike nonhumans, people may choose not to be sexual or may be sexual without emotional or erotic feelings. Finally, as cognitive beings in a complex social environment, people may identify with a certain sexuality without being sexually active. A practical theory of sexual orientation must account for all these elements.

A Neurohormonal/Stress-Diathesis Model

Pioneer sexologists Milton Diamond (1965; 1968; 1979) and John Money (1988, 1991) have presented the most accepted interactive theory of sexual orientation to date. For many years, Money's numerous and creative contributions have shaped and directed the field of sexology, and, consequently, many have been reluctant to examine his ideas critically. (For a writer who has been critical, see Diamond 1979, 1982).

Money (1988) claimed that sexuality exactly parallels native language development. A wealth of data suggests that humans are biologically predisposed, or hardwired, for language but dependent on a nurturing environment for development and expression. Of course, a predisposition for language does not specify which language or accent will be expressed; many forms of verbalization are viable. Money applied a similar relativism to the development of sexual orientation. It is surprising, then, and a little puzzling that he focused on only two "languages" (heterosexuality and homosexuality), giving little attention to the richness of bisexuality, and viewed heterosexuality as the "basal language" (Money & Russo 1979; Money 1988).

A biologic hardwiring or predisposition is hypothesized to be set by prenatal hormonalization. From data on sexual differentiation in laboratory animals and from his work with genetic and hormonal aberrations in humans, Money proposed that the male brain and genitalia are "masculinized" by fetal gonadal release of testosterone, while those same structures are

"defeminized" by release of the müllerian inhibiting hormone. Testosterone is presumed to masculinize the brain by first being transformed to an estrogen-related substance. Only transformed estrogen can "masculinize" brain development. The female brain and genitalia are "feminized" by the presence or absence of estrogen, and those structures are "demasculinized" by the absence of androgen. Typical androgenic exposure in males is assumed to predispose attraction to females, while the absence of androgens in females is thought to favor an erotic interest in males, although how this is done is not discussed.

Sometimes something goes "wrong." Money (1988, 1991) postulated that biologic defects, certain prenatal events, or both may cause fetal males not to "masculinize," or "masculinization" and "feminization" may occur simultaneously, resulting in homosexuality. For example, high levels of maternal stress or indulgence in drugs or alcohol during critical or sensitive periods of development may dislodge prenatal hormonalization from its typical path. Money's stress-diathesis model of homosexuality predicts that mothers who are particularly stressed during pregnancy are more likely to produce gay male children. How or if this process differs for female children is unclear.

Only recently have we begun to be concerned about fetal effects of alcohol and drug use by expectant mothers and have begun to emphasize prenatal health care. If Money's maternal stress theory is correct, one would expect to find with the advent of better prenatal care a greater prevalence of adult heterosexuals and a marked decrease in the numbers of gay men and lesbians. Furthermore, children of poor and disadvantaged mothers, who probably experienced great stress and received inadequate health care during pregnancy, should be more likely to be gay or lesbian as adults. We know of no data to support this supposition.

Given that prenatal hormonalization may establish an inclination toward homosexuality, Money (1988) further proposed that expression of the disposition depends on environmental events. Like learning theorists, Money hypothesized that positive same-sex adult reactions to aroused infant genitalia may reinforce a predisposition toward homosexuality or set up an acquired disposition. In addition, adult interference with childhood (hetero) sexual play may alter sexual development. Money asserted that childhood (hetero) sexual play is necessary rehearsal for successful adult heterosexual identity and sexual behavior. Social or moral prohibitions against heterosexual play may result in inept heterosexuals or may unwittingly encourage homosexuality. Apparently childhood homosexual play does not produce healthy and happy gay people, because healthy homosexual development is never detailed by Money. Furthermore, no data are provided to support the claim that childhood heterosexual play is requisite for healthy adult heterosexuals, that childhood homosexual play interferes with adult heterosexuality, or that heterosexual play is more common than homosexual play among children. Money places a great deal of weight on adult reactions to infant genitals and on childhood sexual play in promoting homosexuality, while ignoring the larger influence of the heterosexist Western culture geared toward producing heterosexuals in thought, word, and deed.

What is more, Money's maternal stress-homosexuality hypothesis was tested by Bailey and colleagues (1991) and was not supported. Researchers recruited 116 gay men (and 83 of their mothers), 25 lesbians (19 mothers), 84 heterosexual men (60 mothers), and 72 heterosexual women (53 mothers). Mothers reported that their most common stressor during pregnancy was "moved residence." For males, mothers' level of stress while pregnant was not related to their sons' adult sexual orientation. However, a small but significant correlation for mother's stress and daughter's adult homosexuality was found. Specifically, reported stress during the first and second trimester of pregnancy was associated with daughter's lesbianism. This finding was not predicted by the maternal stress theory and remains difficult to explain.

Although Money has gone further than most others in explicating the interaction of biologic and environmental factors, his theory nevertheless fails to account for nondysfunctional human development. In addition, Money's heterosexual gender role bias contributes to conceptual problems of assigning culturally defined social roles to hormonalization. To assert that androgens "masculinize" is to imply that they make the organism "masculine" or a "man," and nothing else. What of the "man" who acts like a "woman"? Did "masculinization" occur, or is he a "woman"? Money's reliance on gender classification reinforces stereotypes about men and women. Note that prenatal hormonalization is a matter of degree, timing, and duration and androgens and estrogens are present in both genetic males and females, although in markedly different proportions. Hormonal exposure should predict a complex and rich set of outcomes rather than one or two. What is more, reliance on gender classification has another untoward effect: lack of parsimony. For example, to account for the abstruse phenomenon of gay male transsexuals, Money (1988) adopted a series of mind-numbing cross-gender transpositions that have little explanatory value.

Finally, Money's theory has a decidedly Western flavor. His maternal stress model of homosexuality and obstruction of childhood heterosexual play is an inadequate explanation for ritualized same-sex sexual behavior among men in Sambia, societal bisexuality among the privileged class in ancient Japan or ancient Greece, "mummy-baby" relationships (older-younger females) among women in the Basotho of southern Africa, or the existence of third-gender persons who engage in same-sex sexual activity, such as Indonesian *waria* or Indian *hijra*. An attempt to apply such an explanation imposes Western values translated into theoretical concepts on non-Western cultures.

An Epigenetic/Bisexual Potentiality Model

This section outlines our sociobiological interactionist model of sexual orientation. We think this perspective best incorporates research on sexual orientation and cross-culture observations of sexuality. The reasoning that led us to this model is highlighted below. The first four points represent conclusions from current research, and the remaining points and discussion that follow are extrapolations from the data.

1. Nonhuman sexual development and behavior is not homologous to human sexual development and behavior. Reflexive animal sexual behavior

bears little resemblance to a cognitive-affective phenomena like human sexual orientation.

2. A biologic component of human sexual orientation, if it exists at all, is likely to be at the higher levels of brain functions. Owing to the variety of human sexual behavior, a sexual orientation, "net" is more likely to be cortical than subcortical.

3. A biologic component of human sexual orientation is largely independent of sexual differentiation of the brain.

4. Hormonalization is a matter of degree, timing, and duration, allowing for an assortment of outcomes. The concept of brain genderization ("masculinization and defeminization" and "feminization and demasculinization") is oversimplistic. Hormones do not determine gender role behavior. Gender and gender roles are social constructions. Gender-typic social behaviors do not predict emotional attraction, erotic fantasies, or sexual behavior.

5. Homosexuality and heterosexuality are variants of human sexuality. Across cultures, bisexual behavior may be more common than either exclusive heterosexuality or homosexuality.

6. Human bisexuality may serve to facilitate and maintain a variety of social relationships with men and women, which may be advantageous to the individual and the species.

7. Prenatal and postnatal hormonalization does not affect sexual orientation directly. Hormones influence the perception and meaning of environmental stimuli and facilitate learned associations that canalize sexual feelings and behaviors.

8. Prenatal hormonalization produces a bisexual potentiality or range of sexual attraction. Behavior within that range depends on the social environment and individual reinforcement history. Those with a restricted range of attraction may have a more inflexible sexual orientation.

9. Plasticity of sexual attraction may decline over time and with consistent reinforcement of habitual behavior. However, plasticity is

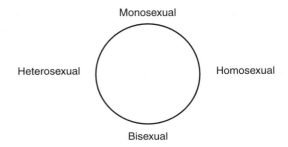

Figure 2   *Circle as Symbol for Sexual Orientation*

probably a function of the breadth of initial range of potentiality. People with a restricted range may have little flexibility; those with a wide range of attraction may retain considerable potentiality through adulthood.

10. Rather than a plane, sexual orientation may be better understood as a circle, with monosexuality at the top and bisexuality at the bottom (figure 2). Opposite-sex attraction may be placed on the left hemisphere of the circle, and same-sex attraction would fall on the right. The midpoint of the circle would represent asexuality. A circle symbolizes the range and fluidity of sexual orientation and suggests common elements of monosexual attraction.

Structure of the Model   Given the reasoning just presented, a single factor theory of sexual orientation would be inadequate. However, in the past thirty years, a new wave of thinking has begun to conceptualize human development in terms of a nature and nurture interaction. Within this construct, an organism's biologic makeup and environment interact in a reciprocally deterministic manner. An epigenetic developmental model (Gottlieb 1970; Lerner 1976) proposes that genetic structures set a reaction range (Gottesman 1963) or potentiality for expression of a given characteristic. The genetic range of responsiveness for a given characteristic may be narrow or broad. Depending on the range of responsiveness, expression of the characteristic may be relatively fixed, or flexible and open to influence.

Eye color is a characteristic with a narrow range of potentiality and is not known to vary much after birth. Height, however, has a wider range of biologic potentiality, although it is not without limits. Within genetic and physiological constraints, a given individual has a response range for the characteristic of height. Whether that individual eventually falls at the upper or lower end of the range depends upon many environmental factors, such as nutrition, health care, illness, physical injury, and other variables. Intelligence (as measured by standardized tests) appears to be a characteristic that for some people has a wide response range. Barring unusual genetic or hormonal limitations, environmental factors such as health, injury, and cognitive stimulation determine where in the range of potentiality an individual settles. Language is another characteristic with a wide response range, which warrants further examination since Money compared it to development of sexual orientation. Human children appear to have a predetermined period of biologic readiness or sensitivity for spoken language (cf. Bornstein, 1989), during which time they are most able to make use of environmental input and feedback to comprehend and form words. While symbolic representations of objects and verbal skills evolve slowly from birth, children from ages 2 to 5 typically show dramatic and rapid development of language skills. During childhood, accents and verbal colloquialisms develop as supported by the child's social milieu, and verbal skills continue to improve into adulthood. Environmental stimulation prior to the period of readiness produces few noticeable effects, but if the period is missed, a child may be unable to develop spoken language fully beyond limited utterances.

Like language, sexual orientation may be a characteristic with a wide biologic range of potentiality. Individuals with a narrow range of potentiality may be able to respond only to men or to women as objects of emotional, romantic, or sexual interest. A monosexual orientation includes exclusive heterosexuality and homosexuality. While someone with a monosexual orientation may be able to perform sexually with a gender outside their range, that individual would probably find it awkward and unfulfilling. In a society that condemned heterosexuality and promoted homosexuality, a heterosexual woman would understand early that her feelings differed from those of peers and from what is socially approved. Although she may conform to society's rules by engaging in same-sex sexual behavior, it is likely that she would find sex far less rewarding than a casual conversation with a man she finds attractive.

People with a wide range of sexual attraction may be interested in both men and women. A bisexual potentiality may shift or set over time, depending on social pressure, personal reinforcement history, and motivation. Presumably an individual with flexibility in sexual responsiveness could adapt easily (and probably without conscious awareness of adaptation) to a society that prefers one form of gender attraction over another. However, a bisexual who is more attracted to one gender may find it difficult to fit into a society that disapproves of attraction to the nonpreferred gender. While plasticity in gender attraction may be repressed, diminished, or even extinguished over time through differential reinforcement, it seems likely that except in extreme cases, the ability to respond erotically to both genders would not be completely lost.

If biology determines our gender of attraction, why are more people not actively bisexual? Why do monosexuals not find everyone of their preferred gender attractive? How do we develop personal erotic and partner preferences? Here, learning theory is useful. Across cultures and time, the popularity or repulsion for particular sexual acts with particular genders—what we view as "normal" or "deviant"—is a product of social learning. From infants, members of a culture are indoctrinated (i.e., reinforced) to accept without question the rightness or wrongness of certain acts and ways of living. Those who can conform with little cost, such as bisexuals, do so. Similarly, eroticism toward certain physical or imagined stimuli such as hair color, body shapes and sizes, ethnicity, clothing, mannerisms, smells, and sounds in our partner, as well as physical stimulation and fetishes, are most parsimoniously explained as learned associations within a cultural context. Of course, cultures evolve, and accepted practice changes. The recent history of masturbation and oral sex in the United States illustrates this point. Each has shifted from taboo to relatively accepted sexual practice. In essence, biology determines the gender of sexual attraction, and psychosocial factors shape its expression (Diamond 1979).

Biology also may influence which associations are learned. Here, observations of nonhuman animal behavior can provide an understanding of human behavior. Previous theorists have employed comparative laboratory data as homologues (similar in etiology and structure) rather than analogues (similar in function but not in origin) of human experience (Whalen 1991). Comparative observations may offer clues to the function or process of many human sexual behaviors. For example, some species appear to be predisposed to associate particular reinforcers with particular stimuli and, in turn, are resistant to punishment or extinction of those conditioned behaviors (Weinrich 1987, 1990). Pigeons will peck for a reward but not to avoid a shock; newly hatched chicks will not avoid a shock in an effort to be near their mother; rats readily make complex odor discriminations but do poorly with visual cues; and humans are much better at visual discriminations than with odors (Whalen 1991). Furthermore, Whalen has noted that among some animal species, circulating hormones and the presence of relevant environmental stimuli interact to evoke behavior, whereas hormones or external stimuli alone do not. In laboratory studies, a castrated male rat will display lordotic behavior only after injection of progesterone, *and* estrogen "priming," *and* exposure to male urine. Among rats, biologic events may create a context for behavior that depends on the presence of relevant environmental releasing stimuli. Stimuli are not equally evocative.

Whalen (1991) added that a biologic interpretation of events may account for individual preferences in sexual partners observed in dogs, cats, and primates. He suggested that hormones may function to make sense of environmental stimuli rather than to direct behavior and speculated that a similar process may occur for humans. Genetic structure and hormonal context may determine stimuli saliency and detectability and make certain erotic associations more likely. Once an association is well established, the production of behavior is guided by motivation and other factors.

Additional cross-species analogues of human sexual behavior include observations of homosexual and bisexual behavior in nearly all species of animals, both captive and in the wild (Beach 1949; Weinrich 1987). While same-sex activity is usually associated with social positioning or play among nonhuman animals (Gadpaille 1980), there are reports of apparently lifelong affectional bonds and, in some cases, what appears to be preferential same-sex sexual activity among dolphins, monkeys, baboons, rams and goats, rats, dogs, and several species of birds, such as mallards and Western gulls (Money 1991). It is difficult to discount same-sex sexual activity among pair bonds as social play when opposite-sex partners are available and ignored or when same-sex pair live as isolates and mount reciprocally.

With humans as with nonhumans, characteristics that exist and thrive must be adaptive and serve some function. Therefore, homosexuality and bisexuality, which exist and thrive, must be adaptive to humans, or these characteristics, being unstable, would have diminished or disappeared over time. Trivers (1972, 1974) hypothesized that if people with same-sex erotic interests acted altruistically, they would increase the reproductive success of relatives and make a case for a biologic predisposition of homosexuality. An example might be the third-gender people of Native American cultures: male Berdache who have sexual relationships with men and female Amazons who have relationships with women (Williams 1986). Berdache are able to perform heavier work than women for the household, provide additional resources to kin, and do not compete for wives or produce children like other men. Amazons do men's work, and both Berdache and Amazons perform unique spiritual duties for the service of the community. In a modern, less-kinship-oriented society, it may be more difficult to make this argument. However, gay people do not compete for heterosexual mates, produce fewer children, and have more time, money, and creative resources to invest in the community.

Bisexual potentiality in romantic feelings, fantasies, and sexual behavior may offer another evolutionary advantage to humans. Within small social bands, at least, the ability to have emotional and erotic feelings, or both, for both men and women could facilitate social bonding, increase cooperation, and decrease competition and community infighting. However, in large and impersonal societies, this would be difficult to maintain, and same-sex affection could be used for political advantage. Imagine a matriarchal society that views men as erotically (and emotionally) interesting but distrusts and subordinates them to maintain social power. The holding of political power by some women would not mean that all women are advantaged. Women on the low end of the economic and class spectrum may experience few benefits from the matriarchy. However, a social glue of homoerotic feelings, fantasies, symbols, and rituals could be directed to temper intergender competition and distrust among women. More than sexual, a homo-*eros* (Greek for "love") adhesive represents a deep desire to identify with, be in the company of, derive affection from, and care for other members of the same gender. In patriarchal Western societies, much has been written on the function of homoeroticism to unify and regulate male behavior in pre-Nazi Germany and Hitler's Nazi party (Oosterhuis & Kennedy 1991), warfare and military institutions (Dundes 1985; Kauth & Landis 1994), and competitive sports (Pronger 1990). Although it is not in the interests of a patriarchy for women to form strong social bonds, homoerotic rituals may be evident among women in southern U.S. families, churches, and some professions. Fear of female bonding may account for the negative reaction many men display toward feminists, lesbians, and strong women.

Up to this point, men and women of any sexual orientation have been discussed as though they ex-press sexuality similarly. However, significant gender differences exist. For example, lesbians may perceive sexual orientation in terms of political views and affectional relationships, while gay men view orientation through erotic fantasy and sexual behavior (Golden 1990; Gonsiorek 1988). Feminist influences aside, differences between gay men and lesbians appear similar to Western gender roles in which women are socialized to be emotionally oriented and interested in forming relationships and men are reinforced to be sexual and nonmonogamous. Cross-cultural observations suggest that most characteristics associated with one or the other gender are social constructions (Mead 1935). Whether straight, gay, bisexual, or asexual, women may have more in common with other women than they have with men, and vice versa. A theory of biologic bisexual potentiality does not contradict and is consistent with observed social and sexual gender differences. However, the biologic mechanisms that produce a bisexual potential may differ for men and women and are as yet unclear.

CONCLUSIONS

Theories are products of their cultural environment and bound by its biases and assumptions. Previous theories of sexual orientation have espoused a heterosexual gender role bias and often focused only on homosexuality. A general theory of human sexual orientation requires examination of sexual attraction across cultures and history, comparison across theoretical paradigms, and conceptualization of development as an evolving and active interaction between biology and environment. A biologic bisexual potentiality model may best meet this goal.

Our intent was to propose a new way of conceptualizing sexual orientation and to open a dialogue on sexuality. It now will be up to our critics and future theorists to take us beyond this paradigm and into the next.

REFERENCES

Allen, L. S., Hines, M., Shryne, J. E., & Gorski, R. A. (1989). Two sexually dimorphic cell groups in the human brain. *Journal of Neuroscience, 9,* 497–506.

Bailey, M. J., & Pillard, R. D. (1991). A genetic study of male sexual orientation. *Archives of General Psychiatry, 48,* 1089–1096.

Bailey, M. J., Pillard, R. D., Neale, M. C., & Agyei, Y. (1993). Heritable factors influence sexual orientation in women. *Archives of General Psychiatry, 50,* 217–223.

Bailey, M. J., Willerman, L., & Parks, C. (1991). A test of the maternal stress theory of human male homosexuality. *Archives of Sexual Behavior, 20*(3), 277–293.

Barlow, D. H., & Agras, W. S. (1973). Fading to increase heterosexual responsiveness in homosexuals. *Journal of Applied Behavior Analysis, 6,* 355–366.

Beach, F. A. (1949). A cross-species survey of mammalian sexual behavior. In P. H. Hoch & J. Zubin (Eds.), *Psychosexual development in health and disease.* New York: Grune & Stratton.

Bell, A. P., & Weinberg, M. S. (1978). *Homosexuality: A study of diversity among men and women.* New York: Simon & Schuster.

Bell, A. P., Weinberg, M. S., & Hammersmith, S. K. (1981). *Sexual preference: Its development in men and women.* Bloomington: Indiana University Press.

Benedict, R. (1938). Continuities and discontinuities in cultural conditioning. *Psychiatry, 1,* 161–167.

Beral, V., & Colwell, L. (1981). Randomized trial of high doses of stilboestrol and norethisterone in pregnancy: Longterm follow-up of the children. *Journal of Epidemiology and Community Health, 35,* 155–160.

Bergler, E. (1947). Differential diagnosis between spurious homosexuality and perversion homosexuality. *Psychiatric Quarterly, 31,* 399–409.

Berube, A. (1990). *Coming out under fire: The history of gay men and women in World War Two.* New York: Free Press.

Bhide, P. G., & Bedi, K. S. (1984). The effects of a lengthy period of environmental diversity on well-fed and previously undernourished rats, II: Synapse to neuron ratios. *Journal of Comparative Neurology, 227,* 305–310.

Bieber, I., Dain, H. J., Dince, P. R., Drellich, M. G., Grand, H. G., Gundlach, R. H., Kremer, M. W., Rifkin, A. H., Wilber, C. B., & Bieber, T. B. (1962). *Homosexuality: A psychoanalytic study of male homosexuals.* New York: Basic Books.

Bornstein, M. H. (1989). Sensitive periods in development: Structural characteristics and causal interpretations. *Psychological Bulletin, 105*(2), 179–197.

Boswell, J. (1980). *Christianity, social tolerance, and homosexuality.* Chicago: University of Chicago Press.

Boswell, J. (1994). *Same-sex unions in premodern Europe.* New York: Villard Books.

Bullough, V. L. (1976). *Sexual variance in society and history.* New York: Wiley.

Byne, W., & Parsons, B. (1993, March). Human sexual orientation: The biologic theories reappraised. *Archives of General Psychiatry, 50,* 228–239.

Diamond, M. (1965). A critical evaluation of the ontogeny of human sexual behavior. *Quarterly Review of Biology, 40,* 147–175.

Diamond, M. (1968). Genetic-endocrine interaction and human psychosexuality. In M. Diamond (Ed.), *Perspectives in reproduction and sexual behavior.* Bloomington: Indiana University Press.

Diamond, M. (1979). Sexual identity and sex roles. In V. Bullough (Ed.), *The frontiers of sex research* (pp. 35–56). Buffalo, NY: Prometheus.

Diamond, M. (1982). Sexual identity, monozygotic twins reared in discordant sex roles and a BBC follow-up. *Archives of Sexual Behavior, 11*(2), 181–186.

Dittman, R. W., Kappes, M. E., & Kappes, M. H. (1992). Sexual behavior in adolescent and adult females with congenital adrenal hyperplasia. *Psychoneuroendocrinology, 17,* 153–170.

Dorner, G., Rhode, W., Stahl, F., Krell, L., & Masius, W. G. (1975). A neuroendocrine predisposition for homosexuality in men. *Archives of Sexual Behavior, 4,* 1–8.

Dover, K. J. (1978). *Greek homosexuality.* Cambridge, MA: Harvard University Press.

Dundes, A. (1985). The American game of "smear the queer" and the homosexual component of male competitive sport and warfare. *Journal of Psychoanalytic Anthropology, 8*(3), 115–129.

Ehrhardt, A. A., Meyer-Bahlburg, H. F., Feldman, J. F., & Ince, S. E. (1984). Sex-dimorphic behavior in childhood subsequent to prenatal exposure to exogenous progestogens and estrogens. *Archives of Sexual Behavior, 13,* 457–477.

Feldman, M. P., & MacCulloch, M. J. (1971). *Homosexual behavior: Therapy and assessment.* Oxford: Pergamon Press.

Freud, S. (1905). Three essays on the theory of sexuality. In J. Strachey (Ed.), *The standard edition of the complete psychological works of Sigmund Freud* (Vol. 7, pp. 123–246). London: Hogarth, 1953.

Freud, S. (1920). The psychogenesis of a case of homosexuality in a woman. In J. Strachey (Ed.), *The standard edition of the complete psychological works of Sigmund Freud* (Vol. 18, pp. 155–172). London: Hogarth, 1955.

Friedman, R. C., & Downey, J. (1993). Psychoanalysis, psychobiology, and homosexuality. *Journal of the American Psychoanalytic Association, 41*(4), 1159–1198.

Gadpaille, W. J. (1980). Cross-species and cross-cultural contributions to understanding homosexual activity. *Archives of General Psychiatry, 37*(3), 349–356.

Gladue, B. A., Green, R., & Hellman, R. E. (1984). Neuroendocrine response to estrogen and sexual orientation. *Science, 225,* 1496–1499.

Golden, C. (1990, August). *Our politics and our choices: The feminist movement and sexual orientation.* Paper presented at the American Psychological Association, Boston.

Gonsiorek, J. C. (1988). Mental health issues of gay and lesbian adolescents. *Journal of Adolescent Health Care, 9,* 114–122.

Gooren, L. (1986a). The neuroendocrine response of luteinizing hormone to estrogen administration in heterosexual, homosexual, and transsexual subjects. *Journal of Clinical Endocrinological Metabolism, 63,* 583–588.

Gooren, L. (1986b). The neuroendocrine response of luteinizing hormone to estrogen administration in the human is not sex specific but dependent on the hormonal environment. *Journal of Clinical Endocrinological Metabolism, 63,* 589–593.

Gooren, L. (1990). Biomedical theories of sexual orientation: A critical examination. In D. P. McWhirter, S. A. Sanders, & J. M. Reinisch (Eds.), *Homosexuality/heterosexuality: Concepts of sexual orientation* (pp. 71–87). New York: Oxford University Press.

Gottesman, I. I. (1963). Genetic aspects of intelligent behavior. In N. Ellis (Ed.), *Handbook of mental deficiency: Psychological theory and research.* New York: McGraw-Hill.

Gottlieb, G. (1970). Conceptions of prenatal development. In L. R. Aronson, E. Tobach, D. S. Lehrman, & J. S. Rosenblatt (Eds.), *Development and evolution of behavior: Essays in memory of T. C. Schneirla.* San Francisco: Freeman.

Green, R. (1985). Gender identity in childhood and later sexual orientation: Follow-up of seventy-eight males. *American Journal of Psychiatry, 142,* 339–341.

Green, R. (1987). *The "sissy boy syndrome" and the development of homosexuality.* New Haven, CT: Yale University Press.

Greenspoon, J., & Lamal, P. A. (1987). A behavioristic approach. In L. Diamant (Ed.), *Male and female homosexuality: Psychological approaches* (pp. 109–128). New York: Hemisphere Publishing Corporation.

Haldeman, D. C. (1991). Sexual orientation conversion therapy for gay men and lesbians: A scientific examination. In J. C. Gonsiorek and J. D. Weinrich (Eds.), *Homosexuality: Research implications for public policy* (pp. 149–160). Newbury Park, CA: Sage.

Halperin, D. M. (1990). *One hundred years of homosexuality and other essays on Greek love.* New York: Routledge.

Hamer, D. H., Hu, S., Magnuson, V. L., Hu, N., & Pattatucci, A. M. L. (1993, July 16). A linkage between DNA markers on the X chromosome and male sexual orientation. *Science 261,* 321–327.

Herdt, G. H. (1981). *Guardians of the flutes: Idioms of masculinity.* New York: McGraw-Hill.

Herdt, G. H. (1984). *Ritualized homosexuality in Melanesia.* Berkeley: University of California Press.

Hines, M. (1982). Prenatal gonadal hormones and sex differences in human behavior. *Psychological Bulletin, 92,* 56–80.

Hooker, E. (1956). The adjustment of the male overt homosexual. In H. M. Ruittenbeck (Ed.), *The problem of homosexuality in modern America* (pp. 141–161). New York: Dutton.

Isay, R. (1989). *Being homosexual.* New York: Farrar, Strauss & Giroux.

Kauth, M. R., & Landis, D. (1994, July). *The U.S. military's "Don't ask; Don't tell" personnel policy: Fear of the open homosexual.* Presented at Second International Congress on Prejudice, Discrimination and Conflict, Jerusalem, Israel.

Kester, P., Green, R., Finch, S. J., & Williams, K. (1980). Prenatal "female hormone" administration and psychosexual development in human males. *Psychoneuroendocrinology, 5,* 269–285.

Kinsey, A. C., Pomeroy, W. B., & Martin, C. E. (1948). *Sexual behavior in the human male.* Philadelphia: W. B. Saunders.

Kinsey, A. C., Pomeroy, W. B., Martin, C. E., & Gebhard, P. H. (1953). *Sexual behavior in the human female.* Philadelphia: W. B. Saunders.

Kraemer, G. W., Ebert, M. H., Lake, C. R., & McKinney, W. T. (1984). Hypersensitivity to d-amphetamine several years after early social deprivation in rhesus monkeys. *Psychopharmacology, 82,* 266–271.

Kuhn, T. S. (1970). *The structure of scientific revolutions* (2nd ed.). Chicago: University of Chicago Press.

Lerner, R. M. (1976). *Concepts and theories of human development.* Reading, MA: Addison-Wesley.

LeVay, S. (1991). A difference in hypothalamic structure between heterosexual and homosexual men. *Science, 253,* 1034–1037.

McWhirter, D. P., & Mattison, A. M. (1984). *The male couple: How relationships develop.* Englewood Cliffs, NJ: Prentice-Hall.

Marks, I. M., & Gelder, M. G. (1967). Transvestism and fetishism: Clinical and psychological changes during faradic aversion. *British Journal of Psychiatry, 113,* 711–729.

Masters, W. H., & Johnson, V. E. (1979). *Homosexuality in perspective.* Boston: Little, Brown.

Mead, M. (1935). *Sex and temperament in three primitive societies.* New York: William Morrow & Co.

Meyer-Bahlburg, H. F. (1984). Psychoendocrine research on sexual orientation: Current status and future opinions. *Progressive Brain Research, 61,* 375–398.

Money, J. (1988). *Gay, straight, and in-between: The sexology of erotic orientation.* New York: Oxford University Press.

Money, J. (1991). The development of sexuality and eroticism in humankind. In M. Haug, P. F. Brain, & C. Aron (Eds.), *Heterotypical behaviour in man and animals* (pp. 127–166). London: Chapman and Hall.

Money, J., & Russo, A. J. (1979). Homosexual outcome of discordant gender activity role in childhood: Longitudinal follow-up. *Journal of Pediatric Psychology, 4,* 29–49.

Money, J., Schwartz, M., & Lewis, V. G. (1984). Adult erotosexual status and fetal hormonal masculinization and demasculinization: 46, XX congenital virilizing adrenal hyperplasia and 46, XY androgen-insensitivity syndrome compared. *Psychoneuroendocrinology, 9,* 405–414.

Oosterhuis, H., & Kennedy, H. (1991). *Homosexuality and male bonding in pre-Nazi Germany.* New York: Harrington Park Press.

Peplau, L. A., & Amaro, H. (1982). Understanding lesbian relationships. In W. Paul et al. (Eds.), *Homosexuality: Social, psychological and biological issues.* Beverly Hills, CA: Sage.

Pillard, R. C., & Weinrich, J. D. (1986). Evidence for a familial nature of male homosexuality. *Archives of General Psychiatry, 43,* 808–812.

Pronger, B. (1990). *The arena of masculinity: Sports, homosexuality, and the meaning of sex.* New York: St. Martin's Press.

Rado, S. (1940). A critical examination of the concept of bisexuality. *Psychosomatic Medicine, 2,* 459–467.

Ross, M. W. (1987). A theory of normal homosexuality. In L. Diamant (Ed.), *Male and female homosexuality: Psychological approaches* (pp. 237–259). New York: Hemisphere Publishing Corporation.

Shilts, R. (1993). *Conduct unbecoming: Gays and Lesbians in the U.S. military.* New York: Fawcett Columbine.

Socarides, C. (1968). *The overt homosexual.* New York: Grune & Stratton.

Socarides, C., & Volkan, V. (1990). *The homosexualities: Reality, fantasy, and the arts.* Madison, CT: International University Press.

Trivers, R. L. (1972). Parental investment and sexual selection. In B. Campbell (Ed.), *Sexual selection and the descent of man, 1871–1971* (pp. 136–179). Chicago: Aldine.

Trivers, R. L. (1974). Parent-offspring conflict. *American Zoologist, 14,* 249–264.

Turner, A. M., & Greenough, W. T. (1985). Differential rearing effects on rat visual cortex synapses, I: Synaptic and neuronal density and synapses per neuron. *Brain Research, 329,* 195–203.

Weinberg, M. S., Williams, C. J., & Pryor, D. W. (1994). *Dual attractions: Understanding bisexuality.* New York: Oxford University Press.

Weinrich, J. D. (1987). *Sexual landscapes: Why we are what we are, why we love whom we love.* New York: Charles Scribner's Sons.

Weinrich, J. D. (1990). The Kinsey scale in biology, with a note on Kinsey as a biologist. In D. P. McWhirter, S. A. Saunders, & J. M. Reinisch (Eds.), *Homosexuality/heterosexuality: Concepts of sexual orientation* (pp. 115–137). New York: Oxford University Press.

Whalen, R. E. (1991). Heterotypical behaviour in man and animals: Concepts and strategies. In M. Haug, P. F. Brain, & C. Aron (Eds.), *Heterotypical behaviour in man and animals* (pp. 215–227). London: Chapman and Hall.

Wiedeman, G. H. (1974). Homosexuality: A survey. *Journal of American Psychoanalytic Association, 22,* 651–696.

Willerman, L., & Cohen, D. (1990). *Psychopathology.* New York: McGraw-Hill.

Williams, W. L. (1986). *The spirit and the flesh: Sexual diversity in American Indian culture.* Boston: Beacon Press.

CHECKPOINTS

1. Traditional explanations of sexual orientation have described sexual orientation using heterosexuality as a normative and prescriptive model. To develop a more inclusive model of sexuality, one must account for social, historical, cultural, and contextual factors.

2. Kauth and Kalichman propose an interactive model that accounts for a wide array of romantic feelings, erotic attractions, and sexual behaviors.

To prepare for reading the next section, think about these questions:

1. Do you think love and intimacy are necessary for sexuality?

2. What is the relationship between gender roles, intimate relationships, and sexuality?

Intimate Relationships and the Creation of Sexuality

PHILIP BLUMSTEIN AND PEPPER SCHWARTZ

The study of human sexuality has been dominated by the presumption that male and female behavior is biologically programmed, and much research has concerned itself with understanding what these programs are and to what extent biological predispositions are modified by social forces. Another prominent assumption posits that each individual has a *true* sexual core self which does not change. Some researchers emphasize that this self emerges over time, through a process of socialization, while others stress that desires are genetic and/or hormonal in origin, but both perspectives share a belief in the immutable core disposition.

The combined force of these two research traditions in the study of human sexuality has almost dismissed from serious scholarly discussion what we believe to be the true nature of human sexuality: that sexuality is situational and changeable, modified by day-to-day circumstances throughout the life course. In our perspective there are few absolute differences between male and female sexuality. What differences we observed are primarily the result of the different social organization of women's and men's lives in various cultural contexts. "Essentialist" theories, that is, theories which assume immutable selves, ignore data which would disturb the assumption. One startling example of the field's willingness to be misled is the unfortunate interpretation of the ground-breaking

We would like to thank Mary Rogers Gillmore, Judith A. Howard, and Barbara Risman for their helpful comments on an earlier draft of this paper. Blumstein, P., and Schwartz, P., "Intimate Relationships and the Creation of Sexuality," in *Homosexuality/ Heterosexuality: Concepts of Sexual Orientation,* D. P. McWhirter, S. A. Sanders, J. M. Reinisch, Eds. (New York: Oxford University Press), to be published in 1989 by Oxford University Press. Reprinted by permission of the Kinsey Institute for Research, Indiana University.

Kinsey studies and the misuse of the Kinsey heterosexuality/homosexuality scale (Kinsey, Pomeroy & Martin 1948; Kinsey, Pomeroy, Martin & Gebhard 1953). In this scale, Kinsey and his colleagues categorized individuals not as heterosexual versus homosexual, but on a continuum between exclusively heterosexual and exclusively homosexual. We would like to reexamine the scale, using it to direct research away from essentialist reifications and more in the direction we believe Kinsey himself would have preferred: toward a kinetic model of sexual desire and away from a static and categorical model.

Unfortunately when the Kinsey group constructed the scale of zero to six, they unintentionally endorsed and extended essentialist ways of thinking by establishing a typology allowing for seven kinds of sexual beings instead of only two. After Kinsey there were such people as *Kinsey 4s* instead of simply heterosexuals and homosexuals. While the seven-point scale does enormously more justice to the range and subtlety of human sexuality, in its common usage it does not do justice to Kinsey's own belief in the changeability and plasticity of sexual behavior. Because researchers have inevitably used Kinsey's scale as a shorthand system of sexual identification, they have refined the person as a sexual type. His or her "real" sexuality is discovered and seen as an essence that has been uncovered. It is the final summation of the person's sexual behavior and "psychic reactions."

Such essentialist thinking allows one to ignore concrete behaviors in assigning people to sexual categories. Even the verbal descriptions made by respondents and patients of their *own* behavior and feeling states may be swept aside in an essentialist judgment. As Katz (1975, p. 1371) has written on this general subject, "Persons conceive of essences as inherent qualities which may be manifested, reflected, indicated, or represented by, but do not exist in, conduct. . . . [E]ssences exist independent of observable behavior." Essentialism also allows one to capture the actor with one great biographical sweep, for example, "She is a homosexual," or "He is a bisexual." The Kinsey scale, as it is frequently used to aggregate behavior over a finite length of time or even over a lifetime, encourages the categorization of an actor's biography; for example, "She is a Kinsey 3."

The application of the Kinsey scale is hardly unique in this respect. Essentialism has dominated both lay and professional thinking about sexuality. Sexuality has been perceived as emanating from a core or innate *desire* that directs an individual's sex life. Before Kinsey, this desire had to be either homosexual or heterosexual; after Kinsey this desire could be ambisexual. But in either case, it originated in constitutional factors or in the person's early experience and was a fixed part of the person. This desire has been seen as so powerful that even though behavior might vary over a lifetime, many psychotherapists and sex researchers have continued to believe in the existence of a basic predisposition reflecting the true nature of each individual's sexuality.

We do not deny that there are men and women who come to a therapist with unacted-upon homosexual desires which they believe reflect their true sexual selves. Nor do we deny that most Americans who call themselves heterosexual or homosexual feel strongly that their sexuality is highly channeled. They feel that they have only *categorical desire,* that is, desire for people of only one specific gender.[1] But the commonly held belief in the generality of this pattern has not been challenged to see if it reflects a truly universal experience. And indeed there is evidence to call that belief into question (Blumstein & Schwartz, 1976a; 1976b).

It is our position that it is not primarily categorical desire that determines whether people's sex partners are male or female. Fundamental categorical desire may not even exist. Rather it is culture that creates understandings about how people are sexual and thus determines whether people will be able to have only one sexual focus, to eroticize both sexes, or to experience categorical desire for one sex at one point of

their life and categorical desire for the other sex at another point in their life (Herdt, 1981). In our society, because virtually everyone partakes of the dominant essentialist theory of sexuality, large numbers of people experience categorical sexual desire and see it as determining their sexual life. But it is critical not to confuse this particular cultural pattern with scientific confirmation that is a core sexual orientation within every human being. In our society there are also people whose fundamental sexual desire seems to be produced within the context of a relationship, rather than by an abstract preference for women or men, or whose sense of sexual self never becomes consistently organized. The essentialist understanding of sexuality skirts questions of what experiences and understandings lead to the behaviors that create a sense of self. Essentialism ignores the *process* of the creation of a sense of self.[2]

But it is not only the essentialist nature of the Kinsey scale to which we object. The Kinsey scale, particularly as it is presently used in lax scientific discourse, is limited because it was based on a single cultural model of sexuality. The Kinsey group inadvertently took the dominant model of middle-class male sexuality as a guide for understanding human sexual behavior, when other models, also cultural, but perhaps ultimately more productive, could have been utilized. In the male model, behavior provides the critical data used to categorize core sexual selves. This is because in the modern Western world, men and their observers have used behavior as the indicator of internal psychic processes. This has been particularly true in the analysis of homosexuality because homosexual behavior so violates cultural proscriptions that it has been assumed that such behavior must surely demonstrate an irrepressible core sexual self. Thus, once homosexual acts were discussed scientifically, the use of behavior as an indicator of an individual's true sexuality became more important.[3] Oddly enough, however, homosexual acts tend to be given greater weight than any heterosexual acts which the individual might also perform. In most cases, it is assumed that "psychic reaction" is the crucial factor to resolve any empirical oddities. If psychic arousal is more dramatic in homosexual relations, then a homosexual core self is adduced. How cross-situationally consistent such psychic arousal might be, however, is seldom contemplated.

The cross-cultural record amply suggests that the essentialist model of human sexuality has far from universal fit. Indeed one does not need a cross-cultural perspective; if one looks at the relatively ignored facts of modern Western female sexuality, the essentialist model's inadequacies become clear. As we have observed elsewhere (Blumstein & Schwartz 1976a; 1977), female sexuality in our culture does not justify an essentialist position. Women are less likely than men to view their sexual acts as a revelation of their "true sexual self," and female sexual choice seems to be based as much on situational constraints as on categorical desire. Desire seems to be aroused frequently by emotionally intimacy rather than by abstract erotic taste.

Our sociological vision of sexuality is far different from the essentialist approach of many other sex researchers. Our thesis is simply that desire is created by its cultural context. Sexuality emerges from the circumstances and meanings available to individuals; it is a product of socialization, opportunity, and interpretation. For example, male sexuality in our culture-view is shaped by the scripts boys are offered almost from birth, by the cultural lessons they learn throughout the life course, among them the belief in a sometimes overpowering male sex drive and the belief that men have immutable sexual needs which are manifest over and above individual attempts at repression.

Our approach leads to a different question than the one posed by essentialists. As sociologists we do not wish to proliferate sexual categories, but rather ask, "What circumstances create the possibility for sexual behavior—either homosexual or heterosexual?" This question cannot be approached fruitfully when one is relying on the seven-point Kinsey scale, since concrete behaviors are lost in the data aggregation process used in applying the scale to people's lives.

Within a specific cultural setting there are many factors which facilitate or deter sexual behavior, both homosexual and heterosexual. The two key factors, which we shall concentrate on in this paper, are (1) the *gender roles* culturally available, and (2) the *social organization of opportunities*.

Biological sex is constrained and directed by the roles society offers men and women. Expectations of role performance organize male and female sexuality. Thus in order to understand human sexual behavior and the meaning of that behavior to people, it is crucial to know what members of each sex have learned is appropriate to feel and to do, and what sanctions exist for inadequate or noncompliant role performance.

While there is still much to be understood about the subtle relationship between sexuality and gender, we are substantially more ignorant about the second factor, the social organization of opportunity. By this we mean how society does or does not offer circumstances that permit certain behaviors to occur. These circumstances may be as concrete as a woman being unable to have heterosexual experience because her interactions with men are always chaperoned, or as subtle as her being unable to have sexual relations outside of her marriage because she is a suburban housewife who, in the course of her typical day, never finds herself in the company of men. Even a wife who is propositioned may not have a real opportunity if the cost of giving in to temptation is ostracism from her community, expulsion from her marriage, and a future of being unacceptable to any other loving partner. Similarly, a boy who goes to all-male schools will have different sexual opportunities than one who is never in an all-male adolescent peer group, and a salesman who travels constantly is more likely to have extramarital temptations than a man who never leaves his small hometown.

Opportunity is also shaped in a less objective fashion by the meanings the culture makes available. A wife may not be able to be sexually responsive even if she is alone with a man other than her husband, if she has learned that a healthy woman has little sexual appetite and that what appetite she has can only be aroused in the context of her role as wife and companion to her husband. A man may have difficulty experiencing homosexual desire in himself if he has been taught that such attractions do not exist in typical heterosexually active men.

From these examples it should be clear that we are not describing forces that affect individuals idiosyncratically, but rather we are focusing on the way society organizes social life. This does not mean that everyone acts according to a single cultural mandate. Sometimes social directives are in flux or they are actually in conflict with one another and leave room for individual choice. For example, when women in large numbers were first allowed a college education, there was no deliberate social plan to make them men's equals, nor certainly for them to have sexual appetites resembling men's. The same can be said of the development of safe and effective contraceptive technologies. The latent consequence of men and women having more similar lives, however, has been that attitudes and norms which had functioned well to maintain very different sex lives for women and men were no longer able to sustain their potency and legitimacy.

We would argue that understanding the dynamics of gender roles and social opportunities is a more fruitful approach to the question of why sexual behavior occurs and under what circumstances sexual identities are adopted than is the essentialist paradigm. We do not in this paper perform a larger sociological task of developing a theory of how social opportunities arise in sexual life. Rather we proceed from the idea that social opportunities exist, and examine one type of opportunity structure in depth in order to show the utility of the concept. The source of opportunities we focus on here is intimate relationships, which we see as profoundly important in determining what behaviors will take place.

As an immediate caveat, we must say that in our culture this is truer for women than for men. If Kinsey had used female sexuality as a model, his scale might have been conceptualized not so much in terms of accumulated acts and psychic preoccupations but rather in terms of intensity and frequency of love relationships, some of which might have only incidental, overt erotic components.

Women have been so effectively socialized to link love and attachment, love and sex, that eroticization is more often a consequence of emotional attraction than the trigger for the involvement. In cases where eroticization comes first, it is unlikely to continue without a relationship context; if the attraction is powerful, a relationship may have to be invented in order to sustain and justify continuing the liaison. Whether this attraction process is the result of women's relatively low position in the social structure (de Beauvoir 1953), or whether it is a response to cultural themes governing female sexuality (Laws & Schwartz 1977), or whether women's erotic cues are biologically different from men's (Symons 1979; van den Berghe 1979), is a large question; and we are unable to put it to rest in this paper. We can, however, show that in our culture women's sexuality is organized by other than physical cues. For modern Western women, the recognition of love or admiration or the pleasure in companionship or deep friendship most often leads to erotic attraction and response. While women are not incapable of seeking sex for its own sake, this pattern of sexual behavior is relatively rare among them (Blumstein & Schwartz 1983). Our research indicates that it is overwhelmingly more common for the relationship (or the desire for such a relationship) to establish itself first.

This pattern is less common among men in our culture. While homosexual and heterosexual erotic feelings can develop in an intimate relationship, it is much more common for a man to have sexual attractions (as early as adolescence) to a number of specific persons (some or all of whom may be total strangers), or to a generalized other, or to fantasized persons. If an opportunity exists, and any personal or cultural interdictions can be overcome, he may seek to realize his erotic preferences in one or more concrete sexual contacts. An intimate or committed relationship is not necessary for excitation, and in some cases may even be counterproductive to sexual arousal. Nonetheless most men do form intimate relationships, and this leads us to ask what is the relevance of such relationships for their subsequent sexual behavior and self-identification?

This is a complex question since in some cases the relationship, for example, marriage to a woman, seems to organize the man's sexual behavior and identity, while in other cases, such as the self-defined homosexual man who is married to a woman, it is less central. The husband who has sexual experiences with other men may feel torn, dishonest, and fearful of exposure, but frequently he also feels a need to have a family and an approved social identity (H. Ross 1971; M. Ross 1983). He also finds the attraction of conventionality more compelling than the opportunity to have a less compromised homosexual sex life. A different but related example is a man with a previously exclusively homosexual life who decides that heterosexual marriage is important to him and that his homosexuality is too costly. We interviewed such a man, who decided to learn how, in his words, to "be heterosexual" in order to facilitate having children and, as he saw it, stability and respectability. While we cannot say that twenty years after this decision he would experience no residual homosexual desire, we can certainly claim that his attachment to a heterosexual relationship changed his behavior and, we believe, his self-identification.

How it is possible for men such as these to organize their lives in these ways is a question that needs and deserves further research. There is, however, some relevant information in the anthropological and historical records on the interaction of appetites, intimate relationships, and sexual self-identity. It is far from culturally universal to expect intimate relationships to be the major or sole outlet for the expression of sexual feelings or appetites. The modern Western desire for sexual, emotional, and lifestyle coherence is probably a rare accommodation. In the ancient world, for example, a gentleman was expected to marry and father children, regardless of his attraction to males; and even in modern times, there are numerous examples of homosexual behavior occurring in the private lives of married men (Humphreys 1970; H. Ross 1971; M. Ross 1983). This homosexual behavior has not exempted men from performing the male role of their time.

An interesting question is whether the separation of family and sexuality has been possible because of innate sexual flexibility or because men are socialized to be able to separate sexual, loving, and obligation impulses so that they can accomplish sex within whatever format is necessary. Or has this ability led to the existence of dual lives so that the appetite could be fulfilled without threatening home and family? Thus, homosexual behavior could occur without

homosexual self-identification, thereby inhibiting the development of an exclusively homosexual lifestyle.

An important question is why is there now such great emphasis on shaping one's life on the basis of one's intimate relationships. Perhaps the same social forces that helped create a bond between love and family and sex for women are starting to apply to men as well. Moreover, recent cultural themes of individual fulfillment and personal growth encourage and shape sexuality by giving people the impression that any disjunction between parts of the self is unhealthy and ultimately an inappropriate way to live. In addition, the ability to identify oneself as a homosexual man or lesbian and be viewed as gay by friends and acquaintances probably diminishes ability to identify with or practice heterosexual desire. The predominance of the essentialist paradigm leads men and women to create a coherent package of behavior, identity, and community, and they are thus more motivated to form same-sex relationships.

While sex role differences are a critical factor in understanding the impact of intimate relationships on sexuality, it is also important to consider the type of relationship. Sexuality is different in marriage as compared to heterosexual cohabitation, and opposite-sex relationships have a different sexual dynamic from same-sex relationships (Blumstein & Schwartz, 1983). An individual's sense of self is in part created by the relationship she or he is in, and most individuals find a transition that might occur, that is, from cohabitation to marriage or from an opposite-sex to a same-sex partner, has an enormous impact on their identity. For example, a man whom we interviewed had married his childhood sweetheart and had what he considered a happy, fulfilling, and monogamous marital sex life until his wife died unexpectedly. This man subsequently, in his words, "became in touch with" early homoerotic feelings and entered into a relationship with a man. He describes himself as having been "obsessed" with his new partner, but also feels that he had been equally taken with his wife. While this man could be labeled as a Kinsey 3, or for that matter as a Kinsey 0 who changed to a Kinsey 6, we argue that it would be more fruitful to look at the circumstances that shaped his sexuality, courtships, marriage, and homosexual relationship. One might also want to know why this man, unlike most men in his society, was sexually galvanized by a tender relationship, rather than by independent erotic desire.

Another example is the case of a woman, unhappily married for twenty-three years, who felt a profound absence of a real "soulmate." She met a woman at her son's college graduation ceremony, and, over a long period of time, the two women gradually fell in love and left their husbands. Not only did the respondent's sense of self change, but so did her sexual habits and desires. Again, instead of trying to determine who the "real person" is, we think it more productive to discover how changing relationships produced some new forms of behavior.

All of this would be theoretically trivial if we were only talking about individual histories. What makes these stories more compelling to a social scientist is that they are reflections of twentieth-century Western opportunities. The manner in which the intimate relationships are conducted is a cultural and historical phenomenon, which, when studied in the aggregate, can show us how sexuality is created.

The organization of opportunity in modern life is formed by the instability of marriage, a high remarriage rate, the ability to survive as an independent unmarried person, and the possibility of meeting eligible sex partners of either sex in institutions that have developed expressly for the purpose of bringing people together. The scenarios described in this paper are uniquely twentieth-century stories and would not have been possible, for example, in nineteenth-century America. There would have been few opportunities for divorce, little ability to live a single or private life, and no conceptualization of the importance of sexual fulfillment or entry into a gay lifestyle. In fact *lifestyle* is a uniquely modern concept. Lifestyle incorporates the notion of sexual choice, and choice has simply not existed for most people in most historical periods. Furthermore, how people behaved within marriage or with a same-sex partner would have been entirely different from the way they would act today. A same-sex relationship in the nineteenth century would probably not be perceived as an appropriate public lifetime commitment.[4]

We are not historians and cannot do justice to the meanings and constructions of everyday sexuality in periods other than our own. We have, however, gathered data in the 1970s and 1980s which show how sexuality is shaped by the available relationship scripts. Our observations are based on two pieces of research: (1) the study of the antecedents of sexual identity and bisexuality, based on a sample of 150 interviews (Blumstein & Schwartz 1976a; 1976b; 1977); and (2) the study of same-sex and opposite-sex couples, involving questionnaire, interview, and observational data, the over-all sample representing approximately 1000 male homosexual couples, 800 lesbian couples, 3600 heterosexual marriages, and 650 heterosexual cohabitation relationships (Blumstein & Schwartz 1983).

Two areas of couples' sexual lives—sexual frequency and monogamy—are presented to illustrate the contention that intimate relationships shape sexuality.

SEXUAL FREQUENCY

In all four groups of couples, frequency declines with the duration of the relationship (see Table 1). From this we infer that there is some habituation effect in all kinds of couples that serves to reduce sexual appetite.[5] Within heterosexual couples, this pattern varies by the simple fact of whether or not the pair is legally married. People who live together without marriage are surely different from those who marry, and these differences may in some measure account for the differences in sexual frequency. But they probably do not account entirely for the differences. Rather, we suggest, it is the differences between marital and nonmarital heterosexual relationships themselves that create different opportunities and different motivations for sexual expression.

When we look at the three groups in our study which include women, we notice that those in relationships with men (both married and unmarried)

TABLE 1   Couples Reporting Sex Three Times a Week or More

Years Living Together	Married Couples		Cohabiting Couples		Male Couples		Female Couples	
2 or less	45%	(344)	61%	(349)	67%	(309)	33%	(357)
Between 2 and 10	27%	(1505)	38%	(288)	32%	(472)	7%	(350)
10 or more	18%	(1754)	———		11%	(169)	1%	(61)

Note: Numbers in parentheses are the number of couples on which the percentages are based. Very few of the cohabitors were together more than ten years.

have a greater sexual frequency than those in relationships with other women. We also note that the sexual frequencies in male homosexual relationships come closer to the heterosexual frequencies. The probable reason for these differences in sexual profiles is that men in our culture are allowed and encouraged to desire and demand more sex. They have fewer costs for experiencing or acting on sexual desires (that is, no reduced marketability, no fear of becoming pregnant), and therefore they establish a fairly high sexual frequency in both heterosexual and homosexual relationships. We do not think women in heterosexual relationships have essentially different sexual appetites from women in lesbian relationships, since both groups of women have had similar sexual socialization and have learned similar inhibitions. If the heterosexual women in our study were suddenly put into a same-sex relationship, their sexual frequency would probably resemble lesbians' sexual frequency. The reduction in sexual frequency would occur because the norms of lesbian relationships are different from those of heterosexual relationships and because two women bring different cultural scripts to a sexual relationship than a man and a woman.[6]

In our study, men initiated sex more than women in opposite-sex relationships.[7] Men are assigned this role, and women in our society are taught to be receptive rather than aggressive in sexual matters.[8] It makes sense, then, that in lesbian couples, where both partners have experienced female sexual socialization, there would be a mutual reluctance to take the sexual lead. Such inheritance of social conditioning might contribute to lesbians' having an overall lower

initiation rate than other couples and hence a lower rate of sexual activity.

Their reluctance to initiate, however, does not simply stem from the internalization of sexual prohibitions directed at women. Additionally, themes in some lesbian subcultures stigmatize sexual aggressiveness as "powerplays" and male-type sexuality, and place a lower premium on genital sexuality, with a corresponding emphasis on other forms of physical intimacy. Moreover, higher standards of relationship satisfaction are demanded in order to legitimate sexual intimacy. Relationship dynamics, rather than essential core sexuality, orient the individual's sexual frequency and sexual pattern.

The internal dynamics of the relationship can affect sexual experience in subtle ways. For example, among all four of the groups of couples in our study, the greater power one partner has, the more likely he or she is to refuse a sexual overture (Blumstein & Schwartz 1983, pp. 219–221). And among the women in heterosexual couples, the more power they have, the less likely the couple's intercourse is to be restricted to the male prone-female supine position (Blumstein & Schwartz 1983, pp. 229–230).

On the basis of these findings, and with every indication that there will be greater equality between the sexes in the future, one might hypothesize that the sexual patterns of heterosexual couples will change in response to a more liberated female sexuality. In some couples frequency may increase and in others it may decrease, but in either event these changes will be responses to the structure of the relationship between the partners, not to some inherent capacity of women.

TABLE 2   **Respondents Reporting at Least One Nonmonogamous Instance in the Previous Year**

Husbands	11% (1510)
Wives	9% (1510)
Male cohabitors	25% (288)
Female cohabitors	22% (288)
Homosexual males	79% (943)
Lesbians	19% (706)

Note: Numbers in parentheses are the number of respondents on which the percentages are based. Respondents are partners in couples who have lived together between two and ten years.

MONOGAMY

The rules of monogamous conduct provide insight into how male sexuality is affected by intimate relationships. With the exception of the male homosexual couples, the majority of each group of couples feels that the rules of monogamous conduct are a cornerstone of the relationship and should not be broken.[9] Homosexual men, while presently intimidated by the risk of contracting AIDS, nonetheless have a long history of separating sexual desire from intimacy and love, and have evolved a norm of having relationships that allow either occasional or a great deal of sex with persons other than one's partner.

Heterosexual men, both married and cohabiting, have frequently mentioned in our interviews that they would like greater permission for "recreational" sex in their relationships, but the data show that they tend not to pursue it (see Table 2). If these men were in a same-sex relationship, they would have a higher rate of nonmonogamy because the rules of acceptability would be altered.[10] Thus, an element of their sexuality is constructed by their female partner's wishes and by the norms that are shaped by the institution of marriage. Compliance to the norm is, of course, not perfect; many husbands do have extramarital sex, and sex outside their relationship is even more common among male cohabitors. The latter face less stringent guidelines within their relationship and are merely asked to comply with their partner's wishes rather than with the directives of marital vows. Looking at the difference between married men's and cohabiting men's extrarelationship sex tells us how much the norms of marriage organize sexuality.

This cursory look at sexual expression in intimate relationships is not intended as more than an illustration of the analytic mileage to be gained by conceptualizing sex within the context of social circumstances. Even by looking at relatively crude survey data we can see that sexual behavior is created by relationship expectations and traditions rather than by sexual essences. If we were to look more microscopically within relationships we could see the subtle ways in which intimate interaction affects participants. We could see how friends, neighborhoods, community, law, and other constraints affect sexual conduct. If research on sexuality were to proceed in this direction, if more attention were paid to opportunity structure—of which intimate relationships are but one—we would uncover the social construction of sexuality.

In sum, we look forward to research where situational variables and cultural meanings are seen as the foundation of sexuality. But new research needs to avoid androcentrism so that opportunity structures are not chosen because of their relevance only to men's lives. A useful approach will take into account individual biography without producing a static and individualistic explanation of sexuality. Sexuality is best comprehended by noting and understanding the *processes* which encourage the occurrence of acts and the reason for their discontinuance. We should focus on the act, behaving not as accountants tabulating frequencies, but as behavioral scientists looking at the meaning of the act for the actors. If we continue as we have in the past, focusing on the individual, rather than on the social context that creates his or her behavior, we may end up with interesting biographies but relatively little ability for further prediction or theory construction. We then run the risk of thinking we understand something merely because we have given it a number on a scale.

NOTES

1. We would also argue that for most members of contemporary Western society, because of the hegemony of sexual essentialism, once an individual develops a sexual identity, it funnels much of his or her social experience into erotic and nonerotic circumstances which continually reinforce a subjective sense of categorical desire.

2. On the social construction of sexuality, see, among others, Gagnon and Simon (1973), McIntosh (1968), Plummer (1975), and Weinberg (1978; 1983).

3. The Kinsey scale was originally aimed at both behavior and "psychic reactions." The inclusion of the latter construct implicitly acknowledged ways in which purely behavioral tabulations could mislead. However, the conceptual and measurement problems associated with psychic reactions have remained largely unresolved.

4. It is important to note that homosexual behavior leads to the existence of gay male and lesbian couple relationships only under extremely rare historical and cultural circumstances. This means that most homosexuality occurs in very different contexts than much (we do not know how much) heterosexuality. This fact, as obvious as it is, has important implications. Most sensible researchers would be wary of equating heterosexual intercourse between two strangers (for example, a man with a female prostitute) with that in a twenty-five-year marriage. Neither situation reflects an "essence of heterosexuality." Researchers have been less sensitive in the case of homosexual behavior, as though the slogan were "sodomy is sodomy is sodomy. . . ." It is critical to see human sexual behavior as context embedded rather than as a simple expression of the underlying sexuality of the individual.

5. Two other interpretations of these data come immediately to mind. First is the argument that physical aging, which is correlated with relationship duration, is the real causal factor. Multivariate statistical analyses allowed an evaluation of the aging effects net of duration and the duration effects net of aging. Based on these analyses we concluded that physical aging and habituation independently reduce sexual frequency. The other interpretation to consider is that couples with relatively low sexual frequency have greater likelihood of longevity. While we have no direct empirical test of this causal hypothesis, it seems implausible in light of substantial positive correlations between sexual frequency and sexual happiness and substantial negative correlations between sexual happiness and relationship durability.

6. Another way of looking at these data is to imagine a woman living in a heterosexual relationship for ten years followed by a homosexual relationship of the same duration. In the typical case, the total number of sexual acts in the heterosexual relationship would be much greater than the total number of acts within the lesbian relationship. Ought we label such a woman a Kinsey 3 because she was in two ten-year relationships. Or would she be a Kinsey 1 because her sexual activity was more frequent in the heterosexual union? Or would we label her a Kinsey 5 or 6 because of her most recent sexual life, especially if asserted that this relationship was permanent? These data suggest caution in the use of a scale that does not take into account the context and changing meaning of people's emotional and sexual lives.

7. Fifty-one percent of husbands say they initiate sex more than their wives as compared to 16 percent who say the reverse pattern holds true; the remainder say initiation is equal ($N = 3612$). While the wives are not in perfect agreement with their husbands, they are very close (48 percent and 12 percent. $N = 3616$). Thirty-nine percent of male cohabitors say they initiate more and 19 percent say their female partner initiates more ($N = 646$). The female percentages are 39 and 15 percent ($N = 648$).

8. Sociobiologists have argued that this difference is a reflection of the different reproductive strategies of men and women. Indeed Symons (1979) has applied this argument to the sexual behavior of lesbians. His discussion, however, does not adequately deal with the influence of cultural learning.

9. We asked respondents how important they felt it is that they themselves be monogamous. The percentages saying it is important are husbands, 75 percent ($N = 3635$); wives, 84 percent ($N = 3640$); male cohabitors, 62 percent ($N = 650$); female cohabitors, 70 percent ($N = 650$); lesbians, 71 percent ($N = 1559$); and male homosexuals, 36 percent ($N = 1924$).

10. It should be noted that the percentages in Table 2 are based on data gathered just before the AIDS crisis began to receive widespread attention in the gay community.

REFERENCES

Blumstein, P., & Schwartz, P. (1976a). Bisexuality in women. *Archives of Sexual Behavior 5,* 171–181.

———. (1976b). Bisexuality in men. *Urban Life 5:* 339–358.

———. (1977). Bisexuality: Some social psychological issues. *Journal of Social Issues 33*(2): 30–45.

———. (1983). *American couples: Money, work, and sex.* New York: William Morrow.

de Beauvoir, S. (1953). *The second sex.* New York: Knopf.

Gagnon, J. H., & Simon, W. (1973). *Sexual conduct: The social sources of human sexuality.* Chicago: Aldine.

Herdt, G. H. (1981). *Guardians of the flutes: Idioms of masculinity.* New York: McGraw-Hill.

Humphreys, L. (1970). *Tearoom trade: Impersonal sex in public places.* Chicago: Aldine.

Katz, J. (1975). Essences as moral identities: Verifiability and responsibility in imputations of deviance and charisma. *American Journal of Sociology 80,* 1369–1390.

Kinsey, A. C., Pomeroy, W. B., & Martin, C. E. (1948). *Sexual behavior in the human male.* Philadelphia: W. B. Saunders.

Kinsey, A. C., Pomeroy, W. B., Martin, C. E., & Gebhard, P. H. (1953). *Sexual behavior in the human female.* Philadelphia: W. B. Saunders.

Laws, J. L., & Schwartz, P. (1977). *Sexual scripts: The social construction of female sexuality.* Hinsdale, Ill: Dryden Press.

McIntosh, M. (1968). The homosexual role. *Social Problems 16,* 182–192.

Plummer, K. (1975). *Sexual stigma: An interactionist account.* London: Routledge & Kegan Paul.

Ross, H. L. (1971). Modes and adjustments of married homosexuals. *Social Problems 18,* 385–393.

Ross, M. W. (1983). *The married homosexual man.* London: Routledge & Kegan Paul.

Symons, D. (1979). *The evolution of human sexuality.* New York: Oxford University Press.

van den Berghe, P. L. (1979). *Human family systems: An evolutionary view.* New York: Elsevier.

Weinberg, T. S. (1978). On "doing" and "being" gay: Sexual behavior and homosexual male self-identity. *Journal of Homosexuality 4,* 143–156.

———. (1983). *Gay men, gay selves: The social construction of homosexual identities.* New York: Irvington.

CHECKPOINTS

1. Using a social constructionist perspective, Blumstein and Schwartz show how gender defines opportunity and constructs sexuality.

2. The dynamic interaction between sexual partners predicts sexual frequency and monogamy across heterosexual, gay, and lesbian couples.

Gender and Sexuality

QUESTIONS FOR REFLECTION

1. What advice should adolescents be given about the relationship between gender and sexuality that would help them make responsible decisions about sexual behavior?
2. According to Tiefer and Kring, gender provides the best prediction of sexual feelings and behavior. Based on your reading of these articles, explain what they mean and provide some evidence that this is true.

CHAPTER APPLICATION

1. Find one book in a local bookstore or library that offers advice for people on sexual matters. How are sexual problems characterized—as biological, medical, interpersonal, psychological? What models of sexuality are portrayed in this advice? Could this advice be used by someone who identifies themselves as gay, lesbian, bisexual, or transgendered?

Gendered Behavior in a Social Context

QUESTIONS TO THINK ABOUT

- **How do we understand sex differences in social behavior?**
- **What is the role of stereotypes in predicting sex differences?**
- **What concerns are there about the research on sex differences in social behavior?**
- **Why are social context and gender belief systems important in understanding social behavior?**
- **What are the similarities and differences for men and women in emotion?**
- **What are the similarities and differences for men and women in aggression?**
- **What are the similarities and differences for men and women in altruism?**
- **What evidence is there for the minimizer versus maximizer views of social behavior?**

THE QUESTION OF DIFFERENCE

The question of sex differences in social behavior is at the heart of much of the research on gender.[1] Do men and women behave similarly or differently in social situations? This question is very general, and to answer it, we must know what social situations are being studied, what behaviors are of interest, and how the similarity or difference is measured. By examining the research on sex differences, we can begin to answer these questions, although this research reveals that sex differences in behavior are inconsistent and generally unstable. To complicate matters further, we find that most individuals believe

men and women are substantially different (Deaux and Major, 1987). Two issues can help us resolve this contradiction between behavioral observations of differences and people's belief in differences. The first issue is the methods by which psychologists study differences (see chapter 2), and the second is the role of stereotypes in people's everyday understanding of gender (see chapter 5).

Minimizers versus Maximizers?

Researchers vary as to whether they are searching for differences or similarities and whether they believe these differences or similarities to be significant or relatively inconsequential. This is the distinction between maximizers and minimizers that we referred to in earlier chapters. Maximizers believe that sex differences are significant, and often they believe that sex differences cut across a variety of cultural and social circumstances. Researchers who tend to endorse the maximizer perspective may not pay careful attention to the particular circumstances of their research, believing that sex differences would hold across different conditions. For example, researchers might generalize from an experiment in a laboratory to similar, naturally occurring conditions outside the lab setting. Minimizers believe that sex differences are either insignificant or only occur in limited circumstances. From this perspective, it would be important to delineate the specific conditions under which a particular sex difference might or might not occur. For example, does a sex difference that is found under controlled laboratory conditions also exist in real-life settings? As you will read in the article by Alice Eagly, *Gender and Altruism* in many laboratory studies of altruism, male participants are more likely to help than female participants. Does this finding mean that, in real life, men are more helpful than women? Eagly's analysis examines the specific features of both laboratory research and field research and considers the specific circumstances related to male and female helpfulness.

Stereotypes and Social Behavior

Stereotypes also play a role in our understanding of social behavior. As we argued in chapter 5, gender role norms and cultural expectations are both significant elements of stereotypes. People are likely to expect a sex difference in behavior when there is a strong cultural norm for men and women to behave differently. It may not be so surprising that people would believe in sex differences, even when people's actual behavior is somewhat inconsistent. To understand these beliefs better, we need to identify the cultural norms for gendered behavior that might be operating. By understanding the relationship between culture and gender roles, we might be able to predict more accurately when sex differences will or will not occur, and we may also recognize the basis for people's general belief in sex differences.

Three of the articles in this chapter are reviews of the evidence for sex differences in important areas of social behavior: emotion, aggression, and altruism. We have chosen these three areas of social behavior because they represent three aspects of behavior for which our stereotyped sex differences are very salient. As you read the evidence for sex differences in emotion, aggression, and altruism, you will want to keep in mind the difference between an essentialist and social constructionist position. Essentialist arguments about sex differences view the characteristics of interest as residing within individuals. Remember that an essentialist would view these as qualities that people embody—one is either more or less emotional, more or less aggressive, more or less altruistic. The implication is that the degree of the quality that individuals possess will predict their behavior across a variety of circumstances. A social constructionist view suggests that social behaviors result from social and cultural circumstances, not characteristics of individual people. Particular situations lead to greater or lesser emotion, aggression, or altruism. As you read the three reviews, you should try to identify examples of essentialist versus social constructionist explanations by looking for evidence that individuals' behavior is consistent across situations (essentialist) or for evidence that individuals' behavior varies depending on the situation (social constructionist). You should also consider the role of culture in defining emotion, aggression, and altruism. Are there cultural gender roles for the expression of emotion, aggression, and altruism that are common across cultures, or do cultures vary in their gender roles in the areas of emotion, aggression, and altruism? Understanding the role of culture helps to distinguish essentialist versus social constructionist explanations, because essentialist arguments are supported by observations of cross-cultural similarities while observations of cultural differences support a social constructionist viewpoint.

A MODEL OF GENDER AND SOCIAL CONTEXT

To understand gender, we must understand context. Thus far in this book we have examined the biological, cultural, and developmental context of gender. Social psychology provides another level of analysis of context, with its focus on the particular aspects of one's immediate social context. This focus includes elaborating on both the setting in which a behavior occurs and the specific features of the participants in a social interaction. Models of social cognition also are concerned with features that reflect how people perceive and interpret social information. In relationship to gender, we have discussed gender schemas, social scripts, and gender roles as cognitive processes that reflect social and cultural aspects of gender. The social psychological analysis that we will emphasize focuses on the *display* of gender-related behavior and on the immediate factors that influence the occurrence of the behavior, including the context and individuals' understanding and interpretation of the ongoing events (Deaux and Major, 1987).

Research on sex differences in social behavior is abundant. As we have already suggested, the proliferation of empirical studies that compare males and females on a specific behavioral dimension has created substantial problems of interpretation. You read in the articles in chapter 2 that the debate about the interpretation of sex differences involves many complex issues, including the conceptual meaning of sex differences, the measurement of the behavior under consideration, and the magnitude of group differences (with sex as the independent variable) versus individual differences. Deaux and Major (1987) have constructed a model of gender and social behavior that provides a coherent framework for explaining the multitude of findings about sex differences. They claim that their model accounts for two critical aspects of gender and social behavior. First, the model explicates the complex pattern of sex differences found in the social psychological research literature. Second, the model predicts the behavior of individuals in specified social contexts. Their model uses the available data on sex differences, analyzes the contextual factors that are relevant to this research, and

elaborates on a set of social cognitive processes that contribute to an understanding of the particulars of individual behavior. Thus, although the model is drawn from literature on sex differences, its goal is to clearly articulate the conditions under which differences will or will not occur and therefore to be able to predict individual behavior in various social contexts.

Kay Deaux and Brenda Major describe their theory of gender in social contexts in the first article in this chapter, titled *A Social-Psychological Model of Gender*.[2] They recognize that the behavior of women and men is variable across time and is flexible in response to the particular circumstances. Unlike theories of development that focus on the origins of gender-related behavior, Deaux and Major are concerned with the *display* of gender-related behaviors. Furthermore, they emphasize the *proximal* (immediate) conditions of behavior rather than either past events or intrapsychic experiences (neither of which are directly observable). Finally, they are concerned with the conditions that affect the likelihood that particular men or particular women will behave in gendered ways (rather than focus on group differences between men and women).

Deaux and Major propose that the presence or absence of sex differences in behavior will be influenced by the gender role beliefs of the individual, the gender role beliefs of other participants in the situation, and the particular features of the immediate context. In the description of their model, Deaux and Major detail the features of gender role beliefs held by both the actor and the other participants in a social interaction as well as the aspects of the context that will influence the likelihood that individuals will respond in gendered ways. In particular, the model describes the interaction between one individual's gender information processing, the other participant's information processing, and the social situation. The model portrays the relationship between individuals and the social context as dynamic—meaning that they exert mutual influence on each other.

The foundation of the model is the activation of gender schemas, or knowledge structures about

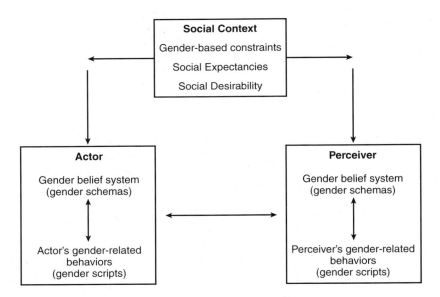

Figure I   *Illustration of the relationship between social context and individual gender role beliefs and scripts.*

gender, and the relationships of these knowledge structures to individual identity. Belief systems about gender might include the degree to which an individual believes that certain behaviors or responses are more appropriate for men versus women and the degree to which an individual believes that gendered responses are more appropriate for themselves. A gender belief system therefore has a component to represent *cognitions* (thoughts or beliefs about gender roles) and a *behavioral* component, sometimes called gender *scripts,* that would represent typical patterns of behaviors under various circumstances.

The model examines variations in the social context and how these variations influence the likelihood of sex differences. The context can include such things as the setting (location), cultural norms for behavior, and social structures (e.g., power, intimacy) that determine the relationship between the participants. In a workplace interaction, for example, we would identify the setting as the particular features of where the interaction takes place (supervisor's office), the cultural norms as the role prescriptions that govern each person's behavior (supervisor

is assertive and directive, employee is deferential and responsive), and the social structure as the norms that govern this type of interaction (supervisor holds power to direct employee's behavior). This model predicts that sex differences in behavior will be *maximized* under the following conditions: when men and women have different expectations for themselves, when other participants in a social interaction have highly gender stereotyped beliefs, or when the context is heavily prescribed with gender expectations. The model predicts that sex differences will be *minimized* under the following conditions: when men and women share similar expectations or beliefs, when few stereotypes apply to the situation, or when the context is neutral with regard to gender.

Figure I portrays a schematic outline of the dynamic relationship among an individual, another participant, and the context for the purpose of understanding the role of gender in a social interaction. This schematic outline is loosely adapted from the key elements presented in the article by Deaux and Major in this chapter.[3] We identify one person as the actor and the other person as the perceiver; however, you should realize that this identification is somewhat arbitrary because in any dynamic social interaction these roles are interchangeable. Our rationale for using these labels is that they enable us to discuss separately the perceptions, beliefs, and behavior of each participant. Like that of Deaux and Major, our schematic outline portrays each participant with a set of gender role beliefs that affect their perception of themselves and of the other person. The perceptions and behaviors of each person are triggered by social and cultural expectations elicited by particular interactions and specific settings. Some social settings are more likely to trigger gendered expectations, for example, searching for a sales clerk in the women's lingerie department, meeting the high school wrestling coach, or planning a birthday party for a five-year-old boy or girl. In each of these examples, we are likely to hold beliefs about the sex of the participants and anticipate certain aspects of their behavior. In addition, we are likely to alter our behavior in accord with these expectations. A recent experience of mine (A.L.) illustrates how we respond when a situation elicits gendered expectations, which, of course, are often not confirmed. I took my daughters to a local shopping mall to have my ten-year-old's recently pierced ears checked by one of the salespeople at the ear-piercing booth. Walking past and seeing only a man at the booth, the ten-year-old commented, "Well, I guess we'll have to come back." I responded that that probably wasn't necessary, and we went over and told the male clerk why we were there. As he was checking her sister's ears, my six-year-old daughter looked at the male clerk, noted his many earrings, and commented, "Well, I guess you only have to have pierced ears to work here." Obviously, both girls thought that piercing ears was a job most likely to be held by a woman and, without some prodding, would have avoided the interaction with a man in that setting. It was fascinating to observe how quickly they realized that having pierced ears seemed to be a more relevant qualification. The interaction ended in a conversation with the clerk about what style earrings he would recommend and his preferences for gold versus silver. We left with some alterations, we hope, in our "gender lenses," as Bem might suggest.

The next three articles in this chapter all concern areas of social behavior for which there are powerful cultural stereotypes: emotion and the expression of emotions, aggression, and altruism. Most people believe that men and women are different in each of these areas. We believe that the model described by Deaux and Major is an extremely useful tool for comparing stereotypes about each social behavior to what we actually know about behavior and the factors that influence behavior. The Deaux and Major model allows us to understand the conditions under which a specific gender stereotype is likely to be observed less likely to be observed. The model is a powerful tool for organizing empirical evidence with regard to the actual conditions that will minimize or maximize the likelihood of sex differences. We illustrate the use of the model for each of the three areas that you learn about in the chapter's readings.

GENDER AND EMOTION

You probably have some ideas about how children are socialized with regard to the expression of emotion. At a fairly young age, boys are taught to control their emotions, especially to not cry, while young girls are allowed to express their emotions openly. With regard to anger, boys are given more latitude in aggressive outbursts while girls are taught other means for expressing anger. By preschool, children hold gender-stereotyped beliefs about emotion, such that they associate anger with males and happiness, sadness, and fear with females (Birnbaum, Nosanchuk, & Croll, 1980). What are the consequences of these differences in expectation for the expression of emotion? Do men and women express emotions differently? Do men and women define emotions differently? Or do men and women feel the same emotions and express them in similar fashion? Studying sex differences by comparing men and women on either the perception or display of emotion had yielded inconsistent and unstable results. Researchers have concluded that one's sex plays little consistent role in emotion display or intensity (Shields, 1987).

In her article in this chapter, *Gender in the Psychology of Emotion: A Selective Research Review*, Stephanie Shields, suggests that an analysis of gender and its relationship to emotion explains the complexities in the research on sex differences in emotion. She uses a social constructionist approach to explore the social contextual variables that influence the display of emotion. By using this strategy, the emphasis shifts from treating emotion as a relatively stable quality that resides within individuals to an analysis that emphasizes the factors that differentially affect men's versus women's perceptions of their own or other's emotions.

Shields examines the limitations of the existing research literature on emotions and reviews a large body of research on gender. According to Shields, one methodological limitation of this research is that it has been conducted with white, middle-class research subjects, often of college age. Two important features of the Deaux and Major model are the role of cultural prescriptions and the individual belief system about gender, however, we should not expect these two features to be the same across race, ethnicity, social class, or age. Researchers should be exploring the ways in which gender prescriptions and expectations vary as a function of other aspects of one's identity—but little research addresses this question. So although the model allows for variation as a function of ethnicity, race, social class, or age, there is unfortunately very little data to tell us exactly *how* gender prescriptions vary. One pervasive limitation of the research that will be reviewed by Shields[4] is the limited population of research participants that have been studied.

Sex Differences in Emotion?

Beliefs about emotion are acquired early and persist throughout life. The emotions of sadness and fear are deemed feminine while happiness and anger are deemed masculine. One of the most comprehensive studies on the acquisition of emotion stereotypes is the research by Fabes and Martin (1991), who conclude that stereotypes about emotion are organized to fit children's rigid notions about males—children are more likely to notice counterstereotypic behavior by boys, are more likely to distort their recollection of boys' violations of stereotypes, and are more likely to judge harshly boys who violate emotion stereotypes. This research suggests that males are expected to adhere closely to narrow prescriptions about the display of emotion and that both boys and girls are more likely to identify and remember when boys violate these prescriptions. Evidence shows that people hold the expectation that women are less likely to express negative emotions such as anger. According to Shields, there is evidence that beliefs about gender and emotion vary across situations. Both adolescents and adults seem to believe that women experience and express more emotion in interpersonal situations, while men's emotions are related more to circumstances that reflect personal autonomy or possessions. As the Deaux and Major model would predict, situations can be more or less gendered with regard to behaviors, and in this case, some circumstances may trigger expectations of emotional expression for either men or women. Also, many circumstances are neutral with regard to the display of emotions.

An additional component of the model includes gender scripts that might organize an individual's cognitions about stereotypes and behavior. In research that uses self-report methods—in which subjects are asked to report on their own emotional experiences—it seems that reported experiences of emotional intensity vary in accord with cultural stereotypes. Shields suggests that emotion stereotypes may act as an internal standard against which individuals judge their particular experiences. For example, knowing that women are supposed to be emotionally expressive, a woman may judge her own behavior as highly expressive. This point demonstrates the interaction between gender beliefs and gender scripts that is illustrated in figure 8.1. In this case, women reporting on their emotions may be reflecting their culturally based beliefs about women's expression of emotion and may enact these beliefs in a scripted way that reflects this stereotype.

Using the evidence in Shields's article and the model of Deaux and Major, we can predict the following sex differences in emotion: Interpersonal or family interactions will elicit the display of emotion by women, whereas public and work settings will elicit the display of emotion by men. Sex differences would be minimal in other settings that are neutral with regard to gender expectations for emotion. We would further expect sex differences in the display of emotions that are highly stereotyped (e.g., anger, happiness, sadness, or fear), but minimal or no sex differences in the display of other emotions (e.g., humor, frustration, love) that are not highly stereotyped. We would expect sex differences in emotion when the prevailing situation elicits well-developed gender scripts for emotional display; that is, we predict that women's display of strong emotion would include crying and men's display of strong emotion would include angry outbursts (Shields, 1987). Finally, because this model represents the mutual effect of two individuals engaged in a social interaction, we would expect that each person's gender beliefs and scripts would interact with the other. Gender differences should be maximized when the actor's cognitions are consistent with the behavior of the other participant, and gender differences should be minimized when gender norms are violated. This analysis moves us far beyond simplistic questions such as are women more emotional than men or do men and women experience emotions differently.

GENDER AND AGGRESSION

Perhaps no other area of social behavior elicits stronger beliefs in the existence of sex differences than the area of aggression. Explanations for aggressive behavior are often essentialist in character. They focus on the universality of male aggression and treat aggression as a personality factor that resides within an individual. The classic review of sex differences research by Maccoby and Jacklin (1974), which determined that in general sex differences are small and inconsistent, concluded, however that aggression remains the one area in which sex differences

are pervasive. In the third article in this chapter, *Deconstructing the Myth of the Nonaggressive Woman*, Jacqueline White and Robin Kowalski report that more recent analyses support the belief that men are more aggressive than women.

White and Kowalski challenge the conclusion that women are not aggressive. According to these authors, the research on aggression has had a distinctly male bias—the choice of research participants, the definitions of aggression, and the context or setting are all more likely to elicit male rather than female aggression. White and Kowalski point out that most research on aggression has defined aggression as behavior intended to harm another and most particularly as forms of physical violence. They contend that aggression needs to be defined more broadly to include retaliatory aggression and nonphysical forms of aggression.

According to White and Kowalski, the circumstances within which women are likely to be aggressive are much narrower than the circumstances in which men are likely to be aggressive. In particular, women are less likely than men to be aggressive toward strangers. Women's aggression is controlled by more social sanctions and prohibitions. For example, girls are discouraged from fighting (they are often not even allowed to engage in rough-and-tumble play). Women's aggression is judged more harshly. Aggression in men is often viewed as socially appropriate, as in sporting events or displays of assertive aggression in the workplace, whereas similar behaviors by women under similar circumstances lead to the portrayal of women as deviant or psychologically out of control. The key point of White and Kowalski's analysis is that these situational and gender role constraints should not be used as evidence that women do not behave aggressively.

Sex Differences in Aggression?

White and Kowalski's review of the literature on aggression can be understood using the model presented by Deaux and Major. Of particular interest are men and women's belief systems about aggression, sex differences in situational prescriptions with regard to gender, and differences in interpretation of the other person's behavior. This analysis will challenge your assumptions about women and aggression. As we previously stated, the most salient element in both men and women's belief systems about aggression is the belief that women are not aggressive. Not only does this translate into a gender role prescription for women, it also shapes the interpretation given to women's behavior by both men and women. Some behaviors by women, such as aggression in response to a threat or verbal aggression, may not be perceived and labeled as aggressive behavior. Aggression in men is not only tolerated but in many situations it is encouraged, for example, in competitive situations, business, driving in the car, or defending oneself against a threat or insult. White and Kowalski argue that the social role of nurturance, caring, and empathy prescribed for women acts against the interpretation of women's behavior as aggressive, whereas the social role of men as assertive, controlling, and independent acts in favor of their behavior being interpreted as aggressive. The same or similar behaviors, therefore, may take on different meanings. One example the authors give to illustrate this point is the use of physical discipline by parents. This behavior by mothers is often viewed as an extension of their maternal role, and the aggressive elements of the behavior may be minimized. In reality, women are found guilty of child abuse more often than men.[5] If we include aggression in the home and within intimate relationships, sex differences in aggression are substantially reduced if not eliminated. Sex differences in aggression are maintained by strong cultural constraints against women's aggression, by limited circumstances in which women might behave aggressively, and by the differing interpretations given to women's and men's aggressive behavior.

The findings about aggression that we have just described are limited to the Western cultural context with which we are most familiar. One interesting comparison you can make is between aggression as described in this article and the aggression described by Lepowsky in the article you read in chapter 4. Lepowsky describes a society in which aggression is rare but equally common for men or women. Her explanation of this phenomenon rests on the degree of equality and power shared by women and men. White and Kowalski agree that norms for the exercise of power govern the use of aggression; however, they claim that in our patriarchal society in which power is not shared, the myth of the nonaggressive woman supports male power.

Using the Deaux and Major model, we can clearly see how varying cultural experiences shape gender schemas as well as expectations and attributions about others. In many Western cultures, women's aggression is carefully controlled by social norms (e.g., women should not express anger, women should not engage in physical aggression, women should not publicly display aggression), whereas in Vanatinai these social norms do not apply and there are no sex differences in the expression of aggression. It is important to remember that Vanatinai society places many social constraints on the expression of aggression in general, and thus very little interpersonal aggression is exhibited by either males or females. Expressions of anger and aggression are controlled through magic and sorcery. Using careful observations across cultures and using a contextual and dynamic model of gender, we can understand cultural variations in behaviors such as aggression. These observations help us avoid the naive and simplistic assumption that there are pervasive and universal sex differences in aggression.

GENDER AND ALTRUISM

Altruism is defined as helpfulness, or willingness to engage in self-sacrificial behavior. Some types of altruism involve little cost or risk to an individual, such as giving up a close parking place for an elderly person or buying warm lemonade from a group of neighborhood children. Other altruistic acts involve real personal cost or potential risk, such as running into a burning building to save a child or offering to lend a friend a great deal of money. The study of altruism emerged from questions about why and when people would help someone in need. Much of the research on altruism has focused on studying people's willingness to help in simulated emergencies in a laboratory setting, although a few classic studies have explored helping behavior in real-life situations such as when someone has a flat tire or is robbed on the subway.

Alice Eagly, in the last article in this chapter, argues that altruism does not reside within men and women but emerges from differing opportunities, circumstances, and the type of behavior being examined. Understanding the relationship between opportunities and specific types of altruistic behaviors is the key to understanding the relationship between gender and altruism.

Sex Differences in Altruism?

Again we can apply the Deaux and Major model to understand the findings about altruism. According to Eagly, there are different belief systems for altruism and different situations in which helpfulness is appropriate for women and men. In general, women are encouraged to be self-sacrificial and men are encouraged to be heroic. Self-sacrificial behaviors may be embedded in nurturing and caring for others, whereas heroic behavior may occur in circumstances of helpfulness to strangers and in which there is potential physical harm to oneself. We can see the role that gender schemas play in interpreting altruistic behaviors because there is considerable evidence that people are more likely to be helpful in areas in which they perceive themselves to be competent. In one study, college-age participants were asked to respond to a scenario depicting a high school friend who asks for help in deciding whether to drop out of college. Female participants were more likely to choose encouraging the friend to talk, whereas male participants more often chose problem-solving strategies such as listing the pros and cons of the decision (Belansky & Boggiano, 1994). Individuals develop more detailed scripts for helpfulness in those areas in which they have gained experience and, as a result, have come to believe themselves capable. Sex differences, therefore, should occur in circumstances in which there would be strong sex differences in perceived

competence. Men might be expected to stop and help a stranded motorist fix a flat tire more often than women would, and women might be expected to offer to care for a neighbor's children more often than men would.

Eagly's careful review of the research on helpfulness reveals that researchers have tended to examine situations that involve helping a stranger or that involve potential harm. Thus, the available research has been biased toward situations in which men may be more helpful. This research does not reveal that men are more helpful than women but that, under certain circumstances, there will be sex differences in helpfulness. Two features of the social setting influence the occurrence of sex differences. First, men are more likely to behave altruistically in public settings with an audience, whereas women's altruism is more likely to occur in private settings in the context of an ongoing relationship. Second, women and men are differentially sensitive to particular features of the opportunity to be helpful. Men are more likely to take risks whereas women are more likely to respond to requests for help. These circumstances predict sex differences, but the absence of these features, or their lesser occurrence, is related to minimal or no sex differences in the likelihood of helping.

As you read the Eagly article, keep in mind the variations in gender belief systems and the variations in the circumstances within which altruism might occur. Based on this premise, you should be able to understand and predict the factors that predict the likelihood of sex differences or similarity in altruism.

BEHAVIOR IN A SOCIAL CONTEXT— SIMILARITIES OR DIFFERENCES?

The search for sex differences is considerably more complex than you might have imagined. Although it is sometimes tempting to use our firsthand experience as evidence, we can see that this evidence does not have the breadth of differing viewpoints and circumstances that allow us to accurately know whether men and women are more similar or different. The readings in this chapter show you that even careful, empirical analysis can be subject to flaws in data collection, definition of variables, and interpretation of findings. Each review that you read takes a critical approach to analyzing a large number of research findings.

All the articles in this chapter contain elements of the social constructionist point of view. Each focuses on the context within which behavior occurs and emphasizes diversity in social behavior as opposed to overgeneralized universals about sex differences. We hope that reading these articles helps you to appreciate the complexity of social behavior and its dynamic and evolving relationship to gender. The remainder of this book examines gender in some important social contexts: school, family, intimate relationships, work,

physical health, and mental health care settings. The most important argument of this chapter is that questions about sex differences or sex similarities are likely to present only part of the picture of gender. We encourage you to use the Deaux and Major model to understand the circumstances under which sex differences are either maximized or minimized. Sex differences have been studied in many other aspects of social behavior (e.g., nurturing, communication, nonverbal behavior, intimacy). As you learn more about those additional aspects, we encourage you to simultaneously consider the social context of any particular behavior as well as the belief systems of the actor and observer in order to differentiate stereotypes from actual behavior.

NOTES

1. In keeping with the distinction we made in chapter 1, we will use the term *sex* in this chapter and in chapter 9 to refer to all of the research that has focused on differences between males and females as the subject of study. Some of the authors in the articles in these chapters use the term *gender* in places in which we use the term *sex*.

2. The article in this book is an abbreviated version of a much longer paper by Deaux and Major (1987).

3. In their original presentation of this model, Deaux and Major (1987) use a more complex diagram of the relationships between gender and social behavior. In particular, we have not represented the details of the factors that trigger an individual's belief systems with regard to gender, and we have condensed the interactions within an individual that govern their

"self-system." These self-system processes include such factors as the individual's self-concept with regard to gender or the relative salience of specific aspects of gender role within individuals.

4. This point also holds for the research reviewed by White and Kowalski and by Eagly.

5. The research provided by White and Kowalski does not account for the different amount of exposure to children of mothers versus fathers and the disproportionate number of single-mother families. These sex differences need to be interpreted with caution, although they do illustrate the more general point intended by White and Kowalski that there are circumstances in which women behave aggressively.

REFERENCES

Belansky, E. S., & Boggiano, A. K. (1994). Predicting helping behaviors: the role of gender and instrumental/expressive self-schemata. *Sex Roles, 30,* 647–661.

Birnbaum, D. W., Nosanchuk, T. A., & Croll, W. L. (1980). Children's stereotypes about sex differences in emotionality. *Sex Roles, 6,* 435–443.

Deaux, K., & Major, B. (1987). Putting gender into context: An interactive model of gender-related behavior. *Psychological Review, 94,* 369–389.

Deaux, K., & Major, B. (1990). A social-psychological model of gender. In D. Rhode (Ed.), Theoretical perspectives on sexual differences (pp. 89–99). New Haven, CT: Yale University Press.

Eagly, A. H. (1996). Gender and altruism. In J. C. Chrisler, C. Golden, & P. D. Rozee (Eds.), *Lectures on the psychology of women* (pp. 43–60). New York: McGraw-Hill.

Fabes, R. A., & Martin, C. J. (1991). Gender and age stereotypes of emotionality. *Personality and social psychology bulletin, 17,* 532–540.

Maccoby, E., & Jacklin, C. N. (1974). *The psychology of sex differences.* Stanford, CA: Stanford University Press.

Shields, S. (1987), Women, men and the dilemma of emotion. In P. Shaver & C. Hendrick (Eds.) *Sex and Gender: Vol. 7 Review of personality and social psychology* (pp. 229–250), Beverly Hills, CA: Sage.

Shields, S. (1991). Gender in the psychology of emotion: A selective research review. In K. T. Strongman (Ed.), *International review of studies on emotion, vol. 1* (pp. 227–245). Chichester, England: Wiley.

White, J. W., & Kowalski, R. M. (1994). Deconstructing the myth of the nonaggressive woman. *Psychology of Women Quarterly, 18,* 487–508.

A Social-Psychological Model of Gender

KAY DEAUX AND BRENDA MAJOR

Psychology's record of considering gender has been, with too few exceptions, a tradition of sex differences.[1] Taking sexual dimorphism as a starting point, investigators have tried to establish, or in some cases refute, the existence of differences between women and men. Whichever conclusion is sought or reached, the debate has its origin in an implicit oppositional model.

This tendency to create oppositions between elements that can be dichotomized is a seductive feature of human thought. In a fascinating study by Barnes,[2] parents were asked to describe their children. Parents who had three or more children described each child in separate terms: for example, Jane is intellectual, Bill is sociable, and Pamela is athletic. Parents of two children, in contrast, succumbed to oppositional thinking: If Jane was a leader, Bill was a follower; if Bill was more sociable, Jane was less sociable. This tendency toward bipolar contrasts is probably exaggerated in the case of males and females, where there is consensus as to what the two categories are and where the categories serve as significant markers in most societies. Dualistic assumptions about gender may also preclude other relevant categories—race, class, age—from entering the analysis.

Those who conclude that there are differences between women and men often assume that these differences are stable. This stability is implicit, we would argue, whether nature or nurture is invoked as the cause. The "different voice" that Carol Gilligan[3] describes with reference to moral reasoning, for example, is attributed primarily to differences in socialization experiences. Yet as the historian Joan Scott[4] has suggested in analyzing the dualism expressed in this work, assumptions of differential experience often fall victim to a certain slippage, in which the original premise, namely, "Women are this way be-

cause of different experience" becomes "Women are this way because they are women." In Scott's words, "Implied in this line of reasoning is the ahistorical, if not essentialist, notion of women."[5]

As a group, psychologists have a pernicious tendency to develop a concept, devise a way to measure it, and then assume its reality. This reification creates a belief that people are, if their assessment scores so reveal, compulsive people, dependent people, aggressive people, and the like. These descriptions, in turn, connote both generality across situations and stability across time (despite numerous disputes within the discipline as to whether those assumptions are justified). In addition, the hypothesized dimensions often take on causal properties, as they are used to explain and justify actions that may seem consistent with the characterization.

This general tendency to infer causality from stability is particularly evident in analyses of sex differences, for which the explanatory concepts tend to be global. As the prototypical case, the conceptualization of "masculinity" and "femininity" was intended to represent the psychological essence of being male and female. It was not linked directly to biological sex but was capable of predicting those behaviors that tend to be associated with gender.[6] Slightly less broad at first glance, but equally pervasive in their implications, are such concepts as "instrumentality" and "expressiveness," or "justice" versus "caring." Like masculinity and femininity, these characteristics or behavioral styles are seen to reside primarily in one or the other sex and to dictate a wide range of outcomes and life choices.

Such diagnostic categories at most assess potentials and estimate probabilities. They do not dictate outcomes. As Hubbard suggests elsewhere in this volume, human nature as an abstract concept means very little.[7] To give this concept meaning, we need to look at the things people actually do. The viewpoint this represents may be too behaviorist for some. Yet while pure behaviorism is as out of fashion in psychology as in the wider intellectual community, Hubbard's injunction provides a useful antidote to the more global diagnoses some psychological and psychoanalytic models make. The analysis of gender is ill served by a reliance on inflexible and often ephemeral conceptions of the nature of woman and man. Attention to actual behavior, in contrast, demands a model that recognizes variability and similarity—as well as stability and difference.

A SOCIAL-PSYCHOLOGICAL PERSPECTIVE ON GENDER

Our analysis is informed by a social-psychological perspective. In contrast to more traditional psychological analyses of gender that tend toward essentialism, a social-psychological perspective emphasizes the varying forces that influence women and men. Social psychology considers the situational influences on human behavior as a defining characteristic, assigning them a priority over individual traits and personality dispositions. From this perspective we ask quite different questions about sex differences in human behavior.[8]

Our model takes as its point of departure the behavior of women and men in dyadic interaction. Such social interactions can involve many forms of behavior—for example, leadership, social influence, moral choices, cooperation, and competition. Although the basis for our analysis is the empirical literature of psychology, we believe that the implications of the analysis go considerably beyond this domain. The emphasis is not on structural constants that program behavior but on conditions that foster variability and change. In contrast to developmental models of gender that deal with the acquisition of gender-linked behavior, our model is concerned with gender as experienced and enacted in a particular social context. The model is intended to supplement, not supplant, earlier theoretical models that stress the origins of specifiable tendencies and habits.

Fundamental to our perspective is the assumption that gender-related behavior is marked by flexibility, fluidity, and variability. Without denying that there may be some regularities in male and female behavior that are the result of biological propensity or socialization experience, we believe it is essential to recognize evidence of changes over time and circumstance. Acknowledging this variation makes the task of analysis more complex—but it is a complexity we need to confront.

A second assumption that underlies the current perspective is that women and men make choices in their actions. In contrast to the deterministic models offered by both psychoanalysis and behaviorism, our framework presumes a repertoire of possibilities from which individual men and women choose different responses on varying occasions with varying degrees of self-consciousness. In other words, gender-related behaviors are a process of individual and social construction. A number of commentators in other disciplines have argued a similar position. Scott, as one recent example, states that "there is room for a concept of human agency as the attempt (at least partially rational) to construct an identity, a life, a set of relationships, a society with certain sets of limits and with language."[9] The sociologists Gerson and Peiss describe gender as a set of "socially constructed relationships which are produced and reproduced through people's actions."[10] In both of these statements, as in our own model, an active dynamic replaces a passive determinism.

To assume flexibility and choice in an analysis of gender requires an appreciation of context. Choices are not made in a vacuum but are shaped by such transitory factors as the other people involved and the prevailing societal norms. In the present analysis, we reflect our disciplinary bias by emphasizing the immediate interpersonal context. Within such situations, individuals simultaneously react to others and present themselves. Social interaction can be viewed as a process of identity negotiation where individuals pursue particular goals for the interaction.[11]

Our view of gender-related behavior in terms of negotiated social interaction draws heavily on two theoretical perspectives in social psychology. Research on expectancy confirmation—sometimes called self-fulfilling prophecy—focuses on the active role of observers in maintaining or creating social reality through their cognitions or behaviors toward a particular individual. This process involves a sequence in which individuals take actions on the basis of their beliefs, and these actions then influence the behavior of the recipient, leading to a confirmation of the initial belief.[12] In applying this analysis here, we consider how the gender belief system of another can impact upon the individual woman, channeling her behavior in ways that support the stereotypic beliefs.

A second theoretical tradition concerns the factors that motivate an individual to vary how she presents herself to others. On the one hand, concerns with self-verification may lead the person to emphasize those underlying beliefs and characteristics that define a stable self-identity. On the other, external pressures may encourage the choice of self-presentation strategies that increase the likelihood of positive reactions from another. In either case the person shows a freedom of choice to select some facet of self from among a number of possible alternatives.

The model that we are developing attempts to deal both with the variation between people and with the variation in a given individual across situations and time. Clearly people confronted with the same situational pressures vary in their responses. Similarly, a single person may take a different course of action depending on the context in which the choice occurs. Dyadic interaction is our chosen testing ground, although our model has implications for other domains as well. In the model, two individuals bring specific beliefs and identities to an interaction, and their interaction occurs within a specifiable context. We do not assume that gender is always salient in these interactions. One of the objectives of our formulation is to specify and to predict just when gender substantially shapes the course of an interaction and when its influence is more muted. To make these predictions, we look at three influences: first, the individual woman or man; second, other individuals with whom the person interacts; and third, the context or setting in which the interaction takes place.

GENDER IDENTITY AND GENDER-BASED ACTION

Gender identity, as the term is typically used by psychologists, refers to a "fundamental, existential sense of one's maleness or femaleness, an acceptance of one's gender as a social-psychological construction that parallels acceptance of one's biological sex."[13] This sense of maleness or femaleness is acquired early in most people's lives. As Spence has stated, "It is inarguable . . . that gender is one of the earliest and most central components of the self concept and serves as an organizing principle through which many experiences and perceptions of self and other are filtered."[14]

Although the concept of gender identity is universal, substantial individual differences occur in the characteristics of these identities. First, people differ in the degree to which gender is a salient aspect of their identity. Chodorow, for example, has suggested that gender identity is differentially important to women and to men.[15] Data from a recent study of self-definition support this suggestion. When asked what identities were important to them, women were more likely than men either to mention gender spontaneously or to acknowledge gender as a central identity when questioned by the interviewer.[16] (Such findings are consistent with the argument that dominant groups have less need to be self-reflective than do groups who must define themselves vis-à-vis a more powerful other.)

A second way in which gender identities differ among individuals concerns the particular features associated with those identities. People may think of themselves as womanly, feminine, or feminist; within any of these general categories, the beliefs and behaviors associated with the label can differ dramatically. Two individuals who are equally conscious of their identities as women may, by virtue of experience or belief, have markedly different conceptions of what that identity means.

The influence of gender on social interaction depends heavily on the degree to which associations with gender are invoked, either consciously or unconsciously. In cognitive psychologists' terms, we can talk about the *accessibility* of gender identity—the degree to which concepts of gender are actively involved in a particular experience or are part of what has been called the "working self-concept."[17] Accessibility is affected by at least two sets of factors: the strength or centrality of that aspect of the self and features of the immediate situation that make gender salient.

For some people, gender will always be part of the working self-concept, an ever-present filter for experience. Individuals differ in how much gender is a chronically accessible aspect of self, and the prominence of gender identity can differ for the same individual across different situations and stages of life. Gender is more likely to shape a woman's experience, for example, when she has her first child or when she receives a diagnosis of breast cancer than it is on other less gender-linked occasions.

External cues can also evoke gender identity, moving it into the working self-concept. In a laboratory demonstration of gender awareness, for example, college students mentioned gender more often when their sex was a minority in a group situation than when it was a majority.[18] Kanter has vividly described how in other work environments gender becomes salient for the individual who is a token in an organizational setting.[19]

Not always recognized in feminist analyses is the fact that people have identities other than gender. A person may think of herself not only as a woman, but as a Black, a professor, an Easterner, or any of numerous other identities. These various senses of self may exist as independent units having little implication for each other. Or two identities may have different implications for action in the same setting and hence prove contradictory. Which identity is dominant in a situation in which both might be accessible depends both on the individual (the relative prominence of a particular identity in some hierarchy of identities) and on the situation (the degree to which circumstances make a particular identity salient). Gender is most likely to dominate interaction, by this account, when it is an identity of primary importance and when the situation contrives to make gender relevant.

Awareness of gender does not automatically dictate action. Instead people choose how to present themselves to others, with the choices reflecting a variety of motivations. Choices may be based on conscious intentions to present a particular stance or to convey a particular image; individuals may cut for the sake of goals that are not clearly recognized in conscious thought. The motives of actions vary. One line of psychological investigation has stressed the degree to which individuals act to verify self-concepts, choosing actions that will be consistent with previous definitions of self.[20] An alternative perspective stresses the degree to which people are sensitive to the social significance of their conduct and strive to present themselves in ways that will ensure social rewards.[21] These two processes are not necessarily contradictory.[22] Rather, concerns with self-verification and self-presentation may be interwoven in any social interaction, as the individual uses both internal and external standards to monitor and shape behavioral choice.

Some empirical investigations have shown how general concerns can alter the image one presents. In one study, for example, women presented descriptions of themselves to a man who was believed to hold either traditional or liberal views of the appropriate roles for women and men.[23] When the target of their presentation was a man possessing socially desirable characteristics (e.g., not in a steady dating relationship, attractive, wealthy), women modified their presentation to approximate the man's alleged views. In contrast, when the man was described as having traits that would presumably not motivate goals of continued interaction (e.g., currently engaged, unattractive, limited career goals), the women did not alter their presentation from what it had been at an earlier assessment. Such alterations are evident in men confronting women as well.[24] Another empirical study of self-presentational shifts found that women ate fewer available snacks when they were interacting with a desirable male partner as compared to a less desirable one. In extending their analysis, the investigators suggested that such eating disorders as anorexia and bulimia might be linked to self-presentational concerns, as women attempting to appear feminine choose behaviors that they believe are consistent with societal norms of femininity.[25]

THE INFLUENCE OF OTHERS

Social interaction occurs in a context in which certain expectations are conveyed by participants toward each other. Within a given setting, whether the dyadic case emphasized in our model or in a larger arena, the individual is generally aware of what is expected, prescribed, or typical in that setting. These expectations can shape the interaction so as to constitute a self-fulfilling prophecy. People interacting with each other may come to manifest the previously held beliefs of their companions.

We know, from both extensive research and common observation, that gender stereotypes are pervasive.[26] People typically believe that men and women differ in a wide range of personality traits, physical characteristics, role behaviors, and occupational positions.[27] Traits related to instrumentality, dominance, and assertiveness, for example, are believed more characteristic of men, while such traits as warmth, expressiveness, and concern for other people are thought more characteristic of women. These beliefs are not all-or-nothing ascriptions; rather, people make judgments about the relative likelihood that women and men will exhibit various characteristics.[28]

People not only have beliefs about women and men at the most general level. They also have clear images of certain types of women and men, such as businesswomen or blue-collar working men.[29] These types correspond to roles that men and women occupy in society and are often described in terms of physical features as well as personality traits. A macho man, for example, is most frequently characterized as being muscular, having a hairy chest and a moustache. Images of sexy women include references to the woman's hair, figure, clothes, facial appearance, and nail polish.[30] These beliefs, operating at various levels of specificity, serve as a framework or orientation for the individual approaching any particular interaction, and because information about physical appearance is both readily available and promi-nently coded, stereotypic thinking may be triggered quite early in initial encounters.

Of course individuals differ in the degree to which they endorse these beliefs and in the attributes they associate with gender categories. Some people may, as Bem has argued, be gender schematic, readily imposing stereotypical beliefs and making sharp distinctions between male and female. Aschematic people eschew such distinctions.[31] More generally, one can think of people as varying along a range of stereotypy, showing greater or lesser propensity to endorse the pervasive cultural beliefs.[32] It seems quite unlikely, however, that many people in contemporary society are unencumbered by some gender-linked expectations and beliefs.

As in the case of self, we do not believe that gender is always salient to the observer or that gender-related beliefs are necessarily activated in social interaction. Yet the obviousness of a person's sex in most instances makes it very likely to influence implicit assumptions. Kessler and McKenna argue that gender attribution is universal, taking precedence over many other forms of categorization.[33]

Both parties in an interaction can influence the likelihood of gender schemata's being activated. Specific features of a person's appearance can trigger a subset of gender beliefs in the mind of the observer, for example, shifting the expectancies from those associated with women and men in general to those linked to more particular subtypes. A woman with a briefcase elicits different associations for most people than does a woman in an apron and housedress. A woman with a low-cut blouse, slit skirt, and high-heeled shoes elicits more attributions of sexiness and seductiveness than does her more conservatively dressed counterpart.[34] Predispositions in the observer may lower the threshold for seeing gender relevance or influence the way in which a particular behavior is interpreted. Men, for example, are more likely than women to assume sexual intent in the friendly behavior of a woman.[35] An analysis of these beliefs is important because of their consequences. The expectancy confirmation sequence describes processes linking beliefs to actions. This link manifests itself in a number of ways, including active avoidance or termination of an interaction. A person can avoid individuals who are presumed undesirable, and such avoidance allows the retention of beliefs in the (untested) attributes of the undesirable one. More typically, perhaps, expectancies shape the form of interaction that occurs. To take an example from the employment realm, consider the case of a female manager whose supervisor believes her to be unfit for leadership positions. The supervisor might engage in such actions toward the woman as shunting her into a subordinate role that allows no room for the display of leadership qualities. The woman's subordinate behavior would then confirm the supervisor's initial belief independent of the woman's actual qualities.

SITUATION AND CONTEXT

The context in which an interaction takes place, like the characters of the actors, shapes the outcome. Context can be considered at many levels, from cultural norms and societal structures to the more immediate circumstances of an interaction. Although our analysis emphasizes immediate circumstances, we do not suggest that others are insignificant, for these more general forces shape, modify, and often limit the range of behaviors available to the individual actor.

Certain situations make gender more salient, increasing the likelihood that each of the participants will bring gender scripts to bear. Some environments, such as a nursery school or an automobile repair shop, are closely linked to gender. Other situations make gender salient because of the particular participants, as Kanter's analysis of tokenism illustrates.[36] Established norms can make gender more or less appropriate as an organizing principle.

To predict whether sex differences will be the rule or the exception, one must analyze the total set of influencing factors. The actual behavior of women and men in a situation depends on the relative weight of the three elements: the self-definitions and goals of each participant, the beliefs and expectations of the other, and the context in which the interaction takes place. By this analysis, sex differences, that is, observed differences in the actions of women and men,

are one of several possible outcomes. In most cases this outcome could be altered relatively easily if one or more elements were changed.

The most straightforward predictions for observed behavior are possible when all forces press toward the same outcome. Using as an example a pair of entry-level managers in a corporation, we can describe conditions of maximal and minimal likelihood for the appearance of sex differences. Sex differences will be most likely, according to our analysis, when:

(1) The man and the woman have different conceptions of themselves as managers and different goals for their corporate experience.
(2) The supervisor holds strong stereotypic beliefs about women and men and is prone to act on those beliefs, creating different experiences for women and men.
(3) The situation is one in which men and women have traditionally assumed different roles and in which the organizational structure is based on a premise of different activities for women and men.

In contrast, sex differences should be rare when the opposite influences prevail. If women and men bring similar experiences and self-conceptions to a situation, if they aspire to the same outcomes, and if they are acting in a context within which sex discrimination is minimal, relatively few differences should be observed.

Both of these scenarios represent pure cases, in which the various influences converge toward a single outcome. In reality cases are rarely that simple. Women with identities and aspirations that match men's encounter situations that press for differentiation. Contexts that are seemingly neutral may still provide a venue for display of sharp differences between particular women and men. When two sources of influence produce contradictory pressures—one fostering difference and the other stressing similarity—what form does behavior take?

To deal with the complexity of frequently conflicting messages and pressures, we turn to a microlevel analysis of the social-psychological process involved in interaction. Rather than offering general statements of sex difference or similarity, we suggest that many dynamic factors must be considered. In each general domain—individual self-systems, expectancies of others, and contextual influences—the range of alternatives is great. With reference to the self-system, for example, people vary in the importance they attach to pleasing others versus verifying internal truths. If pleasing others is more important, situational factors should be much more influential. Characteristics of the other's expectancy that can be important include the desirability of the advocated behavior for the individual and the certainty with which that message is sent. *Who* is conveying the expectation also matters a great deal. A person is far more likely to confirm the expectations of those who are powerful, likable, and control rewards and outcomes than of those whose resources are more limited. Confirmation of another person's expectancies is more likely in public situations than in private, and more common in novel situations than in familiar ones.

The enactment of gender is a dynamic, not a static, phenomenon. People choose (although not necessarily at a conscious level) to act out gender-related behaviors and to vary their behavior with circumstances. Their choices reflect the joint contribution of cognitive factors like the accessibility of relevant beliefs and self-definitions, and motivational factors that relate to one's objectives for a particular interaction. Although we *use* observable behavior as a criterion, we *recognize* the determinants of these behaviors in mental acts. The actions of individual women and men cannot be understood without reference to social context. Changes in context mean changes in outcome, belying the stability of male-female differences so often posited.

The present analysis is more microlevel than some. We are concerned less with human nature than with human actions; with where the repertoires of behavior come from than with how people make choices within those repertoires. Our framework does not deny the usefulness of other formulations, but we believe that the social-psychological perspective is a valuable one. It offers little in the way of ultimatums. What it does, and does in a way lacking in many previous accounts, is to affirm the range of human behavior available to both women and men. By so doing, it moves us away from the oppositional thought that has guided so much previous work.

This essay was written while Kay Deaux was a Fellow at the Center for Advanced Study in the Behavioral Sciences, Stanford, where she was supported in part by the John D. and Catherine T. McArthur Foundation and received additional support from a grant by the National Science Foundation (BNS–8604993). Both authors would like to thank Jane Atkinson, Deborah Rhode, and Anne Firor Scott for their comments on earlier versions of this chapter.

NOTES

1. The meanings associated with the terms *gender* and *sex* vary as a function of both academic discipline and political stance. In this article, we adopt the position defined by Deaux in "Sex and Gender" (*Annual Review of Psychology 36* [1985]: 49–81.) *Sex* refers to the biologically based categories male and female. *Gender* refers to the psychological characteristics associated with those biological states, assigned either by observers or by the individual. In this usage, the term *sex differences* does not make any assumptions about causality (i.e., whether assumed or observed differences are biologically or experientially based) but refers to a categorization of individuals on the basis of biological features.

2. This study is reported in an unpublished doctoral dissertation from the Harvard Graduate School of Education (W. S. Barnes, "Sibling Influences within Family and School Contexts," 1984) and is described in Deborah Belle, "Ironies in the Contemporary Study of Gender," *Journal of Personality 53* (June 1985): 400–05.

3. Carol Gilligan, *In a Different Voice* (Cambridge: Harvard University Press, 1982).

4. Joan W. Scott, "Gender: A Useful Category of Historical Analysis," *American Historical Review 91* (1986): 1053–75.

5. Scott, "Gender," 1065.

6. For an excellent historical analysis of the assumptions underlying research on masculinity and femininity, see J. G. Morawski, "The Measurement of Masculinity and Femininity: Engendering Categorical Realities," in Abigail J. Stewart and M. Brinton Lykes, eds., *Gender and Personality: Current Perspectives on Theory and Research* (Durham: Duke University Press, 1985), 108–35.

7. See Ruth Hubbard's essay in this volume.

8. A full treatment of this model is presented in Kay Deaux and Brenda Major. "Putting Gender into Context: An Interactive Model of Gender-Related Behavior." *Psychological Review* 94 (July 1987): 369–89.

9. Scott, "Gender," 1067.

10. Judith M. Gerson and Kathy Peiss, "Boundaries, Negotiation, Consciousness: Reconceptualizing Gender Relations," *Social Problems* 32 (April 1985): 327.

11. For more discussion of negotiation of self in social interaction, see Michael Athay and John M. Darley, "Toward an Interaction-Centered Theory of Personality," in Nancy Cantor and John F. Kihlstrom, eds., *Personality, Cognition, and Social Interaction* (Hillsdale, N.J.: Lawrence Erlbaum, 1981), 281–308; also William B. Swann, Jr., "Quest for Accuracy in Person Perception: A Matter of Pragmatics," *Psychological Review 91* (October 1984): 457–77.

12. For more extensive reviews of the empirical literature on expectancy confirmation, see John M. Darley and Russell H. Fazio, "Expectancy Confirmation Processes Arising in the Social Interaction Sequence," *American Psychologist* 35 (October 1980): 867–81; and Dale T. Miller and William Turnbull, "Expectancies and Interpersonal Processes," *Annual Review of Psychology 37* (1986): 233–56.

13. Janet T. Spence, "Masculinity, Femininity, and Gender-Related Traits: A Conceptual Analysis and Critique of Current Research," *Progress in Experimental Personality Research 13* (1984): 84. For more traditional discussions of gender identity, see Richard Green, *Sexual Identity Conflict in Children and Adults* (New York: Basic, 1974); John Money and Anke A. Ehrhardt, *Man and Woman, Boy and Girl* (Baltimore: Johns Hopkins University Press, 1972); Robert J. Stoller, *Sex and Gender: On the Development of Masculinity and Femininity* (New York: Science House, 1968).

14. Janet T. Spence, "Gender Identity and Its Implications for Concepts of Masculinity and Femininity," In T. Sondregger, ed., *Nebraska Symposium on Motivation* (Lincoln: University of Nebraska Press, 1985).

15. See Nancy Chodorow's essay in . . . [*Theoretical perspectives on sexual differences* (New Haven, CT: Yale University Press, 1990)].

16. For a preliminary report of these data, see Kay Deaux, "Incipient Identity" (paper presented as the Carolyn Wood Sherif Award Lecture at the meeting of the American Psychological Association, Atlanta, August 1988).

17. For more discussion, see E. Tory Higgins and Gillian King, "Accessibility of Social Constructs: Information-Processing Consequences of Individual and Contextual Variability," in Nancy Cantor and John F. Kihlstrom, eds., *Personality, Cognition, and Social Behavior* (Hillsdale, N.J.: Lawrence Erlbaum, 1981), 69–121; also Hazel Markus and Ziva Kunda, "Stability and Malleability of the Self-Concept," *Journal of Personality and Social Psychology 51* (October 1986): 858–66.

18. Albert A. Cota and Kenneth L. Dion, "Salience of Gender and Sex Composition of Ad Hoc Groups: An Experimental Test of Distinctiveness Theory," *Journal of Personality and Social Psychology 50* (April 1986): 770–76.

19. Rosabeth Moss Kanter, *Men and Women of the Corporation* (New York: Basic, 1977).

20. See William B. Swann, Jr., "Self-Verification: Bringing Social Reality into Harmony with the Self," in Jerry Suls and Anthony Greenwald, eds., *Psychological Perspectives on the Self* (Hillsdale, N.J.: Lawrence Erlbaum, 1983) 2:33–66.

21. Erwin Goffman made the classic statement of this position in *The Presentation of Self in Everyday Life* (New York: Anchor, 1959).

22. For a thorough discussion of this point, see Philip E. Tetlock and A. S. R. Manstead, "Impression Management versus Intrapsychic Explanations in Social Psychology: A Useful Dichotomy?" *Psychological Review 92* (January 1985): 59–77.

23. Mark Zanna and Susan J. Pack, "On the Self-Fulfilling Nature of Apparent Sex Differences in Behavior," *Journal of Experimental Social Psychology 11* (November 1975): 583–91.

24. Rona Fried and Brenda Major, "Self-Presentation of Sex-Role Attributes to Attractive Others" (paper presented at the meeting of the Eastern Psychological Association, Hartford, 1980).

25. DeAnna Mori, Shelly Chaiken, and Patricia Pliner, " 'Eating Lightly' and the Self-Presentation of Femininity," *Journal of Personality and Social Psychology 53* (October 1987): 693–702.

26. For a review of the psychological literature on the gender belief system, see Kay Deaux and Mary E. Kite, "Thinking about Gender," in Beth B. Hess and Myra Marx Ferree, eds., *Analyzing Gender: A Handbook of Social Science Research* (Beverly Hills, Calif.: Sage, 1987), 92–117.

27. For the classic study of gender stereotypes, see Paul Rosenkrantz, Susan Vogel, Helen Bee, Inge Broverman, and Donald M. Broverman, "Sex-Role Stereotypes and Self-Concepts in College Students," *Journal of Consulting and Clinical Psychology 32* (1968): 286–95. For more recent analyses of gender stereotypes among U.S. college students, see Kay Deaux and Laurie L. Lewis, "The Structure of Gender Stereotypes: Interrelationships among Components and Gender Label," *Journal of Personality and Social Psychology 46* (April 1984): 991–1004; and in an international sample, John E. Williams and Deborah L. Best, *Measuring Sex Stereotypes: A Thirty Nation Study* (Beverly Hills, Calif.: Sage, 1982).

28. In recognizing that people have certain beliefs about gender, we do not assume that there is no basis in reality for these beliefs. Research indicates that *on the average* men score higher on measures of instrumentality and women score higher on measures of expressiveness. But these observed differences tend to be relatively small, generally smaller than assessed beliefs about the differences.

29. For discussions of gender subtypes, see: Richard D. Ashmore, Frances K. Del Boca, and David Titus, "Types of Women and Men: Yours, Mine, and Ours" (paper presented at meeting of American Psychological Association, Toronto, 1984); A. Kay Clifton, Diane McGrath, and Bonnie Wick, "Stereotypes of Women: A Single Category?" *Sex Roles 2* (June 1976): 135–48; Kay Deaux, Ward Winton, Maureen Crowley, and Laurie L. Lewis, "Level of Categorization and Content of Gender Stereotypes," *Social Cognition 3* (1985): 145–67; Dorothy Holland and Debra Davidson, "Labeling the Opposite Sex: Metaphors and Themes in American Folk Models of Gender" (Paper presented at the Institute for Advanced Study, Princeton, 1983); Cathryn Noseworthy and Albert J. Lott, "The Cognitive Organization of Gender-Stereotypic Categories," *Personality and Social Psychology Bulletin 10* (September 1984): 474–81.

30. Deaux et al., "Gender Stereotypes."

31. Sandra L. Bem, "Gender Schema Theory: A Cognitive Account of Sex Typing," *Psychological Review 88* (July 1981): 354–64.

32. Carol Lynn Martin, "A Ratio Measure of Sex Stereotypes," *Journal of Personality and Social Psychology 52* (March 1987): 489–99.

33. Suzanne J. Kessler and Wendy McKenna, *Gender: An Ethnomethodological Approach* (New York: John Wiley, 1978).

34. See Antonia Abbey, Catherine Cozzarelli, Kimberly McLaughlin, and Richard J. Harnish, "The Effects of Clothing and Dyad Sex Composition on Perceptions of Sexual Intent: Do Women and Men Evaluate These Cues Differently?" *Journal of Applied Social Psychology 17* (February 1987): 108–26.

35. See Antonia Abbey, "Sex Differences in Attributions for Friendly Behavior: Do Males Perceive Females' Friendliness?" *Journal of Personality and Social Psychology 42* (May 1982): 830–38.

36. Kanter, *Men and Women of the Corporation.*

CHECKPOINTS

1. Deaux and Major believe that social behavior is flexible, is influenced by individual choice, and is affected by social context.

2. They propose that predictions of social behavior should be based on recognition of factors related to gender identity and gender scripts, to the expectations held by people for others' behavior, and to social context.

To prepare for reading the next section, think about this question:

1. In your experience, how are men and women similar in emotional expressiveness?

Gender in the Psychology of Emotion: A Selective Research Review

STEPHANIE A. SHIELDS

Department of Psychology, University of California, Davis, CA 95616, USA

In 1601 Thomas Wright presented a humoral theory of individual differences in *The Passions of the Minde*. Like others who undertook similar projects, he discussed differences between women and men. His list of women's emotional attributes included, on the positive side, inclinations to mercy and pity, piety and devotion, and less tendency to emotional incontinence than men. On the negative side were pride, envy, proclivity for slander, and inconstancy (Wright, 1601/1973, p. 74). The last, he believed, has the same source as the instability that characterizes the imprudence of young men who tend to "resolve rashly and performe rarely" (p. 76). Wright's list is interesting, not only because it diverges somewhat from contemporary gender stereotypes, but also because, at the same time as he engages in sweeping generalizations, this seventeenth-century writer understands that generalizations do not provide an invariant, comprehensive description of all men or all women. Humors, he notes, vary with age, physique, complexion, and "race,"[1] and so account for group similarities as well as individual variation from the norm: "because women have sundrie complexions, so they bee subject to sundry passions. Even as in like sorte, I could say of men; for some are more prone to one passion than an other" (p. 78).

Just as Wright was required to couch his "common sense" assertion about sex-related differences within cautions about the limits of those assertions, any late-twentieth-century attempt to list sex-related differences in emotion would require an even longer list of caveats and qualifications. Empirical studies of the relationship between gender and emotion have focused almost exclusively on the identification of sex-related differences. Analysis of emotions data by subject sex almost invariably fails to reveal stable or theoretically important gender differences. The list of small, unstable, and typically stereotype-consistent sex-related differences which this strategy yields has led many to conclude that gender is not particularly important to the study of the psychology of human emotion. Consequently, sociologists (eg Hochschild, 1983; Cancian, 1987) and anthropologists (eg Lutz, 1988a,b; Rosaldo, 1984; Abu-Loghoud, 1986) have taken the lead in investigating the link between gender and emotion.

In this chapter I will examine why the "sex-differences" approach has been fairly unproductive in the psychology of emotion, and discuss the need to distinguish between isolated sex-related differences and the pervasive influence of gender. First, however, a note on terminology is in order. Among psychologists who study gender, it is general practice to differentiate between the biologically based categories of female and male (sex) and the psychological features associated with biological states which involve social rather than biological categories (gender) (Unger, 1979; Deaux, 1985; Lorber, 1987). Thus, "sex" is used to refer to the physical fact of primary and secondary sex characteristics, "gender" to refer to a psychological and cultural construct. Gender is manifested in the public social world (as in culturally defined standards of sex-appropriate behavior) and within the individual's consciousness (as in one's identification of oneself as male or female).[2] In psychological research, gender (rather than sex) is usually the variable of interest, but the component or quality of "gender" that is of interest is not measured directly; instead, gender is inferred from subject sex. Subject sex is thus a "marker" for gender and obtained sex-related differences are interpreted as reflecting gender differences. Therefore, I will use "sex-related difference" to refer to the results of studies that report a comparison of subjects by sex and "gender difference" to refer to the inferences drawn from those results.

A distinction can be drawn between the aims and methods of what I will term a sex-differences model of research and research strategies that focus on gender-in-context. The sex-differences model (more properly the "sex-related differences" model) typically assesses quantitative differences between male and female research participants within a single research setting. When the obtained difference is statistically significant, there is a tendency to overinterpret it as a stable, fixed, and enduring trait which is often presumed to be biologically based (Unger, 1979; Jacklin, 1989). Dissatisfaction with an uninformed sex-differences approach to gender (and the accompanying reification of masculinity/femininity, eg Lewin, 1984a,b; Morawski, 1987) has been growing for some time.[3]

The most promising alternative research strategy is to view gender as it operates within the social context (eg Deaux & Major, 1987; Unger, 1988; West & Zimmerman, 1987). A gender-in-context perspective differs primarily from the sex-differences model by emphasizing the sensitivity of observed sex-related differences to social and cognitive aspects of the situation/environment (eg Deaux & Major, 1987; Unger, 1989). The emphasis shifts from a description of presumptively stable differences to an exploration of the variables that exaggerate or attenuate the occurrence of differences. Gender exerts an effect as an interaction among actor, observer, and situational variables, hence a gender-in-context perspective takes the position that research should not focus on *whether* differences exist but aim to identify the variables that exaggerate or attenuate these differences. Applying this strategy to the case of emotion, for example, results in replacing the question of whether women or men are more emotional with a strategy designed to identify the variables that differentially affect women's and men's judgments about their own or others' emotionality.

THE LIMITATIONS OF "SEX DIFFERENCES"

Jacklin (1981) discussed a number of limitations of the sex-differences research strategy, three of which stand out as having particular relevance to emotion research. (1) Because gender has largely been studied as a variable of empirical rather than theoretical significance, the level of analysis tends to be descriptive rather than explanatory, or *post hoc* rather than theory driven. (2) Research is largely guided by the assumption that sex-related differences should be invariant in form, stable over time, and biological in origin. (3) When sex is treated as a subject variable (as opposed to a stimulus variable), results vary inconsistently across experimental contexts. I would like briefly to consider each of these limitations as it bears on the psychology of emotion.

Post-Hoc Explanation

In her extensive and comprehensive review of gender differences in emotional development, Leslie Brody (1985) notes that investigation of gender has largely occurred outside of any organizing theoretical framework. Most of this work is not grounded in any theory of gender, but is rather like a catalog of loosely connected themes and particularistic findings. Rarely is gender *per se* of focal interest in emotions research; instead, statistical analyses for sex-related differences are undertaken in order to rule out (or serendipitously reveal) the importance of gender as a causal influence on the experiment's outcome (Manstead, in press). Add a publication bias towards statistically significant results, and the result is largely a literature of inconsistent conclusions.

Presumed Biological Origin

The sex-differences model, by virtue of being limited to assessment of the quantity of emotion expressed or reported, implies that psychologically relevant emotional phenomena (insofar as gender is concerned) should be viewed as fixed capacities of the individual. A sex-related difference in emotion-relevant behavior is therefore taken as an indication that one sex possesses "more" of a given emotional attribute. The sex-differences perspective regards "emotionality," for example, as a quantitatively fixed characteristic of the person, whereas a gender-centered analysis views emotionality as defined, at least in part, by the interpersonal negotiations that occur within particular contexts. The conceptual difference between the sex-differences and gender-in-context models of research is in whether the presumption is made that gender effects are due to stable traits and so ought to manifest *constancy* across contexts within individuals, or whether gender effects are better represented in dynamic, process terms and so ought to *vary predictably* across contexts. The emphasis is thus shifted from the actor's sex *per se* to the actor's beliefs (whether or not they can be verbally articulated) about what gender means within a situation.

The past two decades of gender research have seen the development of increasingly sophisticated views of the concept of gender. The explanatory limits of cataloging putative differences are widely recognized, as are the epistemological and broadly political consequences of adopting assumptions about the sources and social significance of gender differences and similarities (eg Crawford & Maracek, 1989; Hare-Mustin & Maracek, 1988; Morawski, 1987). Yet outside of this area of specialization it is still not uncommon to find that sex-related differences are inferred as being based in—and thereby explained by— subject sex. An example, published within the last few years in a prestigious social psychology journal, illustrates this widespread practice. In the experiment, women and men who reported fear of spiders were presented with a task in which they were to get as close as they could to a tarantula in a Plexiglass box. Dependent measures included proximity to spider, rate of approach to spider, self-report of fearfulness, and psychophysiological measures. The authors found sex-related differences on nearly all measures and then found that those differences were nonsignificant when women and men matched for phobia scores were compared. They also consistently found significant differences between high fearful and moderate fearful women. (None of the male participants

scored as high as the high fearful women, so no comparable within-sex assessment of male subjects could be made.) On the basis of these findings the authors conclude that "these differences [in dependent measures] were due to a sex-linked difference in fear" (from the authors' abstract). The infelicitous wording suggests that the authors believe they have identified a gender difference that reflects a stable, biologically based trait. A more parsimonious interpretation would be that high fearful (phobic?) *individuals* respond differently to specific fear elicitors than do moderately fearful individuals, but this explanation was not considered in the paper.

Sex as a Subject Variable versus Sex as a Stimulus Variable

Cataloging the differences between males and females is neither a good route to an explanation of gender nor does it yield a very reliable set of results. Sex as a subject variable is a now-you-see-it/now-you-don't phenomenon (Unger, 1981). Sex as a stimulus variable, however, exerts sometimes striking and often stable effects (Matlin, 1987).

Analyses of sex-related differences in the efficacy of various mood induction techniques is a good example of the instability of sex as a subject variable. In a pilot study of his original mood induction technique, Velten found a trend towards sex-related differences and so used females only in the final study (Lewis & Harder, 1988). Since then, others have reported significant differences (eg Strickland, Hale & Anderson, 1975) while others have not (eg Buchwald, Strack & Coyne, 1981), and still others find them only in interaction effects, such as interaction with experimenter (Lewis & Harder, 1988). The effects of mood on cognition have yielded similarly mixed results. Studies of the effects of mood on children's memory, for example, do not find consistent effects of sex of subject (eg Potts *et al.*, 1986; Masters, Ford & Arend, 1983; Barden *et al.*, 1985).

Sex as a stimulus variable, in contrast, yields more stable results. This is particularly true of stereotypes. In a series of studies, Birnbaum and her colleagues showed that beliefs about gendered emotion are learned by early childhood and persist in adulthood even when they conflict with other gender-related values. In one study, preschoolers as well as college students associated anger with males and happiness, sadness and fear with females (Birnbaum, Nosanchuk & Croll, 1980); in another, preschool children similarly associated angry statements with boys, happy statements with girls, and sad statements with neither sex (Birnbaum & Chemelski, 1984). Among working class parents and college students, males were associated with anger and females with sadness and fear (Birnbaum & Croll, 1984). The only difference between the groups was that the working class parents believed this difference was natural but the college students hoped that standards would change.

A SELECTIVE REVIEW

The following is not intended as a comprehensive review, but as a brief overview of three topical areas in which most of the gender-related research has been done: (a) understanding and application of emotion concepts (ie beliefs about emotion or specific emotions), including attributions regarding the causes and consequences of emotion; (b) encoding and decoding of facial expressions of emotion; (c) self-reports of experienced and expressed emotion. Other emotion-relevant topics (not discussed in this chapter) in which sex-related differences have been examined include clinical depression (Nolen-Hoeksema, 1987), intimate relationships (eg Gottman & Levenson, 1988), empathy (Eisenberg & Lennon, 1983), symptom sensitivity and reporting (Manstead, in press), and endocrine-aggression relationships (eg Jacklin, 1989).

Emotion Concepts and Attributions

Included in this general category of topics are studies which typically employ sex as a stimulus variable, particularly emotion-relevant stereotypes, and studies which typically employ sex as a subject variable, most of which focus on knowledge of the antecedents, constituents, and consequences of emotion

episodes or specific emotions. The stability of findings when sex is a stimulus variable compared to the inconsistent results of sex as a subject variable is particularly pronounced.

Sex as a Stimulus Variable   In addition to Birnbaum's studies discussed above, other investigators have also demonstrated the robustness of emotion "master stereotypes," some of which are tacitly held (eg Shields & Koster, 1989). The expectation that women should and will display less socially negative affect is particularly pronounced. Undergraduates asked to imagine a female friend and a male friend in emotionally salient situations believed that female friends would experience more of all types of emotion and would express more socially valued positive emotion but that male friends would display more self-oriented, socially less desirable emotions (Johnson & Schulman, 1988). Women whose affective experience is described as highly negative are judged to be less likeable than men who are similarly described (Sommers, 1984). These values vary cross-nationally. Sommers and Kosmitski (1988) found different patterns in the United States and West Germany. For example German women report that rage need not be concealed whereas American women believe that it should be.

Fabes and Martin have thus far undertaken the most comprehensive study of gendered emotion stereotypes (Fabes, 1989). A study of preschoolers revealed that children's recall of images was affected by how well that image conformed to gender stereotypes (Martin *et al.*, 1990). Children were three times more likely to recall the sex of the person expressing an emotion incorrectly when the emotion was counterstereotypic (eg boy crying) than when it was stereotypic (eg boy angry). Interestingly, boys were more likely to distort than were girls and there was more distortion for boy targets than for girl targets. Furthermore, children were more likely to recall sex-consistent emotions as being more intense than sex-inconsistent emotions, even though pictures did not objectively differ in intensity of expression. A follow-up study measured the degree to which preschool children believe adult and children can experience stereotypic versus non-stereotypic emotions. Both boys and girls report that girls and women can sometimes get angry, but that boys and men (in particular) are unlikely to experience sadness. On the basis of these results, Fabes suggests that children's stereotypes about emotions are based primarily on their extreme beliefs about males rather than their beliefs about emotions. That is, young children's stereotypes about emotions may reflect the rigidity of their typing for males, with typing for females being more flexible: moms can get angry but dads can't get sad.

Fabes and Martin (1990a,b) have also compared adults' gendered emotion stereotypes as they are related to the age of the target. They find that sex of target by age of target interactions vary predictably with the emotion rated and whether capacity for experience, control, or expression of the emotion is rated. Their results suggest that adults' gender-emotion stereotypes are based on the belief that males do not show what they feel and that this exaggerated discrepancy between felt emotion and expressed emotion is largely a phenomenon of adolescence and adulthood that is emotion-specific. For example, the experience of sadness is believed to be similar for both sexes across ages, while expression is believed to decrease significantly as control increases, especially for males. When specific problematic negative emotions are considered, female targets are perceived to experience and express emotions related to internalized defenses (guilt, anxiety, depression) and males externalized defenses (hate). In studies of emotion concepts that employ sex as a subject variable, a very different picture of gendered emotion emerges. The large majority of studies that report an analysis for sex-related differences find none for adults (eg Heise & Thomas, 1989; Clark & Teasdale, 1985; Shields, 1984; Lubin, Rinck & Collins, 1986) or for children (eg Covell & Abramovitch, 1988; Thompson, 1989). When differences do occur it is usually within a context that makes gender salient, such as asking subjects to imagine emotion scenarios that highlight social roles or relationships. For example, Egerton (1988) examined accounts of anger and weeping episodes that subjects provided while imagining themselves in the emotion-evoking scenario.

Most notable of the sex-related differences obtained for the two types of emotion scenario was women's greater reported conflict about the anger episode (descriptions of the anger as effective, but upsetting and costly) and men's more frequent use of "passion schemas" (representations of the anger as externally caused and uncontrollable) for the anger episode.

Differences are also likely to be found when subjects have an opportunity to introduce the social or interpersonal aspects of emotion's context into their responses. Carlson and Carlson (1984) asked subjects to write scripts about excitement, fear, joy, and shame. Women used interpersonal themes for all emotions, while men used interpersonal themes only for joy and shame. O'Leary and Smith (1988) examined beliefs about what causes would lead to the experience of each of 10 emotions and found that women were more likely to attribute emotions to relational or internal sources, men to external stimuli. In these and other studies that report sex-related differences, interpersonal aspects of the situation appear to have been more salient for women research participants (eg Brabeck & Weisgerber, 1988).

Results in studies with children are very similar to those employing adults. Strayer (1986), for example, interviewed four–five and seven–eight year old children regarding their beliefs about the antecedents of particular emotions. Girls mentioned more interpersonal themes as instigators of emotion than did boys. Trepanier-Street and Romatowski (1986) looked at stories written by girls and boys (grades 1 and 2, 3 and 4, and 5 and 6) and found that children used more emotion statements with reference to their own sex than the other sex. Older children ascribed more emotion statements to characters than did younger children and this was especially true of the oldest group of girls. Feshbach and Hoffman (1978) interviewed kindergarten, second, third, fourth, and sixth graders of diverse ethnic backgrounds regarding situations that children believe elicit several emotions. The only significant sex-related difference they found was in the tendency for girls to describe emotions as occurring within family and social contexts, while boys were more self-oriented, manifesting greater preoccupations with possessions, competence, and autonomy.

The special significance of the social and interpersonal aspects of emotion's context for gender is particularly striking in Saarni's studies of the acquisition and use of emotion display rules. Although she finds no sex-related differences in children's *knowledge* about effective display rules and the conditions for dissembling (Saarni, 1979, 1989), sex-related differences in *performance* occur, particularly in older children (Saarni, 1984; Cole, 1986). In one study, for example, children in three age groups (6–7, 10–11, and 13–14 years of age) were interviewed regarding their beliefs about emotional dissembling (Saarni, 1988). A few sex-related differences emerged, primarily because the oldest girls were unique in several of their beliefs. Specifically, they reported that dissembling works and that they value honest expression of emotion to peers. They also used more complex reasoning in explaining the relationship between felt and expressed emotion.

The general pattern of these results suggests that the interpersonal causes and consequences of emotion may be more salient to girls and women. However, it is impossible on the basis of available research to separate the "uncensored" on-line reaction that constitutes a gender-based conceptual system from the more self-conscious knowledge of the "gender-correct" response. This is not to suggest that research participants' reports are based on self-presentation concerns, but rather that they may be the non-deliberative reflection of a deeply ingrained gender belief system. Until research is designed directly to sort out the relationship of these two (or other) variables contributing to this apparent gender difference, no conclusion about the "real" basis of the performance difference is possible.

Encoding and Decoding Expression

The great majority of this research has dealt with the processes involved in producing (spontaneous or posed) and judging others' facial expressions of emotion. Of all emotions research it is in this area that the most consistent performance differences between male and female subjects occur. Some studies report women as better at decoding posed or spontaneous expressions (eg Kirouac & Dore, 1985; Sogon & Izard, 1987) or at encoding (eg Haviland & Lieberman, 1990; Wagner, MacDonald & Manstead, 1986; Noller & Gallois, 1986; Gallois & Callan, 1986). The rare studies that find men more accurate at encoding or decoding find greater accuracy for anger (Rotter & Rotter, 1988; Wagner, MacDonald & Manstead, 1986; Walbott, 1988), but this effect is related to cultural background (McAndrew, 1986).

The most extensive reviews and evaluations of this literature have been provided by Judith Hall (1978, 1984, 1987). Her most comprehensive review of the literature concluded that females are better at decoding non-verbal cues, at recognizing faces, and at expressing emotions via non-verbal communication than are males. Females also have more expressive faces, smile more (except, apparently, children), gaze more, receive more gaze (adults at least), employ smaller approach distances when observed unobtrusively, and are approached closer by others. Women use body movements and positions that appear to be less restless, less expansive, more involved, more expressive, and more self-conscious than men do. Finally, they emit fewer speech errors and filled pauses (1984, p. 143).

The size of most of these differences is moderate, and meta-analyses have since suggested that a very small portion of the variance accounted for overall is attributable to subject sex (Hall, 1987). This certainly suggests that characteristics of the experimental situation may be moderating the effects of subject sex. Hall (1987), in fact, notes an important mitigating factor in interpreting these data: the contexts in which expressive behavior is measured tend to be settings in which there are demand characteristics for gender-appropriate behavior. She observes that laboratory studies, conducted largely with college students in contexts that imply or encourage conversation with strangers, "are probably marked by strong implicit demands to be nice, by self-consciousness, and by social anxiety in the presence of strange experimenters and fellow subjects" (Hall, 1987, p. 183).

The signal complexity that is possible when affective channels carry a message different from that expressed linguistically suggests the possibility for a richer, more complex medium of communication (Hall, Mroz & Braunwald, 1983; Halberstadt, Hayes & Pike, 1988). Skilled communicators take advantage of the fact that humans can simultaneously "multiplex" as senders *and* as receivers of communications. The capacity to smile while conveying negative messages need not simply be a deceptive device but can be used as a strategy for maintaining the positive affective side of the relationship while negotiating conflicting goals. von Salisch (1988) examined children's patterns of smiling during structured quarrels in the social psychology laboratory. Like Hall and Halberstadt (1986), she found a weak and non-significant tendency for higher smiling frequency ("genuine" smiling as opposed to social smiling) in girls. Much more striking, however, was the interaction between gender and closeness of friendship: girls who were close friends smiled significantly more and had a higher proportion of synchronous smiles than boys who were close friends. Boys were generally more distant in their communication style. They expressed comparatively few reproaches, smiled significantly fewer genuine smiles and showed more nonverbal signs indicating tension or unrest (eg lip bites, wiggling in their chairs). That complex affective communications may have a relationship-building outcome is suggested in the way adult men and women talk about their friendships. Women (in the United States and New Zealand) report that they are more intimate and emotional in their same-sex friendships than do men; men report deriving more emotional support from friendships with women than with men (Aukett, Ritchie & Mill, 1988).

Reported Experience and Expressiveness

To obtain information about the subjective component of emotion we must rely largely on self-report measures. This technique is not inherently flawed; unfortunately, however, self-report measures are often poorly constructed, inappropriately employed, or grossly misinterpreted. Because self-report reflects belief, it is important to keep in mind that subjects' notions of what "ought" to be true or is "typically" true can be the foundation of the response, particu-

larly when they are asked to make aggregate retrospective self-assessments. When concurrent or highly specific accounts are obtained, the subject's report is better able to reflect beliefs about ongoing experience or factual occurrences. Studies of mood and the menstrual cycle illustrate this point. Global retrospective reports, which are heavily influenced by beliefs about what "ought" to occur or what is "typical," tend to yield "classic" patterns of mood variation over the cycle, whereas concurrent diaries or daily mood checklists show no such pattern (eg Parlee, 1973; Slade, 1984). McFarlane, Martin and Williams (1988), for example, obtained daily mood self-ratings for undergraduates for an extended period (70 days). Mood for both sexes varied as a function of day of the week and mood was equally stable over time for women and men. The concept of emotion, which is larded with stereotypes and tacit beliefs, may be particularly sensitive to different methods of obtaining self-report.

Self-report frequently yields sex-related differences whether subjects are asked about the experience and expression of emotion generally or about specific emotions. The difference typically takes the form of women reporting greater frequency or intensity of the emotion in question (eg Balswick & Avertt, 1977). One notable exception to this pattern is anger. Allen and Haccoun (1976) used a questionnaire method to obtain self-reports about experiencing, expressing, and valuing anger, fear, joy, and sadness in a small sample of college students. Women reported more expression of all four emotions and greater intensity of experience for all emotions except anger, for which there was no difference in women's and men's reports. Allen and Haccoun's finding that women and men report similar intensities of anger has been observed by several other investigators. Averill (1983) obtained college students' self-reports concerning anger episodes. He found no sex-related differences in frequency, intensity, expression, or causes of anger. Stoner and Spencer (1987), using the Anger Expression Scale (Spielberger, Johnson & Jacbos, 1982) found no difference between women's and mens reports about feelings or expressions of anger in 21–83 year old midwestern adults. Spielberger and his colleagues had originally found differences in a high-school sample, with males reporting more unexpressed anger. Janisse, Edguer and Dyck (1986), also using Spielberger's scale, found that type A males gave higher ratings of stated anger, more vivid anger imagery, and lower perceived self-control ratings than type B males or either type A or B females. Burrowes and Halberstadt (1987) obtained self-ratings on a questionnaire regarding the expression and experience of anger in social situations from college students and non-student adults. A subset of their sample was also rated on expressivity via a brief questionnaire given to a friend or family member. These investigators found no significant sex-related differences on any measure.

Laboratory manipulations of anger tend to be equally effective for subjects of both sexes, although Frodi (1978) noted that verbalization of reactions to and feelings towards a research partner who had provoked the subject's anger tended to have different consequences for each sex. Women instructed to write down their thoughts downplayed anger and aggression, whereas men "tended to preoccupy themselves with thoughts of anger or 'stirring themselves up' " (p. 347). When these men were given an opportunity to retaliate (via delivery of noxious sounds), they delivered sounds of significantly greater intensity than did men who had not been instructed to ruminate on the event.

Research participants' reports about their own experience and expressive behavior reflect their understanding of cultural and personal values and their beliefs about their own behavior, and it is not typically possible to discern the extent to which norms and self-observation each contribute to that report. For example, Malatesta and Kalnok (1984) surveyed non-student adults in three age groups and found that men were more likely to agree with the belief that men should conceal their feelings, but when reporting on their own behavior, it was women rather than men who reported more inhibition of emotional expression. Sex-related differences in self-report tend to be consistent with emotion stereotypes, as if some comparison of oneself to an emotional standard is operative in generating a response: "I must be emo-

tional, after all I'm a woman" or "I must be inexpressive, after all I'm a man." The link between people's beliefs about emotion as gendered and their own conceptualization of gender role is further demonstrated in a study that grouped subjects on the basis of gender role self-concept (Ganong & Coleman, 1985). College students completed a measure of gender role self-concept (Bem Sex-Role Inventory; BSRI) and a self-report measure of emotional expressiveness. "Androgynous" students—those rating themselves as possessing a high degree of both "masculine" and "feminine" characteristics on the BSRI—rated themselves as most expressive. "Masculine" students—those rating themselves as possessing a high degree of "masculine" characteristics only—rated themselves as least expressive. Gender role self-concept appears to play a significant role in emotion-related self-evaluation processes and perhaps can explain why sex-related differences in self-report do not occur for anger (a "masculine" emotion) but are routinely obtained for "emotionality" (Deiner, Sandvik & Larsen, 1985; Flett et al., 1986; Kircaldy, 1984), other individual emotions (eg Stapley & Haviland, 1989), and emotion-related behaviors such as empathy (Eisenberg & Lennon, 1983; Strayer, 1989).

Tacit beliefs about the relationship between emotion and gender account for many of the differences obtained in self-report studies, and these beliefs may play a prominent role in how the individual regulates his or her emotional life *vis-à-vis* others. In the course of developing an Emotional Self-Disclosure Scale, Snell, Miller and Belk (1988) found that reported tendency to disclose emotion to another was a function of the personal characteristics of the disclosure recipient as well as the sex of the speaker. Both women and men were less willing (and about equally so) to discuss their emotions with men friends than women friends, and women were more willing to disclose a variety of emotions to women friends and spouses/lovers than were men. Among college students, women and men hold different expectations about the likelihood that they would express particular emotions and the kinds of reactions that others would have to their expressions (eg Dosser, Balswick

& Halverson, 1983). Like adults, children also seem to have gender-based beliefs about their own expressiveness and others' responses to it. Fuchs and Thelen (1988) reported that less positive expectancies and lower likelihood of expression were particularly pronounced for older boys (grade 6 compared to grades 1 and 4). These explicitly held beliefs are reflected in conversational content outside of the laboratory. Shimanoff (1983) found that in natural conversation between friends, college student women and men talked equally about emotion, although men used more affect words and talked more about their own emotions when they were in opposite-sex dyads. Sex of conversation partner did not affect the emotive references of women conversationalists.

Strategies for Studying the Psychology of Gender and Emotion

This brief and selective review suggests that the greatest effect of gender lies less in what each sex knows about emotion than in what each sex is likely to do with that knowledge, particularly in contexts in which gender is salient. A discrepancy between knowledge and practice has been observed for other behaviors that are gender-coded. For example, boys' and girls' knowledge about babies and caregiving is equivalent (Fogel & Melson, 1986), but by age four boys and girls respond quite differently when instructed to "take care of" an infant (Berman, 1987). Furthermore, by age 10, girls have acquired a caregiving "script" that they employ while caregiving, whether or not the script matches the particular needs of the baby (Berman, 1987). The effect is particularly pronounced when instructions to subjects make gendered standards of behavior salient, that is, when the research participant's response may wholly or in part be influenced by his or her sense of what is "correct" or "desirable" behavior. For example, sex-related differences in adults' avowed attraction to infants are exaggerated when self-reports are obtained in public, mixed-sex setting and attenuated when the self-report is private and anonymous (Berman, 1980).

A recurring theme in this review is the robust effect of sex as a stimulus variable. There is clear evidence that beliefs about gender and emotionality influence interactions between infants and caregivers and other adults' communication with the infant. A number of investigators have shown that babies' emotional displays are differentially evaluated solely on the basis of sex. Haviland (1977) had judges rate the expressions of babies in segments of videotape. Some judges were told the correct sex of the infant, others were told that the baby was of the other sex, and still other judges were asked to guess the baby's sex. Babies believed to be boys were seen as expressing fear, anger, and distress much more often than those who were believed to be girls; those believed to be girls were seen as joyful more often than boys. Condry and Condry (1976) similarly found that subjects who saw a child labeled as a boy displaying an ambiguous negative response interpreted the response as anger, while those who saw the same videotape with the child labeled a girl saw the emotion as fear. Even the earliest interactions with the caregiver are characterized by the caregiver's differential responsiveness to the specific emotional expressions of female and male infants (Haviland & Malatesta, 1981; Malatesta & Haviland, 1982).

While the research participant's susceptibility to a gender-based "response bias" adds horrifying complexity to research design, it at least offers a point of origin for the development of testable explanations of apparently ephemeral effects of gender. Paradoxically, instead of demonstrating the insignificance of gender effects in emotions research, it shows how powerfully a tacitly held standard can deploy its effects. It also makes clear the boundaries for generalizing from effects observed within a single measurement context. To infer anything about gender, comparisons of male and female subjects must include consideration of the measurement context as a variable. Such a strategy is exemplified in Hall and Halberstadt's (1986) examination of the conditions of social smiling in adults. To test the extent to which situational variables moderate sex-related differences in smiling frequency, they blind-rated several dimensions of situations (face-to-face involvement, situational friendliness, social tension, and relative status) in which subjects' expressive behavior had been observed. They found that in situations characterized by a friendly tone, inspiring more nervousness, or involving face-to-face involvement women smiled significantly more frequently than men; the individual's relative status in the situation was unrelated to smiling frequency. Another example can be drawn from Gottman and Levenson's (1988) longitudinal investigation of marital interaction, which has revealed some striking and apparently stable sex-related differences. A complete model will require examining how the effect of subject sex is moderated by the role relationship and context. For example, do lesbian or gay male couples show the same behavioral asymmetry and physiological patterning that Gottman and Levenson find in heterosexual couples? Are prototypes of the married couple pattern found in nonintimate heterosexual or same-sex relationships based on role-governed power inequities (eg boss-worker) or on equality (eg close co-workers)?

The effects of beliefs about gender are sufficiently consistent and powerful to deserve greater attention in emotions research. A key set of questions revolves around the relationship between the constructs of expressiveness (variation in behavioral tempo) and emotionality, constructs which are generally conflated in emotion theories.[4] Buck (cited in Hall, 1984) defines facial expressiveness in terms of "breakpoints," that is, the observer's judgment that something meaningful has happened on the face of the expressor. If expressiveness can be conceptualized as a communication, what, then, is "emotionality"? Is it conceptually, expressively, or experientially distinct from the occurrence of specific emotions? For example, to what extent is emotionality inferred by observers in the *absence* of FACS and MAX-codable expressions? More specifically, to what extent is the expectation that different kinds of emotions are expressed by males and females based on actual differences in their expression?

In conclusion, a "gendered" approach to the study of human emotion brings to light assumptions about the operation of emotion in social life. Saarni (1989, p. 182) proposes that "Emotional development occurs *because* we exist within interpersonal systems." To this we can add the proposition that, within these interpersonal systems, sex (as a stimulus variable) serves as one of the most powerful regulators of emotional transactions.

NOTES

1. For the seventeenth-century writer "races" were Italians, Germans, Jews, Spaniards, etc. Like Wright, I must qualify the generalizations that I make in this chapter by noting that they are largely based on the North American research literature. Gender as a social variable is, of course, moderated by class, ethnicity, and historical era.

2. By distinguishing between "sex" and "gender," the phenomena referenced by sex/gender labels are more clearly identified. For example, "gender role" is a more accurate term than "sex role" to apply to a culture's expectations regarding sex-appropriate behaviors, beliefs and attitudes. "Core gender identity," one's identification of oneself as male or female, clearly refers to the individual's beliefs about identity rather than genital appearance alone. The sex/gender distinction is not meant to imply that an independent reality can be or ought to be ascribed to each; rather, the semantic distinction is explicitly concerned with furthering theory development and increasing the conceptual sophistication of empirical research. To adopt the sex/gender distinction is neither to suggest that one is derivative of the other nor that the two are necessarily causally linked. Some continue to use the terms sex and gender interchangeably (eg Maccoby, 1988). For a discussion of the analogy between sex/gender and the biological and cultural manifestations of emotion see Shields (1990).

3. See, for example, Hare-Mustin and Maracek's (1988) analysis of the intellectual consequences of models that emphasize sex differences or sex similarities.

4. Recently, Halberstadt (in press) has developed a model of socialization of expressiveness within the family that successfully disembeds these two constructs.

REFERENCES

Abu-Lughod, L. (1986). Honor and the sentiments of loss in a Bedouin society, *American Ethnologist,* 12, 245–261.

Allen, J. G., & Haccoun, D. M. (1976). Sex differences in emotionality: A multidimensional approach. *Human Relations,* 29(8), 711–722.

Aukett, R., Ritchie, J., & Mill, K. (1988). Gender differences in friendship patterns. *Sex Roles,* 19(1/2), 57–66.

Averill, J. R. (1983). Studies on anger and aggression: Implications for theories of emotion. *American Psychologist,* 38(11), 1145–1160.

Balswick, J., & Avertt, C. P. (1977). Differences in expressiveness: Gender, interpersonal orientation, and perceived parental expressiveness as contributing factors. *Journal of Marriage and the Family,* 39, 121–127.

Barden, R. C., Garber, J., Lieman, B., Ford, M., & Masters, J. C. (1985). Factors governing the effective remediation of negative affect and its cognitive and behavioral consequences. *Journal of Personality and Social Psychology,* 49, 1040–1053.

Berman, P. W. (1980). Are women more responsive than men to the young? A review of developmental and situational variables. *Psychological Bulletin,* 88, 668–695.

Berman, P. (1987). Children caring for babies: Age and sex differences in response to infant signals and to the social context. In N. Eisenberg (Ed.), *Topics in Developmental Psychology.* New York: Wiley, pp. 141–164.

Birnbaum, D. W., & Chemelski, B. E. (1984). Preschoolers' inferences about gender and emotion: The mediation of emotionality stereotypes. *Sex Roles,* 10(7/8), 505–511.

Birnbaum, D. W., & Croll, W. L. (1984). The etiology of children's stereotypes about sex differences in emotionality. *Sex Roles,* 10(9/10), 677–691.

Birnbaum, D. W., Nosanchuk, T. A., & Croll, W. L. (1980). Children's stereotypes about sex differences in emotionality. *Sex Roles,* 6(3), 435–443.

Brabeck, M. M., & Weisgerber, K. (1988). Responses to the Challenger tragedy: Subtle and significant gender differences. *Sex Roles,* 19(9/10), 639–650.

Brody, L. (1985). Gender differences in emotional development: A review of theories and research. *Journal of Personality,* 53(2), 102–149.

Buchwald, A., Strack, S., & Coyne, J. (1981). Demand characteristics and the Velten mood induction procedure. *Journal of Consulting and Clinical Psychology,* 49, 478–479.

Burrowes, B. D., & Halberstadt, A. G. (1987). Self- and family-expressiveness styles in the experience and expression of anger. *Journal of Nonverbal Behavior,* 11(4), 254–268.

Cancian, F. (1987). *Love in America: Gender and Self-Development.* New York: Cambridge University Press.

Carlson, L., & Carlson, R. (1984). Affect and psychological magnification: Derivations from Tomkins' script theory. *Journal of Personality,* 52(1), 36–45.

Clark, D. M., & Teasdale, J. D. (1985). Constraints on the effects of mood on memory. *Journal of Personality and Social Psychology,* 48(6), 1595–1608.

Cole, P. M. (1986). Children's spontaneous control of facial expression. *Child Development,* 57, 1309–1321.

Condry, J. C., & Condry, S. (1976). Sex differences: A study of the eye of the beholder. *Child Development,* 47, 812–819.

Covell, K., & Abramovitch, R. (1988). Children's understanding of maternal anger: Age and source of anger differences. *Merrill-Palmer Quarterly,* 34(4), 353–368.

Crawford, M., & Maracek, J. (1989). Psychology reconstructs the female: 1971–1988. *Psychology of Women Quarterly,* 13(2), 147–165.

Deaux, K., (1985). Sex and gender. *Annual Review of Psychology,* 36, 49–82.

Deaux, K., & Major, B. (1987). Putting gender into context: An interactive model of gender-related behavior. *Psychological Review,* 94(3), 369–389.

Deiner, E., Sandvik, E., & Larsen, R. J. (1985). Age and sex effects for emotional intensity. *Developmental Psychology,* 21(3), 542–546.

Dosser, D. A., Balswick, J. O., & Halverson, C. F. (1983). Situational context of emotional expressiveness. *Journal of Counseling Psychology,* 30, 375–387.

Egerton, M. (1988). Passionate women and passionate men: Sex differences in accounting for angry and weeping episodes. *British Journal of Social Psychology,* 27, 51–66.

Eisenberg, N., & Lennon, R. (1983). Sex differences in empathy and related capacities. *Psychological Bulletin,* 94, 100–131.

Fabes, R. (1989, May). Stereotypes of emotionality. Paper presented at the Nags Head Conference on Sex and Gender, Nags Head, NC.

Fabes, R. A., & Martin, C. L. (1990a). Gender and age stereotypes of emotionality. Paper presented at the meeting of the American Psychological Society, Dallas, Texas.

Fabes, R. A., & Martin, C. L. (1990b). Gender stereotypes of problematic negative emotions. Submitted for publication.

Feshbach, N. D., & Hoffman, M. A. (1978). Sex differences in children's reports of emotion-arousing situations. In D. McGuinnes (Chair), Sex differences: Commotion, motion, or emotion: Psychological gender differences. Symposium conducted at the meeting of the Western Psychological Association, San Francisco, California.

Flett, G. L., Boase, P., McAndrews, M. P., Pliner, P., & Blankstein, K. R. (1986). Affect intensity and the appraisal emotion. *Journal of Research in Personality,* 20, 447–459.

Fogel, A., & Melson, G. F. (1986). *Origins of Nurturance: Developmental, Biological, and Cultural Perspectives on Caregiving.* Hillsdale, NJ: Erlbaum.

Frodi, A. (1978). Experiential and physiological responses associated with anger and aggression in women and men. *Journal of Research in Personality* 12, 335–349.

Fuchs, D., & Thelen, M. H. (1988). Children's expected interpersonal consequences of communicating their affective state and reported likelihood of expression. *Child Development,* 59, 1314–1322.

Ganong, L. H., & Coleman, M. (1985). Sex, sex roles, and emotional expressiveness. *The Journal of Genetic Psychology,* 146(3), 405–411.

Gallois, C., & Callan, V. J. (1986). Decoding emotional messages: Influence of ethnicity, sex, message type, and channel. *Journal of Personality and Social Psychology,* 51(4), 755–762.

Gottman, J. M., & Levenson, R. W. (1988). The social psychophysiology of marriage. In P. Noller & M. A. Fitzpatrick (Eds), *Perspectives on Marital Interactions.* San Diego: College Hill Press, pp. 182–200.

Halberstadt, A. G. (in press). The ecology of expressiveness: Family socialization in particular and model in general. In R. S. Feldman & B. Rimé (Eds), *Fundamentals in Nonverbal Behavior.* New York: Cambridge University Press.

Halberstadt, A. G., Hayes, C. W., & Pike, K. M. (1988). Gender and gender role differences in smiling and communication consistency. *Sex Roles,* 19(9/10), 589–603.

Hall, J. A. (1978). Gender effects in decoding nonverbal cues. *Psychological Bulletin,* 85(4), 845–857.

Hall, J. A. (1984). *Nonverbal Sex Differences: Communication Accuracy and Expressive Style.* Baltimore, Md: Johns Hopkins University Press.

Hall, J. A. (1987). On explaining gender differences: The case of nonverbal communication. In P. Shaver & C. Hendrick (Eds), *Sex and Gender, Volume 7: Review of Personality and Social Psychology.* Beverly Hills, Ca: Sage, pp. 177–200.

Hall, J. A., & Halberstadt, A. G. (1986). Smiling and gazing. In J. S. Hyde & M. C. Linn (Eds), *The Psychology of Gender: Advances Through Meta-Analysis.* Baltimore, Md: Johns Hopkins University Press.

Hall, J. A., Mroz, B. J., & Braunwald, K. G. (1983). Expressions of affect and locus of control. *Journal of Personality and Social Psychology,* 45, 156–162.

Hare-Mustin, R. T., & Maracek, J. (1988). The meaning of difference: Gender theory, postmodernism, and psychology. *American Psychologist,* 43(6), 455–464.

Haviland, J. M. (1977). Sex-related pragmatics in infant nonverbal communication. *Journal of Communication,* 27, 80–84.

Haviland, J. M., & Lieberman, M. S. (1983). Individual factors relating encoding and decoding of facial affect: Gender and personality. Unpublished manuscript.

Haviland, J. M., & Malatesta, C. Z. (1981). Fallacies, facts and fantasies: A description of the development of sex differences in nonverbal signals. In C. Mayo & N. Henley (Eds), *Gender and Nonverbal Behavior.* New York: Springer.

Heise, D. R., & Thomas, L. (1989). Predicting impressions created by combinations of emotion and social identity. *Social Psychology Quarterly,* 52, 141–148.

Hochschild, A. R. (1983). *The Managed Heart.* Berkeley, Ca: University of California Press.

Jacklin, C. N. (1981). Methodological issues in the study of sex-related differences. *Developmental Review,* 1, 266–273.

Jacklin, C. N. (1989). Female and male: Issues of gender. *American Psychologist,* 44(2), 127–133.

Janisse, M. P., Edgner, N., & Dyck, D. G. (1986). Type A behavior, anger expression, and reactions to anger imagery. *Motivation and Emotion,* 10(4), 371–386.

Johnson, J. T., & Shulman, G. A. (1988). More alike than meets the eye: Perceived gender differences in subjective experience and its display. *Sex Roles,* 19(1/2), 67–79,

Kirkcaldy, B. D. (1984). The interrelationship between state and trait variables. *Personal and Individual Differences,* 5(2), 141–149.

Kirouac, G., & Dore, F. Y. (1985). Accuracy of the judgment of facial expression of emotions as a function of sex and level of education. *Journal of Nonverbal Behavior,* 9(1), 3–7.

Krokoff, L. J. (1987). The correlates of negative affect in marriage: An exploratory study of gender differences. *Journal of Family Issues,* 8(1), 111–135.

Lewin, M. (1984a). "Rather worse than folly?" Psychology measures femininity and masculinity, 1: From Terman and Miles to the Guilfords. In M. Lewin (Ed.), *In the Shadow of the Past: Psychology Portrays the Sexes.* New York: Columbia University Press, pp. 155–178.

Lewin, M. (1984b). Psychology measures femininity and masculinity, 2: From "13 gay men" to the instrumental–expressive distinction. In M. Lewis (Ed.), *In the Shadow of the Past: Psychology Portrays the Sexes.* New York: Columbia University Press, pp. 179–204.

Lewis, S. J., & Harder, D. W. (1988). Velten's mood induction technique: "Real" change and the effects of personality and sex on affect state. *Journal of Clinical Psychology,* 44(3), 441–444.

Lorber, J. (1987). From the editor. *Gender & Society,* 1, 123–124.

Lubin, B., Rinck, C. M., & Collins, J. F. (1986). Intensity ratings of mood adjectives as a function of gender and age group. *Journal of Social and Clinical Psychology,* 4(2), 244–247.

Lutz, C. (1988a). Engendered emotion: Gender, power and the rhetoric of emotional control in American discourse. Paper presented for the Workshop Accounts of Human Nature, Windsor, England.

Lutz, C. (1988b). *Unnatural Emotions: Everyday Sentiments on a Micronesian Atoll and Their Challenge to Western Theory.* Chicago: University of Chicago Press.

Maccoby, E. F. (1988). Gender as a social category. *Developmental Psychology,* 24(6), 755–765.

Malatesta, C. Z., & Haviland, J. M. (1982). Learning display rules: The socialization of emotion expression in infancy. *Child Development,* 53, 991–1003.

Malatesta, C. Z., & Kalnok, M. (1984). Emotional experience in younger and older adults. *Journal of Gerontology,* 39(3), 301–308.

Manstead, A. S. R. (in press). Gender differences in emotion. In M. A. Gale & M. W. Eysenck (Eds), *Handbook of Individual Differences: Biological Perspectives.* Chichester: Wiley.

Martin, C. L., Fabes, R. A., Eisenbud, L., Karbon, M. M., & Rose, H. A. (1990). Boys don't cry: Children's distortions of others' emotions. Paper presented at the meeting of the Southwestern Society for Research in Human Development, Tempe, Arizona.

Masters, J. C., Ford, M. E., & Arend, R. A. (1983). Children's strategies for controlling affective responses to aversive social experience. *Motivation and Emotion,* 7, 103–116.

Matlin, M. W. (1987). *The Psychology of Women.* New York: Holt, Rinehart & Winston.

McAndrew, F. T. (1986). A cross-cultural study of recognition thresholds for facial expressions of emotion. *Journal of Cross-Cultural Psychology,* 17(2), 211–224.

McFarlane, J., Martin, C. L., & Williams, T. M. (1988). Mood fluctuations: Women versus men and menstrual versus other cycles. *Psychology of Women Quarterly,* 12, 201–223.

Morawski, J. G. (1987). The troubled quest for masculinity, femininity and androgyny. In P. Shaver & C. Hendrick (Eds), *Sex and Gender, Volume 7: Review of Personality and Social Psychology.* Beverly Hills, Ca: Sage, pp. 44–69.

Nolen-Hoeksema, S. (1987). Sex differences in unipolar depression: Evidence and theory. *Psychological Bulletin,* 101(2), 259–282.

Noller, P., and Gallois, C. (1986). Sending emotional messages in marriage: Non-verbal behaviour, sex and communication clarity. *British Journal of Social Psychology,* 25, 287–297.

O'Leary, V. E., & Smith, D. (1988). Sex makes a difference: Attributions for emotional cause. In D. Smith (Chair), Two different worlds: Women, men, and emotion. American Psychological Association Convention, Atlanta, Georgia.

Parlee, M. B. (1973). The premenstrual syndrome. *Psychological Bulletin,* 83, 454–465.

Potts, R., Morse, M., Felleman, E., & Masters, J. C. (1986). Children's emotions and memory for affective narrative content. *Motivation and Emotion,* 10(1), 39–57.

Rosaldo, M. (1984). Toward an anthropology of self and feeling. In R. Shweder & R. Levine (Eds), *Culture Theory: Essays on Mind, Self, and Emotion.* New York: Cambridge University Press.

Rotter, N. G., & Rotter, G. S. (1988). Sex differences in the encoding and decoding of negative facial emotions. *Journal of Nonverbal Behavior,* 12(2), 139–148.

Saarni, C. (1979). Children's understanding of display rules for expressive behavior. *Developmental Psychology,* 15, 424–429.

Saarni, C. (1984). An observational study of children's attempt to monitor their expressive behavior. *Child Development,* 55, 1504–1513.

Saarni, C. (1988). Children's understanding of the interpersonal consequences of dissemblance of nonverbal emotional–expressive behavior. *Journal of Nonverbal Behavior,* 12(4), 275–294.

Saarni, C. (1989). Children's understanding of strategic control of emotional expression in social transactions. In C. Saarni & P. L. Harris (Eds), *Children's Understanding of Emotion.* Cambridge: Cambridge University Press, pp. 181–208.

Shields, S. A. (1984). Distinguishing between emotion and non-emotion: Judgements about experience. *Motivation and Emotion,* 8, 355–369.

Shields, S. A. (1990). Conceptualizing the biology–culture relationship in emotion: an analogy with gender. *Cognition and Emotion,* 4, 359–374.

Shields, S. A., & Koster, B. A. (1989). Emotional stereotyping of parents in child rearing manuals, 1915–1980. *Social Psychology Quarterly,* 52, 44–55.

Shimanoff, S. B. (1983). The role of gender in linguistic references to emotive states. *Communication Quarterly,* 30(3), 174–179.

Slade, P. (1984). Premenstrual emotional changes in normal women: Fact or fiction? *Journal of Psychosomatic Research,* 28, 1–7.

Snell, Jr., W. E., Miller, R. S., & Belk, S. S. (1988). Development of the emotional self-disclosure scale. *Sex Roles,* 18(1/2), 59–73.

Sogon, S., & Izard, C. E. (1987). Sex differences in emotion recognition by observing body movements: A case of American students. *Japanese Psychological Research,* 29(2), 89–93.

Sommers, S. (1984). Reported emotions and conventions of emotionality among college students. *Journal of Personality and Social Psychology,* 46(1), 207–215.

Sommers, S., & Kosmitski, C. (1988). Emotion and social context: An American-German comparison. *British Journal of Social Psychology,* 27, 35–49.

Spielberger, C. D., Johnson, E. H., & Jacobs, C. A. (1982). *Anger Expression Scale Manual.* Tampa, Fl: Human Resources Institute, University of South Florida.

Stapley, J. C., & Haviland, J. M. (1989). Beyond depression: Gender differences in normal adolescents' emotional experiences. *Sex Roles,* 20(5/6), 295–308.

Stoner, S. B., & Spencer, W. B. (1987). Age and gender differences with the anger expression scale. *Educational and Psychological Measurement,* 47(2), 487–492.

Strayer, J. (1986). Children's attributions regarding the situational determinants of emotion in self and others. *Developmental Psychology,* 22(5), 649–654.

Strayer, J. (1989). What children know and feel in response to witnessing affective events. In C. Saarni & P. L. Harris (Eds), *Children's Understanding of Emotion.* Cambridge: Cambridge University Press, pp. 259–289.

Strickland, B. R., Hale, D. W., & Anderson, L. K. (1975). Effect of induced mood states on activity and self report affect. *Journal of Consulting and Clinical Psychology, 43,* 57.

Thompson, R. A. (1989). Causal attributions and children's emotional understanding. In C. Saarni & P. L. Harris (Eds), *Children's Understanding of Emotion.* Cambridge: Cambridge University Press, pp. 117–150.

Trepanier-Street, M. L., & Romatowski, J. A. (1986). Sex and age differences in children's creative writing. *Journal of Humanistic Education and Development, 25*(1), 18–27.

Unger, R. K. (1979). Toward a redefinition of sex and gender. *American Psychologist, 34*(11), 1085–1094.

Unger, R. K. (1981). Sex as a social reality: Field and laboratory research. *Psychology of Women Quarterly, 5,* 645–653.

Unger, R. K. (1988). Psychological, feminist, and personal epistemology: Transcending contradiction. In M. M. Gergen (Ed.), *Feminist Thought and the Structure of Knowledge.* New York: New York University Press, pp. 124–141.

Unger, R. K. (1989). Sex, gender, and epistemology. In M. Crawford, M. Gentry (Eds), *Gender and Thought: Psychological Perspectives.* New York: Springer-Verlag, pp. 17–35.

von Salisch, M. (1988). Girls' and boys' ways of arguing with a friend. Paper presented at the Third European Conference on Developmental Psychology, Budapest, Hungary.

Wagner, H. L., MacDonald, C. J., & Manstead, A. S. R. (1986). Communication of individual emotions by spontaneous facial expressions. *Journal of Personality and Social Psychology, 50*(4), 737–743.

Wallbott, H. G. (1988). Big girls don't frown, big boys don't cry—gender differences of professional actors in communicating emotion via facial expression. *Journal of Nonverbal Behavior, 12*(2), 98–106.

West, C., & Zimmerman, D. H. (1987). Doing gender. *Gender & Society, 1,* 125–151.

Wright, T. (1973/1601). *The Passions of the Minde.* New York: Verlag.

CHECKPOINT

1. Our understanding of emotion is confounded by the fact that emotional experience is inherently private whereas emotional expression is public. Gender norms govern the public expression of emotion and may influence individuals' private interpretation of their feelings.

To prepare for reading the next section, think about this question:

1. What beliefs and social norms support the stereotype that women are not aggressive?

Deconstructing the Myth of the Nonaggressive Woman: A Feminist Analysis

JACQUELYN W. WHITE

University of North Carolina at Greensboro

ROBIN M. KOWALSKI

Western Carolina University

One of the most pervasive and undisputed gender stereotypes is that men are more aggressive than women. However, this stereotype has, until recently, led researchers to conclude that women are non-aggressive and, therefore, to ignore the topic of female aggression as a distinct phenomenon. The basis of the myth, factors supporting its maintenance, and theories of female aggression are examined. A feminist reinterpretation of aggression that views women's and men's aggressive behavior within social structural arrangements that create and sustain differential power relations is presented.

The evidence seems clear. Violence and aggression belong to the domain of men. Official crime statistics tell us that men are more likely to be perpetrators and victims of a wide range of criminal acts. For example, in 1990 the 50,000 women arrested for aggravated assault constituted only 13.3% of all such arrests (U.S. Department of Justice, Federal Bureau of Investigation, 1992). There are two notable exceptions to this pattern. Girls and women are by far more frequently and seriously sexually victimized. And, within intimate relationships, women and men self-report equivalent levels of verbal and physical aggression, though women are far more likely to be seriously injured or murdered by their combative partners. In spite of what appears to be unequivocal gender-related patterns of

Address correspondence and reprint requests to: Jacquelyn W. White, Ph.D., Department of Psychology, University of North Carolina at Greensboro, Greensboro, NC 27412.

aggression, a number of questions remain. One question is whether women are really as nonaggressive as the stereotype would have us believe. The present paper examines the myth of the nonaggressive female, considers relevant research data, and provides a feminist interpretation of female aggression. For our purposes feminism is defined as ". . . a form of oppositional knowledge, aimed at disrupting accepted notions of women's behavior and women's proper place, and challenging customary categories and meanings that constitute our knowledge of gender" (Marecek & Hare-Mustin, 1990, p. 1).

In reviewing the literature for this paper, we found that aggression was defined as any behavior directed toward another person (or a person's property) with the intent to do harm, even if the aggressor was unsuccessful. The behavior could be physical or verbal, active or passive, direct or indirect (i.e., aggressor could remain anonymous), and the consequence for the target could be physical or psychological (Buss, 1961). Also, we considered offensive and defensive forms of aggression, recognizing that in the judgment of some, defensive forms of aggression are conceptually distinct from offensive aggression. For example, Tedeschi, Smith, and Brown (1974) reported that participants were reluctant to label self-defensive behaviors as aggression. We deemed it appropriate to consider all forms of harm-doing behavior because in some cases, such as domestic violence, it is difficult to distinguish retaliative from self-defense motives (Saunders, 1988). Also, aggression was broadly defined in order to examine more fully the broad range of harm-doing behaviors available to human beings. It is our contention that female harm-doing has been ignored in part because of a narrow focus on physical forms of aggression. As will be seen, much female aggression has gone unnoticed and thus unnamed. For this reason, female physical aggression seems more unexpected, becomes labeled irrational, and is denied legitimacy.

Although the primary focus of this paper is on aggressive behavior, we also examined the literature on female criminality because sociological considerations of female aggression often occur in the context of criminality. Thus, the distinctions between violent behavior and other criminal acts, such as property crimes, are not always drawn. Some of the theories assume underlying connections between various forms of criminal behavior, usually based on stereotypical assumptions about female deviance (Chesney-Lind, 1987).

THE MYTH OF THE NONAGGRESSIVE WOMAN

People around the world hold a number of stereotypes regarding women and men. For example, relative to women, men are considered to be more competitive and more assertive (Block, 1976). Women, on the other hand, are rated higher than men on measures of empathy and nurturance (Eisenberg & Lennon, 1983). Williams and Best (1982), in a study of sex-stereotyping in 30 nations, found aggression to be one of five traits that was more consistently associated with men than women (the other traits were dominance, autonomy, achievement, and endurance; see also Best & Williams, 1993). Although recent research has suggested that gender differences are not as great as they once appeared (Hyde & Linn, 1986) and that within-group differences may be greater than between-group differences, one stereotype about gender has remained virtually unchallenged: Men are perceived to be more aggressive than women (Eron, Huesmann, Lefkowitz, & Walder, 1972; Geen, 1990; Gladue, 1991a, 1991b; Maccoby & Jacklin, 1974; McCabe & Lipscomb, 1988; Segall, 1989; Simon & Landis, 1991; Towson & Zanna, 1982; White, 1983).

Aggressiveness in men has been implicated in men's greater success in competitive environments such as sports and the work place. In contrast, nonviolence is seen as part of the passive, gentle nature of women, suiting them well for their roles as wife and mother, while rendering them unfit for competitive roles of warrior and leader (Bjorkqvist & Niemela, 1992; Richardson, Bernstein, & Taylor, 1979). Macaulay (1985) identified seven beliefs associated with aggression in women: women are nonaggressive, "sneaky" in their expression of aggression, unable to express anger, prone to outbursts of "fury," psychologically distressed if they are aggressive, aggressive in defense of their children, and motivated to aggress by jealousy.

These purported gender differences in aggressiveness have been reported in relation to physical and verbal aggression and apply across a range of situations and cultures (Maccoby & Jacklin, 1974). According to Maccoby and Jacklin (1974), this gender difference in aggression is evident as early as age 2 and continues to be observed throughout the college years. Meta-analytic studies also have provided partial support for the observed gender differences in aggression, reporting an effect size of .50 (Hyde, 1986).

Evidence of Female Aggression

Although it is beyond the scope of the present paper to review the extant literature on gender differences in aggression, an examination of available data provides many examples of female aggression. In four comprehensive reviews of the literature, the authors in each instance argued that the conclusion that men are always more aggressive than women cannot be substantiated (Eagly & Steffen, 1986; Frodi, Macaulay, & Thome, 1977; Hyde & Linn, 1986; White, 1983). Recently, female coercion in sexual relationships (Craig, 1988) and female sexual abuse of children (Finkelhor & Russell, 1984) have been documented. Although these latter occur with considerably less frequency than male aggression against women, even the small numbers indicated that women can be aggressive. Two recent books have catalogued numerous instances of female aggression

(Bjorkqvist & Niemela, 1992; Haug, Benston, Brain, Mos, & Olivier, 1991). Finally, reports of female aggression in intimate relationships (to be discussed more fully in a subsequent section) also defy the stereotype of the nonaggressive woman.

The findings suggest that women have as much potential as men to be aggressive and that, given the appropriate circumstances, are as likely to display aggression as men (Frodi et al., 1977; White, 1983). For example, Towson and Zanna (1982) presented female and male research participants with vignettes describing a frustration with either a traditionally masculine or feminine task. Responses regarding the appropriateness of aggressive responses in the described situations revealed that men advocated more aggression than women in the masculine task condition, whereas gender differences disappeared in the feminine task condition. Furthermore, cultures in which aggression by women and nurturance by men are accepted show a reversal of the traditional "male as aggressor" paradigm (Mead, 1935). Although a discussion of gender differences in aggression in various animal species is beyond the scope of this paper, it is worth noting that even in this research domain the assumption of the nonaggressive woman is being questioned. For example, Cairns, Santoyo, and Holly (1994) stated, "The same genetic pathway was involved in males and females [mice]. . . . The linkage has been obscured in the literature because of the failure to employ gender-relevant assessments" (p. 9); that is, past research has not considered the contexts within which female and male animals are likely to aggress. Similarly, Hrdy and Williams (1983) have challenged the "myth of the passive female" in accounts of primate behavior.

Factors Maintaining the Myth of the Nonaggressive Woman

Lerner's (1986) historical analysis of the origins of patriarchy argues that male aggression is rooted in a warrior culture. Because of women's biological vulnerability in childbirth, more men than women occupied the role of warrior. Men assumed, with women's cooperation, the right to protect women and children from captivity by warring forces. This led to the treatment of women as possessions, with inherent weaknesses. In addition to these historical factors, a number of other factors contribute to the stereotype of the nonaggressive woman.

First, crime statistics may distort the actual incidence of female crime in the general population. In order for a crime to be included within crime statistics, there must first be not only a victim of the crime, but also a victim who is willing to report and prosecute the crime (Morris, 1987). In the case of certain types of female aggressiveness (i.e., violence in intimate relationships), the victim (spouse or child) may not report the crime because of the lack of ability, lack of perceived seriousness, or fear of being stigmatized. Furthermore, until quite recently, female perpetrators of crime were more likely to be treated leniently by the criminal justice system. Aggressive women were labeled pathological rather than criminal. Thus, many of their crimes were unlikely to be incorporated into official crime statistics. Rather, they were more likely to be counted among the mentally ill (Anderson, 1993).

From a methodological standpoint, a number of biases in research procedures contribute to the myth of the nonaggressive woman. These biases include choice of research participants, operational definitions of aggression, and context of aggression.

Because of the notion that aggression is a predominantly male attribute, researchers have disproportionately used male as opposed to female participants in their research studies (Bjorkqvist & Niemela, 1992; Frodi et al., 1977; Morris, 1987; Paul & Baenninger, 1991; Yoder & Kahn, 1993). In the period 1967–1974, only 8% of the published studies examined female aggression, whereas 54% focused exclusively on men (Frodi et al., 1977).

Even when female aggression has been the research focus, the conceptualization and operationalization of aggression has stemmed from the "male" perspective on aggression (Bjorkqvist & Niemela, 1992). For example, much of the research on aggression has focused specifically on physical aggression. Typically, this work involved the teacher-learner paradigm in which the participant, acting as teacher, punishes the "learner" with electric shocks for incorrect responses (Bjorkqvist & Niemela, 1992). Research has shown, however, that women perceive electric shock more negatively and as a less effective deterrent than do men; thus, they are more reluctant than men to administer it (Bjorkqvist & Niemela, 1992; Miller, Gillen, Schlenker, & Radlove, 1974). The use of this particular paradigm "directly pits empathy against aggression, thereby facilitating sex differences. . . . Experiments which have placed empathy for the victim in direct contest with the subject's willingness to shock a victim . . . have left us with a body of literature that attests to the unaggressiveness of females" (Paul & Baenninger, 1991, pp. 404–405). Research demonstrating gender differences in aggression might be reflecting gender differences in a willingness to express physical aggression rather than the potential for aggression (Balkan, Berger, & Schmidt, 1980; Frodi et al., 1977).

A continued focus on types of aggression in which men consistently emerge as more aggressive than women fails to examine those situations in which women might aggress and the modes of aggression they might adopt. Bjorkqvist and Niemela (1992) suggested that because the majority of researchers have been male, they have chosen questions and contexts regarding aggression of greatest personal relevance. For example, women appear to be more likely than men to use indirect methods of aggression, such as sabotaging another's performance (Bjorkqvist, Lagerspetz, & Kaukiainen, 1992; Lagerspetz, Bjorkqvist, & Peltonen, 1988). However, gender differences in indirect aggression only recently have received empirical attention. Cross-cultural research too has identified an extraordinary range of harm-doing behaviors committed by women. Burbank (1987) documented eight categories of aggressive acts in 317 societies in the Human Relations Area Files. Although her data were limited to female aggression directed toward other adults in the context of home or neighborhood (what she labeled "domestic aggression"), a great deal of aggression was recorded. The behaviors studied included verbal, nonverbal, and physical aggression, passive-aggressive behaviors (i.e., nonperformance of duties), property damage, and locking someone out of the house. In our search of the literature, we could not find any studies that examined a comparable range of behaviors in men.

In brief, the notion of the nonaggressive woman is a myth perpetuated by sociohistorically rooted cultural attitudes and values, reified by data based on statistical and methodological biases and flaws. Although women are reported to commit fewer crimes than men, this does not imply that they are not aggressive. Rather, because of opportunities, resources, and socialization pressures, the situations in which women will display aggressive behaviors appear to be more circumscribed, limited specifically to situations in which opportunities and social sanctions for aggressive behavior are present.

Advantages of the Myth of the Nonaggressive Woman for Men

The stereotype of gender differences in aggression has been advantageous to men in maintaining a position of power over women. We argue that all men benefit from the myth, even those individual men who reject misogynist views of women, do not desire power over women, and conduct their personal lives in ways supportive of women. Being male has unavoidable advantages in this context. These can be seen in at least five ways.

First, perceived gender differences in aggression maintain women's subordination to, dependence on, and fear of men. If women are weak and nonaggressive, they must depend on men for protection and fear harm from men against whom they cannot defend themselves.

Second, a corollary of women's fear of men's power and men's disdain for women's weakness has been suggested by Campbell (1993). Knowledge that the man is almost certain to win in a physical confrontation with a woman creates an invisible barrier between women and men in intimate relationships and reinforces the man's power. Intimacy is threatened, and antagonism prevails. The distance created, Campbell argues, is one factor that increases women's vulnerability to abuse.

Third, because aggression is assumed to be correlated with assertiveness and competitiveness, women conveniently are denied access to arenas in which these attributes are valued—not surprisingly, those most associated with power such as politics, business, and the military. Adams (1992) suggested that the belief that "male monopolization of warfare is evidence that war is a product of biology" (p. 18) is a politically useful myth that has allowed men monopoly over the tools of war and ultimately led to economic and political control of the state. Hoffman and Hurst (1990) have argued that stereotypes rationalize the distribution of the sexes into different social roles, especially when it is assumed that the roles are biologically based.

Fourth, aggressive women are labeled more deviant and pathological than are comparably aggressive men. This naming process not only denies aggressive women the opportunity to be heard, but also serves to deter aggressive behavior out of fear of punishment. The possibility that women's aggression is justified is reduced, and the legitimacy of their behavior is discounted. Women thus develop feelings of anxiety and guilt about expressing their anger and frustration in aggressive ways. Given that deviance is commonly defined as behavior that departs from cultural norms and that violence is not socially condoned, it is hardly surprising that "aggressive" women have been labeled more deviant than "aggressive" men (Anderson, 1993). As with many other phenomena, the perspective of men is the yardstick against which the behavior of women is measured (Morris, 1987). In Campbell's (1993) discussion, culture deems male aggression rational; a means-ends analysis is appropriated by men to justify their behavior, whereas women's aggression is seen as irrational and emotional.

Fifth, until recently, the stereotype of the nonaggressive woman has led many to ignore female aggression as a phenomenon in and of itself (Bjorkqvist & Niemela, 1992). According to Paul and Baenninger (1991), "believing that males aggress more than females promotes an implicit ignorance and lack of interest about the situations in which females do aggress, the characteristics of their aggressive behavior, and the profiles of those who are their victims" (p. 403).

Thus, the myth of the nonaggressive woman sustains male power. Women's voices are silenced. Men do not have to listen to women's reasons for aggression, nor attempt to solve the problems that lead to female aggression. This is particularly convenient because data indicate that female aggression is frequently in response to an abusive partner's behavior. The power women have to control others does not have to be acknowledged, even to women.

Female Aggression in Intimate Relationships

Research indicates that women are as likely as men to aggress in situations that are congruent with their gender role orientation, such as family settings (Towson & Zanna, 1982). Strong support appears evident in studies reporting women to be as aggressive, if not more so, than men in intimate relationships (Archer & Ray, 1989; Bookwala, Frieze, Smith, & Ryan, 1992; Johnson, 1990; Malone, Tyree, & O'Leary, 1989; O'Leary et al., 1989; Paul & Baenninger, 1991; White & Koss, 1991). However, most research on female aggression in intimate relationships has been examined via self-reports of aggressive behavior in marital relationships. Although it is beyond the scope of this paper to critique fully this literature, several cautions should be noted (see Yllo & Bograd, 1988, for more extensive information). Because most of the data are self-reports, it would be premature to accept these data as accurate reflections of the amount of aggression in intimate relationships. Women may be more willing to report negative behaviors than men (Inwald, quoted in Adler, 1993); there may be gender-related differences in the salience of memories for certain verbal and physical behaviors; and the criteria that women and men use for labeling a certain action a yell or slap may be gender-related. Biernat, Manis, and Nelson (1991) have shown that gender stereotypes influenced objective (i.e., providing numerical estimates), but not subjective (i.e., Likert scale ratings) estimates. Research has documented that women are more accurate decoders of nonverbal behavior than men (Hall, 1984). Also, it has been documented that the same body movements are more likely to be labeled aggressive (de Meijer, 1991) or dominant (Henley & Harmon, 1985) when performed by a man than by a woman.

In keeping with the notion of the nonaggressive woman, the first studies published about spousal abuse perpetrated by women were met with mixed reviews (Gelles & Cornell, 1985). Many argued that women were too passive to perpetrate abusive acts against their spouses. Others suggested that men, because of their typically larger physiques, were not capable of being abused by their wives. Still others proposed that women were less capable than men of inflicting serious harm or injury on a man and that, therefore, physical violence by women against their spouse was more acceptable (Arias & Johnson, 1989). Researchers cited as evidence the relatively small number of men who reported spousal abuse (Steinmetz & Lucca, 1988).

A national survey conducted on spousal abuse in 1975 revealed not only that women were more likely than men to report physically abusing their spouses, but that "wives committed an average of 10.3 acts of violence against their husbands during 1975, whereas their husbands averaged only 8.8 acts against their wives" (Steinmetz & Lucca, 1988, pp. 237–238). In another study, among married couples assessed 18 months after marriage, 36% of the women and 25% of the men indicated that they had physically aggressed against their spouse (O'Leary et al., 1989). Female aggression in relationships, however, is not limited to marital relationships. O'Leary et al. (1989) found that 44% of the women compared to 31% of the men reported physically aggressing against their dating partner to whom they were engaged. Using a national sample of higher education students, White and Koss (1991) found that over 80% of the women and men reported inflicting as well as sustaining verbal aggression, and approximately 36% reported inflicting physical aggression, with 39% of the men and 32% of the women sustaining some physical aggression. Bookwala et al. (1992) reported slightly higher figures for physical aggression directed toward dating partners (59% for women and 55% for men).

Despite the fact that women are as likely as men to report engaging in physical aggression against their spouse or dating partner, we would be remiss if we did not point out that women are more likely to sustain serious injury than are men. The primary reason for women's visits to emergency rooms is injury due to battering by a male partner. Also, men are more likely to murder their partner than are women: "In 1991, when some 4 million women were beaten and 1,320 murdered in domestic attacks, 622 women killed their husbands or boyfriends" (Booth, McDowell, & Simpson, 1993).

Although women have been reported to initiate acts of violence against their spouses as frequently as men (Steinmetz & Lucca, 1988; Stets & Straus, 1990), the motives of women and men for aggression differ. In self-reports of reasons for spousal homicide, the most frequently cited reason among women is self-defense, whereas among men the most common justification is sexual jealousy and/or the wife threatening to terminate the relationship (Cazenave & Zahn, 1992). Women who initiate acts of violence frequently do so in anticipation of an abusive attack from their partner.

Traditionally, gender roles confined women to the domestic sphere. The resultant opportunity to engage in violence against husbands and children was greater than the opportunity to aggress in the public sphere. Childcare duties present women with one of the primary arenas for aggressive behavior. Thus, the high rates of female involvement in child abuse are not surprising. Some studies suggest that women are more likely than men to physically abuse their children (Johnson, 1990; Steinmetz & Lucca, 1988).

Towson and Zanna (1982) suggested possible reasons for heightened female aggression in gender-role congruent situations. First, they argued that situations such as the home may be more central to a woman's self-concept than other situations. Thus, any threat to this aspect of their self-definition may provoke the expression of aggressive feelings. Second, they suggested that society may be more accepting of women aggressing in situations that are feminine. A third possibility is opportunity. Some situations are more conducive to violence than others. The home offers a private sanctuary with few external restraints on violence. A fourth possibility, not mentioned by Towson and Zanna, is power. The home is the realm where women are expected to hold and exercise authority, thus to the extent that power corrupts men, it may also corrupt women.

Research on female aggression in intimate relationships should not be taken to indicate, however, that women are not aggressive in nonfamily situations. An examination of crime statistics, although supporting the idea that women are, indeed, less aggressive than men in most realms, suggests that women are not passive. For example, according to the Uniform Crime Reports (U.S. Department of Justice, Federal Bureau of Investigation, 1990), women accounted for 10.4% of all arrests for murder and non-negligent manslaughter, and for 13.3% of all arrests for aggravated assaults.

Thus, both in and out of the domestic realm, women have been shown to commit acts of aggression. That women equal or exceed men in the number of reported aggressive acts committed within the family suggests two things. First, it suggests, again, that the notion of the nonaggressive woman is a myth. Second, it provides an impetus for increased study into the topic of female aggression as a distinct and legitimate phenomenon.

Increased Attention to Female Aggression

With the realization that the notion of the nonaggressive woman is a myth, researchers in recent years have devoted increased attention to the patterns and causes of female aggression and violence. "By the 1970s and 1980s, women's aggression had become harder and harder to ignore. Female criminologists began to write about this taboo subject, and national surveys revealed women's high level of aggression in the home" (Campbell, 1993, p. 143). Part of this increased attention stems from a group of scholars interested in the phenomenon of female aggression—scholars who were willing to dismiss the myth of the nonaggressive woman on empirical grounds.

However, this interest has met with resistance and created its own problems. Campbell (1993) noted,

"Instead of putting a spotlight on the new findings, however, these uncomfortable events trigger the minimization phase. . . . Men preferred not to dwell on women's aggression because it was an ugly sign of potential resistance" (p. 143). According to Chesney-Lind (1987), nonfeminist researchers have muddied the waters, lending "support for those who are seeking scientific legitimacy for patterns of personal and institutional sexism" (p. 208). Research on female aggression may be used to blame women for instigating their own abuse. Prosecutors, for example, have argued that some women are using the Battered Women Syndrome (Walker, 1984) as an excuse to cover up the premeditated murder of their husbands in order to avoid divorce and to gain financially (Booth et al., 1993). In fact, some argue that increased attention to female aggression is undermining the women's movement. "Women's groups colluded with them [men]; to recognize its existence would draw attention away from men's far more lethal aggression as well as highlighting undesirably assertive qualities in a group they wanted to depict as victims. Most violent offenders were men, so women's aggression was not a serious problem" (Campbell, 1993, p. 143).

Alternatively, the recent attention to women's aggression may represent a backlash in response to the women's movement. In 1975, attention to female criminality was first publicized when Freda Adler wrote *Sisters in Crime* in which she stated that the rise in female crime was a result of the women's movement and reflected the darker side of liberation. In other words, women were becoming like men. Ann Jones (1980) in her book *Women Who Kill* countered by arguing that the women's movement created a great deal of anxiety in people threatened by women's freedom. One result of this, she proposed, was an increased awareness of women's aggressive behavior and law enforcement's greater willingness to arrest and prosecute women—a crackdown precipitated not by a crime wave but by a fear of women's struggle for freedom. The chivalry hypothesis, as it has been called, implicates the women's movement by suggesting that women's push for equality implies equality in the justice system as well (Simon & Landis, 1991). Proponents of this theory argue that female crime is no more frequent than in the past, but that women are now more likely to be brought to the attention of the criminal justice system and convicted for their crimes. Of all female criminals, women who murder their spouse have the shortest criminal histories. However, women who murder are typically given more severe penalties for spousal homicide than men who murder their spouses (Browne, 1988). For example, a woman who commits spousal homicide is likely to receive a sentence of 15–20 years, whereas the sentence for a man who kills his spouse is only 2–6 years (Booth et al., 1993).

Another reason for increased interest in female aggression is that many women are attaining greater power in their relationships. That is, there may have been some truth in the myth of women's submissiveness and weakness in the past, but women themselves are now changing. The women's movement has increased awareness of the victimization of women within intimate relationships. Women are acknowledging that being hit, kicked, and slapped are abusive acts, no matter who the batterer. Women realize that acceptance and forgiveness are not their only options; anger, defiance, and fighting back are also avenues for them. Women who kill abusive partners have suffered more serious abuse than women who do not kill an abusive spouse and are more likely to have children who have been abused (Ewing, cited in Booth et al., 1993). One national survey of homicides in urban areas found that, as the number of shelters for abused women increased, the number of women killing spouses declined. On the other hand, the presence of shelters does not seem to alter the rate at which men kill their partners (Zahn, 1993).

On the basis of evidence, therefore, several conclusions can be drawn. First, men are more likely than women to express their aggression publicly and physically. Part of this stems from fewer social restrictions placed on men in the expression of aggression relative to women. Women's aggression is restricted primarily to the home and to more indirect modes of expression. In addition, close examination of the means and standard deviations reported in some studies for aggressive acts perpetrated by boys and girls or men and women suggests that there are, in fact, as many within-group differences as there are between-group differences (see Archer, Pearson, & Westeman, 1988, for an example).

Theories of Female Aggression

A traditionalist account of aggression assumed that men have always been aggressive because of God's design and/or biological determinants; men's aggressiveness was seen as universal and natural (Lerner, 1986).[1] On the basis of this long-standing belief, scientific theories developed. These theories have been catalogued variously as biological, social, cultural, anthropological, political, and psychological. Although it is beyond the scope of this paper to review fully all the various theories, several exemplars will be described. What is critical in examining these theories is that those who have power define what constitutes aggression and violence.

The first "modern" theory of aggression was Freudian. Male aggression was rooted in resolution of the Oedipal complex. Aggression directed toward others was seen as normal and as a compensation for the frustration of childhood sexual instincts. Reinterpretation of Freudian theory into learning terms led Dollard, Doob, Miller, Mowrer, and Sears (1939) to posit the frustration-aggression hypothesis. Although this hypothesis has undergone many transformations, it remains an exemplar of the individualistic paradigm that has dominated discourses about human aggression. This paradigm focuses on individual behavior devoid of social context, and has been at the center of feminist critiques of research methods in psychology (Wallston & Grady, 1985). This paradigm is reflected in the major laboratory formats developed in the 1960s to study aggression (Berkowitz, 1962; Buss, 1961; Taylor & Epstein, 1967). Macaulay (1985) has argued that in this dominant paradigm, "The preferred explanation for aggressive behaviors is individual . . . There is no place in this model for an interactive person-norms-situation process;" furthermore, the paradigm ". . . specifies various external and internal variables that shape aggression. They may deflect it, mute it, determine the specific behavior, and even cause flight or passivity rather than fighting, but they are still seen as variables acting on an expected, reliable response . . . The model comprehends control of aggression but not nonaggressive action as a full-fledged normal or usual response" (p. 209). The major theoretical models reflecting this paradigm were models of men's behavior. It was assumed that women were less prone to frustration or anger, hence less aggressive.

When instances of female aggression were observed, attempts were made to account for it. Theories of female aggression can be categorized as male-centered theories (i.e., extensions of theories of male aggression), sex-specific theories, and feminist theories.

Male-Centered Theories   Once the reality of female aggression was recognized, explanations of aggression obtained from studies of men were assumed to generalize to the population of women as well (Morris, 1987). These theories began with the premise that the underlying motivation for aggression and the processes of acquiring aggressive behavior are the same for women and men, but that gender-related factors affect the quantity and quality of the expressed behavior. Because these theories were originally formulated to account for instances of male aggression, they reflect an underlying "male-as-normative" perspective. This perspective ignores a wide range of aggressive behaviors and perpetuates myths about female aggression.

Some contemporary psychoanalysts have suggested that women and men possess the same drives and impulses, but "differ exclusively in how drives and aggressive impulses are worked through and expressed . . . [and] may to a large extent be explained on the basis of forms and practices of child rearing" (Mitscherlich, 1987, p. 224). This results in men's turning aggression outward and women's turning aggression inward. Similarly, social/environmental theories stress the differential socialization experiences of men and women. The mechanisms of social learning (including rewards, punishments, and modeling) result in different behavioral outcomes for women and men. Although social learning theory appears situation-centered, even its major proponent reflects underlying male-centered assumptions about women: "low aggressive modeling by females reflects differential inhibition rather than differential learning of aggression" (Bandura, 1973, as discussed in Macaulay, 1985). This male-as-norm approach assumes that as role expectations of women and men become more similar, female and male patterns of aggressive behavior will become more similar. Three specific hypotheses reflect this expectation. They are the masculinization, opportunity, and marginalization hypotheses.

According to the masculinization hypothesis, as women take on more masculine characteristics and take advantage of opportunities traditionally open only to men, they, too, will show more aggressive behaviors (Adler, 1975). However, mixed support for this idea has been obtained. On the one hand, comparisons of incarcerated women with nonincarcerated controls suggest that women in prison maintain more traditional attitudes than control women (Simon & Landis, 1991). On the other hand, a number of studies have suggested that masculine gender role orientation is a better predictor of aggression than is gender (Kogut, Langley, & O'Neal, 1992; Thompson, 1991). Results may be mixed because some women commit crimes in collaboration with men; these women may hold more traditional gender role attitudes than other women who commit crimes.

Simon and Landis (1991), in discussing the opportunity hypothesis of female crime, suggest that many crimes are limited to particular situations. For example, unless one is involved in the work force, it is very difficult to commit work-related crimes. The implication is that as more women move into the labor force there will be an increase in such crimes. Similarly, as women become more economically self-sufficient, they will be less likely to assume the role of victim (Simon & Landis, 1991). Furthermore, borrowing from social learning theory, proponents of the opportunity hypothesis argue that, as more women move into the work place, they will experience role strain. The stress, anger, and frustration resulting from this role strain will exacerbate their tendency to engage in physical acts of violence against their spouses (O'Leary, 1988).

In contrast to the opportunity theory, the economic marginalization theory suggests that the lack of opportunities open to women has contributed to the rise in female aggression and crime. Because many women live at or below the poverty line, they perform aggressive criminal acts to acquire money and property for their family (Simon & Landis, 1991).

Sex-Specific Theories   Failure of male-centered theories to explain adequately female behavior suggested the need for separate female theories of aggression. These approaches suggested that the nature, motives, and manner of aggression are distinctly different for women and men. Sex-specific explanations of female aggression begin with the assumption that normal women are nonaggressive because of innate characteristics. Sex-specific theories include evolutionary and biologically based explanations. Biological theories of aggression proposed that men are more aggressive than women because of higher testosterone levels (Johnson, 1972). Any deviation from the normal female personality (i.e., nurturant, nonviolent) is associated with deviant, but sex-linked personality characteristics such as being overly emotional, impulsive, or "blinded by love." These theories suggest that female violence is linked to an inability to control emotions, but not linked to social factors. Thus, women who do aggress have a problem with their biologically based gender identity (Balkan et al., 1980). See Salzman (1979) for a critique of the biologically based accounts of gender differences in aggression.

Sociobiological theories also suggest different genetic/hormonal paths to aggression (see Ellis, 1991 for an application of this approach to gender differences in sexual aggression). According to sociobiological accounts, to increase reproductive fitness, women behave aggressively when necessary to acquire the most desired mate and to keep that mate once acquired. This has contributed to the stereotype that motives for female crimes are predominantly of a sexual nature (Anderson, 1993; Omodei, 1981).

Similarly, some sociologists have suggested that women suffer from relational frustration (i.e., obstacles to maintaining positive affective relationships), whereas men experience status frustration (i.e., obsta-cles to economic power and status) (Omodei, 1981). In other words, women who commit crimes are women who have had their goal of acquiring and maintaining satisfactory relationships thwarted, a formulation consistent with revised models of the frustration-aggression hypothesis (Miller, 1941).

Feminist Theories   In response to earlier approaches, feminist models are being developed that explicitly acknowledge the socially constructed meanings of aggression. Such meanings constrain the acknowledgment of female aggression, as well as its expression (Campbell, 1993). Feminist analyses of power relations indicate that men have defined who can be legitimately aggressive—effectively silencing women with regard to their aggression in response to frustration, anger, and instrumental goals. Patriarchy has hidden women's "anger from them by their belief in the naturalness of their subordination to men" (Campbell, 1993, p. 142). Mitscherlich (1987) stated, "those who dominate define what constitutes violence . . . those in power can alone stipulate whose job it is to be maternal and gentle and when" (p. 10). Campbell (1993) argued that control of women's aggression has taken three forms: concealment, denial, and redefinition by men. Male power has allowed men to declare the "correct" interpretation of an event. She argued that a "masculine" instrumental view of aggression has led to a reinterpretation of other forms of expression of anger. Campbell's analysis suggests that instrumental forms of aggression have attained legitimacy, whereas more expressive forms have not. She used this approach to explain the controversy surrounding the legal treatment of battered women who kill, the psychiatric labeling of aggressive women, and aggression as part of premenstrual syndrome. In each case, because an androcentric rational means-ends analysis fails to account fully for a woman's aggressive behavior, "female aggression remains shrouded in mystery—capricious, irrational, arbitrary . . . violent women must be either trying to be men or just crazy" (p. 144).

Feminist theories emphasize the need to understand female violence in terms of the status of women in society—to reveal, acknowledge, and define it from the woman's perspective, including the instrumental and expressive. The intersection of race, class, and gender is of central importance to these theories. Feminists agree with the assertions of social learning theorists regarding the effects of social arrangements, including stress, on women's and men's aggressive behavior. However, feminists push the analysis further to bring patriarchy to center stage, with its attendant differential status and power. Female aggression is judged more harshly by society than male aggression, because it reflects a greater departure from social norms (Paul & Baenninger, 1991). The power differences between women and men, along with women's restricted opportunities and resources, contribute to an increased likelihood of female aggression occurring in interpersonal relationships rather than in other contexts.

Feminists also analyze community responses to female aggression, noting that the "official" response reflects a male perspective. Presently, self-defense is not judged an adequate legal defense for aggression unless a woman was in imminent danger at the time of the violence (Booth et al., 1993). The feminist perspective recognizes the inequality of the relationship (i.e., men's greater power and physical stature) in explaining why a woman would wait until a partner was vulnerable before attacking.

Feminists are less concerned with who is more aggressive, women or men, and are more focused on the outcome. The search for differences perpetuates the subordination of women and encourages biology-based theories and victim-blaming (Fine & Gordon, 1991). The problem of female aggression is located within interpersonal and institutionalized patterns of a patriarchal society. Violence is examined from a woman's perspective—what are her circumstances and options? A woman's violence is understood, though not condoned, by considering her limited options. Until alternative means to safety and security are provided, a woman's aggression in the context of an abusive relationship is seen as a survival response—a response to circumstances, not a manifestation of personal pathology.

One Theory or Two?   We argue that a single theory of aggression is adequate, when gender is defined as a socially constructed process (Unger & Crawford, 1992) and is central in the theory. A single feminist theory that applies to both women and men is recommended. It recognizes the central role of patriarchy in two senses. First, historical and sociocultural factors have coalesced to create multiple messages and consequences that support male aggression and deny female aggression. Second, hierarchical arrangements endorsed by patriarchy support the general message that some people, by virtue of their sex, race, age, socioeconomic status, and other markers of power, have the right to dominate, control, and hurt others. This message allows patriarchical accounts of violence to play central roles in models of female aggression (including women's aggression toward children and lesbian aggression). Aggression is a result more of power than of personality differences.

Recent data illustrate the value of single models to account for female and male aggression. In studies of marital violence (Malone et al., 1989) and dating violence (White, Koss, & Kissling, 1991), it has been found that the same factors predict female and male aggression, although the paths (i.e., the relative weights of each factor) differ. Applying the same model to female and male data made it possible to determine when one factor was relatively more important than another in the prediction of aggression. Similarly, White (1988) and White and Roufail (1989) demonstrated that women and men hold similar preferences for the use of various influence strategies, with physical aggression being a last resort choice. Furthermore, situational factors determined choice of strategies.

Because aggression and violence are complex, multiply determined phenomena, sociocultural explanations alone are inadequate to account for individual differences. Not all men are aggressive and not all women are nonaggressive. Not all men rape, and not all abused women kill their abusers. A feminist account must be sufficiently rich to account for these individual differences. An adequate model must incorporate intrapersonal and interpersonal psychological mechanisms. Also, a person's understanding of appropriate norms must be part of the model. Data indicate that boys approve of aggression significantly more than do girls (Huesmann, Guerra, Zelli, & Miller, 1992). Boys also expect more rewards and fewer punishments for behaving aggressively than girls (Perry, Perry, & Weiss, 1989). Self-presentational studies of aggression have found that women are more likely than men to make derogatory self-statements regarding their aggressive episodes to avoid incurring negative reactions from an audience (Campbell & Muncer, 1987). Finally, a developmental perspective that examines how children learn aggressive behavior in the context of interactions with major social institutions (i.e., family, peer group, media, religion) will help our understanding of gender-related patterns of behavior and the difficulty of changing patterns of aggression.

Dutton's embedded perspective, developed to account for the domestic assault of women, and adopted by White and Koss (1993) to account for male sexual aggression, provides a good example of a model for understanding gender-related patterns of aggression. The model proposes that behavior is the result of the interplay of individual characteristics and various social and cultural factors. Thus, aggression can be best understood by considering the interaction of factors at several levels, the ontogenetic (intrapsychic), microsystems (dyadic level of interaction), exosystems (social structures that define appropriate behaviors), and macrosystems (the larger social context, including cultural norms and values).

CONCLUSION

Acknowledging the reality of female aggression is not inconsistent with feminist goals. A primary feminist goal is eliminating the oppression of women. This oppression is most dramatically seen in the high levels of violence against women in intimate relationships—incest, dating violence, wife abuse, sexual assault, rape, and murder. The fact that women

report being aggressive in these very same relationships does not undermine in any way the seriousness of their own victimization or that of their children. Historical evidence and current statistics document high levels of female victimization. Recognition of this fact does not mean that individual women are weak and helpless. History is replete with examples of the power women garnered from recognizing their victimization. Empowerment comes from the knowledge gained by naming. Once victimization of women was named for what it was (i.e., rape, battering), women could band together to protest it. Women can emerge from being victims with a sense of entitlement and efficacy. Many protest movements gained their energy from collective anger.

The debate today about the proper attention to women's aggression vis-à-vis women's victimization must be understood in the context of a contradiction created by women's historical circumstance. Lerner (1986) argued that women's victimization is the result of exclusion from history-making as well as other forms of subordination to men, but that "it is a fundamental error to try to conceptualize women primarily as victims" (p. 5). She argued that the dialectic created by the "contradiction between women's centrality and active role in creating society and their marginality in the meaning-giving process" (p. 5) has moved women forward. It is only when we look at violence against women from an androcentric point of view that we equate violence against women with female weakness. By deconstructing the myth of the nonaggressive woman, the trap of gendered dualism (male/female : powerful/weak : perpetrator/victim) is recognized and the advantages of the myth to men is diminished. Violence in the United States is recognized as a major problem facing this country today. Other than in intimate relationships, where wives are murdered 2.4 times more than husbands (U.S. Department of Justice, FBI, 1992), men are the targets of murder more often than women. Yet no one is claiming that these high rates of victimization render an image of men as weak and helpless. Debating whether attention to women's aggression denies women's victimization is a distraction from the important analysis of patriarchy's contribution to women's and men's aggression and victimization. Thus, the question is not who is more aggressive. In fact, available data do not provide a clear answer to this question. Rather, the important questions concern the cultural, social, and psychological circumstances surrounding incidents of aggression by women and men.

Appreciation is expressed to Barrie Bondurant, Patricia L. N. Donat, Karlee Hoecker, and students in the first author's seminar on the development of gender-related patterns of aggression for comments on an earlier draft of this paper. Appreciation is expressed also to two anonymous reviewers for their insightful comments.

NOTE

1. Lerner (1986) posited another historical account of male aggression. A Marxist-economic analysis argued that male aggression was based on the overthrow of earlier female dominance or equality.

REFERENCES

Adams, D. (1992). Biology does not make men more aggressive than women. In K. Bjorkqvist & P. Niemela (Eds.), *Of mice and women: Aspects of female aggression* (pp. 17–26). New York: Academic Press.

Adler, F. (1975). *Sisters in crime: The rise of the new female criminal.* New York: McGraw-Hill.

Adler, T. (1993, January). Separate gender norms on tests raise questions. *APA Monitor,* p. 6.

Anderson, M. L. (1993). *Thinking about women: Sociological perspectives on sex and gender.* New York: Macmillan.

Archer, J., Pearson, N. A., & Westeman, K. E. (1988). Aggressive behavior of children aged 6–11: Gender differences and their magnitude. *British Journal of Social Psychology, 27,* 371–384.

Archer, J., & Ray, N. (1989). Dating violence in the United Kingdom: A preliminary study. *Aggressive Behavior, 15,* 337–343.

Arias, I., & Johnson, P. (1989). Evaluations of physical aggression among intimate dyads. *Journal of Interpersonal Violence, 4,* 298–307.

Balkan, S., Berger, R. J., & Schmidt, J. (1980). *Crime and deviance in America: A critical approach.* Belmont, CA: Wadsworth.

Berkowitz, L. (1962). *Aggression: A social psychological analysis.* New York: McGraw-Hill.

Best, D. L., & Williams, J. E. (1993). Cross-cultural viewpoint. In A. E. Beall & R. J. Sternberg (Eds.), *The psychology of gender* (pp. 215–247). New York: Guilford Press.

Biernat, M., Manis, M., & Nelson, M. M. (1991). Stereotypes and standards of judgment. *Journal of Personality and Social Psychology, 60,* 485–499.

Bjorkqvist, K., Lagerspetz, K. M. J., & Kaukiainen, A. (1992). Do girls manipulate and boys fight? Developmental trends in regard to direct and indirect aggression. *Aggressive Behavior, 18,* 117–127.

Bjorkqvist, K., & Niemela, P. (1992). New trends in the study of female aggression. In K. Bjorkqvist & P. Niemela (Eds.), *Of mice and women: Aspects of female aggression* (pp. 3–16). New York: Academic Press.

Block, J. H. (1976). Issues, problems, and pitfalls in assessing sex differences. *Merrill-Palmer Quarterly, 22,* 283–308.

Bookwala, J., Frieze, I. H., Smith, C., & Ryan, K. (1992). Predictors of dating violence: A multivariate analysis. *Violence and Victims, 7,* 297–311.

Booth, C., McDowell, J., & Simpson, J. C. (1993, January). Til death do us part. *Time,* pp. 38–45.

Browne, A. (1988). Family homicide: When victimized women kill. In V. B. Van Hasselt, R. L. Morrison, A. S. Bellack, & M. Hersen (Eds.), *Handbook of family violence* (pp. 271–292). New York: Plenum Press.

Burbank, V. K. (1987). Female aggression in cross-cultural perspective. *Behavior Science Research, 21,* 70–100.

Buss, A. (1961). *The psychology of aggression.* New York: Wiley.

Cairns, R. B., Santoyo, C., & Holly, K. A. (1994). Aggressive escalation: Toward a developmental analysis. In M. Potegal & J. Knutson (Eds.), *The dynamics of aggression* (pp. 227–253). Hillsdale, NJ: Erlbaum.

Campbell, A. (1993). *Men, women, and aggression.* New York: Basic Books.

Campbell, A., & Muncer, S. (1987). Models of anger and aggression in the social talk of women and men. *Journal for the Theory of Social Behavior, 17,* 489–511.

Cazenave, N. A., & Zahn, M. A. (1992). Women, murder, and male domination: Police reports of domestic homicide in Chicago and Philadelphia. In E. C. Viano (Ed.), *Intimate violence: Interdisciplinary perspectives* (pp. 83–97). New York: Hemisphere.

Chesney-Lind, M. (1987). Female offenders: Paternalism revisited. In L. L. Crites & W. L. Hepperle (Eds.), *Women, the courts, and equality* (pp. 114–139). Newbury Park, CA: Sage.

Craig, M. (1988, November). *The sexually coercive college female: An investigation of attitudinal and affective characteristics.* Paper presented at the meeting of the Society for the Scientific Study of Sex, San Francisco, CA.

DeMeijer, M. (1991). The attribution of aggression and grief to body movements: The effect of sex stereotypes. *European Journal of Social Psychology, 21,* 249–259.

Dollard, J., Doob, L., Miller, N., Mowrer, O., & Sears, R. (1939). *Frustration and aggression.* New Haven: Yale University Press.

Eagly, A. H., & Steffen, V. J. (1986). Gender and aggressive behavior: A meta-analytic review of the social psychological literature. *Psychological Bulletin, 100,* 309–330.

Eisenberg, N., & Lennon, R. (1983). Sex differences in empathy and related capacities. *Psychological Bulletin, 94,* 100–131.

Ellis, L. (1991). A synthesized (biosocial) theory of rape. *Journal of Consulting and Clinical Psychology, 59,* 631–642.

Eron, L. D., Huesmann, L. R., Lefkowitz, M. M., & Walder, L. O. (1972). Does television violence cause aggression? *American Psychologist, 27,* 253–263.

Fine, M., & Gordon, S. M. (1991). Effacing the center and the margins: Life at the intersection of psychology and feminism. *Feminism & Psychology, 1,* 19–27.

Finkelhor, D., & Russell, D. (1984). Women as perpetrators: Review of the evidence. In D. Finkelhor, (Ed.), *Child sexual abuse: New theory and research* (pp. 171–187). New York: Free Press.

Frodi, A., Macaulay, J., & Thome, P. R. (1977). Are women less aggressive than men? A review of the experimental literature. *Psychological Bulletin, 84,* 634–660.

Geen, R. G. (1990). *Human aggression.* Pacific Grove, CA: Brooks/Cole.

Gelles, R. J., & Cornell, C. P. (1985). *Intimate violence in families.* Beverly Hills, CA: Sage.

Gladue, B. A. (1991a). Aggressive behavioral characteristics, hormones, and sexual orientation in men and women. *Aggressive Behavior, 17,* 313–326.

Gladue, B. A. (1991b). Qualitative and quantitative sex differences in self-reported aggressive behavioral characteristics. *Psychological Reports, 68,* 675–684.

Hall, J. A. (1984). *Nonverbal differences: Communication accuracy and expressive style.* Baltimore, MD: Johns Hopkins.

Haug, M., Benston, D., Brain, P. B., Mos, J., & Olivier, B. (Eds.). (1991). *The aggressive female.* Weesp: Duphar Publications.

Henley, N. M., & Harmon, S. (1985). The nonverbal semantics of power and gender: A perceptual study. In L. Ellyson & F. Dovidio (Eds.), *Power, dominance, and nonverbal behavior.* New York: Springer.

Hoffman, C., & Hurst, N. (1990). Gender stereotypes: Perceptions or rationalization? *Journal of Personality and Social Psychology, 58,* 197–208.

Hrdy, S. B., & Williams, G. C. (1983). Behavioral biology and the double standard. In S. K. Wasser (Ed.), *Social behaviors of female vertebrates* (pp. 3–17). New York: Academic Press.

Huesmann, L. R., Guerra, N. G., Zelli, A., & Miller, L. (1992). Differing normative beliefs about aggression for boys and girls. In K. Bjorkqvist & P. Niemela (Eds.), *Of mice and women: Aspects of female aggression* (pp. 77–87). New York: Academic Press.

Hyde, J. S. (1986). Gender differences in aggression. In J. S. Hyde & M. C. Linn (Eds.), *The psychology of gender: Advances through meta-analysis* (pp. 51–56). Baltimore: Johns Hopkins Press.

Hyde, J. S., & Linn, M. C. (1986). *The psychology of gender: Advances through meta-analysis.* Baltimore: Johns Hopkins Press.

Johnson, E. H. (1990). *The deadly emotions: The role of anger, hostility, and aggression in health and emotional well-being.* New York: Praeger.

Johnson, R. N. (1972). *Aggression in man and animals.* Philadelphia: Saunders.

Jones, A. (1980). *Women who kill.* New York: Fawcett Crest.

Kogut, D., Langley, T., & O'Neal, E. C. (1992). Gender role masculinity and angry aggression in women. *Sex Roles, 26,* 355–368.

Lagerspetz, K. M. J., Bjorkqvist, K., & Peltonen, T. (1988). Is indirect aggression typical of females? Gender differences in 11- to 12-year old children. *Aggressive Behavior, 14,* 403–414.

Lerner, G. (1986). *The creation of patriarchy.* New York: Oxford University Press.

Macaulay, J. (1985). Adding gender to aggression research: Incremental or revolutionary change? In V. O'Leary, R. K. Unger, & B. S. Wallston (Eds.), *Women, gender, and social psychology* (pp. 191–224). Hillsdale, NJ: Erlbaum.

Maccoby, E. E., & Jacklin, C. N. (1974). *The psychology of sex differences.* Stanford: Stanford University Press.

Malone, J., Tyree, A., & O'Leary, K. D. (1989). Generalization and containment: Different effects of past aggression for wives and husbands. *Journal of Marriage and the Family, 51,* 687–697.

Marecek, J., & Hare-Mustin, R. T. (1990, August). *Toward a feminist poststructural psychology: The modern self and the postmodern subject.* Paper presented at the meeting of the American Psychological Association, Boston, MA.

McCabe, A., & Lipscomb, T. J. (1988). Sex differences in children's verbal aggression. *Merrill-Palmer Quarterly, 34,* 389–401.

Mead, M. (1935). *Sex and temperament in three primitive societies.* New York: Morrow.

Miller, A. G., Gillen, B., Schlenker, B. R., & Radlove, S. (1974).The prediction and perception of obedience to authority. *Journal of Personality, 42,* 23–42.

Miller, N. E. (1941). The frustration-aggression hypothesis. *Psychological Review, 48,* 337–342.

Mitscherlich, M. (1987). *The peaceable sex: On aggression in women and men.* New York: Fromm.

Morris, A. (1987). *Women, crime, and criminal justice.* Worchester: Billing & Sons.

O'Leary, K. D. (1988). Physical aggression between spouses: A social learning theory perspective. In V. B. Van Hasselt, R. L. Morrison, A. S. Bellack, & M. Hersen (Eds.), *Handbook of family violence* (pp. 31–56). New York: Plenum Press.

O'Leary, K. D., Barling, J., Arias, I., Rosenbaum, A., Malone, J., & Tyree, A. (1989). Prevalence and stability of physical aggression between spouses: A longitudinal analysis. *Journal of Consulting and Clinical Psychology, 57,* 263–268.

Omodei, R. (1981). The myth interpretation of female crime. In S. K. Mukherjee & J. A. Scutt (Eds.), *Women and crime* (pp. 51–69). London: George Allen & Unwin.

Paul, L., & Baenninger, M. (1991). Aggression by women: Mores, myths, and methods. In R. Baenninger (Ed.), *Targets of violence and aggression* (pp. 401–441). North Holland: Elsevier Science Publishers.

Perry, D. G., Perry, L. C., & Weiss, R. J. (1989). Sex differences in the consequences that children anticipate for aggression. *Developmental Psychology, 25,* 312–319.

Richardson, D. C., Bernstein, S., & Taylor, S. P. (1979). The effect of situational contingencies on female retaliative behavior. *Journal of Personality and Social Psychology, 37,* 2044–2048.

Salzman, F. (1979). Aggression and gender: A critique of the nature-nurture question for humans. In R. Hubbard & M. Lowe (Eds.), *Genes and gender II: Pitfalls in research on sex and gender* (pp. 71–89). New York: Gordian Press.

Saunders, D. G. (1988). Wife abuse, husband abuse, or mutual combat? A feminist perspective on the empirical findings. In K. Yllo & M. Bograd (Eds.), *Feminist perspectives on wife abuse* (pp. 90–113). Newbury Park, CA: Sage.

Segall, M. H. (1989). Cultural factors, biology, and human aggression. In J. Groebel & R. Altinde (Eds.), *Aggression and war: Their biological and social bases* (pp. 173–185). Cambridge, England: Cambridge University Press.

Simon, R. J., & Landis, J. (1991). *The crimes women commit, the punishments they receive.* Lexington, MA: D. C. Heath.

Steinmetz, S. K., & Lucca, J. S. (1988). Husband battering. In V. B. Van Haaselt, R. L. Morrison, A. S. Bellack, & M. Hersen (Eds.), *Handbook of family violence* (pp. 233–246). New York: Plenum Press.

Stets, J. E., & Straus, M. A. (1990). Gender differences in reporting marital violence and its medical and psychological consequences. In M. A. Straus & R. J. Gelles (Eds.), *Physical violence in American families* (pp. 151–166). New Brunswick: Transaction.

Taylor, S. P., & Epstein, S. (1967). Aggression as a function of the interaction of the sex of the aggressor and the sex of the victim. *Journal of Personality, 35,* 474–496.

Tedeschi, J. T., Smith, R. B., & Brown, R. C. (1974). A reinterpretation of research on aggression. *Psychological Bulletin, 81,* 540–562.

Thompson, E. H., Jr. (1991). The maleness of violence in dating relationships: An appraisal of stereotypes. *Sex Roles, 24,* 261–278.

Towson, S. M. J., & Zanna, M. P. (1982). Toward a situational analysis of gender differences in aggression. *Sex Roles, 8,* 903–914.

Unger, R., & Crawford, M. (1992). *Women and gender.* New York: McGraw-Hill.

U.S. Department of Justice, Federal Bureau of Investigation. (1990). *Uniform Crime Reports.* Washington, DC: Government Printing Office.

U.S. Department of Justice, Federal Bureau of Investigation. (1992). *Uniform Crime Reports.* Washington, DC: Government Printing Office.

Walker, L. (1984). *The battered woman syndrome.* New York: Harper & Row.

Wallston, B. S., & Grady, K. E. (1985). Integrating the feminist critique and the crisis in social psychology: Another look at research methods. In V. O'Leary, R. K. Unger, & B. S. Wallston (Eds.), *Women, gender, and social psychology* (pp. 7–34). Hillsdale, NJ: Erlbaum.

White, J. W. (1983). Sex and gender issues in aggression research. In R. G. Geen & E. I. Donnerstein (Eds.), *Aggression: Theoretical and empirical reviews* (pp. 1–26). New York: Academic Press.

White, J. W. (1988). Influence tactics as a function of gender, insult, and goal. *Sex Roles, 18,* 433–448.

White, J. W., & Koss, M. P. (1991). Courtship violence: Incidence in a national sample of higher education students. *Violence and Victims, 6,* 247–256.

White, J. W., & Koss, M. P. (1993). Adolescent sexual aggression within heterosexual relationships: Prevalence, characteristics, and cause. In H. E. Barbaree, W. L. Marshall, & S. M. Hudson (Eds.), *The juvenile sex offender.* New York: Guilford.

White, J. W., Koss, M. P., & Kissling, G. (1991, June). *An empirical test of a theoretical model of courtship violence.* Paper presented at the meeting of the American Psychological Society, Washington, DC.

White, J. W., & Roufail, M. (1989). Gender and influence strategies of first choice and last resort. *Psychology of Women Quarterly, 13,* 175–189.

Williams, J. E., & Best, D. L. (1982). *Measuring sex stereotypes: A thirty-nation study.* Beverly Hills: Sage.

Yllo, K., & Bograd, M. (1988). *Feminist perspectives on wife abuse.* Newbury Park, CA: Sage.

Yoder J. D., & Kahn, A. S. (1993). Working toward an inclusive psychology of women. *American Psychologist, 48,* 846–850.

Zahn, M. (1993, April). *Homicide in the United States.* Talk given at University of North Carolina at Greensboro, Greensboro, NC.

CHECKPOINTS

1. Biases in the culture and in the research process have led to the deeply entrenched belief that women are not aggressive.
2. The inclusion of indirect and nonphysical definitions of aggression and the recognition of the interpersonal and family context for aggression reveal much higher levels of female aggression than our cultural stereotype would predict.

To prepare for reading the next section, think about this question:

1. Does who you are, as a male or female, influence how and when you help others?

GENDER AND ALTRUISM

Gender and Altruism

ALICE H. EAGLY

Does gender influence how helpful people are to one another? The issue I will consider here is the extent to which women and men are different or similar in their tendencies to help others and, more generally, to behave in ways that would be considered altruistic. I hope to convince you that there is no such thing as a sex that is helpful or altruistic. Rather, there are circumstances under which women tend to be more helpful than men and circumstances under which men tend to be more helpful than women. Gender is very important in relation to altruism, but its impact depends on the context and the particular type of altruistic behavior that we examine.

WHAT IS ALTRUISM?

Psychologists generally define altruism as behavior that is intended to help or benefit other people. To be considered truly altruistic, this behavior should be performed voluntarily and not be coerced or induced by

some external pressure. For example, if you mow your neighbor's lawn and are adequately paid for this service, you would not be altruistic. Also, to be considered altruistic, the helpful act should be performed as an end in itself and not as a means to fulfilling an ulterior personal motive. For example, if you help someone prepare for a math exam only because you want this person to feel obligated to help you write a history paper, your behavior would not be considered altruistic (but expedient or perhaps even manipulative). If you instead help this person merely because you want to be helpful or believe that helping is the "right thing to do," you would be considered genuinely altruistic. Not surprisingly, this definition of altruism contrasts sharply with psychologists' definitions of aggression. Whereas altruism is behavior intended to *help* others, aggression is behavior intended to *harm* others. Altruism and aggression are thus opposites—the good and the bad of interpersonal behavior.

Some psychologists have questioned whether behavior is ever *truly* altruistic if we take seriously the idea that altruistic acts do not fulfill some personal goal of the altruistic person. After all, helpful behavior that does not provide any obvious extrinsic (or external) gain for the helper can provide some intrinsic (or internal) gain. People may feel good or moral when they are helpful and feel bad or guilty when they fail to help. To the extent that people have internalized moral rules about appropriate behavior, they can give themselves internal psychological rewards for conforming to these rules and punishments for deviating from them. Some psychologists maintain that people behave altruistically *in order to* feel good and moral (or avoid feeling bad and guilty) and thus are actually behaving egoistically when they seem to be behaving altruistically. In contrast, other psychologists argue that people can be genuinely altruistic because, at least sometimes, feeling good about oneself is only a by-product of altruistic acts that are intended only to be helpful to others. I will not attempt to resolve this fundamental philosophical and psychological issue but suggest that we consider as altruistic any helpful behaviors that are not coerced or intended to obtain some external reward or avoid some external punishment.

GENDER ROLES' MESSAGES ABOUT ALTRUISM

To understand whether and how altruistic behavior may be shaped by gender in Western society, we need to consider the messages about helping and altruism that are embedded in gender roles. Both the female gender role and the male gender role have the potential to foster altruistic behavior.

Female Gender Role

I will first consider the female gender role because its implications for helpful behavior are probably somewhat more obvious than those of the male gender role. Think for a moment about the female gender role—that is, about society's rules about how to be a good and admirable woman. Do these rules encompass a demand to behave altruistically? Certainly they do—women are expected to be kind, nurturant, compassionate, and caring. Selfishness and lack of compassion are considered serious deficiencies in the character of women. Many social scientists and feminist writers have argued that women are expected to place the needs of others, especially those of family members, before their own. These obligations include caring for the emotional needs of others—being a dedicated listener who bolsters others' morale and sympathizes with their troubles. These burdens may also include delivering routine forms of personal service, such as doing favors and running errands. More generally, the female role includes the demand to facilitate the progress of other people toward their goals, especially the progress of friends, intimates, and family members.

There is an abundance of empirical evidence that women are expected to be caring and compassionate. In particular, studies of gender stereotypes have shown that women are rated as more helpful than men and also as kinder, more compassionate, and more able to devote themselves to others. This aspect of the female stereotype is prescriptive, as shown by the fact that kind and compassionate personality attributes are rated as *desirable* in women and as more desirable in women than men. In general, people think about women as kind and compassionate and believe that it is a good thing for women to have these characteristics.

Male Gender Role

What about the male gender role? What are its messages about altruism? Although men do not have the burden of being kind, nurturant, and compassionate to the same extent that women do, they are expected to be altruistic in other ways. There are two altruistic themes that are particularly salient to the male gender role: I will refer to these themes as *heroism* and *chivalry*. There also seems to be a demand for men to be helpful in practical ways that involve fixing things and solving certain kinds of practical, technical problems.

Let us first consider heroism because it is a theme that Western culture has long incorporated into its images of ideal male behavior. The ideal man, as described in literature and myth, is very often the noble hero. The hero is someone who engages in the altruistic action of saving others from harm or of fighting for the general good; the hero performs these behaviors at some risk to himself of injury or death. The prototypical hero is the man who takes great risks in battle, especially if he is successful in reaching his objective or in saving others from harm. Although heroes are extremely important in warfare, peacetime offers some opportunities for heroism. Thus, a peacetime hero might rescue others in one of many types of life-threatening situations, such as an auto crash, a house or apartment fire, or a potential drowning.

Direct empirical evidence that men are expected to be heroic is not easy to find, probably because opportunities to be heroic are rare in most people's lives. Most of you will live your whole life without, for example, having an opportunity to rescue someone from a car crash or carry someone from a burning building. Because heroism is by definition unusual behavior carried out in an extreme situation, the term "heroic" does not appear to be stereotypic of men. However, research on gender stereotypes has found that male-stereotypic traits include certain tendencies that would provide a potential for heroic behavior. For example, willingness to take risks, adventurousness, calmness in a crisis, and ability to stand up well under pressure are characteristics that are ascribed to men more than women and are viewed as more desirable in men.

Now, to turn to the second of my two themes about masculine altruism, let us consider chivalry. The term "chivalry" may seem somewhat medieval—wasn't it knights in shining armor who were expected to be chivalrous? The Oxford English Dictionary (1971) defines chivalrous behavior as "characterized by pure and noble gallantry, honor, courtesy, and disinterested devotion to the cause of the weak or oppressed." This definition seems quite dated. The tradition of male chivalry had its origins in the chivalric code taken by medieval knights. These knights took oaths that included vows to protect the weak and defenseless, to respect the honor of women, to fight for the general welfare of all, to live for honor and glory, and so forth. The influence of this chivalric tradition on conceptions of ideal male behavior in Western society has been well documented by historians.

If rules of chivalrous conduct are to some extent alive and well in contemporary society, these rules should induce men to engage in certain specific types of helpful behavior. Particularly relevant to an analysis of gender is the stipulation in the chivalric code that men direct courteous and protective acts toward women because it was presumed that women were weak and defenseless and deserved protection. Of course, the knight in shining armor did not extend his protection to *all* women but to women (or "ladies") of his own social class.

In modern society, where might we observe social norms or conventions that obligate men to be especially protective and respectful of women? Consider commonplace rules about what behavior is polite or courteous. These rules have been written down in twentieth-century etiquette handbooks by such people as the redoubtable Emily Post and Amy Vanderbilt and the more contemporary Miss Manners (whose humorous column on etiquette is carried by many newspapers). These authors describe the sort of behavior that is considered good and proper in "polite society." In these books, you could read that a man is expected to open the car door for a woman, especially when on a date. Emily Post's 1984 statement on this practice is the following: "The custom of a man's opening the door and assisting a woman into a car is still correct—in fact some women feel slighted if the gesture is not made." Is the woman in this situation too weak to perform this action for herself? Well, not exactly. Instead, the man and woman are engaging in a stylized behavior that they probably consider "polite."

Consider too that rules of etiquette say that the man is supposed to walk on the outside of the sidewalk next to the street, ostensibly to protect his female companion from splashes or other dangers that might come from that direction. On this subject, Miss Manners (Martin, 1990) wrote: "When they are walking outdoors, American ladies take the side away from the street." A man is also supposed to help a woman put on her coat; he is supposed to open the doors of buildings for her, and even order for her in restaurants and pay for her meal. Traditionally, men stand up when a woman enters a room and stay standing until she sits down. A woman is not supposed to pour her own alcoholic drink when one or more men are present. On this subject, Miss Manners (Martin, 1990) wrote: "Ladies do not pour their own wine when gentlemen are present. They hold their empty wine glasses casually in front of their noses while staring fixedly at the nearest gentleman, who then falls all over himself to do it for them." Rules such as these have eroded considerably in modern society and were practiced much more fully by people who were higher in the social-class system.

Empirical evidence that these rules of chivalrous conduct are still intact to some extent can be found in a recent questionnaire study by Mary Harris (1992). In this study female and male university students reported on their experiences of giving and receiving courteous behaviors. Harris's findings confirmed that even now it is men rather than women who are expected to engage in at least certain courteous behaviors, particularly opening doors for another person and paying for someone (for example, for the person's meal).

Feminists have often criticized these chivalrous rules of polite conduct. The reasons for this disapproval may be fairly obvious to you. Such rules seem to imply that women are the weaker sex, the sex that needs protection and special favors. These behaviors place men in a more dominant and controlling role— as the person who opens doors, orders in restaurants, initiates dates, and so forth. Merely showing "good manners" in the traditional model may thus help preserve the imbalance of power and authority between the sexes and foster passivity in women.

Do you approve or disapprove of chivalrous courtesy? Although some women agree with feminist objections to chivalrous conduct, other women disagree. In fact, female students who have taken this course in the past have sometimes been very vocal in their support of men's chivalrous behavior. These women often argued that they prefer that men show good manners in these ways because they signify *respect* for a woman. The reasoning is that a man who opens doors, holds a woman's coat, and obeys the traditional rules of polite behavior displays that he is respectful of the women he accompanies. Moreover, many people maintain that these behaviors are merely polite and should be performed equally by both sexes. However, few women in fact hold coats for able-bodied men or open car doors for them.

The Harris questionnaire examined university students' agreement or disagreement with the feminist analysis. Harris found some tendency for these respondents to rate polite behaviors as condescending or patronizing, particularly one sequence of restaurant behavior, namely, having a companion ask you what you want to eat in a restaurant and then ordering for you. Although regarding courteous behaviors as patronizing would be in keeping with the feminist analysis, Harris's research suggested that most students view most courteous behaviors as merely courteous and not as condescending or patronizing.

It is easy to get into arguments about chivalry because chivalrous behavior conveys two kinds of meanings simultaneously: a superiority and dominance on the part of the person who behaves chivalrously and a true helpfulness and respect for the person the act is directed toward. This dual meaning makes many women ambivalent about chivalrous behavior. It is thus possible for a woman to both resent *and* appreciate chivalrous behaviors that are directed toward her. In addition, women may disapprove of chivalry on the job, where gender is supposed to be irrelevant, yet approve of it on a date, where gender is more likely to be important. And many men are aware that women may have reservations about the desirability of these forms of etiquette; therefore, men sometimes express confusion about whether they should follow the traditional rules of polite behavior.

Predictions from Analysis of Gender Roles

Given our analysis of the rules that gender roles convey about altruistic behavior, what might a psychologist predict about sex-related differences in altruistic behavior? I doubt that anyone who thinks about the full range of possible altruistic behaviors would predict that one sex is *generally* more helpful than the other sex. The absence of such a simple, general prediction does not of course mean that gender is unimportant. Rather, gender roles may shape altruistic behavior so that women and men specialize in different types of helpfulness and are especially helpful in different types of situations. Consistent with the female gender role, women might tend to be compassionate and self-sacrificing in close relationships—with friends, partners, and family members. Women might specialize in nurturing others and caring for their emotional needs. They may more often reach out to people who are ill, depressed, or lonely. Certainly, not all women would behave in these ways, of course; but these tendencies may be more common in women than men.

What forms of altruism might be more common in men than women? Men might be self-sacrificing in emergency situations that allow for heroism. They may be somewhat more willing to place themselves in danger of physical injury or even death, in order to rescue another person. In addition, men might behave in polite, protective ways, especially toward women of their own social group. Men might also be helpful in practical ways—fixing things around the house and solving practical problems.

EMPIRICAL RESEARCH ON ALTRUISTIC BEHAVIOR

Now I will consider empirical evidence that women and men specialize in different forms of altruism. As I will show, some traditions of psychological research tend to display women's helpfulness, and other traditions display men's helpfulness.

Research on Close Relationships Reveals Female Emotional Suppportiveness

To find evidence of the helpfulness of women, where might we look? If there is truth to the cultural stereotype that women are kind and compassionate, these tendencies might play out most clearly in friendships, marital and partner relationships, and close relationships more generally. Women might provide more social support and sympathy in such relationships because this is what compassion and kindness are all about.

Evidence of this supportiveness can be found, first of all, in studies of friendship. Many researchers have compared same-sex friendships among women with those among men. They have found that women's friendships with other women tend to be more cooperative, intimate, and emotionally expressive than men's friendships with one another. Men's friendships, in contrast, tend to be built around somewhat competitive activities such as career-related activity and sports to a greater extent than women's friendships are. In men's friendships, trust and empathy are important too, but their priorities seem to be somewhat different than women's, with greater emphasis on shared activities. Thus, the prototype of male friendship is business associates who play golf or tennis together. The prototype of female friendship is women who get together to talk, perhaps at a restaurant or one of their homes. Women tend to spend time with female friends in ways that provide opportunities for lots of talking and sharing of experiences. It follows that women are more likely to provide one another with emotional support and informal counseling for personal problems. This same point about women's supportiveness has also been made by studies of college roommates. Female students report a higher level of social support from their roommates than male students do from their roommates.

In a typical study of same-sex friendships (Davidson & Duberman, 1982), unmarried women and men ranging in age from 18 to 35 described their relationship with their best friend and gave detailed accounts of their typical conversations with the best friend. Although all of the participants in this study were white, they came from all social classes. Analysis of these records showed that the men talked mainly about topical issues, such as current events, work, sports, movies, or politics. The women talked less about topical issues than the men and somewhat more about personal problems and considerably more about the relationship with the best friend. In general, men seem to emphasize companionship and carrying out activities together over self-disclosure and emotional expressiveness.

Psychologists have also examined married couples in order to determine the extent to which spouses provide emotional support to one another. Of course spouses generally do support each other emotionally, as long as their marriage is not very troubled. However, husbands report more support and affirmation from their wives than wives do from their husbands. It seems that in marriages as in friendships, women are the social-support experts, and people turn to them when they are distressed. The emphasis in the male role on independence, autonomy, and emotional control makes it difficult for men to be providers of social support (see Barbee et al., 1993). Consequently, women apparently rely a good deal on their female friends and relatives for social support and only to some extent on their husbands; married men tend to turn to their wives.

These differences in male and female behavior have also been reflected in studies of self-disclosure—the sharing of intimate, personal information with another person. People differ in the extent to which they share personal information with others and, of course, are generally more willing to share personal details with family members and "best friends." A recent review of research on self-disclosure found that in general women disclosed more intimate information to their female friends than men disclosed to their male friends (Dindia & Allen, 1992). This disclosure of intimate information often contributes to emotional supportiveness in relationships.

Experiments on Helping Behavior Display Male Heroism and Chivalry

Now let's turn to another, very different type of empirical research. For many years, experimental social psychologists have carried out research on what they call *helping behavior*. Although the term "helping behavior" might seem to be quite inclusive, what in fact has been studied by these investigators are mainly two types of behaviors: (1) rescuing or intervention behavior in emergency situations in which another person is in need (sometimes called studies of bystander intervention) and (2) everyday polite behaviors such as opening doors and picking up something that a person has inadvertently dropped. These behaviors have been examined almost exclusively in brief encounters with strangers in field and laboratory situations and not in long-term role relationships

within families, small groups, or organizations. These two types of helping behavior, bystander intervention and stylized polite behaviors, should remind you of the two altruistic themes that I have emphasized in relation to the male gender role, namely, heroism and chivalry. The heroic man can be a bystander who intervenes; the chivalrous man is polite in certain specific ways, especially toward women. Given the link between bystander intervention and heroism and between chivalry and polite behaviors, you probably will not be surprised when I show you that in general this type of research tends to display ways in which men tend to be more helpful than women.

Examples of Laboratory and Field Experiments on Helping Behavior This tradition of research on helping behavior started with a study by Darley and Latané, which was published in 1968. This experiment was inspired by the case of Kitty Genovese, who was murdered by a man armed with a knife. The attack took place outside of her apartment building in 1964 in a middle-class area of Queens, New York. At least 38 of her neighbors heard or actually watched this attack, which continued for 35 minutes, but none of them called the police until her attacker had departed. This particular tragic incident became famous in part because of an award-winning story about it that appeared in *The New York Times*. Unfortunately, incidents of this type, involving a shocking failure of people to help, have continued to occur from time to time. You have probably read descriptions of such incidents in newspapers.

Darley and Latané conducted a laboratory experiment in order to examine the willingness of bystanders to help someone in need. They designed the experiment to emulate those features of the Kitty Genovese incident that they believed inhibited people from helping. In particular, they thought that having many potential helpers in the situation would decrease helping because no individual would feel uniquely obligated to intervene and in addition each person would reason that someone else must have already taken appropriate action. In the experiment, each subject believed that he or she was a participant in a discussion group whose members were separated

TABLE 1   Percentages of Bystanders Giving Help to Confederate Who Dropped Coins or Pencils in an Elevator

Sex of Bystanders	Sex of Confederate	Columbus, OH	Seattle, WA	Atlanta, GA
Female	Male	23%	16%	7%
	Female	23%	26%	26%
Male	Male	25%	32%	12%
	Female	32%	39%	70%

Source: Adapted from Latané and Dabbs (1975).

in cubicles but listening to one another by means of earphones. Actually they were listening to a recording on which another person who was ostensibly part of the discussion group became very distressed as he went into an epileptic seizure and called for help. The appropriate altruistic action for the subject would be to leave the cubicle and seek out the distressed person. The main finding of interest to Darley and Latané was that the larger the group that was participating in the discussion, the longer it took for the victim to receive help. Their interpretation of this effect of group size was that a *diffusion of responsibility* to help takes place among groups of people. From the perspective of our analysis of gender and altruism, it is important to know that the male subjects were somewhat more likely to help the seizure victim than the female subjects were.

Now let me give you an example of an experiment by Latané and Dabbs (1975) that construed helping as polite behavior, namely, picking up pencils or coins that a person dropped in an elevator. In these field experiments, female and male students who were confederates of the researchers went to elevators in office buildings in three cities: Columbus, Ohio; Seattle, Washington; and Atlanta, Georgia. These confederates dropped coins or pencils, seemingly by accident. The other people riding in the elevator became the subjects. The confederates merely kept track of how many people helped pick up these objects; they also recorded the sex of the persons who helped and did not help.

As you should note in Table 1, men helped more than women in this situation, and women received more help, especially from men. However, these trends were weak in Columbus, stronger in Seattle, and very strong in Atlanta. This research examined a helping act that seems to be as appropriate for women as men and that poses no barriers of skill or danger. Still, the study revealed some typically sex-related aspects of findings from field experiments on everyday polite behavior: specifically, this sort of helping is most commonly directed by men toward women and is less common in other types of dyads (that is, directed by men toward men, women toward women, or women toward men). In this experiment, the regional difference in the extent to which these acts were sex-related is remarkable; perhaps the Atlanta data tell us that a more traditional form of gendered politeness prevails in the South (or prevailed when this study was conducted in the 1970s).

Review of Research on Gender and Helping Behavior
Working with Maureen Crowley, I reviewed 172 studies of helping behavior to examine the extent to which these behaviors were sex-related (Eagly & Crowley, 1986). We believed that we would find men somewhat more helpful than women if we averaged across all of these studies because, as I have explained, this research consists primarily of studies of bystander intervention and polite behavior in relationships between strangers. As we have already seen, the helpfulness of women is particularly apparent in close relationships, which are not studied in this particular research tradition.

The experiments that we located examined a very wide array of helping behaviors (and included the studies that I have already mentioned to illustrate this tradition). For example, studies of bystander intervention examined helping a man who fell in the subway, stopping a brutal fight between two subjects, helping a person with car trouble on a busy street, stopping someone from stealing a student's belongings in the library, reporting someone who had shoplifted at a store, helping a woman who was apparently sexually assaulted in a campus building, and helping a female student who was apparently choking on something. Studies of polite behaviors examined helping a woman whose groceries had fallen at a store, helping a woman pick up packages she had dropped, returning the act of opening doors in a building, mailing a stamped letter left in a phone booth, calling a garage for a person with car problems, telling the time to someone who requested it in a public place, and helping a deaf person make a phone call. Other experiments involved donation behaviors such as donating money to the Leukemia Society to a woman who comes to the door, giving money to a panhandler on campus, and donating blood to a hemophiliac who has been injured. Still other experiments examined acts of volunteerism: Research participants had opportunities to volunteer to spend time with retarded children, to bake cookies or give money for an ecology project, and to be a subject in a psychology experiment.

As we expected, we found that in general in this research literature men helped more than women did and that people were more helpful to women than men. Especially strong in these studies was the tendency for men to be helpful to women. Nevertheless, the findings of these experiments varied quite a lot. In fact, in 38 percent of the experiments, the sex difference in helping went in the female direction, with women helping more than men, and in the other 62 percent of the experiments, men helped more than women.

As you might guess, certain circumstances fostered the tendency for men to be especially helpful. In some situations, women tended to feel less competent than men to perform the helping act (for example, changing a tire) or thought that some of these acts would put them in danger (for example, picking up a hitchhiker). In our review, we were able to show that the tendency for men to be more helpful than women was stronger to the extent that women felt less competent to help or less comfortable in helping or they believed that they would place themselves in danger if they helped.

There were some other very interesting findings in our review of this research. Specifically, men tended to be more helpful than women to the extent that onlookers were present. Sometimes the helper was merely alone with the victim or person who requested help; sometimes there were onlookers—for example, in a subway car or on a city street. Although the presence of many people may inhibit helping, as suggested by the idea that responsibility can be diffused among a group of people, the presence of an audience seems to foster a sex difference in helping behavior. We believe that tendency for men to be especially more helpful than women with onlookers present makes sense because the presence of an audience should make social norms about helping more powerful influences on behavior. In other words, people are more likely to "do the right thing" if they are under surveillance by others. Because most of these experiments involved behaviors that are mildly heroic or merely polite and the male gender role has particularly salient rules about these types of behaviors, an audience should encourage men to help in ways that are consistent with the masculine role.

Another finding in our review was that men tended to be more helpful than women if the opportunity to help came in the form of a need that presented itself rather than an explicit request. For example, a need is merely present if you observe someone who seems to be ill or has dropped something. In contrast, a request to help might consist of a person asking for a charity donation or asking for someone to make a phone call. In the situation in which a need is present, a helper has to take some initiative or show some assertiveness to intervene, whereas in the situation in which a request is made, the helper can merely acquiesce or be compliant. It is thus possible that this tendency for men to be especially more helpful than women in the presence of a need rather than a request may reflect some greater assertiveness on the part of men.

I have described some of the conditions that make it likely that men help more than women in experimental research on helping behavior. When one or more of these conditions are absent, the tendency for men to be especially helpful weakens and may reverse so that women are more helpful than men. Thus, when women feel at least as competent and comfortable to help as men do and think that the helping situation is not dangerous, they may help as much as or more than men. For example, in particular studies included in our review, women were shown to be more helpful than men in volunteering to spend time with retarded children, helping a man with a neck brace who fell in a campus building, and calling a garage for a person with car trouble.

Awards from the Carnegie Hero Fund Commission Display Male Heroism

I have located some archival data on heroism that yield additional insight into the extent to which heroic behavior is sex-related (see Eagly & Crowley, 1986). These data consist of the records of the Carnegie Hero Fund Commission, which was established by Andrew Carnegie in 1904 to recognize outstanding acts of heroism performed in the United States or Canada. A hero was defined for these purposes as someone who risked or sacrificed his or her life in saving or attempting to save someone's life. These acts of heroism are much more extreme and remarkable than the bystander interventions studied in social psychologists' field experiments. Bystander intervention rarely places a helper in serious danger. In contrast, to win a Carnegie medal, a person must have truly risked his or her life.

The winners each receive a Carnegie Medal and under some circumstances a monetary award or a grant for education or training. It is noteworthy that the Carnegie Hero Fund excludes from awards certain classes of people. Specifically, they exclude people such as firefighters whose duties in their regular vocations require heroism, and they similarly exclude people in military service. Excluded also are parents who rescue family members, except in unusual or very outstanding cases. They also exclude children

who are deemed too young to understand the risks that are involved.

Women were explicitly included as potential recipients of these awards from the beginning. Contained in the original charter of the Carnegie Hero Fund Commission was the following statement: "Whenever heroism is displayed by man or woman in saving human life, the Fund applies" (Carnegie, 1907, p. 11). We cannot be sure that these medals were awarded on a gender-fair basis, but it seems that Andrew Carnegie intended that they be so awarded.

Most of the heroic incidents of Carnegie medalists involved acts such as rescuing people from drowning, fires, or physical assault. A typical incident is the following:

Carnegie Medal awarded to John Rex Fidler, who saved Paul J. Twyman and others from burning, Bridgeville, California, March 10, 1982. Paul, 9, and his four brothers and sisters were in their bedroom when fire broke out in an adjoining room. Fidler, 31, mechanic, was alerted and ran to the house, where he broke a window of the bedroom and pulled one of the children out. He entered the room through the window and found three more of the children, whom he handed outside to their father. After climbing outside, Fidler then re-entered the house three more times to search for the fifth child. Dense smoke and intense heat forced him out each time. The fifth child died in the fire; Paul and the other children were not burned. Fidler was treated for smoke inhalation, but he recovered. (*Carnegie Hero Fund Commission Annual Report,* 1983, #6672)

Here is another incident.

Carnegie Medal awarded to Helen Gail Shuler, who saved Benjamin E. Wolf from assault, Collegeville, Pennsylvania, August 24, 1982. A man armed with a 12-inch butcher knife entered a lounge and threatened the five persons present, including Wolf, 54, who required crutches. The others, including Miss Shuler, 36, waitress, fled. Wolf fell as he attempted to flee the assailant, who then poised himself over Wolf, raising the knife. Miss

Shuler ran back to the assailant and grabbed his arm and waist, screaming. The assailant broke away, cutting Miss Shuler as he did so. He ran from the lounge. Miss Shuler recovered. (*Carnegie Hero Fund Commission Annual Report,* 1983, #6720)

When I obtained data from the Carnegie Hero Commission in 1986, they informed me that they had warded 6,955 medals, of which 161 (or 9 percent) had been awarded to women. Men had received 91 percent of the awards. These data suggest that extraordinary heroism is very sex-linked, with men more commonly being the risk-takers. Women do sometimes risk their lives in these ways, but it is less common.

Distributions of the Sexes into Altruistic Social Roles May Display Female and Male Altruism

We have so far looked at altruism that is not part of one's occupational life. However, many people help others because their job requires that they do so. For example, most people who enter burning buildings are ineligible for Carnegie medals because they are firefighters, whose jobs require that they do so. People with occupations involving serious risk of death or injury would include law enforcement officers and members of the armed forces as well as firefighters. Most, if not all, paid occupations that entail a very direct threat to one's life are male-dominated. There has been considerable resistance to allowing women to enter these occupations—for example, to serve in combat roles in the military. In contrast, women are especially well represented in paid occupations that focus on some form of routine personal service. Over half of all women are in clerical and service occupations, and women with professional positions are predominantly in teaching, nursing, and social work.

Whether behavior that is part of one's job should be considered altruistic is an interesting question. Our definition of altruism excluded behavior that brings an external reward. Of course, the fire fighter and nurse receive paychecks, although these occupations are not very highly paid. Physicians *are* highly paid, yet they also help the sick. Should we consider nurses

more altruistic than physicians because they are paid considerably less for their efforts? I won't attempt to resolve this kind of question, but I want you to notice that most occupations that require personal service *for relatively low pay* are female-dominated.

When thinking about altruism and social roles, we must remember that the domestic role is highly service-oriented. The occupant of this role devotes herself (or himself) to caring for family members, particularly for children, and keeping the household running for the benefit of a family. Because the role is unpaid, it might be regarded as particularly altruistic. The role of husband and father ordinarily involves a considerably smaller burden of direct, personal service to family members. As we learn when we study the division of labor in the home, housework and childcare are performed mainly by women, even when they are employed outside the home. Yet, among the tasks that husbands and fathers do perform is the occasional "fixing" chore such as repairing the lawn mower or perhaps the toaster or the car. The tendency for people to think of men as helping by carrying out these types of practical chores thus has some basis in fact.

Family roles often encompass caring for family members who are ill. Especially among middle-aged and older adults, these responsibilities may include caring for chronically ill relatives. Women are more common as caregivers for the sick or disabled. For example, a recent study of primary caregivers for family members who were diagnosed with Alzheimer's disease found that 71 percent of the caregivers were female (Schulz, Williamson, Morycz, & Biegel, 1992).

Community service in volunteer roles is also very relevant to understanding altruism. Many citizens perform community service, donate money to altruistic causes, and join organizations that provide public service or engage in advocacy on social issues. Especially in earlier decades, when women were not employed outside the home as commonly as they are now, many women performed substantial amounts of volunteer work. Of course, many employed people also volunteer for community service, and students volunteer as well. Community service remains important to many citizens, men as well as women.

REASONS WHY WOMEN AND MEN SPECIALIZE IN DIFFERENT FORMS OF ALTRUISM

I have reviewed evidence of several types showing that women and men specialize in somewhat different forms of altruistic behavior. Gender is very important in the altruistic domain, even though it is not sensible to claim that there is a general sex difference in altruism. To the extent that people regard men or women as the helpful sex, they are probably bringing to mind particular types of helping behavior and particular types of situations. If they think that women are altruistic, they may be thinking about the emotional supportiveness of friends or the domestic role; if they think that men are altruistic, they may be thinking about heroic or chivalrous behaviors. Yet, the evidence that I have given you that particular forms of altruism are sex-related raises the deeper issue of *why* altruism is gendered. Why don't men specialize in emotional support as much as women do? Why don't women risk their lives as much as men do in emergency situations?

One approach to answering these questions involves taking moral rules into account. When people are truly altruistic, they help others because they believe that helping is the right thing to do. Perhaps the behavioral differences in altruism reflect the fact that men and women define "the right thing" differently; in other words, they may to some extent have a different set of moral principles.

The issue of gender and morality is an old one in psychology. One of Freud's claims was that women have a less-developed superego (or conscience) because girls do not go through the same psychosexual stages that boys do. In a relatively recent analysis of morality, Carol Gillian proposed that there are two ways of thinking about moral issues: a system of morality based on rights and abstract principles, and a system based on caring and responsibility to others (e.g., Gilligan & Attanucci, 1988). These two systems are sometimes called the *justice* and the *care* perspectives. Gilligan argued that men adopt the justice orientation more often than women do and that women adopt the care orientation more often than men do. Gilligan further argued that these orienta-

tions are equally admirable and that neither is superior: A concern with justice does not reflect a higher type of morality than a concern with care, as it did in Kohlberg's system. To support her claim that women are relatively more concerned with care and men with justice, Gilligan examined the decisions of people facing real-life dilemmas, such as women facing a decision about abortion.

Gilligan's work has proven to be quite controversial, with Gilligan and some other psychologists producing research supporting her analysis and other psychologists producing less-supportive research. Whatever the empirical support for the claim that women and men differ in their moral orientations, Gilligan's theory is provocative and relevant to the sex differences that we have observed in altruistic behavior. The care orientation toward morality may underlie women's tendency to be emotionally supportive in close relationships. Moreover, the care orientation may be one determinant of women's tendency to choose social roles that entail direct service to others: for example, the domestic role, helping professions, and community service.

Interesting as Gilligan's analysis is, it may beg the question of why women and men differ in their altruistic behavior because her analysis merely says that women and men differ in their underlying moral orientations. But why should moral orientations be related to gender? Are there more ultimate causes of sex differences in both altruism and morality?

The more ultimate cause that I have emphasized throughout this lecture is *gender roles,* the rules that a society has for behaving as a woman or man. Gender roles convey important messages about altruism—messages that are different for women and men. I regard the moral orientations that Gilligan has described, justice and care, as one aspect of gender roles. Thus, Gilligan's care orientation is consistent with the communal themes of the female gender role, and the justice orientation may be consistent with the agentic themes of the male gender role.

One particularly important aspect of gender roles is the support they lend to a general difference in status and power between the sexes. Because the specific roles that men occupy in organizations and in families have more power and authority than the roles occupied by women, gender roles include rules that encourage men to act as more dominant people and women to act as more submissive people. The messages about status and power that are embedded in gender roles in turn have implications for altruistic behavior. For example, as I have already noted, the patterning of chivalrous behaviors reflects status and power relations between women and men. Men's chivalrous behaviors are dominant and controlling and reflect their higher status. Women's acceptance of these behaviors may reflect their subordination and need for protection.

This analysis in terms of sex differences in power and status is relevant to other aspects of altruism as well. Preserving friendly social relationships, as reflected in women's emotional supportiveness, may be more important to women than men because of women's lesser power. Women may need to cement bonds with others through kindness and compassion, given their relative lack of other forms of power over others. Gilligan's care orientation to morality may also reflect women's lesser power and status rather than gender *per se.*

To explain why women and men specialize in different forms of altruistic behavior, many psychologists would point to socialization. In general, people are socialized to accept the gender role that the society prescribes for them. In particular, many feminist psychologists have argued that female socialization features an emphasis on learning to be caring and responsible to other people (Chodorow, 1978; Miller, 1976). In contrast, male socialization may emphasize as-

sertiveness, which may prepare men for bystander intervention, and chivalrous protectiveness, which may prepare them for certain types of polite behaviors.

Evolutionary psychologists would make still other arguments about the origins of sex-related altruistic behavior. In particular, they would argue that men have the occasional burden of endangering their own lives because they are the more expendable sex in terms of the maintenance of a society. Women must be preserved as the childbearers if the society itself is to be preserved. Another factor underlying the physical risk often required to behave heroically is women's lesser physical strength. The average woman is less able than the average man to successfully perform rescuing behaviors that are extremely demanding physically (for example, carrying an adult from a burning building).

There are probably several reasons why altruism is related to gender, and it would be dogmatic to claim that any one reason is the key to understanding why many of these behaviors are correlated with sex. Because we do not know the ultimate reasons why many altruistic behaviors are gendered, it is difficult to predict whether women and men will become more similar in these aspects of their behavior. If these sex differences reflect primarily status and power relations between the sexes, then as women gain more equal status to men, these behaviors should become less sex-related. To the extent that altruistic behaviors reflect more intrinsic sex differences (for example, men's greater physical strength), men and women may continue to specialize in different forms of altruism.

REFERENCES

Barbee, A. P., Cunningham, M. R., Winstead, B. A., Derlega, V. J., Gulley, M. R., Yankeelov, P. A., & Druen, P. B. (1993). Effects of gender role expectations on the social support process. *Journal of Social Issues, 49*(3), 175–190.

Carnegie, A. (1907). Deed of trust. In Carnegie Hero Fund Commission, *Annual report* (pp. 9–11). Pittsburgh, PA: Author.

Chodorow, N. (1978). *The reproduction of mothering: Psychoanalysis and the sociology of gender.* Berkeley: University of California Press.

Darley, J. M., & Latané, B. (1968). Bystander intervention in emergencies: Diffusion of responsibility. *Journal of Personality and Social Psychology, 8*, 377–383.

Davidson, L. R., & Duberman, L. (1982). Friendship: Communication and interfactional patterns in same-sex dyads. *Sex Roles, 8,* 809–822.

Dindia, K., & Allen, M. (1992). Sex differences in self-disclosure: A meta-analysis. *Psychological Bulletin, 113,* 106–124.

Eagly, A. H., & Crowley, M. (1986). Gender and helping behavior: A meta-analytic review of the social-psychological literature. *Psychological Bulletin, 100,* 283–308.

Gilligan, C., & Attanucci, J. (1988). Two moral orientations: Gender differences and similarities. *Merrill-Palmer Quarterly, 34,* 223–237.

Harris, M. B. (1992). When courtesy fails: Gender roles and polite behavior. *Journal of Applied Social Psychology, 22,* 1399–1416.

Latané, B., & Dabbs, J. M., Jr. (1975). Sex, group size and helping in three cities. *Sociometry, 38,* 180–194.

Martin, J. (1990). *Miss Manners' guide for the turn-of-the-millennium.* New York: Simon & Schuster.

Miller, J. B. (1976). *Toward a new psychology of women.* Boston: Beacon Press.

Post, E. L. (1984). *Emily Post's etiquette* (14th ed). New York: Harper & Row.

Schulz, R., Williamson, G. M., Morycz, R. K., & Biegel, D. E. (1992). Costs and benefits of providing care to Alzheimer's patients. In S. Spacapan & S. Oskamp (Eds.). *Helping and being helped: Naturalistic studies* (pp. 153–181). Newbury Park, CA: Sage.

SUGGESTED READINGS

Eagly, A. H., & Crowley, M. (1986). Gender and helping behavior: A meta-analytic review of the social-psychological literature. *Psychological Bulletin, 100,* 283–308.

Gilligan, C., & Attanucci, J. (1988).Two moral orientations: Gender differences and similarities. *Merrill-Palmer Quarterly, 34,* 223–237.

Harris, M. B. (1992). When courtesy fails: Gender roles and polite behavior. *Journal of Applied Social Psychology, 22,* 1399–1416.

Martin, J. (1990). *Miss Manners' guide for the turn-of-the-millennium.* New York: Simon & Schuster.

CHECKPOINTS

1. Women's helpfulness is often underestimated because the measurement of altruism has focused on scenarios in which men are more likely to help others.

2. Women are more likely to be helpful in private settings, in interpersonal relationships, when help is requested, or when physical risk is minimized. Men show greater rates of helping in public settings, in settings with potential risk, or in settings with strangers. Both men and women are more likely to offer help in areas in which they are competent.

Gendered Behavior in a Social Context

QUESTIONS FOR REFLECTION

1. In what ways is the study of sex differences in behavior central to understanding gender?
2. Think of another area that contains stereotypes about sex differences. What aspects of circumstances, gender beliefs, and gender scripts might predict differences versus similarities?

CHAPTER APPLICATION

1. Choose one of the areas of social behavior discussed in this chapter, and for two days, keep track of all the examples you encounter of the target behavior. Identify how you defined the target behavior, the settings in which the examples occurred, and any relevant gender role prescriptions. Does the Deaux and Major model explain your examples?

CHAPTER NINE

Gender, Cognition, and Education

QUESTIONS TO THINK ABOUT

1. How do we define and measure cognitive abilities?
2. Why is it important to take diversity into account when defining and measuring cognitive abilities?
3. Why is the study of sex differences in cognitive abilities controversial?
4. What is the research evidence for sex differences in math achievement?
5. Why is math seen as a masculine endeavor?
6. How can the educational environment be changed to promote math achievement for girls?
7. What is the status of gender equity in American education?
8. How does gender bias in education impact the classroom experiences of boys and girls?
9. What solutions have been proposed to reduce gender bias in education?

"In the most intelligent races, as among the Parisians, there are a large number of women whose brains are closer in size to those of gorillas than to the most developed male brains. This inferiority is so obvious that no one can contest it for a moment; only its degree is worth discussion. All psychologists who have studied the intelligence of women, as well as poets and novelists, recognize today that they represent the most inferior forms of human evolution and that they are closer to children and savages than to an adult, civilized man. They excel in fickleness, inconstancy, absence of thought and logic, and incapacity to reason. Without doubt there exist some distinguished women, very superior to the average man, but they are as exceptional as the birth of any monstrosity, as, for example, of a gorilla with two heads; consequently, we may neglect them entirely . . . A desire to give them the same education, and as a consequence, to propose the same goals for them, is a dangerous chimera . . . The day when, misunderstanding the inferior occupations which nature has given her, women leave the home and take part in our battles; on this day a social revolution will begin, and everything that maintains the sacred ties of the family will disappear." (Le Bon as quoted in Gould, 1980, p. 155)

Most of us would agree that the sentiment expressed by Gustave Le Bon in 1879 represents an extreme attack on women and their abilities (as well as on members of minority groups). We might think Le Bon was some crank who just did not think well of women. In fact, Le Bon was a prominent scientist, a founder of social psychology known for his work on crowd behavior (Gould, 1980). On what evidence did Le Bon base his argument about the inherent "inferiority" of women? According to Gould (1980), Le Bon used data gathered by Paul Broca, the leading medical clinician of his time and consummate practitioner of craniometry, the measurement of the skull.[1] There is little doubt that one of the goals of this method was to "prove" the superiority of white European men by measuring the size of the brain of various groups (Shields, 1975). What Broca found was that women's brains on average weighed less than men's brains. What Broca did not account for was the correlation between height, body weight, and brain size, which could easily account for such differences. This was not a methodological oversight for Broca. According to Gould, Broca was well aware of the implications of not accounting for body size but because he so strongly believed that women were intellectually inferior to men, Broca actually used the difference in body weight to buttress his argument by claiming "the relatively small size of the female brain depends in part upon her physical inferiority and in part upon her intellectual inferiority" (Gould, 1980, p. 154). Both Le Bon and Broca are graphic examples of how researchers' findings are influenced, in this case not even subtly, by their ideological beliefs. But more seriously, Le Bon's statement shows how claims about inferiority are linked to denials of equal opportunity, an issue we will return to later in this chapter.

This chapter explores how current research has conceptualized sex and gender differences in cognitive abilities. As you read about the various findings and explanations of sex differences in cognition, you should remember the issues about epistemological perspectives and the social nature of the research process that were raised in chapter 2. One issue often linked to findings of sex differences concerns the types of educational opportunities provided to girls and boys. What is the nature of the educational environment experienced by boys and girls, and in what ways can it be altered to allow all children to reach their full potential?

COGNITIVE ABILITIES—WHAT ARE THEY?

There is perhaps no more contentious area of research in the study of sex and gender differences than the question of cognitive differences.[2] As you have just learned, there is a long and ignominious history of trying to demonstrate male intellectual superiority using a variety of flawed methods. Most of these researchers did not have a definition of intelligence but rather focused on the issue of the measurement of intelligence, which we will discuss shortly. When you think about intelligence, what definition comes to mind? You might think: the ability to do well in school, the ability to use words fluently and reason quantitatively, the ability to solve practical problems, or the ability to communicate effectively and get along well with others. All these answers are partly correct and each represents one aspect of intelligence, but none is sufficient to capture all aspects of intelligence.[3] Intelligence is a multidimensional concept that entails many different types of cognitive abilities—it is an array of abilities that includes verbal, spatial, and quantitative skills. Should cognitive abilities be thought of as aptitudes that individuals possess or achievements that reflect what individuals know through learning? The answer to this question depends on one's underlying beliefs about the meaning of ability. Essentialists view ability as a quality that resides in individuals, expressed as an aptitude relatively imperious to learning. In contrast, social constructionists see ability as something individuals achieve through experiences, opportunities, and cultural expectations. For researchers who believe in aptitude, especially those interested in the measurement of human intelligence, the distinction between aptitude and achievement is very important. Other researchers argue that such a distinction is impossible to make, because cognitive abilities are socially constructed in a matrix of education, experience, expectations, and beliefs.

COGNITIVE ABILITIES—HOW ARE THEY MEASURED?

Obviously, there is no clear and agreed upon definition of what constitutes cognitive ability. This lack of definition has not stopped researchers from trying to measure cognitive abilities. Accompanying the search for sex differences in intelligence has been the search for a unitary measure of intelligence. We will not recite this history here (see Gould, 1981, 1996 for a fascinating account of the history of intelligence testing) except to point out that the prevailing ideology of the testing enterprise has been the belief that intelligence is a unitary concept that can be measured with a numerical value. Such a belief has lead some researchers to pay more attention to measurement issues, in which the goal is to develop a reliable and efficient measurement of cognitive ability rather than to define intelligence. Numerous tests of general intelligence (e.g., Stanford-Binet; Wechsler Intelligence Test) as well as tests of specific mental ability (e.g., visual, verbal, spatial) have been used to differentiate individuals and groups. Standardized testing has a large following, not only within psychology but in society in general. Standardized tests are widely used to make important decisions, especially in work and educational settings, and producing standardized tests is a billion-dollar-a-year industry.

What are the consequences of the use of these tests for the study of sex differences? When the question is asked about whether a sex difference exists, the answer is often offered in terms of how men and women differ on standardized test scores. But we know of other ways to think about cognitive ability. For example, grades in school are a highly reliable measure of cognitive ability but are often ignored in the discussion of sex differences. Two important points should be recognized here. As you no doubt recall from all your previous reading, how researchers ask questions and how they measure the phenomenon of interest very much depends on what epistemological viewpoint they hold. Second, how something is measured will directly influence the results obtained and, most especially, how those results are interpreted. For example, it is widely believed that the quantitative skills of females are not as proficient as those of males. This belief is supported if you compare the performance of girls and boys on the quantitative component of the Scholastic Achievement Test (SAT). When you look at a different measure—grades in mathematics courses—girls outperform boys (Kimball, 1989). What conclusions can we draw? Which measure is a more accurate reflection of quantitative ability? These questions do not have simple answers, and the readings for this chapter present you with differing viewpoints on this issue. This example makes it clear that the conclusions of any research need to be understood in the context of the measurement used and the researcher's rationale for that measurement.

No matter which measurement of cognitive ability a researcher adopts, there is an additional complication. No ability can ever be fully and directly assessed by any measurement technique. What we actually measure is the performance of individuals, and we hope that it is a good indicator of their ability. We do know both from research evidence and our own practical experience that performance can be affected by many variables. Some researchers argue that standardized tests are a better measure of cognitive ability because they believe such tests are less susceptible to performance factors. Of course, this point is debatable for anyone who has taken a standardized test with only a few hours of sleep or in a room that has distracting noises or is too hot or cold. Standardized tests are generally timed, another factor that elicits anxiety in many individuals, which can have detrimental effects on performance. Social-structural factors also can affect performance. For instance, research by Eccles and her colleagues has shown that parents' expectations and beliefs about their children's math ability were related to mathematical achievement (Eccles, 1989; Eccles & Jacobs, 1986; Jacobs & Eccles, 1992; Yee & Eccles, 1988). Parents reported that their daughters had to work harder than their sons at math, even though both the girls and boys in this study did equally well in math in school. Furthermore, when asked about the importance of taking mathematics and science courses, both mothers and fathers rated these courses as more important for their sons than for their daughters. Parents were also more likely to encourage their sons rather than their daughters to take advanced math courses. Interestingly, parents do not lack confidence in their daughters' general academic ability, because they realize that their daughters received better grades overall than did their sons. Rather, parents' lack of confidence only pertains to their daughters' quantitative skills. Not only do parents' beliefs affect their children's perceptions of themselves, but parents with such beliefs are less likely to encourage their daughters to take advanced math courses, which are a necessary precursor to careers in science and math fields. Eccles (1989) suggests that parents, often unwittingly, play a major role in the emergence of sex differences in mathematical achievement. As we discuss later in this chapter, teachers also have a strong influence on children's motivation and beliefs about their cognitive abilities. One lesson that we can learn from the controversy about measuring cognitive ability is the difficulty of equating ability with its measurement; otherwise we run the risk that our measurement tool becomes an end in itself rather than as a instrument of understanding.

COGNITIVE ABILITIES—WHO GETS TESTED?

Besides questioning how we define and measure cognitive abilities, we need to look at the individuals who are tested in all these research studies. If our interest is in the study of sex differences, then it seems reasonable that the groups we would test are males and females. At a cursory level, this reasoning seems intuitive but it hides a more important question: Which males and which females? We know that individuals differ in many other ways in addition to sex, such as age, educational level, social class, race, or ethnicity. As Diane Halpern points out in the first article in this chapter, *Cognitive Gender Differences: Why Diversity Is a Critical Research Issue* (1995), most of the research

that has been conducted to study questions of sex differences has used students, primarily college students. Consequently, we know little about the cognitive ability of the vast majority of the population Why is this a problem? Halpern contends that if we want to use the construct of sex or gender to explain cognitive differences, such differences should appear in the widest spectrum of the population, representing a breadth of age, class, education, ethnicity, and cultural groups. Only with this information can we have any confidence that the factor of sex or gender (or something related to these factors) is responsible for any findings of cognitive differences. This is, however, the very information that is missing from most of the research literature on sex differences, and according to Halpern, the failure to consider diversity leads to bias. Studies investigating gender differences in cognitive ability often use highly select samples. For instance, Benbow and Stanley (1982), whose work on mathematically precocious children touched off a maelstrom of debate, included only children who scored in the top 3 percent on the Scholastic Aptitude Test–Mathematics subscale (SAT-M) and found that boys consistently outperform girls at this level. A significant difference of opinion exists about what these results tell us about the causes of sex differences in mathematical ability, but the one thing the results do not reflect is the nature of sex differences in the general population of children. For instance, children at the low end of the continuum for verbal ability are often not included in studies looking at gender differences. Halpern contends that this exclusion depresses the results of most meta-analyses, leading researchers to assert that there is little or no difference between males and females in verbal ability. Because the largest differences between males and females are found for learning disabilities such as stuttering and dyslexia, with boys far exceeding girls, the female advantage in verbal ability may be underestimated. In contrast, gender differences may be overestimated when we use narrowly defined populations. By using white, middle-class students as our main testing group, we ignore how other factors such as age, social class, or education might interact with sex to produce similarities rather than differences in cognitive ability. Halpern suggests that in adulthood, math performance for males and females might converge due to life experiences, and therefore, sex differences might decrease or disappear. With more data about math performance at different ages, this question could be answered. Without a broader range of subjects, however, such trends are difficult to discover.

Information about cognitive abilities in other cultures, especially non-Western cultures, is relatively sparse. This lack of research evidence has several consequences. Halpern indicates that various theories that posit a biological basis for gender differences in cognitive functioning share a basic deficiency—without evidence of a similar pattern of gender differences across cultures, such theories remain speculative. Even more problematic is that what little evidence is available suggests that sex differences in cognition are not universal. For some researchers, an even more fundamental issue is the bias inherent in traditional Western definitions of cognitive functioning (Cole, 1996). As you learned in chapter 4, cultural context is essential in understanding the meaning of any behavior. Yet our research approach has utilized a narrow definition of intelligence. When we conduct cross-cultural research, measuring individuals with our narrowly defined tests of cognitive ability, we only exacerbate issues of universality. Serpell (1994) found that Zambian children, who performed poorly on standardized Western tests of cognitive ability, did demonstrate highly abstract thinking on tasks such as wire modeling, that could be related to the ecological needs of their culture. Findings such as Serpell's are an important reminder that knowledge about cognitive ability will entail much richer notions of cognition, including culturally derived theory and measurements, than we presently have before we can claim to fully understand cognitive processes.

THE DEBATE OVER COGNITIVE DIFFERENCES

As we have emphasized, there is significant disagreement among researchers who study sex differences about how to define, measure, and test cognitive abilities. You read several articles in chapter 2, including one by Diane Halpern, that debated the question of whether we should study sex differences. Many of the issues that were raised in that chapter are relevant for understanding how to evaluate evidence about the prevalence and meaning of sex differences in cognitive ability; you may want to refer back to those articles. In both her articles, Halpern highlights the concern of many researchers that if sex differences in cognitive ability are discovered, these findings might well be used to discriminate against women and certain minority groups, especially in education and work settings. Part of this fear rests on how information about sex differences has been portrayed in the popular press. Anyone who has picked up a recent newspaper or magazine can attest that sex differences are often glamorized whereas findings showing sex similarity do not even make the back pages. Even more problematic, the intricacies of research findings, with their many qualifications, are rarely reported in the popular press. In addition, findings of sex differences frequently translate into statements of deficiency. Halpern rightly asserts that differences should not be viewed as deficiencies. In our culture, sex differences that favor males are magnified, whereas sex differences that favor females are minimized or ignored altogether. For instance, sex differences on certain visual-spatial tasks (favoring men) are often used to explain why women are poor map readers. The sex differences in verbal ability (favoring females) are never used to suggest that men are poorer in writing or public speaking.

How cognitive abilities are measured may also lead people to focus on group deficiencies. Because cognitive abilities are generally measured in quantifiable units, those numbers can be used to rank people's performance, making it easier to see such performance as less or more of some entity rather than as a difference in skill or a particular test. Although we agree with Halpern that it is society that decides what value to place on these measurements, we also believe it is important not to overlook the history of sex difference research, which has most often favored males. You need to remain aware of the power asymmetry that exists in our society as you evaluate findings on sex differences in cognitive ability.

UNDERSTANDING SEX DIFFERENCES IN COGNITIVE ABILITIES

In considering the question of sex differences in cognitive ability, you should keep in mind the issues of definition, measurement, and test subjects that we raised earlier in this chapter. Furthermore, as you think about the evidence for sex differences in cognitive ability, you should remember that most studies report average differences between a group of males and a group of females. We cautioned you in chapter 2 that a difference between the mean scores of the male and female groups does not give you any indication of how any specific male or female will perform. Many of the results you read in this chapter are based on the statistics of meta-analysis. In chapter 2, we provided you with some rules of thumb to use when considering the results of meta-analyses. Remember that there is not universal agreement about how to interpret the findings of any particular meta-analysis, and different researchers may choose to emphasize different aspects of a study. Although the use of meta-analysis has brought greater coherence to the enormous body of research on sex differences (Hyde & Linn, 1986), it has not ended debate about the meaning of particular sex differences. The articles in this chapter illustrate that this lack of meaning can lead researchers to very different conclusions about whether a sex difference exists for a particular phenomenon. This problem is compounded by the absence of agreed-upon definitions for each cognitive ability. Researchers agree that the components of cognition—such as verbal, visual-spatial, and quantitative—are themselves not unitary concepts. So, for instance, when we ask whether there is a sex difference in verbal ability, we need to know exactly what aspect of verbal ability a researcher has tested. As Halpern's article indicates, if we measure verbal ability in terms of anagrams or speech fluency, then according to the results of a meta-analysis, women perform better than men. In contrast, if we measure it as the ability to solve analogies, men perform better than women. The overall d value ($d = .11$) for all the effect sizes, however, suggests little or no sex differences in verbal ability between men and women (Hyde & Linn, 1986).

Similar issues arise when we look at the research on sex differences in visual-spatial abilities. According to Caplan, MacPherson, and Tobin (1985), the results in this area have been plagued with significant definitional problems. Researchers have used numerous tests to assess spatial skills, and it appears that there may be several different elements that constitute visual-spatial ability. The four factors that have been most extensively studied are: (a) spatial visualization, the ability to see the relationship of objects in space; (b) spatial perception, the ability to locate horizontal or vertical in the presence of distracting information; (c) mental rotation, the ability to visualize how objects change if they are rotated in space; (d) spatio-temporal judgment, the ability to judge moving visual displays (Halpern, 1992). The most consistent sex differences, showing a male advantage, have been found for tests of spatial perception and mental rotation, although the exact meaning of these results is in contention. For example, one question that we can ask is whether there are other ways to measure visual-spatial abilities that relate better to real-world phenomena (e.g., finding one's way along a route), than do the presently used abstract and decontextualized measures (Caplan et al., 1985).

In the second article in this chapter, *Gender and Math: What Makes a Difference?*, Meredith Kimball presents the results of numerous meta-analyses for sex differences in mathematics. These results show another complicated pattern. Given the publicity surrounding this topic, you might be surprised to learn that, looking at the general population, few sex differences in ability emerge. However, some sex differences are evident when we look at different types of mathematics problems. For example, until about age 15, girls appear to have an advantage in computation problems; whereas after about age 15, boys appear to have an advantage in the area of problem solving. In addition, male performance on the SAT-M (math subtest) has been consistently better than female performance (e.g., the mean difference in 1989 was 46 points, Halpern, 1992). We have already discussed the dramatic sex difference for precocious youth (seventh-grade children) as measured by their SAT-M scores. By shifting the criterion to grades in school, we find a different pattern—girls at all grade levels consistently receive better grades in math than boys.

How can we make sense of this tangled web of findings, and what do they tell us about sex differences in cognitive ability? Experts do not always agree on how to interpret any particular sex difference. Researchers may disagree about whether a particular finding is reliable. Two researchers may look at exactly the same data from a meta-analysis and conclude that an effect size is small or moderate. Judgments about the meaningfulness of a finding can be even more contentious. What does a difference of 46 points mean on the SAT-M? Do tests of analogies give us a better measure of verbal ability than do tests of anagrams? Do tests of mental rotation tell us about someone's potential to be an engineer? Are standardized math tests better measures of quantitative ability than grades in math courses? There is not universal agreement about the answers to any one of these questions; they all involve making judgments. If experts do not agree on what the findings mean, do not be surprised that you find the results confusing. In almost every case, conclusions about sex differences need to be qualified by careful attention to how the ability is being defined, the type of cognitive ability that is being measured, what measures are being used, what samples are being tested (e.g., age, class, education, ethnicity), who is doing the testing, and when a study was conducted. Thinking about these issues should make you better at evaluating the claims of the different research studies you will encounter as well as prepare you when reading popular press accounts of these issues.

EXPLANATIONS OF SEX DIFFERENCES IN COGNITIVE ABILITY

Researchers have had difficulty coming to any clear consensus about the meaning of sex differences in cognition, but there is even less agreement about the causes of any proposed sex difference. The explanations given for sex differences run the gamut from the biological to the social-environmental accounts that you already have read in this book.

Biological Accounts

The more biologically oriented accounts of sex differences in cognitive ability focus on hormonal factors and brain organization. You already know from chapter 2 that the so-called sex hormones play a significant role in physical and sexual dimorphism. Researchers speculate that these hormones both prenatally and postnatally influence the sexual differentiation of human cognitive abilities (Kimura, 1992). According to Berenbaum, Korman, and Leveroni (1995), evidence from studies of individuals born with various endocrine diseases or prenatally exposed to hormones with masculinizing effects, along with studies of typical individuals, suggests that moderate to high levels of androgen in the prenatal and early postnatal period are related to the development of high spatial abilities. For adults, the relationship between hormones and cognitive functioning may be even more complex. For example, low-testosterone men perform better than high-testosterone men on spatial tasks, whereas high-testosterone women perform better than low-testosterone women on these tasks (Gouchie & Kimura, 1991). These results suggest the lack of a simple and direct relationship between hormones and cognitive functioning, and that for adults, there may be an optimal level of androgen needed for maximal spatial processing. Evidence also shows that verbal and spatial abilities vary during the female menstrual cycle. Kimura (1992) found that women's spatial ability is higher at the time of menstruation when both estrogen and progesterone levels are at their lowest. Conversely, women's verbal ability appears to be highest at midcycle when both estrogen and progesterone are at their highest. This work may give us a clue as to which hormones are related to verbal skills; it also shows us that the effects of hormones might not be limited to early development. Kimura points out that although research on the effects of hormonal influence on cognitive ability is intriguing, this approach is based on correlational data that suggests relationships between factors rather than a direct causal connection. We need to study the effects of hormones throughout an individual's life and more precisely understand how environmental factors (e.g., prenatal and postnatal stress) might influence hormone production and cognition performance.

Another approach to studying the role of biology in sex differences in cognition is to investigate brain organization and how structural differences might explain differential cognitive ability. Work in this area has proceeded along multiple tracks with several competing and often contradictory theories. The one that you may be most familiar with is the hypothesis that male and female brains are differentially lateralized. Lateralization refers to the degree of task specialization that occurs in each hemisphere of the brain. Research has shown that the left hemisphere of the brain is generally specialized for many language functions and that the right hemisphere is generally specialized for spatial and perceptual processing in typical right-handed individuals (Gazzaniga, 1983). According to Halpern (1992), several researchers have proposed that women are more likely to be less lateralized, using both hemispheres to process language and having less space for the development of spatial abilities in the nondominant hemisphere. In contrast, men are more lateralized for cognitive functioning, using their dominant hemisphere for language processing and their nondominant hemisphere for spatial processing. This greater hemispheric specialization enhances men's performance on spatial tasks. Geschwind and Galaburda (1987) claim that prenatal hormones are responsible for cerebral specialization along with many other developmental consequences (e.g., handedness, allergies). The hypothesis that men's brains are more laterally organized and women's brains are more bilaterally organized is quite appealing in its simplicity. This simplicity obscures some contradictions, however. For instance, if men's brains are more specialized, why do men not perform uniformly better on all spatial tasks as well as verbal tasks. These problems have not been adequately addressed by this approach. Halpern also notes that many of the predictions of cerebral lateralization and sex differences have received only weak support. Researchers have begun to posit a more complicated relationship be-

tween hemispheric specialization and cognitive functioning in which handedness and sex are moderated by the effects of reasoning ability; these findings help resolve some of the inconsistencies in the laterality research.

Other researchers have focused their attention on different aspects of brain organization as a way of explaining sex differences. Kimura (1992) contends that instead of sex differences in hemispheric specialization, there are differences in how each hemisphere functions for men and women. The complexities of these differences are beyond the scope of this chapter and these findings are certainly controversial, but Kimura does have a wealth of clinical data from brain-damaged patients to support her hypothesis. As we mentioned in chapter 3, Kimura's theory of sex-dimorphic brain organization is tied to her view of the different evolutionary pressures that men and women faced as a result of sex selection. Another area of the brain targeted by numerous researchers as demonstrating sex differences in structure is the corpus callosum, the connecting fibers between the two hemispheres. The main idea of this research is that the degree of connection between the two hemispheres may help explain differences in cognitive performance. Some initial support was reported by showing that the splenium—the posterior portion of the corpus callosum—was larger in women, but subsequent results have failed to replicate these findings (Kimura, 1992; Fausto-Sterling, 1992).

Although some intriguing findings suggest possible biological connections to sex differences in cognitive functioning, we urge caution in not overinterpreting these theories as proving the biological basis of sex differences. That certain biological factors play a role in cognitive abilities is obvious, but there is too much conflicting evidence to precisely specify what the nature of that role might be or how or whether these biological connections can be extended to sex differences. First, until the debate about the nature and the extent of sex differences in cognitive functioning is resolved, any explanation for cognitive differences is speculative. Second, even if we accept some of the findings from the research on brain organization, we need to be mindful that the findings of brain structure do not necessarily demonstrate differences in function. As Hyde (1996) states, demonstrating sex differences in brain laterality and also on tests of spatial ability does not demonstrate that laterality *causes* the differences in spatial ability, it only suggests that they may be related in some way. A key point to remember is that finding a relationship between two variables (a correlation) does not allow you to assume that one factor caused the other. Finally, an adequate biological theory of sex differences needs to account for the mosaic of findings about cognitive ability as well as for the instances of sex similarities in cognitive functioning.

A different biological approach to explaining sex differences in cognitive functioning comes from evolutionary psychology. As we have already detailed in chapter 3, evolutionary psychology postulates that sex differences are mainly the result of sexual selection (Buss, 1995). Mate selection, which according to evolutionists is necessary for survival, leads men and women to develop different adaptive strategies. Evolutionary theory predicts that there should be sex differences only in the areas that exert differential pressure on reproduction. From your knowledge of evolutionary psychology, what sex differences in cognitive ability would you predict to exist? What types of cognitive skills do men and women need to maximize their reproductive success? If your concern as a man is to mate and reproduce, and by providing food and protection you are more likely to attract a woman, then hunting and warfare skills become paramount. According to Geary (1995), the spatial skills of visualizing objects in three dimensions, throwing objects far and accurately, tracking objects, and navigating can be directly related to hunting and combat behaviors. As we already know, these abilities are the cognitive skills that show the greatest sex differences. Visual spatialization, which involves locating objects in only two dimensions, does not show any sex difference because both men and women need this skill to successfully navigate their normal environment. A similar contention is made about the minimal sex differences found for verbal or quantitative skills. Evolutionary theorists claim that data showing women to have better spatial location memory further supports their position. According to Silverman and Eals (1992), this female advantage is tied to the foraging skills used by women in prehistoric times as they gathered food. You are already familiar with many of the criticisms of evolutionary theory. Those criticisms equally apply to evolutionary psychology's explanation for sex differences in cognition.

Sociocultural Accounts

Given the highly visible impact of gender on much of our lives, there are any number of social and cultural explanations for how sex differences in cognitive abilities might have arisen. Some of these explanations will be familiar to you from earlier chapters, including differential treatment by parents and teachers, different toy preferences of boys and girls, and gender segregation. We now know that these factors play a role in how boys and girls develop along different paths, with certain interests and skills reinforced and others either tacitly ignored or actively discouraged.

We can look to the formal and informal experiences of boys and girls to help account for sex differences in cognition. Several studies have shown that boys are interested in and engage in activities that promote spatial skills. For example, boys are more likely to play with toys such as blocks and action figures that have a spatial component (Connor & Serbin, 1985). As part of their play behavior, boys use more space in their free play and have wider play boundaries, that is, the distance they can travel from home (Herman, Heins, & Cohen, 1987), and they engage in activities that have more of a spatial component, such as ball throwing (Halpern, 1992). Girls who engage in more masculine tasks and whose personality is classified as more masculine have better spatial skills (Baenninger & Newcombe, 1995). Taken together, these results suggest that informal experiences play a role in facilitating the acquisition of spatial knowledge. We need to be careful in not interpreting these results as causal; it may well be that individuals (both male and female) choose spatial activities precisely because they excel in related abilities. Geary (1995), in his evolutionary account of sex differences in spatial ability, suggests that children's play experiences act along with prenatal and postnatal hormones to explain how differential spatial skills evolved. In this account, these two factors act together to produce the sex differences in spatial ability that we observe today.

Researchers have identified several specific factors that they believe might explain sex differences in cognitive performance. From your own test-taking experiences, you know that the more you understand about the test, the better chance you have of doing well on the test. Learning good test-taking strategies is important to bolstering test performance. Kimball points out in this chapter's article that girls are more likely to leave out questions, especially difficult ones, when taking tests and that this practice may handicap them. Girls are also more deliberate in their decision-making process, which may also disadvantage them in many standardized tests. Learning how to make quick, educated guesses is a critical test-taking strategy, especially for timed multiple choice tests, a strategy that can significantly improve performance and that is taught in SAT prep courses. Acquiring such test-taking strategies is essential if girls are going to perform optimally on measures of cognitive ability. Practice also seems to significantly improve performance. Consider athletics for a minute. We know that repeated practice and instruction can have a tremendous effect on the acquisition and development of athletic skills. The same effect appears to be true for cognitive abilities. You might remember the many books that were published a few years ago aimed at improving memory. When I (D.A.) taught a class with 180 students several years ago, I used some of these techniques to remember the names of all the students in my class, sometimes with startling success, but other times with embarrassing mix-ups. The research on how training affects cognitive performance has a better track record. In several meta-analyses of spatial ability training studies, Baenninger and Newcombe (1995) found that training both for different types of tasks and for different time periods led to increased

performance on a variety of spatial tasks for both boys and girls. These results clearly show that spatial ability has an important learning component, but they do not necessarily explain why there are sex differences in spatial ability in the first place because both groups benefited equally from instruction.

What effect might factors such as classroom experience have on sex differences? Boys take more math classes than girls, especially as they get older (Benbow & Stanley, 1982; Kimball, 1989). This lack of experience certainly puts girls at a disadvantage, especially for those areas of study (e.g., science, engineering, architecture) in which advanced mathematics courses are a prerequisite. The number and type of courses taken can account for some findings of sex differences in mathematical ability, although this factor does not eliminate sex differences (Kimball, 1989). Of course, there may be more subtle factors at work here. We already mentioned the work of Eccles and her colleagues in showing how parents provide an interpretative framework for their children's course choices. As Kimball suggests in her article in this chapter, boys and girls do not necessarily receive the same type of support even when they take the same course. For example, teachers consistently interact more with boys. Although this lack of attention may not directly affect the grades that girls get in those courses, it could have a serious impact on their interest in pursuing additional courses or careers in mathematics.

Are there other factors that explain why girls, whose grades are as good as boys', stop taking math courses? Kimball suggests several reasons linked to the idea that mathematics is perceived as a masculine domain; you want to give careful attention to these reasons as you evaluate different sociocultural accounts of sex differences in math performance. Just look at our image of a typical mathematician to understand the power of one stereotype. There is a pervasive view of math as being masculine, and therefore, female mathematicians are portrayed as unfeminine and deviant. Clearly, such images are not likely to encourage girls to take math courses or pursue professions related to mathematics. In chapter 6, you learned how adolescence is a time of heightened gender identity. The unflattering images associated with math may have the most severe consequences for adolescent girls, who adhere most rigidly to traditional gender roles and are most concerned with concepts of physical attractiveness. Girls may come to believe that interest in math is unfeminine and will make them unappealing. Some researchers have suggested that it is not a coincidence that sex differences in the problem-solving aspects of mathematical ability are at their greatest during this time period.

The amount of self-confidence that individuals feel about their abilities and what value or interest they have in certain subjects relates to their performance on cognitive tasks. Eccles (1989) and colleagues have conducted extensive research on these issues and have proposed a model of educational and occupational choice that can be used to understand sex differences in cognitive performance. According to this model, achievement-related choices are most directly related to an individual's expectations for success and the subjective value placed on achievement. Many other variables, including individual characteristics (e.g., temperament, aptitudes), cognitive characteristics (e.g., goals and schemas), cultural milieu (e.g., gender role stereotypes), and social forces (e.g., parents and teachers) moderate how one's expectations and values will be expressed. Why do women take fewer math courses, and why are they underrepresented in science and math fields while overrepresented in fields related to verbal ability (e.g., teaching, broadcast journalism)? These outcomes, according to Eccles, are the result of women's lack of confidence in their math abilities and the relatively low value women place on math as a subject to take in school or as a career to pursue. Although the Eccles model does not explain all the proposed sex differences in cognitive ability, it does focus our attention on how individual, social, and cultural variables rather than a lack of cognitive abilities might account for the gross underrepresentation of women in the fields of math, engineering, and the physical sciences. Based on the results of the meta-analyses for sex differences in math problem solving, Hyde (1996) estimates that 1.38 percent of men and .7 percent of women have the highest level of math-

ematical ability, which translates into a ratio of approximately 2 males for every 1 female. This ratio falls far short of the current estimate of tenured women faculty in science, which is around 12 percent. Explanations based on sex differences cannot explain this discrepancy. Structural barriers related to gender, such as sex discrimination and a hostile work environment, may make it difficult for women to enter such professions. The individual and social factors proposed by Eccles may explain why many women do not even choose such fields to begin with. Can we change this situation? Eccles suggests that although both parents and teachers play an important role in changing girls' perceptions of their cognitive abilities and in redirecting girls' interests to a wider array of career options, teachers are in a pivotal position to institute change. The role of teachers and the structural variables in classrooms that might reduce gender inequity are the focus of the next section of this chapter.

A plethora of research has explored how sociocultural factors might account for sex differences in cognitive ability. The results of these studies certainly provide a window into understanding the many ways in which the acquisition and maintenance of cognitive skills are influenced by individual, interpersonal, and social-structural factors (Crawford, Chaffin, & Fitton, 1995). We previously argued that the factors identified by biological theories, while suggestive as partial explanations of sex differences in cognitive abilities, have not yet passed the test of causality by linking brain structure to specific cognitive functions. Most of the sociocultural factors that have been proposed to explain possible sex differences in cognitive performance face the same problem. For example, showing that boys and girls play with different toys could explain why boys have better spatial skills for mental rotation or spatial perception (although you would still need to explain why there are no sex differences on some spatial measures), but the explanation could just as easily be that because boys have strong spatial skills, they choose to play with toys that have spatial elements.

Where does this dilemma leave us in trying to understand cognitive differences? We propose that, at present, neither biological nor sociocultural accounts of sex differences in cognitive abilities adequately explain the complex and often contradictory research about cognitive ability. As we stated in chapter 3, we believe that reciprocal models that specify the effects of both biological and sociocultural factors in dynamic interaction with one another represent the most fruitful approach to understanding both sex and gender differences. Do such theories exist? Although there are no fully specified accounts of the reciprocal interaction of biological and sociocultural factors, several researchers have proposed such approaches under the rubric of biopsychosocial models (see Halpern, 1992, for a detailed account of this approach). The main elements of such a model would include at the very least genes; hormones; brain organization; gender role schemas; parental, school, and peer influences; and overarching cultural forces. The model must also specify the independent and joint effects of these variables and how the effects of such factors might change across the life span of an individual. As you already know, the findings of sex differences in cognitive performance represent a complex, often contradictory, and changing picture. A model explaining sex differences in cognitive performance faces enormous challenges because there is so much disagreement about the phenomena. To create this model, we may need to work on developing measures of cognitive ability that have both theoretical and real-life validity because of the significant ramifications of any findings of sex differences, especially for our educational system.

GENDER, COGNITION, AND EDUCATION

The recognition that social factors, especially social interactions, might play a role in the development of sex differences in cognition has led to a body of research examining the classroom environment and its treatment of boys and girls. Early research by Serbin and colleagues (Serbin, O'Leary, Kent, & Tonick, 1973; Serbin & O'Leary, 1975; Serbin & Conner, 1979) established the view that boys and girls have different experiences in school beginning as preschoolers. These researchers studied patterns of social rewards and attention given by teachers and concluded that boys receive a disproportionate share of attention, both rewards and reprimands; they receive more constructive feedback to requests for help; they are more likely to be rewarded for calling out answers; and they are more likely to be publicly rebuked for misbehaviors. Serbin et al. viewed these factors as a pattern that could establish lifelong differences in classroom behavior: girls, rewarded for good behavior, come to be classroom pleasers who listen carefully and are good citizens; whereas boys, rewarded for interrupting, offering suggestions, and asking for help and publicly reprimanded for misbehavior, come to be active, demanding of attention, quick to offer answers, and confident. Education researchers turned their attention to the quality of instruction given to girls and boys and concluded that similar differences existed in teacher treatment and that the differences could be related to specific facets of the quality of education. Boys receive higher quality instruction consisting of more open-ended questions, more spontaneous interaction with teachers, more formal instruction, more problem-solving interactions, and more hints (Jones, 1989; Meece, 1987). In particular, education researchers Sadker and Sadker (AAUW, 1992; Frazier & Sadker, 1973; Sadker & Sadker, 1985, 1986, 1994) revolutionized the study of gender equity in the classroom by providing the kind of empirical evidence and case studies that educators could use to evaluate their classrooms and to make changes to improve their treatment of students. This area of research, known as gender equity research, examines microprocesses in the social and instructional environment for equity in the treatment and experiences of boys and girls and often makes recommendations for improvement.

In 1995, I (A.L.) was invited to speak at a large suburban high school in honor of Women's History Month. I arrived prepared to talk about women's education and self-esteem, and was greeted by the head of the mathematics department, who had arranged my talk. As we walked the corridors of the school, she told me the story of her treatment as an educator and the circuitous path she had taken to become the female head of a math department. Our conversation certainly confirmed my belief that women are not always welcome in traditionally male domains. Because I had about thirty minutes before the scheduled assembly, I sat in on her advanced placement calculus class. I was pleased to see that nearly half the students were female; perhaps the situation had changed more than I realized. I was immediately impressed by the skill and classroom presence of this teacher; she was fluent and dynamic, a wonderful role model for young women. I then turned my attention to the classroom interactions. There was a constant flow of ideas and information as the teacher simultaneously solved problems and guided the students through several examples. The students had their notebooks open, were attentive, and were being constantly challenged, but it wasn't long before I became aware of something else—not one girl said a word the entire time I was there. There was a constant interchange between the teacher and the male students—they were questioned; they were reminded to pay attention; they asked frequent questions; the teacher walked to their desks to look at their notes and homework; she commented on their behavior; and she maintained their interest and attention throughout. Perhaps the girls were just as interested and motivated, but my observations could not confirm it.[4] You may notice several ironies in this example that illustrate the complexity of understanding gender inequity and efforts to improve education. The teacher was a woman, well aware of the barriers to women's success in math and science. She had been treated inequitably in her own career, and she knew it. She knew that I was in the back of the classroom watching her teach. Close to half the students were female in a highly select group of advanced math students, high school sophomores and juniors taking advanced placement calculus. The administrators, and this teacher in particular, were interested in gender and education issues; after all, they had invited me to speak on just that topic.

Gender Equity and Girls' Education

The observations given in the previous example so directly mirror the reported results of formal observations that the incident could have been a staged demonstration of these interaction patterns (but of course it wasn't). Such classroom treatment is offered as evidence of girls' disadvantages in school, and conclusions focus especially on girls' math and science experiences and achievement. This chapter's article by Susan Bailey, *The Current Status of Gender Equity Research in American Schools,* summarizes the research and emphasizes the consequences for girls. Bailey reviews the evidence about gender equity for the following issues: sex differences in teacher interaction patterns with students; interactions among students, especially with reference to gender segregation; the treatment of women, and girl's and women's issues, in the curriculum; structural features of education, such as school and classroom organization; and standardized testing.

Although Bailey and others make the argument that girls and boys do not experience the same educational environment and may be treated inequitably, it is equally clear that effective programs for change must understand the complexity of these findings. One important factor to consider is that the same or similar experiences do not have the same meaning for everyone; for example, what one student interprets as a challenging exchange of questions and answers with a teacher may be perceived by another student as a threat or disagreement. Not every student will thrive in an environment of constant attention to behavior, and indeed, there is evidence that some boys come to internalize a negative view of education early because of the focus on behavioral conformity.

Researchers have extended the questions posed by gender equity research to describe the experiences of African American students in the classroom and have found an interaction between race and sex (Pollard, 1993). Although some factors for both African American and White students were related to success— variables such as high self-esteem, problem-solving skills, and a positive perception of teachers and the school environment—these positive experiences were not uniform across all groups of students. Despite the fact that the African American students were in a low-income area and in a school with fewer resources, the high-achieving African American girls in Pollard's sample had greater confidence in their abilities than did high-achieving White girls. African American boys, by contrast, reported the lowest levels of academic support and the highest levels of reliance on peers for advice. According to Pollard, these results are consistent with other research, which suggests that the benefits for boys in school may not extend to African American boys and that African American boys may be the least likely to utilize sources of academic support. These findings, which are consistent with other evidence, show that for African American girls, self-confidence accompanies acadmic success. Compared to African American boys, African American girls show greater satisfaction with the support they have received from their teachers. These results clearly make the point that experiences in school must be understood in terms of the larger context and other dimensions of cultural socialization. Pollard suggests that socialization for African American girls stresses self-reliance and family and community support for achievement, which may be the basis for the girls' strong self-confidence. School performance, school achievement, and a child's self-perception as a student develop jointly in the school, family, and community environment.

Education, Equity, and Achievement

Much of the research on equity points to consistent patterns of differential treatment, which may be modified by other student characteristics such as race. These patterns are linked to differing levels of self-esteem among students and different levels of participation in school and classroom interactions. The school environment can also be related to differential patterns of achievement between boys and girls. As mentioned earlier in this chapter, Kimball's article emphasizes that math and science are strongly stereotyped as masculine. One consequence of this, which Kimball details in her article,

are the ways that teachers reflect this stereotype. There is evidence that teachers, with a class of students of equal ability, are more likely to remember and single out the male students as most gifted in math, to nominate male students for advanced placement tests in math (and, in fact, to significantly overestimate the abilities of some boys), to make more negative comments about girls and math, and to advise female students in ways that discourage them from pursuing advanced math and science classes (Kimball, 1995; Baenninger & Newcombe, 1995). Teachers with negative attitudes toward math have been shown to organize their classroom in a more teacher dependent way, perhaps strengthening their own math stereotypes and communicating those stereotypes to students. In hundreds of hours of observation of teacher behavior, only a few examples were noted of teachers mentioning the value of math in life or for careers (Meece, Wigfield, & Eccles, 1990). Stereotypes about math and science may translate to differences in experience and opportunity, which themselves serve to further beliefs in these stereotypes.

Boys and Gender Equity

It is also clear that inequitable treatment does not necessarily create a system of advantages for boys. What are the consequences for boys of differential experiences in the classroom? Evidence indicates that only a small number of boys receive measurable benefits from differential treatment. A few boys become stars in school, either through their academic or athletic achievements. Teachers are more likely to remember the names of these stars, and their peers are more likely to admire them and emulate them. Rarely do girls take on this star role (Safir, Hertz-Lazarowitz, BenTsui-Mayer, & Kupermintz, 1992). Teachers are also more likely to identify boys as problems in the classroom and target them for negative attention. Sometimes the physical behavior of boys results in negative labels (e.g., behavior problem, conduct disorder), whereas at other times, boys' behavior is offered as an explanation for why teachers give more attention to boys. You may notice the circularity of this reasoning—teachers reward boys with attention when they misbehave, boys misbehave to receive attention, teachers pay more attention to boys because they misbehave. None of these events *explains* this pattern of student-teacher interaction. One suggestion is that maleness triggers stereotyped responses about boys, such that boys are viewed as more active and aggressive; not only is boys' behavior judged accordingly, but they are treated in ways that may exacerbate this behavior and reinforce the stereotype.

Another area of clear disadvantage for boys is in the perception that boys are less attentive and more distractible. Despite the fact that boys receive more attention from teachers, boys' grades are, on average, lower than girls' grades, and they are more likely to be placed in classes for learning disabled students (71%) and emotionally disturbed students (80%). In results reported by Shaywitz, Shaywitz, Fletcher, and Escobar (1990), boys were more likely to be identified as reading disabled when the initial screening was conducted by a classroom teacher, whereas more objective measures of reading ability showed an almost equal number of boys and girls who might benefit from specialized intervention. Shaywitz et al. suggest that teacher stereotypes about boys' poor verbal skills and an overemphasis on boys' activity level can help explain these findings. Sadker and Sadker (1994) believe that the cultural value of masculinity, with its attendant privileges, also extracts a cost from boys as students—in expectations for high achievement in academics and athletics, in peer interactions that stress competition, and in disappointment for the many boys who do not achieve star status.

Changes in Education

The articles in this chapter offer differing perspectives on social change with reference to sex differences in cognition. The last article, *Anita Hill Is a Boy: Tales from a Gender-Fair Classroom* by Peggy Orenstein, describes the author's observations of a sixth-grade class through the course of a school year, a class in which the teacher has made a myriad of alterations in her teaching, in the curriculum and in the classroom environment in order to create a gender-fair classroom. Not only do Orenstein's observa-

tions give you an opportunity to imagine a different kind of education, but you also will read about the reactions of the students to these alterations.

Changes in education have been in the forefront of explicit efforts to create social change in relation to traditional gender arrangements. Perhaps the most significant barrier is the continued bifurcation of male and female. As long as we perceive masculine and feminine as nonoverlapping categories, changes will be perceived as trade-offs, portraying gender equity as a win-lose proposition. Gender dichotomies would have us believe that increased attention to girls in school and related changes in the curriculum would detract from the opportunities for boys—add feminine, subtract masculine. This misguided analysis of social change pits women and men, boys and girls, against each other as though they were in competition for a limited resource. If they are to be successful, programs of social change need to recognize that gender is socially constructed, related to cultural and social stereotypes, and created from gendered institutions such as school.

We began this chapter with a quote from Le Bon expressing the worst of misogyny guised in a scientific analysis. Clearly we have moved beyond the nineteenth century in our views of women and intelligence; however, we still live in a culture that perpetuates distortions of gender and cognitive ability. The few sex differences that exist are magnified and often treated as essential qualities. Despite more than twenty-five years of efforts to create equity in educational institutions, the results of such changes have been varied and have often been met with resistance. It is our belief that a restructuring of our gender schemas—so that we begin to emphasize and adopt what Bem (1993) would call an "individual differences" schema—would go a long way toward redressing gender equity. People differ in the pattern and magnitude of their cognitive abilities. We need to educate all our children to achieve to the best of their individual level of abilities. Should we be able to create an education system devoted to the goals of identifying individual strengths and weaknesses, educating for abilities, and sustaining children's motivation despite cultural stereotypes, we might realize higher achievement from all students.

NOTES

1. Many of Broca's discoveries of brain function, especially those related to language, are still used by researchers today.
2. Although researchers make a distinction between the terms **intelligence** and **cognitive ability**, we are using them as interchangeable concepts.
3. For two prominent and provocative theories of intelligence, see Sternberg (1985) and Gardner (1983).

4. I have told this story many times, and people have offered many explanations: the teacher only liked male students; boys dominate the classroom and have to be challenged; girls really do not have any confidence in math; it is better to sit still and pay attention; perhaps the girls were better students so they didn't need much attention; and so on. We hope you can see the fallacies in these explanations.

REFERENCES

AAUW. (1992). *How schools shortchange girls: The AAUW report.* Washington, DC: American Association of University Women Education Foundation.

Baenninger, M., & Newcombe, N. (1995). Environmental input to the development of sex-related differences in spatial and mathematical ability. *Learning and Individual Differences, 7,* 363–377.

Bailey, S. M. (1993). The current status of gender equity research in American schools. *Educational Psychologist, 28,* 321–339.

Bem, S. L. (1993). *The lenses of gender: Transforming the debate on sexual inequality.* New Haven: Yale University Press.

Benbow, C. P., & Stanley, J. C. (1982). Consequences in high school and college of sex differences in mathematical reasoning ability: A longitudinal perspective. *American Educational Research Journal, 19,* 598–622.

Berenbaum, S. A., Korman, K., & Leveroni, C. (1995). Early hormones and sex differences in cognitive abilities. *Learning and Individual Differences, 7,* 303–321.

Buss, D. M. (1995). Psychological sex differences: Origins through sexual selection. *American Psychologist, 50,* 164–168.

Caplan, P. H., MacPherson, G. H., & Tobin, P. (1985). Do sex-related differences in spatial abilities exist? *American Psychologist, 40,* 786–799.

Cole, M. (1996). *Cultural psychology: A once and future discipline.* Cambridge, MA: Harvard University Press.

Connor, J. M., & Serbin, L. A. (1985). Visual-spatial skill: Is it important for mathematics? Can it be taught? In S. Chipman, L. Brush, & D. Wilson (Eds.), *Women and mathematics: Balancing the equation* (pp. 151–174). Hillsdale, NJ: Erlbaum.

Crawford, M., Chaffin, R., & Fitton, L. (1995). Cognition in social context. *Learning and Individual Differences, 7,* 341–362.

Eccles, J. S. (1989). Bringing young women to math and science. In M. Crawford & M. Gentry (Eds.), *Gender and thought: Psychological perspectives* (pp. 36–58). New York: Springer-Verlag.

Eccles, J. S., & Jacobs, J. E. (1986). Social forces shape math attitudes and performance. *Signs, 11,* 367–380.

Fausto-Sterling, A. (1992). *Myths of gender: Biological theories about women and men* (2nd ed.). New York: Basic Books.

Frazier, N., & Sadker, M. (1973). *Sexism in school and society.* New York: Harper & Row.

Gardner, H. (1983). *Frames of mind: The theory of multiple intelligences.* New York: Basic Books.

Gazzaniga, M. S. (1983). Right hemisphere language following brain bisection: A 20-year perspective. *American Psychologist, 38,* 525–537.

Geary, D. C. (1995). Sexual selection and sex differences in spatial cognition. *Learning and Individual Differences, 7,* 289–301.

Geschwind, N., & Galaburda, A. M. (1987). *Cerebral lateralization: Biological mechanisms, associations, and pathology.* Cambridge, MA: MIT Press.

Gouchie, C., & Kimura, D. (1991). The relationship between testosterone levels and cognitive ability patterns. *Psychoneuroendocrinology, 16,* 323–334.

Gould, S. J. (1980). *The panda's thumb: More reflections in natural history.* New York: W. W. Norton.

Gould, S. J. (1981). *The mismeasure of man.* New York: W. W. Norton.

Gould, S. J. (1996). *The mismeasure of man, revised and expanded.* New York: W. W. Norton.

Halpern, D. F. (1992). *Sex differences in cognitive abilities* (2nd ed.). Hillsdale, NJ: Erlbaum.

Halpern, D. (1995). Cognitive gender differences: Why diversity is a critical research issue. In H. Landrine (Ed.), *Bringing cultural diversity to feminist psychology* (pp. 77–92). Washington, DC: American Psychological Association.

Herman, J. F., Heins, J. A., & Cohen, D. S. (1987). Children's spatial knowledge of their neighborhood environment. *Journal of Applied Developmental Psychology, 8,* 1–15.

Hyde, J. (1996). Where are the gender differences? Where are the gender similarities? In D. M. Buss & N. M. Malamuth (Eds.), *Sex, power, conflict: Evolutionary and feminist perspectives* (pp. 107–118). New York: Oxford University Press.

Hyde, J. S., & Linn, M. C. (Eds.). (1986). *The psychology of gender: Advances through meta-analysis.* Baltimore: Johns Hopkins University Press.

Jacobs, J. E., & Eccles, J. J. (1992). The impact of mothers' gender-role stereotypic beliefs on mothers' and children's ability perceptions. *Journal of Personality and Social Psychology, 63,* 932–944.

Kimball, M. M. (1989). A new perspective on women's math achievement. *Canadian Psychology, 35,* 388–404.

Kimball, M. M. (1995). *Gender and math: What makes a difference? Feminist visions of gender similarities and differences* (pp. 83–104). New York: Harrington Park Press.

Kimura, D. (1992, September). Sex differences in the brain. *Scientific American*, pp. 119–125.

Meece, J. L., Wigfield, A., & Eccles, J. S. (1990). Predictors of math anxiety and its influence on young adolescents' course enrollment intentions and performance in math. *Journal of Educational Psychology, 82*, 60–70.

Orenstein, P. (1994). Anita Hill Is a Boy: Tales from a Gender-Fair Classroom. In P. Orenstein (Ed.), *School girls: Young women, self-esteem, and the confidence gap* (pp. 245–274). New York: Doubleday, Anchor Books.

Pollard, D. S. (1993). Gender, achievement, and African-American students' perceptions of their school experience. *Educational Psychologist, 28*, 341–356.

Sadker, D., & Sadker, M. (1985). The treatment of sex equity in teacher education. In S. S. Klein (Ed.), *Handbook for achieving sex equity in education* (pp. 145–161). Baltimore: Johns Hopkins University Press.

Sadker, M., & Sadker, D. (1986). Sexism in the classroom: From grade school to graduate school. *Phi Delta Kappan, 67*(7), 512–515.

Sadker, M., & Sadker, D. (1994). *Failing at fairness: How our schools cheat girls.* New York: Simon & Schuster.

Safir, M., Hertz-Lazarowitz, R., BenTsui-Mayer, S., & Kupermintz, H. (1992). Prominence of girls and boys in the classroom: School-children's perceptions. *Sex Roles, 27* 439–453.

Serbin, L. A., & Connor, J. M. (1979). Sex-typing of children's play preferences and patterns of cognitive performance. *Journal of Genetic Psychology, 134*, 315–316.

Serbin, L. A., & O'Leary, K. D. (1975, December). How nursery schools teach girls to shut up. *Psychology Today, 9*, 56–58, 102–103.

Serbin, L. A., O'Leary, K. D., Kent, R., & Tonick, I. (1973). A comparison of teacher response to the preschool preacademic and problem behavior of boys and girls. *Child Development, 44*, 796–804.

Serpell, R. (1994). The cultural construction of intelligence. In W. Lonner & R. Malpass (Eds.), *Psychology and culture* (pp. 157–163). Needham Heights, MA: Allyn & Bacon.

Shaywitz, S. E., Shaywitz, B. A., Fletcher, J. M., & Escobar, M. D. (1990). Prevalence of reading disability in boys and girls. *Journal of the American Medical Association, 264*, 998–1002.

Shields, S. A. (1975). Functionalism, Darwinism, and the psychology of women: A study in social myth. *American Psychologist, 30*, 739–754.

Silverman, I., & Eals, M. (1992). Sex differences in spatial abilities: Evolutionary theory and data. In J. Barkow (Ed.), *The adapted mind: Evolutionary psychology and the generation of culture* (pp. 539–549). New York: Oxford University Press.

Sternberg, R. J. (1985). *Beyond IQ: A triarchic theory of human intelligence.* New York: Cambridge University Press.

Yee, D. K., & Eccles, J. S. (1988). Parent perceptions and attributions for children's math achievement. *Sex Roles, 19*, 317–333.

Cognitive Gender Differences: Why Diversity Is a Critical Research Issue

DIANE F. HALPERN

Reports of research on cognitive gender differences have made front page news in virtually all major newspapers over the past several years. The prestigious "above the fold" section of the front page has been used, for example, for headlines reporting that few girls are among the most mathematically gifted youth (Benbow, 1988), that women's fine motor and cognitive performance vary over the menstrual cycle (Hampson & Kimura, 1988), that toddlers' toy preferences are mediated by prenatal sex hormones (Berenbaum & Hines, 1992), and that females and males use different parts of their brains when they think (Begley, 1995). It seems that editors must believe that news of sex differences, like sex itself, sells. The effect of sensationalized news coverage on public opinion is difficult to assess, but it is certain that the popular press provides a distorted view of what psychologists know and do not know about cognitive gender differences.

It is easy to dismiss the "sound bite" and simplistic coverage given to complex issues by the popular press and other media, but a reasoned analysis of the original research also reveals serious flaws in the empirical literature. One of the greatest problems in interpreting and generalizing results from these studies involves the way participants are selected for psychological studies of human cognition, the branch of psychology concerned with the way people think, learn, and remember.

CONTROVERSIES AND POLITICAL AGENDAS

The many questions about cognitive gender differences are among the most controversial issues in contemporary psychology. Whether, when, and how much women and men differ in thinking abilities is a charged topic that has sparked stormy debates and tens of thousands of journal and text pages. The reason for the acrimony is apparent: If psychologists were to decide that women and men differ in their cognitive abilities, then these results could be used to justify discrimination, affirmative action based on gender, or both. For this reason, many people (especially feminists) are suspicious of any research that supports the notion that women and men are different in any way that is not directly related to their reproductive roles. They are justifiably concerned that if differences are emphasized, then the greater number of similarities between women and men will go unnoticed.

For many, the questions of similarities and differences in the cognitive abilities of women and men are highly emotional. There is a modal response to any research that examines questions pertaining to gender similarities and differences that goes something like this: (a) There are no differences; any differences that are found are attributable to flaws in the experimental design, researcher bias, or both. If this explanation should fail, than a second argument is offered. (b) If differences are found, they are too small in magnitude to be of any practical importance. However, with an increasing number of large effect sizes being reported (e.g., effect sizes greater than 1 SD such as the female advantage in verbal fluency reported by Hines, 1990, and similar size effects favoring males on mental rotation tasks as reported by Master & Sanders, 1993), a third response is given. (c) If large differences are found, they are caused solely by gender-differentiated rearing practices. This line of reasoning is frequently offered by those who are legitimately concerned with the chilling possibility that gender differences research could be and has been misused (Halpern, 1994; Hare-Mustin & Maracek, 1994). One reason that diverse subject pools are needed in interpreting findings of cognitive gender differences concerns the "tug" between biological and psychosocial explanations of these differences. If psychologists find that cognitive differences are influenced by other variables such as socioeconomic status or level of education, then the interactive effects of both biology and environmental variables must be considered in understanding why and how these differences arise.

DIFFERENCES ARE NOT DEFICIENCIES

There is an unstated assumption by those who are opposed to gender differences research. The tacit assumption is that every time a difference is found, there is a "winner" and a "loser." However, gender differences research is not a "zero sum game," and what does it really mean to say that there are gender differences with respect to some variable? There is nothing inherent in this conclusion to suggest that either women or men have "better" abilities overall. Inherent in this reasoning is a fallacy that I have called *the women have less fallacy*. It refers to the mistaken and often unspoken fear that if the "truth" were known, women would be found to be "less"—less smart, less strong, or less of whatever society values—than men (Halpern, 1992).

Differences do not imply deficiencies. Few would argue against the idea that women and men have different genitals, and most agree that it would be ludicrous to argue which gender has the better genitals. Yet, when the topic is cognitive abilities, there is a rush to assume that whenever differences are found, it is the woman who will have less ability. The reasons for this concern are grounded in the way data have historically been interpreted. It was less than 100 years ago when scientists "discovered" that women had inferior brains and that if women engaged in weighty thoughts, then the blood that was needed for normal menstruation would be used

in thinking with unfortunate biological consequences (cited in Gould, 1978).

The fact that research has been used to justify discrimination and support the prevailing social view is precisely why sound empirical research is needed. If researchers find that society consistently values those traits that are associated with being a man and devalues those traits that are associated with being a woman, then the fault lies in the society in which researchers are participants, not in the research that demonstrates that there are gender differences. Consider a similar example from another domain to clarify this point. It is well-known that people with light-colored skin are at greater risk for skin cancer than people of color. Yet, I have never heard anyone interpret this as evidence that white skin is pathological or "less good" than dark skin or that this research must be wrong. Similarly, researchers know that men die an average of approximately 6 years earlier than women (Halpern & Coren, 1991), yet I know of no researcher who has concluded that being a man is a life-threatening handicap and no one who has insisted that the research results must be wrong or biased by experimenter expectations. Data of these sort show that there are group differences; it is society that decides when differences are deficiencies and it is society that can change the way these value judgments are made.

It is *because* of the politicized nature of gender differences research and the very real possibility that results will be misused that careful empirical research is needed. This point was made eloquently by Eagly (1987, 1995). Carefully controlled research on the ways in which women and men are different and are similar does not create gender role stereotypes or discrimination. These social ills exist in the absence of data-based research. The only way to debunk myths about the ways in which women and men differ is by empirically demonstrating that they are myths. It is important to realize that silence does not rebut stereotypes and that ignorance does not promote equality. Feminists have more to lose by censorship, even self-imposed censorship, than they have to gain.

DIVERSITY IN COGNITIVE GENDER RESEARCH

It is interesting that the mountains of research that have been conducted in both the traditional and nontraditional modes have failed to consider the fact that the world is diverse. All of the psychological theories about how, why, and when women and men differ in their thinking abilities pertain to all females and all males. Yet, most of the research designed to answer questions about gender differences in cognitive abilities has used students, especially college students, as their respondents. Researchers cannot legitimately generalize to all women and men from such a biased sample. Researchers know very little about the cognitive skills of the vast majority of the population. Do the cognitive gender differences that are found with college-bound high school seniors (e.g., from data from the Scholastic Aptitude Test [SAT]) appear among high school dropouts? What about cognitive gender differences for the majority of adults who never serve as research participants (e.g., mechanics, postal employees, homemakers, janitors, secretaries, and Third World people)? If there are gender cognitive differences that are related to either biologically mediated mechanisms, social construction, or the interaction between them, then such differences should be found in the entire diversity of the population. In other words, if the differences are caused by some variable that is directly related to femaleness and maleness, then cognitive gender differences should be found in women and men of various ages, socioeconomic classes, countries, education levels, and across the entire range of human diversity. Despite this requirement, researchers have ignored most of the world in their studies. The information that is needed before reaching any meaningful conclusion about cognitive gender differences is missing from the research literature.

HOW FAILURE TO CONSIDER DIVERSITY LEADS TO BIAS

There are numerous examples of the way failures to consider diversity has led to biased and erroneous conclusions. Consider, for instance, the following examples.

Example 1: The Problems With Meta-Analysis

Meta-analysis has been hailed as a "methodological revolution" (Eagly, 1986, p. 162). As readers probably know, meta-analysis is a statistical method for synthesizing and quantifying experimental results from multiple studies (Hyde & Linn, 1986). It involves the computation of a directional effect size statistic (d) that can be used as a standard of comparison. d is computed by subtracting the mean of one group (e.g., men) from the mean of another group (e.g., women) and dividing this mean distance score by the pooled standard deviation. Mathematically, this is

$$d = \frac{M\ (\text{women}) - M\ (\text{men})}{SD}$$

Thus, d is a measure of effect size that is quantified in standard deviation units. If $d = -1$, then the mean of the women's group is 1 SD below the mean of the men's group. Similarly, a positive d value indicates that women score higher than men on whatever is being measured, and a negative d value indicates that men score higher than women on whatever is being measured (assuming that the mean for the men is subtracted from the mean for the women). d values can be aggregated across studies to yield a single number summarizing any number of independent studies.

Although meta-analysis has many desirable properties (i.e., it is based on the results of several studies rather than just a few), it is subject to many of the same problems that plague traditional research analyses. The greatest problem is that although it provides an effect size statistic, it cannot answer the most fundamental research question: When does an effect size become large enough to be meaningful or important? Cohen (1969) suggested that .2 SD units is a small effect size, .5 SD is a medium effect size, and .8 SD is a large effect size. However, there is no valid rationale for accepting these guidelines, and, like all difficult questions, a better answer is that it depends on what is being assessed and the values of the researcher. An effect size of .2 can mean thousands of lives saved if the research concerns drug effects on some dread disease. Thus, *small* is not synonymous with *unimpor-*

tant. Furthermore, Riefer (1991) found that more than 58% of all effect size statistics published in the contemporary literature in psychology (including developmental psychology, memory and cognition, and perception) are less than .2. If one were to accept Cohen's heuristic that .2 is a small effect size, then one must also accept the fact that most of the psychology deals with small effects.

There has been a great flurry of meta-analytic reviews in the gender differences literature in the past 5 years (e.g., Hyde, Fennema, & Lamon, 1990; Masters & Sanders, 1993). Yet, few of them have addressed the fact that most of the studies that are included in meta-analyses have involved restricted samples and yet have made generalizations about all women and all men.

Consider, for example, an extensive meta-analytic review of the literature on gender differences in verbal ability (Hyde & Linn, 1988). The researchers divided experiments on the basis of the participants' age and type of verbal ability assessed—all tests, vocabulary tests, and tests of reading comprehension. They found differences that depended on the type of test and the participants' age, with virtually no gender differences in vocabulary ($d = .02$), reading comprehension ($d = .03$), essay writing ($d = .09$), and the Verbal portion of the SAT ($d = -.03$, with the negative value indicating that men tend to score higher); differences were found, however, in anagrams ($d = .22$), general and mixed verbal abilities ($d = .20$), analogies ($d = -.16$, indicating a male advantage), and speech production ($d = .33$). When the mean of all of the effect sizes was computed, the overall d value was .11. They concluded from these results that "gender differences in verbal ability no longer exist" (Hyde & Linn, 1988, p. 53). I do not believe that this conclusion is supported by their own data. The 165 studies that they reviewed showed no gender differences for some verbal abilities, small differences for others (with some results favoring men), and moderately large differences for at least one component of verbal ability. It makes little sense to conclude from this mixed pattern of results that, overall, there are no differences. More important, however, the literature on which the meta-analysis was based was highly biased by the nature of the participants included in the studies.

The majority of the researchers who have addressed the question of cognitive gender differences studied a narrow range of participants. Virtually all of the studies involve students, and beyond 9th or 10th grade, these samples become increasingly unrepresentative of the population of all males and females in the United States (or other industrialized countries). The size of the gender differences effect in verbal abilities would be much larger if the experiments that were included in the meta-analysis had involved more participants from the low end of the abilities distribution—a group that is rarely included in gender differences research. The largest verbal ability effects are found in areas of stuttering (Skinner & Shelton, 1985), dyslexia, and other extreme forms of reading disabilities (Bannatyne, 1976; Sutaria, 1985), with males exhibiting more of these problems than females. In addition, men are substantially overrepresented in certain categories of mental retardation (e.g., Coren, 1990). If more of the studies included in the meta-analysis had included samples selected from the low end of the distribution, the overall effect size favoring women would have been much larger. Gender ratios are highly disparate in the low end of the verbal abilities distribution, and the systematic exclusion of low-ability participants has led researchers to conclude that the female verbal advantage is smaller than it actually is. Furthermore, large differences favoring women ($d = 1.2$!) have been found on tests of associational (finding synonyms) and generational fluency (naming words that begin with a particular letter; Hines, 1990). The largest differences favoring males occur with moving stimuli, another research paradigm that is rarely used (Law, Pellegrino, & Hunt, 1993). Relatively few studies have included these tests that show the largest between-gender differences. Thus, it is more accurate to conclude that gender differences are sometimes large, sometimes small, and sometimes nonexistent, and that the size of the difference depends on how verbal ability is assessed and who serves as the participants. Thus, any meta-analysis is only as good as the studies that it summarizes. As long as the research literature is based on a narrow selection of participants and assessment procedures, the results of any analysis will be biased.

Example 2: The Problem of Null Results

It is difficult to estimate the number of studies of cognitive gender differences that have failed to show any statistically significant differences between the women and men. The problem with null results is that they are difficult to interpret. Unfortunately, studies that show null results cannot be used to "cancel" studies that show statistically significant differences. There are many ways to obtain null results in any study. A low power design (e.g., too few participants) can virtually ensure that significant differences will not be found even if large differences do exist. Furthermore, plain old sloppy research can be the cause of null results.

Consider the problem of null results in a less politicized area. Suppose that a researcher read that 50 studies were conducted on the effect of a certain drug on blood pressure and that half of them showed that the drug causes a dangerous increase in blood pressure, whereas half showed no effect of the drug on blood pressure. Would that researcher feel confident in concluding that the drug does not affect blood pressure? Most people can understand that the null cannot be used to cancel the drug studies that found differences especially when the significant results are all found in the same direction (i.e, increase). Yet, when the topic is gender differences, many people believe that null results should be given equal weight to studies that find differences. A more fruitful approach is to examine those studies that showed differences and those that did not to see how the two types of studies differ. Similarly, reports of cognitive gender differences should be examined to determine the circumstances under which differences do and do not appear.

Example 3: Biological Theories of Cognitive Gender Differences

There is a large class of theories that posits that biological indexes and correlates of gender are the origin of cognitive gender differences. These theories concern variables such as prenatal hormones, maturation rate, brain organization and structure, and hormones available at puberty. (See Halpern, 1992, in press-a, for a review of these theories). Some of these theories specifically concern the possibility that the male brain (on the average) is organized most optimally for good visual-spatial ability (e.g., Levy, 1976; McGlone, 1980). The strength of the data in support of these hypotheses is varied. Yet, they all share a common weakness: The biology of femaleness and maleness is the same the world over, yet the gender differences that are found in cognition are not universal.

In the United States, more than two thirds of the bachelor's degrees and 80% of the doctorates in mathematics are earned by Asian and White men (Steen, 1987). If biological variables are involved in determining mathematical ability (or any other ability), their effects are much too small to account for gender differences of this magnitude. Nor can such biological variables explain the scarcity of men from other ethnic groups in higher mathematics. There are no theories arguing that African American men or Hispanic men differ from White and Asian men in their biological indicators of sex (e.g., concentrations of sex hormones, gonads, genitals, brain structures). If researchers would take a broader, more culturally diverse view, they would see that the success in mathematics is related to Gender × Ethnicity interactions and not to the main effect of sex per se.

Similarly, research that supports the notion that men are better in higher mathematics than women is based on data from Western industrialized nations. The International Mathematics Olympiad, for example, is a mathematics competition that involves the most mathematically gifted individuals from many countries. When one looks at Western industrialized countries, one finds that virtually all of the participants are men, yet when one examines the composition as a function of gender of the team from China, one finds that Chinese teams have contained several women who have been gold and silver award winners (Stanley, 1990). The conclusion that there is a "universal" absence of women from international mathematics competition is obviously shown to be wrong when one includes data from non-Western countries. Thus, even though some of the gender differences with regard to quantitative ability are found in other countries, the size of the gender effects varies across countries. It is clearly not a biologically fixed ability that is tied to the biological correlates or causes of one's sex.

Example 4: Main Effects and Interactions

One of the principal problems with relying on data collected from a narrow range of the population is that results that really may be interactions appear as main effects. Suppose, for example, that virtually all of the researchers on mathematical ability had students as their participants. (This should not be too hard to imagine because it is true.) In general, students are either children (preschool through 12th grade) or adults in their late teens or 20s. Only a small percentage of undergraduates are in their 30s or older.

One of the largest gender differences is found on the Mathematics section of the SATs. Since the late 1960s, men have scored an average of 46–47 points higher than women (National Education Association, 1989). Of course, such data do not indicate why there is a consistent difference of this magnitude, a critical question that cannot be addressed in this chapter because it requires a careful analysis of massive amounts of data. Putting aside the problem of why there are such large differences, consider the fact that it exists.

A descriptive conclusion is that women are scoring much lower than men on a standardized test that is used, in part, to determine eligibility for higher education. In the language of data analysis, this means that there is a "main effect" for gender. That is, the gender of the test taker makes a difference, on the average, in how well test takers score on this test. Unfortunately, because test takers tend to be relatively homogenous, important interactions are masked. I doubt, for example, that mathematical gender differences of this magnitude or of any magnitude would be found among middle-age and older adults. Unfortunately, there are not enough data to support the Gender × Age interaction that I am suggesting. Similarly, the majority of those who plan to attend college tend to be of middle and higher socioeconomic status.

In fact, there is some evidence that men who take the SATs are from a higher socioeconomic class than women (Ramist & Arbeiter, 1986). It seems likely that Sex × Socioeconomic Status interactions also would be found if the appropriate data were collected. Other interactions also are likely. One obtains a much difference picture of cognitive gender differences when low socioeconomic status participants are included in research than when they are excluded, again suggesting that it is the interaction of other variables (class and age) with gender that are the most important mediators of results that appear as main effects for gender.

Example 5: The Changing Nature of Populations

Consider again data from the SATs to illustrate the importance of diversity in the kinds of results researchers obtain. Other examples are possible, but the SATs are well-known and widely used and are therefore convenient for making several points. Consider the data shown in Figure 1, which depicts average scores for women and men on the Verbal portion of the SATs since 1967.

As shown in Figure 1, it appears that women have "lost" verbal ability over time relative to men. Part of this "apparent decline" can be explained by considering the differential dropout rates for girls and boys in junior and senior high school. Prior to 1980, girls dropped out of secondary school at higher rates than boys, with gender differences in dropout rates narrowing throughout the 1970s (Center for Education Statistics, 1987a). Currently, the dropout rate for students who enrolled as high school sophomores is 18.2% for men and 14.6% for women (Center for Education Statistics, 1987b). The inclusion in testing of a greater proportion of below-average girls and fewer below-average boys over the past several decades has diminished the female advantage on the Verbal portion of the SATs. Once again, failure to include data from groups other than current students can be misleading, and what may appear as a loss for women can be explained as a function of the changing nature of the high school population.

SCORE

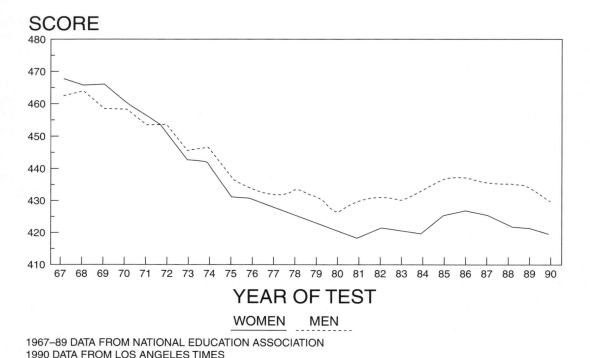

YEAR OF TEST

WOMEN   MEN

1967–89 DATA FROM NATIONAL EDUCATION ASSOCIATION
1990 DATA FROM LOS ANGELES TIMES

Figure 1   *Scholastic Aptitude Tests Scores—Verbal for college-bound high school seniors: 1967–1990. From Halpern (1992). Reprinted with permission of the publisher.*

Example 6: Poverty as a Diversity Issue

It is well-known that a disproportionate number of families living below the poverty level are composed of people of color (U.S. Bureau of the Census, 1990). Families headed by women also are disproportionately overrepresented among the poor. Thus, the weight of poverty in America tends to be borne largely by minority groups and women. Harold L. Hodgkinson, a demographer (cited in National Research Council, 1989), made this point succinctly when he noted that "every day in America, 40 teenage girls give birth to their third child" (p. 19). Given this fact, is it any wonder that researchers find that people of color and women in general tend to perform more poorly on standardized tests of ability

or achievement? Men score an average of approximately 50 points higher than women on the SAT (National Education Association, 1989). The difference in scores between African Americans and White students is close to 200 points. (The mean score in 1989 was 737 for African Americans and 935 for White students; "How Students Fare," 1989, p. 6c). When these data are considered separately from the covariance among gender, race, and poverty, they seem ominous. Yet, when one adds the fact that 50% of African American children are growing up in households whose income is below the poverty level, these numbers seem to say less about gender and race than they do about the crushing effects of poverty on standardized tests of scholastic achievement. When poverty is considered as a diversity issue, the main effects of ethnicity and the Gender × Ethnicity interaction are further modified and explained. The relative absence of the poor from psychological studies of cognitive gender differences has led researchers to overestimate the effect of gender on indicators of cognitive performance.

KNOWLEDGE AS EMPOWERMENT

How can data such as these be interpreted and used? I do not believe that researchers should eliminate tests that show these discrepancies or downplay their importance. Quite the contrary. The needs of women or ethnic minority groups are not served by suppressing these data. Rather, researchers need to know that these discrepancies exist if they are ever to address or redress them. One does not improve the condition of women and minorities by pretending that there are no differences. There are some tests that show large gender differences (such as the SATs, as described earlier). It is important that researchers continue the many debates about when, where, and why these differences are found, but researchers cannot have these debates unless they examine the many variables that affect these data. It is not the purpose of this chapter to provide pat answers to these questions. Instead, my purpose is to ensure that readers ask and consider these questions every time these issues are discussed, every time there is a front page news story about gender differences, and every time value judgments are made about the nature of gender differences research.

RECOMMENDATIONS AND CAVEATS FOR THOSE CONCERNED WITH DIVERSITY

If you are concerned that the psychology we study is genuinely a psychology of all people, then keep the following recommendations in mind when you are planning, reading, and interpreting research (Halpern, in press-b):

1. Are the appropriate generalizations being made? For example, are inferences being made about all women and all men when only college students were subjects?

2. Are main effects being moderated by unidentified interactions? For example, is the main effect of gender or ethnicity really the effect of socioeconomic status on gender or ethnicity? Would the effects of gender, for example, change if different age groups had been included as subjects? What other variables are confounded with gender and ethnicity? For example, African Americans in the United States take fewer college preparatory courses in high school than White students. Given the confounding of these variables, would at least part of the differences that are found be attributable to differential course-taking patterns?

3. Were the hypotheses clearly stated before the data were collected? Is there a plausible and falsifiable theory that can explain these data? Have the critical experiments been conducted that would allow the proposed theory to be found false? Have you considered ways in which experimenter bias could be responsible for the obtained results?

4. Were tests of significance followed with effect size statistics? How does the obtained effect size compare with others in the literature? How were decisions about the importance of an effect size determined? Were results that were not in accord with the researcher's worldview labeled as "small" and those that were in accord with the researcher's worldview described as "large" when there were, in fact, quite similar in size?

5. Were there enough participants in the study to be representative of the population from which they were sampled? Small samples yield inaccurate estimates of what is true in the population and large samples virtually assure statistical significance. Have you considered the way sample size could have affected the results?

6. Are different levels of evidence being used for results that either support or fail to support the researcher's hypothesis? For example, do studies

that show significant relationships have more statistical power (e.g., larger sample size or more sensitive measurement) than studies that fail to show significant relationships?

7. Are meta-analyses based on studies that have involved a wide range of participants? For example, would the conclusions change if there had been more studies that included participants from the low end of the ability distribution, or if a different measure had been used?

8. Are you careful to scrutinize your own willingness to accept evidence to determine whether it has been tainted by personal bias? Are you able to maintain an open mind even when the results do not support your favored hypothesis?

9. Do you understand why null results cannot be used to cancel studies that show significant relationships?

10. Are you careful to distinguish between research results and interpretations of research results? For example, the finding that women and men show different patterns of scores on the SATs does not necessarily mean that there are gender ability differences. All it does mean is at this time and with this test, there are "on the average" between-gender differences. Results of this sort indicate nothing about the cause of the differences.

11. Do you avoid and require others to avoid stereotypic generalizations? For example, are you consciously correcting the mistaken belief that because differences are sometimes found between groups on the average, this does not mean that all the members of one group are different from all the members of another group?

12. Have you maintained an amiable skepticism? Do you scrutinize new research carefully and require independent replications before you are willing to place too much faith in the findings?

13. Are there changes in the nature of the population or the instrument that could be mediating results that look like changes over time?

It is likely that media headlines reporting cognitive gender differences will continue to be published because the general public is fascinated with this topic. Cultural and other types of diversity are rarely addressed in this area of research, yet results are inappropriately generalized to all females and all males. The next time you read or hear about such a study, will you remember to ask the critical questions that were just posed? We live in a diverse and complex world. The type of answer one gets to questions about the ways in which the genders differ with regard to cognitive abilities will depend on a host of other variables that include ethnicity, age, socioeconomic status, native language, educational level, life experiences, nutrition, and the biology of femaleness and maleness. There can be no simple gender effects for complicated questions.

REFERENCES

Bannatyne, A. (1976). *Language, reading, and learning disabilities: Psychology, neuropsychology, diagnosis, and remediation.* Springfield, IL: Charles C Thomas.

Begley, S. (1995, March 27). Gray matters. *Newsweek,* 48–54.

Benbow, C. P. (1988). Sex differences in mathematical reasoning ability in intellectually talented preadolescents: Their nature, effects, and possible causes. *Behavioral and Brain Sciences, 11,* 169–232.

Berenbaum, S. A., & Hines, M. (1992). Early androgens are related to childhood sex-typed toy preferences. *Psychological Science, 3,* 203–206.

Center for Education Statistics. (1987a). *Digest of education statistics: 1987.* Washington, DC: U.S. Government Printing Office.

Center for Education Statistics. (1987b). *The condition of education: 1987.* Washington, DC: U.S. Government Printing Office.

Cohen, J. (1969). *Statistical power analysis for the behavioral sciences.* San Diego, CA: Academic Press.

Coren, S. (Ed.). (1990). *Left-handedness: Behavioral implications and anomalies.* Amsterdam: North-Holland.

Eagly, A. H. (1986). Some meta-analytic approaches to examining the validity of gender-difference research. In J. S. Hyde & M. C. Linn (Eds.), *The psychology of gender: Advances through meta-analysis* (pp. 159–177). Baltimore: Johns Hopkins University Press.

Eagly, A. H. (1987). *Sex differences in social behavior: A social-role interpretation.* Hillsdale, NJ: Erlbaum.

Eagly, A. H. (1995). The science and politics of comparing women and men. *American Psychologist, 50,* 145–158.

Gould J. S. (1978). Women's brains. *Natural History, 87,* 44–50.

Halpern, D. F. (1992). *Sex differences in cognitive abilities* (2nd ed.). Hillsdale, NJ: Erlbaum.

Halpern, D. F. (1994). Stereotypes, science, censorship and the study of sex differences. *Feminism & Psychology, 4,* 523–530.

Halpern, D. F. (in press-a). Psychological and psychobiological perspectives on sex differences in cognition [Special double issue]. *Learning and Individual Differences.*

Halpern, D. F. (in press-b). *Thought and knowledge: An introduction to critical thinking* (3rd ed.) Hillsdale, NJ: Erlbaum.

Halpern, D. F. & Coren, S. (1991). Handedness and life span. *New England Journal of Medicine, 324,* 998.

Hampson, E., & Kimura, D. (1988). Reciprocal effects of hormonal fluctuations on human motor and perceptual-spatial skills. *Behavioral Neuroscience, 102,* 456–495.

Hare-Mustin, R. T., & Maracek, J. (1994). Asking the right questions: Feminist psychology and sex differences. *Feminism & Psychology, 4,* 531–537.

Hines, M. (1990). Gonadal hormones and human cognitive development. In J. Balthzart (Ed.), *Hormones, brain and behavior in vertebrates: 1. Sexual differentiation, neuroanatomical aspects, neurotransmitters and neuropeptides* (pp. 51–63). Basel, Switzerland: Karger.

How students fare on SAT, ACT tests (1989, January 17). *USA Today,* p. 6c.

Hyde, J. S., Fennema, E., & Lamon, S. J. (1990). Gender differences in mathematical performance: A meta-analysis. *Psychological Bulletin, 107,* 139–155.

Hyde, J. S., & Linn, M. C. (Eds.). (1986). *The psychology of gender: Advances through meta-analysis.* Baltimore: John Hopkins University Press.

Hyde, J. S., & Linn, M. C. (1988). Gender differences in verbal ability: A meta-analysis. *Psychological Bulletin, 104,* 53–69.

Law, D., Pellegrino, J. W., & Hunt, E. B. (1993). Comparing the tortoise and the hare: Gender differences and experience in dynamic spatial reasoning tasks. *Psychological Science, 4,* 35–41.

Levy, J. (1976). Cerebral lateralization and spatial ability. *Behavior Genetics, 6,* 171–188.

Masters, M. S., & Sanders, B. (1993). Is the gender difference in mental rotation disappearing? *Behavior Genetics, 23,* 337–341.

McGlone, J. (1980). Sex differences in human brain asymmetry: A critical survey. *Behavioral and Brain Sciences, 3,* 215–227.

National Education Association. (1989). *The NEA 1989 almanac of higher education.* Washington, DC: Author.

National Research Council. (1989). *Everybody counts: A report to the nation on the future of mathematics education.* Washington, DC: National Academy Press.

Ramist, L., & Arbeiter, S. (1986). *Profiles, college-bound seniors, 1985.* New York: College Entrance Examination Board.

Reifer, D. (1991). *Effect size statistics.* Unpublished manuscript, California State University, San Bernardino.

Skinner, P. H., & Shelton, R. L. (1985). *Speech, language, and hearing: Normal processes and disorders* (2nd ed.). New York: Wiley.

Stanley, J. (1990, January 10). We need to know why women falter in math [Letter to the editor]. *Chronicle of Higher Education,* p. B4.

Steen, L. A. (1987). Mathematics education: A predicator of scientific competitiveness. *Science, 237,* 251–252.

Sutaria, S. D. (1985). *Specific learning disabilities: Nature and needs.* Springfield, IL: Charles C Thomas.

Task Force on Women, Minorities, and the Handicapped in Science and Technology. (1988, September). *Changing America: The new face of science and education.* Washington, DC: Author.

U.S. Bureau of the Census. (1990). *Statistical abstracts of the United States, 1989* (109th ed.). Washington, DC: U.S. Government Printing Office.

CHECKPOINTS

1. Halpern outlines several problems with research on cognitive sex differences and how the failure to incorporate diversity has biased the existing research.

2. She provides a number of recommendations for planning, reading, and interpreting research on cognitive sex differences.

To prepare for reading the next section, think about these questions:

1. Who is better at math and why?

2. What experiences have you had with mathematics in school?

Gender and Math: What Makes a Difference?

MEREDITH M. KIMBALL

THE ONE GIRL AT THE BOYS' PARTY

When I take my girl to the swimming party
I set her down among the boys. They tower and
bristle, she stands there smooth and sleek,
her math scores unfolding in the air around her.
They will strip to their suits, her body hard and
indivisible as a prime number,
they'll plunge in the deep end, she'll subtract
her height from ten feet, divide it into
hundreds of gallons of water, the numbers
bounding in her mind like molecules of chlorine
in the bright blue pool. When they climb out,
her ponytail will hang its pencil lead
down her back, her narrow silk suit
with hamburgers and french fries printed on it
will glisten in the brilliant air, and they will
see her sweet face, solemn and
sealed, a factor of one, and she will
see their eyes, two each,
their legs, two each, and the curves of their sexes,
one each, and in her head she'll be doing her
wild multiplying, as the drops
sparkle and fall to the power of a thousand
    from her body

Sharon Olds
The Dead and the Living, 1992, p. 79

Debates about gender similarities and differences in mathematics achievement have been central for many feminist researchers. Women's alleged lower ability in mathematics has been used to explain and justify their low participation in the physical sciences and engineering. Consistent with the similarities tradition, feminist psychologists and educators have focused on the overlap in male and female scores on mathematics achievement measures; the specific contexts in which differences occur; the relationship of girls' mathematics achievement to internal factors such as attitudes and to external factors such as parents' attitudes or teachers' behavior; and the development of intervention programs (Fennema, 1993; Linn & Hyde, 1989). Gender as an analytical tool is applied to understanding and changing the development of individual women and men. In keeping with this tradition, in the first section of this chapter I will focus on the definition and measurement of mathematics achievement and the search for ever more precise information that either destroys, or sharply limits, the myth of women's inferiority in mathematics. However, after 20 years of excellent research the myth remains alive and well. In order to explore why the empirical evidence generated by feminist researchers should be so ineffective in changing beliefs, I turn in my second section to an examination of cultural beliefs that symbolize mathematics as masculine, including the belief that men should be better at math. In my concluding section, I attempt to outline how each of these visions can contribute to the development of equality and equity in mathematics training and education.

GENDER AND MATHEMATICS ACHIEVEMENT

In the empirical studies of mathematics achievement, two definitions of achievement have been used: (1) standardized tests, and (2) classroom grades. By far the greatest bulk of work has been and continues to be concerned with the examination of performance on standardized tests of mathematics achievement. Janet Hyde and her colleagues provide the most thorough review of these studies in a meta-analysis of gender differences. By calculating effect sizes they were able to examine the magnitude of the difference between male and female means expressed in standard deviation units. Their examination of over 250 effect sizes yielded an average effect size of .2. In other words, this is an average mean difference equivalent to 20 percent of the combined standard deviation. Of much more interest than this small overall difference is the way in which effect sizes are distributed across different contexts. In summary, differences favoring males increase with the age of the sample, the selectivity of the sample, and the kind of mathematics problem that is studied. Specifically, in tests of computation, differences favor females up to the age of 15 (15–10 years, $d = -.20$, and 11–14 years, $d = -.22$) with no difference appearing in older samples. In tests of mathematical concepts there is no systematic male or female advantage at any age. In tests of problem solving there is no difference until the age of 15 after which males have an advantage (15–18 years, $d = .29$ and, 19–25 years, $d = .32$). If only samples representative of the general population are included, there is a negligible difference favoring females ($d = -.05$) (Hyde, Fennema, & Lamon, 1990). In another meta-analysis, Lynn Friedman (1989) found a similarly small difference favoring females ($d = -.024$) in representative samples. In highly select samples of mathematically precocious youth, small to medium differences appear favoring males ($d = .54$ and .41). Furthermore, the average effect size is smaller for studies published after 1974 ($d = .14$) than before ($d = .31$) (Hyde, Fennema, & Lamon, 1990).

A disproportionate amount of research and media attention in the U.S. has been focused on studies involving mathematically precocious youth, often without acknowledging the highly restricted nature of the samples (Hyde, Fennema, & Lamon, 1990). These samples are obtained by inviting Grade 7 and 8 students who score at or above the ninety-seventh percentile on national normative tests to take the Scholastic Aptitudes Test-Quantitative Subtest (SAT-M) (Benbow & Stanley, 1980; Benbow & Lubinski, 1993). Similarly selected younger students (Grades 2–6) are invited to take the Preliminary Scholastic

Aptitudes Test-Quantitative Subscale (PSAT-M) (Mills, Ablard, & Stumpf, 1993). Across the samples of highly select students who do take these timed, multiple-choice tests, which are designed for older students, males consistently perform better than females with effect sizes around .4, and these differences have remained consistent over time (Benbow & Lubinski, 1993). Larger differences favoring males also have been found among the top students in Singapore (Kaur, 1990) and Australia (Willis, 1989, pp. 10–11).

One problem with the studies of precocious youth that may exaggerate gender differences is the process of sample selection. Students scoring above the ninety-seventh percentile are notified by school personnel that they are eligible to take the SAT-M. Those who choose to participate take the SAT-M at a regular sitting of the exam which takes place outside of school hours, in an unfamiliar setting, and includes many older students who are taking the exam as a university admission requirement. The authors of these studies do not report what proportion of those eligible are notified by school officials or what proportion of those notified actually take the SAT-M (B. Becker, 1990). To the extent that the very best girls may be less likely than the very best boys to be notified by school personnel and/or may be more reluctant to take the SAT-M, the observed gender differences would be exaggerated. Because it is possible to prepare for the SAT-M with published practice tests, it would also be interesting to know if the students invited to take the SAT-M practice beforehand and if there is a gender difference in the tendency to practice (S. Chipman, personal communication, October 10, 1993).

Although there may be selection processes in the study of precocious youth that tend to exaggerate gender differences, the phenomenon of more males than females at the very highest levels of mathematics achievement appears to be empirically valid. Given even a small mean difference, the distribution of males and females will be more unbalanced at the extremes of the distribution than in the middle. If, in addition to a mean difference favoring males, there is also a larger male variability, as appears to be the case for the PSAT-M and SAT-M, then males will comprise an even larger proportion of the students with very high scores (Feingold, 1992). However, a focus on such select samples is problematic for the study of gender differences in mathematics achievement. It is highly inaccurate to generalize from samples of precocious youth to gender differences in high school and university populations from which mathematics-related professions draw their future members. One does not have to be in the top one to three percent of the population in mathematics achievement to be a successful mathematician, scientist, or engineer. For example, the average SAT-M scores of entering engineering students in the United States was 558 for females and 549 for males (McIlwee & Robinson, 1992, p. 47). It is interesting to note the slightly higher scores of the females, however, the most important point here is that these scores would mean that the vast majority of engineering students' mathematics achievement would not place them close to the achievement levels of the precocious samples.

If one shifts the definition of mathematics achievement from scores on standardized tests to grades in mathematics classrooms, then females rather than males appear to have a small advantage. The pattern of girls' higher grades and boys' higher standardized scores has been found for the U.S. and Canada (Kimball, 1989), Sweden (Grevholm & Nilsson, 1993), Spain, England, and Wales (Burton, 1994). This is consistent with the finding that girls tend to get higher grades than boys in all academic areas (Marsh, 1989; Stockard & Wood, 1984), although girls' advantage in high school mathematics classes is less than in their other classes (Bridgeman & Wendler, 1991; Felson & Trudeau, 1991). Furthermore, this female advantage in grades is found in samples of precocious youth, where the largest male advantage is found on standardized tests (Benbow, 1992; Benbow & Arjmand, 1990). At the university level, among students taking the same mathematics courses, females achieve the same or higher grades than males whose SAT-M scores are higher (Bridgeman & Wendler, 1991). Even among students in the same mathematics course who receive the same letter grade, females' SAT-M scores are 21 to 55 points

lower than males (Wainer & Steinberg, 1992). A similar pattern is found in high school mathematics courses where girls and boys with the same grade in algebra and geometry classes differ in their scores on the PSAT-M with males scoring higher (Fry, 1990). Clearly, in their mathematics classrooms girls achieve as much or more than do their male peers who achieve more on standardized tests.

In contrast to small gender differences in mathematics achievement, differences among ethnic groups, countries, or schools are much larger. Sandra Marshall (1984) found small gender differences among Grade 6 students in California on a statewide test with girls performing better on computation problems and boys on problem solving. These gender differences were consistent across social class and ethnic groups; however, the gender differences were dwarfed by class and ethnic differences. Students from a higher social class background performed better, and Asian students scored higher than whites who scored higher than Hispanics. When Janet Hyde and her colleagues (1990) looked at different ethnic groups in the United States they found a small difference favoring males among white ($d = .13$) students, a small difference favoring females among Asian ($d = -.09$) students, and no gender difference for either black or Hispanic students. Interestingly, if the SAT-M data are included, then a difference favoring males appears for each ethnic group (from $d = .23$ for blacks to $d = .41$ for whites). In each comparison the largest male advantage is for white students (Hyde, Fennema, & Lamon, 1990). It is also important to note that although Asian students and white students receive almost equivalent SAT scores, American Indians, Hispanics, and blacks receive much lower scores (Carson, Huelskamp, & Woodall, 1993) and that these ethnic differences are larger than the gender differences within each group. Gender differences in high achieving samples also vary by ethnicity. In one talent search in the U.S., 27 percent of the white and 47 percent of the Asian winners were female (Willis, 1989, p. 16).

Cross-cultural comparisons of mathematics achievement consistently show small or nonexistent gender differences within cultures and large differences across cultures. Harold Stevenson and his colleagues studied elementary school children from the United States, Japan, and China. Although within each country girls and boys performed equally well, there were striking differences among the countries with Japanese children receiving the highest scores and children in the U.S. the lowest. By Grade 5, the lowest classroom average in Japan was higher than the highest classroom average in the United States (Stevenson, Lee, & Stigler, 1986). Similarly, Corinna Ethington (1990) found that differences among countries in mathematics achievement of Grade 8 students were much larger than gender differences. Using a sample of Grade 12 students from 15 countries, Gila Hanna and her colleagues found a significant country by sex interaction. Specifically, students from countries with a small gender difference experienced more parental encouragement to study math than students from countries with a large gender difference (Hanna, Kundiger, & Larouche, 1990). The mean effect size for studies in Canada ($d = .09$) and Australia ($d = .11$) indicate a very small male advantage (Hyde, Fennema, & Lamon, 1990).

Within countries, it is common to find larger differences among schools than between girls and boys within any particular school. Looking at differences across four high schools in Shanghai, Jinni Xu and Edwin Farrell (1992) found larger school than gender differences. In an examination of mathematics education and achievement in England, Valerie Walkerdine (1989) consistently found school and social class differences in achievement that dwarfed gender differences. In Australia, the percent of students from different mainland states in Year 8 who went on to complete Year 12 math ranged between 16 percent and 55 percent for females and 21 percent and 50 percent for males (Willis, 1989, pp. 11–13). Similarly, a study of high school calculus course completion in the United States found much larger differences across schools than between women and men, with figures ranging from 7 percent to 42 percent for females and 5 percent to 41 percent for males (Dick and Rallis, 1991). The correlation between social class and mathematics achievement is considerably smaller ($r = .20$) when the individual students is the unit of analysis than when the school is the unit of

analysis ($r = .70$). This differences is accounted for by curriculum differences. In schools serving higher socioeconomic populations, more higher level mathematics courses are offered, whereas in those in lower socioeconomic neighborhoods, more remedial and lower level courses are offered (Matthews, 1984; Reyes & Stanic, 1988). Thus, achievement differences among schools most likely reflect both ethnic and social class differences among individual students and curriculum differences among schools.

In summary, gender differences often are not found. When they are found, typically they are small, and if anything, have been getting smaller over time (Friedman, 1989; Hyde, Fennema, & Lamon, 1990; Linn & Hyde 1989). School, ethnic, class, and cultural differences in mathematics achievement are consistently much larger than gender differences.[1] So why all the fuss about gender? Why is the amount of research attention on gender out of proportion to the magnitude of the observed differences? Part of the answer to these questions lies in the bias toward studying largely white, middle-class, urban or suburban samples from the United States. Thus gender is the most obvious group difference to draw the researchers' attention. Clearly an important direction for future research on mathematics achievement is a change in focus from gender as a unitary variable to the interaction of gender with race, ethnicity, class, and cultural diversity.

In addition to this bias in the choice of research samples, I would argue that the focus on gender differences in mathematics achievement reflects the persistent symbolization of mathematics as masculine. In an attempt to reduce, undermine, or destroy this belief, feminist researchers have produced strong and consistent data which demonstrate that females and males achieve very similar mathematical skills. However, these data have had a relatively small impact on the belief predominant in North America that men are better at math than women. In order to understand why this is so, it is important to understand the cultural viability of the symbolic gender system which is largely independent of the individual gender system. Both systems have their own realities and it is to the reality of the masculine symbolism of mathematics that I now wish to turn.

GENDER AND THE SYMBOLIZATION OF MATHEMATICS

In spite of the fact that on many achievement tests and in mathematics classrooms girls and boys have similar achievement patterns, there remains in Eurocentric cultures a persistent belief that mathematics belongs to the realm of the masculine. I am speaking here of what Evelyn Fox Keller calls "the symbolic work of gender" (1992b, p. 17) and Sandra Harding describes as the symbolic sex-gender system (1986, pp. 52–57). In this analysis, gender is an analytical tool that can be applied to all culturally constructed human endeavors including mathematics. Although in certain contexts a cultural analysis may overlap partially with an analysis of individual gender systems, the two systems are also logically, and to a large extent empirically, independent. Thus it is possible for mathematics to be gendered symbolically even though women and men may do equally well at mathematics. What I want to do here is explore, on several different levels, from obvious to more subtle, the results of mathematics as a masculine symbol system.

On the most obvious or conscious level is the stereotype of mathematics as a male domain. This is one of the scales on the Fennema-Sherman Mathematics Attitudes Scale which has been widely used (Fennema & Sherman, 1976). The 12 items on this scale are quite transparent, e.g., "It's hard to believe a female could be a genius in mathematics" and "Females are just as good as males in geometry." Thus one can assume that most children answering these questions are aware of the purpose of the scale. Therefore it is not surprising that both girls and boys tend to express disagreement with the stereotyped view that women are not as good at math as men. In spite of this general tendency to reject or disagree with the stereotype, large gender differences have been found on this scale with girls being much more extreme in their rejection of the stereotype. In a meta-analysis of gender differences in mathematics attitudes, Janet Hyde and her colleagues found that the average gender differences for math as a male domain ($d = .90$) was larger than any of the other atti-

tude scales (Hyde, Fennema, Ryan, Frost, & Hopp, 1990). Furthermore, this gender difference was much larger than the largest gender differences in mathematics achievement ($d = .40$), which are found only with highly select samples and with a single achievement measure, the SAT-M. In an area of investigation where gender differences are so small, this difference in stereotyping stands out. What are the girls trying to say in their almost total rejection of the stereotype of math as a male domain? I would suggest that they are expressing a strong objection to their possible exclusion from a culturally masculine endeavor. On the other hand, boys, by not rejecting this stereotype as strongly as girls, may be expressing a reluctance to give up mathematics as a male territory. Given their male peers' significantly greater willingness to endorse the stereotype of math as a male domain, girls will be exposed to a number of subtle or not-so-subtle comments over the years, the cumulative effect of which will be to reinforce their sense of not belonging. In math intervention programs, drawing girls' attention to the sexist nature of math increased their anxiety (Fennema, 1993).

Individual girls and women consistently express the belief that they are not very good in mathematics in spite of their equal or superior performance in classrooms and on tests. This pattern begins with elementary school children. Deborah Stipek and Heidi Gralinski (1991) found that elementary and junior high school girls were less confident than boys that they would do well on a mathematics test they were just about to take. In a study of Australian students in Grades 3–10, Gilah Leder (1990) found that 65 percent of the boys and 20 percent of the girls thought they had above average math ability. This pattern continues through professional training. Women in graduate programs in science, engineering, and medicine at Stanford consistently assessed themselves as less competent in mathematics than did the men in similar programs (Zappert & Stansbury, 1984, cited in Gottheil, 1987).

Both male and female teachers express their belief that males are better at math in their judgements of students who are particularly successful or unsuccessful at math. These judgements often do not match the students' performance on achievement tests. It is interesting that this bias exists cross-culturally and across an age range of students. Israeli elementary teachers were significantly more likely to name males when asked to nominate the three most eminent math students they had taught (BenTsvi-Mayer, Hertz-Lazarowitz, & Safir, 1989). In England in a study of students nominated to take the O levels in mathematics, Valerie Walkerdine found that fewer females than males were nominated from a group of students who did not differ by gender on a mathematics achievement test. In contrast, almost all students were encouraged to take O levels in English, even though girls are perceived to do better in this subject (Walkerdine, 1989, pp. 165–186). In the United States, Elizabeth Fennema and her colleagues found that Grade 1 teachers were significantly more likely to nominate boys than girls as their most successful students in math. Boys were 79 percent of the teachers' first choices and 58 percent of their second choices. They were also more likely to be nominated as the least successful student although not to such an extreme degree, indicating perhaps that when these teachers thought about mathematics they thought about boys. When the teachers' nominations were compared to the students' achievement scores, the largest group of students inaccurately assigned were boys described as most successful, indicating an overestimation of males' mathematics achievement (Fennema, Peterson, Carpenter, & Lubinski, 1990). Consistent with this overestimation of male achievement, Barry Kissane (1986) found an underestimation of female achievement. Australian teachers were much less accurate in nominating girls who would do well on the SAT-M than they were in nominating similarly achieving boys.

At a more subtle level, I want to examine the persistent bias in the achievement literature that the kind of math men do is better, higher level mathematics. In order to do this I want to return to the distinction between computation and problem solving. Janey Hyde and her colleagues report a gender difference that favors young girls in computation, and advantage that disappears with age. On the other hand, a lack of gender difference in problem solving in young children

changes to a male advantage after the age of 15. Tests of mathematical concepts show no gender difference at any age (Hyde, Fennema, and Lamon, 1990).

Examples of the assumption that girls prefer routine math whereas boys prefer complex problem solving abound. Girls studying for A levels in Ireland reported liking math that was straightforward and disliking difficult problems where procedures were not so obvious, whereas boys reported liking variety in math and disliking what was boring. Teachers of these girls also described them as liking routine, perhaps generating a self-fulfilling prophecy (Rodgers, 1990). In her studies, Valerie Walkerdine (1989) found that girls' good performance in math was constantly played down by teachers as rule-following and passive learning, whereas boys' poor performance and disobedience were seen as an indication of active learning, set breaking, and real understanding. Typically, females' lesser performance on standardized tests of problem solving is seen as a lesser ability to do higher level mathematics critical for autonomous learning of mathematics (Fennema & Peterson, 1985) and for success in engineering and physical sciences (Hyde, Fennema, & Lamon, 1990).

I would argue that privileging problem solving is correlated with the symbolizing of mathematics as masculine. I want to explore this assumption through the consideration of four questions. First, how clear is the distinction between girls' better performance on computation items and boys' better problem solving? Like all dichotomies, a closer look reveals complexities that blur an easy linking of gender with different mathematical skills. For *both* sexes computation items are easier than word problems and the differences across kinds of items are larger than gender differences (Marshall, 1984; Marshall & Smith, 1987). Girls do better than boys on some kinds of word problems. For example, among mathematically gifted junior high students, girls performed better than boys on problems that required them to determine if there was sufficient information to solve a problem, and on problems that required solving logical puzzles (B. Becker, 1990). In a representative sample of younger children, girls did better than boys on noncomputational verbal problems which required them to identify relevant and irrelevant information (Marshall & Smith, 1987). Thus an easy linking of males with higher level or complex math skills and girls with lower level or computational skills is consistent with the cultural norm of math as a masculine domain but much less consistent with the complexity of girls' and boys' skill patterns.

My second question is closely related to my first one. Why do girls perform less well, when they do, on problem-solving tests? Frequently, the assumption is made that girls lack problem-solving skills. Specifically, girls' skills at computation, memorization, and rule following may not be the skills that are the most useful for problem solving. Therefore, when girls behave in an appropriately feminine way, they may not get experience and confidence in working out alternative solutions on their own (Barnes, personal communication, January 17, 1994; Fennema & Peterson, 1985; Willis, 1989, pp. 20–24).

Another reason girls sometimes do less well on tests of problem solving is a lack of good test-taking strategies. In particular, they tend more than boys to omit items, especially difficult ones (B. Becker, 1990; Chipman, Marshall, & Scott, 1991). Thus it may be that boys in some situations have better strategies for taking timed tests rather than better problem-solving skills. For example on the SAT-M there is a correction or penalty for guessing in which the number of wrong items is divided by four and subtracted from the number of correct items (B. Becker). The advice given to students preparing to take the SAT-M by the Education Testing Service is not to guess (Jackson, 1990). However, guessing is a bad strategy only if all four multiple choice alternatives seem equally likely. If even one of the possibilities can be eliminated as incorrect, then guessing among the remaining three alternatives is a better strategy than leaving the item blank. That rapid intelligent guessing is a better strategy than applying and solving the correct formulas is emphasized by special courses that train students to increase their overall SAT performance by as much as 150 points (Jackson, 1990; Linn & Hyde, 1989). Thus girls' greater tendency to omit items they are not sure of may contribute to gender differences on the SAT-M.

My third question centers on the use of math in mathematics-related professions. Clearly, mathematicians engage directly in mathematical problem solving. To what extent, however, is in the use of math by professional scientists a mathematical problem-solving activity and to what extent is it an application of algorithms or rules to a specific situation? Engineers report that they use very little of the higher level math that they are required to take in university in their daily work. Most of the mathematics they use involves basic algebra (McIlwee & Robinson, 1992, p. 27). As a psychologist, I have a fair amount of training in statistics and use math in order to analyze data. However, I would describe what I do as required the right or best application of an existing formula to my data. There *are* problems to be solved, i.e., which is the best analysis to use and whether the data meet the criteria of the test, but these are analytical not mathematical problems. Once I make the decision, the formula is available for my use, usually in the form of a computer program.

My fourth question involves a thought experiment: How could a reversed pattern of performance be interpreted to the advantage of males? Imagine that males do better as young students on computations but there is no difference among older student, and that females do better on tests of problem solving after they become teenagers. Furthermore, imagine that boys get better classroom grades although they do more poorly on standardized tests. It is possible to imagine that educators and researchers would worry about why males lose their early advantage in computation and explore what happens in classrooms that might relate to this loss. Furthermore, accuracy in computation would be seen as a "concern with, attention to, and appreciation of numerical detail or competence in handling numerical systems and their operators" (Damarin, 1993, p. 8), whereas a relative advantage on problem solving would be seen as fooling around or playing with math instead of really doing it. Much would be made of boys' better grades as more realistic measures of mathematics achievement and girls would be labeled underachievers with their pattern of higher scores on standardized tests and lower classroom performance. I am not seriously advocating that problem solving is less important or lower level that computation. But I agree with Valerie Walkerdine that both applying and understanding rules are important skills and that we may overvalue one partly because of its association with the male in a symbolically masculine field (1989, pp. 116–134.).

Another aspect of the symbolization of mathematics as masculine is the underlying assumption in much of the research that men should do better in math. Involvement with this assumption can be expressed as either strong acceptance of the assumption or angry rejection (Gottheil, 1987). Given the socially unacceptable nature of such a belief, one needs to look for indirect evidence of this assumption. I will consider three kinds of evidence that point to this underlying assumption. First is the evidence from women mathematicians of active discouragement of their career choice that increases as they reach higher levels of study (J. Becker, 1990; Luchins, 1979). Some women mathematicians continue to experience hostility when they identify themselves as mathematicians (Damarin, 1993; Selvin, 1992). In contrast, men almost never report active discouragement or hostility when they choose mathematics as a career. Women are much less welcome as colleagues than men at the top universities. Although they received 22 percent of the PhDs in mathematics, they made up only 6 percent of the tenure-track assistant professors at the top ten universities in the U.S. in 1992 (Selvin).

Second, the disproportionate emphasis on standardized tests, especially the SAT-M, exists partly because these are the measures of achievement that reinforce the view that men are better at mathematics. The status of the SAT-M and its association with the largest gender differences is telling. When Janet Hyde and her colleagues removed the SAT-M studies from the total sample of effect sizes, the overall difference favoring males was reduced from $d = .20$ to $d = .15$. And, as I pointed out earlier, this gender difference favoring males is smaller or nonexistent in all ethnic groups in the United States if the SAT-M data are excluded (Hyde, Fennema, & Lamon, 1990). The controversy around the changing of items in the early

1970s on the verbal subtest of the SAT (SAT-V) to eliminate the male disadvantage and even create a small advantage, while, at the same time, not working to eliminate the male advantage on the SAT-M also can be read to indicate an underlying assumption that men should be better at math (Goldberg, 1990; Jackson, 1990: Mandula, 1990). It has been shown clearly that the SAT in general underpredicts women's and overpredicts men's average course grades (Striker, Rock, & Burton, 1991), and their grades in specific mathematics courses (Bridgeman & Wendler, 1991; Wainer & Steinberg, 1992). The solution to this problem is usually seen as including both SAT and high school grades in scholarship and selection procedures but not changing the SAT-M to include more of the kinds of items on which women do better. On the contrary, data sufficiency items which favor females are no longer used on the SAT-M (Chipman, 1988).

Third, the overemphasis, especially in the popular media, on the studies of mathematically precocious youth occurs partly because these are the samples in which the male advantage on standardized tests (almost exclusively the SAT-M) is the largest. Even in these highly select samples, girls get higher grades in math and science courses (Benbow, 1992; Benbow & Arjmand, 1990), a fact discrepant with the assumption that men should be better in math and therefore seldom reported in the popular press. Furthermore, the popular press reports do not always accurately report the highly select nature of these samples leaving open the possibility that the results are misinterpreted as applying to males and females in general, and the further implication that the differences are due to biology (Hyde, Fennema, & Lamon, 1990).

Of course the belief that men should do better in math does not include all men. In addition to the gender symbolization of math there is also a clear hierarchical symbolization that only the elite can truly understand math (Willis, 1989, pp. 26–28). Mathematics is hard and to understand math is to gain a superiority over those who do not. Thus there are unspoken racial and class assumptions in the hierarchical symbolization of mathematics; it is the privileged white male who should do better in math. And just as the small or nonexistent gender differences do not destroy the belief of masculine superiority, the high achievement of Asians (Marshall, 1984; Stevenson, Lee, & Stigler, 1986; Willis, 1989, pp. 16–17) does little to destroy the belief that superior math ability belongs to those who are white. The symbolization of math as belonging to an elite also reinforces the status of and overgeneralization from the studies of mathematically precocious youth.

The final level at which I wish to examine mathematics as masculine is in the language of mathematics. In our technological culture, mathematics is described as rational, detached (Gottheil, 1987), and aggressive (Luchins, 1979; Damarin, 1990). Mathematics has been described as involving the manipulation, dissection, and destruction of figures (Luchins, 1979). Goals of mastery include mathematical power in which the learner attacks problems by applying strategies, using drills, and engaging in competition. Misconceptions are torpedoed, and concepts are arranged in hierarchies. In contrast, feminine symbolic language such as beautiful or elegant proofs or nice solutions often refer to completed processes rather than the activity of doing mathematics (Damarin, 1990). The overwhelmingly masculine nature of the military language used to describe the process of doing mathematics is clearly illustrated by the contrast of possible alternative descriptions. As Suzanne Damarin (1990) suggests, one could speak of internalization of knowledge rather than mastery, instead of attacking a problem one could interact with it, hierarchies could become networks, and one could resolve instead of torpedo a misconception. Sexist remarks and humor convey the message that mathematics is masculine in an even more direct and hurtful way. Claudie Solar (1995) reports a joke told among French mathematicians which states that the worst thing that can happen to a mathematician is to spend the night with an unknown and not find the solution. In French, the unknown is feminine and what makes this a joke is the assumption that the mathematician is male, the unknown female, and the solution is intercourse.

It is easy as feminists to get caught up in attacking the assumption that men should be better in math or that mathematics is a male domain. Consequently much of our energy as feminist researchers has been

spent producing empirical evidence that contradicts these assumptions. Valuable as this task is, it is not sufficient in itself to destroy the cultural assumptions of mathematics as masculine, because they were never based on data in the first place. It is my contention that in addition to exposing these assumptions indirectly through the production of empirical evidence that contradicts them, it is vital for feminists to engage in a direct analysis of how the assumptions are expressed and supported in the cultural and linguistic institutions of mathematics.

GENDER AND MATHEMATICS: WHERE TO GO FROM HERE?

Given the discrepancy between the nonexistent or very small and very limited gender differences in mathematics achievement and the belief that mathematics is a male domain, what will bring about effective social change? Clearly a demonstration of empirical similarity is not enough. One must also work to change the symbolic masculinization of mathematics and reflect this change in the classroom. Effective social change requires both equality and equity of mathematics education. Walter Secada (1989) describes equality as a quantitative concept and equity as a qualitative one. Thus equality is determined by the absence of a difference among demographic groups, or a search for the null hypothesis. One can measure equality as opportunity to learn, access to educational resources, or educational outcomes (Fennema, 1990). An example of an inequality that affects both women and minorities is the practice of assigning beginning or disfavored teachers to general math classes and the best teachers to advanced classes (Secada, 1990).

Clearly, an educational context that results in inequality is inequitable. However, equity includes and goes beyond measurable inequalities. Equality within a system that is symbolically masculine is both difficult to achieve and insufficient to ensure equity. Equity involves fairness and requires a focus not only on the distribution of existing resources, but also on the inclusiveness of what is being taught. Important questions include: is what is being distributed worth having? (Secada, 1990); are measures of what is being learned culture-fair? It is important to notice that in these questions there is a shift from an exclusive focus on empirical inequalities to include questions of the subjective meaningfulness of mathematics for all learners (Jungwirth, 1993).

Most children learn most of the mathematics they know in the classroom. Thus the process, and content in mathematics classrooms become important equality and equity concerns. In focusing on classroom process, researchers have examined both the amount of the teacher's time and attention devoted to females and males and what kinds of classroom structures lead to equivalent outcomes for girls and boys. Girls' treatment in the classroom tends to be one of relative deprivation, particularly in having fewer interactions with mathematics teachers (Eccles, 1989; Kimball, 1989; Leder, 1990). Although girls receive fewer interactions, it is not clear how this relates to their performance as they often receive higher grades and only some of the time perform more poorly on standardized tests.

In an attempt to specify the qualitative aspects of classrooms that support females' mathematics learning, researchers have examined specific classes where girls' performance, mathematics confidence, or interactions with the teacher are similar to or greater than boys', and compared them to classrooms where girls are more disadvantaged. Jacquelynne Eccles and her colleagues identified girl-friendly classrooms, i.e., ones in which girls and boys had similar confidence levels, as involving less social comparison, less competition, more teacher stress on the importance of math, and a warmer, fairer teacher (Eccles-Parsons, Kaczala, & Meece, 1982; Eccles & Blumenfeld, 1985; Eccles, 1989). Within the girl-friendly classroom, a challenging atmosphere may be an important facilitator of girls' learning. Mary Koehler (1990) found that girls' performance in a beginning algebra class increased more in a classroom in which they were encouraged to solve problems on their own than in a classroom in which all their questions were answered. Pat Rogers (1990) chose to study the mathematics department at SUNY Potsdam because of the high percentage of graduating math majors (60 percent) who were women. What she found was a department dominated by male faculty who challenged their students to think precisely and were often described by students as scary but excellent teachers. It is important to distinguish between challenge and competition. It may be that sufficient challenge to think and work on problems on one's own is important for learning math. However, challenge does not have to occur in a highly public and competitive context.

An important related variable may be whether the classroom is teacher-centered or student-centered with the teacher facilitating learning. In a study of Grade 4 and 6 mathematics teachers. Karen Karp (1991) found that teachers with negative attitudes toward math constructed their classrooms in a very teacher-dependent manner which involved students in very little interaction in contrast to teachers with positive attitudes towards math who encouraged interaction with their students. Furthermore, teachers can learn to focus on the individual cognitive styles of each of their students, resulting in better learning for all students. Thomas Carpenter and his colleagues found that a four-week training program in Cognitively Guided Instruction for Grade 1 teachers made a significant difference in the way they taught math and resulted in consistent modest improvement in their students' mathematics performance over students in the control teachers' classrooms (Carpenter et al., 1989). As more is learned about the match between teaching styles and learning styles, it may well be that a focus on styles that are student friendly in the sense of encouraging all students to achieve mathematics competence and excellence are the styles that ensure both equality and equity for minority students and females.

In addition to their interactions and teaching styles, teachers have an opportunity to make a difference in the content they present to their students. Unfortunately, it appears that few of them do so, often reinforcing sex-differentiated and hierarchical values, if not directly, then by their silence (Eccles, 1989). For example, in 400 hours of classroom observations in one study, teachers mentioned fewer than a dozen instances of the value of math in everyday life, math as personally meaningful, or the value of math for careers (Meece, Wigfield, & Eccles, 1990). Furthermore, elementary texts seldom illustrate mathematics careers and even when they represent girls and boys in equal numbers they tend to show girls in helping and subservient roles (Garcia, Harrison, & Torres, 1990; Walkerdine, 1989, pp. 187–197). Most students experience math as rule-bound, involving operations, and lacking in creativity and imagination (Isaacson, 1990; Schoenfeld, 1989; Stodolsy, Salk, & Glaessner, 1991). For example, in one survey high school students reported spending an average of two minutes on a typical homework problem and that they would spend an average of 12 minutes on a problem before deciding it was impossible (Schoenfeld, 1989). In another study, Grade 5 children saw math as a subject that they liked or disliked based on how hard it was, as a subject one could not learn on one's own, and as very unchangeable. All of these views were held in contrast to social studies which one like or disliked based on how interesting the material was, that one could learn on one's own, and that was open to student input and influence (Stodolsky, Salk, & Glaessner, 1991).

A number of innovative attempts have been made to make the content of mathematics courses gender inclusive. Sometimes this involves the adaptation of traditional feminine activities to the classroom such as the use of embroidery to teach border symmetry (Verhage, 1990). In other cases this is done by including examples familiar and interesting to a wide range of students including women. Thus, in a calculus course, problems of population growth, radioactive waste, spread of disease, the absorption of drugs and alcohol into the blood stream (Barnes & Copeland, 1990), the rate of temperature change in a dead body, or measuring the area of deforestation from an aerial map (Barnes, 1994) can be used instead of the typical abstract problems that are of very little interest to the majority of students, both male and female. The inclusion of many examples of the use of mathematics in careers and in everyday life, and an active advertisement campaign to promote

mathematics courses are also important (Blum-Anderson, 1992). One could even make issues of equality directly relevant to learning by bringing sets of data that examine gender or ethnicity differences on various achievement measures, and use them to illustrate statistical and mathematical concepts, including a critique of how they may be distorted (Damarin, 1990). For example, in a mathematics class for mature women in Australia, Vicky Webber focused a series of classes around an article attacking single mothers' welfare payments as a burden to the Australian taxpayer. Fueled by anger, the women developed a sophisticated mathematical analysis of the misuse of numerical data in the article (Webber, 1987/88). Marilyn Frankenstein (1990) has developed a critical mathematical literacy curriculum that presents mathematical problems in a context that emphasizes existing race, gender, and class inequalities in income and resources.

In addition to inclusive content the students' emotional responses to mathematics are important and should be acknowledged. Women mathematics teachers write about the importance of acknowledging mathematics anxiety, emphasizing that frustration is a normal part of problem solving and teaching how to cope with it, recognizing that mathematics confidence is unstable, and developing teaching styles to maintain or build confidence (Blum-Anderson, 1992; Damarin, 1990; Willis, 1989, pp. 20–24).

Finally, it is important to consider how mathematics achievement is assessed. That girls do better in classroom assessment and boys on standardized tests raises important questions (Burton, 1994; Grevholm & Nilsson, 1993; Kimball, 1989). In the United States the exclusive reliance on standardized test results such as the SAT in determining college admissions and scholarships clearly discriminates against females (Mandula, 1990) and as a result many colleges use both SAT results and high school grades, a procedure which reduces the overprediction of male and the underprediction of female performance in university (Striker, Rock, & Burton, 1991). The issue of balancing assessment between classroom performance and standardized exams has been raised as well in Europe (Burton, 1994) and

Australia (H. Forgasz, personal communication, October 11, 1993; Willis, 1989, pp. 34–37). The inclusion of course work as a component of the national or provincial assessment for high school students has had the result of raising all students' scores, especially those of girls, who did as well or better than boys on the course work component, but less well on the standardized exams. Interestingly, there also has been a significant political opposition to the inclusion of course work based on charges of lowered standards and cheating. Assumptions underlying this debate include a symbolization of standardized tests as tough, detached, hard, objective, i.e., masculine and elite; and classroom grades as soft, easy, subjective, deceptive, i.e., feminine and mediocre. Contrast these arguments with the existence of tutoring programs that coach white privileged U.S. students on the SAT raising scores by as much as 150 points (Jackson, 1990; Linn & Hyde, 1989). This is not seen as cheating, although it gives an unfair advantage to a small group of students.

In establishing more equitable methods of assessment based on different patterns of achievement by females and males, a benefit may also accrue to minority students who are disadvantaged by traditional assessment procedures. What is important is that assessment measures are sought that reflect fairly the mathematical knowledge of all students.

A problem with much of the research that has focused on gender equality and equity in mathematics is that the samples studied have been largely limited to U.S. white middle-class elementary and high school students. In these populations gender is highlighted as a marker of disadvantage. However, it is clear that when other ethnic groups and cultures are included, these differences are usually larger than gender. Therefore, if the goal is a truly equitable mathematics education, it must be equitable not only for white middle-class females, but for all students. The establishment of gender-inclusive curricula and gender-fair assessment is one place to begin and such changes may benefit many male students as well. Conversely, teaching styles, content and assessment patterns that work for most students will of necessity benefit female learners. Both of these attempts are worthy of feminist attention.

NOTE

1. It is not always easy to compare the size of various differences. The ideal way would be to have effect sizes for gender and other differences so the size of the difference could be directly compared. Unfortunately, the data necessary to calculate effect sizes are not always presented. However, some comparison is usually possible. For example Harold Stevenson, Shin-Ying Lee, and James Stigler (1986) reported that sex differences in all three countries at all three grades were nonsignificant, but data are not given separately for each gender making it impossible to calculate effect sizes for gender. The effect sizes for differences between countries range from a low of .05 to a high of 1.29. The largest country differences at each grade level are .88 (Kindergarten), .76 (Grade 1), and 1.29 (Grade 5). Although effect sizes for gender cannot be calculated, given that they are statistically nonsignificant and that the number of subjects are large (over 200 students in each country at each grade level), the effect sizes should be smaller than all but one of the nine comparisons between countries. Jinni Xu and Edwin Farrell (1992) present some of the most complete data comparing mathematics achievement across schools in China. The smallest effect sizes for gender are .004 and .046. The largest effect sizes for gender are .34 and .43. The smallest effect size differences between schools are .05 and .49. The largest effect sizes are 2.16 and 3.03.

Two other studies make size of difference comparisons using statistics other than effect sizes. In a comparison of mathematics achievement across eight countries, Corrina Ethington (1990) used a median polish analysis and found gender effects in all cases to be smaller than country effects. For example for the whole test the gender effect was .16. The smallest country effect was 1.41 (France) and the largest country effect was 13.07 (Japan). Sandra Marshall (1984) compared students' mathematics achievement in California ethnic groups (Hispanic, Oriental, and Caucasian), social class (unskilled, semi-skilled, semi-professional, and professional), kind of problem (computation and story problems), and gender. Comparing the probability of a current response across groups, she found that average gender differences ranged from zero to 5 percent. Social class differences ranged from 6 percent to 27 percent. Ethnic differences ranged from 8 percent to 30 percent.

REFERENCES

Barnes, M. (1994). Investigating change: A gender-inclusive course in calculus. *Zentrallblatt für Didaktik der Mathematick. (International Reviews in Mathematics Education), 26*(2), 49–56.

Barnes, M., & Copeland, M. (1990). Humanizing calculus: A case study in curriculum development. In L. Burton (Ed.), *Gender and Mathematics: An International Perspective* (pp. 72–80). New York: Cassell

Becker, B. J. (1990). Item characteristics and gender differences on the SAT-M for mathematically able youths. *American Educational Research Journal, 27,* 65–87.

Benbow, C. P. (1992). Academic achievement in mathematics and science of students between ages 13 and 23: Are these differences among students in the top one percent of mathematical ability? *Journal of Educational Psychology, 84,* 51–61.

Benbow, C. P., & Arjmand, O. (1990). Predictors of high academic achievement in mathematics and science by mathematically talented students: A longitudinal study. *Journal of Educational Psychology, 82,* 430–441.

Benbow, C. P., & Lubinski, D. (1993). Consequences of gender differences in mathematical reasoning ability and some biological linkages. In M. Haug (Ed.), *The Development Of Sex Differences and Similarities in Behavior: Proceedings of the NATO Advanced Research Workshop, Chateau de Bonas, Gers, France, July 14–18, 1992* (pp. 87–109). The Netherlands: Kluwer Academic Publishers.

Benbow, C. P., & Stanley, J. C. (1980). Sex differences in mathematical ability: Fact or artifact? *Science, 210,* 1262–1264.

BenTsvi-Mayer, S., Hertz-Lazarowitz, R., & Safir, M. P. (1989). Teachers' selections of boys and girls as prominent pupils. *Sex Roles, 21,* 231–246.

Blum-Anderson, J. (1992). Increasing enrollment in higher-level mathematics classes through the affective domain. *School Science and Mathematics, 92,* 433–436.

Bridgeman, B., & Wendler, C. (1991). Gender differences in predictors of college mathematics course grades. *Journal of Educational Psychology, 83,* 275–284.

Burton, L. (1994). Differential performance in assessment in mathematics at the end of compulsory schooling: A European comparison. In L. Burton (Ed.), *Who Counts? Mathematics Achievement in Europe* (pp. 1–21). Stoke-on-Trent, Staffordshire: Trentham Books.

Carpenter, J. P., Fennema, E., Peterson, P. L., Chiang, C., & Loef, M. (1989). Using knowledge of children's mathematics thinking in classroom teaching: An experimental study. *American Educational Research Journal, 26,* 499–531.

Carson, C. C., Huelskamp, R. M., & Woodall, T. D. (1993). Standardized tests. *Journal of Educational Research, 86,* 267–272.

Chipman, S. F. (1988, April). *Word Problems: Where Sex Bias Creeps In.* Paper presented at the meeting of the American Educational Research Association, New Orleans, LA (ERIC Document Reproduction Service No. TM 012 411).

Chipman, S. F., Marshall, S. P., & Scott, P. A. (1991). Content effects on work problem performance: A possible source of test bias? *American Educational Research Journal, 28,* 897–915.

Damarin, S. K. (1990). Teaching mathematics: A feminist perspective. In T. J. Cooney & C. R. Hirsch (Eds.), *Teaching and Learning Mathematics in the 1990s: 1990 Yearbook* (pp. 144–151). Reston, VA: National Council of Teachers of Mathematics.

Damarin, S. K. (1993, October). *Gender and Mathematics from a Feminist Standpoint.* Paper presented at ICMI Study 93, Gender and Mathematics Education, Höör, Sweden.

Dick, T. P., & Rallis, S. F. (1991). Factors and influences on high school students' career choices. *Journal for Research in Mathematics Education, 22,* 281–292.

Eccles, J. S. (1989). Bringing young women to math and science. In M. Crawford & M. Gentry (Eds.), *Gender and Thought, Psychological Perspectives* (pp. 36–58). New York: Springer-Verlag.

Eccles-Parsons, J. E., Kaczala, C. M., & Meece, J. L. (1982). Socialization of achievement attitudes and beliefs: Classroom influences. *Child Development, 53,* 322–339.

Ethington, C. A. (1990). Gender differences in mathematics: An international perspective. *Journal for Research in Mathematics Education, 21,* 74–81.

Feingold, A. (1992). Sex differences in variability in intellectual abilities: A new look at an old controversy. *Review of Educational Research, 62,* 61–84.

Felson, R. B., & Trudeau, L. (1991). Gender differences in mathematics performance. *Social Psychology Quarterly, 54,* 113–126.

Fennema, E. (1993, October). *Mathematics, Gender, and Research.* Paper presented at ICMI Study 93, Gender and Mathematics Education, Höör, Sweden.

Fennema, E., & Peterson, P. (1985). Autonomous learning behavior: A possible explanation of gender-related differences in mathematics. In L. C. Wilkinson & C. B. Marrett (Eds.), *Gender Influences in Classroom Interaction* (pp. 17–35). Orlando, FL: Academic Press.

Fennema, E., Peterson, P. L., Carpenter, T. P., & Lubinski, C. A. (1990). Teachers' attitudes and beliefs about girls, boys, and mathematics. *Educational Studies in Mathematics, 21,* 55–69.

Fennema, E., & Sherman, J. A. (1976). Fennema-Sherman Mathematics Attitudes Scales: Instruments designed to measure attitudes toward the learning of mathematics by females and males. *JSAS Catalog of Selected Documents in Psychology, 6,* 31. (Ms. No. 1225).

Frankenstein, M. (1990). Incorporating race, gender, and class issues into a critical mathematical literacy curriculum. *Journal of Negro Education, 59,* 336–347.

Friedman, L. (1989). Mathematics and the gender gap: A meta-analysis of recent studies on sex differences in mathematical tasks. *Review of Educational Research, 59,* 185–213.

Fry, C. J. (1990, April). *Learning Style Factors and Mathematics Performance: Sex-Related Differences.* Paper presented at the meeting of the American Educational Research Association, Boston, MA.

Garcia, J., Harrison, N. R., & Torres, J. L. (1990). The portrayal of females and minorities in selected elementary mathematics series. *School Science and Mathematics, 90,* 2–12.

Goldberg, S. (1990). Numbers don't lie: Men do better than women. *Alumnus: City College of New York, 85* (1), 16–17.

Gottheil, E. (1987). *Psychoanalysis, Female Ability and Mathematics.* Unpublished manuscript, Stanford University Medical Center, Stanford, CA.

Grevholm, B., & Nilsson, M. (1993). *Gender Differences in Mathematics in Swedish Schools.* Unpublished manuscript, Teacher Training College, Malmo, Sweden.

Hanna, G., Kundiger, E., & Larouche, C. (1990). Mathematical achievement of grade 12 girls in fifteen countries. In L. Burton (Ed.), *Gender and Mathematics: An International Perspective* (pp. 87–98). New York: Cassell.

Harding, S. (1986). *The Science Question in Feminism.* Ithaca, NY: Cornell University Press.

Hyde, J. S., Fennema, E., & Lamon, S. J. (1990). Gender differences in mathematics performance: A meta-analysis. *Psychological Bulletin, 107,* 139–155.

Hyde, J. S., Fennema, E., Ryan, M., Frost, L. A., & Hopp, C. (1990). Gender comparisons of mathematics attitudes and affect. *Psychology of Women Quarterly, 14,* 299–324.

Isaacson, Z. (1990). 'They look at you in absolute horror': Women writing and talking about mathematics. In L. Burton (Ed.), *Gender and Mathematics: An International Perspective* (pp. 20–28). New York: Cassell.

Jackson, M. (1990). SATs ratify white male privilege. *Alumnus: City College of New York, 85* (1), 17–18.

Jungwirth, H. (1993). Reflections on the foundations of research on women and mathematics. In S. Restivo, J. P. Van Bendegem, & R. Fisher (Eds.), *Math Worlds: Philosophical and Social Studies of Mathematics and Mathematics Education* (pp. 134–149). Albany, NY: State University of New York Press.

Karp, K. S. (1991). Elementary school teachers' attitudes toward mathematics: The impact on students' autonomous learning skills. *School Science and Mathematics, 91,* 265–270.

Kaur, B. (1990). Girls and mathematics in Singapore: The case of GCE 'O' level mathematics. In L. Burton (Ed.), *Gender and Mathematics: An International Perspective* (pp. 98–112). New York: Cassell.

Keller, E. F. (1992b). *Secrets of Life Secrets of Death: Essays on Language, Gender, and Science.* New York: Routledge.

Kimball, M. M. (1989). A new perspective on women's math achievement. *Psychological Bulletin, 105,* 198–214.

Kissane, B. V. (1986). Selection of mathematically talented students. *Educational Studies in Mathematics, 17,* 221–241.

Koehler, M. S. (1990). Classrooms, teachers, and gender differences in mathematics. In E. Fennema & G. C. Leder (Eds.), *Mathematics and Gender* (pp. 128–148). New York: Teachers College Press.

Leder, G. C. (1990). Teacher/student interactions in the mathematics classroom: A different perspective. In E. Fennema & G. C. Leder (Eds.), *Mathematics and Gender* (pp. 149–168). New York: Teachers College Press.

Linn, M. C., & Hyde, J. S. (1989). Gender, mathematics, and science. *Educational Researcher, 18* (8), 17–19, 22–27.

Luchins, E. H. (1979). Sex differences in mathematics: How *not* to deal with them. *American Mathematical Monthly, 86,* 161–168.

Mandula, B. (1990). Is the SAT unfair to women? *Association for Women in Science Newsletter, 19* (1), 8–16.

Marsh, H. W. (1989). Sex differences in the development of verbal and mathematics constructs: The high school and beyond study. *American Educational Research Journal, 26,* 191–225.

Marshall, S. P. (1984). Sex differences in children's mathematics achievement: Solving computations and story problems. *Journal of Educational Psychology, 76,* 194–204.

Marshall, S. P., & Smith, J. D. (1987). Sex differences in learning mathematics: A longitudinal study with item and error analysis. *Journal of Educational Psychology, 79,* 372–383.

Matthews, W. (1984). Influences on the learning and participation of minorities in mathematics. *Journal for Research in Mathematics Education, 15,* 84–95.

McIlwee, J. S., & Robinson, J. G. (1992). *Women in Engineering: Gender, Power, and Workplace Culture.* Albany, NY: State University of New York Press.

Meece, J. L., Wigfield, A., & Eccles, J. S. (1990). Predictors of math anxiety and its influence on young adolescents' course enrollment intentions and performance in mathematics. *Journal of Educational Psychology, 82,* 60–70.

Mills, C. J., Ablard, K. E., & Stumpf, H. (1993). Gender differences in academically talented young students' mathematical reasoning: Patterns across age and subskills. *Journal of Educational Psychology, 85,* 340–346.

Olds, S. (1992). *The Dead and the Living.* New York: Alfred A. Knopf.

Reyes, L. H., & Stanic, G. M. (1988). Race, sex, socioeconomic status, and mathematics. *Journal for Research in Mathematics Education, 19,* 26–43.

Rodgers, M. (1990). Mathematics: Pain or pleasure? In L. Burton (Ed.), *Gender and Mathematics: An International Perspective* (pp. 29–37). New York: Cassell.

Rogers, P. (1990). Thoughts on power and pedagogy. In L. Burton (Ed.), *Gender and Mathematics: An International Perspective* (pp. 38–46). New York: Cassell.

Schoenfeld, A. M. (1989). Explorations of students' mathematical beliefs and behavior. *Journal for Research in Mathematics Education, 20,* 338–355.

Secada, W. G. (1989). Educational equity vs. equality of education: An alternative conception. In W. G. Secada (Ed.), *Equity in Education* (pp. 66–88). New York: Falmer Press.

Secada, W. G. (1990). The challenges of a changing world for mathematics education. In T. J. Cooney & C. R. Hirsch (Eds.),

Teaching and Learning Mathematics in the 1990s: 1990 Year-book (pp. 135–143). Reston, VA: National Council of Teachers of Mathematics.

Selvin, P. (1992). Profile of a field: Mathematics. *Science, 255,* 1382–1383.

Solar, C. (1995). An inclusive pedagogy in mathematics education. *Educational Studies in Mathematics, 28,* 311–333.

Stevenson, H. W., Lee, S., & Stigler, J. W. (1986). Mathematics achievement of Chinese, Japanese, and American children. *Science, 231,* 693–699.

Stipek, D. J., & Gralinski, J. H. (1991). Gender differences in children's achievement-related beliefs and emotional responses to success and failure in mathematics. *Journal of Educational Psychology, 83,* 361–371.

Stockard, J., & Wood, J. W. (1984). The myth of female under-achievement: A re-examination of sex differences in academic achievement. *American Educational Research Journal, 21,* 825–838.

Stodolsky, S. S., Salk, S., & Glaessner, B. (1991). Student views about learning math and social studies. *American Educational Research Journal, 28,* 89–116.

Striker, L. J., Rock, D. A., & Burton, N. W. (1991). *Sex Differences in SAT Predictions of College Grades* (College Board Report No. 91–2). New York: College Entrance Examination Board. (ETS RR No. 91–38).

Verhage, H. (1990). Curriculum development and gender. In L. Burton (Ed.), *Gender and Mathematics: An International Perspective* (pp. 60–71). New York: Cassell.

Wainer, H., & Steinberg, L. S. (1992). Sex differences in performance on the mathematics section of the Scholastic Aptitude Test: A bidirectional validity test. *Harvard Educational Review, 62,* 323–336.

Walkerdine, V., & The Girls and Mathematics Unit (1989). *Counting Girls Out.* London: Virago Press.

Webber, V. (1987/88, Summer). Maths as a subversive activity. *Education Links,* No. 32, 6–9.

Willis, S. (1989). *Real Girls Don't Do Maths: Gender and the Construction of Privilege.* Geelong, Victoria: Deakin University Press.

Xu, J., & Farrell, E. (1992). Mathematics performance of Shanghai high school students: A preliminary look at gender differences in another culture. *School Science and Mathematics, 92,* 442–444.

CHECKPOINT

1. Kimball argues that gender differences in mathematics are small to nonexistent and reflect cultural beliefs and treatment in school.

To prepare for reading the next section, think about these questions:

1. Do you remember boys and girls being treated differently in school, either by teachers or peers?

2. How would you feel if you were in a classroom in which the achievements of one sex were exclusively taught?

The Current Status of Gender Equity Research in American Schools

SUSAN McGEE BAILEY
Wellesley College
Center for Research on Women

Girls and boys are still far from equal in U.S. elementary and secondary schools. Research on teacher-to-student and student-to-student classroom interaction patterns, reviews of curricular materials, and data on participation in extracurricular activities suggest that the school climate is less encouraging for girls and young women than it is for their male classmates. Even testing and assessment procedures give an inaccurate picture of girls' abilities and thereby limit their options. This article reviews current research and makes specific recommendations for actions to create a more gender equitable environment in the nation's schools.

Title IX of the Education Amendments of 1972 states that no person shall be discriminated against on the basis of sex in any educational program receiving federal funds. Title IX has been the law of the land for 20 years. It has been a powerful force for change in many school systems, but as extensively documented in The AAUW Report: *How Schools Shortchange Girls* (Wellesley College Center for Research on Women [WCCRW], 1992), girls and boys are still far from equal footing in U.S. elementary and secondary schools. Research on teacher-to-student and student-to-student classroom interaction patterns, reviews of curricular materials and data on participation in extracurricular activities suggest that the school climate is less encouraging for girls and young women than it is for their male classmates. Even testing and assessment procedures may give an inaccurate picture of girls' abilities and thereby limit their options.

Furthermore, we live in an economic environment in which a mother's earnings are critically important to the support of her family whether she is a single parent or part of a two-parent household. Over 70% of all women between the ages of 20 and 64 are working outside the home (United States Department of Commerce, Bureau of the Census, 1991). In two-parent families, wives' wages account for 50% of African American family income, 40% of Hispanic family income and 35% of White family income (United States Department of Commerce, Bureau of the Census, 1990). Boys and young men must begin to acquire the child-care, community-building, and homemaking skills that were long thought of as "women's roles." Gender equitable education is more than equal access for girls to the opportunities boys enjoy. Achieving gender equity in education means equally recognizing and rewarding the achievements of both boys and girls. It means providing boys and young men with equal opportunities to pursue training, career paths, and life choices traditionally considered to be more appropriate for women. A wider range of choices will be genuinely available to girls only when an equally wide and nontraditional range of choices is available to boys as well.

This article reviews research conducted over the past decade on classroom interaction patterns, curricular content and school context, and climate as it relates to gender equity. The review concludes with recommendations for action that can provide the base we need to move forward toward a genuinely gender equitable education for all our students.

TEACHER-STUDENT INTERACTION PATTERNS

The amount and the kind of attention students receive from teachers has long been a topic of interest to researchers. Numerous studies specifically have looked at gender differences in the patterns of these interactions (Eccles, Kaczala, & Meece, 1982; Lockheed, 1984; M. Sadker & D. Sadker, 1984; Wilkerson & Marrett, 1985). Unfortunately, only a few studies have also examined the data in terms of race, ethnicity, and socioeconomic status as well as sex (Damico & Scott, 1988; Grant, 1984; Scott-Jones & Clark, 1986).[1] Thus, the patterns revealed by the majority of research on classroom interaction are basically the patterns of middle-class White students.

Twenty years ago, researchers documented that greater amounts of teacher attention were directed toward boys in preschool classrooms than toward girls—in fact, girls were often ignored unless they happened to be physically close to the teacher (Serbin, O'Leary, Kent, & Tronick, 1973). Ten years later, early childhood researchers were still reporting imbalances in favor of boys (Ebbeck, 1984).

Research conducted during the past decade has focused not on the preschool level but on students in elementary and secondary school classrooms and university lecture halls. The pattern at each of these levels has been similar—more overall teacher attention to boys and more active participation by boys (Hall & Sandler, 1982; Jones, 1989: Krupnick, 1985; D. Sadker & M. Sadker, 1985a). Research that delves carefully into the possible causes and/or conditions under which this "overattention" to boys occurs suggests interesting avenues for further research and for specific actions that teachers and school administrators can take. For example, although boys receive more attention than do girls, this attention is not necessarily evenly distributed among all males in the classroom. D. Sadker and M. Sadker (1985b) reported that a few "star" male students receive the bulk of the teacher attention and that, in fact, one or two students often account for as much as 20% of teacher attention. Eccles (1989) reported that in her study of mathematics classes, a few male students in each class received particular attention to the exclu-

sion of all other students, female or male. Furthermore, several studies noted that boys demand more attention than do girls. Boys are more apt to call out answers, and when they do, the teacher is more likely to respond than when the call-out comes from a girl. In fact, girls are often reprimanded for calling out rather than responded to on the basis of the content of their response (M. Sadker & D. Sadker, 1984).

There is evidence that the imbalances in the amount of teacher attention boys and girls receive are particularly marked in science classes (Jones & Wheatley, 1990; Morse & Handley, 1985). Kahle and Meece (in press) reported that although survey responses from teachers indicated that they held similar expectations for girls and boys in science, observations of science classrooms contained data suggesting differential expectations. Baker (1986) found that teachers in science lecture classes questioned boys on the subject matter 80% more often than they did the girls. Another study found that 79% of classroom science demonstrations were conducted by boys (Tobin & Garnett, 1987). Lee and her colleagues (Lee, Marks, & Knowles, 1991) reported that they discovered the most blatant examples of sexism in chemistry classes and that over two thirds of all sexist incidents in the coeducational schools they studied occurred in chemistry classes, although only 20% of their observations were in these classes. Given the fact that girls are not participating or achieving equally with boys in many areas of science (see Kahle, Riley, Parker, & Rennie, 1993), these patterns deserve particular attention.

As mentioned earlier, there is limited research on teacher-student interaction patterns that distinguishes among students on the basis of both race and sex and even fewer than control for socioeconomic status. Damico and Scott (1988) reported that teachers tend to positively reinforce African American girls for social behavior whereas they tend to reinforce academic behavior among White girls. Grant (1985) reported that White girls:

> had warmer and more positive contacts with teachers than did other students [and that] [o]n measures of feedback for classroom behavior boys

had fewer positive interactions than girls. Black boys . . . stood out from other race-gender groups as having largely negative interactions with teachers around such issues. (p. 68)

Other research reports that White females receive the lowest level of overall communication of any race/sex group (Irvine, 1985, 1986). African American girls may have a particular role in desegregated classrooms. Grant (1984) described the go-between role and the consequent enhancement of social skills, possibly at the cost of academic skills. These results suggested that the interaction of racism and sexism is particularly complex and that further research is needed to document the problems and point the way to effective solutions (Pollard, 1993).

Few studies on teacher-student interaction patterns have been conducted within the last 2 or 3 years, years during which a great deal of attention has focused on restructuring schools and classrooms. Many restructuring efforts are designed to place the teacher in a facilitative rather than an authoritative role (Sizer, 1992). Whether these new classroom configurations will result in more equitable patterns of interaction between teachers and students is an open question and one that deserves careful investigation.

Inservice teacher training programs such as Gender/Ethnic Expectations/Student Achievement (Grayson & Martin, 1990) are beginning to gather data which can indicate whether such training is effective in modifying gender imbalances in teacher-student interaction patterns. The training involves not only sensitizing teachers to the issues but also providing practical techniques such as deliberate turn-taking, increasing the wait-time before calling on students (which often increases the number of female volunteers), and suggesting a variety of ways that teachers can get feedback on the interaction patterns in their own classrooms. However, further research is needed to determine the most effective ways to modify existing patterns of teacher-student interactions in order to achieve more gender and race equitable patterns.

STUDENT-TO-STUDENT INTERACTIONS

The ways students interact with each other are an important aspect of the school day. These interactions are a significant part of the informal curriculum, and much of the learning that takes place in school is embedded within them.

Friendship Patterns

Research on friendship patterns during elementary and middle school years reveals that friendships during these years tends to be same-sex ones and that play groups in school yards are often sex segregated (Best, 1983; Etaugh & Liss, 1992; Maccoby & Jacklin, 1987; Thorne, 1986, 1993). In a recent review of this research, Maccoby (1990) concluded:

Fairly distinctive styles of interaction develop in all-boy and all-girl groups. Thus, the segregated play groups constitute powerful socialization environments in which children acquire distinctive interaction skills that are adapted to same-sex partners . . . the distinctive patterns developed by the two sexes at this time have implications for the same-sex and cross-sex relationships that individuals form as they enter adolescence and adulthood. (p. 516)

They also have implications for school policies and classroom teaching strategies.

Small Group Learning Situations

The attitudes and dispositions developed in informal settings carry over to the classroom and must be considered in planning educational strategies. Research on situations in which small groups of students work together suggests that when these groupings are mixed-sex, the positive effects for girls may be limited by the ways in which girls are silenced or placed in traditional sex-stereotyped roles by the boys within the group. Linn and Burbules (in press) reported that often the idea generated by the student with the greatest status is pursued by the group and that other students report feeling pressured by the group to move along rather than consider alternatives. Furthermore, when things do not work out well, the group may resort to stereotypes such as "that proves girls cannot do science."

Other researchers report that boys in small groups usually receive help from girls when they ask for it but that boys often ignore girls' requests for assistance (Wilkinson, Lindow, & Chiang, 1985). Lockheed and Harris (1984) reported that although mixed-sex small groups provide leadership opportunities for boys, girls are often viewed as merely followers. Thus, the research on group learning strategies suggests that peer-to-peer instructional settings may do little more than foster the same patterns of less attention to girls and less active involvement by girls that researchers find in many teacher-to-student classroom interactions.

Students have strong preferences for same-sex work partners (Nelson-Le Gall & DeCooke, 1987). Lockheed (1986) reported that in an experimental setting in which teachers were encouraged to use small mixed-sex instructional groups in their classrooms, increased cross-sex student interactions did occur in comparison to those in a control group of classes. However, these cross-sex interactions did not result in significant changes in students' preferences for same-sex work partners or their evaluations of cross-sex classmates. She suggested that more than simply desegregating work groups may be needed if the goal is to encourage significant and sustained positive interactions between girls and boys.

Furthermore, there are serious questions about the relative merits for girls and boys of cooperative versus competitive instructional strategies. Because small group learning situations can be structured competitively or collaboratively, it is important to consider these variables when looking at research on small group settings. Peterson and Fennema (1985) reported that participation in competitive mathematics activities facilitated the achievement of boys, particularly on lower level mathematics activities but that competitive teaching strategies did not help and may, in fact, have hindered girls' achievement. In contrast girls' mathematics achievement on both lower level and higher level tasks was positively related to participation in cooperative mathematics activities, whereas boys' engagement in such activities was negatively related to their higher level mathematics achievement. Obviously further research on small group instructional settings is needed to understand those settings that facilitate learning for students of both sexes and those in which gender equitable interactions are most apt to be fostered.

Sexual Harassment

Evidence of sexual harassment in schools and classrooms can no longer be ignored. In one of the earliest surveys to address the issue, Stein (1986) reported that young women were more likely to be sexually harassed than were their male classmates, that such harassment was a problem in both academic and vocational schools, and that peer-to-peer harassment was more prevalent than teacher-to-student harassment. Recent data reinforce these points.

Only 4% of the girls and young women responding to a recent survey on sexual harassment in schools cited incidents of teacher-to-student harassment when asked to describe the most serious harassment they had experienced during the last school year. These same respondents reported that in over two thirds of the incidents, others—either classmates or teachers—were present, but even when girls report the harassment to school officials, in 45% of the cases no action was taken (Stein, Marshall, & Tropp, 1993). Furthermore, as documented in a recent Harris Poll, harassment is often an issue for boys as well (Harris/Scholastic Research, 1993).

When harassment occurs in full view of others, but adults in positions of responsibility do not intervene, the message to both girls and boys is a damaging one. The clear implication is that such behavior is somehow appropriate, something girls need to get used to and boys can take part in with impunity. States such as Minnesota and California have developed specific state legislation to deal with sexual harassment in schools, but a great deal more needs to be done.

THE CONTENT OF THE CURRICULUM MATERIALS AND PROGRAMS

The content of formal school curricular materials sends powerful messages to students. These are, after all, the materials their teachers have chosen for them to study, and thus what textbooks and other supplemental materials include and do not include about the world and its people signal to students what is and is not valued by the schools they are attending.

During the 1970s and early 1980s, considerable attention was devoted to analyzing the content of school textbooks and to the development of gender-fair, multicultural, curricular materials. The Council on Interracial Books for Children, The Feminist Press, and later, Educational Equity Concepts, as well as the Women's Educational Equity Act Program of the U.S. Department of Education all encouraged and supported the development of curricular materials that not only used gender-fair language but that included more information on the roles and contributions of women in our society. Although federal support for research and action on both gender and race equity has declined significantly during the past decade (Meece & Eccles, 1993), these early initiatives resulted in publishers' guidelines on nonsexist language, in state guidelines such as the California guidelines on gender and race equity, and in state laws such as those in Iowa and Minnesota requiring school systems to develop gender-fair, multicultural, curricular materials.

Some progress has been made, but students of both sexes are still exposed to gender stereotyping in too many of the materials they study in school: the textbooks (not all schools buy the very newest), the videos, the computer software (Huff & Cooper, 1987) and a wide range of supplementary materials. A 1989 survey of the books most frequently taught in high school English courses included only one by a White woman and none by people of color among the 10 most frequently assigned books (Applebee, 1989). A 1987 survey of over 250 elementary school teachers reveals a similar pattern. Of the top 10 books these teachers were most likely to read to their classes, 8 had males as the main characters (Smith, Greenlaw, & Scott, 1987).

Thus, what is taught via these formal curricular materials reinforces once again, for both girls and boys, a subordinate role for girls in our schools and our society. Furthermore, many of the things that are not taught, that are evaded, avoided, and denied in our schools contribute to a school climate that is inequitable and counterproductive not only for girls and young women but for boys and young men as well.

Education about sex and sexuality is a key element in the evaded curriculum (WCCRW, 1992). Despite strong public support for sex education in schools (Hayes, 1987), few schools have comprehensive sex education courses that begin in the elementary grades and continue through high school (Kirby, 1984). Furthermore, as Fine (1988) pointed out, those sex education courses that do exist tend to focus on sexuality as a question of violence, victimization, and individual morality but rarely as desire or pleasure. This denies the full reality of the experiences of young women as well as of young men (Tolman, 1991).

Furthermore, as AIDS and other sexually transmitted diseases pose an increasing danger for all young people, there is increasing evidence that adolescent girls are at particularly high risk (Dunkle & Nash, 1991; Irwin & Shafer, 1991). The U.S. has the highest rate of teenage childbearing in the industrialized world. Roughly half of the young women who drop out of school cite pregnancy as the reason (Ekstrom, Goertz, Pollack, & Rock, 1986). We can no longer afford to deny students an opportunity to learn about, to understand, and to value their bodies. Schools need to take a broader, more comprehensive, and more gender-equitable approach to sex education (Sapon-Shevin & Goodman, 1992; Stubbs, 1990).

School-based health clinics, child-care programs for the children of students who have not completed their education, and case managers located in schools to connect young mothers with social services outside the education system are all approaches that have proven successful in helping young mothers stay in school (Fraser, Roach, & Kysilko, 1987; Marx, 1987; Marx, Bailey, & Francis, 1988). Further research on effective programmatic approaches may aid in the successful implementation in more schools.

GENDER BIAS IN TESTING

Testing and assessment procedures are at the center of many of today's education reform discussions. Gender-equity issues related to various forms of assessment are less often heard (Bailey & Campbell, 1992–1993). However, research points clearly to a number of problems in our current tests and testing procedures.

The scores of females as a group and males as a group differ on a variety of standardized tests, but these group differences on tests do not always equate with differences in performance in courses or on the job. For example, Wainer and Steinberg (1992) reported that women who had taken the same college math classes and received the same math grade as men had scored on average 33 points lower on the SAT-M than the men. Test scores are used to counsel students about appropriate courses and careers as well as about admission to college and the awarding of college scholarships. Writing about vocational aptitude tests, which also show marked differences between females and males, Connor and Vargas (1992) concluded that "rather than expanding vocational options, aptitude tests and inventories heighten the other systematic pressures that make a young woman's pursuit of nontraditional vocational training extremely unlikely" (p. 24).

There are data indicating that the format of a test influences students' scores differentially on the basis of sex. Girls tend to do better on essay exams; boys do better on multiple-choice tests (Mazzeo, Schmitt, & Bleistein, 1991; Petersen & Livingston, 1982). The content and context of a test item can also favor girls or boys. For example, testing reading ability with an item about baseball batting averages tends to give boys an edge, whereas an item of similar difficulty but focusing on child care may favor girls (Pearlman, 1987; Wendler & Carlton, 1987). Further research on gender-equitable tests, tests in which individual girls and boys may score differently but in which there are

no significant differences between the scores of girls as a group and boys as a group, is needed.

SCHOOL ORGANIZATION FACTORS

The ways schools organize students can have powerful and differential effects on girls and boys; conversely, the sex of the student is sometimes a factor in the school's organizing patterns. Placements in special education classes are disproportionately male (U.S. Department of Education, Office of Civil Rights, 1988). Research by Hallinan and Sorensen (1987) documented that a student's sex influences the assignment to high- and low-ability groups in mathematics: Boys are more often assigned to the high group. Oakes (1990) reported that tracking—placing students systematically in different course sequences—has the cumulative effect of exacerbating, rather than ameliorating, differences among various groups of students. Vocational education course enrollments, despite specific sex-equity legislation and years of work by state-level vocational education sex-equity coordinators, remain highly sex segregated (Wirt, Muraskin, Goodwin, & Meyer, 1989).

School staffing patterns themselves reflect and enforce a gendered organization model. High school science teachers are predominantly male (Weiss, 1987), and in vocational education, women teach over 90% of all home economics classes and only 4% of industrial arts courses (U.S. Department of Education, Office of Educational Research and Improvement, 1992). Seventy-two percent of all classroom teachers are female, but only 28% of school principals and less than 5% of district superintendents are women (American Association of School Administrators, 1990; National Education Association, 1992).

Educators have focused considerable attention recently on early adolescents—students in the so-called middle grades—sixth, seventh, and eighth (Eccles & Midgley, 1990; Mac Iver & Epstein, 1991). Simmons and Blyth (1987) studied the affect on students of moving from elementary to junior high to high school. They reported that girls fare better in situations in which there is a single transition rather than two.

In terms of self-esteem the K–6/JH/SH girls never recover from the seventh-grade drop in self-esteem . . . they respond more, not less, negatively to the transition into senior high school than does the cohort who has to make only one change at a more mature age. (p. 227)

Researchers have documented that junior high school classrooms (Feldlaufer, Midgley, & Eccles, 1988) provide less interaction among students and that student-teacher relationships are less strong in junior high school than in elementary school. Others have noted that the change from the more personal environment of elementary school to the more impersonal environment of junior high school may be particularly difficult for girls (Jackson & Hornbeck, 1989).

However, much of the research on middle school organization and climate does not address gender directly (Midgley, Feldlaufer, & Eccles, 1989). There is a need for further research on the ways in which various school organizational patterns may affect girls and boys differentially.

EXTRACURRICULAR ACTIVITIES AND SPORTS

Research on student participation in extracurricular activities and the impact this may have on academic achievement and on classroom participation is extremely limited. But these activities obviously provide opportunities for leadership and teamwork, opportunities that should be equally available to girls and boys. The data that are available on athletic participation by sex, and in a few cases by race and ethnicity, are incomplete; what is available reveals progress at the same time that it illustrates the need for further improvement. In 1972, the year Title IX was passed, approximately 4% of girls in U.S. public high schools participated in interscholastic sports; today the figure is closer to one third (National Federation of State High School Associations, 1990). However, boys still participate at almost twice the rate of girls. Furthermore, the percentage of women coaching secondary school teams has decreased since 1972 (Isaac & Shafer, 1989).

In one of the few studies examining participation in sports by gender and race/ethnicity, The Women's Sports Foundation Report (1989) found that although Hispanic girls have a low sports participation rate, they, more than any other minority subgroup "were most likely to reap benefits from participating in high school athletics . . . [and] more apt than nonathletes to improve their academic standing while in high school, to graduate and to attend college following high school" (p. 14). Those who believe that Title IX has solved the problems girls and young women face in terms of equal opportunities to participate in school athletics need to look at the data again. Furthermore, research is needed that can help educators better understand the link between athletics and academic achievement and the ways in which gender and race/ethnicity affect this relationship.

A review of over 1,300 research studies, reports, and presentations addressing issues related to the status of girls in public elementary and secondary schools revealed an almost total lack of research on school-sponsored curricular activities and their affect on girls and boys (WCCRW, 1992). However, data on pregnant and parenting students collected in conjunction with a review of Title IX compliance raises questions about the extent to which school personnel may be using eligibility rules for participation in school-sponsored activities to reinforce gender-stereotyped assumptions.

Title IX clearly prohibits differential treatment of pregnant and parenting students, but a 1990 survey of state educational equity practices noted that several states have attempted to bar pregnant students from honor societies but have not exerted similar prohibitions against student fathers (Berrien, 1990).

Although research on extracurricular activities is limited, evaluation data from organizations such as Girls Inc. and the Girl Scouts suggest their programs may have a positive impact on girls and provide an important supplement to the school curriculum. An ethnographic study of Operation SMART (Nicholson & Frederick, 1991) found that "while girls showed some initial reluctance when faced with the unfamiliar [in science], with minimal encouragement and modeling, they soon set to exploring everything from snakes to environmental chemistry" (p. viii). In the words of one participant in Project Eureka, an out-of-school summer science program for girls:

> In Eureka science we get to do experiments every day and discuss and help our peers, but in school science you can't talk among your friends about the work or you will get into trouble . . . you can't experiment every day in school because you are supposed to have covered a certain amount of work by the end of the year. (Campbell, 1990).

Researchers concerned with gender equity in education may want to turn their attention to those after-school activities that appear to be particularly successful for girls in order to provide direction for in-school activities.

RESEARCH ON SINGLE-SEX ENVIRONMENTS

One frequent response to research that reveals inequitable treatment, unequal participation, or lower achievement for girls in coeducational school is to posit single-sex schools and classrooms as the solution. The difficulty in addressing this issue from a research perspective is that virtually all public elementary and secondary schools in the U.S. are coeducation.[2] Single-sex schools are either parochial or private and as such, they draw students from particular segments of society rather than from all racial, ethnic, class, and economic backgrounds. Nevertheless, research conducted in single-sex schools should be considered when reviewing the status of research on gender equity in education, for this work points to important variables and critical issues that should not be overlooked.

Research on single-sex Catholic schools in the U.S. (Lee & Bryk, 1986; Marsh, 1989; Riordan, 1985, 1990) suggests that although there are some academic advantages for girls in a single-sex setting, the advantages for boys are more mixed in comparison to boys in coeducational settings.

Researchers with the Harvard Project on the Psychology of Women and the Development of Girls (Brown & Gilligan, 1992; Gilligan, Lyons, & Harm-

mer, 1990; Rogers & Gilligan, 1988) have been studying girls' development for the past decade. The majority of their published work refers to students in selective single-sex schools. This work raises serious questions about the automatic advantages of single-sex environments for young women. Researchers reported that even though these selective schools were originally designed specifically to foster girls' education, girls are increasingly silenced as they mature. Gilligan (1990) noted that "sometime between the ages of 11 and 12 there is a change. . . . By midadolescence, many girls come to question the validity of their own perceptions or feelings" (pp. 5, 6).

In one of the most comprehensive studies to date of single-sex and coeducational environments (Lee, Marks, & Knowles, 1991), researchers collected data in 86 classrooms in 21 independent schools. They reported that classes in all-girls schools were more often rated as gender equitable but that in many of these classrooms, lack of academic vigor was also found. Lee et al. reported that strong, clearly worded policies that are monitored and enforced play a crucial role in promoting gender-equitable educational environments.

Further research that documents the extent of sexist practices and the methods that are most effective in overcoming them is obviously needed. Studies of schools that have moved from single sex to coeducation may provide important insights into the complex dynamics of creating a truly coeducational environment (Russell, in press).

NEXT STEPS

At the beginning of this article, gender-equitable education was defined, in part, as an education that provides a wide range of choices for students of both sexes. Minow (1992) at the Harvard Law School wrote of the "erroneous view that choice is either all-present or all-absent" (p. 2094). This all-or-nothing approach to choice is a fallacious one; she wrote, "a more fruitful conception locates human choices within varying degrees of constraints" (p. 2094). Educational researchers must examine the constraining factors within our educational system that inhibit girls and boys from making gender-equitable choices about their lives and schooling.

Such research begins with an understanding of the school and its classrooms as social systems within which students learn both from what is taught explicitly—the formal curriculum, as well as from what is evaded; social systems in which the interpersonal interactions between and among teachers, students, and school staff carry powerful lessons; and places where we can prepare girls and boys for the 21st century or where we can attempt to hold them within the constraints of outmoded roles, expectations, and choices.

The research reviewed in this article suggests several steps educators can take now to promote gender-equitable teaching practices and school environments.

1. Establish clearly worded widely disseminated, and strictly enforced policies requiring gender-equitable treatment for all students and staff (including procedures for dealing with sexual harassment).

2. Support faculty development programs that help educators acquire teaching techniques that address the imbalances in the amounts and types of attention and instruction that girls and boys receive.

3. Develop state and local evaluation criteria for teachers and administrators that specifically focus on demonstrating competence in creating gender-equitable schools and classrooms, and tie these evaluations directly to certification, salaries, and promotions.

4. Review curricular materials and testing procedures for gender and racial bias. Not all school districts can afford the newest materials, but by reviewing materials periodically the most outdated can be eliminated and the data generated by the review can serve as an effective argument for additional state and local funding for curricular materials.

5. Gather data by sex and race/ethnicity on course enrollments, achievement levels and extracurricular activities within the school and school district. Study these data to determine whether imbalances exist that may signal inequitable expectations and/or treatment of students in terms of course placements, special referrals, or extracurricular opportunities.

NOTES

1. There are virtually no data on classroom interaction patterns that provide comparisons for disabled and nondisabled girls and boys. However, national data reveal that over two thirds of the students in special education classes are boys (U.S. Department of Education, 1988), despite medical data indicating roughly equal proportions of girls and boys with learning disabilities (Shaywitz, Shaywitz, Fletcher, & Escobar, 1990). Wagner (1992) reported that "data indicate that females in secondary special education represented a different combination of abilities and disabilities than males. As a group, females were more seriously impaired . . . " (p. 34). School personnel appear to be using sex-based criteria when referring students for special education services.

2. Only two public all-girl high schools remain, one in Philadelphia and one in Baltimore.

REFERENCES

American Association of School Administrators. (1990). *Women and minorities in school administration: Facts and figures 1989–1990.* Arlington, VA: Author.

Applebee, A. (1989). *A study of book length works taught in high school English courses.* Albany: State University of New York Press.

Bailey, S., & Campbell, P. (1992–1993). Gender equity: The unexamined basic of school reform. *Stanford Law & Policy Review, 4,* 73–86.

Baker, D. (1986). Sex differences in classroom interactions in secondary science. *Journal of Classroom Interaction,22,* 212–218.

Berrien, J. (1990). *Equal educational opportunities for pregnant and parenting students: Meshing the rights with the realities.* New York: Women's Rights Project of the American Civil Liberties Union and the American Civil Liberties Union Foundation in cooperation with the American Association of University Women Educational Foundation and the American Association of University Women.

Best, R. (1983). *We've all got scars: What boys and girls learn in elementary school.* Bloomington: Indiana University Press.

Brown, L. M., & Gilligan, C. (1992). *Meeting at the crossroads: Women's psychology and girls' development.* Cambridge, MA: Harvard University Press.

Campbell, P. (1990). *Douglass science institute: Three years of encouraging young women in math, science, engineering.* Groton, MA: Campbell-Kibler Associates.

Connor, K., & Vargas, E. (1992). The legal implications of gender bias in standardized testing. *Berkeley Women's Law Journal, 7,* 13–89.

Damico, S., & Scott, E. (1988). Behavior differences between Black and White females in desegregated schools. *Equity and Excellence, 23,* 63–66.

Dunkle, M., & Nash, M. (Eds.). (1991). *Beyond the health room.* Washington, DC: Council of Chief State School Officers, Resource Center on Educational Equity.

Earle, J., Fraser, K., Roach, V., & Kysilko, D. (1987). *What's promising: New approaches to dropout prevention for girls.* Alexandria, VA: National Association of State Boards of Education.

Ebbeck, M. (1984). Equity for some boys and girls: Some important issues. *Early Child Development and Care, 18,* 119–131.

Eccles, J. S. (1989). Bringing young women to math and science. In M. Crawford & M. Gentry (Eds.). *Gender and thought: Psychological perspectives* (pp. 36–58). New York: Springer-Verlag.

Eccles, J. S., Kaczala, C. M., & Meece, J. (1982). Socialization of achievement attitudes and beliefs: Classroom influences. *Child Development, 53,* 322–339.

Eccles, J. S., & Midgley, C. (1990). Changes in academic motivation and self-perception during early adolescence. In R. Montemayor, G. Adams, & T. Gullotta (Eds.), *From childhood to adolescence: A transitional period?* (pp. 134–155). Newbury Park, CA: Sage.

Ekstrom, R., Goertz, M., Pollack, J., & Rock, D. (1986). Who drops out of high school and why: Findings from a national study. *Teachers College Record, 87,* 356–373.

Etaugh, C., & Liss, M. (1992). Home, school, and playroom: Training grounds for adult gender roles. *Sex Roles, 26,* 129–147.

Feldlaufer, H., Midgley, C., & Eccles, J. (1988). Student, teacher, and observer perceptions of the classroom environment before and after the transition to junior high school. *Journal of Early Adolescence, 8,* 133–156.

Fine, M. (1988). Sexuality, schooling, and adolescent females: The missing discourse of desire. *Harvard Educational Review, 58,* 29–53.

Gilligan, C. (1990). Girls at 11: An interview with Carol Gilligan. *Harvard Education Letter, 6,* 5–7

Gilligan, C., Lyons, N., & Hammer, T. (1990). *Making connections.* Cambridge, MA: Harvard University Press.

Grant, L. (1984). Black females' 'place' in desegregated classrooms. *Sociology of Education, 57,* 98–111.

Grant, L. (1985). Race-gender status, classroom interaction, and children's socialization in elementary school. In L. Wilkinson & C. Marrett (Eds.), *Gender influences in classroom interaction* (pp. 55–75). Orlando, FL: Academic.

Grayson, D. A., & Martin, M. D. (1990). *Gender/ethnic expectations and student achievement (GESA): Teacher handbook.* Earlham, IA: GrayMill.

Hall, R. M., Sandler, B. R. (1982). *The classroom climate: A chilly one for women?* Washington, DC: Association of American Colleges.

Hallinan, M., & Sorensen, A. (1987). Ability grouping and sex differences in mathematics achievement. *Sociology of Education, 60,* 63–72.

Harris/Scholastic Research. (1993). *Hostile hallways.* Washington, DC: American Association of University Women.

Hayes, C. D. (Ed.). (1987). *Risking the future: Adolescent sexuality, pregnancy, and childbearing* (Vol. I). Washington, DC: National Academy Press.

Huff, C., & Cooper, J. (1987). Sex bias in educational software: The effects of designer's stereotypes on the software they design. *Journal of Applied Social Psychology, 17,* 519–532.

Irvine, J. (1985). Teacher communication patterns as related to the race and sex of students. *Journal of Educational Research, 78,* 338–345.

Irvine, J. (1986). Teacher-student interactions: Effects of student race, sex, and grade level. *Journal of Educational Research, 78,* 14–21.

Irwin, C., & Shafer, M. (1991, February). *Adolescent sexuality: The problem of a negative outcome of a normative behavior.* Paper presented at the conference "Adolescents at Risk: Medical and Social Perspectives," Cornell University Medical College, Ithaca, NY.

Isaac, T., & Shafer, S. (1989). *Sex equity in sports leadership: Implementing the game plan in your community.* Lexington: Eastern Kentucky University.

Jackson, A., & Hornbeck, D. (1989). Educating young adolescents: Why we must restructure middle grade schools. *American Psychologist, 44,* 831–836.

Jones, G. (1989). Gender bias in classroom interactions. *Contemporary Education, 60,* 216–222.

Jones, G., & Wheatley, J. (1990). Gender differences in teacher-student interactions in science classrooms. *Journal of Research in Science Teaching, 27,* 861–874.

Kahle, J. B., & Meece, J. L. (in press). Research on girls in science: Lessons and applications. In D. Gabel (Ed.), *Handbook of research in science teaching & learning.* Washington, DC: National Science Teachers Association.

Kahle, J. B., Riley, D., Parker, L. H., & Rennie, L. J. (1993). Gender differences in science education: Building a model. *Educational Psychologist, 28,* 379–404.

Kirby, D. (1984). *Sexuality education: An evaluation of programs and their effects.* Santa Cruz, CA: Network Publications.

Krupnick, C. (1985). Women and men in the classroom. *On Teaching and Learning, 12,* 18–25.

Lee, V., & Bryk, A. (1986). Effects of single-sex secondary schools on student achievement and attitudes. *Journal of Educational Psychology, 78,* 381–395.

Lee, V., Marks, H., & Knowles, T. (1991, August). *Sexism in single-sex and coeducational secondary school classrooms.* Paper presented at the annual meeting of the American Sociological Association, Cincinnati.

Linn, M., & Burbules, N. (in press). Construction of knowledge and group learning. In K. Tobin (Ed.), *Constructivism and applications in mathematics and science.* Washington, DC: American Association for the Advancement of Science.

Lockheed, M. (1984). *Final report: A study of sex equality in classroom interaction.* Washington, DC: National Institute of Education.

Lockheed, M. (1986). Reshaping the social order: The case of gender segregation. *Sex Roles, 14,* 617–618.

Lockheed, M., & Harris, A. (1984). Cross-sex collaborative learning in elementary classrooms. *American Educational Research Journal, 21,* 275–294.

Maccoby, E. (1990). Gender and relationships: A developmental account. *American Psychologist, 45,* 513–520.

Maccoby, E., & Jacklin, C. (1987). Gender segregation in childhood. In H. Reese, L. Lipsitt, & C. Spiker (Eds.), *Advances in child development and behavior* (Vol. 20, pp. 239–288). New York: Academic.

MacIver, D., & Epstein, J. (1991, August). Responsive practices in the middle grades: Teacher teams, advisory groups, remedial instruction, and school transition programs. *American Journal of Education, 99,* 587–622.

Marsh, H. (1989). Effects of attending single-sex and coeducational high schools on achievement, attitudes, behaviors, and sex differences. *Journal of Educational Psychology, 81,* 70–85.

Marx, F. (1987). *The role of day care in serving the needs of school-age parents and their children: A review of the literature.* Wellesley, MA: Wellesley College Center for Research on Women.

Marx, F., Bailey, S., & Francis, J. (1988). *Child care for the children of adolescent parents: Findings from a national survey and case studies.* Wellesley, MA: Wellesley College Center for Research on Women.

Mazzeo, J., Schmitt, A., & Bleistein, C. (1991, April). *Do women perform better, relative to men, on constructed response tests or multiple choice tests? Evidence from the Advanced Placement Examinations.* Paper presented at the meeting of the National Council on Measurement in Education, Chicago, IL.

Meece, J. L., & Eccles, J. S. (1993). Introduction: Recent trends and future directions in research on gender and education. *Educational Psychologist, 28,* 313–319.

Midgley, C., Feldlaufer, H., & Eccles, J. S. (1989). Student/teacher relations and attitudes toward mathematics before and after the transition to junior high school. *Child Development, 60,* 981–992.

Minow, M. (1992). Choices and constraints: For Justice Thurgood Marshall. *The Georgetown Law Journal, 80,* 2093–2108.

Morse, L., & Handley, H. (1985). Listening to adolescents: Gender differences in science classrooms interaction. In L. Wilkinson & C. Marrett (Eds.), *Gender influences in classroom interaction* (pp. 37–56). Orlando, FL: Academic.

National Education Association. (1992). *Status of the American public school teacher 1990–1992.* Washington, DC: Author.

National Federation of State High School Associations. (1990). *1990 handbook.* Kansas City, MO: National Federation of State High School Associations.

Nelson-Le Gall, S., & DeCooke, P. (1987). Same-sex and cross-sex help exchanges in the classroom. *Journal of Educational Psychology, 79,* 67–71.

Nicholson, H., & Frederick, J. (1991). *The explorer's pass: A report card on case studies of girls and math, science and technology.* New York: Girls Incorporated.

Oakes, J. (1990). *Lost talent: The underparticipation of women, minorities, and disabled persons in science.* Santa Monica, CA: The RAND Corporation.

Pearlman, M. (1987, April). *Trends in women's total score and item performance on verbal measures.* Paper presented at the annual meeting of the American Educational Research Associates, Washington, DC.

Petersen, N., & Livingston, S. (1982). *English composition test with essay: A descriptive study of the relationship between essay and objective scores by ethnic group and sex.* Princeton, NJ: Educational Testing Service.

Peterson, P., & Fennema, E. (1985). Effective teaching, student engagement in classroom activities, and sex-related differences in learning mathematics. *American Educational Research Journal, 22,* 309–335.

Pollard, D. S. (1993). Gender, achievement, and African-American students' perceptions of their school experience. *Educational Psychologist, 28,* 341–356.

Riordan, C. (1985). Public and Catholic schooling: The effects of gender context policy. *American Journal of Education, 93,* 518–540.

Riordan, C. (1990). *Girls and boys in school: Together or separate.* New York: Columbia University, Teachers College.

Rogers, A., & Gilligan, C. (1988). *Translating girls' voices: Two languages of development.* Cambridge, MA: Harvard University Graduate School of Education, Harvard Project on the Psychology of Women and the Development of Girls.

Russell, J. (in press). Going coed in the 90s and the search for core values: Valuing the feminine, finding the good. *Feminist Teacher.*

Sadker, D., & Sadker, M. (1985a). Is the ok classroom ok? *Phi Delta Kappan, 55,* 358–367.

Sadker, D., & Sadker, M. (1985b). Sexism in the schoolroom of the 80s. *Psychology Today, 19,* 54–57.

Sadker, M., & Sadker, D. (1984). *Year 3: Final report, promoting effectiveness in classroom instruction.* Washington, DC: National Institute of Education.

Sapon-Shevin, M., & Goodman, J. (1992). Learning to be the opposite sex: Sexuality education and sexual scripting in early adolescence. In J. Sears (Ed.), *Sexuality and the classroom: The politics and practices of sexuality education* (pp. 89–105). New York: Teachers College Press.

Scott-Jones, D., & Clark, M. (1986). The school experiences of Black girls: The interaction of gender, race, and socioeconomic status. *Phi Delta Kappan, 67,* 520–526.

Serbin, L., O'Leary, K., Kent, R., & Tronick, I. (1973). A comparison of teacher responses to the pre-academic and problem behavior of boys and girls. *Child Development, 44,* 796–804.

Shaywitz, S., Shaywitz, B., Fletcher, J., & Escobar, M. (1990). Prevalence of reading disability in boys and girls: Results of the Connecticut longitudinal study. *Journal of American Medical Association, 264,* 998–1002.

Simmons, R., & Blyth, D. (1987). *Moving into adolescence: The impact of pubertal change and the school context.* New York: Aldine de Gruyter.

Sizer, T. (1992). *Horace's school: Redesigning the American high school.* Boston: Houghton Mifflin.

Smith, N., Greenlaw, M., & Scott, C. (1987). Making the literate environment equitable. *Reading Teacher,* 400–407.

Stein, N. (1986). Sexual harassment: Its existence and effects in Massachusetts high schools. In N. Stein (Ed.), *Who's hurt and who's liable: Sexual harassment in Massachusetts schools* (4th ed., pp. 1–6). Quincy: The Commonwealth of Massachusetts, Department of Education.

Stein, N., Marshall, N., & Tropp, L. (1993). *Secrets in public: Sexual harassment in our schools.* Wellesley, MA: Wellesley College Center for Research on Women and the National Organization for Women Legal Defense and Education Fund.

Stubbs, M. (1990). *Bodytalk.* Wellesley, MA: Wellesley College Center for Research on Women.

Thorne, B. (1986). Girls and boys together . . . but mostly apart: Gender arrangements in elementary schools. In W. Hartup & Z. Rubin (Eds.), *Relationships and development* (pp. 167–184). Hillsdale, NJ: Lawrence Erlbaum Associates, Inc.

Thorne, B. (1993). *Gender play: Girls and boys in school.* New Brunswick, NJ: Rutgers University Press.

Tobin, K., & Garnett, P. (1987). Gender related differences in science activities. *Science Education, 71,* 91–103.

Tolman, D. (1991). Adolescent girls, women, and sexuality: Discerning dilemmas of desire. In C. Gilligan, A. Rogers, & D. Tolman (Eds.), *Women, girls and psychotherapy: Reframing resistance* (pp. 55–69). New York: Harrington Park Press.

U.S. Department of Commerce, Bureau of the Census. (1990). *Statistical abstract of the U.S.: 1990.* Washington, DC: Author.

U.S. Department of Commerce, Bureau of the Census. (1991). *Statistical abstract of the United States: 1991.* Washington, DC: Author.

U.S. Department of Education, Office of Civil Rights. (1988). *Elementary and Secondary School Civil Rights Survey.* Washington, DC: U.S. Government Printing Office.

U.S. Department of Education, Office of Educational Research and Improvement. (1992). *A comparison of vocational and non-vocational public school teachers of grades 9–12.* Washington, DC: U.S. Government Printing Office.

Wagner, M. (1992). *Being female—A secondary disability? Gender differences in the transition experiences of young people with disabilities.* Bethesda, MD: SRI International, National Longitudinal Transition Study.

Wainer, H., & Steinberg, L. (1992). Sex differences in performance on the mathematics section of the Scholastic Aptitude Test: A bidirectional validation study. *Harvard Educational Review, 62,* 323–336.

Weiss, I. (1987). *Report of the 1985–86 National Survey of Science and Mathematics Education.* Research Triangle Park, NC: Research Triangle Institute.

Wellesley College Center for Research on Women. (1992). *How schools shortchange girls.* Washington, DC: American Association of University Women Educational Foundation.

Wendler, C., & Carlton, S. (1987, April). *An examination of SAT verbal items for differential performance by women and men: An exploratory study.* Paper presented at the annual meeting of the American Educational Research Association, Washington, DC.

Wilkerson, L., & Marrett, C. (1985). *Gender differences in classroom interaction.* Orlando, FL: Academic.

Wilkerson, L., Lindow, J., & Chiang, C. (1985). Sex differences and sex segregation in student's small-group communication. In L. Wilkerson & C. Marrett (Eds.), *Gender influences in classroom interaction* (pp. 185–208). Orlando, FL: Academic.

Wirt, J., Muraskin, L., Goodwin, D., & Meyer, R. (1989). *Summary of findings and recommendations: National assessment of vocational education.* Washington, DC: U.S. Department of Education.

The Women's Sports Foundation Report. (1989, August). *Minorities in sports: The effect of varsity sports participation on the social, educational, and career mobility of minority students.* New York: Women's Sports Foundation.

Anita Hill Is a Boy: Tales from a Gender-Fair Classroom

PEGGY ORENSTEIN

There is no single magic formula that will help girls retain their self-esteem. Scores of educators around the country are working to develop gender-fair curricula in all subjects and reexamining traditional assumptions about how children best learn. Some educators are developing strategies to break down gender and race hierarchies in cooperative learning groups.[1] Others are experimenting with the ways that computers, if used to their best advantage, can enhance equity in math and science courses.[2] Individually, teachers find that calling on students equitably, or simply waiting for a moment rather than recognizing the first child who raises his hand, encourages girls to participate more readily in class. On a national level, the Gender Equity in Education Act, which should be implemented in 1995, includes provisions for improved data gathering, for the development of teacher training programs, for programs to encourage girls in math and science, and for programs to better meet the needs of girls of color.

In trying to address the thornier issues of the hidden curriculum, some school districts have offered self-defense classes for girls, introduced aspects of sexuality education as early as kindergarten, or developed curricula that explicitly take on sexual harassment.[3] A few principals in embattled urban neighborhoods have recast their schools as round-the-clock community centers, offering recreational activities, adult education, medical care, and a flotilla of social services.[4] Others have begun mentoring programs or sponsored mother-daughter activities to help raise educational attainment rates and career aspirations among girls of color.[5]

Meanwhile, heated debate has arisen over whether mere reform—such as adding a few prominent women to existing texts or what has been called the "add women and stir" approach to gender equity[6]—is, indeed, adequate. In science, for instance, educators question the merits of a repackaged, "girl-friendly" curriculum versus a more radical examination of the very nature of objectivity and evidence collection.[7] Is it enough to simply call on girls more often or to introduce cooperative learning without changing the core of the male-dominated curriculum? Is it enough to change the substance of the curriculum but retain traditional classroom structures?

My own gender journey ends where it began, in the classroom of one teacher who is trying not only to practice equity but to teach it, to change both boys' and girls' perspectives on the female self. Judy Logan has been teaching for twenty-six years, twenty-two of them at San Francisco's Everett Middle School, where she currently coordinates the Gifted and Talented Education Program (GATE). Her students are an ethnically diverse lot, and although her classes have the highest proportion of white children in the school, about 40 percent of the pupils are Latino, Filipino, Asian American, or African American. As sixth graders, they spend three hours each morning with Ms. Logan learning language arts and social studies. Over the next two years, the students take quarter-long required and elective courses from all four GATE teachers which combine English and history. But whether she is teaching classes on Greek mythology or world cultures, American history or English literature, Ms. Logan has an agenda beyond the standard lesson plan: she aims to blast the hidden curriculum wide open.

Stepping into Ms. Logan's classroom from the drab hallways of Everett is somewhat of a shock. There are images of women everywhere: the faces of Abigail Adams, Rachel Carson, Faye Wattleton, and even a fanciful "Future Woman" smile out from three student-made quilts that are draped on the walls. Reading racks overflow with biographies of Lucretia Mott, Ida B. Wells, Emma Goldman, Sally Ride, and Rigoberta Menchú. There is a book on Jewish holidays and one on Muslim women. There is a section on Pele, the Hawaiian goddess of volcanoes, and a coffee table book on artist Judy Chicago's famed "Dinner Party." On the back wall, there is a display of student submissions to this year's city-wide National Organization for Women (NOW) essay contest on "Women We Admire." For the eighth year in a row, Ms. Logan's students—an equal number of girls and boys—won first or second prizes in all three grades. A giant computer-paper banner spans the width of another wall proclaiming, "Women are one-half of the world's people; they do two-thirds of the world's work; they earn one-tenth of the world's income; they own one one-hundredth of the world's property."

It almost seems wrong. Looking around Ms. Logan's classroom, I find myself wondering, 'Where are the men?' Then it dawns. This is a classroom that's gone through the gender looking glass. It is the mirror opposite of most classrooms that girls will enter, which are adorned with masculine role models, with male heroes, with books by and about men—classrooms in which the female self is, at best, an afterthought. This is what a classroom would look like if women were the dominant sex. Educator Emily Style has written that the curriculum should be both a window and a mirror for students, that they should be able to look into others' worlds, but also see the experiences of their own race, gender, and class reflected in what they learn.[8] In Ms. Logan's class, girls may be dazzled by the reflection of the women that surround them. And, perhaps for the first time, the boys are the ones looking in through the window.

WHEN BOYS ARE GIRLS

Forty-one sixth graders crowd into Ms. Logan's classroom each morning, and when I visit on a mid-February day, there isn't an extra chair in the house. Normally, the students sit at long, low tables arranged in vertical rows, but today those have been pushed aside, and the sixth graders have turned their child-sized chairs toward the front of the classroom. Ms. Logan sits among them, a fiftyish woman, with a round, pleasant face made owlish by her red plastic-framed glasses. She is dressed casually in an oversized African print shirt, leggings, and knee-high boots.

Today is the culmination of their African American history class. As a final project, each student has researched the lives of two prominent African Americans (past or present) and must now perform brief dramatic monologues as those people. The students have gone to great lengths to fulfill their assignment: the room is awash with costumes, props, audiotapes, books, and athletic gear. Although they had the option to recite their piece alone for Ms. Logan, most have chosen the limelight, and the posterity of the video camera, which is positioned at the back of the room.

Before class began, Ms. Logan told me that the first year she introduced this project she assigned only one monologue, but she noticed that while girls opted to take on either male or female personae, the boys chose only men. "It disturbed me that although girls were willing to see men as heroes, none of the boys would see women that way," she said. This was no surprise: I recall observing the same phenomenon among the student-written myths from Weston's English classes. At the time I wondered how the boys, who could only see male experience as relevant, would ever learn to see girls as equals.

Faced with the same concern, Ms. Logan decided to add her own hidden curriculum to the assignment. She began requiring two reports, one from the perspective of a man and one presented as a woman. To ask a group of boys, most of whom are white, to take on the personae—to actually *become*—black women forces an unprecedented shift in their mind-set. Yet Ms. Logan found they accepted the assignment without question.

"As long as it's required, they accept it," she explained. "But it wouldn't occur to them to choose it."

When the students have settled into their chairs or onto pillows on the floor, Ms. Logan asks for volunteers to begin. Jeremy is among the first to perform his female monologue. He saunters up to the stool that Ms. Logan has placed at the front of the room, a gangly white boy whose loose gait and rubbery features remind me of a Muppet. Like many of the boys, he has minimized the indignity of being required to "become" a woman by performing without a costume: he wears an orange baseball jacket, jeans, and untied sneakers.

He looks around uncomfortably. "To understand the blues," he begins, "you have to understand black history. When we were slaves, the only way we could express our pain was to sing, so we started singing about racism and about love. And that was the blues. To sing the blues, you have to live them, and I'm an example of that. My name is Etta James."

There is muffled tittering from the class.

James goes on to detail her life, starting with her discovery at age fifteen by R&B front man Johnny Otis, and including an incident in which she was threatened at gunpoint in a Texas restaurant for using a whites-only rest room. She touches on her heroin addiction and descent into petty crime, then finishes up with her recent triumphant comeback.

"It wasn't that we wanted to sing the blues," James concludes. "We women had to. And even though men owned the record companies, even though men were the deejays and they controlled the world, we had to sing and be heard. And we were so strong, we women singers—it was scary."

James walks to one side of the classroom, where she has stashed a small tape recorder. She presses a button, returns to center stage, and begins to lip-sync to a bluesy ballad. This is too much for the class to handle, and the disbelief they've so valiantly suspended for the past five minutes comes crashing down. A boy begins to laugh and more join in, as do some of the girls. James tries to keep a straight face, but even she knows that the image of an eleven-year-old white boy syncing the blues is ridiculous, and a struggle for control ensues: Etta briefly gives way to Jeremy, who starts to giggle. Then she regains the upper hand for a moment before losing out to the boy once more. The whole performance ends up more comedic than respectful, and although Jeremy receives a vigorous hand when it is over, he has opened the door for the boys to make a mockery out of the feminine part of their assignment.

"Ms. James," Ms. Logan says when the applause dies down, "did you apologize when the restaurant owner threatened to kill you?"

"Yes," James answers, hopping back onto the stool.

"And how did that feel?"

"I felt really bad about it," James says. "I guess I wasn't used to racism."

Ms. Logan nods her head. "I'd like to ask Ms. James to step aside now and let me ask Jeremy a question."

Jeremy jumps off the stool, takes a few steps and turns around, now himself.

"Was it hard for you when you got up here to sing because some of the people were laughing?" Ms. Logan asks.

Jeremy shrugs. "Sort of," he says.

"Was it different when you practiced it at home?"

"It was more serious at home," Jeremy answers, ducking his head. "I did it seriously."

"Class, I'd like you to understand the interaction between the audience and the performer," Ms. Logan says. "If you laugh, it's very hard for Jeremy to stay in character, but if you support him, he can take risks. How you respond has tremendous impact on what a performer can and can't do. Jeremy, you took some real risks up there and I thought that was great."

As Jeremy returns to his seat, one of the boys turns to another, who had instigated the laughter. "I didn't think it was funny until you had to go and laugh like that," he says. "I would give him an A if I was grading."

A third boy says, "Me, too," and slaps Jeremy five as he walks by.

As the reports proceed, it becomes clear that the subtexts of Ms. Logan's lessons are not just about gender, nor, in fact, are they about race. Muhammad Ali's monologue sparks a discussion about the price one pays for success. West Indian writer Jamaica Kincaid inspires comment about noninvasive tourism. And when Charles, a shy African American boy costumed in gym shorts and a sleeveless jersey, finishes his report as Michael Jordan after a near-disastrous stumble partway through, Ms. Logan steps to the fore and puts a hand on his shoulder.

"I'd like to ask you as Charles," she says, "how did it feel for you to stand up here like this?"

"I didn't like it," he says, his voice trembling slightly. "It was hard for me. I didn't like it at all."

"And how could we, as your audience, have helped you out?"

"You were fine," he says. "You listened and didn't laugh when I messed up. It was me. I'm sorry."

Ms. Logan addresses the students. "How many of you have one thing in this class that's really, really hard for you?" she asks.

Most of the sixth graders raise their hands.

She turns to a small, alert-looking, boy. "What's your hard thing?" she asks.

"I don't know," the boy replies, "but I'm sure there is one."

"Well, okay," Ms. Logan says, turning to a girl who has raised her hand. "What's yours?"

"Stage fright," the girl says, giving a mock shudder.

"How many of you have stage fright, a little bit or a lot?"

About a third of the students raise their hands.

"And what can we, as an audience, do to help?"

"Don't laugh," says Charles.

"Listen," says a girl.

"Smile and look encouraging," says another girl.

"Yes," says Ms. Logan, "show expressions of support. Charles, it was really brave of you to get up here and do this when you had the option not to. You have nothing to apologize for. I know how hard it was, and it took a lot of courage."

Charles leaves the stage smiling. Although this mini-lesson on the value of supportiveness and appropriate risk taking was conducted surrounding a boy's experience, it seemed especially relevant for girls. I thought about the exaggerated fear of humiliation among the young women I have met, a fear so acute that they often silenced themselves in class. Like Weston's history teacher, Ms. Nellas, who stressed that "'dumb' questions lead to learning," Ms. Logan has confronted her students' anxieties and taken the shame out of imperfection.

Later, when a minute Asian American girl begins lip-syncing "What a Difference a Day Makes" as Dinah Washington, the class begins to giggle again and she falters.

"Remember what we learned about the audience and performers, class," Ms. Logan warns, and the students simmer down. By the end of the piece, the girl's performance is so precise that the class is mesmerized, and they finish out the last chorus along with her: "What a difference a day makes, and the difference is you!" (I'm surprised that they know the words, until I remember that the song is also the advertising jingle for the California state lottery.)

Over the course of the next few mornings the students are visited by nearly eighty-four prominent African Americans. Ida B. Wells talks at breakneck speed, reeling off an account of her life as a journalist, an activist, and co-founder of the National Association for the Advancement of Colored People (NAACP). Jackie Robinson discusses the difficulty and rewards of breaking the color barrier in baseball. The class is introduced to a fiery Angela Davis and a very nervous Frederick Douglass. Sculptor Richmond Barthé informs them, "You probably don't know me because certain people who write certain history books didn't put me in them because of my certain color," and poet Paul Laurence Dunbar recites his "Ode to Ethiopia." There are flashes of humor, as when Miles Davis' tape recorder goes on the fritz and Ms. Logan suggests that someone else step in until the trumpeter is ready.

"You know how temperamental these artists can be," she confides to the class.

There are also moments of true poignancy. Maya Angelou, for instance, in the guise of a freckle-faced white boy, discusses the trauma of being raped by a supposed family friend. When the man was subsequently murdered, she explains, looking sorrowfully at the class, "I didn't know whether to laugh or cry, whether to feel sorrow or joy." (Later, when recalling her first pregnancy, Ms. Angelou also asserts that "the pain of childbirth is overrated.")

After two hours of reports, the sixth graders take a fifteen-minute break, during which they have a snack and read to themselves. I join three girls in a corner who are chatting quietly over apples and boxes of juice. Holly wears glasses, has a precocious expression, and speaks in a clipped voice. I ask how she has enjoyed her year in Ms. Logan's class. "I like that Ms. Logan does things on women and women's rights," she answers. "She never, never discriminates against girls, and I'm glad that someone finally got that idea." She takes a bite of apple and chews thoughtfully. "But sometimes I think the boys don't like it."

Jill, a chubby-cheeked girl with dark eyebrows, who seems meek in Holly's presence, pipes up. "My older brother had Ms. Logan," she says. "And he said all she ever talked about was women, women, women. He didn't like her."

"I guess it's because all the other teachers ignore women," Holly says. "But sometimes I worry about the boys, that they get kind of ignored."

"Look at this room," complains Dana, who is Chinese American. The girls turn and scrutinize the walls. "There's all this stuff on women everywhere."

"That's true," says Holly. "But I'm still glad someone finally got the idea that we're all the same. I mean except for a few things, of course. That's good, I guess."

As the girls talk, I recall what a teacher at Weston once told me, that "boys perceive equality as a loss." Apparently, girls are uneasy with it, too. Even these girls, whose parents have placed them in this class in part because of Ms. Logan's sensitivity to gender issues have already become used to taking up less space, to feeling less worthy of attention than boys.

I wander to the back of the room, where Mindy, who is an eighth grader, lolls near the video camera. Mindy is a model of grunge chic, dressed in a faded plaid shirt, battered jeans, and purple Converse sneakers. She has lank brown hair which hangs to her jaw, and a pair of oval granny glasses balanced on her snub nose. Mindy has been in Ms. Logan's class for three years, and is taping today's proceedings as a favor to her teacher. I ask her opinion, as a veteran of the class, about Ms. Logan's attempts at gender-fair teaching.

"The boys definitely resent it," she says matter-of-factly. "They think Ms. Logan is sexist. But you know what I think? I think that it's the resentment of losing their place. In our other classes, the teachers just focus on men, but the boys don't complain that *that's* sexist. They say, 'It's different in those classes because we're focusing on the important people in history, who just happen to be men.'"

Mindy rolls her eyes and adopts a long suffering expression. "The girls like having all the women's history stuff, though," she continues, "unless they like some guy and worry about what *he* thinks about it. But I don't think that's so true by eighth grade. In sixth grade the girls are nervous about what the boys think because they're not used to it yet. But now I enjoy it, and a lot of the other girls do, too."

Of all the African American history monologues Nick's which is performed just after the break, makes the strongest impression. Nick is a thin boy with carrot-colored hair, milky skin, and freckles. He performs as Anita Hill and, like many of the boys, has chosen to proceed without the aid of a costume. Unlike some of the other female monologues delivered by males, there is complete silence as Professor Hill relates her personal history and her now notorious encounters with her onetime boss, Clarence Thomas. The sixth graders are old enough to remember seeing Hill on television when she testified before the Senate Judiciary Committee, and they watch intently, recognizing the importance of her words. Hill declines to go into detail about what, precisely, Judge Thomas said to her, because, she explains, "in the end, no one will really know what happened between us, except us."

Hill ends her report by looking straight into the video camera. "I had to have the courage to speak out against sexual harassment for other women in this country," she says solemnly. "So they could speak out, too, and become strong."

When she is finished, Professor Hill blushes to the roots of her red hair.

"Dr. Hill, I'm a great admirer of yours," Ms. Logan says, "and I'd like to know whether, even though Judge Thomas was confirmed, you feel some good came out of the hearings?"

Hill nods her head. "I showed other women that they can come forward," she responds. "They don't have to take that kind of behavior from *anyone*."

"Give her a hand, everyone," Ms. Logan says, and even though she is gesturing to a boy—who in most cases would undoubtedly be ashamed to be called "her" in front of forty peers—no one even flinches. Instead, the students burst into applause. And Nick, who has, if only for a few minutes, lived the experience of a sexually harassed woman, takes his seat.

EDUCATION THAT INCLUDES US ALL

After the bell rings, and the students leave for lunch, Ms. Logan and I sit across from each other at one of the low tables. "This is learning from the inside out," she explains enthusiastically. "They do the research, they connect into that other life, and they really *become* the person. People always ask me how you can get boys to stop being so totally male-oriented. I say, 'You just do it, and they'll pick it up as you go.' If you do a project like this, they really have to take on a female persona in a serious way, in a way that's respectful to the woman and her role in history. "It's a thrill for me to hear the way boys stand up for women's rights in their monologues. And I think it's meaningful for them, too."

I tell Ms. Logan about my conversation with the sixth-grade girls, about how, in spite of their gratitude toward her for treating them fairly, they worry that equity excludes boys. Before I can even finish my thought, she begins to smile. This is a comment she's heard before.

"It's true," she says. "Sometimes the kids resist the idea of gender equity, and it isn't always the boys either. One year, during a quilt project, a sixth-grade girl said, 'Why do we always study women, Ms. Logan? I feel like I'm not learning anything about men and I don't think that's right.' But she waited to say that until we were in the library and the librarian *and* the principal were listening. Later, I took her aside and said, 'We've done the NOW essay contest and this quilt, and I don't think that's so much considering that women are half of humanity. This is your history we're talking about!' It turned out that she was concerned that the boys would feel left out by those lessons."

Ms. Logan explains that, in fact, only two of her sixth-grade projects focus exclusively on women. Others, such as the African American history reports, simply ensure that women are given equal time. "But because I do that," she explains, "because I *include* women, I'm seen as extreme. If I took those lessons out and concentrated only on men's experience for a whole year, *that* would be 'normal.'"

Ms. Logan can't pinpoint exactly when she began teaching what she calls an "inclusive curriculum." "I never had a moment of 'Aha!'" she says thoughtfully. "I wish I could say I did, that I knew exactly when I started to think this way or teach this way. I do know that if you grow as a person, you grow as a teacher. So, in the 1970s, when I took some classes and started learning more about women myself, women came into the classroom."

For years, Ms. Logan taught her unconventional curriculum gingerly, keeping, as she says, "my mouth and my classroom door shut," to avoid undue notice. Then, at a 1986 women's history conference, she met Peggy McIntosh, a former middle school teacher. Now associate director of the Wellesley College Center for Research on Women, McIntosh had developed a five-phase curricular model based on the changes she'd seen educators go through when trying to teach inclusively.[9] Using history as an example, McIntosh describes Phase One as "Womanless and All-White History," which most of us learned as children. In Phase Two, teachers notice that there are no white women or people of color in the curriculum, and they cast about for a few exceptional achievers to sprinkle in. During Phase Three, the politics of the curriculum are unmasked and the focus is on issues: sexism, racism, classism, and victimization. Phase Four heralds a new era, in which the daily lives of women and minority men are themselves considered worthwhile subjects of intellectual inquiry. Only when those four phases are combined does Phase Five become possible: "History Redefined and Reconstructed to Include Us All." In McIntosh's ideas, Ms. Logan found confirmation of her unorthodox approach to education. In Ms. Logan's teaching, McIntosh found her theories brought to life. The two quickly became friends and colleagues.

Inclusive education, as defined by both Ms. Logan and McIntosh, turns the conventional student-teacher relationship on its head. Students may become the "experts," producing their own curriculum, as in the African American history class, and teachers become learners. Like many educational philosophers, McIntosh and Ms. Logan also question the grounding of classroom interactions in competition rather than cooperation, in individual "right" and "wrong" answers rather than a collective search for meaning. In her own book, *Teaching Stories,* Ms. Logan writes that, during lessons that explore gender roles, which can easily turn into opportunities to cast blame for inequities, emphasizing tolerance is especially important. "If my class seems anxious at the beginning of a 'woman's unit,' I reassure them that women's studies is not about 'ruling over,' it is about 'existing with,' " she writes. "It is important to be explicit with these reassurances right away. Feminist teaching is not about allowing a win/lose situation to develop between boys and girls."[10]

On the other hand, sitting in her classroom today, Ms. Logan admits that delicacy has its limits. "I present women's lives without apology," she says. When I question her again about occasional student resistance she shrugs. "I usually find that boys only resist studying women when they're presented as 'lesser,'" she says. "And if they're presented as 'lesser,' girls don't want to study women either. And I can't blame them.'' . . .

STITCHING IT ALL TOGETHER

For the last four years, as a final, unifying project, Ms. Logan's sixth-grade class makes a quilt with a women's history theme. Like the essays for the NOW competition, most of the quilts feature "Women We Admire." The students each pick a woman—who may be fictional or actual, past or present, famous or anonymous—and create a muslin quilt square in her honor. Some of the students draw faces, others draw symbols of their honorees' achievements: a gorilla for Dian Fossey, a double helix for Rosalind Franklin, a family tree commemorating a beloved great-grandmother. An adult volunteer (usually someone's mother) then sews the squares together and the children help by ironing the seams and knotting the back of the quilt to the front through the cotton-batting center. They also compose essays about the women they have honored. Last year, Ms. Logan, who is adding science to her sixth-grade curriculum, asked her students to make a quilt entitled "Some Women in Science." In the center of the piece there is a large muslin square, painted blue and decorated with the phases of the moon. It bears a quote by nineteenth-century astronomer Maria Mitchell which encapsulates Ms. Logan's educational philosophy: "In my younger days," it reads, "when I was pained by the half-educated, loose and inaccurate ways that we [women] had, I used to say, 'How much women need exact science.' But since I have known some workers in science who were not always true to the teachings of nature, who have loved self more than science, I have now said, 'How much science needs women.'"

When I visit them during the last week of the school year, the sixth graders are busily finishing their quilt squares. Ms. Logan is engaged in a discussion with one of the boys, Jimmy, who has represented tennis star Monica Seles by drawing a bloody knife lying across a tennis racket.

"What do you admire about Monica Seles?" she asks.

Jimmy shrugs. "She was in the paper," he says. "She got stabbed."

"This quilt is about honoring women we admire," Ms. Logan responds. "It's okay to choose her because you admire her, but it's not okay to do a square on her because she was stabbed."

Jimmy begins to sulk. "But without being stabbed she's just another tennis player!" he complains.

"This quilt is not about violence toward women," Ms. Logan says firmly. "You can make a square with tennis rackets if you want to."

I've noticed that, during each of the projects I've observed—the African American history monologues, the American Women Making History class, and the quilt project—the boys who are most resistant to studying the female experience choose to focus on women in sports, especially tennis or track.

When I mention this to Ms. Logan, she nods." That's what they can best relate to," she says. "When boys feel like they're being forced to admire women they try to pick one that they think behaves sort of like a man. It's a step in the right direction. If they don't go beyond that at any point, I guess I'd see it as a failure, but sometimes you have to meet children where they're ready to learn."

I continue walking around the room, glancing at the student's work. Holly has chosen Kristi Yamaguchi, while her friend Dana has chosen Polly Bemis, the Chinese American heroine of the book *A Thousand Pieces of Gold.* Several students have decided to honor the subjects of their African American history monologues and still others have chosen to honor relatives. One Latino boy is drawing a picture of his aunt. "She's a single mom," he explains, "and her baby is in the hospital and she has two other kids at home. She has to work really hard, so I admire that."

A number of Ms. Logan's students are focusing on women in the arts. One of the boys tells me that Frida Kahlo is a big inspiration to him. One of the girls, a redhead named Kristi, has chosen the Japanese artist Mayumi Oda. Oda's paintings depict women as goddesses, as founts of power. They are described in one collection as "a feminine view of the positive self." Kristi tells me she just thinks they're "neat."

Jimmy stares despondently at his new square, which looks rather stark with just a tennis racket. "I've decided to do Billie Jean King instead of Monica Seles," he says. "But I thought it was kind of important, a tennis player getting stabbed just so she wouldn't win. I don't know why that's not appropriate."

Jeremy is sitting on the floor near the door, putting the finishing touches on a square commemorating Rosa Parks, whom he first learned about in elementary school. His journey this year has taken him from Anita Hill, whom he wrote about in the NOW essay contest, to Etta James to Parks. He shrugs when I mention this, more intent on the fact that one of the girls is laughing at his rendition of Ms. Parks's face—the eyes seem, somehow, to have gotten slightly crossed. When I press him further, Jeremy turns to me in exasperation.

"I don't see what the big deal is about women," he says, and I prepare to hear him say that he's tired of Ms. Logan's unfair focus on the female sex. But I've judged Jeremy too quickly. "I mean, as long as they're interesting, what's the difference if they're women? Women are people, too, you know."

Jeremy completes his square and brings it to Ms. Logan. She places it with several others that will be sewn together later and smiles. "This is how you teach about gender," Ms. Logan says to me as Jeremy sifts through the finished squares. "You do it one stitch at a time."

NOTES

1. Elizabeth G. Cohen, *Designing Groupwork: Strategies for the Heterogeneous Classroom,* 2nd ed., with a foreword by John J. Goodlad, New York: Teachers College Press, 1994.
2. Marcia C. Linn, "Gender Differences in Educational Achievement," in *Sex Equity in Educational Opportunity, Achievement, and Testing,* Princeton, NJ: Proceedings of the 1991 Invitational Conference of the Educational Testing Service, 1992; "MMAP: Middle-School Mathematics Through Applications Project," Palo Alto, CA: Documentation from the Institute for Research on Learning, 1993.
3. Suzanne Alexander, "New Grade-School Sexuality Classes Go Beyond Birds and Bees to Explicit Basics," *The Wall Street Journal,* April 2, 1993, p. B1; [Susan Strauss], *Sexual Harassment to Teenagers: It's Not Fun/It's Illegal—A Cur-* *riculum for Identification and Prevention of Sexual Harassment for Use with Junior and Senior High School Students,* St. Paul, MN: Minnesota Department of Education Equal Educational Opportunities Section, 1988.
4. Michael Winerip. "Public School Offers a Social-Service Model," New York *Times,* December 8, 1993, p. A1; Michael Winerip, "In School: A Public School in Harlem That Takes the Time, and the Trouble, to Be a Family," New York *Times,* January 26, 1994, p. A19. For more on integrating values of home and community into the school setting, see Jane Roland Martin, *The Schoolhome: Rethinking Schools for Changing Families,* Cambridge, MA: Harvard University Press, 1992.

5. Josefina Villamil Tinajero, Maria Luisa Gonzalez, and Florence Dick, *Raising Career Aspirations of Hispanic Girls,* Bloomington, IN: Phi Delta Kappa Educational Foundation, 1991; "Facts and Figures on Hispanic Americans, Women, and Education," in *The Broken Web: The Educational Experience of Hispanic American Women,* Teresa McKenna and Flora Ida Ortiz, eds., Berkeley CA: Floricanto Press, 1988, pp. 195–209.

6. Judy Logan, *Teaching Stories,* with a foreword by Peggy McIntosh, St. Paul, MN: Minnesota Inclusiveness Program, 1993, p. x. Logan wrote *Teaching Stories* with the aid of an American Association of University Women Eleanor Roosevelt grant.

7. Di Bentley and Mike Watts, "Courting the Positive Virtues: A Case for Feminist Science," *European Journal of Science Education,* 8 (1986), pp. 121–23. See also Sue Rosser, *Biology & Feminism: A Dynamic Interaction,* New York: Twayne Publishers, 1992; Evelyn Fox Keller, *Reflections on Gender and Science,* New Haven: Yale University Press, 1985; Ruth Bleier, *Science and Gender: A Critique of Biol-ogy and Its Theories and Women,* New York: Pergamon Press, 1984; Evelyn Fox Keller, *A Feeling for the Organism: The Life and Work of Barbara McClintock,* San Francisco: W. H. Freeman and Co., 1983.

8. Emily Style, "Curriculum as Window and Mirror," in *Listening for All Voices: Gender Balancing the School Curriculum,* proceedings of a conference held at Oak Knoll School, Summit, NJ, June 1988, p. 6.

9. Peggy McIntosh, "Interactive Phases of Curricular Re-Vision: A Feminist Perspective," Working Paper No. 124, Wellesley, MA: Wellesley College Center for Research on Women, 1983; Peggy McIntosh, "Interactive Phases of Curricular and Personal Re-Vision with Regard to Race," Working Paper No. 219, Wellesley, MA: Wellesley College Center for Research on Women, 1990. McIntosh's phases are meant to be applied across the curriculum.

10. Logan, *Teaching Stories,* p. 44.

11. Jamaica Kincaid, "Girl," in *At the Bottom of the River,* New York: Plume Contemporary Fiction, 1992, p. 3.

CHECKPOINTS

1. Bailey finds that girl's experiences at elementary and secondary schools are less than optimal in areas such as teacher-student interactions, peer interactions, extracurricular activities, and testing and assessment.

2. Orenstein describes her experiences observing a gender-fair classroom in which boys slowly learn to appreciate the inclusion of women in the curriculum.

Gender, Cognition, and Education

QUESTIONS FOR REFLECTION

1. Why are people so interested in whether there are sex differences in cognition? What is the basis for people's beliefs in either biological or sociocultural explanations?
2. Is it possible to create a gender-fair education system?

CHAPTER APPLICATIONS

1. Construct a plan for observing the treatment of males and females in a classroom. Make sure your research plan takes diversity into account and includes the sex of the teacher. If possible, conduct your observations and summarize the results.
2. Find five popular press accounts for sex differences in cognitive abilities. Analyze the language used to present the research and decide whether the results are shown as a difference or a deficiency.

CHAPTER TEN

The Paradox of Relationships

QUESTIONS TO THINK ABOUT

- **What is intimacy?**
- **What is the role of intimacy in relationships?**
- **Are there different cultural prescriptions for men and women in relationships?**
- **For individuals, what factors related to gender influence their intimate relationships?**
- **What is gender segregation and what is its role in relationships?**
- **How do traditional gender roles influence satisfaction in relationships?**
- **What individual and cultural stereotypes influence relationships?**
- **What are the differences between people's beliefs about friendship and the realities of friendships?**
- **In what ways are gay, lesbian, and heterosexual romantic relationships similar and different?**
- **How do cultures vary in their constructions of intimacy and love?**
- **How does the social constructionist perspective lead to a reconceptualization of relationships?**

GENDER AND RELATIONSHIPS

We live in a world in which gender is a basic category into which people are sorted. As you learned in chapter 6, gender operates as a schema to organize our experiences, our feelings, our sense of self, and how we view others. Just as we live in a gendered world, we also live in a world of relationships. Although relationships take many forms and exist in many variations, they are a given in our world. From the moment of our birth, both gender and relationships are constant factors in our lives (Winstead & Derlega, 1993). Gender is expressed in the context of relationships, and various relation-

ships evolve from gender identity, roles, and norms. Many of the topics in this book provide insight into the role of gender and relationships. Fiske and Stevens (1993) in chapter 5 point out that one characteristic of gender as a social stereotype that distinguishes it from other stereotypes is that men and women are continuously enmeshed with one another in intimate relationships. Similarly, Blumstein and Schwartz (1989) contend in chapter 7 that sexuality emerges out of intimate relationships and the meaning of sexuality is embedded in such relationships. In chapter 11, several of the articles stress the importance of gender in influencing individuals' behaviors within the context of particular family relationships. Relationships are also rooted in social institutions, and in chapter 12, you will be introduced to the links among gender, violence, and relationships.

The very pervasiveness of gender is part of what masks its role in every aspect of our lives and the way in which it influences us. As we pointed out in chapter 1, certain categories are considered to be normative in our culture and they operate as the un-marked category. You saw how concepts of being white, male, or heterosexual are constructed to be the standard-bearer for cultural meanings (Franken-burg, 1993). In a similar vein, Wood (1996) argues that men and masculinity are often used as the stan-dard from which all comparisons about relationships are made. The attitudes, feelings, and activities of white, heterosexual men become, albeit uncon-sciously, the definition of normal, and all other types of relationships and characteristics of those relation-ships are judged in accord with these definitions. The many variations of relationships that we know to exist, although perhaps not considered abnormal, are still judged in comparison to these norms rather than in their own right. We need to be careful not to essentialize certain aspects of relationships. For example, men's loyalty and willingness to use physical means to defend their friends is often defined as the prototype for friendship. As we all know, however, there are other important dimensions to friendship that operate depending on the who, when, and why of a particular friendship.

One argument we make in this chapter is that gender and relationships operate as social construc-tions and that as we come to understand the power of gender, many paradoxes concerning relationships emerge. How people communicate and what they communicate has the power to create and sustain different gendered relationships. Concepts such as mother and father, which you read about in the next chapter, have evolving meanings that need to be un-derstood in relationship to particular social and his-torical contexts. The gender roles associated with communal and agenic qualities of Eagly's social role theory (1987) may be a central characteristic of rela-tionships. These gender roles only exist in the con-text of social relationships. Individual characteristics such as sex, age, race, ethnicity, education, class, and sexual orientation influence the nature of relation-ships that we form and influence the gender roles we assume in relationships. These characteristics inter-act in both obvious and subtle ways. Many of our friendships are formed through school or work, and because most of us live in segregated neighborhoods, we may not have the opportunity to interact with in-dividuals of different ethnic groups or social classes. Is it any surprise that most of us develop relation-ships with others who we think are like us? For ex-ample, cross-race friendships are not very common (Duck, 1991). Although the rarity of these relation-ships is partially attributable to patterns of work and neighborhood segregation, these relationships also reflect some of the same processes that result from gender segregation in play groups. We know that through multiple experiences, we develop styles of interactions as well as beliefs and expectations about other groups that are often difficult to transcend.[1] In addition to personal styles of interaction, issues re-lated to racial identity and racism can impede the de-velopment of cross-race friendships (Rose, 1996). Because relationships provide a backdrop for social and work activities, the social context and individual characteristics often provide prescriptions about gendered behaviors, which will determine the nature and type of relationships we form.

Intimacy in Relationships

The concept of intimacy, for many researchers, is central to their analysis of human relationships. Inti-macy is one of the three basic components of Stern-berg's (1986) theory of love, and it involves a close at-tachment to another person. For other researchers, additional dimensions such as self-disclosure, emo-tional expressiveness, and unconditional support are critical in an understanding of intimacy (Monsour, 1992). Although intimacy is often used as a eu-phemism for sexuality, it has a far broader meaning. Monsour, in a study of the meaning of intimacy in both cross-sex and same-sex friendships, found that sexual contact was given as a meaning only in the context of cross-sex relationships. Of the seven aspects of meaning for intimacy that Monsour had subjects rate as important, sexual contact was rated among the lowest dimensions. This rating suggests that for most individuals, contrary to popular myth, sexual contact is not a necessary nor important dimension of many intimate relationships.

As you know, intimate relationships can take many forms. Numerous relationships exist within families—between husband and wife, between parents and children, among siblings, among members of extended families (e.g., grandparents, aunts, uncles, cousins). As you will learn in more detail in the next chapter, each of these relationships elicits a specific set of gender roles, which change over the life cycle of the family and with cultural and historical trends. Married couples are one type of relationship in which sexual intimacy and commitment are important elements. Couples with the same type of relationship may live together but choose not to marry or may be prohibited from marrying due to societal restrictions. Couples in a committed relationship, living together, will face a variety of decisions about the allocation of resources and the division of labor. For some heterosexual couples, these decisions fall into traditional gender categories, with men being the primary breadwinner and women being in charge of the home, whereas for many other couples, a more flexible pattern has emerged with both individuals employed outside the home and sharing housework. For heterosexual relationships, the division of labor in household chores is more easily apportioned as a function of gender. According to research done by Kurdek (1993), which you will read about in more detail in the next chapter, gay and lesbian couples exhibit a different pattern, one in which household responsibilities are more equitably divided. This pattern of greater equality is expressed differently, however, in that in gay households, tasks are divided so that the same person always performs them, whereas in lesbian households, tasks are allocated so that they are alternated or completed together.

Friendships also occur in many forms with some notable gender effects for both same-sex and cross-sex relationships. If you think of some common stereotypes about women's and men's friendships, what comes to mind? We typically think that women's friendships with other women involve more intimacy and emotional expressiveness and that men's friendships with other men are mostly focused on doing things together. In fact, considerable evidence suggests that on several important dimensions, men's and women's friendships differ. But, as Karen Walker suggests in this chapter's first article, titled *Men, Women, and Friendship: What They Say, What They Do,* there also may be greater similarity in male and female friendships than appears on the surface. We discuss later in the chapter how cultural prescriptions may be at odds with individual behaviors. The point that we emphasize here is that although friendship relationships are often rooted in gender roles, these roles can be fluid and multidetermined. Cross-sex friendships add even greater complexity to an analysis of gendered relationships. There are numerous barriers to the formation and maintenance of cross-sex relationships, making them far less common than same-sex relationships (O'Meara, 1989). Many of the obstacles to such relationships are related to cultural prescriptions about gender roles that have their roots in childhood gender segregation and to a heterosexist culture that assumes that cross-sex relationships must have a sexual element (West, Anderson, & Duck, 1996). Most cross-sex friendships do not involve sex, but an inherent ambiguity regarding sexual boundaries makes such friendships difficult to sustain. On a positive note, Swain (1992) argues that cross-sex friendships can disrupt traditional gender roles by teaching men and women how the other sex views and expresses intimacy. An added value of such relationships is that they may help men move beyond rigid concepts of masculinity to embrace more androgynous notions of friendship.

Because questions about sex often arise in discussions of cross-sex friendships, another question to ask is, what role does sexuality play in gay and lesbian same-sex friendships? Nardi's (1992) study of gay and lesbian friendships sheds some light on this question. He found that gays, in contrast to lesbians, were more likely to have sex with either casual and close friends. The vast majority of gay men, contrary to popular myth, reported that their best friend was a gay or bisexual man, and about half these men said they were currently attracted to their best friend (although only 20 percent were sexually involved with that friend). Nardi suggests that sexual involvement establishes a framework for friendship among gay men, whereas for lesbians, relationships are based on intimacy and sharing rather than on sex. Based on these findings, Nardi hypothesizes that gay male friendships show conformity to traditional male behavior by using sexual behaviors as a way to foster intimacy.

Gender Segregation in Relationships

In chapter 6, you were introduced to Maccoby's (1990) account of how gender segregation occurs in development. There is ample evidence that boys and girls prefer to play in same sex groups, and one consequence of this segregation, according to Maccoby, is that boys and girls develop different interactional styles. As we have already stated, many researchers use this difference in development to explain gender differences in male and female relationships. Girls' friendship groups tend to be smaller and more intimate and to foster cooperation and sensitivity to the needs of others, whereas boys' friendship groups tend to be larger, to be based on a dominance hierarchy, and to foster competitiveness. Related to these play styles are different ways of communicating; boys' language is direct and focused on winning the point, whereas girls use conversation as a way to initiate and maintain intimacy and social relationships. These developmental differences help us understand why women's friendships are more focused on interpersonal elements and emotional expressiveness and men's friendships are more focused on shared interests and activities or discussions of less personal topics such as sports or politics. Leaper (1994) argues that although gender segregation does lead to different preferences for social interaction styles and to preferences for same-sex friends, boys and girls also show evidence for similar needs in relationships, but those needs are expressed differently. For example, girls' peer groups may express aggression through

ostracizing others and through social alienation, whereas boys may demonstrate affiliation through shared goal setting and team competition. For Leaper, these and other examples demonstrate that boys' and girls' peer groups each develop different norms for affiliation and assertion, which may have consequences for adult cross-sex relationships.

Researchers have also suggested that men may display less intimacy and emotional expressiveness with other men because they assume intimacy is related to homosexuality (Nardi, 1992). This false assumption, as we have described in earlier chapters, stems from the homophobia that exists in our culture. Herek (1987) contends that the male gender role is socially constructed around heterosexual masculinity, characterized by attributes such as independence, aggressiveness, and dominance. The behaviors of expressing emotions or displaying intimacy are associated with stereotypic feminine or homosexual attributes, and men come to believe that they should avoid these behaviors so as not to be labeled homosexual. A study by Pleck, Sonenstein, and Ku (1993), which looked at the impact of masculine ideology on adolescents' heterosexual relationships, is related to this phenomenon. Masculine ideology represents beliefs about the importance of conforming to cultural prescriptions of male gender roles. Pleck et al. found that males who strongly adhere to masculine ideology were more likely to have numerous sexual partners in a year, to have a less intimate relationship with their current partner, to hold a more antagonist view of the relationship between men and women, and to be less willing to accept responsibility for pregnancy prevention. Adherence to such stereotyped views of masculinity may be an extreme example of the divergent styles that develop from gender segregation.

CULTURAL PRESCRIPTIONS ABOUT GENDER AND RELATIONSHIPS

Whereas interest in same-sex friendship persists throughout the life span, during adolescence we begin to see a redefinition of cross-sex relationships as interest in dating grows. These redefined relationships, full of cultural prescriptions about male and female behaviors (e.g., girls should be coy and flirtatious, boys should be successful and confident), impact on the many situations such as school and sports in which boys and girls must interact. Adolescents learn clear heterosexual social scripts for dating that are based on gender. Rose and Frieze (1989) found well-specified male scripts (e.g., initiating and paying for date) and female scripts (e.g., sustaining conversation and controlling sexual overtures) for first dates, and the researchers further found that these scripts demonstrate power inequities, because generally men control initiation and women manage the response (Rose & Frieze, 1993).

Given that many of these scripts embody highly stereotyped gender behaviors and roles, an important question to consider is how traditional gender roles affect the development and maintenance of relationships. According to an analysis by Ickes (1993), traditionally masculine men are attracted to traditionally feminine women and vice versa. It appears that the enactment of traditional gender roles heightens the attractiveness of a potential partner of the other sex. This initial attraction is not always maintained into a positive long-term relationship. Dyads of masculine men and feminine women are the least happy in cohabitation and marriage relationships, generally less happy than androgynous men and women. This finding leads to a fundamental paradox in which the very behaviors that create and sustain initial attraction seem to undermine the ongoing optimal functioning of a relationship. To explain this paradox, Ickes analyzes evolutionary and cultural explanations of how gender roles originated. From your previous readings, you are already familiar with these accounts and how they offer different perspectives on gender differences. Ickes suggests that each perspective provides a partial answer to this contradiction. He speculates that there is a conflict between current cultural ideals of relationship equality and traditional attitudes and behaviors that are rooted in our biological and cultural heritage (e.g., stereotyped male behaviors such as dominance and stereotyped female behaviors such as nurturance

that were adapted by evolutionary and cultural pressures). Although highly stereotyped gender characteristics may promote initial sexual attractiveness, they are decidedly unhelpful if one is trying to foster a relationship in which power is shared through equitable division of resources and labor. Think about your own relationships. What characteristics do you seek in a mate, and have any of these characteristics led to any relational discord? Ickes' speculation of a conflict between the values of traditionalism and the values of equality may help us account for the relationship miscommunication that can lead to dissatisfaction and, ultimately, dissolution. You may be wondering, what qualities do contribute to the success of relationships? According to Ickes' review, marital satisfaction appears to require at least one partner who exhibits communal qualities such as nurturance, affection, and caring in the context of the relationship. A note of caution about Ickes's analysis: He reviews research dealing with heterosexual, romantic relationships; his research does not address the impact of traditional gender roles within gay and lesbian relationships or within friendships. It appears that both gay men and lesbians are less likely to base their relationships on traditional gender stereotypes than are heterosexual couples (Wood, 1994). Research reported by Anne Peplau in the second article in this chapter, *Lesbian and Gay Relationships,* shows that most lesbians and gay men do not accept traditional husband-wife or masculine-feminine labels as the basis for their long-term relationships.

THE ROLE OF STEREOTYPES IN RELATIONSHIPS

There are many gender stereotypes about the behavior of women and men in relationships. We expect men and women to differ in their relationship beliefs, behaviors, and experiences. Here are some stereotypes you may have heard: Men do not share their feelings with friends; women gossip with their friends; women take care of the nurturing aspects of a relationship; men take charge in relationships with women. Research has found significant sex and gender differences in relationships that conform to many of our stereotypes about men and women. For example, gender appears to play a significant role in the social support process (Barbee et al., 1993). As you would expect, the sensitive, nurturing characteristics associated with women encourage the giving and receiving of emotional support in relationships, whereas the more autonomous and controlled qualities connected with men act as deterrents to the support process. Even this robust finding, however, needs to be qualified by a closer examination of situational factors. Barbee et al. found some evidence that males can be better at providing instrumental support in situations that capitalize on their competence. You may recall that this point is also supported by the evidence reviewed in the chapter 8 article by Eagly, which suggests that sex differences in helping can be explained by examining social context and perceived competence. Women may perceive themselves as competent at listening and offering advice, whereas men may perceive themselves as competent at solving problems. Because social support is traditionally defined as listening and offering advice, the evidence may favor women. Including instrumental problem solving as a type of social support challenges this stereotype. This discrepancy suggests that we need to look carefully at even the most obvious examples of gender stereotypes to discover greater gender complexity.

Each of the articles in this chapter addresses prevailing stereotypes about gender and relationships. Each article provides a context for understanding ways in which gender differences do not fit stereotypes. One way to think about stereotypes is to consider the model of gender and social context proposed by Deaux and Major (1990) that you read about in chapter 8. The Deaux and Major model provides a framework for understanding how stereotypes are used and maintained. According to Deaux and Major, the actual behavior of men and women is related to the gender role beliefs and expectations of both the actor and the participant in a social interaction and to a set of situational variables that are likely to elicit stereotyped behaviors. The following example should help explicate how this model explains a specific relationship interaction. A

woman and man with egalitarian views about relationships and marriage decide to be married. Because this situation evokes many highly traditional expectations, how would each individual's egalitarian principles be integrated into our culture's gender prescriptions about engagement and marriage? One possibility is that the couple do not change their individual beliefs about, for example, a woman keeping her own name, the type of wedding vows they will speak, or the importance of both partner's careers, but they do modify their behaviors to cope with the social pressures associated with a wedding and marriage. Another possibility is that the couple maintain their beliefs and alter the traditions of the gender behaviors that are most important to them. Yet another possibility is that they change their belief system and conform to the gender prescriptions that this situation elicits. Of course we could describe many other scenarios, especially ones in which the beliefs or responses of the two individuals diverge, but our purpose is to help you see how individual expectations and beliefs combine with different contextual factors to either attenuate or heighten stereotyped behaviors in relationships.

Walker's article in this chapter examines both individuals' beliefs about friendships and their actual experiences with friends. Walker's article has two special aspects we would like you to note. First, it provides both a qualitative and quantitative analysis of gender and friendship, and second, it considers how social class interacts with gender to affect friendship arrangements. Walker found that men and women believe that there are sex differences in friendships that conform to our cultural ideology— men engage in activities together and women share feelings and experience intimacy as friends. When their actual friendship relationships were examined, however, men and women's friendships often did not conform to the cultural prescriptions. Most men and women characterized their friendships as containing elements of both shared activities and shared intimacy. Social class plays a role in how friendships are developed and maintained by influencing opportunities for shared activities, encounters with others, and time for meaningful talk. Intimacy was more difficult to achieve in friendship for middle-class individuals who were occupationally or geographically mobile. Working-class males and females tended to know their friends very well and to be comfortable sharing intimacies, although economic constraints often prevented them from engaging in many activities together. Walker's research on friendship points out a large disparity between our stereotypes about behavior and our actual experiences, and she provides some speculations about the divergence. How might the approach of Deaux and Major help explain the complex dynamic of cultural ideology and friendship behaviors? Although individuals certainly bring specific gendered beliefs about friendship to their relationships, particular interactions are also shaped by contextual variables. For example, many of Walker's working-class respondents saw their friends in their homes or neighborhoods, where barriers to intimacy may be less likely to exist for both males and females. Problems such as marital discord or finances are not as easy, nor as necessary, to hide in such surroundings, so men in particular may feel less need to conform to cultural stereotypes about friendships. In this way, friendships that have developed over a long period and that provide us with significant information about the other party may, at a behavioral level, be less stereotyped even as we maintain our cultural prescriptions about gendered friendships. This dichotomy is consistent with the model of Deaux and Major, which predicts less reliance on gender stereotypes and prescriptions when people in an interaction have more detailed knowledge of each other and greater reliance on stereotypes and prescriptions in interactions in which we have little knowledge other than the sex of the other person. In the latter situation, the sex of the other person acts as a stimulus to trigger the gender stereotypes. Interestingly, intimate relationships, under some conditions, may mitigate against gender stereotypes.

Stereotypes also abound in our views about the relationships of gay and lesbian individuals, not surprising considering only one third of American adults believe that they know anyone who is openly gay (Herek, 1995). This belief helps explain why there are so many misperceptions about gay and lesbian relationships. Peplau's article in this chapter provides research to evaluate several myths and stereotypes about gay and lesbian relationships. Before reading the article, ask yourself what you believe to be true about the following issues: (a) Homosexuals are not interested in permanent relationships and cannot achieve that goal; (b) Gay relationships are dysfunctional and deviant; (c) The role of husband and wife are universal roles in relationships; (d) Gay and lesbian social support systems are not well developed. As you read Peplau's analysis, try to evaluate the evidence she uses to assess and contradict these stereotypes. Peplau shows how models that have been successful in understanding heterosexual relationships can be applied to the study of gay and lesbian relationships. Social exchange theory, for example, can be used to disentangle the effects of gender and power by showing that individuals who see themselves as more powerful, regardless of sexual orientation or gender, tend to rely on reasoning techniques rather than on emotional or withdrawing strategies for conflict resolution. In this case, power becomes a salient situational variable that according to Deaux and Major acts to override typical gender expectations. Like heterosexual couples, significant variation characterizes gay and lesbian couples, and this diversity is related to both gender and individuality. Peplau also maintains that certain research questions may not fit into a preexisting theory (e.g., coming out publicly about one's sexual orientation, the impact of losing a partner to AIDS) but that such issues must be understood to fully appreciate the complexity of gay and lesbian relationships.

One of the myths about gay and lesbian relationships that Peplau debunks in her article is the assumption of universal traditional gender roles. What other assumptions about relationships do we hold that reflect cultural hegemony? When you think about romantic love, what scenario comes to mind? Do you think, girl meets boy, they fall in love, they marry, they live on their own and have children? In the last article in this chapter, titled *Individualistic and Collectivistic Perspectives on Gender and the Cultural Context of Love and Intimacy*, Karen Dion and Kenneth Dion claim that this depiction is premised on a very specific view of how individuals behave toward one another, of what gender role expectations they have, and of how culture prescribes certain normative practices. This depiction, an example of a socially constructed stereotype about heterosexual love and intimacy, is designed to meet particular psychological, sociological, and economic needs of our culture. Other cultures might portray a very different set of events; in fact, they might well question the very idea of romantic love as a necessary prerequisite for a close relationship. We argued in chapter 4 that cultural variables are essential to fully understand the impact of gender in our lives. Dion and Dion propose that individualism and collectivism are two constructs that vary among cultures in how they influence the form and expression of love and intimacy. What is meant by individualism and collectivism? These concepts stand in contrast to one another as differing orientations toward self (individual) and others (family, community, society). Individualism is generally associated with characteristics of self-interest, individual rights, personal autonomy, and independence, whereas collectivism is associated with loyalty to group, sensitivity to the needs of others, and interdependence. Using these two perspectives, Dion and Dion present several predictions for how love and intimacy are construed in different cultures: Romantic love, especially as a basis for marriage, will be emphasized more in cultures that stress individualism; psychological intimacy in marital relationships will be valued more in individualistic cultures; certain aspects of individualism will hinder intimacy. These propositions lead to an interesting paradox about the connection between cultural orientation and the success of relationships. Although romance and personal fulfillment are deemed important in cultures stressing individualism, particular psychological aspects on individualism make such outcomes difficult to achieve. In contrast, in collectivist cultures in which intimacy is nurtured, it is generally not focused on a particular individual. Considering Ickes's (1993) findings and what we know about gender differences in relationships, can you hypothesize about which type of culture and which gender might experience more distress about intimacy? Think of a tra-

ditional relationship (e.g., female exhibiting communal qualities, male exhibiting agenic qualities) in an individualistic society in which attributes of independence take precedence in the relationship so that intimacy becomes defined in agenic terms—would you not expect women to experience greater dissatisfaction? Dion and Dion's article provides an analysis to help us understand how cultures differ on some important dimensions and why cultural variables are crucial to fully appreciate the intricacies of gender and relationships.

DOING RELATIONSHIPS—A SOCIAL CONSTRUCTIONIST APPROACH

Most of the evidence about relationships that we have presented to you in this chapter suggests that relationships are complex entities that develop and change in different cultural context. In many cases, traditional gender differences, cultural ideology and prescriptions, individual belief systems, and situational factors all work together to create a variety of interactional patterns within relationships, and these relationships interact with a cultural context that defines and perhaps redefines the relationship. A social constructionist framework posits that gender emerges out of relationships as relationships simultaneously create the possibility for new gender arrangements. From this perspective, relationships and gender are evolving.

The paradoxes of gender and relationships suggest that within an interpersonal context may lie the solution to narrow gender prescriptions and stereotypes. For example, the evidence shows that intimacy, defined as affiliation, exists in boys' friendships but has been overlooked in favor of emphasis on competition, whereas dominance among girls has similarly been overlooked by a failure to consider peer pressure and ostracizing as evidence of ranking in friendships. Therefore, increased understanding of gendered interactional patterns can be gained through increased analysis of the levels of meaning of particular behaviors. This increase in understanding has a practical benefit, because in recent years we have been overexposed to rhetoric that suggests that men and women are so different in their interactional styles as to render them akin to different species (Gray, 1992). Clearly, there are plenty of successful cross-sex relationships, just as there are failed same-sex relationships.

Another paradox that leads us to speculate on the evolving nature of gender roles is the evidence provided by Ickes (1993) suggesting that attraction to opposite-sex partners with traditional gender role attributes is not matched by long-term success in the relationship when both partners are highly gender role typed. Not only do we see high levels of intimacy among couples in which both partners are androgynous or feminine but also among gay and les-

bian couples, who define their relationships explicitly outside the boundaries of traditional gender role expectations. The accumulating evidence is that intimacy is an important component of successful relationships. As gender roles change, we might expect to see increases in expressed intimacy and increased chances for successful relationships.

In the next two chapters, we pay more attention to questions about social change as we examine the family and social institutions. Interpersonal interactions and relationships are critical elements of both the family and social institutions. As we piece together the elements that sustain cultural gender traditions, we also begin to foresee a future of shifting roles and increased equity.

NOTE

1. Specific aspects of same-race or same-ethnicity styles of interaction for men are described in detail in Lazur and Major's article in chapter 4.

REFERENCES

Barbee, A. P., Cunningham, M. R., Winstead, B. A., Derlega, V. J., Gulley, M. R., Yankeelon, P. A., & Druen, P. B. (1993). Effects of gender role expectations on the social support process. *Journal of Social Issues, 49,* 175–190.

Blumstein, P., & Schwartz, P. (1989). Intimate relationships and the creation of sexuality. In B. J. Risman & P. Schwartz (Eds.), *Gender in intimate relationships: A microstructural approach* (pp. 120–129). Belmont, CA: Wadsworth.

Deaux, K., & Major, B. (1990). A social-psychological model of gender. In D. Rhode (Ed.), *Theoretical perspectives on sexual differences* (pp. 89–99). New Haven: Yale University Press.

Dion, K., & Dion, K. L. (1993). Individualistic and collectivistic perspectives on gender and the cultural context of love and intimacy. *Journal of Social Issues, 49,* 53–69.

Duck, S. (1991). *Understanding relationships.* New York: Guilford Press.

Eagly, A. H. (1987). *Sex differences in social behavior: A social role interpretation.* Hillsdale, NJ: Erlbaum.

Fiske, S. T., & Stevens, L. E. (1993). What's so special about sex? Gender stereotyping and discrimination. In S. Oskamp & M. Costanzo (Eds.), *Gender issues in contemporary society* (pp. 173–196). Beverly Hills, CA: Sage.

Frankenburg, R. (1993). *White women, race matters: The social construction of whiteness.* Minneapolis: University of Minnesota Press.

Gray, J. (1992). *Men are from Mars, women are from Venus.* New York: HarperCollins.

Herek, G. (1987). On heterosexual masculinity: Some psychical consequences of the social construction of gender and sexuality. In M. Kimmel (Ed.), *Changing men: New directions in research on men and masculinity* (pp. 68–82). Newbury Park, CA: Sage.

Herek, G. M. (1995). Psychological heterosexism in the United States. In A. R. D'Augelli & C. J. Patterson (Eds.), *Lesbian, gay, and bisexual identities over the lifespan: Psychological perspectives* (pp. 321–346). Washington, DC: American Psychological Association.

Ickes, W. (1993). Traditional gender roles: Do they make, and then break our relationships? *Journal of Social Issues, 49,* 71–85.

Kurdek, L. A. (1993). The allocation of household labor in gay, lesbian, and heterosexual couples. *Journal of Social Issues, 49,* 127–139.

Leaper, C. (1994). Exploring the consequences of gender segregation on social relationships. In C. Leaper (Ed.), *Childhood gender segregation: Causes and consequences* (pp. 67–86). San Francisco, CA: Jossey-Bass.

Maccoby, E. (1990). Gender and relationships: A developmental account. *American Psychologist, 45,* 513–520.

Monsour, M. (1992). Meanings of intimacy in cross- and same-sex friendships. *Journal of Social and Personal Relationships, 9,* 277–295.

Nardi, P. M. (Ed.). (1992). *Men's friendships.* Newbury Park, CA: Sage.

Nardi, P. M. (1992). Sex, friendship, and gender roles among gay men. In P. M. Nardi (Ed.), *Men's friendships* (pp. 173–185). Newbury Park, CA: Sage.

O'Meara, J. D. (1989). Cross-sex friendship: Four basic challenges of an ignored relationship. *Sex Roles, 21,* 525–543.

Peplau, L. A. (1995). Lesbian and gay relationships. In L. D. Garnets & D. C. Kimmel (Eds.), *Psychological perspectives on lesbian and gay male experiences* (pp. 395–419). New York: Columbia University Press.

Pleck, J. H., Sonenstein, F. L., & Ku, L. C. (1993). Masculinity ideology: Its impact on adolescent males' heterosexual relationships. *Journal of Social Issues, 49,* 11–29.

Rose, S. (1996). Who to let in: Women's cross-race friendships. In J. C. Chrisler, C. Golden, & P. D. Rozee (Eds.), *Lectures on the psychology of women* (pp. 210–226). New York: McGraw-Hill.

Rose, S., & Frieze, I. H. (1989). Young singles' scripts for a first date. *Gender & Society, 3,* 258–268.

Rose, S., & Frieze, I. H. (1993). Young singles' contemporary dating scripts. *Sex Roles, 28,* 499–509.

Sternberg, R. J. (1986). A triangular theory of love. *Psychological Review, 93,* 119–135.

Swain, S. O. (1992). Men's friendships with women: Intimacy, sexual boundaries, and the informant role. In P. M. Nardi (Ed.), *Men's friendships* (pp. 153–172). Newbury Park, CA: Sage.

Walker, K. (1994). Men, women, and friendship: What they say, what they do. *Gender and Society, 8,* 246–265.

West, L., Anderson, J., & Duck, S. (1996). Crossing the barriers to friendships between men and women. In J. Wood (Ed.), *Gendered relationships* (pp. 111–127). Mountain View, CA: Mayfield.

Winstead, B. A., & Derlega, V. J. (1993). Gender and close relationships: An introduction. *Journal of Social Issues, 49,* 1–9.

Wood, J. T. (1994). *Gendered lives: Communication, gender and culture.* Belmont, CA: Wadsworth.

Wood, J. T. (1996). Gender, relationship, and communication. In J. T. Wood (Ed.), *Gendered relationships.* Mountain View, CA: Mayfield.

Men, Women, and Friendship: What They Say, What They Do

KAREN WALKER

University of Pennsylvania

Using data from 52 in-depth interviews with working-class and professional men and women, I examine gender differences in friendships. Men and women respond to global questions about friendship in culturally specific ways. Men focus on shared activities, and women focus on shared feelings. Responses to questions about specific friends, however, reveal more variation in same-sex friendships than the literature indicates. Men share feelings more, whereas women share feelings less; furthermore, the extent to which they do so varies by class. I argue that conceptualizing gender as an ongoing social construction explains the data better than do psychoanalytic or socialization accounts.

Stereotypes about friendship represent women's friendships as intimate relationships in which sharing feelings and talk are the most prevalent activities. Men's friendships are represented as ones in which sharing activities such as sports dominate interaction. In this article, however, I argue that the notions that women share intimate feelings whereas men share activities in their friendships are more accurately viewed as cultural ideologies than as observable gender differences in behavior. Using data from in-depth interviews with working- and middle-class men and women, I show that men and women use these ideologies to depict their friendships and to orient their behavior. Responses to global questions about friendship indicate that men and women think about their friendships in culturally specific ways that agree with stereotypes about men's and women's friendships.

Responses to questions about specific friends, however, reveal more variation in same-sex friendships than the stereotypes or the social scientific literature lead one to expect. When men and women discuss friendship they emphasize the behavior that corresponds to their cultural notions of what men and women are like. Men focus on shared activities, and women focus on shared feelings. When specific friendships are examined, however, it becomes clear that men share feelings more than the literature indicates, whereas women share feelings less than the literature indicates; furthermore, the extent to which they do so varies by class. Employed middle-class women indicate that they are sometimes averse to sharing feelings with friends. Working-class men, on the other hand, report regularly sharing feelings and discussing personal problems.

This approach differs significantly from much of the social scientific literature on friendship by closely examining the link between behavior and ideology and seeing gender as an ongoing construction of social life. Many friendship studies over the past decade have emphasized the extent to which men and women have different kinds of friendships; the conclusions concur with the most prevalent stereotypes. Lillian Rubin (1985) has argued that men bond through shared activities, whereas women share intimate feelings through talk. She ascribes these differences to two phenomena. First, socialization of children encourages attention to relationships for girls and competition among boys and men. Second, the psychic development of girls leads girls and women to develop permeable ego boundaries and relational,

Karen Walker is a postdoctoral researcher at the University of Pennsylvania. She is currently working on a study of how parents manage risk and opportunity for their teens in inner-city neighborhoods.

nurturing capacities that encourage them to seek intimacy within friendship with other females. Boys and men, on the other hand, are threatened by having close, intimate friendships. Intimacy threatens their sense of masculinity because it touches that feminine part of their psyche that they were forced to repress in early childhood. According to Rubin, shared activities and competition are compensatory structures for men that prevent them from becoming too intimate.

Other authors differ somewhat on the causes and evaluation of these differences. Scott Swain (1989), for example, argues that perceiving men as deficient in intimate capacities as measured by verbal communication ignores nonverbal intimacy. In a study of intimate friendships among antebellum men, Karen Hansen (1992) has argued that arguments resting on psychic development are essentialist and neglect historical changes in intimate behavior. Other authors attribute observed gender differences in friendships solely to socialization rather than psychic development (Allan 1989; Swain 1989). There is, however, little debate that contemporary men characteristically engage in shared activities, whereas women engage in verbal sharing of feelings with their friends (Bell 1981; Caldwell and Peplau 1982; Eichenbaum and Orbach 1989; Oliker 1989; Sherrod 1987; Swain 1989).

In contrast to the most commonly developed explanations in friendship studies, some sociologists have argued in recent years that gender is constructed on an ongoing basis in social life (Connell 1987; Leidner 1991; West and Zimmerman 1987). There approaches account not only for the variation within same-sex friendships that I observed but also for the strength of the ideologies about friendship. The process of representing themselves as adhering to cultural norms when they discuss friendship is one way men and women create coherent understandings about themselves as gendered humans; furthermore, because social processes of gender construction emphasize the naturalness of gender differences, individuals rarely question the extent to which those differences exist. Leidner observes that even "the considerable flexibility of notions of proper gender enactment does not undermine the appearance of inevitability and naturalness that continues to support the division of labor by gender" (1991, 158). To this I would add that even

when individuals understand gender differences as socially rather than biologically caused, as several of my respondents did, they see those social causes as having shaped their personalities in such a way that change is difficult, if not impossible, to achieve.

In addition to exploring how women and men construct gender-specific understandings of their friendships, I also explore how social class influences men's and women's capacities for conforming to gendered behaviors. Women's or men's material circumstances affect their abilities to conform to gendered norms about friendship. The friendships of women who did not work in the paid labor force or women whose family took priority over their labor market participation generally conformed to a model of intimate friendship. Middle-class men and women who were geographically or occupationally mobile tended to report a lack of intimacy in specific friendships. Working-class women and men who participated in dense social networks and whose resources limited the extent of their social activities often spent time talking to their friends and sharing feelings about events in their lives, thereby creating intimate friendships; thus social class shapes the experiences men and women have with friendship, and it may do so in ways that contradict stereotypes about men's and women's behaviors.

METHOD OF STUDY

My data were gathered from a series of 52 in-depth interviews that I conducted in 1991 and 1992 with working- and middle-class men and women[1] between the ages of 24 and 48. Because I wanted to observe groups of three or four individuals within each group of men and women from a particular class, I asked some of the men and women I interviewed for referrals to their friends, preferably friends who knew each other. All but three respondents, therefore, had at least one other friend in the study. Several had two friends, and two working-class women had three friends in the study. I wished to see what issues were most salient to groups of friends. I also wished to see to what extent friends agree on what their interactions are like.[2]

Many respondents were married; most worked outside the home. Of the 33 women interviewed,

60 percent worked in the labor force either part- or full-time and 75 percent were married or living with men. Of the 19 men, 84 percent were married and 84 percent worked full-time in the labor force. In addition, two working-class men were formally unemployed but working in the informal labor force. Respondents were mostly white but ethnically diverse. Fifteen percent identified themselves as Italian American, 17 percent as Irish American, 45 percent as of Northern European descent, and 17 percent as Jewish (all but one of the Jewish respondents were middle class). One respondent was African American, one was Puerto Rican, and one was Arab American.

Most studies have missed the variation this study found between reports about friendship in general and what respondents say actually occurs in specific friendships. With the exception of network studies (which neglect issues of meaning within friendship), studies exploring gender differences in friendship have tended to ask either global questions about friends (Bell 1981; Caldwell and Peplau 1982; Rubin 1985; Swain 1989) or to focus on best friendships (Oliker 1989). Rebecca Adams (1989), in contrast, reports that the most accurate data about friendship are obtained by asking detailed questions about each member of a network and then calculating summary scores. Asking about a person's friendship in general is not as effective because "global questions require respondents to describe friendships as if they were all similar" (1989, 26).

Responses to global questions, however, are not inaccurate attempts by individuals to answer poorly designed questions. There are striking patterns to these responses that vary by gender. Individuals respond to such general questions as "How do you define friendship?" and "Do you think men's friendships differ from women's friendships?" in culturally specific ways. One gains knowledge of the meaning of friendship to individuals by asking global questions. This knowledge does not emerge by asking detailed questions about specific friendships precisely because there is a gap between individuals' notions of their social world and their actions in it. Both global and detailed questions are thus necessary to understand the interplay between ideology and actions.

ACCOUNTS OF FRIENDSHIP

Definitions of Friendship

Many men's and women's general accounts of friendship agree with the notion that men bond through shared activities, whereas women share intimate feelings. One man, a working-class father in his late twenties, said that men share a lot of things together, such as

> fishing, baseball, you know, maybe playing softball in a field, huntin', you know, just getting together and having a rap session, you know, sit back and relax and just talk and you know, work on cars, talk about, you know, there's different things, more you can share with a male because most of them, you know, know what's going on.

Other men also focused on shared activities as a basis for friendship. Many men reported that they watched sports with friends and did athletics such as running or playing basketball. Others focused less on physical activities and more on discussing politics or sharing political activism as a basis for friendship.

When asked how they defined friendship, most men commented on its affective dimensions and the importance of trust, but they frequently did so in terms of sharing experiences:

> People I consider friends are people who I'm likely to have warm feelings toward, feel like I have some history with, some events together. (middle-class man)

> How do I define friendship? Someone I can trust I would call a friend. Someone I like to spend some time with, you know, I enjoy certain, I enjoy doing certain things with. (working-class man)

These men shared events, they did things together, and they played games together. They also trusted each other and had warm feelings toward each other, but they did not mention the importance of sharing feelings together.

In contrast, most women responded that friendship was characterized by a shared history, giving and receiving support—primarily emotional support—and being able to talk to each other about things. When asked, "How do you define friendship?" two women responded saying,

Sharing, caring, being there for each other. (working-class woman)

It's a special interest in another person, and it shows caring and openness. (middle-class woman)

These responses emphasize support, talk, and sharing feelings. Whereas men also stressed supportiveness in friends, they often indicate that friends "do anything" for them, for example, give financial help or physical support in confrontations with others. Only one man reported that friendship meant being able to "tell anything and everything" to your friends, whereas several women did.

Perceived Differences in Men's and Women's Friendships

In response to questions about whether men's and women's friendships were similar or different, respondents' answers reflected cultural gender ideology. In a conversation immediately preceding our interview, one professional woman, Anna,[3] asked me what my dissertation was about. Told that it was a study of men's and women's friendships, she said that was very interesting: Her friendships were much different than her husband's friendships. Her husband had a friend named Jim whom Tom (Anna's husband) referred to as his "buddy." But even though Jim and Tom had a lot of fun together, Tom could not establish a more intimate friendship with Jim. Jim did not express his feelings. Anna thought this was because Jim was afraid his feelings would overwhelm him.

Although Anna was unique in bringing up the subject of men's and women's differences herself, about 40 percent of the respondents reported that men were not as open as women.[4] When asked "Do you think that men's friendships are different than women's friendships?", one man responded this way:

Well, we know that they are often. But whether that's a result of social construction or genetics I have no idea. [How are they different?] Well, there's a lot more sense of competition between a lot of men. A lot less openness about personal matters. It's just not as personal as being friends, uh, as your women friends. (middle-class man)

Other responses sounded remarkably similar in focusing on openness, the degree of closeness, and intimacy:

Men keep more to themselves. They don't open up the way women do. Some women will spill their guts at the drop of the hat. (working-class man)

I don't think men are as close as women are to each other. I think they're a little more distant with each other. I don't think men tell each other everything. (working-class woman)

Although a focus on intimacy and closeness was the most common response to questions about gender differences in friendships, another 25 percent of the respondents suggested that men and women do different things with their friends. Men play sports and share activities; women talk. Women discuss children and families; men discuss cars, work, and politics. Thus, about 65 percent of the respondents expressed and engaged in the construction of dominant cultural ideology about friendship that women are more intimate and talk in their friendships, whereas men engage in activities and do not share feelings.

Responses of the remaining one-third who gave other answers about men's and women's friendships were fairly evenly divided between those who said that women's friendships showed greater conflict, those who did not know if there were differences, and those who said men's and women's friendships were essentially similar in that loyalty and trust were requisites of all friendships.

Not only did men and women give gendered accounts of friendship, they also assumed that men and women were different. In doing so, they did not necessarily know how men and women differed, but they believed that they did. Individuals sometimes understood the response of someone from the opposite gender as characteristics of that gender if it differed from their own responses. Men and women frequently told me how their spouses were different from them. A lawyer told me how this process worked for him:

> So if Alberta and Deborah, Alberta my friend at work and Deborah my wife, take the same perspective I will say, "Oh, here's another example of women having the same perspective and men having a different perspective."

He assumed that women are different from him and then categorized a shared response by two women as characteristically feminine. Not only did men and women have different cultural notions about how men and women were different, but they created these notions on an ongoing basis using generalizations. Their accounts of their friendships were deeply influenced by these ideas.

EXPERIENCES IN SPECIFIC FRIENDSHIPS

Many respondents gave general accounts of their friendships that agreed with their understandings of what appropriate gendered behavior is. When I asked respondents detailed questions about activities they did with friends and things they talk about, however, I discovered that there was frequently a disparity between general representations that indicated cultural beliefs and specific information.

For instance, the man quoted above who thought that men friends shared activities such as hunting and fishing never went hunting or fishing with friends. His economic resources were severely limited, he worked two jobs, and had little time to socialize except in the evenings. His wife worked part-time in the evenings and on weekends, and while she worked he took care of their two children. Sometimes friends came over, and they watched TV and drank together. Most frequently, however, he socialized with friends at work in a high school where he was a janitor. He and his work friends discussed retirement, their wives, their children, as well as shared interests in sports.

When asked what he had talked about with his closest friend at work that day, he said they had dis-

cussed their wives' preferences for marital courtship. One wife liked to have the scene set before sex. She and her husband went out to eat together, they went shopping together, and there was a period in which they both knew what would happen later in the evening. My respondent told his friend that he and his wife like spontaneity. Preparing for sex through a series of rituals seemed superficial to them. This is the kind of detailed talk about a significant relationship in which women are reputed to engage. It is a far cry from the stereotype of men friends who discuss sports and who do not have intimate discussions. Nor does it fit with my respondent's own perception of what friendships are like.

There were many similar examples. Seventy-five percent of the men reported engaging in nongendered behavior with friends—all of whom reported that they spoke intimately about spouses, other family members, and their feelings. Furthermore, one-third of those men reported that they engaged in other nongendered behavior as well as intimate talk. A lawyer who said that he did not discuss marital issues or personal matters with his friends later reported that he and his friends had talked with some regularity about fertility problems they were having with their wives. They discussed the fact that their wives were much more concerned about their difficulties in conceiving than they were.

Some men reported the impact of divorce on friendship interaction. One professional man told me of at least two men whom he had supported through their divorces, listening to them talk about their feelings. He told me of friends who had helped him through his divorce, men who allowed him to "ventilate." This man repeatedly told me that he was very emotive and expressive and that he complained a lot to friends. That these conversations are disregarded in how men shape their understandings about being men is indicated by what happened later in the interview. He told me that he thought women were more open than men were. He said he had gone to hear Robert Bly talk, and Robert Bly had said that women had an ability to get to the heart of the matter, to really articulate things, whereas men were unable to do so. My respondent said he really thought Bly was right, and he regretted his own inability to be more open. He also said that he never discussed martial problems or issues with his friends. He reported that he and his friends usually discussed sports, even though my respondent did not much care for sports.

Three young lawyers in an open network talked about doing sports with friends—wrestling in college, running as adults, playing basketball. They also talked about going to football games together and discussing sports in telephone calls. These young men seemed to have stereotypically masculine friendships, but when asked for detailed information about how often they saw their friends and under what circumstances, they reported that the most frequent interaction was during the holidays—at parties, going out to dinner, and getting together with their wives. They did get together for one or two sports events a year. In addition, two of the men had run in local foot races together on two occasions. Although these events were symbolically important in terms of these men's images of their friendships, they did not accurately represent the men's common pattern of friendship interaction. Their friendships were largely carried on through bimonthly or sometimes weekly telephone conversations from their offices, during which they said they discussed sports, work, and family. One of these men was involved in a transatlantic relationship. What to do about his relationship had been a serious issue for the month or two prior to our interview. So, when asked what he and specific friends had talked about in their last conversations, he almost always said he talked about what he should do: should he go to England, should he break up with the woman, was she serious in wanting a commitment?

In addition to talking about things that men are reputed not to talk about—feelings and relationships—sometimes men did things that did not fit with their ideas of what men typically did. For instance, both men and women thought of shopping as something women, but not men, do together. Most men, in fact, said they did not shop with friends. The response of Joe, a working-class man, illuminates the meaning of shopping as a gendered activity. He reported that sometimes he went food shopping with a married friend: "Anita gives him the list and we go to the supermarket like two old ladies and we pick out the things, 'Well, this one's cheaper than that one so let's get this.'" Joe seemed a little embarrassed by this activity. He laughed softly as he reported these shopping trips. His married friends, whom I also interviewed, denied that he shopped with friends.

Gene, a middle-class man, said that he was concerned about moisturizer, but he did not discuss it with friends. I asked why not, and he said it was "faggotty" to do so, blushed, and laughed with embarrassment. Then he talked about going to visit a gay friend in another city. The morning after he got there he and his friend went out early to buy moisturizer and vegetable pâté at Neiman-Marcus—activities he thought of as stereotypically gay and not things most heterosexual men do (his friend was in the entertainment industry in Hollywood, and his behavior could just as easily have been ascribed to the demands of a lifestyle valuing appearance and style). Gene's use of the term "faggotty" indicated that there are certain things that he did not do as he constructed his masculinity in everyday interaction. This accords with Carrigan, Connell, and Lee's (1987) discussion about the importance of hegemonic heterosexual masculinity in constructing power relations among men. Men who construct alternative forms of masculinity, such as being gay, are perceived as not masculine. Like the working-class man who did not feel like a man when he shopped for food with his friend, Gene did not feel like a man when he discussed moisturizer, and so he did not do it with straight friends.

Given that gay men are perceived as not masculine, it is interesting to note that Gene's friendship with Al, his gay friend, did not appear to threaten Gene's masculinity. Gene's account of how Al came out to him emphasized friendship over sexual orientation. Longtime college friends, Al told Gene he was gay several years after college, and he added that he knew his coming out might end their friendship. Gene reported being "very insulted" that Al thought he might stop being his friend. Whether or not being friends with Al threatened his masculinity was unimportant compared to Gene's public reaffirmation of the norm of loyalty to friends; furthermore, Gene emphasized joking behavior as important to friendship and connected joking to masculinity. Al, it turned out, had an acerbic and imaginative sense of humor that Gene appreciated.

Even in a situation where behavior contradicts gendered norms, some aspect of the interaction often constructs gender in ways consonant with ideology. Whereas the action of one person may contradict ideology, the response of the other may construct gender in ways conforming to dominant ideology. This pattern of emphasizing friendship activities that fit with their ideologies of masculinity is analogous to what Leidner (1991) observed in her study of men and women interactive service workers who emphasized those aspect of their jobs that they thought of as consonant with their gender identities. For instance, Gene and a friend were sitting together one night:

> And he says, "So, how are things going?" And I, I had been through a real bad period. And I said, "Fuck it, I'm going to tell him." So I told him how everything was wrong in my life, and toward the end of it he said, "Oh, that's the last time I ask you how you're feeling." . . . I mean, he was actually offensively unsupportive.

In this instance, Gene violated gender ideology dictating that he not discuss his problems with his friend. His friend responded by letting Gene know that he did not want to hear Gene's problems. By belittling Gene's disclosures, his friend also constructed masculinity in ways conforming to dominant norms. Gene, who tended to reject the legitimacy of the dominant norms and who self-consciously violated those norms, interpreted his friend's behavior as typically male. Gene used this event to describe masculine behavior to me, even though it also included Gene's own transgressions of gender ideology.

The construction of gender, therefore, is a highly complex process that occurs through behavior, through ideology, and through accounts of both. One person may act in ways that contradict gender ideology, and the response may be disapproval, which reinforces the ideology. In addition, there are many events and forms of interaction that occur simultaneously in one situation, and flexibility in the construction of one aspect of gender may not threaten the overall construction of gender if other interactions, such as joking, reinforce gender ideology.

Nongendered Behavior Among Women

Similar processes of understanding their own behavior in terms of cultural ideologies and norms occurred among women. Women reported that they could tell their friends anything. They readily volunteered that they talked about their husbands and lovers. Few women volunteered that shared activities were essential to friendship; the middle-class women were more likely to do so than the working-class women—they had more resources with which to engage in shared activities. Few women volunteered that they go to spectator sports with friends. Few women volunteered that they engaged in athletic activities with friends.

Just as there were disparities between men's statements about what their friendships were generally like and what their specific experiences were, there were also disparities between what women said their friendships were like generally and what specific friendships were like. About 65 percent of all women reported engaging in behavior that did not conform to gender ideology. Some women, like some men, occasionally went to spectator sporting events with friends, but, with one exception, I only heard about these activities when I asked directly if they went to sporting events or did athletics with friends. Unlike men, women did not volunteer that they did so. About 25 percent of all women worked out together, went to aerobics classes together, or belonged to local sports teams, but they primarily defined these occasions as other times to see each other and talk; the activities themselves were defined as relatively unimportant.

Another 15 percent of the women respondents said that many friendship interactions occurred while they were doing things with friends. Several middle-class women belonged to musical groups where they met friends. A few working-class women went out to clubs together, leaving their spouses at home. Sharing activities, therefore, sometimes provided the basis for women's friendships just as it provided the basis for some men's friendships.

Finally, 25 percent of the women respondents reported that they considered certain information private and would not discuss it with friends. Ilana, the professional woman quoted above who said that friendship entailed showing openness and caring, reported that there were many things about which she would not talk to friends. For instance, she did not discuss her relationships with men with other women.

Ilana indicated that her reticence was unusual, but it did not force her to reconsider her femininity. Instead, she both acknowledged and denied the masculine stereotype of sharing activities without talk. On the one hand, she said, "There are a lot of male friendships based on doing certain male things together without saying much." On the other hand, she said, "There are also men that surprise me in that it seems to me that they like to gossip and talk about women even more than women may want to talk about men." She went on to report:

> I was going out with someone and we were at a video store and met a friend of his. And it was the first time I ever met this friend, it was only the third time I had ever seen the person I was going out with and immediately they were talking about what happened . . . the other guy was basically stood up by a woman and they were talking about it and, you know, just the whole thing. And then I went to dinner with the person I was going out with and he told me the whole story of this friend, of the whole relationship. . . . And it just didn't seem appropriate somehow.

Ilana, who hesitated to speak with people about personal matters, reconstructed masculinity as gossipy, and she reacted in distaste to her companion's openness; furthermore, she contrasted men's to women's gossip, saying that some men like to gossip about women more than women gossip about men. When Ilana herself did not conform to the gender stereotype of feminine openness she still constructed her behavior in opposition to masculine behavior.

Two academic women reported doing very little intimate sharing with friends. One woman reported that she had no friends whatsoever, although she was on friendly relations with many colleagues. She did not discuss her relationship with her husband or her family, or many intimacies with anyone other than her husband. She also did not talk to people about worries or problems because she said she did not like to burden people. The woman who referred me to her told me that she, too, rarely discussed intimate matters with friends. Like the first woman, she said she did not do so because she did not want to impose her problems on others; she did not think they would be interested.

One group of four working-class women defined openness as an essential component to friendship, and three of the women regarded the fourth woman, Susan, as not open enough, a failing they urged her to overcome. Susan concurred with her friends' opinions that she was not open enough, but she chose silence and reserve as a form of rebellion because she was angry with the woman in the group to whom she was closest. Although Susan's behavior did not conform to the ideal of feminine openness and intimacy, the talk of her friends constructed femininity even as they censured Susan for her secrecy.

Several professional women regretted that they did not have close intimate friendships, or they accepted what they took to be the fact that they did not make good friends. They felt like failures for not having friends with whom they could "say anything." On the one hand, they gave me reasons why they did not have those friendships. On the other hand, they felt as if they were unusual and "bad" friends. This belief in their own failure did not emerge in interviews with men. Whereas some men regretted not being able to open up, no men said they were bad for not doing so. For men, it was characteristically masculine to lack the ability to share intimate feelings with friends.

CLASS AND FRIENDSHIP

Sociologists have noted that social class as well as gender influences friendship patterns (Allan 1989; Willmott 1987). In this study, one way social class influenced behavior was that behavior conflicted with popular ideology, particularly for middle-class women. Middle-class women in traditionally male-dominated occupations such as university professors, lawyers, and doctors most frequently reported a lack of intimacy in friendships. Many had been very mobile. They moved from city to city while they pursued their educations. Some reported having intimate friendships when they were in college or graduate school, but indicated that recent friendships were less likely to be so. Whereas some women regularly corresponded with old friends with whom they were intimate, some did not and therefore reported a lack of intimate friendships. One doctor reported:

> Well, pretty much all my life, although I find this sort of dwindling down now . . . but I think for a long time I always had a couple really close friends, like people I'd see almost every day, talk to a lot, and um, would tell virtually anything and everything to.

The same doctor was asked, "How is it different now?" and responded,

> I don't know if I'm so busy or everybody else, everybody has sort of tunnel vision, you tend not to talk to people or feel you don't have time to talk to people about anything but the essentials. . . . You don't have as many peers, basically . . . you're not in a medical school class of 180 of whom a third are women. That's part of it. . . . Maybe I always did look to my peers who were in the training group or whatever for my friends, and the group has gotten smaller. The other thing is the group has gotten more competitive. I mean, to be blunt, I don't particularly like a lot of people that I'm training with. They are very competitive and they're not very friendly, really. There was only one other woman in my year and I think she viewed me as a rival, not as a potential friend.

In addition to being occupationally mobile, this woman, like many of the middle-class respondents, had been geographically mobile. She had infrequent contact with friends who lived in other cities, and she experienced attrition in groups of older friendships from college and medical school; furthermore, she did not replace friends as quickly as she once did. In addition, drawing on the expectation that friends could be drawn from peers with whom she was relatively equal, she found there were fewer equals in her pool of potential friends. Finally, competition at work dictated against the formation of intimate friendships.

Helen Gouldner and Mary Symons Strong (1987) noted similar experiences among executive women who lacked the time to form friendships off the job and hesitated to form friendships with people at work. Time was a major factor in limiting intimate friendships for the employed middle-class women I interviewed. For many, the development of intimacy required some minimal amount of time. Professional women often lacked the time to give to friends, particularly if they were married and had children. Most of their socializing with friends was done with work colleagues with whom they limited the amount of personal information they exchanged or with their husbands and other couples. Socializing with couples was not very intimate, but were occasions when men and women alike reported that they discussed politics, children, and work.

Professional men had similar friendships in these respects. They, too had been mobile. Their groups of college friends had shrunk over the years. Friends had not been replaced as quickly as they had been lost. Time was limited for many men, particularly married men with children. In addition, much of their socializing was also done in couples, when intimate sharing was at a minimum. These constraints on professional men's and women's abilities to form long-lasting friendships with extensive interaction produced friendships resembling the masculine model of friendship more than the feminine model, especially when compared to unemployed women or working-class men and women.

When middle-class respondents had intimate friendships, they tended to have them with longtime friends and levels of intimacy varied over time. Periods of crisis, such as divorce, were most likely to be times when men and women had intimate discussions, but those times tended to be limited, and after the troubles subsided, they returned to their old patterns of interaction.

The middle-class women who had friendships conforming to gender stereotypes of intimacy tended to be those women who stayed at home with small children and had neighborhood friends. They had more opportunities to see friends alone, which increased their opportunities for intimate discussions. In addition, collegial norms against sharing intimate details did not exist for these women.

Working-class respondents' lives were structured differently from those of professional men and women, and their friendships were correspondently different.[5] Only one working-class man was from another state (whereas three-fourths of the middle-class respondents grew up in other states). Working-class men and women tended to know their friends for much longer periods of time—they met in school or in their neighborhoods. They had fewer friends, but they saw them more often. In addition, they frequently saw their friends informally at home or in the neighborhood; as a result, they knew about each other's troubles in a way that professional men and women who socialized occasionally with friends did not. Their social lives were more highly gender segregated, which provided greater opportunities for intimate discussion. Men, as well as women, reported that they talked to their friends about intimate things on a regular basis. Thus nongendered behavior among working-class respondents tended to occur among men who reported frequent intimate discussions ("We're worse than a bunch of girls when it comes to that").

The working-class respondents also had more problems—financial, substance abuse, family, health—and having these problems meant they tended to be topics of conversations with their friends. When professional men and women faced troubles, they also talked to their friends, but their lives were more stable in many respects. As a group the middle-class respondents were affluent, and they reported having few financial difficulties. Middle-class respondents reported that heavy periods of drug and alcohol use tended to have been in their late adolescence and early twenties, times when they were not married. The working-class respondents married young, and drug and alcohol use tended to be a problem because it interfered with marriage and family. Financial problems, drug problems,

and marital problems often seemed to occur together among the working-class respondents with each problem exacerbating the others, whereas middle-class respondents tended to deal with single problems at a time and to emerge from periods of crisis more quickly. To the extent that discussing problems is a mark of intimacy for many individuals, working-class men appeared to have more intimate friendships than professional men and women.

CONCLUSION

I have conceptualized gender as an ongoing social creation rather than as a role individuals learn or a personality type they develop that causes differences in behavior. This approach to gender accounts for many of the differences between how men and women represent their friendships in general and the specific patterns their friendships have. In interviews, men and women gave me general accounts of their friendships based on specific cultural norms of masculinity and femininity. These accounts often came early in the interview when I asked respondents to give me their definition of friendship and to tell me why friendship was important to them, if it was. They also came up toward the end of the interview when I asked them if they thought men's friendships differed from women's friendships. And they often contradicted specific information gathered during the friendship history.

It is not, however, sufficient to understand these processes as the ongoing production of gender. The process of gender construction is universal, but the forms and content of the construction vary. One must, therefore, ask why these particular ideologies about gender differences in friendship dominate rather than others. Earlier ideologies of friendship represented women as incapable of loyalty and true friendship and men as noble friends. Why has a reversal occurred? Asking this question, Barry Wellman (1992) argues that the domestication of the community through suburbanization has decreased the importance of men's public and semipublic social ties, at the same time increasing the importance of private domestic ties, at which women have traditionally excelled; thus men's friendships are beginning to resemble women's friendships in that they are carried out in the home and as "relations of emotional support, companionship, and domestic services" (Wellman 1992, 101). Wellman is effectively addressing a perceived change over time in friendship behavior among men, not the question of why women's friendships are privileged in contemporary culture.

The answer to that lies in the emergence of the women's movement and the self-conscious attempts to valorize women—and the response to that valorization by men. Much of the academic literature about women's friendship patterns is written by feminist social scientists who respond to older cultural ideologies that men were capable of true friendship and women were not (Rubin 1985; Smith-Rosenberg 1975). Rubin's argument, which claims that men are psychically incapable of the kind of intimacy characterizing women's friendships, draws explicitly on Carol Gilligan's and Nancy Chodorow's feminist work. although it is often difficult to determine the source of cultural ideology, the efflorescence of articles and books about women's friendships and relationships occurs after the beginning of second wave feminism, and it is only then that men begin to respond systematically to those works.

In everyday interaction, these cultural ideologies are reproduced through discussions with friends, through the kind of generalizing people come to regarding gender that I mentioned earlier, through socialization, and through exposure to ideas about gender differences by the media. If men and women accept cultural definitions of reality, and many of them do, they interpret their behavior in light of such depictions and feel either deficient or validated depending on whether they fit or not. Many also orient their behavior toward these prescriptions for behavior. The fact that so much of their behavior does not match the cultural prescriptions, however, indicates the limits of those prescriptions for determining behavior. It also calls into question the adequacy of explanations that conclude that women and men are essentially different. Men and women respond to the demands of their lives in a variety of ways; some of those responses may disaffirm those same men's and women's gender ideologies.

In addition to asking why ideologies about women's openness and men's activities dominate other ideologies, one may also ask why men and women accept the stereotypes when their own behavior differs significantly from them. Several reasons account for this. First, friends sometimes frown on men's and women's gender-inappropriate behaviors. Such disapproval reinforces gender norms, and is interpreted by the one who receives disapproval as an indication that the behavior of the one who disapproves conforms to gender ideologies; therefore, the person whose behavior does not conform comes to see his or her behavior as anamolous. Second, women and men sometimes do not see the disparity between behavior and ideology because they do not reflect on their behavior. Given the enormous number of interactions in which people participate in daily life, it is not surprising that they neglect to reflect on behavior that they do not think meaningful in the construction of their identities.

Finally, friendship interactions are very complex, and men and women do gender in a variety of ways in single interactions. Often their behaviors do not conform to gender stereotypes, but other elements of the interaction construct gender along normative lines. The usual outcome of doing gender, buttressed by life's experiences, is that the actors have no doubts about their gender identities as women or men. In the case of friendship and gender stereotypes, men's and women's flexibility in behavior does not threaten their identities as men or women because so many other aspects of interaction reinforce their identities, which they reify. They are not, therefore, normally faced with a problem of gender identity that they must reflect on and solve either through modifying their behaviors or through modifying their ideologies to better reflect behavior. As I noted earlier, the change in ideology from one valorizing men's friendships to one valorizing women's friendships was initiated by feminists who had identified problems and self-consciously acted to solve them. Their success may rest on the fact that, when asked to reflect on their own experiences, others also recognized the problems in the way men's and women's friendships were perceived and the way they were experienced; but it was first necessary to bring the disparities to people's attention.

Even this change did not fundamentally alter the notion that women's friendships are emotionally expressive, whereas men's friendships are not; rather, it altered the *value* of men's and women's friendships.

One must be wary of arguments that posit the early development of gendered personalities that cause differences in friendship; however, provocative, psychoanalytic theories of masculine or feminine personalities cannot account for the variation one sees in men's or women's behaviors. Nor does it account for the disparity between people's general accounts of friendship and their specific experiences, a disparity that makes sense if one understands those general representations as attempts to provide coherence, and understanding, and to find norms by which to live as gendered humans.

NOTES

1. The terms *working class* and *middle class* are used in this article to refer to people who differ in the work they do in the labor force and in their status. Middle-class men and women held professional or managerial jobs. They all had bachelor's degrees, and many had graduate or professional degrees. Most lived in suburbs or in downtown apartments. In contrast, working-class respondents worked in traditional craft, clerical, or low-level service occupations. Most had high school diplomas or less, although one working-class man had a bachelor of arts degree and seven working-class women had one or two years of college. Most lived in twin or row houses in densely populated working-class urban neighborhoods. Individuals not working in the paid labor force at the time of the interview were defined as working or middle class both on the basis of their status and by the kind of work they did when they worked in the labor force; thus the unemployed working-class women had done clerical work or low-level service work (cashiering), whereas the three formally unemployed working-class men reported that they were a tile setter, a plumber, and a cook, respectively. Unemployed middle-class women had worked in mid-level management or professional jobs.

2. Snowball sampling often introduces bias. In this study, I often found that friends had similar life experiences and educational levels, and the fact that friends shared activities with one another limited the effective size of the sample. My ability to generalize, therefore, is limited. Discrepancies between gender ideology and behavior occurred among most individuals, however, and the fact that they did suggests that earlier explanations of gender differences in friendship, as well as the extent of those differences, should be closely examined.

3. All the names of the respondents have been changed.

4. Results about perceived differences in men's and women's friendships are based on responses of 46 individuals. At the beginning of the study, four women and two men were not asked to compare men's and women's friendships.

5. Clyde Franklin makes similar observations about Black men: "While working class black men's same-sex friendships are warm, intimate, and holistic, upwardly mobile black men's same-sex friendships are cool, non-intimate, and segmented" (1992, 212).

REFERENCES

Adams, R. G. 1989. Conceptual and methodological issues in studying friendship of older adults. In *Older adult friendship: Structure and process,* edited by R. G. Adams and R. Blieszner. Newbury Park, CA: Sage.

Allan, G. 1989. *Friendship: Developing a sociological perspective.* Boulder, CO: Westview.

Bell, R. 1981. *Worlds of friendship.* Beverly Hills, CA: Sage.

Caldwell, M. A., and L. A. Peplau. 1982. Sex differences in same-sex friendships. *Sex Roles* 8:721–32.

Carrigan, T., B. Connell, and J. Lee. 1987. Hard and heavy: Toward a new sociology of masculinity. In *Beyond patriarchy: Essays by men on pleasure, power, and change,* edited by M. Kaufman. Toronto: Oxford University Press.

Connell, R. W. 1987. *Gender and power.* Stanford, CA: Stanford University Press.

Eichenbaum, L., and S. Orbach. 1989. *Between women: Love, envy, and competition in women's friendships.* New York: Penguin.

Franklin, C. W., II. 1992. Friendship among Black men. In *Men's friendships,* edited by P. M. Nardi. Newbury Park, CA: Sage.

Gouldner, H., and M. S. Strong. 1987. *Speaking of friendship: Middle class women and their friends,* New York: Greenwood.

Hansen, K. V. 1992. Our eyes behold each other: Masculinity and intimate friendship in antebellum New England. In *Men's friendships,* edited by P. M. Nardi. Newbury Park, CA: Sage.

Leidner, R. 1991. Serving hamburgers and selling insurance: Gender, work, and identity in interactive service jobs. *Gender & Society* 5:154–77.

Oliker, S. 1989. *Best friends and marriage.* Berkeley: University of California Press.

Rubin, L. 1985. *Just friends: The role of friendship in our lives.* New York: Harper & Row.

Smith-Rosenberg, C. 1975. The female world of love and ritual. *Signs* 1:1–29.

Sherrod, S. 1987. The bonds of men: Problems and possibilities in close male relationships. In *The making of masculinities: The new men's studies,* edited by H. Brod. Boston: Allen & Unwin.

Swain, S. 1989. Covert intimacy: Closeness in men's friendships. In *Gender in intimate relationships: A microstructural ap-*proach, edited by B. Risman and P. Schwartz. Belmont, CA: Wadsworth.

Wellman, B. 1992. Men in networks: Private communities, domestic friendships. In *Men's friendships,* edited by P. M. Nardi. Newbury Park, CA: Sage.

West, C., and D. Zimmerman. 1987. Doing gender. *Gender & Society* 1:125–51.

Willmott, P. 1987. *Friendship networks and social support.* London: Policy Studies Institute.

CHECKPOINTS

1. Our stereotypes about men's and women's friendships are not consistent with our experiences with friends.

2. Social class influences the nature of our friendships by structuring different opportunities for shared activities and by mobility.

To prepare for reading the next section, think about these questions:

1. In what ways do you think gay and lesbian relationships are similar to or different from heterosexual relationships?

2. What can gay and lesbian relationships tell us about heterosexual relationships?

GAY AND LESBIAN RELATIONSHIPS: MYTHS AND REALITIES

Lesbian and Gay Relationships

LETITIA ANNE PEPLAU

Public awareness of lesbian and gay couples is growing; attention to homosexuality in the popular media is increasing. Social scientists have also begun to describe and analyze the nature of gay and lesbian relationships. The new scholarship on homosexual relationships is important both to the scientific community and to the general public.

For the emerging science of close relationships (Kelley et al. 1983), research on homosexual couples broadens the existing knowledge base by increasing the diversity of types of relationships studied to include same-sex partnerships. In the past, virtually all research on adult love relationships has focused on heterosexual dating and marriage. New studies of homosexual couples expand the range and generality of scientific knowledge about intimate relationships.

For the growing research literature on homosexuality, studies of gay and lesbian relationships also represent a new direction. Until recently, scholarship on homosexuality focused primarily on questions of pathology, individual psychological adjustment, and etiology. For example, a recent annotated bibliography included close to 5,000 citations from the social sciences, humanities, and popular press (Dynes 1987). Only 36 of these entries were classified as dealing with gay or lesbian "couples." In contrast, there were 207 entries on psychiatry, psychotherapy, "cures," and related topics, and another 155 entries on the experiences of lesbians and gay men in prison or with the police.

For the general public, accurate information about gay and lesbian relationships is also useful. Scientific research can replace biased stereotypes with factual descriptions of the nature and diversity of homosexual couples. Research can also inform the discussion of new legal and public policy issues that arise as gay men and lesbians become a more visible and vocal part of society. This point is illustrated in the following case descriptions, based on recent legal cases.

Case: 1: Emotional Pain and Suffering

A man in a long-term gay relationship was killed by a reckless driver. The surviving partner sued the driver for damages resulting from the grief and psychological distress of losing a spouse-equivalent. The driver's lawyer countered that gay men's relationships bear little resemblance to marriage, and that it would be ridiculous to provide such payment. This case hinges on fundamental questions about the nature of gay men's relationships. How similar are long-term gay partnerships to heterosexual marriage? What is the intensity of love and attachment experienced in enduring gay relationships, and what is the depth of grief that accompanies bereavement?

Case 2: A Lesbian Mother

A young woman married her college sweetheart, had two daughters, divorced her husband, and retained custody of the children. Some time later, she began a lesbian relationship and set up a joint household with her female partner. At this point, her former husband sued to gain custody of the children, claiming that the mother was an "unfit" parent. It was proposed that she might retain custody if she promised to end her lesbian relationship. At issue here are basic questions about the ability of a lesbian mother to provide a healthy family life, the role models provided by partners in a lesbian relationship, and the impact of a lesbian couple on children in the household.

Case 3: The Crime-of-Passion Defense

During a heated argument, a young man bludgeoned his lover to death with a fire iron. The defense acknowledged that the man had committed the murder, but pleaded that the act was committed in a moment of passion—a defense that could potentially lead to a lesser charge than premeditated homicide. The defendant's case rested on showing that gay relationships are as emotionally intense as heterosexual ones, perhaps even more so. The lawyer argued that a threat to a relationship could send a gay man "over the edge" psychologically. In addition, since both partners were recent immigrants from a culture that is highly intolerant of homosexuality, the defense attorney argued that his client was denied the kinds of social support that might have enabled him to cope more effectively with the crisis in his relationship. The case raises questions about the nature of love, passion, and jealousy in gay relationships, and the social support experienced by homosexuals.

Although existing research does not definitively resolve the questions raised by these cases, it does provide beginning answers. This article reviews social science research on gay and lesbian relationships. It begins by summarizing major research findings relevant to four common stereotypes about gay and lesbian relationships in America. Then, theoretical issues raised by the study of lesbian and gay couples are considered. The article concludes with a discussion of the variation and diversity that exists among same-sex relationships.

It is important to emphasize at the outset that most of the available studies of homosexual relationships are based on samples of younger, urban, primarily White individuals. Occasionally, studies have involved fairly large samples (e.g., Blumstein and Schwartz 1983) or have included ethnic samples (e.g., Bell and Weinberg 1978 surveyed both Black and White respondents), but none has been completely representative of either lesbians or gay men. So it is essential to acknowledge this limitation in our newly accumulating body of research.

DEBUNKING STEREOTYPES ABOUT LESBIAN AND GAY RELATIONSHIPS

Empirical social science research on gay and lesbian relationships dates mainly from the mid-1970s. To date, the work has been largely descriptive-seeking to test the accuracy of prevailing social stereotypes about gay and lesbian relationships and to provide more reliable information. (For other reviews, see De Cecco 1988; Harry 1983; Larson 1982; Peplau and Amaro 1982; Peplau and Cochran 1990; Peplau and Gordon 1983; Risman and Schwartz 1988.)

Myth 1: Homosexuals don't want enduring relationships—and can't achieve them anyway.

Homosexuals are often depicted in the media as unhappy individuals who are unsuccessful in developing enduring same-sex ties. Drifting from one sexual liaison to another, they end up old and alone. Existing data sharply counter this stereotype.

Studies of homosexuals' attitudes about relationships find that most lesbians and gay men say they very much want to have enduring close relationships (e.g., Bell and Weinberg 1978). Other studies have investigated the extent to which lesbians and gay men are successful in establishing intimate relationships. In surveys of gay men, between 40 percent and 60 percent of the men questioned were currently involved in a steady relationship (e.g., Bell and Weinberg 1978; Harry 1983; Jay and Young 1977; Peplau and Cochran 1981; Spada 1979). These figures may actually *under*represent the true frequency of enduring relationships because men in long-term relationships tend to be somewhat older and less likely to go to bars—both factors that would reduce the chances of these men being included in current studies (Harry 1983). In studies of lesbians, between 45 percent and 80 percent of women surveyed were currently in a steady relationship (e.g., Bell and Weinberg 1978; Jay and Young 1977; Peplau et al. 1978; Raphael and Robinson 1980; Schafer 1977). In most studies, the proportion of lesbians in an ongoing relationship was close to 75 percent.

These estimates are not completely representative of all lesbians and gay men in the United States. They do indicate, however, that a large proportion of homosexuals have stable close relationships. Research also suggests that a slightly higher proportion of lesbians than gay men may be in steady relationships.

Given that substantial proportions of lesbians and gay men are involved in intimate relationships, a next question concerns the longevity of these partnerships. Lacking marriage records and representative samples, it is hard to make judgments about how long "typical" homosexual relationships last. Most studies have been of younger adults, whose relationships have lasted for a few years, as would be true for heterosexuals in their twenties. The few studies that have included older gay men and lesbians have found that relationships lasting twenty years or more are not uncommon (e.g., McWhirter and Mattison 1984; Raphael and Robinson 1980; Silverstein 1981).

In a short longitudinal study, Blumstein and Schwartz (1983) followed a large sample of lesbian, gay male, cohabiting heterosexual, and married couples over an eighteen-month period. At the time of initial testing, lesbians, gay men, and heterosexuals were about equal in predicting that their current relationship would continue, although both lesbians and gay men speculated that gay men usually have less stable relationships than lesbians. At the eighteen-month follow-up, most couples were still together. Breakups were rare among couples who had already been together for more than ten years: 6 percent for lesbians, 4 percent for gay men, 4 percent for married couples. (None of the heterosexual cohabiting couples had been together for more than ten years.) Among couples who had been together for two years or less, the breakup rate was also fairly low—less than one relationship in five ended during the eighteen-month period. Minor differences were found in rates of breakup among the different types of couples: 22 percent for lesbian couples, 16 percent for gay male couples, 17 percent for cohabiting couples, and 4 percent for married couples. Although these group differences are quite small, they do run counter to the suggestion that lesbians are more likely to have enduring partnerships. More important, however, is the general pattern of relationship continuity found for all groups.

The basic point to draw from these studies is that gay and lesbian relationships are very much a reality in contemporary life.

Myth 2: Gay relationships are unhappy, abnormal, dysfunctional, and deviant.

It is often believed that gay and lesbian relationships are inferior to those of heterosexuals. For example, a study of heterosexual college students found that they expected gay and lesbian relationships to be less satisfying, more prone to discord, and "less in love" than heterosexual relationships (Testa, Kinder, and Ironson 1987). To investigate this stereotype scientifically, researchers have assessed the psychological adjustment of homosexual dyads, and have often used a research strategy of comparing the relationship functioning of matched samples of homosexual and heterosexual couples. The central question has been how well gay and lesbian relationships fare on standard measures of relationship satisfaction, dyadic adjustment, or love.

Illustrative of this research is a study that Susan Cochran and I conducted (Peplau and Cochran 1980). We selected matched samples of fifty lesbians, fifty gay men, fifty heterosexual women, and fifty heterosexual men—all currently involved in "romantic/sexual relationships." Participants were matched on age, education, ethnicity, and length of relationship, and all completed a detailed questionnaire about their current relationship.

Among this sample of young adults, about 60 percent said they were "in love with their partner"; most of the rest indicated they were "uncertain." On Rubin's standardized Love and Liking Scales, lesbians and gay men generally reported very positive feelings for their partners. Lesbians and gay men also rated their current relationships as highly satisfying and very close. No significant differences were found among lesbians, gay men, and heterosexuals on any of these measures of relationship satisfaction.

We also asked lesbians, gay men, and heterosexuals to describe in their own words the "best things" and "worst things" about their relationships. Responses included such comments as these: "The best thing is having someone to be with when you wake up," or "We like each other. We both seem to be get-

ting what we want and need. We have wonderful sex together." Worst things included "My partner is too dependent emotionally," or "Her aunt lives with us!" Systematic content analyses (Cochran 1978) found no significant differences in the responses of lesbians, gay men, and heterosexuals—all of whom reported a similar range of joys and problems. To search for more subtle differences among groups that may not have been captured by the coding scheme, the "best things" and "worst things" statements were typed on cards in a standard format, with information about gender and sexual orientation removed. Panels of judges were asked to sort the cards, separating men and women, or separating heterosexuals and homosexuals. The judges were not able to identify correctly the responses of lesbians, gay men, or heterosexual women and men. (Indeed, judges may have been misled by their own preconceptions; they tended, for instance, to assume incorrectly that statements involving jealousy were more likely to be made by homosexuals than by heterosexuals.)

Other studies have portrayed similar findings, and have extended the range of relationship measures used. In general, most gay men and lesbians perceive their relationships as satisfying. Homosexual and heterosexual couples who are matched on age and other relevant background characteristics do not usually differ in levels of love and satisfaction, nor in their scores on standardized measures such as the Locke-Wallace Scale or Spanier's Dyadic Adjustment Scale (see Cardell, Finn, and Marecek 1981; Dailey 1979; Duffy and Rusbult 1986; Kurdek and Schmitt 1986b, c, 1987a; Peplau, Cochran, and Mays 1986; Peplau, Padesky, and Hamilton 1982).

None of this is to say that all gay and lesbian couples are happy and problem-free. Rather the point is that homosexual couples are not necessarily any more prone to relationship dissatisfactions and difficulties than are heterosexuals. Although the likelihood of relationship problems may be similar regardless of sexual orientation, however, there may nonetheless be differences in the types of problems most commonly faced by gay, lesbian, and heterosexual couples. For example, therapists have suggested that issues of dependency and individuation may be especially salient in lesbian relationships (e.g., Roth 1985; Sang 1985; Smalley 1987). Recently, psychotherapists have begun to develop new programs of couples counseling geared specifically for gay or lesbian couples (e.g., Berzon 1988; Boston Lesbian Psychologies Collective 1987; Gonsiorek 1985; Stein and Cohen 1986).

In summary, research findings indicate that it is no longer useful or appropriate to describe homosexual relationships in the value-laden language of "abnormal relationships" or "deviance." There is growing recognition of the wide diversity of "families" today—single-parent families, "recombinant families" incorporating children from two previous marriages, and so on. Lesbian and gay partnerships should be included among this diverse array of family types.

There is also increasing evidence from historians (e.g., Boswell 1980) and anthropologists (e.g., Herdt 1981) that our own culture's negative evaluation of homosexual couples has not been shared universally. In other times and places, human culture has recognized and approved of gay partnerships. Interesting, too, are recent efforts by sociobiologists to consider ways in which homosexual relationships might be functional rather than dysfunctional for individuals, in the sense of enhancing their reproductive success and causing their genes to influence the direction of evolutionary change. A detailed discussion of this perspective is presented by Weinrich (1987).

Myth 3: "Husband" and "wife" roles are universal in intimate relationships.

C. A. Tripp notes that "when people who are not familiar with homosexual relationships try to picture one, they almost invariably resort to a heterosexual frame of reference, raising questions about which partner is "the man" and which "the woman" (1975:152). This issue has generated a good deal of empirical research (see reviews by Harry 1983; Peplau and Gordon 1983; Risman and Schwartz 1988).

Historical accounts of gay life in the United States suggest that masculine-feminine roles have sometimes been important. For example, Wolf described lesbian experiences in the 1950s in these terms:

The old gay world divided up into "butch" and "femmes" . . . Butches were tough, presented themselves as being as masculine as possible . . . and they assumed the traditional male role of taking care of their partners, even fighting over them if necessary . . . Femmes, by contrast, were protected, ladylike. . . . They cooked, cleaned house, and took care of the "butch." (1979:40)

More recently, there has been a sharp decline in the occurrence of gender-linked roles in gay and lesbian relationships. Some have attributed this change to the effects of the feminist and gay rights movements and to the general loosening of traditional gender norms in American society (Marecek, Finn, and Cardell 1982; Risman and Schwartz 1988; Ross 1983).

Today, however, research shows that most lesbians and gay men actively reject traditional husband-wife or masculine-feminine roles as a model for enduring relationships (see Blumstein and Schwartz 1983; Harry 1983, 1984; Jay and Young 1977; Lynch and Reilly 1986; Marecek, Finn, and Cardell 1982; McWhirter and Mattison 1984; Peplau and Amaro 1982; Saghir and Robins 1973). Currently, most lesbians and gay men are in "dual-worker" relationships, so that neither partner is the exclusive "breadwinner" and each partner has some measure of economic independence. Further, examination of the division of household tasks, sexual behavior, and decision making in homosexual couples finds that clear-cut and consistent husband-wife roles are uncommon. In many relationships there is some specialization of activities, with one partner doing more of some jobs and less of others. But it is rare for one partner to perform most of the "feminine" activities and the other to perform most of the "masculine" tasks. That is, the partner who usually does the cooking does not necessarily also perform other feminine tasks, such as shopping or cleaning. Specialization seems to be based on more individualistic factors, such as skills or interests.

Nonetheless, a small minority of lesbians and gay men do incorporate elements of husband-wife roles into their relationships. This may affect the division of labor, the dominance structure, sexual interactions, the way partners dress, and other aspects of their relationship. In some cases, these role patterns seemed to be linked to temporary situations, such as one partner's unemployment or illness. For other couples, however, masculine-feminine roles may provide a model of choice.

Given that traditional husband-wife roles are not the template for most contemporary homosexual couples, researchers have sought to identify other models or relationship patterns. One model might be based on differences in age, with an older partner acting, in part, as a mentor or leader. In his studies of gay male relationships, Harry (1982, 1984) found that the age-difference pattern characterized only a minority of gay male couples. When it did occur, the actual differences in age tended to be relatively small, perhaps five to ten years. Harry also found that in these couples, the older partner often had more power in decision making. McWhirter and Mattison (1984) also observed age differences among some of the male couples they studied, and reported that age differences of five years or more were characteristics of couples who had been together for thirty years or more.

Finally, another pattern is based on friendship or peer relations, with partners being similar in age and emphasizing companionship, sharing, and equality in the relationship (e.g., Harry 1982, 1983; Peplau et al. 1978; Peplau and Cochran 1981). A friendship script typically fosters equality in relationships. In contrast to marriage, the norms for friendship assume that partners are relatively equal in status and power. Friends also tend to be similar in interests, resources, and skills. Available evidence suggests that most American lesbians and gay men have a relationship script that most closely approximates best friendship.

In summary, contemporary homosexual relationships follow a variety of patterns or models. Most common are relationships patterned after friendship. Among both lesbians and gay men, a minority of couples may incorporate elements of traditional masculine-feminine roles into their relationships. For others, age differences may be central to role patterns. We currently know little about the causal factors responsible for these different patterns. That many lesbians and gay men are able to create satisfying love relationships that are not based on complementary, gender-linked role differentiation challenges

the popular view that such masculine-feminine differences are essential to adult love relationships.

Myth 4: Gays and lesbians have impoverished social support networks.

Although there is growing public awareness of the existence of gay and lesbian communities, stereotypes continue to depict homosexuals as socially isolated and lacking in social support. It is certainly true that in a homophobic society, gays and lesbians may suffer from social alienation and estrangement. We should not minimize the psychological stress that results from social rejection and stigma. What is noteworthy, however, is the extent to which contemporary lesbians and gay men seem able to overcome these obstacles and to create satisfying social networks. This is especially important because of growing evidence that emotional support, guidance, assistance, and other forms of social support contribute to mental and physical health.

Illustrative of research on social support is a comparative study of lesbian and heterosexual women conducted by Aura (1985). She compared the social support experiences of fifty lesbians and fifty heterosexual women. All women were currently in a primary relationship and were matched for age, education, and length of their relationship. None had children in their household. Women filled out detailed questionnaires about many specific types of social support. Results showed that both groups of women held similar values about the importance of social support. In addition, women reported receiving similar total amounts of support from their personal relationships. Lesbians and heterosexuals however, often received support from different sources. In particular, many lesbians depended somewhat less on relatives and more on their partner or friends than did heterosexuals. For example, lesbians and heterosexuals reported receiving similar amounts of material assistance, such as help in moving or getting a ride to the airport, but lesbians relied more on friends and heterosexuals relied more on family.

Research by Lewin investigated the social support experiences of lesbian and heterosexual divorced mothers raising children (Lewin 1981; Lewin and Lyons 1982). Lewin found that both lesbian and heterosexual mothers were equally likely to turn to their parents or other family members for support. About 84 percent of the lesbian mothers said that most or all of their relatives were aware of their homosexuality. Although this initially created stress for many lesbians and their families, over time the families seemed to come to terms with the situation. One woman who had been estranged from her family reported that she now sees her mother daily because her son stays with his grandmother after school. For both lesbian and heterosexual mothers, kinship ties were often of central importance for child care and "to offer a sense of stability, an opportunity to continue family tradition, and emotional comfort" (in Lewin and Lyons 1982:262). Results suggest that the presence of children may increase the similarity in social support experiences of lesbian and heterosexual women.

Kurdek (1988) studied social support among gay men and lesbians in couples. When asked who provided social support, virtually everyone listed not only their partner but also other friends. In addition, 81 percent of the gay men and 86 percent of the lesbians cited a family member as a source of support—most often their mother or a sister. Using the standardized Social Support Questionnaire developed by Sarason and his associates (1983), Kurdek found no differences between gay men and lesbians in the source of support or in satisfaction with support. Overall levels of support received by gays and lesbians were similar to and slightly higher than those reported by Sarason for a college student sample (see also D'Augelli 1987: D'Augelli and Hart 1987; Kurdek and Schmitt 1987b).

In summary, despite potential obstacles to the establishment of meaningful social relations, many lesbians and gay men are able to create supportive social networks.

THEORETICAL ISSUES IN THE STUDY OF GAY AND LESBIAN RELATIONSHIPS

To date, much of the work on gay and lesbian relationships has been descriptive, designed to fill gaps in the existing data base. But newer research has had a stronger theoretical or conceptual focus. Three approaches can be distinguished: a) work that seeks to test the general applicability of relationship theories initially developed with heterosexuals; b) work that uses comparative studies of gay, lesbian, and heterosexual relationships to test ideas about the impact of gender on interaction; and c) work that seeks to create new theories about same-sex relationships.

The General Applicability of Theory: Social Exchange Theory

Most social science concepts, models, and theories of relationships have been based explicitly or implicitly on heterosexual experiences. Efforts to investigate the applicability of such theories to new populations of lesbians and gay men are important to the development of a science of relationships. Evidence that existing theories can usefully be applied to homosexual relationships would also have practical significance, suggesting that work on same-sex couples can build on the existing literature rather than start anew.

Social exchange theory (Burgess and Huston 1979; Kelley and Thibaut 1978) has been one of the most influential theoretical perspectives on relationships. Several studies have now tested predictions derived from exchange theory among lesbian and gay male couples. In general, research has confirmed the generalizability of exchange theory to this new population and has shown the usefulness of exchange concepts in understanding relationship processes.

For example, Mayta Caldwell and I (1984) investigated the balance of power in lesbian relationships. In our sample of young adults, 61 percent of lesbians said that their current relationship was equal in power. We explored two factors that might tip the balance of power away from equality. First, we considered the "principle of least interest"—the prediction that when one person is more dependent, involved, or interested in continuing a relationship, that person is at a power disadvantage. We found strong support for this prediction.

We also investigated the impact of personal resources on power. The prediction here is that when a person has substantially more resources than the partner, he or she will have a power advantage. In our sample, differences in both income and education were significantly related to imbalances of power, with greater power accruing to the lesbian partner who was relatively better educated or earned more money. Studies of gay male relationships by Harry (1984) have also shown that a power advantage can accrue to the partner who has a higher income and who is older. Work by Blumstein and Schwartz (1983), however, raises the possibility that the importance of specific resources, such as money, may differ across groups. In their large-scale study, Blumstein and Schwartz found that money was related to power in heterosexual relationships and was "an extremely important force" in determining dominance in gay male relationships. But for lesbians, income was unrelated to power. This is a good illustration of the notion that personal resources are not universal, but rather depend on the values of the partners in a relationship.

Another way in which research has drawn on exchange principles concerns commitment in gay and lesbian relationships. The question here is whether the forces affecting commitment might be different in homosexual versus heterosexual relationships. As Levinger (1979) and others have pointed out, commitment and permanence in a relationship are affected by two separate types of factors. The first concerns the strength of the positive attractions that make us want to stay in a relationship. Although stereotypes depict gays and lesbians as having weaker attractions to their partners than do heterosexuals, we have already seen that research does not support this view. In general, homosexuals do not appear to differ from heterosexuals in the level of satisfaction and love they feel for their primary partner.

The second factor maintaining the stability of relationships are barriers that make the ending of the relationship costly, in either psychological or material terms. For heterosexuals, marriage usually creates many barriers to dissolution, including the cost of divorce, the wife's financial dependence on her husband, joint investments in property, concerns about children, and so on. Such factors may encourage married couples to "work" to improve a declin-

ing relationship, rather than end it. In contrast, gay and lesbian couples may be less likely to experience comparable barriers to the ending of a relationship—they cannot marry legally, their relatives may prefer that they end their relationship, they are less likely to have children in common, and so on. Another barrier to ending a relationship might be the lack of alternative partners or resources. To the extent that a current partner is the "best available," we are less likely to leave.

This exchange theory analysis suggests that for all types of relationships, the level of commitment should be related to attractions, barriers, and alternatives. Because of differences in the social context of homosexual and heterosexual relationships, lesbian and gay male couples may tend to have fewer barriers than heterosexuals. As a result, possible differences in commitment between heterosexual and homosexual couples may result from barriers to dissolution rather than from attractions to the partner.

Empirical research has investigated these predictions. Kurdek and Schmitt (1986c) compared self-reported attractions, barriers, and alternatives in gay, lesbian, heterosexual cohabiting, and married couples. They found no differences across the groups in attractions. All groups were equally likely to report feelings of love and satisfaction. Barriers—assessed by statements such as "many things would prevent me from leaving my partner even if I were unhappy"—did differ. Married couples reported significantly more barriers than either gays or lesbians reported, and cohabiting heterosexual couples reported the fewest barriers of all. In answering questions about available alternatives to the current relationship, lesbians and married couples reported the fewest alternatives; gay men and heterosexual cohabitors reported the most alternatives. For all groups, love for the partner was significantly related to perceiving many barriers to leaving, few alternatives, and many attractions. In summary, differences between gay, lesbian, and heterosexual couples were found in the barriers they perceived to ending a relationship, not in the quality of the relationship itself. Kurdek and Schmitt did not relate these factors to commitment.

Rusbult (1988) investigated the dynamics of commitment more directly, testing what she calls an "investment model" of commitment based on social exchange principles. After initial tests of her model with heterosexuals, Duffy and Rusbult (1986) conducted a comparative study of homosexual and heterosexual relationships to test the generalizability of her findings. This research found that lesbians, gay men, and heterosexuals all generally described their relationships in quite similar ways. All groups reported strong attraction to their partner (that is, high rewards and low costs from the relationship and high satisfaction), moderately high investments in the relationship, and moderately poor alternatives. All types of couples also reported strong commitment. Consistent with exchange theory principles, commitment was predicted by satisfaction, investments, and alternatives for lesbians, gay men, and heterosexuals.

These studies found somewhat different patterns of results, with Kurdek and Schmitt reporting that sexual orientation was related to differences in barriers and alternatives, and Duffy and Rusbult finding no effects of sexual orientation. Further research will be needed to explore these issues more fully. Nonetheless, available evidence does clearly suggest the usefulness of applying principles from social exchange theory to homosexual relationships. This is an important demonstration of the generalizability of the theory. Equally important, it suggests that those interested in understanding the dynamics of gay and lesbian relationships can at least sometimes take existing theory as a starting point.

The Impact of Gender on Relationships: Contrasting Gender Versus Power Interpretations

Comparative studies of same-sex and cross-sex couples provide a new approach to investigating how gender affects close relationships. For example, by comparing how women behave with male versus female partners, we can begin to disentangle the effects on social interaction of an individual's own sex and the sex of their partner. This comparative research strategy is not identical to an experiment in which participants are randomly assigned to interact with a male or female partner. In real life, individuals are obviously not randomly assigned to have heterosexual or homosexual relationships. Nonetheless, strategically planned comparisons can be informative. This point is illustrated by studies investigating gender versus power interpretations of social interaction patterns.

It has been observed that when trying to influence a partner, women and men tend to use somewhat different tactics. Women may be more likely to use tears and less likely to use logical arguments. Why? One interpretation views this sex difference as resulting from differential gender socialization—women have learned to express emotion, men to use logic. But a second interpretation is also plausible: in male-female relationships, men often have the upper hand in power. Influence tactics may stem from the partner's relative dominance in the relationship, not from male-female differences in dispositions to use particular influence tactics. Several studies have used comparisons of gay, lesbian, and heterosexual relationships to investigate these compelling interpretations.

In a study of influence strategies in intimate relationships, Toni Falbo and I (1980) compared the tactics that lesbians, gay men, and heterosexuals reported using to influence a romantic partner. We also asked questions about the balance of power in the relationship. Our results led to two major conclusions. First, gender affected power tactics, but only among heterosexuals. Whereas heterosexual women were more likely to withdraw or express negative emotions, heterosexual men were more likely to use bargaining or reasoning. But this sex difference did not emerge in comparisons of lesbians and gay men influencing their same-sex partner. Second, consistent with the dominance interpretation, regardless of gender or sexual orientation, individuals who perceived themselves as relatively more powerful in the relationship tended to use persuasion and bargaining. In contrast, partners low in power tended to use withdrawal and emotion.

Howard, Blumstein, and Schwartz (1986) also compared influence tactics in the intimate relationships of homosexuals and heterosexuals. They found that dependent (lower-power) partners in all three types of couples used different influence tactics than did the more powerful. Regardless of sexual orientation, a partner with relatively less power tended to use "weak" strategies, such as supplication and manipulation. Those in positions of strength were more likely to use autocratic and bullying tactics, both "strong strategies." Further, individuals with male partners (i.e., heterosexual women and homosexual men) were more likely to use supplication and manipulation. Similarly, Kollock, Blumstein, and Schwartz (1985) found that signs of conversational dominance, such as interrupting a partner in the middle of a conversation, were linked to the balance of power. Although interruption has sometimes been viewed as a "male" behavior, it was, in fact, more often engaged in by the more powerful person in the relationship, regardless of gender. Taken together, the results of these studies provide considerable support for the dominance interpretation of sex differences in male-female interaction.

These studies demonstrate the potential benefits of using strategic comparisons of same-sex and cross-sex couples to help understand the causes of sex differences in personal relationships. (For an illustration of using comparisons of homosexual and heterosexual couples to test social versus evolutionary theories of partner selection, see Howard, Blumstein, and Schwartz 1987.)

New Theories: Stage Models of the Development of Gay Relationships

There have been several attempts to create models of stages in the development of relationships among gay men (e.g., Harry and Lovely 1979; McWhirter and Mattison 1984) and lesbians (e.g., Clunis and Green 1988). These models have typically been empirically based efforts to generate theory from clinical observations or from research studies of same-sex couples. The goal has been to capture patterns unique to gay or lesbian relationships.

For example, an early model of gay male relationships was proposed by Harry and Lovely (1979), well before the current AIDS epidemic. Observing that sexual exclusivity was uncommon in the relationships of gay men, Harry and Lovely proposed a two-stage model of gay male relationship development.

Initially, they hypothesized, there is a relatively brief "honeymoon" phase of sexual monogamy. Over time, there is a transformation of relationships from sexually closed to open ones (pp. 193–94). Indeed, they suggested that sexual openness may be necessary for the survival of gay relationships over time.

In 1980 David Blasband and I tested this two-stage model with a sample of forty gay male couples (Blasband and Peplau 1985). Our data provided little support for the generality of this model. Of the forty couples, only 20 percent indicated that their relationship was initially closed and later became sexually open. The rest reported other patterns. Roughly 20 percent indicated that their relationship had always been sexually open, 30 percent said it had always been closed, and the rest followed other patterns. Two couples said that they had once had a sexually open relationship but decided to become closed because of problems they were experiencing.

We were not surprised to find such a wide variety of patterns. As research on heterosexual courtship and couple development has shown (Levinger 1983), it is exceedingly difficult to find universal, invariant stages in the development of relationships. Efforts to identify fixed and invariant stages are probably only successful when cultural scripts are rigid and widely accepted. Left to their own devices, humans are more creative in the range of relationship patterns they construct.

More recently, detailed stage models of gay and lesbian relationships have been presented. Based on a study of 156 male couples, McWhirter and Mattison (1984) proposed a six-stage model of development. Their stages, roughly linked to the length of the relationship, are blending, nesting, maintaining, building, releasing, and renewing. Partly building on the McWhirter and Mattison work, Clunis and Green (1988) proposed a six-stage model for the development of lesbian relationships including these stages: prerelationship, romance, conflict, acceptance, commitment, and collaboration. These stage theorists have acknowledged variation among couples. As Clunis and Green comment, "Not every couple starts with the first stage. Some couples never go through all the stages, and certainly not in the order they are presented" (p. 10). Similarly, McWhirter and Mattison caution that "characteristics from one stage also are present in other stages, and they overlap. Remember, too that not all male couples fit this model" (p. 16). These stage models represent innovative attempts to characterize the unique relationship progression of contemporary gay and lesbian relationships. Further research will be needed to assess how well these models apply to other samples of lesbian and gay male couples (e.g., Kurdek and Schmitt 1986a).

In summary, a good deal has been learned about gay and lesbian couples during the past decade. The field has begun to move beyond basic descriptive studies in the direction of theory development and testing. The use of strategic comparisons of same-sex and cross-sex dyads appears to be a useful way to shed light on the impact of sexual orientation and gender on couples. New concepts and models based on lesbian and gay experiences need to be tested and refined, and their possible contribution to more general analyses of human relationships should be explored.

DIVERSITY AMONG GAY AND LESBIAN RELATIONSHIPS

Having debunked old stereotypes about homosexual relationships, we must continue to avoid the tendency to characterize the "typical lesbian couple" or the "typical gay male relationship." There are enormous variations among lesbian couples, as there are among gay male couples. To understand this diversity, two goals are important: first, we need to describe major ways in which homosexual couples differ from one another, for instance in dominance, or patterns of communication, or modes of conflict resolution, or degree of commitment (cf. Bell and Weinberg 1978). Second, we need to identify factors that produce these variations or, more technically, to identify the causal conditions affecting interaction patterns.

Variation Based on Gender

A major source of variation in same-sex relationships appears to be gender. In the 1950s and 1960s, discussions of homosexuality often assumed that there were

many commonalities among the experiences of gay men and lesbians—based on their "deviant" status or "abnormal" sexual orientation. Empirical research has seriously challenged this notion. Gagnon and Somon (1973) first articulated the opposite view, that it is one's socialization as male or female that most profoundly structures one's life experiences. Gagnon and Simon contended that the "female homosexual follows conventional feminine patterns in developing her commitment to sexuality and in conducting not only her sexual career but her nonsexual career as well" (p. 180). Focusing on sexuality, they suggested that lesbian sexuality would tend "to resemble closely" that of heterosexual women, and to differ radically from the sexual activity patterns of both heterosexual men and gay men. Current research clearly supports this assertion.

Although gender differences are evident in many aspects of gay and lesbian relationships, they are perhaps seen most easily in the area of sexuality (cf. Schafer 1977). Results of comparative studies of lesbians, gay male, and heterosexual relationships—including our own work at UCLA and the large-scale study of Blemstein and Schwartz (1983)—converge on three trends.

First, in all three types of relationships, *sexual frequency* declines with the duration of the relationship. In relationships of comparable duration, the frequency of sex with the primary partner is greatest among gay men, intermediate among heterosexuals, and lowest among lesbians.

Second, *sexual exclusivity versus openness* is an issue for all couples. In general, heterosexuals and lesbians are more supportive of sexual monogamy in relationships than are gay men. Their behavior corresponds. Sexual exclusivity in relationships is least common among gay men at all stages in their relationship. For example, Blumstein and Schwartz reported that among couples together for two to ten years or more, 79 percent of gay men have had sex with another partner in the previous year, compared with only 11 percent of husbands and 9 percent of wives. For lesbians, the comparable figure was 19 percent.

Third, levels of *sexual satisfaction* are similar across lesbian, gay male, and heterosexual couples, suggesting that couples in each group find their sexual relations equally gratifying on average (e.g., Masters and Johnson 1979).

The gender differences in these data are large and support the view that men want sex more often than women do and that men more highly value sexual novelty. Heterosexual relationships are, on some measure, a compromise between the preferences of the man and the woman (cf. Symons 1979). In contrast, same-sex partnerships are more extreme—men with male partners have sex more often and are less inclined toward sexual exclusivity. Women with female partners have sex least often, and differ sharply from gay men in their rates of nonmonogamy. Further explorations of the way in which gender affects the relationship experiences of gay and lesbian couples would be useful. (These generalizations are based on research conducted before the AIDS crisis. It remains to be seen how AIDS may alter patterns of sexual behavior.)

Variation Based on Personal Values

Another source of differences among same-sex couples concerns the personal values about intimacy that individuals bring to their relationship. We have begun to explore individual differences in values about the nature of love relationships (Peplau et al. 1978; Peplau and Cochran 1980, 1981). Consistent with discussions in the relationship literature, we have found two basic value dimensions for relationships. These dimensions have sometimes been called intimacy and independence, attachment and autonomy, or closeness and separation. We have conceptualized these distinctions as value orientations and have developed two independent scales, one to assess each orientation.

We have called the first of these orientations *dyadic attachment.* It concerns the value placed on having an emotionally close and relatively secure love relationship. As one gay man described what he wants in a love relationship: "The most important thing . . . is the knowledge that someone loves and needs me. . . . It would be a stabilizing force in my life, and give me a sense of security" (cited in Spada 1979:198). On our measure, a person who scores high on attachment strongly values permanence,

security, shared activities, sexual exclusivity, and "togetherness."

The second theme we have called *personal autonomy,* and it concerns the boundaries that exist between an individual and his or her partner. While some individuals wish to immerse themselves entirely in a relationship to the exclusion of outside interests and activities, others prefer to maintain personal independence. On our measure, a person who scores high on personal autonomy emphasizes the importance of having separate interests and friendships apart from a primary relationship and preserving independence within the relationship by dividing finances equally and making decisions in an egalitarian manner.

Our research has shown that these same two value themes are relevant to the experiences of lesbians, gay men, and heterosexuals. In all samples, the two measures are independent—not polar opposites. Some individuals may want to combine a high degree of togetherness with a high level of independence, others prefer a high degree of togetherness and low independence, and so on. These relationship values are predictive of variations among relationships in such factors as love and satisfaction, perceived commitment, types of problems experienced, and sexual behavior, although these linkages are not always very strong.

An important direction for future research will be to identify other sources of diversity among lesbian and gay male relationships. Other factors worth exploring include the impact of age (or cohort), ethnicity (e.g., Peplau, Cochran, and Mays 1980), length of a relationship, or degree of integration in a lesbian or gay community. Ultimately, we will want to develop a fuller picture of how interaction in gay and lesbian couples is affected by characteristics of the individual partners, by features of the dyad itself, and by social and cultural conditions.

CONCLUSION

This article has reviewed a growing body of scientific research on gay and lesbian relationships. Research has shown that most lesbians and gay men want intimate relationships and are successful in creating them. Homosexual partnerships appear no more vulnerable to problems and dissatisfactions than their heterosexual counterparts, although the specific problems encountered may differ for same-sex and cross-sex couples. Characterizations of gay and lesbian relationships as "abnormal" or "dysfunctional" are not justifiable. Another myth that has been disconfirmed is the belief that most homosexual couples adopt "husband" and "wife" roles. Finally, new work has found that gay men and lesbians do not typically have impoverished social support networks. It is important that mental health practitioners, educators, and the general public become more informed about the realities of same-sex relationships, so that misconception can be replaced with up-to-date scientific knowledge.

Scholars are increasingly emphasizing the rich diversity that exists among gay and lesbian couples. Much needed research remains to be done to describe the varieties of same-sex partnerships, and to understand how such factors as ethnicity, social class, openness about one's sexual orientation, and participation in gay or lesbian communities influence the experiences of lesbian and gay male couples. The debunking of derogatory social stereotypes about homosexual relationships should also clear the way for an open discussion of the special problems that do affect contemporary gay and lesbian couples. The enormous impact of the AIDS epidemic on homosexual relationships is just beginning to receive the attention it deserves (e.g., Carl 1986; Risman and Schwartz 1988). New research investigating the effects on relationships of alcohol abuse (e.g., Weinberg 1986) and physical violence (Leeder 1988; Renzetti 1988; Waterman, Dawson, and Bologna 1989) is also important, and illustrates some of the many useful new directions for future research.

Studies of lesbian and gay couples can contribute to the emerging science of close relationships. The applicability of general theories, such as social exchange theory, to homosexual couples has now been demonstrated in several studies, and further research of this sort would be useful. This work suggests the possibility of developing general theories capable of explaining a wide variety of relationship types. Studies of same-sex partnerships can also provide a new perspective on the impact of gender on close relationships. Comparisons of same-sex and cross-sex couples provide a new research strategy for testing competing interpretations of sex differences in interaction. New theories based on the distinctive experiences of gay and lesbian couples are an important new direction for future work.

Acknowledgments—The author gratefully acknowledges the valuable assistance of Amanda Munoz and Steven L. Gordon in the preparation of this article.

REFERENCES

Aura, J. 1985. Women's social support: A comparison of lesbians and heterosexuals. Doctoral dissertation, University of California, Los Angeles.

Bell, A. P., and M. A. Weinberg. 1978. *Homosexualities: A Study of Diversity Among Men and Women.* New York: Simon and Schuster.

Berzon, B. 1988. *Permanent Partners: Building Gay and Lesbian Relationships that Last.* New York: Dutton.

Blasband, D., and L. A. Peplau. 1985. Sexual exclusivity versus openness in gay male couples. *Archives of Sexual Behavior* 14(5):395–412.

Blumstein, P., and P. Schwartz. 1983. *American Couples: Money, Work, Sex.* New York: Morrow.

Boston Lesbian Psychologies Collective, eds. 1987. *Lesbian Psychologies: Explorations and Challenges.* Urbana: University of Illinois Press.

Boswell, J. 1980. *Christianity, Social Tolerance, and Homosexuality.* Chicago: University of Chicago Press.

Burgess, R. L., and T. L. Huston, eds. 1979. *Social Exchange in Developing Relationships.* New York: Academic Press.

Caldwell, M. A., and L. A. Peplau. 1984. The balance of power in lesbian relationships. *Sex Roles* 10:587–600.

Cardell, M., S. Finn, and J. Marecek. 1981. Sex-role identity, sex-role behavior, and satisfaction in heterosexual, lesbian, and gay male couples. *Psychology of Women Quarterly* 5(3):488–94.

Carl, D. 1986. Acquired immune deficiency syndrome: A preliminary examination of the effects on gay couples and coupling. *Journal of Marital and Family Therapy* 12(3):241–47.

Clunis, D. M., and G. D. Green. 1988. *Lesbian Couples.* Seattle: Seal Press.

Cochran, S. D. 1978. Romantic relationships: For better or for worse. Paper presented at the Western Psychological Association meeting, San Francisco, April.

Dailey, D. M. 1979. Adjustment of heterosexual and homosexual couples in pairing relationships: An exploratory study. *Journal of Sex Research* 15(2):143–57.

D'Augelli, A. R. 1987. Social support patterns of lesbian women in a rural helping network. *Journal of Rural Community Psychology* 8(1):12–21.

D'Augelli, A. R., and M. M. Hart. 1987. Gay women, men, and families in rural settings: Toward the development of helping communities. *American Journal of Community Psychology* 15(1):79–93.

DeCecco, J. P., ed. 1988. *Gay Relationships.* Binghamton, N.Y.: Haworth Press.

Duffy, S. M., and C. E. Rusbult. 1986. Satisfaction and commitment in homosexual and heterosexual relationships. *Journal of Homosexuality* 12(2):1–24.

Dynes, W. R. 1987. *Homosexuality: A Research Guide.* New York: Garland.

Falbo, T., and L. A. Peplau. 1980. Power strategies in intimate relationships. *Journal of Personality and Social Psychology* 38(4):618–28.

Gagnon, J. H., and W. Simon. 1973. A conformity greater than deviance: The lesbian. In *Sexual Conduct,* pp. 176–216. Chicago: Aldine.

Gonsiorek, J. C., ed. 1985. *A Guide to Psychotherapy with Gay and Lesbian Clients.* New York: Harrington Park Press.

Harry, J. 1982. Decision making and age differences among gay male couples. *Journal of Homosexuality* 8(2):9–22.

Harry, J. 1983. Gay male and lesbian relationships. In E. Macklin and R. Rubin, eds., *Contemporary Families and Alternative Lifestyles: Handbook on Research and Theory,* pp. 216–34. Beverly Hills, Calif.: Sage.

Harry, J. 1984. *Gay Couples.* New York: Praeger.

Harry, J., and R. Lovely. 1979. Gay marriages and communities of sexual orientation. *Alternative Lifestyles* 2(2):177–200.

Herdt, G. H. 1981. *Guardians of the Flutes: Idioms of Masculinity.* New York: McGraw-Hill.

Howard, J. A., P. Blumstein, and P. Schwartz. 1986. Sex, power, and influence tactics in intimate relationships. *Journal of Personality and Social Psychology* 51(1):102–9.

Howard, J. A., P. Blumstein, and P. Schwartz. 1987. Social or evolutionary theories? Some observations on preferences in human mate selection. *Journal of Personality and Social Psychology* 53(1):194–200.

Jay, K., and A. Young. 1977. *The Gay Report: Lesbians and Gay Men Speak Out about Sexual Experiences and Lifestyles.* New York: Summit Books.

Jones, R. W., and J. E. Bates. 1978. Satisfaction in male homosexual couples. *Journal of Homosexuality* 3(3):217–24.

Kelley, H. H., E. Berscheid, A. Christensen, J. H. Harvey, T. L. Huston, G. Levinger, E. McClintock, L. A. Peplau, and D. R. Peterson. 1983. *Close Relationships.* New York: W. H. Freeman.

Kelley, H. H., and J. W. Thibaut. 1978. *Interpersonal Relations: A Theory of Interdependence.* New York: Wiley-Interscience.

Kollock, P., P. Blumstein, and P. Schwartz. 1986. Sex and power in interaction: Conversational privileges and duties. *American Sociological Review* 50:34–46.

Kurdek, L. A. 1988. Perceived social support in gays and lesbians in cohabiting relationships. *Journal of Personality and Social Psychology* 54(3):504–9.

Kurdek, L. A., and J. P. Schmitt. 1986a. Early development of relationship quality in heterosexual cohabiting, gay, and lesbian couples. *Developmental Psychology* 22:305–9.

Kurdek, L. A., and J. P. Schmitt. 1986b. Relationship quality of gay men in closed or open relationships. *Journal of Homosexuality* 12(2):85–99.

Kurdek, L. A., and J. P. Schmitt. 1986c. Relationship quality of partners in heterosexual married, heterosexual cohabiting, and gay and lesbian relationships. *Journal of Personality and Social Psychology* 51:711–20.

Kurdek, L. A., and J. P. Schmitt. 1987a. Partner homogamy in married, heterosexual cohabiting, gay, and lesbian couples. *Journal of Sex Research* 23:212–32.

Kurdek, L. A., and J. P. Schmitt. 1987b. Perceived emotional support from family and friends in members of gay, lesbian, and heterosexual cohabiting couples. *Journal of Homosexuality* 14:57–68.

Larson, P. C. 1982. Gay male relationships. In W. Paul, J. D. Weinrich, J. C. Gonsiorek, and M. E. Hotvedt, eds., *Homosexuality: Social, Psychological, and Biological Issues,* pp. 219–32. Beverly Hills, Calif.: Sage.

Leeder, E. 1988. Enmeshed in pain: Counseling the lesbian battering couple. *Women and Therapy* 7(1):81–99.

Levinger, G. 1979. A social psychological perspective on marital dissolution. In G. Levinger and O. C. Moles, eds., *Divorce and Separation,* pp. 37–63. New York: Basic Books.

Levinger, G. 1983. Development and change. In H. H. Kelley, E. Berscheid, A. Christensen, J. H. Harvey, T. L. Huston, G. Levinger, E. McClintock, L. A Peplau, and D. R. Peterson, *Close Relationships,* pp. 315–59. New York: W. H. Freeman.

Lewin, E. 1981. Lesbianism and motherhood: Implication for child custody. *Human Organization* 40(1):6–14.

Lewin, E., and T. A. Lyons. 1982. Everything in its place: The coexistence of lesbianism and motherhood. In W. Paul, J. D. Weinrich, J. C. Gonsiorek, and M. E. Hotvedt, eds., *Homosexuality: Social, Psychology, and Biological Issues,* pp. 249–74. Beverly Hills, Calif.: Sage.

Lynch, J. M., and M. E. Reilly. 1986. Role relationships: Lesbian perspectives. *Journal of Homosexuality* 12(2):53–69.

McWhirter, D. P., and A. M. Mattison. 1984. *The Male Couple.* Englewood Cliffs, N.J.: Prentice-Hall.

Marecek, J., S. E. Finn, and M. Cardell. 1982. Gender roles in the relationships of lesbians and gay men. *Journal of Homosexuality* 8(2):45–50.

Peplau, L. A., and H. Amaro. 1982. Understanding lesbian relationships. In W. Paul, J. D. Weinrich, J. C. Gonsiorek, and M. E. Hotvedt, eds., *Homosexuality: Social, Psychological, and Biological Issues,* pp. 233–48. Beverly Hills, Calif.: Sage.

Peplau, L. A., and S. D. Cochran. 1980. Sex differences in values concerning love relationships. Paper presented at the annual meeting of the American Psychological Association, Montreal, September.

Peplau, L. A., and S. D. Cochran. Forthcoming. A relationship perspective on homosexuality. In D. P. McWhirter, S. A. Sanders, and J. M. Reinisch, eds., *Homosexuality/Heterosexuality: The Kinsey Scale and Current Research.* New York: Oxford University Press.

Peplau, L. A., S. D. Cochran, and V. M. Mays. 1986. Satisfaction in the intimate relationships of Black lesbians. Paper presented at the annual meeting of the American Psychological Association, Washington, D.C., August.

Peplau, L. A., S. Cochran, K. Rook, and C. Padesky. 1978. Women in love: Attachment and autonomy in lesbian relationships. *Journal of Social Issues* 34(3):7–27.

Peplau, L. A., and S. L. Gordon. 1983. The intimate relationships of lesbians and gay men. In E. R. Allgeier and N. B. McCormick, eds., *The Changing Boundaries: Gender Roles and Sexual Behavior,* pp. 226–44. Palo Alto, Calif.: Mayfield.

Peplau, L. A., C. Padesky, and M. Hamilton. 1982. Satisfaction in lesbian relationships. *Journal of Homosexuality* 8:23–35.

Raphael, S. M., and M. K. Robinson. 1980. The older lesbian: Love relationships and friendship patterns. *Alternative Lifestyles* 3(2):207–30.

Renzetti, C. M. 1988. Violence in lesbian relationships. *Journal of Interpersonal Violence* 3(4):381–99.

Risman, B., and P. Schwartz. 1988. Sociological research on male and female homosexuality. *Annual Review of Sociology* 14:125–47.

Ross, M. W. 1983. Femininity, masculinity, and sexual orientation: Some cross-cultural comparisons. *Journal of Homosexuality* 9(1):27–36.

Roth, S. 1985. Psychotherapy issues with lesbian couples. *Journal of Marital and Family Therapy* 11:273–86.

Rusbult, C. E. 1988. Commitment in close relationships: The investment model. In L. A. Peplau, D. O. Sears, S. E. Taylor, and J. L. Freedman, eds., *Readings in Social Psychology,* 2d ed., pp. 147–57. Englewood Cliffs, N.J.: Prentice-Hall.

Saghir, M. T., and E. Robins. 1973. *Male and Female Homosexuality: A Comprehensive Investigation.* Baltimore: Williams and Wilkins.

Sang, B. 1985. Lesbian relationships: A struggle toward partner equality. In T. Darty and S. Potter, eds., *Women-Identified Women,* pp. 51–66. Palo Alto, Calif.: Mayfield.

Sarason, I. G., H. M. Levine, R. B. Basham, and B. R. Sarason. 1983. Assessing social support: The Social Support Questionnaire. *Journal of Personality and Social Psychology* 44:127–39.

Schafer, S. 1977. Sociosexual behavior in male and female homosexuals: A study in sex differences. *Archives of Sexual Behavior* 6(5):355–64.

Silverstein, C. 1981. *Man to Man: Gay Couples in America.* New York: William Morrow.

Smalley, C. 1987. Dependency issues in lesbian relationships. *Journal of Homosexuality* 14(1–2):125–35.

Spada, J. 1979. *The Spada Report: The Newest Survey of Gay Male Sexuality.* New York: Signet.

Stein, T. S., and C. J. Cohen, eds. 1986. *Contemporary Perspectives on Psychotherapy with Lesbians and Gay Men.* New York: Plenum.

Symons, D. 1979. *The Evolution of Human Sexuality.* New York: Oxford University Press.

Testa, R. J., B. N. Kinder, and G. Ironson, 1987. *Journal of Sex Research* 23:163–72.

Tripp, C. A. 1975. *The Homosexual Matrix.* New York: Signet.

Waterman, C. K., L. J. Dawson, and M. J. Bologna. 1989. Sexual coercion in gay male and lesbian relationships: Predictors and implications for support services. *Journal of Sex Research* 26(1):118–24.

Weinberg, T. S. 1986. Love relationships and drinking among gay men. *Journal of Drug Issues* 16(4):637–48.

Weinrich, J. D. 1987. *Sexual Landscapes.* New York: Scribner's.

Wolf, D. G. 1979. *The Lesbian Community.* Berkeley: University of California Press.

CHECKPOINTS

1. Peplau refutes four stereotypes about gay and lesbian relationships.
2. Peplau explains the benefits of comparisons of same-sex and cross-sex relationships for understanding the impact of sexual orientation and gender in intimate relationships.

To prepare for reading the next section, think about these questions:

1. Are love and romance necessary for a satisfying intimate relationship?
2. Do women and men have different views about love and intimacy?

Individualistic and Collectivistic Perspectives on Gender and the Cultural Context of Love and Intimacy

KAREN K. DION AND KENNETH L. DION

University of Toronto

Individualism and collectivism help explain culture-related differences in romantic love and in the importance of emotional intimacy in marriage. Three propositions are suggested: (a) Romantic love is more likely to be an important basis for marriage in individualistic than in collectivistic societies; (b) psychological intimacy in marriage is more important for marital satisfaction and personal well-being in individualistic than in collectivistic societies; and (c) although individualism fosters the valuing of romantic love, certain aspects of individualism at the psychological level make developing intimacy problematic. Evidence pertaining to these propositions is considered based on conceptual and empirical accounts of romantic love and psychological intimacy in marriage in two individualistic societies (Canada and the United States) and three collectivistic societies (China, India, and Japan). In addition, we suggest that consideration of individualism and collectivism as these constructs pertain to gender provides a framework for interpreting gender differences in the reported experience of love and intimacy in North American society.

They met, fell in love, decided to marry (or cohabit), and hoped to live happily ever after. To many North Americans, this depiction of the development of an intimate relationship between a woman and a man has been an enduring prototype, and its features seem very familiar and self-evident. This depiction, however, reflects several assumptions about the nature of intimate, opposite-sex relationships that are culturally based. These assumptions are by no means universally shared, particularly in non-Western societies; even in Western societies, this view of love, intimacy, and marriage has not always prevailed.

We have contended that a cultural perspective is needed to understand the factors contributing to the development of close relationships (Dion & Dion, 1979, 1988). The first step in theory building in this area is to identify conceptual dimensions that have the potential to provide an integrative framework. We believe that the dimensions of individualism and collectivism are key constructs with this potential for the topic of close relationships. These dimensions have been acknowledged by scholars from diverse cultural backgrounds to be of conceptual relevance for under-

Correspondence regarding this article should be addressed to either Karen K. Dion, Division of Life Sciences, Scarborough Campus, University of Toronto, Scarborough, Ontario, Canada M1C 1A4, or Kenneth L. Dion, Department of Psychology, University of Toronto, Toronto, Ontario, Canada M5S 1A1.

KAREN K. DION is Professor of Psychology at the University of Toronto. Her research interests include close relationships, particularly individual difference and sociocultural perspectives, and also adult development and socialization. Stemming from that latter interest, she wrote the chapter on socialization in adulthood for the most recent (third) edition of the *Handbook of Social Psychology*.

KENNETH L. DION is Professor of Psychology at the University of Toronto as well as Consulting Editor to the *Journal of Personality and Social Psychology* (Interpersonal Relations and Group Processes Section) and the *Psychology of Women Quarterly*. He has authored numerous articles on gender, close relationships, and ethnocultural as well as cross-cultural aspects of social psychology. His paper, "Responses to Perceived Discrimination and Relative Deprivation," was commended by SPSSI's Gordon Allport Committee in 1984.

standing the social structuring of relationships. We have previously suggested that there are cultural differences in views of self and that these differences in self-construal have implications for understanding the experience of romantic love and intimacy in heterosexual relationships (Dion & Dion, 1988).

In the present article, we present a more fully elaborated conceptual framework linking individualism and collectivism to culture-related and gender-related differences in close relationships and consider the evidence relevant to three conceptual propositions. We discuss the contrasts in the social construction of love and intimacy in two societies where individualism has been a dominant value orientation (the United States and Canada) and three Asian societies in which a collectivistic orientation has prevailed (China, India, and Japan). Our analysis is therefore most directly applicable to the manifestations of individualism and collectivism in these societies. Moreover, although we focus on the contrasts between individualism and collectivism in this article, as work in this area develops, additional conceptual and empirical analysis of culture and close relationships will be needed to compare different individualistic societies and different collectivistic societies, respectively.

INDIVIDUALISM AND COLLECTIVISM: CULTURAL PERSPECTIVES

The constructs of individualism and collectivism concern the relation between the individual and the group as reflected across many domains of social functioning (Hofstede, 1984). Individualism has been defined as "the subordination of the goals of the collectivities to individual goals" while collectivism involves the opposite, namely, "the subordination of individual goals to the goals of a collective" (Hui & Triandis, 1986, pp. 244–245). These constructs have been conceptualized at the cultural level and at the personal level, and it is important to distinguish these two levels (Kim, 1993). Societies are labeled as "individualistic" or "collectivistic" when these value orientations characterize the majority of individual members (Hui & Triandis, 1986). Within a given so-

ciety, however, individual differences exist in adherence to the prevailing orientation. We have proposed using the terms *societal individualism* and *societal collectivism* to refer to these constructs at the cultural level and *psychological individualism* and *psychological collectivism* to designate these constructs at the individual level (Dion & Dion, 1991).

In his seminal work in this area, Hofstede (1984) proposed that the following features distinguished individualistic as compared to collectivistic societies. In societies characterized by individualism, the emphasis is on promoting one's self-interest and that of one's immediate family. The individual's rights rather than duties are stressed, as are personal autonomy, self-realization, individual initiative, and decision making. Personal identity is defined by the individual's attributes. Prototypic examples of individualistic societies in Hofstede's study were the United States, Australia, Great Britain, and Canada. At the personal level, individualism is characterized by valuing one's independence and showing less concern for other persons' needs and interests (Hui & Triandis, 1986).

In contrast, collectivistic societies, according to Hofstede, are characterized as stressing the importance of the individual's loyalty to the group, which in turn safeguards the interests and well-being of the individual. Other features include reduced personal privacy, a sense of personal identity based on one's place in one's group, a belief in the superiority of group compared to individual decisions, and emotional dependency on groups and organizations. Among the Asian countries and city states in Hofstede's sample characterized by the above features were Taiwan, Singapore, Hong Kong, and Pakistan. At the personal level, collectivism is manifested by concern about interpersonal bonds, greater awareness of and responsiveness to the needs of others reflecting a sense of interconnectedness, and interdependence (Hui & Triandis, 1986).

These contrasts between individualism and collectivism are reflected in the psychological concepts underlying North American compared to Asian analyses of personal and interpersonal functioning. For example, concepts that have been salient in

North American personality and social psychology, such as locus of control, self-actualization, and self-esteem, can be regarded as different manifestations of individualism (Waterman, 1984). As a result of her or his personal choices across the diverse areas of life, the individual can "realize a variety of inherent potentialities and capabilities" and organize personal identity based on these choices (Roland, 1988, p. 330). In this context, a sense of self as independent is likely, characterized by features such as valuing personal uniqueness, self-expression, and the realization of personal goals (Markus & Kitayama, 1991).

Asian scholars have contended that psychological concepts emerging from an individualistic orientation constrain a full understanding of human functioning. (Western scholars, too, have been critical of the pervasive impact of individualism as shown by Bellah et al., 1985; Hogan, 1975; Sampson, 1977, 1985). Asian and some Western behavioral scientists have identified psychological constructs pertaining to interpersonal functioning that are derived from a collectivistic social structure. Based on these analyses, there is evidence that the social construction of self and other differs greatly in individualistic as contrasted with collectivistic societies. Specifically, many important concepts in Asian societies, such as *amae,* are inherently relational (Ho, 1982). They reflect a sense of self as interdependent, rather than independent (Hsu, 1971; Markus & Kitayama, 1991).

To illustrate the emphasis on interdependence that characterizes many constructs from Asian psychology, the Japanese construct of *amae,* which has been discussed extensively by Doi (1962, 1963, 1977, 1988) provides a good example. The verb form of this noun is *amaeru,* which is defined as "to depend and presume upon another's benevolence" (Doi, 1962). A Japanese person who wishes to *amaeru* seeks to be a passive love object and to be indulged by another. The psychological prototype of *amae* is the mother-infant relationship (Doi, 1988). According to Doi (1988) and other scholars (Morsbach & Tyler, 1986), the expression of *amae* is aimed at psychologically denying the fact of one's separation from the mother.

Doi (1988) has used the *amae* concept as a single, sovereign principle for understanding Japanese personality as well as Japanese society. The people one can *amaeru* with impunity define insiders and include one's parents, relatives, close friends, and others with whom one stands in an hierarchical relationship. According to Doi, among outsiders, one must exhibit restraint or *enryo* and suppress the expression of any dependency needs, which Japanese find unpleasant.

A second example of cultural contrasts can be found in Roland's (1988) discussion of the *familial self* in India, which he compared with the North American *individualized self.* In his analysis, the Indian conception of self is basically relational rather than autonomous. Roland suggested that the familial self developed in hierarchical relationships within the extended family in which the following qualities were present: strong emotional interdependence, reciprocal demands for intimacy and support, mutual caring, and a high degree of empathy and sensitivity to another's needs and desires within the family structure.

INDIVIDUALISM AND COLLECTIVISM: GENDER PERSPECTIVES

There are some conceptual parallels between the above discussion of cultural differences in the social construction of self-other relationships and analyses of gender differences in self-other construal within North American society. The characteristics of the relational self hypothesized to be prevalent in various Asian societies are similar to some aspects of self-construal suggested as characterizing many North American women. Various scholars have proposed that the social construction of self for many North American women is relational, while for many men, it is autonomous. Before discussing this hypothesized contrast, it should be acknowledged that individual differences in self-construal *within* gender also seem likely. Nonetheless, hypothesized gender differences in self-construal provide a provocative analytical framework. The following two examples illustrate this viewpoint. (See also Lykes, 1985, and Markus &

Kitayama, 1991, for an additional example and discussion of this issue.)

Chodorow (1978) analyzed the relation between the role of women as primary care givers in the family and the development of a sense of personal identity in their daughters and sons. She argued that primary parenting by women fostered the emergence of a "sense of self . . . continuous with others" for girls, while boys were encouraged to develop a more autonomous and distinct sense of self (Chodorow, 1978, p. 207). She suggested that this autonomous orientation ultimately made satisfying the emotional needs of others more problematic for men than for women.

Bardwick (1980) suggested that the predominant mode of self-construal for women has been either a dependent or an interdependent mode, both of which involve the self defined in the context of relationships. The former involves a sense of dependency, both psychologically and economically, as would be the case in a traditional marriage. The latter type involves both a "sense of self" but at the same time an awareness of the reciprocal aspects of an intimate relationship. With reference to Levinson's (1978) theory of adult development in which individuation is a key developmental task, Bardwick commented that this particular view of development was "very American and very male" and contrasted markedly with a view of adulthood as a time for "meeting responsibilities within relationships" (p. 40). She suggested that an individualistic, egocentric view of self characterized only a small minority of women.

Considered together, the above conceptual analyses suggest that in some individualistic societies there are gender differences in self-construal that in turn may be related to the experience of romantic love and the capacity for intimacy in close relationships. Although the focus here is on gender differences, there are other important individual difference dimensions that also are related to the experience of love and intimacy for both women and men (see Dion & Dion, 1985; Worell, 1988).

Finally, this perspective raises some intriguing questions about the relation between gender and the experience of love and intimacy in collectivistic societies. Specifically, if the mode of self-construal is interdependent for women and for men, this social construction of self should facilitate the capacity for intimacy for both sexes. As will be evident however, in collectivistic societies both gender and cultural factors are related to the expression of intimacy in particular close relationships, such as marriage.

In the remainder of this article, we propose that individualistic societies (the United States and Canada) differ from collectivistic ones (China, India, and Japan) in the social construction of love and intimacy. Moreover, we suggest that gender and cultural differences in the reported experience of love and intimacy in heterosexual relationships are related in part to differences in self-construal.

LOVE AND INTIMACY

Proposition 1: Romantic love is more likely to be considered an important basis for marriage in societies where individualism as contrasted with collectivism is a dominant cultural value.

As noted at the start of this article, marriage based on romantic love may seem like a description of the natural progression of intimacy to many North Americans. It has been suggested, however, that romantic love is most likely to emerge in particular societal contexts. For example, Averill (1985) suggested a relation between aspects of romantic love such as idealization of the lover for his or her unique qualities and "individuation of the self" (Averill, 1985, p. 101). Both during earlier periods of Western history and in some Asian societies, Averill argued that since personal identity was not highly differentiated from the group, the social context did not provide the conditions in which romantic idealization could develop.

The conceptual link between the presence of romantic love and societal individualism has been commented on by other scholars. Bellah and his colleagues discussed the pervasive impact of individualism in both the public and the private domain of American life (Bellah et al., 1985). They used the term "expressive individualism," referring to the need for self-expression and self-realization, to describe the role of individualism in the private domain of life, including intimate relationships. In this context, romantic love provided the chance for exploring and revealing dimensions of oneself, with each member of the couple seeking to share their "real selves" with one another (Bellah et al., 1985).

Interestingly, although undertaken from a very different theoretical perspective on love, similar themes emerged in Sternberg and Grajek's (1984) research on the core components of love, based on adults' completion of several psychometric measures of love across different types of relationships. Among the features of love identified as central by Sternberg and Grajek were several which pertain to intimate self-expression and personal fulfillment such as "sharing of deeply personal ideas and feelings" and "personal growth through the relationship."

In more collectivistic societies, such as China, traditionally, love and intimacy between a woman and a man were less important than other factors as a basis for marriage. Hsu (1981) suggested that the concept of romantic love did not fit particularly well with traditional Chinese society since the individual was expected to take into account the wishes of others, especially one's parents and other family members, when choosing a spouse. The Western ideal of romantic love characterized by intense feelings, disregard of others' views of one's lover, and complete mutual absorption would be regarded as disruptive. Indeed it can be argued that in many collectivistic societies, romantic love as a basis for marriage would be dysfunctional.

Consistent with this line of reasoning, family structure has been found to be related to the occurrence of romantic love as a basis for marriage and autonomous selection of one's marital partner (Lee & Stone, 1980). Analyzing cross-cultural data from 117 nonindustrial societies, Lee and Stone found that marriage based on love and choice of one's own spouse was *less* likely to occur in societies characterized by extended family systems compared to those with nuclear family structures. An extended family system can be viewed as one manifestation of greater societal collectivism.

Among recent cohorts of young adults in some Asian societies, there are signs of change toward greater valuing of love as a basis for marriage. For example in Japan, the number of "love marriages" has increased over the past four decades. However, traditional values in the parents' generation have persisted (Fukada, 1991). As of the early 1980s, Buruma (1984, p. 40) reported that up to 50% of all marriages in Japan were still arranged ones. Survey data for the latter part of the 1980s presented by De Mente (1989), however, seem to indicate stronger pressure for "love" or "love-based" marriages among young Japanese women today. Specifically, 70% of unmarried women in Japan were said to prefer to find their own husband, and an "overwhelming majority" (the exact percentage was not stated) of young Japanese women were described as preferring a love-based marriage. Similarly, in the 1980s (prior to 1989), there were signs of individualistic trends pertaining to choice of spouse in the People's Republic of China (Honig & Hershatter, 1988; Xiaohe & White, 1990).

It is intriguing to speculate about the factors that may contribute to the importance assigned romantic love as a basis for marriage in the People's Republic of China in the future. As a function of the "one child per family" policy, there are now large numbers of families in which there is only one child, and this child occupies a special and favored place in a household where traditionally the needs of the family unit were dominant. It would seem that a sense of personal uniqueness, a desire for personal gratification and fulfillment—in essence a highly individualized sense of self—are likely to develop in many of these children. Paradoxically, in a society where a relational sense of self traditionally has been the cultural norm, the family structure resulting from the "one-child" policy may ultimately foster a generation of individualists who may attach greater importance than earlier cohorts to self-discovery and personal fulfillment in their relationships with opposite-sex peers.

Proposition 2: Psychological intimacy in a marital relationship is more important for marital satisfaction and personal well-being for adults in individualistic societies than for those in collectivistic societies.

Much conceptual analysis and research on dating and marital relationships has been undertaken by researchers in the United States and in Canada. This interest in understanding what factors contribute to satisfaction and to stability in these types of relationships reflects the cultural value placed on marriage or similar types of committed relationships as an important source of personal well-being. The social support, especially the emotional support provided by one's spouse, has been suggested as one important contributor to physical and psychological health (Ross, Mirowsky, & Goldsteen, 1990).

Moreover, gender is related to societal expectations about the responsibility for fostering this desired intimacy in marriage. Based on a content analysis of articles pertaining to marriage in U.S. women's magazines from 1900 to 1979, Cancian and Gordon (1988) found that despite a shift toward emphasizing the importance of self-fulfillment in marriage, the advice given to women still conveyed the expectation that the woman was responsible for the emotional tenor of the marital relationship. It was her role to keep the relationship functioning smoothly.

This valuing of emotional intimacy with one's spouse found in some individualistic societies contrasts with expectations about emotional intimacy in marriage occurring in some traditionally collectivistic societies, such as China, Japan, and India. In the following discussion, we are *not* suggesting that in collectivistic societies couples do not develop affection and caring for each other. We are suggesting that for married couples in collectivistic societies, personal well-being is not as strongly related to psychological intimacy in marriage when compared to married couples in individualistic societies. In China, even after marriage, the primary ties of intimacy in which the individual's psychological well-being was rooted were the family relationships with parents, siblings, and other relatives (Hsu, 1985). Dependency on the family and the virtues of filial piety and devotion were emphasized across the life span (Ho, 1975).

Based on definitions of intimacy provided by North American behavioral scientists, Perlman and Fehr (1987) suggested three major components: degree of self-disclosure, interdependence, and emotional warmth. Interestingly, in Hsu's (1981) description of the traditional Chinese marriage, intimacy, as

defined by reciprocal self-disclosure, sharing of activities, and revealing strong personal feelings, was not emphasized. Hence, there was little, or at least, less concern with issues such as happiness or satisfaction in the marriage since the bond between spouses was not their most important relationship. The man's primary responsibility was to his parents; the woman's primary responsibility after her marriage was to her husband's family.

There is, however, evidence suggesting some change. In Xiaohe and Whyte's (1990) study, the predictors of marital satisfaction among Chinese women were examined. The measure of marital satisfaction mostly assessed different facets of reported psychological intimacy (such as mutual disclosure of thoughts and feelings, affection given to and received from spouse, spouse's concern for wife's problems). The findings indicated that after controlling for a number of other background and family-related variables, degree of freedom of choice was the strongest positive predictor of marital satisfaction. In addition, reflecting the continuing importance of family relationships, parental approval of respondent's marriage, and having a good current relationship with husband's family also positively predicted marital satisfaction. This pattern of findings suggested the importance of individualistic factors (choice) and collectivistic factors (relations with other members of the family system) as correlates of Chinese women's satisfaction with their marital relationship.

According to Honig and Hershatter (1988), the depiction of the Chinese wife's role has begun to change from passive compliance and obedience to her husband and in-laws to a more active role in maintaining good family relations. For example, popular articles advised women that once married, they were expected to be a "skilled emotional manager," responsible for dealing with any friction with in-laws and for the emotional aspects of the relationship with their spouse. This portrayal of the wife's role in maintaining marital and familial harmony has its parallels in Cancian and Gordon's (1988) analysis of women's responsibility for maintaining intimacy, as depicted in advice to North American women in popular magazines throughout several decades of the 20th century.

Traditional Japanese society also illustrated the lesser importance of psychological intimacy in marriage in a collectivistic society. Marriages were generally arranged based on the two families' similarity of rank, occupation, and/or status (Fukada, 1991). Upon marriage, the bride was incorporated and effectively assimilated into her husband's *ie* (i.e., extended household), where she began a lengthy and demanding apprenticeship under the tutelage of her mother-in-law and, to a lesser extent, any sisters-in-law. Given the almost completely separate social spheres of women and men in the *ie* household, the married woman's primary relationships of emotional intimacy were focused primarily upon her children and secondarily with the other married women in the hierarchically structured, extended household (Roland, 1988). Fulfillment of needs for intimacy and nurturance were realized by a feeling of belonging in the context of the family group rather than by "sharing one's intimate self in companionship and communion" with one's spouse (DeVos, 1985, p. 165).

Among contemporary middle-class Japanese couples, it has been suggested that there continues to be relatively little psychological intimacy in the marital relationship for many couples (Roland, 1988). Although the influence of the *ie* extended household weakened in the post-World War II period, for many middle-class men, emotional and psychological needs are grounded in the intricate social relationships of their occupational context. The desire for a more intimate marital relationship on the part of some more educated Japanese women is difficult to realize given their spouse's long hours at work combined with the men's extensive postwork socializing. Thus for many middle-class Japanese women, the relationship with their children and to a lesser extent, long-standing friendships with women who were former classmates, are the principal sources of intimacy (Roland, 1988).

When considering the importance of psychological intimacy with one's spouse in Indian cultural contexts, the existence of religious and regional diversity in India must be kept in mind. In much of India, though there are some exceptions, the family structure is patriarchal, with age and gender defining one's position in the social hierarchy (Desai & Krishnaraj, 1990). A relational sense of self, although applicable to both sexes, has been suggested as more strongly descriptive of Indian women's self-construal (Kumar, 1991). For Hindu women, the complex family system structured women's relationships first in their family of origin, where they were prepared for their eventual roles as wife and mother. After an arranged marriage, they entered their husband's family where their relationships with the husband's mother and other female relatives became important. These relationships with the female relatives were traditionally a major source of concern and attention for married women, rather than the relationship with the spouse. Another source of emotional intimacy was the mother-child, especially the mother-son, relationship (Kumar, 1991).

Derlega (1984) suggested that to develop intimacy, it was important for individuals to accept each other's "true self," which involved in part a willingness to reveal negative as well as positive information about oneself. From this perspective, the findings of a study comparing marital satisfaction and communication in three types of marriages, Indian arranged marriage, Indian "love marriage," and American "companionate" marriage, are of interest (Yelsma & Athappilly, 1988). The data for the American couples were from a previous study and were used for comparison purposes with the Indian sample. For the Indian couples, most marriages were arranged by parents, but in urban areas, there were some "love matches," in which the individuals chose their own partners, sometimes from different religious, caste, or socioeconomic backgrounds. In the case of arranged marriages, both members of the proposed match could decline the choice made by the parents.

Individuals completed a measure of marital satisfaction (the Dyadic Adjustment Scale developed by Spanier, 1976) and a measure of reported interaction with their spouse in three domains (verbal, nonverbal, and sexual). In the North American sample, many aspects of reported marital communication were related to marital satisfaction, while among the Indian couples in arranged marriages, very few reported behaviors were correlated with marital satisfaction. Yelsma and Athappilly (1988) interpreted their findings as suggesting that while "a desire for emotional excitement" contributed to satisfaction in companionate marriages, other variables such as "a sense of lifelong commitment and cultural tradition" were more likely to be related to satisfaction in arranged marriages. Their observation raises an important issue—namely, the criteria for defining a "successful marriage" may well differ for persons from individualistic and collectivistic societies.

Examination of the specific reported behaviors that were correlated with marital satisfaction among the American respondents reveals that many items pertained to psychological intimacy, such as sharing feelings and personal concerns, including discussing personal problems as well as positive topics. Among Indian respondents, some aspects of psychological intimacy, such as "talk about intimate matters" and "can tell what kind of day spouse has had," were related to marital satisfaction for those in love-based marriages but not for those in arranged marriages. However, compared to the American companionate marriages, the pattern of findings suggested that the type of intimacy reported by Indian respondents in the love-based marriages involved less extensive self-disclosure.

This pattern of findings raises an intriguing question about the nature of intimacy in close relationships. What is the role of verbal self-disclosure in the development of a sense of intimacy? Perhaps verbal disclosure is especially important in societal contexts where close relationships must be constantly negotiated, and a sense of mutual dependence and positive regard cannot be assumed, even after the initial formative phases of the relationship. This suggestion leads to our final proposition.

Proposition 3: Although individualism fosters the valuing of romantic love as a basis for marriage, certain aspects (or types of) individualism at the psychological level make developing intimacy problematic.

Problems with developing intimacy in a relationship should be most likely to occur among those persons characterized by "self-contained individualism" described by Sampson (1977), in which the emphasis is on valuing autonomy, personal control over one's life outcomes, and disliking any form of dependency. Attempting to reconcile the needs of two people in a relationship, each of whom is striving for intimacy, yet at the same time trying not to sacrifice personal control, is difficult (see also Bellah et al., 1985).

In our own research, we recently examined the relation between psychological individualism—valuing individualism at the personal level—and romantic love among Canadian respondents (Dion & Dion, 1991). This study illustrates a point made earlier: namely, that within an individualistic society, there are differences in the degree to which people endorse the prevailing value orientation. We reasoned that one component of psychological individualism was a desire to maintain one's personal autonomy, as illustrated by endorsing the following types of items: "My freedom and autonomy mean more to me than almost anything else" or "The best way to avoid trouble is to be as completely self-sufficient as possible." If psychological individualism partly reflects the valuing of personal autonomy, there might be ambivalence about emotional dependence in an intimate relationship. This ambivalence was hypothesized to manifest itself in less reported affective involvement with one's partner and in a less satisfying experience of romantic love.

We found, as predicted, that "self-contained individualism" was negatively related to reported caring, need, and trust of one's partner. "Self-contained" individualists were also less prone to describe their experience of romantic love as rewarding, deep, and tender. They were more likely to view "love as a game," as a test of their skills and power in a love relationship. In essence, our study suggested that psychological individualism, at least the "self-contained" type, was related to emotional detachment in romantic relationships.

Given the above pattern of findings, it is plausible that psychological individualism may be one factor contributing to a high rate of divorce in the United States and in Canada. Cherlin (1981) speculated that an individualistic view of relationships that specifies that a relationship end when either party is dissatisfied, might well contribute to a greater likelihood of divorce. Consistent with this speculation, we found that university students scoring high on psychological individualism indicated a less positive attitude toward marriage and were less opposed to divorce (Dion & Dion, 1993).

There is a marked difference in the evaluation of interpersonal dependency in individualistic vs. collectivistic societies. For example, *amae* psychology in Japan affirms an essentially positive and constructive attitude toward dependency upon others, especially in familial and pseudofamilial social arrangements. *Amae* has generally positive connotations to the Japanese, who use it to describe a variety of positively toned and sentimentalized relationships between parent and child, wife and husband, where one partner depends upon the other to provide indulgent gratification and considerate affection. In contrast, the term "dependency" has primarily negative or ambivalent connotations in Western cultures, such as the United States, which value autonomy and individuality. There is no equivalent word to *amae* or *amaeru* in Western languages, a fact that apparently astonishes Japanese (Doi, 1988).

Research on gender and relationships is also consistent with the proposition that some aspects of individualism may create problems for intimacy in relationships. As noted earlier, it has been suggested that women's construal of self is more relational (that is, more collectivistic) than men's views of self. Hui (1988) found some support for gender differences on his measure of individualism-collectivism in a cross-cultural study comparing university students from the United States and from Hong Kong. Women from both cultural groups scored higher on collectivism with regard to parents and friends than did their male peers.

Gender differences in reported social skills are also consistent with hypothesized gender differences in self-construal. Riggio (1986) found that women reported greater emotional expressivity and sensitivity as well as greater social expressivity and social sensitivity than men, qualities consistent with a relational view of self. Men in contrast reported greater emotional control and social manipulation than did women, qualities consistent with a view of self as autonomous. On another type of social skill that is consistent with a relational view of self, namely, the capacity to take one's partner's perspective, women were perceived both by themselves and by their spouse as more capable on this dimension (Long & Andrews, 1990).

In our research on the relation between gender and the reported experience of romantic love, the pattern of findings indicated that college-age women from the United States and from Canada expressed greater pragmatism than their male peers in their beliefs about love and more caution in their readiness to "fall in love." Once involved in a romantic relationship, however, women reported more intense positive emotions and described their experience as more emotionally involving and rewarding than did men (Dion & Dion, 1985, 1991). We have suggested that these gender differences might reflect greater responsiveness and adeptness on the part of the women in relationships involving psychological intimacy, described by Shaver and Buhrmester (1983) as involving reciprocal self-disclosure, emotional supportiveness, and a low level of defensiveness. All of these qualities are those that one would expect to be associated with a relational sense of self.

After marriage, however, some North American studies on the correlates of marital satisfaction have found greater dissatisfaction reported by wives compared to husbands (see Dion, 1985; Worell, 1988). Of interest here, much of the greater reported dissatisfaction appears to center around the issue of psychological intimacy (e.g., Locksley, 1980; Thurnher, 1976). In an individualistic society, both women and men may expect psychological intimacy in marriage. However, gender-related differences in how self is viewed in relation to others may in turn be related to the capacity for providing psychological intimacy to one's spouse. In a recent review of North American research, Ross et al. (1990) suggested that marriage was related to greater physical and psychological health benefits for men than for women. One of the key factors they proposed as underlying the relation between marriage and personal well-being was providing emotional intimacy and support to one's partner.

CONCLUSIONS

In conclusion, the purpose of this paper is to draw attention to the need to take into account the cultural context in which women's and men's experience of love and intimacy is based. Most theoretical accounts of close relationships in the social psychological literature have not explicitly considered this issue. As we can attest from writing this article, there is relatively little empirical research on close relationships in other cultural contexts, especially non-Western societies. Much of the research that does exist is in other disciplines such as psychological anthropology, family sociology, or comparative family studies.

We have presented three propositions suggesting a relation between individualism and collectivism, on the one hand, and romantic love and emotional intimacy in marriage, on the other. Considered together, these propositions lead to the following paradox: In societies where individualism is prevalent, greater emphasis is placed on romantic love and on personal fulfillment in marriage. However, some features of individualism at the psychological level make the likelihood of realizing these outcomes more difficult. In contrast, collectivism (as illustrated by the examples from three Asian societies) fosters a receptiveness to intimacy, but at the psychological level, this intimacy is likely to be diffused across a network of family relationships.

What are the implications of this conceptual analysis? It can be argued that in some respects, the marital relationship in individualistic societies is under greater pressure than in collectivistic societies because marriage is expected to fulfill a diverse array of psychological needs. It is not coincidental that at both the level of professional services and popular advice, there are numerous individuals and groups proffering advice on how to maintain and improve marriage. Given the high expectations for personal fulfillment in marriage, the rate of divorce is likely to increase as individualism, especially the self-contained type of individualism, increases. It may be that other types of individualism are not as problematic, but this possibility remains to be empirically documented.

We have suggested that some of the gender differences in the reported experience of romantic love and satisfaction with emotional intimacy in marriage within North American society may reflect gender differences in self-construal. It should not, however, be assumed that differences in self-construal are inherent in gender per se. Instead, it seems more plausible that a sense of self as relational or autonomous develops within a particular context of social relationships. Accordingly, cohort differences in self-construal for women and for men, respectively, might well be expected if there were changes in the structure of social relationships at both the personal and the societal levels. One can speculate, for example, that within North American society, there has been a trend for cohorts maturing in the 1970s and 1980s toward more individualistic self-construal. If so, we would expect that this trend might ultimately be related to greater reported dissatisfaction with emotional intimacy in marriage and similar relationships for both sexes compared to earlier cohorts.

Finally, although in recent years individualistic features (most notably, greater freedom of choice of one's spouse) have been present in some collectivistic societies, this particular trend should not necessarily be assumed to be a harbinger of the self-contained type of individualism. More collectivistic factors (such as parental approval of one's choice and maintaining a network of family and kin relationships after one's marriage) continue to be important. However, the analysis in this paper suggests that if some aspects of traditionally collectivistic societies change in the direction of greater individualism, the importance of psychological intimacy in marriage for marital satisfaction and personal well-being will increase.

Preparation of this article was facilitated by a Social Sciences and Humanities Research Council of Canada (SSHRCC) grant to the first author. The authors would like to express their appreciation to Arthur Aron, Val Derlega, Susan Sprecher, and Barbara Winstead for their helpful and constructive comments on earlier versions of this article.

REFERENCES

Averill, J. R. (1985). The social construction of emotion: With special reference to love. In K. J. Gergen & K. E. Davis (Eds.), *The social construction of the person* (pp. 89–109). New York: Springer-Verlag.

Bardwick, J. (1980). The seasons of a woman's life. In D. McGuigan (Ed.), *Women's lives: New theory, research and policy* (pp. 35–55). Ann Arbor: University of Michigan Press.

Bellah, R. N., Madsen, R., Sullivan, W. M., Swidler, A., & Tipton, S. M. (1985). *Habits of the heart: Individualism and commitment in American life.* Berkeley: University of California Press.

Buruma, I. (1984). *A Japanese mirror: Heroes and villains of Japanese culture.* New York: Viking Penguin.

Cancian, F., & Gordon, S. L. (1988). Changing emotion norms in marriage: Love and anger in U.S. women's magazines since 1900. *Gender and Society, 2,* 308–342.

Cherlin, A. J. (1981). *Marriage, divorce and remarriage.* Cambridge, MA: Harvard University Press.

Chodorow, N. (1978). *The reproduction of mothering: Psychoanalysis and the sociology of gender.* Berkeley: University of California Press.

De Mente, B. (1989). *Everything Japanese.* Lincolnwood, IL: Passport Books.

Derlega, V. J. (1984). Self-disclosure and intimate relationships. In V. J. Derlega (Ed.), *Communication, intimacy, and close relationships* (pp. 1–9). Orlando, FL: Academic.

Desai, N., & Krishnaraj, M. (1990). *Women and society in India.* Delhi, India: Ajanta Publications.

DeVos, G. (1985). Dimensions of the self in Japanese culture. In A. J. Marsella, G. DeVos, & F. L. K. Hsu (Eds.), *Culture and self: Asian and Western perspectives* (pp. 141–184). London, England: Tavistock.

Dion, K. K. (1985). Socialization in adulthood. In G. Lindzey & E. Aronson (Eds.), *Handbook of social psychology* (Vol. II, pp. 123–148). New York: Random House.

Dion, K. K., & Dion, K. L. (1985). Personality, gender, and the phenomenology of romantic love. In P. R. Shaver (Ed.), *Self, situations and behavior: Review of Personality and Social Psychology* (Vol. 6, pp. 209–239). Newbury Park, CA: Sage.

Dion, K. K., and Dion, K. L. (1991). Psychological individualism and romantic love. *Journal of Social Behavior and Personality, 6,* 17–33.

Dion, K. L., & Dion, K. K. (1979). Personality and behavioural correlates of romantic love. In M. Cook & G. Wilson (Eds.), *Love and attraction* (pp. 213–220). Oxford, England and New York: Pergamon.

Dion, K. L., & Dion, K. K. (1988). Romantic love: Individual and cultural perspectives. In R. J. Sternberg & M. L. Barnes (Eds.), *The psychology of love* (pp. 264–289). New Haven, CT: Yale University Press.

Dion, K. L., & Dion, K. K. (1993). *Correlates of psychological individualism and collectivism.* Manuscript in preparation.

Doi, T. (1962). AMAE: A key concept for understanding Japanese personality structure. In R. J. Smith & R. K. Beardsley (Eds.), *Japanese culture: Its development and characteristics* (pp. 132–139). Chicago, IL: Aldine.

Doi, T. (1963). Some thoughts on helplessness and the desire to be loved. *Psychiatry, 26,* 266–272.

Doi, T. (1977). The structure of amae. In M. Hyoe & E. G. Seidensticker (Eds.), *Guides to Japanese culture* (pp. 84–88). Tokyo: Japan Cultural Institute.

Doi, T. (1988). *The anatomy of dependence.* Tokyo and New York: Kodansha International.

Fukada, N. (1991). Women in Japan. In L. L. Adler (Ed.), *Women in cross-cultural perspective* (pp. 205–219). Westport, CT: Praeger.

Ho, D. Y. F. (1975). Traditional approaches to socialization. In J. W. Berry & W. J. Lonner (Eds.), *Applied cross-cultural psychology* (pp. 309–314). Amsterdam, Holland: Swets und Zeitlinger.

Ho, D. Y. F. (1982). Asian concepts in behavioral science. *Psychologia, 25,* 228–235.

Hofstede, G. (1984). *Culture's consequences: International differences in work-related values.* Newbury Park, CA: Sage.

Hogan, R. (1975). Theoretical egocentrism and the problem of compliance. *American Psychologist, 30,* 533–540.

Honig, E., & Hershatter, G. (1988). *Personal voices: Chinese women in the 1980's.* Stanford, CA: Stanford University Press.

Hsu, F. L. K. (1971). Psychosocial homeostatis and Jen: Conceptual tools for advancing psychological anthropology. *American Anthropologist, 73,* 23–44.

Hsu, F. L. K. (1981). *Americans and Chinese: Passage to differences* (3rd ed.). Honolulu, HI: The University Press of Hawaii.

Hsu, F. L. K. (1985). The self in cross-cultural perspective. In A. J. Marsella, G. DeVos, & F. L. K. Hsu (Eds.), *Culture and self: Asian and Western perspectives* (pp. 24–55). London, England: Tavistock.

Hui, C. H., & Triandis, H. C. (1986). Individualism-collectivism: A study of cross-cultural researchers. *Journal of Cross-Cultural Psychology, 17,* 225–248.

Hui, C. H. (1988). Measurement of individualism-collectivism. *Journal of Research in Personality, 22,* 17–36.

Kim, U. (1993). *Introduction to individualism and collectivism: Conceptual clarification and elaboration.* Unpublished manuscript.

Kumar, U. (1991). Life stages in the development of the Hindu woman in India. In L. L. Adler (Ed.). *Women in cross-cultural perspective* (pp. 142–158). Westport, CT: Praeger.

Lee, G. R., & Stone, L. H. (1980). Mate-selection systems and criteria: Variation according to family structure. *Journal of Marriage and the Family, 42,* 319–326.

Levinson, D. (1978). *The seasons of a man's life.* New York: Knopf.

Locksley, A. (1980). On the effects of wives' employment on marital adjustment and companionship. *Journal of Marriage and the Family, 42,* 337–346.

Long, E. C. J., & Andrews, D. W. (1990). Perspective taking as a predictor of marital adjustment. *Journal of Personality and Social Psychology, 59,* 126–131.

Lykes, M. B. (1985). Gender and individualistic vs. collectivist bases for notions about the self. *Journal of Personality, 53,* 356–383.

Markus, H. R., & Kitayama, S. (1991). Culture and the self: Implications for cognition, emotion, and motivation. *Psychological Review, 98,* 224–253.

Morsbach, H., & Tyler, W. J. (1986). A Japanese emotion. In R. Harré (Ed.), *The social construction of emotions* (pp. 289–307). New York: Blackwell.

Perlman, D., & Fehr, B. (1987). The development of intimate relationships. In D. Perlman & S. Duck (Eds.), *Intimate relationships: Development, dynamics, and deterioration* (pp. 13–42). Newbury Park, CA: Sage.

Riggio, R. E. (1986). Assessment of basic social skills. *Journal of Personality and Social Psychology, 51,* 649–660.

Roland, A. (1988). *In search of self in India and Japan.* Princeton, NJ: Princeton University Press.

Ross, C. E., Mirowsky, J., & Goldsteen, K. (1990). The impact of the family on health: The decade in review. *Journal of Marriage and the Family, 52,* 1059–1078.

Sampson, E. E. (1977). Psychology and the American ideal. *Journal of Personality and Social Psychology, 35,* 767–782.

Sampson, E. E. (1985). The decentralization of identity: Toward a revised concept of personal and social order. *American Psychologist, 40,* 1203–1211.

Shaver, P., & Buhrmester, D. (1983). Loneliness, sex-role orientation and group life: A social needs perspective. In P. B. Paulhus (Ed.), *Basic group processes* (pp. 259–288). New York: Springer-Verlag.

Spanier, G. B. (1976). Measuring dyadic adjustment: New scales for assessing the quality of marriage and similar dyads. *Journal of Marriage and the Family, 38,* 15–25.

Sternberg, R. J., & Grajek, S. (1984). The nature of love. *Journal of Personality and Social Psychology, 47,* 312–329.

Thurnher, M. (1976). Midlife marriage: Sex differences in evaluation and perspectives. *International Journal of Aging and Human Development, 7,* 129–135.

Waterman, A. S. (1984). *The psychology of individualism.* New York: Praeger.

Worell, J. (1988). Women's satisfaction in close relationships. *Clinical Psychology Review, 8,* 477–498.

Xiaohe, X., & Whyte, M. K. (1990). Love matches and arranged marriages: A Chinese replication. *Journal of Marriage and the Family, 52,* 709–722.

Yelsma, P., & Athappilly, K. (1988). Marital satisfaction and communication practices: Comparisons among Indian and American couples. *Journal of Comparative Family Studies, 19,* 37–54.

CHECKPOINTS

1. According to Dion and Dion, cultures vary in the degree to which they value either individualism or collectivism. This degree of variation predicts differences in the meaning of love and intimacy.

2. Individualistic cultures place great emphasis on love and romance but individualism makes it difficult to fulfill these desires.

The Paradox of Relationships

QUESTIONS FOR REFLECTION

1. How do traditional gender roles both strengthen and undermine our intimate relationships?
2. What would friendships and gay and lesbian romantic relationships be like in a more collectivistic culture?

CHAPTER APPLICATIONS

1. Identify one specific type of relationship—gay, lesbian or heterosexual romance, cross-sex or same-sex friendship, cross-race friendship, or intergenerational relationship—and interview several people about their perceptions and experiences with such relationships. Be sure to include questions about gender. What are your conclusions about stereotypes versus actual experiences?

CHAPTER ELEVEN

Gender and Reconceptualizing the Family

QUESTIONS TO THINK ABOUT

- **What is the importance of names in relationships and families?**
- **What are the essentialist and social constructionist views of the family?**
- **What are the consequences of prescriptive definitions of family?**
- **How has psychology stigmatized divorced women, unmarried women, and African American mothers?**
- **What does fatherhood mean to men?**
- **How do traditional gender roles define mother and father, and how can these roles be reconceptualized?**
- **How do traditional gender roles segregate family labor, and how can this separation be changed?**
- **How are household tasks shared in gay, lesbian, and heterosexual families, and what does this division of labor imply about power in intimate relationships?**
- **How can families become more egalitarian?**

USING NAMES: DEFINING FAMILY

In this chapter's first reading, an essay titled *What We Call Each Other,* Andee Hochman describes a conversation with her elderly grandfather in which he inquires, "So, how's your lady friend?" referring to Hochman's lesbian partner. This inquiry, the meaning of which is unclear to Hochman, leads her to reflect on the meaning and power of names. Before you read this essay, think about who you are within your family, especially the different names you

are known by. Many of us have nicknames left over from childhood. Some of us have pet names given to us by parents, siblings, lovers, or a spouse. Names are sometimes based on particular relationships—grandmother, grandfather, aunt, uncle, cousin—and these names designate who we are within our family. Hochman ponders the implications of names, what they mean to us, and what they communicate to others. Hochman identifies the many names that heterosexual couples have for their relationships, terms that describe increasing intimacy—date, boy/girlfriend, fiancé, spouse. Gay individuals and couples have no convenient names that describe their relationships in ways that convey similar meaning. Often the names used by gay, lesbian, or bisexual individuals or partners are euphemisms that conceal rather than acknowledge their relationships. Names define us, make public our relationships, communicate who is and is not part of our family, and often mark who we are as male and female.

Gender Roles and the Family

Within the family, names carry meaning not only about who we are in relationship to others but also about the roles we play—husband, wife, mother, father, daughter, son—and these names often influence behavior and beliefs about what is appropriate for each family member. Roles within the family are deeply ingrained with meaning about gender. Gender roles, as we have described them, are intimately connected to roles within the family, and for theorists such as Eagly (1987), gender roles originate in the division of labor within the family and society. Eagly argues that the communal role (typically female) derives from activities and relationships within the home, whereas the agenic role (typically male) derives from activities and relationships in the larger community outside the home. Thus the gender roles ascribed to women and men revolve around the extent to which one does or does not engage in family caregiving, child rearing, and wage earning. According to Eagly, social roles function as prescriptions for how one should behave and feel about oneself.

Beliefs about roles within the family, the structure of family, and the organization of family life permeate our culture and have shaped many public and political debates. Public policy issues such as divorce, child custody, abortion, public assistance for poor individuals or families, and the distribution of employee benefits such as insurance or pensions all revolve around contested definitions of the family and its roles and responsibilities. By examining the complex relationship between gender and family, you may gain a new perspective on both the meaning of family and the ongoing debates about the nature and function of family.

The embeddedness of gender roles in the family has impacted how social scientists, especially psychologists and sociologists, have studied the family. The social science perspective has often adopted the view that specialized roles within the family, along with certain family forms, are most natural. The articles in this chapter by Theodore Cohen, *What Do Fathers Provide?*, and Joy Rice, *Reconsidering Research on Divorce, Family Life Cycle, and the Meaning of Family*, look at how traditional research has studied and portrayed the family, particularly the roles of men and women within the family. Cohen is concerned that fathers have been theorized to be oriented toward wage earning and not family life so researchers have rarely studied men's attitudes and values regarding family and work. Rice is concerned that women whose lives do not conform to the pattern of married with children are not only stigmatized publicly but are often viewed by psychological theory as dysfunctional and pathological. Each of these articles presents an analysis that challenges the traditional view of men, women, and the family.

What is a Family?

One view of family, supported by evolutionary psychology, is that the family unit originates in male-female pairs and in the need for reproduction. Daly and Wilson (1996) suggest that in all cultures, women and men enter into individual partnerships that include mutual obligations and shared responsibilities. The evolutionary point of view identifies several key elements of marriage. Marriage often connotes an exclusive sexual relationship between the partners; it determines caregiving responsibilities toward offspring; it influences the sexual division of labor; and it may determine the allocation and inheritance of resources. The evolutionary point of view acknowledges the wide cross-cultural diversity in marriage, such as whether marriage is marked by a public ceremony, considered lifelong, involves one or more than one partner, or involves the cohabitation of marriage partners. For evolutionary theorists such as Daly and Wilson, this diversity does not invalidate the central observation that marriage and family are rooted in reproduction. The evolutionary view of family supports the view that one sort of family— man, woman, and their biological children—is the primary form of human family. Emerging from this perspective are a number of corollary arguments about the sexual division of labor. Evolutionary theorists argue that women invest far more effort in bearing and caring for children and therefore are likely to develop skills related to these activities. As a result of their vulnerability during pregnancy and lactation, women who selected as mates men with the fitness and resources to invest in them and their children would have been more likely to survive (Buss, 1995). Men are hypothesized to seek female partners who are likely to be fertile; therefore men would be attracted to young women. According to Kendrick and Trost (1993), many cultures exhibit this pattern of mate preference in which women prefer men who are older and have resources whereas men across a wide age range prefer women in their twenties and place greater emphasis on attractiveness.

The evolutionary explanation of family roles is an essentialist view of both family and gender roles. It portrays the nuclear family as the natural and favored family form, having evolved as a result of the differences in sexual selection between males and females. The view that the unit of man, woman, child is the fundamental family unit is not limited to evolutionary theory. In studying the family, researchers have typically treated the nuclear family as the model family and have considered variations from this model as deviations from the norm.

The Diversity of Families

An alternative view of family sees it as a socially constructed set of relationships that vary across cultures and of individual roles that vary in meaning across the life span. According to Jackson (1993), there is great diversity in the family form throughout history and cross-culturally. Family forms construct kinship relationships in varying ways that are not always based on the degree of biological relatedness. For example, families may be composed of individuals who are interdependent economically or who cohabitate. Marriage varies worldwide in whether it is

expected to last a lifetime, whether it is monogamous for one or all partners, and whether the marriage occurs in a matriarchal or patriarchal context. The definition of fatherhood and motherhood may vary from culture to culture in terms of responsibility and obligations toward either biological or nonbiological children. Thus the assumption that the triad of mother, father, and child forms the basis for all families is challenged by worldwide variations in the formation and maintenance of families.

Family arrangements are not based solely on procreation, as portrayed by a strict evolutionary perspective. The family, by offering economic interdependence, by providing safety, by establishing emotional attachment and intimacy, and by sharing of skills and resources, serves a multitude of needs. The view of family as a psychological, cultural, and social institution portrays the relationship between gender and the family differently from the view postulated by evolutionary theory. One difference is in the perspective on alternative family arrangements. Evolutionary theory does not provide an adequate explanation for gay or lesbian families, nor does it provide a means to understand paternal nurturance, especially when it occurs in the context of maternal disinterest or abandonment of children. Evidence shows us that not only do these alternative family forms exist but that the variations they represent tell us something important about gender.

Gay and Lesbian Couples as Family

Peplau (1995) describes, in the article you read in chapter 10, many myths about gay and lesbian couples. These relationships are often stereotyped as impoverished in many ways and are cast as weak imitations of heterosexual relationships. As Peplau shows, the evidence does not support these stereotypes, although we can see how gender shapes relationships for both heterosexual and gay and lesbian couples. Regardless of sexual orientation, men claim a greater interest in sexual activity than do women. In a related fashion, women's relationships show higher rates of fidelity and a greater commitment to self-disclosure and sharing within the context of an intimate relationship. Cultural gender roles transcend sexual orientation, and in some ways, women and men are similar in relationships regardless of the sex of their partner. Gay, lesbian, and bisexual individuals seek intimacy and sexuality in relationships and are as likely as heterosexual people to believe that love is important for their overall happiness. Furthermore, despite stereotypes to the contrary, most gay and lesbian people believe in and are interested in developing a sustained love relationship (Peplau, Veniegas, & Campbell, 1996).

Does sexual orientation affect the likelihood that a relationship will last? As you may already know, approximately one in every two marriages will end in divorce. The odds of a romance between heterosexual couples turning into a marriage that lasts a lifetime are relatively low. How likely is it that gay and lesbian relationships will endure? Research by Blumstein and Schwartz (1983), some of which you read in chapter 7, examined the stability of relationships over a period of eighteen months. Among couples who had been together for ten or more years prior to the time this research began, the breakup rates were very low—only 4 percent of gay couples, 6 percent of lesbian couples, and 4 percent of married couples separated during the eighteen-month period. For couples whose relationship at the beginning of the research period was less than two years' duration, the separation rates were higher—22 percent of lesbian couples, 16 percent of gay couples, 17 percent of cohabiting heterosexual couples, and 4 percent of married couples. The important distinction may not be sexual orientation but marital status. Peplau, Veniegas, and Campbell (1996) found that the duration of a relationship is, in part, affected by obstacles to ending the relationship. Heterosexual married couples, more so than other couples, face barriers to ending their relationship, such as legal entanglements, joint property, children, and the public nature of their commitment. In contrast, gay and lesbian couples face many barriers to the inception and continuation of their relationships. In many settings, there is no public acknowledgment of gay and lesbian relationships, and extended families may refuse to acknowledge the relationship. Couples who wish to share economic resources may find it

difficult to do so, and very few civic and religious institutions recognize committed gay and lesbian relationships. Couples who wish to have a public commitment may have to create and celebrate with a ceremony of their own making.[1] The conclusion of Peplau, Veniegas, and Campbell is that heterosexual couples may be less likely to end a marriage because of the structural and emotional barriers to its ending, whereas gay and lesbian individuals may have an easier time ending an unhappy relationship because it is not subjected to as much public scrutiny. Ultimately, however, we do not know how long gay and lesbian relationships last because there are no census data for gay and lesbian couples; therefore, we cannot get an accurate estimate of the length of duration or rate of breakup of committed gay and lesbian couples. Given the high divorce rate among heterosexual couples, we would not be surprised to find that those gay and lesbian relationships that have surmounted the social and structural barriers described earlier have a greater likelihood of success.

Gender Roles and Parenting

To examine the influence of gender roles on parenting, we need to look at parenting arrangements that differ from the standard equation of parent = mother that is prevalent today. The assumption that mothers should be the primary caregiver and moral authority within the family is a recent cultural construction. According to Berry (1993), during colonial times and through the nineteenth century, fathers took primary responsibility for the supervision, education, and moral upbringing of their children. This responsibility differed somewhat by social class and race, because wealthier white fathers had more resources and time to devote to child rearing, whereas poor families were likely to treat their children as an economic resource once children reached the age where their labor could make a contribution to family survival (around the age of 6 or 7). The families of African Americans during slavery were decimated by forced childbearing and separation of families. Despite efforts to destroy the families of slaves, husbands and fathers made material contributions to their families—hunting, fishing, collecting firewood, carving household objects—even when they lived apart from their family. The Civil War brought great changes to American families, black and white, but for different reasons. White women, either left behind or widowed, took on new economic responsibilities for their families, whereas African American women took on the challenge of moving out of slavery and reuniting their families. For both groups, dramatic social and economic changes accompanied the advent of what Berry refers to as the "Mother-Care period," which reflected the growing belief that mothers are best suited to raise their children. During the twentieth century, the view that women should be the sole caregivers of their children has been strongly promoted and institutionalized in public policies. This perspective provides a partial explanation for why the United States has lagged behind other countries in providing parental leave for childbirth or adoption, public- or employer-supported childcare, and early education for children. Despite economic circumstances that require women to be employed in great numbers, our society continues to promote the idea that mothers bear the primary responsibility for their children.

In light of the strong socialization of women as caregivers and of the social and cultural conditions that exclude men from child care activities, we could ask two related questions about the etiology of these rigid gender roles and family life. Does caregiving become an essential quality of women, as the prevailing cultural view would suggest? Does masculine socialization prevent men from assuming the caregiving role in their families? We can address these questions by examining the experiences of men who, through varied circumstances, have become the primary caregivers of their children. Briefly stated, the evidence suggests that caregiving is not a quality held only by women, and when the circumstances place men in the primary caregiving role, they respond much as we might expect women to behave. In a study of 141 single fathers,[2] Risman (1989) provides some evidence about the experiences of single fathers. Risman reports that more than 80 percent of the fathers had no outside help

with household chores. The fathers were responsible for, among other things, cooking, shopping, cleaning, laundry, and yard work. The vast majority (92 percent) had created what Risman refers to as a child-centered home, where the organization of family life was centered on the child or children. These fathers knew their child's homeroom teacher and were involved to some degree in school activities; they knew the names of their child's friends; they had made provisions for accidents and emergencies and made regular visits to the pediatrician and dentist; they took primary responsibility for child care and spent considerable time on household and recreational activities with their children. Nearly all the fathers reported high levels of emotional involvement with their children and high levels of satisfaction with their role as primary caregiver. Although many hoped to remarry, none sought to marry a woman in order for her to take over child care and housekeeping responsibilities. In fact, 38 percent expected to retain primary caregiving themselves, and about half expected to share caregiving should they remarry. These fathers were highly satisfied with their lives and deeply committed to their roles as fathers. Perhaps these results do not surprise you (although we suspect otherwise), but they certainly contradict the notion that there are essential roles for men and women within the family. If the potential behavior of men and women within the family is inherently flexible as opposed to fixed, we might ask what forces sustain the distinctiveness of women's and men's roles within the family.

Cultural Views of Fathers and Mothers and Research on the Family

The two articles in this chapter written by Cohen and Rice look at the relationship between traditional views of the roles of men and women in the family and how researchers have studied the family. Each of these authors believes it is important to understand how the traditional model of the family as mother, father, and child has shaped scholarship on the roles of men and women and the family. Our understanding of men and their roles in the family and of women-headed households is limited because of the reliance on the assumption that the nuclear family is the preferred family form. According to Epstein (1988), although social scientists have long been aware that the idealized nuclear family misrepresented American family life, social science research has continued to perpetuate the belief that the nuclear family is the typical and a preferred family form. Research on the family has often replicated the view of the nuclear family, with its closely prescribed roles for men and women, and has failed to include alternative family arrangements studied on their own terms. For example, researchers typically study parenting by examining the behavior and attitudes of mothers; they limit their study of fathers to the role of playmate, not caregiver.

Cohen's article points out that the role of work in men's lives is central to theories of masculinity. As a consequence, researchers have focused their study of masculinity on men and work and have neglected the role of men in the family. Theories about masculinity and the role of work seem completely consistent with the dominant cultural view that a man's central role in American society is to earn money. As children, boys are taught to aspire to a wide range of adult careers and to value such characteristics as self-reliance, independence, aggressiveness, and goal-directedness (Levant, 1995). The classic social science view of masculinity within the family, as articulated by Bernard (1981), has been called the good-provider role, with an emphasis on accomplishment in the workplace and on earnings as the definition of male success. The underlying assumption is that being a good provider is the essence of being a good father. This view of fatherhood leads to the neglect of the emotional meaning of the role of father and, according to Cohen, to the perceptions that parenting is provided largely by mothers and that full-time fathers are deviant.

There are social consequences of this view of fathers as well. In 90 percent of divorce cases, child custody is awarded to mothers and fathers are under court order to provide monetary support. Many mothers interfere with paternal visitation, and even more fathers fail to provide the full court-awarded child support (Silverstein, 1996). This arrangement, which gives precedence to the role of mother as nurturer and father as provider, replicates a narrow view of mothers and fathers and does not facilitate implementation of successful divorce settlements. In her analysis of fathering, Silverstein urges caution in asserting a traditional patriarchal view of fathers and encourages exploration of the nurturing dimensions of fatherhood. Such a focus might contribute to a more diverse view of families, with father-headed households and gay fathers gaining social legitimacy as healthy, vibrant family forms.

In his article, Cohen reports on his extensive interviews with men during their transitions to marriage and fatherhood. He observes that much of the impact of fatherhood is invisible to those on the outside. The men he interviewed reported dramatic changes in their self-perception and how new meanings emerged for the events in their lives. When asked what made them feel most like fathers, only one of the thirty fathers referred to his financial responsibilities and work. Most of the men, contrary to cultural stereotypes, mentioned nurturing and the expressive dimension of fatherhood as central to their experiences. Cohen suggests that these results, which contradict the traditional view of fathers, occur as a result of his use of qualitative methods, which allow greater exploration of the subjective meaning of the fatherhood role. When researchers limit their study of fathers to measures such as time spent with children or time spent in various child-related activities, they overlook the emotional significance of this role to men. While reading Cohen's article, be alert for the complexities of the role of father and for the multiple meanings of the role of men within the family context.

It is often assumed that a woman's central role in the family is as a wife and mother and that girls are socialized to incorporate these roles into their feminine gender role identity. Although we know that not all women aspire to these roles, it remains true that women are often judged on the degree to which they succeed as wives and mothers. Thus the family setting becomes the playing field for the expression of a woman's gender role identity. Rice's article in this chapter shows that women-headed households have been portrayed by the media, as well as in the work of psychologists and sociologists, as deficient. Rice refers to this portrayal as the deficit comparison model of the family, which emerges from the use of the nuclear family as a normative and prescriptive model. Based on the nuclear view of family, the goals of social intervention and family therapy are to restore the family to a state that includes both mother and father. Mother-headed households, which can occur as a result of nonmarital childbearing or divorce, are portrayed as deficient and dysfunctional. Rice reviews the research on Black female-headed households, single women, and divorced women with children as examples of family structures that have been stigmatized as deviant. Her analysis suggests that these characterizations are not supported by a careful evaluation of the research evidence.

The fastest growing type of family is the woman-headed household, with dramatic increases in both divorced and never-married mothers. According to Baca Zinn (1990), social and economic factors distinguish white, Black, and Latina women-headed households. An increase in employment for white women has contributed to greater economic independence, which is related to women delaying marriage or choosing not to marry. These factors also make it possible for women in unhappy marriages to divorce. Black women have a lower rate of marriage overall, which may be attributed in part to economic and employment hardships among Black men. Latina women have frequently been employed in subsistence wage jobs whereas Latino men have been employed in transient jobs that may force family separations. Baca Zinn suggests that we distinguish the mechanisms that account for the emergence of women-headed households and understand the resultant adaptations within the family. Ethnic minority families rely on extended family and on the development of strategies for integrating employment and motherhood, which places these families in the forefront of creative adaptation to social changes, in contrast to their typical portrayal as deficient families. Baca Zinn further argues that researchers who de-

velop theories of family can learn more by studying family diversity rather than adhering to stereotyped views of family arrangements.

In her analysis of women-headed families, Rice also urges us to consider alternative family structures as adaptive and positive. She argues that researchers have failed to consider that unmarried women may have actively chosen to remain unmarried and that women may actively choose divorce as a more positive alternative to an unsatisfying or abusive marriage. The failure to consider women-headed households as a positive alternative to a heterosexual couple can be related to the kinds of research questions that are asked about marriage and divorce. In particular, researchers have taken a problem-centered approach to divorce, examining how single mothers parent their children and probing for conflict and negative postdivorce consequences among children. Rice describes a meta-analysis of approximately 100 studies on the consequences of divorce for children that shows that children of single mothers fare better psychologically than children in high-conflict homes with both parents.

The articles by Cohen and Rice both suggest that researchers need to examine their assumptions about gender and the family as part of the research process. These articles offer examples of how men and women have been cast into narrow roles within the family and of how research has reproduced and reified these roles by failing to consider alternative models of family organization. Cohen considers the emotional meaning of fatherhood for men, and Rice evaluates the social portrayal of women. From both these analyses, we can learn ways to critically evaluate the relationship between gender and the family.

PUBLIC LIFE AND PRIVATE LIFE

One of the distinguishing features of gender roles is their spheres of influence or expertise. Traditionally, the male gender role is enacted in public, primarily in work settings, whereas the female gender role is reserved for the private life of the family. Recent changes in employment, however, have resulted in the majority of women being employed outside the home during most of their adulthood. In the mid-1990s, 58 percent of women with children under the age of 6 and 74 percent of women with children between the ages of 6 and 16 were employed (U. S. Department of Labor, 1995). Among women with a college degree, employment rates are even higher; rates are also higher for African American and Hispanic women across all levels of education. Today, for all families, the issues of work and family are intertwined despite the segregation of gender roles into family and work arenas. Any explanation of gender and the family must take into account the many ways in which work intersects with family life and decision making. Decisions about living arrangements, child care, daily life, health care, and household chores are all influenced by men's and women's employment and family roles.

Power, the Family, and Employment

Although women are employed outside the home in great numbers, men's employment still holds precedence in most family decision making. Among heterosexual couples, husbands' jobs generally are better paid and have higher status than wives' jobs, and consequently, choices about where to live and how to organize the household may hinge on supporting the husband's employment. In addition, socialization pressures encourage couples to place a differential value on work and family responsibilities for men versus women. This model of work and family applies to heterosexual couples and is embedded in the dynamic of cross-sex relationships. One element of this dynamic is the asymmetry between the roles of women and men, in which masculinity, because it is a more socially valued attribute, accords men higher status. Interacting with the social status of masculinity and femininity is the cultural context of love and romance. Remember the article by Dion and Dion in chapter 10 that characterized our culture as individualistic with an emphasis on independence and achievement. Dion and Dion (1993) contend that one consequence of this orientation is that partners'

expectations for intimacy within a marriage may come into conflict with a psychological view of self as autonomous and with a cultural emphasis on individualism. Dissatisfaction may emerge when a relationship is not able to meet one or both partners' need for intimacy, and yet there is enormous cultural pressure for economic success and achievement—and this pressure affects both partners. Lips (1991) suggests that for traditional couples, power may be mediated by earned income, such that higher wage earners are able to exercise more direct control over decision making while lower wage earners may have their decision making mediated by the more powerful partner. We would expect the power dynamics in marriage to change during a time of considerable social change in which individuals express desire for greater equality in their relationships, in which there are growing economic opportunities for women, and in which marriages succeed and fail at almost equal rates. This contention is supported by recent research from Barnett and Rivers (1996) that suggests that two-earner families are not only increasing, but working to successfully combine, employment and family in a less traditional, more egalitarian fashion.

The Division of Labor Within the Family

Another place to examine power and gender within the family is in household labor. All households depend on substantial family labor,[3] cooking, cleaning, shopping, laundry, child care, home maintenance, car maintenance, and lawn and garden work are required tasks for most families. You may recognize that the first part of this list corresponds to activities typically performed by women and the second half to tasks typically performed by men. In recent years, considerable debate has ensued over whether the traditional division of labor has changed (Barnett & Rivers, 1996; Hochschild, 1989; Lorber, 1994; Pleck, 1993). Division of household labor is a contentious issue, because the evidence speaks to the questions of changing family values and of equity within relationships. We follow this research closely because we all have a keen interest in whether the family is changing and whether there is fairness in marital relationships. The evidence does suggest that women perform more of the day-to-day household chores, especially the mundane, repetitive tasks such as cooking, laundry, cleaning, and shopping. In their review of this issue, Barnett and Rivers conclude that men spend considerably more time on household chores than earlier estimates would suggest and that the absolute amount of time spent on household chores is less important than other dimensions of the division of labor. Barnett and Rivers contend that the nature of household tasks is the most important factor in predicting how people view their participation in such activities. Day-to-day tasks such as planning and preparing meals, laundry, and housecleaning are *demanding* (because of their repetitive nature) and the person who has the responsibility for these chores has *little control* over when the chores are done. This combination of demanding work and little control has been associated with stress-related reactions and with dissatisfaction in both employment and the family setting. Both men and women in Barnett and River's research who found themselves with more responsibility for demanding but low control chores showed lower satisfaction with their marriage and more stress-related symptoms such as self-reports of depression or anxiety. According to Barnett and Rivers, the relationship between stress and repetitive chores is gender-neutral and is not mitigated by quality of marriage, parental status, length of marriage, or gender role ideology (e.g., whether participants believe that chores should be divided along gender lines). An important element that reduces stress and supports marital happiness is perceived control and flexibility in day-to-day activities, which probably results from relationships that are more egalitarian and less dependent on cultural stereotypes.

In this chapter's last article, *The Allocation of Household Labor in Gay, Lesbian, and Heterosexual Married Couples* Lawrence Kurdek, examines the division of household labor for gay, lesbian, and heterosexual married couples. By asking partners in long-term relationships to estimate their degree of responsibility for a number of household tasks,

Kurdek is able to characterize relationships in terms of the degree of sharing of household responsibilities. Couples followed different patterns of allocation of household responsibilities: Gay men divided household chores in accord with skill, interest, or work schedule; lesbians were most likely to share household chores and do them simultaneously or alternately; heterosexual couples divided tasks according to the traditional pattern, with wives doing far more chores. Interestingly, only wives showed significant levels of depression and stress. Kurdek's findings are consistent with the argument of Barnett and Rivers (1996) that responsibility for low control, demanding chores is related to stress. How do the patterns of equality exhibited by gay and lesbian couples develop, and what lessons might there be for heterosexual couples in terms of relationship equality? Peplau, et. al., (1996) found that most gay men and lesbians actively reject traditional gender roles and that each partner is likely to have some measure of economic independence. For these couples, decision making about household responsibilities seems more deliberate and based on a goal of equality. Heterosexual couples may aim for a goal of equality, but traditional gender roles could conflict with this goal, and in working out decisions about the distribution of household labor, couples may unwittingly revert to traditional patterns. The Barnett and Rivers findings point out that stress symptoms occur for either spouse with an unequitable share of responsibilities, but the data also show that men can benefit psychologically from involvement in their home life. Men can derive pleasure from several household activities, such as keeping the house looking nice, doing tasks that let off steam, entertaining guests, or making improvements in the house. Men and women can protect themselves from stress and improve marital happiness by sharing the more pleasurable household activities and minimizing the degree to which any one partner is responsible for the tedious tasks. This clear benefit of egalitarian relationships can be obtained by any couple willing to renegotiate their roles and question traditional stereotypes.

SOCIAL CHANGE AND THE AMERICAN FAMILY

Hochman, in this chapter's essay on family names, challenges the prevailing definitions of family. Developing inclusive language for families that differ from the nuclear family provides a means for many different social arrangements to be recognized as families. We are in an age of rapid social change, in which the family form has been revolutionized; have gender roles changed in accord with these changes in the family?

Social Change and Parenting

In chapter 6, you read an article by Sandra Bem subtitled "raising gender-aschematic children in a gender-schematic society." Bem proposed these suggestions in 1983 as a way of showing how her theory of gender schemas could be used to promote social change, which she believes is essential for dismantling gender stereotypes. Did you wonder if any families ever attempted to alter their child rearing to be less gender stereotyped, and if so, how these altered family attitudes have affected children? Today we have families with traditional attitudes toward women and men and we have families with egalitarian attitudes; researchers are identifying and studying some of these families to understand how gender might be played out in families with differing gender arrangements. We do have some evidence that is related to Bem's suggestion from research that compares traditional and egalitarian families.

In an interesting study by Fagot and Leinbach (1995), children in egalitarian and traditional families were compared for their acquisition of gender labels and gender role knowledge in early childhood. The sample of parents with egalitarian values described themselves as committed to nonsexist, shared parenting and were compared to a matched sample of parents who described themselves in traditional terms. The researchers made observations in the homes of the families when the children were 18 months and 27 months old. Fagot and Leinbach found that fathers in the egalitarian group interacted signifi-

cantly more with their children, whereas mothers in both groups interacted at the same rates. Boys of traditional parents received more negative sanctions than did boys of egalitarian families or girls of either type of family. The evidence for gender learning showed that children of the traditional parents learned gender labels earlier and showed greater gender role knowledge than did children of the egalitarian parents. These findings support Bem's suggestion that the development of gender schemas may be delayed or deterred with intentional efforts to provide alternative child rearing. However, the results bear closer examination. The explicit ideology of nonsexist child rearing appears to have a more dramatic impact on fathers than on mothers, because the behavior of both groups of mothers was not significantly different. Whether the children's differences in gender role knowledge will translate into behavioral differences is unclear, but Fagot and Leinbach speculate that they will not. Although the egalitarian parents, through their nonsexist behavior, have avoided reproducing cultural stereotypes and have delayed the development of rigid gender schemas, Fagot and Leinbach believe that behavioral preferences are controlled more by peer group interactions.[4]

Researchers may characterize families as egalitarian or traditional, but in reality, families vary considerably in how they express traditional gender roles in family life and organization. The dual-income families in the Barnett and Rivers (1996) study all of whom had children were committed to their work and family, and in general, worked collaboratively to integrate all their responsibilities. They may not have thought of themselves as egalitarian and may not have organized their family life around ideology, but both spouses showed a high degree of coordination of responsibilities. Barnett and Rivers conclude that a cluster of related factors provide the greatest rewards in marriage, and when these factors co-occur, both men and women are happy and satisfied with their marriages and their lives. The factors that Barnett and Rivers identified are close emotional connection between partners, a satisfying intimate and sexual life, shared financial responsibilities, and being a part of an extended family. Not only are partners happier in such relationships, but they also show higher levels of good mental health; thus, for men and women, a good marriage has psychological benefits for both married partners and their children. We see these factors as a perfect description of an egalitarian family in which the expressive needs are met by both partners creating emotional connection and the agenic needs are shared via an equitable distribution of family labor and financial responsibilities.

Shifting Social Norms?

We have explained how gender role behaviors can change and why they should. What happens, however, when a couple's gender role beliefs and family behavior are not in agreement? What about wives who wish to share household responsibilities but are married to men who spend 80 hours a week at work? Within this context, we examine the consequences of shifting social norms as they occur within families. A longitudinal study of marriage and family life by McHale and Crouter (1992) identified couples who were incongruent in values and behavior—either wives who expressed nontraditional gender role beliefs but whose family roles were traditional or husbands whose beliefs were traditional but whose family roles were nontraditional. These couples were compared to couples whose values and behavior were congruent. Although the evidence from this research is complex, a few points are revealing about the process of social change. In general, the spouses whose lives showed incongruity between gender role beliefs and family behavior were less happy in comparison to their own spouses and, as a group, less happy in comparison to the couples with congruent attitudes and behavior. The data showed that wives with nontraditional values experienced little change in family gender role ideology or behavior during the three years of the study. This result suggests that wives' shifting values do not have much of an impact on family dynamics. Husbands whose traditional beliefs conflicted with a family distribution of labor in which the husbands shared housework were more

unhappy than other groups of husbands. These husbands became more dissatisfied in the second year of the research, and their dissatisfaction returned to its original level by the third year. McHale and Crouter, reporting from the same group of research participants, describe the consequences of different family patterns on children. From another set of complex results (McHale, Crouter and Bartko, 1992), one finding addresses gender role ideology in fostering emotional intimacy, and the evidence is clear. Children (age 10 and up) report higher levels of shared intimacy with their parents in families where there is equity in family responsibilities, especially when fathers spent more time in child-related activities. Although we can only speculate on what will happen when these children grow up and form their own adult relationships, we would expect the children to carry into adulthood their positive experiences with shared intimacy, which we know to be important to relationship success. Perhaps this path is one way to create successful egalitarian families in the future. McHale and Crouter point out the significance of observing shifts in social attitudes and related behaviors over time, during which we are likely to see changes within couples as well as between types of families. They further emphasize that understanding the consequences for children of shifting gender role ideologies will require an understanding of family dynamics, of the expressed beliefs and gender role behavior of family members, and of the recognition that both values and behavior may change over time.

The impact of variations in gender role ideology on parenting can be observed in gay and lesbian families with children. Our stereotyped notions of gays and lesbians may not include images of parenthood; however, there are an estimated 6 to14 million gay or lesbian parents in the United States (Patterson, 1996). The route to parenthood is varied for lesbians and gays: Some become a parent while in a heterosexual relationship or marriage and then come out as gay or lesbian; some adopt; lesbians may use artificial insemination; gay men may use a surrogate mother; and some are stepparents to the child of a current partner. Gay and lesbian parents may have either a custodial or non-custodial relationship with their child or children. Although our purpose here is to examine the consequences of nontraditional gender role ideology within families, because of the myths surrounding the impact of a parent's sexual orientation on children, we first briefly examine this issue. No evidence supports the view that children of gay or lesbian parents are more likely to become gay, lesbian, or bisexual, and there are no personality or socioemotional differences between children of gay or lesbian parents and children of heterosexual parents. Furthermore, children of custodial lesbian mothers show no evidence of social stigma from their peer group or difficulties in peer relations, there is no evidence that children of gay fathers are at risk for sexual abuse, and children of divorced lesbian mothers have more contact with their noncustodial fathers than do children of divorced heterosexual mothers (Patterson, (1996).

Returning to our examination of nontraditional gender role ideology, we find that children are higher in social adjustment in lesbian families in which the division of child care is viewed as equitable by both partners. Children of lesbian parents see themselves as less aggressive than children of heterosexual parents, and in the same study, the children of lesbian parents are seen by parents and teachers as more lovable, affectionate, and responsive. Although this research is tentative, it does suggest that children may develop less rigid notions of gender roles in homes in which gender role ideology is less apparent. This concept is supported by the research we reviewed earlier of Fagot and Leinbach (1995) and McHale and Crouter (1992) which studied the impact of shifting gender role ideologies on children.

Research on shifting gender roles in the family is in its infancy. The questions are fascinating and they intersect with significant social changes in the organization of family life, but our conclusions must be tentative. It is possible to identify families in which gender roles are nontraditional, either by intention or as a consequence of other aspects of life. The available evidence suggests benefits for adults and children of egalitarian gender roles.

Partners in a relationship can obtain more satisfaction by emphasizing equity in the distribution of responsibilities and congruence between ideology and behavior. Increased involvement in child care by fathers is related to delayed gender role labeling and positive perceptions of parent-child intimacy. Children suffer no harmful effects from gay and lesbian parenting, and indeed they may experience less gender role stereotyped behavior. Many questions about the changing family need to be answered, and we hope that new research will reflect some of the complexity in the relationship between gender and family.

THE ROLE OF GENDER IN RECONCEPTUALIZING THE FAMILY

We have argued that research on gender can lead to a reconceptualized view of the family. Definitions of family can change to reflect the variety of significant relationships in our lives, and roles within the family can be less prescribed by culture and more reflective of individual skills and interests. What we call family can be broadened to include all relationships that involve shared responsibility, intimacy, and commitment. Families can achieve equity, which has a positive mental health benefit for everyone, by increasing shared responsibilities, both financial and family. The evidence suggests that men can "mother" and women can "father" and children benefit through increased psychological security and intimacy. Happy relationships between parents translate into happier and healthier children. Recognizing the myriad forms of the family may help you understand the role of gender in your own life and may help you plan your own prescriptions for intimate relationships and parenting. Recognizing the reconceptualized family would also help researchers avoid the narrow view of men's and women's roles that has dominated social science inquiry on the family and would lead to the creation of research plans that account for the complexity of the family in a world of changing values.

NOTES

1. See Hochman (1994) for vignettes that exemplify feminist, alternative family arrangements and the celebrations of such families.
2. All the single fathers had at least one child under the age of 14 at home. Sixty-two percent of the fathers had been deserted or widowed or their wives had refused custody. The remainder had actively sought custody either through negotiation or against the mother's wishes. The sample was 90 percent white and diverse economically.
3. Although household responsibilities can be performed by hired workers, typically it is only among the wealthiest families that all household work is paid labor.
4. To remind yourself of the complexity of early gender learning, refer back to the Fagot article in chapter 6.

REFERENCES

Baca Zinn, M. (1990). Family, feminism, and race in America. *Gender & Society, 4*, 68–82.

Barnett, R. C., & Rivers, C. (1996). *She works/He works: How two-income families are happier, healthier, and better off.* New York: HarperCollins.

Bernard, J. (1981). The good-provider role: Its rise and fall. *American Psychologist, 36*, 1–12.

Berry, M. F. (1993). *The politics of parenthood.* New York: Penguin Books.

Blumstein, P., & Schwartz, P. (1983). *American couples: Money, work, sex.* New York: Morrow.

Buss, D. M. (1995). Psychological sex differences: Origins through sexual selection. *American Psychologist, 50*, 164–168.

Cohen, T. F. (1993). What do fathers provide? Reconsidering the economic and nuturant dimensions of men as parents. In J. C. Hood (Ed.), *Men, work, and family* (pp. 1–22). Newbury Park, CA: Sage.

Daly, M., & Wilson, M. (1996). Evolutionary psychology and marital conflict. In D. M. Buss & N. M. Malamuth (Eds.), *Sex, power, conflict: Evolutionary and feminist perspectives* (pp. 9–29). New York: Oxford University Press.

Dion, K., & Dion, K. L. (1993). Individualistic and collectivistic perspectives on gender and the cultural context of love and intimacy. *Journal of Social Issues, 49*, 53–69.

Eagly, A. H. (1987). *Sex differences in social behavior: A social role interpretation.* Hillsdale, NJ: Erlbaum.

Epstein, C. F. (1988). *Deceptive distinctions: Sex, gender and the social order.* New Haven: Yale University Press.

Fagot, B. I., & Leinbach, M. D. (1995). Gender knowledge in egalitarian and traditional families. *Sex Roles, 32*, 513–526.

Hochman, A. (1994). What we call each other. In A. Hochman (Ed.), *Everyday acts and small subversions: Women reinventing family, community, and home* (pp. 257–262). Portland, OR: Eighth Mountain Press.

Hochschild, A. R. (1989). *The second shift.* New York: Viking.

Jackson, S. (1993). Women and the family. In D. Richardson & V. Robinson (Eds.), *Thinking feminist: Key concepts in women's studies.* New York: Guilford.

Kendrick, D. T., & Trost, M. R. (1993). The evolutionary perspective. In A. E. Beall & R. J. Sternberg (Eds.), *The psychology of gender* (pp. 148–172). New York: Guilford.

Kurdek, L. A. (1993). The allocation of household labor in gay, lesbian, and heterosexual married couples. *Journal of Social Issues, 49*, 127–139.

Levant, R. F. (1995). *Masculinity reconstructed: Changing the rules of manhood—at work, in relationships, and in the family life.* New York: Dutton.

Lips, H. M. (1991). *Women, men, and power.* Mountain View, CA: Mayfield.

Lorber, J. (1994). *Paradoxes of gender.* New Haven: Yale University Press.

McHale, S. M., & Crouter, A. C. (1992). You can't always get what you want: Incongruence between sex-role attitudes and family work roles and its implications for marriage. *Journal of Marriage and the Family, 54*, 537–547.

McHale, S. M., Crouter, A. C., & Bartko, W. T. (1992). Traditional and egalitarian patterns of parental involvement: Antecedents, consequences, and temporal rhythms. In D. L. Featherman, R. M. Lerner, & M. Permutter (Eds.), *Life-span development and behavior* (Vol. 2). Hillsdale, NJ: Erlbaum.

Patterson, C. J. (1996). Lesbian and gay parents and their children. In R. C. Savin-Williams & K. M. Cohen (Eds.), *The lives of lesbians, gays, and bisexuals: Children to adults* (pp. 274–300). Fort Worth, TX: Harcourt Brace.

Peplau, L. A. (1995). Lesbian and gay relationships. In L. D. Garnets & D. C. Kimmel (Eds.), *Psychological perspectives on lesbian and gay male experiences* (pp. 395–419). New York: Columbia University Press.

Peplau, L. A., Veniegas, R. C., & Campbell, S. M. (1996). Gay and lesbian relationships. In R. C. Savin-Williams & K. M. Cohen (Eds.), *The lives of lesbians, gays, and bisexuals: Children to adults* (pp. 250–273). Fort Worth, TX: Harcourt Brace.

Pleck, J. (1993). Are "family-supportive" employer policies relevant to men? In J. Hood (Ed.), *Men, work, and family.* Newbury Park, CA: Sage.

Rice, J. K. (1994). Reconsidering research on divorce, family life cycle, and the meaning of family. *Psychology of Women Quarterly, 18*, 559–584.

Risman, B. (1989). Can men "mother"? Life as a single father. In B. Risman & P. Schwartz (Eds.), *Gender in intimate relationships: A*

microstructural approach (pp. 155–164). Belmont, CA: Wadsworth.

Silverstein, L. B. (1996). Fathering is a feminist issue. *Psychology of Women Quarterly, 20*, 3–37.

U. S. Department of Labor. (1995). *Women's Bureau of Labor Statistics*. Washington DC: U. S. Department of Labor.

What We Call Each Other

ANDEE HOCHMAN

We'd covered all the routine subjects—the weather in Portland, the weather on the Jersey shore (it was summer in both places). I'd thanked him for sending me a paperback copy of *The Joys of Yiddish*. Then my eighty-nine-year-old grandfather said, "So, how's your lady friend?"

I gulped. It was possible he meant Rachael, and "lady friend" was a quaint attempt to cover up the fact that he'd forgotten her name. But I'd never heard him use that phrase, with its tinge of old-fashioned, coy romance, to describe an acquaintance of mine.

Finally, I mumbled that she was just fine, thanks. "Rachael and John are fine, too." I said, testing. There was no response.

Later, I told my "lady friend" about the comment, and we both laughed. But I still don't know if my grandfather knew what he asked, if he grasped what he heard. Words are like that. They can swab the air clean of illusion, or they can fog the truth in a comfy, opaque veil.

So many of the words for romantic or sexual partners make women mere appendages of men, extend a long-standing power imbalance. What is the term to describe a relationship of equals, two adults trying to make a life together? I like "partner," with its hints of adventure and readiness, the idea of moving together through a love affair or a life. Most of my friends, gay or straight, use it to describe their romantic associates.

But even "partner" isn't perfect. For one thing, it conveys a sense of stability that doesn't apply to all relationships, especially brand new ones. Heterosexual couples have a whole vocabulary that hints at changing degrees of intimacy and intention. First "lovers" or "boyfriend/girlfriend"; then "fiancé/e"; finally "spouse." But unmarried or gay partners have no language to describe those shifts.

The words commonly used in such cases are designed to mask the truth rather than tell it. The euphemisms for gay and lesbian lovers—"constant companion" or "very special friend"—hide the true nature of the relationship under a cloak of decorum. But it's a cloak made to be seen through; everyone knows it's a cover for something else. It indicates that the real thing is too scandalous even for discourse; the word itself can't go out of doors unclad.

One lesbian couple I know dislikes "partner" for the same reasons I'm drawn to it—because it is democratic, gender-neutral. These women refer to each other as "girlfriends," refusing, even in casual conversation to pass.

Slowly, slowly, names gather a new history; the weight of a word can shift. When lesbians and gay men appropriate the language of the mainstream, filling in their partners' names where government forms say "spouse," insisting that they deserve a "family" membership to the YMCA, they force others to reorder their mental maps. Those maps would change even faster if heterosexual couples boycotted marriage and its honorifics, if they, too combed the language for words that more precisely describe their bonds.

Girlfriend. Boyfriend. Mistress. Beau. Old man. Lady friend. Steady. Helpmate. Fiancé/e. Lover. Paramour. Spouse. Domestic partner. Soul mate. Significant other. Homeslice. Sweetie. Co-habitant. Ally. Longtime companion. Live-in. Partner. Collaborator. Consort. Intimate. Confidant/e. Familiar. Alter ego. Mainstay. Second self. Complement. Mate.

Even words that don't carry a gender bias can be suspect, quiet enforcers of the status quo. I used the word "single" to describe women without intimate partners until the irony of the term struck me. I was writing about these women precisely because they'd built networks of support through work, friends, housemates, yet my easy description of them conveyed someone alone and unconnected, with no important social ties.

"Are you in a relationship?" people inquire euphemistically, when what they mean is "Are you sexually involved with someone?" The notion of *a* relationship—primary, intimate, more weighty than the rest—doesn't fit the lives of people who choose celibacy, or who are in nonmonogamous relationships involving two or more significant "others."

Then there's "friend," which doesn't begin to cover enough ground. It describes everyone from the colleague I chat with once a month at a writers' meeting to the woman I've known since infancy but haven't seen for a decade, to Rachael, whom I lived with for more than five years. The word, forced to stand for such a range of connections, erases distinction, implies all friendships are the same.

Names wake us to the particulars of a thing. If I call Diana my mainstay, Pattie my soul mate, and Rachael my sister, I remember that these women have different qualities, that my friendship with each is unique.

I say Rachael is my "sister," and then pause. Why is that the only term that seems to fit? I struggle to describe closeness and am left holding a simile, a stand-in phrase that only gropes at description. "He's like a brother to me," we say, revealing not only the assumed potency of sibling bonds but the dearth of words to describe intense, nonsexual attachments.

There's a level of intimacy that "friend" seems too small to contain. Then we make it even smaller, often denigrating it with the qualifier "just." They're "just friends," we concede, as if friendship were automatic and uninteresting, less full of potential than any romantic pairing. In fact, the vast majority of people in our lives fall into that maligned category; friendship deserves a vocabulary of its own.

Acquaintance. Colleague. Buddy. Bosom-buddy. Sidekick. Chum. Amiga. Compadre. Homegirl. Mate. Pal. Sister. Fellow. Right-hand man. Companion. Compañera. Associate. Cohort. Crony. Aficionado.

Compeer. Confrere. Ally. Comrade. Familiar. Accomplice. Mainstay. Primary. Neighbor. Friend.

I've wrestled, too, with "childless." It's a gender-weighted word—we don't refer, with quite the same sense of anomaly and pity, to "childless" men. And it assumes childbearing is the norm and *not* childbearing a lesser version of life; it defines an existence by what it lacks. "Nonparent" makes the same mistake.

I've seen women use "child-free," which seems tipped in the other direction—as though children were a burden and only people without them have liberty. Besides, many women who choose not to be parents include children in their lives as nieces and nephews, neighbors, clients, friends. I thought about words like "adult-based" or "adult-centered" for women who don't have much to do with children. But I've yet to find a term that expresses, without judgment, the facets of this complicated choice.

And there are relationships, existences we scarcely have language to describe. The words for an unmarried woman—maiden aunt, spinster—are all pejorative. "Old maid," in particular, holds layers of judgment—a woman who contradicts her own nature, at once old and young, a perpetual servant. Thanks to Mary Daly and others, feminists are reclaiming "spinster" as a source of creative pride; one woman I know named her sewing business "Spinster Textiles."

Few terms exist to describe former lovers who now are good friends, or nonbiological parents, or relationships between the childhood families of a gay couple. I've heard a woman explain to her child, conceived through alternative (as opposed to "artificial") insemination, that there are "seed daddies" as well as the kind of daddies who live at home, and a lesbian friend coined "sister-outlaws" to describe her lover's siblings.

The contemporary women's movement and gay and lesbian liberation helped prompt people to create new honorifics, such as "Ms.," and reclaim old names, taking them back from the domain of those who hate. Queer. Dyke. Crone, Cripple. Faggot. Fat person. Fairy. When we use these words for ourselves, we become powerful, filled with the awesome responsibility that is naming. We print the words on buttons, shout them in parades. We repossess the names and, in the process, repossess ourselves.

Language changes from the edges; new terms ripple back to the center. Gradually, I have seen "partner" replace "longtime companion" in news stories about gay men and lesbians. Several papers even have begun listing gay commitment ceremonies. As such events become more popular and public, terms unimagined as yet may enter the lexicon.

Coupling. Espousals. Union. Match. Bond. Pairing. Knot. Joining. Dovetailing. Commitment ceremony. Intention. Dedication. Webbing. Mingling. Intertwining. Weaving. Blending. Braiding. Concord. Alignment. Alchemy. Convergence. Handfasting. Tryst.

What we call each other—how we refer to lovers and friends, partnerships and families—is more than a matter of etiquette. The words tell us who is owned and who is free, who really counts and who is merely secondary.

The language of the nuclear family continues to sway our speech, crowd out equally valid models of living. Homeless teenagers I worked with took the words of the families that failed them and applied them to each other. I heard them use "sister" and "brother" for their friends, but also "mother" and "kid," outlining large and intricate networks of street kin.

The actual people represented by those terms may have abused or abandoned these teenagers, but the words themselves seem to carry an infinitely renewable potency, a hope that someday someone will grow into the legend that is "mother," "sister," or "son."

"Blood family" itself carries that mythic power—"blood," with its symbolism of oath and source, a magical connection that cannot be undone. "Biological family" is less poetic but equally weighted. Married couples aren't related genetically, nor are adopted children. In families formed through remarriage, in foster families and extended families, "blood" connections have little to do with linkage.

I've toyed with "first family," "original family," and "childhood family" to describe the groups we grow up with, and "present family," "chosen family," or "adult family" for those we have now.

But the word "family" itself is loaded. The term can help justify secrecy ("let's keep it in the family") or serve as an argument for public hands-off ("that's a family matter"). And it is used disingenuously, as in "We're all one big happy family here" by businesses that want to promote childlike docility from employees and avuncular rule from bosses.

No mere noun, it's a way of categorizing society, even allocating resources, with "family" memberships and "family" fares on airlines and trains. "Family values" is political shorthand, evoking marriage, patriotism, and obedient children, a code aimed to halt a changing world.

Imagination is larger than language. The names claim who we already are and who we wish to become. We don't require them in order to live, but they make our living known, translatable, turn it into something we can talk about. There is room for more words, for the finest of distinctions, for as many possibilities as our minds can shape.

Someday, the white house in New Jersey will be mine. I cannot imagine selling it. I want it to remain in the family. Families. Meaning me, my cousins, our parents, our children, if we have them. And more than that. The partners and compatriots, lovers and allies, cronies and intimates, all those who share the everyday acts of our lives.

I can see it. Someone will tap on the glass between the front stairs and the kitchen. I will look up, out the window, through the house and the window beyond it, straight out to the ocean we all come from. I will recognize the face, and I will wave.

Welcome, I might say, to my tribe. My group. Cabal. Circle. Club. Nucleus, Team. Neighborhood. Community. Affinity group. Kin. Karass. People. Coalition. League. Assemblage. Confederation. Gang. Clique. Coterie. Set. Crew. Crowd. Cadre. We-group. Affiliates. Relations. Folk. Household. Brood. Collection. Cronies. Network.

Welcome to my company, my clan.

BIBLIOGRAPHY

Cronan, Sheila, "Marriage," in *Radical Feminism,* ed. Anne Koedt, Ellen Levine, Anita Rapone (New York: Quadrangle Books, 1973).

Falk, Marcia, "Notes on Composing New Blessings," in *Weaving the Visions: New Patterns in Feminist Spirituality,* ed. Carol P. Christ and Judith Plaskow (San Francisco: Harper & Row, 1989).

Firestone, Shulamith, *The Dialectic of Sex: The Case for Feminist Revolution* (New York: Bantam, 1970).

Gilman, Charlotte Perkins, *Women and Economics* (Boston: Small, Maynard & Company, 1898).

Kay, Herma Hill, *Text, Cases and Materials on Sex-Based Discrimination* (St. Paul, Minn.: West Publishing Company, 1981).

Kaye/Kantrowitz, Melanie, "Some Notes on Jewish Lesbian Identity," in *Nice Jewish Girls: A Lesbian Anthology,* ed. Evelyn Torton Beck (Trumansburg, N.Y.: The Crossing Press, 1982).

Le Guin, Ursula K., "The Space Crone," in *Dancing at the Edge of the World: Thoughts on Words, Women, Places* (New York: Grove Press, 1989).

Loewenstein, Andrea Freud, "Troubled Times: Andrea Freud Loewenstein Interviews Sarah Schulman," in *The Women's Review of Books* (Vol. VII, Nos. 10–11, July 1990).

CHECKPOINT

1. For Hochman, the language of the nuclear family defines who is included and who is excluded in the social recognition of family and other relationships.

To prepare for reading the next section, think about these questions:

1. How do you define family?

2. Why are divorced women, single women, and single mothers viewed negatively in our society?

3. What is the most important aspect of fatherhood?

Reconsidering Research on Divorce, Family Life Cycle, and the Meaning of Family

JOY K. RICE

University of Wisconsin–Madison

This article analyzes functionalist and normative assumptions about marriage, divorce, family, and gender in developmental models of family life cycle. An interdisciplinary review of the literature in family development, family sociology, and family therapy reveals how a deficit comparison model implicitly informs the discourse in the study of single-parent families, women who are alone, and the adjustment of women and children to divorce. A feminist critique of family life cycle as the prevailing conceptual model in family development and therapy is presented, and postmodern definitions that deconstruct the concept of family are discussed. Future perspectives for research on family life and form are considered in terms of new action theory that considers divorce as a mode of resistance and change for women and families.

Nearly one out of every two marriages in the United States now ends in divorce, a very significant social, economic, and psychological phenomenon that has frequently been addressed in the social science and lay literature of the past decade. Because women are twice as likely as men to initiate divorce, and women increasingly head single-parent households, divorce can also be seen as a significant feminist issue (National Center for Health Statistics, 1989). The emergence of a popular backlash effect is now also apparent, which relates women's new roles and the "breakdown of the family" to a variety of social and psychological ills ranging from juvenile delinquency, drug and alcohol abuse, and male sexual dysfunction to violence against women, social narcissism, and materialism (Dart, 1991; Faludi, 1991; Whitehead, 1993).

I will argue in this paper that divorce can be seen not just as a manifestation of the breakdown of society or the family, a paradigm and conclusion derived from old action theory. Instead divorce can be considered from a feminist perspective, as resistance to the oppression of women in families and as an identifying marker of societal and historical change and transformation. Researchers, however, continue to frame their questions around divorce as a perceived threat to the prevailing social order, for example, adult and children's postdivorce dysfunction, diminished parenting by fractured families, etc.

Using an interdisciplinary approach and drawing upon the literature in family development, family sociology, and family therapy, I will discuss how a deficit comparison model is applied in situations where the dominant family form differs from the so-called "normative" one, that is, intact, White, middle-class, and male-headed, as in the study of Black families headed by women and divorced families headed by single-parent mothers. Such a model generally informs the discourse whenever women by choice or circumstances live without men. The paper then presents a feminist critique of family life cycle (FLC) and its treatment of divorce and gender. FLC theory has been the overreaching conceptual model for the fields of family development and family therapy for the past 45 years but, as will be seen from this review, is a largely mythological framework. Finally I will discuss postmodern feminist approaches that deconstruct the concept of family. Old action theory will be contrasted with new action theory in terms of the implications for research on divorce and family life and form.

Address correspondence and reprint requests to: Joy K. Rice, Department of Educational Policy Studies, University of Wisconsin–Madison, Madison, WI 53706.

A Social Alarm

Before 1939 there were never more than 10,000 divorces per year in the United States. By 1988 divorces climbed to a peak of 1,183,000 and then plateaued (National Center for Health Statistics, 1989). Demographers estimate that currently about two thirds of all first marriages are likely to disrupt (Martin & Bumpass, 1989). Nearly 40% of children under 18 spend a part of their childhood living with a single parent, usually a mother (Norton & Glick, 1986).

The societal upheaval related to our idealized perceptions and expectations of family and marriage has now reached the point where the popular media is sounding an alarm. And the conclusion about family diversity and divorce is dire. In a long, scathing essay on the effects of divorce and family diversity, Whitehead (1993) concludes,

> The social-science evidence is in: Though it may benefit the adults involved, the dissolution of intact two-parent families is harmful to large numbers of children. Moreover, . . . family diversity in the form of increasing numbers of single-parent and step-parent families does not strengthen the social fabric, but rather, dramatically weakens and undermines society. . . . Indeed it is not an exaggeration to characterize (family disruption) as a central cause of many of our most vexing social problems, . . . poverty, crime and declining school performance. . . . These new families are not an improvement on the nuclear family, nor are they even just as good, whether you look at outcomes for children or outcomes for society as a whole. In short, far from representing society progress, family change represents a stunning example of social regress. (pp. 47, 77, 80).

A distressing picture of the traditional American family as an endangered species has been presented, not only by the popular press, but also by some psychologists, sociologists, educators, child activists, and various other researchers testifying before the Senate subcommittee on Children, Families, Alcoholism and Drugs (Dart, 1991).

THE DEFICIT COMPARISON MODEL

This negative portrait of contemporary family life is directly related to our normative and patriarchal proscriptions of marriage and divorce. Divorce typically is seen as socially disruptive and personally devastating because of the intense emotional injury and role loss it usually engenders (Rice & Rice, 1986). The loss is magnified, however, because of how we socially construct the roles of single parents and mothers as well as single women in our society. Single-parent families formed by divorce are still often regarded as deviant, labeled as broken and/or disintegrated, and frequently presumed to promote maladjustment in their members (Warren & Konanc, 1989). Even when families of divorce are not stigmatized, the single-parent family is often regarded as a transitory variation in family structure preceding remarriage. Similarly Knaub (1989) notes that much of stepfamily research is based on a deficit comparison model in which variations from the intact nuclear family are regarded as dysfunctional, problematic, and inadequate. Such a formulation also informs the research on Black female-headed families, women who remain single, and the adjustment of women and children postdivorce.

Black Female-headed Families

Female-headed families account for one half of all poor families, and one half of these are headed by a woman who is divorced or separated (U.S. Bureau of Census, 1987). Black women have been particularly stigmatized as single-parent mothers and heads of households. White, intact families have been the standard by which other families are largely compared, assessed, and studied as witnessed by the special single chapters devoted to the "multiproblem poor Black family," "the ethnically diverse family," and "poor Black families" in texts on FLC (Carter & McGoldrick, 1980, 1989; Hines, 1989).

The experiences of Black families are often considered and subsumed under the general rubric of "ethnicity and families" (Carter & McGoldrick, 1989; McGoldrick, Anderson, & Walsh, 1989; McGoldrick,

Pearce, & Giordano, 1982). When women of color are marginalized into an ethnic variation, the particular effects of racism may be masked, and a White prototypic family as standard implicitly prevails. Such a standard may not account for the rich intergenerational support systems among female-headed Black families, which are not merely economically caused, but culturally rooted (Rodgers-Rose, 1980). If one turned the tables and made the intergenerational extended Black family the so-called normative centerpiece in family development theory and research, the White family might appear inadequate if not deviant (Smith, 1993). The isolation of contemporary nuclear and binuclear families, the heavy reliance on nonfamilial, disinterested providers of care, and the erosion of intimate kinship systems and contact might be seen as deficient in a deficit comparison model turned upside-down.

Biased conceptions of the Black single-parent family as inevitably dysfunctional have been challenged for some time with a new view of Black cultural variation as a strength rather than a handicap in successful family functioning (Jewell, 1988; Staples, 1985). More recent work has attempted to avoid cultural and familial ethnocentrism, while empirically discerning the social support variables that may positively contribute to successful family functioning from those that are negative or benign (Lindblad-Goldberg & Dukes, 1985). The latter authors found little difference in the social support kinship networks of urban single-parent Black, nonclinic families (no history of child or substance abuse, delinquency, criminal charges, chronic illness, physical handicap, social or school problems, or use of mental health services) with those of single-parent Black families who were in treatment for various child and school-related problems. Economic variables, however, were significant, with nonclinic mothers more likely to be employed, to live in and to own their family home, to have fewer dependents at home, and to rely less on a boyfriend or male figure than were clinic mothers.

In terms of family life cycle descriptions, Hines (1989) described Black families as having four distinguishing characteristics: (a) a more truncated cycle, (b) being female-headed and of the extended family type, (c) a life cycle punctuated by numerous unpredictable life events and the associated stress they engender, and (d) few resources available to assist them in coping with these stressors, with an extensive reliance on governmental institutions to meet basic needs. The inadequacy of this snapshot portrait becomes apparent when a life course model is applied to the Black family that considers historical epoch, social, and economic factors. The Black, rural, premodern family was nuclear in form with a strong kinship network (Demos, 1986). The loss of paternal presence in urban poor families between 1950 and 1970 occurred with continuing massive unemployment that affected Black men and their families as they migrated to the urban North. Welfare programs also combined with modern labor markets to marginalize men. Dizard and Gadlin (1990) argued that, given adequate income, jobs, and housing, the phenomenon of large numbers of female-headed Black families might not prevail. The argument is that this family form is not as primarily socially or culturally based as it is economically based.

These frameworks of Black family development attempt to view the female-headed family in positive cultural context as a legitimate family form based on historical and ethnographic data or as a temporary variant due to poverty. Both conceptions still imply deficit comparison, that is, the "good" intact family is damaged by "bad" circumstances. Nor does either framework, the social-cultural or the structural-demographic, account for the variable of choice—women's choice to be separate or live apart from men.

Women Alone

Women who choose to remain single, whether after a divorce or by never marrying, are still regarded with suspicion and disfavor in our society and societies across the world (Moore, 1988). Pervasive negative stereotypes of single women are frequently discussed in feminist literature. Yet nearly two decades of feminist critique of marriage as central to female development has largely failed to erase popular conceptions of the single woman as selfish, immature, angry, and undesirable, even schizoid (Hicks & Anderson, 1989).

A deficit comparison model does not presume that women would choose to be alone, and the statistics pointing to this phenomenon are largely ignored. As early as 1976, reports began to appear that increasing numbers of well-educated and economically self-sufficient women were choosing not to marry at all or to divorce and become single heads of households (Bequaert, 1976). By 1984, 75% of men and 57% of women were single at age 25 compared to 55% and 36%, respectively, in 1970, and approximately 10% of women were choosing not to marry at all (Glick, 1984). Women are not only marrying later and less often, but they are divorcing more frequently across income levels (Greenstein, 1990).

Classic feminist analysis would posit the family as the focal structure of patriarchy and the operation of oppression for women (Bograd, 1986; Hare-Mustin, 1978; Smart, 1984), and research has shown that marriage has a protective effect for men, but a detrimental effect, mentally and physically, for women (Sobel & Russo, 1981). Smart (1984) notes that resistance to marriage is an important feminist strategy, but "it is precisely this resistance which can render feminism so unpopular" (p. 145). Thus another way of considering divorce is as resistance by women to the oppression they do not expect, but come to experience in marriage (Ambrose, Harper, & Pemberton, 1993). This is a conception that is not discussed directly in any of the research literature on divorce, yet is buttressed by a variety of data. Women are far more likely than men to initiate divorce, to list specific problems, and to prefer less contact with their ex-spouses (see review in Diedrick, 1991). Substance abuse and physical abuse are frequently cited by women as reasons for divorce. Within the last two decades, the insidiousness of this phenomenon within marriage has become public with more women seeking legal and social recourse and separation. Conservative estimates range from 10 to 20% of women in marriages experiencing physical battering, verbal abuse, and/or forced sexuality (Bagarozzi & Giddings, 1983; Bograd, 1986).

Not surprisingly then, a large body of research finds that despite a lower financial status, women make greater psychological gains after divorce than men whether measured by constructs of self-reported happiness, self-esteem, adjustment and/or satisfaction, and such effects have been found up to 10 years postdivorce assessment (Diedrick, 1991). Diedrick (1991) suggested that gender differences in postdivorce adjustment may be explained by the fact that women generally have more to gain than men in terms of the personal autonomy that forms a basis for self-esteem. Women also form more positive attitudes toward feminism and egalitarian sex roles after divorce, although such a relationship has not been as conclusively documented (Amato & Booth, 1991).

Women, Children, and Adjustment to Divorce

Social backlash to divorce is evident not only in the popular press, but appears in professional literature in several varying forms. In the sociological literature, for example, one can find discussion of the passing down of divorce proneness from one generation to the next as though it were a disease (Catton, 1988). Others characterize divorce as excessive individualism: "Indeed, many old evils get reframed as positive contributions to maturity and personal growth—divorce becomes a 'developmental stage,' infidelity is transformed into 'open marriage,' children left unattended are being encouraged to be 'autonomous' " (Dizard & Gadlin, 1990, p. 189).

The implicit message of this conceptualization of divorce in this research is that women are selfish to leave their marriages and families, and that the children pay the brunt of the price for the woman's freedom with the burden of guilt laid on mothers. Faludi (1991) has documented how a wide variety of social ills have been laid to feminism, with an implicit theme running through much of the research she cites that women (and/or children) will be penalized for their rebellion (be less likely to marry, be infertile, suffer severely economically). She exposes the major methodological problems in two studies that have been systematically cited over and over again and politically used by the popular press to buttress traditional family ideology: one claims that women suffer dire economic losses after divorce (Weitzman, 1985), and the second that children suffer significant long-term adjustment problems (Wallerstein & Blakeslee, 1989). A review of the literature, both in marriage and family therapy, FLC, family sociology, and divorce, reveals that rarely are the severe methodological problems of these studies discussed, nor is the wealth of other data that contradicts their findings mentioned. Weitzman's highly publicized claim that women suffer a 73% decline in standard of living after divorce was based on a local small sample of Los Angeles divorce cases with a very low response rate, a sample perhaps not even representative of Los Angeles County. Divorce clearly has an important negative economic impact on women, but the costs are not as catastrophic as Weitzman and the media have asserted. National census statistics (Bianchi, 1991) confirm the findings of Duncan and Hoffman, divorce statisticians who have nationally tracked the effects of divorce on income for nearly two decades (Duncan & Morgan, 1976; Hoffman, 1977). Duncan and Hoffman (1985) found a 30% decline in women's living standards after divorce. Five years postdivorce, the average woman's living standard was slightly higher than when she was married to her husband. The average, however, includes both the half who had remarried whose income had improved and the half who had not remarried whose income decline had remained the same.

More backlash and the implicit operation of a deficit comparison model is evident in recent studies that claim to show the inevitable, negative long-term effects of divorce on children (Wallerstein & Blakeslee, 1989; Wallerstein & Kelly, 1980). Like Weitzman, Wallerstein relied on self-report data, employed no comparative or control groups with intact families, and made generalizations from a very small group of 60 urban, middle-class, California Bay area families (now 34 in the follow-up). Despite the obvious major conceptual and methodological problems of this study, it continues to be widely and indiscriminately quoted in the literature more often than any other study on adjustment to divorce, demonstrating the widespread pervasiveness of social stereotype informing research conclusions.

Feminist critique of social science research always includes the observation that social, political, and economic imperatives operate to form the lens through which we construct our methodology and inform the discourse of our interpretation. The literature on the postdivorce adjustment is no exception and has not been immune to such conceptual and methodological bias.

Problem Families We have seen how a deficit model of divorce and single parenting largely dominates the family development and family therapy literature. Thus researchers studying the adjustment of single parents and children to divorce employ a discourse that implicitly compares these families with intact first families, thereby creating a problem-oriented framework that focuses on the difficulties of these families. Amato's (1991) research using expectancy confirmation theory and self-fulfilling prophecy demonstrated that people recall information about children from divorced families in a biased manner. His review of the literature revealed that teachers, parents, and people in general hold negative stereotypes about children of divorce that may lead to expectancies or problems; for example, poorer adjustment, personal character, moral development, ability to cope, and academic performance. Such information is schema-consistent rather than inconsistent with prior stereotypes. In actuality, meta-analysis of nearly 100 studies on children and divorce reveals that children in high-conflict, intact families exhibit lower levels of well-being than do children in divorced families (Amato & Keith, 1991b).

Mothers Responsible Within this problem-oriented discourse, the labeling of these families as "female-headed" or "mother-headed" conceptually wipes out the role of the father and creates an empirical expectation to find problems and solutions through the mothers of these families. Virtually all Census Bureau statistics on divorce and child support are based on interviews with mothers and their self-reports (Haskins, Richey, & Wicker, 1987), a methodology that may lead to discrepancies in estimations of reported contact with fathers and amount of support. The few studies of fathers, not unexpectedly, paint a different picture. Weitzman (1985), for example, found that fathers in her sample reported weekly contact with their children, whereas the mothers said that these very fathers were seeing their children on a less than monthly basis.

Postdivorce adjustment studies are also focused on women's rather than men's adjustment to divorce (Bursik, 1991; Hughes, Good, & Candell, 1993; Wijnberg & Holmes, 1992). The child-rearing strategies of divorced mothers rather than fathers also dominate the literature (Forehand, Thomas, Brody, & Fauber, 1990; Gordon, Burge, Hammen, Adrian, Jaenicke & Hiroto, 1989; Holloway & Machida, 1991; Lowery & Settle, 1985), an emphasis that parallels the dramatic over-representation of mothers in research on child and adolescent psychopathology (Phares & Compas, 1992). The mother is singled out as the most crucial factor in the postdivorce adjustment of the child (Wallerstein & Kelly, 1980) because the father is generally not around. Vincent, Harris, and Plog (1991), for example, discarded an interparental conflict model in explaining children's adjustment postdivorce in favor of a "Maternal Affect & Parenting Model" that lays the burden of adjustment on the mother's adjustment. They conclude, after citing only two studies, that "single parents have been shown to exhibit a host of emotional problems . . . as well as deficits in parenting behavior" (p. 49). The type of parenting a single mother does manage to do alone has been described as "diminished parenting" (Wallerstein & Kelly, 1980), a label with pejorative overtones, intended or not. Paradoxically then, although family researchers may assume and write about women having a greater readiness and aptitude for child-rearing (Wynne, 1986), when they do it alone, it is not good enough.

Such beliefs, expectancies, and language can influence not only how social science researchers look at social phenomena such as divorce and its consequences, but can prescribe what therapists recommend as solutions (e.g., help mothers, continue to ignore fathers). Imber-Black (1986) for example, documented how large social service systems as well as individual therapists generally operate from unquestioned social and cultural norms. Such norms may lead professionals to engage the woman/mother in the treatment process over other family members, to make appointments only with the woman, and to reframe the family problems as belonging to the woman.

Methodological Bias   Past and current thinking about divorce, single parenting, and the effects on adults and children has been affected not only by conceptual bias and social stereotype, but by rampant methodological problems that characterize this literature. Untangling the aspects of the complex divorce process and its effects has been hampered by empirical findings that are largely the effect of methodological artifacts and shortcomings (Rice & Rice, 1986).

In a review of the literature, Lowery and Settle (1985) noted that the typical sampling problems that plague the divorce adjustment literature include very small samples: samples from more highly educated and affluent families, samples from lower SES groups where poverty and education are inextricably confounded with outcome, clinical samples from individuals with prior history of mental health problems, and mother custody only samples. Few studies include control groups of intact families. The data are also generally retrospective, sometimes collected many years later and usually based on self-report. The confounding effects of intervening variables and the reliance of parent and teacher reports are not addressed, and the few longitudinal studies that do exist on divorce adjustment unfortunately have not measured large representative samples before and after changes in family configuration.

Amato and Keith's (1991a) useful meta-analysis of 37 studies of 81,000 individuals suggested two important conclusions. First, the more sophisticated and recent the study, the more tenuous is the connection between parental divorce and later adult well-being. Effect sizes were also significantly stronger (up to five times larger for psychological adjustment) in clinical studies than in studies of more representative community samples. They were also stronger in earlier studies than in more recent studies, and stronger in studies that did not use statistical controls than in those that did. Secondly, the impact of parental divorce has diminished over time. Studies in the '80s show effect sizes in psychological adjustment and the material quality of life that are small in absolute terms; the largest mean effects were around one third of a standard deviation with most on the order of one tenth. Meta-analysis of 92 studies involving 13,000 children revealed similar results (Amato & Keith, 1991b). The effect sizes in the literature on children and divorce adjustment are generally quite weak, and the better and more methodologically sophisticated the study, the weaker the effects.

In sum, it is very simplistic to point to the divorce per se as the causal link in positive or negative adjustment, an approach that may account for why prior studies comparing children from divorced and intact families have found no consistent findings in adjustment (Lowery & Settle, 1985). A host of intervening variables other than the parental separation are involved, including age of child, circumstances and preparation for divorce, availability of support, material resources, interparental conflict, and cultural, familial, and individual beliefs and attitudes (Atwood, 1993; Cashion, 1982), as well as the social expectancies and confirmations set up by researchers and practitioners in the field.

GENDER PERSPECTIVES ON FAMILY LIFE CYCLE

The last 15 years have been remarkable for the applications of feminist theory, approaches and epistemological critique in the field of family research and family therapy. At the most fundamental level of analysis, feminists have insisted that gender, as well as generation, is a basic organizing principle of family life (Avis, 1985; Goldner, 1989; Hare-Mustin, 1978, 1983, 1986; McGoldrick et al., 1989; Walters, Carter, Papp, & Silverstein, 1988). When generation is privileged as an organizing construct in epigenetic models of family development, gender is trivialized or ignored. Feminists have criticized family systems theory for deflecting attention away from the ways in which women are abused in families in service of presumptions of homeostasis and circular causality for family systems maintenance and stability (Ault-Riche, 1986; Goldner, 1985). Bograd (1986) noted, for example,

that there is no mention of violence to women in the classic works of family systems literature.

Similarly, the concept of complementarity of roles (Parsons & Bales, 1955), which has informed family developmental theory and therapy since the field's beginnings, has been critiqued for gender bias and a conserving macrofunctionistic position where the priorities of society take precedence over the needs of women (Ault-Riche, 1986; Goldner, 1985; Hare-Mustin, 1986). Insistence on families as fully integrated into wider systems of economic and political power and a recognition of the conflicting interests of family members have been hallmarks of the most recent feminist critical analysis of family sociology and therapy (Baca Zinn, 1990; Boss & Thorne, 1989; Ferree, 1990).

Taggart (1985) noted that despite its liberal pretensions, family therapy has failed to take feminist critique seriously, and that there is little evidence that mainstream researchers are even aware of what feminists have written. Hare-Mustin (1986) concluded that the field of family therapy has not had any significant impact on our culture or time.

This may be an accurate assessment for several other reasons. First there is very little research in the field, and the writing is almost exclusively nonempirical (Taggart, 1985). Furthermore, unlike the field of family sociology, family therapy has not provided us with significant or provocative ways to reconceptualize family, nor has it deconstructed the concept of the "family" as feminists have deconstructed gender. Almost every model of family therapy has relied very heavily on one paradigm, FLC, as the cornerstone of conceptualization in the field (Breunlin, Schwartz, & Mac Kune-Karrer, 1992; Falicov, 1988), and as this paper will demonstrate, FLC is considered essentially mythological by even its proponents.

FLC and Epigenesis

Evelyn Duvall and Reuben Hill initially conceived a systematic paradigm for the organization of family life. It involved an eight-stage theory with normative age role expectations for the nuclear family, and its members were based on family size, age of oldest child, and change in work status of the spouses (Duvall, 1957; Hill, 1970; Hill & Rogers, 1964). Their work on FLC became the useful conceptual foundation and standard reference work for much of family theory, research, and therapy for over four decades.

FLC theory is based on the epigenetic principle of a schema of stepwise, successive change in development and stages in life cycle. The so-called normative family life cycle referred to by most FLC researchers (Carter & McGoldrick, 1980, 1989; Wynne, 1986) finds root in this paradigm: events of becoming (genesis) build upon (epi) immediately preceding events. Such a model argues that for each stage (Stage I, Beginning family; Stage II, Child-rearing family, etc.), families must master a set of tasks that are specific to that stage, enabling them to go on successfully to the tasks of the next stage and to prevent developmental arrest.

FLC and Normal Development

Late in his career Hill (1986) attempted to consider the far-reaching changes that were occurring in the 1970s in family life and forms, and a paper with Mattessich (1987) discussing single-parent families and life cycle comparisons with "modal two parent nuclear families" (p. 19) was published posthumously. Normative assumptions are apparent in the stated aim of the study: "Looked at against the schedule of phases characteristic of the modal careers of two parent nuclear families, it will be possible to ascertain how badly 'off schedule' the families which experienced female headedness are, and whether they managed to get back 'on schedule' later in the life span" (p. 24). Linguistic analysis reveals the implicit gender, class, and racial bias in descriptions of these families compared to normal families by the use of such phrases as "fractured homes" and "badly off schedule" (p. 24), and "experience deficit financing and life cycle squeeze" (p. 19), and if they remarry, are subject to "even more structural disorder" (p. 28).

Subsequent family researchers have based their descriptions of normative FLC in the tradition of Duvall and Hill as have most of researchers in family development (Ahrons, 1980; Aldous, 1990; Carter &

McGoldrick, 1980, 1989; Peck & Manocherian, 1989). McGoldrick and Carter (1989) acknowledged that the complex process of reorganization of the remarried family system merits adding another phase to the FLC. Similarly, while attempting to dissipate much of the negative terminology of the single-parent and divorced family, Ahrons (1980) uses the term "bi-nuclear" to describe the new stepfamily after divorce and remarriage. Such a discourse forces the family again into an amended version of the nuclear family and therefore, by implication, more normative. In both cases then, divorce is not considered a normative or expected part of the FLC experiences of over half of today's families. Instead, a divorce is viewed as a disruption of FLC that precipitates reorganization and stages of adjustment until the family reestablishes itself and again conforms to the normative FLC described by Hill and Rodgers (1964).

The fact that many families rarely follow FLC stage theory expectations in an orderly or proscribed way (Falicov, 1988) has led to refinement of the more static, linear notion of time in FLC and to the idea that continuous microtransitions in family development may occur under stress. An oscillation in development (e.g., non-age-appropriate behavior by a family member) signals a need to dampen or eliminate it, thus restoring normal development (Bruenlin et al., 1992; Hoffman, 1989; Moen & Howery, 1988). What is important to note here, however, is that the conceptual emphasis is on defining normal by age-appropriate behaviors. Thus, generation is privileged, and gender, class, and race, largely ignored in expectations about appropriate behavior in family development. When the symptomatic child learns to act her or his age, the problem is solved. In a Black single-parent family, however, a 14-year-old brother parenting a 5-year-old sibling could be an oscillation in development that is not age-appropriate, yet could well be functional and normative. In this framework, however, he would be paranormal.

Wijnberg and Holmes (1992) similarly conclude from their study of divorced female heads of families that traditional FLC conceptions do not explain the differences in the processes of adaptation for single-parent families. After becoming divorced, women did not simply resume so-called normative FLC stages and expectations postdivorce. Role theory was a more helpful conceptual model in explaining the changes and adaptations postdivorce. Women with a less traditional marital and work orientation were more likely to alter their role set to mother/breadwinner and to move more quickly into role reorganization and restructuring, whereas traditional women continued to view the mother role as primary and the single-parent family as temporary.

Feminist Critique of FLC

Feminist critique has not been systematically applied to FLC for its gender bias and inadequacies. Even Carter and McGoldrick, feminist family therapists, clung to this model in the revision of their book on family development. They incorporated divorce and separation as temporary disruptions in "normative family structure," but never challenged the whole FLC paradigm for its basic functional, Parsonian, and epigenetic bias (1989). Paradoxically, the authors did acknowledge that their FLC framework for middle-class families is "currently more or less mythological" (p. 12). While briefly mentioning how historical and cultural factors can impact how families go through and are changing FLC, the authors still reified FLC by delineating each of six stages, transitions, and marker events. By noting that divorce and alternative families have made the task of defining the "normal" family life cycle even more difficult, the authors still implicated and maintained normative, middle-class White family ideology by comparison. By saying "no family relationships except marriage are entered into by choice" (p. 7), families that are nonbiologically related are effectively disenfranchised conceptually and empirically in this genre of research. A feminist critique of FLC would thus include these questions:

Who Does It Include? FLC theory is implicitly based on a deficit comparison formulation. This is strikingly highlighted in one of the very few empirically based large-sample studies of FLC of nearly 2700 individuals in over 1000 families (Olson, 1988). The author noted "that the sample could not be considered as completely representative of all U.S. families" (p. 20), for all the families studied were intact and nearly all were middle-class and Lutheran church members. Minority groups were very under-represented. Yet, concluded the author, "this is, however, one of the largest data sets of intact families that has been collected in the U.S. and it provides a unique opportunity to study 'normal' families" (p. 20). The discourse here betrays the schema for normative definition, choice, and inclusion for study. The constructs of cohesion, adaptability, and communication used in the study could well have been fruitfully applied and analyzed with nonstandard North American (Smith, 1993) family forms, but was not. To the present time, the pioneers of the field continue to look to nuclear families for their insights and hypotheses. It is somewhat astounding, for example, that in Minuchin and Nichols' newest book, *Family Healing* (1993), all the case examples fit into a nuclear family form.

Who Does It Not Include? FLC is still treated and reified as a kind of timeless truth, a given that an individual progresses in an almost inevitable developmental sequence from mate selection as a young adult, to marriage and children, through child-bearing or adoption, to the mid-years of rearing children, and to the exiting of children who select mates for themselves and repeat the next generational cycle. There are two points to be made here. One, the almost total reliance on marriage and the presence of children to define family in FLC theory effectively eliminates the legitimacy of choosing not to be married and/or not to have children and still be a family. There is effectively no FLC theory for the adult family. The very names of the stages presuppose marriage, children, and an intact nuclear family or comparisons with such a family.

Secondly, the emphasis on the intact, married nuclear family in most of FLC theory and research minimizes and disenfranchises the experiences of individuals and families who do not conform to these values and stages. These may include poor families, many minority families, and lesbian families. Attempts to acknowledge the severe limitations of this codified framework have led FLC writers to include separate chapters on divorced families, low-income families, and poor Black families, as well as alcoholic families and lesbian couples (Carter & McGoldrick, 1980, 1989; Roth, 1989). Although well-meaning in the attempt at inclusion, the fundamental flaw of isolating these families through language, separate labeling, treatment, and lack of basic integration into the mainstream paradigm of FLC is not recognized. Such families are not only effectively marginalized, but deemed non-normative, if not deviant by comparison.

Slater and Mencher (1991), in their critique of FLC from a lesbian perspective, further document how the FLC promulgated by feminist family therapists is ultimately inapplicable for lesbians because of its conceptual assumptions: (a) its presumption of multigenerational context and support, (b) its reliance on social/legal rituals such as marriage, (c) its child-centered focus, and (d) its consideration of stressors as stage-specific. The fundamental stressor for lesbian families is society's view of the members as unconnected, as nonviable. This stressor is external and is not successfully negotiated by the completion of a developmental stage (e.g., the launching of children). Lesbian mothers may belong to several family systems among a created family of friends in the lesbian community (Roth & Murphy, 1986). Co-mothering, because of society's lack of recognition, is also subject to particular stresses that are different from the co-parenting stresses for a heterosexual couple (Lewin, 1984; Pollack & Vaughn, 1987). In sum, the lesbian bond in the lesbian family receives no social status and has no demarcated stages of development or temporal progress in FLC terms (Slater & Mencher, 1991).

Whose History? Period Effects   FLC does not integrate well the social, historical, and economic realities that have acted upon the family and normatively "constructed" it. The use of demographics (e.g., birth of first child) to establish the stage timetables can ignore how family events are shaped by historical and cultural context (Elder, 1985). Demographers have borrowed the FLC paradigm for aggregate measures to organize census data on American families (Norton, 1980). Critics note that such aggregate measures assume typicality in regard to how families are formed and the course of the life cycle. The use of average age of members in discerning the start and duration of events like the timing of children in census data also tends to obscure and wash out ethnic and class differences. Such structural factors, however, can be considered and incorporated into analysis in family development studies (Norton, 1983).

A life course perspective considers the links between individual life time, social family time, and historical time and is more compatible with a feminist perspective that considers the reality of these forces on family form and function. Thus, changes in family structure and events—length of lives and marriage, timing and number of children, longer workforce participation, shortening of childbearing, and amount of time spent living in families, serial marriages, and nonconjugal marriages—can be studied in historical context.

As Aldous (1990) noted, a life course framework not only forces researchers to consider how societal events have shaped families, but brings to focus outdated findings and the period effects that make even longitudinal studies of limited usefulness in exploring contemporary family phenomena. For example, the assumptions of FLC perspective that: (a) the family evolves universally through fairly predictable stages and that (b) "most of the human race shares similar biologic time clocks or societal expectations . . . and there is little choice about these changes," (Falicov, 1988, p. 13) are directly challenged by the increasing numbers of women that are choosing to delay childbirth until their 30s and 40s.

Generation Over Gender and Class   By privileging the category of generation, FLC theory has minimized the category of gender. Thus, the fact that women work and have always worked in domestic and public domains takes a secondary role to their reproductive and care-taking functions in the stages of FLC growth. As a sociologist, Hill (1970) brought the idea of role complementarity into FLC, which accepts conflict only when it serves the course of presumed positive developmental change. Such a view may be unsympathetic to women pressing for role change and freedom and initiating marital breakup and divorce. As has been previously discussed, the epigenetic discourse informing FLC lays heavy emphasis on the intact family, marriage, and children and on the value of stability over change. The basis of epigenesis is predictable repetition, whereas the essence of learning and evolution is openness and change (Bateson, 1978).

If, as Candib (1989) suggested, the ideological function of the FLC metaphor exists in maintaining the power and privilege of the dominant class, White middle-class men, it is not a surprise that FLC and stage classification has almost exclusively focused on intact families and that the field has not seen divorce as acceptable, conceptually or practically, for family success. Divorce as a means of resistance to traditional power structure within the family challenges the basic patriarchal structure of a society.

FLC also minimizes the effect of class. The assumed universal and timeless sequence of the FLC model implies economic assumptions that the nuclear family can make it on their own if they work hard enough, that competent families are self-sufficient, and that the family operates in a just economic system—a host of underlying presumptions that do not square with the realities for poor and/or minority families in this country nor for many other families. Social class delimits access to economic resources and may dramatically affect ability to marry, timing of parenthood, and correspondingly, entry into job market, delay of marriage and children, and longer educational preparation for the job market (Hurvitz & Straus, 1991). Traditional FLC stages do not fit these rich and important variations in family life across race and culture.

FLC frameworks, which rely so heavily on generation for categorical analysis of function, also fail when we consider how many grandparents have to become parents again for their grandchildren. Current estimates place more than 4 million children in the primary care of senior citizens (Crowley, 1993). This widespread social phenomenon of grandparents reparenting children separated by one and even two

generations hardly fits the FLC normative stage of postparenting in one's 40s and 50s and retirement in the next decades.

Perhaps Keith and Whitaker (1988) best expressed the limitations of FLC. In a deconstructivist stand on FLC, they warned against reifying FLC, but still saw it as a useful metaphor for research and practice with the important recognition that the construct does not become the explanation for understanding family patterns over the life course. Such a caveat has been largely ignored in the decades of research on family development. Similarly they noted that one must focus on a largely symbolic version of family in psychological and sociological analysis as "families are infinite" (p. 433).

POSTMODERN CONCEPTIONS OF FAMILY AND DIVORCE

If one concedes that FLC is largely mythological, what about the so-called family? Are current definitions of what constitutes family also largely mythological? In the final section of this paper an attempt will be made to explore the impact of postmodern thinking on the family and the implications for women, single parents, and divorce. Certainly family researchers, sociologists, and therapists have moved beyond functionist formulations of family definition. Murdock (1949) introduced the term "nuclear family" as a social group characterized by common residence, economic cooperation, and reproduction. It includes adults of both sexes, at least two of whom maintain a socially approved sexual relationship, and one or more children, one's own or adopted of the sexually co-habiting adults" (p. 1). Parsons (1951) and Winch (1963) extended the functionistic format, presenting the family as the basic social structure of society, stabilizer of adult development and socializer of children and mechanism for reproduction. The conjugal family of husband, wife, and children living together as overarching conceptual ideal has dominated family therapy literature (Levin, 1993) as well as sociological and social policy perspectives (Bould, 1993).

The long-standing assumptions in family sociology that families must live together and be related by blood, marriage, or adoption are reflected in the operational definition of the U.S. Bureau of the Census. Critics of this definition note how it informs not only family research, but also the debate over what constitutes a family; how it fails to describe the explosively changing demography of American families; and how it disenfranchises families of single parents, single elders, and lesbian/gay cohabitation (Bould, 1993). On the other hand, a very loose definition of family, based only on personal choice, bonds of affection, or felt commitment, renders the researcher empirically with a very difficult task. Offering one proposal, Bould (1993) suggested a "middle range definition" in which family is conceived within the context of care-taking functions, a behavioral approach that is consistent with census and modern state policy. It is, however, still within a functionalistic tradition, for it asks, who are the children and who are taking care of them: "family is the informal unit where those who cannot take care of themselves can find care in time of need" (p. 138). Such a definition does not depend on genetic link nor on legal ties. Similarly Scanzoni and Marsiglio (1993) offer a model of social exchange and reciprocity for analyzing families based on the assumption that families are essentially dyads operating within a social context.

Deconstructing the Family

A deconstructionist approach to family recognizes first that "family," like the concepts of role and gender, is socially constructed. Deconstruction of the concept of family thus involves analyzing how it has been defined and constructed within a social, political, historical, and cultural context (Collier, Rosaldo, & Yanaesako, 1982). While the past decades of family sociology have been dominated by discussion of family diversity and redefinition beyond Murdock (Dizard & Gadlin, 1990; Trost, 1993; Zinn & Eitzen, 1987), Bernardes (1993) represents the ultimate deconstructivist approach, declaring we should not define the family because it simply does not exist, that the very act of attempting to define it is normative.

The reality and standard, noted Trost (1993), is that "we seem to have reached a dynamic structure in some countries where children can assume or presume that they will cohabit, split up, cohabit again and then marry, divorce, recohabit, split up and recohabit, remarry, and so on" (p. 103).

Postmodern definitions of the family not only recognize the family pluralistic approach, but also that a fundamental cultural shift is taking place in Western society, namely that these increasingly complex and different family forms and experiences are not simply a temporary phase of disorganization. Rather a total reorganization of social life is *not* imminent, nowhere in sight, and unlikely to appear (Stacey, 1990). The postmodern family revolution is a revolution with continuous change, not a transition, not a stage, not a period of disequilibrium, but a kind of "revolving door with no exit" (Cheal, 1993). A postmodern analysis of family form then is quite different from a conceptualization of family form in FLC, where divorce, remarriage, and cohabition are considered temporary disruptions in the cycle which, when successfully transcended, lead to a resumption of the next stage in FLC. Even the suggestion that another stage be added to FLC to accommodate the unique form and timetable of the remarried family (McGoldrick & Carter, 1989) fails to appreciate the family as nonstatic, non-normative, and evolving.

As a social mediating form, family is replicated everywhere in the structures of society from factories and corporations to schools, churches, political parties, fraternities, clubs, governments, and armed forces. The so-called "universality of family life has led to model assumptions that the family has phylogenetic origins and is biologically established as a species specific characteristic" (Stevens, 1982, p. 81). From this perspective it is not surprising that we have such a hard time accepting the conclusion of the deconstructivists that the family does not exist or why traditional family ideology is so implicitly embedded in research on the family.

In this regard, Smith (1993) deftly analyzes the pervasive assumptions about normative family existence and expectations by the use of discursive analysis and considers the standard North-American family (SNAF) as a kind of ideological code. SNAF in this analysis becomes a discursive schema, a set of procedures for selecting the categories, the syntax, the very vocabulary in the writing of our texts, research, and literature and how we order and interpret it. Smith gives many examples of SNAF as ideological discourse. One example describes the sociobiological deployments of SNAF in one text that writes of family life in cities where "during the day the women and children remain in the residential area while the men forage for game or its symbolic equivalent in the form of money" (Wilson, 1978, p. 553). Another example cites SNAF-defined census codes of single-parent-headed families as female-headed that employ no notation for a family member who is not spouse, child, parent, or sibling of the head of household other than "boarder."

In a revealing and helpful personal analysis, Smith (1993) also details how she and her colleagues unwittingly incorporated SNAF-structuring discourse of family-equals-mother into their study of single parents' experiences in schools, both in the design of their inventory and the selection of their interview topics. In asking how mothers kept track of their children's homework and school activities, implicit assumptions were made about their employment, role conflict, and guilt that led to tentativeness in querying work questions if the mothers had young children at home. Moreover it became apparent that the mothers also operated within and expected this interpretative schema of the school-mother discourse. Thus, both the study questions and the responses operated within SNAF code.

New Action Social Theory

SNAF schema dominates "old action theory." Alexander (1988) describes old action theory as the structural functionism that anchored nuclear families into roles and implicitly made this family form normative. Even the label "alternative families" sets up a conceptual dichotomy of comparison reinforcing the functional belief that the old established pattern of family form is better for society, with alternatives more likely to lead to social disorder (Bernardes, 1993). Old action theory is about social reproduction and how individuals learn values and norms and reproduce what they learn. The central research question in old action theory becomes the consequences of those actions, that is, some deviation of (X) for (Y). Within the parameters of this paper, a good example would be studying the effect of divorce on children's or adults' adjustment.

In contrast, new action theory does not reify the family, but treats it as a social arrangement that is constructed (Scanzoni & Marsiglio, 1993).

The central research question is not the effect of a deviation (X) on a presumed norm (Y), but on the conditions, processes, and outcomes related to creativity exploration, and rebellion. Stacey's research (1990) embodies this approach, documenting how people are experimenting and struggling to create new, unheard of family arrangements to better their lives and to cope with the ever-changing conditions of their circumstances.

New action theory is valuable and fits with a feminist perspective on family that conceptualizes divorce not as deviance, but as resistance (Rice & Rice, 1986). A research agenda utilizing this perspective would analyze the ways in which dyads of people interact with each other and cope with political, social, and economic conditions to better their lives and the lives of their families. In new action theory, a woman's choice to depart from an abusive family or oppressive relationship through separation and divorce might be framed as adaptive. Similarly, the intergenerational parenting of Black families can be considered and studied as creative constructions of family that encompass a range of households sharing interdependent social exchanges.

New action theory applied to FLC research would not treat divorce as a temporary event producing temporary disequilibrium. It would not assume a return to reorganization of "normative" marital or family developmental tasks upon successful negotiation of the divorce transition (Hill, 1986). Nor would it presume divorce leads to reorganization before entering a new stage of development and order as, for example, remarriage and the "bi-nuclear" family (Ahrons, 1980; Carter & Mc-Goldrick, 1989). Such a paradigm derives from old action theory. In new action theory, divorce is a process that may not lead to predictable family forms, even in changed or disguised states.

What are the implications of these developments for feminists attempting to do family research?

1. The first consideration in critiquing old action theory and its methodology concerns the assumption and portrayal of a family as real, as existing, as being a relevant category of analysis. This assumption forms the foundation for family ideology embedded in research and policy on divorce and single parenting. The reification of the family has produced a family ideology "so deeply integrated into our consciousness that most people cannot support the idea that the family does not exist for any length of time" (Bernardes, 1993, p. 40). Rarely does academic analysis avoid the conceptual dilemma. A new program for family studies would ask what inspires the family choice and definition and would center on questions of discourse and interpretation, culture, and practice. Such an analysis would help ensure that we did not consciously or unconsciously impose socially approved values and definitions of family on our theory, methods, or analysis.

2. Both conceptions of family and of FLC are heavily value-laden and incorporate the cultural context and norms as well as the developmental preferences of the researcher and therapist that "mythologize" the family. Coontz (1992) in *The Way We Never Were* revealed, for example, that the assumption of stable, happy self-sufficient families in prior decades is largely a myth. Postwar, middle-class, happy families were based on enormous public investment of federal educational and housing benefits, as well as the domestic labor of nearly half of the African-American women who worked outside their homes and had small children. The task of demythologizing family life and recognizing the impact of gender, race, and class is, of course, made more formidable by the privacy and invisibility of much of family life.

3. Dismantling the cloak of impartial observer also makes us face the impact of our role in social policy formation for disenfranchised groups including single parents, divorced families, lesbian parents, and stepchildren. The formula use of census data to buttress family ideology is one obvious example of how this process works. Laws governing alimony, child support, custody, and minimum guaranteed income are all affected by prevalent family sociology and ideology. Welfare policy, currently hotly debated in the public and private sector, is inextricably linked to social constructions and definitions of approved family form. In this regard, there is a pressing need for feminist researchers across the social sciences and professions to place at center stage the needs of families rather than the problems of families. Such an approach recognizes the unity, vitality, and reality of family life that is different from what we once conceived.

4. For the first time in our society, marriage is freely terminable, divorce normative, and family form infinite. We lack the psychological theory to understand these phenomena, however, because child, marital, and family development theory and family sociology all developed within the context of the intact, nuclear family. Some new directions for such an analysis are suggested by recent feminist empiricism, epistemology, and critical pedagogy. As we know from a critical analysis of knowledge production, the position of the observer is key. Divorce, separation, father absence, etc., can be seen then in part as defined by the social meanings that we as psychologists, sociologists of the family, and marital and family therapists devise, perceive, and attribute to these phenomenon. It is convenient to treat marital status, marriage, birth of a child, and onset of divorce as clean demographic variables that can be quantified. Then we can also correlate other events like delinquency, school dropouts and achievement scores with those social markers as though they were the cause. The orthodox way to pursue knowledge is, of course, to look for explanatory measurable phenomena and a legal

divorce provides a convenient marker event for a linear analysis. A different analysis would proceed from a social production model. Such a conceptualization invites, creates, and shapes new life narrative paradigms for women, men, and their children and families that are multiple and nonlinear (Gergin, 1990).

Literary works in modern Western culture are generally linear, sequential, and directional—a progression toward an end point. For women, that end point is usually marriage and children. As Gergin points out, a narrative may be assessed as to its evaluative trajectory, progressive, stable, or regressive. After empty nest, the story for a woman may be seen as regressive, but after divorce, it is even worse. An alternative to this linear, one-dimensional, biological portrayal of the life course might instead view life cycle in terms of multiple and shifting attachments, separations, and reattachments with family, children, friends, spouses, ex-spouses, and significant others. Understanding the multiple meanings and layers of these attachments and separations within marital family life span development is a task that is just beginning for many feminist researchers.

5. By emphasizing the creative or productive element of individuals in families and the choices they make, the structures they conceive, and the resistance they effect, one can consider a "social-cultural production" whereby one looks to the lived culture of the individuals in families as they create it. Such an analysis goes beyond a social reproduction analysis of the family as a mirror reconstruction of the broader patriarchal society, to an analysis that incorporates the experiences and resistance of the participants. Divorce is then seen in yet another light. Divorce is frequently portrayed as a psychological phenomenon, an individual solution or a social problem, but far less frequently, from a feminist perspective as a political struggle to change the patriarchal relationships between men and women, in short, as resistance. Thus, women are not seen merely as passive agents of the discrimination and oppression they face, but as active decision-makers of their fates and lives.

6. The final challenge to be mentioned is to go beyond categorical theory that begins with women and men as uniform categories and instead to account for differences within gender. Theories based on socially defined gender roles such as husband and wife run into immediate problems when the presumed form of the family turns out not to be the form familiar to people from different backgrounds, that is, binuclear, non-nuclear, step, remarried, nonheterosexual. Going beyond categorical theory to practice theory (Holland & Eisenhart, 1990) and examining internal differences and conflicts of interest within families is an approach that may better account for the realities of the rich and variant forms of actual family structure today.

Similarly, attitudes toward divorce and the availability of divorce options as resistance may vary significantly among women, depending on the interaction between gender, generation, and cultural, religious, and ethnic identity. This complex task has barely begun, but as the challenge is met, we will likely redefine what marriage and the family mean in the 21st century.

REFERENCES

Ahrons, C. (1980). Redefining the divorced family: A conceptual framework. *Social Work, 25,* 437–441.

Aldous, J. (1990). Family development and the life course: Two perspectives on family change. *Journal of Marriage and the Family, 52,* 571–583.

Alexander, J. C. (1988). The new theoretical movement. In N. J. Smelser (Ed.), *Handbook of sociology* (pp. 77–102). Newbury Park, CA: Sage.

Amato, P. R. (1991). The "child of divorce" as a person prototype: Bias in the recall of information about children in divorced families. *Journal of Marriage and the Family, 53,* 59–69.

Amato, P. R., & Booth, A. (1991). The consequences of divorce for attitudes toward divorce and gender roles. *Journal of Family Issues, 12,* 306–322.

Amato, P. A., & Keith, B. (1991a). Parental divorce and adult well-being: A meta-analysis. *Journal of Marriage and the Family, 53,* 43–58.

Amato, P. A., & Keith, B. (1991b). Parental divorce and child well-being: A meta-analysis. *Psychological Bulletin, 110,* 26–46.

Ambrose, P., Harper, J., & Pemberton, R. (1993). *Surviving divorce: Men beyond marriage.* Totowa, NY: Rowman & Allanheld.

Atwood, J. D. (1993, Fall). The competent divorce. *The Family Psychologist,* 15–19.

Ault-Riche, M. (1986). A feminist critique of five schools of family therapy. In M. Ault-Riche (Ed.), *Women and family therapy* (pp. 1–15). Rockville, MD: Aspen.

Avis, T. (1985). The politics of functional family therapy: A feminist critique. *Journal of Marital and Family Therapy, 11,* 127–138.

Baca Zinn, M. (1990). Family, feminism and race in America. *Gender and Society, 4,* 68–82.

Bagarozzi, D., & Giddings, C. (1983). Conjugal violence: A critical review of current research and clinical practices. *American Journal of Family Therapy, 11,* 3–15.

Bateson, G. (1978). *Mind and nature.* New York: Dutton.

Bequaert, L. (1976). *Single women: Alone and together.* Boston: Beacon Press.

Bernardes, J. (1993). Responsibilities in studying postmodern families. *Journal of Family Issues, 14,* 35–49.

Bianchi, S. (1991). Family disruption and economic hardship: Survey of income and program participation. U.S. Bureau of the Census, Series P-70, no. 23.

Bograd, M. (1986). A feminist examination of family systems models of violence against women in the family. In M. Ault-Riche (Ed.), *Women and family therapy* (pp. 34–49). Rockville, MD: Aspen.

Boss, P., & Thorne, B. (1989). Family sociology and family therapy: A feminist linkage. In M. McGoldrick, C. M. Anderson, & F. Walsh (Eds.), *Women in families: A framework for family therapy* (pp. 78–96). New York: Norton.

Bould, S. (1993). Familial caretaking: A middle-range definition of family in the context of social policy. *Journal of Family Issues, 14,* 133–151.

Breunlin, D. C., Schwartz, R. C., & Mac Kune-Karrer, B. (1992). *Meta-frameworks: Transcending the models of family therapy.* San Francisco: Jossey-Bass.

Bursik, K. (1991). Correlates of women's adjustment during the separation and divorce process. *Journal of Divorce and Remarriage, 14,* 137–162.

Candib, L. M. (1989). Point and counterpoint. Family life cycle: A feminist critique. *Family Systems Medicine, 7,* 473–487.

Carter, E. A., & McGoldrick, M. (Eds.). (1980). *The family life cycle: A framework for family therapy.* New York: Gardner.

Carter, E. A., & McGoldrick, M. (Eds.). (1989). *The changing family life cycle: A framework for family therapy.* Boston: Allyn and Bacon.

Cashion, B. G. (1982). Female-headed families: Effects on children and clinical implications. *Journal of Marital & Family Therapy, 8,* 77–85.

Catton, W. R. (1988). Family "divorce heritage" and its intergenerational transmission: Toward a system-level perspective. *Sociological Perspectives, 31,* 398–419.

Cheal, D. (1993). Unity and difference in post modern families. *Journal of Family Issues, 14,* 5–19.

Collier, J., Rosaldo, M. Z., & Yanaesako, S. (1982). Is there a family? In B. Thorne & M. Yalom (Eds.), *Rethinking the family* (pp. 25–39). New York: Longman.

Coontz, S. (1992). *The way we never were: American families and the nostalgia trap.* New York: Basic Books.

Crowley, S. L. (1993). Grandparents to the rescue. *National Retired Teachers Association Bulletin, 34*(1), 16–17.

Dart, B. (1991, January 17). Senate given bleak view of U.S. families. Washington, DC: Cox News Service.

Demos, J. (1986). *Past, present, and personal: The family and the life course in American history.* New York: Oxford University Press.

Diedrick, P. (1991). Gender differences in divorce adjustment. *Journal of Divorce & Remarriage, 14,* 33–45.

Dizard, J. E., & Gadlin, H. (1990). *The minimal family.* Amherst: The University of Massachusetts Press.

Duncan, G. J., & Hoffman, S. D. (1985). A reconsideration of the economic consequences of marital dissolution. *Demography, 22,* 485–497.

Duncan, G. J., & Morgan, J. N. (Eds.). (1976). *Five thousand American families: Patterns of economic progress.* Ann Arbor, MI: Institute for Social Research.

Duvall, E. M. (1957 and revised editions, 1962, 1967, 1971, 1977). *Family development.* Philadelphia: Lippincott.

Elder, G. H., Jr. (1985). *Life course dynamics: Trajectories and transitions, 1968–1980.* Ithaca: Cornell University Press.

Falicov, C. J. (1988). Family sociology and family therapy contributions to family development framework: A comparative analysis and thoughts on future trends. In C. J. Falicov (Ed.), *Family transitions, continuity, and change over the life cycle* (pp. 3–53). New York: Guilford.

Faludi, S. (1991). *Backlash, the undeclared war against women.* New York: Crown.

Ferree, M. M. (1990). Beyond separate spheres: Feminism and family research. *Journal of Marriage and the Family, 52,* 866–884.

Forehand, R., Thomas, N., Brody, G., & Fauber, R. (1990). Role of maternal functioning and parental skills in adolescent functioning following parental divorce. *Journal of Abnormal Psychology, 99,* 278–283.

Gergin, M. (1990). Finished at 40: Women's development within the patriarchy. *Psychology of Women Quarterly, 14,* 471–493.

Glick, P. C. (1984). Marriage, divorce and living arrangements. *Journal of Social Issues, 5,* 7–26.

Goldner, V. (1985). Feminism and family therapy. *Family Process, 24,* 31–47.

Goldner, V. (1989). Generation and gender: Normative and covert hierarchies. In M. McGoldrick, C. M. Anderson, & F. Walsh (Eds.), *Women in families: A framework for family therapy* (pp. 42–60). New York: Norton.

Gordon, D., Burge, D., Hammen, C., Adrian, C., Jaenicke, C., & Hiroto, D. (1989). Observations of interaction of depressed women with their children. *American Journal of Psychiatry, 146,* 50–55.

Greenstein, T. N. (1990). Marital disruption and the employment of married women. *Journal of Marriage and the Family, 52,* 657–676.

Hare-Mustin, R. (1978). A feminist approach to family therapy. *Family Process, 17,* 181–193.

Hare-Mustin, R. (1983). Psychology: A feminist perspective on family therapy. In E. Haber (Ed.), *The Women's Annual: 1982–83* (pp. 177–204). Boston: G. K. Hall.

Hare-Mustin, R. (1986). The problem of gender in family therapy. *Family Process, 26,* 15–27.

Haskins, R., Richey, T., & Wicker, F. (1987). Paying and visiting: Child support enforcement and fathering from afar. Unpublished manuscript.

Hicks, S., & Anderson, C. M. (1989). Women on their own. In M. McGoldrick, C. M. Anderson, & F. Walsh (Eds.), *Women in families: A framework for family therapy* (pp. 308–335). New York: Norton.

Hill, R. (1970). *Family development in three generations.* Cambridge, MA: Schenkman.

Hill, R. (1986). Life cycle stages for types of single parent families: Of family development theory. *Family Relations, 35,* 19–29.

Hill, R., & Rogers, R. (1964). The developmental approach. In H. Christensen (Ed.), *Handbook of marriage and the family* (pp. 171–172). Chicago: Rand-McNally.

Hines, P. M. (1989). The family life cycle of poor black families. In E. A. Carter & M. McGoldrick (Eds.), *The changing family life cycle: A framework for family therapy* (pp. 513–544). Boston: Allyn & Bacon.

Hoffman, L. (1989). The family life cycle and discontinuous change. In E. A. Carter & M. McGoldrick (Eds.), *The changing family life cycle: A framework for family therapy* (pp. 91–105). Boston: Allyn & Bacon.

Hoffman, S. D. (1977). Marital instability and the economic status of women. *Demography, 14,* 67–76.

Holland, D. C., & Eisenhart, M. A. (1990). *Educated in romance: Women, achievement, and college culture.* Chicago: University of Chicago Press.

Holloway, S. C., & Machida, S. (1991). Child-rearing strategies of divorced mothers: Relationship to coping strategies and social support. *Journal of Divorce and Remarriage, 14,* 179–199.

Hughes, R., Good, E. S., & Candell, K. (1993). A longitudinal study of the effects of social support on the psychological adjustment of divorced mothers. *Journal of Divorce and Remarriage, 19,* 37–56.

Hurvitz, N., & Straus, R. A. (1991). *Marriage and family therapy: A sociocognitive approach.* New York: Haworth Press.

Imber-Black, E. (1986). Women, families and larger systems. In M. Ault-Riche (Ed.), *Women and family therapy* (pp. 25–33). Rockville, MD: Aspen.

Jewell, K. S. (1988). *Survival of the black family: The institutional impact of U.S. social policy.* New York: Praeger.

Keith, D., & Whitaker, C. (1988). The presence of the past: Continuity and change in the symbolic structure of families. In C. J. Falicov (Ed.), *Family transitions, continuity, and change over the life cycle* (pp. 431–447). New York: Guilford.

Knaub, P. K. (1989). The stepfamily. In M. Textor (Ed.), *The divorce and divorce therapy handbook* (pp. 333–367). London: Jason Aaronson.

Levin, I. (1993). Family as mapped realities. *Journal of Family Issues, 14,* 82–91.

Lewin, E. (1984). Lesbianism and motherhood: Implications for child custody. In T. Darty & S. Potter (Eds.), *Women-identified women* (pp. 163–183). Palo Alto, CA: Mayfield.

Lindblad-Goldberg, M., & Dukes, J. L. (1985). Social support in black, low-income, single parent families. *American Journal of Orthopsychiatry, 55,* 42–58.

Lowery, C. R., & Settle, S. A. (1985). Effects of divorce on children: Differential impact of custody and visitation patterns. *Family Relations, 34,* 455–463.

Martin, T. C., & Bumpass, L. L. (1989). Recent trends in marital disruption. *Demography, 26,* 37–51.

Mattessich, P., & Hill, R. (1987). Life-cycle and family development. In M. B. Sussman & S. K. Steinmetz (Eds.), *Handbook of marriage and the family* (pp. 437–469). New York: Plenum Press.

McGoldrick, M., Anderson, C. M., & Walsh, F. (Eds.). (1989). *Women in families: A framework for family therapy.* New York: Norton.

McGoldrick, M., & Carter, E. A. (1989). Forming a remarried family. In E. A. Carter & M. McGoldrick (Eds.), *The changing family life cycle: A framework for family therapy* (pp. 399–429). Boston: Allyn & Bacon.

McGoldrick, M., Pearce, J. K., & Giordano, J. (Eds.). (1982). *Ethnicity and family therapy.* New York: Guilford.

Minuchin, S., & Nichols, M. P. (1993). *Family healing: Tales of hope and renewal from family therapy.* New York: Free Press.

Moen, P., & Howery, C. B. (1988). The significance of time in the study of families under stress. In D. M. Klein & J. Aldous (Eds.), *Social stress and family development* (pp. 131–156). New York: Guilford.

Moore, H. L. (1988). *Feminism and anthropology.* Minneapolis: University of Minnesota Press.

Murdock, G. P. (1949). *Social structure.* New York: Free Press.

National Center for Health Statistics. (1989). Incidence of divorce: 1975–1988. Washington, DC: U.S. Government Printing Office.

Norton, A. J. (1980). The influence of divorce on traditional life-cycle measures. *Journal of Marriage and the Family, 42,* 63–69.

Norton, A. J. (1983). Family life cycle: 1980. *Journal of Marriage and the Family, 45,* 267–277.

Norton, A. J., & Glick, P. C. (1986). One parent families: A social and economic profile. *Family Relations, 35,* 9–17.

Olson, D. H. (1988). Family types, family stress, and family satisfaction: A family development perspective. In C. J. Falicov (Ed.), *Family transitions, continuity, and change over the life cycles* (pp. 55–79). New York: Guilford.

Parsons, T. (1951). *The social system.* New York: Free Press.

Parsons, T., & Bales, R. F. (1955). *Family socialization, and interaction process.* New York: Free Press.

Peck, J. S., & Manocherian, J. R. (1989). Divorce in the changing family life cycle. In E. A. Carter & M. McGoldrick (Eds.), *The changing family life cycle: A framework for family therapy* (pp. 335–369). Boston: Allyn & Bacon.

Phares, V., & Compas, B. E. (1992). The role of fathers in child and adolescent psychopathology: Make room for Daddy. *Psychological Bulletin, 111,* 387–412.

Pollack, S., & Vaughn, J. (1987). *Politics of the heart: A lesbian parenting anthology.* Ithaca: Firebrand Books.

Rice, J. K., & Rice, D. G. (1986). *Living through divorce: A developmental approach to divorce therapy.* New York: Guilford.

Rodgers-Rose, L. (Ed.). (1980). *The black woman.* New York: Sage.

Roth, S. (1989). Psychotherapy with lesbian couples: Individual issues, female socialization and the social context. In M. McGoldrick, C. M. Anderson, & E. Walsh (Eds.), *Women in families: A framework for family therapy* (pp. 297–307). New York: Norton.

Roth, S., & Murphy, B. C. (1986). Therapeutic work with lesbian clients: A systemic therapy view. In M. Ault-Riche (Ed.), *Women and family therapy* (pp. 78–89). Rockville, MD: Aspen.

Scanzoni, J., & Marsiglio, W. (1993). New action theory and contemporary families. *Journal of Family Issues, 14,* 105–132.

Slater, S., & Mencher, J. (1991). The lesbian family life cycle: A contextual approach. *American Journal of Orthopsychiatry, 61,* 372–382.

Smart, C. (1984). *The ties that bind: Law, marriage and the reproduction of patriarchal relations,* London: Routledge & Kegan Paul.

Smith, D. E. (1993). The standard North American family: SNAF as an ideological code. *Journal of Family Issues, 14,* 50–65.

Sobel, S. B., & Russo, N. F. (1981). Sex roles, equality, and mental health. *Professional Psychology, 12,* 1–5.

Stacey, J. (1990). *Brave new families.* New York: Basic Books.

Staples, R. (1985). Changes in black family structures: The conflict between family ideology and structural conditions. *Journal of Marriage and the Family, 47,* 1005–1013.

Stevens, A. (1982). *Archetype: A natural history of the self.* London: Routledge & Kegan Paul.

Taggart, M. (1985). The feminist critique in epistemological perspective: Questions of context in family therapy. *Journal of Marital & Family Therapy, 11,* 113–126.

Trost, J. (1993). Family from a dyadic perspective. *Journal of Family Issues, 14,* 92–104.

U.S. Bureau of the Census. (1987). *Current population reports,* P-60, No. 157. Washington, DC: U.S. Government Printing Office.

Vincent, J. P., Harris, G. E., & Plog, A. (1991). Divorce and children's adjustment: The role of interparental conflict, maternal affect and parenting. In J. P. Vincent (Ed.), *Advances in family intervention, assessment and theory* (pp. 47–67). London: Jessica Kingsley.

Wallerstein, J. S., & Blakeslee, S. (1989). *Second chances: Men, women and children a decade after divorce.* New York: Ticknor& Fields.

Wallerstein, J. S., & Kelly, J. B. (1980). *Surviving the breakup.* New York: Basic Books.

Walters, M., Carter, E., Papp, P., & Silverstein, O. (1988). *The invisible web: Gender patterns in family relationships.* New York: Guilford.

Warren, N. J., & Konanc, J. T. (1989). Single parent families. In M. Textor (Ed.), *The divorce and divorce therapy handbook* (pp. 303–331). London: Jason Aaronson.

Weitzman, L. (1985). *The divorce revolution: The unexpected social and economic consequences for women and children in America.* New York: Free Press.

Whitehead, B. D. (1993, April). Dan Quayle was right. *Atlantic Monthly, 271*(4), 47–84.

Wijnberg, M. H., & Holmes, T. (1992, March). Adaptation to divorce: The impact of role orientation of family life-cycle perspectives. *The Journal of Contemporary Human Services,* 159–167.

Wilson, E. O. (1978). *On human nature.* Cambridge, MA: Harvard University Press.

Winch, R. F. (1963). *The modern family.* New York: Holt, Rinehart & Winston.

Wynne, L. C. (1986). The epigenesis of relational systems: A model for understanding family development. *Family Process, 23,* 297–318.

Zinn, M. B., & Eitzen, D. S. (1987). *Diversity in families.* New York: Harper & Row.

What Do Fathers Provide?
Reconsidering the Economic and Nurturant Dimensions of Men as Parents

THEODORE F. COHEN

For much of the 20th century, Americans have associated fathers with the act of working and the responsibility of "providing" for their families. This image of fathers arises more from general assumptions about men and the dominant ideologies of gender than from any empirical evidence. As many scholars have noted, men were long typecast in "instrumental," economically derived positions whereby masculinity, male identity, and male role performance all center around work (Brannon, 1976; Cohen, 1987, 1988; Pleck, 1979, 1983). We have "measured masculinity by the size of the paycheck" (Gould, 1976), assumed that men identified themselves with and derived their self-esteem from performance at work (Goetting, 1982; Rubin, 1979), and acted as if the most meaningful male activity took place outside of the family in pursuit of a wage (Parsons, 1942; Zelditch, 1974). Even men's familial roles and responsibilities were seen as discharged outside and away from the family itself as "good providers" or in the "Husband-Economic-Provider-Role" (Bernard, 1983; Grönseth, 1972; Liebow, 1967; Rubin, 1976). Working from such traditional assumptions, researchers studied men's lives almost exclusively in their more public dimensions, as if men's familial experiences had no bearing on their daily realities. Likewise, social scientists studying families have paid little attention to fathers and husbands. Studies of marriage or parenthood relied, instead, on data drawn primarily from wives and mothers (e.g., Blood & Wolfe, 1960; Miller & Swanson, 1958; Safilios-Rothschild, 1969).

A corollary of this oversight was to narrowly portray women's lives as centered primarily on family and maternal responsibilities. This treatment of women is well critiqued by Ann Oakley (1974) in the following excerpt from *The Sociology of Housework:* "By far the largest segment of sociological literature concerning women is focused on their roles as wives, mothers and housewives. . . . Possibly the family and marriage are areas in which [women's] sociological visibility exceeds social presence" (pp. 17–18).

With such "core assumptions" guiding our thinking about gender and family, the specific formulations of parental roles followed accordingly. "Parenting" was culturally perceived as "mothering," in that it implied nurturance, an activity seen as natural to women but foreign to men (Cancian, 1985). Fathers' connections to their children were portrayed as chiefly financial; good fathers were "good providers" and good providers made good fathers (Bernard, 1983). Numerous cultural and scientific implications followed these emphases. For example, maternal employment was perceived as a potentially serious social problem in that it implied the absence of mothers and a lack of nurturing. Because fathers were inexorably associated with providing, their job-induced absence was normal and their sustained, full-time presence (via unemployment, disability, "role reversals") assumed to be problematic. As Joseph Pleck noted, the dominant, though not exclusive, cultural image of 20th-century fathers has been the "father-breadwinner model" (Pleck, 1987), wherein fathers were the ultimate sources of both morality and discipline, but physically, socially, and emotionally removed from the family by their concentration on work.

Given the overwhelming acceptance of the male economic provider role as the model of what men *ought* to be like, it is difficult to know whether there were many men whose parental roles did not conform to the dominant model. Cultural messages about men's roles in the family discouraged much open deviation, and researchers, guided by earlier ideologies of gender, asked questions that assumed compliance with a traditional division of responsibilities (Pleck, 1979). Because men's daily lives were consumed largely at work, their actions seemed to affirm both the earlier traditional functionalist model and the later critical feminist perspectives of men and families. As a result, many questions about the depth and substance of men's parental attachments went unasked.

Recent years have seen an explosion in research on fathering (Bronstein & Cowan, 1988; R. LaRossa, 1988; Lewis & O'Brien, 1987; McKee & O'Brien, 1982). There are indicators of greater male investments and involvements in parenting and child care. Culturally, we herald the emergence of the "new father," noting an increase in both male involvement in parenting and the meaning of fatherhood to men. Ambiguities remain, however. Even late-20th-century "alternative" and more intimately involved styles of fathering have failed to completely replace the father-breadwinner model or challenge its position of cultural dominance (Pleck, 1987). Further, in pointing to the increasing emphasis on nurturant dimensions of fatherhood, Ralph LaRossa cautions that such expectations may say more about changes in motherhood than about shifts in what is truly desired of and by fathers (R. LaRossa, 1988). Thompson and Walker (1989) support this point in their review of literature on gender in families, asserting "Virtually all men believe being a good father means first and foremost being a good provider" (p. 861). Thus, despite much recent attention to men's experience of fathering, it is unclear what contemporary U.S. fathers do or think they should do beyond providing.

It is also uncertain what fathering does to men. If being a father was reducible to being a stable breadwinner, and being an adult male, married or single, meant likewise, the discontinuity between being childless and being a father should not be great, given that men's role repertoire supposedly remained centered around working. If, however, men are adopting broader conceptualizations of fatherhood, they will experience more discontinuity between their childless and parental statuses.

In the following pages I use data drawn from an exploratory study of men's transitions to marriage and fatherhood and their enactments of their marital, parental, and work roles (Cohen, 1986, 1987) to reveal the inadequacy of the traditional father-as-provider ideology. In addition to the "breadwinning" component, I will assess other, more nurturant components of men's paternal role definitions and performances. I will show that neither the impact of fatherhood on my informants nor the way they perceived and performed their roles as fathers can be fully understood by focusing primarily on their activities as economic providers.

SAMPLING AND DATA COLLECTION

The data for this analysis come from semistructured interviews with a nonprobability sample of 30 Boston-area new husbands and fathers. Interviews explained informants' experiences "becoming and being" husbands and fathers, that is, their transitions to marriage and fatherhood and their conceptualizations of and involvements in work, marital, and parental roles. Almost half of the informants were married men without children (14 men), and the rest were married fathers of young children. Because I was interested in both "becoming" and "being" husbands and fathers, I sought informants who were able to speak about their life before marriage or fatherhood and had had time enough to assume their new family roles and speak with some depth about how their life had changed as a result of these role transitions. I therefore restricted the sample to men who were relatively new to each status. The 14 childless men had been married 1 to 3 years (average of 1.9 years); the "new fathers" were married men who had been fathers for 5 years or less (average was 2.1 years of fatherhood and the average length of marriage for fathers was 4.6 years). Of the 14 childless husbands, 4 were "pregnant fathers." They were particularly useful sources of information about the transition to parenthood and the shifts in one's perceptions and expectations of fatherhood as the event grows both nearer and more real.

Because I was interested both in the transitions between statuses and in the way informants experience marriage and fatherhood, I chose to restrict the sample so that most men reported on only one transition to marriage and/or one experience of fatherhood. Ninety percent of the sample were men in first marriages; likewise, 13 of the 16 fathers were first-time parents. These sampling requirements yielded a sample of relatively young men (average age was 29; 26.6 for new husbands, 31.5 for new fathers).

I used a combination of nonprobability sampling strategies to generate my sample of informants. Twelve men were obtained via a variety of agencies and organizations, including church or medical personnel in a working-class community outside of Boston. This group "snowballed," yielding eight more men. The remaining 10 were referred by my own colleagues, friends, or neighbors. To increase the range of variation in my sample, I accepted no more than two referrals from any informant.

I deliberately sought men of varying socioeconomic backgrounds. Informants' occupations ranged from laborer (janitor, warehouseman), through skilled laborer (tool and die maker, mechanic), low-level white-collar worker (computer operator, sales representative) to administrator and professional (architect, college professor). Half of the employed informants worked in traditional blue-collar or low-level white-collar occupations. Four men were not employed; three were full-time students, and one was a househusband. More than two thirds of the sample were husbands of employed women. Of the nine wives who were not employed outside the home, eight were "new mothers" who had recently stopped working upon the birth of their child. Informants' educational backgrounds were more "middle class." Sixty percent of the men, including some of those in blue-collar occupations, had college degrees (nine men) or graduate education (nine men).

Using an interview schedule of more than 100 items, I interviewed each informant once about his experiences becoming and being a husband and/or father as well as about the effects of work on his family life. Men were interviewed alone, in settings convenient to them, for an average of just under 2 hours. I tape-recorded and later transcribed each interview. The transcripts were then analyzed thematically, using the existing literature on men, women, and families as initial sources of themes (Oakley, 1980; R. LaRossa & M. LaRossa, 1981; Rubin, 1976). Other themes emerged from the interview material itself through the "constant comparative method" of qualitative analysis (Glaser & Strauss, 1976). Given the size and nature of this nonprobability sample, the findings presented are offered not for generalization to the population of contemporary U.S. fathers, but rather as suggestions for future research. The findings do, however, indicate the inadequacy of traditional assumptions about the content and meaning of fatherhood. If, as I will show, my informants' experiences extended far beyond their roles as economic providers, then at least some men's experiences as fathers are overlooked or misrepresented by those traditional assumptions.

FINDINGS AND DISCUSSION

Becoming a Father

> I think everything in a personal relationship a baby changes. . . . It's just fantastic . . . it knocked me for a loop. Something creeps into your life and then all of a sudden it dominates your life. It changes your relationship to everybody and everything, and you question every value you ever had. . . . And you say to yourself, "This is a miracle . . ."
>
> (33-year-old municipal administrator)

Contrary to what traditional thinking about fatherhood would lead one to expect, becoming fathers had a dramatic impact on informants' lives, extending far beyond the economic implications of this transition. Repeatedly, in interviews with both fathers and fathers-to-be, I was struck by moving accounts of the consequences of becoming a father. Although all the men did not react in the same way, they did find themselves affected in unexpected ways. Because little of the assessed impact was economic, the most important aspects of entering fatherhood may be lost if one assumes that fathering is nearly synonymous with breadwinning.

To examine men's reactions to fatherhood, I began with their reactions to pregnancy and childbirth, the point at which men become aware of the impending transition. During pregnancy, men begin to anticipate fatherhood and attempt to ready themselves for whatever conceptions of fatherhood they possess.

Few men recalled being surprised by the news that they were to become fathers, and few remembered having any opposition to the idea. When the pregnancy was confirmed, most men recalled reacting in very positive ways, with feelings ranging from "happy" to "absolutely fantastic." Those who acknowledged any ambivalence seemed to be weighing their pleasure against their sense of change and responsibility. For example, this comment came from a 28-year-old sales representative who was an expectant father at the time of the interview:

I was excited. . . . [It] was a very, very exciting time but a nervous time too—no turning back now. . . . It was very early; she was only 2 or 3 weeks pregnant when we found out. It was scary. I'm very excited, okay? But I'm also scared at the same time 'cause it's gonna change things.

Pregnancy quickly triggered feelings and concerns that informants had never before felt. One can see this in their answers to both a general question about their feelings and a series of specific probes into selected areas about which they might have worried during pregnancy. Included among my probes were questions about the pregnancy, the birth process, economic matters, and changes that were expected to accompany parenthood. The two most anxiety-provoking areas for men were the baby's health and the wife's health and safety. Because men have little control over either of these matters, a sense of powerlessness heightened their concern. Thirteen of the 20 fathers and expectant fathers found themselves thinking and worrying about possible birth defects or the pregnancy and birth processes. As a 29-year-old laborer said:

It was all needless worrying, I guess. I was really worried about taking her to the hospital. . . . I though for sure that she would have the baby . . . in traffic, in the car. . . . And of course you do worry about how the baby is gonna come out. You hope the baby is gonna be healthy. I worried about that—If he wasn't, was I gonna be able to handle that?

Twelve men described worrying specifically about their wife's health and safety. For some this worry included a concern for the fetus, although for most the preoccupation was solely with their wife. For example, a 37-year-old architect said:

I worried about my wife, that was all. She had a real concern for the health of the child. I had listened to the child late at night and had seen the ultrasound. I tried, maybe I was blocking that [fear] out. . . . I was just hoping that she wouldn't be knocked around too much.

As a result of these two sets of concerns, many found themselves taking more precautions, even imposing limitations on their wife in an effort to exert some control over the uncontrollable. Occasionally wives experienced these preventive measures as overprotectiveness, and at least one man recalled being unaware of how differently he was treating his wife until she pointed it out to him. Most, however, simply went out of their way to be more conscientious.

The next two most common concerns were also closely interrelated. Would they be good fathers and how would fatherhood affect their life? In both cases, the concerns were exacerbated by men's lack of knowledge. Nine of the 20 fathers and expectant fathers had anxieties about their abilities to be "good enough" fathers as well as doubts about knowing how to father. As they voiced such concerns, it was clear that men's perceptions of fathering extended well beyond providing. The following comments illustrate these worries:

I worry about being a father 'cause I don't know what it will be like. I know how it was for my father to be a father, I know he was always working his ass off, but I don't know how I'm gonna be with my kids.

> (26-year-old material control manager)

Oh yeah, I definitely worried about being a father. . . . I even kept a journal, trying to figure that out. My worries . . . came down to: "What is it that will qualify me to be a father? What am I going to be able to give to him?"

> (30-year-old truck driver)

In a similar vein, eight men talked about not knowing how the presence of a child and the demands of child care might affect their life in general or their relationships with their wife.

> I knew there would be this little person that I didn't know anything about . . . exactly what he or she was going to be like. It was unclear to me. Certainly it was going to take up a lot of time. . . . I worried that my [wife] and I would have a lot less time together.

> (36-year-old househusband)

Most surprising was the relatively low level of anxiety expressed about the economic responsibilities associated with being fathers. Only six men recalled thinking about the economic impact of parenthood. They reported worrying about increased expenses associated with children and reduced income due to wives stopping work. Expecting that the "burden will fall more heavily" onto their shoulders led them to worry about having their "financial end together." One man expressed this in the following terms:

> Most of our worries were out of our financial condition. She made significantly more money than I did and it was obvious that she wasn't going to be working for a while. . . . She felt she wanted to stay home with the baby and I felt guilty about not being able to afford her that opportunity.

> (31-year-old retail manager)

There are a number of explanations for why more men didn't express greater concern with economic aspects of the transition to fatherhood. Although one might assume that the financial component of the fa-

ther role was less salient to these men than other components, one should not conclude that it was unimportant. Given that nearly all of the fathers and expectant fathers were stably employed prior to the birth of their children, it is possible that they worried more about those responsibilities that were unknown to them. Work was something they were used to, wage earning something they were already doing. Many may have simply expected to keep doing what they were doing at work while feeling less confident about, and therefore more preoccupied with, those more immediate changes that fatherhood would trigger.

It is also possible that more attention was not paid to the economic dimensions of fathering because of men's perceptions that they would be able to absorb whatever additional costs might follow. Although this was not a particularly affluent sample, the fact that they were dual-earner couples until the birth of the child may have delayed financial concerns. Three fathers, who admitted that they hadn't worried enough about money, support this interpretation. For example:

> I thought about the future but I didn't think about the real important things. I didn't worry about money . . . I still hadn't thought about that. . . . She worked until just about when he was born . . . [and] I didn't think about what I was gonna be doing about money as far as saving for a new apartment or a house or for [son's] education since she wasn't gonna be working anymore. I never thought about saving, just went along. . . . I bought little gifts for her [and] we did a lot of the same things we had before.

> (29-year-old laborer)

Even men who claimed not to make "great money" thought that they made enough to afford the expenses that they would incur. As a 33-year-old municipal administrator said:

> I don't think I anticipated them [expenses] correctly. Babies are a very expensive commodity today . . . just his daily upkeep and his care, doctor's bills and stuff like that. . . . It's just unbelievable.

Whatever the reasons behind it, the deemphasis on issues of providing is instructive. I did not hear the deep or frequent expression of concern about providing that would be expected if men did indeed perceive fathering as breadwinning.

The Impact of Fatherhood

Going far beyond increased breadwinning responsibilities, men saw changes in the ways in which they perceived themselves, the relationships they maintained with their wife and others, and the kinds and meaning of activities that they engaged in:

> It's almost like I've been completed in a way . . . like a little candle has been lit inside of me. It's there all the time, you can feel its warmth, you can use it for light if you want. . . . It's almost like I have a focus in life. Before, everything I did really didn't matter much, but now everything I do has bearing for the future.
>
> (25-year-old food handler)

Nicely suggested in the previous quote, the impact of fatherhood was broader and more dramatic than men expected. Beginning with the birth of their children, men were acutely affected by becoming fathers. New priorities, less freedom and free time, restricted relationships with peers, and diminished relationships with wives were common outcomes. As one man put it:

> I had to give up everything I knew and was comfortable with; just open up the drawer, put it all in the drawer, and close the drawer.
>
> (35-year-old municipal administrator)

Many of the most widely expressed effects of the transition to fatherhood are invisible to the outsider. Alterations in men's sense of self and life priorities cannot be observed in behavioral changes after children are born. Even men's continued performance of role behaviors initiated long before fatherhood, such as wage earning, took on new meaning. These roles were redefined within the context of parenthood. If fatherhood were reducible to providing, one would not expect either the extent or depth of change these men reported.

In addition to the intrapersonal and interpersonal adjustments men made, they found that their role obligations were affected through both the addition of new responsibilities and the heightening of others. Those tasks associated with child care were, of course, new to men's round of activities. These responsibilities were broader than men had anticipated and therefore required more adjustments. Their activities covered everything from daily physical care to more long-term responsibilities as teachers or nurturers in their child's socialization:

> It's not like a puppy—great when it's small but now [that] it's starting to chew up things . . . get rid of it. It's not like that . . . type of commitment. . . . In effect, you are a butler or maid for them for the first year or two.
>
> (25-year-old food handler)

> I told someone once that I was a manservant for a midget. . . . At the time I was putting my son's coat on. . . . And then simple things, like crossing the street—I have to teach my son how to cross the street. All those things, there's never a moment's rest. You can't just take it out and unplug it like a TV or a radio.
>
> (33-year-old municipal administrator)

The transition to fatherhood also bound men more tightly to their existing occupational role. Because most of the fathers in the sample became sole breadwinners for at least a time after the birth of their first child, it is not surprising that many of them found their work-related concerns heightened. Some worried for the first time about how well they were providing or about either losing their job or having to be "stuck" in jobs that they found ungratifying. What is important about these anxieties is that they were activated by men's transitions to fatherhood. With the arrival of children and the wife's at least temporary departure from the labor force, men who had never before given priority to breadwinning began to feel more like "providers." This shift in role priority is a real though easily misunderstood indicator of the impact of fatherhood on men.

It is easy to overlook the role fatherhood plays in causing men to modify or revise their commitments to their jobs. In fact, because they continue to work as they did before becoming parents, men may seem relatively unaffected by becoming fathers. Any changes in their commitment to work may be interpreted as just that: changes in their commitment to work. Yet when one explores the altered meanings men attach to their activities, one sees that they are initiated by fatherhood. This greater than expected impact of fatherhood in men's lives was matched by broader than anticipated definitions and enactments of the male parenting role.

Being a Father

If the traditional depiction of men in families were accurate and complete, then fathers' roles in their children's lives would center around providing rather than around any other dimension of parenting. It would also follow that breadwinning activities would be what made them most feel like fathers because that would represent the fulfillment of their primary obligation as a parent. My interviews with new fathers suggest that neither of these characterizations can be adequately generalized to all fathers. Although a few fathers in the sample saw their roles in more traditional terms, a majority offered role definitions and attachments that emphasized more nurturant dimensions of parenting.

When asked to define a father's main responsibilities to his children, only 5 of the 16 fathers even mentioned "providing." The only one of these five who restricted his answer to traditional notions of fatherhood said:

> I would say mostly financial. . . . Also, I would be the one to put my foot down when he's disobeying; she threatens him—"I'll get Daddy. . . . Wait till I tell Daddy."
>
> (29-year-old laborer)

The other four fathers who included father's economic provider responsibility listed it as one of a number of both instrumental and expressive responsibilities. A 30-year-old truck driver described fatherhood this way:

> To provide the child with the physical means to live and grow, every father should provide that whether in opulence or poverty. . . . [Also] to teach about the things I enjoy . . . give him my sense of morals . . . do the things that help him to be happy.

By far, the most frequent responses dealt with the father as a role model or teacher in his child's socialization:

> Same as a woman's responsibility—show the child the right way to grow up and stuff.
>
> (27-year-old warehouseman)

> Just to be a parent, to be a role model for behaviors that will help your child master things. . . . It's appealing to me to think that I could be worthy of being a role model.
>
> (37-year-old architect)

Also mentioned repeatedly were fathers' roles as nurturers and as companions or playmates for their children. For instance:

> I think the most important responsibility is that of nurturing the child. I think it's important for fathers to be with a child as much as mothers are, if it's at all possible. If it's not, they ought to try and make it possible, even if it means giving up something.
>
> (31-year-old retail manager)

Despite a question that invited reference to the breadwinner-provider role, less than one third of the fathers even included this role among fathers' "major responsibilities." In a similar vein, when asked what they themselves do that most makes them feel like fathers, only one father, this time a 30-year-old truck driver, referred to the meeting of his breadwinning responsibilities:

> Sometimes, the fulfillment of what I feel are my financial responsibilities will make me feel like a father because I will feel like I'm doing this for him.

Much more common were answers about nurturing activities. For some men this nurturance was expressed through teaching their children certain values or necessary skills; for others it was being emotionally supportive, physically affectionate, or playful with their children. Finally, a few fathers stressed moments when they attempt to discipline their children as occasions when they most feel like fathers.

The combination of answers men gave to the questions described above indicate a much greater emphasis on the nurturant dimensions of the father role than on any other aspect. Men also emphasized nurturing activities in their accounts of what they value most about being a father and in the way they considered themselves most unlike their own fathers. Taken together, it was the importance informants placed on their expressive relationships to their children that most separated the fathers I interviewed from what has traditionally been written or thought about men as parents. As others have noted (Cohen, 1991; McKee & O'Brien, 1982; Pleck, 1983), if we want to know how men think about being and becoming fathers, a qualitative analysis of their own descriptions of fatherhood experiences is more useful than quantitative measures of the amount of time spent in child care activities. Although informants did see a connection between being a father and "providing," they had a much broader idea of what it is that fathers ought to provide. Even examining what informants reported doing as fathers, however, revealed an involvement greater than expected.

Informants' Activities With Their Children

Estimate of fathers' actual time spent with their children have varied considerably, depending on whether one measured total time together (which might include mothers and others) or one-to-one time. Estimates have ranged as low as 37.7 seconds a day (Rebelsky & Hanks, 1971), through Fischman's (1986) finding of an average of 8 minutes a day during the week and 14 minutes a day on weekends, to more optimistic measures of "total time" such as Barnett and Baruch's (1988) 29 hours a week. The wide variability in these and other such estimates of fathers' participation in child care results from a number of factors, including how long ago the study was conducted, the age of the children receiving care, and most important, how father participation was operationalized (e.g., sole responsibility vs. time together) and measured (e.g., time diaries, estimates, etc.).

It is important to note that regardless of the sample or measurement strategies used, estimates of fathers' involvement with their children and responsibility for child care indicate that they spend less time with their children than do mothers. Fathers are also more likely than mothers are to concentrate their time with children in passive and less demanding "secondary child care activities" (Barnett & Baruch, 1988; R. LaRossa, 1988; R. LaRossa & M. LaRossa, 1981).

These same differences surfaced in my informants' accounts of their and their partners' parenting. Although the fathers in my sample displayed a greater attachment to and involvement in their parental roles than even they had expected, all but one were still secondary caretakers when compared to their wives. There were, for example, still some men whose activities consisted almost exclusively of "play" and whose involvement with their children consisted of "secondary" passive child care such as watching their child at play or watching television together (R. LaRossa & M. LaRossa, 1981). Men offered no descriptions of wives employing this same style of parenting, and it is not likely that many can or do. With only one exception, even the most active and involved of the fathers were less active and involved parents than their partners. However, it is equally true that most of the fathers were more active and involved in parenting than men have typically been thought to be.

When asked about the amount of time spent with their children, fathers reported spending a range of time, from relatively little to nearly all of the child care given to the children. The latter father, the 36-year-old full-time househusband, described his primary caretaking responsibilities:

> I don't want to exaggerate my role in the child care. My wife takes care of the kids a lot, she loves

taking care of the kids, but she reaches a point where she's got to go do something else. If I reach that point, I don't have a choice. I just have to keep doing it.

The other end of the spectrum was more common. Five fathers, in keeping with traditional notions of fathering, were struggling to maintain even a low level of involvement in daily child care. This comment from a 28-year-old computer technician is typical of these fathers:

I spend little overall time with them during the week; I'm gone before they wake up and I get home at 5 or 5:30. I spend a little time here in one form or another—playing or eating [together]— Usually my wife and I try and talk too, so I'm not even sure how much time I spend with the kids.

The majority of fathers fell between these two extremes. These men described active daily involvement in day-to-day child care and rather high estimates of actual time spent with their children. When pressed to qualitatively assess their involvements with their children and in child care, these men revealed role relationships that were both active and extensive, encompassing most of the tasks associated with child care. For example:

I get up early in the morning with him. I'm with him for like an hour and a half in the morning, I make him breakfast every morning, play with him before I go to work. . . . When I come home at night, I get home around 6 so I'm with him for about 3 1/2 hours, four times a week. On the weekends, I have him every other weekend for a whole weekend at a time, from 7 in the morning till 7 at night. . . . I've even taken weeks off, a week off on vacation, so that [my wife] could go away and I took care of [him].

(33-year-old municipal administrator)

I'd say we spend 40–50 hours a week together. This comes from having 2 days off and every other weekend. [During that time] I'll wash him, feed him, go for a walk. . . . I could [either] just watch TV and bounce him on my knee or I can take him to the park or to a shopping mall. Maybe because I see a return coming back I [choose not to] just sit there and watch the tube. I change him, feed him, bathe him.

(25-year-old food handler)

In analyzing men's comments about fatherhood, I identified the following three factors accounting for their actual levels of involvement in child care: (a) their commitment to fathering, (b) wives' needs for "down time" (R. LaRossa & M. LaRossa, 1981) and most relevant for the present discussion, (c) their work schedules (see Presser & Cain, 1983). Thus, whereas men's work did not form the substance of informants' responsibilities as fathers, the timing of that work was the strongest determinant of the shape of their parenting activities.

As some of the comments above indicated, men's relationships with their children had to be fitted around their jobs. Men who reported the lowest levels of time with their children also described "having to leave" the house before their children even woke, or "not getting home until" an hour in the evening that left little opportunity to spend time together. As was true of their marital relationships (Cohen, 1987, 1988), occupational constraints on involvement was a source of much discontent or guilt. A 31-year-old retail manager described the conflict between work and family time:

Work eats into our time together. Before, [my wife] worked part-time evenings and I worked part-time days so that we had more time to spend with our daughter and we had weekends to spend all three of us together. Now we have, at most, one day off a week together. . . . I have fantasies about being able to have a livable income off of [business in the home] and spending all day with my daughter. If I could do that, I would like to.

For some fathers, then, attachment to fathering well surpassed the amount of time spent with their children. This being the case, any measure of the former that uses the latter as the sole or major indicator would be suspect.

On the other hand, men's paid work schedules occasionally afforded them unique opportunities to engage in more extensive activity with their children, which itself fostered a greater involvement in parenting. Two fathers who worked nights, a third who as a teacher returned home early from work, and a fourth whose job included two weekdays off all associated their work schedules with higher than expected levels of involvement in child care (Hood & Golden, 1979; Presser & Cain, 1983). Thus, whereas some fathers felt that their jobs restricted their parenting activities, others owed their high levels of involvement to their work schedules. In both directions, work became a dominant influence over the nature of men's relationships with their children.

Retreat From the Provider Role?

I think if you are going to have kids it is important that you interact with them. That is something I didn't have that much with my father because he was working 10 hours a day. . . . But it doesn't have to be that way.

(29-year-old physicist)

Measuring attachment to and performance of the "provider role" is problematic (Hood, 1986). If one defines the provider role as requiring a single-mindedness about working and an identification of work as one's primary contribution to one's family, then informants deliberately rejected attachment to this role. There were three manifestations of this rejection. First, when I asked about the "most important roles" in their lives, men identified more strongly with being a father and husband than with being a worker (Cohen, 1987, 1988). Second, they staked no ideological claim on working and providing. When they were sole supporters of their family, they described this condition as the result of the practical circumstances of having very young children and a wife who had recently left the labor force. This mostly temporary, parentally induced, shift to sole wage earning may have made some men come to see themselves as breadwinners and worry, for the first time, about their role perfor-

mance. It was not, however, a role that they performed and protected with any sense of ownership. When I asked informants how they felt about their wives working outside the home, only one man noted that he "was not happy about it." More typically, men claimed to have positive feelings about their wives' employment. Examples of men's responses were, "It's great, I love it"; "I think it's fine"; and "It doesn't bother me." As the following comments reveal, most informants questioned the whole idea of the father as the provider:

When I was growing up, work was my father's responsibility. That is no longer the case. Everybody works—everybody has to pitch in. It is no longer a husband's position or a wife's position. It's everybody's.

(40-year-old mechanic)

I think it's great that she works. . . . I knew one guy in high school who, when he got married, gave his wife orders that she was to stay home and make his meals. I thought he was a real jackass; I have no respect for people like that. We supposedly got rid of slavery a hundred years ago.

(29-year-old physicist)

Interestingly, whereas only one informant openly objected to his wife working outside the home, four others recalled objecting to the idea of their wives not working.

Finally, and most notably, men seemed to be consciously attempting to avoid replicating with their children the kinds of relationships they recalled having with their own father.

When fathers and expectant fathers were asked to compare themselves to their own father, overwhelmingly men described trying, wanting, or expecting to be unlike their own father. They wanted to be "better" parents, "interact more," be "more involved" with their children, and have better father-child relationships. In their accounts it becomes clear that the deficiencies in their early relationships with their father stemmed from what they saw as excessive job-induced father absence from daily life. Without blaming their fathers for the lack of time or attention they received as children, fathers and expectant fathers embraced a more active version of fathering:

> In a certain sense, my approach is a response to my relationship with my father, who—until I was 10—would be gone for work before I woke up, and not until I was 7 or 8, was he back before I went to bed. I spent little time with him. I still feel little emotional echoes from it . . . so I make an effort with my son.
>
> (42-year-old teacher)

> When I was a kid we hardly saw [my father] because he worked two jobs. That's something that I'd rather not do, not 'cause I don't want to work two jobs or we couldn't use the money, it's just that I'd rather see more of my kids. . . . My father never saw us kids.
>
> (29-year-old laborer)

These comments suggest only that men can, and do, articulate a larger, more involved notion of fathering. Actual relationships between informants and their children may ultimately come to resemble what they recall of relationships with their fathers. Because the men's memories came from later stages of childhood than represented in their current families, it is even possible that their fathers started with similar desires and comparable levels of participation when their children were young, but as the children grew older, shifts in the demands of jobs conspired to reduce their involvements in the sons' childhoods.

If, however, one accepts men's disavowal of the kind of fathering they received, then one must accept, too, the implications of this repudiation. As men themselves noted, it was not their fathers that they were rejecting but the life-style their fathers had to live. In seeking to avoid the same outcome with their children, they were advocating less involvement in the provider role.

Absence of Class Differences

Somewhat unexpectedly, there was little socioeconomic variation in the ways in which informants defined fathering and in the impact becoming a father

had in their lives. Working-class men were as likely to emphasize the nurturing dimensions of fathering as middle-class men. Further, in both the range and extent of child care involvement, social class influences were not apparent. Where economic variation existed in involvement in child care, it manifested itself indirectly through occupational constraints (e.g., schedules, expected levels of commitment) imposed from without rather than differing class-based ideologies of fathering. Only in the meaning attached to work and its relationship to being fathers did social class make a noticeable difference.

More common for working- than middle-class fathers was a sense that one's work was an expression of family roles. It was their status as husbands and especially fathers that frequently led them to take or keep the jobs they were in. They became "locked into" their jobs because the responsibilities of parenthood made occupational change difficult. Additionally, with little intrinsic gratification derived from their jobs, they were more likely to understand their work as part of what they contributed to their families.

Middle-class informants were more likely to see intrinsic rewards in their jobs. Their work was more deeply a part of how they saw themselves and less immediately seen as something they gave their families. Whereas they recognized the contribution their working made to their wife and children, this familial contribution was neither the sole nor most powerful motivation for working (Cohen, 1988).

SUMMARY AND CONCLUSION

The preceding discussion has suggested that traditional work-centered definitions of "fathering" are inadequate for characterizing either informants' beliefs about fathering or their behavior as parents. Despite inferential limitations imposed by sampling, my informants' experiences show that the traditional father-provider role does not fit all men's lives. Few informants advocated the ideology of the father-provider. For the majority, experiences becoming and being fathers stretched far beyond working. Study participants described attachments to the more nurturant dimensions of "parenting" that sounded like endorsements of contemporary, involved fathering. Ralph LaRossa's cautionary assessment of how much substantial change has really occurred in the substance of fatherhood is an important one, especially lest anyone conclude from the foregoing discussion that I'm suggesting fathers are becoming interchangeable with mothers in the caring for children. However, Pleck (1983) makes a persuasive case that if men already possess high levels of psychological involvement in their family roles, there is a greater likelihood of increasing their familial role performance than there would be if they first had to shift their psychological involvement from work to family. In a similar vein, if men accept the ideology of "involved fathering," and if that filters into and is reinforced through the expectations of their spouses, the fathering they do is more amenable to enlargement than it would be if definitions of fathering centered around "providing."

Accepting men's accounts as sincere expressions of a desire for more involvement in more aspects of parenting than the traditional role of father as provider prescribes may require looking beyond their relative allocation of time to work and parenting. By themselves, such temporal distributions may seem to validate the traditional role, because when fathers are "providers," work is an expression rather than a restriction on fathering. If, however, men are enlarging their attachments to more nurturant dimensions of parenting and pushing for or being pushed into more involvement with their children, work will become increasingly defined as a barrier to parenting. Thus, to maximize what men are available for and encouraged to do as parents will require reducing or restructuring what they are required or expected to do as workers. If informants sincerely wish to avoid "the sins of the fathers" by having greater and deeper involvement with their sons and daughters, they will need the time to do so. This need for time may be met through many of the familiar work-family supports—flextime, parental leave, job-sharing, and so on—typically identified as "women's issues." Coupling these family supports with continued and widened cultural reinforcement of the value of more involved fathering will be the most viable combination for creating broader and more fulfilling styles of fathering.

REFERENCES

Barnett, R., & Baruch, G. (1988). Correlates of father's participation in family work. In P. Bronstein & C. Cowan (Eds.), *Fatherhood today: Men's changing role in the family* (pp. 66–78). New York: John Wiley.

Bernard, J. (1983). The good provider role: Its rise and fall. In A. Skolnick & J. Skolnick (Eds.), *Family in transition* (3rd ed., pp. 125–144). Boston: Little, Brown.

Blood, R., & Wolfe, D. (1960). *Husbands and wives.* New York: Free Press.

Brannon, R. (1976). The male sex role: Our culture's blueprint of manhood and what it's done for us lately. In D. David & R. Brannon (Eds.), *The forty-nine percent majority: The male sex role* (pp. 1–48). Reading, MA: Addison-Wesley.

Bronstein, P., & Cowan, C. (Eds.). (1988). *Fatherhood today: Men's changing role in the family.* New York: John Wiley.

Cancian, F. (1985). Gender politics: Love and power in the private and public spheres. In A. Rossi (Ed.), *Gender and the life course* (pp. 253–262). Hawthorne, NY: Aldine.

Cohen, T. F. (1986). *Men's family roles: Becoming and being husbands and fathers.* Doctoral dissertation, Boston University. (University Microfilms No. 86–09272)

———. (1987). Remaking men: Men's experiences becoming and being husbands and fathers and their implications for reconceptualizing men's lives. *Journal of Family Issues, 8,* 57–77.

———. (1988). Gender, work and family: The impact and meaning of work in men's family roles. *Family Perspective, 22,* 293–308.

———. (1991). Speaking with men: Application of a feminist methodology to the study of men's lives. *Men's Studies Review, 8*(4), 4–13.

Fischman, J. (1986, October). The children's hours. *Psychology Today,* pp. 16–18.

Glaser, B., & Strauss, A. (1976). *The discovery of grounded theory.* New York: Aldine.

Goetting, A. (1982). The six stations of remarriage: Developmental tasks of remarriage after divorce. *Family Relations, 31,* 213–222.

Gould, R. (1976). Measuring masculinity by the size of a paycheck. In D. David & R. Brannon (Eds.), *The forty-nine percent majority: The male sex role* (pp. 113–117). Reading, MA: Addison-Wesley.

Grönseth, E. (1972). The breadwinner trap. In L. K. Howe (Ed.), *The future of the family* (pp. 175–191). New York: Simon & Schuster.

Hood, J. (1986, May). The provider role: Its meaning and measurement. *Journal of Marriage and the Family, 48,* 349–359.

Hood, J., & Golden, S. (1979). Beating time/making time: The impact of work scheduling on men's family roles. *Family Coordinator, 28,* 575–592.

LaRossa, R. (1988). Fatherhood and social change. *Family Relations, 37,* 451–457.

LaRossa, R., & LaRossa, M. (1981). *Transition to parenthood: How infants change families.* Beverly Hills, CA: Sage.

Lewis, C., & O'Brien, M. (1987). *Reassessing fatherhood: New observations on fathers and the modern family.* Beverly Hills, CA: Sage.

Liebow, E. (1967). *Tally's corner: A study of Negro streetcorner men.* Boston: Little, Brown.

McKee, L., & O'Brien, M. (Eds.). (1982). *The father figure.* London: Tavistock.

Miller, D., & Swanson, G. (1958). *The changing American parent.* New York: John Wiley.

Oakley, A. (1974). *The sociology of housework.* New York: Pantheon.

———. (1980). *Women confined: Towards a sociology of childbirth.* New York: Schocken.

Parsons, T. (1942). Age and sex in the social structure. *American Sociological Review, 7,* 604–616.

Pleck, J. (1979). Men's family work: Three perspectives and some new data. *Family Coordinator, 28,* 473–480.

———. (1983). Husbands paid work and family roles: Current research issues. In H. Lopata & J. Pleck (Eds.), *Research into the interweave of social roles: Families and jobs* (Vol. 3, pp. 251–333). Greenwich, CT: JAI.

———. (1987). American fathering in historical perspective. In M. Kimmel (Ed.), *Changing men: New directions in research on men and masculinity* (pp. 83–97). Newbury Park, CA: Sage.

Presser, H. B., & Cain, V. (1983). Shift work among dual-earner couples with children. *Science, 219,* 876–879.

Rebelsky, F., & Hanks, C. (1971). Fathers' verbal interaction with infants in the first three months of life. *Child Development, 42,* 63–68.

Rubin, L. (1976). *Worlds of pain: Life in the working class family.* New York: Basic Books.

———. (1979). *Women of a certain age: The search for midlife self.* New York: Harper & Row.

Safilios-Rothschild, C. (1969). Family sociology or wives' family sociology: A cross cultural examination of decision making. *Journal of Marriage and the Family, 31,* 290–301.

Thompson, L., & Walker, A. (1989). Gender in families: Women and men in marriage, work and parenthood. *Journal of Marriage and the Family, 51,* 845–871.

Zelditch, M. (1974). Role differentiation in the nuclear family. In R. Coser (Ed.), *The family: Its structure and functions* (2nd ed., pp. 256–258). New York: St. Martin's.

CHECKPOINTS

1. According to Rice, normative prescriptions about the family stigmatize women, lead to biased research on the family, and construct an inappropriate model for family therapy.

2. According to Cohen, men's subjective experiences during the transition to fatherhood emphasize nurturance.

To prepare for reading the next section, think about this question:

1. How were household tasks divided in your family when you were growing up?

The Allocation of Household Labor in Gay, Lesbian, and Heterosexual Married Couples

LAWRENCE A. KURDEK

Wright State University

This study compared how gay, lesbian, and heterosexual married couples (ns = 95, 61, and 145, respectively) allocated household labor. Partners in each couple lived together without children. Compared to both married and gay couples, lesbian couples tended to share tasks. Compared to lesbian couples, gay couples and married couples were likely to have one or the other partner perform the tasks; in married couples, this was most likely the wife. Compared to married couples, gay couples and lesbian couples were likely to split tasks so that each partner performed an equal number of different tasks. The relation between the extent to which household tasks were performed and personal power, gender role orientation, relationship satisfaction, and psychological symptoms generally varied by partner and type of couple. It is concluded that although gender is a powerful determinant of how household labor gets allocated in heterosexual married couples, no single variable carries as much weight with gay or lesbian couples.

Lawrence A. Kurdek received his Ph.D. in developmental psychology from the University of Illinois at Chicago in 1976. He is currently Professor of Psychology at Wright State University, Dayton, Ohio. His current research interests include the effects of divorce on parents and children, the relation between family structure and children's adjustment, and the development of relationship quality in homosexual and heterosexual couples. He is a member of the Editorial Board of the following periodicals: *Journal of Marriage and the Family, Merrill-Palmer Quarterly, Journal of Family Issues, Journal of Gay and Lesbian Social Services, Psychology of Women Quarterly,* and *Journal of Genetic Psychology.*

There is ample evidence that the study of marital behavior is in large part the study of gender specialization in marital roles (Thompson & Walker, 1989). Because this pattern of gender specialization underscores the relative powerlessness of women (Thompson, 1991), strategies for assigning roles and tasks based on criteria other than gender are of interest. Such strategies are constructed by gay and lesbian couples who cannot use gender to assign roles in their relationships for the obvious reason that both partners are the same gender.

An ideal contribution to this collection of articles on gender and close relationships would be a review of the criteria gay and lesbian couples do use to assign relationship roles. However, studies of gay/lesbian couples are rare, and studies comparing gay/lesbian and heterosexual couples are even more rare. In view of this limited information, the focus of this article is a study of how partners in heterosexual married, gay, and lesbian couples allocate household labor commonly regarded as "women's work" (e.g., housework, cooking, cleaning the bathroom, doing laundry, writing the grocery list, and buying groceries). Before this study is described, background information will be presented on how married heterosexual, gay, and lesbian couples typically allocate such household labor and the variables that have been proposed to explain the pattern of allocation.

Correspondence regarding this article should be addressed to Larry Kurdek, Wright State University, Department of Psychology, Dayton, OH 45435–0001.

HOW DO MARRIED COUPLES ALLOCATE HOUSEHOLD LABOR?

Recent national surveys indicate that the major criterion married couples use to allocate household labor is gender. For example, Blair and Lichter (1991) report that wives do so much of the household labor (e.g., meal preparation, dishes, ironing/washing, and shopping) that husbands would have to reallocate over 60% of their family labor to other chores before gender equality would be achieved in the distribution of time spent on all domestic tasks. Household labor was more likely to be performed by wives than by husbands even in highly educated couples and in couples without children.

Four negative consequences of identifying household labor as "women's work" have been noted. First, because household labor is typically monotonous and highly routinized, it has been cited as one cause of elevated levels of depression in wives (Ross, Mirowsky, & Huber, 1983). Second, because husbands are generally dependent on their wives for running the household, the absence of a wife—for example, through divorce—can lead to men's perceiving household labor as a major stressor (Hetherington, Cox, & Cox, 1982). Third, although labor force participation is becoming an integral part of wives' lives, such participation is often dependent on the couple's need for extra income and the absence of children (Bergen, 1991). Women's dependency on the family context has been seen as limiting their access to economic and social resources, which, in turn, restricts their ability both to contribute resources to the family and to negotiate successfully within the marriage (Bergen, 1991). Finally, a continuing pattern of gender specialization in work means that children will be socialized to choose activities and careers based on gender rather than on interests and skills (Brody & Steelman, 1985).

Two explanations have been provided for why wives do more household labor than husbands. The first explanation is that wives do more household labor than husbands because as individual with little personal power (e.g., low income and low job status) they are relegated to doing menial tasks. In support of this explanation, unemployed wives do more household labor than employed wives (Shelton, 1990). Further, data from the National Survey on Families and Households indicate that wives' employment (representing personal power and personal resources) is positively related to husbands' absolute and proportionate contribution to housework (Blair & Lichter, 1991).

The second explanation for why wives do more household labor than husbands is that the performance of household labor matches an internalized standard of "femininity" (Atkinson & Huston, 1984). Because identifying oneself as a woman means doing "woman-type" things, a wife who has internalized a traditional notion of what a woman should do may not only claim household chores as her own but may also directly or indirectly prevent her husband from helping with household labor because she believes his socialization has not prepared him to do household tasks "the right way."

In support of this explanation, there is evidence that gender role orientation is linked to the performance of household tasks. For example, wives who see themselves as possessing many stereotypic feminine characteristics (e.g., emotional, gentle, and helpful to others) frequently perform household tasks, whereas husbands who see themselves as possessing many stereotypic masculine traits (e.g., independent, competitive, and self-confident) infrequently perform household tasks (Atkinson & Huston, 1984). Because this evidence is correlational, however, it cannot be claimed that gender role orientation is causally linked to the performance of household tasks.

HOW DO GAY/LESBIAN COUPLES ALLOCATE HOUSEHOLD LABOR?

As part of their large-scale study of diverse types of couples, Blumstein and Schwartz (1983) reported that 30% of full-time employed gay partners and 27% of full-time employed lesbian partners did more than 10 hours of housework per week. Although these data suggest few differences in how gay and lesbian couples distribute household labor, Blumstein and

Schwartz (1983) did not compare the actual strategies that gay and lesbian couples used to allocate household labor. Relevant data on such strategies are limited to studies of only gay couples and studies of only lesbian couples.

In their study of gay couples, McWhirter and Mattison (1984) noted that the handling of household chores varied by stage of the relationship. In the first year of the relationship, partners shared almost all chores. Later, however, routines got established as chores were assigned primarily on the basis of each partner's skill and work schedule. In instances where each partner was skilled, partners willingly unlearned previous skills in order to create complementarity and a sense of balance in the relationship.

Unfortunately, relevant data on lesbian couples are more sketchy. Blumstein and Schwartz (1983) noted that lesbian couples were especially careful to divide household labor equally. These authors speculate that lesbians may avoid task specialization in the area of household work because of the low status traditionally associated with the women who do it. Although no supportive data are presented, this position is consistent with other reports that lesbian couples are more likely than either gay or heterosexual couples to follow an ethic of equality (Peplau & Cochran, 1990).

PURPOSES OF THE PRESENT STUDY

The current study addressed how partners in gay, lesbian, and married heterosexual couples allocated household tasks commonly regarded as "women's work." Because gay/lesbian couples differ from heterosexual couples in that they are unlikely to include children, only couples without children were studied. Partners in each type of couple lived together.

The first purpose of the study was to compare married, gay, and lesbian couples on three distinct patterns of allocating household labor. In the *equality pattern,* each partner is equally likely to do household labor. For example, partners in a couple could do the cooking and the laundry together or they could take turns doing each task. In the *balance pattern,* each

partner is responsible for an equal number of household tasks, but not the same household tasks. For example, one partner routinely does the cooking while the other partner routinely does the laundry. Finally, in the *segregation pattern,* one partner in the couple does the bulk of household labor whereas the other partner does little or no household labor.

Based on the previous findings (Bergen, 1991; Blair & Lichter, 1991; Blumstein & Schwartz, 1983), it was predicted that married couples would be more likely than gay or lesbian couples to follow the segregation pattern, with wives doing the bulk of the household labor. Although based on much more limited work (McWhirter & Mattison, 1984; Peplau & Cochran, 1990), it was also expected that gay couples would be more likely than married or lesbian couples to follow a balance pattern and that lesbian couples would be more likely than married or gay couples to follow an equality pattern.

Because these predictions are based on group averages, the frequency of performing household labor was also expected to vary within partners in each type of couple. That is, some married couples would follow an equality or a balance pattern (Ferree, 1991), and some gay and lesbian partners would follow a segregation pattern (Coleman & Waters, 1989). The second purpose of this study was to identify individual-differences variables that were linked to the extent to which a partner performed household labor. Generalizing from previous work done with heterosexual couples (Atkinson & Huston, 1984; Blair & Lichter, 1991; Blumstein & Schwartz, 1983; Ross et al., 1983), it was expected that the partner who typically performed household labor would have low personal power (i.e., low level of education or low personal income), a high feminine gender role orientation, a low masculine gender role orientation, and frequent symptoms of depression and overall poor psychological health.

Although household labor is a daily occurrence in any relationship, the link between the frequency of performing household labor and relationship satisfaction has not been widely investigated in past research on close relationships. There is evidence, however, that women who do not strongly ascribe to traditional female gender role attributes report declines in marital satisfaction over the transition to parenthood when they become primarily responsible for household labor (including childcare) in the postnatal period (Belsky, Lang, & Huston, 1986). The final purpose of this study was to explore the relation between the extent to which household labor is performed and relationship satisfaction in gay, lesbian, and married couples without children.

PLAN OF THE STUDY

Who Participated in the Study?

Heterosexual subjects were both spouses from 145 couples who completed the fourth annual assessment of an on-going longitudinal study of marital satisfaction and marital stability in newlywed couples. Most respondents (97% of husbands and 98% of wives) were white. Couples were recruited from newspaper listings of marriage licenses (see Kurdek, 1991b, for details).

Homosexual subjects were both partners from 95 gay and 61 lesbian couples who were participants in two separate studies. Most respondents (93% of gay partners and 94% of lesbian partners) were white. The first study included 61 gay couples and 31 lesbian couples, and the second included an additional 34 gay couples and 30 lesbian couples. Data on some of the gender role orientation variables and on the psychological symptoms variables were available only from the first subsample. Couples were recruited from advertisements in national gay/lesbian magazines and newsletters as well as from referrals from other participants (see Kurdek, 1991a, for details). Because homosexual partners have no a priori defined roles such as "husband" or "wife," they were randomly assigned to a partner 1 or a partner 2 status.

How Was Information Collected and What Variables Were Measured?

Each couple was sent two identical surveys that included additional measures not of interest to this study. Partners were directed to complete their surveys privately and not to discuss their answers with each other until the forms had been completed and returned in separate postage-paid envelopes.

Demographic and Personal Power Variables   Participants provided information regarding age, race, and the number of months they lived with their spouse/partner. Couples scores throughout this study were derived by averaging partners' scores.

Personal power was assessed by occupation (here coded as unemployed/employed), annual personal income (represented by 12 intervals ranging from $5000 or less to $50,000 or more), and education (represented by eight intervals ranging from completion of less than seventh grade to the award of a doctorate).

Allocation of Household Labor   Subjects used a 5-point scale (1: *much more true of my partner;* 3: *equally true of both of us;* and 5: *much more true of me*) to indicate how true six items were of their partners or themselves. These items were doing housework, doing the cooking, cleaning the bathroom, doing laundry, writing down items on a grocery list, and buying groceries. Items were taken from the household responsibilities domain of the Sex Role Behavior Scale (Orlofsky, 1981).

It is of note that for married, gay, and lesbian couples, partners' summed composite scores were substantially correlated, $rs = -.70, -.82$, and $-.79$, respectively, $p < .01$, meaning that partners generally agreed on how tasks were allocated. These correlations are negative because concordance between partners means that a high score from one partner (e.g., much more true of me) is matched by a low score from the other partner (e.g., much more true of my partner).

Five scores were derived for each partner that facilitated the derivation of couple equality, balance, and segregation pattern scores:

(a) The *extent to which tasks were done by the self (whether shared with the partner or done primarily by the self)* was derived by recoding original values of 1 or 2 (indicating partner did the task) to 0, original values of 3 (task shared) to 1, original values of 4 (task done more by self) to 2, and original values of 5 (task done much more by self) to 3. Thus, 0 indicated that the task was not done by self, 1 indicated that the task was shared, 2 indicated that the task was done more by self, and 3 indicated that the task was done much more by self. Recoded values for the six tasks were summed.

(b) The *number of household tasks shared equally with the partner* was derived by counting the number of times a rating of 3 (task shared) was given for each of the six tasks. Equal sharing could mean turn taking or doing a task together.

(c) The *extent to which tasks were done primarily by one or the other partner* was derived by recoding original values of 3 (task shared) to 0, original values of 4 (task done more by self) or 2 (task done more by partner) to 1, and original values of 5 (task done much more by self) or 1 (task done much more by partner) to 2. Thus, 0 indicated that the task was shared, 1 indicated that the task was done more by one or the other partner, and 2 indicated that the task was done much more by one or the other partner. A composite score was obtained by summing the recoded values for each of the six items.

(d) The *extent to which tasks were done primarily by oneself (and were not shared)* was derived by recoding original values of 1 or 2 (task done more by partner) or 3 (task shared) to 1, original values of 4 (task done more by self) to 2, and original values of 5 (task done much more by self) to 3. Thus, 1 indicated that the task was done more by the partner or was shared, 2 indicated that the task was done more by self, and 3 indicated that the task was done much more by self. Recoded values for the six tasks were summed.

(e) The *extent to which tasks were done primarily by the partner* was derived by recoding original values of 3 (task shared) or 4 or 5 (task done more by self) to 1, original values of 2 (task done more by partner) remained values of 2, and original values of 1 (task done much more by partner) to 3. Thus, 1 indicated that the task was done more by self or shared, 2 indicated that the task was done more by partner, and 3 indicated that the task was done much more by partner. Recoded values for the six tasks were summed.

From these partner scores, three couples scores were derived. An *equality* score was derived by averaging partners' (b) scores. This represented the number of tasks equally shared. A *segregation* score was derived by averaging partners' (c) scores, which measured the degree to which tasks were done primarily by one or the other partner. Finally, a dichotomous *balance* score was derived by categorizing couples as balanced (a score of 1) or not balanced (a score of 0). In order to distinguish the equal pattern from the balance pattern, couples who shared all tasks equally were coded a priori as not balanced (score of 0). The rest of the couples received either a score of 1 (balanced) if the average of partner 1's (d)/(e) ratio (self/partner housework) and partner 2's (e)/(d) ratio (partner/self housework) fell within the interval of 0.75 to 1.33, or a score of 0 (not balanced) if the average of partner 1's (d)/(e) ratio and partner 2's (e)/(d) ratio fell outside of the 0.75 to 1.33 interval.

Scores within the 0.75 to 1.33 interval corresponded to partners in a couple "specializing" (i.e., receiving ratings of 2 or 3) on 3 tasks each. For example, if partner 1 indicated that he/she does 3 tasks and his/her partner does 3 tasks, the (d) and (e) scores would range from 9 to 12 [2 + 2 + 2 (for tasks done more by self) and 1 + 1 + 1 (for tasks done by partner) or 3 + 3 + 3 (for tasks done much more by self) and 1 + 1 + 1 (for tasks done by partner)]. Thus, the couple's (d)/(e) ratio and (e)/(d) ratio would range from 0.75 (9/12) to 1.33 (12/9). In the perfect balance case, each partner does 3 separate tasks, and the (d)/(e) and (e)/(d) ratios are 1.0 (12/12). Couples following a segregation pattern would have scores that reflect that one partner does all the tasks by himself/herself (12–18) and that the other partner does no tasks (6). In this case, the relevant ratios would be 0.33 (6/18) to 0.50 (6/12) or 2.00 (12/6) to 3.00 (18/3). As would be expected, these values fall outside of the critical range of 0.75 to 1.33.

Gender Role Orientation Expressiveness, Masculinity, and Femininity scores were derived from the Bem Sex Role Inventory (Bem, 1974). The Expressiveness score was available for all respondents, and was based on a subset of 12 of the 20 items comprising the Femininity score. This subject was defined by items (e.g., tender, compassionate, warm, sympathetic, and understanding) that were found to cluster together in a factor analysis of the Bem Sex Role Inventory (Kurdek, 1987). Masculinity and Femininity scores were available for all heterosexual couples and from the first subsample of gay/lesbian couples. Cronbach's alpha for the summed composite Expressiveness score across partners ranged from .79 to .90. Similar ranges for the Masculinity and Femininity scores were .77 to .88 and .65 to .80, respectively.

Relationship Satisfaction Relationship satisfaction was assessed by the 10-item Dyadic Satisfaction subscore of the Dyadic Adjustment Scale (Spanier, 1976). Cronbach's alpha for this score ranged from .77 to .86 across partners.

Symptoms of Depression and General Psychological Distress Depressive symptoms and symptoms of general psychological distress were respectively assessed by the Depression and Global Severity scores derived from the Symptom Checklist-90-R (Derogatis, 1983). These scores were available for all married couples, and from the first subsample of gay/lesbian couples. Cronbach's alpha for the Depression score ranged from .62 to .89 across partners, whereas that for the Global Severity score ranged from .95 to .97.

FINDINGS FROM THE STUDY

Were Gay, Lesbian, and Married Couples Equivalent on Background Characteristics?

To see if the three types of couples were equivalent on age, education, proportion employed, income, and months living together, couple scores were submitted to a one-way (type of couple) multivariate analysis of variance. The effect was significant, $F(10, 592) = 13.73$, $p < .001$. Univariate analyses of variance indicated that the three types of couples differed on age, education, income, and months living together, $F(2, 299)$ ranging from 5.55 to 47.07, $p < .05$. Student Newman-Keuls comparisons, $p < .05$ here and below,

showed that gay and lesbian couples were older than married couples, Ms = 40.26, 40.16, and 33.17, respectively; that gay and lesbian couples were better educated than married couples, Ms = 6.33, 6.29, and 5.68, respectively; that gay and lesbian couples had higher joint incomes than married couples, Ms = 7.77, 7.72, and 6.88, respectively; and that gay couples lived together more months than lesbian couples who, in turn, lived together more months than married couples, Ms = 117.47, 83.39, and 43.56, respectively. Given these differences among types of couple, age, education, income, and months living together were used as covariates in subsequent multivariate analyses of covariance (MANCOVAs). However, because these couples likely differed on other variables, this statistical control did not truly equate the three groups.

How Did Partners in Gay, Lesbian, and Married Couples Allocate Household Labor?

To compare how gay, lesbian, and married couples distributed household tasks, the three dependent variables (equality, segregation, and balance scores) were submitted to a one-way (type of couple) MANCOVA with age, education, income, and months living together couple scores as covariates. The type of couple effect was significant, $F(6, 588) = 5.54$, $p < .01$. Univariate analyses of covariance indicated that the multivariate effect was due to the equality, segregation, and balance scores, $F(2, 295) = 12.62$, 10.49, and 10.98, respectively, $p < .01$.

Student Newman–Keuls comparisons ($p < .05$) indicated that lesbian couples had higher equality scores than either married or gay couples, Ms = 2.63, 1.58, and 1.76; that married and gay couples had higher segregation scores than lesbian couples, Ms = 6.49, 6.13, and 4.73, respectively; and that the proportion of balanced couples was higher for gay and lesbian couples than for married couples, Ms = 0.42, 0.57, and 0.20, respectively.

Because married couples had relatively high segregation scores and relatively low balance scores, it was likely that one partner in the couple did the bulk of the household labor. In order to identify this partner, the

TABLE 1.   **Percentage of Husbands and Wives for Whom Household Tasks are Done Primarily by Other Partner, Equally, or Primarily by Self**

	Husband			Wife		
	Partner	*Equally*	*Self*	*Partner*	*Equally*	*Self*
Do housework	63	29	8	2	31	67
Cook	63	29	8	2	31	67
Clean bathroom	67	18	15	10	21	69
Do laundry	62	30	8	7	25	68
Write grocery list	73	21	6	4	22	74
Buy groceries	46	41	13	7	38	55

Note: For husbands and wives, $n = 146$.

percentage of husbands/wives performing each household task primarily by themselves or sharing them with each other is presented in Table 1. Comparisons using scores that reflected the extent to which tasks were performed primarily by husbands or wives showed that wives performed more household tasks than husbands, paired $t(145) = 19.66$, $p < .01$.

Taken together, these findings are consistent with the view that married, gay, and lesbian couples follow different strategies for allocating household labor. As has been reported in other studies (Blair & Lichter, 1991; Thompson & Walker, 1989), married couples allocated household labor primarily on the basis of gender. Simply put, wives did the bulk of the housework. Although partners in gay couples and married couples were equally likely to specialize in task performance, gay couples tended to distribute the pattern of specialization equally so that—unlike married couples—one partner did not do all the work. As McWhirter and Mattison (1984) noted, it is likely that partners in gay couples specialize in task performance on the basis of skill, interest, and work schedule. Finally, lesbian couples allocated household tasks by sharing them. This pattern is consistent with the view that lesbian partners are especially likely to follow an ethic of equality (Blumstein & Schwartz, 1983; Peplau & Cochran, 1990).

Correlates of Performing Frequent Household Tasks

Partial correlations—controlling for number of months living together—were computed between the extent to which household tasks were done by the self [whether performed by the self or with the partner, score (a) above] and personal power (whether or not the respondent was employed, level of education, and level of personal income); gender role orientation (expressivity, femininity, and masculinity); relationship satisfaction; and severity of psychological symptoms (depression and general distress). Findings are presented by partner and type of couple in Table 2.

Although few correlations were significant, several partners are of note: (a) husbands who did household labor tended to be employed, to have low personal income, and to have low masculine gender role orientation. (b) Wives who did household labor were likely to be unemployed, to have low personal income, and to experience symptoms of both depression and general distress. (c) Overall, correlations for gay partners were nonsignificant. (d) Although several significant correlations for partner 1 were not replicated for partner 2, lesbian partners who did household labor were less likely to report symptoms of depression or general distress.

These findings indicate that linking the performance of household labor to personal power and gen-

TABLE 2.   **Partial Correlations Between Extent of Self-Performed Household Labor and Personal Power, Gender Role Orientation, Relationship Satisfaction, and Psychological Symptom Variables for Partners in Each Type of Couple with Control for Number of Months Living Together**

	Married		Gay		Lesbian	
	Husband	*Wife*	*Partner 1*	*Partner 2*	*Partner 1*	*Partner 2*
Employment	.15*	−.19**	−.14	−.02	−.14	−.05
Education	.08	−.05	−.08	.08	−.22*	.10
Income	−.16*	−.20**	−.30**	−.11	−.25*	−.10
Relationship satisfaction	−.08	−.08	−.08	−.08	.26*	−.05
Expressiveness	−.07	.04	.13	−.13	.27*	−.09
Masculinity	−.23**	−.10	−.14	−.15	.34*	−.20
Femininity	−.03	.03	.00	−.19	.34*	−.02
Depression	−.13	.18*	.12	.03	−.32*	−.18
Global distress	−.09	.19*	.10	−.03	−.23	−.33*

Note: For husbands and wives, $n = 146$ for all variables. For coefficients involving masculinity, femininity, depression, and global distress, *ns* for gay and lesbian partners = 61 and 31, respectively; for all other variables, *ns* = 95 and 61, respectively.
*$p < .05$.
**$p < .01$.

der role orientation (Atkinson & Huston, 1984; Blair & Lichter, 1991; Shelton, 1990) works for only married couples. Because, as noted earlier, gay and lesbian couples do not assign all household labor to only one partner, issues involving personal power are unlikely to occur in this domain.

Generally, the performance of household tasks was unrelated to relationship satisfaction. Because wives performed a disproportionate amount of household labor, this finding was surprising. However, Thompson (1991) has discussed women's notion of fairness in the context of family work and notes that although women do the bulk of family work, there is little evidence that they regard this as unfair. It may be that the extent to which partners did household tasks by themselves was unrelated to relationship satisfaction because expectations regarding how labor *should* be distributed were not violated (Belsky et al., 1986). That is, married couples may expect the wife to do household tasks, gay couples may expect to dis-

tribute household tasks in a balanced fashion, and lesbian couples may expect to share household tasks equally. Future studies in this area could directly assess such expectations and link them to how discrepancies between ideal and actual relationships affect relationship satisfaction (Kurdek, 1991a).

Perhaps the most intriguing finding of this study is that although the performance of household labor was *positively* related to the severity of psychological symptoms for wives—consistent with the findings of Ross et al. (1983)—the performance of household labor was *negatively* related to the severity of psychological symptoms for lesbian partners. This pattern of results suggests that it is not the drudgery of household labor that is related to psychological distress, but rather the interpersonal context within which it occurs. It is unlikely that lesbian partners actually enjoy household labor more than wives. However, it is likely that lesbian partners performed household because they chose to do it, unlike wives who did household labor because they felt resigned to do it.

This study has several limitations. Married, gay, and lesbian couples were at different developmental stages in their relationships, and differed on education and income. Further, neither sample can be claimed to be representative. Although traditional "women's work" household tasks were selected, no actual observations were made regarding how household labor was performed, and household tasks not commonly regarded as "women's work" were not sampled.

Nonetheless, this study indicates that close relationships do exist in which criteria other than gender are used to determine how household labor gets allocated. As noted above, it is unlikely that any couple actually enjoys household labor. However, gay and lesbian couples seem to have developed work-able strategies for fairly distributing the work related to one of the less glamorous aspects of a life together. As Blumstein and Schwartz (1983) noted, although gender in heterosexual relationships provides an efficient way of assigning tasks and roles, it typically does so at the expense of change, innovation, and choice by depriving women of power and status. On the other hand, although partners in gay/lesbian relationships stand a good chance of building their relationship on an ethic of fairness, they do so without tried-and-true traditions and guidelines.

I would like to thank the couples who participated in this study, and Barbara Winstead, Val Detlega, Arthur Aron, and Susan Sprecher for helpful comments on previous drafts of the paper.

REFERENCES

Atkinson, J., & Huston, T. L. (1984). Sex role orientation and division of labor early in marriage. *Journal of Personality and Social Psychology, 46,* 330–345.

Belsky, J., Lang, M., & Huston, T. L. (1986). Sex typing and division of labor as determinants of marital change across the transition to parenthood. *Journal of Personality and Social Psychology, 50,* 517–522.

Bem, S. L. (1974). The measurement of psychological androgyny. *Journal of Consulting and Clinical Psychology, 42,* 155–162.

Bergen, E. (1991). The economic context of labor allocation. *Journal of Family Issues, 12,* 140–157.

Blair, S. L., & Lichter, D. T. (1991). Measuring the division of household labor. *Journal of Family Issues, 12,* 91–113.

Blumstein, P., & Schwartz, P. (1983). *American couples.* New York: Morrow.

Brody, C. J., & Steelman, L. C. (1985). Sibling structure and parental sex-typing of children's household tasks. *Journal of Marriage and the Family, 47,* 265–273.

Coleman, M. T., & Walters, J. M. (1989). *Beyond gender role explanations: The division of household labor in gay and lesbian households.* Paper presented at the meeting of the American Sociological Association, San Francisco.

Derogatis, L. R. (1983). *SCL 90-R: Administration, scoring, and procedures manual.* Towson, MD: Clinical Psychometric Research.

Ferree, M. M. (1991). The gender division of labor in two-earner marriages: Dimensions of variability and change. *Journal of Family Issues, 12,* 158–180.

Hetherington, E. M., Cox, M., & Cox, R. (1982). Effects of divorce on parents and children. In M. E. Lamb (Ed.), *Nontraditional families: Parenting and child development* (pp. 233–287). Hillsdale, NJ: Erlbaum.

Kurdek, L. A. (1987). Sex role self schema and psychological adjustment in coupled homosexual and heterosexual men and women. *Sex Roles, 17,* 549–562.

———. (1991a). Correlates of relationship satisfaction in cohabiting gay and lesbian couples. *Journal of Personality and Social Psychology, 61,* 910–922.

———. (1991b). Predictors of increases in marital distress in newlywed couples: A 3-year prospective longitudinal study. *Developmental Psychology, 27,* 627–636.

McWhirter, D. P., & Mattison, A. M. (1984). *The male couple: How relationships develop.* Englewood Cliffs, NJ: Prentice-Hall.

Orlofsky, J. L. (1981). Relationships between sex role attitudes and personality traits and the Sex Role Behavior Scale-1. *Journal of Personality and Social Psychology, 40,* 927–940.

Peplau, L. A., & Cochran, S. D. (1990). A relational perspective on homosexuality. In D. P. McWhirter, S. A. Sanders, & J. M. Reinisch (Eds.), *Homosexuality/heterosexuality: Concepts of sexual orientation* (pp. 321–349). New York: Oxford University Press.

Ross, C. E., Mirowsky, J., & Huber, J. (1983). Dividing work, sharing work, and in-between: Marriage patterns and depression. *American Sociological Review, 48,* 809–823.

Shelton, B. A. (1990). The distribution of household tasks. *Journal of Family Issues, 11,* 115–135.

Spanier, G. B. (1976). Measuring dyadic adjustment. *Journal of Marriage and the Family, 38,* 15–28.

Thompson, L. (1991). Family work: Women's sense of fairness. *Journal of Family Issues, 12,* 181–196.

Thompson, L., & Walker, A. (1989). Gender in families. *Journal of Marriage and the Family, 51,* 845–871.

CHECKPOINT

1. Kurdek presents data that show that gay men divide tasks according to ability, lesbians share tasks, and heterosexual couples follow traditional patterns of the division of labor.

Gender and Reconceptualizing the Family

QUESTIONS FOR REFLECTION

1. How does the evidence from these articles challenge traditional views of family and relationships?
2. How would a more egalitarian family affect the relationship between parents and children?

CHAPTER APPLICATION

1. Identify a social policy that relates to the family, for example, child support, divorce laws, child custody, employee benefits, inheritance laws, parental leave. Research the implementation of this policy, and describe how it treats men and women. Is the policy gender-neutral, gender-specific, or gender-biased? What, if any, changes to the policy would you recommend based on your understanding of family?

CHAPTER TWELVE

Social Institutions and Gender

QUESTIONS TO THINK ABOUT

- What are social institutions?
- How do social institutions maintain gender segregation?
- What are the implications of gender segregation for men and women in institutions?
- What are the formal and informal factors that distinguish the experiences of women and men in social institutions?
- How is power a key to understanding the relationship between gender and social institutions?
- What are the cultural stereotypes that maintain myths about affirmative action?
- In what ways do stereotypes about race and gender create differences in beliefs about affirmative action for Blacks versus women?
- How is gendered violence a social institution?
- How do the elements of sexual terrorism impact both men and women?
- What is the relationship between masculinity and men's violence?
- What efforts have been made to achieve equity in social institutions?

THE GENDERED NATURE OF SOCIAL INSTITUTIONS

You will probably live your life enmeshed in a complex web of social institutions. School, employment, government, organized religion, clubs, and other groups are all examples of formal social institutions. You might be involved simultaneously in several of these organizations. As a typical college student of the late twentieth century, you may attend school full-time, belong to a fraternity or sorority, participate in some student government organizations, have a part-time job at a local coffee bar, volunteer at an after-school program for elementary school children, and occasionally attend worship services.[1] Although you may be less aware of its presence in your life, government exerts a powerful influence over your behavior and choices. If you earn money, you pay a variety of taxes; if you are over age eighteen, you can vote (but may choose not to); your school may use a variety of federal and state programs to support higher education; and you or your family may rely on one of several state or federal programs for college grants and loans. You may have never thought of your friendships and informal interactions as social institutions, but families, neighborhoods, volunteer groups, friendships, cliques, classrooms, and campus clubs, all share some characteristics with formal social institutions. Organizations exert influence on our behavior, set norms and expectations, perpetuate ideologies, and structure time and activities. Organizational behavior may require formal rules such as how to vote in federal elections, when to pay taxes, when to speak at a public meeting, or what time to come to work. Social institutions also exert informal pressures on behavior by setting norms and standards. There is no rule about raising one's hand in a college classroom, yet everyone (except the instructor) does it; friends listen carefully and take turns in conversation; workers are deferential with their supervisors; and we expect everyone to exhibit good team fair play by sharing opportunities. Not all of these informal rules apply at all times, although social pressures exert considerable influence to maintain them. Social institutions vary in the degree to which they exert explicit, as opposed to implicit, control over behavior. The formal rules of taxation exemplify explicit control; the unstated rules of who eats lunch with whom at the office exemplify implicit control. Some social institutions have clearly marked physical spaces while others are symbolic. Institutions differ in the degree of influence they exert and in the degree to which people might conform to their standards. Regardless of institutional variation, we are all involved in multiple social organizations and are therefore subject to a variety of social influences.

Social institutions are a pervasive and often ubiquitous aspect of modern life. Many scholars have concluded that social institutions are also *gendered* (Lorber, 1994b; Martin, 1992; Worrell, 1993), and we agree with this analysis. What does it mean to claim that institutions are gendered? Briefly stated, it means that women and men have different experiences within the same institution. In this introduction, we explain the basis for this argument, and we describe different types of social institutions. We examine how gendered experiences in social institutions are maintained, and we consider the issues of equity and change within social institutions.

Gender and Sex Segregation in the Workplace

In her review of gender and social organizations, Martin (1992) provides a thorough account of some of the factors that contribute to differences in men's and women's experiences within organizations, especially workplace organization.[2] One of the most important factors for this differential experience is the degree of gender segregation in an organization. Sex segregation in employment is extreme. The majority of women are employed in highly segregated, female-dominated occupations: secretaries (99%), receptionists (97%), registered nurses (92%), elementary school teachers (86%), waitstaff (82%), cashiers (81%). Many other jobs are largely male: construction (98%), mechanics (97%), skilled labor (82%), manual labor (82%), engineering (92%), protective services, e.g., police, firefighters (87%), farming/forestry (84%) (U.S. Department of Labor, 1994). Even employment categories in which overall sex ratios are more equal still show considerable segregation by sex. Among teachers, for example, 98 percent of preschool and kindergarten teachers and 86 percent of elementary school teachers are women, while 45 percent of secondary school teachers and 68 percent of college professors are men. Many jobs and careers become gendered as the work itself takes on masculine or feminine qualities. Our belief that teachers of young children should be nurturing while police officers should be strong reflects the embeddedness of work and gender stereotypes in definitions of work-related competences.

Martin (1992) contends that within organizations, many factors further segregate women and men. For instance, similar jobs may be titled differently and located in different facilities; women are almost always supervised by men; labor unions have historically treated women and men differently; informal work groups are almost always sex segregated; male norms and standards may be used to set performance criteria; and managers enforce segregation out of fear of sexual dynamics in the workplace. Martin argues that in many settings such as construction sites, shipyards, military units, and coal mines, women are excluded because of concern about sexuality. Whereas these attitudes may deny women employment opportunities, the behavior of men in these settings is rarely questioned. Martin concludes that gender is ranked, in that males and masculinity hold precedence over women and femininity. This ranking is found especially in work settings in which gender rank is confounded with workplace authority, so that being a supervisor and being male confers on that person additional authority. Women as supervisors are given less respect because they lack the rank of masculinity. As you may remember from the article in chapter 5 by Fiske and Stevens, women cannot earn the rank accorded to masculinity by engaging in nontraditional behavior. Instead, they may be judged even more harshly for being unfeminine. Managers responsible for hiring decisions reflect this bias in their preference for male candidates or, in the absence of clear information about an applicant's sex, their favorable ratings of applications that indicate more masculine interests and characteristics (Glick, Zion, & Nelson, 1988). One's gender rank influences judgments of behavior, qualifications, and performance in the workplace and translates into advantages for men, but most especially for white men.

Compounding the issue of gender segregation is the continuing pay disparities between men and women. Several different types of comparisons demonstrate significant differences in earnings by women and men. Controlling for education and training, length of service with the company, and job title, Gerhart (1990) found that women in one large firm earned 88 percent of men's salaries. White men earn more than any other sex/race group, and within racial or ethnic groups, men earn more than women. A comparison of women's to men's earnings in the 1990s shows that women earn 71.5 percent of what men earn (National Committee on Pay Equity, 1994). The jobs predominantly held by women—secretary, nurse, elementary school teacher—are paid less than comparable jobs more likely to be held by men—construction worker, computer programmer, high school teacher. Even in jobs in which women are the clear majority, men may be paid more. For example,

the 1995 median salary for female nurses was $35,360, and for male nurses, it was $36,868. There is even a 20 percent wage differential between female and male retail cashiers (U.S. Department of Labor, 1995).

The confluence of gender segregation and salary disparities suggests that one important issue about gender in the workplace is why women have not gained parity with men. This issue can be understood by looking at two important questions: What factors perpetuate the segregation of women and men into different jobs and careers, and what factors perpetuate salary disparities, especially among jobs with seemingly similar requirements for education and training?

Gender Segregation in Other Settings

According to Maccoby (1990), whose views on gender segregation you read in chapter 6, gender segregation in the workplace may reflect the play preferences and friendship patterns established in childhood. While acknowledging the importance of social structural factors in maintaining gender segregation and gender hierarchies in the workplace, Maccoby argues that the distinctiveness of male and female cultures and the establishment of preferences for same-sex organizations are entirely consistent with the degree of gender segregation in the workplace. Experiences during childhood and adolescence often limit cross-sex interactions to family encounters (parent or sibling), classroom interactions in school, and dating during adolescence. Not surprisingly, according to Maccoby (1991), men and women adopt patterns of behavior in workplace cross-sex encounters that mimic their early same-sex experiences. These patterns of behavior position men as dominant, that is, demanding, assertive, confident, and oriented toward winning. Women are more likely to be conciliatory, oriented toward persuasion, and interested in intimacy. One result of this mismatch of styles is that men and women often have a strong preference for company of the same sex, so almost all informal work groups—people who share coffee in the morning or go to lunch together, people who volunteer for special projects or form small groups to lobby for changes, people who share activities and socializing after work hours—tend to be same-sex pairs or groups. Martin (1992), referring to these as *identity* groups, suggests that such groups tend to form around a number of status features, such as race, ethnicity, nationality, or age.

Many of these features of gender segregation can be observed in other social organizations besides the workplace. Return to the list of organizations or institutions you are associated with, and determine how many exhibit some degree of gender segregation. If you live on a college campus, observe your living arrangements. Even in coed dorms, many students congregate with same-sex peers for socializing and studying. In clubs and organizations, are you more likely to volunteer to share an activity with someone who is of the same sex? Look at the seating patterns in your school cafeteria—do identity groups congregate in special places? Your answers to these questions may not totally confirm gender segregation, given that while in college people have more cross-sex friends than any other time in their life. The lifestyle and living circumstances of college promote cross-sex friendships. Yet even college students encounter considerable gender segregation in their day-to-day lives. Interpersonal styles and social structures interact to maintain other social institutions as gendered organizations. Both intimate relationships and families, as described in the past two chapters, share characteristics with institutions: They both have formal and informal rules for behavior; they are influenced by the relative power of all participants; and they structure behavioral routines and norms. Other social institutions have struggled with issues of gender, most especially sex segregation. In the military, for example, there is continued, and often rancorous, debate over the inclusion of women in formerly all-male domains—in combat, as pilots, and on naval ships. Religious institutions have also grappled with the full inclusion of women, and many have maintained the tradition of strict sex segregation by rigidly defining the roles of women and men. Many volunteer groups, clubs, civic organiza-

tions, and sports teams segregate men and women. This segregation occurs explicitly in some settings, such as civic groups that have men's and women's branches. Until recently, Lions Clubs and Rotary International were male only, while the Junior League remains a women's group. Or segregation may be implicit in the tasks that men and women choose (e.g., in the Meals on Wheels program, a volunteer meal delivery service for shut-ins, more women prepare the meals while more men drive to deliver the meals). One goal of this chapter is to examine the forces that sustain gender segregation and to explain how social institutions perpetuate gendered relationships among individuals.

The first article in this chapter, *Guarding the Gates: The Micropolitics of Gender* by Judith Lorber, reviews many of the structural factors that maintain the status quo in employment. Although Lorber is concerned largely with workplace dynamics, many of the organizational features she describes apply to other formal and informal institutions. The second article, *Affirmative Action in Theory and Practice* by Jennifer Eberhardt and Susan Fiske, analyzes the results of affirmative action policies implemented to change sex and race imbalances in social institutions. Affirmative action is part of a larger question about creating equitable social institutions in which sex and gender do not play a large part in determining people's opportunities and experiences. Eberhardt and Fiske compare attitudes toward affirmative action based on race and gender. They believe that differences in race and gender stereotypes can help explain differences in public attitudes toward affirmative action for Blacks versus women. The last two readings in this chapter confront the issue of gendered violence. Although gendered violence is often equated with violence against women—an important manifestation of the social inequities that disadvantage women in many contexts—you will see that violence within the family, violence against gays and lesbians, and violence within gay and lesbian relationships all share characteristics with violence against women. The third article, *Sexual Terrorism: The Social Control of Women* by Carole Sheffield posits that violence against women is a form of social control that per-

p. 607

meates the social institutions within which we live. In Sheffield's analysis, violence against women *is* a social institution. The last reading, *Pain Explodes in a World of Power: Men's Violence* by Michael Kaufman introduces you to the notion that violence is a part of the male gender role and that male expressions of violence are widespread and systemic. Kaufman provides some examples of the psychological consequences for men of the social reproduction of violence through the male role.

POWER, GENDER, AND SOCIAL INSTITUTIONS

More than any other feature, social organizations represent institutionalized hierarchies of power. Power is often treated as a limited resource, a commodity that can be hoarded, distributed, or traded; a resource that can influence people, change behavior or circumstances, benefit oneself or others. Power commands respect, confers worth, and secures one's position in the social hierarchy. An alternative view portrays power, not as a commodity, but as a characteristic of relationships. Just as we "do gender" (West & Zimmerman, 1987), we can "do power," with our attempts to influence others, control outcomes, manage our resources, and create change. From this point of view, individuals do not just possess power; rather power emerges in different circumstances and expresses itself differently, depending on the individuals involved. The processes of social influence that we use to exercise power—leadership, negotiation, persuasion, cooperation, resistance, bargaining, compromise, refusal—reflect childhood socialization and, most important from the perspective of this book, our position in the gender hierarchy.

Power may be implied by social position (e.g., wealth is power), conferred by authority (e.g., police are authorized to use force), or socially defined by status (e.g., gender, race). Having access to resources such as money, education, or expertise may give someone power. Power may be demonstrated in the distribution of resources, decision making, efforts to control other's behaviors or choices, or attempts to influence others. Many social institutions

are organized hierarchically, and power is explicit in the positions people hold in the organization. As you might expect, men are more likely to be in positions of power in social organizations.

Power and Gender

For many contemporary theorists, power is one of the keys to understanding gender relations (Epstein, 1988; Lips, 1994; Lorber, 1994b; Worrell, 1993). In this perspective, gendered relationships are viewed as asymmetrical, with females and femininity relatively powerless and devalued within the culture. This perspective has been referred to as **institutionalized sexism,** because it entails systemic, organized differences in power that disadvantage women. While we are enmeshed in social institutions that replicate this power structure, we are largely unaware of the gendered nature of these social systems. Many of the routine assumptions we make about gender and power go unacknowledged. In how many countless ways do we hold beliefs about men and women, within social institutions, that are based solely on gender? For example, as female professors, we have both been mistaken for secretaries or staff members, a mistake never made about our male colleagues. Notice that one, completely unstated implication of this mistake is that the mere perception of an individual as a woman positions that woman at a lower level in the social organization. Without explicit efforts to address this misperception, continued social interactions are likely to support it.

In an intriguing synthesis of research on educational achievement, gender socialization, and power, Lips (1994) concludes that girls are socialized for powerlessness. Her analysis is evidence of adolescent girls' declining self esteem and their adoption of interactional styles that effectively diminish their interpersonal influence. In the context of social institutions that reward masculine styles of interaction and demonstrations of power, these attitudes of self-doubt and expressions of hesitance will be magnified. This argument is supported by Maccoby's (1990) analysis of the effects of gender segregation, which shows that boys use more power assertive and direct strategies to influence others whereas girls use more indirect and polite strategies for social influence. Boys typically are more experienced in competitive interactions, are more likely to take charge, and are more intrusive in conversations. Girls, on the other hand, often engage in more cooperative interactions and use more strategies to facilitate conversation. Evidence reviewed by Lips (1994) reveals that, by adolescence, girls rate themselves as less competent, less effective, and less powerful in comparison to boys.

Kaufman (1994) agrees that men are privileged members of our society, but there are significant costs to men in exchange for their social and institutional power. Kaufman believes that the pain of masculinity is disguised and obscured by the focus on male power. Power can be a source of alienation, especially emotional isolation, because the cost of masculinity is the need to distance oneself from the full range of human emotions. Men are taught to suppress inclinations toward nurturing, empathy, and compassion in order to gain the power of manhood. In Kaufman's analysis, power and pain are two sides of the same coin—masculinity. These elements of masculinity are not tempered by passivity or nurturance, because in our culture masculinity and femininity are viewed as mutually exclusive—one cannot simultaneously be powerful and nurturant. Kaufman says that, for men, this schism from their nurturing, empathic qualities is a source of pain and loss. Kaufman, in this chapter's reading, applies this analysis to male aggression, especially aggression against women. The analyses by Lips and Kaufman suggest that mechanisms in early development predispose men and women to respond differently to social/organizational structures. Ask yourself while you read the articles in this chapter, in what ways do gender-based predispositions interact with gendered features of social institutions?

Power in the Workplace

Lorber's article in this chapter's readings describes many features that maintain the gendered norms within social institutions. According to Lorber, gender segregation and beliefs about leadership and authority that characterize them in traditionally masculine terms sustain the organization of the workplace in ways that disadvantage women. One issue that Lorber pays particular attention to is the informal features that provide channels for communication about the workplace. Lorber argues that rooted in the establishment of trust among men are traditions of informal mentoring and networking that benefit those on the inside track. Typically, access to the inside track is based on similarity among managers and subordinates, so men are more likely to take an interest in and provide these channels of informal access to men like themselves. We would like you to note, especially for the upcoming section on affirmative action, that these informal processes based on perceived similarity also disadvantage men and women of color. Through informal communication, workers are likely to learn a wealth of information about the organizational culture, norms for behavior, who to know and who to avoid, which jobs lead to success and which jobs are dead ends, and other subjective features of workplace organization. Many of the features Lorber describes, such as the glass ceiling, the mommy track, and tokenism, are invisible; therefore, workers in an organization may be oblivious to dimensions of the workplace that are dissimilar for women and men.

An issue that has received substantial attention in research on women and men in organizations is the nature of leadership (Johnson, 1992). In attempts to explain the disproportionately high number of men in leadership positions, theorists have considered various explanations related to leadership style and structural barriers to women's opportunities. Based on what you have read so far in this chapter and on what you have learned from the other readings in this book, you might have some ideas about how gender, leadership, and social organizations interact. Given Maccoby's (1990) description of gender segregation, you might expect men and women to approach leadership with different styles—men as more authoritarian and women as more democratic. Examining the data on the degree of gender segregation, you might not expect to find many female leaders in male-dominated professions, although you may be uncertain about whether female leaders of predominantly male groups would be different from male leaders. Finally, from the evidence about gender segregation in most employment settings, you might predict that women and men are more likely to be differentially associated with specific settings and therefore likely to be differentially successful in settings matched with their sex.

Of all our questions about gender, leadership, and social organizations, the most intriguing might be whether men and women have different leadership styles and how men and women are judged on effective leadership. Not all findings are consistent, but the research evidence suggests overall that women are no more person-centered as leaders than are men; however, there is some evidence that women are more democratic, are more likely to ask for suggestions, and are more open to participatory decision making (Eagly & Johnson, 1991).

A meta-analysis by Eagly and colleagues (Eagly, Karau, & Makhijani, 1995) of research on judgments of leadership effectiveness support a complex interpretation of the relationship between leadership effectiveness and work. Overall, men and women are judged as equally effective leaders; however, men are judged to be better leaders in male-dominated work settings, such as the military, whereas women are judged better leaders in female-dominated settings, such as teaching. Thus, within professions, gender role stereotypes may prevail. Some additional evidence indicates that women prefer to work under a democratic style of leadership, whereas men prefer to work under a more autocratic style—although ironically, women who exercise autocratic leadership are judged more harshly.

Let us summarize this review by considering the predictions made earlier. Men and women leaders are, in general, more similar than they are different. Women typically use and prefer to work under democratic strategies, a finding supported by the evidence about gender differences in socialization, especially girls' and women's greater tendency to use collaboration. Men and women are judged similarly in effectiveness ratings, although women are judged more harshly in nontraditional work settings or when portrayed as possessing autocratic characteristics. These results are consistent with Eagly's social role theory, which argues that agenic behaviors (such as leadership) emerge from opportunities to engage in agenic activities. Presumably a work life in which one prepares for and assumes leadership will lead to the development of agenic qualities—in either women or men. Finally, we see an interaction between sex, leadership style, and work setting based on the observation that certain work settings become highly gender stereotyped, especially when they are predominantly male or female. We can conclude that leadership and power are intimately related, and as the power differentials between women and men change, we expect that the stereotypes about women as leaders will diminish and that people will accept the reality that leadership is not a product of one's sex.

Affirmative Action—Can Power be Redistributed?

Try this short quiz on affirmative action by deciding whether each statement is true or false: Affirmative action policies allow employers to give special preferences to minority and female job candidates; when affirmative action policies are used, often less qualified minority or female employees are hired over more qualified white or male candidates; affirmative action replaces hiring decisions based on merit with hiring based on race or sex. All these statements are false, but they are common misperceptions of affirmative action. This chapter's article by Eberhardt and Fiske answers the question of why misperceptions of affirmative action are so prevalent and looks at how power and stereotypes sustain these beliefs about affirmative action.

Affirmative action is a public policy based on a 1968 Executive Order amendment to the 1964 Civil Rights Act, which prohibits discrimination based on sex. Prior to affirmative action, employers could restrict jobs to only men or only women, so, for example, men were not hired as flight attendants and women were not hired as firefighters. Under affirmative action policy, employers may not specify the sex of employees, may not specify the marital status of employees, may not prevent pregnant women from working, and may not have double standards for evaluation or retirement. It is a violation of federal law to engage in any of these practices. In the 1980s and 1990s the Supreme Court narrowed the scope of affirmative action, and consequently, its impact has been slowed. The number of women employees has increased in many workplace environments, and women have been treated more equitably because of affirmative action.

The policies of affirmative action that are most contentious are the programs used to increase the number of employees in underrepresented groups who are minorities and women (Lindgren & Taub, 1993). According to Eberhardt and Fiske, affirmative action has such a negative reputation because it is a social policy that challenges traditional power structures. Although employers have been under federal mandate to alter their hiring practices, the workplace does not always support these changes in the power hierarchies. Ironically, this attitude is inconsistent with the observation that people in general favor the goals of affirmative action. Eberhardt and Fiske believe this contradiction can be explained in part by the attitudes held toward Blacks and women. The evaluation process of a job candidate's qualifications contains considerable ambiguities, and these ambiguities provide ample opportunity for stereotypes to play a part in hiring decisions. Eberhardt and Fiske compare the stereotypes of Blacks and women to explain the experiences with affirmative action for each group. Typically, Blacks are judged more undeserving when hired through policies of affirmative action. Overall, the effectiveness of affirmative action for women has been judged somewhat successful, whereas the evidence suggests that affirmative action has had less of an impact on job opportunities for Blacks. Stereotypes for both groups intersect with power dynamics in the workplace so that those holding power, typically white men, are accorded higher status and are assumed to be deserving of their position. Affirmative action job candidates who challenge that assumption are believed to be undeserving, unqualified, or unable to make it on their

own. People in power in the workplace (presumably White men) are more likely to have extensive contact with women in other settings, which leads them to be more tolerant of women as beneficiaries of affirmative action. This notion is consistent with the observations that affirmative action stereotypes more often view minorities as beneficiaries and with the fact that women have benefited more from affirmative action. One of the authors (Jennifer Eberhardt) includes a personal account of an encounter with a police officer in which both race and gender stereotypes contributed to a misunderstanding over an expired car inspection that escalated into her arrest. She reflects on the contributions of race, gender, and setting—she was pulled over adjacent to an urban housing project—to this event. This real-life example shows the complexity of teasing apart the influences of stereotypes and of accounting for the perceptions of all individuals involved. We ask in the title of this section whether power can be redistributed. To answer that question, you need to read the articles by Lorber and by Eberhardt and Fiske and you need to ask yourself whether social policies can ever change social institutions.

GENDERED VIOLENCE—ABUSE OF POWER?

One important consequence of the women's movement of the last thirty years has been the public recognition of the extent to which women are victimized by violence, both in the context of intimate relationships and in assaults or rapes by strangers. A feminist analysis of violence against women focuses on its widespread nature and on the extent to which our culture tolerates attitudes and behaviors that sustain violence. More recently, theorists working from the perspective of the men's movement have added their voices to the feminist analysis of men's violence, focusing on intrapsychic factors within men along with cultural attitudes that privilege masculinity (Beneke, 1982; Kaufman, 1993; Messerschmidt, 1993). Even more recently has been added the recognition that much of the violence in the context of these intimate relationships, either heterosexual or homosexual, may be related to the gendered nature of intimate relationships. Our analysis treats gender violence as a social institution, and for our last two readings in this chapter, we have chosen feminist and men's movement analyses that support this view. Both these readings agree that it is essential to expose the social-structural factors that perpetuate violence. Carole Sheffield focuses on culture as a social institution, and Michael Kaufman focuses on the cultural norms that define and maintain masculinity. You need to realize that these analyses are complementary. Both authors agree that gendered violence is a significant social problem and that women are victimized in far greater numbers than are men. We want you to approach this topic with the recognition that this point is not an indictment of all men nor does it assume the victimization of all women—we are not advocating a "he said, she said" analysis. We believe that everyone in this culture must recognize the degree to which gendered violence impacts us all by threatening the quality of our individual and family life.

Gender and Violence

Violence against women includes rape and sexual assault by strangers, date rape, marital rape, incest, spouse or partner abuse, and sexual harassment ranging from unwanted touching to rape. Many of these crimes use sexuality as a weapon of violence (e.g., rape, incest, sexual harassment), and some are physical violence in the context of a gender relationship or social setting (e.g., spouse or partner abuse). Men are also victimized by all these crimes, although in fewer numbers and usually under different circumstances. For example, men are more likely to be raped while they are in prison, whereas women are raped more frequently by men they know. Rape is estimated to be the most underreported crime in the United States. About 105,000 rapes of women were reported in 1993 (U.S. Department of Justice, 1994), but the actual number is estimated to be somewhere between three and ten times as many. Women experience coercive sexual intercourse even more frequently; the results of several surveys of col-

lege-age women suggest that between 25 percent and 44 percent report that they have had unwanted sexual experiences (O'Toole & Schiffman, 1997). Female victims of rape cross over age, race, and ethnicity, although victims are more likely to be young. In one national survey, 61 percent of rape victims were under the age of 18, and 78 percent of the victims knew the rapist (National Victim Center, 1992).

It is nearly impossible to estimate the number of men and boys who are raped because the factors that prevent women from reporting rape (e.g., fear of being disbelieved, embarrassment, social attitudes that blame the victim, stigma, behavior not defined as rape, fear of reprisal from the rapist) are exacerbated for men. The rape of men shares some characteristics of the rape of women. It is a crime of violence, control, and disempowerment of the victim and is a behavioral distortion of masculinity (Kaufman, 1993; Pelka, 1992).

Studies of child abuse show that both boys and girls are physically abused; some evidence suggests that boys are more frequently victimized by severe physical abuse whereas girls are nearly four times more likely to be sexually abused (Herzberger, 1996). Children experience gender violence as victims of incest and molestation, prostitution and pornography, as victims of prenatal injury caused by battering of pregnant women, and as witnesses to the abuse of a parent, most often the mother, by that parent's partner (O'Toole & Schiffman, 1997). These forms of child abuse mirror the gendered nature of violence in adults in that they reflect the patriarchy and power imbalances in our society and within the family. According to Bowker, Arbitell, and McFerron (1988), the intentional abuse of children is one strategy used by men who abuse their partners to control the abused partner. Renzetti (1997) reports the same phenomenon among gay and lesbian couples, in which an abusive partner uses abuse toward children as a means of control.[3] Research by Stahly (1996) indicates that women stay in abusive relationships out of fear that their children will be abducted or abused. Statistics compiled from battered women's shelters in California show that 11 percent of the nearly 100,000 women served by these shelters actually had their children abducted, for a total of 10,687 kidnappings in one year. Abusive husbands and fathers are more likely to seek custody of their children than are nonabusive men. One inescapable explanation for this pattern is that violence toward children in the family is linked to misogyny and to power and control over women.

Between one third and one half of all working women, and about 9 percent of men, have been harassed at some time in their work life (Gutek, 1993). Most harassers are men. Gutek reports that the majority of men (61%) and women (68%) have been the recipient of a sexual comment or activity although they were not interpreted as harassment or did not meet the legal definition of harassment. Although men are not as likely to be harassed, they clearly experience sexual behavior at work, most especially in the form of teasing, comments on clothing, or flirtatious behavior. Men tend to perceive these sexual behaviors as friendly whereas women are more likely to perceive these sexual behaviors as threatening. Environments, therefore, that are highly sexualized—as many male-dominated work environments are—with posters, jokes, calendar pictures, sexual metaphors, and obscene language are likely to be interpreted by women as threatening environments. Remember from the Fiske and Stevens article in chapter 5 that Lois Robinson was working in a highly sexualized environment at the Jacksonville Shipyards. Recall also that Lois Robinson was the recipient of repeated, direct harassing behaviors from her coworkers. Two elements of the Fiske and Stevens analysis of gender stereotypes help us understand the institutionalized nature of gendered violence. First, men and women have differential access to power, and in highly gender-segregated work environments, male power can be virtually unchecked. When you hear about situations like that of Lois Robinson or about less explicit forms of sexual harassment, notice that you also often hear the claim that the behavior is benign or that women need to learn to take a joke. Second, gender stereotypes are highly prescriptive, which implies that men and women are likely to act in conventional ways that reflect these stereotypes. Men who privately object to sexual harassment may ignore or tolerate it out of fear of being thought less masculine. Similarly, women may have internalized the notion of themselves as sex objects, so although they may find the harassment highly unpleasant and threatening, they do not define it as inappropriate. Stereotypes sustain power differentials and internalized notions of gender appropriate behavior, both of which support the institutionalized nature of gender violence. This explanation helps us understand the perpetuation of sexual harassment as well as other forms of gender violence.

Violence also occurs in gay and lesbian relationships, and some of it parallels violence in heterosexual relationships. It is nearly impossible to estimate the extent of violence within gay and lesbian relationships because accurate estimates would depend on full access to the larger population of gay and lesbian couples.[4] For our analysis, it is less important to estimate the extent of gay and lesbian violence than it is to acknowledge its occurrence and to understand its meaning, especially in terms of gender. According to Renzetti (1997), theorists need to be careful about simplistic assumptions that all domestic violence can be based on models derived from observations of heterosexual violence. Domestic violence within lesbian and gay relationships may involve all of the types of abuse observed in heterosexual battering as well as psychological and physical abuse that would not be found among heterosexuals. Notably, this abuse could include threats of outing either to family or employers, and among gay men, AIDS may interact with violence by increasing one's vulnerability to abuse or by inducing guilt, making it more difficult to leave an abusive, HIV positive, or AIDS stricken partner. Another difference, which we have discussed in both chapters 10 and 11, is that power dynamics may differ in gay and lesbian relationships. Additionally, gay and lesbian couples face many more structural barriers to the establishment and maintenance of their relationships, and it may be more difficult for abused individuals to find help from support groups or therapists. Renzetti suggests that we need a more contextualized understanding of violence in intimate relationships. This would provide some evidence of the meanings of violent behaviors given by both the victim and the aggressor, would examine the motivations of each partner, and would take into account race, ethnicity and age as well as gender and sexual orientation. We will have to wait for more research to make such a contextualized account.

Cultural Explanations for Gendered Violence

Sheffield, in her article in this chapter, draws the analogy between violence against women and terrorism. Sheffield believes that our culture supports a climate of sexual terrorism against women, and she draws the following comparisons between political and sexual terrorism. Sexual terrorism is supported by a cultural ideology of patriarchy, in which propaganda maintains biased perceptions about sexual violence. The violence against women is indiscriminant and amoral, and voluntary compliance is provided by a system of socialization that encourages male violence and female self-blame. We encourage you to carefully evaluate the evidence Sheffield provides.

Kaufman's analysis of male violence is consistent with Sheffield's, although he is focused on a very different question—why are men violent? Kaufman claims that male violence is rooted in the nature of masculinity. Manhood is equated with having power, and violence is one manifestation of men's efforts to act on their power. Masculinity is a form of control, and the suppression of emotion, especially fear, pain, sadness, or embarrassment, is the ultimate exercise of self-control and power. Kaufman says that for many men, all emotion is channeled into various forms of aggression, some of which is socially acceptable and some of which is not tolerated or illegal. It does seem axiomatic in our culture that masculinity is defined around denial of feeling and aggression. Kaufman's view is intriguing and will resonant with those of you who see yourself or see people you know in his examples.

Left unanswered is the question of how to explain women's violence in intimate relationships with other women, in instances of sexual harassment, or with a male partner. Certainly women do not become violent because of their internalization of masculine ideology. Can we explain this violent behavior using Sheffield's model? Only partially. Sheffield bases her

analysis of violence against women on the patriarchal nature of our society and the overall denigration of women; therefore, some violence by women may reflect this cultural belief. Neither she nor Kaufman directly address the question of women's violence. You may remember that in chapter 8, White and Kowalski do address this question, and their arguments support our view that gender violence is a social institution.[5] White and Kowalski (1994) suggest that power does influence women's violence because it is more likely to occur in the setting in which women have relatively greater power—the home. White and Kowalski's analysis suggests that power dynamics are partially responsible for the way women's aggression is defined. They suggest that women's use of physical violence in response to abuse is frequently denied or minimized and that this denial becomes a means to perpetuate male dominance by denying that women utilize traditionally masculine approaches to respond to aggression. Finally, these researchers suggest that a more contextualized analysis will shed light on women's violence, and this argument is echoed by others who have examined nontraditional violence (Renzetti, 1997). We should not expect the experience of gendered violence to be the same for everyone. Until we examine the intersections of race, ethnicity, sexual orientation, and age with gender, we cannot fully appreciate the complexity of the dynamics that sustain and/or diminish violence of this sort. Although we have argued that gender violence is a social institution, we would not argue that it is a monolithic institution. Our contention is that gendered violence is an institution supported by cultural traditions, beliefs about gender, and stereotypes and by institutional practices that are amenable to change.

Social Change and Reducing Violence

Public recognition of violence against women has grown and public policies have been enacted to address such violence, but we are often oblivious to the forces that sustain violence. We live in a culture in which publicly sanctioned violence is readily available through television, news, movies, music, sports, and pornography. Every day television broadcasts a "woman in peril" movie, which enacts one of the cultural scripts of violence against women. We become desensitized to violence when it is such an omnipresent feature of our daily lives.

Another critical dimension of gender in our society, which has not been fully exposed, is the degree to which the cultural dichotomy of gender segregates our experiences. For most of us, gender divides people into two categories, which are treated as nonoverlapping. So we assume, and behave as though, the experiences of and expectations for women and men are completely different. If men are aggressive, women must not be. If women are conciliatory, men must not be. We know these prescriptions do not adequately describe people's real behavior, but as long as the bifurcated notion of gender prevails, the issue of gendered violence will continue to be labeled as a feminist or women's issue, which leads to its ultimate devaluation. Only when gendered violence is recognized as a complex human problem affecting all of us can we begin to reduce violence in social institutions. In his first-person account of being raped while hitchhiking, Fred Pelka (1992) suggests that sexual violence is simultaneously a women's and a human problem. "One source of confusion appears to be the distinction between victimization and oppression. . . . feminists see rape as a "man vs. woman" issue, emphasizing the central role male violence plays in stunting and destroying women's lives, and they're right. The distinction is that while many women, and some men, are victimized by rape, all women are oppressed by it, and any victimization of women occurs in a context of oppression men simply do not understand. Being a male rape survivor means I no longer fit our culture's neat but specious definition of masculinity, as one empowered, one always in control" (p. 40).

ACHIEVING EQUITY IN SOCIAL INSTITUTIONS

There is a paradox in asking the question of how to bring about social change. Social institutions are made up of individuals who bring their individual beliefs and values to the organization while at the same time institutions act to constrain an individual's behavior through structural forces that maintain the status quo. Thus the often conflicting nature of individual beliefs and the structural aspects of the institution need to be addressed when proposing social change. The paradox is that we cannot necessarily predict, or even fully understand, the complex dynamic between these two forces. Affirmative action provides one example of this paradox. We learn in the Eberhardt and Fiske reading that policy change (affirmative action) interacts with people's belief systems (stereotypes) in complex ways. Thus, affirmative action has decreased workplace segregation for women but has not had a significant impact on employment opportunities for Blacks; also, affirmative action has not addressed the considerable amount of informal sex segregation. Social change cannot always be brought about by social policy changes.

Other changes in the workplace reflect the increasing number of women in paid employment, most notably, family/work benefits such as child care subsidies, parental leave, and flextime. Pleck (1993) has examined men's utilization of these policies and provides several interesting conclusions. Men spend more time on household and child care responsibilities than in past generations, although the exact amount of increase is contested (Barnett & Rivers, 1996). Men, however, show a surprising reluctance to utilize employer benefits designed for family responsibilities. For example, although unpaid parental leave is available to all employees, only a minority of men take formal parental leave at the birth of a child. Instead, men use informal strategies (e.g., vacation days, accumulated sick leave, or compensatory time) to be home for a few days with their new baby. Pleck attributes this behavior to several factors, including loss of pay and negative perceptions among coworkers and supervisors that a father's parental leave is unmasculine. Even though structural factors have altered workplace policies, these new policies interact with prevailing stereotypes. Pleck concludes that the workplace culture is probably more important than the availability of formal policies. Work environments that minimize sex segregation, that recognize family responsibilities, and that aggressively address sexual harassment are likely to alter the corporate culture and, therefore, counteract the force of stereotyped beliefs and attitudes that maintain gender inequality between women and men. The relationship among institutional, interpersonal, and individual factors is complex and dynamic. Social change will require a greater understanding of this complexity, and changes at all levels of social institutions must reflect a consistent valuing of equity.

We have discussed many of the structural features of social institutions as they relate to gender. There is considerable inequity in our social institutions, maintained by gender segregation, power imbalances, and gender roles that provide prescriptive control over people's behavior. Most of the inequities we have described disadvantage women—in the workplace, clubs and organizations, religions, government, and relationships. These disadvantages for women lead to economic disparities, to the fears and realities of violence, and to limited employment opportunities. The inequities do not, however, necessarily translate into advantages for men. Ironically, only a small minority of men are explicitly privileged by our patriarchal society. Those men at the pinnacle of the social class hierarchy may enjoy advantages not shared by others. For most men, the advantages of masculinity are more symbolic than they are tangible. Minority men, gay men, and poor men may hold the status of masculinity, but the realities of their lives are often constructed around racism and ethnic prejudice, heterosexism, and limited economic opportunities. Without minimizing the damage done to women through our social institutions, we would add that we doubt that most men feel privileged by their masculinity. It is our firm belief that a more equitable society would advantage both women and men.

NOTES

1. Of course, you may be very different from this hypothetical student, so we encourage you to list the institutions you participate in, or interact with, regularly.
2. The examples we use, based on Martin's account, relate to the workplace. Try to compare these workplace examples to the establishment and maintenance of sex segregation in other settings.
3. Throughout this section, we discuss violence among gay and lesbian couples and use these examples to support the argument that these forms of aggression are intimately connected to gender dynamics. However, no evidence suggests that violence among gay and lesbian couples occurs with the same frequency that it is observed within heterosexual couples.
4. Many gay and lesbian partners do not publicly disclose the nature of their relationship, and therefore it is impossible to include such individuals in research studies. Without access to a true random sample of gay and lesbian couples, the rate of violence or any other relevant behavior cannot be accurately estimated.
5. Your initial reading of White and Kowalski may not have led you to undertand how women's violence is related to gendered violence. You may want to reread their article after reading this introduction and while reading the Sheffield and Kaufman articles.

REFERENCES

Barnett, R. C., & Rivers, C. (1996). *She works/he works: How two-income families are happier, healthier, and better off.* New York: HarperCollins.

Beneke, T. (1982). *Men on rape.* New York: St. Martin's Press.

Bowker, L., Arbitell, M., & McFerron, R. (1988). On the relationship between wife beating and child abuse. In K. Yllo & M. Bograd (Eds.), *Feminist perspectives of wife abuse.* Newbury Park, CA: Sage.

Eagly, A. H., & Johnson, B. T. (1991). Gender and leadership style: A meta-analysis. *Psychological Bulletin, 108,* 233–256.

Eagly, A. H., Karau, S. J., & Makhijani, M. G. (1995). Gender and the effectiveness of leaders: A meta-analysis. *Psychological Bulletin, 117,* 125–145.

Eberhardt, J. L., & Fiske, S. T. (1994). Affirmative action in theory and practice: Issues of power, ambiguity, and gender versus race. *Basic and Applied Social Psychology, 15,* 201–220.

Epstein, C. F. (1988). *Deceptive distinctions: Sex gender and the social order.* New Haven: Yale University Press.

Gerhart, B. (1990). Gender differences in current and starting salaries: The role of performance, college major, and job title. *Industrial and Labor Relations Review, 43,* 418–433.

Glick, P., Zion, C., & Nelson, C. (1988). What mediates sex discrimination in hiring decisions? *Journal of Personality and Social Psychology, 55,* 178–186.

Gutek, B. A. (1993). Responses to sexual harassment. In S. Oskamp & M. Constanzo (Eds.), *Gender issues in contemporary society* (pp. 197–216). Newbury Park, CA: Sage.

Herzberger, S. (1996). *Violence within the family: Social psychological perspectives.* Boulder, CO: Westview Press.

Johnson, C. (1992). Gender, formal authority, and leadership. In C. Ridgeway (Ed.), *Gender, interaction, and inequality* (pp. 29–49). New York: Springer-Verlag.

Kaufman, M. (1993). Pain explodes in a world of power: Men's violence. In *Cracking the armour: Power, pain, and the lives of men* (pp. 159–188). New York: Viking Penguin.

Kaufman, M. (1994). Men, feminism, and men's contradictory experiences of power. In H. Brod & M. Kaufman (Eds.), *Theorizing Masculinities* (pp. 142–163). Beverly Hills, CA: Sage.

Lindgren, J. R., & Taub, N. (1993). *The law of sex discrimination.* Minneapolis, MN: West.

Lips, H. (1994). Female powerlessness: A case of "cultural preparedness"? In L. Radtke & H. Stam (Eds.), *Power/gender— Social relations in theory and practice* (pp. 89–107). London: Sage.

Lorber, J. (1994a). Guarding the gates: The micropolitics of gender. In J. Lorber (Ed.), *Paradoxes of gender* (pp. 225–252). New Haven: Yale University Press.

Lorber, J. (1994b). *Paradoxes of gender.* New Haven: Yale University Press.

Maccoby, E. (1990). Gender and relationships: A developmental account. *American Psychologist, 45,* 513–520.

Maccoby, E. (1991). Gender segregation in the workplace: Continuities from childhood to adulthood. In M. Frankenhaeuser, U. Lundberg, & M. Chesney (Eds.), *Women, work and health: Stress and opportunities* (pp. 3–16). New York: Plenum Press.

Martin, P. Y. (1992). Gender, interaction, and inequality in organizations. In C. L. Ridgeway (Ed.), *Gender, interaction, and inequality* (pp. 208–231). New York: Springer-Verlag.

Messerschmidt, J. (1993). *Masculinities and crime: Critique and reconceptualization of theory.* Lanham, MD: Rowman & Littlefield.

National Committee on Pay Equity. (1994). *Newsnotes, 15,* 1–13.

National Victim Center. (1992). *Rape in America: A report to the nation.* Arlington, VA: National Victim Center.

O'Toole, L. L., & Schiffman, J. R. (1997). *Gender violence: Interdisciplinary perspectives.* New York: New York University Press.

Pelka, F. (1992, Spring). Raped: A male survivor breaks his silence. *On the Issues, 22,* 8–11, 40.

Pleck, J. (1993). Are "family-supportive" employer policies relevant to men? In J. Hood (Ed.), *Men, work, and family.* Newbury Park, CA: Sage.

Renzetti, C. M. (1997). Violence in lesbian and gay relationships. In L. L. O'Toole & J. R. Schiffman (Eds.), *Gender violence: Interdisciplinary perspectives* (pp. 285–293). New York: New York University Press.

Sheffield, C. (1987). Sexual terrorism: The social control of women. In M. Ferree & B. Hess (Eds.), *Analyzing gender: A handbook of social science research* (pp. 171–189). Newbury Park, CA: Sage.

Stahly, G. B. (1996). Battered women: Why don't they just leave? In J. C. Chrisler, C. Golden, & P. D. Rozee (Eds.), *Lectures on the psychology of women* (pp. 289–308). New York: McGraw-Hill.

U.S. Department of Justice, F.B.I. (1994). *Uniform crime reports for the United States, 1993.* Washington, DC: U.S. Government Printing Office.

U.S. Department of Labor. (1995). *Women's Bureau of Labor Statistics.* Washington, DC: U.S. Department of Labor.

U.S. Department of Labor. (1994). *1993 handbook on women workers: Trends and issues.* Washington, DC: U.S. Government Printing Office.

West, C., & Zimmerman, D. H. (1987). Doing gender. *Gender & Society, 1,* 125–151.

White, J. W., & Kowalski, R. M. (1994). Deconstructing the myth of the nonaggressive woman. *Psychology of Women Quarterly, 18,* 487–508.

Worrell, J. (1993). Gender in close relationships: Public policy vs. personal prerogative. *Journal of Social Issues, 49,* 203–218.

Guarding the Gates: The Micropolitics of Gender

JUDITH LORBER

You're proposing your interpretation of the universe, and for that you need to have the recognition of your colleagues. You must assert that this is a good idea, the right interpretation, and that you *thought of it, because all three of those things have to be accepted by your colleagues. It doesn't do your career any good to have the theory accepted, without anyone giving you the credit.*

—Harriet Zuckerman, Jonathan R. Cole, and John T. Bruer (1991, 103)

Twenty-five years ago, Muriel F. Siebert bought a seat on the New York Stock Exchange, the first woman to be permitted to do so. In 1992, receiving an award for her accomplishments, she said bluntly that despite the numbers of women coming into high finance, the professions, and government, the arenas of power are still overwhelmingly dominated by men (Henriques 1992). The numbers bear her out.

In 1980 in the United States, only two women were chief executive officers of the largest corporations, the Fortune 500. They were Katherine Graham, chief executive of the Washington Post Company, and Marion O. Sandler, co–chief executive of Golden West Financial Corporation, in Oakland, California. In 1985, there were three: Graham, Sandler, and Elisabeth Claiborne of the Liz Claiborne clothing company. In 1990, there were also three: Graham, Sandler, and Linda Wachner of the Warnaco Group, Inc., New York. In 1992, Charlotte Beers became chief executive of Ogilvie & Mather Worldwide, the fifth largest international advertising agency, with billings of $5.4 billion, making her the world's highest ranking women executive in that field (Elliott 1992). Linda Wachner (earning $3.1 million in 1991) was the first woman in *Fortune*'s "roster of exorbitantly paid executives" (Strom 1992). Thus, in the past decade, in the United States, where women composed between 42.4 and 45.4 percent of the work force, and numbered between 42.1 and 53.5 million, a total of five women were heads of the largest corporations (Marsh 1991).[1] When *Fortune* culled the lists of the highest paid officers and directors of 799 U.S. industrial and service companies, out of 4,012 it found 19 women, or less than one-half of 1 percent (Fierman 1990).

The belief that upward mobility and leadership positions would automatically follow if women increased their numbers in the workplace greatly underestimated the social processes that get some people onto the fast track and systematically derail others. These processes are used by those at the top to ensure that those coming up will be as similar as possible to themselves so that their values and ideas about how things should be done will be perpetuated. The markers of homogeneity are gender, race, religion, ethnicity, education, and social background. The few heterogeneous "tokens" who make it past the gatekeepers first must prove their similarity to the elite in outlook and behavior. The numbers at the bottom in any field have little relation to the numbers at the top, where power politics is played and social policies are shaped.

The gender segregation so evident in the modern work world is exacerbated at the top echelons of business, the professions, and politics by gendered concepts of authority and leadership potential. Women are seen as legitimate leaders only in areas considered of direct concern to women, usually health, education, and welfare. Women's accomplishments in men's fields tend to be invisible or denigrated by the men in the field, and so women rarely

607

achieve the stature to be considered leaders in science or space, for example.[2] The U.S. National Aeronautics and Space Administration put twenty-five women pilots through rigorous physical and psychological testing from 1959 to 1961. Thirteen demonstrated "exceptional suitability" for space flight, but neither they nor seventeen women with advanced science degrees were chosen to be astronauts or space scientists, even though the Russians had sent Valentina Tereshkova into space in 1963 (McCullough 1973). As Gloria Steinem said, recalling these invisible women almost twenty years later, women's demonstrating they have the "right stuff" turns into the "wrong stuff" without the approval of the men in charge (1992).

When a leader is chosen among colleagues, women are often overlooked by the men of the group, and there are usually too few women to support one another. Even where women are the majority of workers, men tend to be favored for positions of authority because women and men will accept men leaders as representing their general interests but will see women as representing only women's interests (Izraeli 1984). As a result, men in occupations where most of the workers are women, such as nursing and social work, tend to be overrepresented in high-level administrative positions, and women in occupations where most of the workers are men rarely reach the top ranks (C. L. Williams 1989, 95–98; Zunz 1991).

When men choose a woman for a position of power and prestige, she is often considered "on probation." For example, an Israeli woman physician who was made head of a prestigious department of obstetrics and gynecology where she was the only woman told me that a year later, the men colleagues who had chosen her told her that they were now enormously relieved. She had not made any serious mistakes, so their decision to choose her as head of the department was validated. She was furious that they had felt she had to prove herself; she had been their colleague and friend for seventeen years, and they surely should have known her worth and her leadership capabilities. At that point, she said, she realized that her men colleagues had never really considered her "one of them."[3]

THE GLASS CEILING

The pervasive phenomenon of women going just so far and no further in their occupations and professions has come to be known as the *glass ceiling*. This concept assumes that women have the motivation, ambition, and capacity for positions of power and prestige, but invisible barriers keep them from reaching the top. They can see their goal, but they bump their heads on a ceiling that is both hidden and impenetrable. The U.S. Department of Labor defines the glass ceiling as "those artificial barriers based on attitudinal or organizational bias that prevent qualified individuals from advancing upward in their organization into management level positions" (L. Martin 1991, 1).

A recent study of the pipelines to power in large-scale corporations conducted by the U.S. Department of Labor found that the glass ceiling was lower than previously thought—in middle management. Members of disadvantaged groups were even less likely than white women to be promoted to top positions, and the upper rungs were "nearly impenetrable" for women of color (L. Martin 1991). A random sample of ninety-four reviews of personnel in corporate headquarters found that of 147,179 employees, 37.2 percent were women and 15.5 percent were minorities. Of these employees, 31,184 were in all levels of management, from clerical supervisor to chief executive officer; 16.9 percent were women and 6 percent were minorities. Of 4,491 managers at the level of assistant vice president and higher, 6.6 percent were women and 2.6 percent were minorities. Thus, in this survey, the higher the corporate position, the smaller the proportion of women; if the numbers of women in the top ranks had been proportional with the number of women in the lower ranks, over a third of the vice presidents, presidents, and executive officers would have been women. There was no separate breakdown of these figures for women of color, but another report cited by the Labor Department indicated that they make up 3.3 percent of the women corporate officers, who make up only 1 to 2 percent of all corporate officers.

Karen Fulbright's (1987) interviews with twenty-five African-American women managers found fifteen who had reached the level of vice president, department head, or division director in oil, automobile manufacturing, telecommunications, and banking, or had moved rapidly up the hierarchy. The factors in their upward mobility were long tenure, a rapidly growing company, or a Black-owned or operated company. The others had experienced blocked mobility, despite positioning themselves on career tracks that were known to be the routes to the top.

Similar attrition in the numbers of women at the top has been found in public-sector jobs in the United States. As of 1990, 43.5 percent of the employees in lower-level jobs were women, but they were only 31.3 percent of the department heads, division chiefs, deputies, and examiners in state and local government agencies (*New York Times* 1992a). African-American women were 9.8 percent of the workers at lower levels, 5.1 percent at the top levels.

The ways that most people move up in their careers are through *networking* (finding out about job opportunities through word-of-mouth and being recommended by someone already there), *mentoring* (being coached through the informal norms of the workplace), and *sponsorship* (being helped to advance by a senior colleague). In civil service bureaucracies, where promotion depends on passing a test or getting an additional credential, those who receive encouragement and advice from senior members of the organization tend to take the qualifying tests or obtain the requisite training (Poll 1978). In the sciences, research productivity depends to a significant degree on where you work, whom you work with, and what resources are available to you.[4] All these processes of advancement depend on the support of colleagues and superiors, which means that in a workplace where men outnumber women and whites outnumber any other racial ethnic group, white women and women and men of disadvantaged racial ethnic groups have to be helped by white men if they are to be helped at all.

An in-depth study of nine Fortune 500 companies with a broad range of products and services located in different parts of the country found that despite differences in organizational structure, corporate culture, and personnel policies, the same practices results in a glass ceiling for women, especially women of color

(L. Martin 1991, 4–5). These practices were recruitment policies for upper-management levels that depended on word-of-mouth networking and employee referrals. When "head hunters" were used, they were not instructed to look for women and men of social groups underrepresented at managerial levels. The few white women and women and men of color who were already hired were not given the opportunity to build up their credentials or enhance their careers by assignment to corporate committees, task forces, and special projects. These are traditional avenues of advancement, since they bring junior members into contact with senior members of the organization and give them visibility and the chance to show what they can do. There was not monitoring of evaluation or compensation systems that determine salaries, bonuses, incentives, or perks to make sure that white women and women and men of color were getting their fair share. In general, "monitoring for equal access and opportunity, especially as managers move up the corporate ladder to senior management levels where important decisions are made, was almost never considered a corporate responsibility or part of the planning for developmental programs and policies" (L. Martin 1991, 4). In short, none of the white men in senior management saw it as their responsibility to sponsor white women or women and men of color to be their replacements when they retired.

Men in traditional women's occupations report the opposite phenomenon. Their minority status turns out to be a career advantage. Christine Williams's study of seventy-six men and twenty-three women in nursing, teaching, librarianship, and social work in the United States, whom she interviewed from 1985 to 1991, found that the men were tracked into the more prestigious, better-paying specialties within the occupation, and urged by their mentors, mostly other men, to move into positions of authority. Most of these men were white, so they were the most advantaged workers.[5] For them not to move up to supervisory and administrative positions was considered inappropriate. As a result, they were on a "glass escalator," Williams says: "Often, despite their intentions, they face invisible pressures to move up in their professions. As if on a moving escalator, they must work to stay in place" (1992, 256). But they sometimes faced a glass ceiling at higher levels. The affirmative action policies of many institutions make the women deans and heads of departments in the women's areas too visible for them to be replaced by men (257).

Although these processes may seem benign, the imbalance of lower-level workers with disadvantaged social characteristics compared to upper-level workers with advantaged social characteristics implies a deliberate, though unstated, policy of hostility and resistance that deepens with each additional mark of disadvantage. Kimberlé Crenshaw presents a graphic analysis of who can make it through the glass ceiling:

> Imagine a basement which contains all people who are disadvantaged on the basis of race, sex, class, sexual preference, age and/or physical ability. These people are stacked—feet standing on shoulders—with those on the bottom being disadvantaged by the full array of factors, up to the very top, where the heads of all those disadvantaged by a single factor brush up against the ceiling. . . . A hatch is developed through which those placed immediately below can crawl. Yet this hatch is generally available only to those who—due to the singularity of their burden and their otherwise privileged position relative to those below—are in the position to crawl through. Those who are multiply-burdened are generally left below. (1991, 65)

Bands of Brothers

Parallel to the formal organization of a large, modern workplace, which is structured as a task-related, bureaucratic hierarchy, is the informal organization, which is based on trust, loyalty, and reciprocal favors (Lorber [1979] 1989a). Because the unspoken rules are often as significant to the way business is conducted as the written rules, colleagues want to work with people who know what goes without saying: "In order that men [*sic*] may communicate freely and confidentially, they must be able to take a good deal of each other's sentiments for granted. They must feel easy about their silences as well as about their utterances. These factors conspire to make colleagues,

with a large body of unspoken understandings, uncomfortable in the presence of what they consider odd kinds of fellows" (Hughes 1971, 146).

Personal discretion and reliability are particularly necessary for those in positions of authority because of the uncertainties they face (Kanter 1977a, 47–68). According to Dianne Feinstein, former mayor of San Francisco who was elected to the U.S. Senate in 1992, women have to bend over backward to prove not only their competence but their trustworthiness:

> Women have to prove themselves effective and credible time and time again. Experience has taught me that the keys to a woman's effectiveness in public office are to be "trustable": to give directions clearly and to follow up, to verify every statement for accuracy, to guard her integrity carefully, and to observe the public's trust one hundred percent. Most important, she must be a team player and build relationships with her colleagues that are based on integrity and respect. (Cantor and Bernway 1992, xv)

Almost twenty years ago, Margaret Hennig and Ann Jardim predicted that conscientious and hardworking women would find it difficult to get out of middle management because their performance was geared to formal training and bureaucratic responsibilities. They felt that if women knew that senior management relies on informal networking, gathering extensive sources of knowledge from areas other than one's own, planning, policy-making, and delegating responsibility to reliable subordinates, they would be able to move up corporate career ladders (1976, 55–68).[6] Career mobility, however, does not depend only on competent performance and other efforts by the ambitious individual. To move up, a young person's worth has to be recognized and encouraged by those in the upper echelons. Promising young men of the right social characteristics are groomed for senior management by "godfathers" or "rabbis"—sponsors who take them under their wing and see to it that they learn the informal organizational rules for getting ahead. Promising young women are left to fend for themselves (Lorber 1981).

Brotherly trust among men who are business associates goes back to the nineteenth century. Before the creation of the impersonal corporation, each partner in an enterprise was personally responsible for raising capital and making a profit. Credit depended on personal trustworthiness; bankruptcy was a personal tragedy (Davidoff and Hall 1987, 198–228; Silver 1990). In these transactions, the active players were all men. Women were passive partners; their money was used by kinsmen and men friends who acted as trustees. In order to cement the brotherly bonds among men who were in business together, women were encouraged to marry cousins or their brothers' partners; two sisters often married two brothers, or a brother and sister married a sister and brother: "Free choice marriage controlled in this way provided a form of security in binding together members of the middle class in local, regional and national networks, a guarantee of congenial views as well as trustworthiness in economic and financial affairs" (Davidoff and Hall 1987, 221).[7]

In twentieth-century businesses, professions, and politics, trust and loyalty are built not through kin ties (which is considered nepotism) but through *homosociality*—the bonding of men of the same race, religion, and social-class background (Lipman-Blumen 1976). These men have the economic, political, professional, and social resources to do each other favors. Women with the same social characteristics may be included in men's circles when they have equivalent wealth, power, and social position (C. F. Epstein 1981, 265–302; Lorber 1984, 57–63). Most men and women, however, relate to each other socially only in familial or sexual roles (G. Moore 1990).

Homosociality starts early. In childhood play, boys separate themselves from girls and become contemptuous of girls' activities in their efforts to keep themselves apart.[8] This segregation, attributed to boys' needs to establish their masculinity, makes friendship between girls and boys difficult because it is discouraged by same-gender peers. Gender grouping is not perfect in mixed-gender schools but is broached by social class and racial ethnic cross-currents and sometimes by the organizing activities of teachers (Thorne 1990).[9] In adulthood, whenever men and women come together as equals, in coed schools and workplaces that are not gender-segregated, cross-gender friendships are undermined by intimations of sexual attraction (O'Meara 1989). One study of white middle-class young adults found that the women preferred same-gender friendships more than the men did because the men were more interested in them sexually than as companions (S. M. Rose 1985). The men invested more time and attention in their friendships with men than they did in their friendships with women, while the women gave as much emotional support to their men friends as they did to their women friends. Letty Cottin Pogrebin (1987, 311–40) feels that the main reason that women and men are rarely intimate friends is that they are rarely true equals.

Many working women are expected as part of their job to smile, be cordial, sympathetic, agreeable, and a bit sexy.[10] Men workers are supposed to display masculine emotions—coolness under fire, rationality, and objectivity, which are part of the performance of power (Sattel 1976). The qualities men want in women in the workplace as well as in the home—sympathy, looking out for the other person, understanding the nuances and cues of behavior, caretaking, flattering them sexually—keep women out of the top ranks of business, government, and the professions. Such qualities are gender-marked as "womanly"; they are also subordinating (Ridgeway and Johnson 1990).

Much of men's workplace small talk is about sports or sex. Replaying the weekend's games gives men the chance to compete and win vicariously (Kemper 1990, 167–206). Sexist jokes establish the boundaries of exclusion, and if the men are of the same race or religion, so do racist and anti-Semitic or anti-Catholic jokes. Sexist joking also keeps men from revealing their emotional bonds with each other and deflects their anger from their bosses onto women.[11] Women who can talk and joke like men may be allowed entry into the men's brotherhood, as honorary men, but then they cannot protest against sexism and sexual harassment, even if they themselves are the victims.[12]

Although men or women may be "odd fellows" in their workplace or job, the pressures of being a woman in a man's job and a man in a woman's job are quite different. Men nurses can talk cars and sports with men physicians. In doing so, they affiliate with a higher status group, affirm their masculinity, and gain a benefit from these informal contacts in more favorable evaluations of their work. Men physicians' status is too high to be compromised by chatting with men nurses (or flirting with women nurses). Men who are openly homosexual, however, may face discrimination from men supervisors (C. L. Williams 1992, 259). Women physicians socialize with women medical students, interns, and residents, but not with women nurses.[13] Women physicians' status is more tenuous, and they end up in a bind. They need to get along with the women nurses so that their work proceeds efficiently, yet they lose status if they bond with a lower-status group as women. Women physicians need to build colleague relationships with the men physicians who are their peers, but these men may not treat them as equals. They also need to seek sponsors among senior men who can help them advance their careers, but these men may not want them as protégées.

Because men know the power of homosocial bonding, they are discomfited when women do the same thing and often accuse such women of lesbianism, particularly because women's attentions are turned to each other and not to them. As Carol Barkalow said of the military:

> They often appear to possess an irrational fear of women's groups, believing that, in their midst, men will be plotted against, or perhaps worst of all, rendered somehow unnecessary. If women soldiers do try to develop a professional support network among themselves, they are faced with the dilemma that something as simple as two women officers having lunch together more than once might spark rumors of lesbianism—a potentially lethal charge, since even rumored homosexuality can damage an officer's career. (1990, 167–68)[14]

Women officers who want to bond without innuendoes of homosexuality often turn to sports, which is as legitimate a place to build trust and loyalty among women as it is among men.[15]

For the most part, as colleagues, friends, and wives, women are relegated to acting as audience or sex objects for men. According to Kathryn Ann Farr (1988), who studied a group of upper-class white men whose bonding preserved their race and class as well as their gender privileges, wives and girlfriends were needed to serve as foils for the men's exclusive sociability. The women listened as the men talked about their exploits. When the men went off on an escapade, their women warned them against getting into too much trouble, prepared food for them, and stayed behind. The men defined the boundaries of their homosocial world by excluding women, just as they maintained its racial and class exclusivity by keeping out the "wrong" kind of men. The irony is that they built their superior status in a direct and immediate way by denying their own wives and girlfriends the privileges of their race and class. In this way, the domination of men over women in their own social group is sustained, and the women collude in the process:

> These men do not view themselves as sexist, and they do not appear to be viewed by the women *with whom they interact* as sexist. In their choice of wives and girlfriends, the majority of these men seem to value independent and intelligent women. Yet their socialization into a male-dominated environment and a culture in which male sociability is highly valued causes them to think and act in ways that conflict with their intellectual assessments of the worth of and the value of social relationships with women. (Farr 1988, 269)[16]

By excluding women who share their social characteristics from their social space, these men never have to treat women as equals or as serious competitors for positions of power.[17]

THE "MOMMY TRACK"

If they could not exclude women completely or relegate them to subordinate positions, men have reduced competition and encouraged turnover by refusing to hire married women or mothers and by encouraging women employees who get married or have children to quit. Marriage bars were used against women schoolteachers, stewardesses, and other occupations in the United States well into the twentieth century and are still used today in other countries (Brinton 1989; Goldin 1990, 160–84). When the marriage bar fell out of use in the United States in the late 1950s, partly because there was a dearth of young single women workers, it was replaced by what Claudia Goldin calls "the pregnancy bar" (1990, 176). The ideology that children need full-time mothering produced turnover not at marriage but at first pregnancy.

Discriminating against women workers and job applicants who are married, pregnant, or mothers is now illegal in the United States; informally, however, these practices have been replaced by a tacit or openly acknowledged "mommy track." Ostensibly intended to make it easier for married women with children to continue managerial and professional jobs, the "mommy track" offers flexible working hours and generous maternity leave to women but not men in dual-career marriages to ameliorate the pressures of family and work (Rodgers and Rodgers 1989). But women are penalized for taking advantage of these policies, because once they do, their commitment to achieving top-level positions is called into question (Kingson 1988). The secondary result and, I would argue, latent function of these "mommy tracks" is to derail women who were on fast tracks to the top. As Alice Kessler-Harris says: "To induce women to take jobs while simultaneously restraining their ambition to rise in them required a series of socially accepted constraints on work roles. Unspoken social prescription—a tacit understanding about the primacy of home roles—remained the most forceful influence. This is most apparent in professional jobs where the potential for ambition was greatest" (1982, 231).

Until quite recently in many Westernized countries, the more prestigious professions, such as medicine, law, and the sciences, and the upper-level managerial sector of business were thoroughly dominated by men.[18] Men were easily able to keep women out because they were gatekeepers in several ways: They determined admissions to professional and managerial training schools; they controlled recruitment to

and from such schools; and they determined promotion policies. With the advent of affirmative action in the United States, many women have become doctors, lawyers, scientists, and administrators, and they have become formidable competition for men. The "mommy track" keeps women professionals and managers in lower-paid, lower-prestige ranks. This exclusion from top-level positions is considered legitimate because they are mothers. The assumption is that women could not possibly handle the responsibility of leadership and the responsibility for their children's welfare at the same time, but they are never given the chance to try (Covin and Brush 1991). It is also taken for granted that mothers, never fathers, will supervise their children's day-to-day care.[19] "Mommy tracks" thus reinforce and legitimate the structural glass ceiling, the processes of exclusion, and the justifying stereotypes.

Paradoxically, "mommy tracks" are not the way most married women professionals and executives with children organize their careers. Such women order their lives so they can be productive.[20] Jonathan Cole and Harriet Zuckerman's interviews with seventy-three women and forty-seven men scientists, eminent and rank and file, who received their doctorates between 1920 and 1979 found little difference in the rates and patterns of publication of the men and women, the married and single women, and the childless women and those with children (1991). A woman with an endowed chair in a major department of behavioral science was married four times, divorced three times, and had four children by three different husbands, but the largest dip in her publication rate came in a year when there were no changes in her personal life (167). The rate of publication for all these scientists depended on stage of career, extent of collaboration, and the completion of projects. The women they interviewed were successful scientists as well as wives and mothers not because of a "mommy track" but because they carefully timed both marriage and childbearing, had child care and household help, and cut out leisure-time activities that had no professional payoff.[21]

When women put their families before their careers, they are often responding to a generalized cultural mandate that is mediated through direct pressures from their husbands at home and other women's husbands in the workplace (Cockburn 1991). These men, according to Mirra Komarovsky, have inconsistent ideas about their women peers:

> Some of the revealed inconsistencies are: . . . the right of an able woman to a career of her choice; the admiration for women who measure up in terms of the dominant values of our society; the lure but also the threat that such women present; the low status attached to housewifery but the conviction that there is no substitute for the mother's care of young children; the deeply internalized norm of male occupational superiority pitted against the principle of equal opportunity irrespective of sex. (1976, 37)

These inconsistencies are resolved by rewarding men's efforts to move up in their careers but not rewarding women's efforts, and both rewarding and punishing women for taking care of their families—rewarding them as women and punishing them as professionals, managers, and politicians. Should any woman not make the appropriate "choice" to put her family before her career, both she and her husband often face subtle and not-so-subtle harassment from their men colleagues. African-American women and men may have more egalitarian norms and expectations about women's ambitions, but these women face discrimination from white men on two counts and may be competing with African-American men for the same few "minority" positions (Fulbright 1987). Women may feel it is their choice to stay home with their small children and to limit their career commitments, but their choices are constrained by real and direct social pressures (Gerson 1985; Komarovsky 1985, 225–68).

THE SALIERI PHENOMENON AND THE MATTHEW EFFECT

What happens when women can't be excluded from the workplace and don't choose to put family before career, but instead become men's competitors? The unspoken practices of the informal organization of work make women particularly vulnerable to the covert undercutting I have called the *Salieri phenomenon,* after the highly placed composer who allegedly sabotaged Mozart's career (Lorber 1984, 8–10). In Peter Shaffer's play *Amadeus,* Salieri never openly criticized Mozart to the emperor who employs both of them; he simply fails to recommend him enthusiastically. Salieri also suggests that Mozart be paid much less than the musician he is replacing. Mozart later thanks Salieri for his help in getting a position; he blames the emperor for the low salary (P. Shaffer 1980, 71–72). Salieri's damning with faint praise is one way women are undermined by their men colleagues and bosses, often without being aware of it.

Nijole Benokraitis and Joe Feagin (1986) describe other ways men subtly undercut women: *condescending chivalry,* where a boss protects a woman employee from what could be useful criticism; *supportive discouragement,* where a woman is not encouraged to compete for a challenging position because she might not make it; *friendly harassment,* such as being joshed in public when visibly pregnant or dressed for a social occasion; *subjective objectification,* or being grouped with "all women"; *radiant devaluation,* when a woman is given extravagant praise for doing what is considered routine when men do it—the "dancing dog" effect; *liberated sexism,* such as inviting a woman for an after-work drink but not letting her pay for a round; *benevolent exploitation,* where a woman is given all the detail work so she can learn the job, but a man takes credit for the final product; *considerate domination,* such as deciding what responsibilities a married woman can and cannot handle, instead of letting her determine how she wants to organize her time; and *collegial exclusion,* thoughtlessly scheduling networking meetings for times women are likely to have family responsibilities. These practices undermine a woman's reputation for competence in the eyes of others and her abilities in her own eyes, making it less likely that she will be visible to gatekeepers or considered a legitimate competitor for a position of power.

Once out of the fast track for advancement, it is very difficult to accrue the necessary resources to perform valued professional activities. Those who have access to personnel, work space, and money have the opportunity to do the kind of work that increases their reputation, brings the approval of superiors, and garners additional rewards and promotions. The circular proliferation of prestige, resources, and power is the *Matthew effect*. As attributed to Christ in the Gospel according to Matthew, those who have faith become more and more favored and those who do not sink lower and lower: "For whosoever hath, to him shall be given, and he shall have more abundance: but whosoever hath not, from him shall be taken away even that he hath." (Bible, King James version, 25:29).

The Matthew effect in science was first described by Robert Merton (1968) and Harriet Zuckerman (1977) to explain the "halo" that winning the Nobel Prize confers. The process of accumulating advantages in science, however, starts with the scientist's working at a prestigious university or laboratory that encourages the kind of research and productivity that wins Nobel Prizes.[22] Women scientists are disadvantaged by positions that give them fewer resources and less encouragement to do high-quality work and by a lesser payoff for their achievements in recognition, rewards, and additional resources. Citations of published papers by others in a field are a form of visibility that adds to the researcher's or scholar's reputation (Astin 1991). According to Marianne Ferber (1986, 1988), women tend to cite other women more than men cite women, and the fewer women in a field, the greater the citations gap. As a result of the accumulation of disadvantages, women often have stop-and-go careers that may start out well, but then founder (Lorber and Ecker 1983).[23]

Two brilliant twentieth-century women scientists who were loners had totally different fates that had little to do with the value of their scientific work. One of them, Rosalind Franklin, was a well-born Jewish woman scientist who launched a productive career in England in the 1950s. Her crucial contribution to the discovery of the double-helix structure of DNA was minimally acknowledged in the initial announcement by James Watson and Francis Crick in 1953.[24] She herself was denigrated by Watson in his widely read book, *The Double Helix* (1968). His description of her and her work is a classic example of the Salieri phenomenon: "Rosy . . . spoke to an audience of about fifteen in a quick, nervous style. . . . There was not a trace of warmth or frivolity in her words. And yet I could not regard her as totally uninteresting. Momentarily I wondered how she would look if she took off her glasses and did something novel with her hair. Then, however, my main concern was her description of the crystalline X-ray diffraction pattern" (68–69).[25] What Franklin was describing was nothing less than a clear X-ray picture of the DNA molecule that actually showed its helical structure! Watson paid little attention to what she had reported for over a year. Working alone, Franklin tried to envisage the three-dimensional structure her photographs of DNA suggested; she alternately played with and rejected a helical model. Watson subsequently was shown her best picture without her knowledge by the man who ran the laboratory she worked in, Maurice Wilkins; to Watson, "the pattern shouted helix" (Judson 1979, 135).

Wilkins could have been the collaborator Franklin needed to help her make an inductive leap, but according to Franklin's biographer, they "hated one another at sight. . . . Only too evidently the antipathy was instant and mutual" (Sayre 1975, 95). Horace Freeland Judson calls the conflict between Wilkins and Franklin "one of the great personal quarrels in the history of science" (1979, 101), noting but underplaying the gendered overtones. Wilkins insisted he hired Franklin to do the X-ray diffractions on DNA; Franklin's friends insisted that she thought she had been given control of the project and "was profoundly angered" by being treated as an assistant rather than a colleague by Wilkins (148).[26] At thirty-one, she was eight years older than Watson and a little younger but "much further along professionally than Crick" (148). Yet Wilkins, Watson, and Crick regularly corresponded, conversed, and ate together (159); Franklin's only associate was a graduate student, and as a woman, "she was denied the fellowship of the luncheon club organized by the senior common room" at King's College, London, where her laboratory was located (148).

Franklin died of cancer in 1958, at the age of thirty-seven; Watson, Crick, and Wilkins were awarded the Nobel Prize in physiology or medicine in 1962. Only in a contrite epilogue to his book, published in 1968, did Watson pay tribute to Franklin:

> The X-ray work she did at King's is increasingly regarded as superb. . . . We both came to appreciate greatly her personal honesty and generosity, realizing years too late the struggles that the intelligent woman faces to be accepted by a scientific world which often regards women as mere diversions from serious thinking. Rosalind's exemplary courage and integrity were apparent to all when, knowing she was mortally ill, she did not complain but continued working on a high level until a few weeks before her death. (225–26)[27]

Another woman scientist, also a loner but luckier because she lived to see her work rewarded with science's highest honor, was Barbara McClintock. She published a landmark paper in 1931 that established the chromosomal basis of genetics and, in 1945, was elected president of the Genetics Society. In the 1950s, the field became dominated by the Watson-Crick model of genetics, in which DNA produces RNA, and RNA produces protein. The research that McClintock published in that decade, which showed that the process was not so straightforward and that genes could "jump," or transpose, was ignored: "In spite of the fact that she had long since established her reputation as an impeccable investigator, few listened, and fewer understood. She was described as 'obscure,' even 'mad' " (Keller 1983, 10).

In 1960, McClintock described the parallels between her own work and that of other scientists, but these scientists did not reciprocate and cite her work. Except for two other women scientists, she was ignored at Cold Spring Harbor Laboratory where she had worked since 1941 (Watson became director in 1968), but she had nowhere else to go. McClintock lived long enough to see "startling new developments in biology that echo many of the findings she described as long as thirty years ago" (Keller 1983, x), and she was awarded the Nobel Prize in medicine in 1983, when she was eighty-one years old. She died on September 2, 1992, at the age of ninety, her work "widely celebrated as prescient" (Kolata 1992b).

The Salieri phenomenon and the Matthew effect are two sides of the same coin. Those who benefit from the Matthew effect receive acknowledgments from their colleagues for good work, which builds their reputation and brings them financial and professional rewards. The work of those subjected to the Salieri phenomenon is not recognized; they do not get credit for good performance, and their careers are stymied. But reputations must be constantly maintained; even those who have built up social credit can lose it, and reversals of fortune are not uncommon. Because women do not have a protective "status shield," they are easy targets for jealous, threatened, or hostile Salieris. Certainly, not all women are future Mozarts, but even those who are may never be heard.[28]

INNER CIRCLES, FRIENDLY COLLEAGUES, AND TOKENS

The discriminatory aspects of the sorting and tracking that occur in every occupation and profession with long career ladders are obscured because colleagues who are not considered for the top jobs are not fired. They simply fail to make it into the inner circle. Colleagues are organized, informally, into three concentric circles—*inner circles, friendly colleagues,* and *isolated loners.*[29] Power is concentrated and policy is made in inner circles, which are usually homogeneous on gender, race, religion, ethnicity, social class, and education or training. Friendly colleagues usually have some, but not all, of the social characteristics members of the inner circle have. Although they are not totally excluded from the informal colleague network, they are rarely groomed to be part of the inner circle. Women with excellent credentials and work performance in occupations and professions dominated by men tend to end up friendly colleagues if they are of the same race and social class as the men of the inner circle and do similar kinds of work; otherwise, they become loners. Women professionals have formed their own separate colleague groups or professional networks, but many ambitious women do not want to be professionally segregated. They often try to fit in with the men or work on their own and hope that their worth will eventually be recognized by the gatekeepers of their profession or occupation.

Although inner circles tend to be homogeneous on gender, religion, race, ethnicity, education, and class background, a few people with different social characteristics may be accepted if they have a respected sponsor and demonstrate that in all other ways, they are just like the others. They are the true "tokens" (J. L. Laws 1975). They are actively discouraged from bringing more of their kind into the inner circle or from competing for the very top positions in the organization. Tokens usually are eager to fit in and not embarrass their sponsor, so they do not challenge these restrictions or the views, values, or work practices of the inner circle. Indeed, they may outdo the others in upholding the prevailing perspectives and exclusionary practices. That is why token women tend to be "one of the boys."

In order to get support from senior men, a senior woman may end up in the paradoxical position of making a stand for women by proving she is just like a man. A woman physician I interviewed was passed over by one set of gatekeepers in favor of her younger brother for the top position in a hospital department. She went over their heads to more powerful men, who vouched for her "manliness." She said:

> I do give a hoot about titles and I'm enough of a feminist not to let them promote my brother over me. I have put in many years more of service, and I'm a far better dermatologist than my brother. They tried to do this to me because I'm a woman. Those, excuse the French, assholes, said to me, "Do you mind us promoting your brother over you? He needs the honor." And I said, "For the sake of the women who follow after me, I mind." . . . And they said, "Well, if you come to our meetings, we can't tell dirty jokes, and we can't take off our shoes." I said, "Bull to that one. I know just as many dirty jokes as you do, and I always take off my shoes." All the board of trustees laughed like hell when they heard about it. They all said, "For God's sake, promote her." Most of them were patients of mine anyway. It's a stupid thing to say to a woman doctor. I don't care for me, but I want to make sure that the next generation gets a fair shake and doesn't get it in the eye. (Lorber 1984, 61–62)

Unfortunately, token junior women cannot afford to be so outspoken.

In 1977, Rosabeth Moss Kanter predicted that as the number of workgroup peers with different characteristics significantly increased, they would lose their token status and characteristics and be better integrated into the group.[30] They would be able to express individual differences and sponsor others with similar social characteristics for leadership positions. When they became almost half of the group, they could become a recognized subgroup, with alternative views and work practices and their own inner circles. Subsequent research on what came to be called the "Kanter hypothesis" showed that as the numbers of women approach 15 percent, paradoxically, they are *more* not less isolated, as she had predicted. They are cut off from organizational information flows, are not able to acquire the loyal subordinates that leaders depend on, and are not central in the organizational structure (Olson and Miller 1983; South et al. 1982a, 1982b). Because they lack the protection of a sponsor that tokens have, they may be subject to open and covert harassment. When the occupation is symbolically masculine, such as police work or the military, additional numbers of women rarely break down the interactional barriers, and they continue to be loners.[31] Being few in number, therefore, may result in a more favorable position than a more balanced gender mix, since an increase may be seen as a threat to those in the majority (Toren and Kraus 1987; Wharton and Baron 1987).

Why are men professionals and managers reluctant to allow substantial numbers of women into elite inner circles or to support the ambitions of more than a select few for leadership positions? Competition is one reason. Yet other men are competitors, too. Catholic and Jewish men physicians, once also subject to discriminatory quotas in American medical schools, are more successfully integrated than women into the prestigious ranks of the medical profession. It could be that men feel their profession will "tip" and become feminized if too many women are in high-paid, high-prestige, and high-power positions (Lorber 1991). Just as one group seems to fear the neighborhood will go downhill when too many of a devalued group move in, men professionals may be afraid that if too many women become leaders, their profession will become women's work, and the men in it will lose prestige, income, and their control over resources (Blum and Smith 1988; Reskin 1988).

People from subordinate social groups do not become half of the work group unless the occupation, profession, or job specialty loses its prestige and power (Carter and Carter 1981). The leaders, however, tend to stay on and continue to choose successors to the top positions who are like themselves, not like the new people who outnumber them. The men in colleague groups of mostly women and the whites in groups of mostly people of color (at least in the United States) tend to remain the supervisors and administrators. As administrators, dominant white men need to keep productivity high and costs low. If the members of formerly excluded groups can be relegated to the necessary lower-paid and less prestigious jobs (such as primary care in medicine), administrators can keep costs down and use the increasing numbers of white women and women and men of color who are highly trained professionals and managers without disturbing the status quo.[32]

GENDER AND AUTHORITY

Are men so much more acceptable in positions of authority because women "do power" differently? There tend to be two models of women's leadership styles: women are exactly like men, and women are different, but equally competent (Adler and Izraeli 1988a).[33] How women or men act does not give the whole picture; women's and men's leadership styles are socially constructed in interaction and heavily influenced by the situational context and how others perceive them. If women in positions of authority tend to be more accessible, to grant more autonomy, but also to be more demanding of subordinates to perform well, the reason may be that they are in weaker positions in the organization and have fewer resources.[34] They need subordinates' help but may be unable to reward them with raises or other perks. As a result, they ask more of subordinates but are also more likely to give concessions to those who are loyal to them, which may be perceived as contradictory behavior.

Authority in a woman is granted in a woman-dominated situation, such as nursing, but questioned where authority is defined as a masculine trait, such as in police work or the military.[35] In 1986, 10.4 percent of all uniformed U.S. Army personnel were women, but they have been underrepresented in the higher ranks. In 1988, there were nine women who were one-star generals in the U.S. military, 1.2 percent of the total, and none of higher rank. Women constituted 2 percent of the colonels, 3.5 percent of the lieutenant colonels, and 7.1 percent of other officer ranks (Barkalow and Raab 1990, 280–81). In 1991, a woman, Midshipman Juliane Gallina, was chosen the U.S. Naval Academy's brigade commander, student leader of 4,300 midshipmen. Ironically, her appointment came six months after a survey found that a "considerable segment" of students, faculty, and staff believed women had no place in the Naval Academy (*New York Times* 1991b).

A woman leader is expected to be empathic, considerate of other's feelings, and attuned to the personal (Lorber 1985). If she is not, she is likely to be called "abrasive." As the editor of the prestigious *Harvard Business Review,* Rosabeth Moss Kanter has been publicly faulted for her confrontational management style by her associates, even though her predecessor, a man, had similar problems in his first year (A. L. Cowan 1991). Her high status as a Harvard Business School professor, corporate consultant, and author of internationally known books on management did not protect her from open criticism by her colleagues.

On the other hand, a more conciliatory style may be criticized by men and women colleagues as insufficiently authoritative. Despite the increase in women managers in the past twenty years, men and women at all career stages, including undergraduate and graduate business students, stereotype the good manager as "masculine" (Powell 1988, 145–50). Nonetheless, there are situations where a nonconfrontational approach is highly appropriate. In medicine and police work, quintessential masculine professions in American society, being able to listen and take the role of the other person may be more productive than a distancing, authoritative stance in eliciting information or deflecting conflict (S. E. Martin 1980; West 1984, 51–70). Conciliation and using the other person's views can be threatening to men in police work who have learned to rely on physical force and to men doctors for whom medical expertise is the ultimate authority.

If the goal for women in men-dominated situations is to be treated as if they were men, they are in a double bind, and so are the men (Chase 1988). If the women act like men, they challenge men's "natural" right to positions of power. If the women act like women, they don't belong in a situation where they have to take charge (that is, act like a man). As Susan Ehrlich Martin says of policewomen on patrol: "The more a female partner acts like a police officer, the less she behaves like a woman. On the other hand, the more she behaves like a woman, the less protection she provides, the less adequate she is as a partner—although such behavior preserves the man's sense of masculinity. The way out of the bind is simple: keep women out of patrol work" (1980, 93–94).[36]

PRODUCING "FACE"

All these processes of legitimation and validation that build the reputations of stature and ability needed by a competitor for a position of power and prestige take place in face-to-face interaction.[37] In everyday encounters, people present themselves the way they would like to be responded to—as powerful leaders, cooperative colleagues, deferential underlings, more or less intimate friends, possible sexual partners. The ways people dress, gesture, talk, act, and even show emotion produce social identities, consciously or unconsciously crafted for different arenas and a variety of occasions.[38] Ritual behavior, such as bows and handshakes, and the rules of protocol—who goes through a door first, who sits where, who calls whom by their first name—reproduce status hierarchy or create status equality. Ordinary conversations become covert battlegrounds: Who talks more, who interrupts, whose interests are discussed, who gets sustained attention or short shrift, all indicate who has the social upper hand.[39] Whom one walks with or stands with—or puts space between—demonstrates affiliation, hostility, or respect, as does eye contact, touching, and other forms of "body politics."[40] These "face" productions are such delicate balances of power and deference that they can easily be disrupted by rudeness or embarrassment (Goffman 1967, 97–112; Scheff 1988). Secret stigmas, such as deviant behavior in the past or present, or even by members of one's family or by intimate friends, can contaminate a seemingly upright identity if revealed (Goffman 1963a). In face-to-face interaction, accidental attributes, such as beauty or height, may add to social status, and obvious physical deformities often detract from it.[41]

These presentations of self take place in social contexts, and the responses of others validate, neutralize, deny, or subvert them. Status signals, whether they are verbal or nonverbal, practical or symbolic, can be understood only in the social context and only by people who have learned their meaning (Hodge and Kress 1988). You need to know the symbolic language of everyday social interaction to be able to tell who is the boss and who is the employee, who are friends and who are enemies. Signals can be manipulated to shore up or subvert the status quo, or they can be used deliberately in open resistance or rebellion.

These status productions are part of "doing gender" (or of doing race, ethnicity, religion, or social class). In doing gender, as West and Zimmerman point out, "men are also doing dominance and women are doing deference" (1987, 146). That is, in face-to-face interaction, what is being produced, reinforced, or resisted is the society's whole system of social stratification. This system endows women and men, people of different racial ethnic groups and religions, and those with greater or lesser economic resources with different social worth. Everyday interaction reenacts these power and prestige differences because people with different status characteristics are seen as legitimately superior or inferior by the others in the situation. When people are evaluated highly, the others take what they have to say seriously, follow their suggestions, and defer to their judgment. Those who have low status in the eyes of the others are not listened to, their advice is ignored, and their bids for leadership are simply not acknowledged. Status superiors are granted the benefit of the doubt if they make a mistake; status inferiors have to prove their competence over and over again.

The pattern of structured power and prestige in face-to-face interaction replicates the ranking of social characteristics in the larger society because people are seen not as individuals but as representatives of their race, religion, gender, education, occupation, and so on. If everyone in a group has the same social characteristics, then natural leaders and followers emerge; in a group of friends, there is usually one person who is the ringleader. But when the social characteristics of people in a group differ, the social characteristics have more salience than personal characteristics—the woman who leads other women follows when men are present. The solo man does not dominate in a group of women, but he is listened to more than the solo woman is in a group of men (Johnson and Schulman 1989). The size of the group, its status mix, endurance, and purpose determine its structure of power and prestige, but the patterns are constant: Status superiors lead because others feel they have the right to lead; they don't have superior status because they lead. Most of the time, the building up and tearing down of "face" goes unnoticed, but conflicts and confrontations reveal that the vital subtext is the social production of prestige and power (Morrill 1991).

PRODUCING POWER

The week I started to write this chapter was the week of the U.S. Senate Judiciary Committee hearings on Professor Anita Hill's allegations of sexual harassment by Judge Clarence Thomas, nominee to the Supreme Court. These encounters dramatized status production and destruction, and the interplay of race, class, and gender with evaluations of performance and social worth. They laid bare the social processes of upward mobility, and how these differ for women and men of the same race. "The scalding contest was not only about race and sex, and women and men. It was about power, and who knows how to use it more effectively" (Dowd 1991c).[42]

Both Clarence Thomas and Anita Hill are African Americans who were born into poverty and segregation, and both received their law degrees from Yale University, one of the most prestigious law schools in the United States, during a time of nationally approved and implemented affirmative action. They met when they worked together in the administration of President Ronald Reagan. Judge Thomas, then thirty-three years old, was at the Department of Education and then head of the Equal Employment Opportunities Commission (EEOC), the body set up to implement the civil rights laws against discrimination. Professor Hill, then twenty-five years old, worked for Judge Thomas in both organizations for several years.

Professor Hill contended that on and off during this time, at both workplaces, she had been subject to Judge Thomas's repeated requests for dates, as well as descriptions of the sexual acts in pornographic movies he had seen, the size of the breasts and penises of the actors in those movies, the size of his own penis, and his own sexual prowess. She had told few people of the incidents—two women friends, a man she was dating who lived in another city, and the dean at a school considering her for an appointment six or seven years later. They testified before the Judiciary Committee that she had been very upset and uncomfortable talking about it, although she had offered none of the graphic details that she was asked to make public at the reconvened hearings.

Judge Thomas denied the allegations categorically and made his own charges that he was the victim of a particularly ugly brand of racism, the stereotyping of African-American men as nothing more than sexual animals. He called it "high-tech lynching," but it was Anita Hill who was verbally lynched by the senators who supported Judge Thomas. The judge's supporters on the Judiciary Committee accused Professor Hill of being a vindictive scorned woman, the tool of anti-Thomas political interests, a fantasizer, and a schizophrenic. The members of the Judiciary Committee who were against confirming Judge Thomas were circumspect when they questioned him, and rambling and disjointed with his witnesses. They did not ask him anything about what was rumored to be his well-known interest in pornography. They called no experts to testify on sexual harassment, its effects, or common responses, but listened respectfully to the rambling, self-serving account of a man who had met Anita Hill at a large party.

Professor Hill's accusation of sexual harassment by Judge Thomas was called into question because she had followed him from the Department of Education to the EEOC and had kept in touch with him professionally after she left the EEOC for a teaching position, once asking him for a needed reference, once to come to her campus as a speaker, and at other times requesting help for others or materials for seminars and grants. She had telephoned him about ten to fifteen times in the decade after she left Washington, D.C. When he came to speak at the school where she had her first teaching job, she participated in the social events around his visit and drove him to the airport. A witness to their interaction said it was very friendly and relaxed.

Judge Thomas's supporters on the Judiciary Committee said over and over that they could not understand why Anita Hill had followed him from one organization to another after he had harassed her. She said that for several months before he took the new position, he had not engaged in lewd talk or pressured her for dates, and he had started seeing someone seriously. After they both moved to EEOC, she said he harassed her again. His relationship had not worked out, and he was also going through a divorce.

Pro-Thomas members of the committee also said they could not understand why she had maintained a cordial professional relationship with him in the ensuing years. One of Professor Hill's witnesses tried to explain why by talking about her own experience, which included "touching," and said that as a Black woman you learn to "grit your teeth and bear it" so that you can get to a position where you do not need the support of your harasser any longer.

Professor Hill said she had followed Thomas to EEOC because she was afraid she could not otherwise find employment commensurate with her credentials and abilities. She had been a corporate lawyer and did not want to return to that sector of law. Although this motivation for continuing a relationship with someone she said had subjected her to disgusting talk was challenged by witnesses for Judge Thomas, the evidence of her career path bears out her restricted opportunities. At the time of the alleged incidents, Professor Hill was an African-American woman professional in her twenties, a graduate of a highly prestigious law school, just beginning her career. The position she went to after she left EEOC was with Oral Roberts University, a small low-status school (now defunct).[43] Judge Thomas was an African-American man in his thirties, appointed by the president to direct a large federal agency. He was being groomed for further appointments in Republican circles and was described by one witness as "a rising star." Professor Hill's continued reliance on Judge Thomas for reference letters, speaking engagements, positions for others, and materials on civil rights enhanced her career and standing at her workplace and in the profession. Despite a high level of professional activities, such as research and attendance at conventions of the American Bar Association, she could not afford to alienate an important professional contact.

The women who testified for Judge Thomas lauded him for his respect for women and the help he gave them; except for one, none was a professional. They called Anita Hill "stridently aggressive," "arrogant," "opinionated," "hard," "tough," "ambitious," and "aloof." They suggested that her motivation was that she resented not being his main assistant at EEOC, as she had been at the Department of Education, or that she "had a crush on him" and was scorned.

As a professional woman, Professor Hill realized too late that Clarence Thomas was more interested in her sexually than professionally and was not going to be helpful in advancing her career at EEOC. She said that he had said when she left EEOC that if she ever talked about what he had done, it would ruin *his* career. She did not talk about it publicly, and in turn, he filled any request from her. She had nothing to gain by going public when she finally did so, and she said she would not have done so had she not been approached by staff of the Judiciary Committee, who had been told of rumors that Judge Thomas had been involved in sexual harassment at EEOC.

The Judiciary Committee was made up of fourteen upper-middle-class white men. The Senate, which had to vote to confirm the nomination, consisted of ninety-eight men, almost all white, and two white women. More of the senators (including the Republican woman) and, according to polls, more of the American people, believed him than her (Kolbert 1991b). After a weekend of testimony by Professor Hill and Judge Thomas and witnesses for and against her and for him, and a day of debate in the full Senate, on October 16, 1991, he was confirmed, 52–48, to a lifetime term on the Supreme Court. Professor Hill went back to her teaching job, with applause from her colleagues and students and later awards from professional women's groups.[44]

SEXUAL HARASSMENT AS DISCRIMINATION

Barbara Gutek (1985) found that 67.2 percent of 393 men would be flattered if asked to have sex by a woman coworker, but 62.8 percent of 814 women would be insulted by a sexual invitation from a male colleague (table 1, p. 96). Demands for sexual relations by superiors as the cost of keeping a job or advancing in it is quid pro quo, a long-standing ugly phenomenon of work life for heterosexual and lesbian women of all classes and races, and also for many women college and graduate students.[45] Most people understand the unfairness when someone who needs a job or a grade is subject to unwanted sexual advances, verbal or physical. But sexual talk, ges-

tures, and other behavior inappropriate to a work environment or to a professional or student-teacher relationship also constitute discrimination against the targets. This concept of sexual harassment as discrimination, first advanced by Catharine MacKinnon (1979), was promulgated in EEOC guidelines in 1980 but was not upheld in the courts in this or other countries until the late 1980s (Lewin 1991a; Weisman 1989).

The concept of harassment as discrimination emerged in the United States when white women and women and men of color were hired in workplaces and accepted in training institutions from which they had been excluded. Women in blue-collar jobs tend to come up against sexual harassment and other forms of interpersonal resistance when they successfully break into white men's work worlds, especially when they are women of color and have low-status jobs (Gruber and Bjorn 1982). The intent of such harassment is to make work life so unpleasant that the woman will quit. Women who enter formerly all-men managerial or professional schools or workplaces are likely to be subject to sexual innuendoes or remarks about their physical appearance, which are aimed at undercutting their poise and work performance. The aim is to induce them to shrink from visibility and assertiveness, the hallmarks of the person who becomes a leader in a field.

Only recently, and only in a very few instances, have formal complaints or grievances been filed and lawsuits instituted over persistent episodes of sexual harassment of women or of homosexual men. The reason for not making the incidents public is that the accuser is often not supported by colleagues or bosses, and in many cases, the harasser is the boss (Schneider 1991). When the incidents, such as embarrassing sexual remarks or jokes at meetings, are between peers, they are frequently condoned or at least not halted or criticized by those present. Neither senior men nor women are likely to put a stop to such incidents while they are happening or to chastise the harasser and offer support to the person harassed in private afterward. Those "microinequities" are not considered serious enough for a lawsuit, but "in the daily lives of working women, it is precisely these small, taken-for-granted comments, jokes, and physical acts, each individually unlikely to force a woman to initiate administrative action, that may accumulate in the long-term feeling and experience of harassment" (Schneider 1985, 104).[46]

Recently, feminists have begun to speak of a continuum that runs from *gender harassment,* which is inappropriately calling attention to women's or men's bodies, sexuality, and marital status, to *sexual harassment,* which is turning a professional, work or student-teacher relationship into a sexual relationship *that is not wanted by one of the people involved and that is coercive because the initiator has some power over the other person.*[47] The defining criterion for gender harassment is that the person's gender or sexual persuasion is used to comment on the individual's capabilities or career commitment. The defining criterion for sexual harassment is that the behavior is *inappropriate* for the situation; what should be a gender-neutral situation is turned into an *unwanted* sexual situation, and the initiator or instigator has *power,* which makes it difficult for those subject to the harassment to protest, leave, complain to others, or take action without jeopardy to their own status. The immediate reaction to gender and sexual harassment is likely to be discomfort, anger, feelings of powerlessness, inability to work, or feeling demeaned. These feelings may be suppressed if the person feels he or she has no choice but to continue in the situation or relationship.

Even senior women have faced such continued harassment. Several months before Anita Hill's allegations, a woman neurosurgeon, Dr. Frances K. Conley, a fifty-year-old full professor at Stanford Medical School and head of the Faculty Senate, resigned after sixteen years on the faculty.[48] She said she had been subject to continuous verbal sabotage of her professional status, such as comments on her breasts at meetings and being called "honey" in front of patients. Dr. Conley was the only woman faculty member in neurosurgery and one of two full professors in the department. The other, the acting head of neurosurgery, was going to be made chair of the department. He was the man she said was constantly insulting to her and to other women. Her women colleagues and the women medical students reported the long-standing practice of men physicians' use of pictures of naked women in lectures. If women complained or argued, they were labeled "premenstrual." Women medical students have always been subject to sexist practices, but women now constitute almost 40 percent of the classes in the United States. Rather than abating, gender and sexual harassment as a means of curbing the ambitions of women has persisted as the number of women in medicine has increased.[49]

"Speak-out" sessions reveal many incidents of gender and sexual harassment and how situations are differently perceived by women and by men. Neither type of harassment is likely to diminish using only formal methods of complaint and censure because both are so pervasive at every level in every workplace where women and men work together. The best remedy is clear indication from senior men, in a public setting, that *all* women employees, trainees, and students are to be treated *neutrally*—which does not mean coldly and distantly, but in a cordial, friendly, but not sexual manner. Most people do know the difference; they make such distinctions all the time in relating to their friends' spouses, for instance.

It takes a very well-established woman to stand up for her professional status successfully, and she needs the support of senior men. Dr. Conley finally agreed to return to the Stanford Medical School faculty because the administration appointed a task force on discrimination and also set up committees to review claims of sexual harassment. A follow-up interview showed that her actions paid off. Mary Roth Walsh (1992) reported that Conley has become the Anita Hill of American medicine, giving speeches all over the country and garnering awards from feminist organizations. Dr. Gerald Silverberg, the chair who had harassed Conley and many other women who were prepared to testify against him, resigned, made a formal apology, and was attending gender sensitivity classes and counseling sessions!

Women who live on the economic margins and women at the beginning of their careers cannot be expected to counter the constant sexist commentary that men use to guard the boundaries of what they feel is their turf. Nor can sympathetic men in similar positions. Not much support can be expected from senior men, who often engage in gender and sexual harassment themselves. So it is up to senior women to use

whatever power they have for social change. They can no longer remain silent: "Woman must put herself into the text—as into the world and into history—by her own movement" (Cixous 1976, 875).[50]

NOTES

1. On women in management cross-culturally, see Adler and Izraeli 1988b, 1993; Antal and Izraeli 1993. On the structural conditions that affect women's entry into and upward mobility in management in Israel, see Izraeli 1993.

2. Nine women won the Nobel Prize in the sciences between 1901 and 1989, 2.2 percent of the 407 awarded. Similar percentages of women were members of the prestigious national academies of science in England (3.2), France (2.3), Germany (2.1), and the United States (3.4) in the 1980s. The percentages of women who obtained doctorates in the sciences in the late 1960s and early 1970s (the feeder pool) was 9.3 percent for England, 19 percent for France, 4.8 percent for Germany, and 9.8 percent for the United States (Zuckerman 1991, 47, table 1.1).

3. Interview with Jardenia Ovadia, M.D., July 26, 1984. For the tentativeness with which women are supported for positions of authority by noncolleagues, see Chase and Bell 1990. For a review and critique of the literature on women and achievement, see Kaufman and Richardson 1982.

4. Cole and Singer 1991; M. F. Fox 1991; Reskin 1978a, 1978b.

5. The interviews took place in California, Texas, Massachusetts, and Arizona. The percentages of men in these occupations in the United States in 1990 were nursing, 5.5; elementary school teachers, 14.8; librarians, 16.7; social workers, 31.8 (table 1, 254). The proportion of Black men is greatest in social work.

6. Also see Dexter 1985; Martin, Harrison, and DiNitto 1983.

7. For a continuance of this pattern of business-family marriages well into the twentieth century in Japan, but with arranged marriages, see Hamabata 1990.

8. Lever 1976, 1978; Luria and Herzog 1991; Maccoby 1990; Thorne 1990, 1993; Thorne and Luria 1986.

9. Some teachers deliberately mix boys and girls, but in other schools, teachers routinely divide a class into boys and girls (for teams, lineup, etc.). For a history of gender practices in the public schools in the United States, see Hansot and Tyack 1988.

10. Gutek 1985, 129–52; Hochschild 1983; Tancred-Sheriff 1989, 52–55.

11. Sexist jokes and sexual remarks about and to women seem to occur among men of all classes, in every work setting, and in many countries. See Collinson 1988; Lyman 1987; Peña 1991. These verbal acts of sexual aggression can easily turn into sexual assault if the woman is alone with a group of men

and physically or psychologically vulnerable. For the concept of a continuum of sexual violence, see Liz Kelly 1987.

12. Barkalow and Raab 1990; Collinson and Collinson 1989; Fine 1987b.

13. For men nurses, see C. L. Williams 1989, 118–19; on women physicians, see Lorber 1984, 60–61.

14. Also see Cockburn 1991, 159–61.

15. See Booth-Butterfield and Booth-Butterfield 1988 for cooperation and support among women teammates.

16. See Remy (1990, 45) for a more general statement of "fratriarchy based . . . on the self-interest of the association of men itself." He equates this age-graded bonding with men's huts, blood brotherhoods, and all-male secret societies.

17. Bourdieu 1989; Coser 1986; C. F. Epstein 1988, 215–31. Because bathrooms are gender-segregated, they are used by women as well as men for networking, but women also use them for letting out anger against "them," and as places of refuge from men (Barkalow 1990, 65; Reskin 1988; Quindlen 1988, 30–33).

18. C. F. Epstein 1981; Kanter 1977a; Lorber 1984; Zuckerman 1991. In some countries, such as the former Soviet Union, most doctors are women because it is not a high-prestige profession; in some Arab countries, women doctors are needed because women patients are not allowed to be examined by men doctors.

19. For domestic arrangements among dual-career couples, see Fava and Deierlein 1989; Hertz 1986; Holmstrom 1972; Lorber 1984, 80–98; Vannoy-Hiller and Philliber 1989. For choice between career and family, see Gerson 1985.

20. Cole and Zuckerman 1991; C. F. Epstein 1981, 342–43; Kaufman 1978; Lorber 1984, 91–93; Zunz 1991.

21. Lorber 1984, 80–98, found that married women physicians tended to combine their social life with networking, and since many were married to physicians, their networks were larger than those of single women.

22. The process actually starts in childhood, with differential treatment of girls and boys in grade schools, and proliferates in the higher grades, with only bright middle-class boys being encouraged to take math and science courses (AAUW Report 1992).

23. On women in science, see Cole 1979; Keller 1983, 1985; Reskin 1978a, 1978b; M. W. Rossiter 1982; Sayer 1975; Zuckerman, Cole, and Brewer 1991; and the *Sage* issue on Black women in science and technology (6 [Fall] 1989). On com-

parisons of women's and men's careers in various professions, see Ahearn and Scott 1981; C. F. Epstein 1971, 1981, 1991; M. F. Fox 1991; Fox and Faver 1985; Judi Marshall 1989; Powell 1988, 175–206.

24. Freeland Judson says that with Linus Pauling, James Watson, and Francis Crick, "she was one of the four people closest to the discovery of the structure of DNA" (1979, 147). His account discusses the personalities and interchanges of all the players (1979, 100–98).

25. "Rosy" was a nickname used behind her back (Judson 1979, 148).

26. Freeland Judson cites a letter that he feels indicates "she had good reason to think she headed an independent team" (103).

27. According to Freeland Judson, Crick and other readers of the manuscript forced the apologia; Wilkins still had feelings of animosity toward his "dear, dead colleague" (1979, 102).

28. Mozart's own sister, Nannerl, was also a pianist, composer, and child prodigy. She and Mozart traveled around Europe together until she was fifteen and married. She may even have written some of the early works attributed to Mozart (Steinem 1992). Actually, Mozart wasn't "Mozart, the great composer," in his own day, nor was he in the nineteenth century. Mozart's high status is a modern phenomenon. The term *status shield* is Hochschild's (1983, 162–81).

29. Oswald Hall (1946, 1948, 1949) developed these concepts for medical communities. I extended them to women physicians' careers (Lorber 1984), but the concepts are valid for all kinds of colleague groups.

30. In 1977a, 206–42; also 1977b. The effects of imbalanced numbers in work situations are boundary maintenance by dominants, role encapsulation (assigning or defining the work tokens do as appropriate), performance pressures because of tokens' heightened visibility, and stereotyped informal roles, such as, for token women, mother, mascot, seductress, and "iron maiden." (I have not seen similar roles identified for token men, such as men nurses, or for Black women or men in white groups or vice versa).

31. Barkalow and Raab 1990; S. E. Martin 1980; C. L. Williams 1989.

32. M. F. Fox 1981, 1984; Lorber 1987a, 1991.

33. For a psychological approach to women's leadership styles, see Cantor and Bernay 1992. For an anthropological perspective, see Power 1991, 166–67, who notes that among chimpanzees in the wild, "a charismatic leader . . . is any of a number of animals of either sex who are, to varying degrees, confident, self-assured, normally nonaggressive, but fearless when roused, tolerant of others, approachable and responsive, with a 'presence' through posture and bearing (rather than through size and strength) and who carry our leader-role related behaviors." For female leadership, see pp. 196–203 and De Waal 1984.

34. England 1979; Hearn and Parkin 1988; Kanter 1977a, 166–205; Powell 1988, 150–56; Wolf and Fligstein 1979a, 1979b.

35. Barkalow and Raab 1990; S. E. Martin 1980; C. L. Williams 1989.

36. Also see C. L. Williams 1990, 48–87, on the official obsession with masculinity and femininity when women entered the Marine Corps.

37. Formal theories and experiments on how status organizes interaction, particularly how beliefs about actors' social characteristics govern evaluation of performance, allocation of rewards, and the structure of power and prestige in small groups, document many of the processes described in this section. For overviews and recent developments in the field, see Fisek, Berger, and Norman 1991; Ridgeway and Berger 1988; Wagner and Berger 1991. For studies specifically on gender, see Carli 1991; Lockheed 1985; Molm 1998; Pugh and Wahrman 1983; Ridgeway 1988; Ridgeway and Diekema 1989; Stewart 1988; Wagner 1988.

38. Deaux and Major 1987; Goffman 1959; Hochschild 1983; Ridgeway 1987; Ridgeway and Johnson 1990; Scheff 1990.

39. Dovidio et al. 1988; Fishman 1978; Kollock, Blumstein, and Schwartz 1985; West 1982; Wiley and Woolley 1988; Zimmerman and West 1975.

40. Goffman 1963b, 1967, 5–95; Henley 1977. When Geraldine Ferraro was Walter Mondale's running mate, there was a whole set of rules about standing, walking, touching, and addressing each other (Dowd 1984).

41. Dabbs and Stokes 1975; F. Davis 1961; Egolf and Corder 1991; C. F. Epstein 1981, 309–14; Goffman 1963a; Hatfield and Sprecher 1986; Unger, Hilderbrand, and Mader 1982; Webster and Driskell 1983.

42. For other *New York Times* reports, columns, and stories documenting the continuing pervasiveness of sexual harassment and the micropolitics of the issue, see Apple 1991; Bray 1991; De Witt 1991; Dowd 1991a, 1991b; Goleman 1991; Kolbert 1991a, 1991b; Lewin 1991b; Quindlen 1991b, 1991c, 1991d; Schafran 1991; Warrock 1991; Wicker 1991; Lena Williams 1991; M. C. Wilson 1991. For articles and features slanted toward men's perspectives, see the special section of the *Wall Street Journal,* Sex and Power in the Office, October 18, 1991, B1–B4.

43. Professor Hill's experiences are not unusual for minority women seeking teaching positions in law schools. A recent survey of 174 of the 176 U.S. law schools found that minority women compared to minority men are more likely to begin in nontenured tracks (44 percent to 29 percent), to teach at lower-prestige law schools (–0.12 to 0.66 on a scale where 0 is average), and twice as likely to teach beginning courses (Merritt and Reskin 1992).

44. The January-February 1992 issue of *Ms. Magazine* featured an article by Anita Hill based on remarks delivered at a panel on sexual harassment and policy-making at the National Forum for Women State Legislators, which had been convened by the Center for the American Woman and Politics at Rutgers University (1992). Also see Sharpe 1992 on the reality of sexual harassment in Washington, D.C.; Williams et al.

1992 for analysis and comment by five African-American feminists. For a rebuttal of right-wing interpretations, see Mayer and Abramson 1993.

45. Dziech and Weiner 1990; Gutek 1985; MacKinnon 1979; Mathews 1991; Paludi 1990; Schneider 1982, 1985, 1991. Consensual sexual relations between equals (and even between a superior and a subordinate) is not harassment, but, in the face of refusal, persistent demands for dates or sexual relations is. Work organizations, schools, and the military usually have written and unwritten rules governing dating and sexual relations among their members, but may be less explicit about what constitutes sexual harassment. See Barkalow 1990; Cockburn 1991, 138–70; Gutek 1985, 149; Powell 1988, 135–37; Schneider 1984.

46. Also see Rowe 1977; Schneider 1982.

47. On the range of verbal and nonverbal types of sexual harassment, see Gruber 1992.

48. See L. Fraser 1991; J. Gross 1991; *Stanford-Observer* 1991 for background stories; *New York Times* 1991c for the news report.

49. Grant 1988; Lenhart et al. 1991; Lorber 1991.

50. Partly as a result of Anita Hill's experiences in front of a panel of white men, after the 1992 election, the number of U.S. senators rose from two to six; one is African-American, Carol Mosely Braun.

REFERENCES

Adler, Nancy J., and Dafna N. Izraeli. 1988a. Women in management world-wide. In *Women in management world-wide,* edited by Nancy J. Adler and Dafna N. Izraeli. Armonk, N.Y.: M. E. Sharpe.

Astin, Helen S. 1991. Citation classics: Women's and men's perceptions of their contributions to science. In Zuckerman, Cole, and Bruer.

Barkalow, Carol, with Andrea Raab. 1990. *In the men's house.* New York: Poseidon Press.

Benokraitis, Nijole V., and Joe R. Feagin. 1986. *Modern sexism: Blatant, subtle, and covert discrimination.* Englewood Cliffs, N.J.: Prentice-Hall.

Blum, Linda M., and Vicki Smith. 1988. Women's mobility in the corporation: A critique of the politics of optimism. *Signs* 13:528–45.

Brinton, Mary C. 1989. Gender stratification in contemporary Japan. *American Sociological Review* 54:549–64.

Cantor, Dorothy W., and Toni Bernay with Jean Stoess. 1992. *Women in power: The secrets of leadership.* Boston: Houghton Mifflin.

Carter, Michael J., and Susan Boslego Carter. 1981. Women's recent progress in the professions or, women get a ticket to ride after the gravy train has left the station. *Feminist Studies* 7:477–504.

Chase, Susan E. 1988. Making sense of "the woman who becomes a man." In *Gender and discourse: The power of talk,* edited by Alexandra Dundas Todd and Sue Fisher. Norwood, N.J.: Ablex.

Cixous, Hélène. 1976. The laugh of the Medusa, translated by Keith Cohen and Paula Cohen. *Signs* 1:875–93.

Cockburn, Cynthia. 1991. *In the way of women: Men's resistance to sex equality in organizations.* Ithaca, N.Y.: ILR Press.

Cole, Jonathan R., and Harriet Zuckerman. 1991. Marriage, motherhood, and re-research performance in science. In Zuckerman, Cole, and Bruer.

Covin, Teresa Joyce, and Christina Christenson Brush. 1991. An examination of male and female attitudes toward career and family issues. *Sex Roles* 25:393–415.

Cowan, Alison Leigh. 1991. Management citadel rocked by unruliness. *New York Times,* Business Section, 26 September.

Crenshaw, Kimberlé. 1991. Demarginalizing the intersection of race and sex: A Black feminist critique of antidiscrimination doctrine, feminist theory, and antiracist politics. In *Feminist legal theory: Readings in law and gender,* edited by Katharine T. Bartlett and Rosanne Kennedy. Boulder, Colo: Westview Press.

Davidoff, Leonore, and Catherine Hall. 1987. *Family fortunes: Men and women of the English middle class, 1780–1850.* Chicago: University of Chicago Press.

Dowd, Maureen. 1991c. Image more than reality became issue, losers say. *New York Times,* 16 October.

Epstein, Cynthia Fuchs. 1991. Constraints on excellence: Structural and cultural barriers to the recognition and demonstration of achievement. In Zuckerman, Cole, and Bruer.

Farr, Kathryn Ann. 1988. Dominance bonding through the good old boys sociability group. *Sex Roles* 18:259–77.

Ferber, Marianne A. 1986. Citations: Are they an objective measure of scholarly merit? *Signs* 11:381–89.

———. 1988. Citations and networking. *Gender & Society* 2:82–89.

Fierman, Jaclyn. 1990. Why women still don't hit the top. *Fortune,* 30 July.

Fulbright, Karen. 1987. The myth of the double-advantage: Black female managers. In *Slipping through the cracks: The status of Black women,* edited by Margaret C. Simms and Julianne Malveaux. New Brunswick, N.J.: Transaction Books.

Gerson, Kathleen. 1985. *Hard choices: How women decide about work, career, and motherhood.* Berkeley: University of California Press.

Goffman, Erving. 1963a. *Stigma.* Englewood Cliffs, N.J.: Prentice-Hall.

————. 1967. *Interaction ritual: Essays in face-to-face behavior.* Hawthorne, N.Y.: Aldine.

Goldin, Claudia. 1990. *Understanding the gender gap: An economic history of American women.* New York: Oxford University Press.

Gruber, James, and Lars Bjorn. 1982. Blue-collar blues: The sexual harassment of women auto workers. *Work and Occupations* 9:271–98.

Gutek, Barbara A. 1985. *Sex and the workplace: The impact of sexual behavior and harassment on women, men, and organizations.* San Francisco: Jossey-Bass.

Hennig, Margaret, and Anne Jardim. 1976. *The managerial woman.* New York: Pocket Books.

Henriques, Diana B. 1992. Ms. Siebert, still on the barricades. *New York Times,* Business Section, 5 July.

Hughes, Everett C. 1971. *The sociological eye.* Chicago: Aldine-Atherton.

Izraeli, Dafna N. 1984. The attitudinal effects of gender mix in union committees. *Industrial and Labor Relations Review* 37:212–21.

Johnson, Richard A., and Gary I. Schulman. 1989. Gender-role composition and role entrapment in decision-making groups. *Gender & Society* 3:355–72.

Judson, Horace Freeland. 1979. *The eighth day of creation: The makers of the revolution in biology.* New York: Simon & Schuster.

Kanter, Rosabeth Moss. 1977a. *Men and women of the corporation.* New York: Basic Books.

Keller, Evelyn Fox. 1983. *A feeling for the organism: The life and work of Barbara McClintock.* New York: W. H. Freeman.

Kemper, Theodore D. 1990. *Social structure and testosterone: Explorations of the socio-biosocial chain.* New Brunswick, N.J.: Rutgers University Press.

Kessler-Harris, Alice. 1982. *Out to work: A history of wage-earning women in the United States.* New York: Oxford University Press.

Kingson, Jennifer A. 1988. Women in the law say path is limited by "mommy track." *New York Times,* 8 August.

Kolata, Gina. 1992b. Dr. Barbara McClintock, 90, gene research pioneer, dies. *New York Times,* 4 September.

Kolbert, Elizabeth. 1991b. Most in national survey say judge is the more believable. *New York Times,* 15 October.

Komarovsky, Mirra. 1976. *Dilemmas of masculinity: A study of college youth.* New York: Norton.

————. 1985. *Women in college: Shaping new feminine identities.* New York: Basic Books.

Laws, Judith Long. 1975. The psychology of tokenism: An analysis. *Sex Roles* 1:51–67.

Lewin, Tamar. 1991a. Nude pictures are ruled sexual harassment. *New York Times,* 23 January.

Lipman-Blumen, Jean. 1976. Toward a homosocial theory of sex roles: An explanation of sex segregation in social institutions. *Signs* 1(Spring, pt. 2):15–31.

Lorber, Judith. 1981. The limits of sponsorship for women physicians. *Journal of the American Medical Women's Association* 36:329–38.

————. 1984. *Women physicians: Careers, status, and power.* London and New York: Tavistock.

————. 1985. More women physicians: Will it mean more humane health care? *Social Policy* 16(Summer):50–54.

————. [1979] 1989a. Trust, loyalty, and the place of women in the informal organization of work. *Women: A feminist perspective,* 2d and 4th eds., edited by Jo Freeman. Mountain View, Calif.: Mayfield.

————. 1991. Can women physicians ever be true equals in the American medical profession? In *Current research occupations and professions,* edited by Judith A. Levy. Vol. 6. Greenwich, Conn.: JAI Press.

Lorber, Judith, and Martha Ecker. 1983. Career development of female and male physicians. *Journal of Medical Education* 58:447–56.

MacKinnon, Catharine A. 1979. *Sexual harassment of working women.* New Haven: Yale University Press.

Martin, Lynn. 1991. *A report on the glass ceiling initiative.* Washington, D.C.: U.S. Department of Labor.

Martin, Susan Ehrlich. 1980. *Breaking and entering: Police women on patrol.* Berkeley: University of California Press.

McCullough, Joan. 1973. The 13 who were left behind. *Ms. Magazine,* September.

Merton, Robert K. 1968. The Matthew effect in science. *Science* 159:56–63.

Moore, Gwen. 1990. Structural determinants of men's and women's personal networks. *American Sociological Review* 55:726–35.

Morrill, Calvin. 1991. Conflict management, honor, and organizational change. *American Journal of Sociology* 97:585–621.

New York Times. 1991b. Woman to lead Annapolis midshipmen. 28 April.

————. 1992a. Few women found in top public jobs. 3 January.

Olson, Jon, and Jon Miller. 1983. Gender and interaction in the workplace. In *Research in the interweave of social roles: Jobs and families.* Vol. 3, edited by Helena Znaniecki Lopata and Joseph H. Pleck. Greenwich, Conn.: JAI Press.

O'Meara, J. Donald. 1989. Cross-sex friendship: Four basic challenges of an ignored relationship. *Sex Roles* 21:525–43.

Pogrebin, Letty Cottin. 1987. *Among friends: Who we like, why we like them and what we do with them.* New York: McGraw-Hill.

Poll, Carol. 1978. No room at the top: A study of the social processes that contribute to the underrepresentation of women on the administrative levels of the New York City school system. Ph.D. diss. City University of New York Graduate School.

Powell, Gary N. 1988. *Women and men in management.* Newbury Park, Calif.: Sage.

Reskin, Barbara F. 1988. Bringing the men back in: Sex differentiation and the devaluation of women's work. *Gender & Society* 2:58–81.

Ridgeway, Cecelia L., and Cathryn Johnson. 1990. What is the relationship between socioemotional behavior and status in task groups? *American Journal of Sociology* 95:1189–1212.

Rodgers, Fran Susser, and Charles Rodgers. 1989. Business and the facts of family life. *Harvard Business Review,* November-December, 121–29.

Rose, Suzanna M. 1985. Same- and cross-sex friendships and the psychology of homosociality. *Sex Roles* 12:63–74.

Sattel, Jack W. 1976. The inexpressive male: Tragedy or sexual politics? *Social Problems* 23:469–77.

Sayre, Anne. 1975. *Rosalind Franklin and DNA.* New York: Norton.

Scheff, Thomas J. 1988. Shame and conformity: The deference-emotion system. *American Sociological Review* 53:395–406.

Schneider, Beth E. 1985. Approaches, assaults, attractions, affairs: Policy implications of the sexualization of the workplace. *Population Research and Policy Review* 4:93–113.

Shaffer, Peter. 1980. *Amadeus.* New York: Harper & Row.

Silver, Allan. 1990. Friendship in commercial society: Eighteenth-century social theory and modern sociology. *American Journal of Sociology* 95:1474–1504.

South, Scott J., Charles M. Bonjean, Judy Corder, and William T. Markham. 1982a. Sex and power in the federal bureaucracy: A comparative analysis of male and female supervisors. *Work and Occupations* 9:233–54.

South, Scott J., Charles M. Bonjean, William T. Markham, and Judy Corder. 1982b. Social structure and intergroup interaction: Men and women of the federal bureaucracy. *American Sociological Review* 47:587–99.

Steinem, Gloria. 1992. Seeking out the invisible woman. *New York Times,* Arts and Leisure Section, 13 March.

Strom, Stephanie. 1992. Fashion Avenue's $100 million woman. *New York Times,* Business Section, 17 May.

Thorne, Barrie. 1990. Children and gender: Constructions of differences. In *Theoretical perspectives on sexual difference,* edited by Deborah L. Rhode. New Haven: Yale University Press.

Toren, Nina, and Vered Kraus. 1987. The effects of minority size on women's position in academia. *Social Forces* 65: 1090–1100.

Walsh, Mary Roth. 1992. Before and after Frances Conley. *Journal of the American Medical Women's Association* 48:119–21.

Watson, James D. 1968. *The double helix: A personal account of the discovery of the structure of DNA.* New York: Atheneum.

Weisman, Steven R. 1989. Tokyo journal. Sex harassment: Glare of light on man's world. *New York Times,* 13 November.

West, Candace. 1984. *Routine complications: Troubles with talk between doctors and patients.* Bloomington: Indiana University Press.

West, Candace, and Don Zimmerman. 1987. Doing gender. *Gender & Society* 1:125–51.

Wharton, Amy S., and James N. Baron. 1987. So happy together? The impact of gender segregation on men at work. *American Sociological Review* 52:574–87.

Williams, Christine L. 1989. *Gender differences at work: Women and men in nontraditional occupations.* Berkeley: University of California Press.

———. 1992. The glass escalator: Hidden advantages for men in the "female" professions. *Social Problems* 39:253–67.

Williams, Patricia J., Barbara Smith, Rebecca Walker, Marcia Ann Gillespie, and Eleanor Holmes Norton. 1992. Refusing to be silenced. *Ms. Magazine,* January-February.

Zuckerman, Harriet. 1977. *Scientific elite: Nobel laureates in the United States.* New York: Free Press.

Zuckerman, Harriet, Jonathan R. Cole, and John T. Bruer (eds.). 1991. *The outer circle: Women in the scientific community.* New York: Norton.

Zunz, Sharyn. 1991. Gender-related issues in the career development of social work managers. *Affilia* 6:39–52.

CHECKPOINTS

1. Lorber identifies the following factors that sustain gender segregation in the workplace: glass ceiling, informal networks, homosocial groups, the "mommy track," the Salieri effect, the Matthew effect, and inner circles.

2. According to Lorber, gender segregation is linked to the distribution of power and authority in the workplace.

To prepare for reading the next section, think about these questions:

1. Do you believe affirmative action is an appropriate mechanism for achieving equity in social institutions?

2. Have you ever been in a situation in which you believe someone's judgment of you was influenced by stereotypes?

Affirmative Action in Theory and Practice: Issues of Power, Ambiguity, and Gender Versus Race

JENNIFER L. EBERHARDT

SUSAN T. FISKE
University of Massachusetts at Amherst

Reactions to affirmative action are, in part, a function of how recipients are perceived in American society as well as how recipients perceive themselves. Affirmative action for relatively powerless groups may be viewed negatively because their group membership is more salient than that of the powerful and because the stereotypes about them serve to perpetuate power asymmetries. Moreover, affirmative action for Blacks may be viewed even more negatively than affirmative action for women because race stereotypes tend to be more simplistic and less prescriptive than gender stereotypes. Black affirmative-action recipients also may understand affirmative-action policies differently than women recipients. Blacks may be more likely than women to feel entitled rather than unfairly helped. As a result, Blacks may be less likely to develop negative self-evaluations due to affirmative action. Regardless of self-perceptions, affirmative-action policies are held suspect. Suspicions sur-rounding recipients' ability to fit in, their competence, their job placements, and their promotions all affect how difficult it will be to implement successfully affirmative-action policies. Researchers have suggested that the most effective method for dealing with these suspicions is to provide more explicit and detailed information regarding affirmative-action policies and recipient qualifications. No research has yet adequately addressed why this information is not being provided, or how this information should be provided.

Affirmative action is an anomaly among political and psychological issues. People's talk is at once expressive and reticent. Teaching a course on psychology and politics, one of us found that the overwhelmingly White and liberal class exploded on the issue of affirmative action. Anecdotes abounded about White male relatives, friends, and immediate family who had allegedly lost jobs or promotions to Black affirmative-action candidates. Yet amidst the clamor, not one person acknowledged knowing anyone who had benefited from affirmative action. Also, although women are beneficiaries of affirmative action, the affirmative-action candidates blamed for job losses were all racial minorities.[1] Women were as likely as men to tell these affirmative-action stories. No Black student told such stories.[2]

These reactions echo the initial themes of this article: First, we suggest that perceptions of affirmative action are overwhelmingly negative in part because group membership is more salient for the powerless (targets of affirmative action) than for the powerful (beneficiaries of the status quo). Second, we suggest that race differs significantly from gender as a stereotypic category, which results in race-based affirmative action being more threatening than gender-based affirmative action hence, all the targets of the stories were Black. Third, Black and female recipients of affirmative action view the program differently, which may explain why White women joined in the stories but Black students did not.

Following these theoretical considerations, we discuss practical considerations of implementation. More specifically, we consider the effects of affirmative action on power relations, strategies that may produce positive effects of affirmative action, and problems that may block the successful implementation of these strategies.

THEORETICAL CONSIDERATIONS

Why People View Affirmative Action Negatively

People view affirmative action negatively in part because they see it as replacing a race-neutral and gender-neutral status quo with a group-based reward system that considers group membership to the exclusion of merit. We argue that group membership becomes salient for disadvantaged groups more than for the powerful, although logically both group memberships matter. Implicit in this dialogue about race and gender is the notion that gender is an attribute and that women "have" and race is an attribute that Blacks "have," more so than their more powerful counterparts. White men are seen as race-free and gender-free such that their group status could not possibly influence any outcome. Such a view ignores the disparities in group power that link race and gender to an ostensibly "neutral" distribution of rewards. The same power asymmetries promote simplistic negative stereotypes of outgroups, which further obscure how power asymmetries inject a group bias into a supposedly neutral system. The rest of this article elaborates these points and serves as a commentary on other articles in this special issue.

Affirmative-action policies are designed to insure equal employment opportunities for members of groups that have been historically underrepresented in valuable positions in society (Crosby, 1994). Organizations have developed numerous strategies for achieving this goal, all of which involve weighing both a candidate's group membership and qualifications in making employment decisions. Contrary to some popular views of affirmative action, the recruiting, hiring, and promoting of employees solely on the basis of group membership is highly atypical and is illegal for most employers (see Crosby, 1994; Taylor, 1994).

Yet lay people commonly perceive affirmative action as preferential treatment (Blanchard & Crosby, 1989) that replaces qualified White males with unqualified minorities and women. Many feel that the existence of these policies gives legal and political backing to "reverse discrimination." Because affirmative action is seen as giving preference to members of protected groups with little regard for merit, people imagine employers carelessly attempting to fill quotas for minorities (and sometimes women), as White males allegedly become more and more disenfranchised.

Although many researchers have examined how the damaging consequences of these misperceptions can be effectively eliminated (see Turner & Pratkanis, 1994), little research has examined why these misperceptions are so prevalent. Aversive racism and procedural-justice frameworks have been extremely useful in illuminating people's reactions to affirmative action policies (see, e.g., Barnes Nacoste, 1994; Murrell, Dietz, Dovidio, Gaertner, & Drout, 1994), yet these theories do not speak directly to why people often fail to understand what these policies entail. People's lack of accurate information becomes especially apparent in comparing perceptions of affirmative action with perceptions of equal opportunity. Generally, people have a good grasp of equal opportunity policies, yet few have a clear understanding of affirmative action (for a more detailed discussion, see Crosby, 1994).

Gross misperceptions of affirmative action may reflect how little attention Americans typically pay to social structural variables such as power relations. If *social power* is defined as the degree of control one group has over another group's outcomes (Dépret & Fiske, 1993), men and Whites can be considered more powerful than women and Blacks. Members of powerful groups tend to have higher status and prestige, they control a greater number of rewards, and people tend to have higher expectations of their performance and competence (Fiske & Stevens, 1993). When people are alerted to the power asymmetries resulting from discriminatory practices and how these asymmetries distort the meritocratic process, they show less resistance to affirmative-action policies (Murrell et al., 1994). People then understand how affirmative action may be needed to counteract the distortions that result from longstanding power asymmetries.

Power asymmetries also promote stereotypes of less powerful groups. Stereotyping occurs less often for members of powerful groups (Fiske, 1993). Because the powerful, by definition, control the outcomes of others, people pay closer attention to them and are less likely to form simplistic judgments about their behavior. In contrast, simplistic and stereotypic judgments are made much more often about members of powerless groups. People may have less concern and less need to be accurate about those considered relatively insignificant to their own outcomes. People are more likely to commit the "ultimate attribution error," attributing the plight of powerless out-groups to negative group characteristics rather than to circumstances (Pettigrew, 1979). In the same vein, recipients of affirmative action are thought to be in that position (i.e., powerless) because they do not have the talent, skills, or drive necessary to become members of the controlling, dominant group. In laboratory studies, when experimenters explicitly inform subjects of the fact that the recipients of affirmative action are indeed "qualified," thus rebutting the presumption the stereotype creates, subjects feel less negative about affirmative-action policies (Major, Feinstein, & Crocker, 1994).

Misperceptions of affirmative action can also affect how social scientists study the issue. Much of the social psychological research on affirmative action compares subjects' responses to selection procedures that take into account only group membership (e.g., gender) to selections based only on merit. Researchers have begun to discuss the fact that solely group-based selections are highly atypical (see, e.g., Major et al., 1994). However, social psychologists have continued to employ group-based conditions in experimental studies because lay people commonly perceive affirmative action primarily as group-based selection. This is doubtless necessary because perceptions of affirmative action can be of equal or greater importance than the realities of the policies. Nevertheless, as lay people become (one hopes) more sophisticated, their perceptions of actual affirmative-action processes (e.g., combining merit and group membership criteria) will be important.

The myth of merit-based selection in the absence of affirmative action further contributes to unfavorable views of affirmative action. Although researchers have attended to the myth of selection procedures based solely on group membership, there is relatively little analysis of the myth of merit-based selection. One erroneous implication of this gap could be the blind acceptance of the idea that, absent an explicit affirmative-action policy targeting minorities and women, the selection criteria are fair, just, and culture-free. The odd assumption may be that there is typically no influence of group membership on selection unless one is, for instance, a Black or a woman. Yet, on careful examination, one sees that perceptions of merit-based qualification fluctuate with the social status of the person being evaluated and are thus necessarily linked to group membership.

Power mediates the perception of merit. Differences in perceptions of merit reflect, in part, underlying power relations. Achievements of powerful group members are thought to be merit based, whereas achievements of less powerful group members are viewed as group-based benefits. This attributional asymmetry may result in powerful group members being less aware than powerless group members of the ways that their achievements are group linked. The reactions of White men to selection procedures across a number of studies illustrate this point (Major et al., 1994; or for a review, see Turner & Pratkanis, 1994). Although White women who are selected for a position because of their gender are likely to have more negative self-evaluations than meritoriously selected women, selection procedure has little to no effect on men's self-evaluations (Turner & Pratkanis, 1994). When men do show an effect for selection procedure, it is in the direction opposite to that for women (Major et al., 1994). For example, White men who have been selected for positions based on gender later show less depressed affect than men selected for positions based on merit (Major et al., 1994). In addition, White men exhibit no difference in task choice as a function of selection procedure, whereas White women who are selected based on gender tend to choose (safer) easier tasks to perform in comparison to those tasks chosen by women selected on merit (Turner & Pratkanis, 1994). Moreover, White men who have been selected for positions based on gender are subsequently less likely than preferentially selected women to perceive gender as having had an effect on their selection (see Major et al., 1994).

White men in these studies are not the only ones who perceive gender as having little effect on their selection. For example, all subjects (male and female) need explicit proof and reassurance of a woman's qualifications for a position before affirmative action can be considered positively, yet proof of a man's qualifications is implicit in his social status and does not require additional explanation (see Major et al., 1994; Turner & Pratkanis, 1994). Gender is perceived as having an overwhelming effect on a female candidate's selection unless stated otherwise, whereas gender is perceived as having little effect on the selection of male candidates. By accepting the traditional notion of merit-based selection as independent of group membership, social scientists may be paying too little attention to how gender benefits males (and race benefits Whites) as well.

Race Versus Gender Stereotypes: Differences and Implications

Perhaps we also need to examine, more carefully, differences between racial and gender stereotypes. Social psychologists, starting with the work on authoritarian personality, have noted correlations among stereotyping of multiple ethnic groups; that is, people prejudiced against one group (e.g., Blacks) are likely to be prejudiced against other groups as well (e.g., Jews; perhaps women also). General processes were thought to underlie the stereotyping of various groups. Although other early work, such as the D. Katz and Braly (1933) checklists and their descendants, instead documented the content of various stereotypes, little linkage was made between the specific contents and differences in the stereotyping process. With the advent of cognitive approaches to stereotyping, forecast by Allport (1954) two decades before they took hold, the focus on process has completely dominated a focus on content or their interaction (for a history, see Ashmore & Del Boca, 1981). This was a useful initial strategy, and in the past two decades, social psychologists have made significant progress in uncovering many of the intricacies of stereotyping processes. Yet studies rarely focus on the manner in which the content of stereotypes may influence the processing of so-

cial information. Thus, we do not know enough about how the specific contents of different stereotypes interact with the processes involved.

We suggest that there are important content differences and important content-process interactions in the perceptions and self-perceptions of Blacks and women, which illuminate reactions to affirmative action. Social psychologists must be particularly careful in generalizing from reactions toward affirmative-action policies for women to reactions toward these policies for Blacks (and vice versa). We argue that racial stereotypes and gender stereotypes differ in fundamental ways that may affect perceptions of affirmative action.

The relation between the stereotyped group and the more powerful members of society differs for Blacks and women. Most important, racial groups are segregated from each other to a much greater degree than are men and women. It is quite possible for a White American to live in this country having almost no contact at all with Black Americans. Some argue that the existence of extreme residential, economic, social, and educational segregation between Blacks and Whites is not simply the residue of America's past prejudices; rather, current individual behaviors, institutional practices, and public policies work to perpetuate it (Massey & Denton, 1993). Moreover, there are few intimate relationships among Black Americans and White Americans. For example, according to the 1980 U.S. Census, only 2 percent of Blacks are married to partners outside their racial group (Lee & Yamanaka, 1990). This figure is extremely low in comparison to other groups, such as Latinos, Chinese Americans, Japanese Americans, or Korean Americans who tend to outmarry at much higher rates (13%, 16%, 34%, and 32%, respectively). Naturally, it goes without saying that there are many more communal relationships between men and women than between individuals of different ethnic and racial groups (especially Blacks).

The relative degree of segregation may directly affect the content and processing of racial stereotypes as compared to gender stereotypes (Fiske & Stevens, 1993). Although all stereotypes contain some descriptive and prescriptive elements, racial stereotypes tend to be primarily descriptive. The descriptive element of stereotypes contains information about what the typical group member is like. Attributes such as unintelligent, criminal, lazy, or musically inclined are primarily descriptive. In contrast, gender stereotypes contain a strong prescriptive element as well as a descriptive element. The prescriptive element contains information about what group members *should* be like. Descriptions of women may include such attributes as emotional, dependent, or weak, whereas prescriptions for women include a number of "shoulds," such as moving in a ladylike fashion, accommodating others, or speaking softly.

Differences in the degree of segregation and the resulting differences in stereotypes affect the level of complexity involved in stereotype processing (Fiske & Stevens, 1993). Because males and females are less segregated throughout their lives and tend to have more experience with one another than do Whites and Blacks, the stereotypes developed about women tend to be more complex, having a great many more subtypes (e.g., the feminist, the temptress, the caregiver, the housewife, or the professional woman; see Deaux & Lewis, 1984), compared to stereotypes about Blacks (Devine & Baker, 1991). Gender stereotypes may also be much more developed, nuanced, and multifaceted because gender categories are acquired much earlier in childhood (24 months) in comparison to racial categories (5 years; Thompson, 1975; Williams & Morland, 1976).

Even though many of the power asymmetries facilitated by gender and race stereotypes are identical (e.g., lower prestige, lower status, lower expectations, minimal control over resource distribution), not all power asymmetries are identical for both groups. For example, although males (the advantaged group) pose a greater threat to females in physical power, this physical threat is reversed for Blacks and Whites. The advantaged group (Whites) fear the disadvantaged group (Blacks, especially Black males) and avoid contact with them (Fiske & Ruscher, 1993; I. Katz, Wackenhut, & Hass, 1986). On the other hand, both Blacks and women can be viewed as sexually dangerous to the more powerful groups.

Gender and race asymmetries pose different threats in other ways as well. Changing norms against the expression of racial stereotypes may result in a difference in the psychological threat posed by Blacks and women. For White Americans who consider themselves and attempt to present themselves as nonprejudiced, threats to their egalitarian self-concept may be heightened with racial stereotypes (Devine, Monteith, Zuwerink, & Elliot, 1991). People are arguably more sensitive about appearing racist than appearing sexist (Fiske & Stevens, 1993). The degree of guilt, embarrassment, and shame brought on by exhibiting discriminatory responses related to Blacks may be greater than that for discriminatory responses related to women.

Differences in the content and processing of racial and gender stereotypes may have a direct impact on perceptions of affirmative-action policies targeted for those groups. Because gender stereotypes are more complex, they offer more avenues for understanding gender-based affirmative action in a nonthreatening manner. The multifaceted nature of the stereotype means that only a small number of (potentially deserving) subtypes are thought to benefit (e.g., career women), not the group as a whole. Moreover, the more frequent communal relationships mean that men may imagine their wives or daughters as beneficiaries of affirmative action in compensation for acknowledged discrimination.

Affirmative action for Blacks may be more threatening because these policies are thought to benefit the entire Black race, not simply a small subset of Blacks. The relatively unidimensional perspective on race may grossly exaggerate the actual benefits that come from these policies because the group is seen as a monolithic entity. Blacks may be seen as a relatively homogeneous out-group whose members are largely unintelligent, unskilled, and therefore, undeserving of group-based rewards. Because the stereotypes are more simplistic, they offer fewer possibilities for perceiving affirmative action in a nonthreatening manner. Nontargets, then, are more likely to perceive affirmative action for Blacks as a dangerous and massive threat to the status quo in comparison to identical policies for women.

According to our theory, the differences in the content and processing of race and gender stereotypes may lead many Whites to perceive Blacks as the primary beneficiaries of affirmative-action policies.

The greater physical and psychological threats posed by Blacks may heighten the negative reactions to affirmative action when Blacks are recipients. For example, aversive racists are much more likely to attack policies that work to decrease discrimination against out-group members than to attack out-group members directly. The Murrell et al. (1994) finding of more resistance to affirmative action for Blacks is certainly consistent with this hypothesis; however, much more work is needed with target groups other than women to further test this theory.

Target-Group Versus Non-Target -Group Views of Affirmative Action

Just as we cannot assume that racial and gender stereotypes function in the same manner, so we cannot assume that target-group and non-target-group members have identical perspectives on affirmative action. Much of the research in this special issue and elsewhere treats affirmative action as a form of help to specific target groups (for a review, see, e.g., Turner & Pratkanis, 1994). Indeed, it appears that most members of nontargeted groups understand affirmative action in this manner as well. It is quite possible, however, that recipients of affirmative action do not share this view. Whether recipients perceive affirmative action as help may greatly depend on the target group one considers.

Whites may consider affirmative action as help because to do so is consistent with the belief that rewards are distributed in a race-neutral manner in the absence of affirmative action. Also, to see Blacks as in need of help fits in nicely with stereotyped perceptions of Blacks as lazy, unintelligent, and morally corrupt. Similarly, to see affirmative action for women as help fits the view of women as dependent and helpless.

However, Blacks themselves may be less likely than Whites to view affirmative action as help, for a number of reasons. First, Blacks are much more likely than Whites to believe that there is systemic discrimination against Blacks (Blauner, 1992; Sigelman & Welch, 1991). In fact, a national survey revealed that more than 74% of Blacks agree that without affirmative action Blacks would not get a "fair shake," and less than 20% of Blacks agree that affirmative action will lead to reverse discrimination (Sigelman & Welch, 1991). But less than 26% of Whites agree that affirmative action is needed to promote fairness, whereas over 40% of Whites agree that these policies will lead to reverse discrimination. Blacks are also more likely to belive that systemic racial discrimination outweighs the affirmative-action policies put in place to deal with existing discrimination (Barnes Nacoste, 1994). Moreover, only 15% of Blacks equate affirmative action with preferential treatments and quotas (Taylor, 1994). Given this, many Blacks may feel entitled to policies that protect their civil rights rather than feel as though they are being helped unfairly and are therefore undeserving.

Women are less likely to feel so entitled. Women tend not to make the most pertinent comparisons, for example in considering fair wages (Major, 1989; Major & Testa, 1989), and as a result seem not to act so entitled to various job benefits. Women as a rule do not have a strong group identity (e.g., Gurin, 1985; Gurin, Miller, & Gurin, 1980), nor do they see themselves personally as targets of discrimination (Crosby, 1994).

In contrast, Blacks may have a more cohesive group identity than do women. Blacks may, therefore, be more aware of the history of discrimination against their group and may have more cultural buffers in place to aid group members in dealing with this. For example, they may have more self-protective strategies safeguarding them from the negative feedback of Whites, even under more subtle circumstances than those that protect women (Crocker, Voelkl, Testa, & Major, 1991). Blacks may shield themselves from the negative feedback associated with affirmative action by attributing the feedback to prejudice or discrimination. To the extent that women do not see themselves as discriminated against (Crosby, 1994), they do not have quite the same defenses available.

Finally, selections based on merit and selections based on group membership may not be seen as inherently conflicting selection procedures for individuals who have a strong group identity. Benefits provided to the group may not be seen as significantly different from benefits provided for individual merit. Members of a group with a strong cohesive group identity may feel personally deserving of group-based rewards.

Whether one views these policies as help or entitlement can have a significant impact on one's social interactions, self-assessments, and achievements in the workplace. Because the vast majority of the studies on recipients' perceptions of affirmative action have examined these perceptions as a function of gender, the question of whether Blacks and women as targeted groups may differ in their perceptions cannot be answered directly. Although a study highlighted by Major et. al. (1994) found that Blacks who were helped by Whites on an intellectual task had lower self-esteem than Whites who were helped by Whites (cf. Schneider, Major, Luhtanen, & Crocker, 1991), that outcome may have been influenced by defining what the White person contributed as "help." Had the Black person been the recipient of an entitlement as opposed to what was clearly defined as help, the outcome may have been different, with little or no negative effect on self-esteem and other self-assessments. Taylor's (1994) field study on the impact of affirmative action for beneficiary groups represents one of few attempts to examine Black recipients' perceptions of affirmative action. She finds little evidence of the negative self-assessments of both Blacks and women reported in laboratory studies. More work needs to be done in this area.

Summary

In sum, we suggest that researchers examine more closely (a) the manner in which power relations may influence perceptions of affirmative action, (b) implications for affirmative action of differences in gender and racial stereotyping, and (c) differences in perceptions of affirmative action by nontargeted and targeted groups. We have gone further to propose specific hypotheses for each of these issues. First, group membership is more salient for powerless groups, and this group saliency may contribute to negative perceptions of affirmative action. Second, affirmative action for Blacks may be viewed as more threatening and less fair than affirmative action for women because racial stereotypes are considerably less complex than gender stereotypes. Third, Blacks may be less likely than Whites or women to view affirmative action as help. This is due to Blacks' awareness of the history of discrimination against their group, the development of self-protective strategies to shield group members from prejudice and discrimination, and the existence of a more cohesive Black group identity.

BARRIERS TO EFFECTIVE IMPLEMENTATION

On a Wednesday afternoon in Boston, I (Eberhardt) was returning with a friend from a trip to the bindery to pick up my dissertation when a police officer turned on his lights signaling us to pull over. We were stopped approximately 50 yards from the entrance to my friend's apartment complex. The apartment complex contains a significant number of welfare recipients and low-income families interspersed with a fair number of middle-income people. The majority of the tenants are Black, including my friend who is conducting anthropological research at the complex. Black teenagers and young adults constantly complain about police misconduct. My friend is actively involved in a task force at the complex designed, in part, to suggest alternative policing techniques to deal with this problem.

The police officer began to approach my car. Because my friend was driving, he asked to see her license and registration. I reached into the glove compartment to pull out my registration which had expired 6 weeks previously. I had been too busy trying to finish my dissertation to go home to Cleveland to get the emissions test required for all Ohio car registrations. The officer began to quiz me about the information contained on the registration I had just handed to him and went back to his patrol car. Apparently he thought the car might be stolen. He spent a considerable amount of time in his patrol car, as we were left wondering what was happening.

Suddenly, a huge tow truck arrived and began to lower its gear in front of the car. The police officer approached the car once again and demanded that we exit the vehicle. When asked why, the officer responded, "I have reason to believe this car is unregistered and uninsured." I responded that the car was indeed insured in Ohio. He demanded again that we exit the vehicle. When it became clear that we were not going to do so without an explanation, he called in a "disorderly" incident and requested back up.

Several White officers arrived on the scene. One, a female officer, called out, "Let's forget this crap. Get your knife and just cut them out of there." I was pulled from the car. I was standing on the sidewalk with my hands behind my back waiting to be handcuffed, when I was body-slammed onto the roof of the car. I had never been arrested before but I knew something was not right, Did I, a 103 lb, 5'3" Black female, pose a physical threat to this man? This was incredible. A number of people were beginning to gather, one person calling out to ask if I was okay.

We were then taken to a police station and handcuffed to the wall, awaiting the jail bondsman. We listened as a number of police officers began to laugh and tease the officer about the great arrest he had made. The arresting officer joined in mocking our facial and verbal expressions indicating our shock and distress over what had just occurred.

I arrived at Harvard's commencement the following morning with six bruises on my arm and swollen cartilage on my sternum near my second, third, and fourth ribs. I did not realize the full extent of my injuries until I lifted the banner I was to carry to lead the PhD recipients in the procession to the Yard where our degrees would be conferred.

The next morning the Dean of Student Affairs, my friend, and I stood before the judge to learn that I was charged with assault and battery on a police officer. The judge, who continued to call me Dr. Eberhardt (this was the first time I had ever been addressed by that title), was just as confused about what had occurred as we were. "Was there some language barrier?" she asked. "I am looking at the report here and this isn't making any sense." She dismissed all the charges and we were free to leave.

The officer in question is Black. Upon describing the incident to other people (Black and White, academics and nonacademics), most assumed that the arresting officer was White. Comments such as "The cops in that city are crazy; they are known to be racists" or "They do that kind of thing to Black people all of the time" were common. When told that the officer was Black, most seemed perplexed. This certainly added another element to the story. Suggestions to eliminate police brutality in Black communities often include diversifying the workforce. Yet, how effective are the affirmative-action policies put in place to achieve this goal? Do these policies actually change role-based power relations? Are there detrimental consequences associated with implementing these policies, for both targeted and nontargeted groups? This section addresses these issues.

Making Room for Change

The goals of affirmative action may be undermined by patterns of social interaction that result from existing power relations. Affirmative-action policies can do a great deal toward eliminating barriers that blatantly discriminate against powerless groups such as women and Blacks (Braddock & McPartland, 1987). Yet affirmative action has considerably less impact on the negative social interactions that result from existing power relations (Barnes Nacoste, 1994; Pettigrew & Martin, 1987). Members of powerless out-groups are often viewed as "not fitting in" (Fiske & Ruscher, 1993). Others do not feel as comfortable working with them because, by virtue of their differences, they evoke attention to rules and assumptions beyond what is required of normal, daily social interactions. Because the sharing of common goals is what primarily defines a group, out-groups are thought to have goals that conflict with those of the in-group. Any differences between out-group members and in-group members in attributes, attitudes, or behaviors—real or imagined—may be perceived as a threat to the existing social order (Fiske & Ruscher, 1993). Simply by their mere membership in powerless out-groups they may be mistrusted and thought to be disruptive.

Because of the lack of control over their own outcomes, the burden is typically placed on the powerless to smooth uncomfortable social interactions (Fiske & Ruscher, 1993). This may create immense pressure for targeted individuals to "fit in" with their nontargeted colleagues. De Vries and Pettigrew (1994), for example, found that Dutch minority police officers with authoritarian supervisors were happier and better liked by their colleagues the more authoritarian they themselves were. Powerless out-group members who attempt to shed their differences by molding themselves to the existing social structure are perceived as less threatening.

Stereotypes facilitate in-group bias by allowing out-group rewards (or lack thereof) to be attributed to group characteristics. The role of power relations in determining the distribution of rewards and defining what is considered merit is obscured. Stereotypes may become particularly pronounced when an affirmative-action recipient has solo status in the organization (Fiske & Stevens, 1993). Solos can attempt to disconfirm the stereotypes, yet stereotype disconfirmation often means exhibiting in exaggerated form the attributes and behaviors of the powerful in-group (Fiske & Ruscher, 1993).

The goal of affirmative-action policies is undermined by pressures on minorities to conform to existing practices in order to be accepted. On the job, recipients may feel a daily strain to adapt. These pressures may also result in a selection bias on behalf of the employer or an anticipatory socialization bias on behalf of potential affirmative-action recipients. Rather than creating diversity and its benefits, suppression of difference maintains the status quo. Therefore, the out-group members who gain access may, by not disrupting the homogeneity of the status quo, perpetuate the same stereotypes and biases that motivated affirmative-action policies in the first place. Ironically, these policies would then be continually needed, not because recipients are becoming less motivated, helpless, and dependent, but because the structure that necessitates these policies simply is not changing.

Clearing the Air

Discrimination is difficult to detect with absolute certainty in isolated cases (Crosby, 1994). None of us has available our own exact control group. For any particular case, a number of alternative explanations may adequately account for the observed behavior. In the police-citizen story, for example, there was a considerable degree of ambiguity around whether this was a racial incident. Would the arresting officer respond to any two other individuals in the same manner? Could gender have been the determining factor? Was the officer simply having a bad day? If the location were different, would the same events have transpired? Could it have been a combination of all these factors? To aid us in clearing up such ambiguity, evidence has to be gathered outside the incident in question. For example, statistics on police brutality as a function of race of officer and race of victim would be helpful. A number of theoretical considerations may also be useful. For instance, when is stereotyping most likely to occur? How can we determine whether or not the police officer was employing stereotypes in that particular incident? Even if the officer does hold stereotypes about Blacks and women, how can we be sure that he acted on the basis of his stereotypes? How might racial and gender stereotypes be combined? If the victims were Black men, White men, or White women, would the officer have acted differently? Because of the difficulty involved in establishing discrimination and because people do not commonly have access to information outside the incident in which they are involved, there is a definite need to have policies in place that "monitor" the behavior of individuals and organizations to protect victims of discrimination (Crosby, 1994).

The presence of ambiguity does make it necessary to have policies such as affirmative action in place. Yet affirmative action may introduce its own brand of ambiguity, one that can have detrimental consequences for the recipients. Because the conditions surrounding a position obtained through affirmative action are often left ambiguous, nontargeted individuals may give their targeted colleagues little credit for the qualifications and talent they bring to the job.

Ironically, targets of affirmative action, rather than facing less discrimination, may be further victimized at the workplace because of their token status. For nontargeted individuals, the mere presence of affirmative-action recipients (especially Blacks) may induce fear and ambivalence about their own positions. They may begin to ask themselves, "Am I the next to be displaced by an affirmative action hiring?" "How difficult will it be for me to secure future employment?" Targets themselves may question whether they were hired simply because of their group affiliations. Women who obtain positions traditionally held by men may ask, "Do I deserve to be here?" When salaries are raised, promotions are given, or evaluations are written, Blacks may continue to ask themselves, "If I were White, would things be different? Could I not have advanced faster?"

What has become clear . . . Is that the effectiveness of affirmative-action policies largely depends on the implementation strategies employed. It is not the case that affirmative-action policies necessarily have detrimental consequences for recipients and nonrecipients. The attributional ambiguity framework put forth by Major et al. (1994) serves as an excellent example. They find that when it is made clear to women that they are being selected for a leadership position due to both merit and gender, women attribute their selection to both merit and gender. Furthermore, the merit-plus-gender condition does not depress the likelihood of women attributing their selection to merit. Because the circumstances surrounding their selection are not left ambiguous, women in this condition are just as likely to attribute their selection to test scores and abilities as are women in merit-only conditions.

A number of other studies . . . point to identical conclusions. When recipients are given explicit, unambiguous, and focused feedback regarding their abilities and qualifications, the detrimental consequences of affirmative action disappear or are greatly reduced (e.g., see Barnes Nacoste, 1994; Major et al., 1994; Turner & Pratkanis, 1994). Feedback has positive effects on nontargets as well. Nontargets are less resistant to affirmative action, report less hostility, and are less likely to feel these policies to be unfair when accurate and detailed information is provided (Major et al., 1994; Murrell et al., 1994). Providing nontargets with more information about affirmative-action policies and recipient qualifications may enormously reduce their fears and suspicions (De Vries & Pettigrew, 1994). This feedback may also provide the impetus needed for more constructive perceptions of targeted out-group members. Targets may no longer represent the resented outsiders who play by unfair rules but welcomed insiders who become appreciated for the differences in attributes, attitudes, and behaviors they may bring (or are presumed to bring) to the organization.

Why Isn't the Air Cleared Yet?

Making affirmative-action policy clear and explicit to its recipients and to the public apparently is all that it takes to have an enormous impact on perceptions. So why is this not being done? Why are people not receiving accurate information on the policies or more explicit information on the recipients of affirmative action? Are employers consistently failing to make policies and selection practices explicit, unambiguous, and focused? Why might this be? We suggest two possibilities: (a) Employers may be hesitant publicly to recognize race and gender categories, and (b) even if accurate and detailed information is provided, people may not believe it.

In today's social climate, employers, like many Americans, may be hesitant to focus on race and gender categories. Because many believe that focusing on these categories will necessarily lead to stereotyping and prejudiced responses, strategies to protect a nonprejudiced self-image include attempting to ignore group differences. To ignore race and gender bolsters people's sense of themselves as not thinking in a prejudiced manner. Affirmative action policies, however, require that employers explicitly take group-based characteristics (such as race and gender) into account (Crosby, 1994). This requirement then, is squarely at odds with the demands of maintaining a nonprejudiced self-image.

One of the few times when it may be culturally appropriate publicly to acknowledge race and gender categories is in situations that are deemed unfair

(Eberhardt, 1993). In these situations, highlighting group differences may not at all pose a challenge to one's egalitarian self-concept because attention to race and gender is justified through reference to "unfairness." Race and gender may be thought of as qualities that unfairly aid Blacks and women. The irony, of course, is that the perception of "unfairness" (used to justify attention given to race and gender) itself results from race and gender stereotypes. Not only are race and gender something that Blacks and women "have" more so than Whites and men (their more powerful counterparts), it is something that Blacks and women allegedly exploit to gain an advantage over their peers. The fact that affirmative action is viewed as unfair by many, coupled with the biases in the group saliency of its recipients, increases the chances of intergroup conflict. Employers may fear that to focus on race and gender categories may make matters worse; they may choose, instead, simply to let the ambivalence and anger surrounding affirmative action go unaddressed.

Even if employers do manage to provide accurate and detailed information regarding recipient qualifications, people may simply refuse to believe it. Positive reactions of laboratory subjects to merit-plus-group-membership conditions may not reflect reactions outside the controlled laboratory experiment. Outside the laboratory, the credentials of Blacks and women may be less credible. Being more skeptical of these credentials may not present a challenge to the egalitarian self-image because, in everyday life, there are many more extraneous variables on which people can hang their rationalizations (Eberhardt, 1993). The likelihood of believing information about recipient qualifications may also be influenced by the content of the stereotype. Complex stereotypes may offer more means of accepting the idea that a particular recipient may indeed be qualified than do simple stereotypes.

Both these issues point to the need to place social psychological processes in their proper sociohistorical context. In this case, the solution becomes not simply that employers should provide unambiguous, explicit feedback. The solution should also incorporate why it is, in these times, and in these particular settings, that this feedback is not being provided. This refocus will aid us in determining how employers might effectively communicate selection procedures to targeted and nontargeted individuals, given the organizational context.

Summary

In sum, we have suggested that there may be significant barriers to the effective implementation of affirmative action. First, because of extreme pressures on minorities and women to conform to traditional practices, the diversity that they could potentially bring to organizations is suppressed, the likelihood is increased that both targets and nontargets will perpetuate existing prejudices and biases, and therefore, the likelihood is increased that affirmative-action policies will be continually needed. Second, because affirmative-action policies may increase the degree of ambiguity surrounding employment decisions for both targets and nontargets, targets may continue to be discriminated against. Yet . . . providing unambiguous and explicit feedback about the policies and the recipients of the policies can circumvent many of the problems associated with affirmative action. In this vein, the final issue we discussed was the potential problems involved in providing the feedback that is so crucial to the effectiveness of affirmative-action policies.

CONCLUSIONS

Reactions toward affirmative action are, in part, a function of how recipients are perceived in American society as well as how recipients perceive themselves. Many perceive recipients as unqualified, undeserving, and, to some extent, unethical. Negative reactions toward affirmative action are strongest when recipients are members of powerless outgroups for which negative, simplistic, and descriptive stereotypes exist. If recipients perceive their status as does the powerful group, they are also likely to view affirmative action negatively. However, if recipients are aware of the manner in which discrimination contributes to their status, they may not be as likely to have such negative perceptions.

Social psychological research on affirmative action is greatly needed. Theoretical analyses and empirical findings reported by social psychologists may prove useful to any organization attempting to implement affirmative-action policies. Research in this area may also allow us to refine our theories of social interaction. . . . We feel encouraged by the recent interest in this area and hopeful that future research will yield further insights for those interested in both policy and social behavior.

NOTES

1. Although several racial and ethnic groups are protected by affirmative-action policies, we concentrate primarily on Black Americans. There is more data on Black Americans in comparison with other groups. Residential, economic, and social segregation is more extreme for Black Americans than for any other ethnic group in the United States. Degree of segregation, as is pointed out in later sections of this article, may have a significant impact on perceptions of affirmative action.

2. We recognize that the term *African American* highlights ethnicity whereas the term *Black* highlights race. But people have responded to and continue to respond to African Americans as a racial group rather than an ethnic group. The stereotypes that arise from this are race stereotypes, not ethnic stereotypes. We use the term *Black* as opposed to African American to reflect this.

REFERENCES

Allport, G. W. (1954). *The nature of prejudice*. Reading, MA: Addison-Wesley.

Ashmore, R. D., & Del Boca, F. K. (1981). Conceptual approaches to stereotypes and stereotyping. In D. L. Hamilton (Ed.), *Cognitive processes in stereotyping and intergroup behavior* (pp. 1–63). Hillsdale, NJ: Lawrence Erlbaum Associates, Inc.

Barnes Nacoste, R. (1994). If empowerment is the goal. . . .: Affirmative action and social interaction. *Basic and Applied Social Psychology, 15*, 87–112.

Blanchard, F. A., & Crosby, F. J. (Eds.) (1989). *Affirmative action in perspective*. New York: Springer-Verlag.

Blauner, B. (1992, Summer). Talking past each other: Black and white languages of race. *The American Prospect*, pp. 55–64.

Braddock, J. H., Jr., & McPartland, J. M. (1987). How minorities continue to be excluded from equal employment opportunities: Research on labor market and institutional barriers. *Journal of Social Issues, 43*(1), 5–40.

Crocker, J., Voelkl, K., Testa, M., & Major, B. (1991). Social stigma: The affective consequences of attributional ambiguity. *Journal of Personality and Social Psychology, 60*, 218–228.

Crosby, F. J. (1994). Understanding affirmative action. *Basic and Applied Social Psychology, 15*, 13–41.

Deaux, K., & Lewis, L. L. (1984). Structure of gender stereotypes: Interrelations among components and gender label. *Journal of Personality and Social Psychology, 46*, 991–1004.

Dépret, E., & Fiske, S. T. (1993). *Perceiving the powerful: Intriguing individuals versus threatening groups*. Manuscript submitted for publication.

Devine, P. G., & Baker, S. M. (1991). Measurement of racial stereotype subtyping. *Personality and Social Psychology Bulletin, 17*, 44–50.

Devine, P. G., Monteith, M. J., Zuwerink, J. R., & Elliot, A. J. (1991). Prejudice with and without compunction. *Journal of Personality and Social Psychology, 60*, 817–830.

De Vries, S., & Pettigrew, T. F. (1994). A comparative perspective on affirmative action: *Positieve aktie* in The Netherlands. *Basic and Applied Social Psychology, 15*, 179–199.

Eberhardt, J. L. (1993). Where the invisible meets the obvious: The effects of stereotyping biases on the fundamental attribution error. *Dissertation Abstracts International, 54*, 06B. (University Microfilms No. 9330903)

Fiske, S. T. (1993). Controlling other people: The impact of power on stereotyping. *American Psychologist, 48*, 621–628.

Fiske, S. T., & Ruscher, J. B. (1993). Negative interdependence and prejudice: Whence the affect? In D. M. Mackie & D. L. Hamilton (Eds.), *Affect, cognition, and stereotyping: Interactive processes in group perception* (pp. 239–268). San Diego: Academic.

Fiske, S. T., & Stevens, L. E. (1993). What's so special about sex? Gender stereotyping and discrimination. In S. Oskamp & M. Costanzo (Eds.), *Gender issues in contemporary society: The Claremont Symposium on Applied Psychology* (pp. 173–196). Newbury Park, CA: Sage.

Gurin, P. (1985). Women's gender consciousness. *Public Opinion Quarterly, 49*, 143–163.

Gurin, P., Miller, A., & Gurin, G. (1980). Stratum identification and consciousness. *Social Psychology Quarterly , 43*, 30–47.

Katz, D., & Braly, K. W. (1993). Racial stereotypes of 100 college students. *Journal of Abnormal and Social Psychology, 28*, 280–290.

Katz, I., Wackenhut, J., & Haas, R. G. (1986). Racial ambivalence, value duality, and behavior. In J. F. Divodio & S. L. Gaertner

(Eds.), *Prejudice, discrimination, and racism* (pp. 35–60). Orlando, FL: Academic.

Lee, S. M., & Yamanaka, K. (1990). Patterns of Asian American intermarriage and marital assimilation. *Journal of Comparative Family Studies, 21*, 287–305.

Major, B. (1989). Gender differences in comparisons and entitlement: Implications for comparable worth. *Journal of Social Issues, 45*(4), 99–115.

Major, B., Feinstein, J., & Crocker, J. (1994). Attributional ambiguity of affirmative action. *Basic and Applied Social Psychology, 15*, 113–141.

Major, B., & Testa, M. (1989). Social comparison processes and judgments of entitlements and satisfaction. *Journal of Experimental Social Psychology, 25*, 101–120.

Massey, D. S., & Denton, N. A. (1993). *American apartheid: Segregation and the making of the underclass.* Cambridge, MA: Harvard University Press.

Murrell, A. J., Dietz-Uhler, B. L., Dovidio, J. F., Gaertner, S. L., & Drout, C. (1994). Aversive racism and resistance to affirmative action: Perceptions of justice are not necessarily color blind. *Basic and Applied Social Psychology, 15*, 71–86.

Pettigrew, T. F. (1979). The ultimate attribution error: Extending Allport's cognitive analysis of prejudice. *Personality and Social Psychology Bulletin, 5*, 461–476.

Pettigrew, T. F., & Martin, J. (1987). Shaping the organizational context for Black American inclusion. *Journal of Social Issues, 43*(1), 41–78.

Schneider, M., Major, B., Luhtanen, R., & Crocker, J. (1991, June). *Social stigma and reactions to help.* Paper presented at the meeting of the American Psychological Society, Washington, DC.

Sigelman, L., & Welch, S. (1991). *Black Americans' views of racial inequality: The dream deferred.* Cambridge, England: Cambridge University Press.

Thompson, S. K. (1975). Gender labels and early sex role development. *Child Development, 46*, 339–347.

Turner, M. E., & Pratkanis, A. R. (1994). Affirmative action as help: A review of recipient reactions to preferential selection and affirmative action. *Basic and Applied Social Psychology, 15*, 43–69.

Williams, J. E., & Morland, K. J. (1976). *Race, color, and the young child.* Chapel Hill: University of North Carolina Press.

CHECKPOINTS

1. There are more negative attitudes about affirmative action for Blacks than for women because the stereotypes about Blacks are more simplistic and less prescriptive.

2. The numerous barriers to the effective implementation of affirmative action may be understood by examining social stereotypes.

To prepare for reading the next section, think about these questions:

1. Why is there violence in intimate relationships?

2. What are the roles of masculinity and femininity in sustaining gendered violence?

Sexual Terrorism:
The Social Control of Women

CAROLE J. SHEFFIELD

William Paterson College

At a time when the media, the political right, and many of my students, male and female, have proclaimed the end of the women's movement, we must ask some hard, direct questions about the status of women in American society. In an era when women are indeed exercising hard-won options in areas such as employment, childbearing, and politics, they often seem to be limited in simpler choices—whether to go to the movies alone, where to walk or jog, whether to answer the door or telephone. Can we measure the success of a social movement for equality if we do not include an assessment of the quality of life of the affected groups? No aspect of well-being is more fundamental than freedom from personal harm motivated by hatred or fear of one's ascribed characteristics, that is, freedom from ideologically justified violence against one's person. Without such freedom it is impossible to implement other choices. To the extent that women's personal freedom is still restricted and denied, we can continue to speak of oppression.

All systems of oppression employ violence or the threat of violence as an institutionalized mechanism for ensuring compliance. "Inferior" peoples— whether they be blacks in South Africa, peasants in South America, or females in the United States—are kept in their place by fear, which is generated by periodic displays of force. Subordination, as described by Dworkin (1985), is a social/political dynamic consisting of hierarchy, objectification, submission, and violence. This [reading] is largely concerned with the last element—violence—as a crucial element in the ongoing process of female subordination.

Sexual terrorism is the system by which males frighten, and by frightening, dominate and control females. It is manifested through actual and implied violence. All females are potential victims—at any age, any time, or any place, and through a variety of means: rape, battery, incest, sexual abuse of children, sexual harassment, prostitution, and sexual slavery. The subordination of women in all other spheres of the society rests on the power of men to intimidate and to punish women sexually.

In this [reading] we will analyze the ways in which male dominance is established and maintained through sexual terrorism, primarily as manifested in our society today. That is, we shall consider terrorism as a crucial strategy in sustaining the power relationships of *patriarchy,* whereby maleness is glorified and femaleness denigrated. As the institutionalized mechanism for the social control of women, sexual terrorism operates at several levels: through (1) the normative dichotomy of good woman/bad woman; (2) the production of fear through expressions of the popular culture—rituals of degradation, music, literature, films, television, advertising, pornography; and (3) providing legitimation and social support for those who act out their contempt for women (e.g., rapists, men who beat "nagging" wives, and so forth).

Thus, while sexual terrorism is the objective condition of female existence—that is, living in fear of bodily harm—it also provides a theoretical framework for examining how patriarchal social orders are created and maintained. The three levels at which sexual terrorism operates—normative, cultural, and social—can be integrated into a boarder conceptual model of terrorism in general, in which five basic components have been identified: ideology, propaganda, indiscriminate violence, "voluntary compliance," and perceptions of victim and oppressor characteristics.

IDEOLOGY

Terrorism must be "explicitly rationalized and justified by some philosophy, theory, or ideology—however crude" (Johnson, 1978: 273), and indeed no bomb thrower or world power is without a claim to a "higher principle" or "greater good." In the case of sexual terrorism, the ideological underpinnings of patriarchal power relationships serve as ample justification for violence against women. If maleness is superior to femaleness, then females must be described in terms of some basic flaw, some trait that makes their subordination both necessary and legitimate. Many feminist thinkers (e.g., Tavris and Wade, 1984) have identified this presumed "basic flaw" as female sexuality itself—tempting and seductive, and therefore disruptive; capable of reproducing life itself, and therefore powerful. Out of their own fear, men have sought to bring this threatening force under control by both physical and psychological means.

Although there is still much debate over the original basis for male dominance and the role of sheer physical force in that equation, by the time of full-fledged archaic states the ideological components were well in place. The story of Adam and Eve, along with its counterparts throughout the world, can stand as the basic cautionary tale of the dire consequences of unfettered female sexuality.

Moreover, if maleness becomes the standard of normality, femaleness (whether manifest by females or males) is necessarily abnormal. The definition of female behavior as somehow non-normative, a neat example of the social construction of deviance (Schur, 1984), sets in motion the process of stigmatization, which in turn becomes the rationalization for both gender stratification (patriarchy) and sexual terrorism.

The concept of female "deviance" reflects—indeed, some structuralists would claim that it is the original instance of—a basic division of the world into dichotomous types: female/male, nature/culture, emotion/reason, body/brains, and so forth. Not only is masculinity defined in opposition to femininity, but males are seen as self-reliant, courageous, competent, and rational. In contrast, females must therefore be dependent, sensual, emotional, and evil. If man is the maker of history, the one who does things, woman is "the mediating force between man and nature, a remainder of his childhood, a reminder of the body, and a reminder of sexuality, passion, and human connectedness . . . the repository of emotional life and of all the nonrational elements of human experience" (Lowe and Hubbard, 1983: 12). To the extent that men must not harbor such traits and must distance themselves from femininity, contempt and fear of femaleness are logical concomitants of this dualistic conception of gender.

Yet another dichotomy lies *within* the construct of femininity itself: between the "good" woman and the "bad" woman. Somehow, some women are going to have to become "good" enough so serve as marriage partners. Apparently, this is achieved by accepting their limitations, controlling their basically evil nature, and placing themselves under the protection of a man. The "good" woman becomes the wife; or more likely, the wife is compelled to have these attributes, as one outcome of the complex historical process whereby women are transformed into private property (Firestone, 1972).

The pressure to achieve "goodness" is a powerful mechanism of social control; one must work constantly to earn the label of "lady," an accolade that can only be bestowed by men (Fox, 1977). Although some women may achieve instant respectability through wealth or lineage, most must strive to acquire and maintain that status. Further, becoming a good woman in order to secure protection from male violence is a rather dubious bargain; the home is hardly a haven from sexual assaults, nor does marriage shield women from nonfamily attacks.

The good woman/bad woman dichotomy has particularly troublesome consequences for black women in our society. In general, racism and sexual violence, particularly rape, are part of the same oppressive structure. Historically, U.S. rape laws were enacted to maintain the property rights of white men and to control black men and women. Although it was a capital offense for a black man to rape a white woman, the rape of a black woman (by either a black or a white man) was not considered a crime. According to the racist ideology, the black woman was inherently inferior and could therefore never achieve goodness. Thus, "to assault her and exploit her sexually . . . carried with it none of the normal sanctions against such behavior" (Lerner, 1973: 163).

Hooks (1981: 108) carries the argument one step further, to suggest that black women have had great difficulty forming alliances with men from either group in order to gain protection from the other. Neither the abolition of slavery nor the 120 years of American history since the Civil War have had much effect on the way in which black women are regarded, especially by white men. Their "blackness" continues to define their sexuality. Given the continued pervasiveness of racism in our society, it is reasonable to assume that women of color experience additional humiliation when they encounter the predominantly male judicial system.

In sum, all aspects of male supremacist ideology provide a justification for sexual terrorism as a means of keeping women in their place and thus reinforcing the gender stratification system of patriarchy across time and place. But the effectiveness of ideologies depends on how broadly and thoroughly they are disseminated and on how they are given concreteness.

PROPAGANDA

The second component of terrorism is propaganda—the methodical dissemination of information promoting this ideology. By definition, the information is biased, even false, designed to present one point of view and to discredit all contrary opinion (LaBelle, 1980). "Terrorism must not be defined only in terms of violence, but also in terms of propaganda. . . . Violence of terrorism is a coercive means for attempting to influence the thinking and actions of people. Propaganda is a persuasive means for doing the same thing" (Watson, 1976: 15).

Other [writings] suggest the degree to which patriarchal ideology has shaped what passes for "knowledge" in such diverse realms as anthropology, sociology, psychology, economics, political science, medicine, and the law. These are all areas in which

the new feminist scholarship has questioned and corrected many misconceptions (although the public remains largely unaware of this reshaping and reconstruction of knowledge).

The avenues of propaganda central to the theme of this [reading] are those of the modern mass media: television, radio, films, music, and advertising. It is not difficult to find telling examples in which the theme of violence toward women dominates. Battered women appear nightly on television (and even the programs presumably devoted to "educating the public" have a high titillation factor). Moviemakers such as Brian DePalma outdo one another in finding ever more gory ways to mutilate female bodies (a recent one being with a power saw). Lyrics for rock music have become offensive enough to elicit an agreement from record companies to provide warning labels. Pictures of women in bondage appear on album covers, in the pages of *Vogue* magazine, and in the windows of Bloomingdale's department store.

But the propaganda of sexual terrorism is most fully embodied in the books and films and paraphernalia exclusively devoted to the sexual degradation of women—pornography. The word itself is derived from the Greek *porne,* referring to the lowest class of sexual slave. Here the line between good and bad women may be erased, as all female bodies and all parts of the body exist for the pleasure of men. To its most severe critics, then, pornography teaches men not only what they can do with/to whores but also what can be done with/to one's wife, lover, or daughter (Barry, 1979; Russell, 1982). This view has received support from recent research on the link between exposure to pornography and subsequent tolerance of violence against women (Donnerstein, 1980; Malamuth, 1981).

There is no question that most pornography today articulates a male fantasy world in which women are typically depicted as depraved and insatiable, and therefore appropriate objects for rape, bondage, mutilation, and even murder. But there is a very heated controversy among feminists about the effects of pornography, the distinction between eroticism and pornography, the threat to civil liberties of antiobscenity campaigns, and the dangers of alliances with antifeminists.[1]

Pornography, however, is more than a sexual—or even legal—issue; it is also about power. Its economic power is immense; it's a multi-billion-dollar industry, involving a network of producers, distributors, retailers, and consumers. Even more important, pornography is about the power of naming, or naming women as body parts and their sexuality as depraved, thus literally "doing the dirty work" in the spread of the ideology of patriarchy.

The ultimate power of pornography is terrorization. Pornography embodies acts of sexual terrorism (rape, battery, incestuous assault, bondage, torture), symbols of sexual terrorism (gun, knife, fist, whip, etc.), and the legend of sexual terrorism (the male as dangerous; Dworkin, 1979). The extreme manifestations of physical violence found in much of contemporary pornography are considered by many people, feminist and antifeminist alike, to pose a threat to the safety of women and girls insofar as these images normalize sexual abuse and raise the level of tolerance for such behavior.

INDISCRIMINATE AND AMORAL VIOLENCE

According to classic theories of political terrorism, an ideology and its spread through propaganda are both necessary *and* sufficient causes of overt violence directed at people who possess a particular ascribed characteristic that legitimates their victimization. As described by Wilkinson (1974: 17), all terrorism involves "indiscriminateness, unpredictability, arbitrariness, ruthless destructiveness and amorality." Sexual terrorism, then, is violence perpetrated on girls and women *simply because they are female,* as when the threat of sexual assault keeps many girls and women in a state of fear, regardless of their actual risks (Warr, 1985).

The element of amorality can be seen in the fact that only rarely do those who commit acts of sexual violence perceive themselves as having done "wrong"—even child molesters and incestuous fathers. Rather, like the rapists studied by Scully and

Marolla (1985), they construct a vocabulary of motives and rationales from the surrounding culture that they feel will be acceptable to others. That this vocabulary is often shared by police officers, lawyers, and judges can be seen in the low rate of prosecution of crimes of sexual violence in our society (Polk, 1985). Indeed, the rationalizations may also be shared by an entire community. In the case of the New Bedford, Massachusetts, gang rape, for example, the largely Portuguese community interpreted the prosecution of the rapists as an incident of ethnic discrimination rather than a response to sexual violence.

Although from the viewpoint of women sexual terrorism could be defined inclusively, public perception will often be based on those acts that fall within the criminal law (keeping in mind that each state defines its own standards of appropriate sexual behavior, and that the federal law may hold to yet another standard). Despite such diversity, there is at least one unifying strand: The laws have been promulgated by male-dominated legislatures and interpreted by a male-dominated judiciary (MacKinnon, 1983; Bart and Scheppele, 1980). Changing these laws to take into account women's own definitions of their experience is perhaps the most difficult yet most crucial task for feminist activists in the coming decades.

At the moment, however, the generally recognized acts of sexual violence that have been prohibited by law include the following: rape, wife assault, sexual abuse of children, sexual harassment, and sexual slavery. And each has been defined from a male point of view.

Rape. The definition of rape, for example, was originally drawn to exclude the possibility of marital sexual assaults on the assumption that a wife's sexual services were part and parcel of the marriage contract (Russell, 1982). That is, the laws were designed precisely to protect a husband's sexual property.

In addition, the description of the forbidden act was based on the traditional model of sexual intercourse (i.e., vaginal-penile penetration), thus obscuring the whole context of violence in which the act takes place. This exclusive focus on the sexual component, then, requires some evidence that the victim was not "willing," in other words, that she resisted. For no other crime is a victim required to prove non-consent; rape, however, is still viewed largely in terms of women's sexuality rather than men's coercion (Stanko, 1985). Women must prove that they resisted, or consent is presumed. Yet at the same time they are warned of the potential bodily harm that their resistance might encourage—a veritable "catch-22": If you fight back you'll get hurt, but if you don't we'll think you welcomed the attack. Yet recent research strongly suggests that women who physically resist are more likely than nonresisters to *avoid* being raped, without necessarily increasing the rapist's level of violence (Bart and O'Brien, 1984).

Redefining rape to include forms of sexual violation other than intercourse would be a first step in directing attention to the inherent violence and degradation of the phenomenon but would not necessarily advance a deeper understanding of the victimization of women. The value of Brownmiller's (1975: 5) claim that rape is a "more or less conscious process of intimidation by which *all* men keep *all* women in a state of fear" is that it draws attention to the power dimension of the act. But power relationships are themselves a function of complex historical/economic processes.

Other social scientists have argued that not all men are potential rapists and not all cultures provide a vocabulary of motives; rather, we should look to the links among socioeconomic inequality, general levels of violence in a society, and variations in gender stratification systems (e.g., Leacock, 1981; Sanday, 1981; Schwendinger and Schwendinger, 1983). The general finding from these reviews of the anthropological and sociological literature is that rape is part of an entire sociocultural complex in which men lose control over their own destinies and in which violence toward women is a response to powerlessness in other spheres of activity.

Yet when looking at contemporary America, Brownmiller's thesis receives qualified support from rape researchers Holmstrom and Burgess (1983: 36), who conclude that while it would have been more accurate to say that "rape is one way in many (but not all) societies that men *as a class* oppress and control

women *as a class*," it is a fact that "macho" values are institutionalized in the United States today and that "male-dominated patterns of aggressive behavior and male-dominated institutions oppress and control women" (1983: 36).

Wife-assault. Here again in dealing with behavior that takes place within the privacy of the marriage, the law—and public opinion—often reflect the traditional assumptions of appropriate gender roles and power relationships. Yet much has changed over the past two decades as certain types of family violence have been redefined as "social problems," with the result that both public opinion and the law are changing.

As analyzed by Breines and Gordon (1983), these changes in the perception and definition of family violence are the result of a number of societal trends, including the feeling that intrafamily violence is a symptom of a deeper "crisis" in the American family; the notion of child-centered parenthood, which makes violence toward children less acceptable than in the past; the feminist emphasis on the family as source of oppression and on the translation of the personal into the public; and the growing acceptance of a "confessional mode" in which people are encouraged to "tell all." It would be a mistake, however, to lump all family violence together, as there are very different historical developments in both the incidence and the recognition of each type as a social problem. Note, however, that as these acts receive public attention they are also being privatized through the use of terms such as "family" or "domestic" violence (i.e., that these are really personal problems of unhappy individuals, and most likely due to a failure on the part of the wife/mother whose task it is precisely to maintain harmony in the home). This language also obscures the primary victims (Bush, 1985). Russell (1982) makes a similar point by suggesting that the term "wife-rape" is preferable to either "marital rape" or "spousal rape" specifically because wife-rape is not gender neutral.

The recognition of wife-assault as a social problem, for example, is primarily a product of the women's movement (Tierney, 1982) and has been the subject of an outpouring of feminist research and analysis over the past 15 years (reviewed in Breines and Gordon, 1983; Pagelow, 1985). The theme has also been taken up by the mass media, although not without an element of voyeurism and typically in a way that emphasizes the psychological problems of the abuser or of the marital pair. So while the personal has become public, it has not yet been transformed into the political. A feminist analysis of gender-power relationships in the wider society is still missing. Instead, violence against women has typically been treated by clinicians, law enforcement personnel, and the judiciary as a consequence of victim characteristics that either arouse or anger the batterers (i.e., the "victim provocation" thesis). It follows from this view that the solution lies in training women to watch themselves—to become, as it were, the monitors of their own actions. This is victimization internalized. Also, the simplistic solution to wife-abuse—that women should leave batterers—suggests that women are to blame if they do not leave. Blame, then, comes back on the victim for "accepting" this behavior. Only rarely, and only in the feminist literature, are the roots of such violence located in culture and social structure—the gender stratification system, the socioeconomic system, or the structure of the family (for this type of analysis see Schechter, 1982; Schwendinger and Schwendinger, 1983).

Yet as women begin to speak out and as others realize the extent of the phenomenon, pressures are generated on lawmakers and judges, who, despite their patriarchal interests, are slowly changing the legal definitions of appropriate marital behavior. Only a few states define wife-abuse as a felony per se, and in most other states the general assault statues apply to violence directed against a wife. But lawmakers are loath to tackle the subject of wife-rape, particularly if the couple is living together, and in a few states a husband cannot be charged even if the couple is legally separated (Russell, 1982).

Although it is difficult to estimate the incidence or prevalence of wife-rape—in part because the wife may not interpret the situation in those terms—it is interesting to note that when researcher Irene Frieze (1983) sought a matched sample to compare with a group of 137 women who had reported being physically assaulted by their husbands, she discovered that close to 30% of the presumably violence-free comparison group had also experienced marital attacks. The findings from this study of wives indicate that wife-rape is strongly associated with other acts of personal violence; that wives do *not* precipitate such incidents by refusing sex or being unfaithful; and that husbands who rape appear to like violent sex and lots of it, and feel they have the right to demand it.

Sexual abuse of children. This category includes a number of different types of behavior, from incest to indecent exposure. Again, the statutes vary from state to state with regard to what acts are included, how they are defined, and how the offense will be treated (as a felony, misdemeanor, or a form of assault). In general, the phrases most often used to describe the sexual abuse of children are the following: (by definition) statutory rape, incest, molestation, carnal knowledge, indecent liberties, and impairing the morals of a minor. It is assumed that a child cannot give informed consent, even though it is possible that some adolescents are willing partners. In the case of incest, Butler (1978) argues that the term "incestuous assault" is more useful because it implies nonconsensual, essentially coercive behavior. Increasingly the use of children as models in pornography is specifically included in the statutes, although this behavior also falls well within several of the existing definitions.

It is impossible to know the true extent of sexual abuse of children; estimates vary from 1% to 10% for man/girl incest to 25% of all females being victims of some form of "sexual molestation" by the time they reach 18 years of age (data reviewed in Breines and Gordon, 1983: 521–522). The sexual abuse of children, unlike child abuse in general, is overwhelmingly committed by men against girls, a fact that the clinical literature succeeded in ignoring until the recent wave of feminist scholarship. By denying the male-dominant nature of incest, for example, the clinical establishment could continue to consider it a problem of individual psychopathology—on the part of the victim who may have acted "seductively," or on the part of the mother who "failed" to protect her daughter or who "collaborated" with her partner in "allowing" the assault—and not on the part of the assailant, who was only following his sexual nature.

Despite the existence of statutory prohibitions (and certain types of incest have always been criminalized), the sexual abuse of children is notoriously difficult to prosecute. The victims, if they recognize themselves as such, are relatively powerless; adults employ denial mechanisms; the perpetrator has the power to punish; and few outsiders can pierce the veil of privacy that protects the modern family. As in the case of wife-assault, the women's movement has given many women the courage to speak out about their own childhood experiences, making it quite clear that they were not willing participants, that it was not pleasurable (a common male fantasy), and that they still bear deep psychological scars. Feminism has also spurred an analysis based on cultural and societal variables, to which gendered power relationships are central. Childhood victimization is a powerful socialization to that fear so essential to the entire system of sexual terrorism.

Sexual harassment. Although coined only recently, "sexual harassment" (Farley, 1978) is a phenomenon with which women were well acquainted before it was named. Sexual harassment refers to a wide range of coercive and intimidating behavior that reinforce the basic fears of women by implying the ultimate use of force.

Although sexual assaults, in the work place or anywhere else, were already covered by the criminal law, other less physical but nonetheless threatening behaviors are now also forbidden. The most common legal definition includes any deliberate, repeated, or unwelcome verbal comments, gestures, or physical contacts of a sexual nature. A specific definition covering academic sexual harassment is that of the National Advisory Council on Women's Educational Programs: "The use of authority to emphasize the sexuality or sexual identity of a student in a manner which prevents or impairs that student's full enjoy-

ment of educational benefits, climate, or opportunities" (Till, 1980: 7).

Under 1980 federal guidelines, sexual harassment has been subsumed under the rubric of discrimination as an unfair impediment to an individual's ability to get the job done or to advance on one's own merits. Many organizations now have written rules spelling out the proscribed conduct and providing channels for handling complaints, which may provide women with some protection or redress. However, the fact that sexual harassment is analogous to rape in that it is less an expression of sexuality than of power and represents a process of intimidation must not be overlooked. Only in the feminist literature and scholarship do we find the link to the larger system of gender stratification.

There is, therefore, some question about the effectiveness of antiharassment laws given the "combined effects of occupational segregation, employment discrimination, and economic dependency [that] force women to remain in workplace situations that are decidedly threatening and coercive" (Schneider, 1985: 26). As Schneider also points out, because workplace harassment occurs almost by definition among people who know one another, the victim has the same problem as the victim of "acquaintance rape" in interpreting the event as totally unprovoked and in being believed by others.

With respect to antiharassment regulations drawn up by universities, Crocker (1983) notes that they cover a wide spectrum of actions, acknowledge the potentially damaging consequences for victims, provide ample warning to possible violators, and also raise community consciousness—all generally constructive outcomes. Yet Crocker also suggests that using the words "inappropriate" or "unwelcome" implies that there are appropriate or welcome leers and pinches that will not be considered harassment. Similarly, the use of words such as "coercion" and "force" implies that unforced sexual favors are acceptable. But is it really possible, given the power of professors over students, that even uncoerced sexual favors are truly willingly bestowed? Then, too, the ranking of offenses—the general assumption that threat of punishment ("fuck or flunk") is a more serious offense than promise of reward ("A for a lay")—makes little difference to the student, who may not even need to have the alternatives articulated in order to protect herself (Crocker, 1983).

In other words, in both the work place and academe, sexual harassment regulations may alert women to their rights, may restrain some men, and may raise the general level of consciousness of all members of the community, but as long as the gender stratification system remains intact, sexual threats will continue to characterize the lives of women outside the family as well as within.

Sexual slavery. Sexual terrorism may well reach its ultimate form in the practice of what Barry (1979) calls "female sexual slavery"—the international traffic in women and forced street prostitution. Although prostitution is illegal in most jurisdictions, our legal conception is actually very limited and misleading. Prostitution was defined as illegal in order to protect men (primarily from disease) and is viewed as a crime that women commit willingly. Barry argues that "female sexual slavery is present in all situations where women or girls cannot change the immediate conditions of their existence; where regardless of how they got into those conditions, they cannot get out; and where they are subject to sexual violence and exploitation" (1979: 33).

Another form of sexual slavery, practiced by individual pimps who employ intimidation or overt violence to force women and girls to sell their bodies for his profit, is more well known. The situation of runaway girls has recently been exploited by the mass media, along with general concern over the potential sexual abuse of "missing children"—both boys and girls (although we suspect that cases of male prostitutes receive disproportionate attention).

Procurers imply a variety of subtle as well as openly coercive techniques to attach their women to them, including both emotional and drug dependencies. Among urban blacks, where so many other forms of achievement are systematically blocked, Bell Hooks (1981: 108) notes that "the male who overtly reveals his hatred and contempt of women is admired," so that the pimp becomes a hero.

The newest pimp may be the broker who arranges marriages between American men and Asian women. These brokers, who sell women for a lifetime rather that for an hour or an evening or who arrange for increasingly popular sex tours of Southeast Asia, combine racism—that is, the stereotypical view of submissive and exotic Asian women—with the traditional view of women as chattel.

Barry (1979) also extends the definition of sexual slavery to include situations where fathers and husbands use force to keep wives and daughters submissive and powerless. As we have noted for other types of family violence, it is often difficult to prove that victims were not volunteers, and the authorities are far more prone to see complicity rather than coercion. Few have asked the crucial question posed by Barry (1979: 70): "Are these women able to change the conditions of their existence?" If not, their complicity cannot be assumed.

VOLUNTARY COMPLIANCE

An institutionalized system of terror requires mechanisms other than sustained violence to achieve its goals. Sexual terrorism is maintained by a system of sex-role socialization that encourages men to be terrorists in the name of masculinity and women to be victims in the name of femininity. Therefore, the fourth element in the model of terrorism, "voluntary compliance," is almost an automatic assumption in cases of sexual terrorism. Not only do women "ask for" this type of treatment, but deep down they really "want it"—a belief bolstered by the pseudo-scientific authority of psychoanalysis. To the extent that the essence of femininity is defined as an innate masochism, coerciveness is rationalized away. This image is perhaps the quintessential aspect of the ideology, the basic theme of so much propaganda, a key to the vocabulary of motives, and an effective means of interjecting fear.

As long as each women clutches her self-doubts to herself, the line between compliance and coercion can be blurred. In one recent study of the responses of victims of sexual violence, Stanko (1985) found three common reactions among women, whether they were raped, battered, harassed, or incestuously assaulted: self-blame, shame, and guilt (responsibility). Such feelings complete the circle of the self-fulfilling prophecy as women internalize the identity of "bad women," the one who must deserve her fate (see also Burgess, 1985). This is also one way to resolve the cognitive dissonance of maintaining the image of a good woman while recognizing that awful things have been done to you: Either you're not all that good or what's happened to you isn't all that bad.

A third possibility is to realize that you are good and that you don't deserve to be attacked—neither perception being nurtured in the patriarchy. And here is precisely where the feminist reconstruction of reality can begin to erode the forces of fear. As Bart and O'Brien (1984) found, the women who resisted rapists also defied the traditional vocabulary of motives, and whether their resistance was successful or not, were less likely than other victims to feel depressed or to blame themselves. It is not quite clear what led to the original decision to resist, but there is no question that the experience of having resisted brought a psychic liberation. If rape is the purest expression of male dominance, than resisting (not just avoiding) rape is a powerful statement of self-worth.

PERCEPTIONS OF VICTIMS AND TERRORISTS

Among the major goals of any system of terror are the erosion of public support for victims and acquisition of respectability for one's own cause. The effectiveness of all the other elements of terrorism can be judged by an examination of societal responses. With regard to sexual terrorism, the evidence is that such acts are the least reported of crimes and that when reported are least likely to be brought to trial or to result in conviction.

In addition, the exclusive focus of the law and the media is on the sexual nature of the crime; and because the victim and terrorist are usually known to one another, sexual assaults are treated as "acquain-tance crimes" (i.e., the result of some personal problem between the individuals involved).

Yet sexual violence is pervasive (Stanko, 1985; Finklehor, 1984; Straus et al., 1980) and cuts across lines of age, religion, ethnicity, and social class. Although some research suggests no relationship to social class (e.g., Adler, 1985), other scholars disagree (e.g., the studies reviewed by Schwendinger and Schwendinger, 1983). These mixed findings reflect, in part, a political agenda. That is, if you see sexual violence as a response to socioeconomic conditions—at the macro and micro levels—you have a vested interest in finding that lower status subgroups are most likely to engage in sexual terrorism. If, conversely, you believe that sexually aggressive behavior is a generalized male trait or that all men in a society benefit from the partriachal system, you will look for support in the finding of no social class effect.

It is always comforting to believe that crimes and other antisocial behaviors are restricted to people unlike those who make and enforce the laws—poor, uneducated, or nonwhite people. And it is easy to deny disconfirming evidence. Thus it seems likely that sexual terrorism is more widely distributed across the social class structure than is commonly assumed. But it is also possible that the proximate causes of sexual violence are disporoportionately experienced by the less affluent.

In any event, whoever commits the crime stands very little chance of having a complaint filed or of being prosecuted. For example, in 1984, over 84,000 rapes were reported to the police (FBI, 1985), a 7% increase over 1983 and 50% increase since 1975. It is doubtful that, in such a short time span, this increase reflects only a greater willingness to report a rape or more effective law enforcement. The FBI calculates that, correcting for under-reporting, a rape occurs every two minutes. Yet rape has the lowest conviction rate of all violent crime.

As with rape, the true prevalence of wife-assault is unknown because the crime is so seldom reported. Although wife-assault is not yet an FBI crime category, federal analysts recognize that it is widespread and estimate that it is three times as common as rape. Russell's (1982) random sample of 644 women revealed that 21% had been subjected to physical violence by a husband. In their national study of violence in American homes, Straus et al. (1980) found husbands violent in 27% of the marriages analyzed. They suggest, however, that the true rate is much higher.

Similarly, the incidence of the sexual abuse of children is unknown. Finklehor (1984) estimates that 75% to 90% of the incidents are never reported. In spite of this, studies clearly suggest that child sexual abuse is of great magnitude. Reviewing the evidence from five surveys on incest between 1940 and the present, Herman (1981) found that one-fifth to one-third of all the respondents reported that they had had some kind of childhood sexual encounter with an adult male; between 4% and 12% reported a sexual experience with a relative, and 1 female in 100 reported having had a sexual experience with her father or step-father. In spite of the acknowledged prevalence of wife-assault and child sexual abuse, arrest and prosecution is arduous and discouraging and convictions are rare.

An identical pattern emerges when examining the data on sexual harassment. While accurate data are impossible to obtain, studies suggest that sexual harassment is pervasive. Farley (1978) found that within the federal government, accounts of sexual harassment are extensive, and that surveys of working women in the private sector suggest a "dangerously high rate of incidence of this abuse." The U.S. Merit System's Protection Board surveyed 23,000 federal employees in 1981 and found that within the two years prior to the survey 42% of the respondents experienced sexual harassment (Stanko, 1985). Moreover, younger, single women reported a higher incidence of harassment. According to Dziech and Weiner's (1984) study of academic sexual harassment, 20% to 30% of female students are victims of sexual harassment during their college years. While victims of sexual harassment are increasingly breaking silence and some are even successful in bringing cases to court, adjudication and conviction in these cases are rare.

CONCLUSIONS

As the task of confronting men's power to intimidate and violate females is manifold, the agenda for feminist research and activism must be diverse and bold. Therefore, in an effort to deepen and broaden our understanding of sexual terrorism, I would like to offer several suggestions for further research.

First, we must expand our understanding of the definitions and scope of sexual violence. Since 1971 when the first speak-out on rape was held, both feminist scholars and courageous survivors of sexual terrorism have broken silence on the darkest aspects of patriarchy. In the past 15 years we have pierced the curtain of ignorance of what W. W. Visser't Hofft (1982) calls "the twilight between knowing and not knowing." The breaking of the tradition of silence surrounding rape, wife-assault, wife-rape, sexual harassment, sexual slavery, incestuous assault, and pornography is truly revolutionary. Because women have been constructed within a male-dominated society, women's experiences of sexual violence have been viewed through a patriarchal lens, resulting in an illusion of at best insignificance, and at worst complicity. What was lost—or rather, what was denied—was a woman-defined understanding of sexual terrorism. As feminist theory comes largely from the experience of women, the breaking of silence has informed and transformed the study of violence against women. While the gap between women's experiences of male violence and men's definition of sexual violence still must be bridged, the recognition that violence must be defined, in large measure, by those who experience it provides a meaningful foundation for future research.

We still need, however, to know more about the actual extent of violence against women. Hence a national random incidence survey is imperative. Such a study should not be limited to the conventional criminal categories, but should include the opportunity for women and girls to provide subjective understanding and definitions.

Second, we need to bring together the various forms of violence against females in order to see the patterns. In furthering our understanding of the commonalities of forms of sexual violence, we can then examine areas of women's oppression that have been previously neglected in the literature on violence. For example, the link between medicine and sexual violence has yet to be fully explored. Corea's (1985) analysis of medicine as a form of social control, and the work of Stark et al. (1979) on the treatment of battered women in a hospital emergency room, represent an important introduction to this uncharted terrain. Additionally, the diagnosis and treatment of women in psychiatric care should be analyzed from the perspective of societal attitudes toward sexual violence and the role of violence in keeping women subordinate in institutions of care.

We need to know more about multiple personality syndrome and its connection to sexual violence. Similarly, an investigation of female self-abusers and studies of suicide and attempted suicide relative to sexual violence are necessary. Research into these areas would not only enlarge the scope of our understanding of sexual violence but would provide insight into the coping/survival strategies of victims and the ways sexual violence is processed by agencies of the culture.

Third, the role of violence in structuring and maintaining male-female relationships remains inadequately considered. This needs to be addressed at the macro level, where force and the threat of violence are functional to male supremacy and provide the foundation for other forms of domination and control. At the micro level we need to study the psychosexual processes that underscore the heterosexual social system. From this perspective, Hammer and Saunders (1984) suggest that we look at the concepts of authority and obedience in personal relationships. Also, we should continue exploring the interconnections between the socially constructed dependencies of women and the further powerlessness engendered by physical intimidation and violence.

Moreover, the study of women should illuminate the study of men. This is generally, and notably, not the case in the study of sexual violence. For example, the majority of offenders are known to the victims, yet the significance of this has yet to be explored. To date, most of the studies involving offenders (Groth, 1979; Scully and Marolla, 1985) have been done with *convicted* sex offenders. Given that victims are least likely to report when the offender is known to them, and acquaintance rapes rarely result in conviction, studies on convicted offenders are limited in their ability to inform us about the complexities inherent in the phenomenon of men committing violence against women and girls whom they profess to love.

Fourth, there is a need for much more research into the legal system and its response to offenders and victims. While there has been both evidentiary and statutory reform in the legal codes, the greater problem in the litigation of sexual violence seems to be discriminatory enforcement. The chasm between legislative reform and women's experiences of the legal process as "the second assailant" (Stanko, 1985) remains wide.

Finally, I believe that the continuing study of the relationships between sexual terrorism and popular culture is crucial. The expressions of popular culture—literature, films, television, music, advertising, and so on—are vehicles for the transmission of patriarchal myths and attitudes.

Furthermore, the level of violence against females is not only at an all-time high, but indications are that it is increasing. To say that it is pervasive is not enough; acts of sexual violence are more severe and brutal than ever before. There is an apparent increase in gang rapes, serial rapes, and murders (which often involve dismemberment of women's bodies). This alarming phenomenon should be analyzed in relation to the propaganda of sexual terrorism and the production of fear.

Strategies to free women must be based on a thorough understanding of the roots and range of the system of sexual terrorism. The task of feminist scholarship is to forward the search for truth and, in so doing, develop a body of knowledge and a new curriculum about women, and to inform public policy. As Kathleen Barry (1979: 11) put it, "knowing the worst frees us to hope and strive for the best."

NOTES

1. This debate on "sex war," as explicated by Ferguson et al. (1981), hinges on two radically different visions of feminist sexual morality. One group, the "radical feminists," perceives not only pornography but all forms of sexuality based on dominance and power inequality as supportive of the patriarchal sex/gender system. The other group—"libertarian feminists"—argues that feminism must stand for liberation from the narrow confines of male-defined traditional sexuality, that women must be allowed to find sexual pleasure in a variety of hitherto forbidden ways, provided only that the relationships are consensual.

   Libertarians claim that the antipornography activists would turn the clock back to a repressive morality in which female sexuality would be once more stifled. The radicals perceive libertarians as reinforcers of brutality in the larger society and among women. The debate among feminists, however, may make it possible to find some third path to defining a female sexuality that is both liberating and noncoercive.

   In addition, many feminists doubt the effectiveness of using the law to control pornography when both are defined by male perspectives . . . Nonetheless, other feminists have written and promoted local ordinances that would define pornography as a threat to women's rights to move freely in the community and to enjoy equal protection of the laws (Blakely, 1985).

   The antifeminists have, of course, an entirely different agenda in their crusade against "obscenity," one that has more to do with a fear of rampant sexuality (echoing the basic patriarchal position) than with the issue of gender power (Diamond, 1980). There is, then, a way in which the suppression of pornography, along with the suppression of contraception and access to abortion, could herald a new wave of puritanism that would once more deny to women the ability to define and control their own sexuality.

REFERENCES

Adler, C. (1985) "An exploration of self-reported sexually aggressive behavior." Crime and Delinquency 31, 2: 306–331.

Barry, K. (1979) Female Sexual Slavery, Englewood Cliffs, NJ: Prentice-Hall.

Bart, P. B. and P. H. O'Brien (1984) "Stopping rape: Effective avoidance strategies." Signs 10, 1: 82–101.

Bart, P. B. and K. L. Scheppele (1980) "There ought to be a law: Women's definitions and legal definitions of sexual assault." Presented at the American Sociological Association meeting.

Blakely, M. K. (1985) "Is one woman's sexuality another woman's pornography?" Ms. (April).

Breines, W. and L. Gordon (1983) "The new scholarship on family violence." Signs 8, 3: 490–531.

Brownmiller, S. (1975) Against Our Will: Men, Women and Rape. New York: Simon & Schuster.

Burgess, A. W. (1985) Rape and Sexual Assault, New York and London: Garland Publishing.

Bush, D. M. (1985) "Doublethink and newspeak in the real 1984: Rationalizations for violence against women." Humanity and Society, 9(3): 308–327.

Corea, G. (1985) The Hidden Malpractice: How American Medicine Mistreats Women. New York: Harper & Row.

Crocker, P. L. (1983) "An analysis of university definitions of sexual harassment." Signs 8, 4: 696–707.

Diamond, I. (1980) "Pornography and repression: A reconsideration of who and what," in Laura Lederer (ed.) Take Back the Night: Women on Pornography, New York: William Morrow.

Donnerstein, E. (1980) "Aggressive erotica and violence against women." Journal of Personality and Social Psychology 39, 2: 269–277.

Dworkin, A. (1979) Pornography: Men Possessing Women. New York: Perigree Books.

Dworkin, A. (1985) "A word people don't understand." Ms. (April).

Dziech, B. W. and L. Weiner (1984) The Lecherous Professor, Boston: Beacon.

Farley, I. (1978) Sexual Shakedown: The Sexual Harassment of Women on the Job. New York: McGraw-Hill.

Ferguson, A. I. Phillipson, I. Diamond, L. Quinby, C. S. Vance, and A. B. Snitow (1984) "The feminist sexuality debates." Signs 10, 1: 102–153.

Finkelhor, D. (1984) Child Sexual Abuse: New Theory and Research. New York: Free Press.

Firestone, S. (1972) The Dialectic of Sex. New York: Bantam.

Fox, G. L. (1977) "Nice girl: Social control of women through a value construct." Signs 2, 4: 805–817.

Frieze, I. H. (1983) "Investigating the causes and consequences of marital rape." Signs 8, 3: 532–553.

Groth. N. (1979) Men Who Rape: The Psychology of the Offender. New York: Plenum.

Hanmer, J. and S. Saunders (1984) Well-Founded Fear: A Community Study of Violence to Women. London: Hutchinson.

Herman, J. I. with L. Hirschman (1981) Father-Daughter Incest. Cambridge, MA: Harvard University Press.

Holmstrom, L. and A. W. Burgess (1983) "Rape and everyday life." Society (July/August): 33–40.

Labelle, B. (1980) "The propaganda of misogyny," in Laura Leder (ed.) Take Back the Night: Women on Pornography. New York: William Morrow.

Hooks. B. (1981) Ain't I A Woman: Black Women and Feminism. Boston: South End Press.

Johnson, C. (1978) "Perspectives on terrorism, in Walter Laqueur (ed.) The Terrorism Reader. Philadelphia: Temple University Press.

Leacock, E. B. [ed.] (1981) Myths of Male Dominance: Collected Articles on Women Cross-Culturally. New York: Monthly Review Press.

Lerner, G. [ed.] (1973) Black Women in White America: A Documentary History. New York: Vintage Books.

Lowe, M. and R. Hubbard (1983) Women's Nature: Rationalizations of Integrity. New York: Pergamon.

Mackinnon, C. A. (1983) "Feminism, Marxism, method and the state: Toward feminist jurisprudence." Signs 8, 4: 635–658.

Malamuth, N. M. (1981) "Rape proclivity among males." Journal of Social Issues 37: 138–157.

Pagelow, M. D. with L. W. Pagelow (1985) Family Violence. New York: Praeger.

Polk, K. (1985) "Rape reform and criminal justice processing." Crime and Delinquency 31, 2: 191–205.

Russell, D. F. H. (1982) Rape in Marriage. New York: Macmillan.

Sanday, P. R. (1981) "The socioculture context of rape." Journal of Social Issues 37, 1.

Schehier, S. (1982) Woman and Male Violence: The Visions and Struggles of the Battered Women Movement. Boston: South End Press.

Schneider, B. E. (1984) "Put up and shut up: Workplace sexual assaults." Presented at the American Sociological Association Meeting.

Schur, F. M. (1984) Labeling Women Deviant: Gender, Stigma, and Social Control. New York: Random House.

Schwendinger, R. J. R. and H. Schwendinger (1983) Rape and Inequality. Newbury Park, CA: Sage.

Scully, D. and J. Marolla (1985) "Riding the bull at Gilley's: Convicted rapists describe the rewards of rape." Social Problems 32, 3: 251–263.

Stanko, F. A. (1985) Intimate Intrusions: Woman's Experience of Male Violence. London: Routlege & Kegan Paul.

Stark, F., A Flitcraft, and W. Fraziew (1979) "Medicine and patriarchal violence: The social construction of a 'private' event." International Journal of Health Services 9, 3: 461–492.

Strauss, M., R. Giles, and S. Steinmetz (1980) Behind Closed Doors. Garden City, NY: Anchor/Doubleday.

Tavris, C. and C. Wade (1984) The Longest War: Sex Differences in Perspectives. New York: Harcourt Brace Jovanovich.

Tierney, K. J. (1982) "The battered women's movement and the creation of the wife beating problem." Social Problems 26, 2: 207–220.

Till, F. J. (1980) Sexual Harassment: A Report on the Sexual Harassment of Students. Washington, DC: National Advisory Council on Women's Educational Programs.

U.S. Department of Justice, Federal Bureau of Investigation (1985) Uniform Crime Report. Washington, DC: U.S. Government Printing Office.

Vissert Hofft, W. W. (1982) The Terrible Secret: The Suppression of the Truth About Hitler's Final Solution, New York: Penguin.

Warr, M. (1985) "Fear of rape among urban women." Social Problems 32, 3: 238–250.

Watson, F. M. (1976) Political Terrorism: The Threat and the Response. Washington, DC: R. B. Luce.

Wilkinson, P. (1974) Political Terrorism. New York: John Wiley.

Pain Explodes In a World of Power: Men's Violence

MICHAEL KAUFMAN

In the dying moments of the 1980s a man named Marc Lepine walked into the Engineering School at the University of Montreal. He wore jeans and a baseball cap. In his hand was a semi-automatic rifle. He climbed the stairs to a second-floor classroom, and calmly ordered the men out of the room. After they left he opened fire. He cruised the room, then a hallway, then another classroom, and by the time he was finished he had killed fourteen women and wounded several others. Witnesses later said he looked like an ordinary sort of guy. Normal, one of them said.

Mass murderers are not common in Canada and, really, by the standards set in the twentieth century, the cynic might say that killing fourteen people hardly counts. Marc Lepine, however, did manage to touch a nerve before he ended his own life. With his finger on the trigger he said simply, "I want the women. You're all a bunch of feminists. I hate feminists."

At first the media covered these events as a random act of violence by a lone and crazed madman. There was no doubt Marc Lepine was crazy. The horrible thing was that he had chosen to express his craziness through violence, using a language that has gained far too much social acceptance. After all, there are lots of ways to be crazy. He could have dedicated his life to collecting recipes for Jell-O salads. He could have run down the street naked, tossing dollar bills to strangers. Instead, the language he chose was the language of violence, and his particular dialect was a hatred of women.

Let's not talk about crazy men. Let's talk about all of us, or at least about something that gets attached to our definitions of masculinity. Of course most men aren't rapists or murderers; we're not batterers or child abusers; we're not army generals who order bombs to be dropped on cities. But all men have experienced some form of violence as a child or adult, as perpetrator or victim, doer or done to.

Men's violence is the most dramatic display of the destructive potential of the hallucination of masculinity set in a real patriarchal world. Combined with the realities of men's social power, such a hallucination is a dangerous thing. The potent mixture of men's pain and men's power nurtures aggression and, all too often, encourages that aggression to be expressed in acts of violence.

THE NURTURING ENVIRONMENT OF VIOLENCE

Men's violence is not just a psychological problem that torments individuals. Although there are bad men, men aren't bad. We aren't born to kill. We are the products of societies led by men in which violence is institutionalized at all levels of social, political, cultural and economic life. It should be no surprise that such societies produce some men who are particularly violent and many others whose lives have been touched by violence. Violence is the preferred means to settle international and individual disputes among men. War is a corporate fortune-maker, the world's biggest business, accounting for trillions of dollars of annual expenditures. Media violence is now the prime form of popular entertainment and also a big money-maker. One estimate suggests that the average North American child has seen depictions of 18,000 murders and violent deaths by the end of high school. Violence is integrated into sports, and sport becomes a metaphor for large-scale violence.

The roots of violence run deep. Some tribal societies had high levels of violence; others had absolutely none, and some only experienced it occasionally. As larger, hierarchical societies developed five to ten thousand years ago, first in parts of the Middle East and Asia, large-scale, organized military violence became a chief means of expansion and survival. The modern world has been built on so much violence that blood has soaked deep into the fabric of society: European colonization, slavery, decimation of indigenous populations, imperial wars, the conquest of nature, the inroads of industrialization into every corner of our lives. Nowadays many forms of violence are barely considered criminal. Think of various types of corporate violence, from the poison of toxic waste, and the daily crush of unsafe and alienating jobs to the activities of the biggest drug cartels on earth—the tobacco companies. Psychological and sometimes physical violence is etched into the body politic of our world through widespread acceptance of discrimination and oppression that casts certain humans as acceptable targets for the wrath of others. Institutionalized and individualized forms of hatred, discrimination and violence based on sex, race, religion, sexual orientation, nationality, physical ability and age are widespread throughout the patriarchal world, from North America to Europe, Africa to Asia, Latin America to the Middle East.

In any act of violence, whether sexual harassment or rape, whether a school-yard tussle, a violent display of temper or a vicious assault, individual men are acting out relations of sexual and social power. One man may be striking out at a woman or a man in order to deny his own social powerlessness; another might be repeating his own treatment as a child. Whatever the case, there is nothing purely individual about these acts. The violent man must be held responsible, but he alone is not to blame, for these actions are a ritualized acting-out of our social relations of power: the dominant and the submissive, the powerful and the powerless, the active and the passive, the masculine and the feminine.

INDIVIDUAL REPRODUCTION OF VIOLENCE

Into this violent environment the individual is born. Here we arrive, spanking new, ready to take it all in. Boys take it in with a vengeance. The starting point is not violence, nor even aggression. It is the boy's unknowing acceptance of the dominant creed of manhood: to be a man we need to shape a personality that can always control and dominate our social and natural environment. It is the way we build our psyches around the active/passive split. The ability to dominate—perhaps only through words or self-control, perhaps through actions—becomes a core feature of masculinity. It is our ability to act *on,* to do *to,* to control and manipulate the world around us, and not to succumb to "weakness" or receptivity. This is our great escape from the childhood experience of powerlessness.

The boy comes to personify activity, developing what Herbert Marcuse calls a "surplus aggressive" character type, although important differences exist between one man and the next. The problem isn't that men are assertive or aggressive in some situations, for these are important and positive human traits; the problem is that aggression is not usually balanced by receptivity and passivity.

Control, along with the aggression that is often required to sustain it, and the rejection of "weakness," together form the dominant values of many patriarchal societies. Those who rise to the top in any niche are those who are most effective, efficient, capable, and in some cases ruthless, in controlling and manipulating their environment. It is this orientation that we men, to a greater or lesser extent, tend to develop, maybe in our work life, maybe in our life in our communities, on the street, at play or at home. Some of us express it in our body language. Ken Kesey captured this in his description of Hank, a central character in *Sometimes a Great Notion:* "Did it take that much muscle just to walk, or was Hank showing off his manly development? Every movement constituted open aggression against the very air through which Hank passed."

Robert is thirty-seven years old. Three months before I met him, he arrived at the door of a treatment program for men who batter. Arrived is a nice way of putting it. He had been ordered by a judge to attend the sixteen-week program or spend the time in jail. Robert works as an accounts manager for a small company. He's rather soft-spoken, not someone you'd guess was a bully or a batterer. Josh is twenty-eight and works as a counsellor in the treatment program. A counselling group is in progress. Some of the material they are covering they've obviously been over before.

Josh: "You beat your wife regularly." (It's a statement, not a question.)

Robert: "Well no, not really, it happened a few times a year." Then he asks angrily, "Why are you asking me again?"

Josh pauses for a moment, letting the tension die down; then asks: "When did it happen?"

Robert: "No time in particular. Things just seem to build up. Get more tense and troubled." (Robert often uses the word troubled.) "Something would happen and I'd feel pushed too far by her."

Another man in the group: "Sure you didn't have a couple?"

Robert: "No, not really. That might be the case with you and some guys here." (There is some hostility in Robert's voice, but other men in the group nod their heads.) "But in my case, no."

The discussion moves on to others and later comes back to Robert.

Robert: "My life felt troubled, I know that now."

Josh: "By what? . . . What about?"

Robert: "Something was missing. Not with Julia. She was really a fine catch for me, I've always known that. It's that I've always felt, since I was a teenager, I guess, that I had a lot bottled up inside. Back in college I worried about it sometimes. As soon as I heard the words 'existential crisis' I started having one. But then that passed and I settled into a job and my marriage."

Josh: "When did the violence start?"

Robert: "A couple of years into the marriage."

Josh: "What was happening around then?"

Robert: "Nothing really. I felt like I had settled into the rest of my life. Like this was it. It kind of troubled me. This was it, that's all, this was all I can expect."

Another man in the group: "Like waking up with a hangover after partying for a week."

Robert: "I had these ideas about what my life would be like. I mean, I never really expected to be rich or famous . . . well, a bit, like everyone else, but I knew I would amount to something. That made me feel good in high school, knowing I'd amount to something."

Josh: "And?"

Robert: "What do you think? I put in my time. I get pats on the back sometimes and dumped on other times. It's a job. It's life. Then my wife comes in chittering about her job or the kids are bugging me about something. And I can't seem to hear myself think and it builds up and then . . ."

Although he hadn't yet found the words for it, what Robert had been experiencing during those years was, in part, a drawn-out crisis of his sense of masculinity. Like many other men and women in our society, he was feeling a sense of disappointment with what his life had become. More than disappointment, he was feeling as if his power had been stripped away. He had little control at work and was alienated from his job. "At work men are powerless," writes sociologist Meg Luxton, "so in their leisure time they want to have a feeling that they control their own lives."

Being a man is supposed to be about having some sort of power and control. Robert wasn't in control of his environment. He felt shunted around by the demands of life. It was as if a demon were whispering in his ear that he hadn't made the grade as a man. So what did he do about it? Society had provided him with a way of compensating for these feelings: it had linked him up with someone who had been defined as less powerful. If masculinity isn't only a set of roles we fit into, but a power relationship between men and women, then asserting his dominance in his relationship with his wife became a means to reassert his sense of self-worth and manhood. This was one reason why he felt terrible after he had hit or beaten his wife, although one can't compare it to what she, the survivor of his rage, felt. Before and during, he had no sense of wrong, but afterwards he knew he had done wrong although he wanted to deny it. Why? Like most men in that situation he was worried his wife would leave him or call the police. There was something else, however, something genuine about his concern. After all, now that he felt strong again he no longer needed to beat his wife. At least not until the next time, several months later, when the same self-doubts and insecurities would build up and he would lash out again.

Part of Robert's problem was that he had learned to suppress a range of emotions and capacities. He was unable to feel what his wife was feeling. Many abusers simply don't recognize the harm they are doing to their son, daughter, lover or wife. Violence may even be experienced as a misshapen image of concern, of love, of caring. As he became a man, his own sense of alienation, self-doubt and confusion was transformed into emotions that he identified with his own sense of masculinity: he started turning a range of feelings into aggression and violence. Aggressiveness is a trait that is part of every person's birthright, but here it rages unbalanced due to an inability to express reciprocity, connection and receptiveness.

Underneath the violence directed at his wife was his own internalized violence—violence directed at himself. Such is the structure of the masculine ego, of the dominant and normal forms of masculinity in most of the world's cultures. The formation of what we think of as normal manhood in our culture does not depend on brute force, but it does require internalized violence. We ask ourselves to continually deny, or at least hold down, the many emotions, feelings and actions men associate with passivity—fear, pain, openness, sadness, embarrassment. Anytime these emotions rear their heads we feel a sense of unconscious dread that warns us to stay away from that feeling. There's a bad smell about these things. It tells us, No trespassing. Off limits to men.

The dampening of these emotions is compounded by the blocking of avenues of emotional release. The expression of fear, hurt and sadness, for example, through crying or trembling, is physiologically and psychologically necessary because these painful emotions fester, especially if they are not con-

sciously felt. Men become pressure cookers. The failure to find safe avenues of emotional expression and release means that a whole range of emotions are transformed into aggression and hostility. You feel sad or hurt or angry, and you strike out. Part of the aggression is directed at yourself in the form of guilt, self-hate and various physiological and psychological symptoms. It isn't simply anger, for anger itself is just an emotion that grows out of a sense, rightly or wrongly, that your needs have not been met. The problem here is the way anger, like other emotions, gets expressed through aggression and violence.

For some men the only safe avenue for letting go is through outbursts of verbal abuse, which may be as subtle as a sarcastic putdown or as clear as a string of insults. Other men will explode in fireworks of anger or physical violence. Many men explode only in a situation where they feel secure and where they can feel confident of winning. This is why so much violence occurs in families, against those whom men love. The family provides an arena for the expression of needs and emotions not considered legitimate elsewhere. It's one of the few places where men feel safe enough to let go, to unwind, to express emotions and to demand that their needs be met. When their emotional dams break, the flood pours out—mostly on women and children.*

---

*Levels of spousal assault (most often assault of women) are horrendous. One study suggests that every year in the United States, one in six couples experiences at least one violent act. According to a national survey by the U.S. Violence Commission, 25 percent of respondents could think of "appropriate circumstances" for spousal hitting. It would be naïve to think that men completely monopolize household violence. Women, too, internalize the values of a violent society, even if to a much lesser extent than men. As primary caregivers, women are often responsible for the physical punishment of children, although the ultimate threat is often, "Wait till your father comes home." In the U.S., roughly the same number of domestic homicides are committed by each sex. In 1975, 8.0 percent of homicides were committed by husbands against wives and 7.8 percent by wives against husbands. But these statistics paper over what Suzanne Steinmetz and others have called the cycle of violence: many of these women are reacting to years of harassment or battering by their husbands.

Violence is not always so intimate. Nor does it come naturally to men. A look at the making of soldiers confirms this. . . .

RAPE

Most of us are lucky: war has not been a regular feature of our lives. Yet the realities of men's violence against women are as everyday as apple pie. In rape, wife assault and child abuse, we see some of the more vicious and common expressions of these patterns of violence.

Rape is not a universal feature of manhood but the product of particular societies. Many tribal societies were free of rape, while only a few had high levels of rape comparable to those in contemporary North America. Those societies where rape was common were those that believed strongly in the inferiority of women and encouraged physical aggression in men.*

Many researchers now estimate that a U.S. or Canadian woman has a one out of four risk of being raped sometime during her life. Most attackers know their victim, and rape is often directed at dates or spouses. Because men are not the principal victims, most of us don't realize the extent of rape, the extent of fear in women's lives because of something that our brothers and sons, our fathers and friends are doing. A pioneering study of rape on college campuses in the United States conducted in the mid-1980s indicated that over half of college women had experienced some sort of unwanted sexual victimization since the time they were fourteen years old. Meanwhile, although one out of four college men admitted to some form of sexual aggression, only 7.7 percent admitted to rape or attempted rape. Many

men refused to own up to the truth: of the men who admitted an assault that met the legal definition of rape, 88 percent insisted that it wasn't really rape.*

There is a much smaller incidence of rape of other men. The chief location for rape of adult men is prison, where it is an institutionalized product of an inhuman environment. Outside prisons, rape of other men and boys goes almost completely unreported because of the immense sense of shame experienced by a raped man, the almost complete lack of social support and the fear of further violence. Not surprisingly, the response of raped men has many of the same characteristics as that described by raped women. One man, reflecting on being raped by a stranger six years earlier, still feels the pain: "I feel a mixture of physical and emotional pain, the sense of the crossing of boundaries which shouldn't be crossed. Someone has crossed the boundary of my skin and stolen the basis of my identity, my ability to control my body. . . . I feel like nothing more than a rag for someone to come in. I go through the paces unaware of my surroundings while I think over and over, 'How could I have let this happen?' "

In the important struggle to reform our criminal codes to bring in harsher penalties for rape and stricter compliance with the law, rape is increasingly recognized as not being about sex, but about control and violence. Some believe it's a violent assault like any other. I agree, but only up to a point. Rape is *always* an act of violence and aggression and has *nothing* to do with sexual pleasure for the victim. But that much said, rape certainly can have something to do with the sexuality of the rapist and with the way sexual relationships have been shaped in our society. After all, the way our sexualities develop always has something of a power play in it, and this is obviously going to be reflected in sexual assault.

---

*In Peggy Sanday's study of ninety-five tribal societies, almost half, 47 percent, were free of rape. Only 18 percent showed what she called a significant incidence of rape. The remaining 35 percent had a very limited amount. Another study of 186 nonindustrialized cultures, by I. L. Weiss, suggests that those societies with strong beliefs in women's inferiority and high levels of male physical aggression were the ones with a higher percentage of rape.

*A study by Mary P. Koss and colleagues reported that 14 percent of women mentioned unwanted touching, 12 percent said they had experienced sexual coercion and over 27 percent had experienced rape or attempted rape. One out of four women in this eighteen- to twenty-four-year-old group had been raped, 84 percent by close acquaintances or dates.

The rape of strangers gives us the clearest example that rape isn't primarily about sex, but rather about control and domination. It is also the rarest type of rape. The testimony of these rapists reveals a bottomless pit of inferiority, powerlessness and anger. While many men might experience these feelings to some degree, a relatively small number choose rape as a way of expressing their power and of making others feel the terror they feel. In doing so, they have chosen three popular refrains of patriarchal culture: that power equals power over another person; that to be a real man you have to have power over women; and that you can't be degraded yourself if you can degrade someone else. The recollections of such men are horrifying. Hal: "I felt very inferior to others. . . . I felt rotten about myself, and by committing rape I took this out on someone I thought was weaker than me, someone I could control." Carl: "I think that I was feeling so rotten, so low, and such a creep." Len: "I feel a lot of what rape is isn't so much sexual desire as a person's feelings about themselves and how that relates to sex. My fear of relating to people turned to sex because . . . it just happens to be the fullest area to let your anger out on, to let your feelings out on."

The vast majority of rapes—of a girlfriend, a date or a spouse—have a different dynamic. Unwanted physical contact often occurs because of attitudes among boys and men that sex is a right, particularly if they are paying the way. Studies of date rapists, such as those by researcher Mary Koss, have shown that these men view sexual aggression as normal. They have conservative beliefs about women staying in their place and about women's sexuality. They accept the myths that women are turned on by coercion and want to be raped, that no means yes. They see heterosexual relationships as game playing. Rape in this instance is not motivated simply by a desire to put a woman in her place; it is also a misguided and destructive attempt to find sexual pleasure.

Two male students once offered to tell me why they didn't think date rape was a problem. "It's not really rape, you know," said an otherwise bright young business student. "I can't stand it when I hear people say that. It's a game. You ask someone out and, you know, it's not like you're asking them to go to a tea party or home to meet the parents. They

know what they're getting into. Why the hell does anyone go out with anyone when you're my age?" He paused for effect. "We're talking the big F." He smiled. He liked his turn of phrase.

A frosh engineering student nodded in agreement. "I think some people are making a mountain out of a molehill. Sure, there might be a problem once in a while. Everyone has heard of those and I certainly don't like that, but we're just trying to have some fun. No law against that, is there?"

"Actually there is," I chimed in.

The gulf between men and women, men's confusion about sexuality, the mystification so many men feel about women, all seem to coalesce in rape. Anti-rape activist Timothy Beneke reports that he often hears men say, "I have been injured by women. By the way they look, move, smell and behave, they have forced me to have sexual sensation I didn't want to have. If a man rapes a sexy woman, he is forcing her to have sexual sensation she doesn't want. It is just revenge." One told him, "Growing up, I definitely felt teased by women . . . I definitely felt played with, used, manipulated, like women were testing their power over me."

In these statements, the masculine fear of unwanted and powerful emotions reaches an extreme. We see the myths about women and about women's desires. At the same time there is also an accurate, even if horrific, acting-out of the active/passive split of masculinity and femininity, of male/female relations of power. Some men's insecurity and a fear of rejection combine with their views of sex as adversarial with terrifying results.

Rape, as a drama where relations of power are acted out, is made possible by the adversarial nature of sex and just about everything else, in our society. Because of the active/passive split, patriarchal society has tended to place sexual assertion and aggression in the hands of men. How can women control and shape their own sexuality? Although many women have reclaimed sexual independence and control, and others have developed a sexual orientation towards other women, many women, particularly while young, have only the tools of refusal and manipulation to meet their needs. Our culture celebrates the resultant game playing, dressing it up in heroic guise—man the hunter, woman the coy prey. It's not wonder that sexual relations often take on an adversarial air or that there is sometimes game playing with words, particularly among the young, where experience and confidence are still low. When you combine this adversarial dynamic with the insecurities of masculinity, with the way sex gets defined as a power relationship, with sexist attitudes towards women, with public shame and misinformation about sex, then the climate becomes ripe for the proliferation of all forms of sexual harassment, from verbal harassment and unwanted contact to coercion and rape.

Establishing that these sexual dynamics are among the factors leading to rape does not suggest that any woman is responsible for being raped. A young woman, any woman, may give off signals that a man may misinterpret. Young, inexperienced, scared, confused, she might just say yes or might say no when she is actually feeling ambivalent and simply needs to wait, or talk, or think things through. It's important for her to learn to express what she wants and for couples to learn to express their needs. No man has the right to decide on her behalf what it is she really wants. Men, too, must learn to express clearly what they want, but also to realize that *no* always means *no,* and that the absence of a clear *yes* also means *no.*

THE ABUSE OF CHILDREN

One of the most terrifying manifestations of a world of violence—and perhaps the greatest, most sustained crime of humanity—is the systematic abuse of young children. In all but some tribal societies, there is an almost uncontested acceptance of the right of parents to hit children. One U.S. study estimates that 84 to 97 percent of parents physically punish their children. Children learn that violence is legitimate if you have power over the person you hit. Children learn that you can simultaneously love someone and be violent, even be violent *because* you love someone. It's high time we recognize hitting a child, no matter what the situation, as an unacceptable form of abuse.

The problem isn't only corporal punishment. It includes the more subtle uses of parental power to enforce discipline in ways that are not necessary for safety, that are rather the result of parental frustration and merely surviving life in an industrialized, hectic, stressful society. In such a society it takes a conscious act of will *not* to be violent. I think of the times I used my superior strength to stop my son from doing something he wanted to do. These weren't moments when his physical safety was at stake. They were the culmination of an escalating battle of wills, usually in the morning before school or at night before bed—times when both of us were overtired, when I thought he was being obstreperous and stubborn and he probably thought I was being the same, when I had other things I desperately had to do, and after I could no longer keep my patience. Of course children must learn there are costs for certain types of actions. But whatever his stubborn behaviour, it couldn't justify my harshly grabbing him. How much this typical family conflict must be magnified in the lives of children who are regularly threatened with physical punishment. Might is right. Somehow we are supposed to be surprised when these children become violent as teenagers or adults. Like the hysteric in the 1950s movies, we expect them to respond to a slap with a grateful, "Thanks, I needed that."

Sometimes the abuse of children takes the form of sexual abuse. Those who work with incest survivors report some cases of abuse by women—relatives, teachers, stepmothers, rarely mothers—but these remain a small minority. Most perpetrators are men. Again, we have a men's issue. It is a men's issue because it is men committing most sexual abuse, and it is a men's issue because the victims include boys as well as girls.

In her autobiographical story, *My Father's House,* novelist Sylvia Fraser writes of her own abuse as a child. Early in life she developed a split personality. It was the second personality that bore the weight of abuse. Throughout her childhood and teenage years her dominant, everyday personality didn't even know her father regularly forced her into having sex, and it wasn't until she reached her forties that she rediscovered her other self and what had happened to her. At one point in her book, Fraser recounts a visit to her bedridden grandmother, "Other Grandmother," as she called her. "Soon, soon will come that unspeakable moment when we line up, in order of size, to kiss Other Grandmother's cheek. I struggle against the heaving of my stomach, the yammering of my heart, trying not to experience, before I have to, that instant when the sweet smell of Other Grandmother's gardenia powder overwhelms me and my lips are swallowed in the decaying pulpiness of her cheek. Why this revulsion for an old woman's kiss? I do not know. I cannot say.

"This truth belongs to my other self, and it is a harsh one. Other Grandmother's caved-in cheek is the same squishy texture as daddy's scrotum."

We talk about these horrors to learn about them and to learn how to interrupt the chains and cycles of violence. I once heard a social worker speak of being in a courtroom where a man was being prosecuted for sexual abuse of a young boy. "I remember," she said, "feeling so much hate and anger for this man throughout the trial. Then he started talking about his past and I realized that in twenty or thirty years the abused little boy at my side might be the one up there on the stand. I wondered when it all would end. The older man was guilty and deserved to be punished, but he was only part of the cycle of violence."

VIOLENCE AS AN ISSUE FOR MEN

Since the rise of the women's liberation movement in the late 1960s, one of feminism's major themes has been the many forms of violence against women. The issue of violence has been brought into popular consciousness and public debate with urgency and in some cases desperation. Women raped and women battered; fear at home, on the streets and at work. Men's violence against women and children isn't a new issue, but we don't often hear it talked about as a men's issue. That's a shame since it may be your brother, your father, your son, your best friend, your neighbor or even you who is carrying out this violence. It's a shame because there might be a man out there who is using violence to reinforce his control over your sister, your mother, your daughter, your friend or your neighbor. It's a shame we haven't seen it as our issue for it affects all of us: as children many men suffered violence at the hands of men or other boys and many witnessed abuse of their mothers; as adults all of us live in a society where women have learned to be afraid of us simply because we are men. It's a shame because, if statistics hold true, every fourth male reader of this book has committed an act of violence—perhaps unwanted touching, perhaps battering, perhaps rape, perhaps verbal abuse—against a girlfriend or spouse.

"For six months," writes Martin Amis in one of his short stories, "she had been living with a man who beat her, lithe little Pat, sinewy, angular, wired very tight. I think she beat him too, a bit. But violence is finally a masculine accomplishment. Violence—now that's man's work."

It now must be men's work to challenge men's violence. We can confidently take up the issue because we know that men are not born to rape and batter. It isn't in our genes, hormones or anatomy. It's lodged in our vision of manhood and the structures of patriarchal power; in many cases it results from the way pain and power combine to make the man. The fact that most men *don't* explode, or do so rarely, is a testimony to some sort of basic human principle that resists the more destructive norms of masculinity. It is a testimony to the uninterrupted unity of activity and passivity that endures, like a whisper in our souls.

CHECKPOINTS

1. Sexual terrorism controls women through cultural ideology, propaganda, indiscriminant and amoral violence, voluntary compliance, and the biased portrayal of victims and terrorists.

2. Kaufman argues that gendered violence is a distorted expression of masculinity based on emotional repression and the need for power and control.

Social Institutions and Gender

QUESTIONS FOR REFLECTION

1. What would a nongendered social institution be like in terms of power and relationships? Can you think of any examples?
2. What conditions would have to exist for affirmative action to be perceived as fair and effective in creating equity?
3. What individual, institutional, and interpersonal changes need to occur in order to reduce gendered violence?

CHAPTER APPLICATIONS

1. Design a program for men aimed at violence prevention.
2. Identify a social institution you are associated with, and list the ways it is gendered. Develop a plan to create gender equity within that institution. Would this plan lead to equity for other social groups (race, ethnicity, religion, age) as well?

CHAPTER THIRTEEN
Gender and Health

QUESTIONS TO THINK ABOUT

- Do men and women have different health concerns?
- Are there racial differences in health care issues?
- Why should we be concerned about using categories such as gender and race to examine biomedical research results?
- In what ways has biomedical research and medical care exhibited gender bias?
- What improvements in medical research and health care would address gender bias?
- What are the important components of a biopsychosocial model of stress and health?
- What lifestyle factors are important in understanding health for men and women?
- How might gender roles be related to stress and health?
- What dimensions of feminine and masculine gender roles might be advantageous in dealing with stress?

UNDERSTANDING GENDER AND HEALTH

You may be familiar with recent controversies over funding for research of health care issues that are sex-specific. It has been charged that breast, cervical, and uterine cancers have been underfunded in health care research in comparison with research for men's health issues such as coronary artery disease. Critics have responded that other men's health issues, such as prostate cancer, have been underfunded relative to the rate of their occurrence. As with many issues tied to gender, this dilemma has been reduced to a battle pitting women against men for, in this case, money to understand diseases that affect more women versus men or men versus

women. Throughout this book, we have tried to emphasize the pitfalls of this win/lose approach to gender, and in this case, the consequences are particularly pernicious. These arguments reduce the relationship among gender, health, and health care to a battle of the sexes. This competition, we would argue, which ignores the importance of good health and health care for everyone, suggests that many health problems are *either* male or female and ignores the intimacies of many cross-sex relationships that would suggest that men and women share an interest in each other's health. The relationship among gender, health, and health care is complex, and several issues are relevant to exploring this interaction.

The first issue examines questions of sex differences. Do men and women have different diseases or health care problems? Do women and men receive or require different treatment? Do men and women experience health and illness differently, and do they respond to treatment similarly? We suggest that these sex difference questions are difficult to answer and that the type of answers that are proposed depend on the view of gender and health that is taken. In this chapter's first reading, *Man-Made Medicine and Women's Health: The Biopolitics of Sex/Gender and Race/Ethnicity*, Nancy Krieger and Elizabeth Fee discuss the implications of the essentialist view of sex and gender whereby the categorization of people as either male or female, and black or white becomes the basis for medical research questions. One important conclusion of their article is that the sex differences approach to health and health care may obscure the similarities between women and men and ignore the interaction between gender and social conditions, such as poverty, as they relate to health.

A second issue involved in understanding the interaction of gender, health, and health care is the issue of discrimination in the health care system. Although we agree that debates about which disease gets how much money may trivialize complex issues, we do believe that many aspects of health care show gender bias (and other forms of bias as well). Women's health care concerns have often been narrowly defined around reproductive health issues, ignoring the many nonreproductive diseases or health-related issues that face women of all ages. Krieger and Fee make it clear that sexist assumptions about women and their presumed inferiority has guided much of twentieth-century medical research. In the second article in this chapter, *Health Issues for Women in the 1990s*, Iris Litt describes some specific aspects of women's health and the nature of gender discrimination in health research and heath care. She provides an important perspective on current issues in women's health.

The final issue examines the interrelationship between the social and psychological dimensions of gender and health and health care. Researchers have investigated how gender roles are related to physical health and then examine the particular role of stress in mediating gender roles and health consequences. Many illnesses, such as the development of coronary artery disease or the progression of different types of cancer, are related to stress. For example, researchers have recently begun to examine how specific features of traditional gender roles are stressful. Is masculinity or femininity "unhealthy"? The last two readings in this chapter address this issue. The article by Victoria Banyard and Sandra Graham-Bermann, *Can Women Cope? A Gender Analysis of Theories of Coping with Stress*, raises questions about existing analyses of the ways women cope with stress and suggests an alternative perspective on women's coping strategies. Richard Eisler, in his article *The Relationship Between Masculine Gender Role Stress and Men's Health Risk: The Validation of a Construct*, reports on efforts to develop a scale to measure the stress-related elements of masculinity. Using this scale, Eisler provides evidence of how masculine gender role stress relates to physical health. Both of these analyses offer a way to examine the relationship between the psychological aspects of gender roles and the physical realm of health.

HEALTH CARE AND THE POLITICS OF CATEGORIES

Social Categories and the Medical Model of Health

To study the rates at which people acquire various illnesses and the effectiveness of alternative treatments, we must examine subpopulations of people. One obvious division is the category of male and female because of the assumption that the physiological differences between males and females might explain, or be linked to, differences in physical health. Two sex differences have been consistently observed in the research literature. First, the **mortality rate** for women at all ages is lower than for men. Women have a longer life expectancy; the average for women is 78.4 years and the average for men is 71.8 years(U.S. Department of Health and Human Services, 1993). In the past 100 years, the gap in mortality rate between males and females has grown significantly. In 1900, the survival advantage for women was about two years; now it is estimated at about seven years. In contrast, the **morbidity rate** for women is higher, meaning that they have higher rates of chronic illnesses such as diabetes, anemia, arthritis, and hypertension, and they seek medical care more often than men do (Strickland, 1988). Some differences in mortality and morbidity for males and females are given in the following examples. Male fetuses are more likely to be miscarried during pregnancy or to die during infancy (the ratio is 146:100); males are more likely at all ages to die of congenital abnormalities (the ratio is 120:100); and men are more likely to die of accidental injury, homicide, or suicide. Women, on the other hand, are more likely to die of stroke, complications from diabetes, and breast cancer (Holden, 1987; U.S. Department of Health and Human Services, 1993). Litt's article contains a detailed review of differences in mortality and morbidity that focuses on changes in risk patterns for women. Biological explanations for disease variations between men and women have focused on the presumed advantages of the second X chromosome of women or on hormonal differences. For example, estrogen is thought to protect women against heart attack, which may be why heart attack rates for women rise after menopause. Biological explanations, however, are not sufficient to account for the complex pattern of differences and similarities that can be observed in comparisons of women and men. Overall, men and women die most frequently of the *same* causes: cancer and cardiovascular disease leading to heart attack or stroke.

Krieger and Fee's article hearkens back to the issues raised in Hubbard's article in chapter 1. Both articles address the categorization of people into sex and race groupings. Krieger and Fee present evidence that race and gender became central elements in many biological theories of the nineteenth century and, like Hubbard, conclude that biological theories were constructed to bolster prevailing views about the social order, especially the dominant social position of white males over women and African Americans. Women, were presumed inferior and were described medically in ways consistent with this view. For example, reproductive functions, especially men-

struation, were assumed to make women vulnerable to a host of frailties and were used to deny women education and voting rights. Darwin's theory of natural selection was used as an explanation for social class hierarchies whereby the predominance of white males in the upper class was viewed as a natural outcome of social evolution. This explanation became a scientific justification for viewing African Americans as well as more recent immigrant groups as biologically inferior based on their social standing. Not only were race and ethnicity treated as natural biological categories, but differences between groups, for example, in the occurrence of tuberculosis, became evidence for the biological inferiority of the affected group. For both women and African Americans, the belief in biological differences became institutionalized as a part of the biomedical research enterprise. Ironically, according to Krieger and Fee and Hubbard, neither sex nor race can be adequately described as a biological category.

One consequence of the essentialist view of race and sex and the consequence of viewing health as intrinsically related to identity within these categories is the overemphasis on the role of reproduction in women's health. Throughout the nineteenth and twentieth centuries, medical views of women's health have been focused on obstetrics and gynecology. Childbirth was altered from a home-centered experience attended by other women—more than 95 percent of births at the turn of the century occurred at home—to a medical procedure by 1980, more than 99 percent of births occurred in a hospital or medical birthing facility. Childbirth became an illness and was treated with a series of interventions; many births during the middle of this century occurred while the mother was completely sedated.[1] Other evidence of the emphasis on women's reproductive systems has been the rise in the number of hysterectomies. This surgical removal of the uterus is the most frequently performed major surgery in the United States, despite evidence that as many as one in seven surgeries is questionable (Muller, 1990). The focus on women's reproductive health establishes a cultural norm for attention to these dimensions of health and neglect of other issues, which may be why women make more use of the health care system. Rodin and Ickovics (1990) suggest that technological interventions in reproductive care may be overutilized, whereas technological diagnostic procedures are less likely to be used with women in other areas of medicine. This underutilization is especially true in cardiac care, even though cardiovascular disease is the number one cause of death for postmenopausal women.

Consistent with the inextricable links drawn between sex and gender roles under the essentialist view of gender and health, considerable research has been done on occupational hazards in predominantly male work environments but health consequences of other sorts of employment, especially those jobs held predominantly by women, have been neglected. This neglect may be related to the emphasis on employment as part of the male gender role, so as medical researchers have become more sensitive to environmental models of disease, they have looked to the male-dominated workplace for answers. It is true that men are more likely to be employed in jobs that risk accidental injury, such as construction work, or in jobs that involve long-term exposure to carcinogens, such as coal mining (Waldron, 1991). Work-related health consequences likely to be experienced by women, such as repetitive motion injuries or exposure to toxic chemicals during the manufacturing of microchips, have only recently been acknowledged as serious health concerns. Not only are these hazards more likely to be experienced by women, but some of these jobs, especially assembly line work, are held predominantly by women of color (Fox, 1991).

A Social Contextual Model of Health and Gender

The search for biological causes of sex differences in mortality and morbidity has obscured the complexity of these differences, especially with regard to social factors that might explain, or provide a context for explaining, similarities and differences. According to Krieger and Fee, recognizing that biological categories are actually social categories should lead us to search for social measures and explanations in health

research. The diversity of women's reproductive health experiences, such as contraception, pregnancy, childbirth, and menopause, illustrates how to develop a contextualized understanding of women's health and health care that considers the interaction of biological and social/psychological factors.

Although pregnancy and childbearing are uniquely female experiences, the experiences of pregnancy and childbirth are not the same for all women. Poor women do not receive as much early prenatal care as do women with greater financial resources. Minority women who are poor are at greater risk for complications during pregnancy or as a result of abortion than are white women or middle-class women. African American women are more likely to die from breast cancer, whereas white women have higher rates of breast cancer but are more likely to survive. African American women also have higher rates of cervical cancer. Poor women have less access to health care, and what care they receive, such as in hospital emergency rooms, usually focuses on an immediate acute illness and not on prevention. One study in New York City showed that only 7 percent of physicians treating predominantly black and Hispanic women, compared to 23 percent of physicians whose patients were predominantly white, recommended mammograms to their patients (Gemson, 1990). These examples suggest that health and health care need to be understood as a complex interaction of biological factors in the context of variables such as race/ethnicity, social class, age, and gender.

A contextualized review of women's reproductive health should help you understand the importance of addressing factors such as poverty, employment status, or social roles in health care research. We would be remiss, however, if we did not remind you that women's health care needs go far beyond reproduction. Some critics have suggested that the focus on reproduction "genitalizes" women and may perpetuate the view that reproduction is the central element of women and their health care (Klonoff, Landrine, & Scott, 1995). We want to reiterate that, overall, men and women have remarkably similar health needs, and that both groups, are impacted by social and cultural factors.

An interactionist model that integrates biological with contextual factors can help explain the difference in longevity between women and men. It has been argued that males are more vulnerable to genetic defects than are females and that estrogen provides a measure of protection against heart disease, the number one killer of men. Interacting with these biological factors are several social factors that are equally important. A variety of lifestyle factors create conditions of greater risk for men than women. Men have higher rates of alcoholism and drug abuse, are more likely to smoke, are more frequently exposed to dangerous work environments, have higher rates of suicide, and are more likely to neglect preventive health care or seek help less often (Kilmartin, 1994). Each of these factors has its own etiology, so we are not equating them, but we are suggesting that many lifestyle factors put men's health at risk in various ways. Please note that although these factors are referred to as lifestyle factors, which are strongly influenced by behavior, lifestyle cannot be interpreted as a matter of equal choice. Conditions of poverty constrain the opportunities of poor people, and limit their health insurance and access to health care. Poverty is related to life circumstances of increased risk such as in urban areas with greater pollution, crowding, and risk of crime. The mortality rates for homicide illustrate the intersections of sex, race, and social class. Men are five times more likely than women to be murdered, and 87 percent of murders are committed by men. However, race and sex interact such that African American females (13%) are more likely to be murdered than are white men (8.9%), with African American males composing nearly 69 percent of all murder victims. Furthermore, murder victims are disproportionately poor (U.S. Department of Justice, 1994).

Interaction of Gender, Sexual Orientation, and Behavior in Understanding the Prevention of the Transmission of HIV/AIDS

AIDS provides another example of the importance of gender in understanding health and health risks. The risk of acquiring AIDS, which is largely transmitted by certain sexual practices or the exchange of blood via used hypodermic needles, involves a complex mix of biology, social/cultural forces, economic class, sexual orientation, and gender roles. Our social awareness of AIDS can be largely credited to the gay male community, which effectively addressed the role of particular sexual practices among gay men in the transmission of the virus and successfully campaigned for changes in sexual behavior that would reduce the transmission of the virus (Paul, Hays, & Coates, 1995). The AIDS epidemic in the United States originated in the gay male community, and consequently, HIV/AIDS in the United States has come to be known as a disease of gay men. This social perception—coupled with a more complex pattern of transmission than was originally recognized and a context of cultural and economic forces that play important roles in establishing the risk factors of HIV transmission—suggests that HIV/AIDS can best be understood by jointly examining health and gender.

Approximately 60 percent of AIDS cases in the United States occur among gay men. The death rate from AIDS, however, is increasing faster among women than among men and is the leading cause of death for women ages 25 to 44 in major urban areas (Gillespie, 1991). An examination of infection rates worldwide shows that about 60 percent of cases occur through infection via heterosexual contact, wherein the rate of infection from male to female is 17 times more likely than is the rate of infection from female to male. Thus the AIDS risks for women are substantial. About 72 percent of all women infected with HIV/AIDS are women of color, who are very likely to be poor (Land, 1994). The risk of transmission from a pregnant women to her fetus is also substantial, about 15 to 30 percent. The transmission of HIV from mother to fetus accounts for 92 percent of pediatric AIDS cases (Davis et al., 1995). Both Krieger and Fee and Litt make the point that the actual number of women with HIV or AIDS is unknown, because the diagnosis has typically been made from criteria drawn from the population of male patients and these criteria may overlook some of the manifestations of the disease for women. For example, cervical cancer is linked to AIDS for women.

Typically, women are diagnosed later in the course of the disease and consequently have a shorter life span after diagnosis than do men (Akeroyd, 1994).

Important lifestyle factors linked to the transmission of AIDS also help distinguish the risks for women versus men. One of the most important modes of transmission for women is through heterosexual sex. Poor women are at greater risk than nonpoor women for a variety of reasons: They are more likely to have sex with habitual intravenous (IV) drug users (who themselves are also more likely to have had multiple sex partners), they are more likely to be IV drug users themselves, they are more likely to have multiple sex partners for money, they are less likely to use condoms, and they may be less able to exert control in their sexual relationships with men (Hammonds, 1992). Among gay men, there have been dramatic behavioral changes in the use of preventive measures to avoid infection (for example, the rate of condom use went from 2 percent in 1981 to 62 percent in 1987), and there have been notable declines in the number of sexual partners reported by gay men (Paul et al., 1995). Behavioral changes among high-risk heterosexuals, especially IV drug users, has not occurred. It is important to identify some of the dynamics that influence sexual behavior for affected populations in order to understand how prevention efforts might be directed.

In general, both partners in a gay male relationship are at risk for HIV infection, and relationship dynamics, while variable, are not necessarily subject to the power dynamics that occur between heterosexual couples. Although gay men as a group have increased their condom use and reduced their number of sexual partners, they still vary in their adherence to practices of safer sex. Older gay men in urban gay communities have made the greatest changes in their sexual practices, whereas younger men, substance abusers, and minority men are more likely to continue risky behavior. Both effective communication skills and peer norms support the continuation of behavioral changes in sexual practices and the use of condoms (Paul et al., 1995). In their article on the impact of HIV/AIDS on the gay male community, Paul et al. discuss how the subjective meaning of sex

as an expression of affiliation, love, and commitment may limit men's willingness to use safer sex practices. These authors point to a number of responses to the AIDS crisis, such as an increased interest in long-term committed relationships, that have influenced the cultural meaning of gay male identity, sexual practices, and community responses to the epidemic. These responses may be related to shifting definitions of sexuality in the context of gay male identity strengthening the role of fidelity, which in turn influence the rate of adherence to safer sex practices.

Understanding the factors that govern sexual practices among heterosexuals is particularly important for understanding the risks faced by women, especially poor minority women, who are more likely to be at risk. According to Krieger and Fee, urban decay and circumstances that support drug addiction and prostitution are at the heart of risk factors for women. Advising these women to increase their use of condoms may be ineffective, unlike in the gay community, where this advice has been largely heeded. Just as male drug users are unlikely to use condoms, women who use drugs are unlikely to insist that their partners use condoms. Women who have sex with IV drug users or who are having sex in exchange for money or drugs are unlikely to convince their partners to use condoms. Power dynamics in sexual practices also influence exposure to risk among heterosexual college students, who evidence high levels of awareness of AIDS and its transmission, but low levels of effective behavior modification. Despite their knowledge, college students are likely to use reputation or intuition to judge whether a partner might be infected with AIDS (Bowen & Michal-Johnson, 1996). Women are more open to condom use and more aware of its role in preventing the spread of AIDS and other sexually transmitted diseases (STDs) but are often unable to persuade their partner to use a condom. Men are less willing to use condoms, are less willing to discuss the risks of STDs and AIDS, and prefer as sexual partners women who defer to their preferences. Bowen and Michal-Johnson also point out that decision making around sexual practices is influenced, often powerfully, by alcohol use and sexual scripts, both of which support impulsive, spontaneous behavior instead of attention to precautions.

This review suggests that understanding the AIDS epidemic requires attention to several interlocking factors. Gender and sexual orientation are both important in understanding sexual practices and adherence to safer sex precautions. The mechanisms of transmission have been identified, but our understanding of the psychological, cultural, social contextual, and economic factors that influence exposure to risk are less well articulated. The effectiveness of intervention depends on understanding all the forces related to the transmission and development of AIDS.

GENDER DISCRIMINATION AND HEALTH CARE

Recent feminist analyses of health care have uncovered the extent to which health care research has distorted or ignored women. The article by Litt reviews specific aspects of women's health and how diagnosis and treatment can be shaped by conditions of discrimination. Tavris (1992) provides some startling examples of biases in health care research. For example, an epidemiological study of more than 22,000 participants found that a small dose of aspirin can prevent heart attack—yet all participants in the research were male. Even more unbelievable is the research project that investigated the effects of diet on rates of breast cancer—using only male participants. In 1990, only 13 percent of the National Institute of Health (NIH) research money was devoted to research on women's health issues. After continued publicity and pressure from women's groups, Congress in 1993 mandated a $500 million women's health project to be conducted by NIH, that examines a wide range of health issues and includes at least 20 percent participation by women of color (Renzetti & Curran, 1995). Treatment of women by the medical establishment shows a similar pattern in which women's health concerns are often discounted, so that physicians spend less time, on average, with their female patients than with their male patients. Women's roles in the health care system have only recently begun to change. Women have

traditionally been the primary caregivers, that is, nurses, hospital aides, home health care workers, or within the family as caregivers, while men have been physicians and medical researchers. These traditional patterns are breaking down. By the middle of this decade, nearly equal numbers of women and men entered medical school. Although there is greater public recognition of gender bias as well as more effort to change these patterns, the legacy of gender bias has left serious gaps in our understanding of diseases and resulted in an institutionalized organization of health care that is often ill prepared to deal with women's health needs.

One important issue that arises in the discussion of gender bias is how to create a gender-fair system, how to recognize differences but not create a system that is constructed solely around differences. Tavris (1992) refers to this dilemma as the "confusion between equality and sameness"(p. 95), in which a social philosophy of equal treatment is reduced to the notion that everyone is the same. You may recognize that this notion is the same simplistic argument used against prejudice by people who claim that everyone is the same, a belief that may erase substantial differences in people's experiences, culture, social class, or race. Tavris argues that in untangling this confusion for gender we must recognize that a gender-fair system would not be premised on the belief that men and women are the same. This belief of sameness is promoted in the body of health care research that is based only on white men and in the medical schools in which little time is spent on issues related to women and women's health. Some differences must be recognized and addressed. Researchers have not included women as subjects in biomedical research because of the belief that the menstrual cycle would interact with data collection and perhaps produce variations in responses related to menstruation. This rationale is what led to the design of the research study on diet and breast cancer using only male subjects. The absurdity of this thinking should be clear, and furthermore, if menstruation interacts with diet, and this interaction is related to breast cancer in some way, certainly it would be important to understand such effects. Research has shown that the menstrual cycle interacts with the course of several diseases, including heart disease, rheumatoid arthritis, and hypertension (Tavris, 1992). In these cases, and perhaps in many more that have gone unrecognized, an emphasis on sameness clearly would be inappropriate. Equality of care would address differences where appropriate but would not place higher value on one sex or one set of experiences over another. Equality would require equal understanding of differences and commitment to equal opportunity for wellness and appropriate health care, regardless of gender, age, race, or social class.

In her article in this chapter, Litt proposes specific changes that would address gender discrimination and create greater equity in health care. Her analysis suggests that consumers and practitioners need to be aware of gender bias in decision making, in referrals, and in ceilings placed on costs for procedures likely to be needed more by males or females that have resulted from the increased use of managed care. Legal and moral issues are entangled in women's reproductive health care because the use of contraception, abortion, and reproductive technologies are as much moral and religious decisions as they are medical. Litt raises concerns about laws that limit access to abortion via controlling the information physicians are allowed or required to give their patients. Finally, Litt argues that medical research procedures need to take women's psychology into account by including women as research participants. In conclusion, equity would include access to health care, understanding health needs via adequate research, and social policies that do not control access to information or services.

GENDER ROLES, STRESS, AND HEALTH

Stress is one of the clearest examples of how one's psychological state can influence one's physical health, and it is a major health issue for both women and men. The psychological dimension of stress includes affective experiences such as frustration, depression, or anxiety. The emotions experienced in response to stress are subjective, and although there may be some commonality of experience, there is considerable variability in the degree to which an individual experiences positive or negative emotions in response to stress. Individuals also vary in the degree to which they define particular circumstances as stressful; an event such as taking an exam can create debilitating levels of anxiety for one individual, whereas another person may have a manageable rise of apprehension. The psychological experience of stress has been linked to a particular set of physiological responses that may themselves be linked to health consequences that will be discussed shortly. From what we presently know about stress, an adequate theory would incorporate individual differences in subjective emotional experience, an understanding of the relationship between the precipitating events surrounding stress responses, and the physiological mechanisms triggered by stress. We would also want to know how social categories such as gender and race would interact with the experience of stress.

Frankenhaeuser (1994) has proposed a biopsychosocial model of stress and gender that incorporates both the subjective emotional elements and social situational factors. Physiological responses to stress have been known since the turn of the century and have played a role in theories linking the psychology of emotion to the physiology of arousal. It is theorized that two hormonal responses are related to stress: cortisol mediated by the pituitary and adrenal cortex and epinephrine mediated by the sympathetic-adrenal system. Both of these hormones are used as a measure of physiological response to stress, but researchers are still investigating the specific nature of the interaction between the neurological systems that produce these two hormones in response to stress. Frankenhaeuser claims that the most widely accepted model views the relationship among the biological, psychological, and social levels of stress as *transactional*, meaning that each influence is presumed to interact with the other.

Not all stress responses are negative. The secretion of epinephrine, but not cortisol, is associated with *positive* stress responses and is related to circumstances that trigger high activity and are accompanied by positive emotions, these responses could be described as productive and happy circumstances. Situations involving low activity and negative emotion, such as high-pressure unpleasant tasks, are associated with increases in both epinephrine and cortisol. In conditions of low activity and positive emotion, described as a state of pleasant relaxation, the production of epinephrine and cortisol are low (Frankenhaeuser, 1994). According to the model presented by Frankenhaeuser, one key to distinguishing positive from negative stress is the degree of control experienced by the individual. Situations of high control, or autonomy, can lead to positive stress responses, whereas situations of low control lead to negative stress responses as measured by increases in both epinephrine and cortisol. This response to stress has been linked to negative health consequences such as heart disease. Using this model as a basis, we can understand how gender influences the interaction of stress, psychological reactions, and health.

Are Traditional Gender Roles Harmful to Your Health?

The biopsychosocial model proposed by Frankenhaeuser (1994) offers some specific ways that gender roles might be related to stress and to the health-related consequences of stress. In particular, we might consider the role of perceived control in mediating opportunities for positive versus passive responses and positive versus negative emotional dimensions of stress. Do masculine and feminine gender roles prescribe different ways of dealing with control or different responses to stressful situations? Do gender roles lead to more positive or negative emotional responses to stress? The two readings we have selected on stress and gender roles address these questions. The article by Banyard and Graham-Bermann in this chapter evaluates theories of coping with stress and concludes that the theories have been biased against coping styles more likely used by women. These two authors present a view of coping that takes into account race, social class, and power imbalances in understanding women's experiences with stress. The article by Eisler presents the theory

of male gender role strain and evaluates the relationship between male gender role and reactions to stress. He concludes that certain elements of adherence to traditional masculinity may be related to negative stress reactions but that not all men will show this pattern and not all stressful events elicit masculine-typed responses.

Both the cognitive assessment of control and one's choice of coping strategies should be related to gender roles (Eisler, 1995; Frankenhaeuser, 1994; Gallant, Coons, & Morokoff, 1994). As you might expect, women are predicted to respond to stressful events with more passive coping strategies, which are thought to be less satisfying in relieving stress-related emotions. The evidence for this prediction is conflicting and suggests that we need to carefully examine the meaning of different coping strategies. According to Banyard and Graham-Bermann, the prevailing view of effective coping with stress involves active problem-solving behavior, actions more likely to be used by men. In contrast, women tend to use coping strategies such as negotiation, forbearance, and reliance on social supports, all of which have been ignored as coping mechanisms or cast as ineffective. By recognizing that power and opportunity will influence the assessment of a stressor and choice of coping mechanism, we can see that women, especially poor women, may react to stress with fewer active solutions. In many social circumstances, women, most especially poor women, find themselves unable to utilize active problem solving, so they may be limited to passive responses. According to Banyard and Graham-Bermann, public institutions are often impervious to individual influence, leading individuals to adopt a passive response style, which may then lead to an unhealthy stress response as predicted by Frankenhaeuser's model. Banyard and Graham-Bermann argue that under such circumstances passive coping should be viewed as an accurate assessment of the fruitlessness of attempts to change an entrenched organization. They suggest that researchers should abandon the view of coping as an essentialist quality removed from an ongoing social context and instead focus on coping as a contextualized response involving gender, race, and cultural norms for behavior.

One persistent dilemma in the study of health and gender is the mortality difference between men and women. Although biological mechanisms may underlie this difference, we have seen that lifestyle factors play a large role in the early deaths of many men; high-risk behavior, addictions, and work-related risks are all disproportionately borne by men. Theorists who have addressed the relationship between the masculine gender role and health have proposed that these sorts of risks reflect gender role prescriptions for bravery, dominance, aggression, and risk taking. Other elements of the masculine gender role may also be related to the health consequences associated with stress. In our culture, masculinity is associated with controlling one's emotions as well as with being successful, both of which are associated with negative responses to stress. Eisler's article reviews the ways in which masculinity might be related to negative stress responses. Relying on Pleck's classic analysis of male gender role strain, Eisler provides a social constructionist analysis of masculinity. Several critical elements of Eisler's approach are the recognition that male gender role behavior varies across situations, that men are held to an unrealistic standard with regard to masculinity, and that some dimensions of masculinity, particularly aggressiveness and overly competitive behavior, are psychologically dysfunctional. Gender role stress is experienced when men believe that they are not living up to the culturally sanctioned prescriptions for masculinity. Part of an individual man's judgment of his own behavior will reflect his internalized identity with regard to masculinity; thus, for some men, masculinity is internalized largely as positive characteristics such as assertiveness, achievement, and self-confidence whereas for other men, negative manifestations of masculinity would include excesses of anger, lack of emotional expressiveness, denial of femininity, or risk-taking behavior.

In an attempt to measure how masculine gender role stress is related to high levels of endorsement of the negative dimensions of masculinity, Eisler developed a scale of items that measures the degree of stress elicited by a wide range of situations. Eisler's scale, known as the Male Gender Role Strain Scale

(MGRSS) differentiates the healthy elements of masculinity, such as assertiveness and self-confidence, from dimensions of masculinity that are problematic, such as anger, anxiety, and poor health habits. Five dimensions of stress-related masculinity emerge from Eisler's research using the MGRSS: physical inadequacy, emotional inexpressiveness, subordination to women, intellectual inferiority, and performance failure. High scores on these dimensions of the MGRSS are correlated with high scores on measures of anger, fear, and risk-taking behavior with low scores of emotional expressiveness. The final point discussed by Eisler is the relationship between scores on the MGRSS and negative arousal, which has been identified as a risk factor for cardiovascular disease. In a series of laboratory investigations, Eisler and his colleagues demonstrated that negative arousal is correlated with high MGRSS scores on stressful tasks typically associated with men, such as pain tolerance. Eisler's evidence suggests that coping strategies used by men are correlated with the negative dimensions of masculinity, for example, aggression and emotional repression, which may elicit negative arousal.

Gender Roles, Health, and Social Context

We noted earlier that perceived control is an important element in managing stress and that women very often find themselves in circumstances in which they cannot gain control. Men, on the other hand, may be more likely to seek to gain control or may be unwilling to concede their lack of control, and these perceptions may generate negative emotional responses. The emotional responses generated by stress may also be an issue for men because masculinity defines appropriate emotional responses narrowly, denying men emotional outlets that may help reduce stress. One area of interest in the study of stress and health is how men and women respond to employment conditions, especially to work that allows for some degree of autonomy and control versus work with very little employee control.

Frankenhaeuser (1994) presents interesting data for men and women in high-control and low-control jobs. Men and women in high-control jobs (i.e., management) showed a complex pattern of response to stress. Stress measured during the work day demonstrated no sex differences, with women showing the patterns of high arousal typical of male responses. In the evening hours after work, however, women showed evidence of continued stress as measured by stress hormones, blood pressure, and reported mood. In contrast, men in management jobs showed a decline in physiological measures of stress after work hours. In contrast to the male managers, female managers were more likely to have smaller social support networks and to perceive a lack of support for their decisions from upper level management. Apparently, the combination of work and family responsibilities causes a negative stress reaction for women, and we might speculate that this negative reaction is jointly related to the little control women have over their household responsibilities, their perceived responsibilities at work, and the meager social support network they have on the job. In chapter 11, we discussed the family division of labor and the tradition of women having responsibility for those chores that involve low control and high demands. In that context, we saw that those marriage partners who have responsibilities for day-to-day chores tend to be the least happy. It is important to note that employment per se is not responsible for the stress reactions shown by women managers; rather, it is the combination of a demanding, high-control job and household responsibilities that typically afford little control. This pattern does not hold for women in clerical jobs in the same workplace setting. These women have a more extensive social support network and do not show negative stress responses. Other research has demonstrated employment's overall health and mental health benefits for women (Rodin & Ickovics, 1990; Waldron, 1991). Although complex, these data show the importance of analyzing the combination of work and family responsibilities and the importance of women's cognitive assessment of their balance between responsibilities and perceived control in understanding health and stress.

Our analysis of stress and health is in accord with the two articles on gender role and stress. The articles suggest that essentialist arguments that treat masculinity and femininity as inherent holistic properties of individuals reduce complex interactions among individuals to simple stereotypes. Both masculine and feminine gender roles do prescribe particular emotions and behaviors to individuals based on gender identity; people, however, do not slavishly recreate these gender roles. Rather, the gendered nature of situations, one's cognitive appraisals of the situation, the behavior of others, and individual interpretations of gender role prescriptions will all affect one's response to stress. A recent research study, conducted as an ongoing analysis of people's daily life, suggests that men's and women's responses to stress are more similar than different; they both prefer actions that are directed toward others, distraction, and redefinition of the problem (Porter & Stone, 1995). The most critical differences found were for the types of situations that men and women consider stressful; women reported more family and child care stress, and men reported more work-related problems. As we have suggested throughout this book, an analysis of gender, rather than a study of sex differences per se, would be more beneficial in understanding stressful situations and distinguishing positive and negative stress responses.

GENDER, HEALTH CARE, AND SOCIAL CHANGE

The primary distinction between the health care needs of men and of women lie in the difference between mortality and morbidity. As we established early in this chapter, the mortality rates for men at every age are higher, whereas the morbidity rates for women are higher. Certainly biology is implicated in these sex differences; however, every viable explanation for these differences must consider the interaction among lifestyle factors, social and cultural roles of women and men, economic conditions, aspects of identity such as race and ethnicity, and gender along with biology. Differences such as greater risk taking by men, and perceived lack of control by women, factors that are both linked to these primary health care issues, are not biological sex differences but rather are reflections of the complex manifestations of gender in our society.

The introduction of a psychological perspective as an alternative to the solely medical model of health advocates the incorporation of a number of individual and social factors into our understanding of disease, health maintenance, illness prevention, and compliance with treatment. Masculine gender roles and feminine gender roles each apply different definitions to behaviors such as lifestyle risk, compliance, perceived stress, coping with health risk and stress, and reliance on social support systems. Also, situations vary in the degree to which they impose particular risks and the degree to which they elicit gender-typical responses. The most essential change for the medical health care system is to recognize the central role of behavior and how social roles such as gender roles influence people's behavior. A second essential change in health care is to address the need for gender equity in research. The first two readings in this chapter point out that not only have women's needs not been adequately repre-

sented in health care research but that race, ethnicity, and social class have not been fully represented either. Equity in research would adequately represent both differences and similarities by recognizing that equity does not require the assumption of sameness. A third essential change in health is to develop a more complex and nuanced model of the relationship among health, stress, and gender. Gender roles, as internalized by the individual and prescribed by social circumstances, influence the perception and interpretation of stress and the physiological and behavioral response that occurs to stress. As you read these articles on gender, health, and stress, reflect on the multiple meanings of gender that we have presented throughout this book and on the importance of integrating these meanings into understanding health and health care. Throughout your life, matters of health will be important to you and those you care about. An understanding of the relationship between psychology, social roles, and health will help you reach a better appreciation of your own health care.

NOTE

1. The view of childbirth as an illness has been strongly challenged, and many changes have been made in the last twenty years to offer a more family-centered birth experience. Nevertheless, 99 percent of births still occur in hospitals, are attended by physicians, and include the use of considerable technology and drug interventions.

REFERENCES

Akeroyd, A. (1994). Gender, race, and ethnicity in official statistics: Social categories and the HIV/AIDS "numbers game." In H. Afshar & M. Maynard (Eds.), *The dynamics of "race" and gender: Some feminist interventions* (pp. 63–81). London: Taylor & Francis.

Banyard, V. L., & Graham-Bermann, S. A. (1993). Can women cope? A gender analysis of theories of coping with stress. *Psychology of Women Quarterly, 17,* 303–318.

Bowen, S. P., & Michal-Johnson, P. (1996). Being sexual in the shadow of AIDS. In J. T. Wood (Ed.), *Gendered relationships* (pp. 177–196). Mountain View, CA: Mayfield.

Davis, S. F., Byers, R. H., Lindegren, M. L., Caldwell, M. B., Karon, J. M., & Gwinn, M. (1995). Prevalence and incidence of vertically acquired HIV infection in the United States. *Journal of the American Medical Association, 274*(12), 952–955.

Eisler, R. M. (1995). The relationship between masculine gender role stress and men's health risk: The validation of a construct. In R. F. Levant & S. Pollack (Eds.), *A new psychology of men* (pp. 207–225). New York: Basic Books.

Fox, S. (1991). *Toxic work.* Philadelphia, PA: Temple University Press.

Frankenhaeuser, M. (1994). A biopsychosocial approach to stress in women and men. In V. J. Adesso, D. M. Reddy, & R. Fleming (Eds.), *Psychological perspectives on women's health.* Washington, DC: Taylor & Francis.

Gallant, S. J., Coons, H. L., & Morokoff, P. J. (1994). Psychology and women's health: Some reflections and future directions. In V. J. Adesso, D. M. Reddy, & R. Fleming (Eds.), *Psychological perspectives on women's health.* Washington, DC: Francis & Taylor.

Gemson, D. H. (1990). Screening for breast cancer: Are physicians doing enough? *New York State Journal of Medicine, 90*, 285–286.

Gillespie, M. A. (1991, January/February). HIV: The global crisis. *MS, 1*, 17–22.

Hammonds, E. (1992). Race, sex, AIDS: The construction of "other." In M. L. Anderson & P. H. Collins (Eds.), *Race, class, and gender: An anthology* (pp. 329–340). Belmont, CA: Wadsworth.

Holden, C. (1987). Why do women live longer than men? *Science, 238*, 158–160.

Kilmartin, C. T. (1994). *The masculine self.* New York: Macmillan.

Klonoff, E. A., Landrine, H., & Scott, J. (1995). Double jeopardy: Ethnicity and gender in health research. In H. Landrine (Ed.), *Bringing cultural diversity to feminist psychology* (pp. 335–360). Washington, DC: American Psychological Association.

Krieger, N., & Fee, E. (1994). Man-made medicine and women's health: The biopolitics of sex/gender and race/ethnicity. *International Journal of Health Services, 24*, 265–283.

Land, H. (1994, June). AIDS and women of color. *Families in Society*, pp. 355–361.

Litt, I. F. (1993). Health issues for women in the 1990s. In S. Matteo (Ed.), *American women in the 90s* (pp. 139–157). Boston: Northeastern University Press.

Muller, C. F. (1990). *Health care and gender.* New York: Russell Sage Foundation.

Paul, J. P., Hays, R. B., & Coates, T. J. (1995). The impact of the HIV epidemic on U.S. gay male communities. In A. R. D'Augelli & C. J. Patterson (Eds.), *Lesbian, gay, and bisexual identities over the lifespan: Psychological perspectives* (pp. 347–397). Washington, DC: American Psychological Association.

Porter, L. S., & Stone, A. A. (1995). Are there really gender differences in coping? A reconsideration of previous data and results from a daily study. *Journal of Social and Clinical Psychology, 14*, 184–202.

Renzetti, C. M., & Curran, D. J. (1995). *Women, men, and society* (3rd ed.). Boston: Allyn & Bacon.

Rodin, J., & Ickovics, J. R. (1990). Women's health. *American Psychologist, 45*, 1018–1034.

Strickland, B. B. (1988). Sex-related differences in health and illness. *Psychology of Women Quarterly, 12*, 381–389.

Tavris, C. (1992). *Mismeasure of women.* New York: Simon & Schuster.

U.S. Department of Health and Human Services. (1993). *Health of the United States, 1993.* Washington, DC: U.S. Government Printing Office.

U.S. Department of Justice, F. B. I. (1994). *Uniform crime reports for the United States, 1993.* Washington, DC: U.S. Government Printing Office.

Waldron, I. (1991). Effects of labor force participation on sex differences in mortality and morbidity. In M. Frankenhaeuser, U. Lundberg, & M. Chesney (Eds.), *Women, work, and health: Stress and opportunities.* New York: Plenum.

Man-Made Medicine and Women's Health: The Biopolitics of Sex/Gender and Race/Ethnicity

NANCY KRIEGER AND ELIZABETH FEE

Glance at any collection of national health data for the United States, whether pertaining to health, disease, or the health care system, and several obvious features stand out (1–5). First, we notice that most reports present data in terms of race, sex, and age. Some races are clearly of more interest than others. National reports most frequently use racial groups called "white" and "black," and increasingly, they use a group called "Hispanic." Occasionally, we find data on Native Americans, and on Asians and Pacific Islanders. Whatever the specific categories chosen, the reports agree that white men and women, for the most part, have the best health, at all ages. They also show that men and women, across all racial groups, have different patterns of disease: obviously, men and women differ for conditions related to reproduction (women, for example, do not get testicular cancer), but they differ for many other conditions as well (for example, men on average have higher blood pressure and develop cardiovascular disease at an earlier age). And, in the health care sector, occupations, just like diseases, are differentially distributed by race and sex.

All this seems obvious. But it isn't. We know about race and sex divisions because this is what our society considers important. This is how we classify people and collect data. This is how we organize our social life as a nation. This is therefore how we structure our knowledge about health and disease. And this is what we find important as a subject of research (6–9).

It seems so routine, so normal, to view the health of women and men as fundamentally different, to consider the root of this difference to be biological sex, and to think about race as an inherent, inherited characteristic that also affects health (10). The work of looking after sick people follows the same categories. Simply walk into a hospital and observe that most of the doctors are white men, most of the registered nurses are white women, most of the kitchen and laundry workers are black and Hispanic women, and most of the janitorial staff are black and Hispanic men. Among the patients, notice who has appointments with private clinicians and who is getting care in the emergency room; the color line is obvious. Notice who provides health care at home: wives, mothers and daughters. The gender line at home and in medical institutions is equally obvious (11–15).

These contrasting patterns, by race and sex, are longstanding. How do we explain them? What kinds of explanations satisfy us? Some are comfortable with explanations that accept these patterns as natural, as the result of natural law, as part of the natural order of things. Of course, if patterns are that way by nature, they cannot be changed. Others aim to understand these patterns precisely in order to change them. They look for explanations suggesting that these patterns are structured by convention, by discrimination, by the politics of power, and by unreasonable law. These patterns, in other words, reflect the social order of people.

In this chapter, we discuss how race and sex became such all-important, self-evident categories in 19th and 20th century biomedical thought and practice. We examine the consequences of these categories for our knowledge about health and for the provision of health care. We then consider alterative approaches to studying race/ethnicity, gender, and health. And we address these issues with reference to a typically suppressed and repressed category: that of social class.

THE SOCIAL CONSTRUCTION OF "RACE" AND "SEX" AS KEY BIOMEDICAL TERMS AND THEIR EFFECT ON KNOWLEDGE ABOUT HEALTH

In the 19th century, the construction of "race" and "sex" as key biomedical categories was driven by social struggles over human inequality. Before the Civil War, the dominant understanding of race was as a natural/theological category—black-white differences were innate and reflected God's will (16–19). These differences were believed to be manifest in every aspect of the body, in sickness and in health. But when abolitionists began to get the upper hand in moral and theological arguments, proponents of slavery appealed to science as the new arbiter of racial distinction.

In this period, medical men were beginning to claim the mantle of scientific knowledge and assert their right to decide controversial social issues (20–22). Recognizing the need for scientific authority, the state of Louisiana, for example, commissioned one prolific proponent of slavery, Dr. Samuel Cartwright, to prove the natural inferiority of blacks, a task that led him to detail every racial difference imaginable—in texture of hair, length of bones, vulnerability to disease, and even color of the internal organs (23–25). As the Civil War changed the status of blacks from legal chattel to bona fide citizens, however, medical journals began to question old verities about racial differences and, as importantly, to publish new views of racial similarities (26, 27). Some authors even attributed black-white differences in health to differences in socioeconomic position. But by the 1870s, with the destruction of reconstruction, the doctrine of innate racial distinction again triumphed. The scientific community once again deemed "race" a fundamental biological category (28–32).

Theories of women's inequality followed a similar pattern (33–36). In the early 19th century, traditionalists cited scripture to prove women's inferiority. These authorities agreed that Eve had been formed out of Adam's rib and that all women had to pay the price of her sin—disobeying God's order, seeking illicit knowledge from the serpent, and tempting man with the forbidden apple. Women's pain in childbirth was clear proof of God's displeasure.

When these views were challenged in the mid-19th century by advocates of women's rights and proponents of liberal political theory, conservatives likewise turned to the new arbiters of knowledge and sought to buttress their position with scientific facts and medical authority (37, 38). Biologists busied themselves with measuring the size of women's skulls, the length of their bones, the rate of their breathing, and the number of their blood cells. And considering all the evidence, the biologists concluded that women were indeed the weaker sex (39–41).

Agreeing with this stance, medical men energetically took up the issue of women's health and equality (42–45). They were convinced that the true woman was by nature sickly, her physiological systems at the mercy of her ovaries and uterus. Because all bodily organs were interconnected, they argued, a woman's monthly cycle irritated her delicate nervous system and her sensitive, small, weak brain. Physicians considered women especially vulnerable to nervous ailments such as neurasthenia and hysteria. This talk of women's delicate constitutions did not, of course, apply to slave women or to working-class women—but it was handy to refute the demands of middle-class women whenever they sought to vote or gain access to education and professional careers. At such moments, many medical men declared the doctrine of separate spheres to be the ineluctable consequence of biology.

At the same time, 19th century medical authorities began to conceptualize class as a natural, biological distinction. Traditional, pre-scientific views held class hierarchies to be divinely ordained; according to the more scientific view that emerged in the early 19th century, class position was determined by innate, inherited ability. In both cases, class was perceived as an essentially stable, hierarchical ranking. These discussions of class usually assumed white or Western European populations and often applied only to males within those populations.

With the impact of the industrial revolution, classes took on a clearly dynamic character. As landowners invested in canals and railroads, as merchants became capitalist entrepreneurs, and as agricultural workers were transformed into an industrial proletariat, the turbulent transformation of the social order provoked new understandings of class relationships (46). The most developed of these theories was that of Karl Marx, who emphasized the system of classes as a social and economic formation and stressed the contradictions between different class interests (47). From this point onward, the very idea of social class in many people's minds implied a revolutionary threat to the social order.

In opposition to Marxist analyses of class, the theory of Social Darwinism was formulated to suggest that the new social inequalities of industrial society reflected natural law (48–51). This theory was developed in the midst of the economic depression of the 1870s, at a time when labor struggles, trade union organizing, and early socialist movements were challenging the political and economic order. Many scientists and medical men drew upon Darwin's idea of "the struggle for survival," first expressed in the *Origin of the Species* in 1859 (52), to justify social inequality. They argued that those on top, the social elite, must by definition be the "most fit" because they had survived so well. Social hierarchies were therefore built on and reflected real biological differences. Poor health status simultaneously was sign and proof of biological inferiority.

By the late 19th century, theories of race, gender, and class inequality were linked together by the theory of Social Darwinism, which promised to provide a scientific basis for social policy (48–51). In the realm of race, for example, proponents of Social Darwinism blithely predicted that the "Negro question" would soon resolve itself—the "Negro" would naturally become extinct, eliminated by the inevitable workings of "natural selection" (29, 53). Many public health officers—particularly in the southern states—agreed that "Negroes" were an inherently degenerate, syphilitic, and tubercular race, for whom public health interventions could do little (54–57). Social Darwinists also argued that natural and sexual selection would lead to increasing differentiation between the sexes (34, 48, 58). With further evolution, men would become ever more masculine and women ever more feminine. As proof, they looked to the upper classes, whose masculine and feminine behavior represented the forefront of evolutionary progress.

Over time, the Social Darwinist view of class gradually merged into general American ideals of progress, meritocracy, and success through individual effort. According to the dominant American ideology, individuals were so mobile that fixed measures of social class were irrelevant. Such measures were also un-American. Since the Paris Commune, and especially since the Bolshevik revolution, discussions of social class in the United States were perceived as politically threatening. Although fierce debates about inequality continued to revolve around the axis of nature versus nurture, the notion of class as a social relationship was effectively banished from respectable discourse and policy debate (48, 59). Social position was once again equated only with rank, now understood as socioeconomic status.

In the early 20th century, Social Darwinists had considerable influence in shaping public views and public policy (48, 59–64). They perceived two new threats to American superiority: the massive tide of immigration from eastern and southern Europe, and the declining birth rate—or "race suicide"—among American white women of Anglo-Saxon and Germanic descent. Looking to the fast-developing field of genetics, now bolstered by the rediscovery of Gregor Mendel's laws and T. H. Morgan's fruit fly experiments (65–68), biological determinists regrouped under the banner of eugenics. Invoking morbidity and mortality data that showed a high rate of tuberculosis and infectious disease among the immigrant poor (69–71), they declared "ethnic" Europeans a naturally inferior and sickly stock and thus helped win passage of the Immigration Restriction Act in 1924 (72–74). This legislation required the national mix of immigrants to match that entering the United States in the early 1870s, thereby severely curtailing immigration of racial and ethnic groups deemed inferior. "Race/ethnicity," construed as a biological reality, became ever more entrenched as the *explanation* of racial/ethnic differences in disease; social explanations were seen as the province of scientifically illiterate and naive liberals, or worse, socialists and Bolshevik provocateurs.

Other developments in the early 20th century encouraged biological explanations of sex differences in disease and in social roles. The discovery of the sex chromosomes in 1905 (75–77) reinforced the idea that gender was a fundamental biological trait, built into the genetic constitution of the body. That same year, Ernest Starling coined the term "hormone" (78) to denote the newly characterized chemical messengers that permitted one organ to control—at a distance—the activities of another. By the mid-1920s, researchers had isolated several hormones integral to reproductive physiology and popularized the notion of "sex hormones" (79–83). The combination of sex chromosomes and sex hormones was imbued with almost magical powers to shape human behavior in gendered terms; women were now at the mercy of their genetic limitations and a changing brew of hormonal imperatives (84, 85). In the realm of medicine, researchers turned to sex chromosomes and hormones to understand cancers of the uterus and breast and a host of other sex-linked diseases (86–90); they no longer saw the need to worry about environmental influences. In the workplace, of course, employers said that sex chromosomes and hormones dictated which jobs women could—and could not—perform (45, 91, 92). This in turn determined the occupational hazards to which women would be exposed—once again, women's health and ill-health were really a matter of their biology.

Within the first few decades of the 20th century, these views were institutionalized within scientific medicine and the new public health. At this time, the training of physicians and public health practitioners was being recast in modern, scientific terms (93–95). Not surprisingly, biological determinists views of racial/ethnic and sex/gender differences became a natural and integral part of the curriculum, the research agenda, and medical and public health practice. Over time, ethnic differences in disease among white European groups were downplayed and instead, the differences between whites and blacks, whites and Mexicans, and whites and Asians were emphasized. Color was now believed to define distinct biological groups.

Similarly, the sex divide marked a gulf between two completely disparate groups. Within medicine, women's health was relegated to obstetrics and gynecology; within public health, women's health needs were seen as being met by maternal and child health programs (8, 45, 96). Women were perceived as wives and mothers; they were important for childbirth, childcare, and domestic nutrition. Although no one denied that some women worked, women's occupational health was essentially ignored because women were, after all, only temporary workers. Outside the specialized realm of reproduction, all other health research concerned men's bodies and men's diseases. Reproduction was so central to women's biological existence that women's non-reproductive health was rendered virtually invisible.

Currently, it is popular to argue that the lack of research on white women and on men and women in nonwhite racial/ethnic groups resulted from a perception of white men as the norm (97–99). This interpretation, however, is inaccurate. In fact, by the time that researchers began to standardized methods for clinical and epidemiologic research, notions of difference were so firmly embedded that whites and nonwhites, women and men, were rarely studied together. Moreover, most researchers and physicians were interested only in the health status of whites and, in the case of women, only in their reproductive health. They therefore used white men as the research subjects of choice for all health conditions other than women's reproductive health and paid attention to the health status of nonwhites only to measure degrees of racial difference. For the most part, the health of women and men of color and the nonreproductive health of white women were simply ignored. It is critical to read these omissions as evidence of a logic of difference rather than as an assumption of similarity.

This framework has shaped knowledge and practice to the present. In the United States, vital statistics present health information in terms of race and sex and age, conceptualized only as biological variables—ignoring the social dimensions of gender and ethnicity. Data on social class are not collected. At the same time, public health professionals are unable adequately to explain or to change inequalities in health between men and women and between diverse racial/ethnic groups. We now face the question: Is there any alternative way of understanding these population patterns of health and disease?

ALTERNATIVE WAYS OF STUDYING RACE, GENDER, AND HEALTH: SOCIAL MEASURES FOR SOCIAL CATEGORIES

The first step in creating an alternative understanding is to recognize that the categories we traditionally treat as simply biological are in fact largely social. The second step is to realize we need social concepts to understand these social categories. The third step is to develop social measures and appropriate strategies for a new kind of health research (10).

With regard to race/ethnicity, we need to be clear that "race" is a spurious biological concept (100–102). Although historical patterns of geographic isolation and migration account for differences in the distribution of certain genes, genetic variation within so-called racial groups far exceeds that across groups. All humans share approximately 95 percent of their genetic makeup (100, p. 155). Racial/ethnic differences in disease thus require something other than a genetic explanation.

Recognizing this problem, some people have tried to substitute the term "ethnicity" for "race" (103, 104). In the public health literature, however, "ethnicity" is rarely defined. For some, it apparently serves as a polite way of referring to what are still conceptualized as "racial"/biological differences. For others, it expresses a new form of "cultural" determinism, in which ethnic differences in ways of living are seen as autonomous "givens" unrelated to the social status of particular ethnic groups within our society (105, 106). This cultural determinism makes discrimination invisible and can feed into explanations of health status as reductionist and individualistic as those of biological determinism.

For a different starting point, consider the diverse ways in which racism operates, at both an institutional and interpersonal level (107–109). Racism is a matter of economics, and it is also more than eco-

nomics. It structures living and working conditions, affects daily interactions, and takes its toll on people's dignity and pride. All of this must be considered when we examine the connection between race/ethnicity and health.

To address the economic aspects of racism, we need to include economic data in all studies of health status (110, 111). Currently, our national health data do not include economic information—instead, racial differences are often used as indicators of economic differences. To the extent that economics are taken into account, the standard approach assumes that differences are either economic or "genetic." So, for those conditions where racial/ethnic differences persist even within economic strata—hypertension and preterm delivery, for example—the assumption is that something biological, something genetic, is at play. Researchers rarely consider the noneconomic aspects of racism or the ways in which racism continues to work within economic levels.

Some investigators, however, are beginning to consider how racism shapes people's environments. Several studies, for example, document the fact that toxic dumps are most likely to be located in poor neighborhoods and are disproportionately located in poor neighborhoods of color (112–114). Other researchers are starting to ask how people's experience of and response to discrimination may influence their health (115–118). A recent study of hypertension, for example, found that black women who responded actively to unfair treatment were less likely to report high blood pressure than women who internalized their responses (115). Interestingly, the black women at highest risk were those who reported *no* experiences of racial discrimination.

Countering the traditional practice of always taking whites as the standard of comparison, some researchers are beginning to focus on other racial/ethnic groups to better understand why, within each of the groups, some are at higher risk than others for particular disease outcomes (119–121). They are considering whether people of color may be exposed to specific conditions that whites are not. In addition to living and working conditions, these include cultural practices that may be positive as well as negative in their effects on health. Some studies, for example, point to the importance of black churches in providing social support (122–124). These new approaches break with monolithic assumptions about what it means to belong to a given racial/ethnic group and consider diversity *within* each group. To know the color of a person's skin is to know very little.

It is equally true that to know a person's sex is to know very little. Women are often discussed as a single group defined chiefly by biological sex, members of an abstract, universal (and implicitly white) category. In reality, we are a mixed lot, our gender roles and options shaped by history, culture, and deep divisions across class and color lines. Of course, it is true that women, in general, have the capacity to become pregnant, at least at some stages of our lives. Traditionally, women as a group are defined by this reproductive potential. Usually ignored are the many ways that gender as a social reality gets into the body and transforms our biology—differences in childhood expectations about exercise, for example, affect our subsequent body build (38, 125).

From a health point of view, women's reproductive potential does carry the possibility of specific reproductive ills ranging from infertility to preterm delivery to cervical and breast cancer. These reproductive ills are not simply associated with the biological category "female," but are differentially experienced according to social class and race/ethnicity. Poor women, for example, are much more likely to suffer from cervical cancer (119, 126). By contrast, at least among older women, breast cancer is more common among the affluent (126, 127). These patterns, which at times can become quite complex, illustrate the general point that, even in the case of reproductive health, more than biological sex is at issue. Explanations of women's reproductive health that ignore the social patterning of disease and focus only on endogenous factors are thus inadequate.

If we turn to those conditions that afflict both men and women—the majority of all diseases and health problems—we must keep two things simultaneously in mind. First are the differences and similarities among diverse groups of women; second are the differences and similarities between women and men.

For a glimpse at the complexity of disease patterns, consider the example of hypertension (128, 129). As we mentioned, working-class and poor women are at greater risk than affluent women; black women, within each income level, are more likely to be hypertensive than white women (5). The risks of Hispanic women vary by national origin: Mexican women are at lowest risk, Central American women at higher risk, and Puerto Rican and Cuban women at the highest risk (130, 131). In what is called the "Hispanic paradox," Mexican-American women have a higher risk profile than Anglo-American women, yet experience lower rates of hypertension (132). To further complicate the picture, the handful of studies of Japanese and Chinese women in the United States show them to have low rates, while Filipino women have high rates, almost equal to those of African Americans (130, 133, 134). Rates vary across different groups of Native American women; those who live in the Northern plains have higher rates than those in the Southwest (130, 135). From all this, we can conclude that there is enormous variation in hypertension rates among women.

If we look at the differences between women and men, we find that men in each racial/ethnic group have higher rates of hypertension than women (129). Even so, the variation among women is sufficiently great that women in some racial/ethnic groups have higher rates than men in other groups. Filipina women, for example, have higher rates of hypertension than white men (5, 133). Obviously, the standard biomedical categories of race and sex cannot explain these patterns. If we want to understand hypertension, we will have to understand the complex distribution of disease among real women and men; these patterns are not merely distracting details but the proper test of the plausibility of our hypotheses.

As a second example, consider the well-known phenomenon of women's longer life expectancy. This difference is common to all industrialized countries, and amounts to about seven years in the United States (136, 137). The higher mortality of men at younger ages is largely due to higher accident rates, and at older ages, to heart disease.

The higher accident rates of younger men are not accidental. They are duet to more hazardous occupations, higher rates of illicit drug and alcohol use, firearms injuries, and motor vehicle crashes—hazards related to gender roles and expectations (136, 137). The fact that men die earlier of heart disease—the single most common cause of death in both sexes—may also be related to gender roles. Men have higher rates of cigarette smoking and fewer sources of social support, suggesting that the masculine ideal of the Marlboro man is not a healthy one. Some contend that women's cardiovascular advantage is mainly biological, due to the protective effect of their hormone levels (138). Interestingly, however, a study carried out in a kibbutz in Israel, where men and women were engaged in comparable activities, found that the life expectancy gap was only four and a half years—just over half the national average (139). While biological differences between men and women now receive much of the research attention, it is important to remember that men are gendered beings too.

Clearly, our patterns of health and disease have everything to do with how we live in the world. Nowhere is this more evident than in the strong social class gradients apparent in almost every form of morbidity and mortality (110, 140–143). Yet here the lack of information and the conceptual confusion about the relationship between social class and women's health is a major obstacle. As previously noted, in this country, we have no regular method of collecting data on socioeconomic position and health. Even if we had such data, measures of social class generally assume male heads of households and male patterns of employment (111, 144). This, indeed, is one of the failures of class analyses—that they do not deal adequately with women (144–147).

Perhaps the easiest way to understand the problems of class measurements and women's health is briefly to mention the current debates in Britain, a country that has long collected social class data (148, 149). Men and unmarried women are assigned a social class position according to their employment; married women, however, are assigned a class position according to the employment of their husbands. As British feminist researchers have argued, this tra-

ditional approach obscures the magnitude of class differences in women's health (149). Instead, they are proposing measures of household class that take into account the occupations of both women and their husbands, and their ownership of household assets.

Here in the United States, we have hardly any research on the diverse measures of social class in relation to women's health. Preliminary studies suggest we also would do well to distinguish between individual and household class (150, 151). Other research shows that we can partly overcome the absence of social class information in U.S. medical records by using census data (126, 152). This method allows us to describe people in terms of the socioeconomic profile of their immediate neighborhood. When coupled with individual measures of social class, this approach reveals, for example, that working-class women who live in working-class neighborhoods are somewhat more likely to have high blood pressure than working-class women who live in more affluent neighborhoods (152). We thus need conceptually to separate three distinct levels at which class operates: individual, household, and neighborhood.

As a final example of why women's health cannot be understood without reference to issues of sex/gender, race/ethnicity, and social class, consider the case of AIDS (153–155). The definition of disease, the understanding of risk, and the approach to prevention are shaped by our failure fully to grasp the social context of disease. For the first decade, women's unique experiences of AIDS were rendered essentially invisible. The first definition of AIDS was linked to men, because it was perceived to be a disease of gay men and those with a male sex-linked disorder, hemophilia. The very listing of HIV-related diseases taken to characterize AIDS was a listing based on the male experience of infection. Only much later, after considerable protest by women activists, were female disorders—such as invasive cervical cancer—made part of the definition of the disease (156, 157).

Our understanding of risk is still constrained by the standard approaches. AIDS data are still reported only in terms of race, sex, and mode of transmission; there are no data on social class (158). We know, however, that the women who have AIDS are overwhelmingly women of color. As of July 1993, of the nearly 37,000 women diagnosed with AIDS, over one half were African American, another 20 percent were Hispanic, 25 percent were white, and about 1 percent were Asian, Pacific Islander, or Native American (158). What puts these women at risk? It seems clear that one determinant is the missing variable, social class. Notably, the women at highest risk are injection drug users, the sexual partners of injection drug users, and sex workers (154). The usual listing of behavioral and demographic risk factors, however, fails to capture the social context in which the AIDS epidemic has unfolded. Most of the epidemiological accounts are silent about the blight of inner cities, the decay of urban infrastructure under the Reagan-Bush administrations, unemployment, the drug trade, prostitution, and the harsh realities of everyday racism (159, 160). We cannot gain an adequate understanding of risk absent a real understanding of people's lives.

Knowledge of what puts women at risk is of course critical for prevention. Yet, just as the initial definitions of AIDS reflected a male-gendered perspective, so did initial approaches to prevention (161). The emphasis on condoms assumed that the central issue was knowledge, not male-female power relations. For women to use condoms in heterosexual sex, however, they need more than bits of latex; they need male assent. The initial educational materials were created without addressing issues of power; they were male-oriented and obviously white—in both the mode and language of presentation. AIDS programs and services, for the most part, still do not address women's needs, whether heterosexual, bisexual, or lesbian. Pregnant women and women with children continue to be excluded from most drug treatment programs. And when women become sick and die, we have no remotely adequate social policies for taking care of the families left behind.

In short, our society's approach to AIDS reflects the larger refusal to deal with the ways in which sex/gender, race/ethnicity, and class are inescapably intertwined with health. This refusal affects not only what we know and what we do about AIDS, but also the other issues we have mentioned—hypertension, cancer, life expectancy—and many we have not (162). As we have tried to argue, the issues of women's health cannot be understood only in biological terms, as simply the ills of the female of the species. Women and men are different, but we are also similar—and we both are divided by the social relations of class and race/ethnicity. To begin to understand how our social constitution affects our health, we must ask, repeatedly, what is different and what is similar across the social divides of gender, color, and class. We cannot assume that biology alone will provide the answers we need; instead, we must reframe the issues in the context of the social shaping of our human lives—as both biological creatures and historical actors. Otherwise, we will continue to mistake—as many before us have done—what is for what must be, and leave unchallenged the social forces that continue to create vast inequalities in health.

REFERENCES

1. National Center for Health Statistics. *Health, United States, 1991.* DHHS Pub. No. (PHS) 92–1232. U.S. Public Health Service, Hyattsville, Md., 1992.

2. National Center for Health Statistics. *Vital Statistics of the United States—1988, Vol. I, Natality.* DHHS Pub. No. (PHS) 90–1100. U.S. Government Printing Office, Washington, D.C., 1990.

3. National Center for Health Statistics. *Vital Statistics of the United States—1987. Vol. II, Mortality, Part A.* DHHS Pub. No. (PHS) 90–1101. U.S. Government Printing Office, Washington, D.C., 1990.

4. National Center for Health Statistics. *Vital Statistics of the United States—1988. Vol. II, Mortality, Part B.* DHHS Pub. No. (PHS) 90–1102. U.S. Government Printing Office, Washington, D.C., 1990.

5. U.S. Department of Health and Human Services. *Health Status of Minorities and Low-Income Groups,* Ed. 3. U.S. Government Printing Office, Washington, D.C., 1991.

6. Krieger, N. The making of public health data: Paradigms, politics, and policy. *J. Public Health Policy* 13:412–427, 1992.

7. Navarro, V. Work, ideology, and science: The case of medicine. In *Crisis, Health, and Medicine: A Social Critique,* edited by V. Navarro, pp. 142–182. Tavistock, New York, 1986.
8. Fee, E. (ed.). *Women and Health: The Politics of Sex in Medicine.* Baywood, Amityville, N.Y., 1983.
9. Tesh, S. *Hidden Arguments: Political Ideology and Disease Prevention Policy.* Rutgers University Press, New Brunswick, N.J. 1988.
10. Krieger, N., et al. Racism, sexism, and social class: Implications for studies of health, disease, and well-being. *Am. J. Prev. Med.,* 9(suppl 2): 82–122, 1993.
11. Butter, I., et al. *Sex and Status: Hierarchies in the Health Workforce.* American Public Health Association, Washington, D.C., 1985.
12. Sexton, P. C. *The New Nightingales: Hospital Workers, Unions, New Women's Issues.* Enquiry Press, New York, 1982.
13. Melosh, B. *The Physician's Hand: Work, Culture and Conflict in American Nursing.* Temple University Press, Philadelphia, 1982.
14. Wolfe, S. (ed.). *Organization of Health Workers and Labor Conflict.* Baywood, Amityville, N.Y., 1978.
15. Feldman, P. H., Sapienza, A. M., and Kane, N. M. *Who Cares for Them? Workers in the Home Care Industry.* Greenwood Press, New York, 1990.
16. Krieger, N. Shades of difference: Theoretical underpinnings of the medical controversy on black/white differences in the United States, 1830–1870. *Int. J. Health Serv.* 17: 256–278, 1987.
17. Stanton, W. *The Leopard's Spots: Scientific Attitudes Towards Race in America, 1815–59.* University of Chicago Press, Chicago, 1960.
18. Stepan, N. *The Idea of Race in Science, Great Britain, 1800–1860.* Archon Books, Hamden, Conn., 1982.
19. Jordan, W. D. *White Over Black: American Attitudes toward the Negro, 1550–1812.* University of North Carolina Press, Chapel Hill, 1968.
20. Rosenberg, C. E. *No Other Gods: On Science and American Social Thought.* Johns Hopkins University Press, Baltimore, Md., 1976.
21. Daniels, G. H. The process of professionalization in American science: The emergent period, 1820–1860. *Isis* 58: 151–166, 1967.
22. Rothstein, W. G. *American Physicians in the 19th Century: From Sects to Science.* Johns Hopkins University Press, Baltimore, Md., 1972.
23. Cartwright, S. A. Report on the diseases and physical peculiarities of the Negro race. *New Orleans Med. Surg. J.* 7: 691–715, 1850.
24. Cartwright, S. A. Alcohol and the Ethiopian: Or, the moral and physical effects of ardent spirits on the Negro race, and some accounts of the peculiarities of that people. *New Orleans Med. Surg. J.* 15: 149–163, 1858.
25. Cartwright, S. A. Ethnology of the Negro or prognathous race—A lecture delivered November 30, 1857, before the New Orleans Academy of Science. *New Orleans Med. Surg. J.* 15: 149–163, 1858.
26. Reyburn, R. Remarks concerning some of the diseases prevailing among the Freed-people in the District of Columbia (Bureau of Refugees, Freedmen and Abandoned Lands). *Am. J. Med. Sci.* (n.s.) 51: 364–369, 1866.
27. Byron, J. Negro regiments—Department of Tennessee. *Boston Med. Surg. J.* 69: 43–44, 1863.
28. Foner, E. *Reconstruction: America's Unfinished Revolution, 1863–1877.* Harper & Row, New York City, 1988.
29. Haller, J. S. Jr. *Outcasts from Evolution: Scientific Attitudes of Racial Inferiority, 1859–1900.* University of Illinois Press, Urbana, 1971.
30. Stocking, G. W. *Race, Culture, and Evolution: Essays in the History of Anthropology.* Free Press, New York, 1968.
31. Lorimer, D. *Colour, Class and the Victorians.* Holmes & Meier, New York, 1978.
32. Gamble, V. N. (ed.). *Germs Have No Color Line: Blacks and American Medicine, 1900–1940.* Garland, New York, 1989.
33. Barker-Benfield, G. J. *The Horrors of the Half-Known Life: Male Attitudes toward Women and Sexuality in Nineteenth-Century America.* Harper & Row, New York, 1976.
34. Fee, E. Science and the woman problem: Historical perspectives. In *Sex Differences: Social and Biological Perspectives,* edited by M. S. Teitelbaum, pp. 175–223. Anchor/Doubleday, New York, 1976.
35. Jordanova, L. *Sexual Visions: Images of Gender in Science and Medicine between the Eighteenth and Twentieth Centuries.* University of Wisconsin Press, Madison, 1989.
36. Ehrenreich, B., and English, D. *Complaints and disorders: The Sexual Politics of Sickness.* The Feminist Press, Old Westbury, N.Y., 1973.
37. Russell, C. E. *Sexual Science: The Victorian Construction of Womanhood.* Harvard University Press, Cambridge, Mass., 1989.
38. Hubbard, R. *The Politics of Women's Biology.* Rutgers University Press, New Brunswick, N.J., 1990.
39. Fee, E. Nineteenth-century craniology: The study of the female skull. *Bull. Hist. Med.* 53: 415–433, 1979.
40. Smith-Rosenberg, C., and Rosenberg, C. E. The female animal: Medical and biological views of woman and her role in 19th century America. *J. Am. Hist.* 60: 332–356, 1979.
41. Gould, S. J. *The Mismeasure of Man.* W. W. Norton, New York, 1981.
42. Smith-Rosenberg, C. Puberty to menopause: The cycle of femininity in nineteenth-century America. *Feminist Stud.* 1: 58–72, 1973.
43. Smith-Rosenberg, C. *Disorderly Conduct: Visions of Gender in Victorian America.* Knopf, New York, 1985.
44. Haller, J. S., and Haller, R. M. *The Physician and Sexuality in Victorian America.* University of Illinois Press, Urbana, 1974.

45. Apple, R. D. (ed.). *Women, Health, and Medicine in America: A Historical Handbook.* Rutgers University Press, New Brunswick, N.J., 1990.

46. Williams, R. *Culture & Society: 1780–1950,* revised edition. Columbia University Press, New York, 1983 [1958].

47. Marx, K. *Capital,* vol. I. International Publishers, New York, 1967 [1867].

48. Hostadter, R. *Social Darwinism in American Thought.* Beacon Press, Boston, 1955.

49. Young, R. M. *Darwin's Metaphor: Nature's Place in Victorian Culture.* Cambridge University Press, Cambridge, U.K., 1985.

50. Kevles, D. J. *In the Name of Eugenics: Genetics and the Uses of Human Heredity.* Knopf, New York, 1985.

51. Chase, A. *The Legacy of Malthus: The Social Costs of the New Scientific Racism.* Knopf, New York, 1977.

52. Darwin, C. *On the Origin of Species by Means of Natural Selection, or the Preservation of Favoured Races in the Struggle for Life.* Murray, London, 1859.

53. Anderson, M. J. *The American Census: A Social History.* Yale University Press, New Haven, Conn., 1988.

54. Hoffman, F. L. *Race Traits and Tendencies of the American Negro.* American Economic Association, New York, 1896.

55. Harris, D. Tuberculosis in the Negro. *JAMA* 41: 827, 1903.

56. Allen, L. C. The Negro health problem. *Am. J. Public Health* 5: 194, 1915.

57. Beardsley, E. H. *A History of Neglect: Health Care for Blacks and Mill Workers in the Twentieth-Century South.* University of Tennessee Press, Knoxville, 1987.

58. Geddes, P., and Thompson, J. A. *The Evolution of Sex.* Walter Scott, London, 1889.

59. Ludmerer, K. M. *Genetics and American Society: A Historical Appraisal.* Johns Hopkins University Press, Baltimore, Md., 1972.

60. Higham, J. *Strangers in the Land: Patterns of American Nativism, 1860–1925.* Rutgers University Press, New Brunswick, N.J., 1955.

61. Haller, M. H. *Fugenics: Hereditarian Attitudes in American Thought.* Rutgers University Press, New Brunswick, N.J., 1963.

62. Pickens, D. K. *Eugenics and the Progressives.* Vanderbilt University Press, Nashville, Tenn., 1968.

63. King, M., and Ruggles, S. American immigration, fertility, and race suicide at the turn of the century. *J. Interdisciplinary Hist.* 20: 347–369, 1990.

64. Degler, C. N. *In Search of Human Nature: The Decline and Revival of Darwinism in American Social Thought.* Oxford University Press, Oxford, 1991.

65. Allen, G. E. *Life Science in the Twentieth Century.* Cambridge University Press, Cambridge, U.K., 1978.

66. Castle, W. E. The beginnings of Mendelism in America. In *Genetics in the Twentieth Century,* edited by L. C. Dunn, pp. 59–76. Macmillan, New York, 1951.

67. Wilkie, J. S. Some reasons for the rediscovery and appreciation of Mendel's work in the first years of the present century. *Br. J. Hist. Sci.* 1: 5–18, 1962.

68. Morgan, T. H. *The Theory of the Gene.* Yale University Press, New Haven, 1926.

69. Kraut, A. M. *The Huddled Masses: The Immigrant in American Society, 1800–1921.* Harlan Davison, Arlington Heights, Ill., 1982.

70. Stoner, G. W. Insane and mentally defective aliens arriving at the Port of New York. *N. Y. Med. J.* 97: 957–960, 1913.

71. Solis-Cohen, S. T. The exclusion of aliens from the United States for physical defects. *Bull. Hist. Med.* 21: 33–50, 1947.

72. Ludmerer, K. Genetics, eugenics, and the Immigration Restriction Act of 1924. *Bull. Hist. Med.* 46: 59–81, 1972.

73. Barkan, E. Reevaluating progressive eugenics: Herbert Spencer Jennings and the 1924 immigration legislation. *J. Hist. Biol.* 24: 91–112, 1991.

74. Kraut, A. M. Silent travelers: Germs, genes, and American efficiency, 1890–1924. *Soc. Sci. Hist.* 12: 377–393, 1988.

75. Farley, J. *Gametes & Spores: Ideas About Sexual Reproduction, 1750–1914.* Johns Hopkins University Press, Baltimore, Md., 1982.

76. Allen, G. Thomas Hunt Morgan and the problem of sex determination. *Proc. Am. Philos. Soc.* 110: 48–57, 1966.

77. Brush, S. Nettie M. Stevens and the discovery of sex determination by chromosomes. *Isis* 69: 163–172, 1978.

78. Starling, E. The Croonian lectures on the chemical correlation of the functions of the body. *Lancet* 2: 339–341, 423–425, 501–503, 579–583, 1905.

79. Lane-Claypon, J. E., and Starling, E. H. An experimental enquiry into the factors which determine the growth and activity of the mammary glands. *Proc. R. Soc. London [Biol.]* 77: 505–522, 1906.

80. Marshall, F. A. *The Physiology of Reproduction.* Longmans, Green and Co., New York, 1910.

81. Oudshoorn, N. Endocrinologists and the conceptualization of sex. *J. Hist. Biol.* 23: 163–187, 1990.

82. Oudshoorn, N. On measuring sex hormones: The role of biological assays in sexualizing chemical substances. *Bull. Hist. Med.* 64: 243–261, 1990.

83. Borrell, M. Organotherapy and the emergence of reproductive endocrinology. *J. Hist. Biol.* 18: 1–30, 1985.

84. Long, D. L. Biology, sex hormones and sexism in the 1920s. *Philos. Forum* 5: 81–96, 1974.

85. Cobb, I. G. *The Glands of Destiny (A Study of the Personality).* Macmillan, New York, 1928.

86. Allen, E. (ed.). *Sex and Internal Secretions: A Survey of Recent Research.* Williams & Wilkins, Baltimore, Md., 1939.

87. Frank, R. *The Female Sex Hormone.* Charles C. Thomas, Springfield, Ill., 1929.

88. Lathrop, A. E. C., and Loeb, L. Further investigations of the origin of tumors in mice. III. On the part played by internal secretions in the spontaneous development of tumors. *J. Cancer Res.* 1: 1–19, 1916.

89. Lane-Claypon, J. E. *A Further Report on Cancer of the Breast, With Special Reference to its Associated Antecedent Conditions,* Reports on Public Health and Medical Subjects, No. 32. Her Majesty's Stationery Office, London, 1926.

90. Wainwright, J. M. A comparison of conditions associated with breast cancer in Great Britain and America. *Am. J. Cancer* 15: 2610–2645, 1931.

91. Chavkin, W. (ed.). *Double Exposure: Women's Health Hazards on the Job and at Home.* Monthly Review Press, New York, 1984.

92. Ehrenreich, B., and English, D. *For Her Own Good: 150 Years of the Experts Advice to Women.* Anchor Books, Garden City, N.Y., 1979.

93. Starr, P. *The Social Transformation of American Medicine.* Basic Books, New York, 1982.

94. Fee, E. *Disease and Discovery: A History of the Johns Hopkins School of Hygiene and Public Health, 1916–1939.* Johns Hopkins University Press, Baltimore, Md., 1987.

95. Fee, E., and Acheson, R. M. (eds.). *A History of Education in Public Health: Health that Mocks the Doctors' Rules.* Oxford University Press, Oxford, 1991.

96. Meckel, R. *Save the Babies: American Public Health Reform and the Prevention of Infant Mortality, 1850–1920.* Johns Hopkins University Press, Baltimore, Md., 1990.

97. Rodin, J., and Ickovics, J. R. Women's health: Review and research agenda as we approach the 21st century. *Am. Psychol.* 45: 1018–1034, 1990.

98. Healy, B. Women's health, public welfare. *JAMA* 266: 566–568, 1991.

99. Kirchstein, R. L. Research on women's health. *Am. J. Public Health* 81: 291–293, 1991.

100. Lewontin, R. *Human Diversity.* Scientific American Books, New York, 1982.

101. King, J. C. *The Biology of Race.* University of California Press, Berkeley, 1981.

102. Cooper, R., and David, R. The biological concept of race and its application to epidemiology. *J. Health Polit. Policy Law* 11: 97–116, 1986.

103. Cooper, R. Celebrate diversity—or should we? *Ethnicity Dis.* 1: 3–7, 1991.

104. Crews, D. E., and Bindon, J. R. Ethnicity as a taxonomic tool in biomedical and biosocial research. *Ethnicity Dis.* 1: 42–49, 1991.

105. Mullings, L. Ethnicity and stratification in the urban United States. *Ann N.Y. Acad. Sci.* 318: 10–22, 1978.

106. Feagin, J. R. *Racial and Ethnic Relations,* Ed. 3. Prentice-Hall, Englewood Cliffs, N.J., 1989.

107. Feagin, J. R. The continuing significance of rare: Anti-black discrimination in public places. *Am. Sociol. Rev.* 56: 101–116, 1991.

108. Essed, P. *Understanding Everyday Racism: An Interdisciplinary Theory.* Sage Publications, Newbury Park, Calif., 1991.

109. Krieger, N., and Bassett, M. The health of black folk: Disease, class, and ideology in science. *Monthly Rev.* 38: 74–85, 1986.

110. Navarro, V. Race or class versus race and class: Mortality differentials in the United States. *Lancet* 2: 1238–1240, 1990.

111. Krieger, N., and Fee, E. What's class got to do with it? The state of health data in the United States today. *Socialist Rev.* 23: 59–82, 1993.

112. Polack, S., and Grozuczak, J. *Reagan, Toxics and Minorities: A Policy Report.* Urban Environment Conference, Washington, D.C., 1984.

113. Commission for Racial Justice, United Church of Christ. *Toxic Wastes and Race in the United States: A National Report on the Racial and Socioeconomic Characteristics of Communities with Hazardous Waste Sites.* United Church of Christ, New York, 1987.

114. Mann, E. *L.A.'s Lethal Air: New Strategies for Policy, Organizing, and Action.* Labor/Community Strategy Center, Los Angeles, 1991.

115. Krieger, N. Racial and gender discrimination: Risk factors for high blood pressure? *Soc. Sci. Med.* 30: 1273–1281, 1990.

116. Armstead, C. A., et al. Relationship of racial stressors to blood pressure and anger expression in black college students. *Health Psychol.* 8: 541–556, 1989.

117. James, S. E., et al. John Henryism and blood pressure differences among black men. II. The role of occupational stressors. *J. Behav. Med.* 7: 259–275, 1984.

118. Dressler, W. W. Social class, skin color, and arterial blood pressure in two societies. *Ethnicity Dis.* 1: 60–77, 1991.

119. Fruchter, R. G., et al. Cervix and breast cancer incidence in immigrant Caribbean women. *Am. J. Public Health* 80: 722–724, 1990.

120. Kleinman, J. C., Fingerhut, L. A., and Prager, K. Differences in infant mortality by race, nativity, and other maternal characteristics. *Am. J. Dis. Child.* 145: 194–199, 1991.

121. Cabral, H., et al. Foreign-born and US-born black women: Differences in health behaviors and birth outcomes. *Am. J. Public Health* 80: 70–72, 1990.

122. Taylor, R. J., and Chatters, L. M. Religious life. In *Life in Black America,* edited by J. S. Jackson, pp. 105–123. Sage, Newbury Park, Calif., 1991.

123. Livingston, I. L., Levine, D. M., and Moore, R. D. Social integration and black interracial variation in blood pressure. *Ethnicity Dis.* 1: 135–149, 1991.

124. Eng, E., Hatch, J., and Callan, A. Institutionalizing social support through the church and into the community. *Health Ed. Q.* 12: 81–92, 1985.

125. Lowe, M. Social bodies: The interaction of culture and women's biology. In *Biological Woman—The Convenient Myth,* edited by R. Hubbard, M. S. Henefin, and B. Fried, pp. 91–116. Schenkman, Cambridge, Mass., 1982.

126. Devesa, S. S., and Diamond, E. L. Association of breast cancer and cervical cancer incidence with income and education among whites and blacks. *J. Natl. Cancer Inst.* 65: 515–528, 1980.

127. Krieger, N. Social class and the black/white crossover in the age-specific incidence of breast cancer: A study linking census-derived data to population-based registry records. *Am. J. Epidemiol.* 131: 804–814, 1990.

128. Krieger, N. The influence of social class, race and gender on the etiology of hypertension among women in the United States. In *Women, Behavior, and Cardiovascular Disease,* proceedings of a conference sponsored by the National Heart, Lung, and Blood Institute, Chevy Chase, Md., September 25–27, 1991. U.S. Government Printing Office, Washington, D.C., 1994, in press.

129. U.S. Department of Health and Human Services. *Report of the Secretary's Task Force on Black & Minority Health, Volume IV: Cardiovascular and Cerebrovascular Disease, Part 2.* Washington, D.C., 1986.

130. Martinez-Maldonado, M. Hypertension in Hispanics, Asians and Pacific Islanders, and Native Americans. *Circulation* 83: 1467–1469, 1991.

131. Caralis, P. U. Hypertension in the Hispanic-American population. *Am. J. Med.* 88(Suppl. 3b): 9s–16s, 1990.

132. Haffner, S. M., et al. Decreased prevalence of hypertension in Mexican-Americans. *Hypertension* 16: 255–232, 1990.

133. Stavig, G. R., Igra, A., and Leonard, A. R. Hypertension and related health issues among Asians and Pacific Islanders in California. *Public Health Rep.* 103: 28–37, 1988.

134. Angel, A., Armstrong, M. A., and Klatsky, A. L. Blood pressure among Asian Americans living in Northern California. *Am J. Cardiol.* 54: 237–240, 1987.

135. Alpert, J. S., et al. Heart disease in Native Americans. *Cardiology* 78: 3–12, 1991.

136. Waldron, I. Sex differences in illness, incidence, prognosis and mortality: Issues and evidence. *Soc. Sci. Med.* 17: 1107–1123, 1983.

137. Wingard, D. L. The sex differential in morbidity, mortality, and lifestyle. *Annu. Rev. Public Health* 5: 433–458, 1984.

138. Gold, E. (ed.). *Changing Risk of Disease in Women: An Epidemiological Approach.* Colbamore Press, Lexington, Mass., 1984.

139. Leviatan, V., and Cohen, J. Gender differences in life expectancy among kibbutz members. *Soc. Sci. Med.* 21: 545–551, 1985.

140. Syme, S. L., and Berkman, L. Social class: Susceptibility and sickness. *Am. J. Epidemiol.* 104: 1–8, 1976.

141. Antonovsky, A. Social class, life expectancy and overall mortality. *Milbank Mem. Fund Q.* 45: 31–73, 1967.

142. Townsend, P., Davidson, N., and Whitehead, M. *Inequalities in Health: The Black Report and The Health Divide.* Penguin, Harmondsworth, U.K., 1988.

143. Marmot, M. G., Kogevinas, M., and Elston, M. A. Social/economic status and disease. *Annu. Rev. Public Health* 8: 111–135, 1987.

144. Roberts, H. (ed.). *Women's Health Counts.* Routledge, London, 1990.

145. Dale, A., Gilbert, G. N., and Arber, S. Integrating women into class theory. *Sociology* 19: 384–409, 1985.

146. Duke, V., and Edgell, S., The operationalisation of class in British sociology: Theoretical and empirical considerations. *Br. J. Sociol.* 8: 445–463, 1987.

147. Charles, N. Women and class—A problematic relationship. *Socil. Rev.* 38: 43–89, 1990.

148. Morgan. M. Measuring social inequality: Occupational classifications and their alternatives. *Community Med.* 5: 116–124, 1983.

149. Moser, K. A., Pugh, H., and Goldblatt, P. Mortality and the social classification of women. In *Longitudinal Study: Mortality and Social Organization, Series I S, No. 6,* edited by P. Goldblatt, pp. 146–162. Her Majesty's Stationery Office, London, 1990.

150. Krieger, N. Women and social class: A methodological study comparing individual, household, and census measures as predictors of black/white differences in reproductive history. *J. Epidemiol. Community Health* 45: 35–42, 1991.

151. Ries, P. Health characteristics according to family and personal income, United States. *Vital Health Stat.* 10(147). DHHS Pub. No. (PHS) 85–1575. National Center for Health Statistics. U.S. Government Printing Office, Washington, D.C., 1985.

152. Krieger, N. Overcoming the absence of socioeconomic data in medical records: Validation and application of a census-based methodology. *Am. J. Public Health* 82: 703–710, 1992.

153. Carovano, K. More than mothers and whores: Redefining the AIDS prevention needs of women. *Int. J. Health Serv.* 21: 131–142, 1991.

154. PANOS Institute. *Triple Jeopardy: Women & AIDS.* Panos Publications, London, 1990.

155. Anastos, K., and Marte, C. Women—The missing persons in the AIDS epidemic. *HealthPAC,* Winter 1989, pp. 6–13.

156. Centers for Disease Control. 1993. Revised classification system for HIV infection and expanded surveillance case definition for AIDS among adolescents and adults. *MMWR* 41: 961–962, 1992.

157. Kanigel, R. U.S. broadens AIDS definition: Activists spur change by Centers for Disease Control. *Oakland Tribune,* January 1, 1993, p. A1.

158. Centers for Disease Control and Prevention. *HIV/AIDS Surveillance Rep.* 5: 1–19, July 1993.

159. Drucker, E. Epidemic in the war zone: AIDS and community survival in New York City. *Int. J. Health Serv.* 20: 601–616, 1990.

160. Freudenberg, N. AIDS prevention in the United States: Lessons from the first decade. *Int. J. Health Serv.* 20: 589–600, 1990.

161. Fee, E., and Krieger, N. Thinking and rethinking AIDS: Implications for health policy. *Int. J. Health Serv.* 23: 323–346, 1993.

162. Fee, E., and Krieger, N. Understanding AIDS: Historical interpretations and the limits of biomedical individualism. *Am. J. Public Health* 83: 1477–1486, 1993.

CHECKPOINTS

1. Krieger and Fee challenge the essentialist tradition of categorizing people into racial and sex groups for purposes of examining the results of biomedical research. They argue that this categorizing obscures the importance of social context, especially socioeconomic class, in understanding health risks.

2. Krieger and Fee use the examples of hypertension, accident rates, and AIDS to illustrate complex interactions among race, sex, social class, and gender roles in understanding health risks.

To prepare for reading the next section, think about this question:

1. In your experience, have women and men been treated equally by the medical establishment?

WOMEN'S HEALTH AND DISCRIMINATION

Health Issues for Women in the 1990s

IRIS F. LITT

HEALTH STATUS OF WOMEN

Women are traditionally viewed as being healthier than men because they live longer, although it is not clear how much of this advantage is due to biologic or social and cultural influences.

While it is true that the average life expectancy of women is seven years longer than that of men,[1] there are many illnesses that are unique to women or affect them more, and others that are more serious in women or for which there are different risk factors or interventions.[2] Moreover, *quantity* of life is different from *quality* of life and it is now apparent that the majority of women who live to old age do so in a state of dependency and disability because of chronic diseases that are more common in women.

As disabled elderly, women are less likely to have a spouse or children available to care for them and are more apt to need long-term health care than are men. Accordingly, women's health must be examined not merely as the absence of disease but in the context of the definition of health, given by the World Health Organization, "the achievement of optimal physical, psychological, economic and social well-being."[3]

Changing social roles and responsibilities interact with biologic features to affect the health and well-being of women. Women have always had dual roles, as wives and mothers. Increasingly, through the 1980s and early 1990s, they have entered the paid labor force and assumed additional responsibilities that carry the risk of additional health problems. Currently, 52 percent of women are employed outside the home. While the majority work in the service fields, there is evidence of diversification and some upward mobility. Consequently, women's work roles are emerging as one of the most important factors concerning their health status.[4]

In this chapter, we will examine the causes, preventive measures, and possible remedies of women's health problems, and consider the implications of these factors for public policy.

TABLE 1   Leading Causes of Death for Women, 1988

Cause of Death	Number of Deaths
1. Heart disease	379,754
(28 percent of all deaths in women)	
2. Cancer	226,960
Lung	55,000 ±
Breast	44,500 ±
Colorectal	13,000 ±
Ovarian	12,500
Endometrial	5,500
Cervical	4,500
3. Cerebrovascular disease	90,758
4. Pneumonia/influenza	40,828
5. Chronic obstructive pulmonary disease	33,914
6. Accidents	31,279
Automotive	
Domestic violence	
7. Diabetes	23,393
8. Atherosclerosis	13,759
9. Septicemia	11,793
10. Nephritis	11,512

Modified from Pharmaceutical Manufacturers Association, *New Medicines in Development for Women* (Washington, D.C.: Pharmaceutical Manufacturers Association, 1991).

GENDER DIFFERENCES IN HEALTH STATUS

Health status is generally monitored by mortality and morbidity statistics. *Mortality* describes the causes of death and *morbidity* describes how frequently a reportable disease occurs in a population.

Mortality

As seen in Table 1, which outlines the ten leading causes of death for women in 1988, 28 percent of deaths among women were caused by heart disease, previously considered almost exclusively a disease of men. In fact, men have heart attacks at an earlier age than women, largely because of the protective effect of estrogen on women. This protection is lost after the menopause unless replacement estrogen is taken.

Thus, for both women and men over age 65, the three leading causes of death are the same: heart disease, cancer, and stroke.

The types of cancer differ between men and women, with the most conspicuous differences related to cancers of the reproductive organs. Contrary to general impressions, however, "female" cancers are no longer common types of cancer in women. Since 1986, there have been more deaths in women from lung cancer than from breast cancer,[5] and more deaths from cancer of the colon and rectum than from cancers of the ovaries, uterus, or cervix. The fact that mortality data are usually collected at a single point in time means that these figures may mask other dramatic changes that have occurred recently with regard to death in women. For example, the death rate from lung cancer in women has increased sixfold in the past

TABLE 2   Prevalence of Health Problems

Health Problem	Prevalence
Gynecologic	
Cancers	
Endometrial	33,000/yr
Cervical	13,000/yr
Ovarian	20,700/yr
Infections	
Pelvic inflammatory disease	(750,000 in 1990)
Human papilloma virus	15% to 40% of women
Vulvovaginal candidiasis	13 million
Amenorrhea	3%
Infertility	4.9 million (15 to 44 years)
Endometriosis	10% to 20% (15 to 44 years)
Postmenopausal symptoms	6.2 million
Breast	176,000

SOURCE: Pharmaceutical Manufacturers Association, *New Medicines in Development for Women* (Washington, D.C.: Pharmaceutical Manufacturers Association, 1991).

30 years. From 1980 to 1986, the rate of lung cancer increased steadily from 28.4 to 37.2 per 100,000 per year for females.[6] During the same period of time, there was a slight fall in the rate of lung cancer for men, suggesting that factors like environmental pollution are not to blame for this increase. Clearly, it is the increase in smoking among women during this period that is responsible for this devastating finding.

Another worrisome mortality statistic is that deaths from AIDS among women are increasing at a much faster rate than in men. It is now the seventh leading cause of death among women of all races in the 25 to 34 year age group and the fourth leading cause of death for black women.[7] In New York City, it is now the leading cause of death among women ages 25 to 44 years.[8] The true number of women with AIDS is, as yet, unknown because the official criteria for diagnosing the disease have been established on the basis of male symptoms. As a result, cervical cancer, a common cause of death among women with AIDS, is not listed in criteria for its diagnosis. The disparity in

rates of increase reflects, in part, the fact that the incidence of AIDS in the heterosexual community has been grossly underestimated in the United States.

Morbidity

Table 2 describes those health problems that are unique to women. These obviously reflect biologic differences between the sexes and focus on those illnesses of reproductive organs and characteristics. The health problems listed in Table 3 are less obvious, but equally important, because they represent the illnesses that are currently recognized as being more common in women than in men. For these, there is no simple biologic explanation for their predilection for women. Research is needed to better understand this phenomenon and eventually to reduce the disproportionate burden of illness faced by women.

Morbidity data are considered in terms of incidence and prevalence. The *incidence* of an illness is its rate of occurrence in a given period of time, usu-

---

TABLE 3   **Health Problems That Are More Common in Women Than in Men**

Health Problems	Number of Women (%)
Musculo-skeletal-connective tissue	37 million
Osteoporosis	20 million (80)
Juvenile rheumatoid arthritis	61,000 (86)
Osteoarthritis	11.7 million (74)
Rheumatoid arthritis	1.5 million (71)
Systemic lupus erythematosus	450,000 (90)
Cardiovascular	
Hyperlipidemia	(82% of women aged 45 to 74 years vs. 71% of men)
Hypertension	16 million (58)
Kidney/urologic	
Incontinence	9.6 million (80)
Neurologic	
Migraine	12 million (70)
Glaucoma	1.5 million (67)
Psychiatric	
Depression	(9.75% of women vs. 4.7% of men)
Bulimia	7 million (87)
Respiratory	
Acute bronchitis	5.3 million (60.5)
Asthma	6.02 million (53)
Influenza	66 million (54)

SOURCE: Pharmaceutical Manufacturers Association, *New Medicines in Development for Women* (Washington, D.C.: Pharmaceutical Manufacturers Association, 1991).

---

ally a year. The *prevalence* is the total number of cases in the population under study at any one point in time. These data are tracked by government agencies interested in public health, as well as by categorical private professional or lay organizations, such as the American Cancer Society, for example. Health-care delivery systems and insurance companies also provide morbidity data. The reliability of these figures depends upon how accurately and conscientiously organizations and agencies report the illnesses they see. While government agencies are subject to penalties for the failure of responsible individuals or institutions to report such figures, other agencies are not. Because not all conditions can be tracked, these data are necessarily limited to those deemed sufficiently important to be reported for public-health or other reasons.

Some data of potential importance to understanding women's health status may, under the current system, be difficult to access. For example, it would not be possible to find the numbers of women with premenstrual syndrome (PMS), eating disorders, or osteoporosis, or who use oral contraceptives, and so on. Even for those conditions that *are* reportable, it is not possible to know how many women have more than one condition. Moreover, since women are less often insured and less likely to receive health care when ill, their illnesses may never get diagnosed and never enter any data base. In addition, because more data are reported from public institutions than from private doctors' offices (particular about sensitive issues such as sexually transmitted diseases and suicide attempts), poor women are more likely to be overrepresented in some data bases. Since there are more poor women reported than affluent, the recorded data about the health of women may be skewed by this reporting bias.

Neither mortality nor morbidity data adequately address the issue of quality of life. Clearly, what might be a relatively minor ailment for an individual with support and resources can become a major problem for a poor single mother or an elderly woman caring for her disabled spouse. In addition, since the quality of a younger woman's life is often determined by the number and spacing of her children, the availability of safe and effective birth control is an important health issue that is not reflected in any data base.

DETERMINANTS OF WOMEN'S HEALTH STATUS

While our knowledge is limited by the inadequacy and accuracy of the methods used to collect information about women's health status, it has grown considerably during the late 1980s and early 1990s. We are now aware that it is an oversimplification to consider the health status of women as if they are a homogenous group. In fact, their health status varies in relation to their socioeconomic status, ethnicity, age, and occupation, as well as being influenced by biologic factors.

Biology

It is clear that the biologic differences between men and women will, in some way, influence their respective health status. But, in addition to illnesses of reproductive organs or hormones, there are other more subtle differences between women and men. These include certain genetic diseases or features that only occur in women (e.g., Turner's syndrome). Other genetically determined diseases are more common in women than men (among these are diabetes mellitus and systemic lupus erythematosus).

Biologic differences are found in terms of physical growth and development. For example, when puberty is completed, women are generally shorter, have more body fat, wider hips, smaller hearts, less lung capacity, looser ligaments, fewer red blood cells, and, therefore, less oxygen-carrying capacity than males. These

differences, for example, affect their athletic capabilities, giving them an advantage in swimming and a disadvantage in long-distance running. These differences may also have less apparent effects. For example, the increase in fatness of puberty in females is normal and healthy, but it interacts with the present societal emphasis on thinness as the supposed ideal for the female form. Clearly, the high rates of dieting and of unhealthy eating behaviors among adolescent women in our society have their origins in this biologic fact.

Socioeconomic Status

Poverty affects health in direct and indirect ways. Not having enough money for the necessities of life like food and shelter will directly impact on health by causing malnutrition, or increasing susceptibility to infectious diseases, exposure, and overcrowding. In the United States, poverty is also associated with receipt of little or no preventive or therapeutic health care. As a result, the poor suffer disproportionately from preventable diseases, have higher infant mortality rates, more disability from chronic illness, and more accidents and violence.[9] Because many women live in poverty, they bear a disproportionate share of these health burdens.

For women, however, having financial resources does not guarantee good health care. Even with private health insurance, it is often difficult to get payment for preventive procedures, like mammograms, or for psychiatric care, which is typically capped on these policies. Moreover, the inadequate research on women's health (as discussed later in this chapter) and the biases among physicians about the health status of women contribute to poorer health care for women of all socioeconomic strata.

Ethnicity

In addition to genetically transmitted diseases that may vary with ethnicity, this variable may affect health in other ways. In our society, however, it is often difficult to disentangle the effects of ethnicity from those of poverty, which for most minority groups in the United States are intertwined.

Language is often a barrier to receiving health care. For example, one study found that Hispanic women who did not speak English were less likely to get a mammogram for early detection of breast cancer than were those who spoke English.[10]

For women, ethnic differences have been reported in the incidence of AIDS (more common in blacks and Latinas), eating disorders (more common in whites), homicides (higher rate in blacks), sexually transmitted diseases (more common in blacks), osteoporosis (less common in blacks than whites), and so on.

Age

During adolescence, gender differences in health emerge that result from the biologic events of puberty, from different psychosocial experiences, and from the interactions of both.

The pubertal differences between the sexes were discussed earlier. Those differences are also responsible for the development of a higher incidence of thyroid disease and scoliosis, as well as the more obvious breast and gynecologic disorders in female adolescents.

Among the psychosocial problems, the higher incidence of eating disorders and depression that continue throughout the life span of women are first seen in the mid-adolescent years. For example, suicidal depression at some time has been reported in 30 percent of adolescent women vs. 10 percent of their male peers. A recent survey of 12- to 14-year-olds showed that 1 in 11 females had already experienced suicidal thoughts, compared with 1 in 25 males.[11]

Physicians begin to prescribe more mood-altering medications, such as tranquilizers and sedatives, to women than men from the time patients are 13 years of age.[12] Drug abuse has, on the other hand, been traditionally viewed as a problem of male adolescents. While it remains true that there is more drug and alcohol use and abuse among teen males, the gender gap is narrowing.[13] In fact, there are now more female adolescent new smokers than males. Because of its significant role in the causation of life-threatening disease in later life, the increase in smoking by adolescent females, which now exceeds that for males, must be regarded as a critical area for preventive research.

Similarly, although there are more violent deaths among male than female adolescents, homicide is one of five leading causes of death among adolescent women. The incidence of sexual, emotional, and physical abuse is much higher in teenaged women. Females are four times more likely to be sexually abused than males (a rate of 3.5/1000).[14]

Pregnancy during adolescence is associated with serious socioeconomic, as well as health, consequences for women and their children. Because of political and religious pressures in the United States, it is difficult for minors to obtain contraception without parental consent. For this reason, the United States has the highest rate of adolescent pregnancy among industrialized countries of the world. A related problem is the high incidence of sexually transmitted disease among adolescents, responsible for acute illness and, often, for sterility in women.

For adult women, health problems often include some of those seen among adolescents, such as problems related to reproductive function, but there is an increased incidence of collagen-vascular diseases, cancers, and diseases of the endocrine or hormonal system at this life stage. For the nearly 50 percent of women who have entered the paid labor force, these preexisting health problems are further complicated by problems related to occupational status. Exposure to industrial hazards, complications of work requiring repetitive motion and use of equipment designed for and by men, and psychologic pressures of environments that may discriminate against women are currently some of the additional health-risk factors for women. In fact, one study found that a woman's satisfaction with her primary work role is the most significant determinant of her health status.[15] Another report shows that occupation is one of the most important causes of premature death among women.[16] Violence has become one of the leading causes of death and disability for women under the age of 34 years, with homicide becoming one of the top five.

For middle-aged women, there is increased health risk from the changes that relate to the menopause. Coronary artery disease, strokes, breast cancer, lung cancer and cancer of the colon and rectum, and the beginning of osteoporosis become significant issues at

TABLE 4   Estimated Cost of Women's Health Problems

Health Problem	Estimated Cost
Arthritis	$36 billion/yr
Osteoporosis	>$10 billion for care of fractures (1987)
Cancers	$104 billion (1990)[1]
Atherosclerosis	$34.2 billion (1987, direct costs)
Congestive heart failure	$4.7 billion (1987, direct costs)
Coronary artery disease	$14 billion (1987, direct costs)
Hypertension	$13.7 billion (1991, estimate)
Stroke	$25 billion/yr
Urinary tract infections	$4.4 billion/yr[2]
Alzheimer's disease	$88 billion (1985)
Migraine	$50 billion +/yr (workdays lost and medical expenses)
Eye disorders	$16 billion +/yr
Depression	$27 billion +/yr[3]
Asthma	$6.8 billion (1986)[4]
Chronic obstructive pulmonary disease	$10.2 billion (1988)
Diabetes	$20.4 billion/yr

[1]Approximately ⅓ for direct medical costs, <⅔ for mortality costs, and ⅒ for lost productivity/morbidity
[2]Includes physician, hospitalization, and lost productivity
[3]15% of this is the amount lost due to suicides
[4]⅓ of this is for direct medical costs
Modified from Pharmaceutical Manufacturers Association, *New Medicines in Development for Women* (Washington, D.C.: Pharmaceutical Manufacturers Association, 1991).

this time in life. One of the most urgent areas for additional research is the prevention of these life-threatening diseases. The role of estrogen-replacement therapy and the prevention or cessation of smoking are two critical factors that require further study.

Older women are at increased risk for a variety of life-threatening diseases, such as congestive heart failure, stroke, myocardial infarction (heart attacks), hypertension (high blood pressure), and chronic obstructive pulmonary disease. The most serious threat to the quality of their lives, however, relates to their increased risk for development of chronic illnesses, such as Alzheimer's disease, parkinsonism, and the sensory deficits such as blindness and deafness. Their increased risk for arthritis and osteoporosis (fractures) further limits their mobility and health status.

Cost

It has been estimated by the Department of Commerce and the Department of Health and Human Services that health-care spending cost $738 billion in 1991. They predict that it will rise to $817 billion in 1992, thus constituting 14 percent of the GNP.[17] This percentage has been rising at a rate of 1 percent each year since 1989. For comparative purposes, the cost of the national health insurance plan for Canada is only 8.6 percent of the GNP. It is reasonable to estimate that health care for women represents about one-half to three-quarters of the total expenditure (based on the 1988 figure of $464 billion given in Table 4). As seen in Table 4, although the total cost of health care for women currently exceeds that spent on men, relatively little is expended on research or prevention efforts. Until this fact is acknowledged and remedied, women will continue to require a disproportionately large share of the health-care dollar in the United States while experiencing a poorer quality of life because of their higher illness burden.

Barriers to Improved Health for Women

Access to Care   Access to health care, according to Pechansky and Thomas,[18] consists of the following five relationships:

1. Availability: the relationship between supply and need
2. Accessibility: the relationship between location and population
3. Affordability: the relationship between service prices and client resources
4. Accommodation: the relationship between organization of the resources and use patterns of clients
5. Acceptability: the relationship between provider and practice characteristics and client attitudes, preferences, and expectations

For each of these relationships, there is evidence that access is problematic for women patients. Most significant among the problems of access, however, is that of cost.

Thirty-seven million Americans have no health insurance and an additional 7,000,000 to 10,000,000 have inadequate coverage.[19] Because insurance coverage is often linked to employment and because women are more likely to be part-time employees, temporary or service workers, or unemployed heads of households, they number prominently among the uninsured. Under the current system in the United States, therefore, in which access to health care is based largely on private insurance provided through employment, women are at a clear disadvantage. In an analysis provided by Hartmann of the system of employer-provided insurance coverage, it was shown that during the 1980s there was a 3 percent decrease in the proportion of married couples with children who had health insurance through their employers, but the drop for single mothers was 10 percent.[20] By 1987, 50 percent of single mothers had no health insurance for their children. Including the insurance provided by Medicaid, which serves twice as many women as men, children of single mothers are twice as likely not to have health insurance as children of married couples. In addition to the obvious psychological implications of lack of health coverage for their children, children's illness is a leading cause of parents' absence from work, a particular problem and reason for job loss for single parents, most of whom are women.

There are many adverse effects of being uninsured, the most studied of which is its impact on pregnancy outcome. Prenatal care is the most important determinant of good pregnancy outcome, including a decrease in stillbirths, miscarriages, prematurity, and maternal anemia. Pregnancy outcome is notoriously worse for adolescents than for older women, one explanation for which is the fact that adolescents get prenatal care late or not at all. Contributing to this problem is the fact that the majority of adolescent females lack health-insurance coverage for maternity-related care, either because of exclusions in their parents' policies, the necessity to notify policy holders and thus violate the adolescent's right to confidentiality, or the absence of any form of health insurance.[21] The cost to society of providing care to sick and premature infants born to mothers unable to access prenatal care for financial reasons far exceeds that which would be required to provide the needed coverage.

Access may also be affected by ethnicity and socioeconomic status. It is obviously difficult to separate the effects of poverty and of acculturation from that of lack of health insurance, but one study showed that Hispanic women who were predominately Spanish speaking and lacked health insurance were one-quarter as likely as English-speaking Hispanic women (who were twice as likely to have health insurance) to have had a mammogram for the early detection of breast cancer.[22]

Any measures that enhance women's employability are important steps toward improving their health status insofar as they enhance the likelihood that they will have access to health insurance. A major step toward achieving this goal is the passage of a universal national health plan, provided there is adequate support for the health needs of women and provided there is nonpoliticized choice of and access to the full range of health-care options and protection of the rights that women require in U.S. society.

HEALTH-CARE RATIONING

When health resources are scarce, decisions about their allocation are necessary. As health cost containment becomes critical, as it is in the early 1990s, there is increasing pressure to limit expenditures. The few data available suggest that women suffer under conditions of health-care rationing. For example, one criterion for the decision to undertake an expensive medical procedure is age. Often, the younger patient will be given preference in allocation of costly or limited resources, such as transplantation. Age is, therefore, one important limiting factor in medical decision making. Because women are disproportionately represented among the elderly, this criterion has a greater impact in disqualifying women than men from care.[23]

Age is not the only explanation, however, for the gender inequality in distribution of costly medical interventions. One study of patients with end-stage kidney disease showed that a female patient had 25 percent less chance than a male with the same disease to receive a kidney transplant.[24] In fact, among those in the 46- to 60-year age category, a woman's chance was half that of a man. In addition, despite the fact that the risk of having coronary artery disease is only three times higher for men than women, women were 6.5 times less likely to be referred by their physicians for cardiac catheterization than men with the same clinical symptoms and findings. Women are less likely to be referred for cardiac bypass surgery when their coronary artery disease is diagnosed, largely because of data showing that they have a greater chance

of dying following the procedure. This poorer outcome results from the fact that women are typically operated on when their disease has progressed further than is the case for men,[25] and should not be used as a reason to limit women's access to this procedure.

Traditional social-value judgments also enter into these decisions. "A general perception that men's social role obligations or their contributions to society are greater than women's may fuel these disparities."[26] Viewed as the primary financial supports of their families, our society has typically placed a greater value on the lives of men and appears more willing to pay to support their health-care costs.

LEGAL AND POLICY ISSUES THAT AFFECT HEALTH-CARE DELIVERY TO WOMEN

Reproductive Rights

Political and religious impediments to access to the necessary range of reproductive options represents one of the most serious health problems facing women in the United States today.

The most recent setback in this long and often-fought battle to allow women to make well-informed decisions about their reproductive health is the U.S. Supreme Court's upholding of the restrictive Title X regulations in the case of *Rust v. Sullivan.*[27] This so-called *gag rule* bars health-care providers in family-planning clinics that receive federal funds (which effectively includes all facilities available to the poor) from mentioning, let alone counseling or referring women for abortions. This decision interferes not only with the right to free speech of physicians and other health workers but also with their professional and moral duty to provide their patients with information about all medical options. Because physicians in the private practice of medicine are not constrained in terms of the information they provide to patients who can afford their care, the gag rule clearly discriminates against poor women and the young who must attend federally funded clinics or get no care at all. Limitation of payment for abortion in federal Medicaid recipients is another way in which the government has interfered with this vital right of women.

States vary in the extent to which they limit reproductive decision making by women; some require spousal notification or parental consent for performance of abortion or prescription of contraceptives to a minor. It is likely that the U.S. Supreme Court will use the restrictive Pennsylvania, Utah, or Louisiana cases as the basis for eventually overturning *Roe v. Wade*.

A pro-choice Congress is the only hope for preservation of the limited reproductive rights women now have. The protections now afforded by *Roe v. Wade* must become codified under federal law. The Freedom of Choice Act has been introduced into both houses of Congress in order to reverse the ban on abortion counseling (the gag rule). It has been passed in the Senate and action in the House is expected soon. Elected officials at every level of local, state, and federal government must support women's health rights, as battles will be fought across this spectrum of the system.

Product Liability Law

Fear of product liability lawsuits, as well as the cost involved, has caused the pharmaceutical industry to withdraw from developing new, safer, forms of contraception. In 1991, Norplant became the first new contraceptive to be introduced in the United States in 20 years. Fear of antichoice extremism has forced the French manufacturers of RU-486, a potentially noninvasive safer method of inducing an early abortion, to withhold the drug from the U.S. market. The 1992 Labor–Health and Human Services–Education Appropriations bill includes funding for the National Institutes of Health (NIH) Women's Health Initiative, one small part of which is for contraceptive research. A model for needed legislation is that of the 1988 Vaccine Injury Compensation Act.

A related issue is the need for better surveillance of products such as breast implants and tampons, which have not received adequate review under past Food and Drug Administration (FDA) procedures.

Research

Half of the U.S. population is female, women's health problems currently constitute more than two-thirds of health-care costs, and women contribute equally with men through their tax dollars to the budget of the NIH, which directs most medical research in the United States; yet, only 13 percent of the medical research in this country is on women's health.

The image of women as the healthy sex (based on their longer life expectancy) has helped to exclude them from much of medical research, except that which relates to "female problems." Those illnesses that affect reproductive function and structure have typically colored the picture of women's health status and guided the content and process of health-care delivery to women, to the detrimental exclusion of other conditions. Indeed, the exclusion of women from research studies has severely limited our knowledge of the extent of health problems in women. Women have been ignored or intentionally excluded from research for a variety of reasons, some of which are well intentioned.

Fear among researchers that a women may be pregnant and not know it or may become pregnant during a study has led to wholesale exclusion of women from research that involves the testing of any drug deemed potentially harmful to an unborn fetus. The possibility of periodic pregnancy testing and that women are capable of giving informed consent with appropriate warnings and safeguards, is not considered, often out of concern about a lawsuit. In other cases, women are excluded from drug research because of concern about the effect of changing hormones during the menstrual cycle and their potential effect on drug metabolism. This is another understandable, but potentially controllable, rationale. Moreover, the effect of hormonal fluctuations on drug metabolism is never considered in the prescribing of drugs. Physicians never consider the stage of the menstrual cycle and adjust the dose accordingly. A recent study underscored the importance of this consideration.[28] It showed that by prescribing the same daily dose of an antidepressant a woman has too high a blood level in the first half of the cycle and a less than therapeutic level in the premenstrual half of the cycle. From this observation, it is appropriate to conclude that drug doses are, indeed, influenced by women's hormone levels. Rather than being the basis for excluding women from research, however, it is imperative that this biologic fact be addressed in both the design of research testing of new drugs to be prescribed ultimately to women and in the prescribing information provided to physicians, as well as to patients. We cannot simply generalize from research on male subjects to female patients.

Increased spending for research on identified health problems of women is a reasonable beginning, but woefully inadequate to redress the deficits of the past. We need exploratory epidemiologic surveys designed to redefine health in ways more consistent with the experience of women. Existing instruments and diagnostic criteria derived from and by males must be reexamined to eliminate bias against women. New paradigms for thinking about women's health are indicated and more women researchers and health-care providers are necessary. Such a large-scale overhaul of the medical research system of this country requires commitment and funding. This funding must come from the public sector, as well as from the pharmaceutical and health-care industries.

INFLUENCING POLICY AND
THE POLITICAL PROCESS

To influence the political process, policymakers as well as candidates for local, state, and federal office must be aware of, sensitive to, and knowledgeable about the health status of women, its improvement, and its implications for their well-being. Accordingly, they must be responsive to questions about access, research needs, and health policy.

In the area of access, they should favor some form of national health insurance, specifically being aware of the need for adequate coverage for preventive procedures such as mammograms, for psychiatric and contraceptive care, and opposed to rationing provisions that are potentially discriminatory against women. They must be sensitive to the need to cover all women at every stage of life and to the importance of not linking health insurance to employment status. They should be aware that tax credits for purchase of private health insurance are inadequate for poor women.

They must be aware of the need to increase the funding for research on women's health problems through federal and private funding, the latter linked to the need for protection against legal suit of pharmacologic companies. A related issue is the importance of bringing more women into the sciences and health fields by increasing role models in leadership positions in these fields in both academic and industrial settings.

When asked what can be done to decrease the problem of adolescent sexually transmitted disease and pregnancy, the candidate should be aware of the importance of improved quality and earlier introduction of sex education in the schools, elimination of parental notification requirements for access to contraception or abortion, and the need for increased funding for research on more effective interventions and improved availability of contraceptives.

The recent relevations about the questionable safety of breast implants has far-reaching implications and mandates that we ensure safe and more effective preventive and therapeutic interventions for women. Accordingly, candidates must be aware of the need to guarantee inclusion of women in drug-research studies; support wider FDA control of devices, products, and drugs used by women; and advocate control of cigarette and alcohol advertising aimed at young women.

As in all other aspects of their well-being, women's participation in the paid labor force has important health implications. Accordingly, the candidate need be sensitive to the need for paid dependent care leave (e.g., support The Family Leave Act) and for adequate child and dependent care and recognize the role of gender bias in hindering advancement and pay equity.

NOTES

1. U.S. Department of Health and Human Services, Public Health Service, Centers for Disease Control, *Monthly Vital Statistics Report* 40(8) Suppl. 2, January 7, 1992.

2. P. Cotton, "Is There Still Too Much Extrapolation from Data on Middle-Aged White Men?" *Journal of the American Medical Association* 263 (1990): 1051–1052.

3. World Health Organization Constitution, WHO Basic Documents (Geneva: World Health Organization, 1948).

4. L. M. Verbrugge, "Work Satisfaction and Physical Health," *Journal of Community Health* 7 (1982): 262–283.

5. *Mortality and Morbidity Weekly Report* 39(48), December 7, 1990: 875, 881.

6. Ibid.

7. H. Hartmann, "Women's Health in the United States," Institute for Women's Policy Research. Presented by the Campaign for Women's Health, July 12, 1991.

8. Department of Health, New York City, 1992 (personal communication).

9. Children's Safety Network, "A Data Book of Child and Adolescent Injury" (Washington, D.C.: National Center for Education in Maternal and Child Health, 1991).

10. J. A. Stein and S. A. Fox, "Language Preference as an Indicator of Mammography Use among Hispanic Women," *Journal of the National Cancer Institute* 21 (1990): 1715–1716.

11. C. Garrison, K. Jackson, C. Addy, et al., "Suicidal Behaviors in Young Adolescents," *American Journal of Epidemiology* 133 (1991): 1005–1014.

12. D. B. Kandel and J. A. Logan, "Patterns of Drug Use from Adolescence to Young Adulthood: 1. Periods of Risk for Initiation, Continued Use, and Discontinuation," *American Journal of Public Health* 74 (1984): 660–666.

13. L. D. Johnston, J. G. Bachman, and P. M. O'Malley, "Drug Use, Drinking, and Smoking: National Survey Results from High School, College and Young Adult Populations, 1975–1988," NIDA, USDHHS, PHS, Alcohol, Drug Abuse, and Mental Health Administration. DHHS Publ. No. (ADM) 89-1638, 1989.

14. National Center on Child Abuse and Neglect, *Study Findings—Study of National Incidence and Prevalence of Child Abuse and Neglect* (Washington, D.C.: USDHHS, 1991).

15. J. H. LaRosa, "Executive Women and Health: Perceptions and Practices," *American Journal of Public Health* 80 (1990): 1450–1454.

16. G. Doebbert, K. R. Riedmiller, and K. Kizer, "Occupational Mortality of California Women, 1979–1981," *Western Journal of Medicine* 149 (1988): 734–740.

17. *New York Times,* January 6, 1992.

18. R. Pechansky and J. W. Thomas, "The Concept of Access: Definition and Relationship to Consumer Satisfaction," *Medical Care* 19 (1981): 127–140.

19. U.S. Congress, Office of Technology Assessment, *Adolescent Health—Volume I: Summary and Policy Options* (OTA-H-468) (Washington, D.C.: U.S. Government Printing Office, April 1991), 25–27.

20. Hartmann, 1991.

21. Ibid.

22. Stein and Fox, 1990.

23. N. S. Jecker and R. A. Pearlman, "Ethical Constraints on Rationing Medical Care by Age," *Journal of the American Geriatrics Society* 37 (1989): 1067–1075.

24. Council on Ethical and Judicial Affairs, American Medical Association, "Gender Disparities in Clinical Decision Making," *Journal of the American Medical Society* 266 (1991): 559–562.

25. Ibid.

26. *Rust v. Sullivan,* 499 U.S., 111 S.C.T.1759, 114 LED.2d 233 (1991).

27. Ibid.

28. *Newsletter of the Association of Women Psychiatrists* 9(1), October 3, 1990.

CHECKPOINTS

1. Litt compares the mortality and morbidity statistics for women and men and suggests the following as special concerns for women: quality of life as related to chronic health issues, employment status, family variables, and poverty.

2. Barriers to improvements in women's health care include access to appropriate care, affordability of care, and an appropriate match between the health care system and social, economic, and psychological needs of the patient.

To prepare for reading the next section, think about this question:

1. Do women and men experience stress differently, and if so, how might this be related to prescriptions imposed by gender roles?

Can Women Cope?
A Gender Analysis of Theories of Coping with Stress

VICTORIA L. BANYARD AND SANDRA A. GRAHAM-BERMANN

University of Michigan

In this article, various feminist theories are used to critique selected psychological theories of coping with stress, a reformulated coping theory is outlined, and recommendations for future research are made. To date, theories of coping often portray women as less able copers than the samples of men with whom they are compared. A reformulated theory, based on different women's experiences, explicitly examines the role of social forces (sexism, racism) and access to power as variables in the coping process rather than solely focusing on the individual. Selected examples of research that contribute to such a revision are given. Revised theories and methodologies will encourage the more accurate appraisal of women's coping abilities and generate information vital to the creation of more inclusive and representative theories of coping.

The issue of gender has received increasing attention in research on human psychology in recent years. There has been growing interest in studying women's lives and the unique circumstances that they face. Theories of stress and coping in particular have been used as a basis for understanding phenomena from rape and domestic violence (Burgess & Holstrom, 1979; Mitchell & Hodson, 1983) to hopelessness (Milburn & D'Ercole, 1991). A closer examination of current research paradigms of coping with stress, however, reveals that they are quite problematic for use with these populations because they do not adequately illuminate the experiences of diverse groups of women. The lack of attention to feminist critiques of social science more generally has resulted in studies of coping that have ignored women altogether or have studied them only in comparison with men,

finding their skills to be inferior to an ideal, male model of coping.

This paper first demonstrates the need for reformulated theories of coping by using a feminist perspective to illuminate the limitations of current theories. The feminist lens, based on theoretical work by Harding (1991), Hare-Mustin and Marecek (1990), and others (e.g., Peplau & Conrad, 1989; Smith, 1987; Unger, 1990), is then used to sketch the outlines of a revised coping theory and to propose the beginnings of a research paradigm for studying the coping strengths of diverse groups of women. Such a research design should more accurately give voice to women's experiences, filling in the gaps of our current understanding and avoiding a recreation in research of the disempowerment that many groups so regularly face in their interactions with society. Grappling with such applications of feminist theories not only extends our understanding of how to incorporate gender into our research but forces us to confront the question of how to include the equally important and problematic issues of race and class.

PROBLEMS WITH EXISTING THEORIES: INVISIBILITY, MARGINALITY, AND GENDER STEREOTYPES

Existing research on coping is diverse in terms of its definition and measurement of what constitutes "coping." Most researchers agree, however, that it is comprised of actions taken to deal with stress (e.g., Billings & Moos, 1981; Folkman & Lazarus, 1980; Pearlin & Schooler, 1978), including both the appraisal of the situation and judgments about one's resources for dealing with the stressor. Although this is a useful definition, the subsequent value judgments placed on coping strategies and the dichotomy created between what is "good" and "bad" coping is problematic for any study of women's lives. Women fall on the lower end of the coping hierarchy. This situation arises in part from the lack of systematic attention to gender in the coping literature to date, from stereotypical assumptions about gender used in formulating both theory and research questions, and from the use of methods that silence women's voices.

Gender is invisible in a large segment of the research on coping with stress. Coping is treated as an abstract concept that is untouched by such individualizing characteristics as gender, race, or class (Bramson, 1985; Flach, 1988; Kobasa & Puccetti, 1983). The studies that fall under this category are ones in which the participants have all been men and it is presumed that the individual possesses numerous resources (power, money, support) to aid in the coping process, enabling the experience of stress to be positive and growth enhancing. Yet coping itself is often attributed to individual personality characteristics rather than viewed as the product of such access to resources. The apparent gender-neutral theories that result are packaged as universal explanations of behavior in spite of being based on the experiences of those in the more privileged strata of society. When the model is applied to other groups, such as women in poverty, their behaviors are found to be deficient. Perhaps it is the models and not the individuals that are lacking.

The more recent trend in theories of coping, however, has been to include the study of both women and men. Furthermore, coping is viewed as a process, rather than a trait, that varies from situation to situation for any one individual rather than remaining constant (Billings & Moos, 1981; Folkman & Lazarus, 1980; Pearlin & Schooler, 1978). This view of coping brings the social context of the individual to the forefront of analysis and would seem to provide interesting possibilities for understanding the impact of social forces on an individual's coping efforts. Yet gender remains a marginal analytic variable and is usually only defined in terms of sex differences. Such

an exclusive focus on these differences results in the deficit view of women's coping. For example, Folkman and Lazarus (1980) studied 100 White women and men in a community and found very few gender differences when participants were asked to describe a recent stressful event and to complete a checklist of strategies they had used to cope with the situation. In spite of this, the discussion highlighted the few differences that were found and put women's functioning in a negative light.

> The most puzzling gender difference was the finding that men used more problem-focused coping than women in situations that had to be accepted. Perhaps men persevere in problem-focused coping longer than women before deciding that nothing can be done; and even when nothing can be done, men may be disposed to think about the problem more than women. (Folkman & Lazarus, 1980, p. 235)

Although no outcome measures were used, their use of language implies that how the men coped was better. Furthermore, there is little critical explanation of the findings.

Similar problems can be seen in the work of other coping theorists, such as Billings and Moos (1981) and Pearlin and Schooler (1978). These researchers used methods similar to those of Folkman and Lazarus (1980). Although their theories seem tolerant of diversity in coping, by talking about the importance of understanding the personal meaning of the stressful event and the context in which it occurs, they continued to revert back to traditional gender models when discussing their results. Questions were posed in terms of how women coped as compared with men. Pearlin and Schooler (1978, p. 15) concluded that

> there is a profound imbalance between the sexes in their possession and use of effective mechanisms. Men more often possess psychological attributes or employ responses that inhibit stressful outcomes of life-problems; and in two of the three instances where women more often employ a response it is likely to result not in less stress, but in more.

No mention is made of the fact that women seem to employ other strategies such as negotiation and forbearance more often than men. Negative judgments were made about women in spite of the observation that sex differences were small. There was no discussion of whether such small levels of difference would appear significant in actual, observable behaviors. A question that remains unasked is whether there might be fewer differences between the coping strategies of women and men of the same race and social class than between women of different races and classes.

There is a body of literature within the area of coping with stress that does focus more specifically on gender (e.g., Biener, 1987; Miller & Kirsh, 1987; Solomon & Rothblum, 1986). This work moves away from the view of women as deficient copers by suggesting that they are not better or worse, just different. These pieces (which are mostly reinterpretations of previous work) move beyond a strict definition of gender as biology and discuss gender as roles assumed in society. Women and men are exposed to different stressors as a result of the different jobs that they perform in society and are thus required to use different coping strategies. This research represents some degree of progress toward a better understanding of women's coping. However, even this work, with its continued emphasis on gender differences, remains somewhat limited in its explanatory value. Differences in the roles played by women and men are often discussed as though both roles are valued and treated equally in society, with little emphasis on the fact that women and men are given access to different amounts of power in those roles. Such role division also diverts attention from the fact that women and men are increasingly fulfilling some of the same roles. In addition, generalizations continue to be made about women as a whole, although these studies are based on racially and culturally limited samples. The result is that what these studies actually have to say about how women cope is as equivocal in this literature as it is in the general coping literature.

Biener's (1987) work on the use of cigarette smoking in coping provides an example. She explored the finding that among certain groups, such as professionals, rates of smoking in response to a negative stressor were higher for women than for men and that measures of psychological job demands and perceived control in one's job were more predictive of smoking behavior in women than in men. She proposed that women and men may engage in smoking behavior for different reasons and that for women cigarettes are used as a coping response to feelings of lack of control. She then linked this use to an assertion that traditional sex-role socialization teaches women to be passive, to accept even uncontrollable situations as beyond their powers of intervention. Women are also more often in subordinate positions in which they really do have little control. The result is that, for women, the goal of coping is emotion-focused adaptation, making them quite susceptible to the use of strategies such as cigarette smoking (Biener, 1987). Although this is a useful observation that serves to reduce some of the individual blame, it still seems to portray women as passive victims of their environments. There is little attention to the findings that women and men use tranquilizers and alcohol in apparently equal numbers for coping, beyond stating that gender differences in substance exposure may account for men more often choosing alcohol and women using medical drugs. In addition, the socialization about which Biener speaks has actually been the socialization experience of one group of women, those in the White middle-class. The role of race and an analysis of differences among women is markedly absent.

Yet another example can be seen in the way in which women's coping is conceptualized largely in terms of social support (Belle, 1987; Brown & Gary, 1985; Solomon & Rothblum, 1986). Although this is an area of research in which women's lives have taken center stage and where many women's strengths have been documented, it reflects general assumptions about the more affiliative nature of women and their primary roles as caretakers of friends and family. Is social support the only way that women cope? This thinking repeats the common trap of studying men in terms of employment and rational, intellectual domains and women in terms of relationships, the home, and the family. Theories based on such rigid stereotyping can hardly be considered explanatory of universal human behavior, as they claim to be.

On the issue of gender, what we supposedly "learn" from looking at the literature is that women do not cope as well as men regardless of the fact that there is little conclusive evidence to show this is the case. What we know has been overly constrained by our tenacious adherence to assumptions about gender differences (Hare-Mustin & Marecek, 1990; Unger, 1990), which is in part the result of linguistic and theoretical tendencies to separate all groups into dichotomous entities based on differences. Value is placed only on one side of that difference, a practice that hinders a discussion of women's strengths. In the process, the concept of gender itself is oversimplified and seen as a unitary biological trait rather than as a process that changes in interaction with its environment (Hare-Mustin & Marecek, 1990; Unger, 1990). This oversimplification creates a number of problems. First, we cannot speak of coping by women and men generally, as Folkman and Lazarus (1980) and Pearlin and Schooler (1978) did, if we are speaking only of White women and men in their particular constellation of roles. The picture remains incomplete. One of the important lessons of recent revisions in coping theories is that coping is highly specific to both the individual and the context (Lazarus & Folkman, 1984; Pearlin & Schooler, 1978). Women inhabit diverse contexts, depending on their race, class, age, and sexual orientation. Therefore, we must investigate a broad range of situations before we can say that we have a general theory of coping or of which types of coping strategies lead to more favorable psychological outcomes.

Second, when explaining gender differences, there is not enough emphasis on the issue of power and how it may act as a mediator in the stress and coping process. This lack of emphasis may be an artifact of the narrow focus on gender alone as the differentiating factor among groups; when discussions of gender are separated from other categories such as race and class, it is more difficult to see the importance of power as a dimension of analysis (Hare-Mustin & Marecek, 1990). There is impressive evidence that access to resources, such as education and income, influences coping, particularly as it is traditionally measured (Pearlin & Schooler, 1978; Singh & Pandly, 1985). According to theories about coping, those with more power do better. Yet power is never talked about as such. It is disguised under the mask of biological or role differences. This treatment must change, particularly if we are to adequately understand all women's lives, including marginalized groups such as women in poverty. This population is at risk because of their lack of access to resources. Without considering power and opportunity, we develop programs designed to diagnose and treat the individual rather than examining the problem of their position in society and then creating avenues to increase the availability of resources.

OTHER LIMITATIONS OF COPING THEORY FOR STUDYING WOMEN

Limitations in coping theory for the study of women go beyond the treatment of gender as a theoretical variable. This section outlines the ways that methodological issues, such as the design of protocols and definition of research variables, compromise the applicability of coping theory to many women's lives.

Methodologically, coping researchers share what some have called a "top down" or nomothetic approach to research (Allport, 1951; Fine, 1985; Unger, 1990). That is, researchers begin to formulate questions and procedures for testing them based on their own notions of what they will find. A list of possible coping responses to a particular situation are presented to participants who are then asked to choose which items describe the ways that they cope. No further inquiry is made as to how the respondents interpreted the items or whether the results adequately reflect how an individual deals with stress. Furthermore, ideas about what the coping process looks like (which have been generated in the minds of researchers from their own experiences and the responses of one group of participants) are assumed to be applicable to everyone who fills out the questionnaire. Some feminist scholars (e.g., Gergen, 1988) have criticized this approach for its disempowerment of respondents. Lists of coping strategies developed by researchers may not include ways of adapting used by particular groups. Furthermore, the meaning of a given strategy's use by a participant may be misinterpreted (Stone & Neale, 1984). For example, the use of avoidance as a strategy is commonly seen as maladaptive. It is true that putting aside a particular problem may carry heavy psychological costs. We miss something, however, if we stop here and do not ask why people have chosen a particular option. We may learn that avoiding certain issues is very much motivated by a need to survive by saving one's energy for dealing with other problems. This is particularly true of impoverished women who must struggle daily to procure the most basic resources for survival. Although some coping theorists have begun to question their own assumptions about such things as the benefits of perceived control and direct action (Folkman, 1984), they have not yet pushed the limits of this idea far enough.

In addition to issues of questionnaire design, our complete understanding of the coping process, and more specifically women's coping, has been hindered by the narrow selection of outcome measures. A closer look at the literature reveals researchers' heavy reliance on both self-report measures and measures of depressive symptomatology. To be coping well means to be relatively free from anxiety and depression. This definition has implications for the study of gender and coping, given that women more often express distress in internalized and depressive symptoms than do men (Miller & Kirsch, 1987; Solomon & Rothblum, 1986). Women have also been found to be more willing than men to report distress. This finding may create a response bias that makes women appear more distressed and less adequate in their ability to cope (Borden & Berlin, 1990).

A further limitation lies in the heavy focus in coping research on the individual as the primary unit of study. Consequently, our knowledge of what coping looks like is constrained by looking only at the actions of one person with one particular stressor. Work such as that conducted by Singh and Pandly (1985) and Gutierrez (1988) introduces the notion of collec-

tive coping, which consists of efforts by multiple persons in conjunction with one another to influence adverse circumstances. Singh and Pandly stated that this form of coping may be particularly important for non-Western cultures, whose belief and value systems have more of a community focus, and for those individuals in highly disempowered positions for whom individual action seldom brings more than frustration. A great deal of important cross-cultural work (e.g., Markus & Kitayama, 1991) has documented the existence of alternatives to the western concept of the autonomous and individual self, positing the existence of views of the self, and the actions taken as a result of that view, that are interdependent and heavily based on a consideration of one's relationship to others. The overvaluation of the independently functioning self is both problematic and misleading and lends to the privileging of some forms of actions (i.e., some forms of coping) over others regardless of context and prevents an accurate appreciation of the true scope of coping activities (Fine, 1985).

Coping researchers' focus on individuals as autonomous copers leads them to consider context only in terms of the individual. When theorists such as Folkman and Lazarus (1980) discuss the importance of differences in context in the coping process, they tend to be speaking about the ways that coping varies with different stressors or with differences in an individual's appraisal of the situation. An interesting question that is often not asked, however, concerns the nature of the social milieu in which a particular stressor is experienced. Do women report coping with problems differently if they are coping in the context of other women or in the presence of men or when they are alone? Theorists believe that gender norms impact coping globally by assigning women and men to different social roles and sanctioning only certain behaviors for each gender. Feminists such as Unger (1990) suggest that gender be defined even more specifically than this. She suggested that gender will look different from situation to situation. Women may behave in a more passive way in groups with men, where stereotyped roles and social norms may be most strictly enforced. These same women may look quite different when acting alone or in a same-sex group. Furthermore, gender also operates in conjunction with race and class to define the context of the situation. Lykes (1983, p. 83) stated,

> A Black woman may cope with problems differently, working within a context where the dominant perspective is articulated and shaped by Whites, than she does while working in a context where the dominant perspective is articulated and shaped by Blacks.

AN ALTERNATIVE MODEL FOR COPING THEORY

The preceding critique indicates that much of what feminists have had to say about psychological research in general can be applied to the coping literature. However, recognizing limitations of the traditional theory is only the beginning of the process. The task now is to move beyond, to explore what a revised theory of coping would look like and how to conduct new research. The work of Harding (1991) and others (Fine, 1992; Hare-Mustin & Marecek, 1990; Marecek, 1989; Peplau & Conrad, 1989; Smith, 1987; Unger, 1990) provides a feminist lens through which to view the outlines of a reformulated theory and recommendations for future coping research that will begin to fill in the gaps in our current knowledge of how women cope.

Harding (1991) asserted that we must go beyond simply adding women to theories and formulations developed by, on, and about men. We need to take a new view, one that starts from the lives and viewpoints of many women. Women's views provide a vantage point from which to gain varied perspectives on the coping process. This approach has been particularly helpful in the study of social support (Belle, 1982; Solomon & Rothblum, 1986). Belle's (1982) work on low-income women has changed our notions of social support as a completely positive, adjustment enhancing resource to an understanding of its profound costs for women through the "contagion of stress" (Belle, cited in Solomon & Rothblum, 1986, p. 199). Belle (1982) found that members of a support network can condone negative and harmful behaviors, such as substance abuse, and bring the added responsibility of dealing with network members' problems. A revised theory of coping would acknowledge that women's lives are a valid place from which to generate knowledge of the stress process.

In addition, such a coping theory would incorporate a complex view of gender itself. Harding (1991) began by discussing gender as a process that cannot be seen as independent from the wider social context. The thoughts and actions of women and men are influenced as much by their race, class, and life experiences as by the biological fact of their sex. A reformulated theory of coping would not assume that female/male differences were the most important but would instead understand that coping occurs in a context shaped by social forces based on gender, race, class, age, and sexual orientation. These forces exert a powerful influence both on how a stressful situation is appraised and on judgments made about what coping resources are available. The experiences of women at the intersections of these various forces challenge us to explicitly examine and account for the impact of such social variables.

The work of Lykes (1983) on African American women coping with discrimination illustrates the need to study race as well as gender and the ways that these variables affect judgments about stressful situations. Lykes analyzed 71 oral histories of successful African American women, rather than the White sample employed in traditional studies. She was primarily interested in how these women coped with discrimination, and she hypothesized that coping would differ depending on the context in which the racist treatment occurred. Lykes was not looking for the correct or best way to cope. She looked, instead, at the variety of ways that women made active choices based on a complex analysis of the forces at play in their environment at the time. In addition, Lykes took the traditional notions of context and situation specificity a necessary step further, examining the role of historical social forces (such as racism) as well as individual personal concerns in coping decisions. Lykes found that the context in which the experience of discrimination took place was an important variable mediating the women's choice of coping strategy. African American women in predominantly White institutions who perceived the outcome to be under their personal control tended to use a high degree of flexibility of coping rather than simply relying on directly instrumental actions. These women tended to selectively ignore the incident, whereas women working in Black institutions relied more on directly confronting the perpetrator of the discrimination. The organizational environment in which these women worked had a direct effect on which strategies were used in coping. The women were able to use a variety of strategies and chose one over another based on characteristics of the institution. Power was a key variable defining that context.

An understanding of power then leads one to think beyond the categories of problem-focused and emotion-focused coping, which have been so dichotomized by the work of traditional coping theorists, and to question the value labels placed on various coping strategies (Folkman & Lazarus, 1980). Many of the women in Lykes's (1983) study reported using emotion-focused or avoidant strategies in a purposeful way. They coped creatively and effectively by choosing not to deal with the stress of discrimination but rather focusing on something else. A woman may lose some sense of personal justice in doing this but sees this as a necessary price to pay for keeping her job and the benefits and paycheck that protect her family. There are times when emotion-focused strategies may be used as problem-focused solutions to a stressful dilemma. This element of complexity may be missed when exclusively studying populations of people who do not confront chronic, overarching stressors, such as racism, which are not immediately amenable to direct behavioral actions.

Incorporating the role of wider social forces into a theory of coping permits us to go beyond the search for individual deficiencies. As stated above, it is no longer meaningful to place stresses in general categories and compare how women and men cope with such things as parenting stress. Such a category will look quite different if one is a White woman, a woman of color, or a White man, because the sociopolitical context creates an experience of parenting that is quite different for each group, necessitating the use of different strategies. A reformulated theory, then, would document women's strengths in the face of oppression, appreciating the constraints of their coping choices because of the power of various social institutions.

The work of Dill, Feld, Martin, Beukema, and Belle (1980) on the lives of low-income women provokes a shift in perspective from the standard views of coping because often what appears to be the best strategy is in fact quite complicated and impossible to carry out. Dill et al. used the example of a woman who wanted very much to be employed. Her job, however, made her ineligible for the welfare benefits she needed to get back on her feet. She was unable to afford daycare and living expenses on her salary and was being pushed back onto public assistance against her will.

> The strategy with which a woman eventually addresses a problem will often be a compromise between what the environment allows and what she is capable of accomplishing, thus her performance may not accurately reflect her ability. When low-income mothers' coping strategies are assessed, the researcher should consider whether or not the optimum strategy would have been possible for the woman to accomplish, given her circumstances. (Dill et al., 1980, p. 507)

They cited examples of the ways that public institutions impeded these women's efforts or were unresponsive to their actions. These negative interactions in turn led the women to feel that they had little control over their lives. Such experiences of frustration have powerful implications for the self-esteem of these women, particularly as they continue to be viewed through an individual lens that blames them for their situation. Looking at the process of coping through these women's lives further shows the ways that the environment can constrain one's choice of coping strategy. This work suggests that we may not be adequately tapping into actual coping ability by using traditional measures that look at only one instance of coping, a technique that does not take these environmental factors enough into account.

A revised theory of coping would also more closely examine what is meant by different categories of coping. Not only will each type of coping strategy have different costs and benefits depending on the individual's social situation, but the meaning and description of strategies will be redefined. For example, the terms "passive strategies" or "avoidance" may mask a variety of actions that are discovered only by looking out through the eyes of various groups of women. In addition, coping will not only be seen as actions taken by and for the self but also those actions used to maximize the survival of others (such as children, family, friends).

Fine's (1985) work on coping with rape addressed these issues. It focused on a case study of a woman named Altemese who was brought into a hospital emergency room after being gang raped. The woman elected not to press charges or to avail herself of the counseling resources available at the hospital. She trusted a higher power to bring justice to those who had wronged her and preferred to put the incident behind her, dealing with it on her own. She was concerned only with getting out of the hospital as soon as they would let her leave so that she could go home to care for her young child. Fine was struck by the ways in which traditional psychology would label this woman as dependent, passive, and helpless. It would label her behavior as "learned helplessness" and would label her as a woman who has no control over her life. Such an analysis masks the very active survival strategies Altemese used and the choices she made, what Fine termed "relational coping." Altemese realistically saw that her friends would not testify on her behalf and that prosecuting those who had raped her would only further endanger her family. She rejected the use of social services, geared to helping the individual bring justice, out of a realistic appraisal of the ineffectiveness of such strategies in dealing with a problem that required structural change. In addition, coping for her was not just about her own survival but about how to keep her children safe. The shift in thinking that this incident promotes requires reexamination of current beliefs about how to define control and problem solving in coping and enables us to conceptualize coping as more than individuals' appraisals of the impact a stressor will have on them. Coping also has to do with evaluating how the stressor and strategies used to deal with it will impact the welfare of others to whom individuals are connected (Fine, 1985).

A reformulated theory of coping reflects changes in all aspects of our current understanding of this phenomenon. The context in which coping occurs is redefined to include the influence of social forces and one's access to resources. These forces play a role in defining both the nature of the stressor to be dealt with and the range of coping options available. A revised theory documents women's strengths, views their lives as a valuable place from which to generate knowledge, and opens up traditional categories of coping strategies to scrutiny and more complex analyses. Coping is not restricted to actions taken by individuals to further their own survival but may be defined in terms of its impact on significant others. Furthermore, gender is viewed as a complicated variable that does not operate independently of age, race, class, or sexual orientation.

DIRECTIONS FOR FUTURE RESEARCH

Ultimately, however, much research is needed to fill in this outline of a reformulated theory of coping. Such a task requires careful examination of how we conduct such studies. Here, too, feminist theory provides some useful guidelines. Using Harding's (1991) standpoint theory helps us to ask the questions that will enable us to analyze the benefits, costs, and consequences of various coping strategies for women in different contexts and to develop a more flexible theory of coping.

Harding (1991) and Smith (1987) discussed the necessity of "thinking from women's lives," beginning our questions and analyses from the perspectives of women in many different places within society. Feminist theory helps us to form different research hypotheses. For example, we can now ask how poverty, racism, and sexism affect the coping process. We can investigate explicitly how coping changes under different conditions of power. Social forces become key variables, and research is not focused solely on individual reasons for coping choices, such as locus of control or individual deficiencies (Kahn & Yoder, 1989). How we see and describe the environment in which coping takes place will be different when viewed through women's lives. For many women, coping with work, for example, entails coping with sexual harassment or the availability of child-care. These pressures will have an effect on how a woman copes with particular situations. She will not just personally appraise stressors differently; there are real pressures on her in her environment that are different for her than for many of the men she may work with. In addition, beginning from women's perspectives permits us to ask questions about what women are doing well because we do not begin with the assumption that women cope less well than men do.

Feminist theory also admonishes us to include different groups of women in our pool of respondents and to refrain from assuming that coping and survival look the same for all women. Looking more closely at the differences within particular groups of women enables us to capture women's strengths and to document the personal costs that various strategies exact without stereotyping and pathologizing the group as a whole (e.g., McAdoo, 1986; Meyers, 1980). Within-group study allows us to appreciate the variations in human experience and is a necessary component to studies that articulate the social context of behavior more fully. Women's strengths will remain hidden if we continue to study women and men as monolithic biological categories.

In addition, feminist theorists such as Harding (1991) assert that science must include a thorough study of itself as well as its participants, with researchers examining the background of beliefs embedded in their pursuits and the process of research itself as well as examining their respondents. They call for descriptions of a researcher's beliefs and social location to ground the reader in the assumptions and values on which the study is based. In this way, scientists and their participants begin to meet as collaborators on the same power plane, quite a change from the top-down approach so prevalent in the cop-

ing literature to date. Researchers also acknowledge the changes in their own belief systems that have occurred as a result of engaging in the research process. Harding (1991) argued that research should teach us as much about ourselves as scientists as it does about participants. Those who study coping must be particularly careful that results are not an artifact of their own biases and must continually check their interpretations against the actual experiences of women. This checking may be done in a variety of ways, including the use of focus groups with participants to discuss any research findings.

Regarding the specifics of research design, a feminist perspective requires the careful scrutiny of all investigative methods to examine them for gender bias but does not restrict researchers to one set of tools or make prescriptions about qualitative or quantitative methods (Jayaratne & Stewart, 1991; Peplau & Conrad, 1989). The key to feminist research on coping seems to lie in the questions that are asked and how analyses are conducted and described. It may be quite useful to use old measures to answer new questions, while working to develop new tools that are more sensitive to women's experiences. For example, the African American Women's Stress Scale (Watts-Jones, 1990) is a quantitative measure that is quite feminist; it has been developed to illuminate the specific experiences of a group of women who have often been left out of other stress checklist measures. The scale includes a list of very important items about stressful encounters with racism and illustrates the ways in which quantitative measures can be modified to include an appreciation of the impact of larger social forces on stress and coping.

A reformulated theory does not completely contradict traditional coping theories. It does, however, provide a different perspective on these theories and how they should be researched. By starting in the lives of women from many different racial, ethnic, and economic backgrounds, such work will gather information that both challenges and adds to our thinking about what the coping process looks like. Although the methods used may be quite diverse, they share a variety of characteristics in common with Harding's (1991) and Smith's (1987) theories of methodology.

Such work starts with a respect for the differing perspectives of multiple lives. It looks to understand coping as these women live and makes no attempts to universalize findings or to speak for all women. Consequently, we are able not only to uncover a wealth of women's strengths, which seem to have been missed by other coping research, but also to make observations about the coping process that extend our understanding of coping by all people.

CONCLUSION

This article has attempted to use feminist theory to illustrate limitations in current coping theories for understanding women. Theoretical work by Harding (1991) and others (Hare-Mustin & Marecek, 1990; Smith, 1987; Unger, 1990) was used to shape the beginnings of a revised theory of coping with stress and to formulate recommendations for future research. To date, much of the complexity of women's lives and the differences among them have been rendered invisible. The stakes are particularly high for those women who are further marginalized because they live in poverty or other difficult circumstances. As social scientists, we are being called upon increasingly to address social problems and to find solutions. We must move beyond paradigms that are ready to label women as individually deficient to capture the larger social forces that are at play in their lives. We need a theory to adequately capture strengths while placing often difficult lives in the proper context, appreciating the costs. We need a methodology that will not be disempowering to participants. Such research is a necessary foundation for the design of more effective policies and services for all groups of women.

REFERENCES

Allport, G. (1951). *The use of personal documents in psychological science.* New York: Social Science Research Council.

Belle, D. (1982). The impact of poverty on social networks and supports. *Marriage and Family Review, 5*(4), 89–103.

Belle, D. (1987). Gender differences in the social moderators of stress. In R. Barnett, L. Biener, & G. Baruch (Eds.), *Gender and stress* (pp. 257–277). New York: The Free Press.

Biener, L. (1987). Gender differences in the use of substances for coping. In R. Barnett, L. Biener, & G. Baruch (Eds.), *Gender and stress* (pp. 330–349). New York: The Free Press.

Billings, A., & Moos, R. (1981). The role of coping responses and social resources in attenuating the stress of life events. *Journal of Behavioral Medicine, 4*(2), 139–157.

Borden, W., & Berlin, S. (1990). Gender, coping, and psychological well-being in spouses of older adults with chronic dementia. *American Journal of Orthopsychiatry, 60,* 603–610.

Bramson, R. (1985). Toward effective coping: Basic steps. In A. Monat & R. Lazarus (Eds.), *Stress and coping* (2nd ed., pp 356–370). New York: Columbia University Press.

Brown, D., & Gary, L. (1985). Social support differences among married and unmarried Black women. *Psychology of Women Quarterly, 9,* 229–241.

Burgess, A., & Holstrom, L. (1979). Adaptive strategies and recovery from rape. *American Journal of Psychiatry, 136,* 1278–1282.

Dill, D., Feld, E., Martin, J., Beukema, S., & Belle, D. (1980). The impact of the environment on the coping efforts of low-income mothers. *Family Relations, 29,* 503–509.

Fine, M. (1985). Coping with rape: Critical perspectives on consciousness. *Imagination, Cognition, and Personality, 3*(3), 249–267.

Fine, M. (1992). *Disruptive voices: The possibilities of feminist research.* Ann Arbor: University of Michigan Press.

Flach, F. (1988). *Resilience.* New York: Fawcett Columbine.

Folkman, S. (1984). Personal control and stress and coping processes: A theoretical analysis. *Journal of Personality and Social Psychology, 46,* 839–852.

Folkman, S., & Lazarus, R. (1980). Analysis of coping in a middle-aged sample. *Journal of Health and Social Behavior, 21,* 219–239.

Gergen, M. (1988). Toward a feminist metatheory and methodology in the social sciences. In M. Gergen (Ed.), *Feminist thought and the structure of knowledge* (pp. 87–104). New York: New York University Press.

Gutierrez, L. (1988). *Coping with stressful life events: An empowerment perspective* (Working Paper 87–88–05). University of Michigan, School of Social Work.

Harding, S. (1991). *Whose science? Whose knowledge? Thinking from women's lives.* Ithaca, NY: Cornell University Press.

Hare-Mustin, R., & Marecek, J. (Eds.). (1990). *Making a difference: Psychology and the construction of gender.* New Haven, CT: Yale University Press.

Jayaratne, T., & Stewart, A. (1991). Quantitative and qualitative methods in the social sciences: Current feminist issues and practical strategies. In M. Fonow & J. Cook (Eds.), *Beyond methodology* (pp. 85–106). Bloomington: Indiana University Press.

Kahn, A., & Yoder, J. (1989). The psychology of women and conservatism: Rediscovering social change. *Psychology of Women Quarterly, 13,* 417–432.

Kobasa, S., & Puccetti, M. (1983). Personality and social resources in stress resistance. *Journal of Personality and Social Psychology, 45,* 839–850.

Lazarus, R., & Folkman, S. (1984). *Stress, appraisal, and coping.* New York: Springer.

Lykes, M. B. (1983). Discrimination and coping in the lives of Black women. *Journal of Social Issues, 39*(3), 79–100.

Marecek, J. (1989). Introduction. *Psychology of Women Quarterly, 13,* 367–377.

Markus, H., & Kitayama, S. (1991). Culture and the self: Implications for cognition, emotion, and motivation. *Psychological Review, 98,* 224–253.

McAdoo, H. (1986). Strategies used by Black single mothers against stress. In M. Simms & J. Malveaux (Eds.), *Slipping through the cracks: The status of Black women* (pp. 153–166). New Brunswick, NJ: Transaction Books.

Meyers, L. (1980). *Black women: Do they cope better?* Englewood Cliffs, NJ: Prentice-Hall.

Milburn, N., & D'Ercole, A. (1991). Homeless women: Moving toward a comprehensive model. *American Psychologist, 46,* 1161–1169.

Miller, S., & Kirsch, N. (1987). Sex differences in cognitive coping with stress. In R. Barnett, L. Biener, & G. Baruch (Eds.), *Gender and stress* (pp. 278–307). New York: The Free Press.

Mitchell, R., & Hodson, C. (1983). Coping with domestic violence: Social support and psychological health among battered women. *American Journal of Community Psychology, 11,* 629–654.

Pearlin, L., & Schooler, C. (1978). The structure of coping. *Journal of Health and Social Behavior, 19,* 2–21.

Peplau, L., & Conrad, E., (1989). Beyond nonsexist research: The perils of feminist methods in psychology. *Psychology of Women Quarterly, 13,* 379–400.

Singh, A., & Pandly, J. (1985). Dimensions of coping with socioeconomic problems. *Social Change, 15,* 51–54.

Smith, D. (1987). *The everyday world as problematic.* Boston: Northeastern University Press.

Solomon. L., & Rothblum, E. (1986). Stress, coping, and social support in women. *Behavior Therapist, 9*(10), 199–204.

Stone, A., & Neale, J. (1984). New measure of daily coping: Development and preliminary results. *Journal of Personality and Social Psychology, 46,* 892–906.

Unger, R. (1990). Imperfect reflections of reality: Psychology constructs gender. In R. Hare-Mustin & J. Marecek (Eds.), *Making a difference: Psychology and the construction of gender* (pp. 102–149). New Haven, CT: Yale University Press.

Watts-Jones, D. (1990). Toward a stress scale for African-American women. *Psychology of Women Quarterly, 14,* 271–275.

The Relationship Between Masculine Gender Role Stress and Men's Health Risk: The Validation of a Construct

RICHARD M. EISLER

MASCULINITY AND HEALTH

The wisdom of relying on traditional masculine gender role beliefs and behavior patterns to ensure men's health and adjustment to life has only recently been critically examined by mental and medical health researchers. In 1976 the popular writer and psychologist Herb Goldberg was one of the first to warn of the emotional and health "hazards of being male." Others, notably Doyle (1989) and Fasteau (1975), have theorized about the stressful and unhealthy aspects of adherence to traditional masculine imperatives, including competitiveness, a focus on obtaining power and control, and being successful at all costs. O'Neil (1982) has hypothesized that culturally sanctioned homophobia and antifemininity are central underlying precepts of masculinity that have produced stifling conformity in men's roles.

Recent epidemiological data on gender-linked differences between men's and women's health have documented sex differences in "premature mortality" and hazardous lifestyles or behavior patterns for men (Cleary, 1987; Harrison, Chin, & Ficarrotto, 1989). In the United States, women live, on average, about seven years longer than men; the rate of death if higher for men than for women at all ages, and for all leading causes of death (Verbrugge, 1985). Some of the data suggest that gender-related lifestyles may impact the differential death rates. For example, between the ages of 15 and 24, men die at three times the rate of women, largely because of the higher rates of violent death among male youth (Cleary, 1987).

Men have nearly twice the premature death rate of women from coronary artery disease. The reasons for that particular higher mortality rate among men are hotly debated between those advocating a biogenetic etiology and those adhering to a psychosocial perspective. What is not debated is the fact that men are nearly three times as likely to die in motor vehicle accidents and three times as likely as women to actually commit suicide (Waldron & Johnson, 1976). Higher death rates in men by homicide, suicide, and accidents have been attributed by some to the paucity of acceptable masculine alternatives for aggressive behaviors in coping with stress. Additionally, data compiled by Waldron and Johnson (1976) showed that men's death rate from lung cancer is nearly six times that of women, and twice as high from cirrhosis of the liver, suggesting that masculine coping styles that incorporate higher rates of smoking and drinking are added health risk factors for men.

Mental Health Issues

Large-scale American epidemiological studies conducted by Robins and her colleagues (Robins, Helzer, Weissman, Orvaschel, Gruenberg, Burke, & Regier, 1984) looked at gender differences in vulnerability to psychiatrically diagnosed mental disorders. The results showed that while women are more prone to anxiety disorders and depression, men show more evidence of antisocial personality disorder and alcohol and drug abuse. Also compelling is the evidence that men, compared with women, are far more likely to be involved in violent crime and in spouse or sexual abuse (Widom, 1984). Thus, it appears that our culturally sanctioned masculine coping styles, including repertoires of toughness, combativeness, and reliance on aggressive responses, may have maladaptive consequences for men and their families. In the context of our culture's sports events, military operations, and business competitions, masculine initiative and shows of force are virtuously applauded. In the context of armed robbery, rape, or sexual harassment, masculine imperatives of aggression and daring are clearly less than welcome.

The Concept of Masculine Gender Role Stress

A central impetus for the measurement of—and the research on—masculine gender role stress reported in this chapter was my assumption that our dominant culture's requirement that men adhere to several aspects of culturally approved masculine ideology and role behavior may have dysfunctional health consequences for many men and for those with whom they come into contact. Unlike some who write about men's issues, I do not believe there is evidence to conclude that all or even most of our most cherished stereotypic masculine qualities in themselves are necessarily detrimental to men's health. For instance, Cook's (1985) extensive review of research on androgynous, masculine, and feminine characteristics showed that many attributes of traditional masculinity, as opposed to traditional femininity, have positive implications for the psychological adjustment of both men and women.

In this chapter, I (a) discuss the theoretical derivation of the masculine gender role stress construct; (b) detail the empirical development of the Masculine Gender Role Stress Scale (MGRSS); (c) present validation of and research with the MGRSS; and finally, (d) discuss the implications of this research for understanding men's health problems.

THEORETICAL NOTIONS UNDERLYING MASCULINE GENDER ROLE STRESS

During the last few decades, there has been increasing interest among those doing research on men in viewing "masculinities" as cultural constructions that are imposed on men by particular social groups and organizations rather than as routine outcomes of bio-psycho-social development. For example, Franklin (1988) has pointed out that, traditionally, men, as distinct from women, have *shared* a culturally designed

and enforced way of seeing things, planning things, and doing things. That is, many American men, whatever their race, politics, ethnic background, and educational or vocational attainment, may have shared a collective "masculine consciousness" or traditional masculinity that is enacted through commitment to socially prescribed masculine gender roles. For example, many men who differ in race or ethnic background commonly value power and dominance in their relationships, approve of a certain degree of aggression and violence in gaining competitive advantage, and disdain "feminine" strategies for coping with life. This antifeminine imperative for men is often manifested through demeaning the importance or utility of self-disclosing emotion or vulnerability in human relationships. Some questions we might ask at this point are: How do men become so deeply committed to particular masculine gender roles? How do these roles become so pervasive among so many men of different ethnic background and status?

Bem's Gender Schema Theory

In contrast to her work on androgynous sex roles (1974), Sandra Bem's more recent theoretical work on cognitive processing differences between sex-typed and non-sex-typed persons (1981) has relevance for our notions about gender role stress. Bem (1981) has proposed a cognitive theory of the development of gender schema to explain the pervasiveness of each sex's affinity for masculine versus feminine gender roles and attitudes. She has proposed that sex-typed masculinity and femininity originate from an individual's general readiness to encode and organize information about the world and himself or herself in terms of the culture's definitions of "maleness" and "femaleness." Thus, a person's self-concept becomes interwoven with culturally approved, sex-typed distinctions.

What Bem's (1981) gender schema theory proposes, then, is that sex-typed attitudes and behaviors are learned when one is willing to process information primarily according to society's mandates of what is appropriate for one's own sex and to ignore information associated with the opposite sex. For example, the adults in a child's world seldom note how nurturant a little boy is or how stoic a little girl is. Therefore, the child learns to apply the same gender schema to himself or herself.

The implications of Bem's gender schema theory for development of the masculine gender role stress model are: (a) men and women to learn to evaluate their adequacy (as persons) based on their ability to regulate their behavior in accord with their learned masculine or feminine gender schema; (b) this self-propagating developmental process becomes stable at an early age; and (c) some men (and some women) become more highly committed than others to regulating their behavior in accord with masculine (or feminine) socially prescribed schema as a way of assessing their self-worth.

One might raise questions at this point about the problems associated with approaching life from such gender-based schemata. Certainly, men acting in predictably masculine ways and women acting in predictably feminine ways provide a certain stable, if not always comfortable, basis for relationships with both the same and the opposite gender. One has to look no further than the current debate about gay men in the military to note the potential havoc many fear will result if some men fail to think or behave in traditionally accepted masculine ways.

To thoroughly explore the complex questions about the disadvantages of men becoming highly committed to culturally stereotypic masculine attitudes and behaviors would require more space than we have here. Certainly, those men and women who have written about and participated in the women's movement against sexism have felt that rigid gender roles were becoming a problem for us all. However, one of the most influential scholars to portray the stressful and unhealthy implications of traditional masculinity was the psychologist Joseph H. Pleck.

Joseph Pleck's View of Masculinity

In the early 1980s, Pleck critically analyzed what he termed the gender role identification (GRI) paradigm in his book *The Myth of Masculinity* (1981). This paradigm had dominated the social sciences' views of

masculine sex typing since the 1930s. According to Pleck, the GRI paradigm held that boys innately need to develop a "masculine" sex role identity to ensure that they develop normally into adult men. From this perspective, mental health problems would arise not from the imposition of culturally inspired gender roles, but rather from the failure of men to learn gender roles appropriate to their biological sex.

To counter the long-held traditional notions that certain features of culturally defined masculinity, such as "dominance," are not only innate but necessary for healthy male development, Pleck (1981) set forth what he termed the gender role strain (GRS) paradigm. Among the assumptions of the GRS paradigm are (a) gender role norms are contradictory and inconsistent; (b) the proportion of individuals who violate traditional gender role norms is high; (c) violating gender role norms leads to social condemnation; (d) violating gender role norms leads to negative and stressful psychological consequences; (e) violating gender role norms has more severe consequences for males than females; and (f) certain consequences prescribed by gender role norms are psychologically dysfunctional. Pleck (1981) also reviewed existing research findings on the effects of gender role violation for men to support his propositions that traditional masculinity often produces deleterious psychological and physical health consequences.

Thus, Pleck's landmark book helped to systematically debunk long-held views that there is something inevitable, natural, or necessary about males developing culturally sanctioned masculine attitudes and role behaviors. On the contrary, the implications of Pleck's work for our notions about masculine gender role stress are that: (a) men have been externally directed by societal expectations to live up to culturally *imposed* definitions of masculinity; (b) the struggle to attain these masculine characteristics may frequently have undesirable consequences for many or even most men; and (c) the routine deployment of masculine strategies for dealing with life's problems may produce dysfunctional solutions and emotional distress for many men.

At this point, we might ask what aspects of traditional masculinity predispose men to being stressed in a manner different from women. Is there something about the way men have been socialized to think and respond differently from women that puts them at greater risk for developing certain types of health problems? How can culturally approved masculine gender role behavior increase or decrease a man's vulnerability to stress? To answer these questions, a measure assessing the kinds of situations that tend to produce more stress in men than in women was needed. But first, a theoretical view of stress that would enable the investigators to focus on gender differences in the cognitive attribution of stress in men compared with women needed to be developed. Richard Lazarus and his colleagues (Lazarus & Folkman, 1984; Lazarus, 1990) provided a model of stress appraisal and coping that we deemed particularly relevant to our development of the notion of masculine gender role stress.

Lazarus's Theory-Based Measurement of Stress

Over time, the concept of stress has evolved as a bio-psycho-social construct in which psychological and biological factors interact with environmental events to produce physical and psychological disorders (Goldberger & Breznitz, 1982; Neufeld, 1989; Selye, 1978). Modern theories that describe the way stressful situations produce illness are based on the notion that cognition links events to arousal. It is realized that the impacts of environmental events are cognitively modified by our perceptions, anticipations, and beliefs about a situation, as well as by our appraisal of the efficacy of our coping responses to them. According to Lazarus and Folkman (1984), "psychological stress is a particular relationship between the person and the environment that is appraised by the person as taxing or exceeding his or her resources and endangering his or her well being" (p. 19). Thus, the interaction between cognitive appraisals of situations and evaluations of one's ability to psychologically and emotionally manage those situations defines the stress process.

While many factors can influence one's appraisal of a situation as challenging or threatening, one's vulnerability to a stressor is partly related, as Lazarus and Folkman (1984) pointed out, to the strength of one's *commitment* to that event. Therefore, if a man becomes extremely committed to being successful at a particular enterprise, his vulnerability to stress and emotional upset should be proportional to the strength of his commitment.

MASCULINE GENDER ROLE STRESS PARADIGM

Borrowing from Bem's theory that gender role schema predispose men to view the world through masculine-tinted cognitive lenses, from Pleck's view that culturally imposed masculinity predisposes men to masculine gender role strain, and from Lazarus and Folkman's views about the roles of cognitive appraisal and commitment in understanding stress, we have developed the following propositions about the masculine gender role stress paradigm to help explain stress arousal and subsequent health problems in men.

1. The sociocultural contingencies that reward masculine attitudes and behaviors while punishing nonmasculine (i.e., feminine) attitudes result in the development of masculine gender role cognitive schema in the vast majority of individuals with XY chromosome patterns. Thus, little boys develop masculine schema that encourage them to attack rather than cry when someone hurts or threatens them, because the former response will be rewarded and the latter will be rejected as unmasculine. This schema is first rewarded by social peers and adults and then operates independently through a self-evaluation process in which a child says to himself, "this is a good [i.e., strong and masculine] way for me to behave."

2. Masculine schema are then employed by men, in varying degrees, to appraise threats and challenges from the environment as well as to evaluate and guide their choice of coping strategies. Masculine schema are lenses that shape men's appraisals of threat along the lines of traditional masculine gender ideology and also guide the selection of a response from a restricted repertoire of masculine coping behaviors. From this perspective, men are more likely to display

aggression when challenged than to employ cooperative or conciliatory responses.

3. Based on their disparate experiences, there are important differences among men as to how *committed* they are to culturally accepted models of masculinity. For a variety of temperamental, psychological, and cultural reasons, men differ in their level of commitment to traditional masculinity and stereotyped masculine behaviors. At one end of the continuum, men may be so committed to masculinity that they behave like certain male firefighters in New York City who, because they believed that women could not possess the skills and abilities essential to working safely with men, harassed female firefighters so that they would quit the department. At the other end of the continuum, men have relinquished their commitment to traditional masculinity by abandoning their careers to stay at home and raise their children.

4. Masculine gender role stress may arise from excessive commitment to and reliance on certain culturally approved masculine schema that limit the range of coping strategies employable in any particular situation. Some men may experience severe stress from losing in a competitive game; others who are less committed to masculine values can cope with the loss more easily, by telling themselves they played well anyway or they got healthy exercise from the competition.

5. Masculine gender role stress may also arise from the belief that one is not living up to culturally sanctioned masculine gender role behavior. Men may experience stress if they feel they have acted in an unmanly or feminine fashion. Many men are doubly stressed by experiencing fear or by feeling that they did not appear successful or tough enough in situations requiring masculine appearances of strength and invincibility.

Development of the MGRSS: Item Generation

A sentence completion task was used to elicit over 200 items from both male and female undergraduate students for both the Masculine Gender Role Stress Scale (MGRSS) for men and the Feminine Gender Role Stress Scale (FGRSS) for women. Only details regarding the gender role stress measure for men will be reported here for women. (See Gillespie & Eisler, 1992, for a description of the FGRSS.) The sentence completion task was designed to elicit sex-typed appraisals from several hundred college students by asking them to separately list what they felt would be the most difficult or most stressful things associated with being either a man or a woman. Additional items regarding the stressful aspects of being a man or woman were taken from various professional books and journals about gender issues. Based on these data, over 100 different items were written for a preliminary version of the men's MGRSS.

The preliminary items were then given to 25 male and 25 female graduate student and faculty judges in the Psychology Department at Virginia Polytechnic Institute and State University. The judges were asked to give their appraisals of how much stress the situations represented by each item would generally be expected to elicit in men and in women on seven-point intensity scales. The items retained for the initial versions of MGRSS had to meet two criteria: (1) the average intensity ratings for *both* male and female raters of men's probable stress intensity had to be assessed in the moderate to high range (4.0 or above on the 7.0 scale), and (2) the mean appraisals of *both* male and female raters had to indicate that the item was significantly *more stressful* for men than for women to be retained for the original MGRSS scale. Only 66 items passed this screen.

Validation

The 66-item version of the MGRSS was administered to another sample of 82 male and 91 female psychology undergraduates. It was deemed important to distinguish masculine gender role stress from purely sex-typed masculinity, in line with our earlier notion that not all adherence to masculine norms is stress-producing. For example, measures of sex-typed masculinity typically assess socially desirable masculine attributes, including autonomy, assertiveness, self-confidence, and so on. For this purpose, the measure of sex-typing in Spence and

Helmreich's (1978) Personal Attributes Questionnaire (PAQ) was administered.

In addition, we felt it was important for this preliminary validation to determine links between masculine gender role stress, emotions frequently associated with stress—including anger and anxiety—and health risk habits. Thus, Siegel's (1986) Multidimensional Anger Inventory and the State-Trait Anxiety Inventory (Spielberger, Gorsuch, Lushene, Vagg, & Jacobs, 1983) were also included in the battery, as were items adapted from the National Health Information Clearinghouse (1984) instrument, which asks subjects about their health habits, including diet, exercise, smoking, drinking, and seat belt use. The results from administering the MGRSS with the above measures follow.

I have to caution our readers at this point that most of the items for our research MGRSS were generated by a young group of predominantly white college males and females who may have differed in their views about gender from other, more diverse educational, ethnic, and cultural groups. Additional validation studies will be needed to compare these results with those of other cultural groups.

Gender, the MGRSS, and Masculinity   Since the MGRSS items were constructed to assess experiences that were more likely to be appraised as stressful for men than for women, it was expected that in a population of "normal" men and women, men would score higher on the preliminary MGRSS than women (Eisler & Skidmore, 1987). This was confirmed in that, on average, men achieved higher MGRSS scores (mean = 265) than women (mean = 240) (p<.01).

Previous research had shown that some aspects of culturally sanctioned masculinity (e.g., assertiveness) play a positive role in the healthy adjustment of both men and women, whereas we were selecting MGRSS items to reflect the appraisal of the stress-inducing aspects of masculinity for men. Thus, we were expecting that the MGRSS would have weak associations with measures of sex-typed masculinity. The results confirmed our hope for the MGRSS in that it failed to correlate significantly with the PAQ measure of stereotypic positive masculine traits (r = .08).

The MGRSS, Anger, and Anxiety   As expected, the MGRSS had significant correlations with anger and anxiety. In this sample, the MGRSS correlated moderately highly with the Siegel anger inventory (.54), and to a lesser degree with state anxiety (.23) and trait anxiety (.22) scores. Just the opposite pattern was found for women. Their scores on the MGRSS correlated more highly with state anxiety (.40) than with anger (.17). Thus, as expected, men who scored high on appraisal of masculine stress were more prone to anger, while women who indicated such stress manifested their stress responses with elevated state anxiety (Eisler, Skidmore, & Ward, 1988). Additionally, in a recent study, Arrindell, Kolk, Pickersgill, and Hageman (1993) found a very strong relationship between MGRSS scores and the self-reported experience of irrational fears, particularly social fears in men.

Masculinity, the MGRSS, and Health Behaviors   Finally, it was predicted that sex-typed masculinity would have a positive association with psychosocial health and adjustment in men, whereas our MGRSS measure would predict high-risk health habits (smoking and high alcohol consumption) in these same men. Multiple regression and correlation analysis showed that, as expected, the PAQ measure of masculinity was negatively associated with anxiety (r = −.42) and anger (r = −.18), but positively associated with good health habits (r = .29) (Eisler, Skidmore, & Ward, 1988). On the other hand, the MGRSS, as previously indicated, was positively associated with anger and anxiety, but also positively associated, albeit weakly, with high-risk health habits.

Thus, our initial investigations with the preliminary version of the MGRSS indicate that masculine gender role stress is a viable construct conceptually and operationally distinct from sex-typed masculinity per se. For this population, MGRSS scores were higher for men than for women, whereas previous research has shown that more typically women admit to greater distress than do men. Additionally, MGRSS scores, but not masculinity, were associated with higher levels of anger and anxiety in the male samples. This is consistent with research on Type A behavior patterns, which has shown that negative emotional traits, such as impatience and hostility are associated with higher Type A health risk (Price, 1982). Finally, these results suggest that while subjects who score high in socially acceptable masculine traits may not be at especially high risk for health problems, those who score high on the MGRSS are more prone to engage in high-risk health behaviors.

The MGRSS and Health Problems   An additional study with employees of a telephone company was undertaken at Washington University Medical Center to determine the association between MGRSS scores and various health practices of employed adults (Watkins, Eisler, Carpenter, Schectman, & Fisher, 1991). The results indicated that high MGRSS scores were moderately associated with Type A coronary-prone behavior, hostility, and elevated blood pressure in both men and women. Also, high-scoring MGRSS participants reported less satisfaction with their lives than low-scoring MGRSS participants. Thus, there was a correlation between masculine gender role stress and cardiovascular health in a population of working adults.

Factor Analysis of the MGRSS

To further refine the MGRSS scale and also to more specifically examine the meaning of the MGRSS itself, individual items were correlated with the total scale scores, using a new sample of 150 college-age males. Also, with this new sample, factor analytic procedures were employed to determine the underlying structure of the instrument (Eisler & Skidmore, 1987).

From these procedures, the initial 66-item version of the scale was reduced to 40 items, owing to either low intercorrelation with the total scale or weak factor loadings of some items. The 40-item version of the MGRSS has the following five interpretable factors.

1. Physical Inadequacy: This group of nine items reflects fears of an inability to meet masculine standards of physical fitness, in sports rivalries or in sexual prowess.

2. Emotional Inexpressiveness: High stress appraisal ratings on these seven items reflect fears of vulnerability in expressing one's emotions, such as love, weakness, or hurt feelings. These items also reflect fear of dealing with other people's vulnerable feelings.

3. Subordination to Women: These nine items reflect fears of being outperformed by women in activities at which men traditionally are expected to excel. Representative items place the male in the position of being outperformed by women at work or in a sports competition.

4. Intellectual Inferiority: Endorsement of these seven items reflects fear of appraisal as unable to think rationally or to be decisive, or as not smart enough to handle a situation.

5. Performance Failure: These eight items reflect men's fear of failure to meet masculine standards in the arenas of work and sexual adequacy. That these two instrumental situations clustered together reflects men's perception that their feelings about their masculine adequacy connect the two areas.

Discussion

The lack of association between MGRSS scores and the PAQ measure of masculinity and the different pattern of these two instruments' associations with indicators of stress, hostility, anxiety, and health risk behaviors were viewed as supportive of the masculine gender role stress construct. First, it appears that men who score high on socially desirable masculine traits are not necessarily at high risk for psychological difficulties or health problems. Being assertive, being decisive, and having the ability to act independently contribute to positive personal adjustment for both genders. It is therefore a mistake to implicate all dimensions of traditional masculinity as the source of the host of stress and personality disorders that occur in men. However, the findings did support the notion that men's commitment or adherence to some aspects of "culturally approved masculinity" may be unhealthy and stress-producing. This was demonstrated in the associations between MGRSS scores and high levels of anger, greater fears, and a propensity for engaging in higher-risk behaviors. The next question addressed was, What are these areas of masculine commitment that are likely to produce stress and/or behavior problems in men? The five dimensions revealed in the factor analytic study of the MGRSS have provided some suggestions.

First, many men place a great deal of emphasis on being able to prevail in situations that require physical strength and physical fitness. Being perceived as weak or sexually below par is a major threat to self-esteem for many men. Second, men tend to be distressed by women who they perceive to be equal or superior to them in traditional masculine domains such as competitive games or earning capacity. Third, it is important for men to view themselves as supremely decisive and self-assured. Men value acting in a rational as opposed to an emotional manner because the latter is viewed as feminine. Fourth, most men are committed to performing well and being perceived as triumphant in two arenas, work achievement and sexual prowess. Finally, many men feel uncomfortable in situations that require expression of tender (read, feminine) emotions because doing so is perceived as a violations of traditional masculine norms. Unfortunately, some men experience little stress when they express anger and violence, which are often sanctioned by some of our culture's most cherished views of masculinity.

The MGRSS and Emotional Expressiveness

Based on our factor analytic study, which showed that both expressing emotion and dealing with the emotions of others were associated with distress in our male samples, we conducted a study looking at the relationship between MGRSS scores and emotional expression in college males who role-played scenes requiring expressions of anger and irritability, on the one hand, and expressions of fear and vulnerability, on the other. Verbal emotional expressions and nonverbal facial expressions were videotaped during the role-plays. Mehrabian's (1972) criteria coding "movements of facial muscles to non-neutral

expressions" (p. 195) were used to rate changes in facial expressions.

The results indicated that all males, irrespective of MGRSS scores, showed less facial expressiveness when they were expected to express fear or tenderness than when they were expected to express anger. Second, the high-scoring MGRSS men were less verbally expressive than the low-scorers in situations that required the expression of tender emotions. There were no differences between the high- and low-scoring MGRSS men in the verbal expression of anger. Taken as a whole, these results supported the notion that masculine gender role fears are related to the suppression of emotional expression.

Whether men's socialized tendency to inhibit emotional expression has deleterious health consequences for them has been debated in the popular literature. Recently, Pennebaker and his associates (Pennebaker, Hughes & O'Heeron, 1987; Pennebaker, Kiecolt-Glaser, & Glaser, 1988) have shown that individuals who do not disclose unpleasant emotions have chronic physiological arousal and poorer immune system functioning. Thus, there is some support for the notion that men, with their greater tendency than women to inhibit feelings of fear or sadness, may be more vulnerable to disorders related to physiological arousal. Should future research with the MGRSS substantiate these findings, it would mean that men highly committed to suppressing their feelings of vulnerability are at greater risk for stress-induced disorders.

THE MGRSS AND CARDIOVASCULAR REACTIVITY

The previously described research on the development and measurement of masculine gender role stress has provided tentative confirmation of our belief that strong commitment to some aspects of masculinity as prescribed by Western cultures may be unhealthy for men.

The positive associations obtained between MGRSS scores and measures of anger arousal and blood pressure have led us to hypothesize that high

MGRSS scores may be associated with the cardiovascular disease process, which has been a leading cause of premature death in male, as compared with female, populations. In this section, I focus on a series of laboratory studies conducted with my student colleagues that have attempted to link gender-related appraisal of stress to the increased incidence of cardiovascular disease in men.

The electronic media and the popular press have often speculated about the relationship between men's economic struggles in the competitive jungles of work and their early demise. It remained for Friedman and Rosenman (1974) to introduce the experimentally verifiable concept of a Type A behavior pattern to postulate linking coronary artery disease in their predominantly male patients to such masculine traits as aggressiveness, competitive drive, and overcommitment to work. Since the development of coronary disease occurs over several decades, designing experimentally sound research that attempts to link it to psychological responses requires that one understand the physiological mechanisms through which behavior patterns may initiate a pathogenic process at the biological level, resulting over time in physical illness.

Cardiovascular Reactivity

Cardiovascular reactivity has received much attention as a potential mechanism for the development of coronary artery disease (Krantz & Manuck, 1984; Manuck, Kaplan, & Clarkson, 1985). According to the cardiovascular reactivity model, chronic and sustained increases in heart rate and blood pressure, activated by high levels of stress through endocrine responses, cause injury to the arterial walls over time. Reviews of the literature on gender differences in cardiovascular reactivity have found that men generally show greater blood pressure reactivity than do women, although the sexes typically do not differ in heart rate responses (Polefrone & Manuck, 1987).

There has been much conjecture that greater cardiovascular reactivity, and hence heart disease, in men as compared with women, is primarily a function of gender-based biological differences, including hormonal differences. However, additional studies

(e.g., Van Egeren, 1979) have shown that when women are placed in some kinds of stressful situations, they exhibit similar or even more reactivity than men. Thus, researchers have speculated that gender differences in reactivity to particular situations may sometimes be a function of gender differences in the "cognitive appraisal of these situations as stressful" (Jorgenson & Houston, 1981; Polefrone & Manuck, 1987).

From this perspective, the heightened cardiovascular responses in males to the laboratory stressors of pain or competition measured in previous research may be understood as men's cognitive appraisal of these challenges as particularly threatening to their masculine self-image, whereas women are less threatened because femininity does not demand that women withstand pain or be as competitive as men.

The next section reports on a series of laboratory studies designed to explore the relationship between MGRSS scores and cardiovascular reactivity, and hence the risk of cardiovascular disease. Also, these studies were designed to determine how men's cognitive appraisals of situations containing masculine challenge situations may produce measurable differences from gender-neutral or feminine stressors.

The MGRSS, Stress, and Reactivity

The first in a series of laboratory studies was designed to evaluate the association between masculine gender role stress appraisal and cardiovascular reactivity. It was conducted by exposing college men with high, medium, or low MGRSS scores to two types of stressors. The first was a standard laboratory induction of "pain" known as the Cold Pressor Stress Test. The subject was required to place his hand in ice water for a period of several minutes. Physiological measures of cardiovascular response were measured before, during, and after the hand was immersed in the cold water. The magnitude of the increases in blood pressure and heart rate response were employed as measures of the men's reactivity to this painful stressor.

The addition to the physical stress of the cold pressor test, high-, medium-, and low-scoring MGRSS subjects were also subjected to the Masculine Threat Interview, a psychologically stressful interview by a female confederate, who frequently challenged the subject's masculinity. The interviewer asked pointed questions based on the masculine gender role stress factors identified by the MGRSS. For example, subjects were challenged to talk about topics such as their academic performance, problems in dating, and ability to express themselves emotionally.

The results, analyzed by multiple regression, indicated that there was a linear relationship between MGRSS scores and systolic blood pressure reactivity to both the Cold Pressor Stress Test and the Masculine Threat Interview. That is, there was a progressive increase in blood pressure reactivity associated with an increasing MGRSS score. The results for the cold Pressor Stress Test and the Masculine Threat Interview were virtually indistinguishable. The stress of both pain and psychological threat to self-esteem had very similar effects in producing greatly increased reactivity for the high-scoring MGRSS men compared with low-scorers. Thus, the nature of the challenge, pain, or psychological threat was found to be less important than the subject's tendency to appraise the situation as a threat to his masculine gender role competence as reflected in his MGRSS score.

The MGRSS, Stress, Reactivity, and Masculine Challenge

The previous study suggested that cardiovascular reactivity in men is in part a function of differences in their cognitive appraisals of threats to their masculinity. That is, high-scoring MGRSS men tend to appraise certain situations involving masculine challenge as more stressful and therefore show greater reactivity than their low-scoring counterparts. In the absence of cognitive threats to masculinity, there should be no differences in the stress responses, and hence in the reactivity of high- and low-scoring MGRSS men. However, when presented with clear evidence of masculine challenge, we expected the high-scoring MGRSS men to be more reactive than the low-scorers.

To test these predictions, we exposed both high- and low-scoring MGRSS men to the previously described cold pressor test under different gender-relevant instructions, to either enhance or reduce the "masculine challenge" of the task (Lash, Eisler, & Schulman, 1990). We wanted to determine whether the greater reactivity of the high-scoring MGRSS men was a function of the pain of the cold water immersion itself or of the particular way these men assessed the implied masculine demand characteristics of the situation, as compared with the low-scoring MGRSS men.

To ensure that high- and low-scoring MGRSS men would assess the stressor differently, male groups were exposed to either a high or low masculine challenge cold pressor test that differed only in that we provided a different rationale for performing the task. In the low masculine challenge test, prior to immersion, the men were told that we simply wanted to obtain physiological measures on people who had their hands in cold water. In the high masculine challenge test, prior to immersion, we emphasized that this was a test of endurance, strength, and ability to withstand pain. The results, as expected, indicated that for the low masculine challenge test, there were no differences in the cardiovascular responses of high-scoring as compared with low-scoring MGRSS men. However, for men in the high masculine challenge groups, large differences in reactivity occurred, with high-scoring MGRSS men showing much more blood pressure reactivity both prior to and during immersion in the cold water. That is, high-scoring MGRSS men were more reactive than the low-scores during both the anticipation of the masculine challenge as well as during exposure to the stressor itself.

Further evidence that gender-determined appraisal plays a role in cardiovascular reactivity was gathered from additional studies we conducted using both male and female subjects exposed to masculine and feminine challenges (Lash, 1991; Lash, Gillespie, Eisler, & Southard, 1991). In these subsequent investigations, it was found that women were more reactive than men if the situation threatened their adequacy in areas in which females are expected to excel, such as nurturance and child-rearing ability. On the other hand, it was found that men were more reactive than women if the situations contained masculine challenges such as competitiveness or ability to withstand pain.

Discussion

It must be recognized that our studies showing relationships between the MGRSS and masculine challenge and cardiovascular reactivity have uncovered far from conclusive evidence linking masculine gender role behavior patterns with the development of coronary artery disease in men. However, I think we have been able to show that some stresses in men are gender-specific, and that by increasing the masculine relevance of tasks, we can increase arousal in susceptible high-scoring MGRSS men. Second, we have shown that in understanding how masculinity predisposes men to appraise and struggle with the environment in certain gender-stereotypic ways, we may better understand the connection between masculine constructions of the self and men's vulnerability to gender-induced health problems.

CONCLUSIONS

Our research with the MGRSS has shown that men tend to experience stress arousal when attempting to deal with emotions they feel are more appropriate for women, or when fearing that women may best them in an activity at which men are expected to excel. Men are also likely to experience stress if they appraise themselves as not performing up to manly standards of achievement in the masculine spheres of work and sexual performance. These appraisals result from pressures men tend to place on themselves to conform to outmoded stereotypes, that is, caricatures of traditional masculine roles.

Overall, the studies we have done with the MGRSS, laboratory stressors, and measures of cardiovascular reactivity have supported a cognitively mediated view of stress based on men's diverse commitments to traditional masculine ideology. High-scoring MGRSS men who were highly committed to traditional masculinity were more likely than others to become excessively emotionally aroused, as measured by their blood pressure, when asked to perform tasks at which men are expected to excel, such as the ability to withstand pain. When the same tasks were presented without the stereotypic expectation that a man would suppress feelings of pain, there were no differences in stress arousal between high- and low-scoring MGRSS men. Additionally, when men were presented with tasks at which females were expected to excel (Lash, 1991), men did not show as much reactivity as the women. These results suggest that men and women are socialized to follow gender-segregated patterns of response based on perceived masculine- and feminine-relevant challenges. Men, for example, are more likely to be stressed by perceived inadequacies in the work environment or deficiencies in strength or mental toughness. Women, on the other hand, may be more stressed by feelings of inadequacy in such areas as the family and relationships (Gillespie & Eisler, 1992).

Future researchers into the health and adjustment problems of men, such as heart disease, hypertension, alcoholism, spouse abuse, and sexual harassment, must become more informed about the pressures and influences of socialized masculine gender roles, which promote unhealthy coping behavior. New programs for men might develop, promote, and evaluate psycho-educational programs on alternative roles and decision-making strategies for men that would expand their range of healthy behaviors.

Finally, it must be recognized that most of the research reported on here was done with relatively young, well-educated, predominantly white men. Nevertheless, there is reason to suspect that there are dysfunctional aspects to the masculinities created by men of other ages, races, and cultural groups as well. Much additional work is needed to generalize the suitability of these findings to men of other ages, races, and cultural backgrounds.

REFERENCES

Arrindell, W. A., Kolk, A. M., Pickersgill, M. J., & Hageman, W. J. (1993). Biological sex, sex role orientation, masculine sex role stress, dissimulation and self-reported fears. *Advances in Behaviour Research and Therapy, 15,* 103–146.

Bem S. (1974). The measurement of psychological androgyny. *Journal of Consulting and Clinical Psychology, 42,* 155–162.

Bem S. (1981). Gender schema theory: A cognitive account of sex typing. *Psychological Review, 88,* 354–364.

Cleary, P. D. (1987). Gender differences in stress related disorders. In R. C. Barnett, L. Biener, & G. K. Baruch (Eds.), *Gender and stress* (pp. 39–72). New York: Free Press.

Cook, E. P. (1985). *Psychological androgyny.* New York: Pergamon.

Doyle, J A. (1989). *The male experience.* Dubuque, IA: William C. Brown.

Eisler, R. M., & Skidmore, J. R. (1987). Masculine gender role stress: Scale development and component factors in the appraisal of stressful situations. *Behavior Modification, 11,* 123–136.

Eisler, R. M., Skidmore, J. R., & Ward, C. H. (1988). Masculine gender-role stress: Predictor of anger, anxiety and health-risk behaviors. *Journal of Personality Assessment, 52,* 133–141.

Fasteau, M. F. (1975). *The male machine.* New York: Dell.

Franklin, C. W. (1988). *Men and society.* Chicago: Nelson-Hall.

Friedman, M., & Rosenman, R. (1974). *Type A behavior and your heart.* Greenwich, CT: Fawcett.

Gillespie, B. L., & Eisler, R. M. (1992). Development of the Feminine Gender Role Stress Scale: A cognitive-behavioral measure of stress, appraisal and coping for women. *Behavior Modification, 16,* 426–438.

Goldberg, H. (1976). *The hazards of being male.* New York: Nash.

Goldberger L., & Breznitz, S. (Eds). (1982). *Handbook of stress: Theoretical and clinical aspects.* New York: Free Press.

Harrison, J., Chin, J., & Ficarrotto, T. (1989). Warning: Masculinity may be dangerous to your health. In M. S. Kimmel & M. A. Messner (Eds.), *Men's lives* (pp. 296–309). New York: Macmillan.

Jorgensen, R. S., & Houston, B. K. (1981). Type A behavior patterns, sex differences, and cardiovascular responses to recovery from stress. *Motivation and Emotion, 5,* 201–214.

Krantz, D. S., & Manuck, S. B. (1984). Acute physiologic reactivity and risk of cardiovascular disease: A review and methodologic critique. *Psychological Bulletin, 96,* 435–464.

Lash, S. J. (1991). *Gender differences in cardiovascular reactivity: Effects of gender relevance of the stressor.* Unpublished doctoral dissertation, Virginia Polytechnic Institute and State University, Blacksburg, VA.

Lash, S. J., Eisler, R. M., & Schulman, R. S. (1990). Cardiovascular reactivity to stress in men. *Behavior Modification, 14,* 3–20.

Lash, S. J., Gillespie, B. L., Eisler, R. M., & Southard, D. R. (1991). Sex differences in cardiovascular reactivity: Effects of the gender relevance of the stressor. *Health Psychology, 6,* 392–398.

Lazarus, R. S. (1990). Theory-based stress measurement. *Psychological Inquiry, 1,* 2–13.

Lazarus, R. S., & Folkman, S. (1984). *Stress, appraisal, and coping.* New York: Springer.

Manuck, S. B., Kaplan, J. R., & Clarkson, T. B. (1985): Stress-induced heart rate reactivity and atherosclerosis in female macaques. *Psychosomatic Medicine, 47,* 90.

Mehrabian, A. (1972). *Nonverbal communication.* Chicago: Aldine.

National Health Information Clearinghouse. (1984). *Health style: A self test.* Washington, DC: U.S. Public Health Service.

Neufeld, R. W. (Ed.). (1989). *Advances in the investigation of psychological stress.* New York: Wiley.

O'Neil, J. M. (1982). Gender role conflict and strain in men's lives: Implications for psychiatrists, psychologists, and other human service providers. In K. Solomon & N. B. Levy (Eds.), *Men in transition: Theory and therapy* (pp. 5–44). New York: Plenum.

Pennebaker, J. W., Hughes, C. F., & O'Heeron, R. C. (1987). The psychophysiology of confession: Linking inhibitory and psychosomatic processes. *Journal of Personality and Social Psychology, 52,* 781–793.

Pennebaker, J. W., Kiecolt-Glaser, J. K., & Glaser, R. (1988). Disclosure of traumas and immune function: Health implications for psychotherapy. *Journal of Consulting and Clinical Psychology, 56,* 239–245.

Pleck, J. (1981). *The myth of masculinity.* Cambridge, MA: MIT Press.

Polefrone, J. M., & Manuck, S. B. (1987). Gender differences in cardiovascular and neuroendocrine response to stressors. In R. Barnett, L. Biener, & G. Baruch (Eds.), *Gender and stress* (pp. 13–38). New York: Free Press.

Price. V. A. (1982) *Type A behavior pattern: A model for research and practice.* New York: Academic Press.

Robins, L. N., Helzer, J. E., Wiessman, M. M., Orvaschel, H., Gruenberg, E., Burke, J. D., & Regier, D. A. (1984). Lifetime prevalence of specific psychiatric disorders in three sites. *Archives of General Psychiatry, 41,* 949–958.

Selye, H. (1978). *The stress of life.* New York: McGraw-Hill.

Siegel, J. N. (1986). The Multidimensional Anger Inventory. *Journal of Personality and Social Psychology, 51,* 191–200.

Spence, J. T., & Helmreich, R. L. (1978). *Masculinity and femininity: Their psychological dimensions, correlates, and antecedents.* Austin: University of Texas Press.

Spielberger, C. D., Gorsuch, R. L., Lushene, R., Vagg, P. R., & Jacobs, G. A. (1983). *Manual for the State-Trait Anxiety Inventory (Form Y).* Palo Alto, CA: Consulting Psychologists Press.

Van Egeren, L. F. (1979). Cardiovascular changes during social competition in a mixed motive game. *Journal of Personality and Social Psychology, 37,* 858–864.

Verbrugge, L. M. (1985). Gender and health: An update on hypothesis and evidence. *Journal of Health and Social Behavior, 26,* 156–182.

Waldron, I., & Johnson, S. (1976). Why do women live longer than men? *Journal of Human Stress, 2,* 19–29.

Watkins, P. L., Eisler, R. M., Carpenter, L., Schechteman, K. B., & Fisher, E. B. (1991). Psychosocial and physiological correlates of male gender role stress among employed adults. *Behavioral Medicine, 17,* 86–90.

Widom, C. S. (Ed). (1984). *Sex roles and psychopathology.* New York: Plenum.

CHECKPOINTS

1. Banyard and Graham-Bermann challenge prevailing psychological theories that suggest that women are less able to cope with stress than are men. They provide an alternative view of stress and coping, which emerges from a contextualized analysis of women's experience, including social forces and access to resources.

2. Eisler proposes a new measurement scale to assess male gender role strain and uses this scale to predict cardiovascular reactivity. The results of this research indicate that certain elements of the male gender role are related to stress responses and may be associated with unhealthy coping responses.

Gender and Health

QUESTIONS FOR REFLECTION

1. How could an understanding of gender improve the approach taken to biomedical research?
2. Should medical specialties be developed for men's health and women's health? If physicians treat both female and male patients, what should they know about gender roles?

CHAPTER APPLICATION

1. Interview several male and female friends about what events they find stressful and how they cope with stress. Do you find any patterns of difference or similarity? Which responses to stress do you think will be most successful, and which might be related to negative arousal and health consequences?

Gender, Mental Health, and Psychopathology

QUESTIONS TO THINK ABOUT

- **Why are definitions of sex and gender important in the study of psychopathology?**
- **Are there sex differences in psychopathology?**
- **What is the relationship of gender roles to psychological distress?**
- **How do individual and sociocultural factors play a role in psychopathology?**
- **What gender biases have existed in the diagnosis and treatment of mental illness?**
- **What other biases exist in the diagnosis and treatment of mental illness, and how do they intersect with gender?**
- **How are diagnostic categories influenced by social stereotypes?**
- **How do gender prescriptions shape perceptions of what are considered normal behaviors or feelings?**
- **What innovations in psychotherapy have resulted from feminist criticism?**
- **What are the major tenets of feminist therapy?**
- **What challenges face feminist therapy in its goal to include men and minorities?**

QUESTIONS OF DEFINITION

What comes to mind when you think of a normal person? Someone who does what everyone else does? Someone who doesn't act crazy? Someone who can function in daily life? Someone who acts "right" or follows the cultural norms? How do we judge whether someone is normal or abnormal? The questions of what defines normal and abnormal and how we judge whether people are normal or abnor-

mal are at the heart of the mental health enterprise. We answer these questions all the time in making informal evaluations of people. Yet for all the research in the mental health field, there is still no standardized definition of abnormal behavior among either professionals or the lay population. Therapists do, of course, take action based on their chosen definitions of normal and abnormal and have developed criteria for treating individuals. The point is that therapists function more on consensus than on proven scientific meaning. The definition of normal or abnormal behavior is always a matter of subjective meaning, and that meaning, as you will read in several of the articles in this chapter, has shifted over time because of changes in social values, political activism, and less frequently, scientific evidence. One premise of this chapter is that questions of definition, especially about mental health, are open questions, provoking disagreement and often contentious debate.

Studying Mental Health and Questions of Sex and Gender

This debate centers around many of the issues you have already been exposed to in this book. In particular, we would like to draw your attention to the meaning of the terms *sex* and *gender* that you read about in chapter 1. The use of these two terms, as you recall, is not simply a semantic debate but reflects the implicit (most often) or explicit (less often) beliefs of researchers about the nature of the phenomena that they are studying. Most of the research in the area of psychopathology has studied *sex* as a subject variable, comparing women and men. Not surprisingly, researchers have not been careful to only use the term *sex,* rather, they use the terms *sex* and *gender* interchangeably. Much less attention has been given to gender-related characteristics such as masculinity and femininity and how these characteristics might influence the findings of research in psychopathology. Lewine (1994) suggests that researchers of psychopathology could benefit from a more clearly defined approach in studying the effects of sex and gender. For example, according to Lewine, most of the schizophrenia research uses sex as an independent variable; however, work in this area could benefit from the inclusion of gender as a way to explore the meaning of gender-based delusions in schizophrenia. Focusing on either the categories of sex or the social construction of gender often reveals a researcher's perspective on the causes of any differences in psychopathology. Those researchers interested in biological explanations of psychopathology see it as a condition or a disorder that resides in individuals,

which reflects the essentialist view that we have described in detail in previous chapters. This perspective uses the medical model approach, in which psychopathology is seen as a disease that has clear biological underpinnings and a well-defined set of symptoms. In contrast, a social constructionist views psychopathology in relationship to social as well as individual characteristics. Pathological behaviors, therefore, must be understood in the context in which they occur and cannot be simply reduced to an abstract set of symptoms. Mental health and mental illness reflect either adaptive or maladaptive responses to particular situations in which gender norms are operative. Instead of conceptualizing all psychological problems as mental disorders, social constructionists are more likely to view many of the problems that are labeled as psychopathological as part of the unequal power distribution that characterizes the conditions of everyday life (Tavris, 1992). Although social constructionists do not deny the seriousness of certain disorders or the need, at times, for chemical interventions (e.g., certain drug treatments), they are united in their belief that psychopathology needs to be understood in terms of the social interpretations given to specific behaviors by both individuals and society.

Diagnosis and Treatment of Mental Health as it Relates to Gender

Serious consequences result from a therapist's definition of psychopathology. How mental disorders are diagnosed and what treatment modalities are deemed appropriate will differ radically depending on which perspective a researcher or a therapist adopts. Several important issues related to diagnosis and treatment will be discussed in this chapter. The first article in this chapter, *Gender and Psychological Distress* by Ellen Cook, describes some of the ways that gender roles are related to psychopathology, both at the psychological and sociocultural levels. Cook provides an overview of several individual disorders in which sex differences in diagnosis have emerged, and she provides an interpretive framework from which to understand such findings. The questions of diagnosis and of how women and members of other marginalized groups have fared in the traditional mental health system is addressed in varying ways by the next three articles. Jeanne Marecek and Rachel Hare-Mustin, in their article titled *A Short History of the Future: Feminism and Clinical Psychology*, describe how women have been treated by the clinical establishment and how different waves of feminism have responded to systematic misdiagnosis, treatment biases, sexual misconduct in therapy, and the misprescribing and overprescribing of psychoactive drugs. For example, behavior consistent with traditional gender roles has been treated as a psychopathological syndrome, known as self-defeating personality disorder, which ultimately stigmatizes women simply for exhibiting behavior that may be expected of them (Caplan, 1993). Terry Kupers, in his article *The Politics of Psychiatry: Gender and Sexual Preference in DSM-IV*, explains that the most current version of the major diagnostic tool used by psychiatrists, psychologists, and social workers still categorizes as pathological those individuals who deviate from gender prescriptions. Many of these prescriptions exist as cultural stereotypes, and women and members of various minority groups are especially vulnerable to both misdiagnosis and ineffective therapy by clinicians. In *Clinical Diagnosis among Diverse Populations: A Multicultural Perspective*, Alison Solomon contends that several factors, such as cultural and clinician bias, poor diagnostic tools, and institutional racism, explain why minorities have so often been the victims of poor evaluation and treatment. As long as the mental health system is controlled by a small power elite, there will be very little impetus for change. The final issue that we address in this chapter concerns therapeutic approaches that challenge the traditional view of mental illness and its treatment and push for greater focus on cultural diversity. The last reading, *The Future of Feminist Therapy* by Laura Brown and Annette Brodsky, explains the basic tenets of feminist therapy and how this approach has evolved to include the diverse experiences of both women and men.

GENDER ROLES AND PSYCHOPATHOLOGY

Gender Role Conformity and Sex Differences in Mental Health

The previous chapters of this book have shown how gender pervades all aspects of our lives. Gender is an essential element in our interpersonal relationships, in how we view ourselves and each other as sexual beings, in how we behave in different social contexts, in how we handle stress and develop coping strategies, and in how social institutions treat us at work and at home. In all these situations, our culture pushes us to acquire and conform to specific gender roles. Your previous readings have shown the negative consequences of gender role conformity: unhappy relationships, unequal distribution of labor in heterosexual families, violence against women, lost educational opportunities. Does such conformity create risks for psychopathology? According to Cook's analysis, substantial evidence indicates that psychological distress is related to the gender roles that males and females adopt and that, while both men and women may develop the same psychological problems, the etiology and expression of certain pathologies may differ markedly in relationship to these gender roles. Cook also argues that understanding male and female responses to particular gender roles is important in situations in which different psychological problems develop in response to life situations. One interesting set of findings shows that gender roles in marriages impact on the mental health of males and females. Married women suffer significantly higher rates of mental illness than do married men. In contrast, single women show lower rates of mental illness than do single men (Walker, Bettes, Kain, & Harvey, 1985). Why? Several researchers contend that the traditional expectations of marriage often place inordinate burdens on women. As you know from your readings in chapter 11, women in heterosexual couples do a disproportionate amount of housework, even though both partners may be employed outside the home (Kurdek, 1993). In addition, women often have little control over when their assigned tasks must be done, which leads to a greater sense of powerlessness (Barnett & Rivers, 1996). Women who stay at home are also disadvantaged, because their identity is often tied to their husband's status. For men, on the other hand, marriage enhances social status; it provides a man with intimacy, a support system, and someone to do the bulk of the household work. In certain ways, men benefit from marriage and women suffer from trying to fulfill too many roles. It is no surprise that gender roles, especially those based on gender inequality, can lead to psychological distress, most notably depression. As Marecek and Hare-Mustin contend in their article, the issues of everyday life can be highly problematic.

Gender Roles and Depression

Depression is an example of a disorder that has been consistently diagnosed more frequently in women than in men. Nolen-Hoeksema (1990) estimates that women are twice as likely as men to be classified as depressed. Depression may have a strong biological component, but factors such as reproductive hormones are not a viable explanation of gender differences in depression (Strickland, 1992). We can look to the stress associated with the female gender role described in the previous section as one reason why women are more depressed. What are some of the identified stressors that women face as a result of gender that might be related to depression? Discrimination (especially in the workplace), unequal household responsibility, unsatisfying interpersonal relationships, poverty, and harassment or violence have all been implicated as contributory factors in depression (McGrath, Keita, Strickland, & Russo, 1990).

Nolen-Hoeksema (1990) contends that an important reason why women may experience depression more than men is that women adopt cognitive strategies that amplify what they are feeling, such as ruminating about their feelings, while men are more likely to engage in self-distracting activities that often divert attention away from their problems. In contrast, Tavris (1992) has suggested that women and men do not actually differ in experiencing depression, but because of differential socialization, they

learn to express their feelings in ways that fit gender stereotypes. The criteria for diagnosing depression, according to Tavris, are more consistent with the ways that women express sadness or loss (e.g., talking about being unhappy, staying in bed, crying), so women are more likely to be classified as depressed. Men's grief behaviors differ markedly and conform to the masculine gender role of acting tough, working frantically, abusing drugs and alcohol, and engaging in high-risk or violent acts. Instead of being classified as depressed, men who engage in these behaviors receive different diagnoses, such as substance-related disorders or intermittent explosive disorders.

The influence of gender roles on depression may begin early in childhood (Nolen-Hoeksema & Girgus, 1994). The ruminating, internal focus more common in females and the cooperative play style designed to foster intimate relationships may leave girls more at risk for feeling inadequate as they face the challenges that occur during adolescence. Feelings of defeat and distress may occur as girls try to manage complex interpersonal relationships and academic challenges while maintaining harmonious relationships with others and being unable to respond aggressively to frustrating situations. These feelings may in turn leave some women more vulnerable to the stresses linked to adult gender roles and so more likely to become depressed. One conclusion we can draw is that the critical factors for both the experience and expression of depression relate to aspects of gender—such as social roles, self-esteem, and power—rather than to sex, so that depression is very much a gendered phenomenon.

Many other disorders are diagnosed at different rates for men and women. Eating disorders, anxiety disorders, and dependent and borderline personality disorders are more commonly diagnosed in women, and antisocial, narcissistic, and paranoid personality disorders are more commonly diagnosed in men. Whether the differential prevalence of males and females in various diagnostic categories reflects sex biases in diagnosis or treatment, exaggerated manifestations of social roles, or sex differences remains a matter of serious debate. We do know, however, that the symptoms associated with certain disorders closely follow many of the commonly held stereotypes not only of women and men but of various minority groups as well.

STEREOTYPES AND DIAGNOSIS

Stereotypes and Diagnostic Categories

What are some of the ways that stereotypes operate in our views of mental illness? Why do so many diagnostic categories reflect gender, ethnic, and racial stereotypes? In a series of intriguing studies, Landrine (1987, 1988, 1989) investigated how gender role prescriptions affect our judgments of descriptions of individuals fitting the symptoms of different personality disorders. In one study, Landrine (1989) asked college students to judge what type of person (e.g., male or female, wealthy or poor, old or young, white or black) would fit a particular diagnostic description from the different personality disorders of the *Diagnostic and Statistical Manual of Mental Disorders* (DSM). She found that students' judgments of many of these profiles matched social stereotypes. For example, the description of the person with antisocial characteristics was most often predicted to be a lower-class male, the profile of the person with dependent characteristics was predicted to be a married, white, middle-class female, and the profile of the person with histrionic characteristics was predicted to be a single, upper- or middle-class woman. Would you expect more knowledgeable individuals, clinicians for example, to exhibit less stereotyped judgments? Landrine (1987) tested the judgment of clinicians by giving them case studies with stereotyped descriptions of individuals, including information about sex, social class, and marital status, and asking them to diagnosis the cases. The clinicians were explicitly cautioned that the cases might be descriptions of normal individuals. The results showed that clinicians also used stereotypes in labeling these cases. They labeled a stereotyped description of a single white female as a histrionic disorder and that of a lower-class male as an antisocial personality disorder; only the upper-class male was rated as normal. Landrine's work shows that the use of diagnostic categories is influenced by stereotypes, and it provides one clue to the question of why males are represented more in certain personality disorder categories and females more in other categories.

Whereas traditional gender roles can lead to stereotyped diagnoses for women, the converse is true for men. Robertson and Fitzgerald (1990) found that lack of adherence to traditional gender roles can have an adverse effect on how men's mental health is assessed. In their study, therapists were asked to diagnose one of two men portrayed on videotape. The same actor portrayed both roles, which were identical except that one individual was depicted as being nontraditional in occupation and family role while the other individual was depicted as being gender traditional on those dimensions. Robertson and Fitzgerald found significant bias concerning gender role; the nontraditional man was diagnosed as having more severe pathology than the traditional man and the reasons given for the nontraditional man's depression focused on his marital and family responsibilities, areas that many of the therapists thought appropriate for therapeutic intervention. These results are a clear illustration that transgression from gender prescriptions is often "pathologized" by the clinical community and seen as behavior that should be changed rather than as behavior worthy of social support.

Contradictions in Clinical Diagnosis and Gender Role Prescriptions

The two studies described in the previous section provide evidence that clinical diagnosis can be significantly influenced by cultural stereotypes. This misdiagnosis puts both sexes in a bind: If women follow their traditional gender roles too well (or if they deviate too much from traditional roles), they may be considered disturbed; if men violate their gender roles, they may be labeled as deviant. We might well ask ourselves, who is the prototype for mental health, and the answer consistently comes out to look like a traditional white man. According to Brown (1992), qualities such as independence, autonomy, and goal setting are considered the epitome of good mental health. As Marecek and Hare-Mustin point out in their article, the process of diagnosis and subsequent treatment very much reflects the values and beliefs of the predominant culture in which clinicians live. From a social constructionist perspective, concepts of mental illness reflect criteria that are based on what a culture deems as appropriate and inappropriate rather than on an objective system of classification of particular disorders derived from scientific evidence. As explained in the articles by both Marecek and Hare-Mustin and Kupers, criteria for diagnosis of many disorders have shifted in accord with changes in social prescriptions for behavior. No matter how seemingly benign, diagnostic categories and therapeutic interventions represent methods of social control, whereby those in power set the standards of behavior for all to follow and deviators are punished, often by being labeled crazy, irrational, or incompetent. In addition, almost all models of mental illness focus on individual or intrapsychic aspects of pathology. Virtually ignored are the contribution of sociocultural factors such as family and community that provide the context for understanding why certain behaviors occur. The readings in this chapter by Marecek and Hare-Mustin, Kupers, and Solomon all provide critiques of how the mental health community has diagnosed and treated women and minority groups. In particular, Kupers provides vivid examples of how the latest version of the *Diagnostic and Statistical Manual of Mental Disorders,* the DSM-IV, continues to pathologize individuals who, as members of marginalized groups, hold little power in our culture or represent alternatives to traditional lifestyles. Although we may no longer live in an era in which a woman wanting a divorce could be institutionalized for mental illness or a runaway slave is diagnosed with drapetomania, or madness caused by the urge to escape slavery, Marecek and Hare-Mustin and Kupers argue that there is still considerable gender, class and racial/ethnic inequality in the mental health establishment and that male behavior is often considered the standard for mental health.

Gender and the DSM-IV

Before we discuss some of the particular ways that individual disorders provide exaggerated views of men and women, we need to understand the system that therapists have developed for diagnosing and treating individuals. The most commonly used system in the United States is the *Diagnostic and Statistical Manual of Mental Disorders* (DSM) (1994). The DSM, now in its fourth edition, is an attempt to provide operational definitions for each diagnostic category to facilitate agreement among clinicians and thereby establish some reliability of judgment about specific disorders. The DSM-IV allows therapists to classify an individual based on a set of concrete diagnostic criteria in which people are assigned to a category based on the presence of a certain number of particular defining features of the category. Five dimensions, or axes, make up the diagnostic system. The first dimension, or axis, focuses on major clinical syndromes such as schizophrenia, depression, and anxiety, while the second axis emphasizes lifelong personality disorders such as dependent personality, antisocial personality, borderline personality, and narcissistic personality. The third axis of the DSM-IV is related to medical conditions, and the fourth axis focuses on psychosocial stressors such as divorce, death in the family, moving, and more enduring traumas such as physical and sexual abuse. The fifth axis provides an overall rating of how well the individual is functioning; the rating extends from 1 to 100, with lower numbers indicating greater impairment. Whereas earlier versions of the DSM (I and II) were based more on clinical intuitions or a theoretical position (psychoanalytic), the later versions (III, III-R, and IV) have a stronger empirical basis and more clearly defined categories of diagnosis (Nathan, 1994). For certain disorders, an additional section provides the clinician with information about how culture, age, and gender factors might affect the symptomatology of the disorder and cautions against making gender-biased assumptions about particular behaviors (Ross, Frances, & Widiger, 1995). Kupers suggests that the DSM-IV is an improvement over earlier versions because it includes a greater diversity of participants, especially women, and because it attends to questions of racial and ethnic stereotyping in diagnosis in greater although not sufficient detail.

As you might expect, the DSM system has been challenged on a number of grounds. One criticism focuses on the entire diagnostic enterprise and sees the attempt to treat psychological disorders like physical disorders as highly problematic. Both Tavris (1992) and Caplan (1995) argue that most psychological difficulties are problems of everyday living, so that even disorders like depression, which may have a biological component, should not be thought of as diseases. Depression, for example, rather than being essentialized, needs to be understood in the context of the stressors that elicit particular behaviors, such as mood changes, fatigue, significant weight loss, and lack of concentration. This problem has also been identified by the authors of the DSM-IV because they concede that the manual does not always permit a clear distinction between mental disorders and normal behavior (Frances, First, & Pincus, 1995). We know that poor women have high levels of depression, and ample evidence links their depression to conditions of poverty, where one has little sense of control and few social support systems (Belle, 1990). As Marecek and Hare-Mustin argue, too much of the focus of the entire mental health system, including the DSM, is on the intrapsychic causes of mental illness and too little attention is given to either stressful life events (e.g., sex discrimination, rape) or stressful life conditions (e.g., poverty). Certain disorders in the DSM system, such as post-traumatic stress syndrome, are defined in relationship to the long-term consequences of traumatic events in life (e.g., stress of war, rape). These types of disorders are not, however, the main focus of the DSM approach, because they have only recently been included.

Another criticism involves the empirical evidence for certain disorders, especially the personality disorders of Axis II. Many of the disorders in this category are not clearly defined (e.g., borderline personality disorder), and there is a significant lack of reliability of diagnosis among clinicians (Tavris, 1992; Brown, 1992). This problem limits the DSM to a de-

scription rather than an explanation of these mental disorders. Even the proponents of DSM recognize that "it is not based on a deep understanding of mental disorders because in most cases we lack that understanding" (Frances et al., 1995, p. 5). A related problem with many of the personality disorders is that they caricature gender stereotypes, notwithstanding the caveats of the DSM-IV about sensitivity to gender bias. There is substantial evidence, including Landrine's work previously discussed, to show that the underlying bases of these categories consist of traditional gender role characteristics that we acquire as part of the normal socialization process. This bias increases the likelihood that certain disorders will be overdiagnosed in men (e.g., antisocial personality disorder) and women (e.g., dependent personality disorder). There is also the possibility of underdiagnosis, in which a man who is severely depressed but covers his feelings by acting out will not get help or a woman's gambling problem is overlooked. Overall, it appears that overdiagnoses occur for women and underdiagnoses occur for men (Redman, Webb, Hennrikus, Gordon, & Sanson-Fisher, 1991). How do traditional gender-based behaviors become mental disorders? Kupers offers a provocative analysis of this question. He contends that diagnostic categories may provide the upper limit for the very behaviors that our culture promotes. Females are taught to be cooperative, caring, and emotional, but when they become too caring are labeled with dependent personality disorders or when they become too emotional are labeled with histrionic personality disorders. Likewise, males are socialized to be aggressive, dominant, rational, and sexually active, but when they become too aggressive are diagnosed with antisocial personality disorders or when they become too rational are considered obsessive-compulsive. Kupers proposes that we rethink the categories that count as pathological and base them on the virtues that emanate from a society that contains true equality among all individuals. In that society, the behaviors that would be considered pathological would include racism, sexism, and homophobia, all behaviors that are impediments to justice and equality.

The Politics of Diagnosis: Gender and Sexual Orientation

Kupers presents several categories of behaviors that were at one time considered pathological, or are presently still being debated, as a way to understand the social and political nature of diagnosis and treatment as evidenced in the DSM system. Two categories, self-defeating personality disorder (masochism) and late luteal phase dysphoric disorder (a variant of premenstrual syndrome), pathologize many behaviors that are part of normal life.[1] Individuals who find themselves in abusive relationships and feel they cannot leave because of children or finances are diagnosed as mentally ill (self-defeating personality disorder) instead of classified as being in a horribly bad situation that affords them little choice. Staying in the relationship is not considered a rational, although difficult, choice even though, as we learned in chapter 12, women and children may face greater risk after leaving an abusive relationship. Both mental health professionals and the public at large unwittingly blame individuals for situations that look self-defeating from the outside instead of recognizing the structural constraints that limit the decisions of such individuals. Ultimately, the authors of the DSM-IV decided that the empirical underpinnings and diagnostic utility of self-defeating personality disorder were not sufficient to warrant its inclusion, even in the appendix in which it had been placed for DSM-III-R (Ross et al., 1995). In contrast, late luteal phase disorder remains a diagnostic category in the appendix of DSM-IV as a disorder that needs further study (Ross et al., 1995).[2] Why are the normal monthly changes connected with menstruation labeled as a mental disorder? There is little evidence that hormonal changes are related to mood shifts (Hamilton & Gallant, 1990), and even the DSM authors recognize the difficulty of providing a reliable definition of premenstrual syndrome (Ross et al., 1995). We cannot deny that some individuals, both males and females, experience mood changes that might affect their behavior. The fundamental question is how to deal with such behaviors, because the evidence for this syndrome as a psychological disorder is tenuous at best. Perhaps our attention would be better directed toward creating a world in which, as Tavris (1992) has suggested, "women and men would regard changes in moods, efficiency, and good humor as expected and normal variations, not as abnormal deviations from the (impossible) male ideal of steadiness and implacability" (p. 168).

Homosexuality was considered a psychological disorder until 1973, when the American Psychiatry Association voted to eliminate it as a diagnostic category. According to Kupers, a substitute category was added to DSM-III in 1980; this category, called ego-dystonic homosexuality, referred to gays and lesbians who are dissatisfied with their sexual orientation. The category was dropped from DSM-IV. On what basis was homosexuality considered a mental illness? As Kupers points out, certain theorists have essentialized homosexuality as a type of pathological personality. A different attempt to label homosexuality as a mental illness assumes that mental health is a normative judgment and that homosexuality, as a nonnormative choice, is a deviant and hence pathological behavior. This conclusion clearly points out the danger of relying on simple dichotomies such as normative and nonnormative as indices of mental health. Other researchers have looked to the scientific literature for evidence that gays and lesbians experience disproportionate mental health difficulties. Although considerable effort has been expended to demonstrate differences in psychological functioning between gay and lesbian and heterosexual individuals, the evidence is clear that sexual orientation does not determine the mental health of individuals (Gonsiorek, 1996). There is no evidence that links sexual orientation and mental health. The essentialism in this approach is significant because the underlying assumption is that any evidence of psychological disturbance would be attributed to sexual orientation. Even though these approaches have been discredited and the category of homosexuality has been removed, Kupers claims that the pathologizing of homosexuality continues, albeit in more subtle forms.

Solomon's article in this chapter describes how ethnic and racial stereotypes affect the diagnosis and treatment of members of various minority groups. These stereotypes should come as no surprise because we have already discussed that the archetype for mental health, especially as represented in the DSM-IV, is a white, middle-class male. Solomon presents data on how race, class, cultural background, and gender may act, separately or in unison, to influence the therapeutic process and lead to misdiagnosis. Solomon identifies four key factors that act in concert and can help us understand why minorities have not fared well in the mental health system. First, not every culture has the same way of expressing emotions and corresponding behaviors, so we cannot assume that the same symptoms will have the same meaning with regard to a particular disorder. Introverted behaviors may be a sign of depression in one culture, whereas acting out might be its indication in another culture. Or a culture may have religious or spiritual beliefs that not only are in marked contrast to our own but would be considered bizarre, if not crazy, to us. Solomon presents an example of a Ghanian woman who, during her clinical assessment, was asked if she heard voices and responded that she had vivid visions of her deceased mother, who constantly told her what to do. Solomon argues that this women was engaged in the process of grief as defined in her culture (e.g., communicating with the dead) and that the diagnosis she received of schizophrenia and treatment with psychotropic medication was inappropriate and came from a lack of understanding of culturally relevant symptoms. We know why the attending physician made this diagnosis because we have seen that the evaluation tools used by clinicians are clearly biased toward a norm of white, middle-class men in Western cultures. Biased evaluation tools are the second problem identified by Solomon, and it relates to the third issue, clinician bias and prejudice. Clinicians are trained to use diagnostic systems such as the DSM-IV, whose focus, as we suggested, is almost exclusively on intrapsychic rather than social and cultural explanations for mental disorders. Perhaps more troubling is that most therapists are unaware of their prejudices and thus unlikely to overcome their biases by questioning their values and perspectives. The final problem that can lead to misdiagnosis is institutional racism and sexism, which is clearly in evidence

in many of the categories of the DSM-IV. All these factors have an impact not only on how an individual is diagnosed but also on how an individual receives treatment. Particularly important are the self-perceptions and understanding that individuals bring to the therapy situation. According to Solomon, the very behaviors that may help African Americans persist in a culture of racism may also prevent them from easily forming a trusting relationship with a therapist. Asian Americans who are socialized to cooperate and respect authority may act in therapy in ways that connote agreement or understanding when, in fact, neither is the case. Therapists must be both knowledgeable and sensitive to cultural variations. They must also be willing to explore a variety of therapeutic forms that might work better for individuals who have different cultural backgrounds. Equally important, however, is to recognize variation within cultures so that a therapist does not trade one type of stereotype or bias for a different one.

In an attempt to rectify some of these biases and to educate therapists, the fourth edition of the DSM has included a section on race, age, and gender features for different disorders. The goal is to help therapists gain a better understanding of different cultural norms. Many researchers, such as Kupers, are skeptical that this type of information can counteract a system whose underlying premise is an essentialist view of psychopathology. Manson (1994) contends that the Western perspective of illness and distress is not necessarily shared by members of other cultures and that such explanations may play a significant role in how individuals understand and respond to the process of therapy. For example, Western psychiatrists understand depression as a disorder that results from the interaction of biochemical and intrapsychic factors, whereas Pentecostal Catholics may see it as a disorder resulting from retribution from God for moral transgressions and Haitian Blacks may see it as connected to supernatural intervention. Without a knowledge of specific cultural norms and contexts, it is impossible to fully understand the meaning of an individual's set of behaviors, and this lack of understanding can lead to misdiagnosis and ineffective treatment.

FEMINIST THERAPIES

The inherent biases and stereotypes as well as the unequal power distribution within the mental health profession have led many individuals to propose alternative forms of therapy. Marecek and Hare-Mustin describe a variety of feminist responses and revisions to conventional therapies. They argue the necessity of recognizing the diversity of voices that characterize feminist therapies, so as not to misrepresent the various therapies as one monolithic approach. Brown and Brodsky, in the last reading in this chapter, offer a similar perspective in their portrayal of feminist therapy. Based on the grassroots effort of the women's movement in the 1960s and 1970s, one key aspect of feminist therapy arose from consciousness-raising groups (CR), the goal of which was to help women find a voice to express their oppression and to recognize the patriarchal nature of society in which power is unequally distributed. One principle of CR was that "the personal is political," and therefore these groups—which were based on an egalitarian structure with no leader—fostered personal empowerment, political activism, and solidarity among women. All these values were incorporated into the therapeutic process by feminist therapists. According to Brown and Brodsky, feminist therapy is a philosophical approach rather than a specific set of therapeutic techniques, and it may be practiced as part of any form of therapy (e.g., psychodynamic, behavioral, cognitive). Although there are many forms of feminist therapy, they all contain certain core principles that define a common vision. These include respecting the variety of experiences of women from all racial, class, age, religious, and sexual orientation groups and not defining women by the norms of traditional therapy; rejecting the view of a power differential between the therapist and client, working instead to establish an egalitarian relationship that fosters empowerment whereby the client has a role in setting the goals for therapy; and recognizing the social and cultural context of behavior, especially the role of traditional gender prescriptions in main-

taining power differentials and harmful self-images. Feminist therapy entails valuing both autonomy and relational competence as important dimensions of healthy functioning and using empirical data from feminist scholarship to inform the therapeutic process. How does feminist therapy differ from therapeutic approaches that profess to be nonsexist? The two are similar in that the major ideas of nonsexist therapy are that the therapeutic process should involve equal treatment for men and women and should avoid gender stereotypes. Feminist therapy, however, takes an explicitly political view that change does not just occur intrapsychically, within the individual, but must be part of a larger personal, social, and political context.

Many questions and issues still present a challenge to the feminist therapy that Brown and Brodsky describe in some detail. We believe that two issues are particularly important to highlight. One issue is the question of multiculturalism. Feminist therapy derives from a belief in the importance of all women's experiences, but its basis is still very much the reality of white, middle-class women, although it has worked to become sensitive to women's diversity. Because so much of the theorizing within feminist therapy is linked to the personal experiences of the researcher or therapist, the types of questions asked are limited by these personal experiences. For example, Brown (1995) notes that white feminists are very interested in questions about mothering and work, sexual harassment and acquaintance rape, the nature of lesbian relationships, and abusive or incestuous relationships. These issues may or may not reflect the concerns and experiences of women of color and poor women, but the lack of diversity of voices contributing to feminist therapy and heard by feminist therapists limits the nature of the questions being asked. This exclusion may not be intentional but the consequence is still the same. As we described in chapter 1, white privilege can lead to the assumption among whites that their experiences represent the experiences of all people. Brown and Brodsky contend that feminist therapy and practice is reacting in positive ways to the challenge of multiculturalism by working to include the visions and realities of women from nondominant groups.

Feminist Therapy and Men

A second and related issue of feminist theories concerns the population that it serves. Because its expressed goal is to improve the position of women in society, feminine therapy is often assumed to have little to offer men, families, or children. If one of the goals of feminist therapy is to redress gender prescriptions and to encourage social and political change, then it must begin to find ways to include all these individuals in the therapeutic process. Just as the diversity of women's experiences will need to be more fully represented as feminist therapy moves into the future, so too will the multiple and often conflicting experiences and concerns of men need careful attention. We have argued throughout this book that gender roles are constraining for both men and women, and such constraints pose risks and challenges that must be understood as part of the larger picture of health and pathology. One cornerstone of the burgeoning Men's Studies research is in understanding the emotional ramifications of the male role (Kaufman, 1993).

Men not only avoid feminist therapy, they avoid therapy in general. Women are twice as likely to seek therapy as men. We have already provided some reasons why women may seek therapy and be overrepresented in the counseling process. The flip side of this question is why men do not seek therapy. Previous readings in this book have described how men experience gender role strain in trying to adhere to the many dimensions of masculinity. As Eisler (1995) suggested in his article in chapter 13, certain aspects of masculinity, such as risk-taking behaviors, suppression of emotions, and denial of femininity, may have serious negative consequences for men. These troubling consequences can lead not only to the types of physical stress identified by Eisler, but also to psychological distress. Specific aspects of traditional gender roles may also make it more difficult for men to seek help. Robertson and Fitzgerald (1992) found that traditional masculine at-

titudes are negatively linked to willingness to seek psychological help. They also found that men with these traditional attitudes respond more positively to counseling interventions that appear to be compatible with traditional masculine gender roles (i.e., a brochure that focused on self-help materials, classes, and workshops). Research also indicates that healthy coping is often defined as behaviors most associated with men, such as confrontation, assertiveness, and active problem solving. Outward behavior that conforms to traditional gender prescriptions may lead counselors to minimize or overlook men's underlying pain or distress. Therefore, therapists' views of appropriate gender behavior may compound men's masculine socialization by preventing men from seeking psychological help or by reinforcing negative elements of masculinity. The challenge for feminist therapy, in including men, is to find ways to help men overcome the masculine mystique (Robertson & Fitzgerald, 1992). Gender aware therapy may provide a way to make men more willing to seek help (Good, Gilbert, & Scher, 1990). Based on many of the principles of feminist therapy, this approach advocates that therapists should be cognizant of the impact of gender in the treatment of all individuals. One aspect of gender aware therapy may be particularly useful in encouraging men to seek help. According to Good et al., the goal of gender aware therapy is to help clients seek whatever behavioral changes are appropriate, even if those changes are consistent with traditional gender roles. Men are, therefore, encouraged to change in ways that are consistent with their internalized notions of masculinity as long as these choices are not harmful. This point is reminiscent of the evidence provided by Eisler that many elements of traditional masculinity lead to productive, active problem solving, which is a good and healthy response to stress. Therapists, and men as clients, would be well served to understand the nuances of gender role based behavior and how it affects both positive and negative life choices and emotional responses. Gender aware therapy does not advocate the eradication of gender as a goal in promoting psychological health.

BACK TO THE FUTURE

Many of the issues of psychopathology mirror the questions raised in chapter 1 and discussed in readings throughout the book. For example, the multiple meanings and lack of consensus about the terms *normal* and *abnormal* are similar to the debates about the most appropriate definitions of *sex* and *gender*. The controversies within the mental health establishment, especially about how men and women are diagnosed and treated, reflects the differing perspectives of essentialism versus social constructionism. We have also seen that the voices of many individuals have not impacted on psychological research and theory, especially the voices of nondominant groups who have been left out or misperceived. We are only beginning to understand how race, class, sexual orientation, age, and gender interact and intersect in the lives of ordinary people. We know that women, women of color, poor women and men, and gays and lesbians often are diagnosed according to stereotypes and receive less than optimal treatment from many mental health professionals. What remains to be seen is whether the discipline of psychology can respond to the diversity of experiences that characterize our lives with more inclusive theo-

ries about the phenomena we have reviewed in this book. The study of psychopathology reminds us that only some individuals in our culture have the power to name categories of mental illness and to design treatments—that power has often been misused to subordinate women and members of various minority groups. On a positive note, therapy also has the power to help us change—at both the individual and societal level.

We hope that the readings in this book have raised questions for you, have answered questions, have made you angry at times, and have helped you understand your experiences in new ways. We hope you agree with us that the answers to questions of gender cannot be provided by reducing gender to sex differences, by looking for ways in which one sex is better than another, or by trying to erase gender with simplistic arguments in favor of sameness. Gender is a complex reality, one that will change along with social, individual, and cultural changes, but we do not expect gender to disappear. We hope the issues raised in this book can help you create a framework to rethink questions of gender and to engage in both individual and social action that you think appropriate. As long as gender is a lens we use to understand ourselves and others, questions of gender will remain.

NOTES

1. See Caplan (1995) for a provocative account of the process by which diagnostic categories are included or excluded from the DSM.

2. In DSM-IV, it was renamed premenstrual dysphoric disorder, the name that had originally been given to it.

REFERENCES

American Psychiatric Association. (1994). *Diagnostic and statistical manual of mental disorders.* Washington, DC: Author.

Barnett, R. C., & Rivers, C. (1996). *She works/he works: How two-income families are happier, healthier, and better off.* New York: HarperCollins.

Belle, D. (1990). Poverty and women's mental health. *American Psychologist, 45,* 385–389.

Brown, L. S. (1992). A feminist critique of personality disorders. In L. S. Brown & M. Ballou (Eds.), *Personality and psychotherapy: Feminist reappraisals* (pp. 206–228). New York: Guilford Press.

Brown, L. S. (1995). Cultural diversity in feminist therapy: Theory and practice. In H. Landrine (Ed.), *Bringing cultural diversity to*

feminist psychology (pp. 143–161). Washington, DC: American Psychological Association.

Brown, L. S., & Brodsky, A. M. (1992). The future of feminist therapy. *Psychotherapy, 29,* 51–57.

Caplan, P. J. (1993). *The myth of women's masochism.* Toronto, Canada: University of Toronto Press.

Caplan, P. J. (1995). *They say you're crazy: How the world's most powerful psychiatrists decide who's normal.* Reading, MA: Addison-Wesley.

Cook, E. P. (1990). Gender and psychological distress. *Journal of Counseling and Development, 68,* 371–375.

Eisler, R. M. (1995). The role between masculine gender role stress and men's health risk: The validation of a construct. In

R. F. Levant & S. Pollard (Eds.), *A new psychology of men* (pp. 207–225). New York: Basic Books.

Frances, A., First, M. B., & Pincus, H. A. (1995). DSM-IV: Its value and limitations. *The Harvard Mental Health Letter, 11,* 4–6.

Gonsiorek, J. C. (1996). Mental health and sexual orientation. In R. C. Savin-Williams & K. M. Cohen (Eds.), *The lives of lesbians, gays, and bisexuals: Children to adults* (pp. 462–478). Forth Worth, TX: Harcourt Brace.

Good, L. E., Gilbert, L. A., & Scher, M. (1990). Gender aware therapy: A synthesis of feminist therapy and knowledge in gender. *Journal of Counseling and Development, 68,* 376–380.

Hamilton, J. A., & Gallant, S. J. (1990). Problematic aspects of diagnosing premenstrual phase dysphoria: Recommendations for psychological research and practice. *Professional Psychology: Research and Practice, 21,* 60–68.

Kaufman, M. (1994). Men, feminism, and men's contradictory experiences of power. In H. Brod & M. Kaufman (Eds.), *Theorizing masculinities* (pp. 142–163). Beverly Hills CA: Sage.

Kupers, T. A. (1995, Summer). The politics of psychiatry: Gender and sexual preference in DSM-IV. *masculinities, 3*(2), 67–68.

Kurdek, L. (1993). The allocation of household labor in gay, lesbian and heterosexual married couples. *Journal of Social Issues, 49,* 127–139.

Landrine, H. (1987). On the politics of madness: A preliminary analysis of the relationship between social roles and psychopathology. *Psychological Monographs, 113,* 341–406.

Landrine, H. (1988). Depression and stereotypes of women: Preliminary empirical analyses of the gender-role hypothesis. *Sex Roles, 19,* 527–541.

Landrine, H. (1989). The politics of personality disorder. *Psychology of Women Quarterly, 13,* 325–339.

Lewine, R. J. (1994). Sex: An imperfect marker of gender. *Schizophrenia Bulletin, 20*(4), 777–779.

Manson, S. M. (1994). Culture and depression: Discovering variations in the experience of illness. In W. J. Lonner & R. Malpass (Eds.), *Psychology and culture* (pp. 285–290). Boston: MA: Allyn & Bacon.

Marecek, J., & Hare-Mustin, R. T. (1991). A short history of the future: Feminism and clinical psychology. *Psychology of Women Quarterly, 15,* 521–536.

McGrath, E., Keita, G. P., Strickland, B. R., & Russo, N. F. (1990). *Women and depression: Risk factors and treatment issues.* Washington, DC: American Psychological Association.

Nathan, P. (1994). DSM-IV: Empirical, accessible, not yet ideal. *Journal of Clinical Psychology, 50,* 103–110.

Nolen-Hoeksema, S. (1990). *Sex differences in depression.* Stanford, CA: Stanford University Press.

Nolen-Hoeksema, S., & Girgus, J. S. (1994). The emergence of gender differences in depression during adolescence. *Psychological Bulletin, 115,* 424–443.

Redman, S., Webb, G. R., Hennrikus, D. J., Gordon, J. J., & Sanson-Fisher, R. W. (1991). The effects of gender on diagnosis and psychological disturbance. *Journal of Behavioral Medicine, 14*(5), 527–540.

Robertson, J., & Fitzgerald, L. F. (1990). The (mis)treatment of men: Effects of client gender role and life-style on diagnosis and attribution of pathology. *Journal of Counseling Psychology, 37,* 3–9.

Robertson, J., & Fitzgerald, L. F. (1992). Overcoming the masculine mystique: Preferences for alternative forms of assistance among men who avoid counseling. *Journal of Counseling Psychology, 39,* 240–246.

Ross, R., Frances, A., & Widiger, T. A. (1997). Gender Issues in DSM-IV. In M. R. Walsh (Ed.), *Women, men, and gender: Ongoing debates* (pp. 348–361). New Haven, CT: Yale University Press.

Solomon, A. (1992, June). Clinical diagnosis among diverse populations: A multicultural perspective. *Families in Society,* pp. 371–377.

Strickland, B. (1992). Women and depression. *Current Directions in Psychological Science, 1,* 132–135.

Tavris, C. (1992). *Mismeasure of women.* New York: Simon & Schuster.

Walker, E., Bettes, B. A., Kain, E. L., & Harvey, P. (1985). Relationship of gender and marital status with symptomatology in psychotic patients. *Journal of Abnormal Psychology, 94,* 42–50.

Gender and Psychological Distress

ELLEN PIEL COOK

Gender is a multidimensional construct that encompasses the many ways society is differentiated on the basis of sex. To understand the role of gender in psychological problems of the sexes, counselors need to be aware of gender-socialized individual characteristics, which may affect what psychological problems people develop, associated symptoms, and how people respond to the problems. It is also important to recognize how the broader sociocultural context presents men and women with different expectations, opportunities, and rewards.

The question of how and why the sexes differ as much as they do is a familiar topic of conversation among men and women, with adults often wryly expressing more puzzlement than their children. Psychological sex differences are more subtle and complicated than they first appear. To some extent, the nature of psychologists' explanations reflects the values of the times, whether affirming the differences as stable and meaningful or minimizing them as ephemeral and illusory (Hare-Mustin & Marecek, 1988). Eagly (1987) exemplifies how psychologists are increasingly turning their attention to analyzing how these subtle but consistent sex differences function and are maintained, after some years of denying or minimizing them.

Gender is a multidimensional construct that encompasses the many ways our society is differentiated on the basis of sex. Psychology has typically emphasized gender as a property of the individual, whether predestined by biology or, as is now believed, primarily learned (e.g., Basow, 1986). The most common explanation for observed psychological sex differences over the years has focused on the sex-typed personality traits, attitudes, and behaviors men and women bring to situations. In this view the

gender socialization process results in two different sets of characteristics in women and men, labeled as *feminine* and *masculine*. Femininity includes such characteristics as emotionality, sensitivity, nurturance, and interdependence, where masculinity denotes assertion, independence, dominance, and goal directedness, among other characteristics (Cook, 1985). These sex-differentiated characteristics are used to explain why the sexes behave the way that they do. Although the androgyny literature has expanded this perspective to recognize varying combinations of masculinity and femininity in individuals, the focus in the sex differences literature has tended to remain on the individual rather than on the context in which he or she behaves (see Cook, 1985; Deaux, 1984).

Recently, attention has turned to how gender is a central organizing principle in society and in everyday social interactions. As Lott (1985) stated, "It is not sex that matters but those life conditions that are systematically related to it by cultural prescription, regulation or arrangement" (p 162). Part of these life conditions refer to the extent to which the sexes face on a daily basis different messages, expectations, resources, and opportunities throughout their lives because of their sex. A related insight is the degree to which sex is in the eye of the beholder. Biological sex functions as a stimulus variable, in that individuals' sex triggers sex-differentiated ways of perceiving and behaving toward themselves in their daily encounters with others (Deaux, 1984; Deaux & Major, 1987; Unger, 1979).

Surprisingly little literature provides careful analyses of how gender as a multidimensional construct is related to psychological problems faced by women and men. Discussions of gender and psychological distress have typically worked backward by noting differences in frequencies of certain types of disorders and then singling out which gender-socialized characteristics seem linked in content to the nature of the disorder. This individualistic view of sex differences is that each sex is predisposed to experience certain psychological problems as a result of gender socialization. To some extent these mental health problems can be predicted by extrapolation from each gender stereotype. Some of this predisposition is attributable to the "dark side" of each set of characteristics—for example, "hostile" masculinity and "servile" femininity (Spence, Helmreich, & Holahan, 1979). This predisposition may also take the form of exaggeration of gender-socialized characteristics into some type of dysfunction—for example, men's dominance and aggression exaggerated into antisocial tendencies. A third form of this predisposition is failure to develop adaptive characteristics and skills because of gender socialization. O'Neil (1981) described this form concisely: "Men and women have each learned only about one-half of the attitudes, skills, and behaviors necessary to cope with life" (p. 64).

This individualistic approach has been valuable in understanding certain aspects of the relationship between gender and psychological adjustment. However, many discussions of gender issues in psychological distress point to factors not directly reducible to individuals' gender-socialized characteristics. Our understanding of gender issues in mental health has also been limited by the common practice of focusing exclusively on one sex at a time in gender analyses. Although such a sex-specific analysis provides some essential clarity, it may also make it difficult to compare how the sexes are different (or alike) in certain respects.

In this article I briefly discuss some of the ways in which gender socialization explanations for psychological distress can be expanded. I will argue that to understand the role of gender in psychological problems, counselors need to be aware of the impact of learned individual characteristics, which may affect in complex ways what particular disorders people develop, symptoms associated with the disorder, and how they respond to the disorder. The literature on depression exemplifies these points. I also discuss

the impact of the broader sociocultural contexts in which men and women live.

THE ROLE OF INDIVIDUAL GENDER-SOCIALIZED CHARACTERISTICS

It appears that the sexes are equally likely to have some form of psychological problem, although there are consistent sex differences in prevalence of individual disorders. Summarizing across numerous epidemiological studies, Cleary (1987) concluded that men are more likely than women to have problems with alcohol and illicit drug abuse, antisocial behaviors, and suicide, whereas depression, phobias and other anxiety disorders, and psychotropic drug abuse are more typical among women than men. Some personality disorders are also diagnosed more commonly in one sex (Kass, Spitzer, & Williams, 1983).

One of the most consistently documented sex differences in incidence of psychological problems is depression. After reviewing a number of studies examining sex differences in diagnosed depression and in self-reported symptoms in the general population, Nolen-Hoeksema (1987) concluded that "women are diagnosed as having a depressive disorder significantly more frequently than men and, with a few exceptions, report more depressive symptoms than do men in most geographical areas of the world . . . The mean female-to-male ratio is 2.02" (p. 265). Because of the pronounced discrepancy in incidence among the sexes, the topic of depression has been more thoroughly analyzed with respect to gender than other disorders.

The similarity between extreme stereotypic feminine characteristics and depressive symptoms is striking. Landrine (1988) reviewed definitions of depression as a caricature of women's traditional role, a role that stresses such qualities as passivity, dependency, lack of self-confidence, and helplessness. Such explanations focusing on women's socialization are intuitively appealing but have the shortcoming of not addressing why one out of three individuals identified as depressed is a man. Also, empirical studies have not provided convincing evidence concerning the relationship of femininity to depression and other indices of psychological adjustment either (Bassoff & Glass, 1982; Cook, 1985; Feather, 1985).

Another possibility is that men and women may become depressed for unique reasons explainable by differences in their socialization. For example, Kaplan (1986) explained women's depression in terms of relationship issues with others. In her view a core strength of women is concern with building and maintaining relationships with others, but this strength is not valued in our society. Women's vulnerability to depression is due to a combination of factors, according to Kaplan: devaluing of their relational capacities; women's frequent disappointments in relationships, especially with men; women's sense of responsibility to maintain relationships at the cost of expressing their own anger, needs, and wishes, further inhibited by their low self-esteem; and their interpretation of relational failures as a failure of the self. In contrast, men's depression is linked to failures of personal goal attainment rather than to relationships with others, but Kaplan does not develop this idea further (see also Warren, 1983). Kaplan's theory builds on central distinctions commonly made between the sexes' characteristics and roles but would seem to imply that relational failure is more frequent and disturbing to women than goal attainment failure is for men. There is no empirical evidence to suggest that this is the case.

Some of the sex differential in rates of depression may be related to social norms regulating how free the sexes feel to express their psychological distress. Men may be prone to avoid, deny, or camouflage their depression because of their gender socialization (Warren, 1983). Vredenburg, Krames, and Flett (1986) suggested that fear of social rejection for admitting depressive symptoms may prompt men to withdraw socially and attempt to cope with depression on their own, to express their symptoms in a socially sanctioned way through work-related problems, or to seek medical intervention for psychosomatic symptoms accompanying depression rather than help for the depression itself. The first and third alternatives may successfully inhibit recogni-

tion of the underlying depression. Or, other men may become alcoholic instead of depressed. Nolen-Hoeksema (1987) cautioned that alcoholism in men should not automatically be considered a symptom of or equivalent to depression, but a different type of response to difficult life circumstances shaped by differing expectations for the sexes.

Research does suggest that there are differences in how men and women report that they cope with affective distress, in ways that are consistent with gender stereotypes. Women are more likely to cry, blame themselves, confront their feelings, eat, and seek support from others; men are more likely to become aggressive, engage in some distracting activity (e.g., walking, sex), and being with others without being singled out as depressed (Chino & Funabiki, 1984; Kleinke, Staneski, & Mason, 1982).

These easily observable differences may be related to more fundamental differences in cognitively coping with stress. Nolen-Hoeksema (1987) argued that women may be more likely than men to ruminate about their negative feelings and to engage in less self-distracting activities. These tendencies would amplify and increase in number women's depressive episodes (see also Ingram, Cruet, Johnson, & Wisnicki, 1988). Such cognitive explanations are compatible with the popularity of cognitive-behavioral conceptualizations and treatment of depression (e.g., Beck, Rush, Shaw, & Emery, 1979). Miller and Kirsch (1987), however, found weak empirical support for sex differences in cognitively coping with stress, except for a tendency for men to use more problem-focused strategies in certain situations. It is not yet established empirically whether how the sexes think about their problems is linked to depression, how such differences originate, and why in these conceptualizations only some individuals of each sex develop serious depression.

Analogous sex differences in how clients express their psychological distress have been noted for victims of sexual abuse. Sexual abuse is a common yet frequently misdiagnosed background factor in individuals requesting psychological help, particularly women (Browne & Finkelhor, 1986; Carmen, Rieker, & Mills,

1984). Because of the much greater prevalence in reported sexual abuse of women by men, nearly all of the literature has focused on the female sexual abuse victim. Many of the psychological symptoms and dynamics that sexual abuse victims present in counseling are similar for the sexes (see Courtois, 1988). There are some interesting sex differences as well.

In discussing responses to criminal victimization, including sexual abuse, Janoff-Bulman and Frieze (1987) argue that female victims may withdraw from others because of the violation of trust, whereas men may actively try to buttress their severely threatened masculine self-concept. Male sexual abuse victims have been widely observed to engage in aggressive and acting-out behaviors more frequently than female victims. A common interpretation of this observation is that male sexual abuse victims attempt to compensate for their sense of powerlessness by controlling or dominating others via aggressive, delinquent, sexually abusive, and violent behavior (Briere, Evans. Runtz, & Wall, 1988; Carmen et al., 1984; Courtois, 1988; Finkelhor & Browne, 1985; Janoff-Bulman & Frieze, 1987). Also, although few sexual abuse victims are willing or able to disclose their history of abuse readily, male victims may be even more likely to withhold or disguise it because of their shame at not protecting themselves or concerns about their sexual orientation (Courtois, 1988; Janoff-Bulman & Frieze, 1987). Counselors thus run the risk of overlooking the possibility of sexual abuse, perhaps labeling clients as antisocial without appreciating the victims' injuries and vulnerabilities.

This brief review suggests that the sexes may develop the same psychological problem for different gender-related reasons, may express these psychological problems in different ways, and may develop different psychological problems in response to life stresses. Although research indicates that men and women tend to learn different ways of expressing and coping with psychological distress, how gender dynamics are involved in producing differences in prevalence is far more complex than implicating certain masculine/feminine characteristics learned by the individual.

THE SOCIOCULTURAL CONTEXT AND PSYCHOLOGICAL DISTRESS

Psychological adjustment is shaped by the broader sociocultural context in which individuals live on a day-to-day basis, as well as on the personal behavioral dispositions that they develop over time. Because of the extensive sex differentiation in our society, the sexes face different expectations, opportunities, and rewards. These life conditions interact with the gender-socialized characteristics of individuals to create what may at its extreme appear to be "different worlds" inhabited by each sex (see Voydanduff, 1988, for a review of Jessie Bernard's classic analysis using this terminology). Eagly (1987) convincingly argued how consensual normative expectations about the sexes' roles and behaviors and actual sex differences in distributions among social roles produce and maintain individual sex differences in behavior.

Women and men are differentially exposed to major stressful life events linked to the development of certain psychological problems, such as battle-related posttraumatic stress disorder. First, in their everyday life as well, men and women are likely to be exposed to different stressors because of the sex stratification of our society (Aneshensel & Pearlin, 1987). Recent statistics indicate that substantial sex differentiation of the work force remains, where the sexes continue to hold different jobs and perform different tasks within the same jobs (LaCroix & Haynes, 1987). Women's domestic and work roles tend to have less status and authority than men's roles (Eagly, 1987), while women face multiple obstacles in their efforts to obtain real power on the job (Ragins & Sundstrom, 1989). Also, although an increasing number of men share home and parenting responsibilities with their partners, women are expected to and do tend to assume more of these responsibilities than their partners (Gilbert & Rachlin, 1987; Pleck, 1987). For men, unquestioned commitment to career, coupled with expectations for aggressive competitiveness may place special burdens on them at work (O'Neil, 1981). Thus, even when the work roles assumed by the sexes

* but what about male normal vs. female normal? If males are more aggressive anyway, this finding is not useful

appear similar, there may be some important differences in responsibilities and frustrations faced by them. Some sex differences in stress and coping patterns may be attributable to women's and men's efforts to operate within functionally different environments shaped by different opportunities and expectations for each sex.

A second way in which the sexes may live in "different worlds" is the arena of interpersonal relationships. Considerable evidence suggests that the nature, intensity, and impact of relationships differ for men and women. On a one-to-one level, intimate conversations appear to be more central to relationships for women, who tend to have more conversations with others than men do about personal feelings and relationships. In contrast, men's conversations tend to focus on work, sports, and other issues external to the individuals (Aries, 1987). Aries characterized men's interactions as "more task oriented, dominant, directive, hierarchical" and women's interactions as "more social-emotional, expressive, supportive, facilitative, cooperative, personal, and egalitarian" (p. 170). Descriptions of the sexes' friendships are consistent with this portrayal: Women's same-sex friendships are more emotionally intense, sharing, and supportive, whereas men's same-sex friendships tend to be more activity-focused (Caldwell & Peplau, 1982; Sherrod, 1987; Williams, 1985). Both sexes may gain more emotional support and intimacy from their friendships with women (Aukett, Ritchie, & Mill, 1988; Buhrke & Fuqua, 1987). These results are consistent with observations about men's tendency to share less of their intimate thoughts and feelings compared with women (Balswick, 1988; O'Neil, 1981).

This role for women as major providers of emotional support continues at home and in the broader social network. Recent reviews of research on relationships and stress suggest that marital and parenting roles may present more burdens for women and more satisfaction for men than is commonly recognized, considering our society's emphasis on family and work as being the core roles for women and men (Barnett & Baruch, 1987). Women tend to be more involved in and emotionally affected by life events

occurring to others outside their immediate family and are more likely to provide emotional support to others in need (Belle, 1987; Wethington, McLeod, & Kessler, 1987). Women are more likely to mobilize a range of social support in times of stress, whereas men are likely to rely exclusively on their wives (Belle, 1987).

Little is known about the impact of these differences on psychological distress. Because of both sexes' reliance on women for emotional support, Belle (1987) suggested that women are more likely than men to suffer from a "contagion of stress" (being affected by the distress of others) and to experience a support gap if they have a lack of support in return from others (see also Wethington et al., 1987). Yet, because of their more intensively emotional involvement with others women may enjoy more stress-buffering effects of social support than men.

Looking at the consequences of men's characteristic interpersonal style, Balswick (1988) and O'Neil (1981) clearly viewed men's relationships as having negative consequences for their emotional functioning. Silverberg (1986) labeled problems in establishing intimacy as instrumental in bringing men into therapy. The purposes and paths to intimacy that men's relationships take, however, may simply be different (Sherrod, 1987). Because of the importance of relationships in all human being's lives, these pervasive differences in relationship patterns need to be better understood.

Finally, eating disorders provide an intriguing example of how broad sociocultural influences in interaction with gender-socialized characteristics can directly shape the nature and prevalence of specific types of psychological disorders. Eating disorders—in particular, anorexia nervosa and bulimia—are much more common in women than in men. The preponderance of eating disorders in women is believed to be related in part to society's strong emphasis on physical attractiveness for women, which today means being thin (Attie & Brooks-Gunn, 1987; Mazur, 1986). Because of the discrepancy between the sociocultural ideal and their actual body size and their heightened sensitivity to body image, women may suffer chronically low self-esteem (Striegel-

Moore, Silberstein, & Rodin, 1986), and some may resort to excessive dieting, exercise, binging, and purging to approximate the ideal body (Attie & Brooks-Gunn, 1987).

Men have traditionally been permitted more latitude in what constitutes a pleasing physique than women have. Although men as well as women feel dissatisfaction and some inadequacy concerning their bodies (Mishkind, Rodin, Silberstein, & Striegel-Moore, 1987), women consistently appear to be less satisfied than men are (Mintz & Betz, 1986) and may suffer more negative consequences if overweight (Stake & Lauer, 1987). However, because maintaining a particular type of physique as an affirmation of a man's masculine identity is becoming more important today, men may be increasingly at risk for developing eating disorders (Mishkind et al., 1987; Striegel-Moore et al., 1986).

The etiology of eating disorders is complex; not everyone exposed to our sociocultural ideals for physical attractiveness develops serious eating disorders. The relationships between increased incidence of eating disorders, differences in standards of attractiveness by sex, and changes in standards of beauty over time do graphically illustrate how broad sociocultural influences can shape the form and intensity of psychological problems in ways not explainable by reference to an individual's gender-related personality characteristics alone.

SUMMARY AND COMMENTARY

In our sex-differentiated society, gender shapes our personal characteristics and views of ourselves, the experiences open to us on a daily basis, and the nature of our interactions with others. It appears reasonable to assume that gender also plays a role in the types of psychological distress that clients present to counselors. Recent theoretical perspectives and research indicate that the impact of gender extends past socializing certain masculine/feminine characteristics predisposing individuals to specific types of distress. Gender-related factors may also be involved in why the sexes may develop the same psychological prob-

lem for different reasons, express psychological distress in different ways, and manifest different types of psychological problems in response to life stresses. The sexes may also face quite different stresses and rewards in the labor force, at home, and in their relationships with others, providing them protection from or increased likelihood of developing psychological distress.

Because the focus of this article was necessarily limited, certain relevant topics were not covered. For example, the sexes may face different role requirements and rewards throughout the life span (Belle, 1987). Other problems have clear gender determinants or implications, such as anxiety disorders (Hafner, 1986) and alcoholism (Wilsnack & Cheloha, 1987). Broad sociodemographic factors such as income and race also are clearly salient in determining the private worlds in which individual men and women live. The distinction made in this article between individual and contextual factors is also somewhat oversimplified and artificial, in that gender-related behavior is the product of a dynamic social interaction between individuals influencing each other in a specific situation (see Deaux & Major, 1987). Finally, it is worth emphasizing that empirical differences between women and men tend to be a matter of degree rather than absolute in nature. As discussions of gender issues have repeatedly pointed out (e.g., Cook, 1985), summary descriptions may or may not fit an individual person very well. These complexities lead us beyond simplistic notions about the sexes to pondering interactions among possible factors.

In this article I have suggested some of the ways in which gender as a multidimensional construct operates across sex-differentiated lines to affect human beings' lives in our society and at this time. Respecting the differences that distinguish the sexes' lives, experts have typically focused on one sex at a time or have reported empirical sex differences without framing them in a broader conceptual framework about how gender has once again, however subtly, affected our lives. What has not been asked betrays something of our interests and values. For instance, studies on stress in men typically have not reported the marital or parental status of their research participants; little is also known about how paid work contributes to men's psychological well-being (Barrett & Baruch, 1987). Much has been learned about the relationship between gender and psychological well-being by asking sex-specific questions to one sex at a time. More can be learned now by posing the same questions to both sexes simultaneously.

REFERENCES

Aneshensel, C. S., & Pearlin, L. I. (1987). Structural contexts of sex differences in stress. In R. C. Barnett, L. Biener, & G. K. Baruch (Eds.), *Gender and stress* (pp. 75–95). New York: Free Press.

Aries, E. (1987). Gender and communication. In P. C. Hendrick (Ed.), *Sex and gender* (pp. 149–176). Newbury Park, CA: Sage.

Attie, I., & Brooks-Gunn, J. (1987). Weight concerns as chronic stressors in women. In R. C. Barnett, L. Biener, & G. K Baruch (Eds.), *Gender and stress* (pp. 219–254). New York: Free Press.

Aukett, R., Ritchie, J., & Mill, K. (1988). Gender differences in friendship patterns. *Sex Roles, 19,* 57–66.

Balswick, J. (1988). *The inexpressive male.* Lexington, MA: Lexington Books.

Barnett, R. C., & Baruch, G. K. (1987). Social roles, gender, and psychological distress. In R. C. Barnett, L. Biener, & G. K. Baruch (Eds.), *Gender and stress* (pp. 122–143). New York: Free Press.

Basow, S. H. (1986). *Gender stereotypes: Traditions and alternatives* (2nd ed.). Monterey, CA: Brooks/Cole.

Bassoff, E. S., & Glass, G. V. (1982). The relationship between sex roles and mental health: A meta-analysis of twenty-six studies. *The Counseling Psychologist, 10,* 105–112.

Beck, A. T., Rush, A. J., Shaw, B. F., & Emery, G. (1979). *Cognitive therapy of depression.* New York: Guilford.

Belle, D. (1987). Gender differences in the social moderators of stress. In R. C. Barnett, L. Biener, & G. K. Baruch (Eds.), *Gender and stress* (pp. 257–277). New York: Free Press.

Briere, J., Evans, D., Runtz, M., & Wall, T. (1988). Symptomatology in men who were molested as children: A comparison study. *American Journal of Orthopsychiatry, 58,* 457–461.

Browne, A., & Finkelhor, D. (1986). Impact of child sexual abuse: A review of the research. *Psychological Bulletin, 99,* 66–77.

Buhrke, R. A., & Fuqua, D. R. (1987). Sex differences in same- and cross-sex supportive relationships. *Sex Roles, 17,* 339–352.

Caldwell, M. A., & Peplau, L. A. (1982). Sex differences in same-sex friendship. *Sex Roles, 8,* 721–732.

Carmen, E., Rieker, P. P., & Mills, T. (1984). Victims of violence and psychiatric illness. In P. P. Rieker & E. Carmen (Eds.), *The gender gap in psychotherapy: Social realities and psychological processes* (pp. 199–211). New York: Plenum.

Chino, A., & Funabiki, D. (1984). A cross-validation of sex differences in the expression of depression. *Sex Roles, 11,* 175–187.

Cleary, P. D. (1987). Gender differences in stress-related disorders. In R. C. Barnett, L. Biener, & G. K. Baruch (Eds.), *Gender and stress* (pp. 39–72). New York: Free Press.

Cook E. P. (1985). *Psychological androgyny.* Elmsford, NY: Pergamon.

Courtois, C. (1988). *Healing the incest wound.* New York: Norton.

Deaux, K. (1984). From individual differences to social categories: Analysis of a decades research on gender. *American Psychologist, 39,* 105–116.

Deaux, K., & Major, B. (1987). Putting gender into context: An interactive model of gender-related behavior. *Psychological Review, 94,* 369–389.

Eagly, A. H. (1987). *Sex differences in social behavior: A social role interpretation.* Hillsdale, NJ: Erlbaum.

Feather, N. T. (1985). Masculinity, femininity, self-esteem, and subclinical depression. *Sex Roles, 12,* 491–500.

Finkelhor, D., & Browne, A. (1985). The traumatic impact of child sexual abuse: A conceptualization. *American Journal of Orthopsychiatry, 55,* 530–541.

Gilbert, L. A., & Rachlin, V. (1987). Mental health and psychological functioning of dual-career families. *The Counseling Psychologist, 15,* 7–49.

Hafner, R. J. (1986). *Marriage and mental illness.* New York: Guilford.

Hare-Mustin, R. T., & Marecek, J. (1988). The meaning of difference: Gender theory, postmodernism, and psychology. *American Psychologist, 43,* 455–464.

Ingram, R. E., Cruet, D., Johnson, B. R., & Wisnicki, K. S. (1988). Self-focused attention, gender, gender role, and vulnerability to negative affect. *Journal of Personality and Social Psychology, 55,* 967–978.

Janoff-Bulman, R., & Frieze, I. H. (1987). The role of gender in reactions to criminal victimization. In R. C. Barnett, L. Biener, & G. K. Baruch (Eds.). *Gender and stress* (pp. 159–184). New York: Free Press.

Kaplan, A. (1986). The "self-in relation": Implications for depression in women. *Psychotherapy, 23,* 234–242.

Kass, F., Spitzer, R. L., & Williams, J. B. W. (1983). An empirical study of the issue of sex bias in the diagnostic criteria of DSM-III Axis II personality disorders. *American Psychologist, 38,* 799–801.

Kleinke, C. L., Staneski, R. A., & Mason, J. K. (1982). Sex differences in coping with depression. *Sex Roles, 8,* 877–889.

LaCroix, A. Z., & Haynes, S. G. (1987). Gender differences in the health effects of workplace roles. In R. C. Barnett, L. Biener, & G. K. Baruch (Eds.), *Gender and stress* (pp. 96–121). New York: Free Press.

Landrine, H. (1988). Depression and stereotypes of women: Preliminary empirical analyses of the gender-role hypothesis. *Sex Roles, 191,* 527–541.

Lott, B. (1985). The potential enrichment of social/personality psychology through feminist research and vice versa. *American Psychologist, 40,* 155–164.

Mazur, A. (1986). U.S. trends in feminine beauty and overadaptation. *Journal of Sex Research, 22,* 281–303.

Miller, S. M., & Kirsch, N. (1987). Sex differences in cognitive coping with stress. In R. C. Barnett, L. Biener, & G. K. Baruch (Eds.), *Gender and stress* (pp. 278–307). New York: Free Press.

Mintz, L. B., & Betz, N. E. (1986). Sex differences in the nature, realism, and correlates of body image. *Sex Roles, 15,* 185–195.

Mishkind, M. E., Rodin, J., Silberstein, L. R., & Striegel-Moore, R. H. (1987). The embodiment of masculinity: Cultural, psychological, and behavioral dimensions. In M. S. Kimmel (Ed.), *Changing men: New directions in research on men and masculinity* (pp. 37–52). Newbury Park, CA: Sage.

Nolen-Hoeksema, S. (1987). Sex differences in unipolar depression: Evidence and theory. *Psychological Bulletin, 101,* 259–282.

O'Neil, J. M. (1981). Male sex role conflicts, sexism, and masculinity: Psychological implications for men, women, and counseling psychology. *The Counseling Psychologist, 9,* 61–80.

Pleck, J. H. (1987). The contemporary man. In M. Scher, M. Stevens, G. Good, & G. A. Eichenfeld (Eds.), *Handbook of counseling and psychotherapy with men* (pp. 16–27). Newbury Park, CA: Sage.

Ragins, B. R., & Sundstrom, E. (1989). Gender and power in organizations: A longitudinal perspective. *Psychological Bulletin, 105,* 51–88.

Sherrod, D. (1987). The bonds of men: Problems and possibilities in close male relationships. In H. Brod (Ed.), *The making of masculinities: The new men's studies* (pp. 213–239). Boston: Allen & Unwin.

Silverberg, R. A. (1986). *Psychotherapy for men: Transcending the male mystique.* Springfield, IL: Charles C Thomas.

Spence, J. T., Helmreich, R. L., & Holahan, C. K. (1979). Negative and positive components of psychological masculinity and femininity and their relationships to self-reports of neurotic and acting out behaviors. *Journal of Personality and Social Psychology, 37,* 1673–1682.

Stake, J., & Lauer, M. L. (1987). The consequences of being overweight: A controlled study of gender differences. *Sex Roles, 17,* 31–47.

Striegel-Moore, R. H., Silberstein, L. R., & Rodin, J. (1986). Toward an understanding of risk factors for bulimia. *American Psychologist, 41,* 246–263.

Unger, R. (1979). Toward a redefinition of sex and gender. *American Psychologist, 34,* 1085–1094.

Voydandoff, P. (1988). Women, work, and family: Bernard's perspective on the past, present, and future. *Psychology of Women Quarterly, 12,* 269–280.

Vredenburg, K., Krames, L., & Flett, G. L. (1986). Sex differences in the clinical expressions of depression. *Sex Roles, 14,* 37–49.

Warren, L. W. (1983). Male intolerance of depression: A review with implications for psychotherapy. *Clinical Psychology Review, 3,* 147–156.

Wethington, E., McLeod, J. D., & Kessler, R. C. (1987). The importance of life events for explaining sex differences in psychological distress. In R. C. Barnett, L. Biener, & G. K. Baruch (Eds.), *Gender and stress* (pp. 144–156). New York: Free Press.

Williams, D. G. (1985). Gender, masculinity-femininity, and emotional intimacy in same-sex friendship. *Sex Roles, 12,* 587–600.

Wilsnack, R. W., & Cheloha, R. (1987). Women's roles and problem drinking across the lifespan. *Social Problems, 34,* 231–348.

CHECKPOINTS

1. Cook argues that in order to understand psychological distress, we must recognize how specific features of gender roles shape individual experience.

2. How we experience gender occurs at two levels. First is the individual level, in which differences in manifestation of distress might be seen in such behaviors as rumination, expressiveness, and coping style. These individual factors then interact with gendered sociocultural factors such as sex stratification, support systems, and interpersonal relationships.

To prepare for reading the next section, think about these questions:

1. How would you identify individuals who are in need of psychological treatment?

2. Is it possible to develop a diagnostic approach that is objective and unbiased?

A Short History of the Future: Feminism and Clinical Psychology

JEANNE MARECEK
Swarthmore College

RACHEL T. HARE-MUSTIN
Villanova University

Since the 19th century, feminists have criticized the mental health establishment and its treatment of women. Issues include the sexist use of psychoanalytic concepts and psychiatric diagnoses, the misuse of medication, and sexual misconduct in therapy. Feminists have also called attention to psychological problems arising from gender inequality in everyday life. Physical and sexual abuse of women is of special concern. Feminist innovations in therapy include consciousness-raising, sex-role resocialization, and new approaches to psychoanalysis and family therapy. We urge feminists to develop a fuller understanding of gender and power, and to use this knowledge to challenge the established theory and practice of clinical psychology.

Every history is a reconstruction of events, told from the vantage point of the teller. When psychology texts recount the history of clinical psychology, they often date the modern era from the time of the humanitarian reforms of Phillippe Pinel and William Tuke at the close of the 18th century. In this account, what is emblematic about the modern era—"our" era—is its humane sensibility, its repudiation of physical coercion and restraint, and its regard for the rights of individuals in treatment. However, although the field may represent itself in this way, others have disputed this view (e.g., Edelman, 1974; Goffman, 1961; Showalter, 1985). Especially when viewed from the perspective of women and members of other marginalized groups, codified diagnoses and accepted treatments too often fall short of these emblematic ideals.

One such accepted treatment was Dr. Isaac Baker Brown's use of clitoridectomy as a cure for masturbation, which he regarded as a "disease" that, he claimed, would reduce women to "idiocy, mania, and death." Brown, practicing in England in the latter part of the 19th century, operated on women whose "symptom" was the wish for divorce, as well as on girls, some only 10 years old, who exhibited "restlessness' (Showalter, 1985). Even more widely acclaimed was Dr. S. Weir Mitchell's so-called cure for female neurasthenia. Mitchell, an American psychiatrist, treated Charlotte Perkins Gilman, Edith Wharton, Jane Addams, and other prominent women of the late 19th century. As depicted in Gilman's autobiographical novella *The Yellow Wallpaper* (1892/1985), Mitchell's prescription involved forced bed rest, deprivation of mental stimulation, enforced isolation from adult company, and constant heavy feeding, leading to weight gains of 50 pounds or more. Gilman's heroine, rather then being restored, is made mad and driven to suicide. Gilman's theme, that sexist treatments cause (or at least exacerbate) psychological difficulties, has been a recurring one in feminist protests against the mental health establishment (e.g., Chesler, 1972: Hare-Mustin, 1983). In this article, we sketch a brief history of feminism in clinical psychology.

PREFEMINIST CLINICAL PSYCHOLOGY

Clinical psychology in the United Stated has a short history. Although the field officially began in 1896 with the founding of Lightner Witmer's Psychological

Clinic (Watson, 1953), the tasks and roles of early applied psychologists bear little resemblance to those of present-day clinical psychologists. "Mental testing" was the primary focus in the early days. This included screening recruits for their suitability for military service and assessing the mental status of children (Korchin, 1983). A number of women psychologists made important, though not specifically feminist, contributions to testing. Among these women were Florence Goodenough (1926), Lauretta Bender (1938), Christiana Morgan (Morgan & Murray, 1935), and, in a later period, Karen Machover (1949). The number of women in applied psychology, although high relative to academic psychology, was small in absolute terms. Moreover, in keeping with gender norms of the day, women were underrepresented in military-related psychology and concentrated in settings, such as child guidance clinics, that focused on children and schools (Bohan, 1990; Furomoto, 1987).

In 1945, large-scale training programs were initiated by the Veterans Administration (VA) to meet heavy demands for mental health services occasioned by World War II. This marked the start of a process by which clinical psychology evolved and expanded into its present form (Korchin, 1983). Despite the high demands, women were not welcomed into early VA clinical training programs. Furthermore, because U.S. military personnel were mostly male, the VA setting offered little opportunity or incentive for therapists to think about the needs of women in treatment.

Psychodynamic Influences

Postwar clinical psychology bears the indelible stamp of psychoanalysis. The history of psychoanalysis is replete with eminent women analysts; many of these women, including Helene Deutsch, Marie Bonaparte, Jeanne Lampl-de-Groot, Joan Riviere, and Frieda Fromm-Reichmann, took up issues of female sexuality and feminine psychology. Although these historical figures did not break with Freudian orthodoxy, a few others did, most notably Karen Horney and Clara Thompson. Horney took issue with the centrality of penis envy in psychoanalytic accounts of female development, pointing out how closely the ideas put forth by psychoanalysts resembled the "naive assumptions" of small boys (1926/1967). Dismayed by psychoanalysts' lack of attention to motherhood, she asserted its importance for women's psychic life; at the same time, she conjectured that women's childbearing ability was at the root of male misogyny. Cultural devaluation of women concealed and served to counter men's unconscious dread of women's power to create new life (1932/1967). Horney also connected women's "overvaluation of love" to their social and economic dependence on men and marriage (1934/1967). Thompson (1942, 1950), too, examined cultural pressures on women such as economic dependence, restricted opportunities, and the derogation of women's sexuality and sexual organs. Although both Horney and Thompson suffered disdain and ostracism at the hands of many of their psychoanalytic colleagues, their thinking presaged the feminist critiques of psychoanalysis of the 1960s and 1970s (Garrison, 1981).

In the postwar years, psychoanalysis dominated the mental health professions. Psychoanalytic ideas about women were served up as scientific evidence for reinstating women in their "proper" domestic place. These ideas included interpreting women's ambition as penis envy, blaming mothers for an extensive array of difficulties and disorders of childhood and adult life, and equating heterosexuality, marriage, and motherhood with psychological maturity (e.g., Lundberg & Farnham, 1947). Thus, it is not surprising that feminists of the late 1960s objected strongly to Freudian psychoanalysis. By devaluing, restricting, and pathologizing women, psychoanalysis helped to create the very unhappiness that it purported to cure (Hare-Mustin, 1983).

FEMINISM AND CLINICAL PSYCHOLOGY

In the past 25 years, feminists have made numerous and varied contributions to clinical psychology as activists, theorists, and practitioners (Brodsky, 1980). There are abundant interconnections among these areas, but we will examine them separately in order to highlight some of the major accomplishments.

Developments have been uneven; nonetheless, feminist issues have been raised throughout this period with considerable moral and intellectual force.

Critique and Activism

Feminism is a form of oppositional knowledge, and its boldest efforts are its challenges to accepted dogma. The dominant discourses in clinical psychology have taken white males as the norm, and thus while women and people of color have been viewed as deviant and inferior. Early on, studies by Broverman and her colleagues (Broverman, Broverman, Clarkson, Rosenkrantz, and Vogel, 1970; Broverman, Vogel, Broverman, Clarkson, & Rosenkrantz, 1972) demonstrated that therapists, who were presumed authorities in human personality and behavior, did not draw their knowledge of women and men from scientific sources, but instead held biases and stereotypes similar to those of the public at large. The work of Broverman and her colleagues opened the way for a large number of subsequent studies (reviewed by Davidson & Abramowitz, 1980; Marecek & Johnson, 1980; Sherman, 1980) that investigated how these biases might influence clinical judgments, diagnoses, and interactions in therapy. In addition, feminist clinicians designed workshops and training exercises to help clinicians become aware of possible biases and modify their practices. Although research on therapy failed to reveal clear and consistent gender effects, it did show that gender enters into the clinical situation in any number of complicated, indirect, and mediated ways, often in interaction with other social categories such as race, age, social class, and sexual orientation (Brodsky & Hare-Mustin, 1980). Thus, this early work pointed the way toward the more complex and nuanced analyses of gender relations in clinical situations that are now being formulated (e.g., Goldner, Penn, Sheinberg, & Walker, 1990; Hare-Mustin, 1991; Holstein, 1987; Walters, Carter, Papp, & Silverstein, 1988).

Diagnosis and Labeling: To What End?   Since the beginning of the present feminist movement, feminists have insisted that diagnosis is not a neutral tool at the clinician's disposal. Some have argued that diagnosis can be a means of discrediting and punishing women who do not conform to men's interests (Chesler, 1972; Task Force on Sex Bias and Sex-Role Stereotyping in Psychotherapeutic Practice, 1975). Others have noted that gender stereotypes can lead therapists to overlook or minimize women's complaints, to trivialize their distress, and thus to withhold needed treatment. Thus, both overdiagnosing and underdiagnosing can result from gender biases, and both can serve as mechanisms of social control over women.

In the early 1970s, feminists were among groups that mounted a protest against the inclusion of homosexuality in the official *Diagnostic and Statistical Manual* (DSM), a protest (that was ultimately successful.[1] Later, arguing on grounds of both scientific adequacy and discriminatory impact on women, feminists challenged certain diagnoses proposed for the DSM-III-R (American Psychiatric Association, 1987), namely, paraphilic rapism, self-defeating personality disorder, and late luteal phase dysphoric disorder (the new psychiatric label for premenstrual syndrome [PMS]) (Sparks, 1985). Diagnoses of sexual dysfunction, which have proliferated in recent DSM revisions, have also come under attack. Critics have noted that definitions of normal sexual functioning are based on an implicit model of male sexual gratification (Tiefer, 1990).

Beyond the battles won and lost regarding specific diagnostic categories, the deeper issue is the political meaning of diagnosis. Far from resting solely on scientific evidence, decisions about what behaviors are acceptable or unacceptable and what behaviors demand intervention or restraint have moral and political dimensions. Diagnostic categories provide the language that therapists speak, and thus, the very framework for their judgments and actions. Moreover, the conventional diagnostic system identifies the individual as the locus of pathology. The influence of the social context—whether family, community, or the broader cultural system—is effectively removed from view. As constructivists, we ask not only *what* ends are served, but, more pointedly, *whose* ends are served. To what extent are diagnoses a means of social control, ensuring conformity to the interests of those in power, and denying the connection between social inequities and psychological distress (Foucault, 1980; Hare-Mustin & Marecek, 1980)?

Sexual Misconduct in Therapy   Sexual abuse by therapists has been another prime target of feminist activism (e.g., Bouhoutsos, Holroyd, Lerman, Forer, & Greenberg, 1983; Hare-Mustin, 1974; Holroyd & Brodsky, 1977). In response to feminist activism, the American Psychological Association (APA) incorporated a direct prohibition against sexual contact between therapist and client in the *Ethical Standards of Psychologists* in 1977. A subsequent revision of the *Ethical Standards* in 1981 added a prohibition against the sexual harassment of students and employees. In addition, feminist psychologists strove to raise the awareness of consumers' rights in therapy more generally (Hare-Mustin, Marecek, Kaplan, & Liss-Levenson, 1979; Liss-Levenson, Hare-Mustin, Marecek, & Kaplan, 1980; National Coalition for Women's Health, Task Force on Consumer Issues in Psychotherapy, 1985). Currently, about half the complaints to state licensing boards against psychologists concern sexual misconduct in therapy, and seven states have now criminalized such behavior (Youngstrom, 1990). Thus, public awareness of clients' rights and of the seriousness of the problem has increased considerably.

Psychiatric Medication   Feminists have also voiced strong concerns about possible misprescribing and overprescribing of psychoactive drugs for women (Cooperstock, 1980; Fidell, 1981; Travis, 1988). When used appropriately, psychoactive drugs have a legitimate and important role in the treatment of certain disorders. Feminist concern has been aroused, however, by the evidence of bias in prescribing practices, by the lack of careful research on women's response to medication, and by sexist depictions of women in pharmaceutical advertising. PMS, which was only recently declared a psychiatric disorder (rather than a disorder of the reproductive system), is a subject of renewed concern. In the eyes of a number of activists, the criteria for diagnosing PMS (or "late luteal phase dysphoric disorder") are shaky at best.

Moreover, as Parlee (1989) noted, the discovery/invention of PMS and the rush to establish it as a diagnostic entity were bankrolled by pharmaceutical firms that were eager to market new drugs to "cure" it.

Breaking the Silence/Reconstructing Knowledge

Voicing what has gone unsaid is the center of feminist scholarship. Echoing Charlotte Perkins Gilman and other early feminists, Betty Friedan (1963) named the "problem with no name," the demoralizing effect that the housewife role had on middle-class women; this statement was a courageous act in its time. This paved the way for psychological research linking disorders prevalent among women, such as depression, agoraphobia, and problems with eating, to traditional femininity and stereotyped role behaviors (Franks & Burtle, 1974; Rawlings & Carter, 1977; Rothblum & Franks, 1983; Widom, 1984).

There is a crucial distinction, however, between social role analyses like those of Friedan and the person-centered analyses that prevail in psychology. The former examines the social relations—especially the distribution of power and other resources—involved in roles such as housewife and mother; the latter has concerned itself with personal attributes thought to be dysfunctional. Thus, these psychological analyses often decontextualize women's experiences and fail to challenge the individualist bias of the discipline.

Everyday Life as Problematic[2]   An important line of research for feminist clinical psychology has been to call attention to how the day-to-day life of women is shaped by gender inequality, and to how relations of inequality give rise to conflict, frustration, and demoralization. Examples include research on stresses in women's family work (Baruch, Biener, & Barnett, 1987; Haavind & Andenaes, 1990; Hochschild, 1989) and in marriage (Hare-Mustin, 1991), the struggles of impoverished women (Belle, 1982), and the burdens that heterosexism and homophobia place on lesbian women (Brown, 1989; Golden, 1987; Krestan & Bepko, 1980; Rohrbaugh, 1990). Works such as these remind us all that clinical interventions must be accompanied by social and political change.

The Abuse of Women: Naming the Problem   Prefeminist clinical psychology was largely silent on the issues of intimate violence and the sexual abuse of women and girls. Feminists have called attention to the prevalence of violence and abuse and to the devastating and protracted psychological consequences that they may have (Koss, 1985; Rush, 1984; Walker, 1979). A core tenet has been that intimate violence and abuse reflect basic themes of masculinity and dominance, and thus cannot be regarded as the aberrant behavior of a few disturbed individuals (Bograd, 1984). Connections have been drawn between sexual abuse and accepted cultural views of male sexuality, male entitlement, and female subordination (Burt, 1980; Herman, 1981; Rush, 1984). Moreover, feminist scholars have shown how presumed experts, such as Freud and Kinsey, failed to recognize (or covered over) evidence of incest, made light of its consequences, and blamed the victims (and sometimes their mothers) rather than the male perpetrators (Lerman, 1986). A recent analysis of clinical literature on incest points out persistent tendencies to deny sexual abuse or minimize its effects, to excuse the perpetrator's behavior, or to shift blame onto the mother (James & MacKinnon, 1990). Moreover, the recent efforts by the psychiatric establishment to introduce the diagnostic category of paraphilic rapism into the DSM demonstrate a continuing attempt to pathologize rape; that is, to label it as the aberrant act of an individual who is out of control. The invention of such a diagnostic category serves to deny that rape is instead an extreme instance of coercion aimed at maintaining male dominance and satisfying male sexual desire.

Feminist Therapies

Of the many activities of feminist clinical psychologists, feminist therapy is the most difficult to characterize. Rather than present a false synthesis, we prefer to describe the heterogeneity of philosophies and approaches. Nearly all the major modes of therapy have generated feminist critiques and corresponding revisions. Moreover, feminist therapies draw on a wide range of feminist philosophies and political stances (Gilbert, 1980; Marecek & Kravetz, 1977; Sturdivant, 1980). Space is too limited to allow us to discuss this diversity in full; instead, we provide a sample of the ideas about feminist practice that have been put forth during the past 20 years.

Consciousness-Raising   The women's liberation movement of the 1960s and 1970s gave rise to the practice of consciousness-raising, which involved thousands of American women (Kravetz, 1978). Consciousness-raising (CR) is akin to the practice of "speaking bitterness," which was widely used in Chinese society during the Maoist revolution. In CR, groups of women met regularly for discussions that were focused on connecting their private troubles to the conditions of society. Discovering that their dissatisfactions were rooted in social injustice in effect helped women see that "the personal is political." Moreover, CR groups, which were leaderless in structure and egalitarian in process, fostered a sense of collective power and responsibility, political solidarity, and sisterhood among members (Kirsh, 1974; Kravetz, Marecek, & Finn, 1983). Some CR groups also engaged in collective political action or community projects.

The vitality of CR attracted many feminist therapists who incorporated CR into their work with clients (Brodsky, 1973; Lerman, 1974). Within therapy, however, the goals of CR shifted from political action to personal change (Kravetz, 1980). Moreover, it was no longer a means of gaining sisterhood and solidarity with a group of women. Nonetheless, as a way of helping individual women relate their difficulties to the social context, CR remains a valuable therapeutic technique.

Sex-Role Resocialization   Sandra Bem's work on psychological androgyny had a strong influence on feminist clinicians' thinking and practice for over a decade (Bem, 1974, 1976). Bem's account focused on conventional prescriptions for masculinity and femininity, which she viewed as rigidly confining and ultimately dysfunctional. In their stead, she proposed psychological androgyny, which involved "liberation" from gender prescriptions; androgyny was expected to lead to greater flexibility, adaptability, and personal fulfillment. Bem's choice of the term *sex-role self-concepts* to refer to masculinity, femininity, and androgyny was unfortunate, as little about societal roles in any strict sense (as opposed to personality traits) was included in their definition. In any case, a number of feminist therapists adopted androgyny as a model of mental health and a goal of therapy. Sex-role resocialization then became a focus of therapy (Kaplan, 1976, 1979).

Much has happened to dampen enthusiasm for androgyny theory and for resocialization as a metaphor for therapy. We refer the reader elsewhere for the trenchant philosophical and theoretical debates that Bem's work inspired (cf. Morawski, 1990; Spence, 1985). We focus instead on the idea of therapy as sex-role resocialization. One example is assertiveness training (AT), a popular approach to personal change developed by behaviorally oriented therapists. We do not doubt that AT can teach clients new and useful interpersonal skills, and that it can foster questioning of gender-role norms (e.g., "Why should women have to play dumb?") as well. However, at the same time as we recognize the value of AT, we also see some problems. One such problem is that many popular publications on assertiveness have presented lack of assertiveness as a "woman's problem." As Gervasio and Crawford (1989) pointed out, the research does not give evidence of a pervasive gender difference in assertiveness. Thus, the popular literature, like much other popular psychology, exaggerates the difference between women and men (Hare-Mustin & Marecek, 1990). Moreover, by assuming that lack of assertiveness is a deficiency to be remedied, this view accepts the idea that it is women who are deficient (Crawford & Marecek, 1989). The question of whether assertiveness is always morally or ethically desirable is sidestepped, as is the issue of whether valuing assertiveness reflects an acceptance of male-centered norms. Moreover, by characterizing assertiveness as a set of individual skills, the AT literature deflects attention from contextual influences. The connection between the lack of domestic, economic, or political power and a lack of assertiveness is overlooked.

Feminist Psychoanalysis   Orthodox psychoanalysis, with its obvious sex bias, was a ready target of the women's liberation movement in the 1960s and early 1970s (e.g., Chesler, 1972). Thus, the development of feminist approaches to psychoanalysis within the past decade has taken many by surprise. In the United States, the impetus was the publication of Nancy Chodorow's *The Reproduction of Mothering* (1978).[3] Chodorow, a sociologist by training, drew on object relations theory and Marxist social theory in an effort to place psychoanalytic ideas about early family life and feminine personality development in a sociocultural context. Many of the subtleties and intricacies of Chodorow's thought have not survived translation into the writings of practitioners. Nonetheless, a recurring idea, which has been echoed by other strains of feminist psychoanalytic thought as well, is that women, owing to experiences during infancy, have a richer emotional life, a deeper sense of connection to others, and an identity rooted in relationships. Readings of Chodorow in the clinical literature usually have focused on the positive aspects of women's "connectedness" or relational self. However, Chodorow emphasized negative aspects of this relationality, such as difficulties in developing a separate sense of identity.

Inaccurate readings or partial borrowings of Chodorow's theory have also been used to bolster dubious claims about women and gender difference. These claims may be appealing because they include the ideas that women *qua* women are better therapists than men, and that all women are endowed with unique capacities for love, care, and empathy. Indeed, some individuals regard such ideas as the cutting edge of feminist therapy. In our view, however, these kinds of claims exaggerate male-female difference and often assume an essential female nature that is unmediated by culture or social circumstances. For us, they come perilously close to reaffirming the "true womanhood" of the past, and in that way contribute to what Judith Stacey (1983) termed "the new conservative feminism." Discussions of these issues have been ongoing among feminist scholars across a variety of disciplines (e.g., Alcoff, 1988; Chodorow, 1979; Scott, 1985).

Feminist psychoanalytic approaches have both virtues and dangers in our view. Most important, they represent efforts to disrupt the blatant sexism of orthodox psychoanalysis and to rewrite the account of women's development in an affirmative, woman-centered way. Moreover, they offer rich possibilities for understanding how gender operates at symbolic levels. Feminist literary criticism, film studies, and cultural theory have used these possibilities to great advantage (e.g., Mulvey, 1975). However, troubling issues remain to be resolved. It seems difficult to avoid mother-blaming, which is so pervasive among orthodox analysts, in therapies that identify early infancy as the determinative period of life. In privileging the intrapsychic as the focus of therapy, therapists may fail to give due importance to the political, social, and interpersonal world. In exploring the dynamics and meaning that domestic violence or sexual abuse have for the victim, therapists may inadvertently convey the idea that the victim is to blame.

Feminist Family Therapy Feminists have criticized traditional family therapy for promoting a patriarchal family structure and traditional gender relations within the family (Hare-Mustin, 1987). Feminist critiques of family therapy have been put forth in increasingly trenchant ways in the 1980s, and they have gained considerable prominence (e.g., Goodrich, Rampage, Ellman, & Halstead, 1988; McGoldrick, Anderson, & Walsh, 1989; Walters, Carter, Papp, & Silverstein, 1988). Feminists' insistence on the importance of context, though at odds with mainstream psychology's focus on the individual, is compatible with the overarching framework of systems theory in family therapy. Indeed, viewing the family as an interrelated system has been the hallmark of family therapy since the 1950s. Moreover, feminists' accounts of the social construction of gender fit with the constructivist stance that is prevalent within family therapy theory. Indeed, the writings of feminist family theorists offer some excellent examples of social constructivism in psychology (e.g., James & MacKinnon, 1990; MacKinnon & Miller, 1987; Taggart, 1985).

FEMINISM AND THE FUTURE OF CLINICAL PSYCHOLOGY

As we read the record, feminist clinical psychology has been a nexus of tension between feminist insistence on social change and psychology's focus on the individual. Indeed, the tension seemed so strong to one feminist psychologist that she flatly proclaimed the term *feminist therapy* an oxymoron (Tennov, 1975).

Clinical psychology often has perpetuated a discourse of self-contained individualism. Like most other branches of psychology in the modern Western world, it is built on a mechanistic, rationalistic, biological model of humankind. Moreover, in recent decades, the mental health field has been undergoing a sweeping re-medicalization (Smith & Kraft, 1989), prompted by technological innovations (Andreasen, 1984), pressures to cut costs, and the resurgence of conservatism in national politics and public policy. Clinical psychology has not escaped these trends, as can be seen in the recent push for prescription privileges ("Psychology and the Pill," 1991). All these developments call for renewed feminist activism against the medicalization of social problems and the possible overuse of medication for women.

The assumption that the reproductive dichotomy of women and men is the root cause of gender differences is so powerful that it has co-opted several intellectual currents that were initially unsympathetic to biologism, such as role theory, psychoanalysis, and even some forms of feminism (Connell, 1987). The focus on male-female differences has pushed the question of male dominance and female subordination to the periphery. In feminist psychology there has been a renewed effort to place questions of gender and power at the center of inquiry (Goodrich, 1991; Haavind, 1984; Kitzinger, 1991). The focus on gender differences also tends so draw attention away from differences among women that arise from their social, cultural, and economic circumstances. The clinical literature has paid scant attention thus far to circumstances that place women at risk of demoralization and victimization—such as recent immigration, poverty, and chronic mental illness (Belle, 1982; Denny, 1986).

CONCLUSION

From the time of Charlotte Perkins Gilman, feminists have offered critiques of the mental health establishment and of treatment for women. Revisiting the history of efforts by feminist clinical psychologists should give us pride in what has been accomplished, but little reason to rest on our laurels. Feminists have produced powerful critiques, a substantial body of research, and a number of models of clinical intervention. Nonetheless, mainstream psychology has resisted feminist thought, as can be seen by the insufficient attention to gender issues in most textbooks in abnormal and clinical psychology, in standard treatment models, and in many training programs. More-

over, as the radicalism of the 1970s has faded, accounts of psychological problems that delineate the effects of the social and political context have been relegated once again to the periphery of the knowledge base and have become irrelevant to conventional individually focused treatment models.

As psychology enters its second century, our hope is that feminist thought can disrupt psychology's gentle slide toward professional quietism. The history of the future should not be like the past. We hope, too, that feminism retains and sharpens its disruptive edge—its courage to break the silence, its willingness to challenge established ways of doing things and accepted categories of meaning, and its determination to call into question the very questions themselves.

NOTES

1. The membership of the American Psychiatric Association voted to expunge homosexuality from the DSM in 1973. DSM-III, which incorporated this change, was published in 1980.
2. The title is taken from a work by Dorothy Smith (1987).

3. There are other strains of feminist psychoanalytic theorizing as well. However, Chodorow's work has had the strongest impact on psychoanalytically oriented feminist clinical psychology in the United States.

REFERENCES

Alcoff, L. (1988). Cultural feminism verus poststructuralism: The identify crisis in feminist theory. *Signs, 13,* 405–436.

American Psychiatric Association. (1987). *Diagnostic and statistical manual of mental disorders* (3rd ed., revised) [DSM-III-R]. Washington DC: Author.

American Psychological Association. (1977). *Ethical standards of psychologists* (revised). Washington, DC: Author.

American Psychological Association. (1981). *Ethical standards of psychologists* (revised). Washington, DC: Author.

Andreasen, N. C. (1984). *The broken brain: The biological revolution in psychiatry.* New York: Harper & Row.

Baruch, G., Biener, L., & Barnett, R. (1987). Women and gender in research on work and family stress. *American Psychologist, 42,* 130–136.

Belle, D., (1982). *Lives in stress.* Beverly Hills, CA: Sage.

Bem, S. L. (1974). The measurement of psychological androgyny. *Journal of Consulting and Clinical Psychology, 42,* 155–162.

Bem, S. L. (1976). Beyond androgyny: Some presumptuous prescriptions for a liberated sexual identify. In J. Sherman & F. Denmark (Eds.), *Psychology of women: Future directions for research* (pp. 1–23). New York: Psychological Dimensions.

Bender, L. (1938). *A visual motor gestalt test and its clinical use.* New York: American Orthopsychiatric Association.

Bograd, M. (1984). Family systems approaches to wife-battering: A feminist critique. *American Journal of Orthopsychiatry, 54,* 558–568.

Bohan, J. S. (1990). Contextual history: A framework for replacing women in the history of psychology. *Psychology of Women Quarterly, 14,* 213–227.

Bouhoutsos, J., Holroyd, J., Lerman, H., Forer, B. R., & Greenberg, M. (1983). Sexual intimacy between psychotherapists and patients. *Professional Psychology: Research and Practice 14,* 185–196.

Brodsky, A. M. (1973). The consciousness-raising group as a model for therapy with women. *Psychotherapy: Theory, Research, and Practice, 10,* 24–29.

Brodsky, A. M. (1980). A decade of feminist influence on psychotherapy. *Psychology of Women Quarterly, 4,* 331–344.

Brodsky, A. M., & Hare-Mustin, R. T. (Eds.). (1980). *Women and psychotherapy.* New York: Guilford.

Broverman, I. K., Broverman, D. M., Clarkson, F. E., Rosenkrantz, P. S., & Vogel, S. R. (1970). Sex-role stereotypes and clinical judgments of mental health. *Journal of Consulting and Clinical Psychology, 34,* 1–7.

Broverman, I. K., Vogel, S. R., Broverman, D. M., Clarkson, F. E., & Rosenkrantz, P. S. (1972). Sex-role stereotypes: A current appraisal. *Journal of Social Issues, 28,* 58–78.

Brown, L. S. (1989). New voices, new visions: Toward a lesbian/gay paradigm for psychology. *Psychology of Women Quarterly, 13,* 479–494.

Burt, M. (1980). Cultural myths and supports for rape. *Journal of Personality and Social Psychology, 38,* 217–230.

Chesler, P. (1972). *Women and madness.* Garden City, NJ: Doubleday.

Chodorow, N. (1978). *The reproduction of mothering: Psychoanalysis and the sociology of gender.* Berkeley: University of California Press.

Chodorow, N. (1979). Feminism and difference: Gender, relation, and difference in psychoanalytic perspective. *Social Review, 9* (4), 51–70.

Connell. R. T. (1987). *Gender and power.* Stanford: Stanford University Press.

Cooperstock. R. (1980). Special problems of psychotropic drug use among women. *Canada's Mental Health, 28,* 3–5.

Crawford, M., & Marecek, J. (1989). Psychology reconstructs the female, 1968–1988. *Psychology of Women Quarterly, 13,* 147–165.

Davidson, C. V., & Abramowitz, S. I. (1980). Sex bias in clinical judgment: Later empirical returns. *Psychology of Women Quarterly, 4,* 377–395.

Denny, P. A. (1986). Women and poverty: A challenge to the intellectual and therapeutic integrity of feminist therapy. *Women and Therapy, 5,* 51–63.

Edelman, M. (1974). The political language of the helping professions. *Politics and Society, 4*(3), 295–310.

Fidell, L. (1981). Sex differences in psychotropic drug use. *Professional Psychiatry, 12,* 156–162.

Foucault, M. (1980). In C. Gordon (Ed.), *Power/knowledge: Selected interviews and other writings, 1972–1977* (Colin Gordon, Leo Marshall, John Mepham, & Kate Soper, Trans.). New York: Pantheon.

Franks, V., & Burtle, V. (Eds.). (1974). *Women in therapy: New psychotherapies for a changing society.* New York: Brunner/Mazel.

Friedan, B. (1963). *The feminine mystique.* New York: Dell.

Furomoto, L. (1987). On the margins: Women and the professionalization of psychology, 1890–1940. In G. A. Mitchell & W. R. Woodward (Eds.), *Psychology in twentieth century thought and society* (pp. 93–113). New York: Cambridge University Press.

Garrison, D. (1981). Karen Horney and feminism. *Signs, 6,* 672–691.

Gervasio, A., & Crawford, M. (1989). The social evaluation of assertiveness: A critique and speech act reformulation. *Psychology of Women Quarterly, 13,* 1–25.

Gilbert, L. A. (1980). Feminist therapy. In A. M. Brodsky & R. T. Hare-Mustin (Eds.), *Women and psychotherapy* (pp. 245–266). New York: Guilford.

Gilman, C. P. (1985). The yellow wallpaper. In S. M. Gilbert & S. Gubar (Eds.), *The Norton anthology of literature by women* (pp. 1148–1160). New York: Norton. (Original work published 1892)

Goffman, E. (1961). *Asylums.* Garden City, NY: Doubleday.

Golden, C. (1987). Diversity and variability in women's sexual identities. In Boston Lesbian Psychologies Collective (Eds.), *Lesbian psychologies* (pp. 18–34). Urbana: University of Illinois Press.

Goldner, V., Penn, P., Sheinberg, M., & Walker, G. (1990). Love and violence: Gender paradoxes in volatile attachments. *Family Process, 29,* 343–364.

Goodenough, F. (1926). *Measurement of intelligence by drawings.* Yonkers-on-Hudson, NY: World Book.

Goodrich, T. J. (Ed.). (1991). *Women and power: Perspectives for therapy.* New York: Norton.

Goodrich, T. J., Rampage, C., Ellman, B., & Halstead, K. (1988). *Feminist family therapy.* New York: Norton.

Haavind, H. (1984). Love and power in marriage. In H. Holter (Ed.), *Patriarchy in a welfare society* (pp. 136–167). Oslo: Universitets Forlaget. (U.S. distribution: Columbia University Press.)

Haavind, H., & Andenaes, A. (1990, June). *Care and the responsibility for children: Creating the life of women creating themselves.* Paper presented at the Fourth Interdisciplinary Congress on Women, New York.

Hare-Mustin, R. T. (1974). Ethical considerations in the use of sexual contact in psychotherapy. *Psychotherapy, 11,* 308–310.

Hare-Mustin, R. T. (1983). An appraisal of the relationship between women and psychotherapy: 80 years after the case of Dora. *American Psychologist, 38,* 593–601.

Hare-Mustin, R. T. (1987). The problem of gender in family therapy. *Family Process, 26,* 15–27.

Hare-Mustin, R. T. (1991). Sex, lies, and headaches: The problem is power. In T. J. Goodrich (Ed.), *Women and power: Perspectives for therapy.* New York: Norton.

Hare-Mustin, R. T., & Marecek, J. (Eds.). (1990). *Making a differences: Psychology and the construction of gender.* New Haven, CT: Yale University Press.

Hare-Mustin, R. T., & Marecek, J., Kaplan, A., & Liss-Levenson, N. (1979). Rights of clients, responsibilities of therapists. *American Psychologist, 34,* 3–16.

Herman, J. L. (1981). *Father-daughter incest.* Cambridge, MA: Harvard University Press.

Hochschild, A. (1989). *The second shift.* New York: Viking.

Holroyd, J. C., & Brodsky, A. M. (1977). Psychologists' attitudes and practices regarding erotic and nonerotic physical contact with patients. *American Psychologist, 32,* 843–849.

Holstein, J. A. (1987). Producing gender effects on involuntary mental hospitalization. *Social Problems, 34*(2), 141–155.

Horney, K. (1967). The dread of women. In *Feminine Psychology* (pp. 133–146). New York: Norton. (Original work published 1926)

Horney, K. (1967). On the genesis of the castration complex in women. In *Feminine Psychology* (pp. 37–53). New York: Norton. (Original work published 1932)

Horney, K. (1967). The overvaluation of love: A study of a common present-day feminine type. In *Feminine Psychology* (pp. 182–213). New York: Norton. (Original work published 1934)

James, K., & MacKinnon, L. (1990). The "incestuous family" revisited: A critical analysis of family therapy myths. *Journal of Marital and Family Therapy, 16,* 71–88.

Kaplan, A. (1976). Androgyny as a model of mental health for women: From theory to therapy. In A. Kaplan & J. Bean (Eds.), *Beyond sex-role stereotypes* (pp. 352–362). Boston: Little, Brown.

Kaplan, A. (1979). Psychological androgyny: Further considerations [Special issue]. *Psychology of Women Quarterly, 3*(3).

Kirsch, B. (1974). Consciousness-raising groups as therapy for women. In V. Franks & V. Burtle (Eds.), *Women in therapy* (pp. 326–354). New York: Brunner/Mazel.

Kintzinger, C. (1991). Feminism, psychology and the paradox of power. *Feminism and Psychology, 1,* 111–129.

Korchin, S. J. (1983). The history of clinical psychology: A personal view. In M. Hersen, A. E. Kazdin, & A. S. Bellack (Eds.), *The clinical psychology handbook* (pp. 5–19). New York: Pergamon.

Koss, M. P. (1985). The hidden rape victim: Personality, attitudinal, and situational characteristics. *Psychology of Women Quarterly, 9,* 193–211.

Kravetz, D. (1978). Consciousness-raising groups in the 1970s. *Psychology of Women Quarterly, 3,* 168–186.

Kravetz, D. (1980). Consciousness-raising and self help. In A. M. Brodsky & R. T. Hare-Mustin (Eds.), *Women and psychotherapy* (pp. 267–284). New York: Guilford.

Kravetz, D., Marecek, J., & Finn, S. (1983). Factors influencing women's participation in consciousness-raising. *Psychology of Women Quarterly, 7,* 257–271.

Krestan, J., & Bepko, C. (1980). The problem of fusion in the lesbian relationship. *Family Process, 19,* 277–289.

Lerman, H. (1974, August) *What happens in feminist therapy.* Paper presented at the meeting of the American Psychological Association, New Orleans.

Lerman, H. (1986). *A mote in Freud's eye: From psychoanalysis to the psychology of women.* New York: Springer.

Liss-Levenson, N., Hare-Mustin, R.T., Marecek, J., & Kaplan, A. (1980). The therapist's role in assuring client rights. *Advocacy Now, 2,* 16–20.

Lundberg, F., & Farnham, M. F. (1947). *Modern woman: The lost sex.* New York: Grossett & Dunlap.

Machover, K. (1949). *Personality projection in the drawing of the human figure.* Springfield, IL: Charles C. Thomas.

MacKinnon, L., & Miller, D. (1987). The new epistemology and the Milan approach: Feminist and sociopolitical considerations. *Journal of Martial and Family Therapy, 13,* 139–155.

Marecek, J., & Johnson, M. (1980). Gender and the process of therapy. In A. M. Brodsky & R. T. Hare-Mustin (Eds.), *Women and psychotherapy* (pp. 67–93). New York: Guilford.

Marecek, J., & Kravetz, D. (1977). Women and mental health: A review of feminist change efforts. *Psychiatry, 40,* 323–329.

McGoldrick, M., Anderson, C. M., & Walsh, F. (Eds.). (1989). *Women in families: A framework for family therapy.* New York: Norton.

Morawski, J. T. (1990). Toward the unimagined. In R. T. Hare-Mustin & J. Marecek (Eds.), *Making a difference: Psychology and the construction of gender* (pp. 150–183). New Haven, CT: Yale University Press.

Morgan, C. D., & Murray, H. A. (1935). A method for investigating fantasies. *Archives of Neurology and Psychiatry, 34,* 289–306.

Mulvey, L. (1975). Visual pleasure and narrative cinema. *Screen, 16*(3), 6–18.

National Coalitions for Women's Health, Task Force on Consumer Issues in Psychotherapy. (1985). *Women and psychotherapy: A consumer handbook.* Temple, AZ: Author.

Parlee, M. B. (1989, March). *The science and politics of PMS research.* Paper presented at the meeting of the Association for Women in Psychology, Newport, RI.

Psychology and the Pill. (1991, March). *The Scientist Practitioner,* pp., 13–21.

Rawlings, E. I., & Carter, D. (1977). *Psychotherapy for women.* Springfield, IL: Charles C. Thomas.

Rohrbaugh, J. B. (1990, August). *Lesbian parenting: Psychological implications of parenting structure.* Paper presented at the meeting of the American Psychological Association, Boston, MA.

Rothblum, E., & Franks, V. (Eds.). (1983). *The stereotyping of women: Its effects on mental health.* New York: Springer.

Rush, F. (1984). *The best-kept secret: Sexual abuse of children.* New York: McGraw-Hill.

Scott, J. W. (1985, December). *Is gender a useful category of historical analysis?* Paper presented at the meeting of the American Historical Association, New York.

Sherman, J. (1980). Therapist attitudes and sex-role stereotyping. In A. M. Brodsky & R. T. Hare-Mustin (Eds.). *Women and psychotherapy* (pp. 35–66). New York: Guilford.

Showalter, E. (1985). *The female malady.* New York: Viking Penguin.

Smith, D. (1987). *The everyday world as problematic.* Boston: Northeastern University Press.

Smith, D., & Kraft, W. A. (1989). Attitudes of psychiatrists toward diagnostic options and issues. *Psychiatry, 52,* 66–78.

Sparks, C. (1985). *Preliminary comment on DSM-III proposed revisions.* Bethesda, MD: Feminist Institute.

Spence, J. T. (1985). Gender identity and its implications for the concepts of masculinity and femininity. In T. B. Sonderegger

(Ed.), *Nebraska Symposium on Motivation 1984: Psychology and gender* (Vol. 32, pp. 59–96). Lincoln, NE: University of Nebraska Press.

Stacey, J. (1983). The new conservative feminism. *Feminist Studies, 9,* 559–583.

Sturdivant, S. (1980). *Therapy with women.* New York: Springer.

Taggart, M. (1985). The feminist critique in epistemological perspective: Questions of context in family therapy. *Journal of Marital and Family Therapy, 11,* 113–126.

Task Force on Sex Bias and Sex-Role Stereotyping in Psychotherapeutic Practice. (1975). Report. *American Psychologist, 12,* 1169–1175.

Tennov, D. (1975). *Psychotherapy: The hazardous cure.* New York: Abelard-Schuman.

Thompson, C. (1942). Cultural pressures in the psychology of women. *Psychiatry, 5,* 331–339.

Thompson, C. (1950). Some effects of the derogatory attitude towards female sexuality. *Psychiatry, 13,* 349–354.

Tiefer, L. (1990, August). *Gender and meaning in the DSM-III-R sexual dysfunctions.* Paper presented at the meeting of the American Psychological Association, Boston.

Travis, C. B. (1988). *Women and health psychology: Mental health issues.* Hillsdale, NJ: Erlbaum.

Walker, L. E. (1979). *The battered woman.* New York: Harper.

Walters, M., Carter, B., Papp, P., & Silverstein, O. (1988). *The invisible web: Gender patterns in family relationships.* New York: Guilford.

Watson, R. I. (1953). A brief history of clinical psychology. *Psychological Bulletin, 50,* 321–346.

Widom, C. S. (Ed.). (1984). *Sex roles and psychopathology.* New York: Plenum.

Youngstrom, N. (October, 1990). Issue of sex misconduct discussed at convention. *APA Monitor,* 20–21.

The Politics of Psychiatry: Gender and Sexual Preference in DSM-IV

TERRY A. KUPERS

The Wright Institute

The Fourth Edition of the Diagnostic and Statistical Manual of Mental Disorders *(DSM-IV), published by the American Psychiatric Association (APA) in 1994, contains the official list of diagnostic categories. It is touted as an improvement over previous editions, more precise in its descriptions of mental disorders, more rigorous in its criteria for establishing diagnoses. There is some effort to take gender and sexual orientation into consideration, as well as race and ethnicity. And there are claims of greater objectivity on account of the improvements, the detail, and the attention to cultural contexts. But is the new edition really an improvement, or merely a more rigorous rationalization for pathologizing non-mainstream behaviors and attitudes? And how successful have the authors been in transcending past gender biases? A meaningful discussion of these questions requires reading between the lines as well as attending to the social and historical context.*

A LONGER, MORE DETAILED LIST OF DIAGNOSTIC CATEGORIES

The first thing to note about the DSM-IV is its size, 886 pages. DSM-I (APA, 1952) contained 130 pages; DSM-II (APA, 1968) contained 134 pages; DSM-III (APA, 1980) contained 481 pages. (A revised DSM-III, DSM-III-R, was published in 1987, but I will leave it out of this summary for simplicity's sake.) In each edition there are new disorders, new groupings of disorders, some deletions, and various revisions in the way well-established disorders are viewed.

For instance, with the publication of the third edition in 1980, Panic Disorder, Post-traumatic Stress Disorder, Social Phobia, and Agoraphobia were added. The last two diagnoses had been lumped under the category Phobias in DSM-II; in DSM-III they, along with Panic Disorder and PTSD, became subtypes of the group of Anxiety Disorders. And with the publications of DSM-III some names were changed, for instance Manic-Depressive Disorder (DSM-II) became Bipolar Disorder (DSM-III); and some categories were dropped, notably homosexuality.

Again, in DSM-IV, there are new categories (Substance-Induced Anxiety Disorder, Sibling Relational Problem, Physical and Sexual Abuse of Adult); there are name changes (Multiple Personality Disorder becomes Dissociative Identity Disorder); there are new groupings (Gender Identity Disorders subsumes what used to be three groupings: Gender Identity Disorder of Childhood, of Adolescence and of Adulthood); and there are deletions (Passive-aggressive Personality Disorder, Transsexualism). Relatively few name categories were added to DSM-IV, the emphasis being on more detail in the descriptions, presumably to increase inter-rater reliability. And the fourth edition makes the diagnostic categories relatively less exclusive so that one does not need to be as careful to rule out one category in order to pin down the diagnosis of another. Consequently a given individual is more likely to be assigned two or more "comorbid" diagnoses, for instance Obsessive Compulsive Disorder with Depression or with Alcohol Dependence.

TWO EXPLANATIONS FOR A LONGER, MORE DETAILED DSM

Why has the DSM grown thicker, the list of disorders longer? There are two basic explanations, one built upon a positivist notion of scientific progress, the other on the notion that our concepts of mental health and mental disorders are socially and historically constructed.

According to the positivist model, which underlies the stance of orthodox psychiatry and rationalizes its current turn toward biologism (for a critique, see Cohen, 1993), advancing technology, and newer research findings permit us to discover mental disorders which always existed, but went undetected until now because our understanding of the brain and mental functioning was not as sophisticated as it is today. Joel Kovel (1980) says it well: "Psychiatry's self-image (is) of a medical profession whose growth is a matter of increasing mastery over a phenomenon, mental illness, which is supposed to be always present, a part of nature passively awaiting the controlling hand of science" (p. 72). The emphasis in DSM-IV on extensive reviews of clinical and research literatures and the conduct of field trials with revised diagnostic categories reflects this assumption. The goal is to see how much consistency can be achieved among diagnosticians.

Then there is the rush to develop "Treatment Guidelines," keyed to DSM-IV categories. For instance, the APA recently released its "Practice Guidelines for the Treatment of Patients With Bipolar Disorder" (APA, 1994b). Treatment guidelines provide medical centers and third party payers with a rationale for allowing some benefits and disallowing others. Thus scientific truth is defined in terms of consensus among certain clinicians, mainly psychiatrists who have clout in the APA about the proper diagnosis and treatment of each disorder.

Confident that their opinions about the existence of mental disorders constitutes a science that is advancing rapidly and unfalteringly, psychiatrists and their collaborators are not very likely to uncover the biases and social interests that determine the path of their scientific endeavors, for instance the fact that a significant part of their research is funded by pharma-

ceutical companies that would like very much to see them identify mental disorders for which the treatment of choice is a pharmaceutical agent.

The social/historical model holds that "the disorder and the remedy are both parts of the same social process, and that they form a unity subject to the total history of the society in which they take place" (Kovel, 1980, p. 72). Our concept of mental health, as well as our categories of mental disorder are socially constructed, and people in power determine what constitutes mental disorder among those they have power over (Conrad, 1980; Foucault, 1965). Jean Baker Miller (1976), building on Hegel's Master/Slave dialectic, points out that in the interest of continuing domination, the dominant group is the model for "normal human relationships" while the subordinate group is viewed as inferior in one way or another (blacks are intellectually inferior, women are "ruled by emotion"). Thomas and Sillen (1974) point out that slaves who ran away from their owners' plantations in the ante-bellum South received the diagnosis "drapetomania," literally "flight-from-home madness" (p. 2).

Elizabeth Packard's husband declared in 1860 that her disagreement with his religious views was evidence of insanity; and because the laws of Illinois as well as the male asylum psychiatrist were on his side, he was able to have her locked in an asylum (Chesler, 1972). Hughes (1990) uncovers some of the gender biases in the testimony of families who had a member admitted to an asylum in late nineteenth century Alabama. Skipping to the present, is it merely coincidental that just when middle-class women are entering the workplace in record numbers, premenstrual syndrome is declared a form of mental disorder?

Social theory provides two related answers to the question why the DSM grows longer and more detailed in successive editions. First, the growth of the mental health industry depends on the expansion of the list of diagnostic categories. The number of psychiatrists, psychologists, and psychotherapists has grown considerably in recent years, as have the variety of psychotropic medications. As clinicians examine and treat a larger proportion of the citizenry, more diagnoses are needed to justify the whole endeavor. I will return to this point in the section on childhood disorders.

Second, our consciousness and everyday lives have become increasingly regimented and administered over the past century, and as a result the average citizen is permitted fewer eccentricities before deviance is declared. The Industrial Revolution required a disciplined work force capable of sufficient delayed gratification to endure long hours at hard labor for less than fair wages. Those who could not work had to be marginalized as criminals, beggars, or lunatics. This was the period when great leaps were made in the description of psychotic conditions such as Dementia Praecox, later to be renamed Schizophrenia. Since the explosive growth of consumerism in the 1920s, newer, milder diagnoses are needed for those who are capable of working, who buy into the promise of ad campaigns that the purchase of one commodity after another will lead to happiness, and yet are unable to attain the kind of happiness portrayed in advertisements and films. The successful but still unhappy people must be neurotic; perhaps they need psychoanalysis, psychotherapy, a tranquilizer or an antidepressant.

While the positivist model directs our attention toward the gathering of ever more empirical data and the evolution of more sophisticated statistical analyses, the social/historical model permits us to understand the way social interests determine our views on psychopathology as well as our views on what constitutes scientific progress.

ABOUT HOMOSEXUALITY

The debate about homosexuality in the late 1960s and early 1970s included mass demonstrations at annual meetings of the APA. The straight male leadership was forced to back down, voting in 1973 to delete the category of homosexuality from the official list of mental disorders. The change was reflected in the next edition, DSM-III, in 1980.

But the stigmatization did not end there. The official list of mental disorders is merely the tip of the iceberg when it comes to pathologizing. Psychoanalysts and psychotherapists pathologize constantly, deciding, for instance, when to intervene in the pa-

tient's story and make an interpretation. There is the decision to interpret something and not to interpret something else, and the clinician's views about normalcy and pathology determine her or his choices. In the 1920s, analysts repeatedly interpreted penis envy in women (for a summary of psychoanalytic views on gender, see Connell, 1994). Why did they not choose instead to interpret the pathology in men's defensive need to exclude women from the halls of power? In the 1960s, analysts interpreted the radical activism of young adults as a sign of psychopathology. Why did they not interpret the inactivism of others (including themselves) in the face of great social upheavals (Kupers, 1993b)?

I do not believe there is anything inherently wrong with pathologizing certain human characteristics. Sedgwick (1982) argues convincingly that the attempt by libertarians and radical therapists in the 60s to get rid of the entire concept of mental illness was misguided at best. The question is which human traits shall be pathologized. Throughout the history of the mental health professions, why has homosexuality consistently been the target for pathologizing while homophobia has never appeared among the list of mental disorders? The unstated biases reflected in these choices do not disappear just because one category of mental disorder is deleted.

Still, in the struggle to transcend homophobia, it is a positive development when homosexuality is removed from the list of mental disorders. In its place, in DSM-III (1980), a new category was added, Ego-Dystonic Homosexuality, designed for gays and lesbians who would prefer to be straight but were having trouble converting their desires. Since this category became, in practice, a substitute for the category of homosexuality, its deletion in DSM-IV is another positive step—likely motivated by the presence of more women and gays on the task force and work groups that developed DSM-IV. The APA even calls for all professional organizations and individuals "to do all that is possible to decrease the stigma related to homosexuality" (APA, 1993, p. 686).

But the pathologization of homosexuality remains. Consider this statement, made two years after the

APA decided to stop diagnosing homosexuality, by Otto Kernberg (1975), a prominent psychoanalyst:

> We may classify male homosexuality along a continuum that differentiates the degree of severity of pathology of internalized object relations. First, there are cases of homosexuality with a predominance of genital, oedipal factors, in which the homosexual relation reflects a sexual submission to the parent of the same sex as a defense against oedipal rivalry. . . . In a second and more severe type, the male homosexual has a conflictual identification with an image of his mother and treats his homosexual objects as a representation of his own infantile self. . . . In a third type of homosexual relation, the homosexual partner is "loved" as an extension of the patient's own pathological grandiose self. . . . This, the most severe type of homosexual involvement, is characteristic of homosexuality in the context of narcissistic personality structure proper, and constitutes the prognostically most severe type of homosexuality. (pp. 328–329)

I am not aware of any disclaimer of this formulation by Kernberg, who is listed as an adviser to the authors of DSM-IV. Even though the diagnosis of homosexuality is no longer officially sanctioned, a clinician, following Kernberg and other prominent experts, might assign a gay man the DSM-IV diagnosis Gender Identity Disorder, Sexually Attracted to Males (APA, 1994a, p. 534) with Narcissistic Personality; or Transvestic Fetishism (p. 530) with Narcissistic Personality Disorder; and other clinicians would get the point. There is also continuing debate about whether the goal in treating homosexuals should be conversion to heterosexuality (Socarides, Kaufman, Gottlieb, & Isay, 1994). In other words, long after the category is removed from the official list and the APA advocates destigmatization, prominent clinicians continue to pathologize homosexuality while showing no interest in creating a category for homophobia.

WOMEN'S DISORDERS

Women have evolved a strong voice within establishment psychiatry. The list of contributors to DSM-II (1968) contains the names of 37 men and 3 women, whereas the equivalent list for DSM-IV (1994a) contains the names of 26 men and 11 women. (It is not as easy to determine how many gays and lesbians were involved.) As a result, there were rancorous debates about the pathologization of women's experiences and characteristics prior to the publication of DSM-IV. Two proposed diagnostic categories were at issue: "Self-defeating Personality" (for women who find themselves repeatedly victimized by abusive men) and "Late Luteal Phase Dysphoric Disorder" (the luteal phase of the menstrual cycle begins at ovulation and ends at menses, and this diagnosis is synonymous with PMS). Feminist psychiatrists and psychologists argued that the former diagnosis stigmatized and blamed the victims of domestic abuse (Caplan, 1987). They prevailed, Self-Defeating Personality was not included in DSM-IV. Meanwhile the categories Sexual Abuse of Adult (APA, 1994a, p. 682) and Physical Abuse of Adult (p. 682) were added to the official list, permitting the clinician to diagnose pathology in their perpetrator.

In regard to Late Luteal Phase Dysphoric Disorder, the question was why pathologize the woman's natural cycles? Why not pathologize instead men's need to avoid all signs of emotion and dependency while maintaining an obsessively steady pace (Spitzer et al., 1989)? I coined the term "pathological arrythmicity" for this disorder in men (Kupers, 1993a). The debate about PMS was not as intense as the one about Self-Defeating Personality. Some women clinicians claimed that a category for PMS might serve to increase sensitivity among male colleagues to the experiences of women. The debate ended in compromise: Premenstrual Dysphoric Disorder is included in an appendix of DSM-IV designated ". . . For Further Study."

But remember, the official manual is merely the tip of the iceberg when it comes to pathologizing. Penis envy was never an official diagnostic category, yet it was frequently diagnosed. Phyllis Chesler (1972) explains how the diagnosis of Hysteria in women has served to maintain their subordination: "Both psychotherapy and marriage enable women to express and defuse their anger by experiencing it as a form of emotional illness, by translating it into hysterical symptoms: frigidity, chronic depression, phobias, and the like" (p. 122). Hysteria is a rare diagnosis today, and women are more likely diagnosed Borderline Character Disorder, Multiple Personality Disorder (there is intense debate about the existence of this disorder, connected with the debate about "recovered memories" of childhood molestation), or Somatization Disorder. Judith Herman (1992) points out that among women assigned these modern diagnostic substitutes for hysteria are a significant number who were molested as girls, but these diagnoses divert attention away from the early traumas and focus the clinician's attention instead on the woman's personal flaws. She proposes that instead of diagnosing Borderline Character Disorder and Somatization Disorder in so many women today, we consider the diagnosis "Complex Post-traumatic Stress Disorder," the residual condition resulting from repeated childhood sexual and physical abuse. Thus far Complex PTSD has not made its way into the DSM.

Another relevant critique of the way women's characteristics are selectively pathologized comes from the staff of the Stone Center at Wellesley College (Jordan, Kaplan, Miller, Stiver & Surrey, 1991). They believe that this culture's over-valuation of autonomy and independence leaves something to be desired in terms of community and the capacity to be intimate, and that a very male notion of independence and autonomy is at the core of traditional clinical descriptions of psychopathology. Women are pathologized because of their emphasis on connection and interdependence. They call for a redrawing of the line between psychopathology and mental health so that women's need for connection and community will be viewed as an admirable trait rather than a symptom.

The APA has not heeded this group's call. The category Dependent Personality Disorder remains in DSM-IV and is assigned disproportionately to women, while no equivalent category has been devised to describe the male dread of intimacy and dependency. The description of Dependent Personality Disorder contains the very bias that clinicians from the Stone Center are concerned about. Consider this sentence: "Individuals with this disorder have difficulty initiating projects or doing things indepen-

dently." (APA, 1994a, p. 666). Often there is a choice between two contrasting ways to handle problems at work: one way being for the individual to come up with a totally independent solution and get credit for doing so at promotion time; another being for several co-workers to brainstorm, work together to figure out a solution collectively and share the credit. It is as if official psychiatry has decided that individual action is preferred and the search for collaborative solutions (more usual for women workers in today's corporate culture) is pathological. Thus, in spite of improvements in DSM-IV regarding gender bias, many problems remain.

WHAT ABOUT THE MEN?

I have already mentioned several diagnoses that might be included in a DSM but are not: homophobia, "pathological arrhythmicity," and the dread of dependency. There are other male behaviors we might wish to pathologize: dependence on pornography, workaholism, friendlessness, the need for sexual conquests, the tendency to react to aging by deserting one's same-age female partner and taking up with someone the age of one's children, and so forth.

There is a brief and very telling statement about the gender distribution of each mental disorder in DSM-IV. Disorders diagnosed more frequently in males include Conduct Disorder in boys and adolescents, Obsessive-Compulsive Personality Disorder (distinct from Obsessive-Compulsive Disorder or OCD which is distributed equally between the sexes), Narcissistic Personality Disorder, Paraphilias, Antisocial Personality Disorder, Intermittent Explosive Disorder, and Pathological Gambling. A comparable list of conditions diagnosed more often in women includes Histrionic Personality Disorder, some forms of Depression, Eating Disorders, Dissociative Identity Disorder, Kleptomania, Panic Disorder, Somatization Disorder, Agoraphobia, and Borderline Personality Disorder.

Could there be a clearer reflection of gender stereotypes? But why are the same qualities that compose the stereotypes—the unfeeling, action-oriented, sexually aggressive, misbehaving male; and the emotional, dependent, weight-conscious, frightened, and sickly woman—so much the basis for pathologizing each gender? Perhaps the diagnostic categories serve to create an upper limit for the very characteristics that are socially encouraged in each gender. Boys are encouraged to be active, rough, aggressive, sexually adventurous, steady, and rational. But when boys become too aggressive they are assigned the diagnosis Conduct Disorder or Intermittent Explosive Disorder, when men become too steady and rational they are diagnosed Obsessive-Compulsive Personality Disorder, when men break the rules too badly in the sexual realm they are considered Paraphiliacs, and so forth. It is a little like the college and pro football teams that encourage players to be hyper-aggressive and then have to discipline some of them when they draw negative publicity by raping women after a game. The mental disorders typically assigned to men, like the fines assigned for the overly aggressive football players, serve to keep the lid on the very behaviors that are being encouraged. Similarly, women are encouraged from early childhood to be emotional and connected with others, but if they are too emotional they are diagnosed Histrionic Personality Disorder, and if they are too connected they are diagnosed Dependent Personality Disorder. There is little if any support for creating new, improved forms of masculinity and femininity in DSM-IV.

CHILDHOOD DISORDERS AND THE SHAPING OF GENDER

The main thing to notice about the section of DSM-IV on childhood and adolescent disorders is that the list of disorders is growing. In DSM-II (1968) there were two subsections containing a total of seven disorders, in DSM-IV (1994a) there are ten subsections and 32 disorders. Most of the enlargement occurred between DSM-II and DSM-III, the authors of DSM-IV being more interested in providing detailed descriptions for established disorders than in adding new ones to the official list. Still, the number of chil-

dren who see mental health professionals and undergo psychotherapy or receive psychotropic medications is growing, and children are being taken to see professionals at younger ages.

Consider three childhood disorders from the list in DSM-IV: Attention Deficit/Hyperactivity Disorder (ADHD), Oppositional Defiant Disorder, and Gender Identity Disorder. What if Oscar Wilde had been given one or more of these diagnoses when he was six or eight years old? What if Ritalin had been prescribed to limit his energy level or he had been given Prozac to control his nonconformist notions about gender and sexuality? What if there had been a way at that time to predict which children might become gay or antisocial (research of this kind is proliferating today,) and preventive treatment had been instituted? Would Wilde's vision have been the same, would he have created great literature? This is not to say that Wilde was mentally disordered, nor that mental disorder is a prerequisite for works of genius. Rather I am selecting Wilde to illustrate the point that earlier diagnosis and treatment of mental disorders in children runs the risk of stigmatizing unusual men and women, creating less tolerance for experimentation in the realm of gender roles, and thereby limiting the historical possibilities for transforming gender relations.

Of course, in some children, for instance those who compulsively pull out their hair or those who cannot sit still long enough to finish a classroom assignment, professional intervention can have positive effects. I am not arguing that any particular child should be denied examination and treatment. But when children in unprecedented numbers are taken to see professionals, there are social ramifications. One is that approaches to social problems are reduced to the search for psychopathology in individual children. For instance, consider the difficulty teachers have maintaining order in classrooms containing even larger numbers of students as budgets for public instruction decline. The teacher cannot reduce the size of the class, but he or she can tell the parents of problematic children that their kids suffer from ADHD and need to be taking Ritalin. In general, it is when we despair about the prospects for social transformation—e.g., making public education a higher social priority—that we tend to reduce social problems to the pathology of individuals. Breggin and Breggin (1994) outline the dangers of this development, though they tend to polarize the discussion by minimizing the positive contributions of child psychiatry and psychotherapy.

Of course, there is money to be made from the quest for earlier detection of mental disorders in children. An even more alarming implication is that society has embarked on the early correction of all deviations from the "straight" path of development. As our lives as workers and consumers become more routinized, and as the gap between the rich and the poor grows wider, concerned parents begin to wonder if their children are going to be among the winners or the losers. This motivates them to watch for early signs of mental disorder and hurry their children off to a mental health professional at the first sign of hyperactivity, school failure, impulsive behavior, or gender impropriety.

There are class and race differences. Diagnosing children in the inner city with Conduct Disorder and Oppositional Defiant Disorder does not usually lead to quality treatment (the public mental health service system is shrinking rapidly); but the diagnoses do serve to rationalize the fact that low-income, inner city children are less likely than their middle class cohorts to find fulfilling work, and are more likely to wind up behind bars. People actually begin to believe it is the psychopathology of poor people, not social inequity, that causes unemployment and criminality. As we pathologize more "off-beat" qualities, we are inadvertently tightening the bounds around what is considered "normal" behavior for boys and girls. Nothing is said about this social inequity in DSM-IV, and this silence is quite worrisome.

CONCLUSION

The DSM-IV is definitely an improvement over previous editions. There is more participation by women in the work group; Homosexuality has been deleted from the list of disorders as has DSM-III's Ego-Dystonic Homosexuality; the proposal to add Self-Defeating Personality has been defeated; and there are sections on racial and ethnic differences (that do not go far enough toward correcting racial bias in the diagnostic process—but I will leave that issue for a future discussion). Meanwhile, the DSM grows longer, the descriptions of mental disorders become more codified, and psychiatry has little or nothing to say about the social ramifications of its pathologizing.

Traditional psychiatry looks backward, diagnosing mental illness in those who do not fit yesterday's prescribed social roles. Emotionality as well as assertiveness in women, rebellion on the part of minority members, and homosexuality have all been pathologized. As previously stigmatized groups gain power within the mental health professions, diagnoses are modified. DSM-IV reflects admirable progress in terms of the inclusion of diverse groups and the concerted effort to minimize gender bias and homophobia wherever it can be identified. Still, the fourth edition of DSM continues to pathologize deviation from yesterday's gender roles.

Instead of a longer, more detailed list of mental disorders, we need a system of psychopathology that is informed by a vision of a better society. We could begin by envisioning that society, one where gender equality reigns and there is no homophobia or any other form of domination. Then, by extrapolating backward from that vision, we could pathologize the qualities that would make a person dysfunctional in that more equitable and just social order. Racism, misogyny, and homophobia would head the list of psychopathologies. This kind of pathologizing might even serve to bring about the vision. Unfortunately, far from solving the problems of gender bias and homophobia, the improvements in DSM-IV will serve largely to appease potential dissenters as the mental health professions evolve an ever more conformist manual of psychopathology.

REFERENCES

American Psychiatric Association. (1952). *Diagnostic and statistical manual of mental disorders.* Washington, DC: Author.

American Psychiatric Association. (1968). *Diagnostic and statistical manual of mental disorders.* (2nd ed.). Washington, DC: Author.

American Psychiatric Association. (1980). *Diagnostic and statistical manual of mental disorders.* (3rd ed.). Washington, DC: Author.

American Psychiatric Association. (1993). Position statement on homosexuality. *American Journal of Psychiatry, 150,* 686.

American Psychiatric Association. (1994a). *Diagnostic and statistical manual of mental disorders.* (4th ed.). Washington, DC: Author.

American Psychiatric Association. (1994b). Practice guidelines for the treatment of patients with bipolar disorder. *American Journal of Psychiatry, 151,* Supplement, 1–36.

Breggin, P. R. & Breggin, G. R. (1994). *The war against children.* New York: St. Martin's Press.

Caplan, P. J. (1987). The psychiatric association's failure to meet its own standards: The dangers of self-defeating personality disorder as a category. *Journal of Personality Disorders, 1,* 178–182.

Chesler, P. (1972). *Women and madness.* New York: Avon.

Cohen, C. (1993). The biomedicalization of psychiatry: A critical overview. *Community Mental Health Journal, 29,* 509–522.

Connell, R. W. (1994) Psychoanalysis on masculinity. In H. Brod & M. Kaufman (Eds.), *Theorizing masculinities* (pp. 11–38). Thousand Oaks, CA: Sage.

Conrad, P. (1980). On the medicalization of deviance and social control. In D. Ingleby (Ed.), *Critical psychiatry* (pp. 102–119). New York: Pantheon.

Foucault, M. (1965). *Madness and civilization.* New York: Pantheon.

Herman, J. (1992). *Trauma and recovery: The aftermath of violence—From domestic abuse to political terror.* New York: Basic Books.

Hughes, J. S. (1990). The madness of separate spheres: Insanity and masculinity in Victorian Alabama. In M. C. Carnes & C. Griffen (Eds.), *Meanings for manhood: Constructions of masculinity in Victorian America* (pp. 67–78). Chicago: The University of Chicago Press.

Jordan, J., Kaplan, A., Miller, J. B., Stiver I. P., and Surrey, J. L. (1991). *Women's growth in connection: Writings from the Stone Center.* New York: Guilford Press.

Kernberg, O. F. (1975). *Borderline conditions and pathological narcissism.* New York: Jason Aronson.

Kovel, J. (1980). The American mental health industry. In D. Ingleby (Ed.), *Critical psychiatry* (pp. 72–101). New York: Pantheon.

Kupers, T. A. (1993a). *Revisioning men's lives: Gender, intimacy and power.* New York: Guilford.

Kupers, T. A. (1993b). Psychotherapy, neutrality and the role of activism. *Community Mental Health Journal, 29,* 523–534.

Miller, J. B. (1976). *Toward a new psychology of women.* Boston: Beacon Press.

Sedgwick, P. (1982). *Psychopolitics: Laing, Foucault, Goffman, Szasz and the future of mass psychiatry.* New York: Harper & Row.

Socarides, C. W., Kaufman, B., Gottlieb, F., & Isay, R. (1994). Letters about reparative therapy. *American Journal of Psychiatry, 151,* 157–159.

Spitzer, R. L., Severino, S. K., Williams, J. B., & Parry, B. L. (1989). Late luteal phase dysphoric disorder and DSM-III-R. *American Journal of Psychiatry, 146,* 892–897.

Thomas, A. & Sillen, S. (1974). *Racism and psychiatry.* Secaucus, New Jersey: Citadel.

Clinical Diagnosis among Diverse Populations: A Multicultural Perspective

ALISON SOLOMON

Abstract: The author discusses four ways in which clinical diagnosis can be detrimental to minority clients: through cultural expression of symptomatology, unreliable research instruments, clinician bias, and institutional racism. Recommendations are offered to minimize misdiagnosis.

Clinicians often assume that issues of discrimination and the improvement of services to minority clients will be addressed by professionals whose work is policy oriented. It is imperative, however, that clinicians who provide direct service to people of all racial and ethnic backgrounds examine their own practice with minority clients. Much has been written about the treatment of minorities in the psychotherapeutic relationship (Hines & Boyd-Franklin, 1982; Boyd-Franklin, 1989; Bryant, 1980; Canino & Canino, 1982; de Anda, 1984; Jue, 1987; Pinderhughes, 1982). Before clients enter such a relationship, however, they are evaluated and diagnosed. This diagnosis is key to the type of treatment they will subsequently receive. Moreover, once a psychiatric label is attached to a client, it often sticks. Thus, a diagnosis of schizophrenia is not usually changed, even if the person no longer show symptoms of the illness. The illness is considered in remission, but the person is not considered cured. It is crucial, therefore, that clinicians be aware not only of racial and cultural bias in the *treatment* of minority members but also of biases inherent in present forms of psychiatric *diagnosis*.

This article highlights and discusses differences in psychiatric diagnoses applied to various racial and ethnic groups. The focus is primarily on instances in which the differences are caused by misdiagnosis. Ways to minimize misdiagnosis are suggested.

CULTURAL DIFFERENCES IN THE LITERATURE

Researchers have described various diagnoses that appear to be connected to the race, class, cultural background, or gender of the client:

- Blacks and Hispanics are more likely to be diagnosed with affective or personality disorders, whereas whites are more likely to be diagnosed with organic disorders (Hines & Boyd-Franklin, 1982; Jones, Gray, & Parson, 1983).
- Blacks and Hispanics are more likely to be misdiagnosed as schizophrenic when they are, in fact, suffering from bipolar affective disorder (Mukherjee, Shukla, & Woodle, 1983).
- African American children are diagnosed as hyperactive more often than are white children, who are, in turn, diagnosed as hyperactive more often than are Asian American children (Sata, 1990).
- Lower-class children are more frequently described in terms of psychosis and character disorder, whereas middle-class children are described as neurotic and normal (Harrison et al., 1965).
- When diagnosed with psychotic or affective disorders, minority clients are more likely to be labeled as having a chronic syndrome than an acute episode (Sata, 1990).
- Adult white males of all ages have a much lower rate of admission to outpatient psychiatric facilities than do white women and nonwhite men and women (Chesler, 1972).
- Research in the 1960s found a higher rate of schizophrenia among Puerto Ricans than among the general population (Padilla & Padilla, 1977).

- Puerto Ricans on the mainland are more likely to be diagnosed with mental illness than are Puerto Ricans in Puerto Rico. Depression is diagnosed more frequently in Puerto Ricans than among other Hispanic groups, including Cuban Americans and Mexican Americans (Canino, 1990).
- Alcohol abuse is at least four times more prevalent among Puerto Ricans in Puerto Rico than it is among the non-Puerto Rican population in the United States (Canino, 1990).
- Studies often show that Puerto Ricans use mental health resources at a higher rate than do "all other populations" or "non-Puerto Rican populations" (Canino, 1990).

Findings such as these require explanations, which in some cases are readily available. For example, Padilla and Padilla (1977) explain the high rate of schizophrenia among Hispanics by the fact that the Hispanic population is poor and psychotic disorders are more prevalent among the poor. Social conditions, migrations, prejudice, and language barriers make Hispanics more vulnerable to psychotic disorders. In a similar vein, Sedgewick (1982) notes that although the factor of racism should not be ignored, labels of psychopathology are social indicators of the stress experienced by populations that lack power; thus, we should expect the oppressed and underprivileged to show more psychopathology.

In addition, behavior that is considered "normal" in one country or ethnic group may be considered pathological or dysfunctional in another country or locale. For example, the consumption of large quantities of alcohol is considered more acceptable in Puerto Rico than it is in the United States. Thus, although alcoholism is a significant problem in Puerto Rico, fewer people are considered "dysfunctional alcoholics" there because Puerto Rican society makes allowances for heavy alcohol use (Canino, 1990).

Although explanations for diagnostic differences are sometimes reasonable, misdiagnosis often occurs. Four basic reasons for misdiagnosis are (1) cultural expression of symptomatology, (2) unreliable research instruments and evaluations inventories, (3) clinician bias and prejudice, and (4) institutional racism.

CULTURAL EXPRESSION OF SYMPTOMATOLOGY

People from different cultures express the same feelings in different ways. Conversely, they also express feelings in ways that may suggest different symptoms in different cultures. For example, in depression one feels unable to cope with daily life; individuals show depression by manifesting symptoms that contradict normal expressivity in a given culture or society. In a culture in which extroversion is valued, depression will be expressed as quiet, introverted behavior. In a culture in which subdued, less expressive behavior is valued, depression is indicated through acting-out behaviors. Moreover, if someone from an "introverted" culture acts out in American culture, he or she is likely to be misdiagnosed with mania or antisocial personality.

In some cultures, the division between psychological and somatic problems is less clearly delineated than it is in American culture. Canino (1988) cites research indicating that Mexicans do not dichotomize or separate emotional illness from somatic diseases. Thus various psychological or emotional disorders that are indicative of grief in Western societies—agitated depression, feelings of helplessness—may be manifested as somatic symptoms among Mexicans (Canino, 1988). Kleinman and Good (1985) note that Asian Indians and Iraqis often present to physicians with somatic complaints rather than affective ones (i.e., "my stomach hurts" rather than "I'm depressed").

In addition, various religions and cultures have quite different ways of expressing grief, including what Westerners might term "hallucinations," "grandiosity," and "hearing voices." Such differences can lead to misdiagnosis. For example,

> S, a Ghanian woman, presented to an outpatient psychiatry service with feelings of apathy, confusion, and depression. S and her husband were in America while he worked on his postdoctoral studies. S had little social life and found caring for her children, which she had previously enjoyed, burdensome. During the mental-status portion of her interview with a psychiatric resident, she was

asked if she ever heard voices other people didn't hear or saw things that other people didn't see. She replied that she had vivid visions of her recently deceased mother, who came to S's room and talked to S. She was asked whether she simply envisioned her mother or literally saw her mother standing before her. S replied that the latter was the case. She was then asked if she ever felt as if someone else controlled her thoughts. S replied that her mother's voice was constantly inside her head, telling her what to do. S mentioned that her mother had died four months earlier but that she and her husband could not afford to go home for the funeral. The attending physician deemed that the sudden and dramatic changes in S's life had triggered a psychotic episode, a form of schizophrenia, and she was started on a course of psychotropic medication.

During this interview, no questions were asked regarding S's spiritual/religious beliefs, nor were cultural aspects of her grieving process examined. Normal grieving in some cultures includes elements that Western culture might view as psychotic (e.g., seeing the dead and communicating with them as they were in life or as transformed into birds, animals, or spirits). Had this aspect of S's reactions been examined, a more appropriate diagnosis of depression or bereavement might have been made.

In discussing cultural variants of depression, Kleinman and Good (1985) provide an excellent argument for the essential importance of considering cultural background in psychiatric diagnosis:

> Because the analytic categories of professional psychiatry so fundamentally share assumptions with popular Western cultures . . . the complaints of patients are viewed as reflecting an underlying pathological phenomenon. From this perspective, culture appears epiphenomenal; cultural differences may exist, but they are not considered essential to the phenomenon itself. However, when culture is treated as a significant variable, for example, when the researcher seriously confronts the world of meaning and experience of members of non-Western societies, many of our

assumptions about the nature of emotions and illness are cast in sharp relief (p. 492).

UNRELIABLE RESEARCH INSTRUMENTS AND EVALUATION INVENTORIES

To recognize symptoms of mental disorder, a normative measure is required. However, whose norm should be employed? As with educational testing, psychiatric testing in America is clearly biased toward the dominant white, male, Western cultural experience and thus is not culturally syntonic for people outside this population. When I was a student doing field practice in an outpatient psychiatric clinic, clients were asked during the mental-status exam if they ever heard things other people didn't hear. In one instance, an educated, middle-class, white male replied, "If you're asking me if I'm schizophrenic, then the answer's no!" In another instance, a 60-year-old working-class African American woman replied, "Well, yes, sometimes when I'm alone in the house, I think I hear voices." Her response led to the question, "And are other people really there?" She said, "No, when I go to look, I never find anyone." Thus, people who are unaware of psychiatric procedures and jargon tend to answer such questions honestly, unaware that they may be setting themselves up for misdiagnosis. People who live in a dangerous neighborhood may indeed hear things other people do not hear. And clients whose grief expression is non-Western may see things other people do not see.

Canino (1990) pointed out that women are more often diagnosed as mentally ill than are men, yet the research instruments measuring mental disorders often do not include items concerning alcohol abuse and antisocial personality ("male" disorders) though they do include anxiety and depression scales ("female" disorders). Canino also pointed out the importance of geography in research on ethnic minorities, noting that studies comparing Hispanics in New York with Cuban Americans in Miami may yield different results because life in New York, especially in the areas where Hispanics typically live, is more difficult than life in Miami. He also pointed out that seeking mental health care is less stigmatizing for Puerto Ricans on the mainland than it is in Puerto Rico, which may explain the higher rate of mental illness among Puerto Ricans here. Moreover, whereas Puerto Ricans may use mental health facilities more, they may use other health facilities less (Canino, 1990). In other words, one must look at their total use of all medical and mental health services offered. Also, the difficulties of intergroup comparisons among persons of the same (or different) ethnic background should not be underestimated. Are immigrant populations compared with nonimmigrant populations? Are people who have come to the United States voluntarily compared with those who were forced to flee their home country?

CLINICIAN BIAS AND PREJUDICE

Misdiagnosis can also be caused by clinician bias. Spurlock (1985) and Gardner (1990) note that many psychiatrists do not perceive African Americans' psyche as being as complex as that of whites. Therefore, the same symptoms that would be labeled emotional or affective disorders among whites are labeled schizophrenic among African Americans. Sata (1990) notes that psychiatry's focus is exclusively on individual pathology and not on social, cultural, and political realities. This focus is inherently racist due to its detrimental effects on clients from the nondominant culture. Gardner (1990) points out that even African American doctors are not immune to such bias—when they don the physician's white coat, they often don its values, too. Language barriers, both obvious and the not so obvious, also exist, complicating the problem of making cross-cultural psychiatric diagnoses. Clearly, immigrants whose English is poor have difficulty making themselves understood. However, even if minority clients speak English well, communication may still be impeded by cultural barriers. For example, Teichner (1981) found that because Puerto Ricans are underrepresented in the mental health professions, professionals' lack of knowledge of Puerto Rican culture is likely to lead to misdiagnosis.

Gardner (1990) takes the problem one step farther, asking whether psychiatrists really want to understand their clients or whether it is easier for most psychiatrists to "blame" clients by labeling them noncompliant or resistant. To examine the meaning behind such labels, one must examine psychiatrists' own values, attitudes, and countertransference issues. Psychiatric training does little to raise awareness of professionals' bias and prejudices. Psychiatric social workers should be aware of this during team diagnosis, and social workers in general should consider the possibility of bias in reports from psychiatric professionals. Most psychiatrists are not aware of their own bias and therefore do not do adequate assessments and history taking.

INSTITUTIONAL RACISM

Institutional racism can also cause misdiagnosis. For example, the *Diagnostic and Statistical Manual of Mental Disorders* (American Psychiatric Association, 1987) claims to be objective and nonpolitical but in fact contains inherent assumptions regarding pathology and mental disease that demonstrate a Western bias. Some of its earlier assumption have been challenged and changed in later editions—for example, it no longer classifies homosexuality as a mental disorder. However, many diagnostic assumptions that affect women and minorities are less overt and have not been adequately questioned. For example, wife-battering is considered a crime but not a psychiatric disorder. If it were labeled a psychiatric disorder, perpetrators could be hospitalized involuntarily. As another example, schizophrenia is characterized by hostility, suspicion, and paranoia. An African American in today's society may manifest all of these emotions in the course of daily survival.

At the other extreme, Spurlock (1985) notes that in their efforts to avoid cultural bias, mental health care providers often miss pathology when they pre-identify it as a cultural trait. Thus, a therapist facing an Asian American who is withdrawn may consider such behavior typical of Asian American peoples instead of recognizing it as a sign of possible depression. Alternatively, if a symptom is dystonic within a particular culture, but not dystonic within the dominant culture, it may not be recognized as pathology. Thus, as noted earlier, Asian American children are often underdiagnosed with hyperactivity because they are measured against the white American cultural norm instead of against their own cultural norm (Sata, 1990).

In a mental-status examination, affect is measured. White Americans may be more open to sharing their feelings than are African Americans, who, although they are very expressive in their mode of communication, may have learned not to share their inner feelings, especially with someone whom they do not know well. Asian Americans learn not to be overtly expressive; thus what appears as blunting of affect to non-Asians may actually represent self-control to Asians. Also, many Asian Americans believe that what is spoken is not as important as that which is left unsaid. Hispanic men verbalize their anger but rarely express fear or anxiety (Jue, 1987). Direct eye contact is viewed as disrespectful in some cultures; thus these clients should not be considered shy or hostile unless these diagnoses are supported by other factors in the interview. Other nonverbal cues, such as the way the client sits, may have less to do with pathology than with cultural dictates. The clinician needs to be familiar with such behaviors if he or she is to interpret them correctly.

TREATMENT ISSUES

Diagnosis may be reached after a single evaluation session or may occur during treatment. Thus, treatment must be evaluated when the possibility of misdiagnosis is considered.

Many authors have discussed the importance of clinician awareness of minority cultures and issues during therapy (Jue, 1987; Hines & Boyd-Franklin, 1982; Boyd-Franklin, 1989; Pinderhughes, 1982; de Anda, 1984). Therapists need to be aware of their own biases and of clients' self-perception and understanding of therapy so that client behaviors can be placed in their proper context. For example, behaviors that help African Americans to survive in the larger society affect their behavior and consequent diagnosis in the therapeutic environment. African Americans may be especially wary of the motives of authority figures and thus may test relationships before allowing themselves to develop a trusting and intimate bond with a therapist. Asian Americans, in contrast, are taught to be cooperative in social relationships and respectful toward authority figures. They may thus maintain a low profile as a survival technique. Hence, in therapy, they may smile and nod in agreement even when they do not agree or understand.

Stereotypes concerning minority clients once permeated the mental health professions and may still influence therapists' behavior in some instances. For example, Hines and Boyd-Franklin (1982) cited various studies indicating that black clients were less likely than were white clients to be in psychotherapy. Black clients were also discharged sooner than were whites. Fewer than one-third of black clients were referred to group or individual therapy, whereas one-half of the white patients were referred to such treatment (Yamamoto, James, & Palley, 1968).

An accusation often leveled against minority clients by clinicians in public health institutions is that they have no respect for time constraints and often are late for or miss appointments (Kuper, 1981). However, therapy appointments are often scheduled to meet the needs of the therapist, not the client. Problems with transportation and babysitting may cause clients to miss appointments. Moreover, poor minority clients' experiences with institutions and services in other areas of their life do not serve as models for responsible behavior. For example, why should a client who typically waits four hours in a welfare line believe that his or her 9:00 A.M. appointment for outpatient psychiatry will be any different?

Depending on cultural background, clients may use Western medicine or psychiatry in conjunction with other forms of healing techniques. Most cultures have spiritual healers—priests, rabbis, shamans, spiritualists—whose advice is sought on mental health issues. In a random sample of Puerto Ricans in New York City, Canino (1990) found that 31% had seen a spiritualist at least once. Canino also found that

73% of a group of outpatients at a New York City mental health clinic reported visiting a spiritualist prior to seeking psychiatric consultation. Clinicians need to be aware that their advice or opinion may conflict with that of the spiritual healer and to respect and integrate differing approaches in the best interests of clients.

RECOMMENDATIONS

How can clinicians ensure that misdiagnosis does not occur when dealing with clients from different cultural backgrounds?

First, clinicians need to examine critically the means used to categorize pathologies and illnesses. Kleinman and Good (1985) recommend that more clinical/descriptive research should be conducted to serve as a bias for evaluating the cross-cultural validity of our current diagnostic categories of mental illness. They also hold that new standards for cross-cultural epidemiological studies should be developed and emphasize that cross-cultural research can help us better understand the relationships among emotions, social influences, causes of illness, cognitions, and somatization. In addition, they believe that serious consideration should be given to adding a cultural axis to the *Diagnostic and Statistical Manual of Mental Disorders* (American Psychiatric Association, 1987).

Perhaps most important, clinicians should focus on the specific personal, familial, and cultural history of the client. Accurate assessment of a client's history includes:

- immigrant-generation status of the client
- level of cultural assimilation—that is, is the client monocultural (e.g., a new immigrant), bicultural (balancing and integrating nondominant culture into the dominant culture), or unicultural (assimilated to the point of no longer identifying with ethnic background)
- level of integration within cultural assimilation (i.e., is the client isolated, marginal, acculturated?)

- religious beliefs
- social class
- child-rearing practices
- school influence

For example, Jones (1985) recommends that clinicians consider the following when assessing the psychological adaptation of African Americans: (1) reactions to racial oppression, (2) influence of the majority culture, (3) influence of African American culture, and (4) individual and family experiences and strengths. The model is interactive; that is, each set of factors has an influence on psychological functioning and an influence on the operation of the other factors. Thus factors such as political activism within the family, personal experience with discrimination, and attendance at a predominantly white or black school and how these factors influence one another would be considered in the assessment.

Some authors have suggested that, depending on the cultural background of the client, one form of therapy may be more culturally syntonic than another. Canino and Canino (1982) recommend goal-oriented, directive, structural family therapy for low-income Hispanic clients. They describe this approach as being appropriate for cultures in which men are expected to assume a dominant role and women and children a passive role. Although clinicians from the dominant culture should not impose their values on those from other cultures, this does not mean that issues of abuse, such as wife-battering or degradation of women, should be overlooked because of different cultural attitudes toward women.

In familiarizing themselves with different cultures, clinicians must note that diversity exists *within* a population as well as between different populations. The term "Middle Eastern" cover peoples from Syria to Algeria to Lebanon. African Americans include Americans whose origins are spread across the whole continent of Africa. Stereotypes of economic class for different populations must also be avoided. Clinicians need to understand the cultural nuances of their clients and remain curious and open to the information that the client presents.

CONCLUSION

Clinical treatment usually follows and is dependent on a given diagnosis. Research has shown that particular racial or ethnic groups are frequently diagnosed as having particular disorders. Although these diagnostic differences are sometimes valid, they can also reflect misunderstandings based on ethnocentric and racist assumptions of the profession.

Cultural background can affect clients' presentation of symptoms. Behaviors that are considered dysfunctional or abnormal in the dominant culture may be considered functional and normal in another culture. Because research instruments and treatment modalities are often based on experiences and needs of the white, male, Western client, they may not reflect the cultural realities of minority clients.

Moreover, studies that examine the cultural differences among particular communities often do not take into account factors such immigrant status, geographical location, and economic status.

Clinician prejudice, bias, and lack of familiarity with different racial and ethnic groups can also result in misdiagnosis. Clinicians need to examine their own potential bias, in that diagnoses are based on deviations from normative measures. If the normative experience of clients from a given cultural background is not considered, diagnosis is likely to reflect the majority culture's bias.

To minimize misdiagnosis, more cross-cultural research is needed. Clinicians must examine their own prejudices and biases so that assessment procedures can better reflect the reality of clients' experience.

REFERENCES

American Psychiatric Association. (1987). *Diagnostic and statistical manual of mental disorders* (3rd ed., rev.). Washington, DC: Author.

Boyd-Franklin, N. (1989). *Black families in therapy*. New York: Guilford.

Bryant, C. (1980). Introducing students to the treatment of inner-city families. *Social Casework, 61*, 629–636.

Canino, G., & Canino, I. (1982). Family therapy: A culturally syntonic approach for migrant Puerto Ricans. *Hospital and Community Psychiatry, 33*, 299–303.

Canino, I. (1988). The clinical assessment of the transcultural child. In C. Kestenbaum & D. Williams (Eds.), *Clinical assessment of children and adolescents*. New York: New York University Press.

Canino, I. (1990, April). *Working with persons from Hispanic backgrounds*. Paper presented at the Cross-Cultural Psychotherapy Conference, Hahnemann University, Philadelphia.

Chesler, P. (1972). *Women and madness*. New York: Doubleday.

de Anda, D. (1984). Bicultural socialization: Factors affecting the minority experience. *Social Work, 29*, 101–107.

Gardner, G. (1990, April). *Working with persons from African American backgrounds*. Paper presented at the Cross-Cultural Psychotherapy Conference, Hahnemann University, Philadelphia.

Harrison, S. I., et al. (1965). Social class and mental illness in children: Choice of treatment. *Archives of General Psychiatry, 13*, 411–417.

Hines, P. M., & Boyd-Franklin, N. (1982). Black families. In M. McGoldrick, J. Pearce, & J. Giordano (Eds.), *Ethnicity and family therapy*. New York: Guilford.

Jones, A. (1985). Psychological functioning in black Americans: A conceptual guide for use in psychotherapy. *Psychotherapy, 22*, 363–369.

Jones, B., Gray, B., & Parson, E. (1983). Manic-depressive illness among poor urban Hispanics. *American Journal of Psychiatry, 140*, 1208–1210.

Jue, S. (1987). Identifying and meeting the needs of minority clients with AIDS. In C. Leukenfeld & M. Fimbres (Eds.), *Responding to AIDS*. Washington, DC: National Association of Social Workers.

Kleinman, A., & Good, B. (Eds.). (1985). *Culture and depression*. Los Angeles: University of California Press.

Kupers, T. A. (1981). *Public therapy*. New York: Free Press.

Mukherjee, S., Shukla, S., & Woodle, J. (1983). Misdiagnosis of schizophrenia in bipolar patients: A multiethnic comparison. *American Journal of Psychiatry, 140*, 1571–1574.

Padilla, E., & Padilla, A. (Eds.). (1977). *Transcultural psychiatry: An Hispanic perspective*. Los Angeles: Spanish Speaking Mental Health Research Center (UCLA).

Pinderhughes, E. (1982). Afro-American families and the victim system. In M. McGoldrick, J. Pearce, & J. Giordano (Eds.), *Ethnicity and family therapy*. New York: Guilford.

Sata, L. (1990, April). *Working with persons from Asian backgrounds*. Paper presented at the Cross-Cultural Psychotherapy Conference, Hahnemann University, Philadelphia.

Sedgewick, P. (1982). *Psycho politics*. New York: Harper and Row.

Spurlock, J. (1985). Assessment and therapeutic intervention of black children. *Journal of American Academy of Child Psychiatry, 24*, 168–174.

Teichner, V. (1981). The Puerto Rican patient. *Journal of the American Academy of Psychoanalysis, 9*, 277.

Yamamoto, J., James, E., & Palley, N. (1968). Cultural problems in psychiatric therapy. *Archives of General Psychiatry, 19*, 45–49.

CHECKPOINTS

1. Maracek and Hare-Mustin conclude that the mental health establishment has marginalized women, and although feminist criticisms have led to the development of many improved therapies, these therapies have not always been incorporated into the mainstream.

2. Kupers suggests that although the DSM-IV is an improvement over earlier versions in its inclusion of women and its elimination of certain gender-biased diagnoses, it continues to perpetuate traditional gender role prescriptions in many of its diagnostic categories.

3. Soloman argues that social stereotypes cause therapists to misperceive and misdiagnose minorities and poor people.

To prepare for reading the next section, think about these questions:

1. What reasons can you give as to why traditional psychotherapy would not be successful for women and minorities?

2. What approaches would you expect from a feminist therapist?

The Future of Feminist Therapy

LAURA S. BROWN

Seattle, Washington

ANNETTE M. BRODSKY

Harbor UCLA Medical Center

This article addresses the development of feminist therapy as a theoretical orientation to practice over the past two decades. The core philosophical principles of feminist therapy are described. Future directions for feminist therapy are conceptualized as including the development of feminist therapy theory, movement toward a more multicultural perspective on feminist therapy, and an expansion of the populations served by feminist therapists. Additionally, the development of formal standards and training in feminist therapy is proposed as an important goal for the future.

It has been barely two decades since a small number of women within the psychotherapy professions profoundly affected by the insights of the women's movement began to use the term *feminist therapy* to describe their work. Feminist therapy is unique among theoretical orientations. It is one of few approaches to psychotherapy whose roots lie outside of the behavioral sciences. It is founded, instead, in the theories and philosophies of the U.S. women's movement of the 1960s and 1970s. As a grass-roots phenomenon, feminist therapy developed through informal exchanges of style, technique, and experience among its practitioners. As with other aspects of the women's movement, feminist therapy has eschewed identified leaders or authority figures. However, this almost organic process had yielded strikingly similar philosophies of treatment among the early feminist therapists that continue to guide feminist therapy theory and practice today.

Much of the direction of the feminist therapy movement arose from the context of consciousness-raising (CR) groups. CR groups were one of the first settings in which feminist therapy concepts saw light as therapists began to apply feminist awareness to their experiences on both sides of the therapy room (Brodsky, 1973).

Conferences, workshops, and feminist therapy collectives sprang up in large numbers in the early 1970s. Papers were written, copied, and passed hand to hand. Although there were some personal and regional variations on the theme, feminist therapy soon came to be characterized by shared concepts. These included the development of egalitarian structures within the therapy relationship; close attention to the effects of social context on the client's problems; and an assumption that environmental pressures, particularly gender roles and gender-based discrimination; these were major factors in determining such aspects of inner experience as identity, cognitive structures, and patterns of interpersonal behavior (Rawlings & Carter, 1977).

Feminist therapy as it currently exists is a philosophy of psychotherapy, not a prescription of technique. It is a hybrid that emerged from the interface between treatment of gender-role-related disorders and application of a process of feminist analysis (Brodsky, 1980). Feminist therapists may practice in a variety of modalities. However, certain core principles are held in common and will inform treatment whether it is cognitive-behavioral or psychodynamic. These principles include

1. Valuing of the diverse and complex experiences of women from all racial, class, religious, age, and sexual orientation groups (Lerman, 1986). Mainstream psychotherapies have privileged the standpoints of dominant groups, which, in this culture, are

the perspectives of white, heterosexual men (Hare-Mustin & Maracek, 1988). Feminist therapists hold that it is essential to rebalance the construction of reality so as to include as normative and valued those experiences and ways of being that inhere to being female in this cultural context, such as nuturance, cooperativeness, and compromise.

2. An attention to power dynamics in the therapy relationship, with the goal of developing egalitarian relationships and structures. Feminist therapists hold that within the essential asymmetry of psychotherapy, those dynamics that unnecessarily lend power to the therapist or take it from the client are inimical to the goals of feminist therapy (American Psychological Association Task Force on Sex Bias and Sex Role Stereotyping in Psychotherapy, 1975).

3. A theory of human behavior that equally attends to intrapsychic and social/contextual variables. Feminist therapists believe that behavior must be understood within the broader social context and that the impact of external realities on internal nonconscious process must be factored into our interpretations of behaviors. As a theory based in feminism, there is special attention paid to the meaning and place of assigned gender role in the individual's social environment and the impact of gender on self-identity.

4. A reliance on the empirical data base arising from feminist scholarship on the psychology of women and gender. Feminist therapy practice itself has been an impetus for the development of research and the growth of bodies of knowledge on disorders of high prevalence in women such as depression, eating disorders, and the sequelae of interpersonal violence and sexual assault (Brodsky & Hare-Mustin, 1980).

5. Valuing a balance of both healthy autonomy and relational competence for all adults, rather than regarding these traits as inevitably gender based and avoiding biological reductionist models of human behavior, particularly gendered behaviors.

6. Seeing the goals of therapy as including both intrapsychic change and a changed perspective on the social/cultural realities that affect clients' lives, whatever the specifics of the context (Brown & Liss-Levinson, 1981). Therapeutic goals for clients are generated cooperatively between therapist and client. There is a focus on empowering the client to change the social, interpersonal, and political environment that has an impact on her or his relationships with others and well-being rather than helping clients to adjust in order to make peace with an oppressive social context. An important aspect of this empowerment process is the rejection of the myth of value-free psychotherapy. Feminist therapists, by making their own biases explicit, facilitate clients' ownership of their own values and choices. Therapy is seen as a cooperative relationship between the two. Both therapist and client perspectives are equally valued although different in nature.

FEMINIST THERAPY LOOKS AT THE FUTURE OF PSYCHOTHERAPY

What can feminist therapy contribute to a vision of the future of the entire field of psychotherapy? It is our sense that feminist therapy already occupies an important position that is a harbinger of the future of psychotherapy. Thus our predictions for therapy overall reflect our perspectives on what is valuable for the practice of psychotherapy, as well as our awareness of the external market forces that may affect achievement of our goals.

Several interesting and challenging visions emerge when we apply a feminist analysis to the future of psychotherapy. One trend, which owes its origins to feminist therapy concepts of empowerment of clients, is that therapy will become more consumer oriented. As the number and variety of practitioners in all disciplines increases, therapists will perforce become more attentive to the specific needs of potential clients. Marketing for the individual with a choice of therapy services and a limited amount of resources leads to shopping for a more defined product. Therapists will need to inform clients more fully as to their approaches, the possible length of therapy, the rates of success that this approach achieves, and the therapist's specific experience with the client's particular problems. More therapists will follow the lead of feminist therapy in offering low-cost initial sessions to clients so as to encourage informed consumers. Feminist therapists have modeled this approach by use of therapy contracts (Brown & Liss-Levinson, 1981). As new forms of service delivery and payment such as health maintenance organizations and managed care networks proliferate, we can predict that in order to survive the 21st century, most approaches to therapy will follow the feminist therapy model and become more consumer oriented.

Culturally sensitive approaches to therapy, another vision of the future pioneered by feminist therapy, will also become essential to the future of general psychotherapy practice. The future of psychotherapy in North America is the future of our population, one that is growing increasingly ethnically and culturally diverse. Feminist therapy, in concert with ethnically sensitive approaches to treatment, has always emphasized the importance of understanding behaviors in their social environments and the necessity of respectful integration of nondominant realities and values into our work. We believe that the future for therapy must include such growing cultural literacy and sensitivity if therapy is to remain relevant for anyone except the ever-smaller white, middle-class population for whom therapy has traditionally been targeted.

FEMINIST THERAPY'S FUTURE

As a relatively new theoretical orientation, feminist therapy is at an exciting and difficult point in the developmental process. We have moved beyond the stage where we needed to clarify what feminist therapists are not (e.g., not an aggressive, man-hating dictator attempting to convert her clients to the same negative characteristics). We also no longer need differentiate feminist therapy as an area of specific standpoint and expertise from simply nonsexist perspectives on treatment (Brodsky, 1975; Rawlings & Carter, 1977). We are now at a point where sufficient work has been done to allow for the articulation of central organizing principles for theory (Lerman, 1986) and the creation of models for understanding development of personality and psychopathology. We

have delineated feminist models of healthy or ideal forms of being and relating (Gilligan, 1982; Jordan, Surrey & Kaplan, 1983; Miller, 1976; Surrey, 1985).

There are, however, several important tasks that lie in the future for feminist therapy as it matures. In keeping with feminist therapy traditions we wish to identify our perspectives on thus our potential biases. Although our views are a fair representation of feminist therapy thought, our own theory makes us aware of the limitations that our experience and demographics impose on us. We are both white, middle-class, U.S. residents, and clinical psychologists. One of us is a lesbian, one over 40, one in full-time practice, one working in a public institutional setting. Neither of us is disabled, foreign born, or male.

The Development of Feminist Therapy Theory

An essential aspect of a future for feminist therapy will be the continued development of central organizing theory. Lerman (1986) has proposed the criteria for such a theory and notes that many current feminist therapy theoreticians are moving toward meeting those criteria. However, a problem for feminist therapy has been our difficulty in clearly differentiating ourselves theoretically from other perspectives. It has been relatively easier to develop models that, for instance, blend feminist analysis with various psychodynamic models (Chodorow, 1970; Eichenbaum & Orbach, 1983; Miller, 1976; Surrey, 1985) or family systems theories (Luepnitz, 1988), for example, than to know what a genuinely feminist paradigm for understanding human behavior and development might be.

An aspect of this problem that is common to feminist theory development in all scholarly disciplines is the difficulty that we have as persons trained within the mainstream and thus intellectually affected by it in getting outside of our own worldviews, which contain the traces of this mainstream intellectual socialization. As radical feminist philosophers such as Mary Daly (1983) and Sonia Johnson (1987, 1989) have pointed out, we become entrapped in the language and forms of patriarchy to such a degree that we can only with difficulty imagine a feminist perspective that is not a blend with or homage to other theories.

Yet we believe that this is a possible and eventually essential aspect of the future of feminist therapy; the creation of visions of human behavior, understandings of development, distress, and healing that are more centrally feminist in their nature. Using a feminist model of drawing upon multiple methodologies and ways of knowing (Ballou, 1990; Belenky et al., 1986) will be an important aspect of this theory development.

Theory development in feminist therapy is tied both politically and conceptually to the feminist process of moving up from the grass roots. We neither have nor want a leader to create a full-blown "correct" theory or practice, choosing instead to follow Lerman's (1986) admonition that we stay "close to the data of experience" in our strategies for theory development. Models for theory development arise from the ranks of practicing feminist therapists who share their insights and innovations and in turn modify their work based on feedback and interchange with other therapists. The therapy collectives of the 1970s have transformed into the larger regional groups in which there is a specific focus on the creation of a theory that is feminist in both process and content. In the work of the Stone Center on personality and relational development (Jordan, Surrey & Kaplan, 1983), the Women's Therapy Centre Institute on eating disorders and mother-daughter relationships (Eichbaum & Orbach, 1983), and the process of the Feminist Therapy Institute in the development of feminist therapy ethical principles (Rave & Larsen, 1990), we can find the legacy of the earlier oral traditions and concrete examples of how theory is built in feminist therapy.

Multiculturalism

The future of feminist therapy will also see the development of a more multicultural, antiracist, and diverse perspective on theory and practice (Brown, 1990). Feminist therapists have always held to an inclusive ideal. However, the reality as feminist therapy finishes its second decade is that it has been primarily a middle-class, American, white women's field (Brown, 1990; Brown & Root, 1990a; Kanuha, 1990). Feminist therapy has been admirable in its inclusion of the realities of white lesbians, many of whom are central figures in the field (Boston Lesbian Psychologies Collective, 1987). Thus it is clear that a feminist therapy model can extend itself outside of the mainstream; however, on issues of color, class, and culture, feminist therapy is only beginning to do so.

Until now, however, much has been lost or ignored regarding the experiences of women of color and ethnic and linguistic minorities within feminist therapy thought and practice. Just as our views of all women have been distorted by viewing behavior through a male paradigm, so, too, have they been limited by the application of a white paradigm. An example of how this distortion excludes some women and limits our ability to conceptualize accurately can be found in the work of Palladino and Stephenson (1990), who point out that theories of women's relational development that are based only or solely in white women's experiences may in consequence be flawed or inadequate to describe *all* women's normal relational development.

Feminist therapy theory and practice have already begun to respond to some degree to this need for a more multicultural perspective with several volumes (Brown & Root, 1990b; Reid & Comas-Diaz, 1990) and projects (Landrine, in press) emerging in the past few years that present images of how a multicultural feminist therapy might be and examples of its applications.

Multiculturalism is a natural and necessary extension of the feminist principle of deconstructing dominant norms and privileging nondominants as a means of newly comprehending dominant experiences. The specific feminist vision of women from nondominant groups (Boyd, 1990; Bradshaw, 1990; Ho, 1990; Hooks, 1981, 1984; Kanuha, 1990; Sears, 1990) and their experiences of what is meant by feminist analysis and values are moving into the mainstream of feminism and feminist therapy (Brown & Root, 1990). As with feminist critique of gender roles and norms, so a feminist analysis of the comparative and interactive effects of gender, race, and class is leading to a more complete and inclusive model of theory and practice for feminist therapy (Brodsky, 1982; Brown & Root, 1990a). A multicultural feminist therapy, by allowing new perspectives on all women's realities, will be of importance to white women as well.

Expanded Populations and New Directions

Feminist therapy has always suffered from the stereotype that it is a therapy for women only. The kernel of truth in this stereotype is that because we began by attempting to correct a lack in regards to women in therapy, adult women have been a primary focus of writing and practice in feminist therapy until very recently. However, feminist therapists have always practiced with a variety of populations, and our future will see a conscious embrace of that expansion. Consequently, a third future vision of feminist therapy is that we will more fully address the needs, concerns, and realities of men, children, families, elders, and people with disabilities. As with multiculturalism, this work is beginning to emerge already. Feminist therapy perspectives on work with men are evolving from the treatment of batterers, as the cultural pairings of sex with violence and dominance with masculinity are being disconnected and applied to work with men in general (Ganley, 1988; Sonkin, Martin & Walker, 1985). Feminist family therapies represent one of the most exciting and energetic dominions of feminist therapy practice today. Along with the inception of a specialty journal on the topic published by the Haworth Press, feminist family therapists are both critiquing existing theories (Bograd, 1984; Goldner, 1987; Luepnitz, 1988) and developing radically feminist revisions of family treatment that eschew traditional models of relating for less heirarchal, more power-equal, and more diversely described pictures of families (Ault-Riche, 1986; Luepnitz, 1988).

Yet another future direction for feminist therapy lies in the area of health and medical issues. Feminist therapists have historically responded to reproductive health concerns of women, exploring the impact of denied reproductive choices and examining the meaning for women of infertility, menstruation, pregnancy, abortion, and menopause (Boston Women's Health Book Collective, 1988; Brodsky, 1987;

Brown, 1991). Beyond the field of women's reproduction, feminist health psychologists are focusing on the necessity of including women as subjects of research on prevention and treatment of disease, adaptation to chronic illness or pain, and coping with the stress of serving as caregivers to the gravely disabled or terminally ill (Grady & Lemkau, 1988).

Children may be the final frontier that has been barely touched by feminist therapy perspectives (Porter, 1989), although the feminist family therapists certainly deal with this group. This in many ways is ironic; feminist therapists were among the most vocal to speak of the sexual abuse of children (Herman, 1981; Rush, 1979) and to address questions of treatments of adult survivors. However, a future feminist therapy will be able to bring our insights about empowerment to work with the least powerful among us and will facilitate the questioning of gender role norms even as they are being formed (Bem, 1983). Additionally, feminist forensic psychologists are increasingly addressing the impact on children of divorce and custody battles, particularly in the context of violence against mothers (Chesler, 1986; Walker & Edwall, 1987).

Standards and Training

The most obvious lack and the most wished-for vision of our future is the establishment of training centers for feminist therapists. The authors of this article, along with most other visible figures who write, train, and practice in the field of feminist therapy, are aware of the demand among therapists in training for opportunities to be taught in settings that offer feminist therapy content and process at the level of graduate and predoctoral internship training.

Feminist therapists can now be found on the faculties of training programs in the mental health disciplines and on the staffs of internship training facilities (American Psychological Association Women's Programs Office, 1990). Feminist research programs are being funded by public agencies (Sayette & Mayn, 1990). Stereotypes that feminist therapists are somehow unscientific, overly political, or unprofessional have diminished to be replaced by an awareness of the rich vistas that a feminist perspective has to offer graduate students, a growing number of whom are interested in pursuing the implications of a feminist therapy model for research and treatment.

Continuing professional education in feminist therapy has also expanded. No longer do only the "true believers" attend workshops by feminist therapists at professional meetings. Many of the topic areas that feminist therapy first addressed in the early 1970s—the sexual exploitation of therapy clients, the sexual abuse of children, domestic violence and its psychological sequelae, sexual harassment in the workplace and academia, dual-career couple relationships—are now considered part of the essential knowledge base for all practitioners and particularly for ethics committees, affirmative action groups, and any therapists considering working with abused populations. Additionally, feminist therapists are constantly searching for opportunities to increase their specifically feminist learning experiences.

But what is available is not yet enough. In consonance with feminist philosophies, few feminist therapy scholars and teachers have promoted themselves and their work at the level of a formal training center, school, or specialty program. Feminist therapy now needs to offer more coherent and intensive training programs. It has become time for the grass to grow tall from its roots.

The beginnings of this move toward more organized training are already in place. The Stone Center at Wellesley College, through their Works in Progress series of lectures and papers, the Women's Therapy Centre Institute in New York, which offers a sequence of courses and practicum experiences in feminist therapy, the Saturday Seminars in the Bay Area, Feminist Therapy Training Associates in Seattle, the Association for Women in Psychology's yearly preconference training workshops, the Psychology of Women Institute of APA's Division 35, which offers annual courses in feminist therapy topics; all of these are evidence of growing response to the need for more training in feminst therapy. The Section on Feminist Professional Training and Practice of APA's Division 35 is working on training offered in schools of professional psychology.

Development of Standards

Along with the promotion of dedicated centers of scholarship and training, feminist therapy is ready for a greater formalization of standards. Standards have been almost taboo for a grassroots movement loathe to restrict those who might identify as a member. In the early 1970s for example, feminist therapist referral roster's simply required self-identification as a feminist therapist, coupled with a statement of one's personal rationale for using the label, to qualify for inclusion (Brodsky, 1970). Over the years, the concepts of both *feminist* and *therapist* have been tightened; the latter due to the introduction of tighter licensing and registration laws, the former in response to what appeared to be greedy attempts on the part of nonfeminists to cash in on the then-cachet and client flow that the title *feminist therapist* conferred in the recession era of the 1970s and early 1980s.

As a consequence, the times now call for standards in feminist therapy. Such standards would address minimum training requirements in the content areas of psychology of women, feminist philosophy and process, and integration of feminist therapy analysis into therapeutic practice. The trend for feminist therapists to develop their standards through inclusionary, consensus models (Rave & Larsen, 1990) means that this process will be a difficult and slow one. We can predict that, as in the area of feminist therapy ethical standards, standards for training and practice will be flexible, process oriented, and respectful of the diverse perspectives contained within feminist therapy.

WHAT FEMINIST THERAPY HAS CONTRIBUTED TO THE FUTURE OF PSYCHOTHERAPY

In recent times, we have found that when feminist therapy is presented to colleagues as a unique method and philosophy of treatment, a prevalent comment is that, "But what you are describing is simply good, ethical practice." We have had to remind our listeners that many ideas that had their genesis in feminist therapy have already been incorporated into the mainstream of psychotherapy practice, because those insights improved the quality of care in other more technically focused treatment systems. Feminist therapy has, in the past two decades, brought the attention of all psychotherapists to the problems of violence and abuse in the family, to the strains of gender roles in a changing culture, to the ethics of practice and the prevention of boundary violations, to precision and care in the application of diagnostic labels, to consideration of the need for fair and unbiased evaluations of all parties in marital and custodial disputes, and to the need for clients to have power over their actions and relationships, including those that occur in the setting of psychotherapy.

It is not that feminist therapy itself had moved into the mainstream. Rather, we have acted as a powerful gadfly, moving the mainstream away from destructive dominant paradigms and into new visions that are shaped by feminist analysis. We will always be a voice for the least powerful and most oppressed in our cultures; we will always be a source of irritation to whatever complacencies about their good intentions that our colleagues may develop about their work with women and members of other disenfranchised and at-risk groups. We will continually challenge mainstream theories and practices to be more inclusive of human diversity, more questioning of their assumptions, more willing to scrutinize their need to be paternalistic with functioning adult clients. We will continue to remind all therapists that gender is an important and highly meaningful category of analysis whose power cannot be denied or minimized at any state of the psychotherapeutic endeavor. We believe that it is this focus, this process of feminist therapy, that presages what our contributions will be in years to come.

REFERENCES

American Psychological Association Task Force on Sex Bias and Sex-Role Stereotyping in Psychotherapeutic Practice. (1975). *Report of the Task Force.* Washington, DC: Author.

American Psychological Association Women's Programs Office. (1990). *Listing of graduate faculty interested in women's issues.* Washington, DC: Author.

Adult-Riche, M. (ed.). (1986). *Women and family therapy.* Rockville, MD: Aspen Systems Corp.

Ballou, M. (1990). Approaching a feminist-principled paradigm in the construction of a personality theory. In L. S. Brown and M. P. P. Root (eds.), *Diversity and complexity in feminist therapy* (pp. 23–40). New York: Haworth Press.

Belenky, M., Clinchy, B., Goldberger, N. & Tarule, J. (1986). *Women's ways of knowing.* New York: Basic Books.

Bem, S. L. (1983). Gender schema theory and its implications for child development: Raising gender-aschematic children in a gender-schematic society. *Signs: Journal of Women in Culture and Society, 8,* 598–616.

Bograd, M. (1984). Family systems approaches to wife-battering: A feminist critique. *American Journal of Orthopsychiatry, 54,* 558–568.

Boston Lesbian Psychologies Collective (eds.). (1987). *Lesbian psychologies: Explorations and challenges.* Champaign, IL: University of Illinois Press.

Boston Women's Health Book Collective (eds.). (1988). *Our bodies, our selves.* New York: Simon & Schuster.

Boyd, J. A. (1990). Ethnic and cultural diversity: Keys to power. In L. S. Brown and M. P. P. Root (eds.), *Diversity and complexity in feminist therapy* (pp. 151–168). New York: Haworth Press.

Bradshaw, C. K. (1990). A Japanese view of dependency; What can amae psychology contribute to feminist theory and therapy? In

L. S. Brown and M. P. P. Root (eds.), *Diversity and complexity in feminist therapy* (pp. 67–86). New York: Haworth Press.

Brodsky, A. M. (1970). *Feminist therapy roster.* Association for Women in Psychology.

Brodsky, A. M. (1973). The consciousness-raising group as a model for therapy with women. *Psychotherapy: Theory, Research, and Practice, 10,* 24–29.

Brodsky, A. M. (1975, April). *Is there a feminist therapy?* Paper presented at the Convention of the Southeastern Psychological Association, Atlanta, GA.

Brodsky, A. M. (1980). A decade of feminist influence on psychotherapy. *Psychology of Women Quarterly, 4,* 331–344.

Brodsky, A. M. (1982). Sex, race, and class issues in psychotherapy research. In M. Parks and J. Harvey (eds.), *Psychotherapy research and behavior change* (pp. 123–150). Washington, DC: American Psychological Association.

Brodsky, A. M. (1987, August). Who should have children? In A. M. Brodsky (Chair), *Donating babies to create families: Psychologists as gatekeepers.* Symposium presented at the Convention of the American Psychological Association, New York:

Brodsky, A. M. & Hare-Mustin, R. (eds.). (1980). *Women and psychotherapy.* New York: Guilford Press.

Brown, L. S. (1991). Therapy with an infertile lesbian client. In C. Silverstein (ed.), *Gays, lesbians, and their therapists: Studies in psychotherapy* (pp. 10–21). New York: Norton.

Brown, L. S. (1990). The meaning of a multicultural perspective for theory-building in feminist therapy. In L. S. Brown and M. P. P. Root (eds.), *Diversity and complexity in feminist therapy* (pp. 1–22). New York: Haworth Press.

Brown, L. S. & Liss-Levinson, N. (1981). Feminist therapy I. In R. Corsini (ed.), *Handbook of innovative psychotherapies* (pp. 299–314). New York: Wiley.

Brown, L. S. & Root, M.P.P. (1990a). Editorial introduction. In L. S. Brown and M.P.P. Root (eds.), *Diversity and complexity in feminist therapy* (pp. i–xiii). New York: Haworth Press.

Brown, L. S. & Root, M.P.P. (eds.). (1990b). *Diversity and complexity in feminist therapy.* New York: Haworth Press.

Chesler, P. (1986). *Mothers on trial.* New York: Doubleday.

Chodorow, N. (1979). *The reproduction of mothering.* Berkeley: Univ. of California Press.

Daly, M. (1983). *Pure lust: Elemental feminist philosophy.* Boston: Beacon Press.

Eichenbaum, L. & Orbach, S. (1983). *Understanding women: A feminist psychoanalytic view.* New York: Basic Books.

Ganley, A. L. (1988). Feminist therapy with male clients. In M. A. Dutton-Douglas and L.E.A. Walker (eds.), *Feminist psychotherapies: Integration of feminist and psychotherapeutic systems* (pp. 186–205). Norwood, NJ: Ablex.

Gilligan, C. (1982). *In a different voice.* Cambridge, MA: Harvard Univ. Press.

Goldner, V. (1987). Instrumentalism, family, and the limits of family therapy. *Journal of Family Psychology, 1,* 109–116.

Grady, K. E. & Lemkau, J. P. (eds.) (1988). Women's health: Our minds, our bodies. *Psychology of Women Quarterly, 12.*

Hare-Mustin, R. & Maracek, J. (1988). The meaning of difference: Gender theory, post-modernism and psychology. *American Psychologist, 43,* 455–464.

Herman, J. L. (1981). *Father-daughter incest.* Cambridge MA: Harvard Univ. Press.

Ho, C. K. (1990). An analysis of domestic violence in Asian American communities: A multicultural approach to counseling. In L. S. Brown and M.P.P. Root (eds.), *Diversity and complexity in feminist therapy* (pp. 129–150). New York: Haworth Press.

Hooks, B. (1981). *Ain't I a woman.* Boston: South End Press.

Hooks, B. (1984). *Feminist theory: From margin to center.* Boston: South End Press.

Johnson, S. (1987). *Going out of our minds: The metaphysics of liberation.* Freedom, CA: The Crossing Press.

Johnson, S. (1989). *Wildfire.* Albuquerque, NM: Wildfire Books.

Jordan, J., Surrey, J. & Kaplan, A. G. (1983). Women and empathy. In *Work in Progress.* Wellesley, MA: Stone Center Working Papers Series.

Kanuha, V. (1990). The need for an integrated analysis of oppression in feminist therapy ethics. In H. Lerman and N. Porter (eds.), *Feminist ethics in psychotherapy* (pp. 24–36). New York: Springer.

Landrine, H. (ed.). (in press). *Diversity in feminist psychology.* New York: Guilford.

Lerman, H. (1986). *A mote in Freud's eye: From psychoanalysis to the psychology of women.* New York: Springer.

Luepnitz, D. A. (1988). *The family interpreted: Feminist theory in clinical practice.* New York: Basic Books.

Miller, J. B. (1976). *Toward a new psychology of women.* Boston: Beacon Press.

Palladino, D. & Stephenson, Y. (1990). Perceptions of the sexual self: Their impact on relationships between lesbian and heterosexual women. In L. S. Brown and M.P.P. Root (eds.), *Diversity and complexity in feminist therapy* (pp. 231–254). New York: Haworth Press.

Porter, N. (1989, August). Feminist perspectives on psychotherapy with sexually abused children. In N. Porter (Chair), *Feminist perspectives on post-traumatic stress disorder.* Symposium presented at the Convention of the American Psychological Association, New Orleans, LA.

Rave, E. J. & Larsen, C. C. (1990). Development of the code: The feminist process. In H. Lerman and N. Porter (eds.), *Feminist ethics in psychotherapy* (pp. 14–23). New York: Springer.

Rawlings, E. & Carter, D. (eds.) (1977). *Psychotherapy for women: Treatment toward equality.* Springfield, IL: Charles C Thomas.

Reid, P. T. & Comas-Diaz, L. (eds.). (1990). Special issue on women of color. *Sex Roles.*

Rush, F. (1979). *The best-kept secret.* New York: Harper & Row.

Sayette, M. A. & Mayne, T. J. (1990). Survey of current clinical and research trends in clinical psychology. *American Psychologist, 45,* 1263–1266.

Sears, V. L. (1990). On being an "only one." In H. Lerman and N. Porter (eds.), *Feminist ethics in psychotherapy* (pp. 102–105). New York: Springer.

Sonkin, D. J., Martin, D. & Walker, L. E. A. (1985). *The male batterer: A treatment approach.* New York: Springer.

Surrey, J. (1985). Self in relation: A theory of women's development. In *Works in Progress.* Wellesley, MA: Stone Center Works in Progress Series.

Walker, L. E. A. & Edwall, G. E. (1987). Domestic violence and determination of visitation and child custody in divorce. In D. J. Sonkin (ed.), *Domestic violence on trial* (pp. 127–154). New York: Springer.

CHECKPOINTS

1. Brown and Brodsky suggest that feminist therapy is a philosophy of psychotherapy that values diversity, attends to power dynamics within the therapeutic relationship, incorporates individual and sociocultural variables, and sees the goal of psychotherapy to be development of independence and autonomy.

2. In order for feminist therapy to meet its goals, it must develop a theoretical base and reach a more diverse population.

Gender, Mental Health, and Psychopathology

QUESTION FOR REFLECTION

1. Can psychotherapy be (re)constructed to eliminate race and gender bias?

CHAPTER APPLICATIONS

1. Construct an interview that would help you identify any potential sources of bias in a therapist.
2. Obtain a copy of the **DSM-IV** and choose one diagnosis. Using the criteria for this diagnosis, make informal observations over the next few days. Under what circumstances do you observe behaviors fitting this diagnosis? What is the difference between normal and pathological behavior?

CREDITS

Chapter 1

pg. 14: "Just what are sex and gender, anyway? A call for a new terminological standard," by D. A. Gentile, *Psychological Science,* 4, 1993, pp. 120–122. Reprinted with the permission of Cambridge University Press, and the author.

pg. 18: "Commentary: Sex and gender—The troubled relationship between terms and concepts," by Rhoda K. Unger & Mary Crawford, *Psychological Science,* 4, 1993, pp. 122–124. Reprinted with the permission of Cambridge University Press.

pg. 21: "Commentary: Sorry, Wrong Number—A reply to Gentile's call," by Kay Deaux, *Psychological Science,* 4, 1993, pp. 125–126. Reprinted with the permission of Cambridge University Press, and the author.

pg. 29: Reprinted, by permission of The Feminist Press at The City University of New York, from Ruth Hubbard, "Race and Sex as Biological Categories," in *Challenging Racism and Sexism: Alternatives to Genetic Explanations,* edited by Ethel Tobach and Betty Rosoff. Copyright © 1994 by Ruth Hubbard.

pg. 35: "Toward a New Vision: Race, Class and Gender as Categories of Analysis and Connection," by P. Hill Collins, *Race, Sex, & Class, I,* 1993, pp. 25–46. Copyright © 1993. Originally published by The Center for Research on Women at The University of Memphis. Reprinted by permission of The Center for Research on Women, and the author.

Chapter 2

pg. 61: "Epistemological Debates, Feminist Voices: Science, Social Values, and the Study of Women," by Stephanie Riger, *American Psychologist,* 47, 1992, pp. 730–738. Copyright © 1992 by the American Psychological Association. Reprinted with permission of the American Psychological Association, and Stephanie Riger, Professor, Psychology and Women's Studies, and Director, Women's Studies Program at The University of Illinois at Chicago.

pg. 76: S. Coltrane, "Theorizing Masculinities in Contemporary Social Science," in H. Brod & M. Kaufman (eds.), *Theorizing Masculinities,* pp. 43–59, copyright © 1994 by Sage Publications, Inc. Reprinted by Permission of Sage Publications, Inc.

pg. 89: Reprinted by permission of Sage Publications Ltd. and the author from Janet S. Hyde, "I. Should Psychologists Study Gender Differences: Yes. With Some Guidelines," *Feminism & Psychology,* 4, 1994, pp. 507–512. Copyright © 1994 by Sage Publications Ltd.

pg. 93: Reprinted by permission of Sage Publications Ltd., and the author from Alice H. Eagly, "II. On Comparing Men and Women," *Feminism & Psychology, 4,* 1994, pp. 513–522. Copyright © 1994 by Sage Publications Ltd.

pg. 99: Reprinted by permission of Sage Publications Ltd. and the author from Diane F. Halpern, "III. Stereotypes, Science, Censorship, and the Study of Sex Differences," *Feminism & Psychology, 4,* 1994, pp. 523–530. Copyright © 1994 by Sage Publications, Ltd.

pg. 104: Reprinted by permission of Sage Publications, Ltd. and the authors from Rachel T. Hare-Mustin and Jeanne Marecek, "IV. Asking the Right Questions: Feminist Psychology and Sex Differences," *Feminism & Psychology, 4,* 1994, pp. 530–537. Copyright © 1994 by Sage Publications, Ltd.

Chapter 3

pg. 120: "Where It All Begins: The Biological Bases of Gender," by H. Devor, *Gender Blending: Confronting the Limits of Duality,* Ch. 1, pp. 1–22. Copyright ©1989. Reprinted by permission of Indiana University Press.

pg. 139: Copyright © 1995 by the American Psychological Association. Reprinted with permission.

pg. 146: "The Political Nature of 'Human Nature'," by R. Hubbard, in D. L. Rhode (ed.), *Theoretical Perspectives on Sexual Difference,* 1990, pp. 63–73. Copyright © 1990. Reprinted by permission of Yale University Press.

Chapter 4

pg. 164: C. Wade and C. Tavris, "The Longest War: Gender and Culture," in W. Lonner & R. Malpass (eds.), *Psychology & Culture.* Copyright © 1994 by Allyn and Bacon. Reprinted by permission.

pg. 170: "Woman, Men and Aggression in an Egalitarian Society," by M. Lepowsky, *Sex Roles, 30,* 1994, pp. 199–211. Reprinted by permission of Plenum Publishing Corporation, and the author.

pg. 179: "MEN OF COLOR: ETHNOCULTURAL VARIATIONS . . ." from A NEW PSYCHOLOGY OF MEN, EDITED by RONALD F. LEVANT and WILLIAM S. POLLACK. Copyright © 1995 by Ronald F. Levant and William S. Pollack. Reprinted by permission of BasicBooks, a division of HarperCollins Publishers, Inc.

Chapter 5

pg. 206: From MASCULINITY/ FEMININITY: BASIC PERSPECTIVES, edited by June Machover Reinisch, et al. Copyright © 1987 by Kinsey Institute. Used by permission of Oxford University Press, Inc.

pg. 216: "Manhood," by D. D. Gilmore. With permission from *Natural History,* June 1990. Copyright the American Museum of Natural History 1990.

pg. 220: APPROXIMATELY 20 PAGES from WOMEN'S ETHNICITIES: JOURNEYS THROUGH PSYCHOLOGY edited by Karen Fraser Wyche. Copyright © 1996 by WestviewPress. Reprinted by permission of WestviewPress.

pg. 232: S. T. Fiske & L. E. Stevens, "What's So Special About Sex? Gender Stereotyping and Discrimination," in *Gender Issues in Contemporary Society* by S. Oskamp & M. Costanzo (eds.), pp. 173–196, copyright © 1993 by Sage Publications, Inc. Reprinted by Permission of Sage Publications, Inc.

Chapter 6

pg. 262: Sandra Lipsitz Bem, "Gender Schema Theory and Its Implications for Child Development: Raising Gender-Aschematic Children in a Gender-Schematic Society," *Signs: Journal of Women in Culture and Society, 8,* 1983, pp. 598–616. Reprinted by permission of The University of Chicago Press, and the author.

pg. 275: "Psychological and Cognitive Determinants of Early Gender-Role Development," by B. I. Fagot, in R. C. Rosen (ed.), *Annual Review of Sex Research,* vol. 6. Copyright © 1995. Reprinted by permission of the Society for the Scientific Study of Sexuality.

pg. 294: "Gender and Relationships: A Developmental Account," by E. Maccoby, *American Psychologist,* 45, 1990, pp. 513–520. Copyright © 1990 by the American Psychological Association. Reprinted with permission of The American Psychological Association, and the author.

Chapter 8

pg. 367: "A Social Psychological Model of Gender," by K. Deaux & B. Major, in D. L. Rhode (ed.), *Theoretical Perspectives on Sexual Difference,* 1990, pp. 89–99. Copyright © 1990. Reprinted by permission of Yale University Press.

pg. 376: "Gender in the Psychology of Emotions: A Selective Research Review," by S. Shields, in K. T. Strongman (ed.), *International Review of Studies on Emotion, Vol. 1,* 1991, pp. 43–59. Copyright © 1991 John Wiley & Sons Limited. Reproduced by permission of John Wiley and Sons Limited.

pg. 390: "Deconstructing the Myth of the Nonaggressive Woman," by Jacquelyn W. White & Robin M. Kowalski, *Psychology of Women Quarterly, 18,* 1994, pp. 487–508. Reprinted with the permission of Cambridge University Press.

Chapter 9

pg. 436: "Cognitive Gender Differences: Why Diversity is a Critical Research Issue," by D. F. Halpern in H. Landine (ed.), *Bringing Cultural Diversity to Feminist Psychology.* Copyright © 1995 by the American Psychological Association. Reprinted with permission.

Fig. 1, pg. 442: From Diane F. Halpern, *Sex differences in cognitive ability,* 2/e. Copyright © 1992. Used by permission of Lawrence Erlbaum Associates, Inc., and the author.

pg. 446: Copyright © 1995 by The Haworth Press, Inc., 10 Alice Street, Binghamtown, NY. "Gender and math: What makes a difference?," by M. M. Kimball, *Feminist visions of gender similarities and differences,* pp. 83–104.

poem, pg. 446: From THE DEAD AND THE LIVING by Sharon Olds. Copyright © 1983 by Sharon Olds. Reprinted by permission of Alfred A. Knopf Inc.

pg. 461: Susan McGee Bailey, "The Current Status of Gender Equity Research in American Schools," *Educational Psychologist, 28,* 1993, pp. 321–339. Copyright © 1993. Reprinted by permission of Lawrence Erlbaum Associates, Inc., and the author.

pg. 473: From SCHOOL GIRLS: YOUNG WOMEN, SELF-ESTEEM AND THE CONFIDENCE GAP by Peggy Orenstein American Assoc. of Univ. Women. Copyright © 1994 by Peggy Orenstein and American Association of University Women. Used by permission of Doubleday, a division of Bantam Doubleday Dell Publishing Group, Inc.

Chapter 10

pg. 493: K. Walker, "Men, Women and Friendship: What They Say, What They Do," *Gender and Society, 8,* copyright © 1994 by Sage Publications, Inc. Reprinted by Permission of Sage Publications, Inc.

pg. 505: from PSYCHOLOGICAL PERSPECTIVES ON LESBIAN AND GAY MALE EXPERIENCES by Linda D. Gamets and Douglas C. Kimmel. Copyright © 1993 by Columbia University Press. Reprinted with permission of the publisher.

pg. 520: Karen K. Dion & Kenneth L. Dion, "Individualistic and Collectivistic Perspectives on Gender and the Cultural Context of Love and Intimacy," *Journal of Social Issues,* Vol. 49, No. 3, pp. 53–69. Copyright © 1993. Reprinted by permission of The Society for the Psychological Study of Social Issues.

Chapter 12

pg. 607: "Guarding the Gates: The Micropolitics of Gender," by J. Lorber, *Paradoxes of Gender,* 1994, Ch. 10, pp. 225–252. Copyright © 1994. Reprinted by permission of Yale University Press.

pg. 629: J. L. Eberhardt and S. T. Fiske, "Affirmative Action in Theory and Practice: Issues of Power, Ambiguity and Gender vs. Race," *Basic and Applied Social Psychology,* 15, pp. 201–220. Copyright © 1994. Reprinted by permission of Lawrence Erlbaum Associates, Inc. and Susan T. Fiske.

pg. 642: "Sexual Terrorism: The Social Control of Women," by C. Sheffield in M. Ferree and B. Hess (eds.), *Analyzing Gender: A Handbook of Social Science Research,* 1987, pp. 43–59, copyright © 1994 by Sage Publications, Inc. Reprinted by Permission of Sage Publications, Inc.

pg. 655: From *Cracking the Armour: Power, Pain and the Lives of Men* by Michael Kaufman. Copyright © Michael Kaufman, 1993. Reprinted by permission of Penguin Books Canada Limited.

Chapter 13

pg. 678: "Manmade Medicine and Women's Health: The Biopolitics of Sex/Gender and Race/Ethnicity by Nancy Krieger & Elizabeth Fee, *International Journal of Health Services, 24,* 1994, pp. 265–283. Reprinted by permission of the publisher, Baywood Publishing Co., Inc., and the author.

pg. 690: From AMERICAN WOMEN IN THE NINETIES: TODAY'S CRITICAL ISSUES, edited, with an Introduction, by Sherri Matteo. Copyright 1993 by Northeastern University Press. Reprinted with the permission of Northeastern University Press.

pg. 702: V. L. Banyard & S. A. Graham-Bermann, "Can Women Cope: A Gender Analysis of Theories of Coping with Stress," *Psychology of Women Quarterly, 17,* 1993, pp. 303–318. Reprinted with the permission of Cambridge University Press, and the author.

pg. 713: CHAPTER 7* BY RICHARD M. EISLER from A NEW PSYCHOLOGY OF MEN, EDITED BY RONALD F. LEVANT and WILLIAM S. POLLACK. Copyright © 1995 by Ronald F. Levant and William S. Pollack. Reprinted by permission of BasicBooks, a division of HarperCollins Publishers, Inc.

*"The Relationship between Masculine Gender Role Stress and Men's Health Risk: The Validation of a Construct."

Chapter 14

pg. 740: Reprinted from "Gender and Psychological Distress," by E. P. Cook, *Journal of Counseling and Development, 68,* 1990, pp. 371–375, © 1990 ACA. Reprinted with permission. No further reproduction authorized without written permission of the American Counseling Association.

pg. 748: "A Short History of the Future: Feminism and Clinical Psychology," by J. Marecek & R. T. Hare-Mustin, *Psychology of Women Quarterly, 15,* 1991, pp. 521–536. Reprinted with the permission of Cambridge University Press.

pg. 759: "The Politics of Psychiatry: Gender and Sexual Preference in DSM-IV," by T. A. Kupers, *Masculinities, 3,* 1995, pp. 67–68. Copyright © 1995. All rights reserved. Reprinted by permission.

pg. 767: "Clinical Diagnosis among Diverse Populations: A Multicultural Perspective," by Alison Solomon, *Families in Society, 73,* June 1992, pp. 371–377. Reprinted by permission of Families International, Inc.

pg. 775: From L. S. Brown & A. M. Brodsky, *Psychotherapy, 29,* 1992, pp. 51–57. Copyright © 1992. Reprinted by permission.

INDEX